EDITION

INTRODUCTION TO
Business Law

Jeffrey F. Beatty
Boston University

Susan S. Samuelson
Boston University

Patricia Sánchez Abril
University of Miami

CENGAGE
Learning®

Australia • Brazil • Japan • Korea • Mexico • Singapore • Spain • United Kingdom • United States

**Introduction to Business Law,
Fifth Edition**

Jeffrey F. Beatty, Susan S. Samuelson,
and Patricia Sánchez Abril

Vice President, General Manager, Social Science &
  Qualitative Business: Erin Joyner

Product Director: Michael Worls

Senior Product Manager: Vicky True-Baker

Senior Content & Media Developer: Kristen Meere

Associate Content Developer: Zachary Fleischer

Product Assistant: Ryan McAndrews

Marketing Director: Kristen Hurd

Marketing Manager: Katie Jergens

Marketing Coordinator: Christopher Walz

Content Project Manager: Megan Guiliani

Manufacturing Planner: Kevin Kluck

Production Service/Compositor: Integra Software
  Services Pvt. Ltd.

Senior Art Director: Michelle Kunkler

Cover and Internal Designer: Beckmeyer Design

Cover Image: Green Sea, Iona, 1920s (oil on canvas),
  Peploe, Samuel John (1871-1935)/The Fleming-Wyfold
  Art Foundation/Bridgeman Art Library

Intellectual Property
  Analyst: Jennifer Nonenmacher
  Project Manager: Betsy Hathaway

Library of Congress Control Number: 2014957071

Student Edition ISBN: 978-1-285-86039-8

Cengage Learning
20 Channel Center Street
Boston, MA 02210
USA

Cengage Learning is a leading provider of customized learning solutions with office locations around the globe, including Singapore, the United Kingdom, Australia, Mexico, Brazil, and Japan. Locate your local office at: **www.cengage.com/global**

Cengage Learning products are represented in Canada by Nelson Education, Ltd.

To learn more about Cengage Learning Solutions, visit **www.cengage.com**

Purchase any of our products at your local college store or at our preferred online store **www.cengagebrain.com**

Printed in the United States of America
Print Number: 02   Print Year: 2015

CONTENTS: OVERVIEW

Preface xv

UNIT 1
The Legal Environment 1

1 Introduction to Law 2
2 Ethics and Corporate Social Responsibility 16
3 International Law 38
4 Constitutional, Statutory, Administrative, and Common Law 57
5 Courts, Litigation, and Alternative Dispute Resolution 78
6 Crime 99

UNIT 2
Torts 119

7 Intentional Torts and Business Torts 120
8 Negligence, Strict Liability, and Product Liability 135
9 Cyberlaw and Privacy 154

UNIT 3
Contracts and the UCC 173

10 Forming a Contract 174
11 Requirements for a Contract 194
12 Performance of a Contract 217
13 Practical Contracts 239
14 Sales 258
15 Negotiable Instruments 275
16 Secured Transactions 292

UNIT 4
Agency and Employment Law 313

17 Agency 314
18 Employment Law 333
19 Employment Discrimination 350
20 Labor Law 370

UNIT 5
The Lifecycle of a Business 387

21 Starting a Business: LLCs and Other Options 388
22 Corporations 407
23 Bankruptcy 431

UNIT 6
Government Regulation 451

24 Securities and Antitrust 452
25 Consumer Protection 471
26 Environmental Law 491
27 Accountants' Liability 509

UNIT 7
Property 527

28 Intellectual Property 528
29 Real Property and Landlord-Tenant Law 546
30 Personal Property and Bailment 567
31 Estate Planning 584
32 Insurance 602

Appendix A
The Constitution of the United States A1

Appendix B
Uniform Commercial Code B1

Appendix C C1

Glossary G1

Table of Cases T1

Index I1

Preface xv

UNIT 1
The Legal Environment 1

1 Introduction to Law 2
2 Ethics and Corporate Social Responsibility 16
3 International Law 38
4 Constitutional, Statutory, Administrative, and Common Law 57
5 Courts, Litigation, and Alternative Dispute Resolution 78
6 Crime 99

UNIT 2
Torts 119

7 Intentional Torts and Business Torts 120
8 Negligence, Strict Liability, and Product Liability 136
9 Cyberlaw and Privacy 154

UNIT 3
Contracts and the UCC 173

10 Introduction to Contracts 174
11 Requirements for a Contract 194
12 Performance of a Contract 212
13 Practical Contracts 229
14 Sales 238
15 Negotiable Instruments 255
16 Secured Transactions 292

UNIT 4
Agency and Employment Law 313

17 Agency 314
18 Employment Law 333
19 Employment Discrimination 350
20 Labor Law 379

UNIT 5
The Lifecycle of a Business 387

21 Starting a Business: LLCs and Other Options 388
22 Corporations 407
23 Bankruptcy 431

UNIT 6
Government Regulation 451

24 Securities and Venture 452
25 Consumer Protection 471
26 Environmental Law 481
27 Accountants' Liability 504

UNIT 7
Property 527

28 Intellectual Property 528
29 Real Property and Landlord-Tenant Law 546
30 Personal Property and Bailment 567
31 Estate Planning 584
32 Insurance 602

Appendix A
The Constitution of the United States A1

Appendix B
Uniform Commercial Code B1

Appendix C C1

Glossary G1

Table of Cases T1

Index I1

CONTENTS

Preface   **xv**

UNIT 1
The Legal Environment   1

Chapter 1 *Introduction to Law*   **2**
1-1 Three Important Ideas about Law   3
    1-1a Power   3
    1-1b Importance   3
    1-1c Fascination   3
1-2 Sources of Contemporary Law   4
    1-2a United States Constitution   4
    1-2b Statutes   5
    1-2c Common Law   5
    1-2d Court Orders   6
    1-2e Administrative Law   6
1-3 Classifications of Law   6
    1-3a Criminal and Civil Law   6
    1-3b Law and Morality   7
1-4 Working with the Book's Features   8
    1-4a Analyzing a Case   8
    1-4b "You Be the Judge"   10

Chapter Conclusion   11
Exam Review   12
Matching Questions   13
True/False Questions   13
Multiple-Choice Questions   13
Case Questions   14
Discussion Questions   15

Chapter 2 *Ethics and Corporate Social Responsibility*   **16**
2-1 Introduction   17
2-2 The Role of Business in Society   18
2-3 Why Be Ethical?   18
    2-3a Society as a Whole Benefits from Ethical Behavior   19
    2-3b People Feel Better When They Behave Ethically   19
    2-3c Unethical Behavior Can Be Very Costly   19
2-4 Theories of Ethics   19
    2-4a Utilitarian Ethics   20
    2-4b Deontological Ethics   20
    2-4c Rawlsian Justice   21

    2-4d Front Page Test   21
    2-4e Moral Universalism and Relativism   21
2-5 Ethics Traps   22
    2-5a Money   22
    2-5b Competition   23
    2-5c Rationalization   23
    2-5d We Can't Be Objective about Ourselves   23
    2-5e Conflicts of Interest   23
    2-5f Conformity   24
    2-5g Following Orders   24
    2-5h Euphemisms and Reframing   24
    2-5i Lost in a Crowd   24
    2-5j Short-Term Perspective   25
    2-5k Blind Spots   25
    2-5l Avoiding Ethics Traps   25
2-6 Lying: A Special Case   25
    2-6a Ethics Case: Truth (?) in Borrowing   26
2-7 Applying the Principles   26
    2-7a Personal Ethics in the Workplace   26
    2-7b Ethics Case: Weird Wierdsma   27
    2-7c The Organization's Responsibility to Society   27
    2-7d Ethics Case: Breathing the Fumes   27
    2-7e The Organization's Responsibility to Its Employees   28
    2-7f Ethics Case: The Storm after the Storm   28
    2-7g The Organization's Responsibility to Its Customers   29
    2-7h Ethics Case: Mickey Weighs In   29
    2-7i The Organization's Responsibility to Overseas Workers   29
    2-7j Ethics Case: A Worm in the Apple   30
2-8 When the Going Gets Tough: Responding to Unethical Behavior   30
    2-8a Loyalty   31
    2-8b Exit   31
    2-8c Voice   31
2-9 Corporate Social Responsibility (CSR)   31
    2-9a Ethics Case: The Beauty of a Well-Fed Child   31

Chapter Conclusion   32
Exam Review   32
Matching Questions   34
True/False Questions   34

v

Multiple-Choice Questions   34
Case Questions   35
Discussion Questions   36

Chapter 3 *International Law*   **38**
3-1 International Law: Public versus Private   39
3-2 Actors in International Law   39
   3-2a The United Nations   39
   3-2b The International Court of Justice   40
   3-2c International Chamber of Commerce   40
   3-2d Sovereign Nations   41
3-3 The World's Legal Systems   41
   3-3a Common Law   41
   3-3b Civil Law   42
   3-3c Islamic Law   42
3-4 Sources of Law   43
   3-4a Treaties   43
   3-4b Custom and General Principles of Law   48
3-5 Extraterritoriality and Foreign Recognition   48
   3-5a Application of U.S. Law Abroad 48
   3-5b U.S. Recognition and Enforcement of
     Foreign Judgments   50
3-6 Essential Clauses in International Contracts   51

Chapter Conclusion   52
Exam Review   52
Matching Questions   54
True/False Questions   54
Multiple-Choice Questions   54
Case Questions   55
Discussion Questions   56

Chapter 4 *Constitutional, Statutory,*
Administrative, and Common Law   **57**
4-1 Constitutional Law   58
   4-1a Government Power   58
   4-1b Power Granted   59
   4-1c Protected Rights   62
   4-1d Fifth Amendment: Due Process and the
     Takings Clause   63
   4-1e Fourteenth Amendment: Equal
     Protection Clause   65
4-2 Statutory Law   66
   4-2a Committee Work   66
4-3 Common Law   67
   4-3a Stare Decisis   67
   4-3b Bystander Cases   68
4-4 Administrative Law   69
   4-4a Rule Making   70
   4-4b Investigation   71
   4-4c Adjudication   71

Chapter Conclusion   71
Exam Review   72
Matching Questions   74
True/False Questions   74
Multiple-Choice Questions   74
Case Questions   75
Discussion Questions   77

Chapter 5 *Courts, Litigation,*
and Alternative Dispute Resolution   **78**
5-1 Three Fundamental Areas of Law   79
   5-1a Litigation versus Alternative Dispute
     Resolution   79
5-2 Alternative Dispute Resolution   79
   5-2a Mediation   79
   5-2b Arbitration   79
5-3 Court Systems   80
   5-3a State Courts   80
   5-3b Federal Courts   83
5-4 Litigation   84
   5-4a Pleadings   84
5-5 Trial   90
   5-5a Adversary System   90
   5-5b Right to Jury Trial   90
   5-5c Opening Statements   90
   5-5d Burden of Proof   90
   5-5e Plaintiff's Case   91
   5-5f Defendant's Case   91
   5-5g Closing Argument   92
   5-5h Verdict   92
5-6 Appeals   92
   5-6a Appeal Court Options   93

Chapter Conclusion   93
Exam Review   94
Matching Questions   95
True/False Questions   96
Multiple-Choice Questions   96
Case Questions   97
Discussion Questions   98

Chapter 6 *Crime*   **99**
6-1 A Civil versus a Criminal Case   100
   6-1a Prosecution   100
   6-1b Burden of Proof   100
   6-1c Right to a Jury   100
   6-1d Felonies and Misdemeanors   101
6-2 Criminal Procedure   101
   6-2a State of Mind   101
   6-2b Gathering Evidence: The Fourth
     Amendment   102
   6-2c After Arrest   104

6-3 Crimes that Harm Businesses (and Their Customers)   106
    6-3a Larceny   106
    6-3b Fraud   106
    6-3c Arson   108
    6-3d Embezzlement   108
    6-3e Hacking   108
6-4 Crimes Committed by Business   109
    6-4a Making False Statements   110
    6-4b RICO   110
    6-4c Money Laundering   111
    6-4d Hiring Illegal Workers   111
    6-4e Foreign Corrupt Practices Act   111
    6-4f Punishing a Corporation   112

Chapter Conclusion   112
Exam Review   113
Matching Questions   115
True/False Questions   116
Multiple-Choice Questions   116
Case Questions   117
Discussion Questions   118

UNIT 2
Torts   119

Chapter 7 *Intentional Torts and Business Torts*   120

7-1 Intentional Torts   122
    7-1a Defamation   122
    7-1b False Imprisonment   123
    7-1c Battery and Assault   124
    7-1d Fraud   124
    7-1e Intentional Infliction of Emotional Distress   124
7-2 Damages   125
    7-2a Compensatory Damages   125
    7-2b Punitive Damages   126
    7-2c Tort Reform and the *Exxon Valdez*   128
7-3 Business Torts   128
    7-3a Tortious Interference with a Contract   128
    7-3b Commercial Exploitation   129

Chapter Conclusion   129
Exam Review   129
Matching Questions   131
True/False Questions   131
Multiple-Choice Questions   131
Case Questions   132
Discussion Questions   134

Chapter 8 *Negligence, Strict Liability, and Product Liability*   135

8-1 Negligence   136
    8-1a Duty of Due Care   137
    8-1b Breach of Duty   139
    8-1c Causation   139
    8-1d Damages   141
8-2 Defenses   142
    8-2a Assumption of the Risk   142
    8-2b Contributory and Comparative Negligence   142
8-3 Strict Liability   143
    8-3a Ultrahazardous Activity   144
    8-3b Product Liability   145
8-4 Contemporary Trends   147

Chapter Conclusion   148
Exam Review   148
Matching Questions   150
True/False Questions   150
Multiple-Choice Questions   150
Case Questions   151
Discussion Questions   152

Chapter 9 *Cyberlaw and Privacy*   154

9-1 Regulation of the Internet   155
    9-1a Net Neutrality   155
    9-1b Regulation of User-Generated Content   155
9-2 Consumer Protection   158
    9-2a The FTC Act   158
    9-2b Spam   159
9-3 Privacy in a Digital World   160
    9-3a How We Lose Our Privacy Online   160
    9-3b Regulation of Online Privacy   161

Chapter Conclusion   166
Exam Review   166
Matching Questions   169
True/False Questions   169
Multiple-Choice Questions   169
Case Questions   170
Discussion Questions   171

UNIT 3
Contracts and the UCC   173

Chapter 10 *Forming a Contract*   174

10-1 Contracts   175
    10-1a Elements of a Contract   175
    10-1b Other Important Issues   176
    10-1c Contracts Defined   176

10-2 Types of Contracts 176
   10-2a Bilateral and Unilateral Contracts 176
   10-2b Executory and Executed Contracts 177
   10-2c Valid, Unenforceable, Voidable, and
     Void Agreements 177
   10-2d Express and Implied Contracts 178
   10-2e Promissory Estoppel and Quasi-
     Contracts 179
   10-2f Promissory Estoppel 180
   10-2g Quasi-Contract 181
10-3 Sources of Contract Law 182
   10-3a Common Law 182
   10-3b Uniform Commercial Code 182
10-4 Agreement 183
   10-4a Meeting of the Minds 183
   10-4b Offer 183
   10-4c Termination of Offers 185
   10-4d Acceptance 186
   10-4e Communication of Acceptance 188

Chapter Conclusion 188
Exam Review 189
Matching Questions 191
True/False Questions 191
Multiple-Choice Questions 191
Case Questions 192
Discussion Questions 193

Chapter 11 *Requirements for a Contract* 194
11-1 Consideration 195
   11-1a What Is Value? 195
   11-1b What Constitutes Exchange? 196
11-2 Legality 197
   11-2a Non-compete Agreements: Sale of a
     Business 198
   11-2b Non-compete Agreements:
     Employment Contracts 198
   11-2c Exculpatory Clauses 199
11-3 Capacity 201
   11-3a Minors 201
   11-3b Mentally Impaired Persons 201
   11-3c Intoxication 202
11-4 Reality of Consent 202
   11-4a Fraud 202
   11-4b Mistake 204
11-5 Contracts in Writing 206
   11-5a The Statute of Frauds 206
   11-5b Contracts that Must Be in Writing 207
   11-5c What the Writing Must Contain 209
   11-5d Sale of Goods 210

Chapter Conclusion 210
Exam Review 211
Matching Questions 212
True/False Questions 213
Multiple-Choice Questions 213
Case Questions 214
Discussion Questions 215

Chapter 12 *Performance of a Contract* 217
12-1 Third Party Beneficiary 218
   12-1a Types of Beneficiaries 218
12-2 Assignment and Delegation 220
   12-2a Assignment 220
   12-2b Delegation of Duties 221
12-3 Performance and Discharge 222
   12-3a Performance 223
   12-3b Good Faith 224
   12-3c Breach 225
   12-3d Impossibility 226
12-4 Remedies 226
   12-4a Expectation Interest 227
   12-4b Reliance Interest 230
   12-4c Restitution Interest 231
   12-4d Other Equitable Interests 231
   12-4e Mitigation of Damages 232

Chapter Conclusion 232
Exam Review 233
Matching Questions 235
True/False Questions 235
Multiple-Choice Questions 235
Case Questions 236
Discussion Questions 237

Chapter 13 *Practical Contracts* 239
13-1 The Lawyer 240
   13-1a Lawyers and Clients 240
   13-1b Hiring a Lawyer 241
13-2 The Contract 241
   13-2a Who Drafts It? 241
   13-2b Mistakes 241
   13-2c The Structure of a Contract 246

Chapter Conclusion 252
Exam Review 252
Matching Questions 254
True/False Questions 254
Multiple-Choice Questions 255
Case Questions 256
Discussion Questions 257

Chapter 14 *Sales*   **258**

14-1 Sales   259
   14-1a Development of the UCC   259
   14-1b Contract Formation   260
   14-1c Performance and Remedies   264
14-2 Warranties   265
   14-2a Express Warranties   265
   14-2b Implied Warranties   266

Chapter Conclusion   269
Exam Review   269
Matching Questions   271
True/False Questions   271
Multiple-Choice Questions   271
Case Questions   272
Discussion Questions   273

Chapter 15 *Negotiable Instruments*   **275**

15-1 Commercial Paper   276
15-2 Types of Negotiable Instruments   276
15-3 The Fundamental "Rule" of Commercial
   Paper   277
   15-3a Negotiability   277
   15-3b Negotiation   281
   15-3c Holder in Due Course   281
   15-3d Consumer Exception   284

Chapter Conclusion   285
Exam Review   285
Matching Questions   288
True/False Questions   288
Multiple-Choice Questions   288
Case Questions   289
Discussion Questions   291

Chapter 16 *Secured Transactions*   **292**

16-1 Secured Transactions   293
   16-1a Scope of Article 9   294
16-2 Attachment of a Security Interest   295
   16-2a Agreement   295
   16-2b Possession   296
   16-2c Value   296
   16-2d Debtor Rights in the Collateral   296
   16-2e Attachment to Future Property   297
16-3 Perfection   297
   16-3a Nothing Less than Perfection   297
   16-3b Perfection by Filing   297
   16-3c Perfection by Possession   299
   16-3d Perfection of Consumer Goods 299

16-4 Protection of Buyers   300
   16-4a Buyers in Ordinary Course of Business   302
16-5 Priorities among Creditors   303
16-6 Default and Termination   304
   16-6a Default   304
   16-6b Termination   306

Chapter Conclusion   306
Exam Review   306
Matching Questions   308
True/False Questions   308
Multiple-Choice Questions   308
Case Questions   309
Discussion Questions   310

UNIT 4
Agency and Employment Law   313

Chapter 17 *Agency*   **314**

17-1 Creating an Agency Relationship   315
   17-1a Consent   315
   17-1b Control   315
   17-1c Fiduciary Relationship   316
17-2 Duties of Agents to Principals   316
   17-2a Duty of Loyalty   316
   17-2b Other Duties of an Agent   318
   17-2c Principal's Remedies when the Agent
     Breaches a Duty   318
17-3 Duties of Principals to Agents   319
17-4 Terminating an Agency Relationship   319
17-5 Liability to Third Parties   320
   17-5a Principal's Liability for Contracts   320
   17-5b Agent's Liability for Contracts   321
   17-5c Principal's Liability for Torts   321
   17-5d Agent's Liability for Torts   326

Chapter Conclusion   326
Exam Review   327
Matching Questions   329
True/False Questions   329
Multiple-Choice Questions   329
Case Questions   331
Discussion Questions   331

Chapter 18 *Employment Law*   **333**

18-1 Introduction   334
18-2 Employment Security   334
   18-2a Family and Medical Leave Act   334
   18-2b Common Law Protections   335
   18-2c Whistleblowing   338

18-3 Workplace Freedom and Safety 339
   18-3a Off-Duty Activities 339
   18-3b Free Speech in the Workplace 340
   18-3c Lie Detector Tests 341
   18-3d Guns 341
   18-3e Workplace Safety 342
18-4 Financial Protection 342
   18-4a Fair Labor Standards Act 342
   18-4b Workers' Compensation 343
   18-4c Health Insurance 343
   18-4d Social Security 343

Chapter Conclusion 343
Exam Review 344
Matching Questions 346
True/False Questions 346
Multiple-Choice Questions 347
Case Questions 348
Discussion Questions 349

Chapter 19 *Employment Discrimination* **350**
19-1 Equal Pay Act of 1963 351
19-2 Title VII of the Civil Rights Act of 1964 351
   19-2a Prohibited Activities 351
   19-2b Religion 355
   19-2c Family Responsibility Discrimination 355
   19-2d Sexual Orientation 356
   19-2e Gender Identity and Expression 356
   19-2f Immigration 356
   19-2g Defenses to Charges of Discrimination 356
   19-2h Affirmative Action 357
19-3 Pregnancy Discrimination Act 358
19-4 Age Discrimination 358
19-5 Americans with Disabilities Act 359
   19-5a The Hiring Process 360
   19-5b Relationship with a Disabled Person 360
   19-5c Obesity 361
   19-5d Mental Disabilities 361
19-6 Genetic Information Nondiscrimination Act 361
19-7 Hiring Practices 361
   19-7a Interviews 361
   19-7b Social Media 362
19-8 Enforcement 363

Chapter Conclusion 364
Exam Review 364
Matching Questions 366
True/False Questions 366
Multiple-Choice Questions 367
Case Questions 368
Discussion Questions 369

Chapter 20 *Labor Law* **370**
20-1 Unions Develop 371
   20-1a Key Statutes 371
   20-1b Labor Unions Today 372
20-2 Organizing a Union 372
   20-2a Exclusivity 372
   20-2b Organizing: Stages 373
   20-2c Organizing: Actions 373
20-3 Collective Bargaining 375
   20-3a Subjects of Bargaining 375
   20-3b Duty to Bargain 375
   20-3c Enforcement 376
20-4 Concerted Action 377
   20-4a Strikes 377
   20-4b Replacement Workers 378
   20-4c Picketing 379
   20-4d Lockouts 380

Chapter Conclusion 380
Exam Review 381
Matching Questions 383
True/False Questions 383
Multiple-Choice Questions 383
Case Questions 384
Discussion Questions 385

UNIT 5
The Lifecycle of a Business 387

Chapter 21 *Starting a Business: LLCs and Other Options* **388**
21-1 Sole Proprietorships 389
21-2 Corporations 389
   21-2a Corporations in General 390
   21-2b Special Types of Corporations 392
21-3 Limited Liability Companies 393
   21-3a Limited Liability 393
   21-3b Formation 394
   21-3c Flexibility 395
   21-3d Transferability of Interests 395
   21-3e Duration 395
   21-3f Going Public 395
   21-3g Piercing the Company Veil 395
   21-3h Legal Uncertainty 396
   21-3i Choices: LLC v. Corporation 397
21-4 Social Enterprises 397
21-5 General Partnerships 398
   21-5a Tax Status 398
   21-5b Liability 398
   21-5c Formation 398

21-5d Raising Capital   398
21-5e Management   398
21-5f Transfer of Ownership   399
21-5g Terminating a Partnership   399
21-6 Limited Liability Partnerships   400
21-7 Professional Corporations   400
21-8 Franchises   400

Chapter Conclusion   402
Exam Review   402
Matching Questions   403
True/False Questions   403
Multiple-Choice Questions   403
Case Questions   404
Discussion Questions   405

Chapter 22 *Corporations*   407
22-1 Promoter's Liability   408
22-2 Incorporation Process   408
    22-2a Where to Incorporate?   409
    22-2b The Charter   409
22-3 After Incorporation   410
    22-3a Directors and Officers   410
    22-3b Bylaws   411
    22-3c Foreign Corporations   411
22-4 Death of the Corporation   412
    22-4a Piercing the Corporate Veil   412
    22-4b Termination   412
22-5 Management Duties   413
22-6 The Business Judgment Rule   413
    22-6a Stakeholders   414
    22-6b Shareholders   414
22-7 Shareholder Rights   418
    22-7a Who Are the Shareholders?   418
    22-7b Right to Information   418
    22-7c Right to Vote   419

Chapter Conclusion   424
Exam Review   424
Matching Questions   427
True/False Questions   427
Multiple-Choice Questions   427
Case Questions   428
Discussion Questions   429

Chapter 23 *Bankruptcy*   431
23-1 Overview of Bankruptcy   432
23-2 Chapter 7 Liquidation   433
    23-2a Filing a Petition   433
    23-2b Trustee   434
    23-2c Creditors   434
    23-2d Automatic Stay   435

23-2e Bankruptcy Estate   436
23-2f Payment of Claims   437
23-2g Discharge   438
23-3 Chapter 11 Reorganization   441
    23-3a Debtor in Possession   441
    23-3b Creditors' Committee   441
    23-3c Plan of Reorganization   442
    32-3d Confirmation of the Plan   442
    23-3e Discharge   442
    23-3f Small-Business Bankruptcy   443
23-4 Chapter 13 Consumer Reorganizations   443
    23-4a Beginning a Chapter 13 Case   443
    23-4b Plan of Payment   443
    23-4c Discharge   443

Chapter Conclusion   444
Exam Review   444
Matching Questions   446
True/False Questions   446
Multiple-Choice Questions   446
Case Questions   447
Discussion Questions   448

**UNIT 6
Government Regulation   451**

Chapter 24 *Securities and Antitrust*   452
24-1 Securities Laws   453
    24-1a What Is a Security?   453
    24-1b Securities Act of 1933   453
    24-1c Securities Exchange Act of 1934   455
    24-1d Insider Trading   457
    24-1e Blue Sky Laws   459
24-2 Antitrust   460
    24-2a The Sherman Act   460
    24-2b The Clayton Act   463
    24-2c The Robinson-Patman Act   464

Chapter Conclusion   465
Exam Review   465
Matching Questions   467
True/False Questions   468
Multiple-Choice Questions   468
Case Questions   469
Discussion Questions   470

Chapter 25 *Consumer Protection*   471
25-1 Introduction   472
25-2 Sales   472
    25-2a Deceptive Acts or Practices   472
    25-2b Unfair Practices   472

25-2c Abusive Acts 472
25-2d Bait-and-Switch 472
25-2e Merchandise Bought by Mail, by
    Telephone, or Online 473
25-2f Telemarketing 473
25-2g Unordered Merchandise 473
25-2h Door-to-Door Sales 474
25-3 Consumer Credit 474
25-3a Payday Loans 474
25-3b Truth in Lending Act 475
25-3c Home Mortgage Loans 475
25-3d Plastic: Credit, Debit, and ATM Cards 476
25-3e Electronic Fund Transfers 478
25-3f Credit Reports 479
25-3g Debt Collection 480
25-3h Equal Credit Opportunity Act 481
25-4 Magnuson-Moss Warranty Act 482
25-5 Consumer Product Safety 483

Chapter Conclusion 484
Exam Review 484
Matching Questions 487
True/False Questions 487
Multiple-Choice Questions 487
Case Questions 488
Discussion Questions 489

Chapter 26 *Environmental Law* **491**
26-1 Introduction 492
26-2 Air Pollution 492
26-2a Clean Air Act 493
26-2b Greenhouse Gases (GHGs) and Global
    Warming 494
26-3 Water Pollution: The Clean Water Act 495
26-3a Coverage 496
26-3b Major Provisions 496
26-4 Waste including Disposal 498
26-4a Resource Conservation and Recovery
    Act (RCRA) 498
26-4b Superfund 499
26-5 Chemicals 500
26-6 Natural Resources 500
26-6a National Environmental Policy Act 500
26-6b Endangered Species Act 501

Chapter Conclusion 503
Exam Review 504
Matching Questions 505
True/False Questions 505
Multiple-Choice Questions 506
Case Questions 507
Discussion Questions 508

Chapter 27 *Accountants' Liability* **509**
27-1 Introduction 510
27-1a Sarbanes-Oxley 510
27-1b Consolidation in the Accounting
    Profession 511
27-1c Audits 511
27-2 Liability to Clients 513
27-2a Contract 513
27-2b Negligence 513
27-2c Common Law Fraud 514
27-2d Breach of Trust 514
27-3 Liability to Third Parties 515
27-3a Negligence 516
27-3b Fraud 517
27-3c Securities Act of 1933 517
27-3d Securities Exchange Act of 1934 517
27-4 Criminal Liability 519
27-5 Other Accountant-Client Issues 520
27-5a The Accountant-Client
    Relationship 520
27-5b Accountant-Client Privilege 520

Chapter Conclusion 521
Exam Review 521
Matching Questions 523
True/False Questions 524
Multiple-Choice Questions 524
Case Questions 525
Discussion Questions 526

UNIT 7
Property 527

Chapter 28 *Intellectual Property* **528**
28-1 Introduction 529
28-2 Patents 529
28-2a Types of Patents 529
28-2b Requirements for a Patent 530
28-2c The Limits of Patentable Subject
    Matter: Living Organisms 531
28-2d Patent Application and
    Issuance 532
28-3 Copyrights 533
28-3a Copyright Term 534
28-3b Infringement 535
28-3c First Sale Doctrine 535
28-3d Fair Use 535
28-3e Digital Music and Movies 536
28-4 Trademarks 537
28-4a Ownership and Registration 537
28-4b Valid Trademarks 538

28-4c Infringement 538
28-4d International Trademark Treaties 539
28-5 Trade Secrets 540

Chapter Conclusion 541
Exam Review 541
Matching Questions 542
True/False Questions 542
Multiple-Choice Questions 542
Case Questions 544
Discussion Questions 545

Chapter 29 *Real Property and Landlord–Tenant Law* **546**
29-1 Nature of Real Property 547
29-2 Concurrent Estates 548
29-2a Tenancy in Common 548
29-2b Joint Tenancy 548
29-3 Adverse Possession 549
29-3a Entry and Exclusive Possession 549
29-3b Open and Notorious Possession 549
29-3c A Claim Adverse to the Owner 549
29-3d Continuous Possession for the Statutory Period 550
29-4 Land Use Regulation 551
29-4a Zoning 551
29-4b Eminent Domain 551
29-5 Landlord-Tenant Law 552
29-5a Three Legal Areas Combined 552
29-5b Lease 552
29-6 Types of Tenancy 553
29-6a Tenancy for Years 553
29-6b Periodic Tenancy 553
29-6c Tenancy at Will 553
29-6d Tenancy at Sufferance 553
29-7 Landlord's Duties 553
29-7a Duty to Deliver Possession 553
29-7b Quiet Enjoyment 554
29-7c Actual Eviction 554
29-7d Constructive Eviction 554
29-7e Duty to Maintain Premises 554
29-8 Tenant's Duties 556
29-8a Duty to Pay Rent 556
29-8b Duty to Mitigate 557
29-8c Duty to Use Premises Properly 557
29-9 Change in the Parties 558
29-9a Sale of the Property 558
29-9b Assignment and Sublease 558
29-10 Injuries 558
29-10a Tenant's Liability 558
29-10b Landlord's Liability 559
29-10c Crime 559

Chapter Conclusion 560
Exam Review 560
Matching Questions 563
True/False Questions 563
Multiple-Choice Questions 564
Case Questions 565
Discussion Questions 566

Chapter 30 *Personal Property and Bailment* **567**
30-1 Gifts 568
30-1a Intention to Transfer Ownership 568
30-1b Delivery 568
30-1c *Inter Vivos* Gifts and Gifts *Causa Mortis* 569
30-1d Acceptance 570
30-2 Found Property 571
30-3 Bailment 573
30-3a Control 573
30-3b Rights of the Bailee 575
30-3c Duties of the Bailee 575
30-3d Rights and Duties of the Bailor 576
30-3e Liability for Defects 576
30-3f Common Carriers and Contract Carriers 576
30-3g Innkeepers 577

Chapter Conclusion 577
Exam Review 577
Matching Questions 579
True/False Questions 579
Multiple-Choice Questions 580
Case Questions 581
Discussion Questions 582

Chapter 31 *Estate Planning* **584**
31-1 Introduction 585
31-1a Definitions 585
31-1b Purpose 585
31-1c Probate Law 585
31-2 Wills 586
31-2a Requirements for a Valid Will 586
31-2b Spouse's Share 588
31-2c Children's Share 588
31-2d Digital Assets 590
31-2e Amending a Will 591
31-2f Intestacy 591
31-2g Power of Attorney 591
31-2h Probate 591
31-2i Property Not Transferred by Will 592
31-2j Anatomical Gifts 592
31-2k End of Life Health Issues 592

31-3 Trusts   593
  31-3a Advantages and Disadvantages   593
  31-3b Types of Trusts   594
  31-3c Trust Administration   595
  31-3d A Trust's Term   595

Chapter Conclusion   596
Exam Review   596
Matching Questions   598
True/False Questions   598
Multiple-Choice Questions   598
Case Questions   600
Discussion Questions   600

Chapter 32 *Insurance*   **602**

32-1 Introduction   603
32-2 Insurance Contract   604
  32-2a Offer and Acceptance   604
  32-2b Limiting Claims by the
    Insured   604
  32-2c Bad Faith by the Insurer   607
32-3 Types of Insurance   609
  32-3a Property Insurance   609
  32-3b Life Insurance   609
  32-3c Health Insurance   611

32-3d Disability Insurance   611
32-3e Liability Insurance   611
32-3f Automobile Insurance   612

Chapter Conclusion   612
Exam Review   612
Matching Questions   614
True/False Questions   614
Multiple-Choice Questions   614
Case Questions   616
Discussion Questions   617

Appendix A
The Constitution of the United States   A1

Appendix B
Uniform Commercial Code   B1

Appendix C   C1

Glossary   **G1**

Table of Cases   **T1**

Index   **I1**

Looking for more examples for class? Find all of the latest developments on our blog at bizlawupdate.com. To be notified when we post updates, just "like" our Facebook page at Beatty Business Law or follow us on Twitter @bizlawupdate.

NOTE FROM THE AUTHORS

New to This Edition

Cyberlaw and Privacy

We all face profound issues about how to maintain privacy in a digital world. Yes, we want to use the Internet, but we also want to protect our personal data. The cyberlaw chapter now includes a thorough discussion of privacy both on- and offline. It is essential information for anyone who has ever connected to the Internet or worried that private data could become public. This chapter has been moved to the Torts unit.

International Law

In a global world, students clamor for more international law, and many schools require coverage of international issues in every course. The international law chapter has been completely rewritten to provide students with an understanding of the basic structure and impact of international law. It includes a discussion of (1) how international law is created, (2) major treaties and other sources of international law, (3) the world's different legal systems, (4) the application of U.S. law overseas, and (5) the enforceability of foreign laws and treaties in the United States.

A Focus on Students

We have increased coverage of topics that are of particular interest to students, such as social media and technology. Also, the bankruptcy chapter includes a new section on student loans. The crime chapter explores the application of constitutional standards of privacy to new technology such as DNA tests, digital cameras, social media, cellphones, and computers. The consumer law chapter looks at the legal issues raised when students spend money through direct debit and ATM cards.

Enhanced Digital Content—*MindTap*™

Our goal – and yours – is for the students to learn the material. With that goal in mind, we have created a *MindTap*™ product for this book. *MindTap*™ is a fully online, highly personalized learning experience that is easy to use and benefits both instructors and students. The *MindTap* for our book contains a prebuilt Learning Path consisting of four different activities: Worksheets that test basic knowledge of the chapter, Brief Hypotheticals that require students to apply what they have learned, Video Activities that reinforce course concepts, and Case Problem Blueprints that require critical thinking skills. **As an assurance to you, we (the authors) have reviewed every question in the *MindTap* product to ensure that it meets the high standards of our book.**

When students are assigned (and required) to complete the *MindTap* Worksheet questions prior to class, they will be **prepared** for class discussions, and you will know the topics with which they struggle. Recent research indicates that students who are pretested in this way learn the material more fully and perform better on final exams.

MindTap guides students through their course with ease and engagement. Instructors can personalize the prebuilt Learning Path by customizing Cengage Learning resources and adding their own content via apps that integrate into the *MindTap* framework seamlessly with Learning Management Systems.

We recognize that the online experience is as important to the students—and you—as the book itself. Each and every item in the Learning Path is assignable and gradable. This gives instructors the knowledge of class standings and concepts that may be difficult. Additionally, students gain knowledge about where they stand—both individually and compared to the highest performers in class.

To view a demo video and learn more about *MindTap*, please visit **www.cengage.com/mindtap/**.

The Beatty/Samuelson Difference

Our goal in writing this book was to capture the passion and excitement, the sheer enjoyment, of the law. Business law is notoriously complex, and as authors we are obsessed with accuracy. Yet this intriguing subject also abounds with human conflict and hard-earned wisdom, forces that we wanted to use to make this book sparkle.

Once we have the students' attention, our goal is to provide the information they will need as business people and as informed citizens. Of course, we present the *theory* of how laws work, but we also explain when *reality* is different. To take some examples, traditionally business law textbooks have simply taught students that shareholders elect the directors of public companies. Even Executive MBA students rarely understand the reality of corporate elections. But our book explains the truth of corporate power. The practical contracts chapter focuses not on the theory of contract law but also on the real-life issues involved in making an agreement: Do I need a lawyer? Should the contract be in writing? What happens if the contract has an unclear provision or an important typo? What does all that boilerplate mean anyway?

Nobel laureate Paul Samuelson famously said, "Let those who will write the nation's laws, if I can write its textbooks." As authors, we never forget the privilege—and responsibility—of educating a generation of business law students. Our goal is to write a business law text like no other—a book that is authoritative, realistic, and yet a pleasure to read.

Strong Narrative. The law is full of great stories, and we use them. Your students and ours should come to class curious and excited. Look at Chapter 5, on dispute resolution. No tedious list of next steps in litigation, this chapter teaches the subject by tracking a double-indemnity lawsuit. An executive is dead. Did he drown accidentally, obligating the insurance company to pay? Or did the businessman commit suicide, voiding the policy? The student follows the action from the discovery of the body, through each step of the lawsuit, to the final appeal.

Every chapter begins with a story, either fictional or real, to illustrate the issues in the chapter. Over the years, we have learned how much more successfully we can teach when our students are intrigued. They only learn when they want to learn.

Context. Many of our students were not yet born when Bill Clinton was elected president. They come to college with varying levels of preparation; many arrive from other countries. We have found that to teach business law most effectively we must provide its context. In the chapter on employment discrimination, we provide a historical perspective to help students understand how the laws developed. Only with this background can students grasp the importance and impact of our laws.

Student Reaction. Students have responded enthusiastically to our approach. One professor asked a student to compare our book with the one that the class was then using. This was the student's reaction: "I really enjoy reading the [Beatty/Samuelson] textbook, and I have decided that I will give you this memo ASAP, but I am keeping the book until Wednesday so that I may continue reading. Thanks! :-)"

This text has been used in courses for undergraduates, MBAs, and Executive MBAs, with students ranging in age from 18 to 55. This book works, as some unsolicited comments indicate:

- From Amazon:

  o "Glad I purchased this. It really helps put the law into perspective and allows me as a leader to make intelligent decisions. Thanks."
  o "I enjoyed learning business law and was happy my college wanted this book. THUMBS UP!"

- From undergraduates:

  o "This is the best textbook I have had in college, on any subject."
  o "The textbook is awesome. A lot of the time I read more than what is assigned—I just don't want to stop."
  o "I had no idea business law could be so interesting."

- From MBA students:

  o "Actually enjoyed reading the text book, which is a rarity for me."
  o "The law textbook was excellent through and through."

- From a Fortune 500 vice president, enrolled in an Executive MBA program:

  o "I really liked the chapters. They were crisp, organized, and current. The information was easy to understand and enjoyable."

- From business law professors:

  o "The clarity of presentation is superlative. I have never seen the complexity of contract law made this readable."
  o "With your book, we have great class discussions."

- From a state supreme court justice:

  o "This book is a valuable blend of rich scholarship and easy readability. Students and professors should rejoice with this publication."

Current.   This fifth edition contains more than 30 new cases. Almost all were reported within the last two or three years, and many within the last 12 months. We never include a new court opinion merely because it is recent. Yet the law evolves continually, and our willingness to toss out old cases and add important new ones ensures that this book—and its readers—remain on the frontier of legal developments.

Authoritative.   We insist, as you do, on a law book that is indisputably accurate. A professor must teach with assurance, confident that every paragraph is the result of exhaustive research and meticulous presentation. Dozens of tough-minded people spent thousands of hours reviewing this book, and we are delighted with the stamp of approval we have received from trial and appellate judges, working attorneys, scholars, and teachers.

We reject the cloudy definitions and fuzzy explanations that can invade judicial opinions and legal scholarship. To highlight the most important rules, we use bold print, and then follow with vivacious examples written in clear, forceful English.

We cheerfully venture into contentious areas, relying on very recent decisions. Can a creditor pierce the veil of an LLC? Are stop and frisk policies constitutional? Are employees protected against bullying in the workplace? Where there is doubt about the current (or future) status of a doctrine, we say so. We want you to have absolute trust in this book.

Humor.   Throughout the text, we use humor—judiciously—to lighten and enlighten. Not surprisingly, students have applauded this—but is it appropriate? How dare we employ levity in this venerable discipline? We offer humor because we take law seriously. We revere the law for its ancient traditions, its dazzling intricacy, its relentless though imperfect attempt to give order and decency to our world. Because we are confident of our respect for the law, we are not afraid to employ some levity. Leaden prose masquerading as legal scholarship does no honor to the field.

Humor also helps retention. Research shows that the funnier or more bizarre the example, the longer students will remember it. Students are more likely to remember a contract problem described in a fanciful setting, and from that setting recall the underlying principle. By contrast, one widget is hard to distinguish from another.

Features

We chose the features for our book with great care. Each feature responds to an essential pedagogical goal. Here are some of those goals and the matching feature.

Exam Strategy

GOAL: To help students learn more effectively and to prepare for exams. In developing this feature, we asked ourselves: What do students want? The short answer is—a good grade in the course. How many times a semester does a student ask you, "What can I do to study for the exam?" We are happy to help them study and earn a good grade because that means that they will also be learning.

Several times per chapter, we stop the action and give students a two-minute quiz. In the body of the text, again in the end-of-chapter review, and also in the Instructor's Manual, we present a typical exam question. Here lies the innovation: We guide the student in analyzing the issue. We teach the reader—over and over—how to approach a question: to start with the overarching principle, examine the fine point raised in the question, apply the analysis that courts use, and deduce the right answer. This skill is second nature to lawyers but not to students. Without practice, too many students panic, jumping at a convenient answer, and leaving aside the tools they have spent the course acquiring. Let's change that. Students love the Exam Strategy feature.

You Be the Judge

GOAL: Get them thinking independently. When reading case opinions, students tend to accept the court's "answer." Judges, of course, try to reach decisions that appear indisputable, when in reality they may be controversial—or wrong. From time to time, we want students to think through the problem and reach their own answer. Most chapters contain a "You Be the Judge" feature, providing the facts of the case and conflicting appellate arguments. The court's decision, however, appears only in the Instructor's Manual. Since students do not know the result, discussions are more complex and lively. Students disagree with the court at least half the time. They are thinking.

Ethics

GOAL: Make ethics real. We ask ethical questions about cases, legal issues, and commercial practices. Is it fair for one party to void a contract by arguing, months after the fact, that there was no consideration? What is wrong with bribery? We believe that asking the questions and encouraging discussion reminds students that ethics is an essential element of justice and of a satisfying life.

Cases

GOAL: Bring case law alive. Each case begins with a summary of the facts followed by a statement of both the issue and the decision. Next comes a summary of the court's opinion. We have written this ourselves, to make the judges' reasoning accessible to all readers, while retaining the court's focus and the decision's impact.

In the principal cases in each chapter, we provide the state or federal citation, unless it is not available, in which case we use the LEXIS and Westlaw citations. We also give students a brief description of the court.

End-of-Chapter Exam Review and Questions

GOAL: Encourage students to practice! At the end of the chapters, we provide a list of review points and several additional Exam Strategy exercises in the Question/Strategy/Result format. We also challenge the students with 25 or more problems—Matching, True/False, Multiple-Choice, Case Questions, and Discussion Questions. The questions include the following:

- **You Be the Judge Writing Problem**. The students are given appellate arguments on both sides of the question and must prepare a written opinion.

- **Ethics**. This question highlights the ethical issues of a dispute and calls upon the student to formulate a specific, reasoned response.

- **CPA Questions**. For topics covered by the CPA exam, administered by the American Institute of Certified Public Accountants, the Exam Review includes questions from previous CPA exams.

Answers to all the odd-numbered questions are available in Appendix C of the book.

Author Transition

Jeffrey Beatty fought an unremitting 10-year battle against a particularly aggressive form of leukemia, which, despite his great courage and determination, he ultimately lost. Jeffrey, a gentleman to the core, was an immensely kind, funny, and thoughtful human being, someone who sang and danced, and who earned the respect and affection of colleagues and students alike. In writing these books, he wanted students to see and understand the impact of law in their everyday lives as well as its role in supporting human dignity, and what's more, he wanted students to laugh.

Jeffrey was a hard act to follow. We feel immensely grateful to have found a worthy successor in Patricia Sánchez Abril. A tenured member of the faculty at the University of Miami School of Business Administration, Patricia is a devoted teacher who has won awards for her teaching in both the undergraduate and graduate programs.. She has also published widely in scholarly journals and has won awards for her scholarship. In 2011, the Academy of Legal Studies in Business honored her with its Distinguished Junior Faculty Award and in 2014 awarded her the Outstanding Distinguished Proceedings Paper award.

TEACHING MATERIALS

For more information about any of these ancillaries, contact your Cengage/South-Western Legal Studies in Business Sales Representative for more details, or visit the Beatty *Introduction to Business Law* website at **www.cengagebrain.com**.

MindTap. *MindTap*™ is a fully online, highly personalized learning experience combining readings, multimedia, activities, and assessments into a singular Learning Path. Instructors can personalize the Learning Path by customizing Cengage Learning resources and adding their own content via apps that integrate into the *MindTap* framework seamlessly with Learning Management Systems. To view a demo video and learn more about *MindTap*, please visit **www.cengage.com/mindtap/**.

Instructor's Manual.   The Instructor's Manual, available on the Instructor's Support Site at **www.cengagebrain.com/**, includes special features to enhance class discussion and student progress:

- Exam Strategy Problems. If your students would like more of these problems, there is an additional section of Exam Strategy problems in the Instructor's Manual.

- Dialogues. These are a series of questions-and-answers on pivotal cases and topics.

- The questions provide enough material to teach a full session. In a pinch, you could walk into class with nothing but the manual and use the Dialogues to conduct an exciting class.

- Action learning ideas: interviews, quick research projects, drafting exercises, classroom activities, commercial analyses, and other suggested assignments that get students out of their chairs and into the diverse settings of business law.

- A chapter theme and a quote of the day.

- Current Focus. This feature offers updates of text material.

- Additional cases and examples.

- Answers to You Be the Judge cases from the text and to the Exam Review questions found at the end of each chapter.

Test Bank.   The test bank offers hundreds of essay, short-answer, and multiple-choice problems, and may be obtained online at **www.cengagebrain.com**.

Cognero Testing Software—Computerized Testing Software.   This testing software contains all of the questions in the printed test bank. This easy-to-use test creation software program is compatible with Microsoft Windows. Instructors can add or edit questions, instructions, and answers; they can also select questions by previewing them on the screen, selecting them randomly, or selecting them by number. Cognero gives instructors the ability to create and administer quizzes online, whether over the Internet, a local area network (LAN), or a wide area network (WAN). The Cognero testing software is available online.

Microsoft PowerPoint Lecture Review Slides.   PowerPoint slides are available for use by instructors for enhancing their lectures. Download these slides at **www.cengagebrain.com**.

Business Law Digital Video Library.   This dynamic online video library features more than 90 video clips that spark class discussion and clarify core legal principles. Access to the Business Law Digital Video Library is available as an optional package with each new student text at no additional charge. Students with used books can purchase access to the video clips online. For more information about the Business Law Digital Video Library, visit **www.cengage.com/blaw/dvl**.

Interaction with the Authors.   This is our standard: Every professor who adopts this book must have a superior experience. We are available to help in any way we can. Adopters of this text often call us or email us to ask questions, obtain a syllabus, offer suggestions, share pedagogical concerns, or inquire about ancillaries. One of the pleasures of working on this project has been our discovery that the text provides a link to so many colleagues around the country. We value those connections, are eager to respond, and would be happy to hear from you.

Jeffrey F. Beatty

Susan S. Samuelson
Phone: (617) 353-2033
Email: ssamuels@bu.edu

Patricia Sánchez Abril
Phone: (305) 284-6999
Email: pabril@bus.miami.edu

ACKNOWLEDGMENTS

We are grateful to the following reviewers who gave such helpful comments for the first five editions:

Joseph F Adamo
Cazenovia College

Joan P. Alexander
Nassau College

Victor Alicea
Normandale College

Basil N. Apostle
Purchase College, SUNY

Lee Ash
Skagit Valley College

Loretta Beavers
Southwest Virginia Community College

Theodore R. Bolema
Anderson Economic Group, LLC

Joseph T. Bork
University of St. Thomas

Karen E. Bork
Northwood University

Beverly Woodall Broman
Everest Institute—Pittsburgh, PA

Jeff W. Bruns
Bacone College

E. Katy Burnett
Kentucky Community & Technical College Systems Online

Bruce W. Byars
University of North Dakota

Dianne L. Caron
The Art Institute of Seattle

Amy F. Chataginer
Mississippi Gulf Coast Community College

Tim Collins
Kaplan Career Institute—ICM Campus

Michael Combe
Eagle Gate College

Mark DeAngelis
University of Connecticut

Laura C. Denton
Maysville Community and Technical College

Julia G. Derrick
Brevard Community College

Dr. Joe D. Dillsaver
Northeastern State University

Ted Dinges
Metropolitan Community College—Longview

Nicki M. Dodd
Guilford Technical Community College

Bradley L. Drell
Louisiana College, Pineville

Donna N. Dunn
Beaufort County Community College

Jameka Ellison
Everest University—Lakeland

Traci C. Etheridge
Richmond Community College

Gail S.M. Evans
University of Houston—Downtown

Alfred E. Fabian
Ivy Tech Community College

Jerrold M. Fleisher
Dominican College—Orangeburg, New York

Andrea Foster
John Tyler Community College—Chester Campus

Daniel F. Gant
Savannah River College

Jolena M. Grande
Cypress College, CA

Marina Grau
Houston Community College

Wade T. Graves
Grayson County College

John P. Gray
Faulkner University

Scott R. Gunderson
Dakota County Technical College, MN

Diane A. Hagan
Ohio Business College—Sandusky

Ruth Ann Hall
The University of Alabama

Robert L. Hamilton
Columbia College—Orlando Campus

Jason M. Harris
Augustana College, SD

Toni R. Hartley
Laurel Business Institute

Tony Hunnicutt
Ouachita Technical College

Robert F. Huyck
Mohawk Valley Community College

Christopher R. Inama
Golden Gate University

Joseph V. Ippolito
Brevard College

David I. Kapelner
Merrimack College

Jack E. Karns
East Carolina University

Mark King
Indiana Business College

Hal P. Kingsley
Trocaire College

Kailani Knutson
Porterville College

Samuel Kohn
New York Institute of Technology

Carl Korman
Community College of Vermont

Douglas Kulper
University of California, Santa Barbara

Kimberly S. Lamb
Stautzenberger College

Greg Lauer
North Iowa Area Community College

Dennis G. Lee
Southwest Georgia Technical College

Paul Leiman
Johns Hopkins University

Paulette S. León
Northwestern Technical College—Rock Spring, GA

Leslie S. Lukasik
Skagit Valley College, Whidbey Island Campus

David MacCulloch
Westmont College

Jerome P. McCluskey
Manhattanville College

MarySheila McDonald
Philadelphia University

Arin S. Miller
Keiser University

Ronald K. Minnehan
California Lutheran University

Tonia Hap Murphy
University of Notre Dame

John J. Nader
Davenport University

Terri J. Nix
Howard College

Cliff Olson
Southern Adventist University

Steven C. Palmer
Eastern New Mexico University

Denielle Pemberton
Johns Hopkins University

Nicole Pierone
Yakima Valley Community College

Linda E. Plowman
The Art Institute of Pittsburgh

Matthew B. Probst
Ivy Tech Community College of Indiana
—Lawrenceburg

Anne Montgomery Ricketts
University of Findlay

Sandra Robertson
Thomas Nelson Community College

Bruce L. Rockwood
Bloomsburg University of Pennsylvania

R. J. Ruppenthal
Evergreen Valley College

Mark R. Solomon
Walsh College—Troy, MI

Harilaos I. Sorovigas
Michigan State University

Kim D. Steinmetz
Everest College—Phoenix, AZ

Kenneth R. Taurman, Jr., JD
Indiana University Southeast

Natalie L. Turner
Middle Georgia Technical College—
Warner Robins

Marion R. Tuttle
New Jersey Institute of Technology

Janet M. Velazquez

Kansas City Kansas Community
College

William V. Vetter
Prairie View A&M University

Jamie S. Waldo
Chadron State College

Deborah B. Walsh
Middlesex Community College, MA

David B. Washington
Augsburg College

Albert B. West
Providence College School of Continuing
Ed.—Providence, R.I.

Mathew C. Williams
Clover Park Technical College

Ira Wilsker
Lamar Institute of Technology

Kelly Collins Woodford
University of South Alabama

Gilbert Ybarra
International Business College

John W. Yeargain
Southeastern Louisiana University

Eric D. Yordy
Northern Arizona University

Bruce Yuille
Mid Michigan Community
College

ABOUT THE AUTHORS

Jeffrey F. Beatty was an associate professor of business law at the Boston University School of Management. After receiving his B.A. from Sarah Lawrence and his J.D. from Boston University, he practiced with the Greater Boston Legal Services representing indigent clients. At Boston University, he won the Metcalf Cup and Prize, the university's highest teaching award. Professor Beatty also wrote plays and television scripts that were performed in Boston, London, and Amsterdam.

Susan S. Samuelson is a professor of business law at Boston University's School of Management. After earning her A.B. at Harvard University and her J.D. at Harvard Law School, Professor Samuelson practiced with the firm of Choate, Hall and Stewart. She has written many articles on legal issues for scholarly and popular journals, including the *American Business Law Journal, Ohio State Law Journal, Boston University Law Review, Harvard Journal on Legislation, National Law Journal, Sloan Management Review, Inc. Magazine, Better Homes and Gardens,* and *Boston Magazine.* At Boston University, she won the Broderick Prize for excellence in teaching. For more than a decade, Professor Samuelson was the faculty director of the Boston University Executive MBA program.

Patricia Sánchez Abril is an associate professor of business law at the University of Miami School of Business Administration. Professor Abril's research has appeared in the *American Business Law Journal, Harvard Journal of Law & Technology, Florida Law Review, Houston Law Review, Wake Forest Law Review, Northwestern Journal of Technology and Intellectual Property*, and *Columbia Business Law Journal*, among other journals. In 2011, the *American Business Law Journal* honored her with its Distinguished Junior Faculty Award, in recognition of exceptional early career achievement. In 2014, one of her articles on privacy won the Outstanding Proceedings competition at the annual conference of the Academy of Legal Studies in Business. Professor Abril has won awards for her teaching in both the undergraduate and graduate programs at the University of Miami.

For Jeffrey, best of
colleagues and dearest of
friends.
s.s.s.

The Legal Environment

CHAPTER 1

INTRODUCTION TO LAW

The Pagans were a motorcycle gang with a reputation for violence. Two of its rougher members, Rhino and Backdraft, entered a tavern called the Pub Zone, shoving their way past the bouncer. The pair wore gang insignia, in violation of the bar's rules. For a while, all was quiet, as the two sipped drinks at the bar. Then they followed an innocent patron toward the men's room, and things happened fast.

"Wait a moment," you may be thinking, "are we reading a chapter on business law or one about biker crimes in a roadside tavern?" Both.

Law is powerful, essential, and fascinating. We hope this book will persuade you of all three ideas. Law can also be surprising. Later in the chapter we will return to the Pub Zone (with armed guards) and follow Rhino and Backdraft to the back of the pub. Yes, the pair engaged in street crime, which is hardly a focus of this text. However, their criminal acts will enable us to explore one of the law's basic principles, negligence. Should a pub owner pay money damages to the victim of gang violence? The owner herself did nothing aggressive. Should she have prevented the harm? Does her failure to stop the assault make her liable?

We place great demands on our courts, asking them to make our large, complex, and sometimes violent society into a safer, fairer, more orderly place. The Pub Zone case is a good example of how judges reason their way through the convoluted issues involved. What began as a gang incident ends up as a matter of commercial liability. We will traipse after Rhino and Backdraft because they have a lesson to teach anyone who enters the world of business.

> **Law is powerful, essential, and fascinating.**

© Creative Travel Projects/Shutterstock.com

1-1 THREE IMPORTANT IDEAS ABOUT LAW

1-1a Power

A driver is seriously injured in an automobile accident, and the jury concludes that the car had a design defect. The jurors award her *$29 million*. A senior vice president congratulates himself on a cagey stock purchase but is horrified to receive, not profits, but a prison sentence. A homeless person, ordered by local police to stop panhandling, ambles into court and walks out with an order permitting him to beg on the city's streets. The strong hand of the law touches us all. To understand something that powerful is itself power.

Suppose, some years after graduation, you are a mid-level manager at Sublime Corp., which manufactures and distributes video games. You are delighted with this important position in an excellent company—and especially glad that you bring legal knowledge to the job. Sarah, an expert at computer-generated imagery, complains that Rob, her boss, is constantly touching her and making lewd comments. That is sexual harassment, and your knowledge of *employment law* helps you respond promptly and carefully.

You have dinner with Jake, who has his own software company. Jake wants to manufacture an exciting new video game in cooperation with Sublime, but you are careful not to create a binding deal (*contract law*). Jake mentions that a similar game is already on the market. Do you have the right to market one like it? That answer you already know (*intellectual property law*).

LuYu, your personnel manager, reports that a silicon chip worker often seems drowsy; she suspects drug use. Does she have the right to test him (*constitutional law* and *employment law*)? On the other hand, if she fails to test him, could Sublime Corp. be liable for any harm the worker does (*tort law* and *agency law*)?

In a mere week, you might use your legal knowledge a dozen times, helping Sublime to steer clear of countless dangers. During the coming year, you encounter many other legal issues, and you and your corporation benefit from your skills.

It is not only as a corporate manager that you will confront the law. As a voter, investor, juror, entrepreneur, and community member, you will influence and be affected by the law. Whenever you take a stance about a legal issue, whether in the corporate office, the voting booth, or as part of local community groups, you help to create the social fabric of our nation. Your views are vital. This book will offer you knowledge and ideas from which to form and continually reassess your legal opinions and values.

1-1b Importance

We depend upon laws for safe communities, functioning economies, and personal liberties. An easy way to gauge the importance of law is to glance through any newspaper and read about nations that lack a strong system of justice. Notice that these countries cannot ensure physical safety and personal liberties. They also fail to offer economic opportunity for most citizens. We may not always like the way our legal system works, but we depend on it to keep our society functioning.

1-1c Fascination

Law is intriguing. When the jury awarded $29 million against an auto manufacturer for a defective car design, it certainly demonstrated the law's power. But was the jury's decision right? Should a company have to pay that much for one car accident? Maybe the jury was reacting emotionally. Or perhaps the anger caused by terrible trauma *should* be part of a court case. These are not abstract speculations for philosophers. Verdicts such as this may cause each of us to pay more for our next automobile. Then again, we may be driving safer cars.

1-2 SOURCES OF CONTEMPORARY LAW

It would be nice if we could look up "the law" in one book, memorize it, and then apply it. But the law is not that simple. Principles and rules of law come from many different sources. Why is this so?

We inherited a complex structure of laws from England. Additionally, ours is a nation born in revolution and created, in large part, to protect the rights of its people from the government. Our country's Founders created a national government but insisted that the individual states maintain control in many areas. As a result, each state has its own government with exclusive power over many important areas of our lives. What the Founders created was **federalism**: a double-layered system of government, with the national government and state governments each exercising important but limited powers. To top it off, the Founders guaranteed many rights to the people alone, ordering national and state governments to keep clear. They achieved all of this in one remarkable document: the United States Constitution.

Federalism
A double-layered system of government, with the national and state governments each exercising important but limited powers

1-2a United States Constitution

U.S. Constitution
The supreme law of the United States

America's greatest legal achievement was the writing of the **United States Constitution** in 1787. It is the supreme law of the land, and any law that conflicts with it is void. This federal Constitution does three basic things. First, it establishes the national government of the United States, with its three branches. Second, it creates a system of checks and balances among the branches. And, third, the Constitution guarantees many basic rights to the American people.

Branches of Government

The Founders sought a division of government power. They did not want all power centralized in a monarch or anyone else. And so the Constitution divides legal authority into three pieces: legislative, executive, and judicial power.

Legislative power gives the ability to create new laws. In Article I, the Constitution gives this power to the Congress, which is comprised of two chambers—a Senate and a House of Representatives.

The House of Representatives has 435 voting members. A state's voting power is based on its population. Large states (Texas, California, Florida) send dozens of representatives to the House. Some small states (Wyoming, North Dakota, Delaware) send only one. The Senate has 100 voting members—two from each state.

Executive power is the authority to enforce laws. Article II of the Constitution establishes the president as commander-in-chief of the armed forces and the head of the executive branch of the federal government.

Judicial power gives the right to interpret laws and determine their validity. Article III places the Supreme Court at the head of the judicial branch of the federal government. Interpretive power is often underrated, but it is often as important at the ability to create laws in the first place. For instance, the Supreme Court ruled that privacy provisions of the Constitution protect a woman's right to abortion, although neither the word "privacy" nor "abortion" appears in the text of the Constitution.[1] And at times, courts void laws altogether. For example, in 1995, the Supreme Court ruled that the Gun-Free School Zones Act of 1990 was unconstitutional because it exceeded Congressional power over interstate commerce.[2]

---

[1] Roe v. Wade, 410 U.S. 113 (1973).
[2] United States v. Alfonso Lopez, Jr., 514 U.S. 549 (1995).

Checks and Balances

The authors of the Constitution were not content to divide government power three ways. They also wanted to give each part of the government the power over the other two branches. Many people complain about "gridlock" in Washington, but the government is sluggish by design. The Founders wanted to create a system that, without broad agreement, would tend towards inaction. The president can veto congressional legislation. Congress can impeach the president. The Supreme Court can void laws passed by Congress. The president appoints judges to the federal courts, but these nominees do not serve unless approved by the Senate.

Many of these checks and balances will be examined in more detail later in the text.

Fundamental Rights

The Constitution also grants many of our most basic liberties. For the most part, they are found in the amendments to the Constitution. The First Amendment guarantees the rights of free speech, free press, and the free exercise of religion. The Fourth, Fifth, and Sixth Amendments protect the rights of any person accused of a crime. Other amendments ensure that the government treats all people equally and that it pays for any property it takes from a citizen.

By creating a limited government of three branches and guaranteeing basic liberties to all citizens, the Constitution has become one of the most important documents ever written.

1-2b Statutes

The second important source of law is statutory law. The Constitution gave to the United States Congress the power to pass laws on various subjects. These laws are called **statutes**, and they can cover absolutely any topic at all, so long as they do not violate the Constitution.

Almost all statutes are created by the same method. An idea for a new law—on taxes, health care, texting while driving, or anything else—is first proposed in the Congress. This idea is called a *bill*. The House and Senate then independently vote on the bill. To pass Congress, the bill must get approval from a simple majority of each of these chambers.

If Congress passes a bill, it goes to the White House. If the president signs it, a new statute is created. It is no longer a mere idea; it is the law of the land. If a president *vetoes* a bill, it does not become a statute unless Congress overrides the veto. To do that, both the House and the Senate must approve the bill by a two-thirds majority. At this point, it becomes a statute without the president's signature.

Statute
A law passed by Congress or by a state legislature

1-2c Common Law

Binding legal ideas often come from the courts. Judges generally follow *precedent*. When courts decide a case, they tend to apply the same legal rules that other courts have used in similar cases. **The principle that precedent is binding on later cases is *stare decisis*, which means "let the decision stand."** *Stare decisis* makes the law predictable, and this in turn enables businesses and private citizens to plan intelligently.

It is important to note that precedent is only binding on *lower* courts. If the Supreme Court, for example, decided a case in one way in 1965, it is under no obligation to follow precedent if the same issue arises in 2020.

Sometimes, this is quite beneficial. In 1896, the Supreme Court decided (unbelievably) that segregation—separating people by race in schools, hotels, public transportation, and so on—was legal. In 1954, on the exact same issue, the Court changed its mind.

In other circumstances, it is more difficult to see the value in breaking with an established rule.

Stare decisis
The principle that precedent is binding on later cases

1-2d Court Orders

Judges have the authority to issue court orders that place binding obligations on specific people or companies. An injunction, for example, is a court order to stop doing something. A judge might order a stalker to stay more than 500 yards away from an ex-boyfriend or girlfriend. Courts have the authority to imprison or fine those who violate their orders.

1-2e Administrative Law

In a society as large and complex as ours, the executive and legislative branches of government cannot oversee all aspects of commerce. Congress passes statutes about air safety, but United States senators do not stand around air traffic towers, serving coffee to keep everyone awake. The executive branch establishes rules concerning how foreign nationals enter the United States, but presidents are reluctant to sit on the dock of the bay, watching the ships come in. Administrative agencies do this day-to-day work.

> **Senators do not stand around air traffic towers, serving coffee to keep everyone awake.**

Most government agencies are created by Congress. Familiar examples include the Environmental Protection Agency (EPA), the Securities and Exchange Commission (SEC), and the Internal Revenue Service (IRS), whose feelings are hurt if it does not hear from you every April 15. Agencies have the power to create laws called *regulations*.

1-3 CLASSIFICATIONS OF LAW

We have seen where laws come from. Now we need to classify them. First, we will distinguish between criminal and civil law. Then we will take a look at the intersection between law and morality.

1-3a Criminal and Civil Law

Criminal law
Concerns behavior so threatening that society prohibits it

It is a crime to embezzle money from an employer, to steal a car, and to sell cocaine. **Criminal law concerns behavior so threatening that society outlaws it altogether. Most criminal laws are statutes, passed by Congress or a state legislature**. The government itself prosecutes the wrongdoer, regardless of what the bank president or car owner wants. A district attorney, paid by the government, brings the case to court. The injured party, for example the owner of the stolen car, is not in charge of the case, although she may appear as a witness. The government will seek to punish the defendant with a prison sentence, a fine, or both. If there is a fine, the money goes to the state, not to the injured party.

Civil law
Regulates the rights and duties between parties

Civil law is different, and most of this book is about civil law. **Civil law regulates the rights and duties between parties**. Tracy agrees in writing to lease you a 30,000-square-foot store in her shopping mall. She now has a legal duty to make the space available. But then another tenant offers her more money, and she refuses to let you move in. Tracy has violated her duty, but she has not committed a crime. The government will not prosecute the case. It is up to you to file a civil lawsuit. Your case will be based on the common law of contracts. You will also seek equitable relief—namely, an injunction ordering Tracy not to lease to anyone else. You should win the suit, and you will get your injunction and some money damages. But Tracy will not go to jail.

Some conduct involves both civil and criminal law. Suppose Tracy is so upset over losing the court case that she becomes drunk and causes a serious car accident. She has committed the crime of driving while intoxicated, and the state will prosecute. Tracy may be fined or imprisoned. She has also committed negligence, and the injured party will file a lawsuit against her, seeking money.

1-3b Law and Morality

Law is different from morality, yet the two are obviously linked. There are many instances when the law duplicates what all of us would regard as a moral position. It is negligence to drive too fast in a school district, and few would dispute the moral value of that law. And similarly with contract law: If the owner of land agrees in writing to sell property to a buyer at a stated price, the seller must go through with the deal, and the legal outcome matches our moral expectations.

On the other hand, we have had laws that we now clearly regard as immoral. Seventy-five years ago, a factory owner could legally fire a worker for any reason at all—including, for example, her religion. It is immoral to fire a worker because she is Jewish—and today, the law prohibits it. Finally, there are legal issues where the morality is not so clear. Suppose you serve alcohol to a guest who becomes intoxicated and then causes an automobile accident, seriously injuring a pedestrian. Should you, the social host, be liable? This is an issue of tort liability, which we examine in Chapter 9. As with many topics in this book, the problem has no easy answer. As you learn the law, you will have an opportunity to re-examine your own moral beliefs. One of the goals of Chapter 2, on ethics, is to offer you new tools for that task. But our ethics discussion does not end there. Throughout the text, you will find ethics questions and features, like the one that follows, which ask you to grapple with the moral dimensions of legal questions.

Ethics It was a cold winter's day. In one of New York City's dank, dark subway stations, dozens of people waited for the next train. All of a sudden, a man was shoved onto the subway tracks. He screamed but since no one helped, he was crushed to death by an oncoming train.[3]

Some of the bystanders were so busy on their smartphones, they did not even hear the man's screams for help. Use of technology has changed our awareness of our surroundings and our sense of civility and duty to those around us.

Other witnesses pulled out their phones to capture images and videos of the last minutes of the victim's life. One man sold his picture of the episode to the *New York Post*, which published it on the cover the next day. Others shared their videos on YouTube.

What are the moral obligations of each of these groups of witnesses? Who has acted most unethically (if anyone)? Remember that the decision to help (or not) is one that is made in a split second. What would you have done?

---

[3]Christine Rosen, "The Gadget and the Bad Samaritan," *The Wall Street Journal*, Oct. 26–27, 2013.

1-4 WORKING WITH THE BOOK'S FEATURES

In this section, we introduce a few of the book's features and discuss how you can use them effectively. We will start with cases.

1-4a Analyzing a Case

A law case is the decision a court has made in a civil lawsuit or criminal prosecution. Cases are the heart of the law and an important part of this book. Reading them effectively takes practice. This chapter's opening scenario is fictional, but the following real case involves a similar situation. Who can be held liable for the assault? Let's see.

KUEHN V. PUB ZONE

364 N.J. Super. 301
Superior Court of New Jersey, 2003

CASE SUMMARY

Facts: Maria Kerkoulas owned the Pub Zone bar. She knew that several motorcycle gangs frequented the tavern. From her own experience tending bar, and conversations with city police, she knew that some of the gangs, including the Pagans, were dangerous and prone to attack customers for no reason. Kerkoulas posted a sign prohibiting any motorcycle gangs from entering the bar while wearing "colors"; that is, insignia of their gangs. She believed that gangs without their colors were less prone to violence, and experience proved her right.

Rhino, Backdraft, and several other Pagans, all wearing colors, pushed their way past the tavern's bouncer and approached the bar. Although Kerkoulas saw their colors, she allowed them to stay for one drink. They later moved towards the back of the pub, and Kerkoulas believed they were departing. In fact, they followed a customer named Karl Kuehn to the men's room, where, without any provocation, they savagely beat him. Kuehn was knocked unconscious and suffered brain hemorrhaging, disc herniation, and numerous fractures of facial bones. He was forced to undergo various surgeries, including eye reconstruction.

Although the government prosecuted Rhino and Backdraft for their vicious assault, our case does not concern that prosecution. Kuehn sued the Pub Zone, and that is the case we will read. The jury awarded him $300,000 in damages. However, the trial court judge overruled the jury's verdict. He granted a judgment for the Pub Zone,

meaning that the tavern owed nothing. The judge ruled that the pub's owner could not have foreseen the attack on Kuehn and had no duty to protect him from an outlaw motorcycle gang. Kuehn appealed, and the appeals court's decision follows.

Issue: *Did the Pub Zone have a duty to protect Kuehn from the Pagans' attack?*

Decision: Yes, the Pub Zone had a duty to protect Kuehn. The decision is reversed, and the jury's verdict is reinstated.

Reasoning: Whether a duty exists depends on the foreseeability of the harm, its potential severity, and the defendant's ability to prevent the injury. A court should also evaluate society's interest in the dispute.

A business owner generally has no duty to protect a customer from acts of a third party unless experience suggests that there is danger. However, if the owner could in fact foresee injury, she is obligated to take reasonable safety precautions.

Kerkoulas knew that the Pagans engaged in random violence. She realized that when gang members entered the pub, they endangered her customers. That is why she prohibited bikers from wearing their colors—a reasonable rule. Regrettably, the pub failed to enforce the rule. Pagans were allowed to enter wearing their colors, and the pub did not call the police. The pub's behavior was unreasonable, and it is liable to Kuehn.

Analysis

Let's take it from the top. The case is called *Kuehn v. Pub Zone*. Karl Kuehn is the **plaintiff**, the person who is suing. The Pub Zone is being sued and is called the **defendant**. In this example, the plaintiff's name happens to appear first, but that is not always true. When a defendant loses a trial and files an appeal, *some* courts reverse the names of the parties for the appeal case.

The next lines give the legal citation, which indicates where to find the case in a law library or online.

The *Facts* section provides a background to the lawsuit, written by the authors of this text. The court's own explanation of the facts is often many pages long and may involve complex matters irrelevant to the subject covered in this book, so we relate only what is necessary. This section will usually include some mention of what happened at the trial court. Lawsuits always begin in a trial court. The losing party often appeals to a court of appeals, and it is usually an appeals court decision that we are reading. The trial judge ruled in favor of Pub Zone, but in the appellate decision we are reading, Kuehn won.

The *Issue* section is very important. It tells you what the court had to decide—and why you are reading the case.

The *Decision* section describes the court's answer to the issue posed. A court's decision is often referred to as its **holding**. The court rules that the Pub Zone did have a duty to Kuehn. The court **reverses** the trial court's decision, meaning it declares the lower court's ruling wrong and void. The judges reinstate the jury's verdict. In other cases, an appellate court may **remand** the case; that is, send it back down to the lower court for a new trial or some other action. If this court had agreed with the trial court's decision, the judges would have **affirmed** the lower court's ruling, meaning to uphold it.

The *Reasoning* section explains why the court reached its decision. The actual written decision may be three paragraphs or 75 pages. Some judges offer us lucid prose, while others seem intent on torturing the reader. Judges frequently digress and often discuss matters that are irrelevant to the issue on which this text is focusing. For those reasons, we have taken the court's explanation and cast it in our own words. If you are curious about the full opinion, you can always look it up using the legal citation.

Let us examine the reasoning. The court points out that a defendant is liable only if he has a duty to the plaintiff. Whether there is such a duty depends on the foreseeability of the injury and other factors. The judges are emphasizing that courts do not reach decisions arbitrarily. They attempt to make thoughtful choices, consistent with earlier rulings, which make good sense for the general public.

The court also points out what it is *not* deciding. The court is *not* declaring that all businesses must guarantee the safety of their patrons against acts by third parties. If an owner had no reason to foresee injury from a third party, the owner is probably not liable for such harm. However, if experience indicated that the third party presented serious danger, the owner was obligated to act reasonably. The judges note that Kerkoulas knew the Pagans could be violent and had taken reasonable precautions by prohibiting gang colors. However, the pub failed to enforce its sensible rule and failed even to telephone the police. By the very standard the pub had created, its conduct was unreasonable. The court therefore concludes that the Pub Zone was liable for the Pagans' injury to Kuehn, and the judges reinstate the jury's verdict for the injured man.

Plaintiff
The person who is suing

Defendant
The person being sued

Holding
A court's decision

Reverse
To declare the lower court's ruling wrong and void

Remand
To send a case back down to a lower court

Affirm
To uphold a lower court's ruling

EXAM Strategy

This feature gives you practice analyzing cases the way lawyers do—and the way *you* must, on tests. Law exams are different from most others because you must determine the issue from the facts provided. Too frequently, students faced with a law exam forget that the questions relate to the issues in the text, and those discussed in class. Understandably, students new to law may focus on the wrong information in the problem or rely on material learned elsewhere. The *Exam Strategy* feature teaches you to figure out exactly what issue is at stake and then analyze it in a logical, consistent manner. Here is an example, relating to the element of "duty," which the court discussed in the *Pub Zone* case.

Question: The Big Red Traveling (BRT) Carnival is in town. Tony arrives at 8:00 p.m., parks in the lot, and is robbed at gunpoint by a man who beats him and escapes with his money. There are several police officers on the carnival grounds, but no officer is in the parking lot at the time of the robbery. Tony sues, claiming that brighter lighting and more police in the lot would have prevented the robbery. There has never before been any violent crime—robbery, beating, or other incident—at any BRT carnival. BRT claims it had no duty to protect Tony from this harm. Who is likely to win?

Strategy: Begin by isolating the legal issue. What are the parties disputing? They are debating whether BRT had a duty to protect Tony from an armed robbery committed by a stranger. Now ask yourself: How do courts decide whether a business has a duty to prevent this kind of harm? The Pub Zone case provides our answer. A business owner is not an insurer of the visitor's safety. The owner generally has no duty to protect a customer from the criminal act of a third party unless the owner could foresee it is about to happen. (In the *Pub Zone* case, the business owner *knew* of the gang's violent history and could have foreseen the assault.) Now apply that rule to the facts of this case.

Result: There has never been a violent attack of any kind at a BRT carnival. BRT cannot foresee this robbery, and has no duty to protect against it. The carnival wins.

1-4b "You Be the Judge"

Many cases involve difficult decisions for juries and judges. Often both parties have legitimate, opposing arguments. Most chapters in this book will have a feature called "You Be the Judge," in which we present the facts of a case but not the court's holding. We offer you two opposing arguments based on the kinds of claims the lawyers made in court. We leave it up to you to debate and decide which position is stronger or to add your own arguments to those given.

The following case is another negligence lawsuit, with issues that overlap those of the *Pub Zone* case. This time the court confronts a fight that resulted in death. The victim's distraught family sued the owner of a bar, claiming that an employee was partly responsible for the death. Once again, the defendant asked the court to dismiss the case, claiming he owed no duty to protect the victim—the same argument made by the Pub Zone.

But there is a difference—this time, the defendant owned the bar across the street, not the one where the fight took place. Could this neighbor be held legally responsible for the death? You be the judge.

You be the Judge

Facts: In the days before cell phones, a fight broke out at Happy Jack's Saloon. A good Samaritan ran across the street to the Circle Inn, where he asked the bartender to let him use the telephone to call the police. The bartender refused.

Back at Happy Jack's Saloon, the fight escalated, and a man shot and killed Soldano's father. Soldano sued the owner of the Circle Inn for negligence. He argued the bartender violated a legal duty when he refused to hand over the inn's telephone, and that, as the employer of the bartender, O'Daniels was partially liable for his father's death.

The lower court dismissed the case, citing the principle that generally, a person does not have a legal responsibility to help another unless he created the dangerous situation in the first place. Soldano appealed.

You Be the Judge: *Did the bartender have a duty to allow the use of the Circle Inn's telephone?*

Argument for the Defendant: Your honors, my client did not act wrongfully. He did nothing to create the danger. The fight was not even on his property. We sympathize with the plaintiff, but it is the shooter, and perhaps the bar where the fight took place, who are responsible for his father's death. Our client was not involved. Liability can be stretched only so far.

The court would place a great burden on the citizens of California by going against precedent. The Circle Inn is Mr. O'Daniel's private property. If the court imposes potential liability on him in this case, would citizens be forced to open the doors of their homes whenever a

SOLDANO V. O'DANIELS
141 Cal. App. 3d 443
Court of Appeal of California, 1983

stranger claims an emergency? Criminals would delight in their newfound ability to gain access to businesses and residences by simply demanding to use a phone to "call the police."

The law has developed sensibly. People are left to decide for themselves whether to help in a dangerous situation. They are not legally required to place themselves in harm's way.

Argument for the Plaintiff: Your honors, the Circle Inn's bartender had both a moral and a legal duty to allow the use of his establishment's telephone. The Circle Inn may be privately owned, but it is a business open to the public. Anyone in the world is invited to stop by and order a drink or a meal. The good Samaritan had every right to be there.

We do not argue that the bartender had an obligation to break up the fight or endanger himself in any way. We simply argue he had a responsibility to stand aside and allow a free call on his restaurant's telephone. Any "burden" on him or on the Circle Inn was incredibly slight. The potential benefits were enormous. The trial court made a mistake in concluding that a person *never* has a duty to help another. Such an interpretation makes for poor public policy.

There is no need to radically change the common law. Residences can be excluded from this ruling. People need not be required to allow strangers into their homes. This court can simply determine that businesses have a legal duty to allow the placement of emergency calls during normal business hours.

Chapter Conclusion

We depend upon the law to give us a stable nation and economy, a fair society, a safe place to live and work. But while law is a vital tool for crafting the society we want, there are no easy answers about how to create it. In a democracy, we all participate in the crafting. Legal rules control us, yet we create them. A working knowledge of the law can help build a successful career—and a solid democracy.

EXAM REVIEW

1. **FEDERALISM**   Our federal system of government means that law comes from a national government in Washington, D.C., and from 50 state governments.

2. **SOURCES OF LAW**   The primary sources of contemporary law are:

   - United States Constitution

   - Statutes, which are drafted by legislatures

   - Common law, which is the body of cases decided by judges, as they follow earlier cases, known as *precedent*

   - Court orders, in which a judge which place binding obligations on specific people or companies, and

   - Administrative law, the rules and decisions made by federal and state administrative agencies.

3. **CRIMINAL AND CIVIL LAW**   Criminal law concerns behavior so threatening to society that it is outlawed altogether. Civil law deals with duties and disputes between parties, not outlawed behavior.

EXAM Strategy

Question: Bill and Diane are hiking in the woods. Diane walks down a hill to fetch fresh water. Bill meets a stranger, who introduces herself as Katrina. Bill sells a kilo of cocaine to Katrina, who then flashes a badge and mentions how much she enjoys her job at the Drug Enforcement Agency. Diane, heading back to camp with the water, meets Freddy, a motorist whose car has overheated. Freddy is late for a meeting where he expects to make a $30 million profit; he's desperate for water for his car. He promises to pay Diane $500 tomorrow if she will give him the pail of water, which she does. The next day, Bill is in jail, and Freddy refuses to pay for Diane's water. Explain the criminal law/civil law distinction and what it means to Bill and Diane. Who will do what to whom, with what results?

Strategy: You are asked to distinguish between criminal and civil law. What is the difference? Criminal law concerns behavior that threatens society and is therefore outlawed. The government prosecutes the defendant. Civil law deals with the rights and duties between parties. One party files a suit against the other. Apply those different standards to these facts. (See the "Result" at the end of this section.)

3. Result: The government will prosecute Bill for dealing in drugs. If convicted, he will go to prison. The government will take no interest in Diane's dispute. However, if she chooses, she may sue Freddy for $500, the amount he promised her for the water. In that civil lawsuit, a court will decide whether Freddy must pay what he promised; however, even if Freddy loses, he will not go to jail.

MATCHING QUESTIONS

Match the following terms with their definitions:

___A. Statute   1. Law created by judges

___B. Administrative agencies   2. Let the decision stand

___C. Common law   3. A law passed by Congress or a state legislature

___D. *Stare decisis*   4. The supreme law of the land

___E. United States Constitution   5. The IRS; the EPA; the FCC; the SEC

TRUE/FALSE QUESTIONS

Circle true or false:

1. T F The idea that current cases must be decided based on earlier cases is called legal positivism.
2. T F Civil lawsuits are brought to court by the injured party, but criminal cases must be prosecuted by the government.
3. T F Congress established the federal government by passing a series of statutes.
4. T F The federal government has three branches: executive, legislative, and administrative.
5. T F Law is different from morality, but the two are closely linked.

MULTIPLE-CHOICE QUESTIONS

1. More U.S. law comes from one country than from any other. Which country?
   (a) France
   (b) England
   (c) Germany
   (d) Spain
   (e) Canada

2. Under the United States Constitution, power that is not expressly given to the federal government is retained by:
   (a) the courts.
   (b) the Congress.
   (c) the Founders.
   (d) the states and the people.
   (e) international treaty.

3. Judges use precedent to create what kind of law?
   (a) Common law
   (b) Statutes
   (c) National law
   (d) Local law
   (e) Empirical law

4. If the Congress creates a new statute with the president's support, it must pass the idea by a _____ majority vote in the House and the Senate. If the president vetoes a proposed statute and the Congress wishes to pass it without his support, the idea must pass by a _____ majority vote in the House and Senate.
   (a) simple; simple
   (b) simple; two-thirds
   (c) simple; three-fourths
   (d) two-thirds; three-fourths

5. What part of the Constitution addresses most basic liberties?
   (a) Article I
   (b) Article II
   (c) Article III
   (d) The Amendments

CASE QUESTIONS

1. Union organizers at a hospital wanted to distribute leaflets to potential union members, but hospital rules prohibited leafleting in areas of patient care, hallways, cafeterias, and any areas open to the public. The National Labor Relations Board (NLRB) ruled that these restrictions violated the law and ordered the hospital to permit the activities in the cafeteria and coffee shop. The NLRB cannot create common law or statutory law. What kind of law was it creating?

2. The stock market crash of 1929 and the Great Depression that followed were caused in part because so many investors blindly put their money into stocks they knew nothing about. During the 1920s, it was often impossible for an investor to find out what a corporation was planning to do with its money, who was running the corporation, and many other vital facts. Congress responded by passing the Securities Act of 1933, which required a corporation to divulge more information about itself before it could seek money for a new stock issue. What kind of law did Congress create? Explain the relationship between voters, Congress, and the law.

3. **ETHICS** The greatest of all Chinese lawgivers, Confucius, did not esteem written laws. He believed that good rulers were the best guarantee of justice. Does our legal system rely primarily on the rule of law or the rule of people? Which do you instinctively trust more?

4. Burglar Bob breaks into Vince Victim's house. Bob steals a flat-screen TV and laptop and does a significant amount of damage to the property before he leaves. Fortunately, Vince has a state-of-the-art security system. It captures excellent images of Bob, who is soon caught by police.

   Assume that two legal actions follow, one civil and one criminal. Who will be responsible for bringing the civil case? What will be the outcome if the jury believes that Bob did in fact burgle Vince's house? Who will be responsible for bringing the criminal case? What will the outcome be this time if the jury believes that Bob did in fact burgle Vince's house?

5. *Kuehn v. Pub Zone* and *Soldano v. O'Daniels* both involve attacks in a bar. Should they come out in the same way? If so, which way—in favor of the injured plaintiffs or owner-defendants? Or, should they have different outcomes? What are the key facts that lead you to believe as you do?

DISCUSSION QUESTIONS

1. Do you believe that there are too many lawsuits in the United States? If so, do you place more blame for the problem on lawyers or on individuals who go to court? Is there anything that would help the problem, or will we always have large numbers of lawsuits?

2. In the 1980s, the Supreme Court ruled that it is legal for protesters to burn the American flag. This activity counts as free speech under the Constitution. If the Court hears a new flag-burning case in this decade, should it consider changing its ruling, or should it follow precedent? Is following past precedent something that seems sensible to you: always, usually, sometimes, rarely, or never?

3. When should a business be held legally responsible for customer safety? Consider the following statements, and circle your opinion.

   a. A business should keep customers safe from its own employees.

   strongly agree   agree   neutral
   disagree   strongly disagree

   b. A business should keep customers safe from other customers.

   strongly agree   agree   neutral
   disagree   strongly disagree

   c. A business should keep customers safe from themselves. (Example: an intoxicated customer who can no longer walk straight.)

   strongly agree   agree   neutral
   disagree   strongly disagree

   d. A business should keep people outside its own establishment safe if it is reasonable to do so.

   strongly agree   agree   neutral
   disagree   strongly disagree

4. In his most famous novel, *The Red and the Black*, the French author Stendhal (1783–1842) wrote: "Prior to laws, what is natural is only the strength of the lion, or the need of the creature suffering from hunger or cold, in short, need." Do you agree with Stendhal? Without laws, would society quickly crumble?

5. Should judges ignore their life experiences, political leanings, and feelings when making judicial decisions? Do you think it is possible?

CHAPTER 2

ETHICS AND CORPORATE SOCIAL RESPONSIBILITY

© Creative Travel Projects/Shutterstock.com

Eating is one of life's most fundamental needs and greatest pleasures. Yet all around the world many people go to bed hungry. Food companies have played an important role in reducing hunger by producing vast quantities of food cheaply. So much food, so cheaply that, in America, one in three adults and one in five children are obese. Some critics argue that food companies bear responsibility for this overeating because they make their products too alluring. Many processed food products are calorie bombs of fat (which is linked to heart disease), sugar (leading to diabetes), and salt (causing high blood pressure).

What obligation do food producers and restaurants have to their customers? After all, no one is forcing anyone to eat. Do any of the following examples cross the line into unethical behavior?

> **Food with high levels of fat, sugar, and salt not only taste better, they are also more addictive.**

1. *Increasing addiction.* Food with high levels of fat, sugar, and salt not only taste better, they are also more addictive. Food producers hire neuroscientists who perform MRIs on consumers to gauge the precise level of fat, sugar, and salt that will create the most powerful cravings, the so-called bliss point. To take one example, in some Prego tomato sauces, sugar is the second-most-important ingredient after tomatoes.[1]

2. *Increasing quantity.* Food companies also work hard to create new categories of products that increase the number of times a day that people eat and the amount of calories in each

---

[1]To find nutritional information on this or other products, search the Internet for the name of the product with the word "nutrition."

session. For example, they have created a new category of food that is meant to be more than a snack but less than a meal, such as Hot Pockets. But some versions of this product have more than 700 calories, which would be a lot for lunch, never mind for just a snack.

3. *Increasing calories.* Uno Chicago Grill serves a macaroni and cheese dish that, by itself, provides more than two-thirds of the calories that a moderately active man should eat in one day, and almost three times the amount of saturated fat. Should restaurants serve items such as these? If they do, what disclosure should they make?

4. *Targeting the poor.* To sell Coca-Cola in the slums of Brazil, the company offers small bottles that cost only 20 cents. Said Jeffrey Dunn, the former president and chief operating officer for Coca-Cola in North and South America, "These people need a lot of things, but they don't need a Coke. I almost threw up."[2] When Dunn tried to develop more healthful strategies for Coke, he was fired.

2-1 INTRODUCTION

This text, for the most part, covers legal ideas. The law dictates how a person *must* behave. This chapter examines **ethics**, or how people *should* behave. Any choice about how a person should behave that is based on a sense of right and wrong is an **ethics decision**. This chapter will explore ethics dilemmas that commonly arise in workplaces, and present tools for making decisions when the law does not require or prohibit any particular choice.

Laws represent society's view of basic ethics rules. And most people agree that certain activities such as murder, assault, and fraud are wrong. **However, laws may permit behavior that some feel is wrong, and it may criminalize acts that some feel are right.** For example, assisted suicide is legal in a few states. Some people believe that it is wrong under all circumstances, while others think that it is the right thing to do for someone suffering horribly from a terminal illness

One goal of this chapter is for you to develop your own **Life Principles**. These principles are the rules by which you live your life. As we will see, **research shows that people who think about the right rules for living are less likely to do wrong.**

How do you go about preparing a list of Life Principles? Think first of important categories. A list of Life Principles should include your rules on:

- Lying
- Stealing
- Cheating
- Applying the same or different standards at home and at work
- Your responsibility as a bystander when you see other people doing wrong, or being harmed

Ethics
How people should behave

Ethics decision
Any choice about how a person should behave that is based on a sense of right and wrong

Life Principles
The rules by which you live your life

---

[2]Michael Moss, "The Extraordinary Science of Addictive Junk Food," *The New York Times*, February 20, 2013.

Specific is better than general. Many people say, for example, that they will maintain a healthy work/life balance, but such a vow is not as effective as promising to set aside certain specific times each week for family activities. Another common Life Principle is "I will always put my family first." But what does that mean? That you are willing to engage in unethical behavior at work to make sure that you keep your job? Or live your life so that you serve as a good example?

Some Life Principles focus not so much on right versus wrong but rather serve as a general guide for living a happier, more engaged life: I will keep promises, forgive those who harm me, say "I'm sorry," appreciate my blessings every day, understand the other person's point of view, try to say "yes" when asked for a favor.

It is important to think through your Life Principles now, so that you will be prepared when facing ethics dilemmas in the future.

2-2 THE ROLE OF BUSINESS IN SOCIETY

Nobel Prize-winning economist Milton Friedman is famous for arguing that a corporate manager's primary responsibility is to the owners of the organization, that is, to shareholders. Unless the owners explicitly provide otherwise, managers should make the company as profitable as possible while also complying with the law.[3]

Others have argued that corporations should instead consider all company stakeholders, not just the shareholders. Stakeholders include employees, customers, and the communities and countries in which a company operates. This choice can create an obligation to such broad categories as "society" or "the environment." For example, after the shooting in Newtown, Connecticut, in which 20 first-graders and 6 educators were murdered, General Electric Co. stopped lending funds to shops that sell guns. GE headquarters are near Newtown. Many of its employees lived in the area, and some had children in the Sandy Hook Elementary School where the shooting took place. In this case, GE was putting its employees ahead of its investors.

As we will see in this chapter, managers face many choices in which the most profitable option is not the most ethical choice. When profitability increases and, with it, a company's stock price, managers benefit because their compensation is often tied to corporate results, either explicitly or through ownership of stock and options. That connection creates an incentive to do the wrong thing.

Conversely, making the ethical choice will sometimes lead to a loss of profits or even one's job. For example, Hugh Aaron worked for a company that sold plastic materials.[4] One of the firm's major clients hired a new purchasing agent who refused to buy any product unless he was provided with expensive gifts, paid vacations, and prostitutes. When Aaron refused to comply with these requests, the man bought from someone else. And that was that—the two companies never did business again. Aaron did not regret his choice. He believed that his and his employees' self-respect were as important as profits.

2-3 WHY BE ETHICAL?

An ethical decision may not be the most profitable, but it does generate a range of benefits for employees, companies, and society.

---

[3]He also mentions that managers should comply with "ethical custom" but never explains what that means. Milton Friedman, *The New York Times Magazine*, September 13, 1970.
[4]Virtually all of the examples in this chapter are true events involving real people. Only their first names are used unless the individual has consented or the events are a matter of public record.

2-3a Society as a Whole Benefits from Ethical Behavior

John Akers, the former chairman of IBM, argued that without ethical behavior, a society could not be economically competitive. He put it this way:

> Ethics and competitiveness are inseparable. We compete as a society. No society anywhere will compete very long or successfully with people stabbing each other in the back; with people trying to steal from each other; with everything requiring notarized confirmation because you can't trust the other fellow; with every little squabble ending in litigation; and with government writing reams of regulatory legislation, tying business hand and foot to keep it honest. That is a recipe not only for headaches in running a company, but for a nation to become wasteful, inefficient, and noncompetitive. There is no escaping this fact: The greater the measure of mutual trust and confidence in the ethics of a society, the greater its economic strength.[5]

In short, ethical behavior builds trust, which is important in all of our relationships. It is the ingredient that allows us to live and work together happily.

2-3b People Feel Better When They Behave Ethically

Every businessperson has many opportunities to be dishonest. But managers want to feel good about themselves and the choices they have made; they want to sleep well at night. Their decisions—to lay off employees, install safety devices in cars, burn a cleaner fuel—affect people's lives. Bad decisions are painful to remember.

2-3c Unethical Behavior Can Be Very Costly

Unethical behavior is a risky business strategy—it can harm not only the bad actors but also entire industries and even countries. For example, when VIPshop recently offered its shares publicly in the United States, they plummeted in price. This was the first Chinese company to go public in the United States in nine months, since a series of accounting frauds in other Chinese companies had caused billions of dollars in losses. Although VIPshop had done nothing wrong, investors were skeptical of *all* Chinese companies.

Unethical behavior can also cause other, subtler damage. In one survey, a majority of those questioned said that they had witnessed unethical behavior in their workplace and that this behavior had reduced productivity, job stability, and profits. **Unethical behavior in an organization creates a cynical, resentful, and unproductive workforce.**

Although there is no *guarantee* that ethical behavior pays in the short or long run, there is evidence that the ethical company is more *likely* to win financially. Ethical companies tend to have a better reputation, more creative employees, and higher returns than those that engage in wrongdoing.[6]

But if we decide that we want to behave ethically, how do we know what ethical behavior is?

2-4 THEORIES OF ETHICS

When making ethical decisions, people sometimes focus on the reason for the decision—they want to do what is right. Thus, if they think it is wrong to lie, then they will tell the truth no matter what the consequence. Other times, people think about the outcome of their actions. They will do whatever it takes to achieve the right result, no matter what. This choice—between doing right and getting the right result—has been the subject of much philosophical debate.

---

[5]David Grier, "Confronting Ethical Dilemmas," unpublished manuscript of remarks at the Royal Bank of Canada, September 19, 1989.

[6]For sources, see "Ethics: A Basic Framework," Harvard Business School case 9-307-059.

2-4a **Utilitarian Ethics**

In 1863, Englishman John Stuart Mill wrote *Utilitarianism*. **To Mill, a correct decision was one that maximizes overall happiness and minimizes overall pain, thereby producing the greatest net benefit.** As he put it, his goal was to produce the greatest good for the greatest number of people. Risk management and cost-benefit analyses are examples of utilitarian business practices.

Suppose that an automobile manufacturer could add a device to its cars that would reduce air pollution. As a result, the incidence of strokes and lung cancer would decline dramatically, saving society hundreds of millions of dollars over the life of the cars. But by charging a higher price to cover the cost of the device, the company would sell fewer cars and shareholders would earn lower returns. A utilitarian would argue that, despite the decline in profits, the company should install the device.

Consider this example that a student told us:

During college, I used drugs—some cocaine, but mostly prescription painkillers. Things got pretty bad. At one point, I would wait outside emergency rooms hoping to buy drugs from people who were leaving. But that was three years ago. I went into rehab and have been clean ever since. I don't even drink. I've applied for a job, but the application asks if I have ever used drugs illegally. I am afraid that if I tell the truth, I will never get a job. What should I say on the application?

A utilitarian would ask: What harm will be caused if she tells the truth? She will be less likely to get that job, or maybe any job—a large and immediate harm. What if she lies? She might argue that no harm would result because she is now clean, and her past drug addiction will not have an adverse impact on her new employer.

Critics of utilitarian thought argue that it is very difficult to *measure* utility accurately, at least in the way that one would measure distance or the passage of time. The car company does not really know how many lives will be saved or how much its profits might decline if the device is installed. It is also difficult to *predict* benefit and harm accurately. The recovered drug addict may relapse, or her employer may find out about her lie.

A focus on outcome can justify some really terrible behavior. Suppose that wealthy old Ebenezer has several chronic illnesses that cause him great suffering and prevent him from doing any of the activities that once gave meaning to his life. Also, he is such a nasty piece of work that everyone who knows him hates him. If he were to die, all his heirs would benefit tremendously from the money that they inherited from him, including a disabled grandchild who then could afford medical care that would improve his life dramatically. Would it be ethical to kill Ebenezer?

2-4b **Deontological Ethics**

Deontological

The duty to do the right thing, regardless of the result

Proponents of deontological ethics believe that utilitarians have it all wrong and that the *results* of a decision are not as important as the *reason* for making it. To a **deontological** thinker, the ends do not justify the means. Rather, it is important to do the right thing, no matter the result.

Categorical imperative

An act is only ethical if it would be acceptable for everyone to do the same thing.

The best-known proponent of the deontological model was the eighteenth-century German philosopher Immanuel Kant. He believed in what he called the **categorical imperative**. He argued that you should not do something unless you would be willing to have everyone else do it, too. Applying this idea, he concluded that one should always tell the truth because if *everyone* lied, the world would become an awful place. Thus, Kant would say that the drug user should tell the truth on job applications, even if that meant she could not find work.

Kant also believed that human beings possess a unique dignity and that no decision that treats people as commodities could be considered just, even if the decision tended to maximize overall happiness, or profit, or any other quantifiable measure. Thus, Kant would argue against killing Ebenezer, no matter how unpleasant the man was.

The problem with Kant is that the ends *do* matter. Yes, it is wrong to kill, but a country might not survive unless it is willing to fight wars. Although many people disagree with some of Kant's specific ideas, most people acknowledge that a utilitarian approach is incomplete, and that winning in the end does not automatically make a decision right.

2-4c Rawlsian Justice

How did you manage to get into college or graduate school? Presumably owing to some combination of talent, hard work, and support from family and friends. Imagine that you had been born into different circumstances—say, a country where the literacy rate is only 25 percent and almost all of the population lives in desperate poverty. Would you be reading this book now? Most likely not. People are born with wildly different talents into very different circumstances, all of which dramatically affect their outcomes.

John Rawls (1921–2002) was an American philosopher who referred to these circumstances into which we are born as **life prospects**. In his view, hard work certainly matters, but so does luck. Rawls argued that we should think about what rules for society we would propose if we faced a **veil of ignorance**. In other words, suppose that there is going to be a lottery tomorrow that would determine all our attributes. We could be a winner, ending up a hugely talented, healthy person in a loving family, or we could be poor and chronically ill from a broken, abusive family in a violent neighborhood with deplorable schools and social services.

What type of society would we establish now, if we did not know whether we would be one of life's winners or losers? First, we would design some form of a democratic system that provided equal liberty to all and important rights such as freedom of speech and religion. Second, we would apply the **difference principle**. Under this principle we would *not* plan a system in which everyone received an equal income. Society is better off if people have an incentive to work hard, so we would reward the type of work that provides the most benefit to the community as a whole. We might decide, for example, to pay doctors more than baseball players. But maybe not *all* doctors—perhaps just the ones who research cancer cures or provide care for the poor, not cosmetic surgeons operating on the affluent. Rawls argues that everyone should have the opportunity to earn great wealth so long as the tax system provides enough revenue to provide decent health, education, and welfare for all. In thinking about ethical decisions, it is worth remembering that many of us have been winners in life's lottery and that the unlucky are deserving of our compassion.

2-4d Front Page Test

There you are, trying to decide what to do in a difficult situation. How would you feel if your actions went viral—on YouTube, the Huffington Post, all over Facebook, or the front page of a national newspaper? Would that help you decide what to do?

The Front Page test is not completely foolproof—there are times you might want to do something private for legitimate reasons. Some states prohibit the videotaping of mistreated farm animals. You would not want everyone to know that you had done so, even if you thought it the right thing to do.

2-4e Moral Universalism and Relativism

For many ethics dilemmas, reasonable people may well disagree about what is right. However, some people believe that particular acts are always right or always wrong, regardless of what others may think. This approach is called **moral universalism**. Alternatively, others believe that it is right to be tolerant of different viewpoints and customs. And, indeed, a decision may be acceptable even if it is not in keeping with one's own ethical standards. This approach is referred to as **moral relativism**. For example, Pope Benedict XVI

Life prospects
The opportunities one has at birth, based on one's natural attributes and initial place in society

Veil of ignorance
The rules for society that we would propose if we did not know how lucky we would be in life's lottery

Difference principle
Rawls' suggestion that society should reward behavior that provides the most benefit to the community as a whole

Moral universalism
A belief that some acts are always right or always wrong

Moral relativism
A belief that a decision may be right even if it is not in keeping with our own ethical standards

wrote that homosexuality is "a strong tendency ordered toward an intrinsic moral evil," while his successor, Pope Francis took a different approach, saying, "If someone is gay and he searches for the Lord and has good will, who am *I* to judge?"[7] Pope Benedict's view reflects a moral universalism—he believes that homosexuality is always wrong—while Pope Francis is taking a more relativistic approach—under certain circumstances, he will not judge.

There are at least two types of moral relativism: cultural and individual. To cultural relativists, what is right or wrong depends on the norms and practices in each society. For example, some societies permit men to have more than one wife, while others find that practice abhorrent. A cultural relativist would say that polygamy is an ethical choice in societies where such practice is long-standing and culturally significant. And, as outsiders to that society, who are we to judge? In short, culture defines what is right and wrong.

To individual relativists, people must develop their own ethical rules. And what is right for *me* might not be good for *you*. Thus, I might believe that monogamy is bad because it goes against human nature. Therefore, I might decide that it is right for me to have relationships with many partners, while you believe that being faithful to one partner is the cornerstone of an ethical life.

Like so much in ethics, none of these approaches will always be right or wrong. It is, however, ethically lazy simply to default to moral relativism as an excuse for condoning any behavior.

2-5 Ethics Traps

Very few people wake up one morning and think, "Today I'll do something unethical." Then why do so many unethical things happen? Sometimes our brains trick us into believing wrong is right. It is important to understand the ethics traps that create great temptation to do what we know to be wrong or fail to do what we know to be right.

2-5a Money

Money is a powerful lure because most people believe that they would be happier if only they had more. But that is not necessarily true. Good health, companionship, and enjoyable leisure activities all contribute more to happiness than money does.

Money *can*, of course, provide some protection against the inevitable bumps in the road of life. Being hungry is no fun. It is easier to maintain friendships if you can afford to go out together occasionally. So money can contribute to happiness, but research indicates that this impact disappears when household income exceeds $75,000. Above that level, income seems to have no impact on day-to-day happiness. Indeed, there is some evidence that higher income levels actually *reduce* the ability to appreciate small pleasures.

Money is also a way of keeping score. If my company pays me more, that must mean I am a better employee. So although an increase in income above $75,000 does not affect *day-to-day* happiness, higher pay can make people feel more satisfied with their lives. They consider themselves more successful and feel that their life is going better.

In short, the relationship between money and happiness is complicated. Above a certain level, more money does not make for more day-to-day happiness. Higher pay can increase general satisfaction with life but when people work so hard or so dishonestly that their health, friendships, and leisure activities suffer, it has the reverse effect.

---

[7]Rachel Donadio, "On Gay Priests, Pope Francis Asks, 'Who Am I to Judge,'" *The New York Times*, July 30, 2013.

2-5b Competition

Deep down, we all want to be better than the other fellow. In one telling experiment, young children elected to get *fewer* prizes for themselves, as long as they still got more than other participants. For example, a child chose to get one prize for herself and zero for the other person, rather than two for herself and two for the other participant.

2-5c Rationalization

Virtually any foul deed can be rationalized. Some common rationalizations:

- If I don't do it, someone else will.
- I deserve this because …
- They had it coming.
- I am not harming a *person*—it is just a big company.
- This is someone else's responsibility.
- Just this once.

> **Deep down, we all want to be better than the other fellow.**

For example, Duke professor Dan Ariely has found in his research that almost everyone is willing to cheat, at least on a small scale. We all want to get the greatest benefit but we also want to think of ourselves as being honest. If we cheat—just a little—then we can tell ourselves that it does not really count. Ariely did an experiment in which he paid people for solving math problems. Participants averaged four correct answers. But when people were allowed to grade the tests themselves without anyone checking up on them, all of a sudden they began averaging six correct answers. You can imagine how they might have rationalized that behavior—"I was close on this one. Today was an off day for me." Surprisingly, when the participants were paid a lot for each correct answer ($10 as opposed to $0.50) they cheated *less*. Presumably, they would have felt worse about themselves if they stole a lot of money rather than a little.

2-5d We Can't Be Objective About Ourselves

Do you do more than your fair share of work at home? In your study group? Of course you do! At least, that is what most people think. **In reality, people are not objective when comparing themselves to others.** Many studies looking at groups as various as married couples, athletes, MBA students, and organizational behavior professors have found a tendency for people to overestimate their own contribution to a group effort. Another experiment showed that, when dividing up work, people tend to assign themselves the easiest tasks, but still rate themselves high on a fairness scale. In making a decision that affects you, it is important to remember that you are unlikely to be objective.

2-5e Conflicts of Interest

Suppose that your doctor is writing a prescription for you. Do you care that she does so with a pen given to her by a pharmaceutical company? You should. The evidence is that doctors are influenced by gifts, and, indeed, small gifts are surprisingly influential because the recipients do not make a conscious effort to overcome any bias these tokens may create. With larger gifts, the recipients are more aware and, therefore, take more effort in overcoming their biases. Doctors are not alone in their reaction. For everyone, the bias created by a conflict of interest tends to be unconscious and unintentionally self-serving. In short, if ethical decisions are your goal, it is better to avoid all conflicts of interest—both large and small. No one—including you—is good at overcoming the biases that these conflicts create.

2-5f Conformity

Warren Buffett has been quoted as saying, "The five most dangerous words in business may be: 'Everybody else is doing it.'" Because humans are social animals, they are often willing to follow the leader, even to a place where they do not really want to go. If all the salespeople in a company cheat on their expense accounts, a new hire is much more likely to view this behavior as acceptable.

2-5g Following Orders

When someone in authority issues orders, even to do something clearly wrong, it is very tempting to comply. Fear of punishment, the belief in authority figures, and the ability to rationalize, all play a role. In a true story (with the facts disguised), Amanda worked at a private school that was struggling to pay its bills. As a result, it kept the lights turned off in the hallways. On a particularly cloudy day, a visitor tripped and fell in one of these darkened passages. When he sued, the principal told Amanda to lie on the witness stand and say that the lights had been on. The school's lawyer reinforced this advice. Amanda did as she was told. When asked why, she said, "I figured it must be the right thing to do if the lawyer said so. Also, if I hadn't lied, the principal would have fired me, and I might not have been able to get another job in teaching."

2-5h Euphemisms and Reframing

The term "friendly fire" has a cheerful ring to it, much better than "killing your own troops," which is what it really means. In a business setting, to "smooth earnings" sounds a lot better than to "cook the books" or "commit fraud." "Right-sizing" is more palatable than "firing a whole bunch of people." In making ethical decisions, it is important to use accurate terminology. Anything else is just a variation on rationalization.

Aerospace engineer Roger Boisjoly (pronounced "Bo zho lay") tried to convince his superiors at Morton-Thiokol, Inc. to scrub the launch of the *Challenger* space shuttle. His superiors were engineers, too, so they were qualified to evaluate Boisjoly's concerns. But during the discussion, one of the bosses said, "We have to make a management decision." Once the issue was reframed as "management" not "engineering," their primary concern was to please their customer, NASA. The flight had already been postponed twice, and, as managers, they felt they needed really clear data to justify another postponement. The Morton-Thiokol managers had to be convinced that it was *not* safe to fly. With that clear evidence lacking, these men approved the launch, which ended catastrophically when the spaceship exploded 73 seconds after liftoff, killing all the astronauts on board. If they had asked an engineering question—"Is this spaceship definitely safe?"—they would have made a different decision. In answering a question, it is always a good idea to consider whether the frame is correct.

2-5i Lost in a Crowd

On a busy street, a man picks up a seven-year-old girl and carries her away while she screams, "You're not my dad—someone help me!" No one responds. This incident was a test staged by a news station. It took hours and many repetitions before anyone tried to prevent the abduction.

When in a group, people are less likely to take responsibility, because they assume (hope?) that someone else will. They tend to check the reactions of others, and if everyone else seems calm, they assume that all is right. Bystanders are much more likely to react if they are alone and have to form an independent judgment.

Thus, in a business, if everyone is lying to customers, smoothing earnings, or sexually harassing the staff, it is tempting to go with the flow rather than protest the wrongdoing.

2-5j Short-Term Perspective

Many times, people make unethical decisions because they are thinking short term. Your boss asks you to book sales in this quarter that actually will not happen until next. That "solution" would solve the immediate issue of low sales while potentially creating an enormous long-term problem that could lead to bankruptcy and prison time.

2-5k Blind Spots

As Bob Dylan memorably sang, "How many times can a man turn his head and pretend that he just doesn't see?" We all have a tendency to ignore even blatant evidence that we would rather not know. Just as tobacco manufacturers were very slow to learn that smoking caused cancer, officials at Penn State University overlooked compelling evidence that football coach Jerry Sandusky was molesting children.

   And then there is the case of Barry Bonds, one of the greatest baseball players of all time. Although he quickly gained tremendous weight and muscle mass that was consistent with the illegal use of steroids, neither his team nor baseball executives took any action against him until the federal government began an investigation.[8]

2-5l Avoiding Ethics Traps

Three practices help us avoid these ethics traps:

1. **Slow down.** We all make worse decisions when in a hurry. In one experiment, a group of students at Princeton Theological Seminary (that is, people in training to be ministers) were told to go to a location across campus to give a talk. On their walk over, they encountered a man lying in distress in a doorway. Only one-tenth of those participants who had been told they were late for their talk stopped to help the ill man while almost two-thirds of those who thought they had plenty of time did stop.

2. **Do not trust your first instinct.** You make many decisions without thinking. When sitting down for dinner, you do not ask yourself, "Which hand should I use to pick up the fork? How will I cut up my food?" You use System 1 thinking—an automatic, instinctual, sometimes emotional process. This approach is efficient but can also lead to more selfish and unethical decisions. When taking an exam, System 1 thinking would not get you far. For that, you need System 2 thoughts—those that are conscious and logical.

   Being in a hurry, or in a crowd, being able to rationalize easily, using euphemisms, doing what every else does, receiving an order, being dazzled by money—these can all lead you to make a quick and wrong System 1 decision. Before making an important choice, bring in System 2 thinking.

3. **Remember your Life Principles.** In his research, Ariely found that participants were less likely to cheat if they were reminded of their school honor code or the Ten Commandments. This result was true even if the participants were atheists. It is a good practice to remind yourself of your values.

2-6 LYING: A SPECIAL CASE

We are taught from an early age to tell the truth. Yet research shows that we tell between one and two lies a day. When is lying acceptable? What about white lies to make others feel better: I love your lasagna. You're not going bald. No, that sweater

---

[8]To see the drastic change in Bonds' physique, search the Internet for "steroids, Barry Bonds".

doesn't make you look fat. When Victoria McGrath suffered a terrible wound to her leg in the Boston Marathon bombing, Tyler Dodd comforted her at the scene by telling her that he had recovered from a shrapnel wound in Afghanistan. His story was not true—he had never been in combat or Afghanistan. McGrath was grateful to him for his lie because it gave her strength and hope.

What are your Life Principles on lying? There may indeed be good reasons to lie, but what are they? To benefit other people? To protect children who believe in Santa Claus? It is useful to analyze this issue now rather than to rationalize later.

2-6a Ethics Case: Truth (?) in Borrowing

Rob is in the business of buying dental practices. He finds solo practitioners, buys their assets, signs them to a long-term contract, and then improves their management and billing processes so effectively that both he and the dentists are better off.

Rob has just found a great opportunity with a lot of potential profit. There is only *one* problem. The bank will not give him a loan to buy the practice without checking the dentist's financial record. Her credit rating is fine, but it turns out that she filed for bankruptcy twenty years ago. That event no longer appears on her credit record but the bank asked about *all* bankruptcies on the form it required her to sign. She is perfectly willing to lie. Rob refused to turn in the form with a lie. But when the bank learned about the bankruptcy, it denied his loan even though *her* bankruptcy in no way affects *his* ability to pay the loan. And the incident is ancient history—the dentist's current finances are strong. Subsequently, four other banks also refused to make the loan.

Rob is feeling pretty frustrated. He figures the return on this deal would be 20 percent. Everyone would benefit—the dentist would earn more, her patients would have better technology, he could afford a house in a better school district, and the bank would make a profit. There is one more bank he could try.

Questions

1. Should Rob file loan documents with the bank, knowing the dentist has lied?

2. Who would be harmed by this lie?

3. What if Rob pays back the loan without incident? Was the lie still wrong? Do the ends justify the means?

4. What is your Life Principle about telling lies?

5. Do you have the same rule when lying to protect yourself, as opposed to benefitting others?

2-7 Applying the Principles

Having thought about ethics principles and traps, let's now practice applying them to situations that are similar to those you are likely to face in your life.

2-7a Personal Ethics in the Workplace

Should you behave in the workplace the way you do at home, or do you have a separate set of ethics for each part of your life? What if your employees behave badly outside of work—should that affect their employment? Consider the following case.

2-7b Ethics Case: Weird Wierdsma

Beatrix Szeremi immigrated to the United States from Hungary. But her American dream turned into a nightmare when she married Charles Wierdsma. He repeatedly beat her and threatened to suffocate and drown her. Ultimately, he pleaded guilty to one felony count and went to jail. Despite his son's guilt, Thomas Wierdsma pressured his daughter-in-law to drop the charges and delete photos of her injuries from her Facebook page. When she refused, he threatened her and her lawyer that he would report her to immigration officials. Father and son discussed how they could get her deported. Thomas also testified in a deposition that it was not wrong to lie to a federal agency. "It happens all the time," he said.[9] Thomas Wierdsma is the senior vice president at The GEO Group, Inc.

Research indicates that CEOs who break the law outside of the office are more likely to engage in workplace fraud. Although their legal infractions—driving under the influence, use of illegal drugs, domestic violence, even speeding tickets—were unrelated to their work, they seemed to indicate a disrespect for the rule of law and a lack of self-control.

Questions

1. If you were the CEO of Thomas Wierdsma's company, would you fire him? Impose some other sanction?

2. Which is worse—threatening his daughter-in-law or stating that it is acceptable to lie to a federal agency?

3. Would you fire a warehouse worker who behaved this way?

4. GEO runs prisons and immigration facilities for the government. Does that fact change any of your answers?

5. Wierdsma's woes were reported in major newspapers, and his statement about lying to a federal agency is on YouTube (see footnote). Do these facts change any of your answers?

6. What would Kant and Mill say is the right thing to do in this case? What result under the Front Page test?

7. What ethics traps might Wierdsma's boss face in this situation?

8. What is your Life Principle? What behavior are you willing to tolerate in the interest of profitability?

2-7c The Organization's Responsibility to Society

Many products can potentially cause harm to customers or employees. What is a company's responsibility to those who are injured by its products?

2-7d Ethics Case: Breathing the Fumes

Every other year, the National Institutes of Health publish the *Report on Carcinogens*, which lists products that cause cancer. Among those in the most recent report was formaldehyde, found in furniture, cosmetics, building products, carpets, and fabric softeners. Unless we take heroic efforts to avoid this chemical, we are all exposed to it on a daily basis. Indeed, almost all homes have formaldehyde levels that exceed government safety rules. In an effort to shoot the

[9]Nancy Lofholm, "GEO investigated in son's domestic violence case," *Denver Post*, April 8, 2013. The You Tube video of his admission about lying to a federal agency is at http://www.youtube.com/watch?v=UTi9fbo202M.

messenger, the American Chemistry Council, which is an industry trade group, lobbied Congress to cut off funding for the *Report on Carcinogens*—not improve it, but defund it.

Questions

1. If you were one of the many companies using products that contain formaldehyde, what would you do? What would you be willing to pay to provide a safer product?

2. If you were an executive at Exxon, Dow, or DuPont, all members of the American Chemistry Council, how would you react to this effort to hide the facts on formaldehyde?

3. What would Mill and Kant recommend?

4. What ethics traps would you face in making a decision?

5. What Life Principle would you apply?

2-7e The Organization's Responsibility to Its Employees

Organizations cannot be successful without good workers. But sometimes looking out for employees may not lead to higher profits. In these cases, does an organization have a duty to take care of its workers? The shareholder model says no; the stakeholder model takes the opposite view.

2-7f Ethics Case: The Storm after the Storm

Yanni is the CEO of Cloud Farm, a company that provides online data centers for Internet companies. Because these data centers are enormous, they are located in rural areas where they are often the main employer. A series of tornados has just destroyed a data center near Farmfield, Arkansas, a town with a population of roughly 5,000 people. Farmfield is a two-hour drive from the nearest city, Little Rock.

Here is the good news: The insurance payout will cover the full cost of rebuilding. The bad news? Data centers are much more expensive to build and operate in the United States than in Africa, Asia, or Latin America. Yanni could take the money from the insurance company and build three data centers overseas. He has asked Adam and Zoe to present the pros and cons of relocating.

Adam says, "If we rebuild overseas, our employees will never find equivalent jobs. We pay $20 an hour, and the other jobs in town are mostly minimum-wage. And remember how some of the guys worked right through Christmas to set up for that new client. They have been loyal to us—we owe them something in return. Going overseas is not just bad for Farmfield or Arkansas, it's bad for the country.

Zoe responds, "That is the government's problem, not ours. We'll pay to retrain the workers, which, frankly, is a generous offer. Our investors get a return of 4 percent; the industry average is closer to 8 percent. If we act like a charity to support Farmfield, we could all lose our jobs. It is our obligation to do what's best for our shareholders— which, in this case, happens to be what's right for us, too."

Questions

1. Do you agree with Zoe's argument that it is the government's responsibility to create and protect American jobs and that it is a CEO's job to increase shareholder wealth?

2. Imagine that you personally own shares in Cloud Farm. Would you be upset with a decision to rebuild the data center in the United States?

3. If you were in Yanni's position, would you rebuild the plant in Arkansas or relocate overseas?

4. What ethics traps does Yanni face in this situation?

5. What is your Life Principle on this issue? Would you be willing to risk your job to protect your employees?

2-7g The Organization's Responsibility to Its Customers

Customers are another group of essential stakeholders. A corporation must gain and retain loyal buyers if it is to stay in business for long. But when, if ever, does an organization go too far?

2-7h Ethics Case: Mickey Weighs In

Disney announced recently that only healthy foods can be advertised on its children's television channels, radio stations, and websites. Candy, fast food, and sugared cereals are banned from Mickey land. Kicked to the curb are such childhood favorites as Lunchables and Capri Sun drinks. In addition, sodium must be reduced by one quarter in food served at its theme parks. Nor does Disney permit its characters to associate with unhealthy foods. No more Mickey Pop-Tarts or Buzz Lightyear Happy Meals. Said Disney chairman, Robert Iger, "Companies in a position to help with solutions to childhood obesity should do just that."[10]

Disney's revenue from advertising, licensing fees, and food sales may decline. On the other hand, this healthy initiative will enhance its reputation, at least with parents, who increasingly seek healthy food options for their children. And Disney will profit from new license fees it receives for the use of a Mickey Check logo on healthy food in grocery aisles and restaurants.

Questions

1. What is Disney's obligation to its young customers?

2. Does this information make you more likely to buy Disney products or allow your children to watch Disney TV?

3. What would Mill or Kant have said? What result with the Front Page test?

4. What ethics traps does Disney face?

5. What is your Life Principle? How much profitability (or income) are you willing to give up to protect children you do not know?

2-7i The Organization's Responsibility to Overseas Workers

What ethical duties does an American manager have overseas, to stakeholders in countries where the culture and economic circumstances are very different? Should American companies (and consumers) buy goods that are produced in sweatshop factories?

---

[10]Brooks Barnes, "Promoting Nutrition, Disney to Restrict Junk-Food Ads," *The New York Times*, June 5, 2012.

Industrialization has always been the first stepping stone out of dire poverty—it was in England in centuries past, and it is now in the developing world. Eventually, higher productivity leads to higher wages. The results in China have been nothing short of remarkable. During the Industrial Revolution in England, per-capita output doubled in 58 years; in China, it took only 10 years.

During the past 50 years, Taiwan and South Korea welcomed sweatshops. During the same period, India resisted what it perceived to be foreign exploitation. Although all three countries started at the same economic level, Taiwan and South Korea today have much lower levels of infant mortality and much higher levels of education than India.[11]

In theory, then, sweatshops might not be all bad. But are there limits? Consider the following case.

2-7j Ethics Case: A Worm in the Apple

"Riots, Suicides and More," blares an Internet headline about a FoxConn factory where iPhones and other Apple products are assembled. Apple is not alone in facing supplier scandals. So have Nike, Coca-Cola, and Gap, among many others. Do companies have an obligation to the employees of their suppliers? If so, how can they, or anyone, be sure what is really going on in a factory on the other side of the world? Professor Richard Locke of MIT has studied supply chain issues.[12] His conclusions:

- The first step that many companies took to improve working conditions overseas was to establish a code of conduct and then conduct audits. These coercive practices do not work, and compliance is at best sporadic.

- A more collaborative approach worked better—when the auditors sent by multinationals saw their role as less of a police officer and more as a partner, committed to problem-solving and sharing of best practices.

What would you do if you were a manager in the following circumstances:

- In clothing factories, workers often remove the protective guards from their sewing machines, because the guards slow the flow of work. As a result, many workers suffer needle punctures. Factories resist the cost of buying new guards because the workers just take them off again. Is there a solution?

- Timberland and Hewlett-Packard have recognized that selling large numbers of new products creates great variation in demand and therefore pressure factory workers to work overtime. What can a company do to reduce this pressure?[13]

2-8 WHEN THE GOING GETS TOUGH: RESPONDING TO UNETHICAL BEHAVIOR

If you find yourself working for a company that tolerates an intolerable level of unethical behavior, you face three choices.

---

[11]The data in this and the preceding paragraph are from Nicholas D. Kristof and Sheryl Wu Dunn, "Two Cheers for Sweatshops," *The New York Times Magazine*, Sept. 24, 2000, p. 70.

[12]"When the jobs inspector calls," *The Economist*, March 31, 2012

[13]These examples are from Richard Locke, Matthew Amengual, and Akshay Mangla, "Virtue out of Necessity?: Compliance, Commitment and the Improvement of Labor Conditions in Global Supply Chains," available at Princeton.edu.

2-8a Loyalty

It is always important to pick one's battles. For example, a firm's accounting department must make many decisions about which reasonable people could disagree. Just because their judgment is different from yours does not mean that they are behaving unethically. Being a team player means allowing other people to make their own choices sometimes. However, the difference between being a team player and starting down the slippery slope can be very narrow. If you are carrying out a decision, or simply observing one, that makes you uncomfortable, then it is time to consult your Life Principles and review the section on ethics traps.

2-8b Exit

When faced with the unacceptable, one option is to walk out the door quietly. You resign "to accept an offer that is too good to refuse." This approach may be the safest for you because you are not making any enemies. But a quiet exit leaves the bad guys in position to continue the unsavory behavior. For example, the CEO was sexually harassing Laura, but she left quietly for fear that if she reported him, he would harm her career. So the CEO proceeded to attack other women at the company until finally a senior man got wind of what was going on and confronted the chief. In short, the braver and better option may be to exit loudly—reporting the wrongdoing on the way out the door.

2-8c Voice

Wrongdoing often occurs because everyone just goes along to get along. One valiant soul with the courage to say, "This is wrong," can be a powerful force for the good. But confrontation may not be the only, or even the best, use of your voice. Learning to persuade, cajole, or provide better options are all important leadership skills. For example, Keith felt that the CEO of his company was about to make a bad decision, but he was unable to persuade the man to choose a different alternative. When Keith turned out to be correct, the CEO gave him no credit, saying, "You are equally responsible because your arguments weren't compelling enough." Keith thought the man had a point.

2-9 CORPORATE SOCIAL RESPONSIBILITY (CSR)

So far, we have largely been talking about a company's duty not to cause harm. But do companies have a **corporate social responsibility**—that is, an obligation to contribute positively to the world around it? Do businesses have an affirmative duty to do good?

Harvard Professor Michael Porter has written that CSR often benefits a company. For example, improving economic and social conditions overseas can create new customers with money to spend. However, in Porter's view, a company should not undertake a CSR project unless it is profitable for the company in its own right, regardless of any secondary benefits the company may receive from, say, an improved reputation. Thus, for example, Yoplait has periodically run a "Save Lids to Save Lives" campaign. For every Yoplait lid mailed in, the company makes a donation to a breast cancer charity. During these campaigns, Yoplait gains market share. Should companies be willing to improve the world even if their efforts *reduce* profitability?

Corporate social responsibility
An organization's obligation to contribute positively to the world around it

2-9a Ethics Case: The Beauty of a Well-Fed Child

Cosmetic companies often use gift-with-purchase offers to promote their products. For example, with any $45 Estee Lauder purchase at Bloomingdale's, you can choose a free gift of creams and makeup valued at over $165, plus a special-edition cosmetic bag.

But Clarins has put a new spin on these offers with what it calls "gift with *purpose*." Buy two Clarins items and you will receive six trial-size products *and* the company will pay the United Nations World Food Program enough for 10 school meals. Clarins hopes that cosmetic buyers, many of whom are women with children, will find this opportunity to feed children particularly compelling.

Questions

1. If you were an executive at Clarins, what would you want to know before approving this promotion?

2. Would you approve this promotion if it were not profitable on its own account? How much of a subsidy would you be willing to grant?

Chapter Conclusion

Many times in your life, you will be tempted to do something that you know in your heart of hearts is wrong. Referring to your own Life Principles and being aware of potential traps, will help you to make the right decisions. But it is also important that you be able to afford to do the right thing. Having a reserve fund to cover six months' living expenses makes it easier for you to leave a job that violates your personal ethics. Too many times, people make the wrong, and sometimes the illegal, decision for financial reasons.

Exam Review

1. **ETHICS**   The law dictates how a person *must* behave. Ethics governs how people *should* behave.

2. **LIFE PRINCIPLES**   Life Principles are the rules by which you live your life. If you develop these Life Principles now, you will be prepared when facing ethical dilemmas in the future.

3. **THE ROLE OF BUSINESS IN SOCIETY**   An ongoing debate about whether managers should focus only on what is best for shareholders or whether they should consider the interests of other stakeholders as well.

4. **WHY BE ETHICAL?**

   - Society as a whole benefits from ethical behavior.

   - People feel better when they behave ethically.

   - Unethical behavior can be very costly.

5. THEORIES OF ETHICS

- Utilitarian thinkers such as John Stuart Mill believe that the right decision maximizes overall happiness and minimizes overall pain.

- Deontological thinkers such as Immanuel Kant believe it is important to do the right thing, no matter the result.

- With his categorical imperative, Kant argued that you should not do something unless you would be willing to have everyone else do it, too.

- John Rawls asked us to consider what type of society we would establish if we did not know whether we would be one of life's winners or losers. He called this situation "the veil of ignorance."

- Under the Front Page test, you ask yourself what you would do if your actions were going to be reported publicly on or offline.

6. ETHICS TRAPS

- Money
- Competition
- Rationalization
- We can't be objective about ourselves
- Conflicts of interest
- Conformity
- Following orders
- Euphemisms and reframing
- Lost in a crowd
- Short-term perspective
- Blind spots

7. To avoid ethics traps:

- Slow down.
- Do not trust your first instinct.
- Remember your Life Principles.

8. WHEN THE GOING GETS TOUGH When faced with unethical behavior in your organization, you have three choices:

1. Loyalty
2. Exit (either quiet or noisy)
3. Voice

9. CORPORATE SOCIAL RESPONSIBILITY An organization's obligation to contribute positively to the world around it.

MATCHING QUESTIONS

Match the following terms with their definitions:

___A. Shareholder model

___B. Stakeholder model

___C. Utilitarianism

___D. Deontological ethics

___E. John Rawls

1. requires doing "the greatest good for the greatest number"

2. thought that society should try to make up for people's different life prospects

3. requires business decisions that maximize the owners' return on investment

4. focuses on the reasons for which decisions are made

5. requires business leaders to consider employees, customers, communities, and other groups when making decisions

TRUE/FALSE QUESTIONS

Circle true or false:

1. T F Immanuel Kant was a noted utilitarian thinker.

2. T F The shareholder model requires that business leaders consider the needs of employees when making decisions.

3. T F Modern China has experienced slower economic growth than did England during the Industrial Revolution.

4. T F John Stuart Mill's ideas are consistent with business use of risk management and cost-benefit analyses.

5. T F John Rawls believed that everyone should have the same income.

MULTIPLE-CHOICE QUESTIONS

1. Milton Friedman was a strong believer in the _____ model. He _____ argue that a corporate leader's sole obligation is to make money for the company's owners.

(a) shareholder; did

(b) shareholder; did not

(c) stakeholder; did

(d) stakeholder; did not

2. Which of the following wrote the book *Utilitarianism* and believed that ethical actions should "generate the greatest good for the greatest number"?

    (a) Milton Friedman

    (b) John Stuart Mill

    (c) Immanuel Kant

    (d) John Rawls

3. Which of the following believed that the dignity of human beings must be respected and that the most ethical decisions are made out of a sense of obligation?

    (a) Milton Friedman

    (b) John Stuart Mill

    (c) Immanuel Kant

    (d) John Rawls

4. Kant believed that:

    (a) it is ethical to tell a lie if necessary to protect an innocent person from great harm.

    (b) it is ethical to tell a lie if the benefit of the lie outweighs the cost.

    (c) it is wrong for some people to be wealthier than others.

    (d) it is wrong to tell a lie.

5. The following statement is true:

    (a) Most people are honest most of the time.

    (b) Even people who do not believe in God are more likely to behave honestly after reading the Ten Commandments.

    (c) When confronted with wrongdoing, most people immediately recognize the problem.

    (d) People make their best ethical decisions instinctively, rather than thinking through a problem.

Case Questions

1. The Senate recently released a report on wrongdoing at JP Morgan Chase. It found that bank executives lied to investors and the public. Also, traders, with the knowledge of top management, changed risk limits to facilitate more trading and then violated even these higher limits. Executives revalued the bank's investment portfolio to reduce apparent losses. JP Morgan's internal investigation failed to find this wrongdoing. Into what ethics traps did these JP Morgan employees fall? What options did the executives and traders have for dealing with this wrongdoing?

2. Located in Bath, Maine, Bath Iron Works builds high tech warships for the Navy. Winning Navy contracts is crucial to the company's success—it means jobs for the community and profits for the shareholders. Navy officials held a meeting at Bath's offices with its executives and those of a competitor to review an upcoming bid. Both companies desperately wanted to win the contract. After the meeting, a Bath worker realized that one of the Navy officials had left a folder on a chair labeled: "Business Sensitive." It contained information about the competitors' bid that would be a huge advantage to Bath. William Haggett, the Bath CEO, was notified about the file just as he was walking out the door to give a luncheon speech. What should he do? What traps did he face? What result if he considered Mill, Kant, or the Front Page test?

3. I oversee the internal audit function at my company. We hold periodic bid competitions to get the lowest price we can. At the moment, we are using Firm A. Recently, one of the partners at A offered me box seats to a Red Sox game. I love the Red Sox, and even more importantly, I could have taken my father who, even though he has always been a big Sox fan, has never been to a game. However, I knew that we would soon be asking A to bid against the other Big Four firms for the right to do next year's audit. I was torn about what I should do.

What traps does this person face? Would something as minor as Red Sox tickets affect his decision about which audit firm to use?

4. Each year, the sale of Girl Scout cookies is the major fund-raiser for local troops. But because the organization was criticized for promoting such unhealthy food, it introduced a new cookie, Mango Cremes with Nutrifusion. It promotes this cookie as a vitamin-laden, natural whole food. "A delicious way to get your vitamins." But these vitamins are a minuscule part of the cookie. The rest has more bad saturated fat than an Oreo. The Girl Scouts do much good for many girls. And to do this good, they need to raise money. What would Kant and Mill say? What about the Front Page test? What do you say?

5. In Japan, automobile GPS systems come equipped with an option for converting them into televisions so that drivers can watch their favorite shows, yes, while driving. "We can't help but respond to our customers' needs," says a company spokesperson.[14] Although his company does not recommend the practice of watching while driving, he explained that it is the driver's responsibility to make this decision. Is it right to sell a product that could cause great harm to innocent bystanders? What would Mill and Kant say?

DISCUSSION QUESTIONS

1. A vice president from the customer service team told me that the company's largest customer was going to be conducting an on-site audit. The customer would be particularly interested in seeing the dedicated computing equipment that was part of their contract. As it turns out, we did not have any dedicated computing equipment. The VP was incredulous because the past director of my area had, on multiple occasions, told him that there was. As it turned out, the former director had been lying. To survive the audit, the VP asked me to lie and also to put fake labels on some of the machines to show the customer. If I didn't agree, I knew the VP would be furious, and we might lose this client.

   What would Kant and Mill say? What is the difference between a long-term versus short-term perspective?

2. Darby has been working for 14 months at Holden Associates, a large management consulting firm. She is earning $85,000 a year, which *sounds* good but does not go very far in New York City. It turns out that her peers at competing firms are typically

---

[14]Chester Dawson, "Drivers Use Navigation Systems to Tune In," *The Wall Street Journal*, April 23, 2013.

paid 20 percent more and receive larger annual bonuses. Darby works about 60 hours a week—more if she is traveling.

Holden has a policy that permits any employee who works as late as 8:00 p.m. to eat dinner at company expense. The employee can also take a taxi home. Darby is in the habit of staying until 8:00 p.m. every night, whether or not her workload requires it. Then she orders enough food for dinner, with leftovers for lunch the next day. She has managed to cut her grocery bill to virtually nothing. Sometimes she invites her boyfriend to join her for dinner. As a student, he is always hungry and broke. Darby often uses the Holden taxi to take them back to his apartment, although the cab fare is twice as high as to her own place. Darby has also been known to return online purchases through the Holden mailroom on the company dime. Many employees do that, and the mailroom workers do not seem to mind.

Is Darby doing anything wrong? What ethics traps is she facing? What would your Life Principle be in this situation?

3. Steve supervises a team of account managers. One night at a company outing, Lawrence, a visiting account manager, made some wildly inappropriate sexual remarks to Maddie, who is on Steve's team. When she told Steve, he was uncertain what to do, so he asked his boss. She was concerned that if Steve took the matter further and Lawrence was fired or even disciplined, her whole area would suffer. Lawrence was one of the best account managers in the region, and everyone was overworked as it was. She told Steve to get Maddie to drop the matter. Just tell her that these things happen, and Lawrence did not mean anything by it.

What should Steve do? What ethics traps does he face? What would be your Life Principle in this situation? What should Maddie do?

4. Many people enjoy rap music at least in part because of its edgy, troublemaking vibe. The problem is that some of this music could cause real trouble, Thus, Ice-T's song "Cop Killer" generated significant controversy when it was released. Among other things, its lyrics celebrated the idea of slitting a policeman's throat. Rick Ross rapped about drugging and raping a woman. Time Warner Inc. did not withdraw Ice-T's song but Reebok fired Ross over his lyrics. One difference: Time Warner was struggling with a $15 billion debt and a depressed stock price. Reebok at first refused to take action, but then singing group UltraViolet began circulating an online petition against the song and staged a protest at the main Reebok store in New York.

What obligation do media companies have to their audiences? What factors matter when making a decision about content?

5. You are negotiating a new labor contract with union officials. The contract covers a plant that has experienced operating losses over the past several years. You want to negotiate concessions from labor to reduce the losses. However, labor is refusing any compromises. You could tell them that, without concessions, the plant will be closed, although that is not true.

Is bluffing ethical? Under what circumstances? What would Kant and Mill say? What result under the Front Page test? What is your Life Principle?

CHAPTER 3

INTERNATIONAL LAW

© Creative Travel Projects/Shutterstock.com

In the early 1990s, a Dutch and British conglomerate named Royal Dutch Petroleum (RDP) operated oil production facilities in Ogoni, a region of Nigeria. When Ogoni residents began protesting the oil giant's environmental practices, the multinational and the Nigerian government joined forces to halt this resistance. And the two stopped at nothing. Nigerian troops raided 60 Ogoni towns where they hanged nine leaders. They shot, raped, tortured, and beat protesters and their families.

Years later, the victims demanded justice. But where would they find it? Who would enforce it? Certainly not Nigeria's courts. The victims argued that U.S. courts were the fairest and best equipped to hear issues of international law. But could a U.S. court meddle in a conflict that occurred on foreign soil between a sovereign government, British and Dutch companies, and non-U.S. citizens?[1]

> **Years later, the victims demanded justice. But where would they find it? Who would enforce it?**

[1]Kiobel v. Royal Dutch Petroleum Co., 133 S. Ct. 1659 (S. Ct. 2013).

Many people throughout the ages have asked this basic question: What is international law? In Chapter 1, we learned that the law is a system of rules that predictably regulates our behavior. It secures our rights and balances government power. For any legal system to thrive, it must have clear rules, shared values, and a system of enforcement that its subjects acknowledge and respect.

International law is different. It has no single source of law or enforcement mechanism. It is a hodge-podge of different actors, legal systems, and cultures. Many times, exiles like the Ogoni victims struggle to find justice anywhere in the world. For these reasons, some people have wondered whether international law exists at all. But it does exist, and is important to study, because our globalized world is more and more dependent on it each day.

3-1 INTERNATIONAL LAW: PUBLIC VERSUS PRIVATE

International law covers a wide array of topics relevant to, well, everything and everyone in the world. **It consists of rules and principles that apply to the conduct of states,[2] international organizations, businesses, and individuals across borders**. It is important to distinguish between two branches of international law: public and private.

Public international law is the law governing relations among governments and international organizations. It includes the law of war (yes, we have to fight fair), the acquisition of territory, and the settlement of disputes among nations. Public international law also has rules governing the globe's shared resources and common elements: the sea, outer space, trade, and communications. Finally, it addresses people: Public international law sets out the basic rules of human rights and laws defining the treatment of refugees, prisoners of war, and international criminals.

Private international law applies to private parties (such as businesses and individuals) in international commercial and legal transactions. It deals with two fundamental issues: Which law applies to a private agreement? How will people from one country settle their private disputes with parties on foreign soil?

Public international law
Rules and norms governing relationships among states and international organizations

Private international law
International rules and standards applying to cross-border commerce

3-2 ACTORS IN INTERNATIONAL LAW

Unlike domestic law—in which the main actors are individuals, businesses, and the government—international law must balance the interests and roles of many different organizations and states.

3-2a The United Nations

After World Wars I and II, people and governments around the world were intent on preventing future conflict. They sought the creation of a supranational organization that could ensure international peace and security, encourage economic and social cooperation, and protect human rights. So, in 1945, 50 nations signed the Charter of the United Nations, binding themselves to its terms and obligations. Today, 193 countries are members of the United Nations.

The UN Charter sets out the organization's governance:

- The **Secretariat** administers the day-to-day operations of the UN.

- The **General Assembly** is the UN's lawmaking body. It is composed of all of its member nations, which propose and vote on resolutions.

---

[2]Throughout the chapter, the authors use "state" to have the same meaning as "country" and "nation."

- The **Security Council** is charged with maintaining international peace. It has 15 member nations. Ten are elected by the General Assembly; five are permanent members: China, France, Russia, the United Kingdom, and the United States. The five permanent members were the primary victors in World War II. They have the right to veto any Security Council resolution.

Much of the UN's work is done through its Specialized Agencies and related organizations, including influential agencies like the World Health Organization (WHO) and the UN Educational, Scientific, and Cultural Organization (UNESCO).

The following agencies, which operate under the UN's umbrella, have great impact on world business:

- The **World Bank's** mandate is to end poverty by encouraging development. Among other activities, it loans money to the poorest countries on favorable terms.

- The **International Monetary Fund** (IMF) aims to foster worldwide economic growth and financial stability.

- The **World Intellectual Property Organization** (WIPO) was established to promote the protection of intellectual property: patents, copyrights, trademarks, and industrial design.

- The **UN Commission on International Trade Law** (UNCITRAL) aims to harmonize international business law by proposing model legislation on such topics as international payments and e-commerce. This agency was responsible for putting forth the UN Convention for the International Sale of Goods (CISG) and the Convention on the Recognition and Enforcement of Foreign Arbitral Awards (New York Convention), both significant business-related treaties discussed later in this chapter.

3-2b The International Court of Justice

International Court of Justice

The judicial branch of the United Nations

The **International Court of Justice (ICJ)**, also known as the World Court, settles international legal disputes and gives advisory opinions to the UN and its agencies. It is comprised of 15 elected judges from 15 countries representing the world's principal legal systems.

In its seven-decade history, the court has heard fewer than 160 cases. The ICJ has not been an important force in resolving international business disputes for several reasons:

- **Only countries can bring a case before the ICJ**, which explains why the Ogoni victims in the chapter opener could not sue Nigeria in this court.

- **The ICJ only has jurisdiction over states that have agreed to be bound by its decisions.** The U.S. had accepted the ICJ's authority—until it lost a case. When the ICJ determined that the U.S. violated international law by secretly supporting Nicaraguan rebels, the U.S. simply withdrew from ICJ jurisdiction. Today the U.S. agrees to ICJ jurisdiction on a case-by-case basis.

- **The court has no enforcement power.**

3-2c International Chamber of Commerce

The International Chamber of Commerce (ICC) is the world's largest global business organization. Its purpose is to facilitate international business. To that end, the ICC advocates on matters of international business policy and develops uniform rules to aid cross-border transactions.

Incoterms

A series of three-letter codes used in international contracts for the sale of goods

In 1936, the organization first proposed the **Incoterms rules**, which define a series of three-letter codes commonly used in international contracts for the sale of goods. No matter what language contracting parties speak, Incoterm "FOB" means that the buyer pays for transportation of the purchased goods. ("FOB" stands for "free on board.")

Note that the ICC does not make law. Instead, it proposes rules whose adoption is voluntary. However, its influence is so widespread that many of its rules like the Incoterms are now accepted as the global standard in international business.

3-2d Sovereign Nations

Last, but certainly not least, we cannot discount the role that countries themselves play in international law. They are its most important and influential actors.

In ancient times, when kings were seen as gods, it was well established that no "god" could interfere in the internal affairs of another. Out of this idea grew the fundamental principle of international law: **sovereignty**, which means that each government has the absolute authority to rule its people and its territory. Under this principle, states are prohibited from interfering in each other's legislative, administrative, or judicial activities.

Sovereign Immunity

Sovereign immunity holds that the courts of one nation lack the jurisdiction (power) to hear suits against foreign governments. Most nations respect this principle. In the United States, the **Foreign Sovereign Immunities Act** (FSIA) provides that American courts generally cannot hear suits against foreign governments. This is a difficult hurdle to overcome, but there are some exceptions:

- **Waiver.** A lawsuit is permitted against a foreign country that voluntarily *agrees to* give up *immunity*.

- **Commercial Activity.** A plaintiff in the United States can sue a foreign country that is engaged in commercial, but not political, activity. An activity is commercial if a business could engage in it (e.g., Iceland purchases helicopters). If, however, the foreign government is doing something that only a government has the power to do (e.g., printing money, making laws), it is a state activity, and the country is immune from related litigation.

3-3 THE WORLD'S LEGAL SYSTEMS

In Chapter 1, we began to explore the origins of our Anglo-American legal tradition. But it is important for every international businessperson to recognize that the great majority—roughly 84 percent—of the world is governed by legal systems that take a very different approach from our own.

3-3a Common Law

As discussed in Chapter 1, we inherited our legal system from England. The United States shares this legacy with most former British colonies, including Australia, Canada, and India. **The hallmarks of the common law are:**

- The use of an adversarial process of dispute resolution presided over by an impartial judge. After the Norman conquest of England, William the Conqueror introduced trial by combat to settle disputes: The winner of the battle was right. This practice formed the basis of the common law's assumption that the role of lawyers is to battle on behalf of the client by making the most persuasive arguments.

- The doctrine of *stare decisis*, which requires judges to base their decisions on prior cases.[3]

- The use of a jury to determine questions of fact.

---

[3]*Stare decisis* is Latin for "to let the decision stand."

Sovereignty

Each government has the absolute authority to rule its people and its territory

Foreign Sovereign Immunities Act

A U.S. statute that provides that American courts generally cannot hear suits against foreign governments

Stare decisis

The principle that legal conclusions must be reached after an analysis of past judgments

3-3b Civil Law

More than 70 percent of the world's population is subject to civil law, including most European countries, Russia, Central and South America, China, large swaths of Asia, and parts of Africa.[4]

The main principle of civil law is that the law is found primarily in the statute books, or codes. The main characteristics of the civil code tradition are:

- The use of an inquisitorial process of dispute resolution, in which the judge acts as interrogator and investigator. Judges rely more on written submissions than on lawyers' oral arguments.

- Courts base their judgments on the code and on the writings of law professors.

- Civil code systems do not use juries.

3-3c Islamic Law

More than one-fifth of the world's population lives under legal systems influenced by the religion of Islam. Islamic law, also known as **shari'a**, is a legal system most commonly found in Africa, Asia, and the Middle East.[5] There is much variation in the interpretation and practice of both Islam and Islamic law.

Shari'a law
Islamic law

Shari'a is based on the Muslim holy book, the Koran, and the teachings and actions of the Prophet Muhammed. Although most of what Westerners hear about *shari'a* law involves harsh criminal punishments, Islamic law covers business relationships, personal and family matters, and daily life. Many of its doctrines are tailored to promote honesty and transparency in business relationships.

The following case may come as a surprise because most people do not realize that U.S. courts can apply foreign law to resolve disputes. The parties filed suit in a U.S. court, even though the dispute was governed by *shari'a* law.

SAUDI BASIC INDUSTRIES CORPORATION V. MOBIL YANBU PETROCHEMICAL COMPANY, INC. AND EXXON CHEMICAL ARABIA, INC.

A.2d 1
Delaware Supreme Court, 2005

CASE SUMMARY

Facts: In the 1970s, SABIC, a corporation owned by the Saudi Arabian government, went into business with Mobil and Exxon. The contracts between SABIC and Mobil and Exxon were governed by Saudi law and forbade the parties from charging each other hidden fees. But SABIC violated this provision for two decades.

ExxonMobil and SABIC sued each other in a Delaware court for breach of contract and tort.[6] Because the

---

[4]Note that "civil law," as referred to in this chapter, is a legal system based on codes (i.e., civil law versus common law systems). In common law systems such as ours, the same term is also used to describe contract, tort, and other areas of private law (i.e., civil law versus criminal law).

[5]*Shari'a* means "path" in Arabic.

U.S. court was required to apply Saudi law, the judge brought in experts in *shari'a* law for instruction.

The jury found SABIC liable for the Saudi tort of wrongful seizure (*ghasb*) and awarded ExxonMobil $416 million. SABIC appealed to the Delaware Supreme Court for a new trial, arguing that that the trial court's application of Saudi law was flawed.

Issue: *Did the U.S. court err in its application of shari'a law?*

Decision: No, the U.S. court applied the law properly.

Reasoning: U.S. courts can apply other nations' laws. In this case, SABIC insisted that a U.S. court hear the case and apply *shari'a* law, but then asked for a new trial, arguing that the judge was not qualified to interpret Islamic law.

Shari'a law is very different from our common law system. It is a religious law based on both the Koran and the model behavior of the Prophet Muhammed. It does not embrace the common law system of binding precedent. In Saudi Arabia, judicial decisions are not in themselves a source of law and are not even open to public inspection.

Instead of determining a single correct answer to the legal question at hand, Saudi judges study Islamic scholarly writings as guides. What determines Saudi law is the judge's study and analysis, or *ijtihad*. The critical inquiry is whether the judge followed proper analytical procedures in reaching the result.

In this case, the American judge conducted an exceptionally in-depth analysis on Saudi law and reasoning. She collected many written reports from different Saudi law experts; she hired her own independent expert, who traveled to Saudi Arabia to perform research; and she heard many hours of expert testimony. Only after this extensive process did she undertake to analyze the Saudi tort of *ghasb*.

Because the judge's process was sound and thorough, the damages are affirmed. SABIC cannot purposefully select the U.S. legal system and then complain that it had no access to a *shari'a* judge.

3-4 SOURCES OF LAW

This section outlines the three major sources of international law: treaties, custom, and general principles of law.

3-4a Treaties

Recall from Chapter 1 that the president makes treaties with foreign nations. According to the Vienna Convention on the Law of Treaties, a **treaty** is an international agreement governed by international law. Since treaties have their own treaty, they also have their own vocabulary:

- A **bilateral treaty** is between two countries—similar to a contract between states. A **multilateral treaty** involves three or more countries.

- A **convention** is a treaty on a specific issue that affects all the participants, like the UN Convention on Contracts for the International Sale of Goods..

- A treaty is said to be **adopted** when those who have drafted it agree that it is in final form.

- A treaty is **ratified** when a nation indicates its intent to be bound by it. **To take effect in the United States, treaties must be approved by at least two-thirds of the United States Senate.**

- A treaty **enters into force** when it becomes legally binding on its signatories. This date may be specified in the treaty or it may be the date on which the treaty receives a certain number of ratifications.

This section examines treaties that are critical to international business.

Ijtihad
The process of Islamic legal and religious reasoning

Treaty
An agreement between two or more states governed by international law

---

[6]Exxon and Mobil entered into separate contracts with SABIC, but by the time of this lawsuit had merged to form one company named ExxonMobil.

GATT

GATT is the General Agreement on Tariffs and Trade. Any discussion of international trade issues must begin with free trade, which has been a contentious issue since David Ricardo first advocated it in the early nineteenth century. He, and economists since him, have argued that citizens of the world will benefit overall if each country produces whatever goods it can make most efficiently and then trades them for goods that other countries make more efficiently. For instance, a developing country with unskilled labor should produce clothing and then trade it to the United States for commercial aircraft and semiconductors (two major categories of U.S. exports).

Such a plan makes great economic sense, unless you happen to work in the clothing business in the United States. So countries are often tempted to impose tariffs and quotas on imports to protect local industries and workers.

GATT is a massive international treaty that has been negotiated on and off since the 1940s as nations have sought to eliminate trade barriers and bolster commerce. To strengthen this treaty, GATT signatories created the **World Trade Organization (WTO)** in 1995. Its mandate is to stimulate international commerce and resolve trade disputes.

GATT and the WTO are founded on the following principles:

World Trade Organization (WTO)
An international organization whose mandate is to lower trade barriers

- **Free Trade.** The major focus of this treaty is to reduce trade barriers.

Most favored nation
WTO/GATT requires that favors offered to one country must be given to all member nations.

- **Most Favored Nation.** Although it sounds like a requirement to give someone special treatment, "**most favored nation**" means that countries must treat every other member nation equally. If WTO-member Greece grants fellow member Laos a special discount on customs duties for certain products, that treatment must be extended to all other WTO members.

National treatment
The principle of nondiscrimination between foreigners and locals

- **National Treatment**. After imported products have entered the country, they must be treated the same as locally produced goods. In other words, countries may not discriminate against foreign goods by imposing additional taxes that do not apply to domestic goods. Japan taxed imported vodka seven times higher than its own domestic version, *shochu*, even though both were distilled similarly. Because this tax violated national treatment provisions, the WTO required that Japan revise its laws.

The WTO tries to promote free trade by limiting countries' efforts to unfairly protect their domestic industries. **Among the techniques that countries use (and the WTO tries to limit) are:**

- **Customs Duties.** Taxes imposed on goods when they enter a country

- **Excise Taxes.** Taxes levied on a particular activity, such as the purchase of wine or cigarettes

- **Nontariff Barriers.** Such as quotas on the amount of a particular good that can be imported.

The WTO is empowered to settle trade disputes between its member states. It may order compliance and impose penalties in the form of trade sanctions. **If a country refuses to comply with the WTO's ruling, affected nations may retaliate by imposing punitive tariffs or other measures.** The United States and four Central American countries filed a complaint with the WTO alleging that the European Union (EU) had placed unfair restrictions on the importation of bananas. The WTO agreed and then granted the United States and Ecuador the right to impose sanctions on EU imports into their countries.

Regional Trade Agreements

Regional trade agreements (RTAs) reduce trade restrictions and promote common trade policies among member nations that are located near each other. Today, RTAs cover more than half of international trade.

The **North American Free Trade Agreement (NAFTA)** is an RTA that has had a large impact on the United States. Signed by the United States, Canada, and Mexico in 1993, its principal goal was to eliminate almost all trade barriers among the three nations. This treaty has been controversial, for all the usual reasons.

Trade between the three nations has increased enormously. Mexico now exports more goods to the United States than do Germany, Britain, and Korea combined. Opponents of the treaty argue that NAFTA costs the United States jobs and lowers the living standards of American workers by forcing them to compete with low-paid labor. Proponents contend that although some jobs are lost, many others are gained, especially in fields with a bright future, such as high technology. They claim that as new jobs invigorate the Mexican economy, consumers there will be able to afford certain categories of American goods for the first time, providing an enormous new market. Also, NAFTA provides American consumers with more, and cheaper, products.

GATS and TRIPs

The **General Agreement on Trade in Services, or GATS**, extends the WTO/GATT principles to transnational services; the **Agreement on Trade Related Aspects of Intellectual Property (TRIPs)** covers intellectual property (IP). The WTO administers both treaties.

The following case is about a tiny country with big dreams of becoming a gambling giant. Without access to the U.S. market, it was just a pipe dream. But would the United States obey the WTO's ruling? Don't bet on it.

Regional Trade Agreements (RTAs)
Treaties that reduce trade restrictions and promote common policies among member nations

North American Free Trade Agreement (NAFTA)
A treaty that reduced trade barriers among Canada, the United States, and Mexico

General Agreement on Trade in Services (GATS)
A treaty on transnational services

Agreement on Trade Related Aspects of Intellectual Property (TRIPs)
A treaty on intellectual property

UNITED STATES – MEASURES AFFECTING THE CROSS-BORDER SUPPLY OF GAMBLING AND BETTING SERVICES

WT/DS285/ARB
WTO Arbitral Body, 2007

CASE SUMMARY

Facts: Antigua is a small Caribbean nation. When it began hosting gambling websites, its economy thrived, boosted by U.S. gamblers. But when the United States started criminally prosecuting Internet gambling, Antigua's profits plummeted. The United States had the right to take this step, but it had to do so consistently—treating foreign and domestic sites the same. The problem was that it allowed Internet betting on horseracing within its borders.

Antigua challenged U.S. gambling laws in the WTO, arguing that they discriminated against foreign betting services. Both the United States and Antigua were members of GATS, under which each agree to free trade (including nondiscrimination and national treatment) in online services.

A WTO panel ruled that the United States' inconsistent gambling laws violated GATS and ordered that it bring them into compliance. Two years passed and the United States did not act.

Frustrated, Antigua requested permission from the WTO to suspend its obligations to the United States under TRIPs. This suspension would mean that Antigua could freely use, reproduce, and distribute any U.S.-copyrighted, trademarked, or patented works—a real blow to the United States entertainment, pharmaceutical, and technology industries. The United States objected and submitted the matter to a panel of WTO experts.

Issue: *When one WTO member refuses to comply with a WTO ruling, can the injured member retaliate by suspending its duties under another treaty?*

Decision: Yes, the injured WTO member may retaliate by suspending another treaty.

Reasoning: When a party that suffers harm from a violation of one treaty seeks to compensate by suspending its duties under another agreement, it must prove that (1) suspending its obligations under the breached treaty is not an effective remedy and (2) the circumstances are serious.

This case involves a dispute between a tiny, developing country and the world's dominant economy. Suspending Antigua's GATS obligations would have virtually no impact on the United States at all. Only Antigua would suffer: Its people would be forced to scramble for replacement services at uncertain cost. Moreover, Antigua imports services from the United States that are worth much less than the $21 million a year that it is owed.

The circumstances of this case are sufficiently serious to allow suspension of TRIPS obligations. For years, the United States has refused to comply with a WTO ruling and has strangled Antigua's trade in services.

This issue has been in dispute for over a decade. As of this writing, Antigua is creating an online platform to openly sell American movies, music, and medications at a discounted price—and keep the profit. Stay tuned.

EXAM Strategy

Question: To limit the number of cars on city streets, Shanghai, China, set up a system under which drivers could only acquire automobile license plates through a monthly auction. But Shanghai ran two different auctions: one for foreign-made cars, in which the government limited the number of license plates to 30 a month and set a high minimum bid and another for Chinese cars, in which 3,000 license plates a month were available, with no minimum bid. The United States complained that Shanghai's system had a direct effect on its imports. Is China in violation of WTO principles?

Strategy: As a signatory to the WTO, China committed to treating imported cars the same as its own domestic products. Does China have the right to impose these restrictions? Is traffic regulation a valid excuse?

Result: National treatment means that a WTO country cannot give special treatment or benefits to its own goods. Even though Shanghai may not have intended its rules to disrupt international trade, it did, because the license auctions had a direct effect on the price of imported cars. Shanghai's rules violated WTO principles.

CISG

The **United Nations Convention on Contracts for the International Sale of Goods (CISG)** aims to make sales law more uniform and predictable—and to make international contracting easier. The United States and most of its principal trading partners (except the United Kingdom) have adopted this important treaty, which governs over two-thirds of the world's trade.

The most important provisions are:

- **The CISG applies to contracts for the sale of commercial goods,** but not to consumer goods bought for personal use.

- **The CISG applies automatically when contracts are formed between two parties located in different signatory countries.** The treaty's application does not depend on nationality, rather on location. If the Starbucks store in Colombia contracts with a seller in Brazil, the CISG automatically applies because both Brazil and Colombia are members of the CISG.

- **Contracting parties can opt out.** If the parties want to be governed by other law, their contract must state clearly that they exclude the CISG and elect another country's law.

- **International sales contracts do not need to be in writing.** Unlike many nations' contract laws, the CISG does not require a writing to prove the existence of a contract.

- **Contracting parties must be flexible and fair.** The CISG requires parties to negotiate in good faith and modify the contract in case of unforeseen circumstances.

- **A buyer can avoid payment under a contract only after giving the seller notice and an opportunity to remedy.** As we will see in Unit 4 on sales, U.S. contract law excuses buyers from paying if the seller's performance is not absolutely perfect. The CISG is much less strict on sellers.

- **Countries may use their own national laws to (1) replace some CISG provisions or (2) fill in the blanks on issues that the CISG does not cover at all.** For example, the CISG does not provide rules for determining whether a contract is fraudulent: This substantive rule is left to the discretion of each country.

In the following case, each country had different contract rules and divergent interpretations of the CISG. The result? A huge mess, in any language. Which law applies?

FORESTAL GUARANI S.A. v. DAROS INTERNATIONAL, INC.

613 F.3d 395
United States Court of Appeals for the Third Circuit, 2010

CASE SUMMARY

Facts: Forestal Guarani, in Argentina, entered into an oral agreement to sell woodworking products to Daros International in New Jersey. Forestal sent Daros all the items, but Daros declined to pay the full amount.

When Forestal sued Daros in the United States for breach of contract, there was confusion about which law applied to the oral contract. Both Argentina and the United States were signatories to the CISG, which allowed for oral contracts, but Argentina opted out of the CISG's no-writing requirement when it ratified the convention. So, did the CISG apply? Or the law of Argentina or New Jersey?

The district court dismissed Forestal's claim because the parties' agreement was not in writing. Forestal appealed.

Issue: *Which law applied to this contract—the CISG, Argentine law, or New Jersey law?*

Decision: Either Argentine or New Jersey law could apply, because Argentina had opted out of the CISG's writing rule.

Reasoning: Because both the United States, where Daros is located, and Argentina, where Forestal is based, are signatories to the CISG and the alleged contract at issue involves the sale of goods, the CISG generally governs the claim.

However, the CISG allows signatories to opt out of some of its rules, and Argentina did indeed opt out of the no-writing requirement. So while the CISG applies generally to this contract, it does not govern the issue of whether the agreement had to be in writing. Either Argentine or New Jersey law will determine the answer to that question. Since the court was not briefed on each jurisdiction's laws, the case is remanded for more information.

3-4b **Custom and General Principles of Law**

Customary international law

International rules become binding through a pattern of consistent, longstanding behavior.

For hundreds of years, until treaties became common, custom was the main way international law was created. A custom is a widely accepted way of doing something. Over time, patterns of states' behavior, action, and inaction crystallized into the compulsory rules of **customary international law**.

Today, courts recognize a custom as binding international law if:

- It is widespread and widely-accepted,
- It is longstanding, and
- Nations follow it out of a sense of obligation to each other.

Customary international law governed behavior on the battlefield and the treatment of prisoners of war until the creation of the Geneva Conventions, which codified these customary practices.

Slavery, genocide, piracy, and torture are often cited as examples of fundamental principles of customary international law that are accepted by all civilized nations.

Ethics Is torture always wrong? That issue has been deeply and bitterly debated in the United States ever since the terrorist attacks of 9/11. On one side of this debate are those who believe that torture should be used if necessary to obtain information that might help prevent other acts of terrorism. They believe that the harsh treatment of suspected terrorists has been successful in keeping America safe. On the other side are those who say that torture is less effective at eliciting useful information than other interrogation methods. The United States' use of brutality, these critics claim, undermines our legal and moral standing worldwide, and gives other countries a license to torture our citizens.

Under what circumstances, if any, should torture be permitted? What would Kant and Mill say?

3-5 EXTRATERRITORIALITY AND FOREIGN RECOGNITION

One of the major legal debates of our time involves the blurring line between sovereignty and international law. While Americans are proud to say that our Constitution has influenced the laws of other countries, the debate becomes considerably more heated when it involves the influence of foreign or international law on the United States.

3-5a **Application of U.S. Law Abroad**

Extraterritoriality

The power of one country's laws to reach activities outside of its borders

Extraterritoriality is the power of one nation to impose its laws in other countries.[7] Many U.S. statutes regulate conduct outside the country. The Foreign Corrupt Practices Act, discussed in Chapter 6 on crime, prohibits bribery abroad. Price-fixing conducted abroad is a violation of the Sherman Act if it has an impact on the United States. **But, as a general rule, U.S. statutes do not apply outside the country, unless they explicitly state that they do.**

In the chapter opener, the Ogoni people sued an oil company for crimes against humanity that occurred in Nigeria. They sued in the United States, under a U.S. statute

---

[7]Extraterritoriality can also refer to exemption from local laws. For example, ambassadors are generally exempt from the law of the nation in which they serve.

passed in 1789 that allowed claims by non-U.S. citizens for certain torts that were violations of international law and occurred in the United States or on the high seas, outside the sovereignty of any country.

The Supreme Court held that, since the statute did not expressly mention extraterritorial application, U.S. courts could not apply it to wrongs committed in another country. As the Court said, "United States law governs domestically but does not rule the world." Any other result could cause confusion and international discord—not to mention danger for U.S. citizens if other countries responded by subjecting them to foreign laws.

Many American companies do business through international subsidiaries—foreign companies that they control. What should happen when an employee of a foreign subsidiary argues that his rights under an American statute have been violated? You make the call.

> **United States law governs domestically but does not rule the world.**

You be the Judge

Facts: Boston Scientific (BSC) was an American company that manufactured medical equipment. The company had its headquarters in Massachusetts but did business around the world through foreign subsidiaries. One of the company's subsidiaries was Boston Scientific Argentina (BSA), and it was there that Ruben Carnero began working. His employment contract stated that Argentine law was to govern the contract. Four years later, Carnero took an assignment to work as a country manager for a different BSC subsidiary, Boston Scientific do Brasil (BSB). Carnero frequently traveled to Massachusetts to meet with company executives, but he did most of his work in South America.

About a year later, BSB fired Carnero, and BSA soon did the same. Carnero claimed that the companies terminated him in retaliation for his reporting to BSC executives that the Argentine and Brazilian subsidiaries inflated sales figures and engaged in other accounting fraud.

Carnero filed suit in federal court in Massachusetts, alleging that his firing violated an American statute, the Sarbanes-Oxley Act of 2002 (SOX). This statute included a "whistleblower" provision designed to protect employees who informed superiors or investigating officials of fraud within the company. The law allows injured employees reinstatement and back pay.

BSC argued that SOX did not apply overseas and the District Court agreed, dismissing the case. Carnero appealed.

You Be the Judge: *Does SOX protect a whistleblower employed overseas by a subsidiary of an American company?*

CARNERO V. BOSTON SCIENTIFIC CORPORATION
433 F.3d 1
United States Court of Appeals for the First Circuit, 2006

Argument for Carnero: Mr. Carnero knew his report would be poorly received but believed he had an ethical obligation to protect his company. For that effort, he was fired, and now Boston Scientific attempts to avoid liability using the technicality of corporate hierarchy.

Yes, Mr. Carnero was employed by BSB and BSA. But both of those companies are owned and operated by Boston Scientific. It is the larger company, with headquarters in the United States, that calls the shots. That is why Mr. Carnero reported to executives in Massachusetts—and why he brought them his unhappy news.

SOX's whistleblower protection is designed to encourage honest employees to come forward and report wrongdoing. By doing so, they protect their company and its shareholders. Mr. Carnero may well have saved his employer from massive losses and public disgrace. Boston Scientific should honor the purpose and intent of SOX by protecting his job.

Argument for Boston Scientific: First, we do not know whether or not there have been any accounting irregularities. Second, the fact that Mr. Carnero is employed by companies incorporated in Argentina and Brazil is more than a technicality. He is asking an American court to go into two foreign countries—sovereign nations with good ties to the United States—and investigate the accounting and employment practices of local companies. That is not a step that the United States should enter into lightly.

If the United States can impose its whistleblowing law in foreign countries, may those nations impose their rules and values here? Suppose that a country forbids women to do certain work. May companies in those nations direct American subsidiaries to reject all female job applicants? Neither the citizens nor courts of this country would find such interference tolerable.

Mr. Carnero's request is also impractical. How would an American court determine why he was fired? Must the trial judge here subpoena Brazilian witnesses and demand documentary evidence from that country?

Finally, SOX does not state that it applies overseas. Congress was well aware that American corporations operate subsidiaries abroad, but made no mention of those companies when it passed this statute.

EXAM Strategy

Question: U.S. citizens Alberto Vilar and Gary Tanaka managed $9 billion in investments through their companies, some of which were located in Panama. The two were arrested in the United States for a massive securities fraud: They had lied to their clients about investments—and used some of the money entrusted to them to repair their homes and buy horses. Vilar and Tanaka claimed that U.S. securities laws did not apply to sales that occurred outside the country. These laws were silent as to their application abroad. Do Vilar and Tanaka have a valid argument?

Strategy: What are the rules on extraterritoriality?

Result: The court agreed with the defendants: When laws do not explicitly state that they cover conduct abroad, judges cannot interpret them to do so. (Unfortunately for the defendants, they still went to jail on other charges.)

3-5b U.S. Recognition and Enforcement of Foreign Judgments

Imagine that you obtain a court judgment for a million dollars against a foreign seller who sent you defective goods. Great news, right? Well, you may not want to celebrate too soon: If the seller has no assets in the country where you won in court, your award may be worthless.

Foreign recognition

Means that a foreign judgment has legal validity in another country

Foreign enforcement

Means that the court system of a country will assist in enforcing or collecting on the verdict awarded by a foreign court

To address this common situation, most major trading nations have rules for recognizing and enforcing foreign judgments within their borders. **Foreign recognition** means that a decision by a another country's court is legally valid domestically. **Foreign enforcement** means that a judgment rendered in a foreign court can be collected domestically as if it were a judgment of the country's own courts.

In the United States, most states have adopted the **Uniform Foreign Money Judgments Recognition Act. This act provides that U.S. courts will recognize foreign judgments if:**

- The award was based on a full and fair trial by an impartial tribunal with proper jurisdiction;

- The defendant was given notice and an opportunity to appear;

- The judgment was not fraudulent or against public policy; and

- The foreign court was the proper forum to hear the case.

The Ecuadorian Supreme Court awarded $9.5 billion to the Ecuadorian victims of a massive, decades-long environmental contamination of an area known as Lago Agrio by oil company Texaco (now Chevron). Since Chevron did not have sufficient assets in Ecuador for the victims to collect, the plaintiffs sought to enforce the judgment in the United States A federal court in New York refused to recognize the award because it found evidence that the corrupt Ecuadorian judges were paid off by the plaintiffs.

Arbitration

Parties who prefer to avoid courts altogether generally opt for arbitration. **Arbitration** is a binding process in which the parties submit their dispute to a neutral private body for resolution. It is especially advantageous when the disputing parties are from different countries because it is generally faster, more private, less expensive, and less political than litigating in foreign courts. International arbitral bodies, such as the ICC, issue arbitral awards, but enforcement depends upon the laws of the individual countries where the parties operate.

The **Convention on the Recognition and Enforcement of Foreign Arbitral Awards** (also known as the **New York Convention**) is an international treaty with 149 signatories that provides common rules for recognizing arbitration agreements. But each country has its own specific requirements. **In the United States, an arbitral award will generally be enforced if:**

- It is enforceable under the local law of the country where the award was granted;

- The arbitral tribunal had proper jurisdiction;

- The defendant was given notice of the arbitration and an opportunity to be heard; and

- Enforcement of the award is not fraudulent or contrary to public policy.

Arbitration

A binding process of resolving legal disputes by submitting them to a neutral third party

New York Convention

Widely accepted treaty on the court enforcement of arbitral awards

3-6 ESSENTIAL CLAUSES IN INTERNATIONAL CONTRACTS

International business brings great reward, but also carries significant risks. Distance, language, politics, culture, and different legal systems all pose potential hurdles to successful transactions.

However, some of these risks can be controlled by carefully thinking about contract terms beforehand. In this chapter, we witnessed what happened to Forestal, an Argentine company that made an oral agreement with a New Jersey buyer. First it was not paid—perhaps due to a miscommunication or cultural difference. Then, it was dragged into a common law court system in a foreign country more than 5,000 miles away, only to spend thousands of American dollars on pricey U.S. lawyers to figure out *which law* applied to their deal. Unfortunately, these outcomes are not uncommon in international business.

To ensure that you do not end up in a similar predicament, be sure to consider the following when you negotiate international deals:

- **Choice of Law: What Law Governs?** When making an agreement, it is *essential* to negotiate which country's law will control. Each side will prefer the law they are most familiar with. How to compromise? Perhaps by using a neutral law. But before reaching any agreement, be sure to seek the advice of an attorney who specializes in the law of that country. It is a good idea to have a trusted legal advisor in any foreign country where you do business.

- **Choice of Forum: Where Will the Case Be Heard?** The parties must decide where disagreements will be resolved. This can be a significant part of a contract because legal and court systems are dramatically different in terms of speed, cost, transparency, and trustworthiness.

- **Choice of Language and Currency.** The parties must select a language for the contract and a currency for payment. Language counts because legal terms seldom translate literally. Currency is vital because the exchange rate may alter between the signing and payment.

Chapter Conclusion

International law is increasingly relevant to our globalized business world. While it was once the domain of nations, today it affects individuals, businesses, and groups all over the world. As the world gets smaller, these issues will become more and more pressing.

EXAM REVIEW

1. **PUBLIC INTERNATIONAL LAW** The law governing relations among governments and international organizations.

2. **PRIVATE INTERNATIONAL LAW** The law governing private parties in international commercial and legal transactions.

3. **INTERNATIONAL COURT OF JUSTICE (ICJ)** The World Court settles international legal disputes among states.

4. **THE INTERNATIONAL CHAMBER OF COMMERCE (ICC)** is the world's largest global business organization.

5. **SOVEREIGN IMMUNITY** Sovereign immunity holds that the courts of one nation lack the jurisdiction (power) to hear suits against foreign governments, unless the foreign nation has waived immunity or is engaging in commercial activity.

6. **COMMON LAW** The legal system based on precedent and adversarial process that was inherited by most British colonies, including the United States and Australia.

7. **CIVIL LAW** The most widespread legal system in the world, whose main principle is that law is found primarily in statutes rather than in judicial decisions.

8. **ISLAMIC LAW** Based on the Koran and the actions and teachings of Mohammad.

EXAM Strategy

Question: No matter where you are in the world, the relationship between landlords and tenants can be a tense one. How would judges in common law, civil law, and Islamic law jurisdictions approach a landlord/tenant controversy?

Strategy: Review the process that judges use to examine and apply the laws in each of these legal systems. (See the "Result" at the end of this section.)

9. **GATT, GATS, AND TRIPS**   The goal of the General Agreement on Tariffs and Trade (GATT) is to lower trade barriers worldwide. The General Agreement on Trade in Services (GATS) and the Trade Related Aspects of Intellectual Property (TRIPs) extend GATT principles to services and intellectual property, respectively.

10. **WTO**   GATT created the WTO, which resolves disputes between signatories to the treaty.

11. **REGIONAL TRADE AGREEMENTS**   Trade agreements promoting common policies among member states.

12. **CISG**   The goal of CISG is to make sales law more uniform and predictable—and to make international contracting easier. A sales agreement between a U.S. company and a foreign company may be governed by U.S. law, by the law of the foreign country, or by the CISG.

EXAM Strategy

> **Question:** Paula, a U.S. citizen, purchased a lamp for her home from Interieures, a lighting website based in Paris. The company's website stated that the governing law would be the law of France and only French courts could hear claims. When the company breached its contract, Paula sought to sue in the United States under the CISG. Does the CISG apply to Paula's claim?
>
> **Strategy:** Review the scope and applicability of the CISG and the section on "Essential Clauses in International Contracts." (See the "Result" at the end of this section.)

13. **CUSTOMARY INTERNATIONAL LAW**   Courts recognize custom as binding international law if it is (1) widespread and widely accepted, (2) longstanding, and (3) nations obey it out of a sense of obligation to each other.

14. **EXTRATERRITORIALITY**   The power of one nation to impose its laws in other countries.

15. **UNIFORM FOREIGN MONEY JUDGMENTS RECOGNITION ACT**   A U.S. act requiring states to recognize foreign judgments under certain conditions.

16. **NEW YORK CONVENTION**   An international treaty that provides rules for the recognition and enforcement of foreign arbitral awards.

> <u>**8. Result:**</u>   The common law judge would hear the arguments of lawyers, who formulate their argument based on prior courts' rulings. The civil law judge would consult the applicable code that deals with landlord and tenant disputes. The Islamic law judge would engage in a process of *ijtihad*, which incorporates legal knowledge with religious reasoning based on the Koran and teachings and actions of Mohammad.
>
> <u>**12. Result:**</u>   Paula is out of luck. First, the CISG only applies to commercial sales contracts, not personal ones. Even if it applied, Interieures has conspicuously opted out of it. The only way U.S. law would have applied is if the two parties had agreed to such a provision.

MATCHING QUESTIONS

Match the following terms with their definitions:

___A. GATT

___B. NAFTA

___C. TRIPS

___D. CISG

___E. ICJ

1. A trade agreement between Mexico, the United States, and Canada

2. The World Court

3. An international convention that governs the sale of goods

4. A treaty that governs trade

5. A treaty that governs intellectual property

TRUE/FALSE QUESTIONS

Circle true or false:

1. T F The ICC makes international law.
2. T F States can opt out of ICJ jurisdiction.
3. T F The CISG requires parties to negotiate internationally in good faith.
4. T F Incoterm rules define terms used in international contracts.
5. T F The WTO settles disputes involving individuals, businesses, or countries.

MULTIPLE-CHOICE QUESTIONS

1. For which of the following activities can a foreign sovereign be sued?

   (a) Operating a factory dangerously

   (b) Issuing a law that discriminates against a certain group

   (c) Suspending the civil rights of its people

   (d) None of the above

2. Outdoor Technologies (an Australian company) obtained a judgment for $500,000 against Silver Star (a Chinese company) in a court in Australia. Silver Star owned property in Iowa so Outdoor filed suit in Iowa to collect the judgment. Which of the following statements is true?

   (a) Outdoor cannot collect in the United States on a judgment that was issued by an Australian court.

   (b) Outdoor cannot collect in the United States because Silver is not an American company.

   (c) Outdoor can collect in the United States if the Australian court was fair and proper.

   (d) Outdoor can collect in the United States, because both the United States and Australia have common law systems.

3. The president negotiates a defense agreement with a foreign government. To take effect, the agreement must be ratified by which of the following?

   (a) Two-thirds of the House of Representatives

   (b) Two-thirds of the Senate

   (c) The Supreme Court

   (d) A and B

   (e) A, B, and C

4. Lynn is an author living in Nevada. She contracted with a company in China, which promised to print her custom children's books. After receiving Lynn's payment, the company disappeared without performing. Lynn wants to sue for fraud, but the contract does not say anything about which country's law will be used to resolve disputes. Both China and the United States are signatories of the CISG. Will the CISG apply in this case?

   (a) Yes, because both countries are signatories.

   (b) Yes, because the parties did not opt out of the CISG.

   (c) No, because the contract does not involve goods.

   (d) No, because the CISG does not establish rules for fraud.

5. Austria, Indonesia, and Colombia are all members of the WTO. If Austria imposes a tariff on imports of coffee beans from Colombia, but not from Indonesia, is it in violation of WTO principles?

   (a) Yes, the WTO prohibits tariffs.

   (b) Yes, the WTO prohibits excise taxes.

   (c) Yes, Austria is violating the WTO's most favored nation rules.

   (d) No, the WTO's most favored nation rules permit Austria to do this.

CASE QUESTIONS

1. A Saudi Arabian government-run hospital hired American Scott Nelson to be an engineer. The parties signed the employment agreement in the United States On the job, Nelson reported that the hospital had significant safety defects. For this, he was arrested, jailed, and tortured for 39 days. Upon his release to the United States, Nelson sued the Saudi government for personal injury. Can Nelson sue Saudi Arabia?

2. The Instituto de Auxilios y Viviendas is a government agency of the Dominican Republic. Dr. Marion Fernandez, the general administrator of the Instituto and Secretary of the Republic, sought a loan for the Instituto. She requested that Charles Meadows, an American citizen, secure the Instituto a bank loan of $12 million. If he obtained a loan on favorable terms, he would receive a fee of $240,000. Meadows did secure a loan, which the Instituto accepted. He then sought his fee, but the Instituto and the Dominican government refused to pay. He sued the government in U.S. federal court. The Dominican government claimed immunity. Comment.

3. Asante, located in California, purchased electronic parts from PMC, whose offices were in Canada. When Asante sued PMC for breach of contract, it alleged that California sales law should apply. PMC argued that the CISG automatically applied because both Canada and the United States have ratified the treaty. Who is right?

4. During the Spanish-American War in 1898, the United States blockaded Cuba. It seized two commercial fishing vessels sailing under a Spanish flag off the Cuban coast. The crew knew nothing about the war and had no arms on board. U.S. officials auctioned off the captured vessels, but their owners protested, claiming that since ancient times countries at war had respected each other's commercial ships. There was no law or treaty on this matter. Do the ship owners have a valid claim?

5. Many European nations are fearful of the effects of genetically modified foods, so they choose to restrict their importation. The EU banned the entry of these foods and subjected them to strict labeling requirements. Does this policy contravene the principles of WTO/GATT?

DISCUSSION QUESTIONS

1. After reading this chapter, do you believe that international law exists? Has your concept of law and legal rules changed?

2. After the 9/11 terrorist attacks, the U.S. government imprisoned suspected terrorists in Guantanamo Bay, Cuba. Officials argued that these detainees did not enjoy constitutional rights because they were not on U.S. soil, even though they were held by Americans. Are the freedoms guaranteed by the U.S. Constitution reserved for U.S. citizens on U.S. soil, or do they apply more broadly?

3. The United Kingdom has not signed the CISG. Until recently, major world traders like Brazil had refused to sign. Imagine that you are a legislator from one of these countries. What might your objections be to ratifying a treaty on sales law?

4. Generally speaking, should the United States pass laws that seek to control behavior outside its borders? Or when in Rome, should our companies and subsidiaries be allowed to do as the Romans do?

5. What responsibility, if any, does the United States have to obey international law? Is it any different from other countries' responsibility to uphold international law? Why or why not?

CHAPTER 4

CONSTITUTIONAL, STATUTORY, ADMINISTRATIVE, AND COMMON LAW

© Creative Travel Projects/Shutterstock.com

> **The wit of man cannot devise a more solid basis for a free, durable and well-administered republic.**

TO MAJOR JOHN CARTWRIGHT.
MONTICELLO, June 5, 1824.

DEAR AND VENERABLE SIR,

I am much indebted for your kind letter…

Our Revolution presented us an album on which we were free to write what we pleased. We had no occasion to search into musty records, to hunt up royal parchments, or to investigate the laws and institutions of a semi-barbarous ancestry. We appealed to those of nature, and found them engraved on our hearts.

We had never been permitted to exercise self-government. When forced to assume it, we were novices in its science. Its principles and forms had entered little into our former education. We established, however, some, although not all its important principles.

The constitutions of most of our States assert that all power is inherent in the people; that they may exercise it by themselves, or they may act by representatives, freely and equally chosen; that it is their right and duty to be at all times armed; that they are entitled to freedom of person, freedom of religion, freedom of property, and freedom of the press.

In the structure of our legislatures, we think experience has proved the benefit of subjecting questions to two separate bodies of deliberants. The wit of man cannot devise a more solid basis for a free, durable and well-administered republic.

[O]ur State and federal governments are coordinate departments of one simple and integral whole. To the State governments are reserved all legislation and administration, in affairs which concern their own citizens only, and to the federal government is given whatever concerns foreigners, or the citizens of other States.

You will perceive that we have not so far [made] our constitutions unchangeable. [W]e consider them not otherwise changeable than by the authority of the people.

Can one generation bind another, and all others, in succession forever? I think not. A generation may bind itself as long as its majority continues in life; when that has disappeared, another majority is in place, holds all the rights and powers their predecessors once held, and may change their laws and institutions to suit themselves. Nothing is unchangeable but the inherent and unalienable rights of man.

Your age of eighty-four and mine of eighty-one years, insure us a speedy meeting. In the meantime, I pray you to accept assurances of my high veneration and esteem for your person and character.

Yours truly,

Thomas Jefferson

4-1 CONSTITUTIONAL LAW

4-1a Government Power

The Constitution of the United States is the greatest legal document ever written. No other written constitution has lasted so long, governed so many, or withstood such challenge. It sits above everything else in our legal system. No law can conflict with it.

In 1783, seven years after declaring it, 13 American colonies *actually gained* surprising independence from Great Britain. Four years later, the colonies sent delegates to craft a new constitution, but they faced conflicts on a basic issue: How much power should the federal government be given? The Framers, as they have come to be called because they made or "framed" the original document, had to compromise. **The Constitution is a series of compromises about power.**

Separation of Powers

One method of limiting power was to create a national government divided into three branches, each independent and equal. Each branch would act as a check on the power of the other two, avoiding the despotic rule that had come from London. Article I of the Constitution created a Congress, which was to have legislative, or lawmaking, power. Article II created the office of president, defining the scope of executive, or enforcement, power. Article III established judicial, or interpretive, power by creating the Supreme Court and permitting additional federal courts.

Consider how the three separate powers balance one another: Congress was given the power to pass statutes, a major grant of power. But the president was permitted to veto legislation, a nearly equal grant. Congress, in turn, had the right to override the veto, ensuring that the president would not become a dictator. The president was allowed to appoint federal judges and members of his cabinet, but only with a consenting vote from the Senate.

Federalism

The national government was indeed to have considerable power, but it would still be *limited* power. Article I, section 8, describes those issues on which Congress may pass statutes. If an issue is not on the list, Congress has no power to legislate. Thus, Congress may create and regulate a post office because postal service is on the list. But Congress may not pass statutes regulating child custody in a divorce: That issue is not on the list. Only the states may legislate child custody issues.

4-1b Power Granted

Congressional Power

Article I of the Constitution creates the Congress, with its two houses. Representation in the House of Representatives is proportionate with a state's population, but each state elects two senators. Congress may perform any of the functions enumerated in Article I, section 8, such as imposing taxes, spending money, creating copyrights, supporting the military, declaring war, and so forth. None of these rights is more important than the authority to raise and spend money (the "power of the purse"), because every branch of government is dependent upon Congress for its money. One of the most important items on this list of congressional powers concerns trade.

Interstate Commerce.   "The Congress shall have power to regulate commerce with foreign nations, and among the several states." This is the **Commerce Clause**: Congress is authorized to regulate trade between states. For example, if Congress passed a law imposing a new tax on all trucks engaged in interstate transportation, the law is valid. Congress can regulate television broadcasts because many of them cross state lines. In the following case, the Supreme Court was faced with a decision that would affect the health care and pocketbook of most Americans: Does the Commerce Clause allow Congress to *force* people into commerce?

Commerce Clause
Gives Congress the power to regulate commerce with foreign nations and among states

NATIONAL FEDERATION OF INDEPENDENT BUSINESS V. SEBELIUS

132 S. Ct. 2566
United States Supreme Court, 2012

CASE SUMMARY

Facts: In 2010, Congress enacted the Affordable Care Act to increase the number of Americans covered by health insurance and decrease the cost of health care. The part of the Act called the "individual mandate" required most Americans to maintain health insurance coverage, or else pay a penalty.

Thirteen states challenged the individual mandate, arguing that Congress had violated the Commerce Clause of the Constitution. The lower courts agreed and the Supreme Court granted *certiorari*.

Issue: *Did the Affordable Care Act violate the Commerce Clause?*

Decision: No. Although Congress does not have the power to make Americans purchase health insurance, it is authorized under the Constitution to impose a tax on the uninsured.

Reasoning: Under the Commerce Clause, Congress may regulate interstate commerce and activities that substantially affect it. The government argued that Congress could order most Americans to buy health insurance because if only the old or sick made this purchase, rates would increase and as a result, affect interstate commerce. But requiring people to buy something is fundamentally different from regulating people who *voluntarily* decide to participate in commerce. Forcing individuals into commerce is beyond the federal government's authority under the Commerce Clause.

However, Congress also has the power to tax. And in many ways, the individual mandate is just a tax on the uninsured. It makes going without insurance just another thing the government taxes, like buying gasoline or earning income. And, like a tax, it is paid to the Treasury and produces some revenue for the government.

In sum, the federal government cannot make people buy health insurance, but it can tax those who do not. The individual mandate is constitutional, because it can reasonably be interpreted as a tax.

Executive Power

Article II of the Constitution defines the executive power. Once again, the Constitution gives powers in general terms. **The basic job of the president is to enforce the nation's laws.** Three of the president's key powers concern appointment, legislation, and foreign policy.

Appointment.   As we see later in this chapter, administrative agencies play a powerful role in business regulation. The president nominates the heads of most of them. These choices dramatically influence what issues the agencies choose to pursue and how aggressively they do so. For example, a president who wishes to push for higher air quality standards may appoint a forceful environmentalist to run the Environmental Protection Agency (EPA), whereas a president who dislikes federal regulations will choose a more passive agency head.

Legislation.   The president and the president's advisors propose bills to Congress and lobby hard for their passage. The executive also has veto power.

Foreign Policy.   The president conducts the nation's foreign affairs, coordinating international efforts, negotiating treaties, and so forth. The president is also the commander-in-chief of the armed forces, meaning that the president heads the military.

Judicial Power

Article III of the Constitution creates the Supreme Court and permits Congress to establish lower courts within the federal court system. Federal courts have two key functions: adjudication and judicial review.

Adjudicating Cases.   The federal court system hears criminal and civil cases. All prosecutions of federal crimes begin in a United States District Court. That same court has limited jurisdiction to hear civil lawsuits, a subject discussed in Chapter 5, on dispute resolution.

Judicial review

Refers to the power of federal courts to declare a statute or governmental action unconstitutional and void

Judicial Review.   Judicial review refers to the power of federal courts to declare a statute or governmental action unconstitutional and void. The courts can examine acts from any branch of federal or state government. If Ohio passed a tax on milk produced in other states, a federal court would declare the law void, as a violation of the Commerce Clause. Exhibit 4.1 illustrates the balance among Congress, the president, and the Court. Is judicial review good for the nation? Those who oppose it argue that federal court judges are all appointed, not elected, and that we should not permit judges to nullify a statute passed by elected officials because that diminishes the people's role in their government. Those who favor judicial review insist that there must be one cohesive interpretation of the Constitution and the judicial branch is the logical one to provide it.

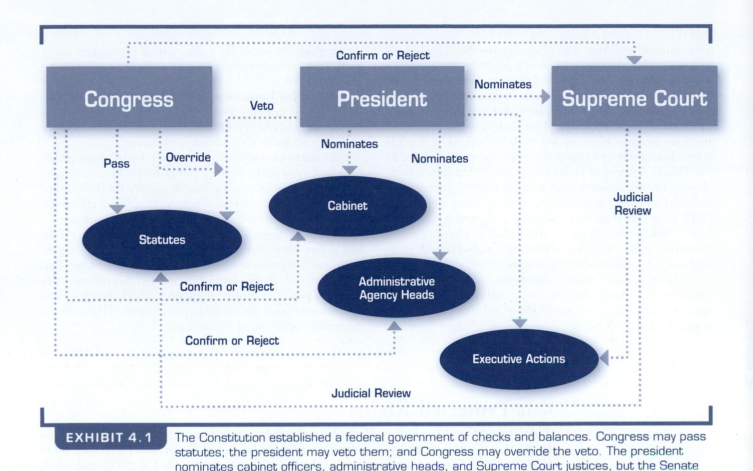

| EXHIBIT 4.1 | The Constitution established a federal government of checks and balances. Congress may pass statutes; the president may veto them; and Congress may override the veto. The president nominates cabinet officers, administrative heads, and Supreme Court justices, but the Senate must confirm the nominees. Finally, the Supreme Court (and lower federal courts) exercise judicial review over statutes and executive actions. |

You be the **Judge**

Facts: Patrick Kennedy raped his eight-year-old stepdaughter. A forensic expert testified that the girl's physical injuries were the most severe he had ever witnessed. The jury also heard evidence that the defendant had raped another eight-year-old. Kennedy was convicted of aggravated rape because the victim was under 12 years of age.

The jury voted to sentence Kennedy to death, which was permitted by the Louisiana statute. The state supreme court affirmed the death sentence, and Kennedy

KENNEDY V. LOUISIANA
554 U.S. 407
United States Supreme Court, 2008

appealed to the United States Supreme Court. He argued that the Louisiana statute was unconstitutional. The Eighth Amendment prohibits cruel and unusual punishment, which includes penalties that are out of proportion to the crime. Kennedy claimed that capital punishment was out of proportion to rape and violated the Eighth Amendment.

Six states had passed laws permitting capital punishment for child rape, though the remaining 44 states had not. Louisiana argued that the statute did not violate the amendment and that the voters must be allowed to express their abhorrence of so evil an act.

You Be the Judge: *Did the Louisiana statute violate the Constitution by permitting the death penalty in a case of child rape? Is it proper for the Supreme Court to decide this issue?*

Argument for Kennedy: The court's interpretation of the Constitution must evolve with society. The Eighth Amendment requires that punishment be proportionate to the crime. A national consensus opposes the death penalty for any crime other than murder. Capital punishment exists in 36 states, but only six of those states allow it for child rape. No state has executed a defendant for rape since 1964. As horrifying as child rape is, society merely brutalizes itself when it sinks to the level of capital punishment for a crime other than murder.

There are also policy reasons to prohibit this punishment. Children may be more reluctant to testify against perpetrators if they know that a prosecution could lead to execution. Also, a young child may be an unreliable witness for a case where the stakes are so high. It is the responsibility of this court to nullify such a harmful law.

Argument for Louisiana: Child rape is one of the most horrifying of crimes. The defendant damages a young person, destroys her childhood, and terrifies a community. Only the severest of penalties is sufficient.

Six states have recently passed statutes permitting capital punishment in these cases. It is possible that a consensus is developing *in favor* of the death penalty for these brutal assaults. If the court strikes down this law, it will effectively stifle a national debate and destroy any true consensus.

Kennedy argues that capital punishment might be bad policy—but that is a question for voters and legislatures, not for courts. Obviously, the citizens of Louisiana favor this law. If they are offended by the statute, they have the power to replace legislators who support it. The court should leave this issue to the citizens. That is how a democracy is intended to function.

4-1c Protected Rights

The original Constitution was silent about the rights of citizens. This alarmed many, who feared that the new federal government would have unlimited power over their lives. So in 1791, the first 10 amendments, known as the Bill of Rights, were added to the Constitution, guaranteeing many liberties directly to individual citizens.

The amendments to the Constitution protect the people of this nation from the power of state and federal government. The **First Amendment** guarantees rights of free speech, free press, and religion; the **Fourth Amendment** protects against illegal searches; the **Fifth Amendment** ensures due process; the **Sixth Amendment** demands fair treatment for defendants in criminal prosecutions; and the **Fourteenth Amendment** guarantees equal protection of the law. We consider the First, Fifth, and Fourteenth Amendments in this chapter and the Fourth, Fifth, and Sixth Amendments in Chapter 6, on crime.

The "people" who are protected include citizens and, for most purposes, corporations. Corporations are considered persons and receive most of the same protections. The great majority of these rights also extend to citizens of other countries who are in the United States.

Constitutional rights generally protect only against governmental acts. The Constitution generally does not protect us from the conduct of private parties, such as corporations or other citizens. Constitutional protections apply to federal, state, and local governments.

First Amendment
Protects freedom of speech

Fourth Amendment
Protects against illegal searches

Fifth Amendment
Ensures due process

Sixth Amendment
Demands fair treatment for defendants in criminal prosecutions

Fourteenth Amendment
Guarantees equal protection of the law

First Amendment: Free Speech

The First Amendment states that "Congress shall make no law … abridging the freedom of speech…." In general, we expect our government to let people speak and hear whatever they choose. The Framers believed democracy would work only if the members of the electorate were free to talk, argue, listen, and exchange viewpoints in any way they wanted.

If a city government prohibited an antiabortion group from demonstrating, its action would violate the First Amendment. Government officers may not impose their political beliefs on the citizens. The government may regulate the *time*, *place*, and *manner* of speech, for example, by prohibiting a midnight rally or insisting that demonstrators remain within a specified area. But outright prohibitions are unconstitutional.

"Speech" includes symbolic conduct. Does that mean flag burning is permissible? The following case is about that issue.

TEXAS V. JOHNSON

491 U.S. 397
United States Supreme Court, 1989

CASE SUMMARY

Facts: Outside the Republican National Convention in Dallas, Gregory Johnson participated in a protest against policies of the Reagan administration. Participants gave speeches and handed out leaflets. Johnson burned an American flag. He was arrested and convicted under a Texas statute that prohibited desecrating the flag, but the Texas Court of Criminal Appeals reversed on the grounds that the conviction violated the First Amendment. Texas appealed to the United States Supreme Court.

Issue: *Does the First Amendment protect flag burning?*

Decision: The First Amendment protects flag burning.

Reasoning: The First Amendment literally applies only to "speech," but this Court has already ruled that the Amendment also protects written words and other conduct that will convey a specific message. For example, earlier decisions protected a student's right to wear a black armband in protest against American military actions. Judged by this standard, flag burning is symbolic speech.

Texas argues that its interest in honoring the flag justifies its prosecution of Johnson, since he knew that his action would be deeply offensive to many citizens. However, if there is a bedrock principle underlying the First Amendment, it is that the government may not prohibit the expression of an idea simply because society finds it offensive.

The best way to preserve the flag's special role in our lives is not to punish those who feel differently, but to persuade them that they are wrong. We do not honor our flag by punishing those who burn it, because in doing so we diminish the freedom that this cherished emblem represents.

4-1d Fifth Amendment: Due Process and the Takings Clause

Ralph is a first-semester senior at State University, where he majors in finance. With a 3.6 grade point average and outstanding recommendations, he has an excellent chance of admission to an elite law school—until his life suddenly turns upside down. Professor Watson, who teaches Ralph in marketing, notifies the school's dean that the young man plagiarized material that he included in his recent paper. Dean Holmes reads Watson's report and sends Ralph a brief letter: "I find that you have committed plagiarism in violation of school rules. Your grade in Dr. Watson's marketing course is an 'F.' You are hereby suspended from the University for one full academic year."

Ralph is shocked. He is convinced he did nothing wrong, and wants to tell his side of the story, but Dean Holmes refuses to speak with him. What can he do? The first step is to read the Fifth Amendment.

Two related provisions of the Fifth Amendment, called the Due Process Clause and the Takings Clause, prohibit the government from arbitrarily depriving us of our most valuable assets. Together, they state: "No person shall be … deprived of life, liberty, or property without due process of law; nor shall private property be taken for public use, without just compensation." We will discuss the civil law aspects of these clauses, but due process also applies to criminal law. The reference to "life" refers to capital punishment. The criminal law issues of this subject are discussed in Chapter 6.

Procedural Due Process

The government deprives citizens or corporations of their property in a variety of ways. The Internal Revenue Service (IRS) may fine a corporation for late payment of taxes. The Customs Service may seize goods at the border. As to liberty, the government may take it by confining someone in a mental institution or by taking a child out of the home because of parental neglect. The purpose of **procedural due process** is to ensure that before the government takes liberty or property, the affected person has a fair chance to oppose the action.[1]

Procedural due process
Ensures that before the government takes liberty or property, the affected person has a fair chance to oppose the action

The Due Process Clause protects Ralph because State University is part of the government. Ralph is entitled to due process. Does this mean that he gets a full court trial on the plagiarism charge? No. **The type of hearing the government must offer depends upon the importance of the property or liberty interest.** The more important the interest, the more formal the procedures must be. Regardless of how formal the hearing, one requirement is constant: The fact finder must be neutral.

In a criminal prosecution, the liberty interest is very great. A defendant can lose his freedom or even his life. The government must provide the defendant with a lawyer if he cannot afford one, adequate time to prepare, an unbiased jury, an opportunity to present his case and cross-examine all witnesses, and many other procedural rights.

A student faced with academic sanctions receives less due process but still has rights. State University has failed to provide Ralph with due process. The school has accused the young man of a serious infraction. The school must promptly provide details of the charge, give Ralph all physical evidence, and allow him time to plan his response. The university must then offer Ralph a hearing, before a neutral person or group, who will listen to Ralph (as well as Dr. Watson) and examine any evidence the student offers. Ralph is not, however, entitled to a lawyer or a jury.

The Takings Clause

Kabrina owns a 10-acre parcel of undeveloped land on Lake Halcyon. She plans to build a 20-bedroom inn of about 35,000 square feet—until the state environmental agency abruptly halts the work. The agency informs Kabrina that, to protect the lake from further harm, it will allow no shoreline development except single-family houses of 2,000 square feet or less. Kabrina is furious. Does the state have the power to wreck Kabrina's plans? To learn the answer, we look to another section of the Fifth Amendment.

Takings Clause
Prohibits a state from taking private property for public use without just compensation

The **Takings Clause** prohibits a state from taking private property for public use without just compensation. A town wishing to build a new football field *does* have the right to boot you out of your house. But the town must compensate you. The government takes your land through the power of eminent domain. Officials must notify you of their intentions and give you an opportunity to oppose the project and to challenge the amount the town offers to pay. When the hearings are done, though, the town may write you a check and grind your house into goalposts, whether you like it or not.

---

[1]In criminal cases, procedural due process also protects against the taking of life.

If the state actually wanted to take Kabrina's land and turn it into a park, the Takings Clause would force it to pay the fair market value. However, the state is not trying to seize the land—it merely wants to prevent large development.

"My land is worthless," Kabrina replies. "You might just as well kick me off my own property!" **A regulation that denies *all beneficial use* of property is a taking and requires compensation.** Has the government denied Kabrina all beneficial use? No, it has not. Kabrina retains the right to build a private house; she just can't build the inn she wants. The environmental agency has decreased the value of the land, but it owes her nothing. Had the state forbidden *all* construction on her land, it would have been obligated to pay Kabrina.

4-1e Fourteenth Amendment: Equal Protection Clause

Shannon Faulkner wanted to attend The Citadel, a state-supported military college in South Carolina. She was a fine student who met every admission requirement that The Citadel set except one: She was not a man. The Citadel argued that its long and distinguished history demanded that it remain all male. Faulkner responded that she was a citizen of the state and ought to receive the benefits that others got, including the right to a military education. Could the school exclude her on the basis of gender?

The Fourteenth Amendment provides that "No State shall … deny to any person within its jurisdiction the equal protection of the laws." This is the **Equal Protection Clause**, and it means that, generally speaking, all levels of government must treat people equally. Unfair classifications among people or corporations will not be permitted. **Regulations based on gender, race, or fundamental rights are generally void.** Shannon Faulkner won her case and was admitted to The Citadel. The Court found no justification for discriminating against women. Any regulation based on race or ethnicity is *nearly certain* to be void; one based on gender is *likely* to be void. Similarly, all citizens enjoy the *fundamental right* to travel between states. If Kentucky limited government jobs to those who had lived in the state for two years, it would be discriminating against a fundamental right, and the restriction would be struck down.

Equal Protection Clause
Requires that the government must treat people equally

EXAM Strategy

Question: Megan is a freshman at her local public high school; her older sister, Jenna, attends a nearby private high school. Both girls are angry because their schools prohibit them from joining their respective wrestling teams, where only boys are allowed. The two girls sue based on the U.S. Constitution. Discuss the relevant law and predict the outcomes.

Strategy: One girl goes to private and one to public school. Why does that matter? Now ask what provision of the Constitution is involved and what legal standard it establishes.

Result: The Constitution offers protection from the *government*. A private high school is not part of the government, and Jenna has no constitutional case. Megan's suit is based on the Equal Protection Clause. Regulations based on gender are generally void. The school will probably argue that wrestling with stronger boys will be dangerous for girls. However, courts are increasingly suspicious of any sex discrimination and are unlikely to find the school's argument persuasive.

4-2 STATUTORY LAW

Statutes
Laws passed by Congress or state legislatures

Most new law is statutory law. **Statutes** affect each of us every day, in our business, professional, and personal lives. When the system works correctly, this is the one part of the law over which we the people have control. We elect the local legislators who pass state statutes; we vote for the senators and representatives who create federal statutes. If we understand the system, we can affect the largest source of contemporary law. If we live in ignorance of its strengths and pitfalls, we delude ourselves that we participate in a democracy.

As we saw in Chapter 1, there are many systems of government operating in the United States: a national government and 50 state governments. Each level of government has a legislative body. In Washington, D.C., Congress is our national legislature. Congress passes the statutes that govern the nation. In addition, each state has a legislature, which passes statutes for that state only. In this section, we look at how Congress does its work creating statutes. State legislatures operate similarly, but the work of Congress is better documented and obviously of national importance.

4-2a Committee Work

Bill
A proposed statute

Congress is organized into two houses, the House of Representatives and the Senate. Either house may originate a proposed statute, which is called a **bill**. After a bill has been proposed, it is sent to an appropriate committee.

If you visit either house of Congress, you will probably find half a dozen legislators on the floor, with one person talking and no one listening. This is because most of the work is done in committees. Both houses are organized into dozens of committees, each with special functions. The House currently has about 27 committees (further divided into about 150 subcommittees), and the Senate has approximately 20 committees (with about 86 subcommittees). For example, the Armed Services committee of each house oversees the huge defense budget and the workings of the armed forces. Labor committees handle legislation concerning organized labor and working conditions. Banking committees develop expertise on financial institutions. Judiciary committees review nominees to the federal courts. There are dozens of other committees, some very powerful, because they control vast amounts of money, and some relatively weak.

When a bill is proposed in either house, it is referred to the committee that specializes in that subject. Why are bills proposed in the first place? For any of several reasons:

- **New Issue, New Worry.** When some employers began requesting that job candidates disclose their Facebook passwords as a condition of employment, a public outcry ensued. Various members of Congress proposed legislation designed to end this new practice.

- **Unpopular Judicial Ruling.** If Congress disagrees with a judicial interpretation of a statute, the legislators may pass a new statute to modify or "undo" the court decision. For example, if the Supreme Court misinterprets a statute about musical copyrights, Congress may pass a new law correcting the Court's error.

- **Criminal Law.** When legislators perceive that social changes have led to new criminal acts, they may respond with new statutes. The rise of Internet fraud has led to many new statutes outlawing such things as computer trespass and espionage, fraud in the use of cell phones, identity theft, and so on.

Congressional committees hold hearings to investigate the need for new legislation and consider the alternatives. Suppose a congressperson believes that a growing number of American corporations locate their headquarters offshore to escape taxes. She requests committee hearings on the subject, hoping to discover the extent of the problem, its causes, and possible remedies. After hearings, she proposes a bill she believes will remedy the problem. If the committee votes in favor of the bill, it goes to the full body, meaning either the House of Representatives or the Senate. If the full body approves the bill, it goes to the other house.

The bill must be voted on and approved by both branches of Congress. If both houses pass the bill, the legislation normally must go to a conference committee, made of members from each house, to resolve differences between the two versions. Assuming both houses then pass the same version of the bill, the bill goes to the president . If the president signs the bill, it becomes law. If the president opposes the bill, he will veto it, in which case it is not law. When the president vetoes a bill, Congress has one last chance to make it law: an override. Should both houses re-pass the bill, each by a two-thirds margin, it becomes law over the president's veto.

4-3 COMMON LAW

What, if anything, must you do if you see someone in danger? Are you required to help? We will examine this issue to see how the common law works.

The **common law** is judge-made law. It is the sum total of all the judicial decisions that have not been overturned by appellate courts. The common law of Pennsylvania consists of all cases decided by the courts in that state. The Illinois common law of bystander liability is all the cases on that subject decided by Illinois appellate courts. Two hundred years ago, almost all the law was common law. Today, most new law is statutory. But common law still predominates in tort, contract, and agency law, and it is very important in property, employment, and some other areas.

We focus on appellate courts because they are the only ones to make rulings or determinations of law. In a bystander case, it is the job of the state's highest court to say what legal obligations, if any, a bystander has. The trial court, on the other hand, must decide facts: Was this defendant able to see what was happening? Was the plaintiff really in trouble? Could the defendant have assisted without peril to himself?

Common law
Legal precedents created by appellate courts

> **What, if anything, must you do if you see someone in danger? Are you required to help?**

4-3a Stare Decisis

Nothing perks up a course like Latin. ***Stare decisis*** means "let the decision stand." It is the essence of the common law. The phrase indicates that once a court has decided a particular issue, it will generally apply the same rule in future cases. Suppose the highest court of Arizona must decide whether a contract for a new car, signed by a 16-year-old, can be enforced against him. The court will look to see if there is precedent; that is, whether the high court of Arizona has already decided a similar case. The Arizona court looks and finds several earlier cases, all holding that such contracts may not be enforced against a minor. The court will apply that precedent and refuse to enforce the contract in this case. Courts do not always follow precedent but they generally do: *stare decisis*.

Two words explain why the common law is never as easy as we might like: *predictability* and *flexibility*. The law is trying to accommodate both goals. The need for predictability is apparent: People must know what the law is. If contract law changed daily, an entrepreneur who leased factory space and then started buying machinery would be uncertain if the

Stare decisis
Means "let the decision stand" and describes the practice of courts following prior decisions

factory would actually be available when she was ready to move in. Will the landlord slip out of the lease? Will the machinery be ready on time? The need for predictability created the doctrine of *stare decisis*.

Yet there must also be flexibility in the law, some means to respond to new problems and changing social mores. We cannot be encumbered by ironclad rules established before electricity was discovered. These two ideas may be obvious, but they also conflict: The more flexibility we permit, the less predictability we enjoy. We will watch the conflict play out in the bystander cases.

4-3b Bystander Cases

This country inherited from England a simple rule about a bystander's obligations: You have no duty to assist someone in peril unless you created the danger. In *Union Pacific Railway Co. v. Cappier*,[2] through no fault of the railroad, a train struck a man, severing an arm and a leg. Railroad employees saw the incident happen but did nothing to assist him. By the time help arrived, the victim had died. In this 1903 case, the court held that the railroad had no duty to help the injured man. The court declared that it was legally irrelevant whether the railroad's conduct was inhumane.

As harsh as this judgment might seem, it was an accurate statement of the law at that time in both England and the United States: Bystanders need do nothing. With a rule this old and well established, no court was willing to scuttle it. What courts did do was seek openings for small changes.

Eighteen years after the Kansas case of *Cappier*, the court in nearby Iowa found the basis for one exception. Ed Carey was a farm laborer, working for Frank Davis. While in the fields, Carey fainted from sunstroke and remained unconscious. Davis simply hauled him to a nearby wagon and left him in the sun for an additional four hours, causing serious permanent injury. The judges said that was not good enough. Creating a modest exception to the bystander rule, the court ruled that when an employee suffers a serious injury *on the job*, the employer must take reasonable measures to help him. Leaving a stricken worker in the hot sun was not reasonable, and Davis was liable.[3]

Remember the *Soldano v. O'Daniels* case from Chapter 1, in which the bartender refused to call the police? As in the earlier cases we have seen, this case presented an emergency. But the exception created in *Carey v. Davis* applied only if the bystander was an employer. Should the law require the bartender to act—that is, should it carve a new exception? Here is what the California court decided:

> Many citizens simply "don't want to get involved." No rule should be adopted [requiring] a citizen to open up his or her house to a stranger so that the latter may use the telephone to call for emergency assistance. Such an action may be fraught with danger. It does not follow, however, that use of a telephone in a public portion of a business should be refused for a legitimate emergency call.
>
> We conclude that the bartender owed a duty to [Soldano] to permit the patron from Happy Jack's to place a call to the police or to place the call himself. It bears emphasizing that the duty in this case does not require that one must go to the aid of another. That is not the issue here. The employee was not the good samaritan intent on aiding another. The patron was.

And so, courts have made several subtle changes to the common law rule.

---

[2]66 Kan. 649 (1903).
[3]Carey v. Davis, 190 Iowa 720 (1921).

EXAM Strategy

Question: When Rachel is walking her dog, Bozo, she watches a skydiver float to earth. He lands in an enormous tree, suspended 45 feet above ground. "Help!" the man shouts. Rachel hurries to the tree and sees the skydiver bleeding profusely. She takes out her cell phone to call 911 for help, but just then Bozo runs away. Rachel darts after the dog, afraid he will jump in a nearby pond and emerge smelling of mud. She forgets about the skydiver and takes Bozo home. Three hours later, the skydiver expires.

The victim's family sues Rachel. She defends by saying she feared that Bozo would have an allergic reaction to mud, and that in any case, she could not have climbed 45 feet up a tree to save the man. The family argues that the dog is not allergic to mud, that even if he is, a pet's inconvenience pales compared to human life, and that Rachel could have phoned for emergency help without climbing an inch. Please rule.

Strategy: The family's arguments might seem compelling, but are they relevant? Rachel is a bystander, someone who perceives another in danger. What is the rule concerning a bystander's obligation to act? Apply the rule to the facts of this case.

Result: A bystander has no duty to assist someone in peril unless she created the danger. Rachel did not create the skydiver's predicament. She had no obligation to do anything. Rachel wins.

4-4 ADMINISTRATIVE LAW

Before beginning this section, please return your seat to its upright position. Stow the tray firmly in the seat back in front of you. Turn off any cell phones, laptops, or other electronic devices. Sound familiar? Administrative agencies affect each of us every day in hundreds of ways. They have become the fourth branch of government. Supporters believe that they provide unique expertise in complex areas; detractors regard them as unelected government run amok.

Many administrative agencies are familiar. The Federal Aviation Administration, which requires all airlines to ensure that your seats are upright before takeoff and landing, is an administrative agency. The IRS expects us to report in every April 15. The EPA regulates the water quality of the river in your town. The Federal Trade Commission (FCC) oversees the commercials that shout at you from your television set.

Other agencies are less familiar. You may never have heard of the Bureau of Land Management, but if you go into the oil and gas industry, you will learn that this powerful agency has more control over your land than you do. If you develop real estate in Palos Hills, Illinois, you will tremble every time the Appearance Commission of the City of Palos Hills speaks, since you cannot construct a new building without its approval. If your software corporation wants to hire an Argentine expert on databases, you will get to know the complex workings of Immigration and Customs Enforcement: No one lawfully enters this country without its nod of approval.

Administrative agencies use three kinds of power to do the work assigned to them: They make rules, investigate, and adjudicate.

> **Before beginning this section, please return your seat to its upright position. Stow the tray firmly in the seat back in front of you.**

4-4a Rule Making

One of the most important functions of an administrative agency is to make rules. In doing this, the agency attempts, prospectively, to establish fair and uniform behavior for all businesses in the affected area. To create a new rule is to promulgate it. Agencies promulgate two types of rules: legislative and interpretive.

Legislative Rules

These are the most important agency rules, and they are much like statutes. Here, an agency is changing the law by requiring businesses or private citizens to act in a certain way. For example, the FCC promulgated a rule requiring all cable television systems with more than 3,500 subscribers to develop the capacity to carry at least 20 channels and to make some of those channels available to local community stations. This legislative rule has a heavy financial impact on many cable systems. As far as a cable company is concerned, it is more important than most statutes passed by Congress. Legislative rules have the full effect of a statute.

Interpretive Rules

These rules do not change the law. They are the agency's interpretation of what the law already requires. But they can still affect all of us.

In 1977, Congress amended the Clean Air Act in an attempt to reduce pollution from factories. The act required the EPA to impose emission standards on "stationary sources" of pollution. But what did "stationary source" mean? It was the EPA's job to define that term. Obscure work, to be sure, yet the results could be seen and even smelled, because the EPA's definition would determine the quality of air entering our lungs every time we breathe. Environmentalists wanted the term defined to include every smokestack in a factory so that the EPA could regulate each one. The EPA, however, developed the "bubble concept," ruling that "stationary source" meant an entire factory, but not the individual smokestacks. As a result, polluters could shift emission among smokestacks in a single factory to avoid EPA regulation. Environmentalists howled that this gutted the purpose of the statute, but to no avail. The agency had spoken, merely by interpreting a statute.

You be the Judge

R. J. REYNOLDS TOBACCO CO. V. FOOD AND DRUG ADMINISTRATION
696 F.3d 1205
District of Columbia Circuit Court of Appeals, 2012

Facts: Congress instructed the FDA to issue regulations on cigarette packaging that would convey the negative consequences of smoking. The FDA's final rules required tobacco companies to include the following on the top half of every cigarette package: written warnings ("Smoking causes cancer"), the phone number of an antismoking hotline, and graphic images, such as an autopsy and a man exhaling smoke out of a hole in his neck.

Tobacco companies challenged the FDA regulation, claiming that the rule violated the First Amendment by requiring them to speak against their will. The FDA argued it was just educating the public with factual information.

You Be the Judge: *Could the FDA force tobacco companies to put emotionally charged warning labels on cigarettes?*

Argument for the FDA: Cigarettes are the deadliest, most addictive product sold in America. The tobacco industry has a history of hiding these risks from customers—particularly the young and uneducated. We are simply ending this history of deception by requiring companies to disclose factual and uncontroversial information. Smokers have not been deterred by the current text-only warnings, so these powerful images are the obvious next step in trying to influence them. The fact that the warnings are powerful does not make them a violation of the First Amendment. Nor does the Constitution prohibit us from requiring that lethal and addictive products carry informative warning labels. Moreover, Congress instructed us to proceed with these requirements so we are obligated to do so.

Argument for Tobacco Companies: Your honors, look at these pictures. These awful images do not educate or protect consumers from deception—they just scare them into quitting. The FDA is treating every single pack of cigarettes as a mini-billboard for their antismoking agenda. The pictures are neither factual nor accurate: They *symbolize* the bad effects of smoking, which is something very different from providing facts. Rather than educating, the FDA is simply trying to disgust consumers into quitting. *Advocating* that the public should not purchase a legal product is not the same as *educating* consumers. If it wants to promote an antismoking message, the government should do so through advertising or increased cigarette taxes, not by making tobacco companies speak.

4-4b Investigation

Agencies do a wide variety of work, but they all need broad factual knowledge of the field they govern. Some companies cooperate with an agency, furnishing information and even voluntarily accepting agency recommendations. For example, the United States Product Safety Commission investigates hundreds of consumer products every year and frequently urges companies to recall goods that the agency considers defective. Many firms comply. Other companies, however, jealously guard information, often because corporate officers believe that disclosure would lead to adverse rules. To force disclosure, agencies use subpoenas and searches. A **subpoena** is an order to appear at a particular time and place to provide evidence. A **subpoena** *duces tecum* requires a person to produce certain documents or things.

4-4c Adjudication

To **adjudicate** a case is to hold a hearing about an issue and then decide it. Agencies adjudicate countless cases. The FCC adjudicates which applicant for a new television license is best qualified. The Occupational Safety and Health Administration (OSHA) holds adversarial hearings to determine whether a manufacturing plant is dangerous.

Most adjudications begin with a hearing before an **administrative law judge (ALJ)**. There is no jury. After all evidence is taken, the ALJ makes a decision. The losing party has a right to appeal to an appellate board within the agency. A party unhappy with that decision may appeal to federal court.

Subpoena
An order to appear at a particular time and place

Subpoena *duces tecum*
An order to require a person to produce certain documents or things

Adjudicate
To hold a formal hearing about an issue and then decide it

Administrative law judge
An agency employee who acts as an impartial decision maker

Chapter Conclusion

The legal battle over power never stops. When may a state outlaw waterfront development? Prohibit symbolic speech? Other issues are just as thorny, such as when a bystander is liable to assist someone in peril, or whether a government agency may subpoena corporate documents. Some of the questions will be answered by that extraordinary document, the Constitution, while others require statutory, common law, or administrative responses. There are no easy answers to any of the questions because there has never been a democracy so large, so diverse, or so powerful.

Exam Review

1. **CONSTITUTION**   The Constitution is a series of compromises about power.

2. **CONSTITUTIONAL POWERS**   Article I of the Constitution creates the Congress and grants all legislative power to it. Article II establishes the office of president and defines executive powers. Article III creates the Supreme Court and permits lower federal courts; the article also outlines the powers of the federal judiciary.

3. **COMMERCE CLAUSE**   Under the Commerce Clause, Congress may regulate interstate trade. A state law that interferes with interstate commerce is void.

EXAM Strategy

Question: Maine exempted many charitable institutions from real estate taxes but denied this benefit to a charity that primarily benefited out-of-state residents. Camp Newfound was a Christian Science organization, and 95 percent of its summer campers came from other states. Camp Newfound sued Maine. Discuss.

Strategy: The state was treating organizations differently depending on the states their campers come from. This raised Commerce Clause issues. What does that clause state? (See the "Result" at the end of this section.)

4. **PRESIDENTIAL POWERS**   The president's key powers include making agency appointments, proposing legislation, conducting foreign policy, and acting as commander-in-chief of the armed forces.

5. **FEDERAL COURTS**   The federal courts adjudicate cases and also exercise judicial review, which is the right to declare a statute or governmental action unconstitutional and void.

6. **FIRST AMENDMENT**   The First Amendment protects most freedom of speech, although the government may regulate the time, place, and manner of speech. In recent years, the Supreme Court has significantly expanded the free speech rights of organizations.

7. **PROCEDURAL DUE PROCESS**   Procedural due process is required whenever the government attempts to take liberty or property.

8. **TAKINGS CLAUSE**   The Takings Clause prohibits a state from taking private property for public use without just compensation.

9. **EQUAL PROTECTION CLAUSE**   The Equal Protection Clause generally requires the government to treat people equally.

10. **LEGISLATION**   Bills originate in congressional committees and go from there to the full House of Representatives or Senate. If both houses pass the bill, the legislation normally must go to a conference committee to resolve differences between the two versions. If the president signs the bill, it becomes a statute; if he vetoes it, Congress can pass it over his veto with a two-thirds majority in each house.

11. *STARE DECISIS*   *Stare decisis* means "let the decision stand," and it indicates that once a court has decided a particular issue, it will generally apply the same rule in future cases.

12. **COMMON LAW**   The common law evolves in awkward fits and starts because courts attempt to achieve two contradictory purposes: predictability and flexibility.

13. **BYSTANDER RULE**   The common-law bystander rule holds that, generally, no one has a duty to assist someone in peril unless the bystander himself created the danger. Courts have carved some exceptions during the last 100 years, but the basic rule still stands.

14. **ADMINISTRATIVE AGENCIES**   Congress creates federal administrative agencies to supervise many industries. Agencies promulgate rules and investigate and adjudicate cases.

EXAM Strategy

Question: Hiller Systems, Inc. was performing a safety inspection on board the M/V *Cape Diamond,* an oceangoing vessel, when an accident occurred involving the fire extinguishing equipment. Two men were killed. OSHA attempted to investigate, but Hiller refused to permit any of its employees to speak to OSHA investigators. What could OSHA do to pursue the investigation? What limits would there be on OSHA's work?

Strategy: Agencies makes rules, investigate, and adjudicate. Which is involved here? (Investigation.) During an investigation, what power has an agency to force a company to produce data? What are the limits on that power? (See the "Result" at the end of this section.)

3. Result: The Commerce Clause holds that a state statute that discriminates against interstate commerce is almost always invalid. Maine was subsidizing charities that served in-state residents and penalizing those that attracted campers from elsewhere. The tax rule violated the Commerce Clause and was void.

14. Result: OSHA can issue a subpoena *duces tecum,* demanding that those on board the ship, and their supervisors, appear for questioning and bring with them all relevant documents. OSHA may ask for anything that is (1) relevant to the investigation, (2) not unduly burdensome, and (3) not privileged. Conversations between one of the ship inspectors and his supervisor are clearly relevant; a discussion between the supervisor and the company's lawyer is privileged due to attorney-client privilege.

MATCHING QUESTIONS

Match the following terms with their definitions:

___A. Statute

___B. Equal Protection Clause

___C. Judicial review

___D. Takings Clause

___E. *Stare decisis*

___F. Promulgate

1. The power of federal courts to examine the constitutionality of statutes and acts of government

2. The part of the Constitution that requires compensation in eminent domain cases

3. The rule that requires lower courts to decide cases based on precedent

4. The act of an administrative agency creating a new rule

5. A law passed by a legislative body

6. Generally prohibits regulations based on gender, race, or fundamental rights

TRUE/FALSE QUESTIONS

Circle true or false:

1. T F The government may not prohibit a political rally, but it may restrict when and where the demonstrators meet.

2. T F The Due Process Clause requires that any citizen is entitled to a jury trial before any right or property interest is taken.

3. T F The government has the right to take a homeowner's property for a public purpose.

4. T F A subpoena is an order punishing a defendant who has violated a court ruling.

5. T F A bystander who sees someone in peril must come to that person's assistance, but only if he can do so without endangering himself or others.

6. T F Administrative agencies play an advisory role in the life of many industries but do not have the legal authority to enforce their opinions.

MULTIPLE-CHOICE QUESTIONS

1. Colorado passes a hotel tax of 8 percent for Colorado residents and 15 percent for out-of-state visitors. The new law:

(a) is valid, based on the Supremacy Clause.

(b) is void, based on the Supremacy Clause.

(c) is valid, based on the Commerce Clause.

(d) is void, based on the Commerce Clause.

(e) is void, based on the Takings Clause.

2. Suppose a state legislature approves an education plan for the next year that budgets $35 million for boys' athletics and $25 million for girls' athletics. Legislators explain the difference by saying, "In our experience, boys simply care more about sports than girls do." The new plan is:

    (a) valid.

    (b) void.

    (c) permissible, based on the legislators' statutory research.

    (d) permissible, but probably unwise.

    (e) subject to the Takings Clause.

3. Congress has passed a new bill, but the president does not like the law. What could happen next?

    (a) The president must sign the bill whether he likes it or not.

    (b) The president may veto the bill, in which case it is dead.

    (c) The president may veto the bill, but Congress may attempt to override the veto.

    (d) The president may ask the citizens to vote directly on the proposed law.

    (e) The president may discharge the Congress and order new elections.

4. Which of these is an example of judicial review?

    (a) A trial court finds a criminal defendant guilty.

    (b) An appeals court reverses a lower court's ruling.

    (c) An appeals court affirms a lower court's ruling.

    (d) A federal court declares a statute unconstitutional.

    (e) A congressional committee interviews a potential Supreme Court justice.

5. What is an example of a subpoena?

    (a) A court order to a company to stop polluting the air.

    (b) A court order requiring a person being deposed to answer questions.

    (c) A federal agency demands various internal documents from a corporation.

    (d) The president orders troops called up in the national defense.

    (e) The president orders Congress to pass a bill on an expedited schedule.

CASE QUESTIONS

1. In the early 1970s, President Richard Nixon became embroiled in the Watergate dispute. He was accused of covering up a criminal break-in at the national headquarters of the Democratic Party. Nixon denied any wrongdoing. A United States District Court judge ordered the president to produce tapes of conversations held in his office. Nixon knew that complying with the order would produce damaging evidence, probably destroying his presidency. He refused, claiming executive privilege. The case went to the Supreme Court. Nixon strongly implied that even if the Supreme Court ordered him to produce the tapes, he would refuse. What major constitutional issue did this raise?

2. In 1996 California legalized the medical use of marijuana, even though it was still illegal under federal law. Californians Angel Raich and Diane Monson used homegrown medical marijuana. When federal agents destroyed their plants, Monson and Raich sued, claiming, among other things, that the Commerce Clause did not permit the federal government to regulate activities that took place in their backyards and homes. The federal government argued that since consuming locally-grown marijuana for medical purposes affects the interstate market for marijuana, the federal government may regulate—and prohibit—such consumption. Whose argument should prevail?

3. *YOU BE THE JUDGE* **WRITING PROBLEM:** An off-duty, out-of-uniform police officer and his son purchased some food from a 7-Eleven store and were still in the parking lot when a carload of teenagers became rowdy. The officer went to speak to them and the teenagers assaulted him. The officer shouted to his son to get the 7-Eleven clerk to call for help. The son entered the store, told the clerk that a police officer needed help, and instructed the clerk to call the police. He returned 30 seconds later and repeated the request, urging the clerk to say it was a Code 13. The son claimed that the clerk laughed at him and refused to do it. The policeman sued the store. **Argument for the Store:** We sympathize with the policeman and his family, but the store has no liability. A bystander is not obligated to come to the aid of anyone in distress unless the bystander created the peril, and obviously the store did not do so. The policeman should sue those who attacked him. **Argument for the Police Officer:** We agree that, in general, a bystander has no obligation to come to the aid of one in distress. However, when a business that is open to the public receives an urgent request to call the police, the business should either make the call or permit someone else to do it.

4. Carter was an employee of the Sheriff's office in Hampton, Virginia. When his boss, Sheriff Roberts, was up for reelection against Adams, Carter "liked" the Adams campaign's Facebook page. Upon winning reelection, Sheriff Roberts fired Carter, who then sued on free speech grounds. Is a Facebook "like" protected under the First Amendment?

5. The federal Defense of Marriage Act (DOMA) defined marriage as a union between a man and a woman. As a result, same-sex couples were not eligible for the federal marriage benefits given to heterosexual couples. Edith Windsor and Thea Spyer had been together for 40 years, and married for two, when Spyer died. Because of DOMA, the federal government did not treat Windsor as a surviving spouse for purposes of estate taxes, so she was presented with a tax bill of $363,000. If she had been married to a man, she would not have owed any taxes. Windsor challenged the statute, claiming the government had violated her right to equal protection. Should she win?

DISCUSSION QUESTIONS

1. Consider the doctrine of *stare decisis*. Should courts follow past rulings, or should they decide cases anew each time, without regard to past decisions? For example, should *Texas v. Johnson* stand because it is precedent, or should the justices take a "fresh look" at the issue of flag burning?

2. Should administrative agencies be able to "tell business what to do"? Do you favor administrative regulations on the environment, safety, and discrimination, or do they amount to "big government"?

3. Gender discrimination currently receives "intermediate" Fourteenth Amendment scrutiny. Is this right? Should gender receive "strict" scrutiny as does race? Why or why not?

4. During live national coverage of a Super Bowl half-time show, Justin Timberlake tore off part of Janet Jackson's shirt, exposing her breast for nine-sixteenths of a second. Television network CBS called it a "wardrobe malfunction," but the "malfunction" coincidentally occurred just as Timberlake was singing the lyrics, "Gonna have you naked by the end of this song." The FCC fined CBS $550,000, but the network challenged the fine in court. The appeals court held that CBS did not have to pay because the FCC did not have a clear policy on momentary displays of nudity. Do you agree with this conclusion? Do you think the incident was intentional or truly accidental? If it was intentional, should CBS have known better, regardless of FCC policies? If it was accidental, should CBS still be held accountable? Should it matter if it was intentional or accidental?

5. Suppose you were on a state supreme court and faced with a restaurant-choking case. Should you require restaurant employees to know and employ the Heimlich maneuver to assist a choking victim? If they do a bad job, they could cause additional injury. Should you permit them to do nothing at all? Is there a compromise position? What social policies are most important?

CHAPTER 5

COURTS, LITIGATION, AND ALTERNATIVE DISPUTE RESOLUTION

© Creative Travel Projects/Shutterstock.com

Tony Caruso had not returned for dinner, and his wife, Karen, was nervous. She put on some sandals and hurried across the dunes to the ocean shore a half mile away. She soon came upon Tony's dog, Blue, tied to an old picket fence. Tony's shoes and clothing were piled neatly nearby. Karen and friends searched frantically throughout the evening. A little past midnight, Tony's body washed ashore, his lungs filled with water. A local doctor concluded he had accidentally drowned.

Karen and her friends were not the only ones distraught. Tony had been partners with Beth Smiles in an environmental consulting business, Enviro-Vision. They were good friends, and Beth was emotionally devastated. When she was able to focus on business issues, Beth filed an insurance claim with the Coastal Insurance Group. Beth hated to think about Tony's death in financial terms, but she was relieved that the struggling business would receive $2 million on the life insurance policy.

Several months after filing the claim, Beth received this reply from Coastal: "Under the policy issued to Enviro-Vision, we are liable in the amount of $1 million in the event of Mr. Caruso's death. If his death is accidental, we are liable to pay double indemnity of $2 million. But pursuant to section H(5), death by suicide is not covered. After a thorough investigation, we have concluded that Anthony Caruso's death was an act of suicide. Your claim is denied in its entirety." Beth was furious. She was convinced Tony was incapable of suicide. And her company could not afford the $2 million loss. She decided to consult her lawyer, Chris Pruitt.

> **A little past midnight, Tony's body washed ashore, his lungs filled with water.**

5-1 THREE FUNDAMENTAL AREAS OF LAW

This case is a fictionalized version of several real cases based on double indemnity insurance policies. In this chapter, we follow Beth's dispute with Coastal from initial interview through appeal, using it to examine three fundamental areas of law: the structure of our court systems, litigation, and alternative dispute resolution (ADR).

When Beth Smiles meets with her lawyer, Chris Pruitt brings a second attorney from his firm, Janet Booker, who is an experienced *litigator*; that is, a lawyer who handles court cases. If they file a lawsuit, Janet will be in charge, so Chris wants her there for the first meeting. Janet probes about Tony's home life, the status of the business, his personal finances, everything. Beth becomes upset that Janet doesn't seem sympathetic, but Chris explains that Janet is doing her job: She needs all the information, good and bad.

5-1a Litigation versus Alternative Dispute Resolution

Janet starts thinking about the two methods of dispute resolution: litigation and alternative dispute resolution. **Litigation** refers to lawsuits, the process of filing claims in court, trying the case, and living with the court's ruling. **Alternative dispute resolution** is any other formal or informal process used to settle disputes without resorting to a trial. It is increasingly popular with corporations and individuals alike because it is generally cheaper and faster than litigation.

Litigation
The process of resolving disputes in court

Alternative dispute resolution
Resolving disputes out of court, through formal or informal processes

5-2 ALTERNATIVE DISPUTE RESOLUTION

Janet Booker knows that even after expert legal help, vast expense, and years of work, litigation may leave clients unsatisfied. If she can use alternative dispute resolution (ADR) to create a mutually satisfactory solution in a few months, for a fraction of the cost, she is glad to do it. In most cases the parties *negotiate*, whether personally or through lawyers. Fortunately, the great majority of disputes are resolved this way. Negotiation often begins as soon as a dispute arises and may last a few days or several years.

5-2a Mediation

Mediation is the fastest-growing method of dispute resolution in the United States. Here, a neutral person, called a mediator, attempts to guide the two disputing parties toward a voluntary settlement.

A mediator does not render a decision in the dispute but uses a variety of skills to move the parties toward agreement. Mediators must earn the trust of both parties, listen closely, defuse anger and fear, explore common ground, cajole the parties into different perspectives, and build the will to settle. Good mediators do not need a law degree, but they must have a sense of humor and low blood pressure.

Of all forms of dispute resolution, mediation probably offers the strongest "win-win" potential. Because the goal is voluntary settlement, neither party needs to fear that it will end up the loser. This is in sharp contrast to litigation, where one party is very likely to lose. Removing the fear of defeat often encourages thinking and talking that are more open and realistic than negotiations held in the midst of a lawsuit. Studies show that more than 75 percent of mediated cases do reach a voluntary settlement.

Mediation
A form of ADR in which a neutral third party guides the disputing parties toward a voluntary settlement

5-2b Arbitration

In this form of ADR, the parties agree to bring in a neutral third party, but with a major difference: The arbitrator has the power to impose an award.

Arbitration
A form of ADR in which a neutral third party has the power to impose a binding decision

The arbitrator allows each side equal time to present its case and, after deliberation, issues a binding decision, generally without giving reasons. Unlike mediation, arbitration ensures that there will be a final result, although the parties lose control of the outcome. Arbitration is generally faster and cheaper than litigation.

Judge Judy and similar TV shows are examples of arbitration. Before the shows, people involved in a real dispute sign a contract in which they give up the right to go to court over the incident and agree to be bound by the host's decision. Parties in arbitration give up many rights that litigants retain, including discovery. *Discovery*, as we see below, allows the two sides in a lawsuit to obtain documentary and other evidence from the opponent before trial. Arbitration permits both sides to keep secret many files that would have to be divulged in a court case, potentially depriving the opposing side of valuable evidence. A party may have a stronger case than it realizes, and the absence of discovery may permanently deny it that knowledge.

Janet Booker proposes to Coastal Insurance that they use ADR to expedite a decision in their dispute. Coastal rejects the offer. Coastal's lawyer, Rich Stewart, insists that suicide is apparent.

It is a long way to go before trial, but Janet has to prepare her case. The first thing she thinks about is where to file the lawsuit.

5-3 COURT SYSTEMS

The United States has more than 50 systems of courts. One nationwide system of *federal* courts serves the entire country. In addition, each individual *state*—such as Texas, California, and Florida—has its own court system. The state and federal courts are in different buildings, have different judges, and hear different kinds of cases. Each has special powers and certain limitations.

5-3a State Courts

The typical state court system forms a pyramid, as Exhibit 5-1 shows.

Trial Courts

Almost all cases start in trial courts, the ones commonly portrayed on television and in film. There is one judge, and there will often (but not always) be a jury. This is the only court to hear testimony from witnesses and receive evidence. **Trial courts** determine the facts of a particular dispute and apply to those facts the law given by earlier appellate court decisions.

In the Enviro-Vision dispute, the trial court will decide all important facts that are in dispute. How did Tony Caruso die? Did he drown? Assuming he drowned, was his death an accident or a suicide? Once the jury has decided the facts, it will apply the law to those facts. If Tony Caruso died accidentally, contract law provides that Beth Smiles is entitled to double indemnity benefits. If the jury decides he killed himself, Beth gets nothing.

Jurisdiction refers to a court's power to hear a case. A plaintiff may start a lawsuit only in a court that has jurisdiction over that kind of case. Some state trial courts have very limited jurisdiction, while others have the power to hear almost any case. In Exhibit 5-1, notice that some courts have power only to hear cases of small claims, domestic relations, and so forth. Courts must have two types of jurisdiction.

Subject-matter jurisdiction means that a court has the authority to hear a particular type of case. In addition to subject-matter jurisdiction, courts must also have personal jurisdiction over the defendant. Personal jurisdiction is the legal authority to require the defendant to stand trial, pay judgments, and the like. Personal jurisdiction generally exists if:

- The defendant is a resident of the state in which a lawsuit is filed; or

- The defendant files documents in court, such as an answer to the complaint; or

Trial courts
First level of courts to hear disputes

Jurisdiction
A court's power to hear a case and bind the parties to its determination

- A **summons** is *served* on a defendant. A summons is the court's written notice that a lawsuit has been filed against the defendant. The summons must be delivered to the defendant when she is physically within the state in which the lawsuit is filed; or

- A **long-arm statute** applies. These statutes typically claim jurisdiction over someone who does not live in a state but commits a tort, signs a contract, causes foreseeable harm, or conducts "regular business activities" there. Under the Due Process Clause of the Constitution, courts can use long-arm statutes only if a defendant has had minimum contacts with a state. In other words, it is unfair to require a defendant to stand trial in another state if he has had no meaningful interaction with that state.

Summons
The court's written notice that a lawsuit has been filed

Long-arm statute
Statutes that may broaden a state court's jurisdiction

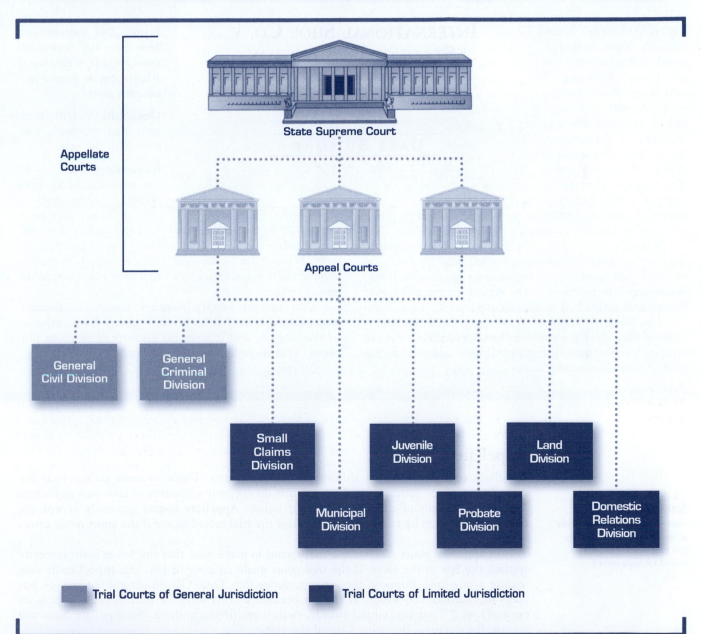

EXHIBIT 5.1   A trial court determines facts, while an appeals court ensures that the lower court correctly applied the law to those facts.

In the following Landmark Case, the Supreme Court explains its views on this important constitutional issue.

Landmark Case

INTERNATIONAL SHOE CO. V. STATE OF WASHINGTON

326 U.S. 310
Supreme Court of the United States, 1945

CASE SUMMARY

Facts: Although International Shoe manufactured footwear only in St. Louis, Missouri, it sold its products nationwide. It did not have offices or warehouses in the state of Washington, but it did send about a dozen salespeople there. The salespeople rented space in hotels and businesses, displayed sample products, and took orders. They were not authorized to collect payment from customers.

When the State of Washington sought contributions to the state's unemployment fund, International Shoe refused to pay. Washington sued. The company argued that it was not engaged in business in the state and, therefore, that Washington courts had no jurisdiction over it.

The Supreme Court of Washington ruled that International Shoe did have sufficient contacts with the state to justify a lawsuit there. International Shoe appealed to the United States Supreme Court.

Issue: *Did International Shoe have sufficient minimum contacts in the state of Washington to permit jurisdiction there?*

Decision: Yes, the company had minimum contacts with the state.

Reasoning: Agents for International Shoe have operated continuously in Washington for many years. Their presence has been more than occasional or casual. And the agents' activities have generated a significant number of sales for the company. Washington's collection action is directly related to commercially valuable activities that took place within the state's borders.

Due process merely requires reasonable fairness. International Shoe has benefitted greatly from activities in Washington, and it faces no injustice if this suit proceeds. The minimum contacts doctrine is satisfied. Affirmed.

Appellate Courts

Appellate courts
Higher courts, which generally accept the facts provided by trial courts and review the record for legal errors

Appellate courts are entirely different from trial courts. Three or more judges hear the case. There are no juries, ever. These courts do not hear witnesses or take new evidence. They hear appeals of cases already tried below. **Appellate courts** generally accept the facts given to them by trial courts and review the trial record to see if the court made errors of law.

An appellate court reviews the trial record to make sure that the lower court correctly applied the law to the facts. If the trial court made an error of law, the appeal court may require a new trial. Suppose the jury concludes that Tony Caruso committed suicide but votes to award Enviro-Vision $1 million because it feels sorry for Beth Smiles. That is an error of law; if Tony committed suicide, Beth is entitled to nothing. An appellate court will reverse the decision, declaring Coastal the victor.

The party that loses at the trial court generally is entitled to be heard at the intermediate court of appeals. The party filing the appeal is the **appellant**. The party opposing the appeal (because it won at trial) is the **appellee**. A party that loses at the court of appeals may *ask* the state supreme court to hear an appeal, but the state's highest court may choose not to accept the case.

5-3b Federal Courts

As discussed in Chapter 1, federal courts are established by the United States Constitution, which limits what kinds of cases can be brought in any federal court. For our purposes, two kinds of civil lawsuits are permitted in federal court: federal question cases and diversity cases.

Federal Question Cases

A claim based on the United States Constitution, a federal statute, or a federal treaty is called a **federal question case**. Federal courts have jurisdiction over these cases. If the Environmental Protection Agency (EPA), a part of the federal government, orders Logging Company not to cut in a particular forest, and Logging Company claims that the agency has wrongly deprived it of its property, that suit is based on a federal statute (a law passed by Congress) and is thus a federal question. Enviro-Vision's potential suit merely concerns an insurance contract. The federal district court has no federal question jurisdiction over the case.

Diversity Cases

Even if no federal law is at issue, federal courts have jurisdiction when (1) the plaintiff and defendant are citizens of different states and (2) the amount in dispute exceeds $75,000. The theory behind diversity jurisdiction is that courts of one state might be biased against citizens of another state. To ensure fairness, the parties have the option to use a federal court as a neutral playing field.

Enviro-Vision is located in Oregon, and Coastal Insurance is incorporated in Georgia. They are citizens of different states and the amount in dispute far exceeds $75,000. Janet could file this case in United States District Court based on diversity jurisdiction.

Trial Courts

United States District Courts are the primary trial courts in the federal system. The nation is divided into about 94 districts, and each has a district court. States with smaller populations have one district, while those with larger populations have several. There are also specialized trial courts such as Bankruptcy Court, Tax Court, and others, which are, you will be happy to know, beyond the scope of this book.

Appellate Courts

United States Courts of Appeals. These are the intermediate courts of appeals. They are divided into "circuits," most of which are geographical areas. For example, an appeal from the Northern District of Illinois would go to the Court of Appeals for the Seventh Circuit.

United States Supreme Court. This is the highest court in the country. There are nine justices on the Court. One justice is the chief justice, and the other eight are associate justices. When they decide a case, each justice casts an equal vote.

Appellant
The party filing an appeal of a trial verdict

Appellee
The party opposing an appeal

Federal question case
A claim based on the United States Constitution, a federal statute, or a federal treaty

Diversity case
A lawsuit in which the plaintiff and defendant are citizens of different states *and* the amount in dispute exceeds $75,000

Appellate courts
Higher courts, which generally accept the facts provided by trial courts and review the record for legal errors

EXAM Strategy

Question: Mark has sued Janelle based on the state common law of negligence. He is testifying in court, explaining how Janelle backed a rented truck out of her driveway and slammed into his Lamborghini, doing $82,000 in damages. Where would this take place?

A. State appeals court

B. United States Court of Appeals

C. State trial court

D. Federal district court

E. Either state trial court or federal district court

Strategy: The question asks about trial and appellate courts, and also about state versus federal courts. One issue at a time, please. What are the different functions of trial and appellate courts? *Trial* courts use witnesses, and often juries, to resolve factual disputes. *Appellate* courts never hear witnesses and never have juries. Applying that distinction to these facts tells us whether we are in a trial or appeals court.

State trial courts may hear lawsuits on virtually any issue. *Federal district courts* may only hear two kinds of cases: federal question (those involving a statute or constitutional provision); or diversity (where the parties are from different states *and* the amount at issue is $75,000 or higher). Apply what we know to the facts here.

Result: We are in a trial court because Mark is testifying. Could we be in federal district court? No. The suit is based on state common law. This is not a diversity case because the parties live in the same state, and this is not an appeal of a previous trial, so this is not an appeals court.

Janet Booker decides to file the Enviro-Vision suit in the Oregon trial court. She thinks that a state court judge may take the issue more seriously than a federal district court judge.

5-4 LITIGATION

5-4a Pleadings

The documents that begin a lawsuit are called the **pleadings**. The most important are the complaint and the answer.

Complaint

The plaintiff files in court a **complaint**, which is a short, plain statement of the facts she is alleging and the legal claims she is making. The purpose of the complaint is to inform the defendant of the general nature of the claims and the need to come into court and protect his interests.

Janet Booker files the complaint, as shown below. Because Enviro-Vision is a partnership, she files the suit on behalf of Beth, personally.

Pleadings

The documents that begin a lawsuit, consisting of a complaint, the answer, and sometimes a reply

Complaint

The pleading that starts a lawsuit, this is a short statement of the facts alleged by the plaintiff and his or her legal claims

STATE OF OREGON
CIRCUIT COURT

Multnomah County

Civil Action
No. _____

_____

Elizabeth Smiles,
Plaintiff

JURY TRIAL DEMANDED

v.

Coastal Insurance Company, Inc.,
Defendant

_____

COMPLAINT

Plaintiff Elizabeth Smiles states that:

1. She is a citizen of Multnomah County, Oregon.
2. Defendant Coastal Insurance Company, Inc., is incorporated under the laws of Georgia and has as its usual place of business 148 Thrift Street, Savannah, Georgia.
3. On or about July 5, 2015, plaintiff Smiles ("Smiles"), Defendant Coastal Insurance Co, Inc. ("Coastal") and Anthony Caruso entered into an insurance contract ("the contract"), a copy of which is annexed hereto as Exhibit "A." This contract was signed by all parties or their authorized agents, in Multnomah County, Oregon.
4. The contract obligates Coastal to pay to Smiles the sum of two million dollars ($2 million) if Anthony Caruso should die accidentally.
5. On or about September 15, 2015, Anthony Caruso accidentally drowned and died while swimming.
6. Coastal has refused to pay any sum pursuant to the contract.
7. Coastal has knowingly, willingly and unreasonably refused to honor its obligations under the contract.

WHEREFORE, plaintiff Elizabeth Smiles demands judgment against defendant Coastal for all monies due under the contract; demands triple damages for Coastal's knowing, willing, and unreasonable refusal to honor its obligations; and demands all costs and attorney's fees, with interest.

ELIZABETH SMILES,
By her attorney,
[Signed]
Janet Booker
Pruitt, Booker & Bother
983 Joy Avenue
Portland, OR
October 18, 2015

Answer

Coastal has 20 days in which to file an answer. Coastal's **answer** is a brief reply to each of the allegations in the complaint. The answer tells the court and the plaintiff exactly what issues are in dispute. Since Coastal admits that the parties entered into the contract that Beth claims they did, there is no need for her to prove that in court. The court can focus its attention on the issue that Coastal disputes: whether Tony Caruso died accidentally.

If the defendant fails to answer in time, the plaintiff will ask for a **default judgment**, meaning a decision that the plaintiff wins without a trial. Recently, two men sued Pepsi, claiming that the company stole the idea for Aquafina water from them. They argued that they should receive a portion of the profits for every bottle of Aquafina ever sold.

Pepsi failed to file a timely answer, and the judge entered a default judgment in the amount of $1.26 billion. On appeal, the default judgment was overturned, and Pepsi was able to escape paying the massive sum, but other defendants are sometimes not so lucky.

It is important to respond to courts on time.

Answer
The defendant's response to the complaint

Default judgment
A decision that the plaintiff in a case wins without going to trial

Class Actions

Suppose Janet uncovers evidence that Coastal denies 80 percent of all life insurance claims, calling them suicide. She could ask the court to permit a **class action**. If the court granted her request, she would represent the entire group of plaintiffs, including those who are unaware of the lawsuit or even unaware they were harmed. Class actions can give the plaintiffs much greater leverage, since the defendant's potential liability is vastly increased. Because Janet has no such evidence, she decides not to pursue a class action.

Discovery

Discovery is the critical, pretrial opportunity for both parties to learn the strengths and weaknesses of the opponent's case.

The theory behind civil litigation is that the best outcome is a negotiated settlement and that parties will move toward agreement if they understand the opponent's case. That is likeliest to occur if both sides have an opportunity to examine the evidence their opponent will bring to trial. Further, if a case does go all the way to trial, efficient and fair litigation cannot take place in a courtroom filled with surprises. On television dramas, witnesses say astonishing things that amaze the courtroom. In real trials, the lawyers know in advance the answers to practically all questions asked because discovery has allowed them to see the opponent's documents and question its witnesses. The following are the most important forms of discovery.

Interrogatories.   These are written questions that the opposing party must answer, in writing, under oath.

Depositions.   These provide a chance for one party's lawyer to question the other party, or a potential witness, under oath. The person being questioned is the **deponent**. Lawyers for both parties are present.

Production of Documents and Things.   Each side may ask the other side to produce relevant documents for inspection and copying; to produce physical objects, such as part of a car alleged to be defective; and for permission to enter on land to make an inspection, for example, at the scene of an accident.

Physical and Mental Examination.   A party may ask the court to order an examination of the other party, if his physical or mental condition is relevant, for example, in a case of medical malpractice.

Janet Booker begins her discovery with interrogatories. Her goal is to learn Coastal's basic position and factual evidence and then follow up with more detailed questioning during depositions. Her interrogatories ask for every fact Coastal relied on in denying the claim. She asks for the names of all witnesses, the identity of all documents, the description of all things or objects that they considered. She requests the names of all corporate officers who played any role in the decision and of any expert witnesses Coastal plans to call.

Coastal has 30 days to answer Janet's interrogatories. Before it responds, Coastal mails to Janet a notice of deposition, stating its intention to depose Beth Smiles. Beth and Janet will go to the office of Coastal's lawyer, and Beth will answer questions under oath. But at the same time Coastal sends this notice, it sends 25 other notices of deposition. It will depose Karen Caruso as soon as Beth's deposition is over. Coastal also plans to depose all seven employees of Enviro-Vision; three neighbors who lived near Tony and Karen's beach house; two policemen who participated in the search; the doctor and two nurses involved in the case; Tony's physician; Jerry Johnson, Tony's tennis partner; Craig Bergson, a college roommate; a couple who had dinner with Tony and Karen a week before his death; and several other people.

Rich, the Coastal lawyer, proceeds to take Beth's deposition. It takes two full days. He asks about Enviro-Vision's past and present. He learns that Tony appeared to have won their biggest contract ever from Rapid City, Oregon, but that he then lost it when he had a fight with Rapid City's mayor. He inquires into Tony's mood, learns that he was depressed, and probes in every direction he can to find evidence of suicidal motivation. Janet and Rich argue frequently over questions and whether Beth should have to answer them. At times, Janet is persuaded and permits Beth to answer; other times, she instructs Beth not to answer. For example, toward the end of the second day, Rich asks Beth whether she and Tony had been sexually involved. Janet instructs Beth not to answer. This fight necessitates a trip into court. As both lawyers know, **the parties are entitled to discover anything that could reasonably lead to valid evidence**. Rich wants his questions answered, so he files a motion to compel discovery. The judge will have to decide whether Rich's questions are reasonable.

A **motion** is a formal request to the court. Before, during, and after trial, both parties will file many motions. A **motion to compel discovery** is a request to the court for an order requiring the other side to answer discovery. The judge rules that Beth must discuss Tony's romantic life only if Coastal has evidence that he was involved with someone outside his marriage. Because the company lacks any such evidence, the judge denies Coastal's motion.

At the same time, the judge hears one of Beth's **motions for a protective order**. Beth claims that Rich has scheduled too many depositions; the time and expense are a huge burden to a small company. The judge limits Rich to 10 depositions. Rich cancels several depositions, including that of Craig Bergson, Tony's old roommate. As we will see, Craig knows crucial facts about this case, and Rich's decision not to depose him will have major consequences.

Motion
A formal request to the court

E-Discovery. The biggest change in litigation in the last decade is the explosive rise of electronic discovery (e-discovery). Companies send hundreds, thousands, or even millions of emails every day. Many have attachments that are sometimes hundreds of pages long. In addition, businesses large and small have vast amounts of data stored electronically. All this information is potentially subject to discovery.

It is enormously time-consuming and expensive for companies to locate all the relevant material, separate it from irrelevant or confidential matter, and furnish it. A firm may be obligated to furnish *millions* of emails to the opposing party.

Who is to say what must be supplied? What if an email string contains individual emails that are clearly privileged (meaning a party need not divulge them), but others that are not privileged? May a company refuse to furnish the entire string? Many will try. However, some courts have ruled that companies seeking to protect email strings must create a log describing every individual email and allow the court to determine which are privileged.

Social media further complicates discovery. When a Facebook profile or Twitter account is public, opposing parties are free to rummage through the treasure trove of personal information. But what about access to a *private* social media profile? To protect people's privacy, courts require parties to show that the discovery request will to lead to relevant and admissible evidence. But that standard means that private accounts are not really private.

Both sides in litigation sometimes use gamesmanship during discovery. Thus, if an individual sues a large corporation, the company may deliberately make discovery so expensive that the plaintiff cannot afford the legal fees. And if a plaintiff has a poor case, he might intentionally try to make the discovery process more expensive for the defendant than a reasonable settlement offer.

In the following case, it was not just legends that were forever—discovery was, too. Was the plaintiff's failure to cooperate part of a calculated plan to tire Nike into settling or just a costly mistake?

LEGENDS ARE FOREVER, INC. v. NIKE, INC

2013 WL 6086461, 2013 U.S. Dist. LEXIS 164091
U.S. District Court, Northern District, New York, 2013

CASE SUMMARY

Case Summary: Legends are Forever, Inc. (Legends) trademarked its name. When Nike used the name as a slogan in an ad campaign, Legends sued Nike.

During discovery, Legends repeatedly failed to comply with Nike's requests. Ultimately, Nike filed a motion to compel Legends to hand over the requested documents. Nike also asked the court to make Legends pay all of the costs and fees relating to the motion to compel, totaling $25,186.91. This sum included Nike's attorney's fees (ranging from $250 to $450 per hour) and all the travel expenses incurred by the two Nike attorneys who attended the hearing on the motion to compel.

The court agreed with Nike, granting it both discovery and its fees. Legends challenged the order, arguing that a small company should not have to pay for Nike's high-priced lawyers.

Issues: *Should Legends have to pay for its unacceptable behavior during discovery? Was $25,000 too high?*

Decision: Legends uncooperative behavior should be penalized, but at a reasonable rate.

Reasoning: Even though Legends was the plaintiff, it was extremely uncooperative, refusing to meet Nike's legitimate discovery demands. For this reason, it should

pay for Nike's reasonable costs and attorney's fees related to the motion to compel.

But what is "reasonable" when it comes to attorney's fees and costs? Does it matter that Nike is a business giant, with resources and high-end lawyers to spare, while Legends is a small player, which would be hurt by *any* financial penalty?

Attorney's fee awards are determined by multiplying a reasonable hourly rate by the number of reasonably expended hours. Courts consider factors such as the difficulty of the legal questions, and the level of time and expertise required, not the financial position of the actors. In this case, $250 to $350 per hour was appropriate. Because Nike paid for two lawyers when one would have sufficed, the fees and costs will be reduced to $12,332.82.

Despite its size and prominence, Nike was entitled to the same discovery, no more and no less, than any other litigant.

Summary Judgment

Summary judgment
A ruling that no trial is necessary because essential facts are not in dispute

When discovery is completed, both sides may consider seeking summary judgment. **Summary judgment** is a ruling by the court that no trial is necessary because some essential facts are not in dispute. The purpose of a trial is to determine the facts of the case; that is, to decide who did what to whom, why, when, and with what consequences. If relevant facts are not in dispute, then there is no need for a trial.

In the following case, the defendant won summary judgment, meaning that the case never went to trial. And yet, this was only the beginning of trouble for that defendant, Bill Clinton.

JONES V. CLINTON

990 F. Supp. 657
United States District Court for the Eastern District of Arkansas, 1998

CASE SUMMARY

Facts: In 1991, Bill Clinton was governor of Arkansas. Paula Jones worked for a state agency, the Arkansas Industrial Development Commission (AIDC). When Clinton became president, Jones sued him, claiming that he had sexually harassed her. She alleged that in May 1991, the governor arranged for her to meet him in a hotel room in Little Rock, Arkansas. When they were alone, he put his hand on her leg and slid it toward her pelvis. She escaped from his grasp, exclaimed, "What are you doing?" and said she was "not that kind of girl." Upset and confused, she sat on a sofa near the door. She claimed that Clinton approached her, "lowered his trousers and underwear, exposed his penis, and told her to kiss it." Jones was

horrified, jumped up, and said she had to leave. Clinton responded by saying, "Well, I don't want to make you do anything you don't want to do," and pulled his pants up. He added that if she got in trouble for leaving work, Jones should "have Dave call me immediately and I'll take care of it." He also said, "You are smart. Let's keep this between ourselves." Jones remained at AIDC until February 1993, when she moved to California because of her husband's job transfer.

President Clinton denied all the allegations. He also filed for summary judgment, claiming that Jones had not alleged facts that justified a trial. Jones opposed the motion for summary judgment.

Issue: *Was Clinton entitled to summary judgment, or was Jones entitled to a trial?*

Decision: Jones failed to make out a claim of sexual harassment. Summary judgment was granted for the President.

Reasoning: To establish this type of sexual harassment case, a plaintiff must show that her refusal to submit to unwelcome sexual advances resulted in specific harm to her job.

Jones received every merit increase and cost-of-living allowance for which she was eligible. Her only job transfer involved a minor change in working conditions, with no reduction in pay or benefits. Jones claims that she was obligated to sit in a less private area, often with no work to do, and was the only female employee not to receive flowers on Secretary's Day. However, even if these allegations are true, all are trivial and none is sufficient to create a sexual harassment suit. Jones has demonstrated no specific harm to her job.

In other words, the court acknowledged that there were factual disputes but concluded that even if Jones proved each of her allegations, she would still lose the case because her allegations fell short of a legitimate case of sexual harassment. Jones appealed the case. Later the same year, as the appeal was pending and the House of Representatives was considering whether to impeach President Clinton, the parties settled the dispute. Clinton, without acknowledging any of the allegations, agreed to pay Jones $850,000 to drop the suit.

Janet and Rich each consider moving for summary judgment, but both correctly decide that they would lose. There is one major fact in dispute: Did Tony Caruso commit suicide? Only a jury may decide that issue. As long as there is some evidence supporting each side of a key factual dispute, the court may not grant summary judgment.

EXAM Strategy

Question: You are a judge. Mel has sued Kevin, claiming that while Kevin was drunk, he negligently drove his car into Mel's property, destroying his rare trees. Mel's complaint stated that three witnesses, at a bar, saw Kevin take at least eight drinks right before the damage was done. In Kevin's answer, he denied being in the bar that night and causing the damage .

Kevin's lawyer has moved for summary judgment. He proves that three weeks before the alleged accident, Mel sold the lot to Tatiana.

Mel's lawyer opposes summary judgment. He produces a security camera tape proving that Kevin was at the bar, drinking beer, 34 minutes before the damage was done. He produces a signed statement from Sandy, Mel's neighbor. Sandy states that she heard a crash, hurried to the window, and saw Kevin's car weaving away from the damaged trees. Sandy is a landscape gardener and estimates the tree damage at $30,000 to $40,000. How should you rule on the motion?

Strategy: Do not be fooled by red herrings about Kevin's drinking or the value of the trees. Stick to the question: Should you grant summary judgment? Trials are necessary to resolve disputes about essential factual issues. Summary judgment is appropriate when some essential facts are not disputed. Is there an essential fact not in dispute? Find it. Apply the rule. Being a judge is easy!

Result: It makes no difference whether Kevin was drunk or sober, whether he caused the harm, or whether he was at home in bed. Mel did not own the property at the time of the accident. He cannot win. You should grant Kevin's summary judgment motion.

> ## More than 90 percent of all lawsuits are settled before trial.

More than 90 percent of all lawsuits are settled before trial. But the parties in the Enviro-Vision dispute are unable to compromise and are headed for trial.

5-5 TRIAL

5-5a Adversary System

Adversary system

A system based on the assumption that if two sides present their best case before a neutral party, the truth will be established

Our system of justice assumes that the best way to bring out the truth is for the two contesting sides to present the strongest case possible to a neutral fact-finder. Each side presents its witnesses, and then the opponent has a chance to cross-examine. The **adversary system** presumes that by putting a witness on the stand and letting both lawyers question her, the truth will emerge.

The judge runs the trial. Each lawyer sits at a large table near the front. Beth, looking tense and unhappy, sits with Janet. Rich Stewart sits with a Coastal executive. In the back of the courtroom are benches for the public. Today, there are only a few spectators. One is Tony's old roommate, Craig Bergson, who has a special interest in the trial.

5-5b Right to Jury Trial

Not all cases are tried to a jury. As a general rule, both plaintiff and defendant have a right to demand a jury trial when the lawsuit is for money damages. For example, in a typical contract lawsuit, such as Beth's insurance claim, both plaintiff and defendant have a jury trial right whether they are in state or federal court. Even in such a case, though, the parties may waive the jury right, meaning they agree to try the case to a judge. Also, if the plaintiff is seeking an equitable remedy, such as an injunction (an order not to do something), there is no jury right for either party.

Although jury selection for some cases takes many days, in the Enviro-Vision case the first day of the hearing ends with the jury selected. In the hallway outside the court, Rich offers Janet $200,000 to settle. Janet reports the offer to Beth, and they agree to reject it. Craig Bergson drives home, emotionally confused. Only three weeks before his death, Tony had accidentally met his old roommate, and they had had several drinks. Craig believes that what Tony told him answers the riddle of this case.

5-5c Opening Statements

The next day, each attorney makes an opening statement to the jury, summarizing the proof he or she expects to offer, with the plaintiff going first. Janet focuses on Tony's successful life, his business and strong marriage, and the tragedy of his accidental death.

Rich works hard to establish a friendly rapport with the jury. If members of the jury like him, they will tend to pay more attention to his presentation of evidence. He expresses regret about the death. Nonetheless, suicide is a clear exclusion from the policy. If insurance companies are forced to pay claims they did not bargain for, everyone's insurance rates will go up.

5-5d Burden of Proof

Burden of proof

The obligation to convince the jury that a party's version of the case is correct

In civil cases, the plaintiff has the **burden of proof**. That means that the plaintiff must convince the jury that its version of the case is correct; the defendant is not obligated to disprove the allegations.

The plaintiff's burden in a civil lawsuit is to prove its case by a **preponderance of the evidence**. The plaintiff must convince the jury that his or her version of the facts is at least *slightly* more likely than the defendant's version. Some courts describe this as a "51–49" persuasion, that is, that plaintiff's proof must "just tip" credibility in its favor. By contrast, in a criminal case, the prosecution must demonstrate **beyond a reasonable doubt** that the defendant is guilty. The burden of proof in a criminal case is much tougher because the likely consequences are, too. See Exhibit 5-2.

5-5e Plaintiff's Case

Since the plaintiff has the burden of proof, Janet puts in her case first. She wants to prove two things. First, that Tony died. That is easy, since the death certificate clearly demonstrates it and since Coastal does not seriously contest it. Second, in order to win double indemnity damages, she must show that the death was accidental. She will do this with the testimony of the witnesses she calls, one after the other. Her first witness is Beth. When a lawyer asks questions of her own witness, it is **direct examination**. Janet brings out all the evidence she wants the jury to hear: that the business was basically sound, though temporarily troubled, that Tony was a hard worker, why the company took out life insurance policies, and so forth.

Then Rich has a chance to **cross-examine** Beth, which means to ask questions of an opposing witness. He will try to create doubt in the jury's mind. He asks Beth only questions for which he is certain of the answers, based on discovery. Rich gets Beth to admit that the firm was not doing well the year of Tony's death; that Tony had lost the best client the firm ever had; that Beth had reduced salaries; and that Tony had been depressed about business.

Janet uses her other witnesses, Tony's friends, family, and coworkers, to fortify the impression that his death was accidental.

5-5f Defendant's Case

Rich now puts in his case, exactly as Janet did, except that he happens to have fewer witnesses. He calls the examining doctor, who admits that Tony could have committed suicide by swimming out too far. On cross-examination, Janet gets the doctor to acknowledge that he has no idea whether Tony intentionally drowned. Rich also questions several

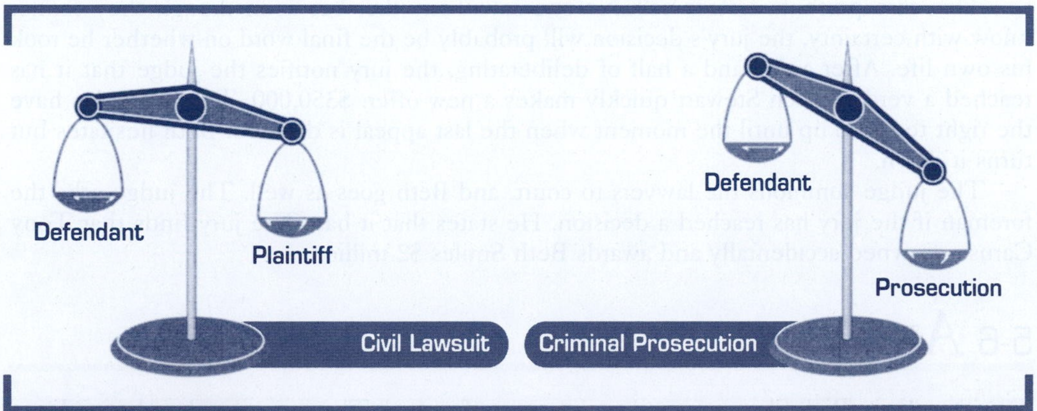

Preponderance of the evidence
The standard of proof required for a civil case

Beyond a reasonable doubt
The government's burden in a criminal prosecution

Direct examination
A lawyer asks questions of his or her own witness.

Cross-examine
A lawyer asks questions of an opposing witness.

EXHIBIT 5.2   *Burden of Proof.* In a civil lawsuit, a plaintiff wins with a mere preponderance of the evidence. But the prosecution must persuade a jury beyond a reasonable doubt in order to win a criminal conviction.

neighbors as to how depressed Tony had seemed and how unusual it was that Blue was tied up. Some of the witnesses Rich deposed, such as the tennis partner Jerry Johnson, have nothing that will help Coastal's case, so he does not call them.

Craig Bergson, sitting in the back of the courtroom, thinks how different the trial would have been had he been called as a witness. When he and Tony had the fateful drink, Tony had been distraught: Business was terrible, he was involved in an extramarital affair that he could not end, and he saw no way out of his problems. He had no one to talk to and had been hugely relieved to speak with Craig. Several times Tony had said, "I just can't go on like this. I don't want to, anymore." Craig thought Tony seemed suicidal and urged him to see a therapist Craig knew. Tony had said that it was good advice, but Craig is unsure whether Tony sought any help.

This evidence would have affected the case. Had Rich Stewart known of the conversation, he would have deposed Craig and the therapist. Coastal's case would have been far stronger, perhaps overwhelming. But Craig's evidence will never be heard. Facts are critical. Rich's decision to depose other witnesses and omit Craig may influence the verdict more than any rule of law.

5-5g Closing Argument

Both lawyers sum up their case to the jury, explaining how they hope the jury will interpret what they have heard. Judge Rowland instructs the jury as to its duty. He tells them that they are to evaluate the case based only on the evidence they heard at trial, relying on their own experience and common sense.

He explains the law and the burden of proof, telling the jury that it is Beth's obligation to prove her case. If Beth has proven that Tony died by means other than suicide but not by accident, she is entitled to $1 million; if she has proven that his death was accidental, she is entitled to $2 million. However, if Coastal has proven suicide, Beth receives nothing. Finally, he states that if they are unable to decide between accidental death and suicide, there is a legal presumption that it was accidental. Rich asks Judge Rowland to rephrase the "legal presumption" part, but the judge declines.

5-5h Verdict

The jury deliberates informally, with all jurors entitled to voice their opinion. Some deliberations take two hours; some take two weeks. Many states require a unanimous verdict; others require only, for example, a 10–2 vote in civil cases.

This case presents a close call. No one saw Tony die. Yet even though they cannot know with certainty, the jury's decision will probably be the final word on whether he took his own life. After a day and a half of deliberating, the jury notifies the judge that it has reached a verdict. Rich Stewart quickly makes a new offer: $350,000. The two sides have the right to settle up until the moment when the last appeal is decided. Beth hesitates but turns it down.

The judge summons the lawyers to court, and Beth goes as well. The judge asks the foreman if the jury has reached a decision. He states that it has: The jury finds that Tony Caruso drowned accidentally and awards Beth Smiles $2 million.

5-6 Appeals

Two days later, Rich files an appeal to the court of appeal. The same day, he phones Janet and increases his settlement offer to $425,000. Beth is tempted but wants Janet's advice. Janet says the risks of an appeal are that the court will order a new trial, and they would start all over. But to accept this offer is to forfeit over $1.5 million. Beth is unsure what to do. The firm desperately needs cash now, and appeals may take years. Janet suggests they wait until oral argument, another eight months.

Rich files a brief arguing that there were two basic errors at the trial: First, that the jury's verdict is clearly contrary to the evidence; and second, that the judge gave the wrong instructions to the jury. Janet files a reply brief, opposing Rich on both issues. In her brief, Janet cites many cases that she claims are **precedent**: earlier decisions by the state supreme court on similar or identical issues.

5-6a Appeal Court Options

The court of appeal can **affirm** the trial court, allowing the decision to stand. The court may **modify** the decision, for example, by affirming that the plaintiff wins but decreasing the size of the award. (That is unlikely here; Beth is entitled to $2 million or nothing.) The court might **reverse and remand**, meaning it nullifies the lower court's decision and returns the case to the trial court for a new trial. Or it could simply **reverse**, turning the loser (Coastal) into the winner, with no new trial.

Janet and Beth talk. Beth is very anxious and wants to settle. She does not want to wait four or five months, only to learn that they must start all over. With Beth's approval, Janet phones Rich and offers to settle for $1.2 million. Rich snorts, "Yeah, right." Then he snaps, "$750,000. Take it or leave it. Final offer." After a short conversation with her client, Janet calls back and accepts the offer.

Precedent
Earlier decisions by a court on similar or identical issues, on which subsequent court decisions can be based

Affirm
To allow a court decision to stand as is

Modify
To let a court decision stand, but with changes

Reverse and remand
To nullify a lower court's decision and return a case to trial

Reverse
To rule that the loser in a previous case wins, with no new trial

---

LITIGATION

1. PLEADINGS	2. DISCOVERY	3. PRETRIAL MOTIONS
Complaint	Interrogatories	Class action
Answer	Depositions	Summary judgment
	Production of documents and things	
	Physical and mental examinations	

4. TRIAL	5. JURY'S ROLE	6. APPEALS
Jury selection	Judge's instructions	Affirm
Opening statements	Deliberation	Modify
Plaintiff's case	Verdict	Reverse
Defendant's case		Remand
Closing argument		

Chapter Conclusion

No one will ever know for sure whether Tony took his own life. Craig Bergson's evidence might have tipped the scales in favor of Coastal. But even that is uncertain, since the jury could have found him unpersuasive. After two years, the case ends with a settlement and uncertainty—both typical lawsuit results. The vaguely unsatisfying feeling about it all is only too common and indicates why litigation is best avoided—by reasonable negotiation.

EXAM REVIEW

1. **ALTERNATIVE DISPUTE RESOLUTION** Alternative dispute resolution (ADR) is any formal or informal process to settle disputes without a trial. Mediation and arbitration are the two most common forms.

2. **COURT SYSTEMS** There are many systems of courts, one federal and one in each state. A federal court will hear a case only if it involves a federal question or diversity jurisdiction.

3. **TRIAL AND APPELLATE COURTS** Trial courts determine facts and apply the law to the facts; appellate courts generally accept the facts found by the trial court and review the trial record for errors of law.

EXAM Strategy

Question: Jade sued Kim, claiming that Kim promised to hire her as an in-store model for $1,000 per week for eight weeks. Kim denied making the promise, and the jury was persuaded: Kim won. Jade has appealed, and she now offers Steve as a witness. Steve will testify to the appeals court that he saw Kim hire Jade as a model, exactly as Jade claimed. Will Jade win on appeal?

Strategy: Before you answer, make sure you know the difference between trial and appellate courts. (See the "Result" at the end of this section.)

4. **PLEADINGS** A complaint and an answer are the two most important pleadings; that is, documents that start a lawsuit.

5. **DISCOVERY** Discovery is the critical pretrial opportunity for both parties to learn the strengths and weaknesses of the opponent's case. Important forms of discovery include interrogatories, depositions, production of documents and objects, physical and mental examinations, and requests for admission.

6. **MOTIONS** A motion is a formal request to the court.

7. **SUMMARY JUDGMENT** Summary judgment is a ruling by the court that no trial is necessary because some essential facts are not in dispute.

8. **RIGHT TO A JURY** Generally, both plaintiff and defendant may demand a jury in any lawsuit for money damages.

9. **BURDEN OF PROOF** The plaintiff's burden of proof in a civil lawsuit is preponderance of the evidence, meaning that its version of the facts must be at least slightly more persuasive than the defendant's. In a criminal prosecution, the government must offer proof beyond a reasonable doubt in order to win a conviction.

Question: In Courtroom 1, Asbury has sued Park, claiming that Park drove his motorcycle negligently and broke Asbury's leg. The jury is deliberating. The jurors have serious doubts about what happened, but they find Asbury's evidence slightly more convincing than Park's. In Courtroom 2, the state is prosecuting Patterson for drug possession. The jury in that case is also deliberating. The jurors have serious doubts about what happened, but they find the government's evidence slightly more convincing than Patterson's. Who will win in each case?

Strategy: A different burden of proof applies in the two cases. (See the "Result" at the end of this section.)

10. **VERDICT**   The verdict is the jury's decision in a case.

11. **APPELLATE COURT RULINGS**   An appeal court has many options. The court may affirm, upholding the lower court's decision; modify, changing the verdict but leaving the same party victorious; reverse, transforming the loser into the winner; or reverse and remand, sending the case back to the lower court.

3. Result: Trial courts use witnesses to help resolve factual disputes. Appellate courts review the record to see if there have been errors of law. Appellate courts never hear witnesses, and they will not hear Steve. Jade will lose her appeal.

9. Result: In the civil lawsuit, Asbury must merely convince the jury by a preponderance of the evidence. He has done this, so he will win. In the prosecution, the government must demonstrate proof beyond a reasonable doubt. It has failed to do so, and Patterson will be acquitted.

MATCHING QUESTIONS

Match the following terms with their definitions:

___A. Arbitration
___B. Diversity jurisdiction
___C. Mediation
___D. Interrogatories
___E. Deposition

1. A pretrial procedure involving written questions to be signed under oath
2. A form of ADR in which the parties themselves craft the settlement
3. A pretrial procedure involving oral questions answered under oath
4. The power of a federal court to hear certain cases between citizens of different states
5. A form of ADR that leads to a binding decision

True/False Questions

Circle true or false:

1. T F One advantage of arbitration is that it provides the parties with greater opportunities for discovery than litigation does.
2. T F In the United States, there are many separate courts, but only one court *system*, organized as a pyramid.
3. T F If we are listening to witnesses testify, we must be in a trial court.
4. T F About one-half of all lawsuits settle before trial.
5. T F In a lawsuit for money damages, both the plaintiff and the defendant are generally entitled to a jury.

Multiple-Choice Questions

1. A federal court has the power to hear:
   (a) any case.
   (b) any case between citizens of different states.
   (c) any criminal case.
   (d) appeals of any cases from lower courts.
   (e) any lawsuit based on a federal statute.

2. Before trial begins, a defendant in a civil lawsuit believes that even if the plaintiff proves everything he has alleged, the law requires the defendant to win. The defendant should:
   (a) request arbitration.
   (b) request a mandatory verdict.
   (c) move for recusal.
   (d) move for summary judgment.
   (e) demand mediation.

3. In a civil lawsuit:
   (a) the defendant is presumed innocent until proven guilty.
   (b) the defendant is presumed guilty until proven innocent.
   (c) the plaintiff must prove her case by a preponderance of the evidence.
   (d) the plaintiff must prove her case beyond a reasonable doubt.
   (e) the defendant must establish his defenses to the satisfaction of the court.

4. Mack sues Jasmine, claiming that she caused an automobile accident. At trial, Jasmine's lawyer is asking her questions about the accident. This is:
   (a) an interrogatory.
   (b) a deposition.
   (c) direct examination.
   (d) cross-examination.
   (e) opening statement.

5. Jurisdiction refers to:
   (a) the jury's decision.
   (b) the judge's instructions to the jury.
   (c) pretrial questions posed by one attorney to the opposing party.
   (d) the power of a court to hear a particular case.
   (e) a decision by an appellate court to send the case back to the trial court.

CASE QUESTIONS

1. State which court(s) have jurisdiction as to each of these lawsuits:
   (a) Pat wants to sue his next-door neighbor Dorothy, claiming that Dorothy promised to sell him her house.

   (b) Paula, who lives in New York City, wants to sue Dizzy Movie Theatres, whose principal place of business is Dallas. She claims that while she was in Texas on holiday, she was injured by their negligent maintenance of a stairway. She claims damages of $30,000.

   (c) Phil lives in Tennessee. He wants to sue Dick, who lives in Ohio. Phil claims that Dick agreed to sell him 3,000 acres of farmland in Ohio, worth over $2 million.

   (d) Pete, incarcerated in a federal prison in Kansas, wants to sue the United States government. He claims that his treatment by prison authorities violates three federal statutes.

2. **ETHICS** Trial practice is dramatically different in Britain. The lawyers for the two sides, called *solicitors*, do not go into court. Courtroom work is done by different lawyers, called *barristers*. The barristers are not permitted to interview any witnesses before trial. They know the substance of what each witness intends to say but do not rehearse questions and answers, as in the United States. Which approach do you consider more effective? More ethical? What is the purpose of a trial? Of pretrial preparation?

3. Claus Scherer worked for Rockwell International and was paid over $300,000 per year. Rockwell fired Scherer for alleged sexual harassment of several workers, including his secretary, Terry Pendy. Scherer sued in United States District Court, alleging that Rockwell's real motive in firing him was his high salary.
   Rockwell moved for summary judgment, offering deposition transcripts of various employees. Pendy's deposition detailed instances of harassment, including comments

about her body, instances of unwelcome touching, and discussions of extramarital affairs. Another deposition, from a Rockwell employee who investigated the allegations, included complaints by other employees as to Scherer's harassment. In his own deposition, which he offered to oppose summary judgment, Scherer testified that he could not recall the incidents alleged by Pendy and others. He denied generally that he had sexually harassed anyone. The district court granted summary judgment for Rockwell. Was its ruling correct?

4. Annie and Bart are coworkers. In fact, they share a cubicle wall. Recently, they were involved in a fender-bender in the company parking lot. Each blames the other for the accident, and the two have stopped speaking. Would you advise them to try to settle their dispute through arbitration, mediation, or with a traditional lawsuit? Why?

5. Raul lives in Georgia. He creates custom paintings and sells them at a weekly art fair near Atlanta. Sarah lives in Vermont. While on vacation in Georgia, she buys one of Raul's paintings for $500. Soon after she returns home, she decides the painting is ugly, calls Raul, and demands a refund. Raul refuses. Sarah wants to sue him in Vermont. Raul has never been to Vermont and has never sold a painting to anyone else from Vermont. Do Vermont courts have personal jurisdiction over Raul? Why or why not?

DISCUSSION QUESTIONS

1. The burden of proof in civil cases is fairly low. A plaintiff wins a lawsuit if he is 51 percent convincing, and then he collects 100 percent of his damages. Is this result reasonable? Should a plaintiff in a civil case be required to prove his case beyond a reasonable doubt? Or, if a plaintiff is only 51 percent convincing, should he get only 51 percent of his damages?

2. Many employees sign mandatory arbitration agreements in employment contracts. Courts usually uphold these clauses. Imagine that you signed a contract with an arbitration agreement, that the company later mistreated you, and that you could not sue in court. Would you be upset? Or would you be relieved to go through the faster and cheaper process of arbitration?

3. Imagine a state law that allows for residents to sue "spammers"—those who send uninvited commercial messages through email—for $30. One particularly prolific spammer sends messages to hundreds of thousands of people.

   John Smith, a lawyer, signs up 100,000 people to participate in a class action lawsuit against a spammer. According to the agreements with his many clients, Smith will keep one-third of any winnings. In the end, Smith wins a $3,000,000 verdict and pockets $1,000,000. Each individual plaintiff receives a check for $20.

   Is this lawsuit a reasonable use of the court's resources? Why or why not?

4. Usually, both a plaintiff and defendant can demand a jury trial in cases asking for cash damages. If you were involved in a trial with $50,000 at stake, would you *want* a jury trial? Would you trust a group of strangers to arrive at a fair verdict, or would you prefer a judge to decide the case? Would your answer depend upon whether you were the plaintiff or defendant?

CHAPTER 6

© Creative Travel Projects/Shutterstock.com

CRIME

Crime can take us by surprise. Stacey tucks her nine-year-old daughter, Beth, into bed. Promising her husband, Mark, that she will be home by 11:00 p.m., she jumps into her car and heads back to Be Patient, Inc. She connects her iPhone to the Bluetooth device in her $100,000 sedan and tries to relax by listening to music. Be Patient is a health care organization that owns five geriatric hospitals. Most of its patients use Medicare, and Stacey supervises all billing to their largest client, the federal government.

She parks in a well-lighted spot on the street and walks to her building, failing to notice two men, collars turned up, watching from a parked truck. Once in her office, she goes straight to her computer and works on billing issues. Tonight's work goes more quickly than she expected, thanks to new software she helped develop. At 10:30, she emerges from the building with a quick step and a light heart, walks to her car—and finds it missing.

A major crime has occurred during the 90 minutes Stacey was at her desk, but she will never report it to the police. It is a crime that costs Americans countless dollars each year, yet Stacey will not even mention it to friends or family. Stacey is the criminal.

> **A major crime has occurred during the 90 minutes Stacey was at her desk, but she will never report it to the police.**

When we think of crime, we imagine the drug dealers and bank robbers endlessly portrayed on television. We do not picture corporate executives sitting at polished desks. "Street crimes" are indeed serious threats to our security and happiness. They deservedly receive the attention of the public and the law. But when measured only in dollars, street crime takes second place to white-collar crime, which costs society *tens of billions* of dollars annually.

The hypothetical about Stacey is based on many real cases and is used to illustrate that crime does not always dress the way we expect. Her car was never stolen; it was simply towed. Two parking bureau employees, watching from their truck, saw Stacey park illegally and did their job. It is Stacey who committed a crime—Medicare fraud. Every month, she has billed the government about $10 million for work that her company has not performed. Stacey's scheme was quick and profitable—and a distressingly common crime.

Crime, whether violent or white-collar, is detrimental to all society. It imposes a huge cost on everyone. Just the *fear* of crime is expensive—homeowners buy alarm systems, and businesses hire security guards. But the anger and fear that crime engenders sometimes tempt us to forget that not all accused people are **guilty**. Everyone suspected of a crime should have the protections that you yourself would want in that situation. As the English jurist William Blackstone said, "Better that ten guilty persons escape than that one innocent suffer."

Thus, criminal law is a balancing act—between making society safe and protecting us all from false accusations and unfair punishment.

Guilty
A judge or jury's finding that a defendant has committed a crime

6-1 A CIVIL VERSUS A CRIMINAL CASE

In civil cases, the wrongdoing has harmed the safety or property of the parties, but it is not so serious that it threatens society as a whole. **Conduct becomes criminal when *society* outlaws it.** If a state legislature or Congress concludes that certain behavior harms *public* safety and welfare, it passes a statute forbidding that behavior; in other words, declaring it criminal. Medicare fraud, which Stacey committed, is a crime because Congress has outlawed it.

6-1a Prosecution

Suppose the police arrest Roger and accuse him of breaking into a store and stealing 50 computers. The owner of the store has been harmed, so he has the right to sue the thief in civil court to recover money damages. But **only the government can prosecute a crime and punish Roger by sending him to prison.** The government may also impose a fine on Roger, but it keeps the fine and does not share it with the victim. (However, the court will sometimes order **restitution**, meaning that the defendant must reimburse the victim for the harm suffered.)

Restitution
When a guilty defendant must reimburse the victim for the harm suffered

6-1b Burden of Proof

In a civil case, the plaintiff must prove her case only by a preponderance of the evidence.[1] But because the penalties for conviction in a criminal case are so serious, **the government has to prove its case beyond a reasonable doubt**. In all criminal cases, if the jury has any significant doubt at all that Roger stole the computers, it *must* acquit him.

Beyond a reasonable doubt
The very high burden of proof in a criminal trial, demanding much more certainty than required in a civil trial

6-1c Right to a Jury

The facts of a case are decided by a judge or jury. **A criminal defendant has a right to a trial by jury for any charge that could result in a sentence of six months or longer.** The defendant may choose not to have a jury trial, in which case, the judge decides the verdict. When the judge is the fact finder, the proceeding is called a **bench trial**.

Bench trial
There is no jury; the judge reaches a verdict

---

[1]See the earlier discussion in Chapter 5, on dispute resolution.

6-1d Felonies and Misdemeanors

A **felony** is a serious crime, for which a defendant can be sentenced to one year or more in prison. Murder, robbery, rape, drug dealing, money laundering, wire fraud, and embezzlement are felonies. A **misdemeanor** is a less serious crime, often punishable by a year or less in a county jail. Public drunkenness, driving without a license, and shoplifting are considered misdemeanors in many states.

6-2 CRIMINAL PROCEDURE

The title of a criminal case is usually the government versus someone: *The United States of America v. Simpson* or *The State of Illinois v. Simpson*, for example. This name illustrates a daunting thought—if you are Simpson, the vast power of the government is against you. Because of the government's great power and the severe penalties it can impose, **criminal procedure** is designed to protect the accused and ensure that criminal trials are fair. Many of the protections for those accused of a crime are found in the first 10 amendments to the United States Constitution, known as the Bill of Rights.

6-2a State of Mind

Voluntary Act

A defendant is not guilty of a crime if she was forced to commit it. In other words, she is not guilty if she acted under duress. However, the defendant bears the burden of proving by a preponderance of the evidence that she did act under duress. In 1974, a terrorist group kidnapped heiress Patricia Hearst from her college apartment. After being tortured for two months, she participated in a bank robbery with the group. Despite opportunities to escape, she stayed with the criminals until her capture by the police a year later. The State of California put on her on trial for bank robbery. One question for the jury was whether she had voluntarily participated in the crime. This was an issue on which many people had strong opinions. Ultimately Hearst was convicted, sent to prison, and then later pardoned.

Entrapment

When the government induces the defendant to break the law, the prosecution must prove beyond a reasonable doubt that the defendant was predisposed to commit the crime. The goal is to separate the cases where the defendant was innocent before the government tempted him from those where the defendant was only too eager to break the law.

Kalchinian and Sherman met in the waiting room of a doctor's office where they were both being treated for drug addiction. After several more meetings, Kalchinian told Sherman that the treatment was not working for him and he was desperate to buy drugs. Could Sherman help him? Sherman repeatedly refused, but ultimately agreed to help end Kalchinian's suffering by providing him with drugs. Little did Sherman know that Kalchinian was a police informer. Sherman sold drugs to Kalchinian a number of times. Kalchinian rewarded this act of friendship by getting Sherman hooked again and then turning him in to the police. A jury convicted Sherman of drug dealing, but the Supreme Court overturned the conviction on the grounds that Sherman had been entrapped. The Court felt there was not enough evidence that Sherman was predisposed to commit the crime.

Conspiracy

Jeen and Sunny Han were 22-year-old identical twin sisters with a long history of physical and verbal fights. One day, Jeen and two teen-age boys purchased gloves, twine, tape, Pine Sol, and garbage bags. While Jeen waited outside Sunny's apartment, the boys forced their way in, tied

Felony

A serious crime, for which a defendant can be sentenced to one year or more in prison

Misdemeanor

A less serious crime, often punishable by less than a year in a county jail

Criminal procedure

The process by which criminals are investigated, accused, tried, and sentenced up Sunny and her roommate, and put them in the bathtub. Luckily, Sunny had had a chance to dial 911 as she heard the boys breaking in. When the police arrived, the two boys fled. This case raises several questions: Has Jeen committed a crime? Are the boys guilty of anything more than breaking into Sunny's apartment? How did this family go so terribly wrong? (Because this is a business law text, we can only answer the first two questions.)

If the police discover a plot to commit a crime, they can arrest the defendants before any harm has been done. It is illegal to conspire to commit a crime, even if that crime never actually occurs. **A defendant can be convicted of taking part in a conspiracy if:**

- A conspiracy existed,

- The defendants knew about it, and

- Some member of the conspiracy voluntarily took a step toward implementing it.

In the Han case, the jury convicted Jeen and the two boys of a conspiracy to murder her sister. As the court asked: What was she planning to do with the Pine Sol and plastic bags, given that she did not have a home?[2] She was sentenced to 26 years to life in prison. The two boys got lesser (but still substantial) sentences because the judge believed Jeen had masterminded the crime.

6-2b Gathering Evidence: The Fourth Amendment

If the police suspect that a crime has been committed, they will need to obtain evidence. **The Fourth Amendment to the Constitution prohibits the government from making illegal searches and seizures of individuals, corporations, partnerships, and other organizations.** The goal of the Fourth Amendment is to protect individuals and businesses from the powerful state.

Warrant

Warrant
Written permission from a neutral officer to conduct a search

As a general rule, the police must obtain a warrant before conducting a search. A **warrant** is written permission from a neutral official, such as a judge or magistrate, to conduct a search.[3] **The warrant must specify with reasonable precision the place to be searched and the items to be seized.** Thus, if the police say they have reason to believe that they will find bloody clothes in the suspect's car in his garage, they cannot also look through his house and confiscate file folders.

Probable Cause

Probable cause
It is likely that evidence of a crime will be found in the place to be searched

The magistrate will issue a warrant only if there is **probable cause**. Probable cause means that based on all the information presented, it is likely that evidence of a crime will be found in the place to be searched.

Searches without a Warrant

There are seven circumstances under which police may search without a warrant.

Plain view.   When Rashad Walker opened his door in response to a police officer's knock, he was holding a marijuana joint in his hand. The court held that the police did not need a warrant to make an arrest because evidence of the crime was in plain view.

Stop and frisk.   None of us wants to live in a world in which police can randomly stop and frisk us on the street anytime they feel like it. The police do have the right to stop and frisk, but only if they have a clear and specific reason to suspect that criminal activity may be afoot and that the person may be armed and dangerous.

---

[2]The People v. Han, 78 Cal. App. 4th 797 (Ct. Appeal, CA, 2000).
[3]A magistrate is a judge who tries minor criminal cases or undertakes primarily administrative responsibilities.

Emergencies.   If the police believe that evidence is about to be destroyed, they can search without a warrant. For example, if they suspect someone is using illegal drugs in an apartment, they can enter without a warrant because, in the time it would take to contact a magistrate, the drugs might be gone.

Automobiles.   If police have lawfully stopped a car and then observe evidence of other crimes in the car, such as burglary tools, they may search.

Lawful arrest.   Police may always search a suspect they have arrested. The goal is to protect the officers and preserve evidence.

Consent.   Anyone lawfully living in a dwelling can allow the police in to search without a warrant. If your roommate gives the police permission to search your house, that search is legal.

No Expectation of Privacy.   The police have a right to search any area in which the defendant does not have a reasonable expectation of privacy. For example, Rolando Crowder was staying at his friend Bobo's apartment. Hearing the police in the hallway, he ran down to the basement. The police found Crowder in the basement with drugs nearby. Crowder argued that the police should have obtained a warrant, but the court ruled that Crowder had no expectation of privacy in Bobo's basement.

Technology and social media have created new challenges in determining what is a reasonable expectation of privacy. For example, **police do need a warrant to:**

- Search the digital contents of your cellphone or personal computer.

- Intercept email in transit.

- Read *private* Facebook profiles and postings.

- Attach a GPS tracking device to your car.

They do *not* need a warrant to:

- Perform a DNA test on anyone they have arrested for a serious crime.

- Find out whom you have emailed.

- Find out what websites you have visited.

- Search your online chat messages.

- Check your online dating profiles.

- Read your Twitter posts.

The courts are divided on whether police must obtain a warrant to access a cell phone's location data or a list of numbers called.

Exclusionary Rule

Under the exclusionary rule, any evidence the government acquires illegally may not be used at trial. The Supreme Court created the exclusionary rule to prevent governmental misconduct. The theory is simple: If police and prosecutors know in advance that illegally obtained evidence cannot be used in court, they will not be tempted to make improper searches or engage in other illegal behavior. Is the exclusionary rule a good idea?

Opponents of the rule argue that a guilty person may go free because one police officer bungled. They are outraged by cases like *Coolidge v. New Hampshire.* Pamela Mason, a 14-year-old babysitter, was brutally murdered. Citizens of New Hampshire were furious, and the state's attorney general personally led the investigation. Police found strong evidence that Edward Coolidge had committed this terrible crime. They took the evidence to the attorney general, who personally issued a search warrant. After a search of Coolidge's car uncovered incriminating evidence, he was found guilty of murder and sentenced to life in prison. But the United States Supreme Court reversed the conviction. The warrant had not been issued by a neutral magistrate. A law officer may not lead an investigation and simultaneously decide what searches are permissible. Ultimately, Coolidge pleaded guilty to second-degree murder and served many years in prison.

In fact, very few people do go free because of the exclusionary rule. One study showed that this rule led to the release of a defendant in only 0.7 percent of all prosecutions.[4]

6-2c After Arrest

Indictment

Grand jury
A group of ordinary citizens that decides whether there is probable cause the defendant committed the crime with which she is charged

Once the police provide the prosecutor with evidence, he presents this evidence to a **grand jury** and asks its members to indict the defendant. Only the prosecutor presents evidence, not the defense attorney, because it is better for the defendant to save her evidence for the trial jury. Just because a defendant is indicted does not mean she is guilty.

If the grand jury determines that there is probable cause that the defendant committed the crime with which she is charged, an **indictment** is issued. An indictment is the government's formal charge that the defendant has committed a crime and must stand trial. Because the grand jury never hears the defendant's evidence, it is relatively easy for prosecutors to obtain an indictment. In short, an indictment is not the same thing as a guilty verdict.

Indictment
The government's formal charge that the defendant has committed a crime and must stand trial

Arraignment

At an arraignment, a clerk reads the formal charges of the indictment. The defendant must enter a plea to the charges. At this stage, most defendants plead not guilty.

Plea Bargaining

A **plea bargain** is an agreement between prosecution and defense that the defendant will plead guilty to a reduced charge, and the prosecution will recommend to the judge a relatively lenient sentence. About 97 percent of all federal prosecutions end in a plea bargain. Such a high percentage has led to some concern that innocent people may be pleading guilty to avoid the risk of tough mandatory sentences. A judge need not accept the bargain but usually does.

> **In the federal court system, about 97 percent of all prosecutions end in a plea bargain.**

Plea bargain
An agreement in which the defendant pleads guilty to a reduced charge, and the prosecution recommends to the judge a relatively lenient sentence

Trial and Appeal

When there is no plea bargain, the case must go to trial. It is the prosecution's job to convince the jury beyond a reasonable doubt that the defendant committed every element of the crime charged. Convicted defendants have a right to appeal.

Double Jeopardy

Double jeopardy
A criminal defendant may be prosecuted only once for a particular criminal offense.

The prohibition against **double jeopardy** means that a defendant may be prosecuted only once for a particular criminal offense. The purpose is to prevent the government from destroying the lives of innocent citizens with repetitive prosecutions.

---

[4]See Justice Brennan's dissent in United States v. Leon, 468 U.S. 897 (S. Ct. 1984).

Punishment

The Eighth Amendment prohibits cruel and unusual punishment. Courts are generally unsympathetic to claims under this provision. For example, the Supreme Court has ruled that the death penalty is not cruel and unusual as long as it is not imposed in an arbitrary or capricious manner.

The Fifth Amendment: Self-Incrimination

The Fifth Amendment bars the government from forcing any person to provide evidence against himself. This provision means that an accused cannot be forced to testify at trial. Indeed, many criminal defendants do not. After all, the burden of proof is on the prosecution, so the defendant may not testify if his lawyer feels the prosecution has not met this burden.

In addition, this provision means that the police may not use mental or physical coercion to force a confession or any other information out of someone. Society does not want a government that engages in torture. Such abuse might occasionally catch a criminal, but it would grievously injure innocent people and make all citizens fearful of the government that is supposed to represent them. Also, coerced confessions are inherently unreliable. The defendant may confess simply to end the torture. If the police do force a confession, the exclusionary rule prohibits the evidence from being admitted in court.

In the following landmark case, the Supreme Court established the requirement that police remind suspects of their right to protection against self-incrimination—with the very same warning that we have all heard so many times on television shows.

Landmark Case

Facts: Ernesto Miranda was a mentally ill, indigent citizen of Mexico. The Phoenix police arrested him at his home and brought him to a police station, where a rape victim identified him as her assailant. The police did not tell him that he had a right to have a lawyer present during questioning. After two hours of interrogation, Miranda signed a confession that said that it had been made voluntarily.

At Miranda's trial, the judge admitted this written confession into evidence over the objection of defense counsel. The officers testified that Miranda had also made an oral confession during the interrogation. The jury found Miranda guilty of kidnapping and rape. After the Supreme Court of Arizona affirmed the conviction, the U. S. Supreme Court agreed to hear his case.

MIRANDA V. ARIZONA
384 U.S. 436
United States Supreme Court, 1966

CASE SUMMARY

of cases decided by this Court, the police resorted to physical brutality—beating, hanging, whipping—and to lengthy questioning in secret. Our goal is to prevent this type of wrongdoing on the part of the government. To maintain a fair balance between state power and individual rights, and to respect human dignity, our system of criminal justice demands that the government seeking to punish an individual produce the evidence against him by its own independent labors rather than by the cruel, simple expedient of compelling it from his own mouth.

Issue: *Was Miranda's confession admissible at trial? Should his conviction be upheld?*

Decision: Neither his written nor his oral confession was admissible. His conviction was overturned.

Reasoning: In a series

Therefore, once the police take a suspect into custody or otherwise deprive him of his freedom, they are required to protect his constitutional right to avoid self-incrimination. To do so, they must warn him that he has a right to remain silent, that any statement he does make may be used as evidence against him, and that he has a right to the presence of an attorney, either retained or appointed. If the police do not inform the accused of these rights, then nothing he says or writes can be admitted in court.

The defendant may waive these rights, provided the waiver is made voluntarily, knowingly, and intelligently. If, however, he indicates in any manner and at any stage of the process that he does not want to be interrogated or wishes to consult with an attorney before speaking, then the police cannot question him. The mere fact that he may have answered some questions or volunteered some statements on his own does not deprive him of the right to refrain from answering any further inquiries until he has consulted with an attorney.

The Sixth Amendment: Right to a Lawyer

As we have seen in the *Miranda* case, the Sixth Amendment guarantees the **right to a lawyer** at all important stages of the criminal process. Because of this right, the government must *appoint* a lawyer to represent, free of charge, any defendant who cannot afford one.

6-3 CRIMES THAT HARM BUSINESSES (AND THEIR CUSTOMERS)

Businesses must deal with five major crimes: larceny, fraud, arson, embezzlement, and hacking.

6-3a Larceny

It is holiday season at the mall, the period of greatest profits—and the most crime. At the Foot Forum, a teenager limps in wearing ragged sneakers and sneaks out wearing Super Sneakers, valued at $145. Down the aisle at a home furnishing store, a man is so taken by a $375 power saw that he takes it. Sweethearts swipe sweaters, pensioners pocket produce. All are committing larceny.

Larceny

The trespassory taking of personal property with the intent to steal it

    Larceny is the trespassory taking of personal property with the intent to steal it. "Trespassory taking" means that someone else originally has the property. The Super Sneakers are personal property (not real estate), they were in the possession of the Foot Forum, and the teenager deliberately left without paying, intending never to return the goods. That is larceny. By contrast, suppose Fast Eddie leaves Bloomingdale's in New York, descends to the subway system, and jumps over a turnstile without paying. Larceny? No. He has "taken" a service—the train ride—but not personal property.

6-3b Fraud

Robert Dorsey owned Bob's Chrysler in Highland, Illinois. When he bought cars, the First National Bank of Highland paid Chrysler, and Dorsey—supposedly—repaid the bank as he sold the autos. Dorsey, though, began to suffer financial problems, and the bank suspected he was selling cars without repaying his loans. A state investigator notified Dorsey that he planned to review all dealership records. One week later, a fire engulfed the dealership. An arson investigator discovered that an electric iron, connected to a timer, had been placed on a pile of financial papers doused with accelerant. Dorsey was convicted and imprisoned for committing two crimes that cost businesses billions of dollars annually—fraud (for failing to repay the loans) and arson (for burning down the dealership).

Fraud refers to various crimes, all of which have a common element: **deception for the purpose of obtaining money or property**. Robert Dorsey's precise violation was bank fraud, because he had taken money from the bank even after he knew he could not pay it back. It is bank fraud to use deceit to obtain money, assets, securities, or other property under the control of any financial institution.

Fraud
Deception for the purpose of obtaining money or property

Wire Fraud and Mail Fraud

Wire and mail fraud are additional federal crimes involving the use of interstate mail, telegram, telephone, radio, or television to obtain property by deceit. For example, if Marsha makes an interstate phone call to sell land that she does not own, that is wire fraud.

Internet Fraud

Online scams are common and include the sale of merchandise that is either defective or nonexistent, the so-called Nigerian letter scam,[5] billing for services that are touted as "free," and romance fraud (you meet someone online who wants to visit you but needs money for travel expenses).

Other common forms of Internet fraud include the following.

Auctions. Internet auctions are the number one source of consumer complaints about online fraud. Wrongdoers either sell goods they do not own, provide defective goods, or offer fakes.

Identity Theft. In identity theft, thieves steal the victim's social security number and other personal information such as bank account numbers and mother's maiden name, which they use to obtain loans and credit cards. The **Identity Theft and Assumption Deterrence Act of 1998** prohibits the use of false identification to commit fraud or other crime, and it also permits the victim to seek restitution in court. In addition, the **Aggravated Identity Theft** statute imposes a mandatory additional sentence of two years on anyone who engages in identity theft during the commission of certain crimes. Also, many states have their own identity theft statutes.

Phishing. In this crime, a fraudster sends a message directing the recipient to enter personal information on a website that is an illegal imitation of a legitimate site. The message might be an email telling you that you need to update your email or bank account information, or it might be an online message that appears to be from a friend suggesting that you click on a link to a great article.

---

[5]Victims receive an email from someone alleging to be a Nigerian government official who has stolen money from the government. He needs some place safe to park the money for a short time. The official promises that, if the victim will permit her account to be used for this purpose, she will be allowed to keep a percentage of the stolen money. Instead, of course, once the "official" has the victim's bank information, he cleans out the account.

EXAM Strategy

Question: Eric mails glossy brochures to 25,000 people, offering to sell them a one-month time-share in a stylish apartment in Las Vegas. To reserve a space, customers need only send in a $2,000 deposit. Three hundred people respond, sending in the money. In fact, there is no such building. Eric, planning to flee with the cash, is arrested and prosecuted. His sentence could be as long as 20 years. (1) With what crime is he charged? (2) Is this a felony or misdemeanor prosecution? (3) Does Eric have a right to a jury trial? (4) What is the government's burden of proof?

Strategy: (1) Eric is deceiving people, and that should tell you the *type* of crime. (2, 3) The potential 20-year sentence determines whether Eric's crime is a misdemeanor or felony and whether or not he is entitled to a jury trial. (4) We know that the government has the burden of proof in criminal prosecutions—but *how much* evidence must it offer?

Result: Eric has committed fraud. A felony is one in which the sentence could be a year or more. The potential penalty here is 20 years, so the crime is a felony. Eric has a right to a jury, as does any defendant whose sentence could be six months or longer. The prosecution must prove its case beyond a reasonable doubt, a much higher burden than that in a civil case.

6-3c Arson

Arson
The malicious use of fire or explosives to damage or destroy real estate or personal property

Robert Dorsey, the Chrysler dealer, committed a second serious crime. **Arson** is the malicious use of fire or explosives to damage or destroy any real estate or personal property. It is both a federal and a state crime. Dorsey used arson to conceal his bank fraud. Most arsonists hope to collect on insurance policies. Every year, thousands of buildings are burned as owners try to extricate themselves from financial difficulties. Everyone who purchases insurance ends up paying higher premiums because of this wrongdoing.

6-3d Embezzlement

Embezzlement
The fraudulent conversion of property already in the defendant's possession

This crime also involves illegally obtaining property, but with one big difference: The culprit begins with legal possession. **Embezzlement** is the fraudulent conversion of property already in the defendant's possession.

There is no romance in this story: For 15 years, Kristy Watts worked part time as a bookkeeper for romance writer Danielle Steele, handling payroll and accounting. During that time, Watts stole $768,000 despite earning a salary of $200,000 a year. Watts said that she had been motivated by envy and jealousy. She was sentenced to three years in prison and agreed to pay her former boss almost $1 million.

6-3e Hacking

Hacking
Gaining unauthorized access to a computer system

During the 2008 presidential campaign, college student David Kernell guessed vice presidential candidate Sarah Palin's email password, accessed her personal Yahoo account, and published the content of some of her emails. To some, his actions seemed like an amusing prank. The joke turned out not to be so funny when Kernell was sentenced to one year in prison.

Gaining unauthorized access to a computer system is called **hacking**. It is a crime under the federal Computer Fraud and Abuse Act of 1986 (CFAA). This statute applies to any computer, cell phone, or other gadget attached to the Internet. **The CFAA prohibits:**

- Accessing a computer without authorization and obtaining information from it

- Intentional, reckless, and negligent damage to a computer, and

- Trafficking in computer passwords.

In the following case, a former employee clearly violated his company's policies, but did he commit a crime? You be the judge.

You be the Judge

Facts: David Nosal worked for an executive search firm, Korn/Ferry (K/F). Shortly after he left the company to start a competing business, he convinced some of his former colleagues to log into the company's confidential database and give him customer information. K/F had authorized the employees to access the database, but not to disclose confidential client information to outsiders.

The government charged Nosal with aiding and abetting his former colleagues in violating a provision of the CFAA that prohibits employees from exceeding their authorized access to a computer with intent to defraud.

You Be the Judge: *Did Nosal commit a crime when he aided and abetted others in violating a workplace policy on computer use?*

Argument for the Defendant: This provision of the CFAA can mean one of two things: Either (1) it is just a crime to access unauthorized *data* or, (2) it is also a crime to access data legally but then use it in an unauthorized *manner.* The K/F employees did access the data legally, but used it in an unauthorized manner when they sent it to Nosal.

UNITED STATES V. NOSAL
676 F.3d 854
United States Court of Appeals
for the Ninth Circuit, 2012

Computers give employees new ways to procrastinate, by g-chatting with friends, playing games, shopping, or watching sports highlights. Such activities are routinely prohibited by many company computer-use policies. Under this broad interpretation of the CFAA, such minor violations would become federal crimes. How will an employee know the difference between a minor personal use and a criminal act?

Argument for the Government: This statute explicitly requires an intent to commit fraud. Therefore, it has nothing to do with watching ESPN.com, playing Sudoku, or checking email. Instead, the K/F employees knowingly exceeded their access to a protected company computer and they did so with an intent to defraud.

This distinction is not complicated. A bank teller is entitled to access money for legitimate banking purposes, but not to take the bank's money for himself. A new car buyer may be entitled to take a vehicle around the block on a test drive but not to drive it to Mexico on a drug run.

6-4 CRIMES COMMITTED BY BUSINESS

A corporation can be found guilty of a crime based on the conduct of any of its agents, who include anyone undertaking work on behalf of the corporation. An agent can be a corporate officer, an accountant hired to audit financial statements, a sales clerk, or almost any other person performing a job at the company's request.

If an agent commits a criminal act within the scope of his employment and with the intent to benefit the corporation, the company is liable.[6] This means that the agent himself must first be guilty. If the agent is guilty, the corporation is, too.

Some critics believe that the criminal law has gone too far. It is unfair, they argue, to impose *criminal* liability on a corporation, and thus penalize employees and shareholders, unless high-ranking officers were directly involved in the illegal conduct. Others argue that subjecting companies to criminal liability protects the public, deters wrongdoing, and publicizes the importance of complying with the law. Indeed, they argue that corporation fines are too small, that they should be large enough to take all the profitability out of criminal acts.

[6]New York Central & Hudson River R.R. Co. v. United States, 212 U.S. 481 (S. Ct., 1909). Note that what counts is the intention to benefit, not actual benefit. A corporation will not escape liability by showing that the scheme failed.

6-4a Making False Statements

It is illegal to make false statements or engage in a cover up during any dealings with the United States government. Sometimes this provision is used to charge someone who is suspected of committing a complex crime that may itself be difficult to prove. In the most famous case, the government accused Martha Stewart, the celebrity homemaker and entrepreneur, of engaging in insider trading. At trial, that charge was thrown out, but the jury nevertheless convicted her of lying to the officers who had investigated the alleged insider trading. Stewart ultimately served five months in prison. However, the Justice Department recently announced that it would only use this statute against defendants who knew their conduct was illegal.

6-4b RICO

Racketeer Influenced and Corrupt Organizations Act (RICO)

A powerful federal statute, originally aimed at organized crime, now used in many criminal prosecutions and civil lawsuits

The **Racketeer Influenced and Corrupt Organizations Act (RICO)** is one of the most powerful and controversial statutes ever written. Congress passed the law primarily to prevent gangsters from taking money they earned illegally and investing it in legitimate businesses. But RICO has expanded far beyond the original intentions of Congress and is now used more often against ordinary businesses than against organized criminals. Some regard this wide application as a tremendous advance in law enforcement, but others view it as an oppressive weapon used to club ethical companies into settlements they should never have to make.

RICO prohibits using two or more racketeering acts to accomplish any of these goals: (1) investing in or acquiring legitimate businesses with criminal money; (2) maintaining or acquiring businesses through criminal activity; or (3) operating businesses through criminal activity.

What does that mean in English? It is a two-step process to prove that a person or an organization has violated RICO:

Racketeering acts

Any of a long list of specified crimes, such as embezzlement, arson, mail fraud, and wire fraud

1. The prosecutor must show that the defendant committed two or more **racketeering acts**, which are any of a long list of specified crimes: embezzlement, arson, mail fraud, wire fraud, and so forth. Thus, if a gangster ordered a building torched in January and then burned a second building in October, that would be two racketeering acts. If a stockbroker sold a fake stock to two customers, that would be two racketeering acts.

2. The prosecutor must then show that the defendant used these racketeering acts to accomplish one of the three *purposes* listed above. If the gangster committed two arsons and then used the insurance payments to buy a dry cleaning business, that would violate RICO.

The government may prosecute both individuals and organizations for violating RICO. For example, the government may prosecute a mobster, claiming that he has run a heroin ring for years. It may also prosecute an accounting firm, claiming that it lied about corporate assets in a stock sale to make the shares appear more valuable than they really were. If the government proves its case, the defendant can be hit with large fines and a prison sentence of up to 20 years. And the court may order a convicted defendant to hand over any property or money used in the criminal acts or derived from them.

In addition to criminal penalties, RICO also creates civil law liabilities. The government, organizations, and individuals all have the right to file civil lawsuits seeking damages and, if necessary, injunctions. For example, a physician sued State Farm Insurance, alleging that the company had hired doctors to produce false medical reports that the company used to cut off claims by injured policy holders. As a result of these fake reports, the company refused to pay the plaintiff for legitimate services he performed for the policy holders. RICO is powerful (and for defendants, frightening) in part because a civil plaintiff can recover **treble damages**, that is, a judgment for three times the harm actually suffered, as well as attorney's fees.

Treble damages

A judgment for three times the harm actually suffered

6-4c Money Laundering

Money laundering consists of taking the proceeds of certain criminal acts and either (1) using the money to promote crime or (2) attempting to conceal the source of the money.

Money laundering is an important part of major criminal enterprises. Successful criminals earn enormous sums, which they must filter back into the flow of commerce in a way that allows their crimes to go undetected. Laundering is an essential part of the corrosive traffic in drugs. Profits, all in cash, may mount so swiftly that dealers struggle to use the money without attracting the government's attention. For example, Colombian drug cartels set up a sophisticated system in which they shipped money to countries such as Dubai that do not keep records on cash transactions. This money was then transferred to the United States disguised as offshore loans. Prosecution by the U.S. government led to the demise of some of the banks involved.

> **Money laundering**
> Using the proceeds of criminal acts either to promote crime or conceal the source of the money

---

EXAM Strategy

Question: Explain the difference between embezzlement and money laundering. Give an example of each.

Strategy: Both crimes involve money illegally obtained, but they are very different. In embezzlement the important question is: How did the criminal obtain the funds? In a laundering case, ask: To what use is the criminal trying to put the cash?

Result: Embezzlement refers to fraudulently taking money that is already in the defendant's possession. For example, if a financial advisor, *lawfully entrusted* with his client's funds for investing, uses some of the cash to buy himself a luxurious yacht, he has embezzled the client's money. Money laundering consists of taking *illegally obtained* money and either using the funds to promote additional crimes or attempting to *conceal* the source of the cash. Thus, an arms dealer might launder money so that he can use it to finance a terrorist organization.

6-4d Hiring Illegal Workers

It is illegal knowingly to employ unauthorized workers. Thus, employers are required to verify their workers' eligibility for employment in the United States. Within three days of hiring a worker, the employer must complete an I-9 form, documenting each worker's eligibility. The government has the right to arrest employees working illegally and to bring charges against the business that hired them.

6-4e Foreign Corrupt Practices Act

The Foreign Corrupt Practices Act (FCPA) prohibits the bribery of foreign officials. Under this statute:

- It is illegal for any employee or agent of a U.S. company (and some foreign companies) to give anything of value to any foreign official for purposes of influencing an official decision.

- A facilitating payment for a routine governmental action does not count as a bribe and is legal. Examples of routine governmental action include processing visas or supplying utilities such as phone, power, or water. To be legal, these payments must simply be hastening an inevitable result that does not involve discretionary action. Thus, for example, "paying an official a small amount to have the power turned on at a factory might be a facilitating payment; paying an inspector to ignore the fact that the company does not have a valid permit to operate the factory would not be."[7]

- All publicly traded companies—whether they engage in international trade or not—must keep accurate and detailed records to prevent hiding or disguising bribes.

Punishments for violations of this act can be severe. A company may face large fines and the loss of profits earned as a result of illegal bribes. In 2011, Johnson & Johnson agreed to pay $77 million to settle an FCPA action. In addition to financial penalties, individuals who violate the FCPA can face up to five years in prison.

6-4f Punishing a Corporation

Fines

The most common punishment for a corporation is a fine. This makes sense, in that a major purpose of a business is to earn a profit, and a fine, theoretically, hurts. But most fines are modest by the present standards of corporate wealth. For example, BP, the oil company formerly known as British Petroleum, was found guilty of two serious legal violations. In Alaska, company pipelines spilled 200,000 gallons of crude oil onto the tundra. In Texas, a catastrophic explosion at a refinery killed 15 people and injured 170 more. The total fine for both criminal violations was $62 million, which sounds like a large number. But it was not enough, evidently, to change BP's practices. The company pleaded guilty to criminal charges in connection with a 2010 oil rig explosion in the Gulf of Mexico, which killed 11 workers and caused the largest marine oil spill ever. The rig that exploded had many safety violations. Will the $4.5 billion fine in that case change BP's business practices?

Compliance Programs

Federal Sentencing Guidelines
The detailed rules that judges must follow when sentencing defendants convicted of federal crimes

Compliance program
A plan to prevent and detect improper conduct at all levels of a company

The **Federal Sentencing Guidelines** are the detailed rules that judges must follow when sentencing defendants convicted of federal crimes. The guidelines instruct judges to determine whether, at the time of the crime, the corporation had in place a serious **compliance program**, that is, a plan to prevent and detect criminal conduct at all levels of the company. A company that can point to a detailed, functioning compliance program may benefit from a dramatic reduction in the fine or other punishment meted out. Indeed, a tough compliance program may even convince federal investigators to curtail an investigation and to limit any prosecution to those directly involved rather than attempting to convict high-ranking officers or the company itself.

Chapter Conclusion

Crime has an enormous impact on business. Companies are victims of crimes, and sometimes they also commit criminal actions. Successful business leaders are ever vigilant to protect their company from those who wish to harm it, whether from inside or out.

[7]U.S. Department of Justice and the U.S. Securities Exchange Commission, "A Resource Guide to the U.S. Foreign Corrupt Practices Act," http://www.justice.gov/criminal/fraud/fcpa/guide.pdf.

EXAM REVIEW

1. **BURDEN OF PROOF** In all prosecutions, the government must prove its case beyond a reasonable doubt.

> **Question:** A fire breaks out in Arnie's house, destroying the building and causing $150,000 damage to an adjacent store. The state charges Arnie with arson. Simultaneously, Vickie, the store owner, sues Arnie for the damage to her property. Both cases are tried to juries, and the two juries hear identical evidence of Arnie's actions. But the criminal jury acquits Arnie, while the civil jury awards Vickie $150,000. How did that happen?
>
> **Strategy:** The opposite outcomes are probably due to the different burdens of proof in a civil and criminal case. Make sure you know that distinction. (See the "Result" at the end of this section.)

2. **RIGHT TO A JURY** A criminal defendant has a right to a trial by jury for any charge that could result in a sentence of six months or longer.

3. **FELONY** A felony is a serious crime for which a defendant can be sentenced to one year or more in prison.

4. **VOLUNTARY ACT** A defendant is not guilty of a crime if she committed it under duress. However, the defendant bears the burden of proving by a preponderance of the evidence that she acted under duress.

5. **ENTRAPMENT** When the government induces the defendant to break the law, the prosecution must prove beyond a reasonable doubt that the defendant was predisposed to commit the crime.

6. **CONSPIRACY** It is illegal to conspire to commit a crime, even if that crime never actually occurs.

7. **FOURTH AMENDMENT** The Fourth Amendment to the Constitution prohibits the government from making illegal searches and seizures of individuals, corporations, partnerships, and other organizations.

8. **WARRANT** As a general rule, the police must obtain a warrant before conducting a search, but there are seven circumstances under which the police may search without a warrant: plain view, stop and frisk, emergencies, automobiles, lawful arrest, consent, no expectation of privacy.

9. **PROBABLE CAUSE** The magistrate will issue a warrant only if there is probable cause. Probable cause means that it is likely that evidence of a crime will be found in the place to be searched.

10. **THE EXCLUSIONARY RULE**   Under the exclusionary rule, evidence obtained illegally may not be used at trial.

11. **FIFTH AMENDMENT**   The Fifth Amendment bars the government from forcing any person to provide evidence against himself.

12. **SIXTH AMENDMENT**   The Sixth Amendment guarantees criminal defendants the right to a lawyer.

13. **DOUBLE JEOPARDY**   A defendant may be prosecuted only once for a particular criminal offense.

14. **EIGHTH AMENDMENT**   The Eighth Amendment prohibits cruel and unusual punishment.

15. **LARCENY**   Larceny is the trespassory taking of personal property with the intent to steal.

16. **FRAUD**   Fraud means deception for the purpose of obtaining money or property.

17. **IDENTITY THEFT**   The Identity Theft and Assumption Deterrence Act of 1998 prohibits the use of false identification to commit fraud or other crime, and it also permits the victim to seek restitution in court. The Aggravated Identity Theft statute imposes a mandatory additional sentence of two years on anyone who engages in identity theft during the commission of certain crimes.

18. **ARSON**   Arson is the malicious use of fire or explosives to damage or destroy real estate or personal property.

19. **EMBEZZLEMENT**   Embezzlement is the fraudulent conversion of property already in the defendant's possession.

20. **HACKING**   The federal Computer Fraud and Abuse Act of 1986 prohibits hacking. It is illegal, among other things, to access a computer without authorization and to obtain information from it.

21. **CORPORATE LIABILITY**   If a company's agent commits a criminal act within the scope of her employment and with the intent to benefit the corporation, the company is liable.

22. **MAKING FALSE STATEMENTS**   It is illegal to make false statements or engage in a cover up during any dealings with the United States government.

23. **RICO**   RICO prohibits using two or more racketeering acts to accomplish any of these goals: (1) investing in or acquiring legitimate businesses with criminal money; (2) maintaining or acquiring businesses through criminal activity; or (3) operating businesses through criminal activity.

24. **MONEY LAUNDERING**   Money laundering consists of taking profits from a criminal act and either using them to promote crime or attempting to conceal their source.

25. **IMMIGRATION LAW**   It is illegal knowingly to employ unauthorized workers.

26. **FOREIGN CORRUPT PRACTICES ACT**   The Foreign Corrupt Practices Act (FCPA) prohibits the bribery of foreign officials.

EXAM Strategy

Question: Splash is a California corporation that develops resorts. Lawrence, a Splash executive, is hoping to land a $700 million contract with a country in Southeast Asia. He seeks your advice. "I own a fabulous beach house in Australia. What if I allow a government official and his family to stay there for two weeks? That might be enough to close the resort deal. Would that be wrong? Should I do it?" Please advise him.

Strategy: What law governs Lawrence's proposed conduct? Is Lawrence legally safe, given that the land is foreign and the contract will be signed overseas? Are there any circumstances under which this house loan would be legal? (See the result at the end of this section.)

<u>**1. Result:**</u>   The plaintiff offered enough proof to convince a jury by a preponderance of the evidence that Arnie had damaged her store. However, that same evidence, offered in a criminal prosecution, was not enough to persuade the jury beyond a reasonable doubt that Arnie had lit the fire.

<u>**26. Result:**</u>   If Lawrence gives anything of value (such as rent-free use of his house) to secure a government contract, he has violated the FCPA. It makes no difference where the property is located or the deal signed. He could go to jail, and his company could be harshly penalized. The loan of the house would be legal if the official was simply in charge of turning on utilities in the area where the resort would be built.

MATCHING QUESTIONS

Match the following terms with their definitions:

___A. Larceny

___B. RICO

___C. Money laundering

___D. Phishing

___E. Embezzlement

1. A statute designed to prevent the use of criminal proceeds in legitimate businesses

2. Fraudulently keeping property already in the defendant's possession

3. Using the proceeds of criminal acts to promote crime

4. Directing someone to enter personal information on a website that is an illegal imitation of a legitimate site

5. The trespassory taking of personal property

TRUE/FALSE QUESTIONS

Circle true or false:

1. T F Both the government and the victim are entitled to prosecute a crime.
2. T F If police are interrogating a criminal suspect in custody and he says that he does not want to talk, the police must stop questioning him.
3. T F A misdemeanor is a less serious crime, punishable by less than a year in jail.
4. T F Corporate officers can be convicted of crimes; corporations themselves cannot be.
5. T F An affidavit is the government's formal charge of criminal wrongdoing.

MULTIPLE-CHOICE QUESTIONS

1. Cheryl is a bank teller. She figures out a way to steal $99.99 per day in cash without getting caught. She takes the money daily for eight months and invests it in a catering business she is starting with Floyd, another teller. When Floyd learns what she is doing, he tries it, but is caught in his first attempt. He and Cheryl are both prosecuted.
   (a) Both are guilty only of larceny.
   (b) Both are guilty of larceny and violating RICO.
   (c) Both are guilty of embezzlement; Cheryl is also guilty of violating RICO.
   (d) Both are guilty of embezzlement and violating RICO.
   (e) Both are guilty of larceny and violating RICO.

2. In a criminal case, which statement is true?
   (a) The prosecution must prove the government's case by a preponderance of the evidence.
   (b) The criminal defendant is entitled to a lawyer even if she cannot afford to pay for it herself.
   (c) The police are never allowed to question the accused without a lawyer present.
   (d) All federal crimes are felonies.

3. Henry asks his girlfriend, Alina, to drive his car to the repair shop. She drives his car, all right—to Las Vegas, where she hits the slots. Alina has committed:
   (a) fraud.
   (b) embezzlement.
   (c) larceny.
   (d) a RICO violation.

4. Which of the following elements is required for a RICO conviction?
   (a) Investment in a legitimate business
   (b) Two or more criminal acts
   (c) Maintaining or acquiring businesses through criminal activity
   (d) Operating a business through criminal activity

5. Probable cause means:

   (a) substantial evidence that the person signing the affidavit has legitimate reasons for requesting the warrant.

   (b) substantial likelihood that a crime has taken place or is about to take place.

   (c) trustworthy evidence that the victim of the search is known to have criminal tendencies.

   (d) that based on all of the information presented, it is likely that evidence of crime will be found in the place mentioned.

CASE QUESTIONS

1. *YOU BE THE JUDGE* **WRITING PROBLEM** An undercover drug informant learned from a mutual friend that Philip Friedman "knew where to get marijuana." The informant asked Friedman three times to get him some marijuana, and Friedman agreed after the third request. Shortly thereafter, Friedman sold the informant a small amount of the drug. The informant later offered to sell Friedman three pounds of marijuana. They negotiated the price and then made the sale. Friedman was tried for trafficking in drugs. He argued entrapment. Was Friedman entrapped? **Argument for Friedman**: The undercover agent had to ask three times before Friedman sold him a small amount of drugs. A real drug dealer, predisposed to commit the crime, leaps at an opportunity to sell. **Argument for the government**: Government officials suspected Friedman of being a sophisticated drug dealer, and they were right. When he had a chance to buy three pounds, a quantity only a dealer would purchase, he not only did so, but he bargained with skill, showing a working knowledge of the business. Friedman was not entrapped—he was caught.

2. Conley owned video poker machines. Although they are outlawed in Pennsylvania, he placed them in bars and clubs. He used profits from the machines to buy more machines. Is he guilty of money laundering?

3. Shawn was caught stealing letters from mailboxes. After pleading guilty, he was sentenced to two months in prison and three years' supervised release. One of the supervised release conditions required him to stand outside a post office for eight hours wearing a signboard stating, "I stole mail. This is my punishment." He appealed this requirement on the grounds that it constituted cruel and unusual punishment. Do you agree?

4. Karin made illegal firearm purchases at a gun show. At her trial, she alleged that she had committed this crime because her boyfriend had threatened to harm her and her two daughters if she did not. Her lawyer asked the judge to instruct the jury that the prosecution had an obligation to prove beyond a reasonable doubt that Karin had acted freely. Instead, the judge told the jury that Karin had the burden of proving duress by a preponderance of the evidence. Who is correct?

5. While driving his SUV, George struck and killed a pedestrian. He then fled the scene of the crime. A year later, the police downloaded information from his car's onboard computer, which they were able to use to convict him of the crime. Should this information have been admissible at trial?

6. While conducting a valid search of a computer for evidence of a murder, a police officer discovered child pornography. Is that evidence admissible, even though the warrant was limited to a search relating to the murder?

7. *The New York Times* reported that Walmart paid bribes to obtain building permits in Mexico. If true, would these acts violate the FCPA?

DISCUSSION QUESTIONS

1. Under British law, a police officer must now say the following to a suspect placed under arrest: "You do not have to say anything. But if you do not mention now something which you later use in your defense, the court may decide that your failure to mention it now strengthens the case against you. A record will be made of anything you say, and it may be given in evidence if you are brought to trial." What is the goal of this British law? What does a police officer in the United States have to say, and what difference does it make at the time of an arrest? Which approach is better?

2. In some countries, bribery is common and widely accepted. What is wrong with bribery, anyway? Why should it be illegal for American companies to pay bribes in countries where everyone else is?

3. **ETHICS** You are a prosecutor who thinks it is possible that Louisa, in her role as CEO of a brokerage firm, has stolen money from her customers, many of whom are not well off. If you charge her and her company with RICO violations, you know that she is likely to plea bargain because otherwise, her assets and those of the company may be frozen by the court. As part of the plea bargain, you might be able to get her to disclose evidence about other people who might have taken part in this criminal activity. But you do not have any hard evidence at this point. Would such an indictment be ethical? Do the ends justify the means? Is it worth it to harm Louisa for the chance of protecting thousands of innocent investors?

4. California passed a "three strikes" law, dramatically increasing sentences for repeat offenders. If defendants with two or more serious convictions were convicted of a third felony, the court had to sentence them to life imprisonment. Such a sentence required the defendant to actually serve a minimum of 25 years, and in some cases much more. Gary Ewing, on parole from a nine-year prison term, was prosecuted for stealing three golf clubs worth $399 each. Because he had prior convictions, the crime, normally a misdemeanor, was treated as a felony. Ewing was convicted and sentenced to 25 years to life. Did Ewing's sentence violate the Eighth Amendment's prohibition against cruel and unusual punishment?

5. Ramona was indicted on charges of real estate fraud. During a legal search of her home, the police found a computer with encrypted files. Would it be a violation of her Fifth Amendment right against self-incrimination to force her to unencrypt these files?

6. Suppose two people are living together: the suspect and a tenant. If the tenant consents to a police search of the premises, then the police are not required to first obtain a warrant. What if the suspect and the tenant disagree, with the tenant granting permission while the suspect forbids the police to enter? Should the police be required to obtain a warrant before searching? Or what if the suspect denies permission to enter but the police go back later and the tenant consents?

7. Hiring relatives of foreign officials for no-show jobs is a violation of the FCPA. But what about hiring children of government officials into real jobs? Is that also a violation? The U.S. government is investigating J.P. Morgan Chase's practice of hiring the children of top Chinese officials in Hong Kong. What are the rules in this situation? What should they be?

Torts

CHAPTER 7

INTENTIONAL TORTS AND BUSINESS TORTS

They say politics can get ugly. *Doubt it?* Just ask John Vogel and Paul Grannis. Both men started off as candidates for public office in California—and then learned about defamation the hard way. They had no defense when mean and nasty statements were posted about them online. Here is their story.

Joseph Felice ran a website that listed "Top Ten Dumb Asses." Vogel and Grannis earned the honor of being number 1 and 2 on that list. Felice's site also claimed that Vogel was "WANTED as a Dead Beat Dad" because he was behind on his child support payments. When users clicked on Vogel's name, they were led to another website—www.satan.com—which included a picture of him altered to look like a devil.

Grannis did not fare any better. Felice's site declared Grannis "Bankrupt, Drunk & Chewin' Tobaccy." It stated that he had "bankrupted many businesses throughout California." Grannis's name was hyperlinked to a website with the address www.olddrunk.com that accused him of criminal, fraudulent, and immoral conduct.

Understandably offended, Vogel and Grannis sued Felice for libel. But they soon learned that filing such a lawsuit is easier than winning it.

> **They had no defense when mean and nasty statements were posted about them online.**

This odd word "tort" is borrowed from the French, meaning "wrong." And that is what it means in law: A tort is a wrong. More precisely, a **tort** is a violation of a duty imposed by the *civil* law. When a person breaks one of those duties and injures another, it is a tort. The injury could be to a person or her property. Libel, which the politicians in the opening scenario alleged, is one example of a tort. A surgeon who removes the wrong kidney from a patient commits a different kind of tort, called *negligence*. A business executive who deliberately steals a client away from a competitor, interfering with a valid contract, commits a tort called *interference with a contract*. A con artist who tricks you out of your money with a phony offer to sell you a boat commits fraud, yet another tort.

Because tort law is so broad, it takes a while to understand its boundaries. To start with, we must distinguish torts from criminal law.

It is a crime to steal a car, to embezzle money from a bank, to sell cocaine. As discussed in Chapter 1, society considers such behavior so threatening that the government itself will prosecute the wrongdoer, whether or not the car owner or bank president wants the case to go forward. A district attorney, who is paid by the government, will bring the case to court, seeking to send the defendant to prison, fine him, or both. If there is a fine, the money goes to the state, not to the victim.

In a tort case, it is up to the injured party to seek compensation. She must hire her own lawyer, who will file a lawsuit. Her lawyer must convince the court that the defendant breached some legal duty and ought to pay money damages to the plaintiff. The plaintiff has no power to send the defendant to jail. Bear in mind that a defendant's action might be both a crime *and* a tort. A man who punches you in the face for no reason commits the tort of battery. You may file a civil suit against him and will collect money damages if you can prove your case. He has also committed a crime, and the state may prosecute, seeking to imprison and fine him.

Tort

A violation of a duty imposed by the civil law

EXAM Strategy

Question: Keith is driving while intoxicated. He swerves into the wrong lane and causes an accident, seriously injuring Marta. Who is more likely to file a tort lawsuit in this case, Marta or the state? Who is more likely to prosecute Keith for drunk driving? Could there be a lawsuit and a prosecution at the same time? In which case is Keith more likely to be found *guilty*, a civil suit or a criminal prosecution?

Strategy: Only one of these parties can prosecute a criminal case and in only one kind of case can a defendant be found guilty.

Result: Only the government prosecutes criminal cases. Marta may urgently request a prosecution, but the district attorney will make the final decision. And only in a criminal case can a defendant be found guilty. However, Marta is free to sue Keith civilly for the injuries he has caused, even if he is simultaneously prosecuted criminally. In her civil case, she can recover money damages for her injuries, whether or not Keith is found guilty in the criminal case.

Intentional torts
Involve harm caused by deliberate action

Tort law is divided into categories. In this chapter, we consider **intentional torts**, that is, harm caused by a deliberate action. When Paula hits Paul, she has committed the intentional tort of battery. In the next chapter, we examine negligence and strict liability, which involve injuries and losses caused by neglect and oversight rather than by deliberate conduct.

7-1 INTENTIONAL TORTS

7-1a Defamation

The First Amendment guarantees the right to free speech, a vital freedom that enables us to protect other rights. But that freedom is not absolute.

Libel
Written defamation

Slander
Oral defamation

The law of defamation concerns false statements that harm someone's reputation. Defamatory statements can be written or spoken. Written defamation is called **libel**. Suppose a newspaper accuses a local retail store of programming its cash registers to overcharge customers, when the store has never done so. That is libel. Oral defamation is **slander**. If Professor Wisdom, in class, refers to Sally Student as a drug dealer when she has never sold drugs, he has slandered her.

Element
A fact that a plaintiff must prove to win a lawsuit

There are four elements to a defamation case. An **element** is something that a plaintiff must prove to win a lawsuit. The plaintiff in any kind of lawsuit must prove all the elements to prevail. The elements in a defamation case are:

1. **Defamatory statement**. This is a statement likely to harm another person's reputation. Since opinions are not factual, they do not generally count as defamatory statements. In the case from the opening scenario, the judge found that "dumb ass" was not a defamatory statement. The court interpreted that slang phrase as a general expression of contempt, not a fact. On the other hand, the accusations that Vogel owed child support payments and Grannis was bankrupt *were* facts that could be proven true or false.

2. **Falsity**. The statement must be false. Felice, the website's author, was ultimately successful in his defense because he proved that Vogel did in fact fail to pay child support and Grannis had filed for bankruptcy. Making a true statement, no matter how cruel, is not defamation.

3. **Communicated**. The statement must be communicated to at least one person *other than the plaintiff*. It stands to reason: If no one else receives the defamatory message, there is no harm done. Defamation protects against injury to reputation, not hurt feelings.

4. **Injury**. The plaintiff must show some injury, unless the case involves false statements about sexual behavior, crimes, contagious diseases, and professional abilities. In these cases, the law is willing to *assume* injury without requiring the plaintiff to prove it. Lies in these four categories amount to **slander per se** when they are spoken and **libel per se** when they are published.

The following case involves libel per se, *The New York Times*, and alleged police brutality. Set in Alabama during the racially charged 1960s, this landmark Supreme Court decision changed the rules of the defamation game for all public personalities.

Landmark Case

NEW YORK TIMES CO. V. SULLIVAN

376 U.S. 254
United States Supreme Court, 1964

CASE SUMMARY

Facts: In 1960, *The New York Times* (NYT) ran a full-page advertisement paid for by civil rights activists. The ad described a series of abuses by the police of Montgomery, Alabama, against civil rights protesters. It also accused the police of bombing the home of Dr. Martin Luther King, Jr. and unjustly arresting him seven times. Most of the ad's statements were true, but a few were not. The NYT did not check the ad's accuracy before publishing it.

Montgomery's police commissioner (L.B. Sullivan) sued the NYT under Alabama's law on libel per se.

An Alabama court awarded Sullivan $500,000. The Supreme Court of Alabama affirmed. The NYT appealed to the U.S. Supreme Court, arguing that the ad was protected by the First Amendment's freedom of speech.

Issue: *Does the First Amendment protect defamatory criticism of public officials?*

Decision: Yes. To win a defamation case, a public official must prove that the harmful statement was made with malice.

Reasoning: First Amendment protection does not depend on the truth, popularity, or social utility of the ideas expressed. Debate on public issues should be uninhibited, robust, and wide-open. Sometimes it will include unpleasantly sharp attacks on government and public officials. Sometimes it may even include inaccurate and defamatory statements.

The NYT advertisement was protected by the First Amendment, even though it contained falsehoods. To preserve free debate about the official conduct of public officials, it is necessary to limit their ability to recover damages in defamation suits. To recover for defamation, a public official must prove that the defamatory statement was made with "actual malice." That is, with knowledge that it was false or with reckless disregard for the truth.

There is no evidence that the NYT acted with malice. The evidence suggests that the NYT was at most negligent in failing to catch the inaccuracies.

The judgment of the Supreme Court of Alabama is reversed.

Now we see another reason why the politicians from our chapter opener lost their defamation case. As candidates for public office, the politicians had to prove their critic's malice—and they could not do so. The *New York Times* rule has been extended to all public figures, like actors, business leaders, and anyone else who assumes an influential and visible role in society.

7-1b False Imprisonment

False imprisonment is the intentional restraint of another person without reasonable cause and without consent. False imprisonment cases most commonly arise in retail stores, which sometimes detain employees or customers for suspected theft. Most states now have statutes governing the detention of suspected shoplifters. **Generally, a store may detain a customer or worker for alleged shoplifting provided there is a reasonable basis for the suspicion and the detention is done reasonably.** To detain a customer in the manager's office for 20 minutes and question him about where he got an item is lawful. To chain that customer to a display counter for three hours and humiliate him in front of other customers is unreasonable and false imprisonment.

False imprisonment
The intentional restraint of another person without reasonable cause or consent

7-1c Battery and Assault

Battery
A harmful or offensive bodily contact

Assault and battery are related but not identical. **Battery** is an intentional touching of another person in a way that is harmful or offensive. There need be no intention to hurt the plaintiff. If the defendant intended to do the physical act and a reasonable plaintiff would be offended by it, battery has occurred.

If an irate parent throws a chair at a referee during his daughter's basketball game, breaking the man's jaw, he has committed battery. But a parent who cheerfully slaps the winning coach on the back has not committed battery because a reasonable coach would not be offended.

Assault
An action that causes another person to fear an imminent battery

Assault occurs when a defendant performs some action that makes a plaintiff fear an imminent battery. It is assault even if the battery never occurs. Suppose Ms. Wilson shouts "Think fast!" at her husband and hurls a toaster at him. He turns and sees it flying at him. His fear of being struck is enough to win a case of assault, even if the toaster misses. If the toaster happens to strike him, Ms. Wilson has also committed battery.

EXAM Strategy

Question: Patrick owns a fast food restaurant that is repeatedly painted with graffiti. He is convinced that 15-year-old John, a frequent customer, is the culprit. The next time John comes to the restaurant, Patrick locks the men's room door while John is inside. Patrick calls the police, but because of a misunderstanding, the police are very slow to arrive. John shouts for help, banging on the door, but Patrick does not release him for two hours. John sues for assault, battery, and false imprisonment. A psychiatrist testifies that John has suffered serious psychological harm. Will John win?

Strategy: The question focuses on the distinctions among three intentional torts. Battery: an offensive touching. Assault: causing an imminent fear of battery. False imprisonment: A store may detain someone if it does so reasonably.

Result: Locking John up for two hours, based on an unproven suspicion, was clearly unreasonable. Patrick has committed false imprisonment, and John will win. However, Patrick did not touch John, so there has been no battery or assault.

7-1d Fraud

Fraud
Injuring someone by deliberate deception

Fraud is injuring another person by deliberate deception. It is fraud to sell real estate knowing that there is a large toxic waste deposit underground of which the buyer is ignorant. Fraud is a tort, but it typically occurs during the negotiation or performance of a contract, and it is discussed in detail in Unit 2, on contracts.

7-1e Intentional Infliction of Emotional Distress

Intentional infliction of emotional distress
Extreme and outrageous conduct that causes serious emotional harm

A credit officer was struggling in vain to locate Sheehan, who owed money on his car. The officer finally phoned Sheehan's mother, falsely identified herself as a hospital employee, and said she needed to find Sheehan because his children had been in a serious auto accident. The horrified mother provided Sheehan's whereabouts, which enabled the company to seize his car. But Sheehan himself spent seven hours frantically trying to locate his supposedly injured children, who in fact were fine. He was not injured physically, but he sued for his emotional distress—and won. The **intentional infliction of emotional distress** results from extreme and outrageous conduct that causes serious emotional harm. The credit company was liable for the intentional infliction of emotional distress.[1] The following case arose in a setting that guarantees controversy—an abortion clinic.

JANE DOE AND NANCY ROE V. LYNN MILLS

536 N.W.2d 824
Michigan Court of Appeals, 1995

CASE SUMMARY

Facts: Late one night, an antiabortion protestor named Robert Thomas climbed into a dumpster located behind the Women's Advisory Center, an abortion clinic. He found documents indicating that the plaintiffs were soon to have abortions at the clinic. Thomas gave the information to Lynn Mills. The next day, Mills and Sister Lois Mitoraj created signs, using the women's names, indicating that they were about to undergo abortions and urging them not to "kill their babies."

Doe and Roe (not their real names) sued, claiming intentional infliction of emotional distress (as well as breach of privacy, discussed later in this chapter). The trial court dismissed the lawsuit, ruling that the defendants' conduct was not extreme and outrageous. The plaintiffs appealed.

Issue: *Have the plaintiffs made a valid claim of intentional infliction of emotional distress?*

Decision: The plaintiffs have made a valid claim of intentional infliction of emotional distress.

Reasoning: A defendant is liable for the intentional infliction of emotional distress only when his conduct is outrageous in character, extreme in degree, and utterly intolerable in a civilized community. A good test is whether the average member of the community would respond to the defendant's conduct by exclaiming, "Outrageous!"

These defendants have a constitutional right to protest against abortions, but they have no such right to publicize private matters. Their behavior here might well cause the average person to say, "Outrageous!" The plaintiffs are entitled to a trial, so that a jury can decide whether the defendants have inflicted emotional distress.

7-2 DAMAGES

7-2a Compensatory Damages

Mitchel Bien, a deaf mute, enters the George Grubbs Nissan dealership, where folks sell cars aggressively. Very aggressively. Luke Maturelli, a salesman, and Bien communicate by writing messages back and forth. The two agree to test drive a 300ZX, and Maturelli takes Bien's own car keys. After the test drive, Bien indicates he does not want the car, but Maturelli escorts him back inside and fills out a sales sheet. Bien repeatedly asks for his keys, but Maturelli only laughs, pressuring him to buy the new car. Minutes pass. Hours pass. Bien becomes frantic, writing a dozen notes, begging to leave, threatening to call the police. Maturelli mocks Bien and his physical disabilities. Finally, after four hours, the customer escapes.

Bien sues for the intentional infliction of emotional distress. Two former salesmen from Grubbs testify that they have witnessed customers cry, yell, and curse as a result of the aggressive tactics. Doctors state that the incident has traumatized Bien, dramatically reducing his confidence and self-esteem and preventing his return to work even three years later.

---

[1]Ford Motor Credit Co. v. Sheehan, 373 So.2d 956 (Fla. Dist. Ct. App. 1979).

> **Bien becomes frantic, writing a dozen notes, begging to leave, threatening to call the police.**

The jury awards Bien damages. But how does a jury calculate the Money? For that matter, why should a jury even try? Money can never erase pain or undo a permanent injury. The answer is simple: Money, however inexact and ineffective, is the only thing a court has to give. A successful plaintiff generally receives **compensatory damages**, meaning an amount of money that the court believes will restore him to the position he was in before the defendant's conduct caused an injury. Here is how damages are calculated.

First, a plaintiff receives money for medical expenses that he has proven by producing bills from doctors, hospitals, physical therapists, and psychotherapists. If a doctor testifies that he needs future treatment, Bien will offer evidence of how much that will cost. The **single recovery principle** requires a court to settle the matter once and for all, by awarding a lump sum for past and future expenses.

Second, the defendants are liable for lost wages, past and future. The court takes the number of days or months that Bien has missed (and will miss) work and multiplies that times his salary.

Third, a plaintiff is paid for pain and suffering. Bien testifies about how traumatic the four hours were and how the experience has affected his life. He may state that he now fears shopping, suffers nightmares, and seldom socializes. To bolster the case, a plaintiff uses expert testimony, such as the psychiatrists who testified for Bien. In this case, the jury awarded Bien $573,815, calculated as in the following table:[2]

Compensatory damages
Are intended to restore the plaintiff to the position he was in before the defendant's conduct caused injury

Single recovery principle
Requires a court to settle a legal case once and for all, by awarding a lump sum for past and future expenses

Past medical	$ 70.00
Future medical	6,000.00
Past rehabilitation	3,205.00
Past lost earning capacity	112,910.00
Future lost earning capacity	34,650.00
Past physical symptoms and discomfort	50,000.00
Future physical symptoms and discomfort	50,000.00
Past emotional injury and mental anguish	101,980.00
Future emotional injury and mental anguish	200,000.00
Past loss of society and reduced ability to interact socially with family, former fiancée and friends, and hearing (i.e., nondeaf) people in general	10,000.00
Future loss of society and reduced ability to socially interact with family, former fiancée and friends, and hearing people	5,000.00
TOTAL	$573,815.00

7-2b Punitive Damages

Punitive damages
Punishment of the defendant for conduct that is extreme and outrageous

Here we look at a different kind of award, one that is more controversial and potentially more powerful: punitive damages. Punitive damages are not designed to compensate the plaintiff for harm because compensatory damages will have done that. **Punitive damages** are intended to

---

[2]The compensatory damages are described in George Grubbs Enterprises v. Bien, 881 S.W.2d 843, 1994 Tex. App. LEXIS 1870 (Tex. Ct. App. 1994). In addition to the compensatory damages described, the jury awarded $5 million in punitive damages. The Texas Supreme Court reversed the award of punitive damages, but not the compensatory. Id., 900 S.W.2d 337, 1995 Tex. LEXIS 91 (Tex. 1995). The high court did not dispute the appropriateness of punitive damages, but it reversed because the trial court failed to instruct the jury properly as to how it should determine the assets actually under the defendant's control, an issue essential to punitive damages, but not to compensatory damages.

punish the defendant for conduct that is extreme and outrageous. Courts award these damages in relatively few cases. When an award of punitive damages is made, it is generally in a case of intentional tort. The idea behind punitive damages is that certain behavior is so unacceptable that society must make an example of it. A large award of money should deter the defendant from repeating the mistake and others from ever making it.

Although a jury has wide discretion in awarding punitive damages, the U.S. Supreme Court has ruled that a verdict must be reasonable. In awarding punitive damages, a court must consider three "guideposts":

1. The reprehensibility of the defendant's conduct.

2. The ratio between the harm suffered and the award. Generally, the punitive award should not be more than nine times the compensatory award. The Supreme Court, it is important to stress, does not completely prohibit punitive damages that exceed the 9-to-1 ratio. The justices merely state that such awards should be reserved for rare cases of unusually reprehensible conduct.

3. The difference between the punitive award and any civil penalties used in similar cases.[3]

A California Court of Appeals decided the following case after the establishment of the three guideposts. How should it implement the Supreme Court's guidelines? You be the judge.

---

[3]The U.S. Supreme Court applied the guideposts in State Farm v. Campbell. In the case, the Campbells suffered emotional distress but no physical injuries. The Utah Supreme Court awarded them $1 million in compensatory damages and $145 million in punitive damages. The U.S. Supreme Court found the punitive award excessive and remanded the case, ordering the Utah Supreme Court to hold to a single-digit ration between compensatory and punitive damages.

You be the Judge

BOEKEN V. PHILIP MORRIS, INCORPORATED
127 Cal. App.4th 1640
California Court of Appeals, 2005

Facts: In the mid-1950s, Richard Boeken began smoking Marlboro cigarettes at the age of 10. Countless advertisements, targeted at boys aged 10 to 18, convinced him and his friends that the "Marlboro Man" was powerful, healthy, and manly. At the time, scientists uniformly believed that cigarette smoking caused lung cancer, but Philip Morris and other tobacco companies waged a long-term campaign to convince the public otherwise. Philip Morris also added ingredients to its cigarettes to increase their addictive power.

Boeken saw the Surgeon General's warnings about the risk of smoking, but he trusted the company's statements that cigarettes were safe. Beginning in the 1970s, he tried many times to stop but always failed. Finally, in the 1990s, he quit after he was diagnosed with lung cancer but resumed smoking again once he had recovered from the surgery.

Boeken filed suit against Philip Morris for fraud and other torts. He died of cancer before the case was concluded.

The jury found Philip Morris liable for fraudulently concealing that cigarettes were addictive and carcinogenic. It awarded Boeken $5.5 million in compensatory damages and also assessed punitive damages—of $3 *billion*. The trial judge reduced the punitive award to $100 million. Philip Morris appealed.

You Be the Judge: *Was the punitive damage award too high, too low, or just right?*

Argument for Philip Morris: The court should substantially reduce the $100 million punitive award because it is totally arbitrary. The Supreme Court has indicated that punitive awards should not exceed compensatory damages by more than a factor of 9. The jury awarded Mr. Boeken $5.5 million in compensatory damages, which means that punitive damages should absolutely not exceed $49.5 million. We argue that they should be even lower.

Cigarettes are a legal product, and our packages have displayed the Surgeon General's health warnings for decades. Mr. Boeken's death is tragic, but his cancer was not necessarily caused by Marlboro cigarettes. And even if cigarettes did contribute to his failing health, Mr. Boeken chose to smoke throughout his life, even after major surgery on one of his lungs.

Argument for Boeken: The Supreme Court says that cases may exceed the 9-to-1 ratio if the defendant's behavior is particularly bad. Phillip Morris created ads that targeted children, challenged clear scientific data that its products caused cancer, and added substances to its cigarettes to make them more addictive. Does it get worse than that?

The behavior of Phillip Morris has caused terrible harm. The plaintiff died a terrible death from cancer. The company's cigarettes kill 200,000 American customers each year, while its *weekly* profit is roughly $100 million. At a minimum, the court should keep the punitive award at that figure. But we ask that the court reinstate the jury's original $3 billion award.

7-2c Tort Reform and the *Exxon Valdez*

Some people believe that jury awards are excessive and need statutory reform, while others argue that the evidence demonstrates excessive awards are rare and modest in size. About one-half of the states have passed limits. The laws vary, but many distinguish between **economic damages** and **non-economic damages**. In such a state, a jury is permitted to award any amount for economic damages, meaning lost wages, medical expenses, and other measureable losses. However, non-economic damages—pain and suffering and other losses that are difficult to measure—are capped at some level, such as $500,000. In some states, punitive awards have similar caps. These restrictions can drastically lower the total verdict.

In the famous *Exxon Valdez* case, the U.S. Supreme Court placed a severe limit on a certain type of punitive award. The ship's captain had been drunk, and when the *Exxon Valdez* ran aground, it caused massive, permanent environmental damage. The jury awarded $5 billion in punitive damages, which the Supreme Court reduced to $507 million, equivalent to the compensatory damages awarded. However, it is unclear how influential the decision will be. The case arose in the isolated area of maritime law, which governs ships at sea. Courts may decide not to apply the *Exxon Valdez* reasoning in other cases.

7-3 BUSINESS TORTS

7-3a Tortious Interference with a Contract

Competition is the essence of business. Successful corporations compete aggressively, and the law permits and expects them to. But there are times when healthy competition becomes illegal interference. This is called **tortious interference with a contract**. To win such a case, a plaintiff must establish four elements:

Tortious interference with a contract

Occurs when a defendant deliberately harms a contractual relationship between two other parties

1. There was a contract between the plaintiff and a third party;

2. The defendant knew of the contract;

3. The defendant improperly induced the third party to breach the contract or made performance of the contract impossible; and

4. There was injury to the plaintiff.

Because businesses routinely compete for customers, employees, and market share, it is not always easy to identify tortious interference. There is nothing wrong with two companies bidding against each other to buy a parcel of land, and nothing wrong with one corporation doing everything possible to convince the seller to ignore all competitors. But once a company has signed a contract to buy the land, it is improper to induce the seller to break the deal. The most commonly disputed issues in these cases concern elements 1 and 3: Was there a contract between the plaintiff and another party? Did the defendant improperly induce a party to breach it? Defendants will try to show that the plaintiff had no contract.

7-3b Commercial Exploitation

Commercial exploitation prohibits the unauthorized use of another person's likeness or voice for commercial purposes. For example, it would be illegal to run a magazine advertisement showing reality star Kim Kardashian holding a can of soda, without her permission. The ad would imply that she endorsed the product. Someone's identity is her own, and it cannot be used for commercial gain unless she permits it. Ford Motor Company hired a singer to imitate singer Bette Midler's version of a popular song. The imitation was so good that most listeners were fooled into believing that Midler was endorsing the product. That, ruled a court, violated her right to be free from commercial exploitation.

Commercial exploitation
Prohibits the unauthorized use of another person's likeness or voice for business purposes

Chapter Conclusion

This chapter has been a potpourri of misdeeds, a bubbling cauldron of conduct best avoided. Although tortious acts and their consequences are diverse, two generalities apply. First, the boundaries of intentional torts are imprecise, the outcome of a particular case depending to a considerable extent upon the fact-finder who analyzes it. Second, the thoughtful executive and the careful citizen, aware of the shifting standards and potentially vast liability, will strive to ensure that his or her conduct never provides that fact-finder an opportunity to give judgment.

EXAM REVIEW

1. **TORT**   A tort is a violation of a duty imposed by the civil law.

2. **DEFAMATION**   Defamation involves a defamatory statement that is false, uttered to a third person, and causes an injury.

EXAM Strategy

Question: Benzaquin had a radio talk show. On the program, he complained about an incident in which state trooper Fleming had stopped his car, apparently for lack of a proper license plate and safety sticker. Benzaquin explained that the license plate had been stolen and the sticker had fallen onto the dashboard, but Fleming refused to let him drive away. Benzaquin and two young grandsons had to find other transportation. On the show, Benzaquin angrily recounted the incident, then described Fleming and troopers generally: "arrogants wearing trooper's uniforms like tights"; "we're not paying them to be dictators and Nazis"; "this man is an absolute barbarian, a lunkhead, a meathead." Fleming sued Benzaquin for defamation. Comment.

Strategy: Review the elements of defamation. Can these statements be proven true or false? If not, what is the result? Look at the defenses. Does any of them apply? (See the "Result" at the end of this section.)

3. **FALSE IMPRISONMENT**   False imprisonment is the intentional restraint of another person without reasonable cause and without consent.

4. **BATTERY AND ASSAULT**   Battery is an intentional touching of another person in a way that is unwanted or offensive. Assault involves an act that makes the plaintiff fear an imminent battery.

EXAM Strategy

Question: Caudle worked at Betts Lincoln-Mercury, a car dealer. During an office party, many of the employees, including the president, Betts, were playing with an electric auto condenser, which gave a slight shock when touched. Some employees played catch with it. Betts shocked Caudle on the back of his neck and chased him around. The shock later caused Caudle to suffer headaches, to pass out, to experience numbness, and eventually to require nerve surgery. He sued Betts for battery. Betts defended by saying that it was all horseplay and that he had intended no harm. Please rule.

Strategy: Betts argues that he intended no harm. Is intent to harm an element of Caudle's case? (See the "Result" at the end of this section.)

5. **INTENTIONAL INFLICTION OF EMOTIONAL DISTRESS**   The intentional infliction of emotional distress involves extreme and outrageous conduct that causes serious emotional harm.

6. **DAMAGES**   Compensatory damages are the normal remedy in a tort case. In unusual cases, the court may award punitive damages, not to compensate the plaintiff but to punish the defendant.

7. **TORTIOUS INTERFERENCE WITH A CONTRACT**   Tortious interference with a contract involves the defendant unfairly harming an existing contract.

8. **COMMERCIAL EXPLOITATION**   Protects the exclusive right to use one's own name, likeness, or voice.

2. Result: The court ruled in favor of Benzaquin, because a reasonable person would understand the words to be opinion and ridicule. They are not statements of fact because most of them could not be proven true or false. A statement like "dictators and Nazis" is not taken literally by anyone.[4]

4. Result: The court held that it was irrelevant that Betts had shown no malice toward Caudle nor intended to hurt him. Betts intended the physical contact with Caudle, and even though he could not foresee everything that would happen, he is liable for all consequences of his intended physical action.

---

[4]Fleming v. Benzaquin, 390 Mass. 175, 454 N.E.2d 95 (1983).

MATCHING QUESTIONS

Match the following terms with their definitions:

___A. Interference with a contract

___B. Fraud

___C. False imprisonment

___D. Defamation

___E. Punitive damages

___F. Intentional infliction of emotional distress

___G. Commercial exploitation

1. Money awarded to punish a wrongdoer
2. Intentionally restraining another person without reasonable cause
3. Intentional deception, frequently used to obtain a contract with another party
4. Deliberately stealing a client who has a contract with another
5. Violation of the exclusive right to use one's own name, likeness, or voice
6. Using a false statement to damage someone's reputation
7. An act so extreme that an average person would say, "Outrageous!"

TRUE/FALSE QUESTIONS

Circle true or false:

1. T F A store manager who believes a customer has stolen something may question him but not restrain him.
2. T F Becky punches Kelly in the nose. Becky has committed the tort of assault.
3. T F A defendant cannot be liable for defamation if the statement, no matter how harmful, is true.
4. T F In most cases, a winning plaintiff receives compensatory and punitive damages.
5. T F A company that wishes to include a celebrity's picture in its magazine ads must first obtain the celebrity's permission.

MULTIPLE-CHOICE QUESTIONS

1. A valid defense in a defamation suit is:
   (a) falsity.
   (b) honest error.
   (c) improbability.
   (d) opinion.
   (e) third-party reliance.

2. Joe Student, irate that he received a B– on an exam rather than a B, stands up in class and throws his laptop at the professor. The professor sees it coming and ducks just in time; the laptop smashes against the chalkboard. Joe has committed:

   (a) assault.

   (b) battery.

   (c) negligence.

   (d) slander.

   (e) no tort, because the laptop missed the professor.

3. Marsha, a supervisor, furiously berates Ted in front of 14 other employees, calling him "a loser, an incompetent, a failure as an employee and as a person." She hands around copies of Ted's work and mocks his efforts for 20 minutes. If Ted sues Marsha, his best claim will be:

   (a) assault.

   (b) battery.

   (c) intentional infliction of emotional distress.

   (d) negligence.

   (e) interference with a contract.

4. Rodney is a star player on the Los Angeles Lakers basketball team. He has two years remaining on his four-year contract. The Wildcats, a new team in the league, try to lure Rodney away from the Lakers by offering him more money, and Rodney agrees to leave Los Angeles. The Lakers sue. The Lakers will:

   (a) win a case of defamation.

   (b) win a case of commercial exploitation.

   (c) win a case of intentional interference with a contract.

   (d) win a case of negligence.

   (e) lose.

5. Hank and Antonio, drinking in a bar, get into an argument that turns nasty. Hank punches Antonio several times, knocking him down and breaking his nose and collarbone. Which statement is true?

   (a) Antonio could sue Hank, who might be found guilty.

   (b) Antonio and the state could start separate criminal cases against Hank.

   (c) Antonio could sue Hank, and the state could prosecute Hank.

   (d) The state could prosecute Hank, but only with Antonio's permission.

   (e) If the state prosecutes Hank, he will be found liable or not liable, depending on the evidence.

CASE QUESTIONS

1. Caldwell was shopping in a K-Mart store, carrying a large purse. A security guard observed her looking at various small items such as stain, hinges, and antenna wire. On occasion, she bent down out of sight of the guard. The guard thought he saw Caldwell put something in her purse. Caldwell removed her glasses from her purse

and returned them a few times. After she left, the guard approached her in the parking lot and said that he believed she had store merchandise in her pocketbook, but he was unable to say precisely what he thought was put there. Caldwell opened the purse, and the guard testified that he saw no K-Mart merchandise in it. The guard then told Caldwell to return to the store with him. They walked around the store for approximately 15 minutes, while the guard said six or seven times that he saw her put something in her purse. Caldwell left the store after another store employee indicated she could go. Caldwell sued. What kind of suit did she file, and what should the outcome be?

2. Tata Consultancy of Bombay, India, is an international computer consulting firm. It spends considerable time and effort recruiting the best personnel from India's leading technical schools. Tata employees sign an initial three-year employment commitment, often work overseas, and agree to work for a specified additional time when they return to India. Desai worked for Tata, but then he quit and formed a competing company, which he called Syntel. His new company contacted Tata employees by phone, offering more money to come work for Syntel, bonuses, and assistance in obtaining permanent resident visas in the United States. At least 16 former Tata employees left their work without completing their contractual obligations and went to work for Syntel. Tata sued. What did it claim, and what should be the result?

3. For many years, Johnny Carson was the star of a well-known television show, *The Tonight Show.* For about 20 years, he was introduced nightly on the show with the phrase, "Here's Johnny!" A large segment of the television-watching public associated the phrase with Carson. A Michigan corporation was in the business of renting and selling portable toilets. The company chose the name "Here's Johnny Portable Toilets," and coupled the company name with the marketing phrase, "The World's Foremost Commodian." Carson sued. What claim is he making? Who should win, and why?

4. You are a vice president in charge of personnel at a large manufacturing company. In-house detectives inform you that Gates, an employee, was seen stealing valuable computer equipment. Gates denies the theft, but you fire him nonetheless. The detectives suggest that you post notices around the company, informing all employees what happened to Gates and why. This will discourage others from stealing. While you think that over, the personnel officer from another company calls, asking for a recommendation for Gates. Should you post the notices? What should you say to the other officer?

5. Lou DiBella was an executive responsible for programming boxing shows on HBO cable network. DiBella signed Bernard Hopkins, the then-middleweight world boxing champion, to participate in a fight televised by HBO. After DiBella's departure from the network, he and Hopkins entered into an agreement in which Hopkins paid $50,000 for DiBella's promotional services. Months later, Hopkins publicly accused DiBella of taking bribes and "selling" spots in HBO fights, calling him greedy, filthy, and unethical. DiBella sued Hopkins for libel. What did DiBella have to prove to be successful in his claim?

DISCUSSION QUESTIONS

1. In the *Exxon Valdez* case, the Supreme Court limited punitive damages in maritime cases to no more than the compensatory damages awarded in the same case. In cases that do not involve maritime law, the ratio is usually limited to 9-to-1. Which is the better guideline? Why?

2. You have most likely heard of the *Liebeck v. McDonalds* case. Liebeck spilled hot McDonald's coffee in her lap, suffering third degree burns. At trial, evidence showed that her cup of coffee was brewed at 190 degrees, and that, more typically, a restaurant's "hot coffee" is in the range of 140–160 degrees. A jury awarded Liebeck $160,000 in compensatory damages and $2.7 million in punitive damages. The judge reduced the punitive award to $480,000, or three times the compensatory award. Comment on the case, and whether the result was reasonable.

3. The Supreme Court has defined public figures as those who have "voluntarily exposed themselves to increased risk of injury by assuming an influential role in ordering society."

When deciding whether someone is a public figure, courts look at whether this person has received press coverage, sought the public spotlight, and has the opportunity to publicly rebut the accusations. Some have argued that social media makes anyone with a public Facebook profile or a certain number of Twitter followers a public figure. Do you agree? Should courts revisit the definition of "public figure" in light of social media?

4. This chapter described two lawsuits in which juries initially gave awards of $100 million or more. Is there any point at which the raw number of dollars is just too large? Was the original jury award excessive in *Boeken v. Philip Morris* or the *Exxon Valdez* case?

5. Many retailers have policies that instruct employees *not* to attempt to stop shoplifters. Some store owners fear false imprisonment lawsuits and possible injuries to workers more than losses related to stolen merchandise. Are these "don't be a hero" policies reasonable? Would you put one in place if you owned a retail store?

© biletskiy/Shutterstock.com

NEGLIGENCE, STRICT LIABILITY, AND PRODUCT LIABILITY

The story you are about to read is true; not even the names have been changed. The participants were the plaintiff and defendant in a tort case. Do not try this at home.

Connie was very depressed. She felt so "overburdened," she decided to end her life by locking herself inside the trunk of her 1973 Ford LTD.

Fortunately, Connie decided against committing suicide. Unfortunately, not until after she had already closed the trunk. The Ford did not have an internal release latch or other emergency opening mechanism. And these were the days before cell phones. Result? Connie was trapped in her trunk for *nine* days awaiting rescue.

This awful episode caused Connie serious psychological and physical injuries. She sued Ford for damages under negligence and strict liability. According to Connie, Ford was negligent because it had a duty to warn her that there was no latch; and the missing latch was a design defect for which Ford should pay.[1]

But whose fault was it? Was Ford's design defective? Was the car unreasonably dangerous? Or was Connie just unreasonable?

> **Fortunately, Connie decided against committing suicide. Unfortunately, not until after she had already closed the trunk.**

---

[1]Based on Daniell v. Ford Motor Co., 581 F. Supp. 728 (D. Ct. N.M. 1984).

These are all practical questions and moral ones as well. They are also typical issues in the law of negligence, strict liability, and product liability. In these contentious areas, courts continually face one question: *When someone is injured, who is responsible?*

8-1 NEGLIGENCE

We might call negligence the "unintentional" tort because it concerns harm that arises by accident. Should a court impose liability?

Things go wrong all the time, and people are hurt in large ways and small. Society needs a means of analyzing negligence cases consistently and fairly. We cannot have each court that hears such a lawsuit extend or limit liability based on an emotional response to the facts. One of America's greatest judges, Benjamin Cardozo, offered a way to analyze negligence cases more than 80 years ago. In a case called *Palsgraf v. Long Island Railroad*, he made a decision that still influences negligence thinking today.

Landmark Case

PALSGRAF V. LONG ISLAND RAILROAD
248 N.Y. 339
Court of Appeals of New York, 1928

CASE SUMMARY

Facts: Helen Palsgraf was waiting on a railroad platform. As a train began to leave the station, a man carrying a plain package ran to catch it. He jumped aboard but looked unsteady, so a guard on the car reached out to help him as another guard, on the platform, pushed from behind. The man dropped the package, which struck the tracks and exploded—since it was packed with fireworks. The shock knocked over some heavy scales at the far end of the platform, and one of them struck Palsgraf. She sued the railroad.

Issue: *Was the railroad liable for Palsgraf's injuries?*

Holding: No, the railroad was not liable.

Reasoning: No one could foresee that what the guards did would harm someone standing at the far end of the platform. Therefore, it does not matter whether or not the guards were careless. For the railroad to be liable, Palsgraf had to show not just that a wrong took place, but that the wrong was to *her*. Negligence in the air is not enough. For example, if a driver speeds through city streets, it is easy to see that someone may be hurt. But, in this case, even the most cautious mind would not imagine that a package wrapped in a newspaper would spread wreckage throughout the station.

The railroad employees owed Palsgraf a duty to be reasonably cautious and vigilant. They did not owe a duty to prevent all harm, no matter how unlikely.

This case was important in establishing the rules of negligence. Courts are still guided by Judge Cardozo's decision.

To win a negligence case, a plaintiff must prove five elements. Much of the remainder of the chapter will examine them in detail. They are:

- **Duty of due care.** The defendant had a legal responsibility *to the plaintiff*. This is the point from the *Palsgraf* case.

- **Breach**. The defendant breached her duty of care or failed to meet her legal obligations.

- **Factual cause.** The defendant's conduct actually caused the injury.

- **Proximate cause.** It was *foreseeable* that conduct like the defendant's might cause *this type of harm*.

- **Damages**. The plaintiff has actually been hurt or has actually suffered a measureable loss.

To win a case, a plaintiff must prove all of the elements listed above. If a defendant eliminates only one item on the list, there is no liability.

8-1a Duty of Due Care

Each of us has a duty to behave as a reasonable person would under the circumstances. If you are driving a car, you have a duty to all the other people near you to drive like a reasonable person. If you drive while drunk or send text messages while behind the wheel, then you fail to live up to your duty of care.

But how *far* does your duty extend? Most courts accept Cardozo's viewpoint in the *Palsgraf* case. Judges draw an imaginary line around the defendant and say that she owes a duty to the people within the circle, but not to those outside it. The test is generally "foreseeability." If the defendant could have foreseen injury to a particular person, she has a duty to him. Suppose that one of your friends posts a YouTube video of you texting behind the wheel and her father is so upset from watching it that he falls down the stairs. You would not be liable for the father's tumble because it was not foreseeable that he would be harmed by your texting.

Let us apply these principles to a case that involves a fraternity party.

HERNANDEZ V. ARIZONA BOARD OF REGENTS

177 Ariz. 244
Arizona Supreme Court, 1994

CASE SUMMARY

Facts: At the University of Arizona, the Epsilon Epsilon chapter of Delta Tau Delta fraternity gave a welcoming party for new members. The fraternity's officers knew that the majority of its members were under the legal drinking age, but they permitted everyone to consume alcohol. John Rayner, who was under 21 years of age, left the party. He drove negligently and caused a collision with an auto driven by Ruben Hernandez. At the time of the accident, Rayner's blood alcohol level was 0.15, exceeding the legal limit. The crash left Hernandez blind and paralyzed.

Hernandez sued Rayner, who settled the case based on the amount of his insurance coverage. The victim also sued the fraternity, its officers, and national organization, all the fraternity members who contributed money to buy the alcohol, the university, and others. The trial court granted summary judgment for all defendants, and the court of appeals affirmed. Hernandez appealed to the Arizona Supreme Court.

Issue: *Did the fraternity and the other defendants have a duty of due care to Hernandez?*

Decision: Yes, the defendants did have a duty of due care to Hernandez.

Reasoning: Historically, Arizona and most states have considered that *consuming* alcohol led to liability, but not *furnishing* it. However, the common law also has had a long-standing rule that a defendant could be liable for supplying some object to a person who is likely to endanger others. Giving a car to an intoxicated youth is an example of such behavior. The youth might easily use the object (the car) to injure other people.

There is no difference between giving a car to an intoxicated youth and giving alcohol to a young person with a car. Both acts involve minors who, because of their age and inexperience, are likely to endanger third parties. Furthermore, furnishing alcohol to a minor violates several state statutes. The defendants did have a duty of due care to Hernandez and to the public in general. Reversed and remanded.

Special Duty: Landowner's Liability

The common law applies special rules to a landowner for injuries occurring on her property. In most states, the owner's duty depends on the type of person injured.

Trespasser

A person on someone else's property without consent

- **Lowest liability: trespassing adults.** A **trespasser** is anyone on the property without consent. A landowner is liable to a trespasser only for intentionally injuring him or for some other gross misconduct. The landowner has no liability to a trespasser for mere negligence. Jake is not liable if a vagrant wanders onto his land and is burned by defective electrical wires.

- **Mid-Level liability: trespassing children.** The law makes exceptions when the trespassers are *children*. If there is something on the land *that may be reasonably expected to attract children*, the landowner is probably liable for any harm. Daphne lives next door to a day-care center and builds a treehouse on her property. Unless she has fenced off the dangerous area, she is probably liable if a small child wanders onto her property and injures himself when he falls from the rope ladder to the treehouse.

Licensee

A person on property for her own purposes, but with the owner's permission

- **Higher liability: licensee.** A **licensee** is anyone on the land for her own purposes but with the owner's permission. A social guest is a typical licensee. A licensee is entitled to a warning of hidden dangers that the owner knows about. If Juliet invites Romeo for a late supper on the balcony and fails to mention that the wooden railing is rotted, she is liable when her hero plunges to the courtyard.

  But Juliet is liable only for injuries caused by *hidden* dangers—she has no duty to warn guests of obvious dangers. She need not say, "Romeo, oh Romeo, don't place thy hand in the toaster, Romeo."

Invitee

A person who has a right to be on property because it is a public place or a business open to the public

- **Highest liability: invitee.** An **invitee** is someone who has a right to be on the property because it is a public place or a business open to the public. The owner has a duty of reasonable care to an invitee. Perry is an invitee when he goes to the town beach. If riptides have existed for years and the town fails to post a warning, it is liable if Perry drowns. Perry is also an invitee when he goes to Dana's coffee shop. Dana is liable if she ignores spilled coffee that causes Perry to slip.

With social guests, you must have *actual knowledge* of some specific hidden danger to be liable. Not so with invitees. You are liable even if you had *no idea* that something on your property posed a hidden danger. Therefore, if you own a business, you must conduct inspections of your property on a regular basis to make sure that nothing is becoming dangerous.

The courts of some states have modified these distinctions, and a few have eliminated them altogether. California, for example, requires "reasonable care" as to all people on the owner's property, regardless of how or why they got there. But most states still use the classifications outlined above.

Special Duty: Professionals

A person at work has a heightened duty of care. While on the job, she must act as a reasonable person *in her profession*. A taxi driver must drive as a reasonable taxi driver would. A heart surgeon must perform bypass surgery with the care of a trained specialist in that field.

Two medical cases illustrate the reasonable person standard. A doctor prescribes a powerful drug without asking his patient about other medicines she is currently taking. The patient suffers a serious drug reaction from the combined medications. The physician is liable for the harm. A reasonable doctor *always* checks current medicines before prescribing new ones.

On the other hand, assume that a patient dies on the operating table in an emergency room. The physician followed standard medical protocol at every step of the procedure and acted with reasonable speed. In fact, the man had a fatal stroke. The surgeon is not liable. A doctor must do a reasonable and professional job, but she cannot guarantee a happy outcome.

8-1b Breach of Duty

The second element of a plaintiff's negligence case is **breach of duty**. Courts apply the *reasonable person* standard: A defendant breaches his duty of due care by failing to behave the way a reasonable person would under similar circumstances. "Reasonable person" means someone of the defendant's occupation. A taxi driver must drive as a reasonable taxi driver would. An architect who designs a skyscraper's safety features must bring to the task far greater knowledge than the average person possesses.

Breach of duty
A defendant breaches his duty of due care by failing to behave the way a reasonable person would under similar circumstances.

8-1c Causation

We have seen that a plaintiff must show that the defendant owed him a duty of care, and that the defendant breached the duty. To win, the plaintiff must also show that the defendant's breach of duty *caused* the plaintiff's harm. Courts look at two separate causation issues: Was the defendant's behavior the **factual cause** of the harm? Was it the **proximate cause**?[2]

Factual Cause

If the defendant's breach led to the ultimate harm, it is a factual cause. Suppose that Dom's Brake Shop tells a customer his brakes are now working fine, even though Dom knows that is false. The customer drives out of the shop, cannot stop at a red light, and hits a bicyclist crossing the intersection. Dom is liable to the cyclist. Dom's unreasonable behavior was the factual cause of the harm. Think of it as a row of dominoes. The first domino (Dom's behavior) knocked over the next one (failing brakes), which toppled the last one (the cyclist's injury).

Suppose, alternatively, that just as the customer is exiting the repair shop, the bicyclist hits a pothole and tumbles off her cycle. Dom has breached his duty to his customer, but he is not liable to the cyclist—she would have been hurt anyway. This is a row of dominoes that veers off to the side, leaving the last domino (the cyclist's injury) untouched. No factual causation.

Factual cause
The defendant's breach led to the ultimate harm.

Proximate cause
Refers to a party who contributes to a loss in a way that a reasonable person could anticipate

Proximate Cause

For the defendant to be liable, the *type of harm* must have been reasonably *foreseeable*. In the first example just discussed, Dom could easily foresee that bad brakes would cause an automobile accident. He need not have foreseen *exactly* what happened. He did not know there would be a cyclist nearby. What he could foresee was this *general type* of harm involving defective brakes. Because the accident that occurred was of the type he could foresee, he is liable.

By contrast, assume the collision of car and bicycle produces a loud crash. Two blocks away, a pet pig, asleep on the window ledge of a twelfth-story apartment, is startled by the noise, awakens with a start, and plunges to the sidewalk, killing a veterinarian who was making a house call. If the vet's family sues Dom, should it win? Dom's negligence was the factual cause: It led to the collision, which startled the pig, which flattened the vet. Most courts would rule, though, that Dom is not liable. The type of harm is too bizarre. Dom could not reasonably foresee such an extraordinary chain of events, and it would be unfair to make him pay for it. See Exhibit 8.1. Another way of stating that Dom is not liable to the vet's family is by calling the falling pig a *superseding cause*. When one of the "dominoes" in the row is entirely unforeseeable, courts will call that event a superseding cause, letting the defendant off the hook.

---

[2]Courts often refer to these two elements, grouped together, as *proximate cause* or *legal cause*. But, as many courts acknowledge, those terms have created legal confusion, so we use *factual cause* and *foreseeable types of harm*, the issues on which most decisions ultimately focus.

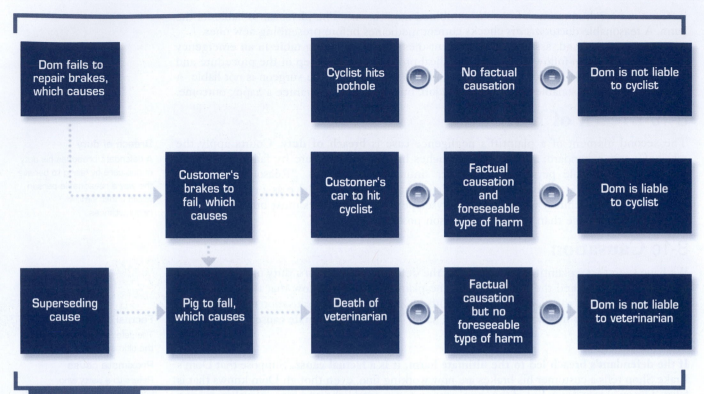

Dom fails to repair brakes, which causes

Cyclist hits pothole = No factual causation = Dom is not liable to cyclist

Customer's brakes to fail, which causes → Customer's car to hit cyclist = Factual causation and foreseeable type of harm = Dom is liable to cyclist

Superseding cause → Pig to fall, which causes → Death of veterinarian = Factual causation but no foreseeable type of harm = Dom is not liable to veterinarian

EXHIBIT 8.1

EXAM Strategy

Question: Jenny asked a neighbor, Tom, to water her flowers while she was on vacation. For three days, Tom did this without incident, but on the fourth day, when he touched the outside faucet, he received a violent electric shock that shot him through the air, melted his sneakers and glasses, set his clothes on fire, and seriously scalded him. Tom sued, claiming that Jenny had caused the damage when she negligently repaired a second-floor toilet. Water from the steady leak had flooded through the walls, soaking wires and eventually causing the faucet to become electrified. You are Jenny's lawyer. Use one (and only one) element of negligence law to move for summary judgment.

Strategy: The four elements of negligence we have examined thus far are duty to this plaintiff, breach, factual cause, and foreseeable type of injury. Which element seems to be most helpful to Jenny's defense? Why?

Result: Jenny is entitled to summary judgment because this was not a foreseeable type of injury. Even if she did a bad job of fixing the toilet, she could not possibly have anticipated that her poor workmanship could cause *electrical* injuries—and violent ones, at that—to anybody.[3]

---

[3]Based on Hebert v. Enos, 60 Mass. App. Ct. 817 (Mass. Ct. App. 2004).

Res Ipsa Loquitur. Normally, a plaintiff must prove factual cause and foreseeable type of harm to establish negligence. But in a few cases, a court may be willing to infer that the defendant caused the harm, under the doctrine of ***res ipsa loquitur*** ("the thing speaks for itself"). Suppose a pedestrian is walking along a sidewalk when an air conditioning unit falls on his head from a third-story window. The defendant, who owns the third-story apartment, denies any wrongdoing, and it may be difficult or impossible for the plaintiff to prove why the air conditioner fell. In such cases, many courts will apply *res ipsa loquitur* and declare that the facts imply that the defendant's negligence caused the accident. If a court uses this doctrine, then the defendant must come forward with evidence establishing that it did not cause the harm.

Because *res ipsa loquitur* dramatically shifts the burden of proof from plaintiff to defendant, it applies only when (1) the defendant had exclusive control of the thing that caused the harm; (2) the harm normally would not have occurred without negligence; and (3) the plaintiff had no role in causing the harm. In the air conditioner example, most states would apply the doctrine and force the defendant to prove she did nothing wrong. The following case applies *res ipsa loquitur* to a prickly problem.

> **Res ipsa loquitur**
>
> Means "the thing speaks for itself" and refers to cases where the facts *imply* that the defendant's negligence caused the harm

BRUMBERG v. CIPRIANI USA, INC.

2013 NY Slip Op 06759
Supreme Court of New York, 2013

CASE SUMMARY

Facts: Cornell professor Joan Jacobs Brumberg attended a university fundraiser catered by Cipriani, where she feasted on fancy appetizers. About 30 minutes later, she felt intense abdominal pain, which did not go away. Weeks later, her doctors removed a 1½–inch piece of wood from her digestive tract. The shard caused internal injuries, which took two surgeries to repair.

Brumberg's physician believed that her injuries were the result of eating wood at Cornell's cocktail party. On that day, she had eaten little else and had experienced no pain until the event, where she ate many appetizers, including shrimp on wood skewers. The doctor supposed that the wood moved through her digestive system for 30 minutes before becoming caught and causing the pain. But when experts compared Brumberg's shard with the wood in Cipriani's toothpicks and skewers, they found that the two were not the same material, eliminating direct evidence of causation.

Brumberg sued Cipriani USA, Inc. for negligence. A lower court dismissed her case on a motion for summary judgment, concluding there was not enough proof that

Cipriani caused Brumberg's injury. The professor appealed, relying on the doctrine of *res ipsa loquitur*.

Issue: *Does res ipsa loquitur apply here?*

Decision: Yes, *res ipsa loquitur* applies.

Reasoning: For *res ipsa loquitur* to apply, (1) the event must be of a kind that would not have occurred in the absence of someone's negligence; (2) it must be caused by something in the defendant's exclusive control; and (3) it must not be the plaintiff's fault.

Without negligence on someone's part, wood does not just end up in food at parties. Someone had to have put the shard there.

Cipriani had exclusive control at the party, which took place at a banquet hall that the company operated. Since its employees were the only ones who prepared and served the food, it was highly unlikely that another guest could have slipped the shard in the food without being seen.

Professor Brumberg did nothing wrong. The injury was caused by the wood, not by her failure to notice it in her food.

Reversed.

8-1d Damages

Finally, a plaintiff must prove that he has been injured or that he has had some kind of measureable losses. In some cases, injury is obvious. For example, Ruben Hernandez suffered grievous harm when struck by the drunk driver. But in other cases, injury is unclear. **The plaintiff must persuade the court that he has suffered harm that is genuine, not speculative.**

Some cases raise tough questions. Among the most vexing are suits involving future harm. Exposure to toxins or trauma may lead to serious medical problems down the road—or it may not. A woman's knee is damaged in an auto accident, causing severe pain for two years. She is clearly entitled to compensation for her suffering. After two years, all pain may cease for a decade—or forever. Yet there is also a chance that in 15 or 20 years, the trauma will lead to painful arthritis. A court must decide today the full extent of present and future damages; the single recovery principle, discussed in Chapter 7, prevents a plaintiff from returning to court years later and demanding compensation for newly arisen ailments. The challenge to our courts is to weigh the possibilities and percentages of future suffering and decide whether to compensate a plaintiff for something that might never happen.

8-2 DEFENSES

8-2a Assumption of the Risk

Good Guys, a restaurant, holds an ice-fishing contest on a frozen lake to raise money for accident victims. Margie grabs a can full of worms and strolls to the middle of the lake to try her luck, but she slips on the ice and suffers a concussion. If she sues Good Guys, how will she fare? She will fall a second time. Wherever there is an obvious hazard, a special rule applies. **Assumption of the risk: A person who voluntarily enters a situation that has an obvious danger cannot complain if she is injured.** Ice is slippery, and we all know it. If you venture onto a frozen lake, any falls are your own tough luck.

Assumption of the risk
A person who voluntarily enters a situation of obvious danger cannot complain if she is injured.

NFL players assume substantial risks each time they take the field, but some injuries fall outside the rule. In a game between the Jets and the Dolphins, Jets assistant coach, standing on the sideline, tripped a Dolphins player during a punt return. The trip was not a "normal" part of a football game, and the "assumption of the risk" doctrine would not prevent the player from recovering damages if injured.

8-2b Contributory and Comparative Negligence

Sixteen-year-old Michelle Wightman was out driving at night, with her friend Karrie Wieber in the passenger seat. They came to a railroad crossing, where the mechanical arm had descended and warning bells were sounding, in fact, had been sounding for a long time. A Conrail train, SEEL-7, had suffered mechanical problems and was stopped 200 feet from the crossing, where it had stalled for roughly an hour. Michelle and Karrie saw several cars ahead of them go around the barrier and cross the tracks. Michelle had to decide whether she would do the same.

> ... the mechanical arm had descended and warning bells were sounding, in fact, had been sounding for a long time.

Long before Michelle made her decision, the train's engineer had seen the heavy Saturday night traffic crossing the tracks and realized the danger. A second train had passed the crossing at 70 miles per hour without incident. SEEL-7's conductor and brakeman also understood the peril, but rather than posting a flagman, who could have stopped traffic when a train approached, they walked to the far end of their train to repair the mechanical problem. A police officer had come upon the scene, told his dispatcher to notify Conrail of the danger, and left.

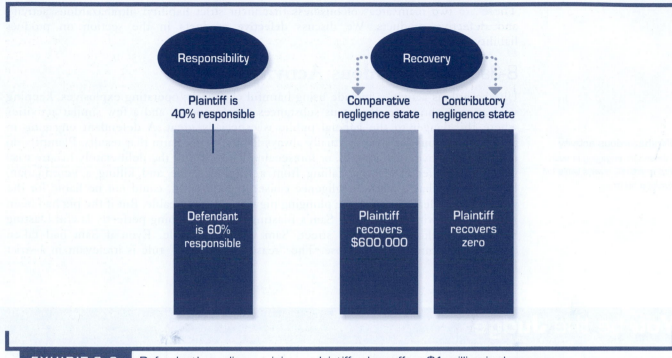

EXHIBIT 8.2 Defendant's negligence injures plaintiff, who suffers $1 million in damages.

Michelle decided to cross the tracks. She slowly followed the cars ahead of her. TV-9, a freight train traveling at 60 miles per hour, struck the car broadside, killing both girls instantly.

Michelle's mother sued Conrail for negligence. The company claimed that it was Michelle's foolish risk that led to her death. Who wins when both parties are partly responsible? It depends on whether the state uses a legal theory called **contributory negligence**. Under contributory negligence., if the plaintiff is even *slightly* negligent, she recovers nothing. If Michelle's death occurred in a contributory negligence state, and the jury considered her even minimally responsible, her estate would receive no money.

Critics attacked this rule as unreasonable. Under those terms, a plaintiff who was 1 percent negligent could not recover from a defendant who was 99 percent responsible. So most states threw out the contributory negligence rule, replacing it with comparative negligence. In a **comparative negligence** state, a plaintiff may generally recover even if she is partially responsible. The jury will be asked to assess the relative negligence of the two parties.

Michelle died in Ohio, which is a comparative negligence state. The jury concluded that reasonable compensatory damages were $1 million. It also concluded that Conrail was 60 percent responsible for the tragedy and Michelle 40 percent. See Exhibit 8.2. The girl's mother received $600,000 in compensatory damages.[4]

Contributory negligence
A plaintiff who is even *slightly* negligent recovers nothing.

Comparative negligence
A plaintiff may generally recover even if she is partially responsible.

8-3 STRICT LIABILITY

Some activities are so naturally dangerous that the law places an especially high burden on anyone who engages in them. A corporation that produces toxic waste can foresee dire consequences from its business that a stationery store cannot. This higher burden is **strict liability**.

Strict liability
A high level of liability assumed by people or corporations who engage in activities that are very dangerous

[4]Wightman v. Consolidated Rail Corporation, 86 Ohio St.3d 431 (Ohio 1999).

There are two main areas of business that incur strict liability: ultrahazardous activity and defective products. We discuss **defective products** in the section on product liability below.

8-3a Ultrahazardous Activity

Ultrahazardous activity
A defendant engaging in such acts is virtually always liable for resulting harm

Ultrahazardous activities include using harmful chemicals, operating explosives, keeping wild animals, bringing dangerous substances onto property, and a few similar activities where the danger to the general public is especially great. A defendant engaging in an **ultrahazardous activity** is virtually always liable for any harm that results. Plaintiffs do not have to prove duty, breach, or foreseeable harm. Recall the deliberately bizarre case we posed earlier of the pig falling from a window ledge and killing a veterinarian. Dom, the mechanic whose negligence caused the car crash, could not be liable for the veterinarian's death because the plunging pig was not foreseeable. But if the pig had been jolted off the window ledge by Sam's Blasting Company, doing perfectly lawful blasting for a new building down the street, Sam would be liable. Even if Sam had taken extraordinary care, he would lose. The "reasonable person" rule is irrelevant in a strict liability case.

You be the Judge

Facts: The Alden Leeds company packages, stores, and ships swimming pool chemicals. The firm does most of its work at its facility in Kearns, New Jersey. At any given time, about 21 different hazardous chemicals are present.

The day before Easter, a fire of unknown origin broke out in "Building One" of the company's site, releasing chlorine gas and other potentially dangerous by-products into the air. There were no guards or other personnel on duty. The fire caused $9 million in damage to company property. Because of the danger, the Department of Environmental Protection (DEP) closed the New Jersey Turnpike and half a dozen other major highways, halted all commuter rail and train service in the area, and urged residents to stay indoors with windows closed. An unspecified number of residents went to local hospitals with respiratory problems.

Based on New Jersey's air pollution laws, the DEP fined Alden Leeds for releasing the toxic chemicals. The appellate court reversed, declaring that there was no evidence the company had caused the fire or the harm. The case reached the state's high court.

NEW JERSEY DEPARTMENT OF ENVIRONMENTAL PROTECTION V. ALDEN LEEDS, INC.
153 N.J. 272
Supreme Court of New Jersey, 1998

You Be the Judge: *Is the company responsible for the harm?*

Argument for Alden Leeds: Alden Leeds did nothing wrong. Why should the company pay a fine? The firm was licensed to use these chemicals and did so in a safe manner. There is no evidence the company caused the fire. Sometimes accidents just happen. Do not penalize a responsible business simply to make somebody pay. The state should go after careless firms that knowingly injure the public. Leave good companies alone so they can get on with business and provide jobs.

Argument for the Department of Environmental Protection: This accident made innocent people sick and caused massive difficulties for tens of thousands. It makes no difference why the accident happened. That is the whole point of strict liability. When a company chooses to participate in an ultrahazardous activity, it accepts full liability for anything that goes wrong, regardless of the cause. If you want the profits, you accept the responsibility. Alden Leeds must pay.

8-3b Product Liability

So far in this chapter, we have discussed how two tort theories—negligence and strict liability—apply when someone's action or inaction harms another. But sometimes products, not people, cause harm. When an exploding cola bottle, a flammable pajama, or a toxic cookie injures, who pays? Someone who is injured by a defective product may have claims in both negligence and strict liability.

Negligence

In negligence cases concerning goods, plaintiffs most often raise one or more of these claims:

- **Negligent design.** The buyer claims that the product injured her because the manufacturer designed it poorly. Negligence law requires a manufacturer to design a product free of *unreasonable* risks. The product does not have to be absolutely safe. An automobile that guaranteed a driver's safety could be made but would be prohibitively expensive. Reasonable safety features must be built in if they can be included at a tolerable cost.

- **Negligent manufacture.** The buyer claims that the design was adequate but that failure to inspect or some other sloppy conduct caused a dangerous product to leave the plant.

- **Failure to warn.** A manufacturer is liable for failing to warn the purchaser or users about the dangers of normal use and also foreseeable misuse. However, there is no duty to warn about obvious dangers, a point evidently lost on some manufacturers. One Batman costume included this statement: "For play only: Mask and chest plate are not protective; cape does not enable user to fly."

Strict Liability for Defective Products

The other tort claim that an injured person can often bring against the manufacturer or seller of a product is strict liability. Like negligence, strict liability is a burden created by the law rather than by the parties. And, as with all torts, strict liability concerns claims of physical harm. But there is a key distinction between negligence and strict liability: In a negligence case, the injured buyer must demonstrate that the seller's conduct was unreasonable. Not so in strict liability.

In strict liability, the injured person need not prove that the defendant's conduct was unreasonable. The injured person must show only that the defendant manufactured or sold a product that was defective and that the defect caused harm. Almost all states permit such lawsuits, and most of them have adopted the following model:

1. One who sells any product in a defective condition unreasonably dangerous to the user or consumer or to his property is subject to liability for physical harm thereby caused to the ultimate user or consumer, or to his property, if

   (a) the seller is engaged in the business of selling such a product, and

   (b) it is expected to and does reach the user or consumer without substantial change in the condition in which it is sold.

2. The rule stated in Section (1) applies although

   (a) the seller has exercised all possible care in the preparation and sale of his product, and

   (b) the user or consumer has not bought the product from or entered into any contractual relation with the seller.

These are the key terms in Section (1):

- **Defective condition unreasonably dangerous to the user.** The defendant is liable only if the product is defective when it leaves his hands. There must be something wrong with the goods. If they are reasonably safe and the buyer's mishandling of the goods causes the harm, there is no strict liability. If you attempt to open a soda bottle by knocking the cap against a counter and the glass shatters and cuts you, the manufacturer owes nothing. A carving knife can produce a lethal wound, but everyone knows that, and a sharp knife is not unreasonably dangerous. On the other hand, prescription drugs may harm in ways that neither a layperson nor a doctor would anticipate. The manufacturer *must provide adequate warnings* of any dangers that are not apparent.

- **In the business of selling.** The seller is liable only if she normally sells this kind of product. Suppose your roommate makes you a peanut butter sandwich and, while eating it, you cut your mouth on a sliver of glass that was in the jar. The peanut butter manufacturer faces strict liability, as does the grocery store where your roommate bought the goods. But your roommate is not strictly liable because he is not in the food business.

- **Reaches the user without substantial change.** Obviously, if your roommate put the glass in the peanut butter thinking it was funny, neither the manufacturer nor the store would be liable.

And here are the important phrases in Section (2).

- **Has exercised all possible care.** This is the heart of strict liability, which makes it a potent claim for consumers. *It is no defense that the seller used reasonable care.* If the product is dangerously defective and injures the user, the seller is liable even if it took every precaution to design and manufacture the product safely. Suppose the peanut butter jar did in fact contain a glass sliver when it left the factory. The manufacturer proves that it uses extraordinary care in keeping foreign particles out of the jars and thoroughly inspects each container before it is shipped. The evidence is irrelevant. The manufacturer has shown that it was not *negligent* in packaging the food, but reasonable care is irrelevant in strict liability cases.

- **No contractual relation.** When two parties are in a contract, they are in privity. Note that privity only exists between the user and the person from whom she actually bought the goods, but in strict liability cases, *privity is not required.* Suppose the manufacturer that made the peanut butter sold it to a distributor, which sold it to a wholesaler, which sold it to a grocery store, which sold it to your roommate. You may sue the manufacturer, distributor, wholesaler, and store, even though you had no privity with any of them.

As we have seen, an injured plaintiff may sue a manufacturer for both negligence and strict liability. Remember Connie from the chapter opener? Let's see how her story ended.

DANIELL V. FORD

581 F. Supp. 728
U.S. District Court, New Mexico 1984

CASE SUMMARY

Facts: See the chapter opener.

Connie Daniell argued that Ford was both (1) negligent because it did not warn her that there was no opening mechanism in the trunk and (2) strictly liable for this design defect. Ford sought summary judgment.

Issue: *Was Ford negligent in failing to warn Connie of the missing latch? Was Ford strictly liable for a design defect?*

Decision: No. Ford was neither negligent nor strictly liable.

Reasoning: A manufacturer only has a duty to address foreseeable risks. When a consumer's unforeseeable use

of a product causes injury, the manufacturer is not liable in negligence or strict liability.

An automobile trunk is used to stow goods. Its design makes it nearly impossible for an adult to enter it and close the lid. The plaintiff's use of the trunk in an attempt to kill herself was unforeseeable. Therefore, Ford had no duty to design an internal release or opening mechanism to prevent suicide.

Ford also did not have a duty to warn the plaintiff of the danger of her conduct. The risk of locking oneself in a trunk is obvious. Neither negligence nor strict liability imposes a duty to warn of known dangers.

Ford's motion for summary judgment is granted.

8-4 CONTEMPORARY TRENDS

If the steering wheel on a brand-new car falls off and the driver is injured as a result, that is a clear case of defective manufacturing, and the company will be strictly liable. Those are the easy cases. But defective design cases have been more contentious. Suppose a vaccine that prevents serious childhood illnesses inevitably causes brain damage in a very small number of children because of the nature of the drug. Is the manufacturer liable? What if a racing sailboat, designed only for speed, is dangerously unstable in the hands of a less experienced sailor? Is the boat's maker responsible for fatalities? Suppose an automobile made of light-weight metal uses less fuel but exposes its occupants to more serious injuries in an accident. How is a court to decide whether the design was defective? Often, these design cases also involve issues of warnings: Did the drug designer diligently detail dangers to doctors? Should a sailboat seller sell speedy sailboats solely to seasoned sailors?

Over the years, most courts have adopted one of two tests for design and warning cases. The first is *consumer expectation*. Here, a court finds the manufacturer liable for defective design if the product is less safe than a reasonable consumer would expect. If a smoke detector has a 3 percent failure rate, and the average consumer has no way of anticipating that danger, effective cautions must be included, though the design may be defective anyway.

Many other states use a *risk-utility test*. Here, a court must weigh the benefits for society against the dangers that the product poses. Principal factors in the risk-utility test include:

- The *value* of the product,
- The *gravity*, or *seriousness*, of the danger,
- The *likelihood* that such danger will occur,
- The mechanical feasibility of a *safer alternative* design, and
- The *adverse consequences* of an alternative design.

EXAM Strategy

Question: Warm, Inc. sells large, portable space heaters for industrial use. Warm sells Little Factory a unit and installs it. The sales contract states, "This heating unit is sold as is. There are no warranties, express or implied." On the third night the unit is used, it causes a fire and burns down the factory. Little sues Warm. At trial, the evidence indicates that a defect in the unit caused the fire, but also that this was unprecedented at Warm. The company employed more than the usual number of quality inspectors, and its safety record was the best in the entire industry. Discuss the effect of the sales contract and Warm's safety record. Predict who will win.

Strategy: The question raises three separate issues: warranty (the disclaimer), negligence (the safety record), and strict liability (the defect). What language most effectively disclaims warranties? What must a plaintiff prove to win a negligence case? To prove a strict liability case?

Result: A company may disclaim almost all warranties by stating the product is sold "as is," especially when selling to a corporate buyer. Warm's disclaimer is effective. The company's safety record is so good that there seems to be no case for negligence. However, Little Factory still wins its lawsuit. The product was unreasonably dangerous to the user. Warm was in the business of selling such heaters and installed the heater itself. In a strict liability case, Warm's safety efforts will not save it.

Chapter Conclusion

Negligence issues necessarily remain in flux, based on changing social values and concerns. A working knowledge of these issues and pitfalls can help everyone—business executive and ordinary citizen alike.

EXAM REVIEW

1. **ELEMENTS OF NEGLIGENCE**   The five elements of negligence are duty of due care, breach, factual causation, proximate causation, and damages.

2. **DUTY**   If the defendant could foresee that misconduct would injure a particular person, he probably has a duty to her.

3. **LANDOWNER'S LIABILITY**   In most states, a landowner's duty of due care is lowest to trespassers; higher to a licensee (anyone on the land for her own purposes but with the owner's permission); and highest of all to an invitee (someone on the property by right).

4. **BREACH**   A defendant breaches by failing to meet his duty of care.

5. **FACTUAL CAUSE**   If an event physically led to the ultimate harm, it is the factual cause.

6. **PROXIMATE CAUSE**   For the defendant to be liable, the type of harm must have been reasonably foreseeable.

7. **DAMAGES**   The plaintiff must persuade the court that he has suffered a harm that is genuine, not speculative.

8. **CONTRIBUTORY AND COMPARATIVE NEGLIGENCE**   In a contributory negligence state, a plaintiff who is even slightly responsible for his own injury recovers nothing; in a comparative negligence state, the jury may apportion liability between plaintiff and defendant.

EXAM Strategy

Question: There is a collision between cars driven by Candy and Zeke. The evidence is that Candy is about 25 percent responsible, for failing to stop quickly enough, and Zeke about 75 percent responsible, for making a dangerous turn. Candy is most likely to win:

(a) A lawsuit for battery.

(b) A lawsuit for negligence, in a comparative negligence state.

(c) A lawsuit for negligence, in a contributory negligence state.

(d) A lawsuit for strict liability.

(e) A lawsuit for assault.

Strategy: Battery and assault are intentional torts, which are irrelevant in a typical car accident. Are such collisions strict liability cases? No; therefore, the answer must be either (b) or (c). Apply the distinction between comparative and contributory negligence to the evidence here. (See the "Result" at the end of this section.)

9. **STRICT LIABILITY** A defendant is strictly liable for harm caused by an ultrahazardous activity or a defective product. Ultrahazardous activities include using harmful chemicals, blasting, and keeping wild animals. Strict liability means that if the defendant's conduct led to the harm, the defendant is liable, even if she exercises extraordinary care.

10. **PRODUCT LIABILITY** Product liability may arise in various ways:

- A seller will be liable if her conduct is not that of a reasonable person.

- A seller may be strictly liable for a defective product that reaches the user without substantial change.

EXAM Strategy

Question: Marko owned a cat and allowed it to roam freely outside. In the three years he had owned the pet, the animal had never bitten anyone. The cat entered Romi's garage. When Romi attempted to move it outside, the cat bit her. Romi underwent four surgeries, was fitted with a plastic finger joint, and spent more than $39,000 on medical bills. She sued Marko, claiming both strict liability and ordinary negligence. Assume that state law allows a domestic cat to roam freely. Evaluate both of Romi's claims.

Strategy: Negligence requires proof that the defendant breached a duty to the plaintiff by behaving unreasonably and that the resulting harm was foreseeable. Was it? When would harm by a domestic cat be foreseeable? A defendant can be strictly liable for keeping a wild animal. Apply that rule as well. (See the "Result" at the end of this section.)

8. Result: In a contributory negligence state, a plaintiff who is even 1 percent responsible for the harm loses. Candy was 25 percent responsible. She can win only in a comparative negligence state.

10. Result: If Marko's cat had bitten or attacked people in the past, this harm was foreseeable and Marko is liable. If the cat had never done so, and state law allows domestic animals to roam, Romi probably loses her suit for negligence. Her strict liability case definitely fails: A housecat is not a wild animal.

MATCHING QUESTIONS

Match the following terms with their definitions:

___A. Breach

___B. Strict liability

___C. Compensatory damages

___D. Negligence

___E. Invitee

1. Money awarded to an injured plaintiff

2. Someone who has a legal right to enter upon land

3. A defendant's failure to perform a legal duty

4. A tort in which an injury or loss is caused accidentally

5. Legal responsibility that comes from performing ultrahazardous acts

TRUE/FALSE QUESTIONS

Circle true or false:

1. T F There are five elements in a negligence case, and a plaintiff wins who proves at least three of them.

2. T F Max, a 19-year-old sophomore, gets drunk at a fraternity party and then causes a serious car accident. Max can be found liable and so can the fraternity.

3. T F Some states are comparative negligence states, but the majority are contributory negligence states.

4. T F A landowner might be liable if a dinner guest fell on a broken porch step, but not liable if a trespasser fell on the same place.

5. T F A defendant can be liable for negligence even if he never intended to cause harm.

6. T F When Ms. Palsgraf sued the railroad, the court found that the railroad should have foreseen what might go wrong.

7. T F Under strict liability, an injured consumer could potentially recover damages from the product's manufacturer and the retailer who sold the goods.

MULTIPLE-CHOICE QUESTIONS

1. In which case is a plaintiff most likely to sue based on strict liability?
   (a) Defamation
   (b) Injury caused on the job
   (c) Injury caused by a tiger that escapes from a zoo
   (d) Injury caused partially by the plaintiff and partially by the defendant
   (e) Injury caused by the defendant's careless driving

2. Martha signs up for a dinner cruise on a large commercial yacht. While the customers are eating dinner, the yacht bangs into another boat. Martha is thrown to the deck, breaking her wrist. She sues. At trial, which of these issues is likely to be the most important?

   (a) Whether the yacht company had permission to take Martha on the cruise

   (b) Whether the yacht company improperly restrained Martha

   (c) Whether Martha feared an imminent injury

   (d) Whether the yacht's captain did a reasonable job of driving the yacht

   (e) Whether Martha has filed similar suits in the past

3. Dolly, an architect, lives in Pennsylvania, which is a comparative negligence state. While she is inspecting a construction site for a large building she designed, she is injured when a worker drops a hammer from two stories up. Dolly was not wearing a safety helmet at the time. Dolly sues the construction company. The jury concludes that Dolly has suffered $100,000 in damages. The jury also believes that Dolly was 30 percent liable for the accident, and the construction company was 70 percent liable. Outcome?

   (a) Dolly wins nothing.

   (b) Dolly wins $30,000.

   (c) Dolly wins $50,000.

   (d) Dolly wins $70,000.

   (e) Dolly wins $100,000.

4. A taxi driver, hurrying to pick up a customer at the airport, races through a 20 mph hospital zone at 45 mph and strikes May, who is crossing the street in a pedestrian crosswalk. May sues the driver and the taxi company. What kind of suit is this?

   (a) Contract

   (b) Remedy

   (c) Negligence

   (d) Assault

   (e) Battery

5. *CPA QUESTION* To establish a cause of action based on strict liability in tort for personal injuries resulting from using a defective product, one of the elements that the plaintiff must prove is that the seller (defendant):

   (a) Failed to exercise due care.

   (b) Was in privity of contract with the plaintiff.

   (c) Defectively designed the product.

   (d) Was engaged in the business of selling the product.

CASE QUESTIONS

1. At approximately 7:50 p.m., bells at the train station rang and red lights flashed, signaling an express train's approach. David Harris walked onto the tracks, ignoring a yellow line painted on the platform instructing people to stand back. Two men shouted to Harris, warning him to get off the tracks. The train's engineer saw him too

late to stop the train, which was traveling at approximately 66 mph. The train struck and killed Harris as it passed through the station. Harris's widow sued the railroad, arguing that the railroad's negligence caused her husband's death. Evaluate the widow's argument.

2. A new truck, manufactured by General Motors Corp. (GMC), stalled in rush-hour traffic on a busy interstate highway because of a defective alternator, which caused a complete failure of the truck's electrical system. The driver stood nearby and waved traffic around his stalled truck. A panel truck approached the GMC truck. Immediately behind the panel truck, Davis was driving a Volkswagen fastback. Because of the panel truck, Davis was unable to see the stalled GMC truck. The panel truck swerved out of the way of the GMC truck, and Davis drove straight into it. The accident killed him. Davis's widow sued GMC. GMC moved for summary judgment, alleging (1) no duty to Davis; (2) no factual causation; and (3) no foreseeable harm. Comment on the three defenses that GMC has raised.

3. Randy works for a vending machine company. One morning, he fills up a vending machine that is on the third floor of an office building. Later that day, Mark buys a can of Pepsi from that machine. He takes the full can to a nearby balcony and drops it three floors onto Carl, a coworker who recently started dating Mark's ex-girlfriend. Carl falls unconscious. Is Randy a cause in fact of Carl's injury? Is he a proximate cause? What about Mark?

4. **ETHICS** Koby, age 16, works after school at FastFood from 4 p.m. until 11 p.m. On Friday night, the restaurant manager sees that Koby is exhausted, but insists that he remain until 4:30 a.m., cleaning up, then demands that he work Saturday morning from 8 a.m. until 4 p.m. On Saturday afternoon, as Koby drives home, he falls asleep at the wheel and causes a fatal car accident. Should FastFood be liable? What important values are involved in this issue?

5. Ryder leased a truck to Florida Food Service; Powers, an employee, drove it to make deliveries. He noticed that the door strap used to close the rear door was frayed, and he asked Ryder to fix it. Ryder failed to do so in spite of numerous requests. The strap broke, and Powers replaced it with a nylon rope. Later, when Powers was attempting to close the rear door, the nylon rope broke and he fell, sustaining severe injuries to his neck and back. He sued Ryder. The trial court found that Powers's attachment of the replacement rope was a superseding cause, relieving Ryder of any liability, and granted summary judgment for Ryder. Powers appealed. How should the appellate court rule?

DISCUSSION QUESTIONS

1. Imagine an undefeated high school football team on which the average lineman weighs 300 pounds. Also, imagine an 0–10 team on which the average lineman weighs 170 pounds. The undefeated team sets out to hit as hard as they can on every play and to run up the score as much as possible. Before the game is over, 11 players from the lesser team have been carried off the field with significant injuries. All injuries were the result of "clean hits"—none of the plays resulted in a penalty. Even late in the game, when the score is 70–0, the undefeated team continues to deliver devastating hits that are far beyond what would be required to tackle and block. The assumption of the risk doctrine exempts the undefeated team from liability. Is this reasonable?

2. Should the law hold landowners to different standards of care for trespassers, social guests, and invitees? Or do the few states that say, "Just always be reasonable" have a better rule?

3. Are strict liability rules fair? Someone has to dispose of chemicals. Someone has to use dynamite if road projects are to be completed. Is it fair to say to those companies, "You are responsible for all harm caused by your activities, even if you are as careful as you can possibly be?"

4. Imagine you are eating at a fast food restaurant when your tooth suddenly and painfully cracks as a result of a piece of bone in your hamburger. Would you sue the restaurant? Why or why not? Would society be better off if lawsuits over such injuries were difficult to win?

5. People who serve alcohol to others take a risk. In some circumstances, they can be held legally responsible for the actions of the people they serve. Is this fair? Should an intoxicated person be the only one liable if harm results? If not, in what specific circumstances is it fair to stretch liability to other people?

CHAPTER 9

CYBERLAW AND PRIVACY

People post all kinds of information on Facebook. And only one thing is certain: No one can be sure where it will go and who will see it.

Just ask Chelsea Chaney: One minute she was goofing around on a family vacation and the next thing she knew, a picture of her in a bikini was part of a PowerPoint presentation to all the students at her high school … and their families. Conveniently, the audience also received copies of the presentation to take home.

Who would do such a cruel thing? A bully? A mean girl? No: It was Curtis Cearley, her high school's technology director. And he was trying to be helpful. When putting together a talk on the dangers of social media, he discovered Chaney's Facebook page, with a picture of her in a red bikini posing with a life-size cutout of rapper Snoop Dogg. Chaney's Facebook settings only allowed her "friends" and "friends of friends" to view her page. But Chaney did not realize that school administrators could be "friends of friends." With "friends" like that, who needs enemies?

On the slide with Chaney's photo was a caption that said, "Once it's there—It's there to stay." In the context of his talk, the implication was clear: Keep your boozy, sexy images to yourself because they may cause embarrassment and grief.

And Cearley was right about one thing: Chaney was absolutely humiliated. Was there anything she could do?

© biletskiy/Shutterstock.com

> **Keep your boozy, sexy images to yourself because they may cause embarrassment and grief.**

The Internet and the World Wide Web comprise one of the great technological developments of modern times. They have brought change to every aspect of our lives—how we do business, buy things, apply for jobs, keep in touch, obtain news, campaign for election, make new friends, and even start revolutions.

This chapter focuses on the business law issues that are unique to the digital world. We discuss three main topics: (1) regulation of the Internet itself (including net neutrality and user-generated content); (2) consumer protection; and (3) privacy in the digital world.

9-1 REGULATION OF THE INTERNET

The "Internet," a term derived from "interconnected network," began in the 1960s as a project to link military contractors and universities. Today, it is a giant network that connects smaller groups of linked computer networks. The World Wide Web, a subnetwork of the Internet, is a decentralized collection of documents containing text, pictures, and sound. Users can move from document to document using links that form a "web" of information.

9-1a Net Neutrality

Internet service providers (ISPs) are companies that connect customers to the Internet. Some customers require more bandwidth than others: It takes much more capacity to watch movies and TV shows than to shop or download books or photos.

ISPs would like to have the option of treating high-capacity users differently—either charging them more or slowing their access to the Internet. But some people worry that ISPs might use access as a way of controlling content. They worry that an ISP like Verizon might, for example, limit access to the USA Today website if it wanted to spike traffic to its own news website, or it might degrade the quality of the connection to Bing if a competitor like Google paid for better access.

The Telecommunications Act of 1996 grants the Federal Communications Commission (FCC) the right to regulate broadband infrastructure. This agency adopted a policy of **net neutrality**: the principle that all information flows on the Internet must be treated equally. Thus, it prohibited ISPs from charging users different fees or providing slower speeds.

Net neutrality is highly controversial. Both those in favor and those opposed argue the same thing: that if their side wins, consumers and innovation will benefit. ISPs also argue that they should be able to control Internet traffic because some websites, like those that deliver telemedicine or emergency services, deserve priority access. As of this writing, courts have held that the FCC does have the right to regulate Internet access but cannot enforce net neutrality until it first rewrites some of its rules. This process will not be quick, easy, or certain, and any change will certainly be challenged in the courts. Stay tuned.

9-1b Regulation of User-Generated Content

User-generated content is information created by end users and shared publicly through the Web. It has changed our lives and our businesses: Customer reviews make shopping easier; wikis help us collaborate; blogs give us a new perspective; and social media keeps us connected. But as Chelsea Chaney (and many of us) have learned, there is a downside to all this information. One role of cyberlaw is to prevent harm.

Internet service providers (ISPs)
Companies like Verizon and Comcast that connect users to the Internet

Net neutrality
The principle that all information flows on the Internet must receive equal treatment

User-generated content
Any content created and made publicly available by end users

The First Amendment

How would you like to be called a cockroach, megascumbag, and crook in front of thousands of people? Or be accused of having a fake medical degree, fat thighs, and poor hygiene? **The First Amendment to the Constitution protects free speech,** and that includes these postings—and worse—that have appeared on Internet message boards and blogs. As upsetting as they may be, they are protected as free speech under the First Amendment so long as the poster is not violating some other law.

In the following case, a teacher received hostile emails. Should the First Amendment protect the anonymous person who sent them?

You be the Judge

JUZWIAK V. JOHN/JANE DOE
415 N.J. Super. 442
Superior Court of New Jersey, Appellate Division, 2010

Facts: Juzwiak was a teacher at Hightstown High School in New Jersey. He received three emails from someone who signed as "Josh." The teacher did not know anyone of that name. These emails said:

1. Subject line: "Hopefully you will be gone permanently"

   Text: "We are all praying for that. Josh"

2. Subject line: "I hear Friday is 'D' day for you"

   Text: "I certainly hope so. You don't deserve to be allowed to teach anymore. Not just in Hightstown but anywhere. If Hightstown bids you farewell I will make it my lifes [sic] work to ensure that wherever you look for work, they know what you have done."

3. Subject line: "Mr. Juzwiak in the Hightstown/East Windsor School System."

   Text: It has been brought to my attention and I am sure many of you know that Mr. J is reapplying for his position as a teacher in this town. It has further been pointed out that certain people are soliciting supporters for him. This is tantamount to supporting the devil himself. I am not asking anyone to speak out against Mr. J but I urge you to then be silent as we can not continue to allow the children of this school system nor the parents to be subjected to his evil ways. Thank you. Josh

It seems that this third email was sent to other people, but it was not clear to whom.

Juzwiak alerted the police, but they took no action. Because Juzwiak did not know who "Josh" was, he filed a complaint against John/Jane Doe, seeking damages for intentional infliction of emotional distress. As part of the lawsuit, he served a subpoena on Yahoo!, asking it to reveal "Josh's" identity. When Yahoo notified "Josh" of the lawsuit, he asked the court not to issue the subpoena.

In a court hearing, Juzwiak testified that the threatening emails had severely disrupted his life, causing deep depression, insomnia, and physical problems.

When the trial court refused to issue the subpoena against Yahoo!, Juzwiak appealed.

You Be the Judge: *Should the trial court have issued the subpoena?*

Argument for Juzwiak: These emails are not entitled to First Amendment protection. First of all, they contained death threats: "Hopefully you will be gone permanently" and "I hear Friday is 'D' day for you." Juzwiak was frightened enough to call the police. He suffered physical and emotional harm.

Furthermore, the emails constituted intentional infliction of emotional distress. They were extreme and outrageous conduct designed to cause harm. They achieved their goal.

In balancing the rights in this case, why would the court protect "Josh," who has deliberately caused harm, rather than the innocent teacher?

Argument for "Josh": These emails are protected free speech under the Constitution. Nothing in them was a realistic threat to the teacher's safety. "Hopefully you will be gone permanently" could easily mean "hope you will move out of town." Juzwiak reported these emails to the police, but they did nothing. Presumably they would have done something if there was a real threat.

Nor did these emails constitute an intentional infliction of emotional distress. They were not so extreme and outrageous. "Josh" did not accuse Juzwiak of vile or criminal acts. The language was not obscene or profane. In short, if Juzwiak is going to teach high school, he needs to develop a thicker skin and a better sense of humor.

The Communications Decency Act of 1996

The Internet is an enormously powerful tool for disseminating information. But what if some of this information happens to be false or in violation of our privacy rights? Is an ISP liable for transmitting it to the world?

Congress reasoned that if ISPs faced the threat of a lawsuit for every problematic posting, the companies would severely restrict content, and the development of the Internet. To prevent this result, Congress passed the **Communications Decency Act of 1996 (CDA)**, which created broad immunity for ISPs and websites.

Under the CDA, end users and anyone who simply provides a neutral forum for information (such as ISPs and website operators), are not liable for content that is provided by someone else. Only content providers are liable. But to avoid liability, the ISP or website must not write, edit, encourage, or influence the content.

The following case lays out the arguments in favor of the CDA, but also illustrates some of the costs of the statute (and of the Internet).

Communications Decency Act of 1996 (CDA)

Provides ISPs and websites immunity from liability when information was provided by an end user

CARAFANO v. METROSPLASH.COM, INC.

339 F.3d 1119
United States Court of Appeals for the Ninth Circuit, 2003

CASE SUMMARY

Facts: Matchmaker.com is an Internet dating service that permits members to post their profiles and to view the profiles of other members. Matchmaker reviews photos for impropriety before posting them but does not examine the profiles themselves.

Christianne Carafano is an actor who uses the stage name Chase Masterson. She had appeared in numerous films and television shows, such as *General Hospital*. Without her knowledge, someone in Berlin posted a fake profile of her in the Los Angeles section of Matchmaker. In answer to the question "Main source of current events?" the person posting the profile put "*Playboy Playgirl*" and for "Why did you call?" responded "Looking for a one-night stand." In addition, the essays indicated that she was looking for a "hard and dominant" man with "a strong sexual appetite" and that she "liked sort of being controlled by a man, in and out of bed." Pictures of the actor, taken off the Internet, were included with the profile. The profile also provided her home address and

an email address, which, when contacted, produced an automatic email reply stating, "You think you are the right one? Proof it !!" [*sic*], and providing Carafano's home address and telephone number.

Unaware of the improper posting, Carafano began receiving sexually explicit messages and threats at her home. Feeling unsafe, Carafano and her son moved out of their home.

When Carafano's assistant learned of the false profile, she contacted Matchmaker on Carafano's behalf, demanding that the profile be removed immediately. The Matchmaker representative refused to remove it then because the assistant herself had not posted it, but two days later, the company blocked the profile from public view, and then deleted it soon after.

Carafano filed suit against Matchmaker alleging invasion of privacy and negligence. Matchmaker argued that it was immune under the CDA, but the district court disagreed on the grounds that the company provided part of the profile content.

Issue: *Does the CDA protect Matchmaker from liability?*

Decision: Matchmaker is not liable.

Reasoning: Under the CDA, Internet publishers are not liable for false or defamatory material if someone else provided the information. In this way, Internet publishers are different from print, television, and radio publishers.

Interactive computer services have millions of users. It would be impossible for these services to screen each of their millions of postings. If they were liable for content, they might choose to severely limit the number and type of messages. To avoid any restriction on free speech, Congress chose to protect computer services from liability if someone else provided the content.

The fact that some of the content in Carafano's fake profile was provided in response to Matchmaker's questionnaire does not make the company liable. The answers to the questions were provided exclusively by the user. No profile has any content until a user actively creates it. In this case, Carafano's home address and the email address that revealed her phone number were transmitted unaltered to profile viewers. Thus, Matchmaker did not play a significant role in creating, developing, or transforming the relevant information.

Despite the serious and utterly deplorable consequences in this case, Matchmaker cannot be sued under the CDA.

Ethics   JuicyCampus.com was a website where college students could anonymously gossip about their schools. To encourage users to "dish dirt," the site promised total anonymity: It did not require a login or username; it assured its users that it was impossible "for anyone to find out who you are and where you are located." The site also instructed users on how to download IP-cloaking software to further ensure anonymity. Most of the Juicy Campus posts were more than just juicy: They ranged from shocking accusations to harassment and revenge. These rumors tarnished reputations, hurt feelings, and tore apart communities. Whether or not it is legally liable, does JuicyCampus.com have an ethical duty to its users? What Life Principles are at stake?

9-2 CONSUMER PROTECTION

9-2a The FTC Act

The Federal Trade Commission Act authorizes the Federal Trade Commission (FTC) to protect consumers. **Section 5 of the FTC Act prohibits unfair and deceptive acts or practices.** The FTC applies this statute to online privacy policies. It does not require websites to have a privacy policy, but if they do have one, they must comply with it, and it cannot be deceptive.

The FTC brought action against Twitter after hackers gained access to its users' accounts through its administrative system. Twitter had allowed any employee access to its system, which was protected by an easy-to-guess password (1234, maybe?). The hackers reset passwords and sent fake tweets. For example, an unauthorized person sent a tweet from Barack Obama's Twitter account offering free gasoline to users who took an Internet poll (which seems benign compared with what the hacker could have done). The FTC found that Twitter had engaged in deceptive acts because its faulty security violated the company's promise to users that it would protect their information from unauthorized access. As part of the settlement, Twitter agreed to strengthen its security practices.

One more FTC issue: Imagine that you are reading a blog that favorably reviews a new Microsoft product. Before clicking on the Buy button, would you want to know that Microsoft had given the blogger a free computer? The FTC thinks you should. Under FTC rules, bloggers face fines as high as $1,000 if they do not disclose all compensation they receive (either in cash or free products) for writing product reviews. Moreover, celebrities must disclose their relationships with advertisers when making endorsements outside of traditional ads, such as on talk shows or in social media.

9-2b Spam

Spam is officially known as *unsolicited commercial email (UCE)* or *unsolicited bulk email (UBE)*. Whatever it is called, it is one of the most annoying aspects of email. It has been estimated that 90 percent of email is spam. And roughly half of these messages were fraudulent—either in content (promoting a scam) or in packaging (the headers or return address are false). Aside from the annoyance factor, bulk email adds to the cost of connecting to the Internet as ISPs increase server capacity to handle the millions of spam emails.

Spam
Unsolicited commercial email

The Controlling the Assault of Non-Solicited Pornography and Marketing Act (CAN-SPAM) is a federal statute that regulates spam, but does not prohibit it. This statute applies to virtually all promotional emails, whether or not the sender has a preexisting relationship with the recipient. **Under this statute, commercial email:**

- May not have deceptive headings (From, To, Reply To, Subject),

- Must offer an opt-out system permitting the recipient to unsubscribe (and must honor those requests promptly),

- Must clearly indicate that the email is an advertisement,

- Must provide a valid physical return address (not a post office box), and

- Must clearly indicate the nature of pornographic messages.

A company can avoid these requirements by obtaining advance permission from the recipients.

CAN-SPAM seems to have had little impact on the quantity of spam (although it has made opt-out provisions more common in legitimate commercial emails). More effective have been the tools developed by online security firms and governments that prevent as much as 98 percent of spam from reaching your email inbox.

EXAM Strategy

Question: Cruise.com operated a website selling cruise vacations. It sent unsolicited email advertisements—dubbed "E-deals"—to prospective customers. Eleven of these "E-deals" went to **inbox@webguy.net**. Each message offered the recipient an opportunity to be removed from the mailing list by clicking on a line of text or by writing to a specific postal address. Has Cruise.com violated the CAN-SPAM Act?

Strategy: Remember that this Act does not prohibit all unsolicited emails.

Result: Cruise.com was not in violation because it offered the recipients a way to unsubscribe. Also, it provided a valid physical return address.

9-3 PRIVACY IN A DIGITAL WORLD

The Internet has vastly increased our ability to communicate quickly and widely. But it also provides a very large window through which the government, employers, businesses, and other invisible audiences can find out more than they should about you and your money, habits, beliefs, and health—so a discussion of privacy is more important than ever.

Issues of privacy occur in many areas of the law including, in this book, crime (in Chapter 6) and employment law (Chapter 18). In this chapter we focus on privacy in cyberspace, including laws specifically tailored to the Internet and others that have been adapted for this use.

9-3a How We Lose Our Privacy Online

Sometimes we voluntarily give up our privacy without considering the consequences; in other cases it is taken from us without our knowledge.

Social Media

The ability to share our opinions, relationship status, and location on social media sites like Facebook, Twitter, and Instagram has weakened our concept of privacy. Much information that, in the past, would have been a closely guarded secret, is now widely shared.

But when someone collects and shares personal information without the knowledge or consent of its subject, much harm can ensue. At its most extreme, people have used social media to harass, bully, and exact revenge on their victims. Malicious postings can cause physical and emotional damage, harm employment prospects, ruin relationships—and have even driven people to suicide.

Data Mining and Behavioral Marketing

Consumers enter the most personal data—credit card numbers, bank accounts, lists of friends, medical information, product preferences—on the Internet, where it is accessed much more extensively than they may realize. The 50 most popular websites in America (which account for 40 percent of all page views) install thousands of **tracking tools** on the computers of people who visit their sites. These tools not only collect data on *all* the websites someone visits, they also record keystrokes to keep track of whatever information the consumer has entered online.

Data mining also leads to **behavioral marketing, or behavioral targeting**. Behavioral marketing is a widespread practice that involves inferring needs and preferences from a consumer's online behavior and then targeting related advertisements to them. If you look at a sweater on the J. Crew website, but do not buy it, you may find that you are repeatedly shown ads for it—and for other items that people who bought that sweater also purchased.

The most troubling aspect of massive information collection is that consumers are often unaware of who has access to what personal information, how it is being used, and with what consequences. One Gmail user reported receiving ads for funeral services after emailing family members about his mother's fatal illness.

In short, Internet users are inadvertently providing intensely personal data to unknown people for unknown uses.

Tracking tools
A computer program that tracks information about Internet users

Behavioral marketing, or behavioral targeting
The practice of aiming certain advertisements at consumers based on their online behavior

Ethics Chitika, Inc., provided online tracking tools on websites. When consumers clicked the "opt-out" button, indicating that they did not want to be tracked, they were not—for 10 days. After that, the software would resume tracking. Is there a legal problem with Chitika's system? An ethical problem? What Life Principles were operating here?

Workplace Privacy

Employers often have access to a wealth of online information about job applicants. And once applicants are hired, technology allows employers to monitor what they do and say on the job and even in their spare time.

Critics of privacy say that it is outdated—or even overrated—and point to the fact that if consumers really cared about it, they would share less information online. Facebook founder Mark Zuckerberg has said that privacy is an outdated social norm.

But people who care about privacy should be worried. Without significant law and oversight, it could well be obliterated.

9-3b Regulation of Online Privacy

The following sections discuss the most important laws and regulations that protect online privacy.

The Fourth Amendment

The Fourth Amendment to the Constitution prohibits unreasonable searches and seizures by the government. As we saw in Chapter 6 on crime, the Fourth Amendment protects the privacy rights of criminal defendants. But these same protections also extend to the relationship between the government and certain of its citizens, including government workers and public school students.

In enforcing this provision of the Constitution, the courts ask whether a person had a reasonable expectation of privacy. **The two requirements for establishing a "reasonable expectation of privacy" are:**

1. **The person had an actual, subjective expectation of privacy.**

2. **Society accepts the person's expectation of privacy as reasonable.**

Courts have generally held that employees do not have a reasonable expectation of privacy in the workplace, especially if using hardware provided by the employer, or if the employee handbook says they may be monitored. When a police officer persistently exceeded his monthly quota of SMS messages, his superior reviewed his texts to determine if they were work-related. It turned out that they were mostly sexts (sexual texts) sent to his mistress. After the officer was disciplined, he filed suit alleging that the department had violated his Fourth Amendment rights. The Supreme Court held that a government employer has the right to review its employee's electronic communications for a work-related purpose.

In the following case from the chapter opener, a bikini-clad teenager claimed she had a reasonable expectation of privacy in her Facebook picture. (Sexts. Bikinis. Who said privacy is boring?)

The Fourth Amendment
Prohibits unreasonable searches and seizures of individuals by the government

---

CHELSEA CHANEY V. FAYETTE COUNTY PUBLIC SCHOOL DISTRICT

2013 U.S. Dist. LEXIS 143030; 2013 WL 5486829
U.S. District Court for the Northern District of Georgia, 2013

CASE SUMMARY

Facts: Review the facts in the chapter opener.

Chelsea Chaney sued, claiming that Cearley and the school district violated her constitutional right to privacy under the Fourth Amendment. The district filed a motion to dismiss.

Issue: *Did Chaney have a reasonable expectation of privacy in her bikini Facebook picture?*

Decision: No, Chaney did not have a reasonable expectation of privacy.

Reasoning: To establish a reasonable expectation of privacy, a person must show: (1) that she had a subjective expectation of privacy and (2) that society is willing to recognize her expectation as legitimate.

Chaney clearly had a subjective expectation of privacy in her Facebook photos—she actually *thought* they were private. But she cannot show that her expectation was reasonable or legitimate.

A person has no legitimate expectation of privacy in information she voluntarily shares. Chaney argues that, by limiting access to "friends and friends of friends" she had intended to keep her page private. But that setting does not ensure privacy because she had no control over her Facebook friends' friends, who may be total strangers and number in the hundreds, if not thousands.

When she posted the picture, Chaney surrendered any reasonable expectation of privacy. She cannot show that society would be willing to recognize her expectation of privacy as legitimate.

Although the Fourth Amendment does not govern private-sector employers, the reasonable expectation of privacy analysis is a guide to judges and lawmakers in every area of privacy law, including the privacy torts, which we discuss next.

Privacy Torts

In 1890, an innovative technology called "photography" allowed the press to meddle in people's affairs in a new way. This changing society inspired later-to-be Supreme Court justice Louis Brandeis to call for the creation of a new right protecting an individual's personal space from intrusion and disclosure. Inspired by his writing, courts created two new torts to protect against violations of privacy: public disclosure of private facts and intrusion.

Public disclosure of private facts

A civil cause of action that may apply when an individual discloses another's private information without consent

Public Disclosure of Private Facts. The tort of public disclosure of private facts applies when people spill the beans: It prohibits the unjustifiable revelation of truthful, but secret, information. **The public disclosure tort requires the plaintiff to show all of the following:**

- **The defendant made public disclosure.** The defendant must have divulged the secret information to a number of people, not just one other person.

- **The disclosed facts had been private.** The person seeking privacy must prove that she had a reasonable expectation of privacy in the information. But courts have held that people cannot have a reasonable expectation of privacy in information that is generally visible or available.

- **The facts were not of legitimate concern to the public.** The First Amendment protects free speech and, therefore, sometimes undermines privacy rights. To protect their privacy, plaintiffs must prove that the revealed secret was not of public concern, that is, that the public was not entitled to know about it.

- **The disclosure is highly offensive to a reasonable person.** Privacy is somewhat subjective. One person's secret is another's reality show. For this reason, defendants must prove that most reasonable people would be offended if the secret was revealed.

As Calvin Green lay dying of a gunshot wound, his mother, Laura, spoke to him in his hospital room, telling him how much she loved him. Reporters from the *Chicago Tribune* were in the hospital reporting on a story about Chicago's homicide rate. They overheard Laura's words to Calvin, which they then printed in the newspaper. When Laura sued, the court ruled that she had stated a claim under the public disclosure tort because the newspaper had (1) printed the information in the newspaper (2) Calvin's hospital room had been private, (3) the facts were not of legitimate concern to the public, and (4) the disclosure of information about this extraordinarily painful incident was highly offensive.

EXAM Strategy

Question: A group of college bullies made a flyer with a fellow student's picture, email address, and phone number—all information found on the university's website. The flyer, posted all around the university campus and online, falsely advertised that he was seeking a male romantic partner. The humiliated victim sued the bullies for public disclosure of private facts—not his sexual orientation but his contact information. What result?

Strategy: Remember that defendants are liable only if they have disclosed secret information.

Result: The bullies committed a horrible act, but they are not liable under the public disclosure tort. The victim's contact information and picture were accessible to all students and faculty via the university's website, so they were not private facts.

Intrusion.   **Intrusion into someone's private life is a tort if a reasonable person would find it offensive.** Peeping through someone's windows or wiretapping his telephone are obvious examples of intrusion. In a famous case involving a "paparazzo" photographer and Jacqueline Kennedy Onassis, the court found that the photographer had invaded her privacy by making a career out of photographing her. He had bribed doormen to gain access to hotels and restaurants she visited, had jumped out of bushes to photograph her young children, and had driven power boats dangerously close to her. The court ordered him to stop. Nine years later the paparazzo was found in contempt of court for again taking photographs too close to Ms. Onassis. He agreed to stop once and for all—in exchange for a suspended contempt sentence.

> **Intrusion**
> A civil cause of action that applies when a person intrudes on another's affairs or space in an offensive way

The tort of intrusion requires the plaintiff to show that the defendant (1) **intentionally intruded, physically or otherwise,** (2) **upon the solitude or seclusion of another or on his private affairs or concerns,** (3) **in a manner highly offensive to a reasonable person.**

In the following case, a nurse was offended when her supervisor snooped on her Facebook postings. But would her Facebook wall be strong enough to protect her privacy?

EHLING V. MONMOUTH-OCEAN HOSP. SERV. CORP.

872 F. Supp. 2d 369
United States District Court for the District of New Jersey, 2012

CASE SUMMARY

Facts: Deborah Ehling was a registered nurse and paramedic at the Monmouth-Ocean Hospital Service Corporation (MONOC). In reaction to a shooting, Ehling posted the following statement on her Facebook page, which limited access to just her "friends."

> An 88 yr old sociopath white supremacist opened fire in the Wash D.C. Holocaust Museum this morning and killed an innocent guard (leaving children). Other guards opened fire. The 88 yr old was shot. He survived. I blame the DC paramedics. I want to say 2 things to the DC medics.

1. WHAT WERE YOU THINKING? and 2. This was your opportunity to really make a difference! WTF!!!! And to the other guards go to target practice.

A hospital supervisor summoned one of Ehling's coworkers, who was her Facebook friend, into an office where she forced him to access his account so that she could view Ehling's post. The supervisor sent a copy of the posting to the boards that regulate nursing and paramedics in New Jersey with a letter saying that the hospital was concerned that this statement showed a disregard for patient safety.

She filed suit against MONOC, alleging intrusion. In her view, these letters were a malicious attempt to damage her reputation and possibly cause her to lose her license. She claimed that she had a reasonable expectation of privacy in her Facebook posting because her comment was disclosed to a limited number of people whom she had individually invited to view a restricted access web-page.

The hospital filed a motion to dismiss, arguing that Ehling did not have a reasonable expectation of privacy in her Facebook posting because the comment was disclosed to dozens of people, including coworkers.

Issue: *Did Ehling have a reasonable expectation of privacy in her Facebook posting?*

Decision: Yes, a jury could find that Ehling's expectation was reasonable.

Reasoning: To state a claim for intrusion, a plaintiff must demonstrate that the defendant intentionally invaded in a highly offensive way. Expectations of privacy are established by general social norms and must be objectively reasonable—a plaintiff's subjective belief that something is private is irrelevant.

There are few hard-and-fast rules for what constitutes a reasonable expectation of privacy. Some courts have held that it is reasonable to share a secret with a limited number of people if the recipients are unlikely to divulge it. Other courts have determined that sharing with just two coworkers invalidates any expectation of privacy.

Privacy determinations are made on a case-by-case basis, in light of the specific circumstances of each case. Here, Ehling stated a plausible claim for invasion of privacy. She actively took steps to protect her Facebook page from public viewing. Whether her expectation was reasonable is a question for the jury to decide.

Fair Information Practices

The FTC has drafted a Code of Fair Information Practices (FIPS) for the Internet. Note that FIPS are recommendations, not law. However, this code is often the basis for online privacy policies and has guided the creation of the statutes we will now discuss. **The core principles of the FIPS are:**

- **Notice/Awareness.** Notice should be given before any personal information is collected;

- **Choice/Consent.** People should be able to control the use and destination of their information;

- **Access/Participation.** People should have the ability to view, correct, or amend any personally identifiable record about them; and

- **Integrity/Security.** Information collectors must take reasonable precautions to ensure that the data they collect are accurate and secure.

Federal Privacy Statutes

In its early days, the Internet was often compared to the Wild West because it was a relatively lawless zone. Little by little, in response to growing concerns and online threats, lawmakers reacted, but in a piecemeal way. Instead of a single comprehensive data privacy law, the United States has a collection of federal privacy laws that apply to particular types of personal data. Diverse laws also apply to the way information is collected and from whom. We will focus on laws covering electronic communications, children, and spies.

Electronic Communications Privacy Act of 1986. The Electronic Communications Privacy Act of 1986 (ECPA) is a federal statute that prohibits unauthorized interception of, access to, or disclosure of wire and electronic communications. The definition of electronic communication includes email, cell phones, and social media. Violators are subject to both criminal and civil penalties. An action does not violate the ECPA if it is unintentional or if either party consents.

Under the ECPA:

- **Any intended recipient of an electronic communication has the right to disclose it.** Thus, if you sound off in an email to a friend about your boss, the (former) friend may legally forward that email to the boss or anyone else.

- **ISPs are generally prohibited from disclosing electronic messages to anyone other than the addressee,** unless this disclosure is necessary for the performance of their service or for the protection of their own rights or property.

- **An employer has the right to monitor workers' electronic communications if (1) the employee consents, (2) the monitoring occurs in the ordinary course of business, or (3) in the case of email, if the employer provides the computer system.**

Thus, an employer has the right to monitor electronic communication even if it does not relate to work activities. This monitoring may include an employee's social media activities. **But one thing employers cannot do is access an employee's social media profile by trickery or coercion.** As we saw earlier in the *Ehling* case, coercion may constitute an invasion of privacy. It may also violate the ECPA. Restaurant employee Brian Pietrylo created a password-protected MySpace group to vent about work-related topics. To gain access, the restaurant's managers coerced another employee into giving them her login information and password. After viewing his posts, the restaurant fired Pietrylo, who then accused the employer of violating the ECPA. Because the worker who provided her password did not act voluntarily, the court found that the employer had violated the ECPA.

The law is evolving, complex, and varies by state, so employees should err on the side of caution and remember that the law often does not protect their electronic lives from employer prying. **You should consider anything you publish on the Internet to be public.**

As for companies, it makes sense to establish policies providing that:

- Employees should never reveal their company's name on a personal blog or social media. Nor should they reveal confidential or proprietary information.

- Personal blogs should contain a disclaimer that "All postings are my opinion and not those of my employer, who has neither vetted nor approved them."

- Online behavior should never be offensive, impolite, or reflect badly on the employer.

Children's Online Privacy Protection Act of 1998. The Children's Online Privacy Protection Act of 1998 (COPPA) prohibits Internet operators from collecting information from children under 13 without parental permission. It also requires sites to disclose how they will use any information they acquire. Enforcement is in the hands of the FTC. Path Inc. had a mobile app that allowed users to create a daily journal and share it with friends. This app permitted children to register without parental permission. Each time users posted a "thought" on the app, they were invited to reveal their location through the geo-tracking feature as well as the names of friends who were with them. When challenged by the FTC, Path agreed to stop this practice and pay a fine of $800,000.

Foreign Intelligence Surveillance Act. Former National Security Agency contractor Edward Snowden set off an international furor when he leaked information revealing the extent of U.S. surveillance on everyone from world leaders to international charities and even U.S. citizens. Angela Merkel, chancellor of Germany and a U.S. ally, was furious to learn that the NSA had been listening in on her cell phone. Snowden reported that, as an NSA agent, he could, sitting at his desk "wiretap anyone, from you or your

Electronic Communications Privacy Act
The ECPA is a federal statute governing the privacy of wire and electronic communications.

The Children's Online Privacy Protection Act
COPPA is a federal statute protecting the privacy of children online.

Foreign Intelligence Surveillance Act
FISA is a federal statute governing domestic spying.

accountant, to a federal judge or even the president, if I had a personal email." According to Snowden, the U.S. government was reading emails, mapping cell phone locations, reviewing browser histories, and monitoring just about everything that anyone does online. Is there a law against this?

The Foreign Intelligence Surveillance Act (FISA) sets out the rules for the use of electronic surveillance to collect foreign intelligence (otherwise known as spying) within the United States. **FISA provides that:**

- To spy on people located in the United States who are communicating abroad, the government does not need a warrant, but it must obtain permission from a secret Foreign Intelligence Surveillance Court (FISC). To obtain this permission, the government need only demonstrate that the surveillance (1) targets "persons reasonably believed to be located outside the United States" and (2) seeks "foreign intelligence information." This standard gives the government broad powers to collect emails, phone calls, and other electronic communications between people in the United States and anyone abroad;

- Government agencies must delete irrelevant and personally identifying data before providing it to other agencies; and

- The government must notify defendants if the evidence being used against them in court was gathered in FISA surveillance.

Chapter Conclusion

The Internet is a thriving ecosystem of knowledge and communication. It can be used for great social benefit and innovation, but the Internet also presents challenges. Although the law rushes to address some of these challenges, technology usually wins the race. Many of the laws that apply to today's Internet were written in the time before cyberspace was part of our daily lives. Courts can apply some of these old laws in new ways, but as legislators and courts learn from experience, new laws will be needed.

EXAM REVIEW

1. **NET NEUTRALITY** The principle that all Internet content and traffic should receive equal treatment.

2. **THE FIRST AMENDMENT** The First Amendment to the Constitution protects speech on the Internet so long as the speech does not violate some other law.

3. **COMMUNICATIONS DECENCY ACT OF 1996 (CDA)** Under the CDA, ISPs and web hosts are not liable for information that is provided by someone else.

Question: Ton Cremers was the director of security at Amsterdam's famous Rijksmuseum and the operator of the Museum Security Network (the Network) website. Robert Smith, a handyman working for Ellen Batzel in North Carolina, sent an email to the Network alleging that Batzel was the granddaughter of Heinrich Himmler (one of Hitler's henchmen) and that she had art that Himmler had stolen. These allegations were completely untrue. Cremers posted Smith's email on the Network's website and sent it to the Network's subscribers. Cremers exercised some editorial discretion in choosing which emails to send to subscribers, generally omitting any that were unrelated to stolen art. Is Cremers liable to Batzel for the harm that this inaccurate information caused?

Strategy: Cremers is liable only if he is a content provider. (See the "Result" at the end of this section.)

4. **THE FTC ACT**   Section 5 of the FTC Act prohibits unfair and deceptive practices. The FTC does not require websites to have a privacy policy, but if they do have one, it cannot be deceptive and they must comply with it.

5. **THE CONTROLLING THE ASSAULT OF NON-SOLICITED PORNOGRAPHY AND MARKETING ACT (CAN-SPAM)**   CAN-SPAM is a federal statute that does not prohibit spam but instead regulates it. Under this statute, commercial email:

   - May not have deceptive headings (From, To, Reply To, Subject),

   - Must offer an opt-out system permitting the recipient to unsubscribe (and must honor those requests promptly),

   - Must clearly indicate that the email is an advertisement,

   - Must provide a valid physical return address (not a post office box), and

   - Must clearly indicate the nature of pornographic messages.

6. **THE FOURTH AMENDMENT**   The Fourth Amendment to the Constitution prohibits unreasonable searches and seizures by the government. This provision applies to computers.

7. **REASONABLE EXPECTATION OF PRIVACY**   There is a reasonable expectation of privacy if (1) the person had a subjective expectation of privacy and (2) society accepts that expectation as reasonable.

8. **PUBLIC DISCLOSURE OF PRIVATE FACTS**   It is a violation of tort law to disclose secret information if disclosure would be highly offensive to a reasonable person and the information is not of legitimate public concern.

9. **INTRUSION**   Intrusion into someone's private life is a tort if a reasonable person would find it offensive.

Question: Every time Dave logs on to his company computer, he clicks "I agree" to the firm's computer usage policy, which states that the employer can monitor everything he does online. On his lunch break, Dave logs on to his Facebook account from his company computer to upload some pictures from his weekend's activities. Can Dave's employer snoop?

Strategy: Does Dave have a subjective expectation of privacy? Given the circumstances, is Dave's expectation of privacy accepted by society? (See the "Result" at the end of this section.)

10. **THE FAIR INFORMATION PRACTICES (FIPS)**   The FIPs include: Notice/Awareness, Choice/Consent, Access/Participation, and Integrity/Security. Although the FIPs are not law, they have had great influence on privacy laws and policy.

11. **THE ELECTRONIC COMMUNICATIONS PRIVACY ACT OF 1986 (ECPA)**   THE ECPA is a federal statute that prohibits unauthorized interception or disclosure of wire and electronic communications. However, it permits an employer to monitor workers' electronic communications if (1) the employee consents, (2) the monitoring occurs in the ordinary course of business, or (3) the employer provides the computer system (in the case of email).

12. **THE CHILDREN'S ONLINE PRIVACY PROTECTION ACT OF 1998 (COPPA)**   COPPA prohibits Internet operators from collecting information from children under 13 without parental permission. It also requires sites to disclose how they will use any information they acquire.

13. **THE FOREIGN INTELLIGENCE SURVEILLANCE ACT (FISA)**   FISA provides the rules for the government's collection of foreign intelligence within the United States.

3. Result: The court found that Cremers was not liable under the CDA.

9. Result: Dave does not have a reasonable expectation of privacy on his work computer, even if he is on break and on his private Facebook page. He consented to employer surveillance when he logged in.

MATCHING QUESTIONS

Match the following terms with their definitions:

___A. ECPA

___B. Fourth Amendment to the
    Constitution

___C. FISA

___D. COPPA

___E. CDA

1. Regulates employers' access to employee email

2. Protects ISPs from liability for content that they
   did not create

3. Regulates collection of information from children

4. Prohibits unreasonable searches and seizures of
   computers

5. Regulates government spying

TRUE/FALSE QUESTIONS

Circle true or false:

1. T F The First Amendment to the Constitution protects bloggers who post insults about other people.

2. T F The government can never legally spy on communications involving U.S. citizens without a warrant.

3. T F The FTC requires websites to establish a privacy policy and then abide by it.

4. T F Any intended recipient of an email may forward it to whomever she wishes.

5. T F Employers can read employees' emails sent on work computers.

MULTIPLE-CHOICE QUESTIONS

1. The following agency is charged with the regulation of electronic communications:
   (a) National Security Agency
   (b) Federal Trade Commission
   (c) Federal Communications Commission
   (d) None of the above.

2. Because Blaine Blogger reviews movies on his blog, cinemas allow him in for free. Nellie Newspaper Reporter also gets free admission to movies.
   Blaine _____ disclose on his blog that he receives free tickets.
   Nellie _____ disclose in her articles that she receives free tickets.
   (a) must; must
   (b) need not; need not
   (c) must; need not
   (d) need not; must

3. An employer has the right to monitor workers' electronic communications if:

   (a) The employee consents.

   (b) The monitoring occurs in the ordinary course of business.

   (c) The employer provides the computer system.

   (d) All of the above

   (e) None of the above

4. Spiro Spammer sends millions of emails a day asking people to donate to his college tuition fund. Oddly enough, many people do. Everything in the emails is accurate (including his 1.9 GPA). Which of the following statements is true?

   (a) Spiro has violated the CAN-SPAM Act because he has sent unsolicited commercial emails.

   (b) Spiro has violated the CAN-SPAM Act if he has not offered recipients an opportunity to unsubscribe.

   (c) Spiro has violated the CAN-SPAM Act because he is asking for money.

   (d) Spiro has violated the CAN-SPAM Act unless the recipients have granted permission to him to send these emails.

5. Sushila suspects that her boyfriend is being unfaithful. While he is asleep, she takes his iPod out from under his pillow and goes through all his playlists. Then she finds what she has been looking for: Plum's Playlist. It is full of romantic songs. Sushila sends Plum an email that says, "You are the most evil person in the universe!" Which law has Sushila violated?

   (a) The First Amendment

   (b) The CDA

   (c) The ECPA

   (d) The CFAA

   (e) None

CASE QUESTIONS

1. **ETHICS** Facebook implemented a new policy on gun sales: It now removes certain posts about guns, notifies gun sellers of gun laws, and limits the visibility of gun posts to users over 18. Proponents contend that Facebook's actions go a long way toward ending illegal firearms sales over social media. But critics worry that Facebook is meddling in legitimate businesses—and a contentious political issue. Is Facebook's gun policy susceptible to legal challenge? Does Facebook have a duty to its users? To its advertisers? To society? What is that duty?

2. Dr. Norman Scott was the head of the orthopedics department at a hospital. His contract with the hospital provided for $14 million in severance pay if he was fired without cause. When the hospital fired him, he filed suit seeking his $14 million. He used the hospital's email system to send emails to his lawyer. The hospital notified him that it had copies of these emails, which it planned to read. He said that, because the emails were protected by the attorney-client privilege, the hospital did not have this right. Could Scott's former employer read his emails?

3. Over the course of 10 months, Joseph Melle sent more than 60 million unsolicited email advertisements to AOL members. What charges could be brought against him? Would you need more information before deciding?

4. **Roommates.com** operated a website designed to match people renting spare rooms with those looking for a place to live. Before subscribers could search listings or post housing opportunities on Roommate's website, they had to create profiles, a process that required them to answer a series of questions that included the subscriber's sex, sexual orientation, and whether he would bring children to a household. The site also encouraged subscribers to provide "Additional Comments," describing themselves and their desired roommate in an open-ended essay. Here are some typical ads:

   - "I am not looking for Muslims."

   - "Not acceptable: freaks, geeks, prostitutes (male or female), druggies, pet cobras, drama queens, or mortgage brokers."

   - "Must be a black gay male!"

   - We are 3 Christian females who Love our Lord Jesus Christ…. We have weekly bible studies and bi-weekly times of fellowship."

   Many of the ads violated the Fair Housing Act. Is **Roommates.com** liable?

5. Barrow was a government employee. Because he shared his office computer with another worker, he brought in his personal computer from home to use for office work. No other employee accessed it, but it was connected to the office network. The computer was not password protected, nor was it regularly turned off. When another networked computer was reported to be running slowly, an employee looked at Barrow's machine to see if it was the source of the problem. He found material that led to Barrow's termination. Had Barrow's Fourth Amendment rights been violated?

DISCUSSION QUESTIONS

1. Marina Stengart used her company laptop to communicate with her lawyer via her personal, password-protected, web-based email account. The company's policy stated:

   E-mail and voice mail messages, Internet use and communication, and computer files are considered part of the company's business and client records. Such communications are not to be considered private or personal to any individual employee. Occasional personal use is permitted; however, the system should not be used to solicit for outside business ventures, charitable organizations, or for any political or religious purpose, unless authorized by the Director of Human Resources.

   After she filed an employment lawsuit against her employer, the company hired an expert to access her emails that had been automatically stored on the laptop. Are these emails private?

2. Eric Schmidt, former CEO of Google, has written:

   The communication technologies we use today are invasive by design, collecting our photos, comments and friends into giant databases that are searchable and, in the absence of outside regulation, fair game for employers, university admissions personnel and town gossips. We are what we tweet.

   Do you consider this a problem? If so, can the law fix it?

3. **ETHICS** Some companies allow people to sell their personal data to companies. One firm offers users $8 a month in return for unrestricted access to their social media accounts and credit card transactions. Critics argue that privacy is an important component of human dignity and that it is wrong to cheapen it by turning it into something that is freely bought and sold—like a car or a cheeseburger. They also contend that these companies are exploiting people, who can never really know how their information may be used against them. Is it ethical to buy people's privacy? Under what conditions? What personal data would you be willing to sell? To whom? For how much?

4. Some European nations are considering the creation of a "right to delete" or "right to be forgotten" online. This right would allow anyone to request that search engines take down their personal information, as long as that information is not in the public interest. For example, a person would be able to request that Facebook delete her unflattering photograph, provided the image is not newsworthy. Is this law a good idea? Do you think it would work? Would U.S. lawmakers ever consider a law like this? Why or why not?

5. Tracking tools give consumers many benefits, but they also carry risks. Should Congress regulate them? If so, what should the law provide?

© Honza Krej/Shutterstock.com

Contracts and the UCC

CHAPTER 10

FORMING A CONTRACT

Chris always planned to propose to his girlfriend, Alissa, at Chez Luc, their favorite ritzy restaurant. When he was ready to pop the question, Chris went on Chez Luc's website to reserve a special table. But the website would not grant him a seating time unless he clicked the box that said: "No one in my party will use a cell phone at Chez Luc." Chris agreed and was issued a booking at his waterfront table of choice.

After Alissa's exuberant "yes" during the appetizer course, the newly engaged couple could not contain their excitement. First they posted selfies on both their Facebook pages. Then they called their parents to share the good news … only to be confronted by the angry *maitre-d'*, who escorted the couple out of the dining room for breaching their contract with the restaurant.

© Honza Krej/Shutterstock.com

The angry maitre d' escorted the couple out of the dining room.

We make promises and agreements all the time—from the casual "*I'll call you later*" to more formal business contracts. These agreements may be long or short, written or oral, negotiable or not. But they are not necessarily enforceable through the legal system. One of the aims of contract law is to determine which agreements are worth enforcing. How do we know if an agreement is "worthy"?

Contract law is based on the notion that you are the best judge of your own welfare. By and large, you are free to make whatever agreements you want, subject to whatever rules you choose, and the law will support you. However, this freedom is not limitless: The law imposes seven requirements, which we will analyze in detail in upcoming chapters.

Contract law is a story of freedom and power, rules and relationships—with drama to spare. It is important to study this story to avoid your own contract drama. Let's start with an introduction to contracts.

10-1 CONTRACTS

10-1a Elements of a Contract

A contract is a legally enforceable agreement. People regularly make promises, but only some of them are enforceable. For a contract to be enforceable, seven key characteristics *must* be present. We will study this "checklist" at length in the next several chapters.

- **Offer.** All contracts begin when a person or a company proposes a deal. It might involve buying something, selling something, doing a job, or anything else. But only proposals made in certain ways amount to a legally recognized offer.

- **Acceptance**. Once a party receives an offer, he must respond to it in a certain way. We will examine the requirements of both offers and acceptances in the next chapter.

- **Consideration**. There has to be bargaining that leads to an *exchange* between the parties. Contracts cannot be a one-way street; both sides must receive some measureable benefit.

- **Legality.** The contract must be for a lawful purpose. Courts will not enforce agreements to sell cocaine, for example.

- **Capacity.** The parties must be adults of sound mind.

- **Consent.** Certain kinds of trickery and force can prevent the formation of a contract.

- **Writing.** While verbal agreements often amount to contracts, some types of contracts must be in writing to be enforceable.

> **Contracts Checklist**
>
> ☐ Offer
> ☐ Acceptance
> ☐ Consideration
> ☐ Legality
> ☐ Capacity
> ☐ Consent
> ☐ Writing

Let's apply these principles to the opening scenario.

Is the "contract" between Chris and Chez Luc legally binding? Can Chez Luc kick out—or even *sue*—Chris for using his phone? In deciding this issue, a judge would consider whether the parties intentionally made an agreement, which included:

- **A valid offer and acceptance.** The restaurant's website set forth its terms, which was an offer. Chris accepted when he clicked the box.

- **Consideration.** A judge would then carefully examine whether the parties exchanged something of value that proved that they both meant to be bound by this agreement. And there was. The restaurant gave up a coveted reservation time in exchange for Chris's promise to stay away from his phone.

- **Capacity and legality.** A judge would also verify that the parties were adults of sound mind and that the subject matter of the contract was legal. It seems that Chris understood what he was doing and was of legal age (we certainly hope so, since he was getting engaged).

- **Consent.** There was no fraud or trickery on the part of the restaurant (the terms were clear, not buried so that Chris was unaware of them).

- **Writing.** The terms were in writing (although they did not have to be.)

Therefore, the agreement was valid and enforceable. Whether kicking out a newly engaged couple is good business practice for a restaurant … now, that's a different story!

10-1b Other Important Issues

Once we have examined the essential parts of contracts, the unit will turn to other important issues.

- **Third-party interests.** If Jerome and Tara have a contract, and if the deal falls apart, can Kevin sue to enforce the agreement? It depends.

- **Performance and discharge.** If a party fully accomplishes what the contract requires, his duties are discharged. But what if his obligations are performed poorly, or not at all?

- **Remedies.** A court will award money or other relief to a party injured by a breach of contract.

10-1c Contracts Defined

Contract

A promise that the law will enforce

We have seen that a **contract** is a promise that the law will enforce. As we look more closely at the elements of contract law, we will encounter some intricate issues, but remember that we are usually interested in answering three basic questions of common sense, all relating to promises:

1. Is it certain that the defendant promised to do something?

2. If she did promise, is it fair to make her honor her word?

3. If she did not promise, are there unusual reasons to hold her liable anyway?

10-2 TYPES OF CONTRACTS

10-2a Bilateral and Unilateral Contracts

Bilateral contract

A contract where both parties make a promise

In a **bilateral contract**, both parties make a promise. Suppose a producer says to Gloria, "I'll pay you $2 million to star in my new romantic comedy, *A Promise for a Promise*, which we are shooting three months from now in Santa Fe." Gloria says, "It's a deal." That is a bilateral contract. Each party has made a promise to do something. The producer is now bound to pay Gloria $2 million, and Gloria is obligated to show up on time and act in the movie. The vast majority of contracts are bilateral contracts.

Unilateral contract

A contract where one party makes a promise that the other party can accept only by doing something

In a **unilateral contract**, one party makes a promise that the other party can accept only by *doing* something. These contracts are less common. Suppose the movie producer tacks a sign to a community bulletin board. It has a picture of a dog with a phone number, and it reads, "I'll pay $100 to anyone who returns my lost dog." If Leo sees the sign, finds the producer, and merely promises to find the dog, he has not created a contract. Because of the terms on the sign, Leo must actually find and return the dog to stake a claim to the $100.

10-2b Executory and Executed Contracts

A contract is **executory** when it has been made, but one or more parties have not yet fulfilled their obligations. Recall Gloria, who agrees to act in the producer's film beginning in three months. The moment Gloria and the producer strike their bargain, they have an executory bilateral express contract. A contract is **executed** when all parties have fulfilled their obligations. When Gloria finishes acting in the movie and the producer pays her final fee, their contract will be fully executed.

Executory contract
A binding agreement in which one or more of the parties has not fulfilled its obligations

Executed contract
An agreement in which all parties have fulfilled their obligations

10-2c Valid, Unenforceable, Voidable, and Void Agreements

A **valid contract** is one that satisfies all of the law's requirements. It has no problems in any of the seven areas listed at the beginning of this chapter, and a court will enforce it. The contract between Gloria and the producer is a valid contract, and if the producer fails to pay Gloria, she will win a lawsuit to collect the unpaid fee.

An **unenforceable agreement** occurs when the parties intend to form a valid bargain but a court declares that some rule of law prevents enforcing it. Suppose Gloria and the producer orally agree that she will star in his movie, which he will start filming in 18 months. The law, as we will see in Chapter 11, requires that this contract be in writing because it cannot be completed within one year. If the producer signs up another actress two months later, Gloria has no claim against him.

A **voidable contract** occurs when the law permits one party to terminate the agreement. This happens, for example, when an agreement is signed under duress or a party commits fraud. Suppose that, during negotiations, the producer lies to Gloria, telling her that Steven Spielberg has signed on to be the film's director. That is a major reason why she accepts the contract. As we will learn in Chapter 11, this fraudulent agreement is voidable at Gloria's option. If she later decides that another director is acceptable, she may choose to stay in the contract. But if she wants to cancel the agreement and sue, she can do that as well.

A **void agreement** is one that neither party can enforce, usually because the purpose of the deal is illegal or because one of the parties had no legal authority to make a contract.

The following case illustrates the difference between voidable and void agreements.

Valid contract
A contract that satisfies all the law's requirements

Unenforceable agreement
A contract where the parties intend to form a valid bargain but a court declares that some rule of law prevents enforcing it

Voidable contract
An agreement that, because of some defect, may be terminated by one party, such as a minor, but not by both parties

Void agreement
An agreement that neither party may legally enforce

You be the Judge

Facts: Mr. W sells fireworks. Under Texas law, retailers may only sell fireworks to the public during the two weeks immediately before the Fourth of July and during the two weeks immediately before New Year's Day. And so, fireworks sellers like Mr. W tend to lease property.

Mr. W leased a portion of Ozuna's land. The lease contract contained two key terms:

> In the event the sale of fireworks on the aforementioned property is or shall become unlawful during the period of this lease and the term granted, this lease shall become void.

MR. W FIREWORKS, INC. v. OZUNA
2009 Tex. App. LEXIS 8237, 2009 WL 3464856
Court of Appeals of Texas, Fourth District, San Antonio, 2009

competition to the Lessee during the term of this lease, *and for a period of ten years after lease is terminated.* [Emphasis added.]

A long-standing San Antonio city ordinance bans the sale of fireworks inside city limits, and also within 5,000 feet of city limits. Like all growing cities, San Antonio sometimes annexes new land, and its city limits change.

Lessor(s) agree not to sell or lease any part of said property including any adjoining, adjacent, or contiguous property to any person(s) or corporation for the purpose of selling fireworks in

One annexation caused the Ozuna property to fall within 5,000 feet of the new city limit, and it became illegal to sell fireworks from the property. Mr. W stopped selling fireworks and paying rent on Ozuna's land.

Two years later, San Antonio's border shifted again. This time, the city *disannexed* some property and *shrank*. The new city limits placed Ozuna's property just beyond the 5,000-foot no-fireworks zone. Ozuna then leased a part of his land to Alamo Fireworks, a competitor of Mr. W.

Mr. W sued for breach of contract, arguing that Ozuna had no right to lease to a competitor for a period of 10 years. The trial court granted Ozuna's motion for summary judgment. Mr. W appealed.

You Be the Judge: *Did Ozuna breach his contract with Mr. W by leasing his land to a competitor?*

Argument for Ozuna: Your honor, as soon as San Antonio's city limits changed and my client's land fell within 5,000 feet of the city, it became illegal to sell fireworks on his property. The lease is quite clear. By its own terms, it became void. Mr. W, therefore, had no continuing right to enforce any part of it.

Mr. W seeks to selectively enforce one portion of a void lease that it finds advantageous. The company shows no desire to pay rent or to live up to any other parts of the lease.

When the city's boundary changed again, my client was free to lease his property to any seller of fireworks he wished.

Argument for Mr. W: Your honor, my client paid for several things when he leased Ozuna's land. He was buying more than the right to sell fireworks; he was also paying for exclusive rights. The fact that selling fireworks became illegal on the property does not require that the court void the non-compete agreement.

Before San Antonio's city limits shifted, Mr. W lived up to its part of the bargain by paying rent each month. Mr. Ozuna has certainly not offered to return those payments. Yet he is trying to get out of his promise not to lease the land to any other fireworks company.

It is Ozuna who seeks to escape selected parts of the contract. He should be held to his agreement, and he should not be permitted to lease his land to a competitor of Mr. W. The court held that the agreement was in fact void, and that Ozuna was free to lease the land to another fireworks seller.

10-2d Express and Implied Contracts

Express contract

An agreement with all important terms explicitly stated

In an **express contract**, the two parties explicitly state all important terms of their agreement. The great majority of binding agreements are express contracts. The contract between the producer and Gloria is an express contract because the parties explicitly state what Gloria will do, where and when she will do it, and how much she will be paid. Some express contracts are oral, as that one was, and some are written.

Implied contract

A contract where the words and conduct of the parties indicate that they intended an agreement

In an **implied contract**, the words and conduct of the parties indicate that they intended an agreement. Suppose every Friday, for two months, the producer asks Leo to mow his lawn, and loyal Leo does so each weekend. Then for three more weekends, Leo simply shows up without the producer asking, and the producer continues to pay for the work done. But on the twelfth weekend, when Leo rings the doorbell to collect, the producer suddenly says, "I never asked you to mow it. Scram." The producer is correct that there was no express contract because the parties had not spoken for several weeks. But a court will probably rule that the conduct of the parties has *implied* a contract. Not only did Leo mow the lawn every weekend, but the producer even paid on three weekends when they had not spoken. It was reasonable for Leo to assume that he had a weekly deal to mow and be paid. Naturally, there is no implied contract thereafter.

Today, the hottest disputes about implied contracts often arise in the employment setting. Many employees have "at will" agreements. This means that the employees are free to quit at any time and the company has the right to fire them at any time, for virtually any reason. Courts routinely enforce at-will contracts. But often a company provides its workers with personnel manuals that guarantee certain rights. The legal issue is whether the handbook implies a contract guaranteeing the specified rights, as the following case demonstrates.

DEMASSE V. ITT CORPORATION

194 Ariz. 500
Supreme Court of Arizona, 1999

CASE SUMMARY

Facts: Roger Demasse and five others were employees at-will at ITT Corporation, where they started working at various times between 1960 and 1979. Each was paid an hourly wage.

ITT issued an employee handbook, which it revised four times over two decades.

The first four editions of the handbook stated that within each job classification, any layoffs would be made in reverse order of seniority. The fifth handbook made two important changes. First, the document stated that "nothing contained herein shall be construed as a guarantee of continued employment. ITT does not guarantee continued employment to employees and retains the right to terminate or lay off employees."

Second, the handbook stated that "ITT reserves the right to amend, modify, or cancel this handbook, as well as any or all of the various policies [or rules] outlined in it." Four years later, ITT notified its hourly employees that layoff guidelines for hourly employees would be based not on seniority but on ability and performance. About 10 days later, the six employees were laid off, though less-senior employees kept their jobs. The six employees sued. ITT argued that because the workers were employees at-will, the company had the right to lay them off at any time, for any reason. The case reached the Arizona Supreme Court.

Issue: *Did ITT have the right unilaterally to change the layoff policy?*

Decision: No, ITT did not have the right unilaterally to change the layoff policy because a valid implied contract prevented the company from doing so.

Reasoning: An employer has the right to lay off an at-will employee for virtually any reason. That means that the employer also has the right unilaterally to change the layoff policy. However, when the words or conduct of the parties establish an implied contract, the employee is no longer at-will.

In deciding whether there is an implied contract concerning job security, the key issue is whether a reasonable person would conclude that the parties intended to limit the employer's right to terminate the employee. A company makes a contract offer when it puts in the handbook a statement about job security that a reasonable employee would consider a commitment. The worker can then accept that offer by beginning or continuing employment. At that point, the parties have created a binding implied contract. Here, the first handbook declared that layoffs would be based on seniority. The employees accepted that offer by working, and from that time on, an implied contract governed the employment relationship. ITT had no right to change the layoff policy unilaterally.

10-2e Promissory Estoppel and Quasi-Contracts

Now we turn away from "true" contracts and consider two unusual circumstances. Sometimes courts will enforce agreements even if they fail to meet the usual requirements of a contract. We emphasize that these remedies are uncommon exceptions to the general rules. Most of the agreements that courts enforce are the express contracts that we have already studied. Nonetheless, the next two remedies are still pivotal in some lawsuits. In each case, a sympathetic plaintiff can demonstrate an injury, but *there is no contract*. The plaintiff cannot claim that the defendant breached a contract because none ever existed. The plaintiff must hope for more "creative" relief.

The two remedies can be quite similar. The best way to distinguish them is this:

1. In **promissory estoppel** cases, the defendant made a promise that the plaintiff relied on.

2. In **quasi-contract** cases, the defendant did not make any promise, but did receive a benefit from the plaintiff.

Promissory estoppel
A doctrine in which a court may enforce a promise made by the defendant even when there is no contract

Quasi-contract
A legal fiction in which, to avoid injustice, the court awards damages as if a contract had existed, although one did not

10-2f Promissory Estoppel

A fierce fire swept through Dana and Derek Andreason's house in Utah, seriously damaging it. The good news was that agents for Aetna Casualty promptly visited the Andreasons and helped them through the crisis. The agents reassured the couple that all the damage was covered by their insurance, instructed them on which things to throw out and replace, and helped them choose materials for repairing other items. The bad news was that the agents were wrong: The Andreasons' policy had expired six weeks before the fire. When Derek Andreason presented a bill for $41,957 worth of meticulously itemized work that he had done under the agents' supervision, Aetna refused to pay.

The Andreasons sued—but not for breach of contract because the insurance agreement had expired. They sued Aetna under the legal theory of promissory estoppel. **Even when there is no contract, a plaintiff may use promissory estoppel to enforce the defendant's promise if he can show that:**

- The defendant made a promise knowing that the plaintiff would likely rely on it;

- The plaintiff did rely on the promise; and

- The only way to avoid injustice is to enforce the promise.

> ### Is enforcing the promise the only way to avoid injustice?

Aetna made a promise to the Andreasons; namely, its assurance that all the damage was covered by insurance. The company knew that the Andreasons would rely on that promise, which they did by ripping up a floor that might have been salvaged, throwing out some furniture, and buying materials to repair the house. Is enforcing the promise the only way to avoid injustice? Yes, ruled the Utah Court of Appeals.[1] The Andreasons' conduct was reasonable, based on what the Aetna agent said. Under promissory estoppel, the Andreasons received virtually the same amount they would have obtained had the insurance contract been valid.

Many promissory estoppel cases involve employment law—bosses make promises that they fail to keep. The following case illustrates what can happen when you bet on the wrong promise.

DONALD L. HARMON V. DELAWARE HARNESS RACING COMMISSION

62 A.3d 1198
Supreme Court of Delaware, 2013

CASE SUMMARY

Facts: The Delaware Harness Racing Commission (Commission) hired Donald Harmon to enforce racetrack rules. After years on the job, Harmon was arrested for improperly changing a judging sheet to favor a horse. The Commission suspended him without pay pending the outcome of the criminal case.

John Wayne (yes, his name was John Wayne) was the executive officer of the Commission. During his suspension,

Harmon asked Wayne to find out from the Commission whether it would reinstate him if he was acquitted. When Wayne asked the commissioners this question, they looked at each other and then said "Yes." The commissioners told Wayne he could relay that message to Harmon. Based on this promise, Harmon decided not to look for other jobs.

Immediately after his acquittal, Harmon asked for his job back. The Commission refused to reinstate him as

---

[1]Andreason v. Aetna Casualty & Surety Co., 848 P.2d 171(Utah App. 1993).

promised. Harmon sued the Commission, claiming promissory estoppel. A trial court sided with Harmon. But the Superior Court reversed, so Harmon appealed to the Supreme Court of Delaware.

Issue: *Was the commissioners' promise to Harmon enforceable?*

Decision: Yes, the commissioners' promise was enforceable under promissory estoppel.

Reasoning: To prevail on his promissory estoppel claim, Harmon had to prove that (1) the Commission made a promise to him; (2) which it reasonably expected him to rely on; (3) he did rely on it, to his detriment; and (4) to avoid injustice, the Commission's promise must be enforced.

All four of these requirements were met:

1. When Wayne asked if Harmon would be reinstated, the commissioners all looked at each other before saying "Yes." This informal vote was clear evidence that a promise was made.

2. The commissioners told Wayne to relay their decision to Harmon. They must have known Harmon would rely on Wayne's word.

3. Harmon did not look for other work. Thus, he suffered a substantial detriment.

4. It would be unfair for Harmon to lose income because he relied on a promise from the commissioners.

10-2g Quasi-Contract

Don Easterwood leased more than 5,000 acres of farmland in Jackson County, Texas, from PIC Realty for one year. The next year he obtained a second one-year lease. During each year, Easterwood farmed the land, harvested the crops, and prepared the land for the following year's planting. Toward the end of the second lease, after Easterwood had harvested his crop, he and PIC began discussing the terms of another lease. As they negotiated, Easterwood prepared the land for the following year, cutting and plowing the soil. But the negotiations for a new lease failed, and Easterwood moved off the land. He sued PIC Realty for the value of his work preparing the soil.

Easterwood had neither an express nor an implied contract for the value of his work. How could he make any legal claim? By relying on the legal theory of a quasi-contract: **Even when there is no contract, a court may use a quasi-contract to compensate a plaintiff who can show that:**

- The plaintiff gave some benefit to the defendant;

- The plaintiff reasonably expected to be paid for the benefit, and the defendant knew this; and

- The defendant would be unjustly enriched if he did not pay.

If a court finds all these elements present, it will generally award the value of the goods or services that the plaintiff has conferred. The damages awarded are called *quantum meruit*, meaning that the plaintiff gets "as much as he deserved." The court is awarding money that it believes the plaintiff *morally ought to have*, even though there was no valid contract entitling her to it. This is judicial activism. The purpose is justice; the term is contradictory.

Quantum meruit

"As much as he deserved." The damages awarded in a quasi-contract case

Don Easterwood testified that in Jackson County it was common for a tenant farmer to prepare the soil for the following year but then move. In those cases, he claimed, the landowner compensated the farmer for the work done. Other witnesses agreed. The court ruled that indeed there was no contract, but all elements of quasi-contract had been satisfied. Easterwood gave a benefit to PIC because the land was ready for planting. Easterwood reasonably assumed he would be paid, and PIC Realty knew it. Finally, said the court, it would be unjust to let PIC benefit without paying anything. The court ordered PIC to pay the fair market value of Easterwood's labors.

10-3 SOURCES OF CONTRACT LAW

10-3a Common Law

Express and implied contracts, promissory estoppel, and quasi-contract were all crafted, over centuries, by courts deciding one contract lawsuit at a time. Many contract lawsuits continue to be decided using common law principles developed by courts.

10-3b Uniform Commercial Code

Business methods changed quickly during the first half of the twentieth century. Transportation speeded up. Corporations routinely conducted business across state borders and around the world. These developments presented a problem. Common law principles, whether related to contracts, torts, or anything else, sometimes vary from one state to another. New York and California courts often reach similar conclusions when presented with similar cases, but they are under no obligation to do so. Business leaders became frustrated that, to do business across the country, their companies had to deal with many different sets of common law rules.

Executives, lawyers, and judges wanted a body of law for business transactions that reflected modern commercial methods and provided uniformity throughout the United States. It would be much easier, they thought, if some parts of contract law were the same in every state. That desire gave birth to the Uniform Commercial Code (UCC), created in 1952. The drafters intended the UCC to facilitate the easy formation and enforcement of contracts in a fast-paced world. The Code governs many aspects of commerce, including the sale and leasing of goods, negotiable instruments, bank deposits, letters of credit, investment securities, secured transactions, and other commercial matters. Every state has adopted at least part of the UCC to govern commercial transactions within that state. For our purposes in studying contracts, the most important part of the Code is Article 2, which governs the sale of goods. **"Goods" means anything movable, except for money, securities, and certain legal rights.** Goods include pencils, commercial aircraft, books, and Christmas trees. Goods do not include land or a house because neither is movable, nor do they include a stock certificate. A contract for the sale of 10,000 sneakers is governed by the UCC; a contract for the sale of a condominium in Marina del Rey is governed by the California common law.

When analyzing any contract problem as a student or businessperson, you must note whether the agreement concerns the sale of goods. For many issues, the common law and the UCC are reasonably similar. But sometimes the law is quite different under the two sets of rules.

And so, the UCC governs contracts for a sale of goods, while common law principles govern contracts for sales of services and everything else. Most of the time, it will be clear whether the UCC or the common law applies. But what if a contract involves both goods and services? When you get your oil changed, you are paying in part for the new oil and oil filter (goods) and in part for the labor required to do the job (services). In a mixed contract, Article 2 governs only if the *primary purpose* was the sale of goods.

Goods
Are things that are movable, other than money and investment securities

---

EXAM Strategy

Question: Leila agrees to pay Kendrick $35,000 to repair windmills. Confident of this cash, Kendrick contracts to buy Derrick's used Porsche for $33,000. Then Leila informs Kendrick she does not need his help and will not pay him. Kendrick tells Derrick that he no longer wants the Porsche. Derrick sues Kendrick, and Kendrick files suit against Leila. What law or laws govern these lawsuits?

Strategy: Always be conscious of whether a contract is for services or the sale of goods. Different laws govern. To make that distinction, you must understand the term *goods*. If you are clear about that, the question is easily answered.

Result: *Goods* means anything movable, and a Porsche surely qualifies. The UCC will control Derrick's suit. Repairing windmills is a primarily a service. Kendrick's lawsuit is governed by the common law of contracts.

Contracts Checklist
- ☑ Offer
- ☐ Acceptance
- ☐ Consideration
- ☐ Legality
- ☐ Capacity
- ☐ Consent
- ☐ Writing

10-4 AGREEMENT

10-4a Meeting of the Minds

Parties form a contract only if they have a meeting of the minds. For this to happen, one side must make an **offer** and the other must make an **acceptance** An offer proposes definite terms, and an acceptance unconditionally agrees to them.

Throughout the chapter, keep in mind that courts make *objective* assessments when evaluating offers and acceptances. A court will not try to get inside anyone's head and decide what she was thinking as she made a bargain.

10-4b Offer

Bargaining begins with an offer. The person who makes an offer is the **offeror**. The person to whom he makes that offer is the **offeree**. The terms are annoying but inescapable because, like handcuffs, all courts use them.

Two questions determine whether a statement is an offer:

1. Do the offeror's words and actions indicate an *intention* to make a bargain?

2. Are the terms of the offer reasonably definite?

Zachary says to Sharon, "Come work in my English-language center as a teacher. I'll pay you $800 per week for a 35-hour week, for six months starting Monday." This is a valid offer. Zachary's words seem to indicate that he intends to make a bargain, and his offer is definite. If Sharon accepts, the parties have a contract that either one can enforce.

Invitations to Bargain

An invitation to bargain is not an offer. Suppose Martha telephones Joe and leaves a message on his answering machine, asking if Joe would consider selling his vacation condo on Lake Michigan. Joe faxes a signed letter to Martha saying, "There is no way I could sell the condo for less than $150,000." Martha promptly sends Joe a cashier's check for that amount. Does she own the condo? No. Joe's fax is not an offer. It is merely an invitation to bargain. Joe is indicating that he would be happy to receive an offer from Martha. He is not promising to sell the condo for $150,000 or for any amount.

Problems with Definiteness

It is not enough that the offeror indicate that she intends to enter into an agreement. **The terms of the offer must also be definite.** If they are vague, then even if the offeree agrees to the deal, a court does not have enough information to enforce it, and there is no contract.

You want a friend to work in your store for the holiday season. This is a definite offer: "I offer you a job as a salesclerk in the store from November 1 through December 29, 40 hours per week at $10 per hour." But suppose, by contrast, you say: "I offer you a job as a

Offer
In contract law, an act or statement that proposes definite terms and permits the other party to create a contract by accepting those terms

Offeror
The party in contract negotiations who makes the first offer

Offeree
The party in contract negotiations who receives the first offer

salesclerk in the store during the holiday season. We will work out a fair wage once we see how busy things get." Your friend replies, "That's fine with me." This offer is indefinite. What is a fair wage? $15 per hour? $20 per hour? What is the "holiday season"? How will the determination be made? There is no binding agreement.

The following case presents a problem with definiteness, concerning a famous television show. You want to know what happened? Go to the place. See the guy. No, not the guy in hospitality. Our friend in waste management. Don't say nothing. Then get out.

BAER V. CHASE

392 F.3d 609
Third Circuit Court of Appeals, 2004

CASE SUMMARY

Facts: David Chase was a television writer-producer with many credits, including a detective series called *The Rockford Files*. He became interested in a new program, set in New Jersey, about a "mob boss in therapy," a concept he eventually developed into *The Sopranos*. Robert Baer was a prosecutor in New Jersey who wanted to write for television. He submitted a *Rockford Files* script to Chase, who agreed to meet with Baer.

When they met, Baer pitched a different idea, concerning "a film or television series about the New Jersey Mafia." He did not realize Chase was already working on such an idea. Later that year, Chase visited New Jersey. Baer arranged meetings for Chase with local detectives and prosecutors, who provided the producer with information, material, and personal stories about their experiences with organized crime. Detective Thomas Koczur drove Chase and Baer to various New Jersey locations and introduced Chase to Tony Spirito. Spirito shared stories about loan sharking, power struggles between family members connected with the mob, and two colorful individuals known as Big Pussy and Little Pussy, both of whom later became characters on the show.

Back in Los Angeles, Chase wrote and sent to Baer a draft of the first *Sopranos* teleplay. Baer called Chase and commented on the script. The two spoke at least four times that year, and Baer sent Chase a letter about the script.

When *The Sopranos* became a hit television show, Baer sued Chase. He alleged that on three separate occasions, Chase had agreed that if the program succeeded, Chase would "take care of" Baer and would "remunerate Baer in a manner commensurate to the true value of his services." This happened twice on the phone, Baer claimed, and once during Chase's visit to New Jersey. The understanding was that if the show failed, Chase would owe nothing. Chase never paid Baer anything.

The district court dismissed the case, holding that the alleged promises were too vague to be enforced. Baer appealed.

Issue: *Was Chase's promise definite enough to be enforced?*

Decision: No, the promise was too indefinite to be enforced.

Reasoning: To create a binding agreement, the offer and acceptance must be definite enough that a court can tell what the parties were obligated to do. The parties need to agree on all of the essential terms; if they do not, there is no enforceable contract.

One of the essential terms is price. The agreement must either specify the compensation to be paid or describe a method by which the parties can calculate it. The duration of the contract is also basic: How long do the mutual obligations last?

There is no evidence that the parties agreed on how much Chase would pay Baer, or when or for what period. The parties never defined what they meant by the "true value" of Baer's services or how they would determine it. The two never discussed the meaning of "success" as applied to *The Sopranos*. They never agreed on how "profits" were to be calculated. The parties never discussed when the alleged agreement would begin or end.

Baer argues that the courts should make an exception to the principle of definiteness when the agreement concerns an "idea submission." The problem with his contention is that there is not the slightest support for it in the law. There is no precedent whatsoever for ignoring the definiteness requirement, in this type of contract or any other.

Affirmed.

10-4c Termination of Offers

As we have seen, the great power that an offeree has is to form a contract by accepting an offer. But this power is lost when the offer is terminated, which can happen in several ways.

Revocation

An offer is **revoked** when the offeror "takes it back" before the offeree accepts. In general, the offeror may revoke the offer any time before it has been accepted. Imagine that I call you and say, "I'm going out of town this weekend. I'll sell you my ticket to this weekend's football game for $75." You tell me that you'll think it over and call me back. An hour later, my plans change. I call you a second time and say, "Sorry, but the deal's off—I'm going to the game after all." I have revoked my offer, and you can no longer accept it.

In the next case, this rule was worth $100,000 to one of the parties.

Revocation
Cancellation of the offer

NADEL v. TOM CAT BAKERY

2009 N.Y. Slip Op 32661
Supreme Court, New York County, 2009

CASE SUMMARY

Facts: A Tom Cat Bakery delivery van struck Elizabeth Nadel as she crossed a street. Having suffered significant injuries, Nadel filed suit. Before the trial began, the attorney representing the bakery's owner offered a $100,000 settlement, which Nadel refused.

While the jury was deliberating, the bakery's lawyer again offered Nadel the $100,000 settlement. She decided to think about it during lunch. Later that day, the jury sent a note to the judge. The bakery owner told her lawyer that if the note indicated the jury had reached a verdict, that he should revoke the settlement offer.

Back in the courtroom, the bakery's lawyer said, "My understanding is that there's a note.... I was given an instruction that if the note is a verdict, my client wants to take the verdict."

Nadel's lawyer then said, "My client will take the settlement. My client will take the settlement."

The trial court judge allowed the forewoman to read the verdict, which awarded Nadel—nothing. She

appealed, claiming that a $100,000 settlement had been reached.

Issue: *Did Nadel's lawyer accept the settlement offer in time?*

Decision: No, the bakery owner's lawyer revoked the offer before acceptance.

Reasoning: An offer definitely existed. And the twice-repeated statement, "My client will take the settlement," indicates a clear desire to accept the proposal. The problem is that the acceptance came too late.

Analyzing the timeline, the bakery owner's attorney indicated that if a verdict had been returned, he revoked the offer. This notice was given before the attempted acceptance. And so, since a verdict had in fact been returned, the offer was no longer open.

The parties did not reach a binding settlement agreement.

Rejection

If an offeree clearly indicates that he does not want to take the offer, then he has **rejected** it. A rejection immediately terminates the offer. Suppose a major accounting firm telephones you and offers a job, starting at $80,000. You respond, "Nah. I'm gonna work on my surfing for a year or two." The next day you come to your senses and write the firm, accepting its offer. No contract. Your rejection terminated the offer and ended your power to accept.

Counteroffer

Counteroffer
An offer made in response to a previous offer

A party makes a **counteroffer** when it responds to an offer with a new and different proposal. Frederick faxes Kim, offering to sell a 50 percent interest in the Fab Hotel in New York for only $135 million. Kim faxes back, offering to pay $115 million. Moments later, Kim's business partner convinces her that Frederick's offer was a bargain, and she faxes an acceptance of his $135 million offer. Does Kim have a binding deal? No. A counteroffer is a rejection. The parties have no contract at any price.

Expiration

When an offer specifies a time limit for acceptance, that period is binding. If the offer specifies no time limit, the offeree has a reasonable period in which to accept.

Destruction of the Subject Matter

A used car dealer offers to sell you a rare 1938 Bugatti for $7.5 million if you bring cash the next day. You arrive, suitcase stuffed with cash—just in time to see a stampeding herd of escaped circus elephants crush the Bugatti. The dealer's offer terminated.

10-4d Acceptance

Contracts Checklist
- ☐ Offer
- ☑ Acceptance
- ☐ Consideration
- ☐ Legality
- ☐ Capacity
- ☐ Consent
- ☐ Writing

As we have seen, when there is a valid offer outstanding, it remains effective until it is terminated or accepted. An offeree accepts by saying or doing something that a reasonable person would understand to mean that he definitely wants to take the offer. Assume that Ellie offers to sell Gene her old iPod for $50. If Gene says, "I accept your offer," then he has indeed accepted, but there is no need to be so formal. He can accept the offer by saying, "It's a deal" or "I'll take it," or any number of things. He need not even speak. If he hands her a $50 bill, he also accepts the offer.

It is worth noting that **the offeree must say or do *something* to accept.** Marge telephones Vick and leaves a message on his answering machine: "I'll pay $75 for your business law textbook from last semester. I'm desperate to get a copy, so I will assume you agree unless I hear from you by 6:00 tonight." Marge hears nothing by the deadline and assumes she has a deal. She is mistaken. Vick neither said nor did anything to indicate that he accepted.

Mirror Image Rule

If only he had known! A splendid university, an excellent position as department chair—gone. And all because of the mirror image rule. The Ohio State University wrote to Philip Foster offering him an appointment as a professor and chair of the art history department. His position was to begin July 1, and he had until June 2 to accept the job. On June 2, Foster telephoned the dean and left a message accepting the position, *effective July 15.* Later, Foster thought better of it and wrote the university, accepting the school's starting date of July 1. Too late! Professor Foster never did occupy that chair at Ohio State. The court held that since his acceptance varied the starting date, it was a counteroffer. And a counteroffer, as we know, is a rejection.[2]

---

[2]*Foster v. Ohio State University*, 41 Ohio App. 3d 86(Ohio Ct. App. 1987).

The common law **mirror image rule** requires that acceptance be on precisely the same terms as the offer. If the acceptance contains terms that add to or contradict the offer, even in minor ways, courts generally consider it a counteroffer.

Mirror image rule
A contract doctrine that requires acceptance to be on exactly the same terms as the offer

The UCC and the Battle of the Forms

Today, businesses use standardized forms to purchase most goods and services. This practice creates enormous difficulties. Sellers use forms they have prepared, with all conditions stated to their advantage, and buyers employ their own forms, with terms they prefer. The forms are exchanged in the mail or electronically, with neither side clearly agreeing to the other party's terms. The problem is known as the "battle of forms." Once again, the UCC has entered the fray, attempting to provide flexibility and common sense for those contracts involving the sale of goods. Under the UCC, an acceptance that adds additional or different terms often *will* create a contract. And, perhaps surprisingly, the additional terms will often become part of the contract.

UCC §2-207 dramatically modifies the mirror image rule for the sale of goods. Under this provision, an acceptance that adds additional or different terms **will often create a contract.** The rule is intricate, but it may be summarized this way:

- For the sale of goods, the most important factor is whether the parties believe they have a binding agreement. If their conduct indicates that they have a deal, they probably do.

- If the offeree *adds new terms* to the offer, acceptance by the offeror generally creates a binding agreement.

- If the offeree *changes* the terms of the offer, a court will probably rely on general principles of the UCC to create a fair contract.

- If a party wants a contract on its terms only, with no changes, it must clearly indicate that.

Suppose Wholesaler writes to Manufacturer, offering to buy "10,000 wheelbarrows at $50 per unit. Payable on delivery, 30 days from today's date." Manufacturer writes back, "We accept your offer of 10,000 wheelbarrows at $50 per unit, payable on delivery. Interest at normal trade rates for unpaid balances." Manufacturer clearly intends to form a contract. The company has added a new term, but there is still a valid agreement.

EXAM Strategy

Question: Elaine faxes an offer to Raoul. Raoul writes, "I accept. Please note, I will charge 2 percent interest per month for any unpaid money." He signs the document and faxes it back to Elaine. Do the two have a binding contract?

Strategy: Slow down—this is trickier than it seems. Raoul has added a term to Elaine's offer. In a contract for services, acceptance must mirror the offer, but not so in an agreement for the sale of goods.

Result: If this is an agreement for services, there is no contract. However, if this agreement is for goods, the additional term *may* become part of an enforceable contract.

Question: Assume that Elaine's offer concerns goods. Is there an agreement?

Strategy: Under UCC §2-207, an additional term will generally become part of a binding agreement for goods, unless … ?

Result: The parties have probably created a binding contract unless Elaine indicated in her offer that she would accept her terms only, with no changes.

10-4e Communication of Acceptance

The offeree must communicate his acceptance for it to be effective. The questions that typically arise concern the method, the manner, and the time of acceptance.

Method and Manner of Acceptance

The "method" refers to whether acceptance is done in person or by mail, telephone, email, or fax. The "manner" refers to whether the offeree accepts by promising, by making a down payment, by performing, and so forth. **If an offer demands acceptance in a particular method or manner, the offeree must follow those requirements.** An offer might specify that it be accepted in writing, or in person, or before midnight on June 23. An offeror can set any requirements she wishes. Omri might say to Oliver, "I'll sell you my bike for $200. You must accept my offer by standing on a chair in the lunchroom tomorrow and reciting a poem about a cow." Oliver can only accept the offer in the exact manner specified if he wants to form a contract.

If the offer does not specify a type of acceptance, the offeree may accept in any reasonable manner and method. An offer generally may be accepted by performance or by a promise, unless it specifies a particular method. The same freedom applies to the method. If Masako faxes Eric an offer to sell 1,000 acres in Montana for $800,000, Eric may accept by mail or fax. Both are routinely used in real estate transactions, and either is reasonable.

Time of Acceptance: The Mailbox Rule

An acceptance is generally effective upon dispatch, meaning the moment it is out of the offeree's control. Terminations, on the other hand, are effective when received. When Masako faxes her offer to sell land to Eric and he mails his acceptance, the contract is binding the moment he puts the letter into the mail. In most cases, this **mailbox rule** is just a detail. But it becomes important when the offeror revokes her offer at about the same time the offeree accepts. Who wins? Suppose Masako's offer has one twist:

- On Monday morning, Masako faxes her offer to Eric.
- On Monday afternoon, Eric writes "I accept" on the fax, and Masako mails a revocation of her offer.
- On Tuesday morning, Eric mails his acceptance.
- On Thursday morning, Masako's revocation arrives at Eric's office.
- On Friday morning, Eric's acceptance arrives at Masako's office.

Outcome? Eric has an enforceable contract. Masako's offer was effective when it reached Eric. His acceptance was effective on Tuesday morning, when he mailed it. Nothing that happens later can "undo" the contract.

Chapter Conclusion

Contracts govern countless areas of our lives, from intimate family issues to multibillion dollar corporate deals. Understanding contract principles is essential for a successful business or a professional career and is invaluable in private life. Courts no longer rubber-stamp any agreement that two parties have made. If we know the issues that courts scrutinize, the agreement we draft is likelier to be enforced. We thus achieve greater control over our affairs—the very purpose of a contract.

EXAM REVIEW

1. **CONTRACTS: DEFINITION AND ELEMENTS** A contract is a legally enforceable promise. Analyzing whether a contract exists involves inquiring into these issues: offer, acceptance, consideration, capacity, legal purpose, consent, and sometimes, whether the deal is in writing.

2. **UNILATERAL AND BILATERAL CONTRACTS** In bilateral contracts, the parties exchange promises. In a unilateral contract, only one party makes a promise, and the other must take some action; his return promise is insufficient to form a contract.

3. **EXECUTORY AND EXECUTED CONTRACTS** In an executory contract, one or both of the parties have not done everything that they promised to do. In an executed contract, all parties have fully performed.

4. **VALID, UNENFORCEABLE, VOIDABLE, AND VOID AGREEMENTS** Valid contracts are fully enforceable. An unenforceable agreement is one with a legal defect. A voidable contract occurs when one party has an option to cancel the agreement. A void agreement means that the law will ignore the deal regardless of what the parties want.

5. **EXPRESS AND IMPLIED CONTRACTS** If the parties formally agreed and stated explicit terms, there is probably an express contract. If the parties did not formally agree but their conduct, words, or past dealings indicate they intended a binding agreement, there may be an implied contract.

6. **PROMISSORY ESTOPPELS AND QUASI-CONTRACTS** A claim of promissory estoppel requires that the defendant made a promise knowing that the plaintiff would likely *rely* on it, and the plaintiff did so. It would be wrong to deny recovery. A claim of quasi-contract requires that the defendant receive a benefit, knowing that the plaintiff would expect compensation, and it would be unjust not to grant it.

EXAM Strategy

Question: The Hoffmans owned and operated a successful small bakery and grocery store. They spoke with Lukowitz, an agent of Red Owl Stores, who told them that for $18,000, Red Owl would build a store and fully stock it for them. The Hoffmans sold their bakery and grocery store and purchased a lot on which Red Owl was to build the store. Lukowitz then told Hoffman that the price had gone up to $26,000. The Hoffmans borrowed the extra money from relatives, but then Lukowitz informed them that the cost would be $34,000. Negotiations broke off and the Hoffmans sued. The court determined that there was no contract because too many details had not been worked out—the size of the store, its design, and the cost of constructing it. Can the Hoffmans recover any money?

Strategy: Because there is no contract, the Hoffmans must rely on either promissory estoppel or quasi-contract. Promissory estoppel focuses on the defendant's promise and the plaintiff's reliance. Those suing in quasi-contract must show that the defendant received a benefit for which it should reasonably expect to pay. Does either fit here? (See the "Result" at the end of this section.)

7. **SOURCES OF CONTRACT LAW** If a contract is for the sale of goods, the UCC is the relevant body of law. For anything else, the common law governs. If a contract involves both goods and services, a court will determine the agreement's primary purpose.

8. **MEETING OF THE MINDS** The parties can form a contract only if they have a meeting of the minds.

EXAM Strategy

Question: Norv owned a Ford dealership and wanted to expand by obtaining a BMW outlet. He spoke with Jackson and other BMW executives on several occasions. Norv now claims that those discussions resulted in an oral contract that requires BMW to grant him a franchise, but the company disagrees. Norv's strongest evidence of a contract is the fact that Jackson gave him forms on which to order BMWs. Jackson answered that it was his standard practice to give such forms to prospective dealers, so that if the franchise were approved, car orders could be processed quickly. Norv states that he was "shocked" when BMW refused to go through with the deal. Is there a contract?

Strategy: A court makes an *objective* assessment of what the parties did and said to determine whether they had a meeting of the minds and intended to form a contract. Norv's "shock" is irrelevant. Do the order forms indicate a meeting of the minds? Was there additional evidence that the parties had reached an agreement? (See the "Result" at the end of this section.)

9. **OFFER** An offer is an act or a statement that proposes definite terms and permits the other party to create a contract by accepting. Offers may be terminated by revocation, rejection, expiration, or destruction of the agreement's subject matter.

10. **ACCEPTANCE** The offeree must say or do something to accept. The common law mirror image rule requires acceptance on precisely the same terms as the offer. Under the mailbox rule, acceptances are effective upon dispatch.

6. Result: Red Owl received no benefit from the Hoffmans' sale of their store or purchase of the lot. However, Red Owl did make a promise and expected the Hoffmans to rely on it, which they did. The Hoffmans won their claim of promissory estoppel.

8. Result: The order forms are neither an offer nor an acceptance. Norv has offered no evidence that the parties agreed on price, date of performance, or any other key terms. There is no contract. Norv allowed eagerness and optimism to replace common sense.

MATCHING QUESTIONS

Match the following terms with their definitions:

___A. Implied contract

___B. Mirror image rule

___C. Offeree

___D. Offeror

___E. Bilateral contract

1. A party that makes an offer

2. An agreement based on one promise in exchange for another

3. A party that receives an offer

4. An agreement based on the words and actions of the parties

5. A common law principle requiring the acceptance to be on exactly the terms of the offer

TRUE/FALSE QUESTIONS

Circle true or false:

1. T F To be enforceable, all contracts must be in writing.

2. T F Abdul hires Sean to work in his store and agrees to pay him $9 per hour. This agreement is governed by the Uniform Commercial Code.

3. T F If an offer demands a reply within a stated period, the offeree's silence indicates acceptance.

4. T F Without a meeting of the minds there cannot be a contract.

5. T F An agreement to sell cocaine is a voidable contract.

MULTIPLE-CHOICE QUESTIONS

1. Mark, a newspaper editor, walks into the newsroom and announces to a group of five reporters: "I'll pay a $2,000 bonus to the first reporter who finds definitive evidence that Senator Blue smoked marijuana at the celebrity party last Friday." Anna, the first reporter to produce the evidence, claims her bonus based on:

   (a) unilateral contract.

   (b) promissory estoppel.

   (c) quasi-contract.

   (d) implied contract.

   (e) express contract.

2. Raul has finished the computer installation he promised to perform for Tanya, and she has paid him in full. This is:

   (a) an express contract.

   (b) an implied contract.

   (c) an executed contract.

   (d) a bilateral contract.

   (e) no contract.

3. Consider the following:

   1. Madison says to a group of students, "I'll pay $35 to the first one of you who shows up at my house and mows my lawn."

   2. Lea posts a flyer around town that reads, "Reward: $500 for information about the person who keyed my truck last Saturday night in the Wag-a-Bag parking lot. Call Lea at 555-5309."
   Which of these proposes a *unilateral* contract?

   (a) I only

   (b) II only

   (c) Both I and II

   (d) None of the above

4. On Monday night, Louise is talking on her cell phone with Bill. "I'm desperate for a manager in my store," says Louise. "I'll pay you $45,000 per year, if you can start tomorrow morning. What do you say?"

   "It's a deal," says Bill. "I can start tomorrow at 8 a.m. I'll take $45,000, and I also want 10 percent of any profits you make above last year's." Just then Bill loses his cell phone signal. The next morning he shows up at the store, but Louise refuses to hire him. Bill sues. Bill will:

   (a) win, because there was a valid offer and acceptance.

   (b) win, based on promissory estoppel.

   (c) lose, because he rejected the offer.

   (d) lose, because the agreement was not put in writing.

   (e) lose, because Louise revoked the offer.

5. Which of the following amounts to an offer?

   (a) Ed says to Carmen, "I offer to sell you my pen for $1."

   (b) Ed says to Carmen, "I'll sell you my pen for $1."

   (c) Ed writes, "I'll sell you my pen for $1," and gives the note to Carmen.

   (d) All of the above

CASE QUESTIONS

1. **ETHICS** John Stevens owned a dilapidated apartment that he rented to James and Cora Chesney for a low rent. The Chesneys began to remodel and rehabilitate the unit. Over a four-year period, they installed two new bathrooms, carpeted the floors, installed new septic and heating systems, and rewired, replumbed, and painted. Stevens periodically stopped by and saw the work in progress. The Chesneys transformed the unit into a respectable apartment. Three years after their work was done, Stevens served the Chesneys with an eviction notice. The Chesneys counterclaimed, seeking the value of the work they had done. Are they entitled to it? Comment on the law and the ethics.

2. Tindall operated a general contracting business in Montana. He and Konitz entered into negotiations for Konitz to buy the business. The parties realized that Konitz

could succeed with the business only if Tindall gave support and assistance for a year or so after the purchase, especially by helping with the process of bidding for jobs and obtaining bonds to guarantee performance. Konitz bought the business, and Tindall helped with the bidding and bonding. Two years later, Tindall presented Konitz with a contract for his services up to that point. Konitz did not want to sign, but Tindall insisted. Konitz signed the agreement, which said: "Whereas Tindall sold his contracting business to Konitz and thereafter assisted Konitz in bidding and bonding, without which Konitz would have been unable to operate, NOW THEREFORE Konitz agrees to pay Tindall $138,629." Konitz later refused to pay. Comment.

3. The Tufte family leased a 260-acre farm from the Travelers Insurance Co. Toward the end of the lease, Travelers mailed the Tuftes an option to renew the lease. The option arrived at the Tuftes' house on March 30 and gave them until April 14 to accept. On April 13, the Tuftes signed and mailed their acceptance, which Travelers received on April 19. Travelers claimed there was no lease and attempted to evict the Tuftes from the farm. May they stay?

4. Sal says to Jennifer, "I'll trim all of your trees if you pay me $300." Jennifer replies, "It's a deal, if you'll also feed my dog next week when I go on vacation." Does the common law or the UCC apply to Sal's proposal? Is Jennifer's reply an acceptance? Why or why not?

5. Raul makes an offer to Tina. He says, "I'll sell you this briefcase for $100." Describe four ways in which this offer might be terminated.

DISCUSSION QUESTIONS

1. Someone offers to sell you a concert ticket for $50, and you reply, "I'll give you $40," The seller refuses to sell at the lower price, and you say, "Okay, okay, I'll pay you $50." Clearly, no contract has been formed because you made a counteroffer. If the seller has changed her mind and no longer wants to sell for $50, she doesn't have to. But is this fair? If it is all part of the same conversation, should you be able to accept the $50 offer and get the ticket?

2. Have you ever made an agreement that mattered to you, only to have the other person refuse to follow through on the deal? Looking at the list of elements in the chapter, did your agreement amount to a contract? If not, which element did it lack?

3. The day after Thanksgiving, known as Black Friday, is the biggest shopping day of the year. One major retailer advertised a "Black Friday only" laptop for $150. On Thanksgiving night, hundreds of people waited for the store to open to take advantage of the laptop deal—only to learn that the store only had two units for sale at the discounted price. Did the retailer breach its contract with the hundreds of consumers who sought the deal? What obligation, if any, does the retailer have to its consumers?

4. Consider promissory estoppel and quasi-contracts. Do you like the fact that these doctrines exist? Should courts have "wiggle room" to enforce deals that fail to meet formal contract requirements, or should the rule be, "If it's not an actual contract, too bad"?

5. Each time employees at BizCorp enter their work computers, the following alert appears: "You are attempting to access the BizCorp network. By logging in, you agree to BizCorp's Computer Usage Policy and certify that your use of this computer is strictly for business purposes. Any activities conducted on this system may be monitored for any reason at the discretion of BizCorp" Once an employee has logged in, have the parties formed a valid contract? Discuss.

CHAPTER 11

REQUIREMENTS FOR A CONTRACT

Soheil Sadri, a California resident, did some serious gambling at Caesar's Tahoe casino in Nevada. And lost. To keep gambling, he wrote checks to Caesar's and then signed two memoranda pledging to repay money advanced. After two days, with his losses totaling more than $22,000, he went home. Back in California, Sadri stopped payment on the checks and refused to pay any of the money he owed Caesar's. The casino sued and recovered ... nothing. Sadri relied on an important legal principle to defeat the suit: A contract that is illegal is void and unenforceable.

© Honza Krej/Shutterstock.com

> **A contract that is illegal is void and unenforceable.**

A gambling contract is illegal unless it is specifically authorized by state statute. In California, as in many states, gambling on credit is not allowed. However, do not become too excited at the prospect of risk-free wagering. Casinos responded to cases like *Sadri* by changing their practices. Most now extend credit only to a gambler who agrees that disputes about repayment will be settled in Nevada courts. Because such contracts are legal in that state, the casino is able to obtain a judgment against a defaulting debtor.

Sometimes parties fail to create a valid contract even when they exchange an offer and acceptance. Sadri's agreement was not a binding contract because of a problem with legality. This is one of five "deal breakers" that we present in this chapter:

1. Consideration: Each party must gain some value from a contract.

2. Legality: Illegal bargains are not enforceable.

3. Capacity: Both parties must have the legal ability to form a contract.

4. Fraud and certain types of mistake make a contract unenforceable.

5. Writing is required for some contracts.

If parties exchange an offer and acceptance, and if there are no problems in any of the five areas presented in this chapter, then a valid contract exists.

11-1 CONSIDERATION

Consideration is the inducement, price, or promise that causes a person to enter into a contract and forms the basis for the parties' exchange. The central idea of consideration is simple: Contracts must be a two-way street. If one side gets all the benefit and the other side gets nothing, then an agreement lacks consideration and is not an enforceable contract. Consideration is proof that the parties intended to be bound to their promises.

There are two basic elements of consideration:

1. **Value.** Both parties must get something of measureable value from the contract. That thing can be money, groceries, agreement promise not to sue, or anything else that has real value.

2. **Exchange.** The two parties must have bargained for whatever was exchanged and struck a deal: "If you do this, I'll do that." If you just decide to deliver a cake to your neighbor's house without her knowing, that may be something of value, but since you two did not bargain for it, there is no contract, and she does not owe you the price of the cake.

Let's take an example: Sally's Shoe Store and Baker Boots agree that she will pay $20,000 for 100 pairs of boots. They both get something of value—Sally gets the boots, Baker gets the money. A contract is formed when the promises are made because a promise to give something of value counts. The two have bargained for this deal, so there is valid consideration.

Let's look at another example. Marvin works at Sally's. At 9 a.m., he is in a good mood and promises to buy his coworker a Starbucks during the lunch hour. The delighted coworker agrees. Later that morning, the coworker is rude to Marvin, who then changes his mind about buying the coffee. He is free to do so. His promise created a one-way street: the coworker stood to receive all of the benefit of the agreement, while Marvin got nothing. Because Marvin received no value, there is no contract.

11-1a What Is Value?

As we have seen, an essential part of consideration is that both parties must get something of value. That item of value can be either an "act," a "forbearance," or a promise to do either of these.

Act

A party commits an **act** when she does something she was not legally required to do in the first place. She might do a job, deliver an item, or pay money, for example. An act does not count if the party was simply complying with the law or fulfilling her obligations under an existing contract. Thus, for example, suppose that your professor tells the university that she will not post final grades unless she is paid an extra $5,000. Even if the university agrees to this outrageous demand, that agreement is not a valid contract because the professor is already under an obligation to post final grades.

Forbearance

A **forbearance** is, in essence, the opposite of an act. A plaintiff forbears if he agrees *not* to do something he had a legal right to do. An entrepreneur might promise a competitor not to open a competing business, or an elderly driver (with a valid driver's license) might promise concerned family members that he will not drive at night.

Promise to Act or Forbear.   A promise to do (or not do) something in the future counts as consideration. When evaluating whether consideration exists, the *promise* to mow someone's lawn next week is the equivalent of actually *doing* the yardwork.

Consideration
The inducement, price, or promise that causes a person to enter into a contract and forms the basis for the parties' exchange

Contracts Checklist
- ☐ Offer
- ☐ Acceptance
- ☑ Consideration
- ☐ Legality
- ☐ Capacity
- ☐ Consent
- ☐ Writing

In the movies, when a character wants to get serious about keeping a promise—*really* serious—he sometimes signs an agreement in blood. As it turns out, this kind of thing actually happens in real life. In the following case, did the promise of forbearance have value? Did a contract signed in blood count? You be the judge.

You be the Judge

KIM V. SON
2009 Cal. App. LEXIS 2011,
2009 WL 597232
Court of Appeal of California, 2009

Facts: Stephen Son was a part-owner and -operator of two corporations. Because the businesses were corporations, Son was not personally liable for the debts of either one.

Jinsoo Kim invested a total of about $170,000 in the companies. Eventually, both of them failed, and Kim lost his investment. Son felt guilty over Kim's losses.

Later, Son and Kim met in a sushi restaurant and drank heroic quantities of alcohol. At one point, Son pricked his finger with a safety pin and wrote the following in his own blood: "Sir, please forgive me. Because of my deeds, you have suffered financially. I will repay you to the best of my ability." In return, Kim agreed not to sue him for the money owed.

Son later refused to honor the bloody document and pay Kim the money. Kim filed suit to enforce their contract.

The judge determined that the promise did not create a contract because there had been no consideration.

You Be the Judge: *Was there consideration?*

Argument for Kim: As a part of the deal made at the sushi restaurant, Kim agreed not to sue Son. What could be more of a forbearance than that? Kim had a right to sue at any time, and he gave the right up. Even if Kim was unlikely to win, Son would still prefer not to be sued.

Besides, the fact that Son signed the agreement in blood indicates how seriously he took the obligation to repay his loyal investor. At a minimum, Son eased his guilty conscience by making the agreement, and surely that is worth something.

Argument for Son: Who among you has not at one point or another become intoxicated, experienced emotions more powerful than usual, and regretted them the next morning? Whether calling an ex-girlfriend and professing endless love while crying or writing out an agreement in your own blood, it is all the same.

A promise not to file a meritless lawsuit has no value at all. It did not matter to Son whether or not Kim filed suit because Kim could not possibly win. If this promise counts as value, then the concept of consideration is meaningless because anyone can promise not to sue any time. Son had no obligation to pay Kim. And the bloody napkin does not change that fact because it was made without consideration of any kind. It is an ordinary promise, not a contract that creates any legal obligation.

11-1b What Constitutes Exchange?

Bargained for

When something is sought by the promisor and given by the promisee in exchange for their promises

The parties must bargain for the consideration. Something is **bargained for** if it is sought by the promisor and given by the promisee in exchange for their respective promises. Eliza hires Joe to be her public relations manager for $15,000 a year. Both Eliza and Joe have made promises to induce the other's action. But what if the going rate for a PR manager with Joe's experience is $65,000?

Joe made a bad deal, but that does not mean it lacked consideration. **Courts do not analyze the economic terms of an exchange to determine whether consideration was adequate.** For consideration to be adequate in the eyes of the law, it must provide some benefit to the promisor or some detriment to the promisee, but these need not amount to much. Here, both Eliza and Joe are promisor and promisee; each receives a benefit and incurs a detriment, so consideration exists.

Law professors often call this the "peppercorn rule," a reference to a Civil War–era case in which a judge mused, "What is a valuable consideration? A peppercorn." Even the tiniest benefit to a plaintiff counts, so long as it has a measureable value.[1]

EXAM Strategy

Question: 50 Cent has been rapping all day, and he is very thirsty. He pulls his Ferrari into the parking lot of a convenience store. The store turns out to be closed, but luckily for him, a Pepsi machine sits outside. While walking over to it, he realizes that he has left his wallet at home. Frustrated, he whistles to a 10-year-old kid who is walking by. "Hey kid!" he shouts. "I need to borrow fifty cents!" "I know you are!" the kid replies. Fiddy tries again. "No, no, I need to *borrow* fifty cents!" The kid walks over. "Well, I'm not going to just give you my last fifty cents. But maybe you can sell me something." 50 Cent cannot believe it, but he really is very thirsty. He takes off a Rolex, which is his least expensive bling. "How about this?" "Deal," the kid says, handing over two quarters. Can 50 Cent get his watch back?

Strategy: Even in extreme cases, courts rarely take an interest in *how much* consideration is given or whether everyone got a "good deal." Even though the Rolex is worth thousands of times more than the quarters, the quarters still count under the peppercorn rule.

Result: After this transaction, 50 Cent may have second thoughts, but they will be too late. The kid committed an act by handing over his money—he was under no legal obligation to do so. And 50 Cent received something of small, but measureable, value. So there is consideration to support this deal, and 50 Cent would not get his watch back.

11-2 LEGALITY

In the opening scenario, we saw that gambling agreements are illegal unless specifically authorized by a state statute. In this section, we examine a type of clause common in employment contracts. A **non-compete agreement** is a contract in which one party agrees not to compete with another in a stated type of business. For example, an anchorwoman for an NBC news affiliate in Miami might agree that she will not anchor any other Miami station's news for one year after she leaves her present employer. Non-competes are often valid, but they are sometimes illegal and void.

Contracts Checklist
- [ ] Offer
- [ ] Acceptance
- [ ] Consideration
- [x] Legality
- [ ] Capacity
- [ ] Consent
- [ ] Writing

Free trade is the basis of the American economy, and any bargain that restricts it is suspect. **To be valid, an agreement not to compete must be ancillary to a legitimate bargain.** "Ancillary" means that the noncompetition agreement must be part of a larger agreement. Suppose Cliff sells his gasoline station to Mina, and the two agree that Cliff will not open a competing gas station within five miles any time during the next two years. Cliff's agreement not to compete is ancillary to the sale of his service station. His noncompetition promise is enforceable. But suppose that Cliff and Mina already had the only two gas stations within 35 miles. They agree between themselves not to hire each other's workers. Their agreement might be profitable to them because each could now keep wages artificially low. But their deal is ancillary to no legitimate bargain, and it is therefore void.

The two most common settings for legitimate noncompetition agreements are the *sale of a business* and an *employment relationship*.

---

[1]Hobbs v. Duff, 23 Cal. 596 (1863).

11-2a Non-compete Agreements: Sale of a Business

Kory has operated a real estate office, Hearth Attack, in a small city for 35 years, building an excellent reputation and many ties with the community. She offers to sell you the business and its goodwill for $300,000. But you need assurance that Kory will not take your money and promptly open a competing office across the street. With her reputation and connections, she would ruin your chances of success. You insist on a non-compete clause in the sale contract. In this clause, Kory promises that for one year, she will not open a new real estate office or go to work for a competing company within a 10-mile radius of Hearth Attack. Suppose, six months after selling you the business, Kory goes to work for a competing realtor two blocks away. You seek an injunction (a court order) to prevent her from working. Who wins?

When a non-compete agreement is ancillary to the sale of a business, it is enforceable if reasonable in time, geographic area, and scope of activity. In other words, a court will not enforce a non-compete agreement that lasts an unreasonably long time, covers an unfairly large area, or prohibits the seller of the business from doing a type of work that she never had done before. Measured by this test, Kory is almost certainly bound by her agreement. One year is a reasonable time to allow you to get your new business started. A 10-mile radius is probably about the area that Hearth Attack covers, and realty is obviously a fair business from which to prohibit Kory. A court will grant the injunction, barring Kory from her new job.

If, on the other hand, the non-compete agreement had prevented Kory from working anywhere within 200 miles of Hearth Attack, and she started working 50 miles away, a court would refuse to enforce the contract.

11-2b Non-compete Agreements: Employment Contracts

When you sign an employment contract, the document may well contain a non-compete clause. Employers have legitimate worries that employees might go to a competitor and take with them trade secrets or other proprietary information. Some employers, though, attempt to place harsh restrictions on their employees, perhaps demanding a blanket agreement that the employee will never go to work for a competitor.

Non-competes limit an individual's right to make a living and choose their work. For this reason, about one-third of states have restrictions on the enforceability of employment-related non-competes. California prohibits them altogether, except when they are tied to the sale of a business or a verifiable trade secret.[2] In other states, employment restrictions are highly scrutinized for fairness.

Generally, a non-compete clause in an employment contract is enforceableonly to the extent necessary to protect (1) **trade secrets,** (2) **confidential information,** or (3) **customer lists developed over an extended period.** In general, other restrictions on future employment are unenforceable.[3]

Suppose that Gina, an engineer, goes to work for Fission Chips, a silicon chip manufacturer that specializes in defense work. She signs a non-compete agreement promising never to work for a competitor. Over a period of three years, Gina learns some of Fission's proprietary methods of etching information onto the chips. She acquires a great deal of new expertise about chips generally. And she periodically deals with Fission Chips' customers, all of whom are well-known software and hardware manufacturers.

Gina accepts an offer from WriteSmall, a competitor. Fission Chips races into court, seeking an injunction to block Gina from working for WriteSmall. This injunction threatens Gina's career. If she cannot work for a competitor or use her general engineering skills, what

---

[2]Edwards v. Arthur Andersen LLP, 44 Cal,.4th 937 (S. Ct. Cal. 2008).

[3]If the agreement restricts the employee from *starting a new business*, a court may apply the more lenient standard used for the sale of business; the non-compete clause will be enforced if reasonable in time, geography, and scope of activity.

will she do? And for exactly that reason, no court will grant such a broad order. The court will allow Gina to work for competitors, including WriteSmall. It will order her not to use or reveal any trade secrets belonging to Fission. She will, however, be permitted to use the general expertise she has acquired, and she may contact former customers because anyone could get their names from the yellow pages.

Was the non-compete in the following case styled fairly, or was the employee clipped?

KING v. HEAD START FAMILY HAIR SALONS, INC.

886 So.2d 769
Supreme Court of Alabama, 2004

CASE SUMMARY

Facts: Kathy King was a single mother supporting a college-age daughter. For 25 years, she had worked as a hairstylist. For the most recent 16 years, she had worked at Head Start, which provided haircuts, coloring, and styling for men and women. King was primarily a stylist, though she had also managed one of the Head Start facilities.

King quit Head Start and began working as manager of a Sports Clips shop, located in the same mall as the store she just left. Sports Clip offered only haircuts and primarily served men and boys. Head Start filed suit, claiming that King was violating the noncompetition agreement that she had signed. The agreement prohibited King from working at a competing business within a two-mile radius of any Head Start facility for 12 months after leaving the company. The trial court issued an injunction enforcing the non-compete. King appealed.

Issue: *Was the non-compete agreement valid?*

Decision: The agreement was only partly valid.

Reasoning: Head Start does business in 30 locations throughout Jefferson and Shelby counties. Virtually every hair-care facility in those counties is located within two miles of a Head Start business and is thus covered by the non-competition agreement. The contract is essentially a blanket restriction, entirely barring King from this business.

King must work to support herself and her daughter. She is 40 years old and has worked in the hair-care industry for 25 years. She cannot be expected at this stage in life to learn new job skills. Enforcing the noncompetition agreement would create a grave hardship for her. The contract cannot be permitted to impoverish King and her daughter.

On the other hand, Head Start is entitled to some of the protection it sought in this agreement. The company has a valid concern that if King is permitted to work anywhere she wants, she could take away many customers from Head Start. The trial court should fashion a more reasonable geographic restriction, one that will permit King to ply her trade while ensuring that Head Start does not unfairly lose customers. For example, the lower court could prohibit King from working within two miles of the Head Start facility where she previously worked, or some variation on that idea.

Reversed and remanded.

11-2c Exculpatory Clauses

You decide to capitalize on your expert ability as a skier and open a ski school in Colorado called "Pike's Pique." But you realize that skiing sometimes causes injuries, so you require anyone signing up for lessons to sign this form:

> I agree to hold Pike's Pique and its employees entirely harmless in the event that I am injured in any way or for any reason or cause, including but not limited to any acts, whether negligent or otherwise, of Pike's Pique or any employee or agent thereof.

The day your school opens, Sara Beth, an instructor, deliberately pushes Toby over a cliff because Toby criticizes her clothes. Eddie, a beginning student, "blows out" his knee attempting an advanced racing turn. And Maureen, another student, reaches the bottom of a steep run and slams into a snowmobile that Sara Beth parked there. Maureen, Eddie, and Toby's families all sue Pike's Pique. You defend based on the form you had them sign. Does it save the day?

Exculpatory clause

A contract provision that attempts to release one party from liability in the event the other party is injured

The form on which you are relying is an **exculpatory clause**, that is, one that attempts to release you from liability in the event of injury to another party. Exculpatory clauses are common. Ski schools use them, and so do parking lots, landlords, warehouses, and daycare centers. All manner of businesses hope to avoid large tort judgments by requiring their customers to give up any right to recover. Is such a clause valid? Sometimes. Courts often—but not always—ignore exculpatory clauses, finding that one party was forcing the other party to give up legal rights that no one should be forced to surrender.

An exculpatory clause is generally unenforceable when it attempts to exclude an intentional tort or gross negligence. When Sara Beth pushes Toby over a cliff, that is the intentional tort of battery. A court will not enforce the exculpatory clause. Sara Beth is clearly liable.[4] As to the snowmobile at the bottom of the run, if a court determines that was gross negligence (carelessness far greater than ordinary negligence), then the exculpatory clause will again be ignored. If, however, it was ordinary negligence, then we must continue the analysis.

An exculpatory clause is generally unenforceable when the affected activity is in the public interest, such as medical care, public transportation, or some essential service. What about Eddie's suit against Pike's Pique? Eddie claims that he should never have been allowed to attempt an advanced maneuver. His suit is for ordinary negligence, and the exculpatory clause probably does bar him from recovery. Skiing is a recreational activity. No one is obligated to do it, and there is no strong public interest in ensuring that we have access to ski slopes.

An exculpatory clause is generally unenforceable when the parties have greatly unequal bargaining power. When Maureen flies to Colorado, suppose that the airline requires her to sign a form contract with an exculpatory clause. Because the airline almost certainly has much greater bargaining power, it can afford to offer a "take it or leave it" contract. But because the bargaining power is so unequal, the clause is probably unenforceable.

An exculpatory clause is generally unenforceable unless the clause is clearly written and readily visible. Thus, if Pike's Pique gave all ski students an eight-page contract, and the exculpatory clause was at the bottom of page 7 in small print, the average customer would never notice it. The clause would probably be void.

EXAM Strategy

Question: Shauna flew a World War II fighter aircraft as a member of an exhibition flight team. While the team was performing in a delta formation, another plane collided with Shauna's aircraft, causing her to crash-land, leaving her permanently disabled. Shauna sued the other pilot and the team. The defendants moved to dismiss based on an exculpatory clause that Shauna had signed. The clause was one paragraph long and stated that Shauna knew team flying was inherently dangerous and could result in injury or death. She agreed not to hold the team or any members liable in case of an accident. Shauna argued that the clause should not be enforced against her if she could prove the other pilot was negligent. Please rule.

Strategy: The issue is whether the exculpatory clause is valid. Courts are likely to declare such clauses void if they concern vital activities like medical care, exclude an intentional tort or gross negligence, or arise from unequal bargaining power.

Result: This is a clear, short clause, between parties with equal bargaining power, and does not exclude an intentional tort or gross negligence. The activity is unimportant to the public welfare. The clause is valid. Even if the other pilot was negligent, Shauna will lose, meaning the court should dismiss her lawsuit.

---

[4] Note that Pike's Pique is probably not liable under agency law principles that preclude an employer's liability for an employee's intentional tort.

11-3 CAPACITY

For Kevin Green, it was love at first sight. She was sleek, as quick as a cat, and a beautiful deep blue. He paid $4,600 cash for the used Camaro. The car soon blew a gasket, and Kevin demanded his money back. But the Camaro came with no guarantee, and Star Chevrolet, the dealer, refused. Kevin repaired the car himself. Next, some unpleasantness on the highway left the car a worthless wreck. Kevin received the full value of the car from his insurance company. Then he sued the dealer, seeking a refund of his purchase price. The dealer pointed out that it was not responsible for the accident, and that the car had no warranty of any kind. Yet the court awarded Kevin the full value of his car. How can this be?

The automobile dealer ignored *legal capacity*. Kevin Green was only 16 years old when he bought the car, and a minor, said the court, has the right to cancel any agreement he made, for any reason. **Capacity** is the legal ability of a party to enter a contract. Someone may lack capacity because of his young age or mental infirmity. Two groups of people usually lack legal capacity: minors and those with a mental impairment.

Contracts Checklist
- ☐ Offer
- ☐ Acceptance
- ☐ Consideration
- ☐ Legality
- ☑ Capacity
- ☐ Consent
- ☐ Writing

Capacity
The legal ability to enter into a contract

11-3a Minors

A minor is someone under the age of 18. Because a minor lacks legal capacity, she normally can create only a voidable contract. **A voidable contract may be cancelled by the party who lacks capacity.** Notice that *only the party lacking capacity* may cancel the agreement. So a minor who enters into a contract generally may choose between enforcing the agreement or negating it. The other party, however, has no such right.

Disaffirmance

A minor who wishes to escape from a contract generally may **disaffirm** it; that is, he may notify the other party that he refuses to be bound by the agreement. Because Kevin was 16 when he signed, the deal was voidable. When the Camaro blew a gasket and the lad informed Star Chevrolet that he wanted his money back, he was disaffirming the contract, which he could do for any reason at all. Kevin was entitled to his money back. If Star Chevrolet had understood the law of capacity, it would have towed the Camaro away and returned the young man's $4,600. At least the dealership would have had a repairable automobile.

Disaffirm
To give notice of refusal to be bound by an agreement

Restitution

A minor who disaffirms a contract must return the consideration he has received, to the extent he is able. Restoring the other party to its original position is called **restitution**. The consideration that Kevin Green received in the contract was, of course, the Camaro. If Star Chevrolet had delivered a check for $4,600, Kevin would have been obligated to return the car.

What happens if the minor is not able to return the consideration because he no longer has it or it has been destroyed? Most states hold that the minor is still entitled to his money back. Kevin Green got his money and Star Chevrolet received a fine lesson.

Restitution
Restoring an injured party to its original position

11-3b Mentally Impaired Persons

A person suffers from a mental impairment if, by reason of mental illness or defect, he is unable to understand the nature and consequences of the transaction.[5] The mental impairment can be insanity that has been formally declared by a court, or mental illness that has never been ruled on but is now evident. The impairment may also be due to some other mental illness, such as schizophrenia, or to mental retardation, brain injury, senility, or any other cause that renders the person unable to understand the nature and consequences of the contract.

---

[5]Reinstatement (Second) of Contracts §15.

A party suffering a mental impairment generally creates only a voidable contract. The impaired person has the right to disaffirm the contract, just as a minor does. But again, the contract is voidable, not void. The mentally impaired party generally has the right to full performance if she wishes.

But the law creates an exception: If a person has been adjudicated insane, then all of his future agreements are void. "Adjudicated insane" means that a judge has made a formal finding that a person is mentally incompetent and has assigned the person a guardian.

11-3c Intoxication

Similar rules apply in cases of drug or alcohol **intoxication**. When one party is so intoxicated that he cannot understand the nature and consequences of the transaction, the contract is voidable.

We wish to stress that courts are *highly* skeptical of intoxication arguments. If you go out drinking and make a foolish agreement, you are probably stuck with it. Even if you are too drunk to drive, you are probably not nearly too drunk to make a contract. If your blood alcohol level is, say, .08, your coordination and judgment are poor. Driving in such a condition is dangerous. But you probably have a fairly clear awareness of what is going on around you.

To back out of a contract on the grounds of intoxication, you must be able to provide evidence that you did not understand the "nature of the agreement" or the basic deal that you made.

11-4 REALITY OF CONSENT

Smiley offers to sell you his house for $300,000, and you agree to buy it in writing. After you move in, you discover that the house is sinking into the earth at the rate of six inches per week. In 12 months, your only access to the house may be through the chimney. You sue, seeking to **rescind**, or cancel, the agreement. You argue that when you signed the contract, you did not truly consent because you lacked essential information. In this section, we look at fraud and mistake.

11-4a Fraud

Fraud begins when a party to a contract says something that is factually wrong. "This house has no termites," says a homeowner to a prospective buyer. If the house is swarming with the nasty pests, the statement is a misrepresentation. But does it amount to fraud? An injured person must show the following:

1. The defendant knew that his statement was false or he made the statement recklessly and without knowledge of whether it was false;

2. The false statement was material; and

3. The injured party justifiably relied on the statement.

Element One: Intentional or Reckless Misrepresentation of Fact

The injured party must show a false statement of fact. Notice that this does not mean the statement was necessarily a "lie." If a homeowner says that the famous architect Stanford White designed her house, but Bozo Loco actually did the work, it is a false statement.

Now, if the owner knows that Loco designed the house, she has committed the first element of fraud. And, if she has no idea who designed the house, her assertion that it was "Stanford White" also meets the first element.

Contracts Checklist
- ☐ Offer
- ☐ Acceptance
- ☐ Consideration
- ☐ Legality
- ☐ Capacity
- ☑ Consent
- ☐ Writing

Rescind
To cancel a contract

Fraud
Intending to induce the other party to contract, knowing the words are false or uncertain that they are true

But, the owner might have a good reason for the error. Perhaps a local history book identifies the house as a Stanford White. If she makes the statement with a reasonable belief that she is telling the truth, she has made an innocent misrepresentation (discussed in the next section) and not fraud.

Opinions and "puffery" do not amount to fraud. An opinion is not a statement of fact. A seller says, "I think land values around here will be going up 20 or 30 percent for the foreseeable future." That statement is pretty enticing to a buyer, but it is not a false statement of fact. The maker is clearly stating her own opinion, and the buyer who relies on it does so at his peril. A close relative of opinion is something called "puffery."

Get ready for one of the most astonishing experiences you've ever had! This paragraph on puffery is going to be the finest part of any textbook you have ever read! "But what happens," you might wonder, "if this paragraph fails to astonish? What if I find the issue dull, the writing mediocre, and the legal summary incomprehensible? Can I sue for fraud?" No. The promises we made were mere puffery. A statement is puffery when a reasonable person would realize that it is a sales pitch, representing the exaggerated opinion of the seller. Puffery is not a statement of fact.

Element Two: Materiality

The injured party must demonstrate that the statement was material, or important. A minor misstatement does not meet this second element of fraud. Was the misstatement likely to significantly influence the decision of the misled party? If so, it was material.

Imagine a farmer selling a piece of his land. He measures the acres himself and calculates a total of 200. If the actual acreage is 199, he has almost certainly not made a *material* misstatement. But if the actual acreage is 150, he has.

Element Three: Justifiable Reliance

The injured party must also show that she actually did rely on the false statement and that her reliance was reasonable. Suppose the seller of a gas station lies through his teeth about the structural soundness of the building. The buyer believes what he hears but does not much care because he plans to demolish the building and construct a day-care center. There was a material misstatement but no reliance, and the buyer may not rescind.

The reliance must be justifiable—that is, reasonable. If the seller of wilderness land tells Lewis that the area is untouched by pollution, but Lewis can see a large lake on the property covered with six inches of oily, red scum, Lewis is not justified in relying on the seller's statements. If he goes forward with the purchase, he may not rescind.

Plaintiff's Remedies for Fraud

In the case of fraud, the injured party generally has a choice of rescinding the contract or suing for damages or, in some cases, doing both. The contract is voidable, which meant that the injured party is not *forced* to rescind the deal but may if he wants. Fraud *permits* the injured party to cancel. Alternatively, the injured party can sue for damages—the difference between what the contract promised and what it delivered.

Nancy learns that the building she bought has a terrible heating system. A new one will cost $12,000. If the seller told her the system was "like new," Nancy may rescind the deal. But it may be economically harmful for her to do so. She might have sold her old house, hired a mover, taken a new job, and so forth. What are her other remedies? She could move into the new house and sue for the difference between what she got and what was promised, which is $12,000, the cost of replacing the heating system.

In some states, a party injured by fraud may both rescind *and* sue for damages. In these states, Nancy could rescind her contract, get her deposit back, and then sue the seller for any damages she has suffered. Her damages might be, for example, a lost opportunity to buy another house or wasted moving expenses.

Innocent Misrepresentation

Misrepresentation
A statement that is factually wrong

If all elements of fraud are present except the misrepresentation of fact was not made intentionally or recklessly, then innocent **misrepresentation** has occurred. So, if a person misstates a material fact and induces reliance, but he had good reason to believe that his statement was true, then he has not committed fraud. Most states allow rescission of a contract, but not damages, in such a case.

11-4b Mistake

A mistake can take many forms. It may be a basic error about an essential characteristic of the thing being sold. It could be an erroneous prediction about future prices, such as an expectation that oil prices will rise. It might be a mechanical error, such as a builder offering to build a new home for $300 when he clearly meant to bid $300,000. Some mistakes lead to voidable contracts; others create enforceable deals. The first distinction is between unilateral and mutual mistakes.

Unilateral Mistake

Unilateral mistake
Occurs when only one party negotiates based on a factual error

A **unilateral mistake** occurs when one party enters a contract under a mistaken assumption; the other is not mistaken. It is not easy for the mistaken party to rescind a contract – the more astute party may simply have made a better bargain. So, to rescind a contract a mistaken party must show something more than just a regrettable deal.

To rescind for unilateral mistake, the mistaken party must demonstrate that he entered the contract because of a basic factual error and that the nonmistaken party knew or had reason to know of the error.

In many contract negotiations, one party knows more, which helps him secure favorable deals. The law of unilateral mistake draws the line where one party takes *unfair* advantage of what he knows to be another's error. **If the nonmistaken party knows or has reason to know of the other party's error, courts will not allow him to profit by snapping it up.**

Fernando is an art dealer who specializes in nineteenth century French painting. At Fiona's flea market stall, he sees a painting that he suspects is by Gustave Courbet. Knowing the painting could be worth millions, Fernando offers Fiona $100 for it. She accepts his offer because she thinks the painting is, at best, by one of Courbet's students. Fernando then does further research, which confirms his guess. He ultimately auctions the masterpiece for $2.4 million. For Fiona to be able to rescind the contract, she must show that Fernando's hunch was much more than a lucky guess, that he had known certainly that the painting was by Courbet. Practically speaking, cases like these are difficult for plaintiffs to win because they must prove that the nonmistaken party knew and that the parties had not assumed the risk of the error.

Mutual Mistake

Mutual mistake
Occurs when both parties negotiate based on the same fundamental factual error

A **mutual mistake** occurs when both contracting parties share the same mistake. **If the contract is based on a fundamental factual error by both parties, the contract is voidable by either one.**

But what types of errors are important enough to warrant rescission? Generally, when the parties are mistaken as to the existence or the identity of the contract's subject matter, the contract is voidable. Believing himself the rightful owner, Arthur contracts to sell a parcel of land to James. When it is later discovered that the land never belonged to Arthur, James can rescind the contract. Both parties were mistaken as to the existence of Arthur's land.

Farnsworth believes he is selling Corbin a topaz; and Corbin thinks he is buying a topaz. In fact, both are wrong: The stone turns out to be a diamond. Since the parties made a material error as to the subject of their contract, there was no valid assent and either one can rescind.

The following classic case illustrates a basic factual mistake as to the subject matter of a contract. When is a cow more than a cow? Answer: When it is two.

Landmark Case

SHERWOOD V. WALKER

66 Mich. 568
Supreme Court of Michigan, 1887

Facts: Hiram Walker & Sons, a cattle breeder, bought a cow named "Rose 2d of Aberlone" for $850. After a few years, Walker realized that Rose was infertile, which made her much less valuable. Based on this assumption, Walker agreed to sell Rose for beef to Sherwood for $80.

But when Sherwood came to collect Rose, the parties realized that (surprise!) she was pregnant, making her now worth about $1,000. Walker refused to part with her, and Sherwood sued for breach of contract. Walker defended, claiming that both parties had made a *mistake* and that the contract was voidable. After the lower court ruled the contract was enforceable, Walker appealed.

Issue: *Does a mutual mistake of fact make a contract voidable?*

CASE SUMMARY

the contract is voidable. If the parties are only mistaken as to a slight difference or quality ("does Rose weigh 1350 or 1400 pounds?), the contract remains binding.

A mistake about a cow's fertility goes to the very substance of the deal: A barren cow and a breeding cow are entirely different animals, used for different purposes. Sherwood and Walker intended to buy and sell a barren cow; instead, she was capable of breeding. There was no contract to sell Rose as she actually was. Walker was entitled to rescind the contract.

Decision: Yes.

Reasoning: Parties may rescind contracts based on mutual mistake of material fact. What is material? When both parties are mistaken as to the subject matter or the whole substance of the sale ("what are we buying?"), then

The defense of mistake is not a cure-all for all bad deals. Courts will not rescind contracts on the basis of a prediction error, a mistaken value, or where the parties assume the risk of error.

Prediction Error. Sherwood and Walker were both wrong about Rose's reproductive ability, and the error was basic enough to cause a tenfold difference in price. Walker, the injured party, was entitled to rescind the contract. Note that the error must be *factual*. Suppose Walker sold Rose thinking that the price of beef was going to drop, when in fact the price rose 60 percent in five months. That would be simply a *prediction* that proved wrong, and Walker would have no right to rescind.

Mistake of Value. Here is one case in which it pays to know less. Suppose that Fiona the flea market vendor sold the nineteenth century masterpiece for $100 to Marguerite, a financial analyst with no inkling of its real worth. Both Fiona and Marguerite shared the same mistake in their estimate of the painting's market value. Sadly for Fiona, Marguerite will reap the benefit of her bargain, because a mistaken value alone is not enough to take back a deal.

Conscious Uncertainty. No rescission is permitted when one of the parties knows he is taking on a risk, that is, he realizes there is uncertainty about the quality of the thing being exchanged. Rufus offers 10 acres of mountainous land to Priscilla. "I can't promise you anything about this land," he says, "but they've found gold on every adjoining parcel." Priscilla, eager for gold, buys the land, digs long and hard, and discovers—mud. She may not rescind the contract. She understood the risk she was assuming, and there was no mutual mistake.

EXAM Strategy

Question: Joe buys an Otterhound named Barky from Purity Dog Shop. He pays $2,500 for the puppy, the high cost due to the certificate Purity gives him, indicating that the puppy's parents were both AKC champions (elite dogs). Two months later, Joe sells the hound to Emily for $2,800. Joe and Emily both believe that Barky is descended from champions. Then a state investigation reveals that Purity has been cheating and its certificates are fakes. Barky is a mixed-breed dog, worth about $100. Emily sues Joe. Who wins?

Strategy: Both parties are mistaken about the kind of dog Joe is selling, so this is an instance of bilateral mistake. What is the rule in such cases?

Result: If the two sides agree based on an important factual error, the contract is voidable by the injured party. A mutt is entirely different from a dog that might become a champion. The parties erred about the essence of their deal. Joe's good faith does not save him, and Emily is entitled to rescind.

11-5 CONTRACTS IN WRITING

> **Perry moved out of their dorm room into a suite at the Ritz and refused to give Oliver one red cent.**

Oliver and Perry were college roommates, two sophomores with contrasting personalities. They were sitting in the cafeteria with some friends, Oliver chatting away, Perry slumped on a plastic bench. Oliver suggested that they buy a lottery ticket, as the prize for that week's drawing was $3 million. Perry muttered, "Nah. You never win if you buy just one ticket." Oliver bubbled up, "OK, we'll buy a ticket every week. We'll keep buying them from now until we graduate. Come on, it'll be fun. This month, I'll buy the tickets. Next month, you will, and so on." Other students urged Perry to do it, and finally, grudgingly, he agreed. The two friends carefully reviewed their deal. Each party was providing consideration, namely, the responsibility for purchasing tickets during his month. The amount of each purchase was clearly defined at one dollar. They would start that week and continue until graduation day, two and a half years down the road. Finally, they would share equally any money won. As three witnesses looked on, they shook hands on the bargain. That month, Oliver bought a ticket every week, randomly choosing numbers, and won nothing. The next month, Perry bought a ticket with equally random numbers—and won $52 million. Perry moved out of their dorm room into a suite at the Ritz and refused to give Oliver one red cent. Oliver sued, seeking $26 million and the return of his blue fleece hoodie.

If the former friends had read this chapter, they would never have slid into such a mess. In the last chapter, we covered the basics of contract law, and now we put the icing on the cake. We will examine which contracts must be in writing, when third parties have rights or obligations under an agreement, what problems arise in the performance of contracts, and the remedies available when a deal goes awry. Oliver and Perry's case involves the Statute of Frauds, the law that tells us which contracts must be written.

Contracts Checklist
- [ ] Offer
- [ ] Acceptance
- [ ] Consideration
- [ ] Legality
- [ ] Capacity
- [ ] Consent
- [x] Writing

11-5a The Statute of Frauds

Statute of Frauds
Requires certain contracts to be in writing

The rule we examine in this chapter is not exactly news. Parliament passed the original **Statute of Frauds** in 1677. The purpose was to prevent lying (fraud) in civil lawsuits. The statute required that in several types of cases, a contract would be enforced only if it was in writing. Almost all states in our own country later passed their own statutes making the same requirements. It is important to remember, as we examine the rules and exceptions, that Parliament and the state legislatures all had a commendable, straightforward purpose in passing their respective statutes of fraud: *to provide a court with the best possible evidence of whether the parties intended to make a contract.*

A plaintiff may not enforce any of the following agreements unless the agreement, or some memorandum of it, is in writing and signed by the defendant. The agreements that must be in writing are those:

- For any interest in **land;**

- That **cannot be performed within one year;**

- To pay the **debt of another;**

- Made by an **executor of an estate;**

- Made in **consideration of marriage;** and

- For the **sale of goods of $500 or more.**

Unenforceable (Sorry, Oliver)

In other words, when two parties make an agreement covered by any one of these six topics, it must be in writing to be enforceable. Oliver and Perry made a definite agreement to purchase lottery tickets during alternate months and share the proceeds of any winning ticket. But their agreement was to last two and one-half years. As the second item on the list indicates, a contract must be in writing if it cannot be performed within one year. The good news is that Oliver gets his hoodie back. The bad news is that he gets none of the lottery money. Even though three witnesses saw the deal made, it is unlikely to be enforced in any state. Perry the pessimist will probably walk away with all $52 million.[6]

11-5b Contracts that Must Be in Writing

Agreements for an Interest in Land

A contract for the sale of any interest in land must be in writing to be enforceable. Notice the phrase "interest in land." This means any legal right regarding land. A house on a lot is an interest in land. A mortgage, an easement, and a leased apartment are all interests in land. As a general rule, leases must therefore be in writing, although many states have created an exception for short-term leases of a year or less.

Exception: Full Performance by the Seller.   If the seller completely performs her side of a contract for an interest in land, a court is likely to enforce the agreement even if it was oral. Adam orally agrees to sell his condominium to Maggie for $150,000. Adam delivers the deed to Maggie and expects his money a week later, but Maggie fails to pay. Most courts will allow Adam to enforce the oral contract and collect the full purchase price from Maggie.

---

[6]Perry might also raise *illegality* as a defense, claiming that a contract for gambling is illegal. That defense is likely to fail. Courts appear to distinguish between the simple purchase of a legal lottery ticket, which friends often share, and the more traditional - and socially dangerous - gambling contracts involving horse racing or casino betting. See, for example, Pando v. Fernandez, 118 A.D.2d 474, 499 N.Y. App. Div. LEXIS 54345 (N.Y. App. Div. 1986), finding no illegality in an agreement to purchase a lottery ticket, even where the purchaser was a minor! Because an illegality defense would probably fail Perry, it is all the more unfortunate that Oliver did not jot down their agreement in writing.

Exception: Part Performance by the Buyer.   The buyer of land may be able to enforce an oral contract if she paid part of the purchase price and either entered upon the land or made improvements to it. Suppose that Eloise sues Grover to enforce an alleged oral contract to sell a lot in Happydale. She claims they struck a bargain in January. Grover defends based on the Statute of Frauds, saying that even if the two did reach an oral agreement, it is unenforceable. Eloise proves that she paid 10 percent of the purchase price, and that in February, she began excavating on the lot to build a house, and that Grover knew of the work. Eloise has established part performance and will be allowed to enforce her contract.

Agreements that Cannot Be Performed within One Year

Contracts that cannot be performed within one year are unenforceable unless they are in writing. This one-year period begins on the date the parties make the agreement. The critical phrase here is "*cannot* be performed within one year." If a contract could be completed within one year, it need not be in writing. Betty gets a job at Burger Brain, throwing fries in oil. Her boss tells her she can have Fridays off for as long as she works there. That oral contract is enforceable whether Betty stays one week or 57 years. It could have been performed within one year if, say, Betty quit the job after six months. Therefore, it does not need to be in writing.[7]

If the agreement will necessarily take longer than one year to finish, it must be in writing to be enforceable. If Betty is hired for three years as manager of Burger Brain, the agreement is unenforceable unless put in writing. She cannot perform three years of work in one year.

Type of Agreement	Enforceability
Cannot be performed within one year. *Example:* An offer of employment for three years.	Must be in writing to be enforceable.
Might be performed within one year, although could take many years to perform. *Example:* "As long as you work here at Burger Brain, you may have Fridays off."	Enforceable whether it is oral or written, because the employee might quit working a month later.

Promise to Pay the Debt of Another

When one person agrees to pay the debt of another as a favor to that debtor, it is called a collateral promise, and it must be in writing to be enforceable. A student applies for a $10,000 loan to help pay for college, and her father agrees to repay the bank if the student defaults. The bank will insist that the father's promise be in writing because his oral promise alone is unenforceable.

---

[7]This rule represents the majority view. In most states, if a company hires an employee "for life," the contract need not be in writing because the employee could die within one year. "Contracts of uncertain duration are simply excluded [from the Statute of Frauds]; the provision covers only those contracts whose performance cannot possibly be completed within a year." Restatement (Second) of Contracts §130, Comment a, at 328 (1981). However, a few states disagree. The Illinois Supreme Court ruled that a contract for lifetime employment is enforceable only if written. McInerney v. Charter Golf, Inc., 176 Ill. 2d 482 (Ill. 1997).

Promise Made by an Executor of an Estate

An executor is the person who is in charge of an estate after someone dies. The executor's job is to pay debts of the deceased, obtain money owed to him, and disburse the assets according to the will. In most cases, the executor will use only the estate's assets to pay those debts, but occasionally she might offer her own money. An executor's promise to use her own funds to pay a debt of the deceased must be in writing to be enforceable.

Promise Made in Consideration of Marriage

This is not the stuff of fairy tales: Barney is a multimillionaire with the integrity of a gangster and the charm of a tax collector. He proposes to Li-Tsing, who promptly rejects him. Barney then pleads that if Li-Tsing will be his bride, he will give her an island he owns off the coast of California. Li-Tsing begins to see his good qualities and accepts. After they are married, Barney refuses to deliver the deed. Li-Tsing will get nothing from a court either, because a promise made in consideration of marriage must be in writing to be enforceable.

11-5c What the Writing Must Contain

Each of the five types of contract described earlier must be in writing in order to be enforceable. What must the writing contain? It may be a carefully typed contract, using precise legal terminology, or an informal memorandum scrawled on the back of a paper napkin at a business lunch. The writing may consist of more than one document, written at different times, with each document making a piece of the puzzle. However, there are some general requirements. The contract or memorandum:

- Must be signed by the defendant, and
- Must state with reasonable certainty the name of each party, the subject matter of the agreement, and all the essential terms and promises.[8]

Signature

A Statute of Frauds typically states that the writing must be "signed by the party to be charged therewith," in other words, the defendant. Judges define "signature" very broadly. Using a pen to write one's name, though sufficient, is not required. A secretary who stamps an executive's signature on a letter fulfills this requirement. Any other mark or logo placed on a document to indicate acceptance, even an "X," will likely satisfy the Statute of Frauds. Electronic commerce creates new methods of signing—and new controversies, discussed later in this chapter.

The Writing Requirement and Electronic Signatures.   Modern life has moved online: We can now buy everything from toothpaste to cars with the click of a mouse. What happens to the writing requirement, though, when there is no paper? The Statute of Frauds requires some sort of "signature" to prove that the defendant committed to the deal. Today, an "electronic signature" could mean a name typed (or automatically included) at the bottom of an e-mail message, a retinal or vocal scan, or a name signed by electronic pen on a writing tablet, among others.

---

[8]Restatement (Second) of Contracts §131.

E-signatures are valid in all 50 states. Almost every state has adopted the Uniform Electronic Transactions Act (UETA), which makes *electronic* contracts and signatures as enforceable as those on paper.[9] In other words, the normal rules of contract formation apply, and neither party can avoid a deal merely because it originated electronically. A federal statute, the **Electronic Signatures in Global and National Commerce Act (E-SIGN)** extends UETA's principles to interstate and foreign commerce.

Note that, in many states, certain documents still require a traditional (non-electronic) signature. Wills, adoptions, court orders, and notice of foreclosure are common exceptions. If in doubt, get a hard copy, signed in ink.

Reasonable Certainty

Suppose Garfield and Hayes are having lunch, discussing the sale of Garfield's vacation condominium. They agree on a price and want to make some notation of the agreement even before their lawyers work out a detailed purchase and sales agreement. A perfectly adequate memorandum might say, "Garfield agrees to sell Hayes his condominium at 234 Baron Boulevard, apartment 18, for $350,000 cash, payable on June 18, 2004, and Hayes promises to pay the sum on that day." They should make two copies of their agreement and sign both.

11-5d Sale of Goods

The UCC requires a writing for the sale of goods priced at $500 or more. This is the sixth and final contract that must be written, although the Code's requirements are easier to meet than those of the common law. In some cases, the Code dispenses altogether with the writing requirement. The basic Statute of Frauds rule is §2-201(1). Important exceptions are found at §§2-201(2) and (3).

The essential UCC rule: A contract for the sale of goods worth $500 or more is not enforceable unless there is some writing, signed by the defendant, indicating that the parties reached an agreement. The key difference between the common law rule and the UCC rule is that the Code does not require all the terms of the agreement to be in writing. The Code demands only an indication that the parties reached an agreement. The two things that are essential are the signature of the defendant and the quantity of goods being sold. The quantity of goods is required because this is the one term for which there will be no objective evidence. Suppose a short memorandum between textile dealers indicates that Seller will sell to Buyer "grade AA, 100% cotton, white athletic socks." If the writing does not state the price, the parties can testify at court about what the market price was at the time of the deal. But how many socks were to be delivered? One hundred pairs or 100,000? The quantity must be written.

Chapter Conclusion

It is not enough to bargain effectively and obtain a contract that gives you exactly what you want. The deal must have consideration or it will not amount to a contract. Bargaining a contract with a non-compete or exculpatory clause that is too one-sided may lead a court to ignore it. Both parties must be adults of sound mind and must give genuine consent. Misrepresentation and mistakes indicate that at least one party did not truly consent. Some contracts must be in writing to be enforceable, and the writing must be clear and unambiguous.

---

[9]Except Illinois, New York, and Washington.

EXAM REVIEW

1. **CONSIDERATION** There are three rules of consideration:

   - Both parties must get something of measureable value from the contract.

   - A *promise* to give something of value counts as consideration.

   - The two parties must have bargained for whatever was exchanged.

2. **ACT OR FORBEARANCE** The item of value can be either an act or a forbearance.

3. **ADEQUACY** The courts will seldom inquire into the adequacy of consideration. This is the "peppercorn rule."

4. **ILLEGAL CONTRACTS** Illegal contracts are void and unenforceable. Claims of illegality often arise concerning non-compete clauses and exculpatory clauses.

EXAM Strategy

Question: The purchaser of a business insisted on putting this clause in the sales contract: The seller would not compete, for five years, "anywhere in the United States, the continent of North America, or anywhere else on Earth." What danger does that contract represent *to the purchaser?*

Strategy: This is a non-compete clause based on the sale of a business. Such clauses are valid if reasonable. Is this clause reasonable? If it is unreasonable, what might a court do? (See the "Result" at the end of this section.)

5. **CAPACITY** Minors, mentally impaired persons, and intoxicated persons generally may disaffirm contracts.

6. **FRAUD** Fraud is grounds for disaffirming a contract. The injured party must prove a false statement of fact, materiality, and justifiable reliance.

7. **MISTAKE** In a bilateral mistake, either party may rescind the contract. In a case of unilateral mistake, the injured party may rescind only in limited circumstances.

8. **WRITING REQUIRED** Contracts that must be in writing to be enforceable concern:

   - The sale of any interest in land,

   - Agreements that cannot be performed within one year,

   - Promises to pay the debt of another,

   - Promises made by an executor of an estate,

   - Promises made in consideration of marriage, and

   - The sale of goods worth $500 or more.

Question: Donald Waide had a contracting business. He bought most of his supplies from Paul Bingham's supply center. Waide fell behind on his bills, and Bingham told Waide that he would extend no more credit to him. That same day, Donald's father, Elmer Waide, came to Bingham's store and said to Bingham that he would "stand good" for any sales to Donald made on credit. Based on Elmer's statement, Bingham again gave Donald credit, and Donald ran up $10,000 in goods before Bingham sued Donald and Elmer. What defense did Elmer make, and what was the outcome?

Strategy: This was an oral agreement, so the issue is whether the promise had to be in writing to be enforceable. Review the list of six contracts that must be in writing. Is this agreement there? (See the "Result" at the end of this section.)

9. **WRITING CONTENTS**   The writing must be signed by the defendant and must state the name of all parties, the subject matter of the agreement, and all essential terms and promises

---

4. Result: "Anywhere else on Earth"? This is almost certainly unreasonable. It is hard to imagine a purchaser who would legitimately need such wide-ranging protection. In some states, a court might rewrite the clause, limiting the effect to the seller's state or some other reasonable area. However, in other states, a court finding a clause unreasonable will declare it void in its entirety—enabling the seller to open a competing business next door.

8. Result: Elmer made a promise to pay the debt of another. He did so as a favor to his son. This is a collateral promise. Elmer never signed any such promise, and the agreement cannot be enforced against him.

MATCHING QUESTIONS

Match the following terms with their definitions:

___A. Fraud

___B. Restitution

___C. Part performance

___D. Exculpatory clause

___E. Consideration

1. A contract clause intended to relieve one party from potential tort liability

2. The idea that contracts must be a two-way street

3. The intention to deceive the other party

4. Restoring the other party to its original position

5. Entry onto land, or improvements made to it, by a buyer who has no written contract

TRUE/FALSE QUESTIONS

Circle true or false:

1. T F A contract may not be rescinded based on puffery.

2. T F An agreement for the sale of a house does not need to be in writing if the deal will be completed within one year.

3. T F Non-compete clauses are suspect because they tend to restrain free trade.

4. T F A seller of property must generally disclose latent defects that he knows about.

5. T F A court is unlikely to enforce an exculpatory clause included in a contract for surgery.

6. T F An agreement for the sale of 600 plastic cups, worth $0.50 each, must be in writing to be enforceable.

MULTIPLE-CHOICE QUESTIONS

1. In which case is a court most likely to enforce an exculpatory clause?
   (a) Dentistry
   (b) Hang gliding
   (c) Parking lot
   (d) Public transportation
   (e) Accounting

2. Sarah, age 17, uses $850 of her hard-earned, summer-job money to pay cash for a diamond pendant for the senior prom. She has a wonderful time at the dance, but decides the pendant was an extravagance, returns it, and demands a refund. The store has a "no refund" policy that is clearly stated on a sign on the wall. There was no defect in the pendant. The store refuses the refund. When Sarah sues, she will:
   (a) win $850.
   (b) win $425.
   (c) win, but only if she did not notice the "no refund" policy.
   (d) win, but only if she did not think the "no refund" policy applied to her.
   (e) lose.

3. Tobias is selling a surrealist painting. He tells Maud that the picture is by the famous French artist Magritte, although in fact Tobias has no idea whether that is true or not. Tobias's statement is:
   (a) bilateral mistake.
   (b) unilateral mistake.
   (c) fraud.
   (d) innocent misrepresentation.
   (e) legal, so long as he acted in good faith.

4. Louise emails Sonya, "I will sell you my house at 129 Brittle Blvd. for $88,000, payable in one month. Best, Louise." Sonya emails back, "Louise, I accept the offer to buy your house at that price. Sonya." Neither party prints a copy of the two emails.

   (a) The parties have a binding contract for the sale of Louise's house.

   (b) Louise is bound by the agreement, but Sonya is not.

   (c) Sonya is bound by the agreement, but Louise is not.

   (d) Neither party is bound because the agreement was never put in writing.

   (e) Neither party is bound because the agreement was never signed.

5. In February, Chuck orally agrees to sell his hunting cabin, with 15 acres, to Kyle for $35,000, with the deal to be completed in July, when Kyle will have the money. In March, while Chuck is vacationing on his land, he permits Kyle to enter the land and dig the foundation for a new cottage. In July, Kyle arrives with the money, but Chuck refuses to sell. Kyle sues.

   (a) Chuck wins because the contract was never put in writing.

   (b) Chuck wins because the contract terms were unclear.

   (c) Kyle wins because a contract for vacation property does not need to be written.

   (d) Kyle wins because Chuck allowed him to dig the foundation.

   (e) Kyle wins because Chuck has committed fraud.

6. Ted's wallet is as empty as his bank account, and he needs $3,500 immediately. Fortunately, he has three gold coins that he inherited from his grandfather. Each is worth $2,500, but it is Sunday, and the local rare-coin store is closed. When approached, Ted's neighbor Andrea agrees to buy the first coin for $2,300. Another neighbor, Cami, agrees to buy the second for $1,100. A final neighbor, Lorne, offers "all the money I have on me"—$100—for the last coin. Desperate, Ted agrees to the proposal. Which of the deals is supported by consideration?

   (a) Ted's agreement with Andrea, only

   (b) Ted's agreements with Andrea and Cami, only

   (c) All three of the agreements

   (d) None of the agreements

Case Questions

1. Brockwell left his boat to be repaired at Lake Gaston Sales. The boat contained electronic equipment and other personal items. Brockwell signed a form stating that Lake Gaston had no responsibility for any loss to any property in or on the boat. Brockwell's electronic equipment was stolen and other personal items were damaged, and he sued. Is the exculpatory clause enforceable?

2. Guyan Machinery, a West Virginia manufacturing corporation, hired Albert Voorhees as a salesman and required him to sign a contract stating that if he left Guyan, he would not work for a competing corporation anywhere within 250 miles of West Virginia for a two-year period. Later, Voorhees left Guyan and began working at Polydeck Corp., another West Virginia manufacturer. The only product Polydeck made was urethane screens, which comprised half of 1 percent of Guyan's business. Is Guyan entitled to enforce its non-compete clause?

3. **ETHICS** Richard and Michelle Kommit traveled to New Jersey to have fun in the casinos. While in Atlantic City, they used their MasterCard to withdraw cash from an ATM conveniently located in the "pit," which is the gambling area of a casino. They ran up debts of $5,500 on the credit card and did not pay. The Connecticut National Bank sued for the money. What argument should the Kommits make? Which party, if any, has the moral high ground here? Should a casino offer ATM services in the gambling pit? If a credit card company allows customers to withdraw cash in a casino, is it encouraging them to lose money? Do the Kommits have any ethical right to use the ATM, attempt to win money by gambling, and then seek to avoid liability?

4. The McAllisters had several serious problems with their house, including leaks in the ceiling, a buckling wall, and dampness throughout. They repaired the buckling wall by installing I-beams to support it. They never resolved the leaks and the dampness. When they decided to sell the house, they said nothing to prospective buyers about the problems. They stated that the I-beams had been added for reinforcement. The Silvas bought the house for $60,000. Soon afterward, they began to have problems with leaks, mildew, and dampness. Are the Silvas entitled to any money damages? Why or why not?

5. Lonnie Hippen moved to Long Island, Kansas, to work at an insurance company owned by Griffiths. After he moved there, Griffiths offered to sell Hippen a house he owned, and Hippen agreed in writing to buy it. He did buy the house and moved in, but two years later, Hippen left the insurance company. He then claimed that at the time of the sale, Griffiths had orally promised to buy back his house at the selling price if Hippen should happen to leave the company. Griffiths defended based on the Statute of Frauds. Hippen argued that the Statute of Frauds did not apply because the repurchase of the house was essentially part of his employment with Griffiths. Comment.

DISCUSSION QUESTIONS

1. During the Gold Rush, John Tuppela bought an Alaskan mine. Sadly, he only found problems there. A court declared him insane and institutionalized him. Four years later, Tuppela emerged to learn that gold had been discovered in his mine, but a court-appointed guardian had already sold it. Tuppela called on his lifelong friend, Embola: "If you will give me $50 so I can go to Alaska, I will pay you $10,000 when I win my property back." Embola accepted the offer, advancing the $50. Tuppela won back his mine, but when he asked his guardian to pay Embola the promised $10,000, the guardian refused. The guardian argued there was insufficient consideration. Embola sued. Was $50 *adequate consideration* to support Tuppela's promise of $10,000?

2. Does the coverage of the Statute of Frauds make sense as it currently stands? Would it be better to expand the law and require that all contracts be in writing? Or should the law be done away with altogether?

3. Imagine that you are starting your own company in your hyper-competitive industry: You are putting your life savings, your professional contacts, and your innovative ideas on the line. As you begin to hire a sales force, you consider binding new employees to non-compete agreements. Outline the ideal terms of your employees' non-competes. What is its duration? What is its geographical radius? Are these terms appropriate for your industry? When you are done, pass your proposed terms to classmates and discuss its enforceability.

4. The Justice Department shut down three of the most popular online poker websites. State agencies take countless actions each year to stop illegal gaming operations. Do you believe that gambling by adults *should* be regulated? If so, which types?

Rate the following types of gambling from most acceptable to least acceptable:

— online poker   — state lotteries   — horse racing

— casino gambling   — bets on pro sports   — bets on college sports

5. Ball-Mart, a baseball card store, had a 1968 Nolan Ryan rookie card in almost perfect condition for sale. Any baseball collector would have known that the card was worth at least $1,000; the published monthly price guide listed its market value at $1,200. Bryan was a 12-year-old boy with a collection of over 40,000 baseball cards. When Bryan went to Ball-Mart, Kathleen, who knew nothing about cards, was filling in for the owner. The Ryan card was marked "1200", so Bryan asked Kathleen if this meant 12 dollars. She said yes and sold it to him for that amount. When Ball-Mart's owner realized the mix-up, he sued to rescind the contract. Who wins?

CHAPTER 12

PERFORMANCE OF A CONTRACT

First, Ronald Schmalfeldt got his teeth knocked out … and then he got his wind knocked out by his dental bills. Here is what happened.

Schmalfeldt was at the Elite Bar playing a pick-up game of pool with another bar patron, whom he did not know. A heated argument ensued. Schmalfeldt tried to walk away, but was struck in the face by the other player, who then fled—never to be heard from again. The brawl caused Schmalfeldt extensive dental damage, to the tune of $1,921. He asked the owner of the Elite Bar to pay his dental expenses, but the owner refused. Schmalfeldt was left with his teeth—and his dental bills—in his hands.

Schmalfeldt sought payment directly from North Pointe, which had issued a commercial liability insurance policy to the owner of the Elite Bar. He claimed that as a pool-playing bar patron he had a right to medical benefits under the policy. In its contract with Elite, North Pointe had agreed to pay up to $5,000 for medical expenses for a bodily injury caused by an accident occurring on Elite's premises, regardless of fault. When North Pointe refused to pay, Schmalfeldt sued.

> **Schmalfeldt was left with his teeth—and his dental bills—in his hands.**

Could Schmalfeldt enforce the bar's contract rights, or did he have to put his money where his mouth was? The basic pattern in third party law is quite simple. Two parties make a contract, and their rights and obligations are subject to the rules that we have already studied: offer and acceptance, consideration, legality, and so forth. However, sometimes their contract affects a third party, one who had no role in forming the agreement itself. The two contracting parties may *intend* to benefit someone else. Those are cases of third party beneficiary. In other cases, one of the contracting parties may actually transfer his rights or responsibilities to a third party, raising issues of assignment or delegation. We consider the issues one at a time. Then we examine issues of contract performance and remedies.

12-1 THIRD PARTY BENEFICIARY

Third party beneficiary
Someone who is not a party to a contract but stands to benefit from it

The two parties who make a contract always intend to gain some benefit for themselves. Often, though, their bargain will also benefit *someone else*. A **third party beneficiary** is someone who was not a party to the contract but stands to benefit from it. Many contracts create third party beneficiaries. A life insurance contract is one example: The person buying life insurance pays premiums to the insurance company so that upon his death, his designated beneficiary will receive a payout. But determining whether someone is a third party beneficiary is not always as clear. In the opening scenario, Schmalfeldt argued that he was a third party beneficiary of the bar's agreement with its insurer. Unfortunately for Schmalfeldt, the court held that since the insurance contract was intended to benefit the bar and made no mention of its patrons, he was not a third party beneficiary and, therefore, could not recover his damages.

As another example, suppose a major league baseball team contracts to purchase from Seller 20 acres of an abandoned industrial site to be used for a new stadium. The owner of a pizza parlor on the edge of Seller's land might benefit enormously. Forty thousand hungry fans in the neighborhood for 81 home games every season could turn her once-marginal operation into a gold mine of cheese and pepperoni.

But what if the contract falls apart? What if the team backs out of the deal to buy the land? Seller can certainly sue because it is a party to the contract. But what about the pizza parlor owner? Can she sue to enforce the deal and recover lost profits for unsold sausage and green pepper?

The outcome in cases like these depends upon the intentions of the two contracting parties. If they *intended* to benefit the third party, she will probably be permitted to enforce their contract. If they did not intend to benefit her, she probably has no power to enforce the agreement.

12-1a Types of Beneficiaries

Promisor
The person who makes the promise

Promisee
The person to whom a promise is made

Creditor beneficiary
When the contracting party intended the benefit in fulfillment of some duty or debt, the beneficiary is a creditor beneficiary.

A person is an *intended beneficiary* and may enforce a contract if the parties intended her to benefit *and if either* (a) enforcing the promise will satisfy a *duty* of the promisee to the beneficiary, or (b) the promisee intended to make a *gift* to the beneficiary. (The **promisor** is the one who makes the promise that the third party beneficiary is seeking to enforce. The **promisee** is the other party to the contract.)

In other words, a third party beneficiary must show two things in order to enforce a contract that two other people created. First, she must show that the two contracting parties were aware of her situation and knew that she would receive something of value from their deal. Second, she must show that the promisee wanted to benefit her for one of two reasons: either to satisfy some duty owed or to make her a gift.

If the promisee is fulfilling some duty, the third-party beneficiary is called a **creditor beneficiary**. Most often, the "duty" that a promisee will be fulfilling is a debt already owed to the beneficiary. If the promisee is making a gift, the third party is a **donee beneficiary**.[1] So long as the third party is either a creditor or a donee beneficiary, she may enforce the contract. If she fails to qualify as a creditor or donee beneficiary, then she is merely an **incidental beneficiary**, and she may not enforce the deal.

John's father, Clarence, has an overgrown lawn. So John enters into a contract with Billy Goat Landscapers for it to mow Clarence's lawn every week. Billy Goat is the promisor and John, the promisee. Although Clarence is not a party to the contract, he is the beneficiary—it is his lawn being cut. John did not owe his father a legal duty, but simply intended to make him a gift, so, Clarence is an intended, donee beneficiary, and can sue the landscaping company to enforce the contract himself.

By contrast, the pizza parlor owner will surely lose. A stadium is a multimillion-dollar investment, and it is most unlikely that the baseball team and the seller of the land were even aware of the owner's existence, let alone that they intended to benefit her. She probably cannot prove either the first element or the second element, and certainly not both.

In the following case, an unlikely plaintiff sues for breach of a state contract. Was the prison inmate an intended beneficiary or was his argument just smoke in mirrors? Who was entitled to sue?

Donee beneficiary

When the contracting party intended the benefit as a gift, the beneficiary is a donee beneficiary.

Incidental beneficiary

A party who benefits from the contract although the contract was not designed for their benefit

RATHKE V. CORRECTIONS CORPORATION OF AMERICA, INC.

153 P.3d 303
Supreme Court of Alaska, 2007

CASE SUMMARY

Facts: The state of Alaska entered into a contract with Corrections Corporation of America (CCA), a private company, to house Alaska's inmates in CCA prisons located in Arizona. The contract required CCA to abide by Alaska's standards and disciplinary procedures.

Gus Rathke was an Alaska inmate at a CCA prison located in Arizona. A routine drug test revealed marijuana in his system. Rathke's level of marijuana was within the limit allowed by Alaska law, but exceeded Arizona's limit. CCA applied the more stringent Arizona standard. As a result, Rathke spent 30 days in segregation and lost his prison job.

Rathke sued CCA for breach of contract, claiming that he was an intended third party beneficiary of the contract between Alaska and CCA. The trial court disagreed. Rathke appealed to Alaska's Supreme Court.

Issue: *Was Rathke an intended beneficiary of the contract between the state of Alaska and CCA?*

Decision: Yes, the prisoner was the intended beneficiary of the prison contract.

Reasoning: To determine if Rathke was an intended beneficiary, we must look to the state of Alaska's intention in entering the prison contract: Did the state intend to give its prisoners the benefit of CCA's performance?

The answer is yes. Alaska owes legal duties to its prisoners. When it contracted with CCA, it was acquiring services that it otherwise would have performed itself: housing inmates. The contract required CCA to step into the state's role, keeping prisons and safeguarding prisoners' rights according to Alaska standards. The services were rendered directly to the prisoners, so it is clear that the contract was for their benefit.

The Alaska/CCA contract is explicit: CCA must apply the standards of Alaska law to Alaska prisoners. When CCA applied Arizona law to discipline Rathke, it breached the contract. Since Rathke is an intended third party beneficiary, he has the right to sue CCA for breach.

---

[1]**Donee** comes from the word **donate**, meaning "to give."

12-2 ASSIGNMENT AND DELEGATION

After a contract is made, one or both parties may wish to substitute someone else for themselves. Six months before Maria's lease expires, an out-of-town company offers her a new job at a substantial increase in pay. After taking the job, she wants to sublease her apartment to her friend Sarah.

A contracting party may transfer his rights under the contract, which is called an **assignment** of rights. Or a party may transfer her obligations under the contract, which is a **delegation** of duties. Frequently, a party will make an assignment and delegation simultaneously, transferring both rights (such as the right to inhabit an apartment) and duties (like the obligation to pay monthly rent) to a third party.

12-2a Assignment

Lydia needs 500 bottles of champagne. Bruno agrees to sell them to her for $10,000, payable 30 days after delivery. He transports the wine to her.

Bruno owes Doug $8,000 from a previous deal. He says to Doug, "I don't have your money, but I'll give you my claim to Lydia's $10,000." Doug agrees. Bruno then *assigns* to Doug *his rights* to Lydia's money, and in exchange Doug gives up his claim against Bruno for $8,000. Bruno is the **assignor**, the one making an assignment, and Doug is the **assignee**, the one receiving an assignment.

Why would Bruno offer $10,000 when he owed Doug only $8,000? Because all he has is a *claim* to Lydia's money. Cash in hand is often more valuable. Doug, however, is willing to assume some risk for a potential $2,000 gain.

Bruno notifies Lydia of the assignment. Lydia, who owes the money, is called the **obligor**; that is, the one obligated to do something. At the end of 30 days, Doug arrives at Lydia's doorstep, asks for his money, and gets it since Lydia is obligated to him. Bruno has no claim to any payment.

What Rights Are Assignable?

Any contractual right may be assigned unless the assignment:

- Would substantially change the obligor's rights or duties under the contract, or
- Is forbidden by law or public policy, or
- Is validly precluded by the contract itself.

Substantial Change.   An assignment is prohibited if it would substantially change the obligor's situation. For example, Bruno is permitted to assign to Doug his rights to payment from Lydia because it makes no difference to Lydia whether she writes a check to one person or another. But suppose that, before delivery, Lydia had wanted to assign her rights to the shipment of 500 bottles of champagne to a business in another country. In this example, Bruno would be the obligor, and his duties would substantially change. Shipping heavy items over long distances adds substantial costs, so Lydia would not be able to make the assignment.

Assignment is also prohibited when the obligor is agreeing to perform **personal services**. The close working relationship in such agreements makes it unfair to expect the obligor to work with a stranger. Warner, a feature film director, hires Mayer to be his assistant on a film to be shot over the next 10 weeks. Warner may not assign his right to Mayer's work to another director.

Assignment
A transfer of contract rights to a third party

Delegation
A transfer of contract duties to a third party

Assignor
The person making an assignment

Assignee
The person receiving an assignment

Obligor
The person obligated to do something under a contract

Personal services
Any service that must be performed by the promisor

Public Policy. Some assignments are prohibited by public policy. For example, someone who has suffered a personal injury may not assign her claim to a third person. Vladimir is playing the piano on his roof deck when the instrument rolls over the balustrade and drops 35 stories before smashing Wanda's foot. Wanda has a valid tort claim against Vladimir, but she may not assign the claim to anyone else. As a matter of public policy, all states have decided that the sale of personal injury claims could create an unseemly and unethical marketplace.

Contract Prohibition. Finally, one of the contracting parties may try to prohibit assignment in the agreement itself. For example, most landlords include in the written lease a clause prohibiting the tenant from assigning the tenancy without the landlord's written permission.

How Rights Are Assigned

An assignment may be written or oral, and no particular formalities are required. However, when someone wants to assign rights governed by the Statute of Frauds, she must do it in writing. Suppose City contracts with Seller to buy Seller's land for a domed stadium and then brings in Investor to complete the project. If City wants to assign to Investor its rights to the land, it must do so in writing.

Rights of the Parties after Assignment

Once the assignment is made and the obligor notified, the assignee may enforce her contractual rights against the obligor. If Lydia fails to pay Doug for the champagne she gets from Bruno, Doug may sue to enforce the agreement. The law will treat Doug as though he had entered into the contract with Lydia.

But the reverse is also true. **The obligor may generally raise all defenses against the assignee that she could have raised against the assignor.** Suppose Lydia opens the first bottle of champagne—silently. "Where's the pop?" she wonders. All 500 bottles have gone flat. Bruno has failed to perform his part of the contract, and Lydia may use Bruno's nonperformance as a defense against Doug. If the champagne was indeed worthless, Lydia owes Doug nothing.

12-2b Delegation of Duties

Garret has always dreamed of racing stock cars. He borrows $250,000 from his sister, Maybelle, in order to buy a car and begin racing. He signs a promissory note in that amount, guaranteeing that he will repay Maybelle the full amount, plus interest, on a monthly basis over 10 years. Regrettably, during his first race, on a Saturday night, Garret discovers that he has a speed phobia. He finally finishes the race at noon on Sunday and quits the business. Garret transfers the car and equipment to Brady, who agrees in writing to pay all money owed to Maybelle. Brady sends a check for a few months, but the payments stop. Maybelle sues Garret, who defends based on the transfer to Brady. Will his defense work?

Most duties are delegable. But delegation does not by itself relieve the delegator of his own liability to perform the contract.

Garret was the **delegator** and Brady was the **delegatee**. Garret has legally delegated to Brady his duty to repay Maybelle. However, Garret remains personally obligated. When Maybelle sues, she will win. Garret, like many debtors, would have preferred to wash his hands of his debt, but the law is not so obliging.

Delegator
A person who gives his obligation under a contract to someone else

Delegatee
A person who receives an obligation under a contract from someone else

Garret's delegation to Brady was typical in that it included an assignment at the same time. If he had merely transferred ownership, that would have been only an assignment. If he had convinced Brady to pay off the loan without getting the car, that would have been merely a delegation. He did both at once.

What Duties Are Delegable

Assignment
A contracting party transfers his rights under a contract to someone else.

The rules concerning what duties may be delegated mirror those about the **assignment of rights.** An obligor may delegate his duties unless:

1. Delegation would violate public policy, or

2. The contract prohibits delegation, or

Obligee
The person who has an obligation coming to her

3. The **obligee** has a substantial interest in personal performance by the obligor.

Public Policy.   Delegation may violate public policy, for example in a public works contract. If City hires Builder to construct a subway system, state law may prohibit Builder from delegating his duties to Subcontractor. A public agency should not have to work with parties that it never agreed to hire.

Contract Prohibition.   The parties may forbid almost any delegation, and the courts will enforce the agreement. Hammer, a contractor, is building a house and hires Spot as his painter, including in his contract a clause prohibiting delegation. Just before the house is ready for painting, Spot gets a better job elsewhere and wants to delegate his duties to Brush. Hammer may refuse the delegation even if Brush is equally qualified.

Substantial Interest in Personal Performance.   Suppose Hammer had omitted the "nondelegation" clause from his contract with Spot. Could Hammer still refuse the delegation on the grounds that he has a substantial interest in having Spot do the work? No. Most duties are delegable. There is nothing so special about painting a house that one particular painter is required to do it. But some kinds of work do require personal performance, and obligors may not delegate these tasks. The services of lawyers, doctors, dentists, artists, and performers are considered too personal to be delegated. There is no single test that will perfectly define this group, but generally when the work will test *the character, skill, discretion, and good faith* of the obligor, she *may not* delegate her job.

12-3 PERFORMANCE AND DISCHARGE

A party is discharged when she has no more duties under a contract. Most contracts are discharged by full performance. In other words, the parties generally do what they promise. Sally agrees to sell Arthur 300 tulip-shaped wine glasses for his new restaurant. Right on schedule, Sally delivers the correct glasses and Arthur pays in full. Contract, full performance, discharge, end of case.

Rescind
To terminate a contract by mutual agreement

Sometimes the parties discharge a contract by agreement. For example, the parties may agree to **rescind** their contract, meaning that they terminate it by mutual agreement. At times, a court may discharge a party who has not performed. When things have gone amiss, a judge must interpret the contract and issues of public policy to determine who in fairness should suffer the loss. We will analyze the most common issues of performance and discharge.

12-3a Performance

Caitlin has an architect draw up plans for a monumental new house, and Daniel agrees to build it by September 1. Caitlin promises to pay $900,000 on that date. The house is ready on time, but Caitlin has some complaints. The living room ceiling was supposed to be 18 feet high, but it is only 17 feet; the pool was to be azure, yet it is aquamarine; the maid's room was not supposed to be wired for cable television, but it is. Caitlin refuses to pay anything for the house. Is she justified? Of course not; it would be absurd to give her a magnificent house for free when it has only tiny defects. And that is how a court would decide the case. But in this easy answer lurks a danger. How much leeway will a court permit? Suppose the living room is only 14 feet high, or 12 feet, or 5 feet? What if Daniel finishes the house a month late? Six months late? Three years late? At some point, a court will conclude that Daniel has so thoroughly botched the job that he deserves little or no money. Where is that point? That is a question that businesses—and judges—face every day.

Strict Performance and Substantial Performance

Strict Performance.   Courts dislike strict performance because it enables one party to benefit without paying and sends the other one home empty-handed. **A party is generally not required to render strict performance unless the contract expressly demands it and such a demand is reasonable.** Caitlin's contract never suggested that Daniel would forfeit all payment if there were minor problems. Even if Caitlin had insisted on such a clause, a court would be unlikely to enforce it because the requirement is unreasonable.

In some cases, strict performance does make sense. Marshall agrees to deliver 500 sweaters to Leo's store, and Leo promises to pay $20,000 cash on delivery. If Leo has only $19,000 cash and a promissory note for $1,000, he has failed to perform, and Marshall need not give him the sweaters. Leo's payment represents 95 percent of what he promised, but there is a big difference between cash and a promissory note.

Substantial Performance.   Daniel, the house builder, won his case against Caitlin because he fulfilled most of his obligations, even though he did an imperfect job. Courts often rely on the substantial performance doctrine, especially in cases involving services as opposed to those concerning the sale of goods or land. **In a contract for services, a party that substantially performs its obligations will receive the full contract price, minus the value of any defects.** Daniel receives $900,000, the contract price, minus the value of a ceiling that is 1 foot too low, a pool the wrong color, and so forth. It will be for the trial court to decide how much those defects are worth. If the court decides the low ceiling is a $10,000 damage, the pool color worth $5,000, and the cable television issue worth $500, then Daniel receives $884,500.

On the other hand, a party that fails to perform substantially receives nothing on the contract itself and will only recover the value of the work, if any. If the foundation cracks in Caitlin's house and the walls collapse, Daniel will not receive his $900,000. In such a case, he collects only the market value of the work he has done, which is probably zero.

When is performance substantial? There is no perfect test, but courts look at these issues:

- How much benefit has the promisee received?

- If it is a construction contract, can the owner use the thing for its intended purpose?

- Can the promisee be compensated with money damages for any defects?

- Did the promisor act in good faith?

EXAM Strategy

Question: Jade owns a straight track used for drag racing. She hires Trevor to resurface it for $180,000, paying $90,000 down. When the project is completed, Jade refuses to pay the balance and sues Trevor for her down payment. He counterclaims for the $90,000 still due. At trial, Trevor proves that all of the required materials were applied by trained workers in an expert fashion, the dimensions were perfect, and his profit margin very modest. The head of the national drag racing association testifies that his group considers the strip unsafe. He noticed puddles in both asphalt lanes, found the concrete starting pads unsafe, and believed the racing surface needed to be ground off and reapplied. His organization refuses to sanction races at the track until repairs are made. Who wins the suit?

Strategy: When one party has performed imperfectly, we have an issue of substantial performance. To decide whether Trevor is entitled to his money, we apply four factors: (1) How much benefit did Jade receive? (2) Can she use the racing strip for its intended purpose? (3) Can Jade be compensated for defects? (4) Did Trevor act in good faith?

Result: Jade has received no benefit whatsoever. She cannot use her track for drag racing. Compensation will not help Jade—she needs a new strip. Trevor's work must be ripped up and replaced. Trevor may have acted in good faith, but he failed to deliver what Jade bargained for. Jade wins all of the money she paid. (As we will see later in this chapter, she may win additional sums for her lost profits.)

12-3b Good Faith

The parties to a contract must carry out their obligations in good faith. The difficulty, of course, is applying this general rule to the wide variety of problems that may arise when people or companies do business. The plaintiff in the following case argued that the owners of a shopping center failed to act in good faith. Did the court agree? Read on.

BRUNSWICK HILLS RACQUET CLUB INC. v. ROUTE 18 SHOPPING CENTER ASSOCIATES

182 N.J. 210
Supreme Court of New Jersey, 2005

CASE SUMMARY

Facts: Brunswick Hills Racquet Club (Brunswick) owned a tennis club on property that it leased from Route 18 Shopping Center Associates (Route 18). The lease ran for 25 years, and Brunswick had spent about $1 million in capital improvements. The lease expired March 30, 2002. Brunswick had the option of either buying the property or purchasing a 99-year lease, both on very favorable terms. To exercise

its option, Brunswick had to notify Route 18 no later than September 30, 2001, and had to pay the option price of $150,000. If Brunswick failed to exercise its options, the existing lease automatically renewed as of September 30, for 25 more years, but at more than triple the current rent.

In February 2000—19 months before the option deadline—Brunswick's lawyer, Gabriel Spector, wrote to

Rosen Associates, the company that managed Route 18, stating that Brunswick intended to exercise the option for a 99-year lease. He requested that the lease be sent well in advance so that he could review it. He did not make the required payment of $150,000.

In March, Rosen replied that it had forwarded Spector's letter to its attorney, who would be in touch. In April, Spector again wrote, asking for a reply from Rosen or its lawyer.

Over the next six months, Spector continually asked for a copy of the lease, or for information, but neither Route 18's lawyer nor anyone else provided any data. In January 2001, Spector renewed his requests for a copy of the lease. Route 18's lawyer never replied. Sadly, in May 2001, after a long illness, Spector died. In August 2001, Spector's law partner, Arnold Levin, wrote to Rosen, again stating Brunswick's intention to buy the 99-year lease and requesting a copy of all relevant information. He received no reply, and the September deadline passed.

In February 2002, Route 18's lawyer dropped the hammer, notifying Levin that Brunswick could not exercise its option to lease because it had failed to pay the $150,000 by September 30, 2001.

Brunswick sued, claiming that Route 18 had breached its duty of good faith and fair dealing. The trial court found that Route 18 had no duty to notify Brunswick of impending deadlines, and it gave summary judgment for Route 18. The appellate court affirmed, and Brunswick appealed to the state supreme court.

Issue: *Did Route 18 breach its duty of good faith and fair dealing?*

Holding: Yes, Route 18 breached its duty of good faith and fair dealing.

Reasoning: Courts generally should not tinker with precisely drafted agreements entered into by experienced businesspeople. Nonetheless, every party to a contract is bound by a duty of good faith and fair dealing in its performance. Good faith is conduct that conforms to community standards of decency and reasonableness. Neither party may do anything that will prevent the other from receiving the contract benefits.

Route 18 and its agents acted in bad faith. Brunswick Hills notified the landlord 19 months before the deadline that it intended to exercise its option to purchase a 99-year lease. Brunswick Hills mistakenly believed that its payment was not due until closing. During that year and a half, Route 18 engaged in a pattern of evasion, sidestepping every request by Brunswick Hills to move forward on closing the lease. After Spector's death, Route 18's lawyer continued to play possum despite the obvious risk to Brunswick Hills. Route 18 acknowledged that it did not want the lease payment because the long-term lease was not in its financial interest.

Neither a landlord nor its attorney is required to act as his brother's keeper. However, there are ethical norms that apply even in the harsh world of commercial transactions. All parties must behave in good faith and deal fairly with the other side. Brunswick Hills' repeated letters and calls to close the lease placed an obligation on Route 18 to respond in a timely, honest manner. The company failed to do that, and Brunswick Hills is entitled to exercise the 99-year lease.

12-3c Breach

When one party *materially* breaches a contract, the other party is discharged. A material breach is one that substantially harms the innocent party. The discharged party has no obligation to perform and may sue for damages. Edwin promises that on July 1 he will deliver 20 tuxedos, tailored to fit male chimpanzees, to Bubba's circus for $300 per suit. After weeks of delay, Edwin concedes he hasn't a cummerbund to his name. This is a material breach, and Bubba is discharged. Notice that a trivial breach, such as a one-day delay in delivering the tuxedos, would not have discharged Bubba.

Statute of Limitations

A party injured by a breach of contract should act promptly. **A *statute of limitations* begins to run at the time of injury and will limit the time within which the injured party may file suit.** Statutes of limitation vary widely. In some states, for example, an injured party must sue on oral contracts within three years, on a sale of goods contract within four years, and on some written contracts within five years. Failure to file suit within the time limits discharges the breaching party.

Statute of limitations
Limits the time within which an injured party may file suit

12-3d Impossibility

"Your honor, my client wanted to honor the contract. He just couldn't. Honest." Does the argument work? It depends. A court will discharge an agreement if performing a contract was truly impossible but not if honoring the deal merely imposed a financial burden. **True impossibility means that something has happened making it utterly impossible to do what the promisor said he would do.** Francoise owns a vineyard that produces Beaujolais Nouveau wine. She agrees to ship 1,000 cases *of her wine* to Tyrone, a New York importer, as soon as this year's vintage is ready. Tyrone will pay $50 per case. But a fungus wipes out her entire vineyard. Francoise is discharged. It is theoretically impossible for Francoise to deliver wine from her vineyard, and she owes Tyrone nothing.

True impossibility is generally limited to these three causes:

1. **Destruction of the subject matter.** This happened with Francoise's vineyard.

2. **Death of the promisor in a personal services contract.** When the promisor agrees personally to render a service that cannot be transferred to someone else, her death discharges the contract.

3. **Illegality.** If the purpose of a contract becomes illegal, that change discharges the contract.

It is rare for contract performance to be truly impossible but common for it to become a financial burden to one party. Suppose Bradshaw Steel in Pittsburgh agrees to deliver 1,000 tons of steel beams to Rice Construction in Saudi Arabia at a given price, but a week later, the cost of raw ore increases 30 percent. A contract once lucrative to the manufacturer is suddenly a major liability. Does that change discharge Bradshaw? Absolutely not. Rice signed the deal *precisely to protect itself against price increases.* The whole purpose of contracts is to enable the parties to control their futures.

12-4 REMEDIES

A remedy is the method a court uses to compensate an injured party. The most common remedy, used in the great majority of lawsuits, is money damages.

The first step that a court takes in choosing a remedy is to decide what interest it is trying to protect. An **interest** is a legal right in something. Someone can have an interest in property, for example, by owning it, or renting it to a tenant, or lending money so someone else may buy it. He can have an interest in a *contract* if the agreement gives him some benefit. There are four principal contract interests that a court may seek to protect:

Interest
A legal right in something

1. **Expectation interest.** This refers to what the injured party reasonably thought she would get from the contract.

2. **Reliance interest.** The injured party may be unable to demonstrate expectation damages but may still prove that he expended money in reliance on the agreement.

3. **Restitution interest.** An injured party may only be able to demonstrate that she has conferred a benefit on the other party. Here, the objective is to restore to the injured party the benefit she has provided.

4. **Equitable interest.** In some cases, something more than money is needed, such as an order to transfer property to the injured party (specific performance) or an order forcing one party to stop doing something (an injunction).

12-4a Expectation Interest

This is the most common remedy. **The expectation interest is designed to put the injured party in the position she would have been in had both sides fully performed their obligations.** A court tries to give the injured party the money she would have made from the contract. If accurately computed, this should take into account all the gains she reasonably expected and all the expenses and losses she would have incurred. The injured party should not end up better off than she would have been under the agreement, nor should she suffer serious loss. If you ever go to law school, you will almost certainly encounter the following case during your first week of classes. It has been used to introduce the concept of damages in contract lawsuits for generations. Enjoy the famous "case of the hairy hand."

Landmark Case

HAWKINS V. MCGEE

84 N.H. 114
Supreme Court of New Hampshire, 1929

CASE SUMMARY

Facts: Hawkins suffered a severe electrical burn on the palm of his right hand. After years of living with disfiguring scars, he went to visit Dr. McGee, who was well known for his early attempts at skin-grafting surgery. The doctor told Hawkins, "I will guarantee to make the hand a hundred percent perfect." Hawkins hired him to perform the operation.

McGee cut a patch of healthy skin from Hawkins's chest and grafted it over the scar tissue on Hawkins's palm. Unfortunately, the chest hair on the skin graft was very thick, and it continued to grow after the surgery. The operation resulted in a hairy palm for Hawkins. Feeling rather...embarrassed...Hawkins sued Dr. McGee.

The trial court judge instructed the jury to calculate damages in this way: "If you find the plaintiff entitled to anything, he is entitled to recover for what pain and suffering he has been made to endure and what injury he has sustained over and above the injury that he had before."

The jury awarded Hawkins $3,000, but the court reduced the award to $500. Dissatisfied, Hawkins appealed.

Issue: *How should Hawkins's damages be calculated?*

Holding: Hawkins should receive the difference between the benefit the contract promised and the benefit he actually received.

Reasoning: The lower court's jury instructions were improper. Damages in contract cases are designed to give the plaintiff the benefit he would have received if the contract had been properly performed.

Pain and suffering are not relevant. Almost any surgery involves some pain and suffering, but the benefits conferred can outweigh such harm. McGee could have performed his obligations perfectly and still caused Hawkins pain.

The correct determination of damages is related instead to the difference in value of the "100 percent perfect" hand Hawkins was promised and the hand as it was after the actual procedure.

Remanded for a new trial to calculate what these damages are.

Now let's consider a more modern example.

William Colby was a former director of the CIA. He wanted to write a book about his 15 years in Vietnam. He paid James McCarger $5,000 for help in writing an early draft and promised McCarger another $5,000 if the book was published. Then he hired Alexander Burnham to co-write the book. Colby's agent secured a contract with Contemporary Books, which included a $100,000 advance. But Burnham was hopelessly late with the manuscript, and Colby missed his publication date. Colby fired Burnham and finished the book without him. Contemporary published *Lost Victory* several years late, and the book flopped, earning no significant revenue. Because the book was so late, Contemporary paid Colby a total of only $17,000. Colby sued Burnham for his lost expectation interest. The court awarded him $23,000, calculated as follows:

	$	100,000	advance, the only money Colby was promised
	−	10,000	agent's fee
	=	90,000	fee for the two authors, combined
divided by 2	=	45,000	Colby's fee (the other half went to the co-author)
	−	5,000	owed to McCarger under the earlier agreement
	=	40,000	Colby's expectation interest
	−	17,000	fee Colby eventually received from Contemporary
	=	23,000	Colby's expectation damages—that is, the amount he would have received had Burnham finished on time

The *Colby* case presented a relatively easy calculation of damages. Other contracts are more complex. Courts typically divide the expectation damages into three parts: (1) direct (or **compensatory damages**), which represent harm that flowed directly from the contract's breach; (2) consequential (or "special") damages, which represent harm caused by the injured party's unique situation; and (3) **incidental damages**, which are minor costs such as storing or returning defective goods, advertising for alternative goods, and so forth.

Note that punitive damages are absent from our list. The golden rule in contracts cases is to give successful plaintiffs "the benefit of the bargain," and not to punish defendants. Punitive damages are occasionally awarded in lawsuits that involve both a contract *and* either an intentional tort (such as fraud) or a breach of fiduciary duty, but they are not available in "simple" cases involving only a breach of contract.

Compensatory damages
Are those that flow directly from the contract

Incidental damages
Are the relatively minor costs that the injured party suffers when responding to the breach

Direct Damages

Direct damages are those that flow directly from the contract. They are the most common monetary award for the expectation interest. These are the damages that inevitably result from the breach. Suppose Ace Productions hires Reina to star in its new movie, *Inside Straight*. Ace promises Reina $3 million, providing she shows up June 1 and works until the film is finished. But in late May, Joker Entertainment offers Reina $6 million to star in its new feature, and on June 1, Reina informs Ace that she will not appear. Reina has breached her contract, and Ace should recover direct damages.

What are the damages that flow directly from the contract? Ace has to replace Reina. If Ace hires Kayla as its star and pays her a fee of $4 million, Ace is entitled to the difference between what it expected to pay ($3 million) and what the breach forced it to pay ($4 million), or $1 million in direct damages.

Consequential damages
Damages that result from the unique circumstances of the plaintiff. Also known as *special damages*.

Consequential Damages

In addition to direct damages, the injured party may seek consequential damages, or as they are also known, "special damages." **Consequential damages** reimburse for harm that results from the *particular* circumstances of the plaintiff. These damages are only available if they are a *foreseeable consequence* of the breach. Suppose, for example, Raould breaches two contracts—he is late picking both Sharon and Paul up for a taxi ride. His breach is the same for both parties, but the consequences are very different. Sharon misses her flight to San Francisco and incurs a substantial fee to rebook the flight. Paul is simply late for the barber who manages to fit him in anyway. Thus, Raould's damages would be different for these two contracts.

The rule comes from a famous 1854 case, *Hadley v. Baxendale.* The Hadleys operated a flour mill, but a shaft broke, and their business ground to a halt. The family hired Baxendale to cart the damaged part to a foundry, where a new one could be manufactured. Baxendale promised to make the delivery in one day, but he was late transporting the shaft, and as a result, the Hadleys' mill was shut for five extra days. They sued for their lost profit—and lost. The court declared: **The injured party may recover consequential damages only if the breaching party should have foreseen them when the two sides formed the contract.** Baxendale had no way of knowing that this was the Hadleys' only shaft, or that his delay in transport would cost them substantial profit. The Hadleys would have won had they *told* Baxendale this was their only shaft. They failed to do that, and they failed to win their profits.

Let us return briefly to *Inside Straight.* Suppose that, long before shooting began, Ace had sold the film's soundtrack rights to Spinem Sound for $2 million. Spinem believed it would make a profit only if Reina appeared in the film, so it demanded the right to discharge the agreement if Reina dropped out. When Reina quit, Spinem terminated the contract. Now, when Ace sues Reina, it will also seek $2 million in consequential damages for the lost music revenue. If Reina knew about Ace's contract with Spinem when she signed to do the film, she is liable for $2 million. If she never realized she was an essential part of the music contract, she owes nothing for the lost profits.

In the following case, the plaintiffs lost not only profits, but their entire business. Can they recover for harm that is so extensive? You decide.

You be the Judge

Facts: Bi-Economy Market was a family-owned meat market in Rochester, New York. The company was insured by Harleysville Insurance. The "Deluxe Business Owner's" policy provided replacement cost for damage to buildings and inventory. Coverage also included "business interruption insurance" for one year, meaning the loss of pretax profit plus normal operating expenses, including payroll.

The company suffered a disastrous fire, which destroyed its building and all inventory. Bi-Economy immediately filed a claim with Harleysville, but the insurer responded slowly. Harleysville eventually offered a settlement of $163,000. A year later, an arbitrator awarded the Market $407,000. During that year, Harleysville paid for seven months of lost income but declined to pay more. The company never recovered or reopened.

Bi-Economy sued, claiming that Harleysville's slow, inadequate payments destroyed the company. The

BI-ECONOMY MARKET, INC. v. HARLEYSVILLE INS. CO. OF NEW YORK

2008 N.Y. Slip Op. 01418
New York Court of Appeals, 2008

company also sought consequential damages for the permanent destruction of its business. Harleysville claimed that it was responsible only for damages specified in the contract: the building, inventory, and lost income. The trial court granted summary judgment for Harleysville. The appellate court affirmed, claiming that when they entered into the contract, the parties did not contemplate damages for termination of the business. Bi-Economy appealed to the state's highest court.

You Be the Judge: *Is Bi-Economy entitled to consequential damages for the destruction of its business?*

Argument for Bi-Economy: Bi-Economy is a small, family business. We paid for business interruption insurance for an obvious reason: In the event of a disaster, we lacked the resources to keep going while buildings were constructed and inventory purchased. We knew that in such a calamity, we would need prompt reimbursement—compensation covering the immediate damage and our ongoing lost income. Why else would we pay the premiums?

At the time we entered into the contract, Harleysville could easily foresee that if it responded slowly, with insufficient payments, we could not survive. They knew that is what we wanted to avoid—and it is just what happened. The insurer's bad faith offer of a low figure, and its payment of only seven months' lost income, ruined a fine family business. When the insurance company agreed to business interruption coverage, it was declaring that it would act fast and fairly to sustain a small firm in crisis. The insurer should now pay for the full harm it has wrought.

Argument for Harleysville: We contracted to insure the Market for three losses: its building, inventory, and lost income. After the fire, we performed a reasonable, careful evaluation and made an offer we considered fair. An arbitrator later awarded Bi-Economy additional money, which we paid. However, it is absurd to suggest that in addition to that, we are liable for an open-ended commitment for permanent destruction of the business.

Consequential damages are appropriate in cases where a plaintiff suffers a loss that was not covered in the contract. In this case, though, the parties bargained over exactly what Harleysville would pay in the event of a major fire. If the insurer has underpaid for lost income, let the court award a fair sum. However, the parties never contemplated an additional, enormous payment for cessation of the business. There is almost no limit as to what that obligation could be. If Bi-Economy was concerned that a fire might put the company permanently out of business, it should have said so at the time of negotiating for insurance. The premium would have been dramatically higher.

Neither Bi-Economy nor Harleysville ever imagined such an open-ended insurance obligation, and the insurer should not pay an extra cent.

Incidental Damages

Incidental damages are the relatively minor costs that the injured party suffers when responding to the breach. When Reina, the actress, breaches the film contract, the producers may have to leave the set and fly back to Los Angeles to hire a new actress. The cost of travel, renting a room for auditions, and other related expenses are incidental damages.

12-4b Reliance Interest

To win expectation damages, the injured party must prove the breach of contract caused damages that can be *quantified with reasonable certainty*. This rule sometimes presents plaintiffs with a problem.

George plans to manufacture and sell silk scarves during the holiday season. In the summer, he contracts with Cecily, the owner of a shopping mall, to rent a high-visibility stall for $100 per day. George then buys hundreds of yards of costly silk and gets to work cutting and sewing. Then in September, Cecily refuses to honor the contract. George sues and easily proves Cecily breached a valid contract. But what is his remedy?

George cannot establish an expectation interest in his scarf business. He hoped to sell each scarf for a $40 gross profit and wanted to make $2,000 per day. But how much would he actually have earned? Enough to retire on—or enough to buy a salami sandwich for lunch? A court cannot give him an expectation interest, so George will ask for *reliance damages*. **The reliance interest is designed to put the injured party in the position he would have been in had the parties *never entered* into a contract.** This remedy focuses on the time and money the injured party spent performing his part of the agreement.

Assuming he is unable to sell the scarves to a retail store (which is probable because retailers will have made purchases long ago), George should be able to recover the cost of the silk fabric he bought and perhaps something for the hours of labor he spent cutting and sewing. However, reliance damages can be difficult to win because *they are harder to quantify*. Judges dislike vague calculations. How much was George's time worth in making the scarves? How good was his work? How likely were the scarves to sell? If George has a track record in the industry, he will be able to show a market price for his services. Without such a record, his reliance claim becomes a tough battle.

12-4c Restitution Interest

Jim and Bonnie Hyler bought an expensive recreational vehicle (RV) from Autorama. The salesman promised the Hylers that a manufacturer's warranty covered the entire vehicle for a year. The Hylers had a succession of major problems with their RV, including windows that wouldn't shut, a door that fell off, a loose windshield, and defective walls. Then they learned that the manufacturer had gone bankrupt. In fact, the Autorama salesman knew of the bankruptcy when he made the sales pitch. The Hylers returned the RV to Autorama and demanded their money back. They wanted restitution.

The restitution interest is designed to return to the injured party a benefit that he has conferred on the other party which would be unjust to leave with that person. Restitution is a common remedy in contracts involving fraud, misrepresentation, mistake, and duress. In these cases, restitution often goes hand in hand with **rescission**, which means to "undo" a contract and put the parties where they were before they made the agreement. The court declared that Autorama had misrepresented the manufacturer's warranty by omitting the small fact that the manufacturer itself no longer existed. Autorama was forced to return to the Hylers the full purchase price, plus the value of the automobile they had traded. The dealer, of course, was allowed to keep the defective RV and stare out the ill-fitting windows.

Rescission
The undoing of a contract, which puts both parties in the positions they were in when they made the agreement

12-4d Other Equitable Interests

Specific Performance

Leona Claussen owned Iowa farmland. She sold some of it to her sister-in-law, Evelyn Claussen, and, along with the land, granted Evelyn an option to buy additional property at $800 per acre. Evelyn could exercise her option any time during Leona's lifetime or within six months of Leona's death. When Leona died, Evelyn informed the estate's executor that she was exercising her option. But other relatives wanted the property, and the executor refused to sell. Evelyn sued and asked for *specific performance*. She did not want an award of damages; she wanted the land itself. The remedy of **specific performance** forces the two parties to perform their contract

A court will award specific performance, ordering the parties to perform the contract, only in cases involving the sale of land or some other asset that is unique. Courts use this equitable remedy when money damages would be inadequate to compensate the injured party. If the subject is unique and irreplaceable, money damages will not put the injured party in the same position she would have been in had the agreement been kept. So a court will order the seller to convey the rare object and the buyer to pay for it.

Historically, every parcel of land has been regarded as unique, and therefore specific performance is always available in real estate contracts. Evelyn Claussen won specific performance. The Iowa Supreme Court ordered Leona's estate to convey the land to Evelyn for $800 per acre. Generally, either the seller or the buyer may be granted specific performance.

Other unique items, for which a court will order specific performance, include such things as rare works of art, secret formulas, patents, and shares in a closely held corporation. By contrast, a contract for a new Jeep Grand Cherokee is not enforceable by specific performance. An injured buyer can use money damages to purchase a virtually identical auto.

Specific performance
Compels parties to perform the contract they agreed to when the contract concerns the sale of land or some other unique asset

EXAM Strategy

Question: The Monroes, a retired couple who live in Illinois, want to move to Arizona to escape the northern winter. In May, the Monroes contract in writing to sell their house to the Temples for $450,000. Closing is to take place June 30. The Temples pay a deposit of $90,000. However, in early June, the Monroes travel through Arizona and discover it is too hot for them. They promptly notify the Temples they are no longer willing to sell and return the $90,000, with interest. The Temples sue, seeking the house. In response, the Monroes offer evidence that the value of the house has dropped from about $450,000 to about $400,000. They claim that the Temples have suffered no loss. Who will win?

Strategy: Most contract lawsuits are for money damages, but not this one. The Temples want the house. Because they want the house itself, and not money damages, the drop in value is irrelevant. What legal remedy are the Temples seeking? They are suing for specific performance. When will a court grant specific performance? Should it do so here?

Result: In cases involving the sale of land or some other unique asset, a court will grant specific performance, ordering the parties to perform the agreement. All houses are regarded as unique. The court will force the Monroes to sell their house, provided the Temples have sufficient money to pay for it.

Injunction

Injunction
A court order to do something or to refrain from doing something

An **injunction** is a court order that requires someone to refrain from doing something. It is another remedy that courts sometimes use when money damages would be inadequate. Bonnie has an employment contract that contains a non-compete clause. If she ever leaves her company, she has promised not to work for a competing firm for six months. But Bonnie breaks her word—she quits her job and immediately takes a job with a competitor. Her old firm might seek an injunction that prohibits her from working for her new firm until her non-compete has expired.

12-4e Mitigation of Damages

Mitigate
To keep damages as low as possible

Note one limitation on *all* contract remedies: **A party injured by a breach of contract may not recover for damages that he could have avoided with reasonable efforts.** In other words, when one party perceives that the other has breached or will breach the contract, the injured party must try to prevent unnecessary loss. A party is expected to **mitigate** his damages—that is, to keep damages as low as he reasonably can.

Chapter Conclusion

A moment's caution! Often that is the only thing needed to avoid years of litigation. Yes, the broad powers of a court may enable it to compensate an injured party, but problems of proof and the uncertainty of remedies demonstrate that the best solution is a carefully drafted contract and socially responsible behavior.

EXAM REVIEW

1. **THIRD PARTY BENEFICIARY** A third party beneficiary is an intended beneficiary and may enforce a contract only if the parties intended her to benefit from the agreement and (1) enforcing the promise will satisfy a debt of the promisee to the beneficiary or (2) the promisee intended to make a gift to the beneficiary.

2. **ASSIGNMENT AND DELEGATION** An assignment transfers the assignor's contract rights to the assignee. A delegation transfers the delegator's duties to the delegatee.

3. **RIGHT TO ASSIGN** A party generally may assign contract rights unless doing so would substantially change the obligor's rights or duties, is forbidden by law, or is validly precluded by the contract.

4. **RIGHT TO DELEGATE** Duties are delegable unless delegation would violate public policy, the contract prohibits delegation, or the obligee has a substantial interest in personal performance by the obligor.

5. **DISCHARGE** Unless the obligee agrees otherwise, delegation does not discharge the delegator's duty to perform.

6. **SUBSTANTIAL PERFORMANCE** Strict performance, which requires one party to fulfill its duties perfectly, is unusual. In construction and service contracts, substantial performance is generally sufficient to entitle the promisor to the contract price, minus the cost of defects.

7. **GOOD FAITH** Good faith performance is required in all contracts.

8. **IMPOSSIBILITY** True impossibility means that some event has made it impossible to perform an agreement.

EXAM Strategy

Question: Omega Concrete had a gravel pit and factory. Access was difficult, so Omega contracted with Union Pacific Railroad (UP) for the right to use a private road that crossed UP property and tracks. The contract stated that use of the road was solely for Omega employees and that Omega would be responsible for closing a gate that UP planned to build where the private road joined a public highway. In fact, UP never constructed the gate; and Omega had no authority to construct the gate. Mathew Rogers, an Omega employee, was killed by a train while using the private road. Rogers's family sued Omega, claiming that Omega failed to keep the gate closed as the contract required. Is Omega liable?

Strategy: Impossibility means that the promisor cannot do what he promised to do. Is this such a case? (See the "Result" at the end of this section.)

9. **REMEDIES**   A remedy is the method a court uses to compensate an injured party.

10. **EXPECTATION INTEREST**   The expectation interest puts the injured party in the position she would have been in had both sides fully performed. It has three components: direct, consequential, and incidental damages.

EXAM Strategy

Question: Mr. and Ms. Beard contracted for Builder to construct a house on property he owned and sell it to the Beards for $785,000. The house was to be completed by a certain date, and Builder knew that the Beards were selling their own home in reliance on the completion date. Builder was late with construction, forcing the Beards to spend $32,000 in rent. Ultimately, Builder never finished the house, and the Beards moved elsewhere. They sued. At trial, expert testimony indicated the market value of the house as promised would have been $885,000. How much money are the Beards entitled to, and why?

Strategy: Normally, in cases of property, an injured plaintiff may use specific performance to obtain the land or house. However, there *is* no house, so there will be no specific performance. The Beards will seek their expectation interest. Under the contract, what did they reasonably expect? They anticipated a finished house, on a particular date, worth $885,000. They did not expect to pay rent while waiting. Calculate their losses. (See the "Result" at the end of this section.)

11. **RELIANCE INTEREST**   The reliance interest puts the injured party in the position he would have been in had the parties never entered into a contract.

12. **RESTITUTION INTEREST**   The restitution interest returns to the injured party a benefit that she has conferred on the other party which would be unjust to leave with that person.

13. **SPECIFIC PERFORMANCE**   Specific performance, ordered only in cases of a unique asset, requires both parties to perform the contract.

14. **INJUNCTION**   An injunction is a court order that requires someone to do something or refrain from doing something.

8. Result: There was no gate, and Omega had no right to build one. This is a case of true impossibility. Omega was not liable.

10. Result: The Beards' direct damages represent the difference between the market value of the house and the contract price. They expected a house worth $100,000 more than their contract price, and they are entitled to that sum. They also suffered consequential damages. Builder knew they needed the house as of the contract date, and he could foresee that his breach would force them to pay rent. He is liable for a total of $132,000.

MATCHING QUESTIONS

Match the following terms with their definitions:

___A. Material

___B. Intended beneficiary

___C. Discharged

___D. Consequential

1. A type of breach that substantially harms the innocent party

2. When a party has no more obligations under a contract

3. Damages that can be recovered only if the breaching party should have foreseen them

4. A third party who should be able to enforce a contract between two others

TRUE/FALSE QUESTIONS

Circle true or false:

1. T F Contract dates and deadlines are strictly enforceable unless the parties agree otherwise.

2. T F Where one party has clearly breached, the injured party must mitigate damages.

3. T F Courts award the expectation interest more often than any other remedy.

4. T F A party who delegates duties remains liable for contract performance.

MULTIPLE-CHOICE QUESTIONS

1. Bob, a mechanic, claims that Cathy owes him $1,500 on a repair job. Bob wants to assign his claim to Hardknuckle Bank. The likeliest reason that Bob wants to do this is:

(a) Cathy also owes Hardknuckle Bank money.

(b) Hardknuckle Bank owes Bob money on a consumer claim.

(c) Hardknuckle Bank owes Bob money on a repair job.

(d) Bob owes Hardknuckle Bank money.

(e) Bob and Cathy are close friends.

2. The agreement between Bob and Cathy says nothing about assignment. May Bob assign his claim to Hardknuckle?

(a) Bob may assign his claim, but only with Cathy's agreement.

(b) Bob may assign his claim, but only if Cathy and Hardknuckle agree.

(c) Bob may assign his claim without Cathy's agreement.

(d) Bob may assign his claim, but Cathy may nullify the assignment.

(e) Bob may not assign his claim because it violates public policy.

3. Jody is obligated under a contract to deliver 100,000 plastic bottles to a spring water company. Jody's supplier has just gone bankrupt; any other suppliers will charge her more than she expected to pay. This is:

   (a) consequential damages.
   (b) impossibility.
   (c) expectation interest.
   (d) substantial performance.
   (e) legally irrelevant.

4. An example of true impossibility is:

   (a) strict performance.
   (b) failure of condition.
   (c) illegality.
   (d) material breach.

5. Museum schedules a major fund-raising dinner, devoted to a famous Botticelli painting, for September 15. Museum then hires Sue Ellen to restore the picture, her work to be done no later than September 14. Sue Ellen is late with the restoration, forcing Museum to cancel the dinner and lose at least $500,000 in donations. Sue Ellen delivers the picture, in excellent condition, two weeks late. Museum sues.

   (a) Museum will win.
   (b) Museum will win if, when the parties made the deal, Sue Ellen knew the importance of the date.
   (c) Museum will win provided that it was Sue Ellen's fault she was late.
   (d) Museum will win provided that it was *not* Sue Ellen's fault she was late.
   (e) Museum will lose.

6. Tara is building an artificial beach at her lakefront resort. She agrees in writing to buy 1,000 tons of sand from Frank for $20 per ton, with delivery on June 1, at her resort. Frank fails to deliver any sand, and Tara is forced to go elsewhere. She buys 1,000 tons from Maureen at $25 per ton and then is forced to pay Walter $5,000 to haul the sand to her resort. Tara sues Frank. Tara will recover:

   (a) Nothing
   (b) $5,000
   (c) $10,000
   (d) $15,000
   (e) $30,000

CASE QUESTIONS

1. Darin bought his fiancée Sarah a three-carat diamond ring for $43,121 from Mandarin Gems. Later, Mandarin supplied the newlyweds with a written appraisal valuing the engagement ring at $45,500. Years later, the couple divorced, and Sarah kept the ring. When she had the ring reappraised, another gemologist assessed its value at only

$20,000. Sarah sued Mandarin for breach of contract, but the jeweler defended by saying that it had never made a contract with her. Does Sarah have contract rights against Mandarin?

2. Nationwide Discount Furniture hired Rampart Security to install an alarm in its warehouse. A fire would set off an alarm in Rampart's office, and the security company was then supposed to notify Nationwide immediately. A fire did break out, but Rampart allegedly failed to notify Nationwide, causing the fire to spread next door and damage a building owned by Gasket Materials Corp. Gasket sued Rampart for breach of contract, and Rampart moved for summary judgment. Comment.

3. Evans built a house for Sandra Dyer, but the house had some problems. The garage ceiling was too low. Load-bearing beams in the "great room" cracked and appeared to be steadily weakening. The patio did not drain properly. Pipes froze. Evans wanted the money promised for the job, but Dyer refused to pay. Comment.

4. Racicky was in the process of buying 320 acres of ranchland. While that sale was being negotiated, Racicky signed a contract to sell the land to Simon. Simon paid $144,000, the full price of the land. But Racicky went bankrupt before he could complete the purchase of the land, let alone its sale. Which of these remedies should Simon seek: expectation, restitution, or specific performance?

5. **ETHICS** The National Football League (NFL) owns the copyright to the broadcasts of its games. It licenses local television stations to telecast certain games and maintains a "blackout rule," which prohibits stations from broadcasting home games that are not sold out 72 hours before the game starts. Certain home games of the Cleveland team were not sold out, and the NFL blocked local broadcast. But several bars in the Cleveland area were able to pick up the game's signal by using special antennas. The NFL wanted the bars to stop showing the games. What did it do? Was it unethical of the bars to broadcast the games that they were able to pick up? Apart from the NFL's legal rights, do you think it had the moral right to stop the bars from broadcasting the games?

DISCUSSION QUESTIONS

1. A manufacturer delivers a new tractor to Farmer Ted on the first day of the harvest season. But the tractor will not start. It takes two weeks for the right parts to be delivered and installed. The repair bill comes to $1,000. During the two weeks, some acres of Farmer Ted's crops die. He argues in court that his lost profit on those acres is $60,000. The jury awards the full $1,000 for the tractor repairs, and $60,000 for the lost crops. Identify the two types of awards. Is it fair that Farmer Ted received 60 times the value of the repair bill for his lost crops?

2. If a person promises to give you a gift, there is usually no consideration. The person can change his mind and decide not to give you the present, and there is nothing you can do about it. But if a person makes a contract with *someone else* and intends that you receive a gift under the agreement, you are a donee beneficiary, and you *do* have rights to enforce the deal. Are these rules unacceptably inconsistent? If so, which rule should change?

3. Imagine that you hire your trusted friend Fran to paint your house and that you do not include a nondelegation clause in the agreement. Fran delegates the job to Sam, who is a stranger to you. The delegation is legal, but should it be? Is it reasonable that you must accept the substitute painter?

4. The death of a promisor in a *personal services* contract discharges an agreement. But if a promisor dies, other kinds of contracts live on. Is this sensible? Would it be better to discharge all kinds of agreements if one of the parties passes away?

5. PepsiCo entered into a contract to sell its corporate jet to Klein for $4.6 million. Before the deal closed, the plane was sent to pick up PepsiCo's chairman of the board, who was stranded at Dulles airport. The chairman then decided that the company should not part with the plane. Klein sued PepsiCo for specific performance, arguing that he could not find a similar jet on the market for that price. Should a court force PepsiCo to sell its plane?

CHAPTER 13

© Honza Krej/Shutterstock.com

PRACTICAL CONTRACTS

Two true stories:

One

Holly (on the phone to her client): So, Judd, Harry's lawyer just emailed me a letter that Harry says he got from you last year. I'm reading from the letter now: "Each year that you meet your revenue goals, you'll get a 1 percent equity interest." Is it possible you sent that letter?

Judd: I don't remember the exact wording, but probably something like that.

Holly: You told me, absolutely, positively, you had never promised Harry any stock. That he was making the whole thing up.

Judd: He was threatening to leave unless I gave him some equity, so I said what he wanted to hear. But that letter didn't *mean* anything. This is a family business, and no one but my children will ever get stock.

> I don't know what the *contract* says—that's just the legal stuff.

Two

Grace (on the phone with her lawyer): Providential has raised its price to $12 a pound. I can't afford to pay that! We had a deal that the price would never go higher than 10 bucks. I've talked to Buddy over there, but he is refusing to back down. We need to do something!

Lawyer: Let me look at the contract.

Grace (her voice rising): I don't know what the *contract* says—that's just the legal stuff. Our *business* deal was no more than $10 a pound!

Businesspeople, not surprisingly, tend to focus more on business than on the technicalities of contract law. However, *ignoring* the role of a written agreement can lead to serious trouble. Both of the clients in this opening scenario ended up being bound by a contract they did not want.

You have been studying the *theory* of contract law. This chapter is different: Its purpose is to demonstrate how that theory operates in *practice* and help you determine if the legal agreement reflects your business deal. We will look at the structure and content of a standard written agreement and answer questions such as the following: What do all these legal terms mean? Are any important provisions missing? By the end of the chapter, you will have a road map for understanding a written contract.[1]

To illustrate our discussion of specific contract provisions, we will use a real movie contract between an actor and a producer. For reasons of confidentiality, however, we have changed the names.

Before we begin our discussion of written contracts, it is important to ask: Do you need a written agreement at all? Oral contracts can certainly be successful, **but there are times when you should *definitely* sign a written agreement:**

1. The Statute of Frauds requires it.

2. The deal is crucial to your life or the life of your business.

3. The terms are complex.

4. You do not have an ongoing relationship with the other party.

Once you decide you need a written contract, then what?

13-1 THE LAWYER

Businesspeople sometimes refer to their lawyers with terms like *business prevention department*. They may be reluctant to ask an attorney to draft a contract for fear of the time and expense that lawyers can inject into the process. And they worry that the lawyers will interfere in the business deal itself, at best causing unnecessary hindrance, at worst killing the deal. Part of the problem is that lawyers and clients have different views of the future.

13-1a Lawyers and Clients

Businesspeople are optimists—they believe that they have negotiated a great deal and everything is going to go well—sales will boom, the company will prosper. Lawyers have a different perspective—their primary goal is to protect their clients by avoiding litigation—now and in the future—or if litigation does occur, making sure their client wins. **For this reason, lawyers are trained to be pessimists—they try to foresee and protect against everything that can possibly go wrong.** Businesspeople sometimes view this lawyering as a waste of time and a potential deal killer, but it may just save them from some dire failure.

Lawyers also prefer to negotiate touchy subjects at the beginning of a relationship, when everyone is on friendly terms and eager to make a deal, rather than waiting until trouble strikes. In the long run, nothing harms a relationship more than unpleasant surprises.

---

[1]For further reading on practical contracts, see Scott Burnham, *Drafting and Analyzing Contracts*, Lexis/Nexis, 2003; Charles M. Fox, *Working with Contracts*, Practical Law Institute, 2008; George W. Kuney, *The Elements of Contract Drafting*, Thomson/West, 2006.

One advantage of using lawyers to conduct these negotiations is that they can serve as the bad guys. Instead of the client raising tough issues, the lawyers do. Many a client has said, "but my lawyer insists …" If the lawyer takes the blame, the client is able to maintain a better relationship with the other party.

Of course, this lawyerly protection comes at a cost—legal fees, time spent bargaining, the hours used to read complex provisions, and the potential for goodwill to erode during negotiations.

13-1b Hiring a Lawyer

If you do hire a lawyer, be aware of certain warning signs. Although the lawyer's goal is to protect you, a good attorney should be a deal maker, not a deal breaker. She should help you achieve your goals and, therefore, should never (or, at least, hardly ever) say, "You cannot do this." Instead, she should say, "Here are the risks to this approach" or "Here is another way to accomplish your goal."

Moreover, your lawyer's goal should not be to annihilate the other side. In the end, the contract will be more beneficial to everyone if the parties' relationship is harmonious. Trying to exact every last ounce of flesh, using whatever power you have to an abusive extreme, is not a sound long-term strategy. In the end, the best deals are those in which all the parties' incentives are aligned.

13-2 THE CONTRACT

In this section, we discuss how a contract is prepared and what provisions it should include.

13-2a Who Drafts It?

Once businesspeople have agreed to the terms of the deal, it is time to prepare a draft of the contract. Generally, both sides would prefer to *control the pen* (that is, to prepare the first draft of the contract) because the drafter has the right to choose a structure and wording that best represents his interests. Typically, the party with the most bargaining power prepares the drafts. In the movie contract, Producer's lawyer was in charge of the first draft. The contract then went to Artist's lawyer, who added the provisions that mattered to his client.

13-2b Mistakes

This author once worked with a lawyer who made a mistake in a contract. "No problem," he said. "I can win that one in court." Not a helpful attitude, given that one purpose of a contract is to *avoid* litigation. In this section, we look at the most common types of mistakes and how to avoid them.

Vagueness

Vagueness means that the parties to a contract deliberately include a provision that is unclear. It may be that they are not sure what they can get from the other side or, in some cases, even what they really want. One party may be trying to get a commitment from the other party without obligating itself. So they create a contract that keeps their options open. This approach is understandable but dangerous. As the following case illustrates: **Vagueness is your enemy.**

Vagueness

When a provision in a contract is deliberately left unclear

You be the **Judge**

QUAKE CONSTRUCTION, INC. v. AMERICAN AIRLINES, INC.
141 Ill. 2d 281
Supreme Court of Illinois, 1990

Facts: Jones Brothers Construction was the general contractor on a job to expand American Airlines' facilities at O'Hare International Airport. Jones verbally accepted Quake's bid to work on the project and promised that Quake would receive a written contract soon. Jones wanted the license numbers of the subcontractors that Quake would be using, but Quake could not furnish those numbers until it had assured its subcontractors that they had the job. Quake did not want to give that assurance until *it* was certain of its own work. So Jones sent a letter of intent that stated, among other things:

> We have elected to award the contract for the subject project to your firm as we discussed on April 15. A contract agreement outlining the detailed terms and conditions is being prepared and will be available for your signature shortly.
>
> Your scope of work includes the complete installation of expanded lunchroom, restaurant, and locker facilities for American Airlines employees, as well as an expansion of American Airlines' existing Automotive Maintenance Shop. A sixty (60) calendar day period shall be allowed for the construction of the locker room, lunchroom, and restaurant area beginning the week of April 22. The entire project shall be completed by August 15.
>
> This notice of award authorizes the work set forth in the attached documents at a lump sum price of $1,060,568.00.

Jones Brothers Construction Corporation reserves the right to cancel this letter of intent if the parties cannot agree on a fully executed subcontract agreement.

The parties never signed a more detailed written contract, and ultimately Jones hired another company. Quake sued, seeking to recover the money it spent in preparation and its loss of anticipated profit.

You Be the Judge: *Was the letter of intent a valid contract?*

Argument for Quake: This letter was a valid contract. It explicitly stated that Jones awarded the contract to Quake. It also said, "This notice of award authorizes the work." The letter included significant detail about the scope of the contract, including the specific facilities Quake would be working on. Furthermore, the work was to commence approximately 4 to 11 days after the letter was written. This short period of time indicates that the parties intended to be bound by the letter so that work could begin quickly. And, the letter contained a cancellation clause. If it was not a contract, why would anyone need to cancel it?

Argument for Jones: This letter was not a contract. It referred several times to the execution of a formal contract by the parties, thus indicating that they did not intend to be bound by the letter. Look at the cancellation clause carefully: It could also be interpreted to mean that the parties did not intend to be bound by any agreement until they entered into a formal contract.

Litigating the meaning of this letter of intent was a disaster for both parties. If you were negotiating for Jones and wanted to clarify negotiations without committing your company, how could you do it? State in the letter that it is *not a contract*, that it is a memorandum summarizing negotiations thus far, but that neither party will be bound until a full written contract is signed.

But what if Quake cannot get a commitment from its subcontractors until they are certain that it has the job? Quake should take the initiative and present Jones with its own letter of intent, stating that the parties *do* have a binding agreement for $1 million worth of work. Insist that Jones sign it. Jones would then be forced to decide whether it is willing to make a binding commitment. If it is not willing to commit, let it openly say so. At least both parties would know where they stood.

The movie contract provides another example of deliberate vagueness. In these contracts, nudity is always a contentious issue. Producers believe that nudity sells movie tickets; actors are afraid that it will tarnish their reputation. Artist's lawyer wanted to include this provision:

Artist may not be photographed and shall not be required to render any services nude below the waist or in simulated sex scenes without Artist's prior written consent.

However, the script called for a scene in which Artist was swimming nude and the director wanted the option of showing him below the waist from the back. Ultimately, the nudity clause read as follows:

> Producer has informed Artist that Artist's role in the Picture might require Artist to appear and be photographed (a) nude, which nudity may include only above-the-waist nudity and rear below-the-waist nudity, but shall exclude frontal below-the-waist nudity; and (b) in simulated sex scenes. Artist acknowledges and agrees that Artist has accepted such employment in the Picture with full knowledge of Artist's required participation in nude scenes and/or in simulated sex scenes and Artist's execution of the Agreement constitutes written consent by Artist to appear in the nude scenes and simulated sex scenes and to perform therein as reasonably required by Producer. A copy of the scenes from the screenplay requiring Artist's nudity and/or simulated sex are attached hereto. Artist shall have a right of meaningful prior consultation with the director of the Picture regarding the manner of photography of any scenes in which Artist appears nude or engaged in simulated sex acts.
>
> Artist may wear pants or other covering that does not interfere with the shooting of the nude scenes or simulated sex scenes. Artist's buttocks and/or genitalia shall not be shown, depicted, or otherwise visible without Artist's prior written consent. Artist shall have the absolute right to change his mind and not perform in any nude scene or simulated sex scene, notwithstanding that Artist had prior thereto agreed to perform in such scene.

What does this provision mean? Has Artist agreed to perform in nude scenes or not? He has acknowledged that the script calls for nude scenes, and he has agreed, in principle, that he would appear in them. However, since he had never worked with this director, he did not want to promise that he would definitely appear in nude scenes. So the contract states that Actor could refuse to shoot nude scenes altogether, or he could shoot them and then, after viewing them, decide not to allow them in the movie. Because of this clause, the director shot different versions of the scene—some with nudity and some without—so that if Artist rejected the nude scene, the director still had options.

The true test of whether a vague clause belongs in a contract is this: Would you sign the contract if you knew that the other side's interpretation would prevail in litigation? In this example, each side was staking out its position and deferring a final negotiation until there was an actual disagreement about a nude scene. If the other side's position is acceptable to you, the vague clause simply defers a fight that you can afford to lose. But if the point is really important to you, it may be wiser to resolve the issue before you sign the contract.

EXAM Strategy

Question: The nudity provision in the movie contract is vague. Rewrite it so that it accurately reflects the agreement between the parties.

Strategy: This is easy! Just say what the parties intended the deal to be.

Result: "The script for the Picture includes scenes showing Artist (a) with frontal nudity from the waist up and with rear below-the-waist nudity (but no frontal below-the-waist nudity); and (b) in simulated sex scenes. However, no scenes shall be shot in which Artist's buttocks and/or genitalia are shown, depicted, or otherwise visible without Artist's prior written consent. Artist shall have the absolute right not to perform in any nude scene or simulated sex scene. If shot, no nude or sex scenes may appear in the Picture without Artist's prior written consent."

Ambiguity

Ambiguity
When a provision in a contract is unclear by accident

Vagueness occurs when the parties do not want the contract to be clear. **Ambiguity** is different—it means that the provision is accidentally unclear. It occurs in contracts when the parties think only about what they want a provision to mean, without considering the literal meaning or the other side's perspective. When reading a contract, try to imagine all the different ways a clause can be interpreted. Because you think it means one thing does not mean that the other side will share your view. For example, suppose that an employment contract says, "Employee agrees not to work for a competitor for a period of three years from employment." Does that mean three years from the date of hiring or from the date of termination? Unclear, so who knows?

What happens if a contract does contain ambiguous language? **Any ambiguity is interpreted against the drafter of the contract**. Although both sides need to be careful in reading a contract—litigation benefits no one—the side that prepares the documents bears a special burden. This rule is meant to:

- Protect laypeople from the dangers of form contracts that they have little power to change. The courts are especially sympathetic to laypeople if a company prepares a form contract and gives the other side only a "take it or leave it" option. (Think insurance policies.)

- Protect people who are unlikely to be represented by a lawyer. Most people do not hire a lawyer to read form contracts. And without an experienced lawyer, it is highly unlikely that an individual would be aware of ambiguities.

- Encourage those who prepare contracts to do so carefully.

Typos

Scrivener's error
A typo

Extell Development Corporation built the Rushmore, a luxury condominium complex in Manhattan. When Extell began selling the units, it agreed to refund any buyer's down payment if the first closing did not occur by September 1, 2009. (The goal was to protect buyers who might not have any place to live if the building was not finished on time.) In the end, the first closing occurred in February 2009. No problem, right? No problem except that the purchase contract had a typo: It said September 1, *2008* rather than *2009*. In the meantime, the Manhattan real estate market tumbled, and many purchasers of Rushmore condominiums wanted to back out. After litigation all the way to the Federal Court of Appeals, purchasers were allowed to cancel their contracts and obtain a refund of their deposits.

What is the law of typos? First of all, the law has a fancier word than *typo*—it is **scrivener's error**. (A scrivener is a clerk who copies documents.) **In the case of a scrivener's error, a court will reform a contract if there is clear and convincing evidence that the alleged mistake does not actually reflect the true intent of the parties.** In the Rushmore case, an arbitrator refused to reform the contract, ruling that there was no clear and convincing evidence that the parties intended something other than the contract term as written.

In the following case, even more money was at stake. What would you do if you were the judge?

You be the Judge

Facts: Heritage wanted to buy a substance called tribasic copper chloride (TBCC) from Phibro but, because of uncertainty in the industry, the two companies could not agree on a price for future years. It turned out, though, that the price of TBCC tended to rise and fall with that of copper sulfate, so Heritage proposed that the amount it paid for TBCC would increase an additional $15 per ton for each $0.01 increase in the cost of copper sulfate over $0.38 per pound.

HERITAGE TECHNOLOGIES, L.L.C. v. PHIBRO-TECH, INC.
2008 U.S. Dist. LEXIS 329, 2008 WL 45380
United States District Court for the Southern District of Indiana, 2008

At the end of a meeting between two top officers of Heritage and Phibro, the Phibro officer hand wrote a document stating the terms of their deal and agreeing to the Heritage pricing proposal. In a subsequent draft of the agreement prepared by Phibro, the $.01 number was changed to $0.10—that is, from 1 cent to 10 cents. In other words, in the original draft, Heritage agreed to an increase in price if copper sulfate went above 39 cents per pound, an additional price rise at 40 cents, and so on. But in the Phibro draft, Heritage's first increase would not occur until the price of copper sulfate went to 48 cents a pound, with a second rise at 58 cents. In short, the Phibro draft was much more favorable to Heritage than the Heritage proposal had been.

At some point during the negotiations, the lawyer for Heritage asked his client if the $0.10 figure was accurate. The Heritage officer said that the increase in this amount was meant to offset other provisions that favored Phibro. There is no evidence that this statement was true. The contract went through eight drafts and numerous changes, but the two sides never again met or discussed the $0.10 figure.

After the execution of the agreement, Heritage discovered a different mistake. When Heritage brought the error to Phibro's attention, Phibro agreed to make the change, even though it was to Phibro's disadvantage to do so.

All was peaceful until the price of copper sulfate went to $0.478 per pound. Phibro believed that because the price was above $0.38 per pound, it was entitled to an increased payment. Heritage responded that the increase would not occur until the price went above $0.48. Phibro then looked at the agreement and noticed the $0.10 term for the first time. Phibro contacted Heritage to say that the $0.10 term was a typo and not what the two parties had originally agreed. Heritage refused to amend the agreement, and Phibro filed suit.

You Be the Judge: *Should the court enforce the contract as written or as the parties agreed in their meeting? Which number is correct—$0.10 or $0.01?*

Argument for Phibro: In their meeting, the two negotiators agreed to a $15 per ton increase in the price of TBCC for each 1-cent increase in copper sulfate price. Then by mistake, the contract said 10 cents. After their first meeting, the two parties never even discussed the 10-cent provision, much less agreed to change it. The court should revise this contract to be consistent with the parties' agreement, which was 1 cent.

Argument for Heritage: The parties conducted negotiations by sending drafts back and forth rather than by talking on the phone. Each party was represented by a team of lawyers. Ultimately, the agreement went through eight drafts, and this pricing term was never altered despite several other changes and additions. Moreover, the change in price was in return for other provisions that benefited Phibro. Certainly, there is no clear and convincing evidence that both parties were mistaken about what the document actually said. Ultimately, the parties agreed to 10 cents, and that is what the court should enforce.

Ethics

When Heritage found a different mistake in the contract, Phibro agreed to correct it, even though the correction was unfavorable to Phibro. But when a mistake occurred in Heritage's favor, Heritage refused to honor the intended terms of the agreement. Is Heritage behaving ethically? Does Heritage have an obligation to treat Phibro as well as Phibro behaved towards Heritage? Is it right to take advantage of other people's mistakes? What Life Principles would you apply in this situation?

What can you do to prevent mistakes? In theory, you should read every contract you sign very carefully. If, for whatever reason, that degree of care is not possible, be sure to at least **read the important terms carefully**. Before signing a contract, check *carefully* and *thoughtfully* the names of the parties, the dates, dollar amounts, and interest rates. If all these elements are correct, you are unlikely to go too far wrong. And, of course, having read this chapter, *you* will never mistake $0.10 for $0.01.

A contract is not only an agreement—it is also a reference document. During the course of your relationship with the other party, you may need to refer to the contract regularly to remind yourself what you agreed to. This brings us to our next topic—the structure of a contract. Once you understand the standard outline of a contract, it will be much easier to find your way through the thicket of provisions.

13-2c The Structure of a Contract

Traditional contracts tended to use archaic words—*whereas* and *heretofore* were common. Modern contracts are more straightforward, without as many linguistic flourishes. Our movie contract takes the modern approach.

Title

The title should be as descriptive as possible—a generic title such as AGREEMENT does not distinguish one contract from another. The title of our movie contract is MEMORANDUM OF AGREEMENT (not a particularly useful name), but in the upper right-hand corner, there is space for the date of the contract and the subject. The subject is Dawn Rising/Clay Parker.

Introductory Paragraph

The introductory paragraph includes the date, the names of the parties, and the nature of the contract. The names of the parties and the movie are defined terms, such as Clay Parker ("Artist"). By defining the names, the actual names do not have to be repeated throughout the agreement. In this way, a standard form contract can be used in different deals without worrying about whether the names of the parties are correct throughout the document.

The introductory paragraph must also include specific language indicating that the parties entered into an agreement. In our contract, the opening paragraph states:

> This shall confirm the agreement ("Agreement") between WINTERFIELD PRODUCTIONS ("Producer") and CLAY PARKER ("Artist") regarding the acting services of Artist in connection with the theatrical motion picture tentatively entitled "DAWN RISING" (the "Picture"),[2] as follows:

Covenants

Now we get to the heart of the contract: What are the parties agreeing to do? Failure to perform these obligations constitutes a breach of the contract and will require the payment of damages. **Covenant** is a legal term that means a promise in a contract.

Covenant
A promise in a contract

At this stage, it is particularly important for lawyer and client to work well together. Clients should figure out what they need for the agreement to be successful. *It is a mistake to assume that everything will work itself out.* Instead, clients need to protect themselves as best they can. Lawyers can help in this negotiation and drafting process because they have worked on other similar deals and they know what can go wrong. Listen to them—they are on your side.

Imagine you are an actor about to sign a contract to make a movie. What provisions would you want? Begin by asking what your goals are for the project. Certainly, to make

---

[2]These are not the parties' real names but are offered to illustrate the concepts.

a movie that critics like and the public wants to see. So you will ask for as much control over the process and product as you can get—selection of the director and co-stars, for instance. Maybe influence on the editing process. But you also want to make sure that the movie does not hurt your career. What provisions would you need to achieve that goal? And shooting a movie can be grueling work, so you want to ensure that your physical and emotional needs are met, particularly when you are on location away from home. Try to think of all the different events that could happen and how they would affect you.

> **Both Artist and Producer want control over the final product. Who will win that battle?**

Now take the other side and imagine what you would want if you were the producer. The producer's goal is to make money—which means creating a quality movie while spending as little as possible and maintaining control over the process and final product. As you can see, some of the goals conflict—both Artist and Producer want control over the final product. Who will win that battle?

Here are the terms of the contract that Actor and Producer ultimately signed.

The Artist negotiated:

1. A fixed fee of $1,800,000, to be paid in equal installments at the end of each week of filming

2. Extra payment if the filming takes longer than 10 weeks

3. 7.5 percent of the gross receipts of the movie.

4. Approval over (but approval shall not be unreasonably withheld):

   a. The director, co-stars, hairdresser, makeup person, costume designer, stand-ins, and the look of his role (although he lists one director and co-star whom he has preapproved)

   b. Any changes in the script that materially affect his role

   c. All product placements, but he preapproves the placement of Snickers candy bars

   d. Locations where the filming takes place

   e. All videos, photos, and interviews of him

5. Approval (at his sole discretion) over the release of any blooper videos

6. His name to be listed first in the movie credits, on a separate card (i.e., alone on the screen)

7. At least 12 hours off duty from the end of each day of filming to the start of the next day

8. First-class airplane tickets to any locations outside of Los Angeles

9. 10 first-class airline tickets for his friends to visit him on location.

10. A luxury hotel suite for himself and a room for his friends

11. A driver and four-wheel-drive SUV to transport him to the set

12. The right to keep some wardrobe items

The Producer negotiated:

1. All intellectual property rights to the movie

2. The right not to make the movie, although he would still have to pay Artist the fixed fee

3. Control over the final cut of the movie

4. That the Artist will show up on a certain date and work in good faith for

   a. 2 weeks in preproduction (wardrobe and rehearsals)

   b. 10 weeks shooting the movie

   c. Two free weeks after the shooting ends, in case the director wants to reshoot some scenes. The Artist must in good faith make himself available whenever the director needs him.

5. The right to fire Artist if his appearance or voice materially changes before or during the filming of the movie

6. That the Artist help promote the movie on dates subject to Artist's approval, which shall not be unreasonably withheld

Breach

Material breach

A violation of a contract that defeats an essential purpose of the agreement

Throughout the life of a contract, there could be many small breaches. Say, Artist shows up one day late for filming or he gains five pounds. **To constitute a violation of the contract, though, the breach must be material.** A **material breach** is important enough to defeat an essential purpose of the contract. Although a court would probably not consider one missed day to be a material breach, if Artist repeatedly failed to show up, that would be material.

Given that one goal of a contract is to avoid litigation, it is can be useful to define in the contract itself what a breach is. The movie contract uses this definition:

> "Artist fails or refuses to perform in accordance with Producer's instructions or is otherwise in material breach or material default hereof," and "Artist's use of drugs [other than prescribed by a medical doctor]."

The contract goes on, however, to give Artist one free pass:

> It being agreed that with regard to one instance of default only, Artist shall have 24 hours after receipt of notice to cure any alleged breach or default hereof.

Reasonably

Ordinary or usual under the circumstances

Good faith

An honest effort to meet both the spirit and letter of a contract

Good Faith.   Note that the covenants in the movie contract use three different standards of behavior: reasonably, in good faith, or with sole discretion. **Reasonably** means ordinary or usual under the circumstances. **Good faith** means an honest effort to meet both the spirit and letter of the contract. A party with **sole discretion** has the *absolute* right to make any decision on that issue. Sole discretion clauses are not entered into lightly.

Sole discretion

The *absolute* right to make any decision on an issue

The following case involves a contract that did not specify which standard of behavior applied. What should the default standard be?

DICK BROADCASTING CO. V. OAK RIDGE FM, INC.

395 S.W.3d 653
Supreme Court of Tennessee, 2013

CASE SUMMARY

Facts: Oak Ridge FM, Inc. and Dick Broadcasting Company (Dick) entered into a contract that gave Dick a right of first refusal to purchase all the assets of Oak Ridge's radio station WOKI-FM. The agreement also provided that:

No party may assign its rights, interests or obligations hereunder without the prior written consent of the other party, and any purported assignment without such consent shall be null and void and of no legal force or effect.

When Dick asked permission to assign its rights to Citadel Broadcasting Company, Oak Ridge refused because it wanted to make its own deal directly with Citadel.

Dick sued Oak Ridge, alleging that it had breached the contract's *implied* covenant of good faith and fair dealing. The trial court dismissed the lawsuit, but the Court of Appeals overturned that decision. The Supreme Court of Tennessee agreed to hear the case.

Issues: *Is a covenant of good faith and fair dealing implied in this contract? In all contracts?*

Decision: In Tennessee (and about half the states), such a covenant is implied in all contracts, unless the parties explicitly agree otherwise. Such a provision was implied in this contract.

Reasoning: Tennessee follows the Restatement (Second) of Contracts, which provides that "every contract imposes upon each party a duty of good faith and fair dealing in its performance and its enforcement."

Oak Ridge argued that (1) the contract clearly gave it the right to withhold its consent for any reason and (2) the courts should not add a good faith provision to the contract because the parties could have included such language, but decided not to.

We disagree. An implied covenant of good faith and fair dealing is not an additional provision. It simply protects the parties' right to receive the benefits of their agreement. If the parties wanted to exclude this covenant, they should have explicitly said so in the contract.

Reciprocal Promises and Conditions. If one party to a contract breaches it, the other parties want to make sure that they can walk away without any further obligation to keep performing their covenants. To ensure this result, the terms of the contract must be *conditional* not *reciprocal*. Suppose that a contract states:

1. Actor shall take part in the principal photography of Movie for 10 weeks, commencing on March 1.

2. Producer shall pay Artist $180,000 per week.

In this case, even if Artist does not show up for shooting, Producer must still pay him. These provisions are **reciprocal promises, which means that they are each enforceable independently.** Producer must make payment and then sue Artist, hoping to recover damages in court.

The better approach is for the covenants to be **conditional**—a party agrees to perform them only if the other side has first done what it promised. In the real movie contract, Producer promises to pay Artist "On the condition that Artist fully performs all of Artist's services and obligations and agreements hereunder and is not in material breach or otherwise in material default hereof."

In short, if you do not expect to perform under the contract until the other side has met its obligations, be sure to say so.

Language of the Covenants. To clarify *who* exactly is doing what, covenants in a contract should use the active, not passive voice. In other words, a contract should say "Producer shall pay Artist $1.8 million," not "Artist shall be paid $1.8 million."

Representations and Warranties

Covenants are the promises the parties make about what they will do in the future. Representations and warranties are statements of fact about the past or present; they are true when the contract is signed (or at some other specific, designated time).[3] These representations and warranties are important—without them, the other party might not have agreed to

Reciprocal promises
Promises that are each enforceable independently

Conditional
Promises that a party agrees to perform only if the other side has first done what it promised

Representations and warranties
Statements of fact about the past or present

---

[3]Although, technically, there is a slight difference between a representation and a warranty, many lawyers confuse the two terms, and the distinction is not important. We will treat them as synonyms, as many lawyers do.

the contract. In the movie contract, Artist warrants that he is a member of the Screen Actors Guild. This provision is important because, if it was not true, Producer would either have to obtain a waiver or pay a substantial penalty.

In a contract between two companies, each side will generally represent and warrant facts such as: They legally exist, they have the authority to enter into the contract, their financial statements are accurate, and they own all relevant assets. In a contract for the sale of goods, the contract will include warranties about the condition of the goods being sold.

EXAM Strategy

Question: Producer does not want Artist to pilot an airplane during the term of the contract. Would that provision be a warranty and representation or a covenant? How would you phrase it?

Strategy: Warranties and representations are about events in the past or present. A covenant is a promise for the future. If, for example, Producer wanted to know that Artist had never used drugs in the past, that provision would be a warranty and representation.

Result: A promise not to pilot an airplane is a covenant. The contract could say, "Until Artist completes all services required hereunder, he shall not pilot an airplane."

Boilerplate

These standard provisions are typically placed in a section entitled *Miscellaneous*. Many people think that the term "boilerplate" is a synonym for "boring and irrelevant," but it is worth remembering that the word comes from the iron or steel that protects the hull of a ship—something that shipbuilders ignore to the passengers' peril. A contract without boilerplate is valid and enforceable, but these provisions do play an important protective role. In essence, boilerplate creates a private law that governs disputes between the parties. Courts can also play this role, and indeed, in the absence of boilerplate, they will. But remember that an important goal of a contract is to avoid court involvement.

Here are some standard, and important, boilerplate provisions.

Choice of law provisions
Determine which state's laws will be used to interpret the contract

Choice of forum
Determines the state in which any litigation would take place

Choice of Law and Forum.   **Choice of law provisions** determine which state's laws will be used to interpret the contract. **Choice of forum** determines the state in which any litigation would take place. (One state's courts can apply another state's laws.) Lawyers often view these two provisions as the most important boilerplate because (1) particular states might have dramatically different laws and (2) it is a lot more convenient and cheaper to litigate a case in one's home courts.

The movie contract states: "This Agreement shall be deemed to have been made in the State of California and shall be construed and enforced in accordance with the law of the State of California." The contract did not, but might have, also specified the forum—that any litigation would be tried in California.

Modification.   Contracts should contain a provision governing modification. The movie contract states: "This Agreement may not be amended or modified except by an instrument in writing signed by the party to be charged with such amendment or modification."

"Charged with such amendment" means the party who is adversely affected by the change. For example, if Producer agrees to pay Artist more, then Producer must sign the amendment. Without this provision, a conversation over beers between Producer and Artist about a change in pay might turn out to be an enforceable amendment.

Assignment of Rights and Delegation of Duties.   An **assignment of rights** is a transfer of the benefits under a contract to another person. Artist might, for example, want to assign his right to receive payment under the contract to his ex-wife.

The movie contract treats the two parties differently on this issue. Producer has the right to *assign* the contract, but he must stay secondarily liable on it. In other words, Producer can transfer to someone else the right to receive the benefits of the contract (that is, to make the movie with Artist), but he cannot transfer his obligations (to pay Artist). If the person who takes over the contract for him fails to pay Artist, then Producer is liable. Artist might be unhappy if another production company makes the movie, but he is still bound by the terms of the contract. At least he knows that Producer is ultimately liable for his paycheck.

Delegation of duties is a transfer of the obligations under a contract. Suppose Artist received an offer to make another movie at the same time. He might want to assign his obligation to act in this movie to some other actor. But it certainly matters to Producer which actor shows up to do the filming. Artist cannot say, "I'm too busy—here's my cousin Jack." So the movie contract provides that Artist cannot delegate his services.

Arbitration.   Some contracts prohibit the parties from suing in court and require that disputes be settled by an arbitrator. The parties to a contract do not have to arbitrate a dispute unless the contract specifically requires it.

Attorney's Fees.   As a general rule, if parties to a contract end up in litigation, they must pay their own legal fees. But contracts may override this general rule and provide that the losing party in a dispute must pay the attorney's fees for both sides. Such a provision tends to discourage the poorer party from litigating with a rich opponent for fear of having to pay two sets of attorney's fees. The movie contract provides:

> Artist hereby agrees to indemnify Producer from and against any and all losses, costs (including, without limitation, reasonable attorney's fees), liabilities, damages, and claims of any nature arising from or in connection with any breach by Artist of any agreement, representation, or warranty made by Artist under this Agreement.

There is no equivalent provision for breaches by Producer. What does that omission tell you about the relative bargaining power of the two parties?

Integration.   During contract negotiations, the parties may discuss many ideas that are not ultimately included in the final version. The point of an integration clause is to prevent either side from later claiming that the two parties had agreed to additional provisions. The movie contract states:

> This Agreement, along with the exhibits attached hereto, shall constitute a binding contract between the parties hereto and shall supersede any and all prior negotiations and communications, whether written or oral, with respect hereto.

Severability.   If, for whatever reason, some part of the contract turns out to be unenforceable, a severability provision asks the court simply to delete the offending clause and enforce the rest of the contract. For example, courts will not enforce *unreasonable* non-compete clauses. (California courts will not enforce *any* non-competes, unless made in connection with the sale of a business.) In one case, a consultant signed an employment contract that prohibited him from engaging in his occupation "anyplace in the world." The court struck down this non-compete provision but ruled that the rest of the contract (which contained trade secret clauses) was valid.

Assignment of rights
A transfer of benefits under a contract to another person

Delegation of duties
A transfer of obligations in a contract

The movie contract states:

> In the event that there is any conflict between any provision of this Agreement and any statute, law, or regulation, the latter shall prevail; provided, however, that in such event, the provision of this Agreement so affected shall be curtailed and limited only to the minimum extent necessary to permit compliance with the minimum requirement, and no other provision of this Agreement shall be affected thereby and all other provisions of this Agreement shall continue in full force and effect.

Force Majeure event

A disruptive, unexpected occurrence for which neither party is to blame that prevents one or both parties from complying with a contract

Force Majeure.   A *force majeure* **event** is a disruptive, unexpected occurrence for which neither party is to blame and that prevents one or both parties from complying with the contract. *Force majeure* events typically include wars, terrorist attacks, fires, floods, or general acts of God. If, for example, a major terrorist event were to halt air travel, Artist might not be able to appear on set as scheduled.

Notices.   After a contract is signed, there may be times when the parties want to send each other official notices—of a breach, an objection, or an approval, for example. In this section, the parties list the addresses where these notices can be sent. For Producer, it is company headquarters. For Artist, there are three addresses: his agent, his manager, and his lawyer. The notice provision also typically specifies when the notice is effective: When sent, when it would normally be expected to arrive, or when it actually does arrive.

Closing.   To indicate that the parties have agreed to the terms of the contract, they must sign it. When a party to the contract is a corporation, the signature lines should read like this:

Winterfield Productions Inc.

By: _____
Name:
Title:

In the end, both parties signed the contract and made the movie. According to Rotten Tomatoes, the online movie site, professional reviewers rated it 7.9 out of 10.

Chapter Conclusion

You will sign many contracts in your life. The goal of this chapter is to help you understand the structure and meaning of the most important provisions so that you can negotiate and analyze contracts more effectively.

Exam Review

1. **AMBIGUITY**   Any ambiguity in a contract is interpreted against the party that drafted the agreement.

2. **SCRIVENER'S ERROR**   A scrivener's error is a typo. In the case of a scrivener's error, a court will reform a contract if there is clear and convincing evidence that the mistake does not reflect the true intent of the parties.

Question: Martha intended to transfer one piece of land to Paul. By mistake, she signed a contract transferring two parcels of land. Each piece was accurately described in the contract. Will the court reform this contract and transfer one piece of land back to her?

Strategy: Begin by asking if this was a scrivener's error. Then consider whether the court will correct the mistake. (See the "Result" at the end of this section.)

3. **MATERIAL BREACH**   A material breach is important enough to defeat an essential purpose of the contract.

4. **SOLE DISCRETION**   A party with sole discretion has the absolute right to make any decision on that issue.

Question: A tenant rented space from a landlord for a seafood restaurant. Under the terms of the lease, the tenant could assign the lease only if the landlord gave her consent, which she had the right to withhold "for any reason whatsoever, at her sole discretion." The tenant grew too ill to run the restaurant and asked permission to assign the lease. The landlord refused. In court, the tenant argued that the landlord could not unreasonably withhold her consent. Is the tenant correct?

Strategy: A sole discretion clause grants the absolute right to make a decision. Are there any exceptions? (See the "Result" at the end of this section.)

5. **REASONABLY**   Reasonably means ordinary or usual under the circumstances.

6. **GOOD FAITH**   Good faith means an honest effort to meet both the spirit and letter of the contract.

7. **STRUCTURE OF A CONTRACT**   The structure of a contract looks like this:

1. Title
2. Introductory Paragraph
3. Definitions
4. Covenants
5. Breach
6. Conditions
7. Representations and Warranties

   i. Covenants are the promises the parties make about what they will do in the future.

   ii. Representations and warranties are statements of fact about the present or past—they are true when the contract is signed (or at some other specific, designated time).

8. BOILERPLATE

  i. Choice of Law and Forum
  ii. Modification
  iii. Assignment of Rights and Delegation of Duties
  iv. Arbitration
  v. Attorney's Fees
  vi. Integration
  vii. Severability
  viii. *Force Majeure*
  ix. Notices
  x. Closing

---

2. Result: The court ruled that it was not a scrivener's error because it was not a typo or clerical error. Therefore, the court did not reform the contract, and the land was not transferred back to Martha.

4. Result: The court ruled for the landlord. She had the absolute right to make any decision, as long as the decision was legal. The moral: Sole discretion clauses are serious business. Do not enter into one lightly.

MATCHING QUESTIONS

Match the following terms with their definitions:

___A. Assignment of rights

___B. Delegation of duties

___C. Covenant

___D. Reciprocal promise

___E. Conditional promise

___F. Representation

1. Promises that a party agrees to perform only if the other side has first done what it promised
2. Promises that are each enforceable independently
3. Statement of fact about the past or present
4. Transfer of obligations under a contract
5. Promise about what a party will do in the future
6. Transfer of benefits under a contract

TRUE/FALSE QUESTIONS

Circle true or false:

1. T F The same states must be named in the Choice of Law and Choice of Forum provisions.
2. T F For a modification to a contract to be valid, both parties must sign it.
3. T F A severability provision asks the court simply to delete the offending clause and enforce the rest of the contract.
4. T F A *force majeure* clause indicates who has the authority to write the first draft of the contract.

5. T F Unless the contract provides otherwise, both sides in a contract dispute pay their own legal fees.

Multiple-Choice Questions

1. Daniel and Annie signed a contract providing that Daniel would lend $50,000 to Annie's craft beer business at an interest rate of 8 percent. During negotiations, Daniel and Annie agreed that the interest rate would go down to 5 percent once she had sold 25,000 cases. This provision never made it into the contract. After the contract was signed, Daniel agreed to reduce the interest rate to 6 percent once volume exceeded 15,000 cases. The contract had an integration provision but no modification clause. Annie has sold 30,000 cases. What interest rate must she pay?

(a) 8 percent

(b) 6 percent

(c) 5 percent

(d) The contract is void because the terms are unclear.

2. A contract states (1) that Buzz Co. legally exists and (2) will provide 2,000 pounds of wild salmon each week.

Which of the following statements is true?

(a) Clause 1 is a covenant, and Clause 2 is a representation.

(b) Clause 1 is a representation, and Clause 2 is a covenant.

(c) Both clauses are representations.

(d) Both clauses are covenants.

3. The following list provides reasons why a party would strongly consider putting a contract in writing. Which of these reasons is *least* important?

(a) The Statute of Frauds requires it.

(b) The deal is crucial to your life or the life of your business.

(c) The terms are complex.

(d) The parties do not have an ongoing relationship.

(e) The parties reside in different jurisdictions.

4. Michael and Scarlett cannot agree on the price he will pay her to manage his hotels in the third year of their contract. They agree to a provision stating that the price will be "reasonable." This provision is —————— . Parties should never include such a provision in a contract unless —————— .

(a) ambiguous; they are sure they will be able to reach an agreement later

(b) vague; they are sure they will be able to reach an agreement later

(c) ambiguous; they would not mind if the other side's interpretation prevails in litigation

(d) vague; they would not mind if the other side's interpretation prevails in litigation

5. Liesl purchased an insurance policy on her house. The policy stated that the insurance company was not liable for any damage to her house caused by vandalism or burglary. An arsonist burned down Liesl's house. Is the insurance company liable?

   (a) No, because arson is a form of vandalism.

   (b) Yes, because arson is not a form of vandalism.

   (c) Yes, because the language is ambiguous and should be interpreted against the insurance company.

   (d) No, because the language is vague and should be interpreted against Liesl.

6. A contract provided, "On January 5, Purchaser shall provide Seller with a certified check in the amount of $100,000. Seller shall transfer a deed for the Property to Purchaser." What is wrong with this provision?

   (a) It is not clear who Purchaser and Seller are.

   (b) The number $100,000 should be written in words.

   (c) The promises are reciprocal.

   (d) The promises are conditional.

CASE QUESTIONS

1. Zoe has been offered a job as CIO at Appsley Co, but first she has to negotiate a contract with the CEO, Phil. Do a role play with another student in your class in which one of you takes the role of Zoe and the other is Phil. What terms do you each want? Draft the contract. Now compare your results with others in the class. Who has negotiated the best deal? Who has written the best contract?

2. List three provisions in a contract that would be material, and three that would not be.

3. Slimline and Distributor signed a contract which provided that Distributor would use reasonable efforts to promote and sell Slimline's diet drink. Slimline was already being sold in Warehouse Club. After the contract was signed, Distributor stopped conducting in-store demos of Slimline. It did not repackage the product as Slimline and Warehouse requested. Sales of Slimline continued to increase during the term of the contract. Slimline sued Distributor, alleging a violation of the agreement. Who should win?

4. *YOU BE THE JUDGE* **WRITING PROBLEM** Chip bought an insurance policy on his house from Insurance Co. The policy covered damage from fire but explicitly excluded coverage for harm caused "by or through an earthquake." When an earthquake struck, Chip's house suffered no fire damage, but the earthquake caused a building some blocks away to catch on fire. That fire ultimately spread to Chip's house, burning it down. Is Insurance Co. liable to Chip? **Argument for Insurance Co.:** The policy could not have been clearer or more explicit. If there had been no earthquake, Chip's house would still be standing. The policy does not cover his loss. **Argument for Chip:** His house was not damaged by an earthquake; it burned down. The policy covered fire damage. If a contract is ambiguous, it must be interpreted against the drafter of the contract.

5. Laurie's contract to sell her tortilla chip business to Hudson contained a provision that she must continue to work at the business for five years. One year later, she quit. Hudson refused to pay her the amounts still owing under the contract. Laurie alleged that he is liable for the full amount because her breach was not material. Is Laurie correct?

DISCUSSION QUESTIONS

1. In the movie contract, which side was the more successful negotiator? Can you think of any terms that either party left out? Are any of the provisions unreasonable?

2. In a contract, should sole discretion clauses be enforced if the party with the discretion behaves unreasonably? Should everyone have an obligation to behave reasonably?

3. What are the advantages and disadvantages of hiring a lawyer to draft or review a contract?

4. ETHICS Sophia negotiated a contract with Pete under which she would buy his company for $10 million plus the amount of the company's outstanding debt (approximately $1 million). But when Pete sent a draft of the contract, it stated that the purchase price would be $10 million *less* the company's debt. What is Sophia's ethical obligation to Pete? Should she tell him about the mistake? What Life Principles would you apply in this situation?

5. Blair Co.'s top officers asked an investment bank to find a buyer for the company. The bank sent an engagement letter to Blair with the following language:

> If, within 24 months after the termination of this agreement, Blair is bought by anyone with whom Bank has had substantial discussions about such a sale, Blair must pay Bank its full fee.

Is there any problem with the drafting of this provision? What could be done to clarify the language?

CHAPTER 14

SALES

He Sued, She Sued. Harold and Maude made a great couple because both were compulsive entrepreneurs. One evening, they sat on their penthouse roof deck, overlooking the twinkling Chicago skyline. Harold sipped a decaf coffee while negotiating, over the phone, with a real estate developer in San Antonio. Maude puffed a cigar as she bargained on a different line with a toy manufacturer in Cleveland. They hung up at the same time. "I did it!" shrieked Maude, "I made an incredible deal for the robots—five bucks each!" "No, *I* did it!" triumphed Harold, "I sold the 50 acres in Texas for $300,000 more than it's worth." They dashed indoors.

Maude quickly scrawled a handwritten memo, which read, "Confirming our deal—100,000 Psychopath Robots—you deliver Chicago—end of summer." She didn't mention a price, or an exact delivery date, or when payment would be made. She signed her memo and faxed it to the toy manufacturer. Harold took more time. He typed a thorough contract, describing precisely the land he was selling, the $2.3 million price, how and when each payment would be made, and what the deed conveyed. He signed the contract and faxed it, along with a plot plan showing the surveyed land. Then the happy couple grabbed a bottle of champagne, returned to the deck—and placed a side bet on whose contract would prove more profitable. The loser would have to cook and serve dinner for six months.

Neither Harold nor Maude ever heard again from the other parties. The toy manufacturer sold the robots to another retailer at a higher price. Maude was forced to buy comparable toys elsewhere for $9 each. She sued. And the Texas property buyer changed his mind, deciding to develop a Club Med in Greenland and refusing to pay Harold for his land. He sued. Only one of the two plaintiffs succeeded. Which one?

© Honza Krej/Shutterstock.com

> "Confirming our deal—100,000 Psychopath Robots—you deliver Chicago—end of summer."

14-1 SALES

The adventures of Harold and Maude illustrate the Uniform Commercial Code (UCC) in action. The Code is the single most important source of law for people engaged in commerce and controls the vast majority of contracts made every day in every state. The Code is old in origin, contemporary in usage, admirable in purpose, and flawed in application. "Yeah, yeah, that's fascinating," snaps Harold, "but who wins the bet?" Relax, Harold, we'll tell you in a minute.

14-1a Development of the UCC

In the middle of the twentieth century, contract law required a reinvention. Two problems had become apparent in the United States.

1. Old contract law principles often did not reflect modern business practices.

2. Laws had become different from one state to another.

On many legal topics, contract law included, the national government has had little to say and has allowed the states to act individually. Texas decides what kinds of agreements count as contracts in Texas, and next door in Oklahoma, the rules may be very different. On many issues, states reached essentially similar conclusions, and contract law developed in the same direction. But sometimes the states disagreed, and contract law took on the aspect of a patchwork quilt.

The UCC was created as an attempt to solve these two problems. It was a proposal written by legal scholars, not a law drafted by members of Congress or state legislatures. The scholars at the American Law Institute and the National Conference of Commissioners on Uniform State Laws had great ideas, but they had no legal authority to make anyone do anything.

Over time, lawmakers in all 50 states were persuaded to adopt many parts of the Uniform Commercial Code (UCC). They responded to these persuasive arguments:

- Businesses will benefit if most commercial transactions are governed by the modern and efficient contract law principles that are outlined in the UCC.

- Businesses everywhere will be able to operate more efficiently, and transactions will be more convenient, if the law surrounding most of their transactions is the same in all 50 states.

This chapter will focus on Article 2 of the UCC, which applies to the sale of goods. A **good** is any moveable physical object except for money and securities (like stock certificates). A house is not a good, but the *stuff* in the house—the car in the garage, the televisions, the furniture, and the paintings hanging on the wall—is. Article 2 applies to contracts that sell goods, and also to contracts that sell a mix of goods and services if the *predominant purpose* of the deal is to sell goods.

Goods
Any moveable physical object

Assume that you take your car to a mechanic for repairs and that there are problems with the work. If a lawsuit ensues, a court will have to determine whether the predominant purpose of the contract was the parts (goods) that were replaced or the labor (service) involved in the work.

It is worth noting that the UCC is not a total replacement for older principles in contract law. Contract lawsuits not involving goods are still resolved using the older common law rules.

Harold and Maude, Revisited

Harold and Maude each negotiated what they believed was an enforceable agreement, and both filed suit: Harold for the sale of his land; Maude for the purchase of toy robots. Only one prevailed. The difference in outcome demonstrates why everyone in business needs a working knowledge of the Code. As we revisit the happy couple, Harold is clearing the dinner dishes. Maude sits back in her chair, lights a cigar, and compliments her husband on the apple tart.

Harold's contract was for the sale of land and was governed by the common law of contracts, which requires any agreement for the sale of land to be in writing and *signed by the defendant*, in this case the buyer in Texas. Harold signed it, but the buyer never did, so Harold's meticulously detailed document was worth less than a five-cent cigar.

Maude's quickly scribbled memorandum, concerning robot toys, was for the sale of goods and was governed by Article 2 of the UCC. The Code requires less detail and formality in a writing. Because Maude and the seller were both merchants, the document she scribbled could be enforced *even against the defendant*, who had never signed anything. The fact that Maude left out the price and other significant terms was not fatal to a contract under the UCC, though under the common law, such omissions would have made the bargain unenforceable.

Merchants

The UCC evolved to provide merchants with rules that would meet their unique business needs. However, while the UCC offers a contract law that is more flexible than the common law, it also requires a higher level of responsibility from the merchants it serves. Those who make a living by crafting agreements are expected to understand the legal consequences of their words and deeds. Thus, many sections of the Code offer two rules: one for "merchants" and one for everybody else.

Merchant

Someone who routinely deals in the particular goods involved

UCC Section 2-104: A merchant is someone who routinely deals in the particular goods involved, or who appears to have special knowledge or skill in those goods, or who uses agents with special knowledge or skill in those goods. A used car dealer is a "merchant" when it comes to selling autos because he routinely deals in them. He is not a merchant when he goes to a furniture store and purchases a new sofa.

The UCC frequently holds a merchant to a higher standard of conduct than a non-merchant. For example, a merchant may be held to an oral contract if she received written confirmation of it, even though the merchant herself never signed the confirmation. That same confirmation memo, arriving at the house of a non-merchant, would not create a binding deal.

14-1b Contract Formation

The common law expected the parties to form a contract in a fairly predictable and traditional way: The offeror made a clear offer that included all important terms, and the offeree agreed to all terms. Nothing was left open. The drafters of the UCC recognized that businesspeople frequently do not think or work that way and that the law should reflect business reality.

Formation Basics: Section 2-204

UCC Section 2-204 provides three important rules that enable parties to make a contract quickly and informally:

1. **Any manner that shows agreement.** The parties may make a contract in any manner sufficient to show that they reached an agreement. They may show the agreement with words, writings, or even their conduct. Lisa negotiates with Ed to buy 300 barbecue grills. The parties agree on a price, but other business prevents them from finishing the deal. Six months later, Lisa writes, "Remember our deal for 300 grills? I still want to do it if you do." Ed does not respond, but a week later, a truck shows up at Lisa's store with the 300 grills, and Lisa accepts them. The combination of their original discussion, Lisa's subsequent letter, Ed's delivery, and her acceptance all adds up to show that they reached an agreement. The court will enforce their deal, and Lisa must pay the agreed-upon price.

2. **Moment of making is not critical.** The UCC will enforce a deal even though it is difficult, in common law terms, to say exactly when it was formed. Was Lisa's deal formed when they orally agreed? When he delivered? She accepted? The Code's answer: It does not matter. The contract is enforceable.

3. **One or more terms may be left open.** The common law insisted that the parties clearly agree on all important terms. The Code changes that. **Under the UCC, a court may enforce a bargain even though one or more terms were left open.** Lisa's letter never said

when she required delivery of the barbecue grills or when she would pay. Under the UCC, the omission is not fatal. As long as there is some certain basis for giving damages to the injured party, the court will do just that. If Lisa refused to pay, a court would rule that the parties assumed she would pay within a commercially reasonable time, such as 30 days.

In the following case, we can almost see the roller coasters, smell the cotton candy—and hear the carnival owners arguing.

JANNUSCH V. NAFFZIGER

883 N.E. 2d 711
Illinois Court of Appeals, 2008

CASE SUMMARY

Facts: Gene and Martha Jannusch owned Festival Foods, which served snacks at events throughout Illinois and Indiana. The business included a truck, servicing trailer, refrigerators, roasters, chairs, and tables.

Lindsey and Louann Naffziger orally agreed to buy Festival Foods for $150,000, the deal including all the assets and the opportunity to work at events secured by the Jannuschs. The Naffzigers paid $10,000 immediately, with the balance due when they received their bank loan. They took possession the next day and operated Festival Foods for the remainder of the season.

In a pretrial deposition, Louann Naffziger acknowledged orally agreeing to buy the business for $150,000. (Her admission under oath made the lack of a written contract irrelevant.) However, she could not recall making the agreement on any particular date. Gene Jannusch suggested the parties sign something, but the Naffzigers replied that they were "in no position to sign anything" because they had received no loan money from the bank and lacked a lawyer. Lindsey admitted taking possession of Festival Foods, receiving the income from the business, purchasing inventory, replacing equipment, and paying taxes and employees.

Two days after the business season ended, they returned Festival Foods to the Jannuschs, stating that the income was lower than expected. The Jannuschs sued. The trial court ruled that there had been no meeting of the minds and hence no contract. The Jannuschs appealed.

Issue: *Did the parties form a contract?*

Decision: Yes, the parties formed a contract.

Reasoning: The Naffzigers argue that nothing was said in the contract about a price for good will, a covenant not to compete, the value of individual assets, release from earlier liens, or the consequences should their loan be denied.

Under the UCC, a contract may be enforced even though some contract terms are missing or left to be agreed upon. However, if the essential terms are so uncertain that a court cannot decide whether the agreement has been broken, there is no contract.

The essential terms were agreed upon. The purchase price was $150,000, and the parties specified all assets to be transferred. No essential terms remained to be agreed upon. The only action remaining was the performance of the contract, and the Naffzigers took possession and used all items as their own.

Louann Naffziger could not recall making the oral agreement on any particular date, but parties may form a binding agreement even though the moment of its making is undetermined. Returning the goods at the end of the season was not a rejection of the Jannuschs' offer to sell; it was a breach of contract.

The parties agreed to a sale of Festival Foods for $150,000, and the Naffzigers violated the agreement. Reversed and remanded.

Based on the UCC, the Jannuschs won a case they would have lost under the common law. Next, we look at changes the Code has made in the centuries-old requirement of a writing.

Statute of Frauds

UCC Section 2-201 requires a writing for any sale of goods priced $500 or more. However, under the UCC, the writing need not completely summarize the agreement. The Code only requires a writing *sufficient to indicate* that the parties made a contract. In other words, the

UCC Statute of Frauds
The UCC requires a writing for any sales of goods priced $500 or more.

writing need not be a contract. A simple memo is enough, or a letter or informal note, mentioning that the two sides reached an agreement.

In general, the writing must be signed by the defendant—that is, whichever party is claiming there was no deal. Dick signs and sends to Shirley a letter saying, "This is to acknowledge your agreement to buy all 650 books in my rare book collection for $188,000." Shirley signs nothing. A day later, Louis offers Dick $250,000. Is Dick free to sell? No. He signed the memo, it indicates a contract, and Shirley can enforce it against him.

Now reverse the problem. Suppose that after Shirley receives Dick's letter, she decides against rare books in favor of original scripts from the *South Park* television show. Dick sues. Shirley wins because she signed nothing.

Enforceable Only to Quantity Stated.

Because the writing only has to indicate that the parties agreed, it need not state every term of their deal. But one term is essential: quantity. **The Code will enforce the contract only up to the quantity of goods stated in the writing.** This is logical since a court can surmise other terms, such as price, based on market conditions. Buyer agrees to purchase pencils from Seller. The market value of the pencils is easy to determine, but a court would have no way of knowing whether Buyer meant to purchase 1,000 pencils or 100,000; the quantity must be stated.

Merchant Exception.

This is a major change from the common law. **When two merchants make an oral contract, and one sends a confirming memo to the other within a reasonable time, and the memo is sufficiently definite that it could be enforced against the sender herself, then the memo is also valid against the merchant who receives it unless he objects within 10 days.** Laura, a tire wholesaler, signs and sends a memo to Scott, a retailer, saying, "Confm yr order today—500 tires cat #886—cat price." Scott realizes he can get the tires cheaper elsewhere and ignores the memo. Big mistake. Both parties are merchants, and Laura's memo is sufficient to bind her. So it also satisfies the Statute of Frauds against Scott unless he objects within 10 days.

EXAM Strategy

Question: Marko, a sporting goods retailer, speaks on the phone with Wholesaler about buying 500 footballs. After the conversation, Marko writes this message by hand: "Confirming our discussion—you will deliver to us 'Pro Bowl' model footballs—$45 per unit— arrival our store no later than July 20 this year." Marko signs and faxes the note to Wholesaler. Wholesaler reads the fax but then gets an order from Lana for the same model football at $51 per unit. Wholesaler never responds to Marko's fax and sells his entire supply to Lana. Two weeks later, Marko is forced to pay more from another seller and sues Wholesaler. Marko argues that under merchant exception, his fax was sufficient to satisfy the Statute of Frauds. Is he right?

Strategy: These two parties are merchants, and the merchant exception applies. Under this exception, a memo that could be enforced against the sender himself may bind the merchant who receives it. Could this memo be enforced against Marko? Make sure that you know what terms must be included to make a writing binding.

Result: The writing must indicate that the two parties reached an agreement. Marko's memo does so because he says he is confirming their discussion. Even if some terms are omitted, the writing may still suffice. However, the memo will be enforced only to the quantity of goods stated. Marko stated no quantity—a fatal error. His writing fails to satisfy the Statute of Frauds, and he loses the suit.

Added Terms: Section 2-207

Under the common law's mirror image rule, when one party makes an offer, the offeree must accept those exact terms. If the offeree adds or alters any terms, the acceptance is ineffective, and the offeree's response becomes a counteroffer. In one of its most significant modifications of contract law, the UCC changes that outcome. **Under Section 2-207, an acceptance that adds or alters terms will often create a contract.** The Code has made this change in response to *battles of the form*. Every day, corporations buy and sell millions of dollars of goods using preprinted forms. The vast majority of all contracts involve such documents. Typically, the buyer places an order by using a preprinted form, and the seller acknowledges with its own preprinted acceptance form. Because each form contains language favorable to the party sending it, the two documents rarely agree. The Code's drafters concluded that the law must cope with real practices.

Intention. The parties must still *intend* to create a contract. Section 2-207 is full of exceptions, but there is no change in this basic requirement of contract law. If the differing forms indicate that the parties never reached agreement, there is no contract.

Additional or Different Terms. An offeree may include a new term in his acceptance and still create a binding deal. Suppose Breeder writes to Pet Shop, offering to sell 100 guinea pigs at $2 each. Pet Shop faxes a memo saying, "We agree to buy 100 g.p. We receive normal industry credit for any unhealthy pig." Pet Shop has added a new term, concerning unhealthy pigs, but the parties have created a binding contract because the writings show they intended an agreement. Now the court must decide what the terms of the contract are because there is some discrepancy. The first step is to decide whether the new language is an *additional term* or a *different term*.

Additional terms are those that raise issues not covered in the offer. The "unhealthy pig" issue is an additional term because the offer said nothing about it. **When both parties are merchants, additional terms generally become part of the bargain.**[1] Both Pet Shop and Breeder are merchants, and the additional term about credit for unhealthy animals does become part of their agreement.

Different terms *contradict* those in the offer. Suppose Brilliant Corp. orders 1,500 cell phones from Makem Co., for use by Brilliant's sales force. Brilliant places the order by using a preprinted form stating that the product is fully warranted for normal use and that seller is liable for compensatory and consequential damages. This means, for example, that Makem could be liable for lost profits if a salesperson's phone fails during a lucrative sales pitch. Makem responds with its own memo stating that in the event of defective phones, Makem is liable only to repair or replace and is not liable for consequential damages, lost profits, or any other damages.

Makem's acceptance has included a different term because its language contradicts the offer. **Different terms cancel each other out.** The Code then supplies its own terms, called **gap-fillers**, which cover prices, delivery dates and places, warranties, and other subjects. The Code's gap-filler about warranties does permit recovery of compensatory and consequential damages. Therefore, Makem would be liable for lost profits.

Additional terms
Raise issues not covered in the offer

Different terms
Contradict those in the offer

Gap-fillers
UCC rules for supplying missing terms

---

[1]There are three circumstances in which additional terms do *not* become part of the agreement: when the original offer *insisted on its own terms;* when the additional term *materially alters* the offer—that is, makes a dramatic change in the proposal; and when the offeror *promptly objects* to the new terms.

14-1c Performance and Remedies

The Code's practical, flexible approach also shapes its rules about contract performance and remedy. As always, our goal in this chapter is to highlight doctrines that demonstrate a change or an evolution in common law principles.

Buyer's Remedies

Conforming goods
Satisfy the contract terms

A seller is expected to deliver what the buyer ordered. **Conforming goods satisfy the contract terms. Nonconforming goods do not.**[2] Frame Shop orders from Wholesaler a large quantity of walnut wood, due on March 15, to be used for picture frames. If Wholesaler delivers, on March 8, high-quality *cherry* wood, it has shipped nonconforming goods.

A buyer has the right to *inspect the goods* before paying or accepting[3] and may *reject non-conforming goods* by notifying the seller within a reasonable time.[4] Frame Shop may lawfully open Wholesaler's shipping crates before paying and is entitled to refuse the cherry wood. However, when the buyer rejects nonconforming goods, **the seller has the right to cure,** by delivering conforming goods before the contract deadline.[5] If Wholesaler delivers walnut wood by March 15, Frame Shop must pay in full. The Code even permits the seller to cure *after* the delivery date if doing so is reasonable. Notice the UCC's eminently pragmatic goal: to make contracts work.

Cover
To reasonably obtain substitute goods because another party has not honored a contract

Cover. If the seller breaches, the buyer may cover by reasonably obtaining substitute goods; it may then obtain the difference between the contract price and its cover price, plus incidental and consequential damages, minus expenses saved.[6] Retailer orders 10,000 pairs of ballet shoes from Shoemaker, at $55 per pair, to be delivered August 1. When no shoes dance through the door, Shoemaker explains that its workers in Europe are on strike and no delivery date can be guaranteed. Retailer purchases comparable shoes elsewhere for $70 and files suit. Retailer will win $150,000, representing the increased cost of $15 per pair.

Consequential damages
Damages resulting from the unique circumstances of the injured party

Incidental and Consequential Damages. An injured buyer is generally entitled to incidental and consequential damages. Incidental damages cover such costs as advertising for replacements, sending buyers to obtain new goods, and shipping the replacement goods. Consequential damages are those resulting from the unique circumstances of *this injured party*. They can be much more extensive and may include lost profits. **A buyer expecting to resell goods may obtain the loss of profit caused by the seller's failure to deliver.** In the ballet shoes case, suppose Retailer has contracts to resell the goods to ballet companies at an average profit of $10 per pair. Retailer is also entitled to those lost profits.

Seller's Remedies

Of course, a seller has rights, too. Sometimes a buyer breaches before the seller has delivered the goods, for example, by failing to make a payment due under the contract. If that happens, **the seller may refuse to deliver the goods.**[7]

> *Of course, a seller has rights, too.*

If a buyer unjustly refuses to accept or pay for goods, the injured seller may resell them. **If the resale is commercially reasonable, the seller may recover the difference between the resale price and contract price, plus incidental damages, minus expenses saved.**[8]

---

[2] UCC Section 2-106(2).
[3] UCC Section 2-513.
[4] UCC Section 2-601, 602.
[5] UCC Section 2-508.
[6] UCC Section 2-712.
[7] UCC Section 2-705.
[8] UCC Section 2-706.

Incidental damages are expenses the seller incurs in holding the goods and reselling them, costs such as storage, shipping, and advertising for resale. The seller must deduct expenses saved by the breach. For example, if the contract required the seller to ship heavy machinery from Detroit to San Diego, and the buyer's breach enables the seller to market its goods profitably in Detroit, the seller must deduct from its claimed losses the transportation costs that it saved.

Finally, the seller may simply sue **for the contract price** if the buyer has accepted the goods *or* if the goods are conforming and resale is impossible.[9] If the goods were manufactured to the buyer's unique specifications, there might be no other market for them, and the seller should receive the contract price.

14-2 WARRANTIES

A **warranty** is a promise that goods will meet certain standards. Normally a manufacturer or a seller gives a warranty, and a buyer relies on it. A warranty might be explicit and written: "The manufacturer warrants that the light bulbs in this package will illuminate for 2,000 hours." Or a warranty could be oral: "Don't worry. This machine can harvest any size of wheat crop ever planted in the state."

Sometimes a manufacturer offers a warranty as a means of attracting buyers: "We provide the finest bumper-to-bumper warranty in the automobile industry." Other times, the law itself imposes a warranty on goods, requiring the manufacturer to meet certain standards whether it wants to or not. We will begin with the first option—when the seller voluntarily provides a warranty.

Warranty
A contractual assurance that goods will meet certain standards

14-2a Express Warranties

An express warranty is one that the seller creates with his words or actions.[10] Whenever a seller *clearly indicates* to a buyer that the goods being sold will meet certain standards, she has created an express warranty. For example, if the sales clerk for a paint store tells a professional house painter that "this exterior paint will not fade for three years, even in direct sunlight," that is an express warranty, and the store is bound by it. The store is also bound by express warranty if the clerk gives the painter a brochure making the same promise or a sample that indicates the same thing.

In the following case, did Sony make an express warranty or was it just playing with its customers? You be the judge.

Express warranty
A guarantee, created by the words or actions of the seller, that goods will meet certain standards

---

[9]UCC Section 2-709.
[10]UCC Section 2-313.

You be the Judge

Facts: The PlayStation 3 (PS3) gaming system had two innovative capabilities: access to online gaming and an "Other OS" feature, which enabled users to use it as a personal computer. When Sony introduced the PS3, it stated in promotional materials that it expected the PS3 to have a "ten year life cycle." But the product license agreement informed

IN RE SONY PS3 "OTHER OS" LITIGATION
2014 U.S. App. LEXIS 187, 2014 WL 31217
United States Court of Appeals
for the Ninth Circuit, 2014

consumers that updates could result in loss of some functionality.

Four years later, Sony released a PS3 software update that posed a dilemma for PS3 owners. Installing the update would improve online gaming, but disable the Other OS feature; declining it would maintain the Other OS, but disable access to online gaming.

A group of disgruntled owners sued Sony, claiming breach of express warranty. The district court dismissed the claim, reasoning that Sony's statements were not express warranties about the features. The plaintiffs appealed.

You Be the Judge: *Did Sony's statements about the PS3 create an express warranty?*

Argument for Sony: Your honors, Sony only promised a 10-year lifespan for the PS3 itself. That statement is not the same as a promise that all of the PS3's features would be available for that entire time period. It was also clear from Sony's license agreement that updates could cause some loss of functionality. Sony's express warranty did not extend to all of the product's features.

Argument for PS3 Owners: Sony explicitly touted the PS3 as having a 10-year life cycle—as what, a bookend? Any reasonable consumer would interpret Sony's promise to include all of the PS3's features. This promise was the basis of the bargain between Sony and the PS3 purchasers. Sony changed the fundamental nature of the PS3 after it was in the consumer's hands. And that switch-up is a breach of an express warranty.

14-2b Implied Warranties

Emily sells Sam a new jukebox for his restaurant, but the machine is so defective it never plays a note. When Sam demands a refund, Emily scoffs that she never made any promises. She is correct that she made no express warranties but is liable nonetheless. Many sales are covered by implied warranties. **Implied warranties are those created by the Code itself, not by any act or statement of the seller.**

Implied warranties
Guarantees created by the Uniform Commercial Code and imposed on the seller of goods

Implied warranty of merchantability
Goods must be of at least average, passable quality in the trade.

Implied Warranty of Merchantability

The **implied warranty of merchantability** is the most important warranty in the Code. **Unless excluded or modified, a warranty that the goods shall be merchantable is implied in a contract for their sale if the seller is a merchant with respect to goods of that kind.** *Merchantable* means that the goods are fit for the ordinary purposes for which they are used.[11] This rule contains several important principles:

- *Unless excluded or modified* means that the seller does have a chance to escape this warranty. A seller may disclaim this warranty, provided he actually mentions the word *merchantability.*

- *Merchantability* requires that goods be fit for their normal purposes. A ladder, to be merchantable, must be able to rest securely against a building and support someone who is climbing it. The ladder need not be serviceable as a boat ramp.

- *Implied* means that the law itself imposes this liability on the seller.

- *A merchant with respect to goods of that kind* means that the seller is someone who routinely deals in these goods or holds himself out as having special knowledge about these goods.

Dacor Corp. manufactured and sold scuba diving equipment. Dacor ordered air hoses from Sierra Precision, specifying the exact size and couplings so that the hose would fit safely into Dacor's oxygen units. Within a year, customers returned a dozen Dacor units, complaining that the hose connections had cracked and were unusable. Dacor recalled 16,000 units and refit them at a cost of $136,000. Dacor sued Sierra and won its full costs. Sierra was a merchant with respect to scuba hoses because it routinely manufactured and sold them. The defects were life-threatening to scuba divers, and the hoses could not be used for normal purposes.[12]

---

[11]UCC Section 2-314(1).
[12]Dacor Corp. v. Sierra Precision, 19 F.3d 21 (7th Cir. 1994).

The scuba equipment was not merchantable because a properly made scuba hose should never crack under normal use.

What if the product being sold is food, and the food contains something that is harmful—yet quite normal?

GOODMAN V. WENCO FOODS, INC.

333 N.C. 1
Supreme Court of North Carolina, 1992

CASE SUMMARY

Facts: Fred Goodman and a friend stopped for lunch at a Wendy's restaurant in Hillsborough, North Carolina. Goodman had eaten about half of his double hamburger when he bit down and felt immediate pain in his lower jaw. He took from his mouth a triangular piece of cow bone, about one-sixteenth to one-quarter inch thick and one-half inch long, along with several pieces of his teeth. Goodman's pain was intense, and his dental repairs took months.

The restaurant purchased all of its meat from Greensboro Meat Supply Company (GMSC). Wendy's required its meat to be chopped and "free from bone or cartilage in excess of 1/8 inch in any dimension." GMSC beef was inspected continuously by state regulators and was certified by the United States Department of Agriculture (USDA). The USDA considered any bone fragment less than three-quarters of an inch long to be "insignificant."

Goodman sued, claiming a breach of the implied warranty of merchantability. The trial court dismissed the claim, ruling that the bone was natural to the food and that the hamburger was therefore fit for its ordinary purpose. The appeals court reversed this, holding that a hamburger could be unfit even if the bone occurred naturally. Wendy's appealed to the state's highest court.

Issue: *Was the hamburger unfit for its ordinary purpose because it contained a harmful but natural bone?*

Decision: Even if the harmful bone occurred naturally, the hamburger could be unfit for its ordinary purpose. Affirmed.

Reasoning: When an object in food harms a consumer, the injured person may recover even if the substance occurred naturally, provided that a reasonable consumer would not expect to encounter it. A triangular, one-half-inch bone shaving may be inherent to a cut of beef, but whether a reasonable consumer would anticipate it is normally a question for the jury.

Wendy's hamburgers need not be perfect, but they must be fit for their intended purpose. It is difficult to imagine how a consumer could guard against bone particles, short of removing the hamburger from its bun, breaking it apart, and inspecting its small components.

Wendy's argues that since its meat complied with federal and state standards, the hamburgers were merchantable as a matter of law. However, while compliance with legal standards is evidence for juries to consider, it does not ensure merchantability. A jury could still conclude that a bone this size in hamburger meat was reasonably unforeseeable and that an injured consumer was entitled to compensation.

Implied Warranty of Fitness for a Particular Purpose

The other warranty that the law imposes on sellers is the **implied warranty of fitness for a particular purpose**. This cumbersome name is often shortened to the *warranty of fitness*. **Where the seller at the time of contracting knows about a particular purpose for which the buyer wants the goods and knows that the buyer is relying on the seller's skill or judgment, there is (unless excluded or modified) an implied warranty that the goods shall be fit for such purpose.**[13]

Implied warranty of fitness for a particular purpose
If the seller knows that the buyer plans to use the goods for a particular purpose, the seller generally is held to warrant that the goods are in fact fit for that purpose.

---

[13]UCC Section 2-315.

Notice that the seller must know about some special use the buyer intends and realize that the buyer is relying on the seller's judgment. Suppose a lumber sales clerk knows that a buyer is relying on his advice to choose the best wood for a house being built in a swamp. The Code implies a warranty that the wood sold will withstand those special conditions.

Disclaimers

Disclaimer
A statement that a particular warranty does not apply

To make life easier, the UCC permits a seller to make a **disclaimer** of *all* warranties by conspicuously stating that the goods are sold "as is" or "with all faults." But, as is often the case, we must point out two exceptions:

First, written express warranties generally *cannot* be disclaimed.

Second, many states prohibit a seller from disclaiming implied warranties in the sale of *consumer goods*. In these states, if a home furnishings store sells a bunk bed to a consumer and the top bunk tips out the window on the first night, the seller is liable.

As the following case illustrates, courts tend to impose high standards on defendants who try to disclaim warranties.

CCB Ohio, LLC v. Chemque, Inc.

649 F. Supp. 2d 757
United States District Court for the Southern District of Ohio, 2009

CASE SUMMARY

Facts: CCB Ohio specializes in upgrading power lines in a way that makes it possible to offer broadband service over an electrical grid. Chemque manufactures Q-gel.

Transformers reduce the 100,000 or more volts flowing through a typical power line to the 120 volts that actually arrive at the outlets in your home. But unfortunately, transformers completely block digital signals. And so, to offer broadband over an electrical grid, data must take a detour around transformers. Couplers allow for this detour.

CCB and its contractors purchased Q-gel. This substance was supposed to create a waterproof seal that would bind newly installed couplers to power lines. Unfortunately, the gel did not gel, at least not for long. Within 18 months, 40 percent of CCB Ohio's couplers were leaking liquefied Q-gel. Ultimately, 90 percent of the couplers throughout the Cincinnati area leaked and caused millions of dollars in losses.

CCB Ohio sued for breach of warranty. Chemque argued that it had disclaimed all implied warranties by giving CCB a specification sheet that read, "All information is given without warranty or guarantee." Chemque moved for summary judgment.

Issue: *Should Chemque's motion for a summary judgment on CCB's warranty claims be granted?*

Decision: No, the motion for summary judgment should not be granted.

Reasoning: In this state, companies that sell consumer goods may not disclaim implied warranties. However, the contract at issue here does not involve consumer goods.

To disclaim implied warranties for other kinds of transactions, the seller must show that the buyer actually received the disclaimer and that it was so conspicuous, a reasonable person would have noticed it. There is no evidence in the record that CCB did get the specification sheet in question. The company also argues that, even if it did receive the sheet, the disclaimer was not clear and conspicuous.

With these significant issues in dispute and unresolved, it would be inappropriate to grant Chemque's motion for summary judgment.

Motion for summary judgment denied.

Chapter Conclusion

The development of the UCC was an enormous and ambitious undertaking. Its goal was to facilitate the free flow of commerce across this large nation. By any measure, the UCC has been a success. Remember, though: The terms of the UCC are precise. Failure to comply with these exacting provisions can close opportunities—and open courtroom doors.

EXAM REVIEW

1. **THE UCC**   The Uniform Commercial Code is designed to modernize commercial law and make it uniform throughout the country. Article 2 applies to the sale of goods.

2. **MERCHANTS**   A merchant is someone who routinely deals in the particular goods involved, or who appears to have special knowledge or skill in those goods, or who uses agents with special knowledge or skill.

3. **CONTRACT FORMATION**   UCC Section 2-204 permits the parties to form a contract in any manner that shows agreement.

4. **WRITING REQUIREMENT**   For the sale of goods worth $500 or more, UCC Section 2-201 requires some writing that indicates an agreement.

Question: To satisfy the UCC Statute of Frauds, which of the following must generally be in writing?

a. Designation of the parties as buyer and seller

b. Delivery terms

c. Quantity of the goods

d. Warranties to be made

Strategy: The question illustrates two basic points of UCC law: First, the Code allows a great deal of flexibility in the formation of contracts. Second, there is one term for which no flexibility is allowed. Make sure you know which it is. (See the "Result" at the end of this section.)

5. **MERCHANT EXCEPTION**   A merchant who receives a signed memo confirming an oral contract may become liable if he fails to object within 10 days.

6. **UCC §2-207**   UCC Section 2-207 governs an acceptance that does not "mirror" the offer. *Additional* terms usually become part of the contract. *Different* terms contradict the offer and are generally replaced by the Code's own gap-filler terms.

Question: Cookie Co. offered to sell Distrib Markets 20,000 pounds of cookies at $1 per pound, subject to certain specified terms for delivery. Distrib replied in writing as follows: "We accept your offer for 20,000 pounds of cookies at $1 per pound, weighing scale to have valid city certificate." Under the UCC:

a. A contract was formed between the parties.

b. A contract will be formed only if Cookie agrees to the weighing scale requirement.

c. No contract was formed because Distrib included the weighing scale requirement in its reply.

d. No contract was formed because Distrib's reply was a counteroffer.

Strategy: Distrib's reply included a new term. That means it is governed by UCC Section 2-207. Is the new term an additional term or a different term? An additional term goes beyond what the offeror stated. Additional terms become a part of the contract except in three specified instances. A different term contradicts one made by the offeror. Different terms generally cancel each other out. (See the "Result" at the end of this section.)

7. **REMEDIES** An injured seller may resell the goods and obtain the difference between the contract and resale prices. An injured buyer may buy substitute goods and obtain the difference between the contract and cover prices.

8. **EXPRESS WARRANTY** A party may create an express warranty with words or actions.

9. **IMPLIED WARRANTY OF MERCHANTABILITY** The UCC implies that goods will be fit for the purpose for which they are sold.

10. **IMPLIED WARRANTY OF FITNESS FOR A PARTICULAR PURPOSE** If the seller knows that the buyer plans to use the goods for a particular purpose, the seller generally is held to warrant that the goods are in fact fit for that purpose.

---

4. Result: (C). The contract will be enforced only to the extent of the quantity stated.

6. Result: The "valid city certificate" phrase raises a new issue; it does not contradict anything in Cookie's offer. That means it is an additional term, and it becomes part of the deal unless Cookie insisted on its own terms, the additional term materially alters the offer, or Cookie promptly rejects it. Cookie did not insist on its terms, this is a minor addition, and Cookie never rejected it. The new term is part of a valid contract, and the answer is "a."

MATCHING QUESTIONS

Match the following terms with their definitions:

___A. Additional terms

___B. Written express warranties

___C. Merchantability

___D. Different terms

1. An implied warranty that goods are fit for their ordinary purpose

2. Generally become part of a contract between merchants

3. Cannot be disclaimed

4. Generally cancel each other out

TRUE/FALSE QUESTIONS

Circle true or false:

1. T F In a contract for the sale of goods, the offer may include any terms the offeror wishes; the offeree must accept on exactly those terms or reject the deal.

2. T F Sellers can be bound by written warranties but not by oral statements.

3. T F The description of products in promotional materials can create express warranties.

4. T F A contract for the sale of $300 worth of decorative stone must be in writing to be enforceable.

MULTIPLE-CHOICE QUESTIONS

1. Which one of the following transactions is *not* governed by Article 2 of the UCC?

(a) Purchasing an automobile for $35,000

(b) Leasing an automobile worth $35,000

(c) Purchasing a stereo worth $501

(d) Purchasing a stereo worth $499

2. Marion orally agrees to sell Ashley her condominium in Philadelphia for $700,000. The parties have known each other for 20 years and do not bother to put anything in writing. Based on the agreement, Marion hires a moving company to pack up all her goods and move them to a storage warehouse. Ashley shows up with a cashier's check, and Marion says, "You're going to love it here." But at the last minute, Marion declines to take the check and refuses to sell. Ashley sues and wins:

(a) nothing.

(b) the condominium.

(c) $700,000.

(d) the difference between $700,000 and the condominium's market value.

(e) damages for fraud.

3. Seller's sales contract states that "The model 8J flagpole will withstand winds up to 150 mph, for a minimum of 35 years." The same contract includes this: "This contract makes no warranties, and any implied warranties are hereby disclaimed." School buys the flagpole, which blows down six months later in a 105-mph wind.

   (a) Seller is not liable because it never made any express warranties.

   (b) Seller is not liable because it disclaimed any warranties.

   (c) Seller is liable because the disclaimer was invalid.

   (d) Seller is liable because implied warranties may not be disclaimed.

4. Manufacturer sells a brand-new, solar-powered refrigerator. Because the technology is new, Manufacturer sells the product "as is." Plaintiff later sues Manufacturer for breach of warranty and wins. Plaintiff is probably:

   (a) A distributor with no understanding of legal terminology.

   (b) A retailer who had previously relied on Manufacturer.

   (c) A retailer who had never done business before with Manufacturer.

   (d) A retailer who failed to notice the "as is" label.

   (e) A consumer.

5. **CPA QUESTION** Which of the following conditions must be met for an implied warranty of fitness for a particular purpose to arise?

   I. The warranty must be in writing.

   II. The seller must know that the buyer was relying on the seller in selecting the goods.

      (a) I only

      (b) II only

      (c) Both I and II

      (d) Neither I nor II

CASE QUESTIONS

1. Nina owns a used car lot. She signs and sends a fax to Seth, a used car wholesaler who has a huge lot of cars in the same city. The fax says, "Confirming our agrmt—I pick any 15 cars fr yr lot—30% below blue book." Seth reads the fax, laughs, and throws it away. Two weeks later, Nina arrives and demands to purchase 15 of Seth's cars. Is he obligated to sell?

2. **YOU BE THE JUDGE WRITING PROBLEM** United Technologies advertised a used Beechcraft Baron airplane for sale in an aviation journal. Attorney Thompson Comerford spoke with a United agent who described the plane as "excellently maintained" and said it had been operated "under §135 flight regulations," meaning the plane had been subject to airworthiness inspections every 100 hours. Comerford arrived at a Dallas airport to pick up the plane, where he paid $80,000 for it. He signed a sales agreement stating that the plane was sold "as is" and that there were "no representations or warranties, express or implied, including the condition of the

aircraft, its merchantability, or its fitness for any particular purpose." Comerford attempted to fly the plane home but immediately experienced problems with its brakes, steering, ability to climb, and performance while cruising. (Otherwise, it was fine.) He sued, claiming breach of express and implied warranties. Did United Technologies breach express or implied warranties? **Argument for Comerford:** United described the airplane as "excellently maintained," knowing that Mr. Comerford would rely. The company should not be allowed to say one thing and put the opposite in writing. **Argument for United Technologies:** Comerford is a lawyer, and we assume he can read. The contract clearly stated that the plane was sold as is. There were no warranties.

3. Lewis River Golf, Inc., grew and sold sod. It bought seed from the defendant, O. M. Scott & Sons, under an express warranty. But the sod grown from the Scott seeds developed weeds, a breach of Scott's warranty. Several of Lewis River's customers sued, unhappy with the weeds in their grass. Lewis River lost most of its customers, cut back its production from 275 acres to 45 acres, and destroyed all remaining sod grown from Scott's seeds. Eventually, Lewis River sold its business at a large loss. A jury awarded Lewis River $1,026,800, largely for lost profits. Scott appealed, claiming that a plaintiff may not recover for lost profits. Comment.

4. Boboli Co. wanted to promote its "California-style" pizza, which it sold in supermarkets. The company contracted with Highland Group, Inc., to produce 2 million recipe brochures, which would be inserted in the carton when the freshly baked pizza was still very hot. Highland contracted with Comark Merchandising to print the brochures. But when Comark asked for details concerning the pizza, the carton, and so forth, Highland refused to supply the information. Comark printed the first lot of 72,000 brochures, which Highland delivered to Boboli. Unfortunately, the hot bread caused the ink to run, and customers opening the carton often found red or blue splotches on their pizzas. Highland refused to accept additional brochures, and Comark sued for breach of contract. Highland defended by claiming that Comark had breached its warranty of merchantability. Please comment.

5. When the Whitehouses decided to breed horses, they went horse shopping at the Lange's ranch. Although the Whitehouses had owned horses, they had no experience in horse breeding. Knowing the buyers would breed the horse, the Langes suggested a particular mare. After the sale, the Whitehouses discovered that this mare was infertile and sued for breach of warranty. Will the buyers win? If so, under which UCC warranty?

DISCUSSION QUESTIONS

1. Hasbro manufactured a toy called "Wonder World Aquarium." The toy included a powder that, when mixed with water, formed a gel that filled a plastic aquarium to create underwater scenes. Cloud Corporation supplied the powder to Hasbro. The toy sold poorly, and Hasbro's need for the powder diminished.

The two companies discussed changing the powder's formula. Cloud believed the conversation amounted to an indication that Hasbro would continue to buy powder, so it produced large quantities. Although it did not receive an order from Hasbro, Cloud sent an order acknowledgment for 9.5 million packets to Hasbro. Hasbro made no objection to it.

Did the order acknowledgment create an enforceable agreement? What specific facts determine your answer?

2. A seller can disclaim all implied warranties by stating that goods are sold "as is" (or by using other, more specific language). Is this fair? The UCC's implied warranties seem reasonable—that goods are fit for their normal purposes, for example. Should it be so easy for sellers to escape their obligations?

3. After learning more about implied warranties and disclaimers, would you ever buy an item sold "as is"? Imagine a car salesman who offers you a car for $8,000, but who also says that he can knock the price down to $6,500 if you will buy the car "as is." If you live in a state that does not give consumers special protections, which deal would be more appealing?

4. Under the UCC's Statute of Frauds, sale-of-goods contracts for $500 or more must be in writing to be valid. But since Article 2 only covers sale-of-goods contracts, agreements to sell services are not subject to the rule. Should the common law change so that *all* contracts valued at $500 or more have a writing requirement, or would that place an undue burden on businesses?

5. When an acceptance contains additional terms, the UCC and the common law contain different rules. The common law's mirror image rule makes the acceptance ineffective, and no contract is formed. But the UCC rules "save" the contract. Which rule do you think is more sensible?

CHAPTER 15

© Honza Krej/Shutterstock.com

NEGOTIABLE INSTRUMENTS

With graduation looming, Chaz needs to rent an apartment and buy a car. Responding to an online ad, he finds the perfect place to rent. True, it is more expensive than he had planned, but he will surely get a raise soon. With nervous hands, he writes out a big check for three month's rent (first month, last month, and security deposit). Then he goes to Trustie Car lot to buy a used car. He cannot afford the entire purchase price, so he makes a down payment and signs a promissory note for the balance due.

With growing excitement, Chaz loads all his worldly possessions into his car and heads over to his new apartment. When he arrives, though, his key does not work and a stranger answers his knock. It turns out that someone else is living in his apartment. Chaz has been scammed—the person he gave his check to had no right to the apartment. Stunned, Chaz gets back in his car to head over to a friend's place where he can crash for a few days. But his car will not start. With his head in his hands, Chaz tries to remember what he learned about negotiable instruments in his business law class.

> **When he arrives, his key does not work and a stranger answers his knock.**

Let's take the rent check first. When Chaz's bank paid the scammer on the check, it became a holder in due course. Chaz has no valid defenses against the bank. So that rent money is just gone, unless Chaz can recover from the thief (not likely). But he has better luck with the car. Because Trustie still holds the promissory note, it is not a holder in due course. If the car is defective, Chaz will not have to pay back the full amount of the Trustie loan. What is the difference, you ask? Read on to save yourself from Chaz's mistakes.

15-1 COMMERCIAL PAPER

As Chaz learned, the law of commercial paper is important to anyone who writes checks or borrows money. Historically speaking, however, commercial paper is a relatively new development. In early human history, people lived on whatever they could hunt, grow, or make for themselves. Imagine what your life would be like if you had to subsist only on what you could make yourself. Over time, people improved their standard of living by bartering for goods and services that other people could provide more efficiently. But traders needed a method for keeping track of who owed how much to whom. That was the role of currency. Many items have been used for currency over the years, including silver, gold, copper, and cowry shells. These currencies have two disadvantages—they are easy to steal and difficult to carry.

Paper currency weighs less than gold or silver, but it is even easier to steal. As a result, money had to be kept in a safe place, and banks developed to meet that need. However, money in a vault is not very useful unless it can be readily spent. Society needed a system for transferring paper funds easily. Commercial paper is that system. Electronic alternatives may ultimately dominate the marketplace, but for now, paper is still king.

15-2 TYPES OF NEGOTIABLE INSTRUMENTS

There are two kinds of commercial paper: negotiable and non-negotiable instruments. Article 3 of the Uniform Commercial Code (UCC) covers only negotiable instruments; non-negotiable instruments are governed by ordinary contract law. There are also two categories of negotiable instruments: notes and drafts.

A **note** (also called a **promissory note**) is your promise that you will pay money. A promissory note is used in virtually every loan transaction, whether the borrower is paying for a multimillion-dollar company, a TV, or college tuition. For example, when Krystal borrows money from the government to pay her college tuition, she signs a note stating, "I promise to pay to the Department of Education all loan amounts disbursed under the terms of this Promissory Note, plus interest and other charges and fees that may become due as provided in this Promissory Note." She is the **maker** because she is the one who has made the promise. The Department of Education is called the **payee** because it expects to be paid.

Promissory note
The maker of the instrument promises to pay a specific amount of money

Maker
The issuer of a promissory note

Payee
Someone who is owed money under the terms of an instrument

PROMISSORY NOTE

1,000.00 florins   Verona

16 . 2 . 1595

On or before the fifteenth day of April in the Year of Our Lord, 1595, the undersigned promises to pay to the order of Juliet, daughter of the house of Capulet, in Verona, the sum of 1,000 florins, with interest from the date hereof at five percent per annum, until paid.

_____
Romeo

In this note, Romeo is the maker and Juliet is the payee.

A **draft** is an order directing someone else to pay money for you. A **check** is the most common form of a draft—it is an order telling a bank to pay money. In a draft, three people are involved: the **drawer** orders the **drawee** to pay money to the payee. Now before you slam the book shut in despair, let us sort out the players. Suppose that Serena Williams wins the River Oaks Club Open. River Oaks writes her a check for $500,000. This check is simply an order by River Oaks (the drawer) to its bank (the drawee) to pay money to Williams (the payee). The terms make sense if you remember that, when you take money out of your account, you *draw* it out. Therefore, when you write a check, you are the drawer, and the bank is the drawee. The person to whom you make out the check is being paid, so she is called the payee.

The following table illustrates the difference between notes and drafts. Even courts sometimes confuse the terms *drawer* (the person who signs a check) and *maker* (someone who signs a promissory note). **Issuer** is an all-purpose term that means both maker and drawer.

	Who Pays	Who Plays
Note	You make a promise that you will pay.	Two people are involved: maker and payee.
Draft	You order someone else to pay.	Three people are involved: drawer, drawee, and payee.

Draft
The drawer of this instrument orders someone else to pay money.

Check
An instrument in which the drawer orders the drawee bank to pay money to the payee

Drawer
The person who issues a draft

Drawee
The person who pays a draft. In the case of a check, the bank is the drawee.

Issuer
The maker of a promissory note or the drawer of a draft

15-3 THE FUNDAMENTAL "RULE" OF COMMERCIAL PAPER

The possessor of a piece of commercial paper has an unconditional right to be paid, so long as (1) the paper is *negotiable*; (2) it has been *negotiated* to the possessor; (3) the possessor is a holder in due course; and (4) the issuer cannot claim a valid defense.

Holder in due course
Someone who has given value for an instrument, in good faith, without notice of outstanding claims or other defenses

15-3a Negotiability

To work as a substitute for money, commercial paper must be freely transferable in the marketplace, just as money is. In other words, it must be *negotiable*.

The possessor of *non*-negotiable commercial paper has the same rights—no more, no less—as the person who made the original contract. With non-negotiable commercial paper, the transferee's rights are *conditional* because they depend upon the rights of the original party to the contract. If, for some reason, the original party loses his right to be paid, so does the transferee. The value of non-negotiable commercial paper is greatly reduced because the transferee cannot be absolutely sure what his rights are or whether he will be paid at all.

As long as Trustie keeps Chaz's promissory note, Chaz's obligation to pay is contingent upon the validity of the underlying contract. Because the car is defective, Chaz might not be liable to Trustie for the full amount of the note. Trustie, however, does not want to keep the note. He needs the cash *now* so that he can buy more cars to sell to other customers. Reggie's Finance Co., is happy to buy Chaz's promissory note from Trustie, but the price Reggie is willing to pay depends upon whether the note is negotiable.

If Chaz's promissory note is non-negotiable, Reggie gets exactly the same rights that Trustie had. As the saying goes, he steps into Trustie's shoes. Other people's shoes may not be a good fit. Trustie lied about the car's condition. As a result, it is worth only $6,000—not the $15,000 Chaz paid. Under contract law, Chaz owes *Trustie* only $6,000, so that is all he has to pay *Reggie*, even though the note *says* $15,000.

The possessor of *negotiable* commercial paper has *more* rights than the person who made the original contract. With negotiable commercial paper, the transferee's rights are *unconditional*. He is entitled to be paid the full amount of the note, regardless of the relationship between the original parties. If Chaz's promissory note is a negotiable instrument, he must pay the full amount to whoever has possession of it, no matter what complaints he might have against Trustie.

Exhibit 15.1 illustrates the difference between negotiable and non-negotiable commercial paper.

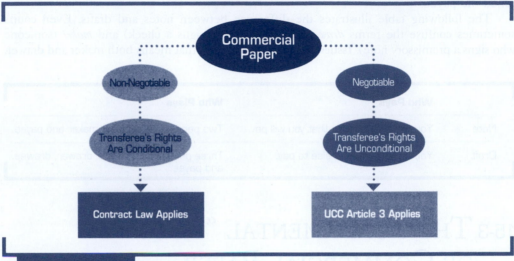

Because negotiable instruments are more valuable than non-negotiable ones, it is important for buyers and sellers to be able to tell, easily and accurately, if an instrument is indeed negotiable. **To be negotiable:**

1. **The instrument must be in *writing*.**

2. **The instrument must be *signed* by the maker or drawer.**

3. **The instrument must contain an *unconditional promise* or *order to pay*.** If Chaz's promissory note says, "I will pay $15,000 as long as the car is still in working order," it is not negotiable because it is making a conditional promise. The instrument must also contain a promise or order to pay. It is not enough simply to say, "Chaz owes Trustie $15,000." He has to indicate that he owes the money and also that he intends to pay it. "Chaz promises to pay Trustie $15,000" would work.

4. **The instrument must state a *definite amount* of money that is clear "within its four corners."** "I promise to pay Trustie one-third of my income this year" would not work because the amount is not definite. If Chaz's note says, "I promise to pay $15,000 worth of diamonds," it is not negotiable because it does not state a definite amount of *money*.

5. **The instrument must be payable on *demand* or at a *definite time*.** A demand instrument is one that must be paid whenever the holder requests payment. If an instrument is undated, it is treated as a demand instrument and is negotiable. An instrument can be negotiable even if it will not be paid until some time in the future, provided that the payment date can be determined when the document is made. A graduate of a well-known prep school wrote a generous check to his alma mater, but for payment date he put, "The day the headmaster is fired." This check is not negotiable because it is payable neither on demand nor at a definite time.

6. **The instrument must be payable to *order* or to *bearer*. Order paper** must include the words "Pay to the order of" someone. By including the word "order," the maker is indicating that the instrument is not limited to only one person. "Pay to the order of Trustie Car Lot" means that the money will be paid to Trustie *or to anyone Trustie designates*. If the note is made out "To bearer," it is **bearer paper** and can be redeemed by *any* holder in due course.

Order paper

An instrument that includes the words "pay to the order of" or their equivalent

Bearer paper

An instrument payable "to bearer"

The rules for checks are different from those for other negotiable instruments. If properly filled out, checks are negotiable. And sometimes they are negotiable even if not filled out correctly. Most checks are preprinted with the words "Pay to the order of," but sometimes people inadvertently cross out "order of." Even so, the check is still negotiable. Checks are frequently received by consumers who, sadly, have not completed a course on business law. The drafters of the UCC did not think it fair to penalize them when the drawer of the check was the one who made the mistake.

EXAM Strategy

Question: Sam had a checking account at Piggy Bank. Piggy sent him special checks that he could use to draw down a line of credit. When Sam used these checks, Piggy did not take money out of his account; instead, the bank treated the checks as loans and charged him interest. The interest rate was not apparent from the face of the check. When Sam wrote checks, Piggy sold them to Wolfe. Were the checks negotiable instruments?

Strategy: When faced with a question about negotiability, begin by looking at the list of six requirements. In this case, there is no reason to doubt that the checks are in writing, signed by the issuer, and with an unconditional promise to pay to order at a definite time. But do the checks state a definite amount of money? Can the holder "look at the four corners of the check" and determine how much Sam owes?

Result: Sam was supposed to pay Piggy the face amount of the check *plus* interest. Wolfe does not know the amount of the interest unless he reads the loan agreement. Therefore, the checks are not negotiable.

Interpretation of Ambiguities

Perhaps you have noticed that people sometimes make mistakes. Although the UCC establishes simple and precise rules for creating negotiable instruments, people do not always follow these rules to the letter. It might be tempting simply to invalidate defective documents (after all, money is at stake here). But instead, the UCC favors negotiability and has rules to resolve uncertainty and supply missing terms.

Notice anything odd about the check pictured on the next page? Is it for $1,500 or $15,000? **When the terms in a negotiable instrument contradict each other, three rules apply:**

1. Words take precedence over numbers.

2. Handwritten terms prevail over typed and printed terms.

3. Typed terms win over printed terms.

According to these rules, Krystal's check is for $15,000 because, in a conflict between words and numbers, words win.

In the following case, the amount of the check was not completely clear. Was it a negotiable instrument?

You be the Judge

Facts: Christina Blasco borrowed $500 from the Money Services Center (MSC). To repay the loan, she gave MSC a check for $587.50, which it promised not to cash for two weeks. This kind of transaction is called a "payday loan" because it is made to someone who needs money to tide them over until the next paycheck. (Note that in this case, Blasco was paying 17.5 percent interest for a two-week loan, which is an annual compounded interest rate of 6,500 percent. This is the dark side of payday loans—interest rates are often exorbitant.)

Before MSC could cash the check, Blasco filed for bankruptcy protection. Although MSC knew about Blasco's filing, it deposited the check. It is illegal for creditors to collect debts after a bankruptcy filing, except that creditors are entitled to payment on negotiable instruments.

Ordinarily, checks are negotiable instruments, but only if they are for a definite amount. This check had a wrinkle: The numerical amount of the check was $587.50, but the amount in words was written as "five eighty-seven and 50/100 dollars." Did the words mean "five hundred eighty-seven" or "five thousand eighty-seven" or perhaps "five million eighty-seven"? Was the check negotiable despite this ambiguity?

You Be the Judge: *Was this check for a definite amount? Was it a negotiable instrument?*

BLASCO V. MONEY SERVICES CENTER
352 B.R. 888
United States Bankruptcy Court for the Northern District of Alabama, 2006

Argument for Blasco: For a check to be negotiable, two rules apply:

1. The check must state a definite amount of money, which is clear within its four corners.

2. If there is a contradiction between the words and numbers, words take precedence over numbers.

Words prevail over numbers, which means that the check is for "five eighty-seven and 50/100 dollars." This amount is not definite. A holder cannot be sure of the precise amount of the check. Therefore, the check is not a negotiable instrument, and MSC had no right to submit it for payment.

Argument for MSC: Blasco is right about the two rules. However, she is wrong in their interpretation. If there is a contradiction between the words and numbers, words take precedence over numbers. In this case, there was no contradiction. The words were ambiguous, but they did not contradict the numbers. If the words had said "five thousand eighty-seven," that would have been a contradiction. Instead, the numbers simply clarified the words. Even someone who was a stranger to this transaction could safely figure out the amount of the check. Therefore, it is negotiable and MSC is not liable.

15-3b Negotiation

Negotiation means that an instrument has been transferred to the holder by someone *other than the issuer*. If the issuer has transferred the instrument to the holder, then it has not been negotiated, and the issuer can refuse to pay the holder if there was some flaw in the underlying contract. Thus, if Jake gives Madison a promissory note for $800 in payment for a new tablet computer, but the tablet crashes and burns the first week, Jake has the right to refuse to pay the note. Jake was the issuer, and the note was not negotiated. But if, before the tablet self-destructs, Madison indorses and transfers the note to Kayla, then Jake is liable to Kayla for the full amount of the note, regardless of his claims against Madison. **To be negotiated, order paper must first be *indorsed* and then *delivered* to the transferee. Bearer paper must simply be *delivered* to the transferee; no indorsement is required.**[1]

An **indorsement** is the signature of the payee. Tess writes a rent check for $600 to her landlord, Larnell. If Larnell signs the back of the check and delivers it to Patty, he has met the two requirements for negotiating order paper: indorsement and delivery. If Larnell delivers the check to Patty but forgets to sign it, the check has not been indorsed and therefore cannot be negotiated—it has no value to Patty.

> If the computer crashes and burns the first week, Jake has the right to refuse to pay the note.

Negotiation
An instrument has been transferred to the holder by someone other than the issuer

Indorsement
The signature of the payee

EXAM Strategy

Question: Antoine makes a check out to cash and delivers it to Barley. She writes on the back, "Pay to the order of Colin." He signs his name. Is this check bearer paper or order paper? Has it been negotiated?

Strategy: To be negotiated, order paper must be indorsed and delivered; bearer paper need only be delivered, but in both cases by someone other than the issuer.

Result: This check changes back and forth between order and bearer paper, depending on what the indorsement says. When Antoine makes out a check to cash, it is bearer paper. When he gives it to Barley, it is not negotiated because he is the issuer. When Barley writes on the back "Pay to the order of Colin," it becomes order paper. When she gives it to Colin, it is properly negotiated because she is not the issuer and she has both indorsed the check and transferred it to him. When Colin signs it, the check becomes bearer paper. And so it could go on forever.[2]

15-3c Holder in Due Course

The fundamental rule of this chapter tells us that **a holder in due course has an automatic right to receive payment for a negotiable instrument (unless the issuer can claim a valid defense).** If the possessor of an instrument is not a holder in due course, then his right to

---

[1] §3-201. The UCC spells the word *indorsed*. Outside the UCC, the word is more commonly spelled *endorsed*.

[2] Even when all the space on the back of the check is filled, the holder can attach a separate paper for indorsements, which is called an **allonge**.

payment depends upon the relationship between the issuer and payee. He inherits whatever claims and defenses arise out of that contract. Clearly, then, holder in due course status dramatically increases the value of an instrument because it enhances the probability of being paid. Thus, it is very important to understand what it takes to be a holder in due course.

Requirements for Being a Holder in Due Course

A holder in due course is a *holder* who has given *value* for the instrument, in *good faith*, *without notice* of outstanding claims or other defects.[3] Let's define these terms.

Holder.   For order paper, a **holder** is anyone in possession of the instrument if it is payable to or indorsed to her. For bearer paper, a holder is anyone in possession. Tristesse gives Felix a check payable to him. Because Felix owes his mother money, he indorses the check and delivers it to her. This is a valid negotiation because Felix has both indorsed the check (which is order paper) and delivered it. Therefore, Felix's mother is a holder.

Value.   A holder in due course must give value for an instrument. **Value** means that the holder has *already* done something in exchange for the instrument. Felix's mother has already lent him money, so she has given value.

Good Faith.   There are two tests to determine if a holder acquired an instrument in good faith. **The holder must meet** *both* **these tests:**

1. **Subjective test.** Did the holder *believe* the transaction was honest in fact?

2. **Objective test.** Did the transaction *appear* to be commercially reasonable?

   Felix persuades his elderly neighbor, Faith, that he has invented a fabulous beauty cream guaranteed to remove wrinkles. She gives him a $10,000 promissory note, payable in 90 days, in return for exclusive sales rights in Pittsburgh. Felix sells the note to his old friend, Griffin, for $2,000. Felix never delivers the sales samples to Faith. When Griffin presents the note to Faith, she refuses to pay on the grounds that Griffin is not a holder in due course. She contends that he did not buy the note in good faith.

   Griffin fails both tests. Any friend of Felix knows he is not trustworthy, especially when presenting a promissory note signed by an elderly neighbor. Griffin did not believe the transaction was honest in fact. Also, $10,000 notes are not usually discounted to $2,000; $8,000 or $9,000 would be more normal. This transaction is not commercially reasonable, and Griffin should have realized immediately that Felix was up to no good.

Notice of Outstanding Claims or Other Defects.   In certain circumstances, a holder is on notice that an instrument has an outstanding claim or other defect:

1. **The instrument is overdue.** An instrument is overdue the day after its due date. At that point, the recipient ought to wonder why no one has bothered to collect the money owed. A check is overdue 90 days after its date. Any other demand instrument is overdue (1) the day after a request for payment is made or (2) a reasonable time after the instrument was issued.

2. **The instrument is dishonored.** To dishonor an instrument is to refuse to pay it. For example, once a check has been stamped "Insufficient Funds" by the bank, it has been dishonored, and no one who obtains it afterward can be a holder in due course.

3. **The instrument is altered, forged, or incomplete.** Anyone who knows that an instrument has been altered or forged cannot be a holder in due course. Suppose Joe wrote a check to Tony for $200. While showing the check to Liza, Tony cackles to himself and says, "Can you believe what that goof did? Look, he left the line blank

---

Holder
For order paper, anyone in possession of the instrument if it is payable to or indorsed to her. For bearer paper, anyone in possession

Value
The holder has *already* done something in exchange for the instrument

---

[3]UCC §3-302.

after the words 'two hundred.'" Taking his pen out with a flourish, Tony changes the zeroes to nines and adds the words "ninety-nine." He then indorses the check over to Liza, who is definitely not a holder in due course.

4. **The holder has notice of certain claims or disputes.** No one can qualify as a holder in due course if she is on notice that (1) someone else has a claim to the instrument or (2) there is a dispute between the original parties to the instrument. Matt hires Sheila to put aluminum siding on his house. In payment, he gives her a $15,000 promissory note with the due date left blank. They agree that the note will not be due until 60 days after completion of the work. Despite the agreement, Sheila fills in the date immediately and sells the note to Rupert at American Finance Corp., who has bought many similar notes from Sheila. Rupert knows that the note is not supposed to be due until after the work is finished. Usually, before he buys a note from her, he demands a signed document from the homeowner certifying that the work is complete. Not only that, but he lives near Matt and can see that Matt's house is only half finished. Rupert is not a holder in due course because he has reason to suspect there is a dispute between Sheila and Matt.

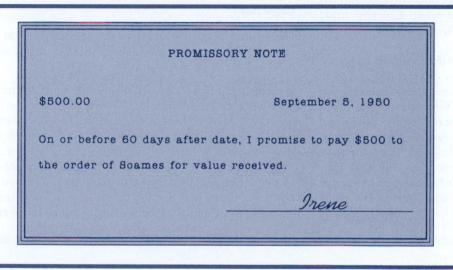

PROMISSORY NOTE

$500.00   September 5, 1950

On or before 60 days after date, I promise to pay $500 to

the order of Soames for value received.

_____ *Irene*

The holder of this note should realize that there may be a problem.

Defenses Against a Holder in Due Course

Negotiable instruments are meant to be a close substitute for money, and, as a general rule, holders expect to be paid. **However, the issuer of a negotiable instrument is not required to pay if:**

1. His signature on the instrument was forged.

2. After signing the instrument, his debts were discharged in bankruptcy.

3. He was underage (typically younger than 18) at the time he signed the instrument.

4. The amount of the instrument was altered after he signed it. (However, if he left the instrument blank, he is liable for any amounts later filled in.)

5. He signed the instrument under duress, while mentally incapacitated, or as part of an illegal transaction.

6. He was tricked into signing the instrument without knowing what it was and without any reasonable way to find out.

The following case illustrates the value of being a holder in due course. Remember that to be a holder, you must be in possession of the instrument.

CREATIVE VENTURES, LLC v. JIM WARD & ASSOCIATES

195 Cal. App. 4th 1430
Court of Appeal of California, 2011

CASE SUMMARY

Facts: Creative Ventures, LLC (Creative) borrowed nearly $3 million from defendant Jim Ward & Associates (JWA) to buy property in California. Creative signed promissory notes, payable to JWA. Thereafter, JWA sold this entire loan to 54 individual investors (Investors). JWA kept possession of the notes but when Creative made payments under the loan to JWA, it paid the Investors their share.

Under the California usury statute, the interest rate on a loan cannot be greater than 8 percent, except in certain circumstances. Those circumstances include loans by a licensed real estate broker. JWA claimed that it was such a broker, but it was not. When Creative discovered this lie, it sued JWA and the Investors to obtain a refund of all interest it had paid under the loan, as is permitted under California law. The Investors argued that they were entitled to keep the interest because, as holders in due course, they had taken the note free of the claim against JWA.

The trial court found for the Investors and Creative appealed.

Issues: *Were the Investors holders in due course? Were they entitled to keep the interest that Creative had paid on the illegal loan?*

Decision: The Investors were not holders in due courses and had no right to keep the interest Creative had paid them.

Reasoning: To be a holder of an instrument, one must be in possession of it. In this case, JWA was in possession of the notes, so it was the holder. Because the Investors were not holders, they could not be holders in due course. Because they were not holders in due course, they had the same rights as the person who made the original contract—that is, JWA. Because JWA violated usury laws, Creative does not have to pay him interest on the loans. Therefore, the Investors must return all the interest that they received.

15-3d Consumer Exception

The most common use for negotiable instruments is in consumer transactions. A consumer pays for a refrigerator by giving the store a promissory note. The store promptly sells the note to a finance company. Even if the refrigerator is defective, under Article 3 the consumer must pay full value on the note because the finance company is a holder in due course. To solve this problem, some states require promissory notes given by a consumer to carry the words "consumer paper." Notes with this legend are non-negotiable.

Meanwhile, the Federal Trade Commission (FTC) has special rules for consumer credit contracts. A **consumer credit contract** is one in which a consumer borrows money from a lender to purchase goods and services *from a seller who is affiliated with the lender*. If Sears loans money to Gerald to buy a 3-D TV at Sears, that is a consumer credit contract. It is not a consumer credit contract if Gerald borrows money from his cousin Vinnie to buy the TV from Sears. The FTC requires all promissory notes in consumer credit contracts to contain the following language:

ANY HOLDER OF THIS CONSUMER CREDIT CONTRACT IS SUBJECT TO ALL CLAIMS AND DEFENSES WHICH THE DEBTOR COULD ASSERT AGAINST THE SELLER OF GOODS OR SERVICES OBTAINED WITH THE PROCEEDS HEREOF.

Consumer credit contract
A contract in which a consumer borrows money from a lender to purchase goods and services from a seller who is affiliated with the lender

The UCC, provides that no one can be a holder in due course of an instrument with this language.[4] If the language is omitted from a consumer note, it is possible to be a holder in due course, but the seller is subject to a fine.

In the following case, consumers found that a home improvement contract, far from improving their home, almost caused them to lose it.

ANTUNA V. NESCOR, INC.

2002 Conn. Super. Lexis 1003
Superior Court of Connecticut, 2002

CASE SUMMARY

Facts: NESCOR was, in theory, a home improvement company. One of its salespeople signed a contract with the Antunas to install vinyl siding and windows. The contract contained the required FTC language: "Any holder of this consumer credit contract is subject to all claims and defenses which the debtor could assert against the Seller of the goods or services pursuant hereto or with the proceeds hereof." NESCOR assigned this contract to The Money Store (TMS).

Under Connecticut law, a home improvement contract is invalid and unenforceable if it is entered into by a salesperson or contractor who has not registered with the state. The NESCOR salesperson was unregistered.

Unhappy with NESCOR's work, the Antunas stopped making payments under the contract. TMS filed suit, seeking to foreclose on their house. The Antunas moved for summary judgment, arguing that TMS could not enforce the contract because it was not a holder in due course.

Issues: *Was TMS a holder in due course? Does it have the right to foreclose on the Antunas' home?*

Decision: TMS has no right to foreclose because it was not a holder in due course.

Reasoning: Because the NESCOR salesperson was not registered, state law gives the Antunas the right to invalidate the home improvement contract with NESCOR. The FTC language explicitly gives the Antunas the right to assert against TMS whatever defenses they have against NESCOR. Accordingly, because the home improvement contract is invalid, neither NESCOR nor TMS can benefit from it. TMS may not enforce the consumer credit contract by foreclosing on the Antunas' house.

Chapter Conclusion

Commercial paper provides essential grease to the wheels of commerce. It is worth remembering, however, that the terms of the UCC are precise and that failure to comply with these exacting provisions can lead to unfortunate consequences.

EXAM REVIEW

1. **NEGOTIABILITY** The possessor of non-negotiable commercial paper has the same rights—no more, no less—as the person who made the original contract. The possessor of negotiable commercial paper has more rights than the person who made the original contract.

---

[4]UCC §3-106(d).

2. THE FUNDAMENTAL RULE OF COMMERCIAL PAPER   The possessor of a piece of commercial paper has an unconditional right to be paid, so long as:

- The paper is negotiable,

- It has been negotiated to the possessor,

- The possessor is a holder in due course, and

- The issuer cannot claim a valid defense.

3. REQUIREMENTS FOR NEGOTIABILITY   To be negotiable, an instrument must:

- Be in writing,

- Be signed by the maker or drawer,

- Contain an unconditional promise or order to pay,

- State a definite amount of money that is clear "within its four corners,"

- Be payable on demand or at a definite time, and

- Be payable to order or to bearer.

4. AMBIGUITY   When the terms in a negotiable instrument contradict each other, three rules apply:

- Words take precedence over numbers.

- Handwritten terms prevail over typed and printed terms.

- Typed terms win over printed terms.

5. NEGOTIATION   To be negotiated, order paper must first be indorsed and then delivered to the transferee. Bearer paper must simply be delivered to the transferee; no indorsement is required.

6. HOLDER IN DUE COURSE   A holder in due course is a holder who has given value for the instrument, in good faith, without notice of outstanding claims or other defects.

EXAM Strategy

Question: After Irene fell behind on her mortgage payments, she answered an advertisement from Best Financial Consultants offering attractive refinancing opportunities. During a meeting at a McDonald's restaurant, a Best representative told her that the company would arrange for a complete refinancing of her home, pay off two of her creditors, and give her an additional $5,000 in spending money. Irene would only have to pay Best $4,000. Irene signed a blank promissory note that was filled in later by Best representatives for $14,986.61. Best did not fulfill its promises to Irene, but within two weeks, it sold the note to Robin for just under $14,000. Irene refused to pay the note, alleging that Robin was not a holder in due course. Is Irene liable to Robin?

Strategy: Review the requirements for being a holder in due course. Is this person a *holder* who has given *value* for the instrument, in *good faith*, without *notice* of outstanding claims or other defects? (See the "Result" at the end of this section.)

7. **DEFENSES**   The issuer of a negotiable instrument is not required to pay if:

- His signature was forged.

- After signing the instrument, his debts were discharged in bankruptcy.

- He was underage (typically under 18) at the time he signed the instrument.

- The amount of the instrument was altered after he signed it.

- He signed the instrument under duress, while mentally incapacitated, or as part of an illegal transaction.

- He was tricked into signing the instrument without knowing what it was and without any reasonable way to find out.

8. **CONSUMER EXCEPTION**   The Federal Trade Commission requires all promissory notes in consumer credit contracts to contain language preventing any subsequent holder from being a holder in due course.

EXAM Strategy

Question: Gina and Douglas Felde purchased a Chrysler car with a 70,000-mile warranty. They signed a loan contract with the dealer to pay for the car in monthly installments. The dealer sold the contract to the Chrysler Credit Corp. The car soon developed a tendency to accelerate abruptly and without warning. Two Chrysler dealers were unable to correct the problem. The Feldes filed suit against Chrysler Credit Corp., but the company refused to rescind the loan contract. The company argued that, as a holder in due course on the note, it was entitled to be paid regardless of any defects in the car. How would you decide this case if you were the judge?

Strategy: Whenever consumers are involved, consider the possibility that there is a consumer credit contract. The plaintiffs in this case are consumers who have borrowed money from a lender to purchase goods from a seller who is affiliated with the lender (both seller and lender are owned by Chrysler). Thus, the contract is a consumer credit contract. (See the "Result" at the end of this section.)

6. Result: In this case, Robin is a holder who has given value. Did she act in good faith? We do not know if she actually believed the transaction was honest, but the court held that the transaction did not appear to be commercially reasonable because Robin's profit was so high. She paid $14,000 for a note worth $14,986.61. Thus, Robin was not a holder in due course, and Irene was not liable to her.

8. Result: Chrysler Credit was not a holder in due course. Therefore, it is subject to any defenses the Feldes might have against the dealer, including that the car was defective.

MATCHING QUESTIONS

Match the following terms with their definitions:

___A. Drawer

___B. Drawee

___C. Issuer

___D. Maker

___E. Holder

1. Someone who issues a promissory note

2. The person who issues a draft

3. The person who pays a draft

4. Anyone in possession of an instrument if it is indorsed to her

5. The maker of a promissory note or the drawer of a draft

TRUE/FALSE QUESTIONS

Circle true or false:

1. T F The possessor of a piece of commercial paper always has an unconditional right to be paid.

2. T F Three parties are involved in a draft.

3. T F To be negotiable, bearer paper must be indorsed and delivered to the transferee.

4. T F Negotiation means that an instrument has been transferred to the holder by the issuer.

5. T F A promissory note may be valid even if it does not have a specific due date.

MULTIPLE-CHOICE QUESTIONS

1. **CPA QUESTION** In order to negotiate bearer paper, one must:
   (a) indorse the paper.
   (b) indorse and deliver the paper with consideration.
   (c) deliver the paper.
   (d) deliver and indorse the paper.

2. The possessor of a piece of order paper does *not* have an unconditional right to be paid if:
   (a) the paper is negotiable.
   (b) the possessor is the payee.
   (c) the paper has been indorsed to the possessor.
   (d) the possessor is a holder in due course.
   (e) the issuer changed his mind after signing the instrument.

3. An instrument is negotiable unless:

(a) it is in writing.

(b) it is signed only by the drawee.

(c) it contains an order to pay.

(d) it is payable on demand.

(e) it is payable only to bearer.

4. Chloe buys a motorcycle on eBay from Junior. In payment, she gives him a promissory note for $7,000. He immediately negotiates the note to Terry. After the motorcycle arrives, Chloe discovers that it is not as advertised. One week later, she notifies Junior. She still has to pay Terry because:

(a) on eBay, the rule is "buyer beware."

(b) Terry's rights are not affected by Junior's misdeeds.

(c) Terry indorsed the note.

(d) Chloe is the drawee.

(e) Chloe waited too long to complain.

5. Donna gives a promissory note to C. J. Which of the following errors would make the note non-negotiable?

(a) The instrument was written on a dirty sock.

(b) The instrument promised to pay 15,000 euros.

(c) The note stated that Donna owed C. J. "$1,500: One thousand and five dollars."

(d) Donna signed the note without reading it.

(e) The due date was specified as "three months after Donna graduates from college."

CASE QUESTIONS

1. Kay signed a promissory note for $220,000 that was payable to Investments, Inc. The company then indorsed the note over to its lawyers to pay past and future legal fees. Were the lawyers holders in due course?

2. Shelby wrote the check shown on the next page to Dana. When is it payable and for how much?

```
                                                                    4201
SHELBY CASE
3020 CREST DRIVE                                    July 27, 2014
ALVIN, TX                                  August 3,  20 13

PAY TO THE
ORDER OF   Dana Locke                              $  352. 00

    Three Hundred Eighty-Two                             DOLLARS

LAST NATIONAL BANK OF ALVIN
ALVIN, TX 77511
5-14/111
                                              Shelby Case
MEMO

⑈010110456⑈ 286 72566 4201
```

3. In the prior question, who are the drawer, drawee, and payee of this check?

4. Tanya and Jerry entered into a contract with a real estate developer that provided he would build the house of their dreams on a lot that he owned. In payment for the property and the house, the couple signed a promissory note which was payable, "upon closing on sale of the house to be constructed on the below described lot or one year from the date of this Note, whichever event first occurs." Is this note negotiable?

5. Duncan Properties, Inc. agrees to buy a car from Shifty for $25,000. The company issues a promissory note in payment. The car that Duncan bought is defective. If Shifty still has the note, does Duncan have to pay it?

6. Shifty sells that note to Honest Abe for $22,000. Does Duncan have to pay Abe?

7. Abe gives the note to his daughter, Prudence, for her birthday. Is Prudence a holder in due course? Does Duncan have to pay Prudence?

8. Tom was CEO of a company. He stole money from the company by writing a series of checks made out to "Cash" which he deposited in his own personal account at Bank. (Please do not try this at home.) Of course, he then spent the money. The company sued the Bank to get the money back. Was the Bank a holder in due course?

DISCUSSION QUESTIONS

1. Catherine suffered serious physical injuries in an automobile accident and became acutely depressed as a result. One morning, she received a check for $17,400 in settlement of her claims arising from the accident. She indorsed the check and placed it on the kitchen table. She then called Robert, her longtime roommate, to tell him the check had arrived. That afternoon, she jumped from the roof of her apartment building, killing herself. The police found the check and a note from her stating that she was giving it to Robert. Had Catherine negotiated the check to Robert?

2. **ETHICS** In desperate financial trouble and fearful of losing his house, Abbott asked his friend Taylor for help. Taylor had been an officer of the Bank, so she put Abbott in touch with some of her former colleagues there. When a $300,000 loan was ready for closing, Taylor informed Abbott that she expected a commission of $15,000. Taylor threatened to block the loan if her demands were not met. Abbott was desperate, so he agreed to give Taylor $4,000 in cash and a promissory note for $11,000. On what grounds might Abbott claim that the note is invalid? Would this be a valid defense? Even if Taylor was in the right legally, was she in the right ethically? What is her Life Principle?

3. The *Blasco* case involved a payday loan, for which she was paying 6,500 percent interest. Some states outlaw such loans or heavily regulate the interest rates. Should the law permit these loans?

4. Kendall raised hogs. The Grain Company would provide him with hogs and grain and, in return, he would sign a promissory note in an amount equal to the value of these items. Once the pigs were grown, Kendall would sell them and repay the loan. One time, an officer of the Grain Company asked Kendall to sign not only his own but also his wife's name to the promissory note. Kendall did so, but put his initials, KH, after her name to indicate that he was the one who had signed the note. Grain Company sold this note to Bank. It turned out that the Grain Company did not actually own the hogs it had given Kendall and the true owner took them away. Bank sued Kendall for payment on the promissory note. Are Kendall and/or his wife liable on the note?

5. On October 12, James Camp agreed to provide services to Shawn Sheth by October 15. In payment, Sheth gave Camp a check for $1,300 that was postdated October 15. On October 13, Camp sold the check to Buckeye Check Cashing for $1,261.31. On October 14, fearing that Camp would violate the contract, Sheth stopped payment on the check. Also, on October 14, Buckeye deposited the check with its bank, believing that the check would reach Sheth's bank on October 15. Buckeye was unaware of the stop payment order. Sheth's bank refused to pay the check. Buckeye filed suit against Sheth. Was Buckeye a holder in due course? Must Sheth pay Buckeye?

CHAPTER 16

SECURED TRANSACTIONS

To: Allison@credit-help-for-all.com
From: Sam12345@yahoo.com
Hi, Allison.

Look, this just doesn't make any sense. When I got out of school, I paid a guy $18,000 for my Jeep. I made every payment on my loan—*every single one*—for over two years. I paid out over 9,000 bucks for that thing. Then I got laid off and I missed a few payments and the bank repossessed the car. And OK, fair enough, I can see why they have to do that.

So they auctioned off the Jeep and somebody else owns it. But now the bank's lawyer called me and said I still owe $5,000. What is that, a joke? I owe money for a Jeep I don't even have anymore? That can't be right. I look forward to your advice.
Sam

> **I owe money for a Jeep I don't even have anymore?**

To: Sam12345@yahoo.com
From: Allison@credit-help-for-all.com

Dear Sam,

I am sympathetic with your story, but unfortunately the bank is entitled to its money. Here is how the law sees your plight. When you bought the Jeep, you signed two documents: a note, in which you promised to pay the full balance owed, and a security agreement, which said that if you stopped making payments, the bank could repossess the vehicle and sell it.

There are two problems. First, even after two years of writing checks, you might still have owed about $10,000 (because of interest). Second, cars depreciate quickly. Your $18,000 vehicle probably had a market value of about $8,000 thirty months later. The security agreement allowed the bank to sell the Jeep at auction, where prices are still lower. Your car evidently fetched about $5,000. That leaves a deficiency of $5,000—for which you are legally responsible, regardless of who is driving the car.
I hope you have a good weekend.
Allison

16-1 SECURED TRANSACTIONS

We can sympathize with Sam, but the bank is entitled to its money. The buyer and the bank had entered into a secured transaction, meaning that one party gave credit to another, insisting on full repayment and the right to seize certain property if the debt went unpaid. It is essential to understand the basics of this law because we live and work in a world economy based solidly on credit.

Article 9 of the Uniform Commercial Code (UCC) governs secured transactions in personal property. Article 9 employs terms not used elsewhere, so we must lead off with some definitions:

- **Fixtures** are goods that have become attached to real estate. For example, elevators are goods when a company manufactures them, but they become fixtures when installed in a building.

- **Security interest** means an interest in personal property or fixtures that secures the performance of some obligation. If an automobile dealer sells you a new car on credit and retains a security interest, it means it is keeping legal rights in your car, including the right to drive it away if you fall behind in your payments.

- **Secured party** is the person or company that holds the security interest. The automobile dealer who sells you a car on credit is the secured party.

- **Collateral** is the property subject to a security interest. When a dealer sells you a new car and keeps a security interest, the vehicle is the collateral.

- **Debtor** For our purposes, debtor refers to a person who has some original ownership interest in the collateral. If Alice borrows money from a bank and uses her Mercedes as collateral, she is the debtor because she owns the car.

- **Security agreement** is the contract in which the debtor gives a security interest to the secured party. This agreement protects the secured party's rights in the collateral.

- **Repossession** occurs when the secured party takes back collateral because the debtor has defaulted (failed to make payments when due).

- **Perfection** is a series of steps the secured party must take to protect its rights in the collateral against people other than the debtor.

- **Financing statement** is a record intended to notify the general public that the secured party has a security interest in the collateral.

- **Record** refers to information written on paper or stored in an electronic or other medium.

- **Authenticate** means to sign a document or to use any symbol or encryption method that identifies the person and clearly indicates she is adopting the record as her own. You authenticate a security agreement when you sign the papers at an auto dealership. A company may authenticate by using the Internet to transmit an electronic signature.

An Example

Here is an example using the terms just discussed. A medical equipment company manufactures a CT scanner and sells it to a clinic for $2 million, taking $500,000 cash and the clinic's promise to pay the rest over five years. The clinic simultaneously

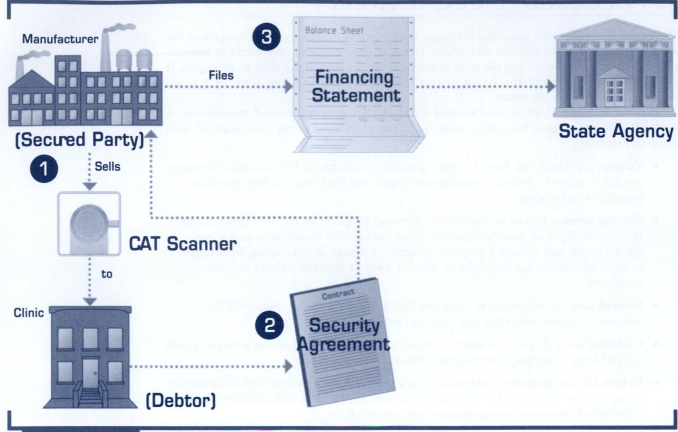

EXHIBIT 16.1 A simple security agreement:
(1) The manufacturer sells a CT scan machine to a clinic, taking $500,000 and the clinic's promise to pay the balance over five years.
(2) The clinic simultaneously authenticates a security agreement.
(3) The manufacturer perfects by electronically filing a financing statement.

authenticates a security agreement, giving the manufacturer a security interest in the CT scanner. The manufacturer then electronically files a financing statement in an appropriate state agency. This perfects the manufacturer's rights, meaning that its security interest in the CT scanner is now valid against all the world. Exhibit 16.1 illustrates this transaction.

If the clinic goes bankrupt and many creditors try to seize its assets, the manufacturer has first claim to the CT scanner. The clinic's bankruptcy is of great importance. When a debtor has money to pay all of its debts, there are no concerns about security interests. A creditor insists on a security interest to protect itself in the event the debtor cannot pay all of its debts.

16-1a Scope of Article 9

Article 9 applies to any transaction intended to create a security interest in personal property or fixtures.

Types of Collateral

The personal property that may be used as collateral includes:

- Goods, which are things that are movable.

- Inventory, meaning goods held by someone for sale or lease, such as all the beds and chairs in a furniture store.

- Instruments, such as drafts, checks, certificates of deposit, and notes.

- Investment property, which refers primarily to securities and related rights.

- Other property, including documents of title, accounts, general intangibles (copyrights, patents, goodwill, and so forth), and chattel paper (for example, a sales document indicating that a retailer has a security interest in goods sold to a consumer). Slightly different rules apply to some of these forms of property, but the details are less important than the general principles on which we shall focus.

Article 9 applies any time the parties intended to create a security interest in any of the items listed above.

16-2 ATTACHMENT OF A SECURITY INTEREST

Attachment is a vital step in a secured transaction. This means that the secured party has taken three steps to create an enforceable security interest:

1. The two parties made a security agreement, and either the debtor has authenticated a security agreement describing the collateral, or the secured party has obtained possession;

2. The secured party has given value to obtain the security agreement; and

3. The debtor has rights in the collateral.[1]

Attachment
A three-step process that creates an enforceable security interest

16-2a Agreement

Without an agreement, there can be no security interest. Generally, the agreement must be either written on paper and signed by the debtor, or electronically recorded and authenticated by the debtor. The agreement must reasonably identify the collateral. For example, a security agreement may properly describe the collateral as "all equipment in the store at 123 Periwinkle Street."

A security agreement at a minimum might:

- State that Happy Homes, Inc., and Martha agree that Martha is buying an Arctic Co. refrigerator, and identify the exact unit by its serial number;

- Give the price, the down payment, the monthly payments, and interest rate;

---

[1]UCC §9-203.

- State that because Happy Homes is selling Martha the refrigerator on credit, it has a security interest in the refrigerator; and

- Provide that if Martha defaults, Happy Homes is entitled to repossess the refrigerator.

16-2b Possession

In certain cases, the security agreement need not be in writing if the parties have an oral agreement and the secured party has possession. For some kinds of collateral, for example stock certificates, it is safer for the secured party actually to take the item than to rely upon a security agreement.

EXAM Strategy

Question: Hector needs money to keep his business afloat. He asks his uncle for a $1 million loan. The uncle agrees, but he insists that his nephew grant him a security interest in Hector's splendid gold clarinet, worth over $2 million. Hector agrees. The uncle prepares a handwritten document summarizing the agreement and asks his nephew to sign it. Hector hands the clarinet to his uncle and receives his money, but he forgets to sign the document. Has a security agreement attached?

Strategy: Attachment occurs if the parties made a security agreement and there was authentication or possession, the secured party has given value, and the debtor had rights in the collateral.

Result: Hector agreed to give his uncle a security interest in the instrument. He never authenticated (signed) the agreement, but the uncle did take possession of the clarinet. The uncle gave Hector $1 million, and Hector owned the instrument. Yes, the security interest attached.

16-2c Value

For the security interest to attach, the secured party must give value. Usually, the value will be apparent. If a bank loans $400 million to an airline, that money is the value, and the bank may therefore obtain a security interest in the planes that the airline is buying.

16-2d Debtor Rights in the Collateral

The debtor can only grant a security interest in goods if he has some legal right to those goods himself. Typically, the debtor owns the goods. But a debtor may also give a security interest if he is leasing the goods or even if he is a bailee, meaning that he is lawfully holding them for someone else.

Result

Once the security interest has attached to the collateral, the secured party is protected against the debtor. If the debtor fails to pay, the secured party may repossess the collateral, meaning take it away.

16-2e Attachment to Future Property

After-acquired property refers to items that the debtor obtains after the parties have made their security agreement. The parties may agree that the security interest attaches to after-acquired property. Basil is starting a catering business but owns only a beat-up car. He borrows $55,000 from the Pesto Bank, which takes a security interest in the car. But Pesto also insists on an after-acquired clause. When Basil purchases a commercial stove, cooking equipment, and freezer, Pesto's security interest attaches to each item as Basil acquires it.

A security agreement automatically applies to proceeds—whatever a debtor obtains who sells the collateral or otherwise disposes of it. The secured party obtains a security interest in the proceeds of the collateral unless the security agreement states otherwise.[2]

After-acquired property
Items that the debtor obtains after the parties have made their security agreement

16-3 PERFECTION

16-3a Nothing Less than Perfection

Once the security interest has attached to the collateral, the secured party is protected against the debtor. Pesto Bank loaned money to Basil and has a security interest in all of his property. If Basil defaults on his loan, Pesto may insist he deliver the goods to the bank. If he fails to do that, the bank can seize the collateral. But Pesto's security interest is valid only against Basil; if a third person claims some interest in the goods, the bank may never get them. For example, Basil might have taken out another loan, from his friend Olive, and used the same property as collateral. Olive knew nothing about the bank's original loan. To protect itself against Olive, and all other parties, the bank must perfect its interest.

There are several kinds of perfection, including:

- Perfection by filing;

- Perfection by possession; and

- Perfection of consumer goods.

In some cases, the secured party will have a choice of which method to use; in other cases, only one method works.

16-3b Perfection by Filing

The most common way to perfect is by filing a financing statement with the appropriate state agency. A financing statement gives the names of all parties, describes the collateral, and outlines the security interest, enabling any interested person to learn about it. Suppose the Pesto Bank obtains a security interest in Basil's catering equipment and then perfects by filing with the secretary of state in the state capital. When Basil asks his friend Olive for a loan, she will check the records to see if anyone has a security interest in the catering equipment. Olive's search uncovers Basil's previous security agreement, and she realizes it would be unwise to make the loan. If Basil were to default, the collateral would go straight to Pesto Bank, leaving Olive empty-handed. See Exhibit 16.2.

Article 9 prescribes one form to be used nationwide for financing statements. The financing form is available online at many websites. Remember that the filing may be done on paper or electronically.

---

[2]UCC §9-204 and §9-203.

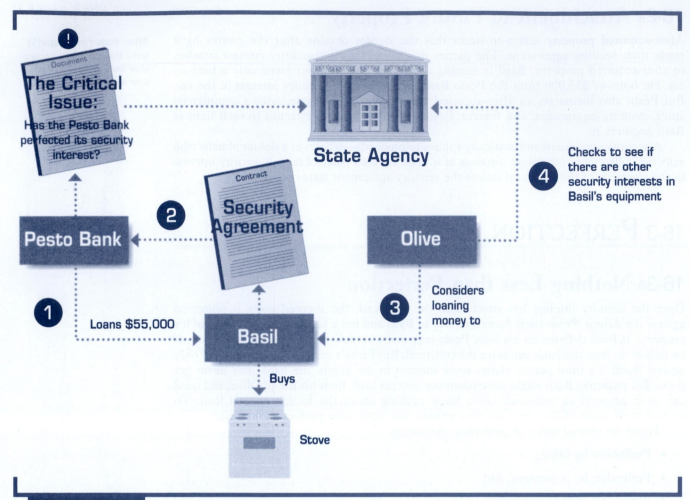

State Agency

Checks to see if there are other security interests in Basil's equipment

Pesto Bank

Security Agreement

Olive

Considers loaning money to

Loans $55,000

Basil

Buys

Stove

EXHIBIT 16.2	The Pesto Bank: (1) Loans money to Basil and (2) Takes a security interest in his equipment. Later, when Olive (3) Considers loaning Basil money, she will (4) Check to see if any other creditors already have a security interest in his goods.

The most common problems that arise in filing cases are (1) whether the financing statement contained enough information to put other people on notice of the security interest; and (2) whether the secured party filed the papers in the right place.

Contents of the Financing Statement

A financing statement is sufficient if it provides the name of the debtor, the name of the secured party, and an indication of the collateral.[3] The name of the debtor is critical because that is what an interested person will use to search among the millions of other financing statements on file. Faulty descriptions of the debtor's name have led to thousands of disputes and untold years of litigation, as subsequent creditors have failed to locate any

---

[3]UCC §9-502(a).

record of an earlier claim on the debtor's property. In response, the Uniform Commercial Code is now very precise about what name must be used. Most states require that individuals use the same name on a financing statement that is on their driver's license or state ID card (for nondrivers).[4] For organizations, the correct name is the one on the "public organic record," defined as any record available for public inspection, including its charter or limited partnership agreement.[5]

Because misnamed debtors have created so much conflict, the Code also offers a straightforward test: A financing statement is effective if a computer search run under the debtor's correct name produces it. That is true even if the financing statement used the *incorrect* name. If the search does not reveal the document, then the financing statement is ineffective as a matter of law. The burden is on the secured party to file accurately, not on the searcher to seek out erroneous filings.[6]

The collateral must be described reasonably so that another party contemplating a loan to the debtor will understand which property is already secured. A financing statement could properly state that it applies to "all inventory in the debtor's Houston warehouse." If the debtor has given a security interest in everything he owns, then it is sufficient to state simply that the financing statement covers "all assets" or "all personal property."

Place and Duration of Filing

Article 9 specifies where a secured party must file. These provisions may vary from state to state, so it is essential to check local law: A misfiled record accomplishes nothing. Generally speaking, a party must file in a central filing office located in the state where an individual debtor lives or where an organization has its executive office.[7]

Once a financing statement has been filed, it is effective for five years (except for a manufactured home, where it lasts 30 years). After five years, the statement will expire and leave the secured party unprotected unless she files a continuation statement within six months prior to expiration. The continuation statement is valid for an additional five years, and a secured party may file such a statement periodically, forever.

16-3c Perfection by Possession

For most types of collateral, in addition to filing, a secured party generally may perfect by possession. So if the collateral is a diamond brooch or 1,000 shares of stock, a bank may perfect its security interest by holding the items until the loan is paid off. **However, possession imposes one important duty: A secured party must use reasonable care in the custody and preservation of collateral in her possession.**[8] Reliable Bank holds 1,000 shares of stock as collateral for a loan it made to Grady. Grady instructs the bank to sell the shares and use the proceeds to pay off his debt in full. If Reliable neglects to sell the stock for five days and the share price drops by 40 percent during that period, the bank will suffer the loss, not Grady.

16-3d Perfection of Consumer Goods

The UCC gives special treatment to security interests in most consumer goods. Merchants cannot realistically file a financing statement for every bed, television, and stereo for which a consumer owes money. To understand the UCC's treatment of these transactions, we need

---

[4]UCC §9-503. If a person has neither kind of state ID card, then her surname and first personal name will be required to perfect by filing.
[5]UCC §102(a)(68).
[6]UCC §9-506(c).
[7]UCC §9-307.
[8]UCC §9-207.

to know two terms. The first is *consumer goods*, which are those used primarily for personal, family, or household purposes. The second term is *purchase money security interest*.

A **purchase money security interest (PMSI)** is one taken by the person who sells the collateral or by the person who advances money so the debtor can buy the collateral.[9] Assume the Gobroke Home Center sells Marion a $5,000 stereo system. The sales document requires a payment of $500 down and $50 per month for the next three centuries and gives Gobroke a security interest in the system. Because the security interest was "taken by the seller," the document is a PMSI. It would also be a PMSI if a bank had loaned Marion the money to buy the system and the document gave the bank a security interest. See Exhibit 16.3.

But aren't all security interests PMSIs? No, many are not. Suppose a bank loans a retail company $800,000 and takes a security interest in the store's present inventory. That is not a PMSI, since the store did not use the money to purchase the collateral.

What must Gobroke Home Center do to perfect its security interest? Nothing. **A PMSI in consumer goods perfects automatically, without filing.**[10] Marion's new stereo is clearly consumer goods because she will use it only in her home. Gobroke's security interest is a PMSI, so the interest has perfected automatically.

The Code provisions about perfecting generally do not apply to motor vehicles, trailers, mobile homes, boats, or farm tractors. These types of secured interests are governed by state law, which frequently require a security interest to be noted directly on the vehicle's certificate of title.

EXAM Strategy

Question: Winona owns a tropical fish store. To buy a spectacular new aquarium, she borrows $25,000 from her sister, Pauline, and signs an agreement giving Pauline a security interest in the tank. Pauline never files the security agreement. Winona's business goes belly up, and both Pauline and other creditors angle to repossess the tank. Does Pauline have a perfected interest in the tank?

Strategy: Generally, a creditor obtains a perfected security interest by filing or possession. However, a PMSI in consumer goods perfects automatically, without filing. Was Pauline's security agreement a PMSI? Was the fish tank a consumer good?

Result: A PMSI is one taken by the person who sells the collateral or advances money for its purchase. Pauline advanced the money for Winona to buy the tank, so Pauline does have a PSMI. Consumer goods are those used primarily for personal, family, or household purposes, so this was *not* a consumer purchase. Pauline failed to perfect and is unprotected against other creditors.

16-4 PROTECTION OF BUYERS

Generally, once a security interest is perfected, it remains effective regardless of whether the collateral is sold, exchanged, or transferred in some other way. Bubba's Bus Co. needs money to meet its payroll, so it borrows $150,000 from Francine's Finance Co., which takes a security interest in Bubba's 180 buses and perfects its interest. Bubba, still short of cash,

---

[9]UCC §9-103.
[10]UCC §9-309(1).

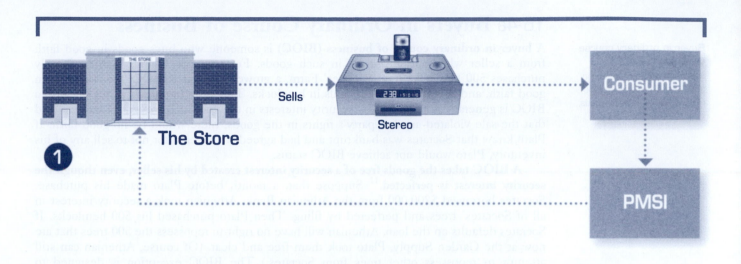

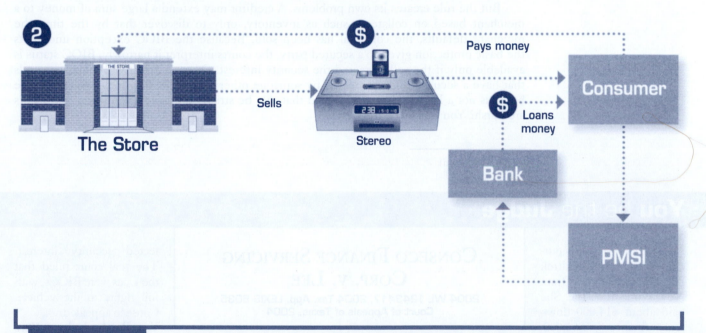

EXHIBIT 16.3 A purchase money security interest can arise in either of two ways. In the first example, a store sells a stereo to a consumer on credit; the consumer in turn signs a PMSI, giving the store a security interest in the stereo. In the second example, the consumer buys the stereo with money loaned from a bank; the consumer signs a PMSI giving the *bank* a security interest in the stereo.

sells 30 of his buses to Antelope Transit. But even that money is not enough to keep Bubba solvent: He defaults on his loan to Francine and goes into bankruptcy. Francine pounces on Bubba's buses. May she repossess the 30 that Antelope now operates? Yes. The security interest continued in the buses even after Antelope purchased them, and Francine can whisk them away.

But there are some exceptions to this rule. The UCC gives a few buyers special protection.

16-4a Buyers in Ordinary Course of Business

Buyer in ordinary course of business (BIOC)

Someone who buys goods in good faith from a seller who routinely deals in such goods

A **buyer in ordinary course of business (BIOC)** is someone who buys goods in good faith from a seller who routinely deals in such goods. For example, Plato's Garden Supply purchases 500 hemlocks from Socrates' Farm, a grower. Plato is a BIOC: He is buying in good faith, and Socrates routinely deals in hemlocks. This is an important status because a BIOC is generally not affected by security interests in the goods. However, if Plato realized that the sale violated another party's rights in the goods, there would be no good faith. If Plato knew that Socrates was bankrupt and had agreed with a creditor not to sell any of his inventory, Plato would not achieve BIOC status.

A BIOC takes the goods free of a security interest created by his seller, even though the security interest is perfected.[11] Suppose that, a month before Plato made his purchase, Socrates borrowed $200,000 from the Athenian Bank. Athenian took a security interest in all of Socrates' trees and perfected by filing. Then Plato purchased his 500 hemlocks. If Socrates defaults on the loan, Athenian will have no right to repossess the 500 trees that are now at the Garden Supply. Plato took them free and clear. (Of course, Athenian can still attempt to repossess other trees from Socrates.) The BIOC exception is designed to encourage ordinary commerce. A buyer making routine purchases should not be forced to perform a financing check before buying.

But the rule creates its own problems. A creditor may extend a large sum of money to a merchant based on collateral, such as inventory, only to discover that by the time the merchant defaults, the collateral has been sold. Because the BIOC exception undercuts the basic protection given to a secured party, the courts interpret it narrowly. BIOC status is available only if the seller created the security interest. Often, a buyer will purchase goods that have a security interest created by someone other than the seller. If that happens, the buyer is not a BIOC. However, should that rule be strictly enforced even when the results are harsh? You make the call.

---

[11]UCC §9-320(a).

You be the Judge

Facts: Lila Williams purchased a new Roadtrek 200 motor home from New World R.V. Inc. She paid about $14,000 down and financed $63,000, giving a security interest to New World. The RV company assigned its security interest to Conseco Finance, which perfected. Two years later, Williams returned the vehicle to New World (the record does not indicate why), and New World sold the RV to Robert and Ann Lee for $42,800. A year later, Williams defaulted on her payments to Conseco.

The Lees sued Conseco, claiming to be BIOCs and asking for a court declaration that they had sole title to the Roadtrek. Conseco counterclaimed, seeking title based on its per-

CONSECO FINANCE SERVICING CORP. V. LEE

2004 WL 1243417, 2004 Tex. App. LEXIS 5035
Court of Appeals of Texas, 2004

fected security interest. The trial court ruled that the Lees were BIOCs, with full rights to the vehicle. Conseco appealed.

You Be the Judge: *Were the Lees BIOCs?*

Argument for Conseco: Under the UCC, a BIOC takes free of a security interest created by the buyer's seller. The buyers were the Lees. The seller was New World. New World did not create the security interest—Lila Williams did. There is no security interest created by New World. The security interest held by Conseco was created by someone else (Williams) and is not affected by the Lees' status as BIOCs. The law is clear, and Conseco is entitled to the Roadtrek.

Argument for the Lees: Conseco weaves a clever argument, but let's look at what they are really saying. Two honest buyers, acting in perfect good faith, can walk into an RV dealership, spend $42,000 for a used vehicle, and end up with—nothing. Conseco claims it is entitled to an RV that the Lees paid for because someone that the Lees have never dealt with, never even heard of, gave to this RV seller a security interest that the seller, years earlier, passed on to a finance company. Conseco's argument defies common sense and the goals of Article 9.

16-5 PRIORITIES AMONG CREDITORS

What happens when two creditors have a security interest in the same collateral? The party who has **priority** in the collateral gets it. Typically, the debtor lacks assets to pay everyone, so all creditors struggle to be the first in line. After the first creditor has repossessed the collateral, sold it, and taken enough of the proceeds to pay off his debt, there may be nothing left for anyone else. (There may not even be enough to pay the first creditor all that he is due, in which case that creditor will sue for the deficiency.) Who gets priority? There are three principal rules.[12]

The first rule is easy: A party with a perfected security interest takes priority over a party with an unperfected interest. This is the whole point of perfecting: to ensure that your security interest gets priority over everyone else's. On August 15, Meredith's Market, an antique store, borrows $100,000 from the Happy Bank, which takes a security interest in all of Meredith's inventory. Happy Bank does not perfect. On September 15, Meredith uses the same collateral to borrow $50,000 from the Suspicion Bank, which files a financing statement the same day. On October 15, as if on cue, Meredith files for bankruptcy and stops paying both creditors. Suspicion wins because it holds a perfected interest, whereas the Happy Bank holds merely an unperfected interest.

The second rule: If neither secured party has perfected, the first interest to attach gets priority. Suppose that Suspicion Bank and Happy Bank had both failed to perfect. In that case, Happy Bank would have the first claim to Meredith's inventory since Happy's interest attached first.

And the third rule follows logically: Between perfected security interests, the first to file or perfect wins. Diminishing Perspective, a railroad, borrows $75 million from the First Bank, which takes a security interest in Diminishing's rolling stock (railroad cars) and immediately perfects by filing. Two months later, Diminishing borrows $100 million from Second Bank, which takes a security interest in the same collateral and also files. When Diminishing arrives, on schedule, in bankruptcy court, both banks will race to seize the rolling stock. First Bank gets the railcars because it perfected first.

Priority

The law sets out three rules to establish which creditors have better claims

March 1	April 2	May 3	The Winner
First Bank lends money and perfects its security interest by filing a financing statement.	Second Bank lends money and perfects its security interest by filing a financing statement.	Diminishing goes bankrupt, and both banks attempt to take the rolling stock.	First Bank, because it perfected first.

---

[12]UCC §9-322(a)(2), UCC §9-322(a)(3), and UCC §9-322(a)(1).

In the example above, it is easy to apply the rules. But sometimes courts must sort through additional complications. We know that a perfected security interest takes priority over others. But sometimes it is not clear exactly when the security interest was perfected. In the following case, the creditor got in just under the wire.

In Re Roser

613 F.3d 1240
United States Court of Appeals for the Tenth Circuit, 2010

CASE SUMMARY

Facts: Robert Roser obtained a loan from Sovereign Bank, which he promptly used to buy a car. Nineteen days later, Sovereign filed a lien with the state of Colorado. The bank expected that with a perfected interest, it would have priority over everyone else.

Unknown to Sovereign Bank, Roser had declared bankruptcy only *12* days after he purchased the car. Later, the bankruptcy trustee argued that he had priority over Sovereign because the bankruptcy filing happened *before Sovereign perfected* its security interest. When the court found for the trustee, Sovereign Bank appealed.

Issue: *Did Sovereign Bank, a PMSI holder, obtain priority over the bankruptcy trustee?*

Decision: Yes, the PMSI holder obtained priority.

Reasoning: On the day that Roser entered bankruptcy, Sovereign Bank had not filed its financing statement, which means that its security interest was not yet perfected. Ordinarily, a bankruptcy trustee would take priority over all security interests that are unperfected on the day that a debtor files a bankruptcy petition. However, there is an exception to this rule: If the creditor files a financing statement for a PMSI within 20 days after the debtor receives the collateral, that security interest is deemed to have been perfected as of the date of the debtor receives the collateral, not the day on which the financing statement was filed. In this case, the bank filed within that 20-day grace period, so its security interest took priority over the bankruptcy trustee.

Reversed and remanded.

16-6 DEFAULT AND TERMINATION

We have reached the end of the line. Either the debtor has defaulted, or it has performed its obligations and may terminate the security agreement.

16-6a Default

The parties define "default" in their security agreement. **Generally, a debtor defaults when he fails to make payments due or enters bankruptcy proceedings.** The parties can agree that other acts will constitute default, such as the debtor's failure to maintain insurance on the collateral. When a debtor defaults, the secured party has two principal options: (1) It may take possession of the collateral; or (2) it may file suit against the debtor for the money owed. The secured party does not have to choose between these two remedies; it may try one after the other, or both simultaneously.

Taking Possession of the Collateral

When the debtor defaults, the secured party may take possession of the collateral.[13] How does the secured party do so? In either of two ways: The secured party can file suit against the debtor to obtain a court order requiring the debtor to deliver the collateral. Otherwise, the secured

---

[13]UCC §9-609.

party may act on its own, without any court order, and simply take the collateral, provided this can be done without a breach of the peace. A **breach of the peace** occurs when the repossession disturbs public tranquility, such as through violent, threatening, or harassing acts.

Breach of the peace
Any action that disturbs public tranquility and order

The repossession in the following case was a disaster, but was it a breach of the peace?

CHAPA V. TRACIERS & ASSOCIATES, INC.

267 S.W.3d 386
Texas Court of Appeals, 2008

CASE SUMMARY

Facts: Marissa Chapa defaulted on her car loan, so Ford Motor Credit Corp. hired Traciers & Associates to repossess her white Ford Expedition. Paul Chambers, Traciers's field manager, staked out the address on file, waiting for a chance to make his move.

One morning, Chambers saw a woman drive a white Expedition out of the driveway and leave it running in the street while she ran back into the house. He made his move, quickly hooking up the car to his tow truck and driving away. Chambers may have been fast, but he was wrong about two things. First, he took the wrong car: This similar vehicle belonged to Marissa's sister-in-law Maria, who was not in default. Second, Maria's two children were in the backseat.

When Maria realized that her car and her children had disappeared, she hysterically dialed 911. Within minutes, Chambers discovered the two Chapa children and immediately returned the kids and the car to a frantic Maria.

Maria sued Ford, the repossession company, and the bank, claiming they had committed a breach of the peace. The trial court dismissed the case and she appealed.

Issue: *Did Chambers commit a breach of the peace in repossessing the car?*

Decision: No, the repo man's error was not a breach of the peace.

Reasoning: When a borrower defaults, a secured party may repossess the collateral without a court order as long as it does not breach the peace. A "breach of the peace" is any conduct that disturbs public order and tranquility, such as violent or forceful action or threats. If the borrower objects during the repossession then, to avoid confrontation, the secured party must immediately desist and pursue its remedy in court.

Here, although Chambers made some mistakes, he did not breach the peace. He removed an apparently unoccupied car from a public street without immediate confrontation, violence, threats, or objection. Chambers returned the vehicle minutes later, as soon as he realized there were children in the car. Chambers's repossession, while very upsetting to Maria, was not a breach of the peace.

Disposition of the Collateral

Once the secured party has obtained possession of the collateral, it has two choices. The secured party may (1) dispose of the collateral or (2) retain the collateral as full satisfaction of the debt. Notice that until the secured party disposes of the collateral, the debtor has the right to redeem it, that is, to pay the full value of the debt and retrieve her property.

A secured party may sell, lease, or otherwise dispose of the collateral in any commercially reasonable manner.[14] Typically, the secured party will sell the collateral in either a private or a public sale. First, however, the debtor must receive reasonable notice of the time and place of the sale so that she may bid on the collateral.

When the secured party has sold the collateral, it applies the proceeds of the sale: first, to its expenses in repossessing and selling the collateral, and second, to the debt. Sometimes the sale leaves a deficiency; that is, insufficient funds to pay off the debt. The debtor remains liable for the deficiency, and the creditor will sue for it. On the other hand, the sale of the collateral may yield a surplus; that is, a sum greater than the debt. The secured party must pay the surplus to the debtor.

---

[14]UCC §9-610.

16-6b Termination

Finally, we need to look at what happens when a debtor does not default, but pays the full debt. (You are forgiven if you have lost track of the fact that things sometimes work out smoothly.) Once that happens, the secured party must complete a termination statement, a document indicating that it no longer claims a security interest in the collateral.[15]

Chapter Conclusion

Secured transactions are essential to modern commerce. Without them, many consumers would never own a car or stereo, and many businesses would be unable to grow. But unless these debts are repaid, the economy will falter. Secured transactions are one method for ensuring that creditors are paid.

EXAM REVIEW

1. **ARTICLE 9** Article 9 applies to any transaction intended to create a security interest in personal property or fixtures.

2. **ATTACHMENT** Attachment means that (1) the two parties made a security agreement and either the debtor has authenticated a security agreement describing the collateral or the secured party has obtained possession; (2) the secured party gave value in order to get the security agreement; and (3) the debtor has rights in the collateral.

3. **PERFECTION** Attachment protects against the debtor. Perfection of a security interest protects the secured party against parties other than the debtor.

4. **FILING** Filing is the most common way to perfect. For many forms of collateral, the secured party may also perfect by obtaining either possession or control.

5. **PMSI** A purchase money security interest is one taken by the person who sells the collateral or advances money so the debtor can buy the collateral. A PMSI in consumer goods perfects automatically.

EXAM Strategy

Question: John and Clara Lockovich bought a 22-foot Chaparrel Villain II boat from Greene County Yacht Club for $32,500. They paid $6,000 cash and borrowed the rest of the purchase price from Gallatin National Bank, which took a security interest in the boat. Gallatin filed a financing statement in Greene County, Pennsylvania, where the bank was located. But Pennsylvania law requires financing statements to be filed in the county of the debtor's residence, and the Lockoviches lived in Allegheny County. The Lockoviches soon washed up in

[15]UCC §9-513.

bankruptcy court. Other creditors demanded that the boat be sold, claiming that Gallatin's security interest had been filed in the wrong place. Who wins?

Strategy: Gallatin National Bank obtained a special kind of security interest in the boat. Identify that type of interest. What special rights does this give to the bank? (See the "Result" at the end of this section.)

6. **BIOC**   A buyer in ordinary course of business takes the goods free of a security interest created by his seller even though the security interest is perfected.

7. **PRIORITY**   Priority among secured parties is generally as follows:

   a. A party with a perfected security interest takes priority over a party with an unperfected interest.
   b. If neither secured party has perfected, the first interest to attach gets priority.
   c. Between perfected security interests, the first to file or perfect wins.

EXAM Strategy

Question: Barwell, Inc., sold McMann Golf Ball Co. a "preformer," a machine that makes golf balls, for $55,000. Barwell delivered the machine on February 20. McMann paid $3,000 down, the remainder to be paid over several years, and signed an agreement giving Barwell a security interest in the preformer. Barwell did not perfect its interest. On March 1, McMann borrowed $350,000 from First of America Bank, giving the bank a security interest in McMann's present and after-acquired property. First of America perfected by filing on March 2. McMann, of course, became insolvent, and both Barwell and the bank attempted to repossess the preformer. Who gets it?

Strategy: Two parties have a valid security interest in this machine. When that happens, there is a three-step process to determine which party gets priority. Apply them. (See the "Result" at the end of this section.)

8. **DEFAULT**   When the debtor defaults, the secured party may take possession of the collateral and then sell, lease, or otherwise dispose of the collateral in any commercially reasonable way, or it may ignore the collateral and sue the debtor for the full debt.

5. Result: Gallatin advanced the money that the Lockoviches used to buy the boat, meaning the bank obtained a PMSI. A PMSI in consumer goods perfects automatically, without filing. The boat was a consumer good. Gallatin's security interest perfected without any filing at all, and so the bank wins.

7. Result: This question is resolved by the first of those three steps. A party with a perfected security interest takes priority over a party with an unperfected interest. The bank wins because its perfected security interest takes priority over Barwell's unperfected interest.

MATCHING QUESTIONS

Match the following terms with their definitions:

___A. Attachment

___B. BIOC

___C. Perfection

___D. PMSI

___E. Priority

1. Someone who buys goods in good faith from a seller who deals in such goods

2. Steps necessary to make a security interest valid against the whole world

3. A security interest taken by the person who sells the collateral or advances money so the debtor can buy it

4. The order in which creditors will be permitted to seize the property of a bankrupt debtor

5. Steps necessary to make a security interest valid against the debtor, but not against third parties

TRUE/FALSE QUESTIONS

Circle true or false:

1. T F A party with a perfected security interest takes priority over a party with an unperfected interest.

2. T F A buyer in ordinary course of business takes goods free of an unperfected security interest but does not take them free of a perfected security interest.

3. T F When a debtor defaults, a secured party may seize the collateral and hold it, using reasonable care, but may not sell or lease it.

4. T F A party may take a security interest in tangible things, such as goods, but not in intangible things, such as bank accounts.

5. T F Without an agreement of the parties, there can be no security interest.

MULTIPLE-CHOICE QUESTIONS

1. **CPA QUESTION** Under the UCC Article 9, perfection of a security interest by a creditor provides added protection against other parties if the debtor does not pay its debts. Which of the following parties is not affected by perfection of a security interest?

   (a) Other prospective creditors of the debtor

   (b) The trustee in a bankruptcy case

   (c) A buyer in the ordinary course of business

   (d) A subsequent personal injury judgment creditor

2. Jim's birth certificate lists him as "James Brown Smith"; his driver's license identifies him as "Jim Smith"; but his business card reads "J.B. Smith"; and his friends call him Jimbo. How should the financing statement list this debtor's name?

(a) James Smith

(b) J.B. Smith

(c) Jim Smith

(d) James Brown Smith

3. *CPA QUESTION* Mars, Inc., manufactures and sells Blu-ray players on credit directly to wholesalers, retailers, and consumers. Mars can perfect its security interest in the goods it sells without having to file a financing statement or take possession of the Blu-ray players if the sale is made to which of the following?

(a) Retailers

(b) Wholesalers that sell to distributors for resale

(c) Consumers

(d) Wholesalers that sell to buyers in ordinary course of business.

4. Which case does *not* represent a purchase money security interest?

(a) Auto Dealer sells Consumer a car on credit.

(b) Wholesaler sells Retailer 5,000 pounds of candy on credit.

(c) Bank lends money to Retailer, using Retailer's existing inventory as collateral.

(d) Bank lends money to Auto Dealer to purchase 150 new cars, which are the collateral.

(e) Consumer applies to Credit Agency for a loan with which to buy a yacht.

5. Millie lends Arthur, her next-door neighbor, $25,000. He gives her his diamond ring as collateral for the loan. Which statement is true?

(a) Millie has no valid security interest in the ring because the parties did not enter into a security agreement.

(b) Millie has no valid security interest in the ring because she has not filed appropriate papers.

(c) Millie has an attached, unperfected security interest in the ring.

(d) Millie has an attached, unperfected security interest in the ring, but she can perfect her interest by filing.

(e) Millie has an attached, perfected security interest in the ring.

CASE QUESTIONS

1. The Copper King Inn, Inc., had money problems. It borrowed $62,500 from two of its officers, Noonan and Patterson, but that did not suffice to keep the inn going. So Noonan, on behalf of Copper King, arranged for the inn to borrow $100,000 from Northwest Capital, an investment company that worked closely with Noonan in other ventures. Copper King signed an agreement giving Patterson, Noonan, and Northwest a security interest in the inn's furniture and equipment. But the financing statement that the parties filed made no mention of Northwest. Copper King went bankrupt. Northwest attempted to seize assets, but other creditors objected. Is Northwest entitled to Copper King's furniture and equipment?

2. Sears sold a lawn tractor to Cosmo Fiscante for $1,481. Fiscante paid with his personal credit card. Sears kept a valid security interest in the lawnmower but did not perfect. Fiscante had the machine delivered to his business, Trackers Raceway Park, the only place he ever used the machine. When Fiscante was unable to meet his obligations, various creditors attempted to seize the lawnmower. Sears argued that because it had a PMSI in the lawnmower, its interest had perfected automatically. Is Sears correct?

3. When Corona leased farmland to a strawberry farmer named Armando Munoz Juarez, it claimed a security interest in his strawberry crop. Corona's financing statement listed the farmer's name as "Armando Munoz," even though his state-issued ID card identified his last name as "Juarez." When the farmer contracted to sell strawberries to Frozsun, it filed its own financing statement securing the strawberries. This statement listed the debtor's name as "Armando Juarez." When the farmer defaulted, both Corona and Frozsun claimed an interest in the same strawberries. Which party prevails—Corona or Frozsun? Why?

4. Alpha perfects its security interest by properly filing a financing statement on January 1, 2014. Alpha files a continuation statement on September 1, 2018. It files another continuation statement on September 1, 2022. When will Alpha's financing statement expire? Why?

5. The state of Kentucky filed a tax lien against Panbowl Energy, claiming unpaid taxes. Six months later, Panbowl bought a powerful drill from Whayne Supply, making a down payment of $11,500 and signing a security agreement for the remaining debt of $220,000. Whayne perfected the next day. Panbowl defaulted. Whayne sold the drill for $58,000, leaving a deficiency of just over $100,000. The state filed suit, seeking the $58,000 proceeds. The trial court gave summary judgment to the state, and Whayne appealed. Who gets the $58,000?

DISCUSSION QUESTIONS

1. Collateral may change categories depending on its holder and how it is being used at the time of default. Classify a refrigerator in the following circumstances:

   a. When sold by an appliance store;

   b. When used by a restaurateur in his business; and

   c. When installed in a homeowner's kitchen.

2. **ETHICS** The Dannemans bought a Kodak copier worth over $40,000. Kodak arranged financing by GECC and assigned its rights to that company. Although the Dannemans thought they had purchased the copier on credit, the papers described the deal as a lease. The Dannemans had constant problems with the machine and stopped making payments. GECC repossessed the machine and, without notifying the Dannemans, sold it back to Kodak for $12,500, leaving a deficiency of $39,927. GECC sued the Dannemans for that amount. The Dannemans argued that the deal was not a lease, but a sale on credit. Why does it matter whether the parties had a sale or a lease? Is GECC entitled to its money? Finally, comment on the ethics. Why did the Dannemans not understand the papers they had signed? Who is responsible for that? Are you satisfied with the ethical conduct of the Dannemans? Kodak? GECC?

3. After reading this chapter, will your behavior as a consumer change? Are there any types of transactions that you might be more inclined to avoid?

4. After reading this chapter, will your future behavior as a businessperson change? What specific steps will you be most careful to take to protect your interests?

5. A perfected security interest is far from perfect. We examined several exceptions to normal perfection rules involving BIOCs, consumer goods, and so on. Are the exceptions reasonable? Should the UCC change to give the holder of a perfected interest absolute rights against absolutely everyone else?

Agency and Employment Law

AGENCY

Lauren Brenner had a great idea for a new kind of fitness studio. Called Pure Power Boot Camp, Brenner's gym was modeled on a U.S. Marine training facility, with an indoor obstacle course, camouflage colors, and a rubber floor designed to look like dirt. Participants (called "recruits") went through a training program ("tour of duty"), which was run by retired marines ("drill instructors").

Brenner hired Ruben Belliard and Alexander Fell as drill instructors. But the two men soon went to war against her: They decided to start their own copycat gym, which was to be called Warrior Fitness Boot Camp. To this end, they rented a nearby gym space. Belliard stole copies of Pure Power's confidential customer list, business plan, and operations manuals. The two men invited Pure Power's clients to a cocktail party to announce Warrior Fitness's launch.

Then one day at Pure Power, Fell openly defied Brenner's instructions, screaming at her that he dared her to fire him. She had little choice but to do so. Two weeks later, Belliard quit without notice, intentionally leaving Brenner with only one drill instructor. Two months later, Fell and Belliard opened Warrior Fitness.

© Creative Travel Projects/Shutterstock.com

> **But the two men soon went to war against her.**

Thus far, this book has primarily dealt with issues of individual responsibility: What happens if *you* knock someone down or *you* sign an agreement? Agency law, on the other hand, is concerned with your responsibility for the actions of others and their obligations to you. What happens if your agent assaults someone or signs a contract in your name? Or tries to take all of your clients? Hiring other people presents a significant trade-off: You can accomplish a great deal more, but your risks increase immensely.

The *Pure Power* case highlights a common agency issue: If your employees decide to leave for greener pastures, what obligation do they owe you in that period before they actually walk out the door? The court's opinion is later in the chapter.

17-1 CREATING AN AGENCY RELATIONSHIP

In an agency relationship, someone (the agent) agrees to perform a task for, and under the control of, someone else (the principal).[1] **To create an agency relationship, there must be:**

- A **principal** and

- An **agent**

- Who mutually consent that the agent will act on behalf of the principal and

- Be subject to the principal's control,

- Thereby creating a fiduciary relationship.[2]

17-1a Consent

To establish consent, the principal must ask the agent to do something, and the agent must agree. In the most straightforward example, you ask a neighbor to walk your dog, and she agrees. Matters were more complicated when Steven James met some friends one evening at a restaurant. After leaving the restaurant, he sped down a highway and crashed into a car that had stalled on the roadway, thereby killing the driver. In a misguided attempt to help his client, James's lawyer took him to the local hospital for a blood test. Unfortunately, the test confirmed that James had indeed been drunk at the time of the accident. The lawyer argued that the blood test was protected by the client-attorney privilege because the hospital had been his agent and therefore a member of the defense team. The court disagreed, however, holding that the hospital employees were not agents for the lawyer because they had not consented to act in that role. James was convicted of murder in the first degree by reason of extreme atrocity or cruelty.[3]

17-1b Control

Principals are liable for an agent's acts because they exercise control over that person. If principals direct their agents to commit an act, it seems fair to hold the principal liable when that act causes harm. How would you apply that rule to the following situation?

William Stanford was an employee of the Agency for International Development. While travelling to Pakistan, his plane was hijacked and taken to Iran, where he was killed. Stanford had originally purchased a ticket on Northwest Airlines but had traded it in for a seat on Kuwait Airways (KA). The airlines had an agreement permitting passengers to

Principal

In an agency relationship, the person for whom an agent is acting

Agent

In an agency relationship, the person who is acting on behalf of a principal

---

[1]The word "principal" is always used when referring to a person. "Principle," on the other hand, refers to a fundamental idea.

[2]§1.01 of the Restatement (Third) of Agency (2006), prepared by the American Law Institute.

[3]Commonwealth v. James, 427 Mass. 312 (S.J.C. 1998).

exchange tickets from one to another. Stanford's widow sued Northwest on the theory that KA was Northwest's agent. The court found, however, that no agency relationship existed because Northwest had no *control* over KA.[4] Northwest did not tell KA how to fly planes or handle terrorists; therefore, it should not be liable when KA made fatal errors.

17-1c Fiduciary Relationship

Fiduciary relationship
One of trust in which a trustee acts for the benefit of the beneficiary, always putting the interests of the beneficiary before his own

A **fiduciary relationship** is one of trust: A trustee acts for the benefit of the beneficiary, always putting the interests of the beneficiary before his own. The beneficiary places special confidence in the fiduciary who, in turn, is obligated to act in good faith and candor, doing what is best for the beneficiary. **Agents have a fiduciary duty to their principals.** Suppose that you hire a real estate agent to help you find a house. She shows you a great house but does not reveal to you the brutal murder that took place there because she is afraid that you would not buy it and she would not receive a commission. She has violated her fiduciary duty to put your interests first.

17-2 DUTIES OF AGENTS TO PRINCIPALS

17-2a Duty of Loyalty

An agent has a fiduciary duty to act loyally for the principal's benefit in all matters connected with the agency relationship.[5] As the following case reveals, the two employees in the opening scenario violated their fiduciary duty to Brenner.

PURE POWER BOOT CAMP, INC. v. WARRIOR FITNESS BOOT CAMP, LLC

813 F. Supp. 2d 489
United States District Court for the Southern District of New York, 2011

CASE SUMMARY

Facts: Based on the facts in the opening scenario, Brenner filed suit against Belliard and Fell, alleging that they had violated their duty of loyalty to her.

Issue: *Did Belliard and Fell violate their duty of loyalty to Brenner?*

Decision: Yes, they did.

Reasoning: In all employment relationships, whether contractual or at-will, an agent owes his employer the utmost good faith and loyalty. Although these employees had the right to make preparations to compete with their employer, even while still working for her, they did not

have the right to do so at her expense, or use her resources, time, facilities, or confidential information. Whether or not they had signed an agreement not to compete, they could not, while still employed by her, solicit her clients, copy her business records for their own use, or actively divert her business for their own personal benefit. And, even in the absence of a trade secret agreement, they were not permitted to copy her client list.

Belliard and Fell's ongoing and deliberate conduct, taking place over the course of several months, constituted a clear breach of the duty of loyalty owed by employees. They must pay her damages of $245,000.

---

[4]Stanford v. Kuwait Airways Corp., 648 F. Supp. 1158 (S.D.N.Y. 1986).
[5]Restatement (Third) of Agency §8.01.

Ethics This case provides an example of agents who competed against their principal. You may well be in this situation at some point in your own life. As we saw in the Ethics chapter, rationalization is a common, and dangerous, trap. Imagine how Belliard and Fell might have rationalized their wrongdoing. What steps can you take to ensure that you do not fall prey to this same ethics trap?

Outside Benefits

An agent may not receive profits unless the principal knows and approves. Suppose that Hope is an employee of the agency Big Egos and Talents, Inc. (BEAT). She has been representing Robert Downey Jr. in his latest movie negotiations.[6] Downey often drives her to meetings in his new Aston Martin. He is so thrilled that she has arranged for him to star in the new movie *Little Men* that he buys her an Aston Martin. Can Hope keep this generous gift? Only with BEAT's permission. She must tell BEAT about the gift; the company may then take the vehicle itself or allow her to keep it.

Confidential Information

The ability to keep secrets is important in any relationship, but especially a fiduciary relationship. **Agents can neither disclose nor use for their own benefit any confidential information they acquire during their agency.** After the Beatles fired their business manager, he passed on to a competitor confidential information about the royalties on a George Harrison song. The court held that the agent's obligation to keep information confidential continued even after the agency relationship ended.[7]

Competition with the Principal

Agents are not allowed to compete with their principal in any matter within the scope of the agency business. Michael Jackson bought the copyright to many of the Beatles' songs. If, before he made that purchase, one of his employees had knowingly bought the songs instead, that employee would have violated her duty to Jackson. Once the agency relationship ends, however, so does the rule against competition. After the employee's job with Jackson ended, she could have bid against him for the Beatles' songs.

Conflict of Interest Between Two Principals

Unless otherwise agreed, an agent may not act for two principals whose interests conflict. Suppose Travis represents both director Steven Spielberg and actress Jennifer Lawrence. Spielberg is casting the title role in his new movie, *Nancy Drew: Girl Detective*, a role that Lawrence covets. Travis cannot represent these two clients when they are negotiating with each other unless they both know about the conflict and agree to ignore it.

Secretly Dealing with the Principal

If a principal hires an agent to arrange a transaction, the agent may not become a party to the transaction without the principal's permission. Suppose that Spielberg hired Trang to read new scripts for him. Unbeknownst to Spielberg, Trang has written her own script. She may not sell it to him without revealing that she wrote it herself. Spielberg may be perfectly

---

[6]Do not be confused by the fact that Hope works as an agent for movie stars. As an employee of BEAT, her duty is to the company. She is an agent of BEAT, and BEAT works for the celebrities.
[7]ABKCO Music, Inc. v. Harrisongs Music, Ltd., 722 F.2d 988 (2d Cir.1983).

happy to buy Trang's script, but he has the right, as her principal, to know that she is the person selling it.

Appropriate Behavior

An agent may not engage in inappropriate behavior that reflects badly on the principal. This rule applies even to *off-duty* conduct. While off-duty (but still in uniform), a coed trio of flight attendants went wild at a hotel bar in London. They kissed and caressed each other, showed off their underwear, and poured alcohol down their trousers. The airline fired two of the employees and gave a warning letter to the third.

17-2b Other Duties of an Agent

Before Taylor left for a five-week trip to Antarctica, he hired Claudia to rent out his vacation house. Claudia neither listed his house on the Multiple Listing Service, used by all the area brokers, nor posted it online, but when the Fords contacted her looking for rental housing, she did show them Taylor's place. They offered to rent it for $750 per month.

Claudia emailed Taylor in Antarctica to tell him. He responded that he would not accept less than $850 a month, which Claudia thought the Fords would be willing to pay. He told Claudia to email him back if there was any problem. The Fords decided that they would go no higher than $800 a month. Although Taylor had told Claudia that he had no cell phone service in Antarctica, she texted him the Fords' counteroffer. Taylor never received it, so he never responded. When the Fords pressed Claudia for an answer, she said she could not get in touch with Taylor. Not until Taylor returned home did he learn that the Fords had rented another house. Did Claudia violate any of the duties that agents owe to their principals?

Duty to Obey Instructions

An agent must obey her principal's instructions unless the principal directs her to behave illegally or unethically. Taylor instructed Claudia to email him if the Fords rejected the offer. When Claudia failed to do so, she violated this duty.

Duty of Care

An agent has a duty to act with reasonable care. In other words, an agent must act as a reasonable person would, under the circumstances. A reasonable person would not have texted Taylor while he was in Antarctica, knowing that he did not have cell phone service.

Duty to Provide Information

An agent has a duty to provide the principal with all information in her possession that she has reason to believe the principal wants to know. She also has a duty to provide accurate information. Claudia knew that the Fords had counteroffered for $800 a month. She had a duty to pass this information on to Taylor.

17-2c Principal's Remedies when the Agent Breaches a Duty

A principal has three potential remedies when an agent breaches her duty:

1. **Damages**. The principal can recover from the agent any damages the breach has caused. Thus, if Taylor can rent his house for only $600 a month instead of the $800 the Fords offered, Claudia would be liable for $2,400—$200 a month for one year.

2. **Profits**. If an agent breaches the duty of loyalty, he must turn over to the principal any profits he has earned as a result of his wrongdoing.

3. **Rescission.** If the agent has violated her duty of loyalty, the principal may rescind the transaction. When Trang sold a script to her principal, Steven Spielberg, without telling him that she was the author, she violated her duty of loyalty. Spielberg could rescind the contract to buy the script.

17-3 DUTIES OF PRINCIPALS TO AGENTS

The principal must (1) pay the agent as required by the agreement, (2) reimburse the agent for reasonable expenses, and (3) cooperate with the agent in performing agency tasks. The respective duties of agents and principals can be summarized as follows:

Duties of Agents to Principals	Duty of Principals to Agents
Duty of loyalty	Duty to pay as provided by the agreement
Duty to obey instructions	Duty to reimburse reasonable expenses
Duty of care	Duty to cooperate with the agent
Duty to provide information	

17-4 TERMINATING AN AGENCY RELATIONSHIP

Here are the options for ending an agency relationship:

- **Term agreement.** The principal and agent can agree in advance how long their relationship will last. Alexandra hires Nicholas to help her purchase guitars previously owned by rock stars. If they agree that the relationship will last two years, they have a term agreement.

- **Achieving a purpose.** The principal and agent can agree that the agency relationship will terminate when the principal's goals have been achieved. Alexandra and Nicholas might agree that their relationship will end when Alexandra has purchased 10 guitars.

- **Mutual agreement.** No matter what the principal and agent agree at the start, they can always change their minds later on, so long as the change is mutual. If Nicholas and Alexandra originally agree to a two-year term, but Nicholas decides he wants to go back to business school and Alexandra runs out of money after only one year, they can decide together to terminate the agency.

- **Agency at will.** If they make no agreement in advance about the term of the agreement, either principal or agent can terminate at any time.

- **Wrongful termination.** An agency relationship is a personal relationship. Hiring an agent is not like buying a book. You might not care which copy of the book you buy, but you do care which agent you hire. If an agency relationship is not working out, the courts

> Hiring an agent is not like buying a book. You might not care which copy of the book you buy, but you do care which agent you hire.

will not force the agent and principal to stay together. Either party always has the *power* to terminate. They may not, however, have the *right*. If one party's departure from the agency relationship violates the agreement and causes harm to the other party, the wrongful party must pay damages. Nonetheless, he will be permitted to leave. If Nicholas has agreed to work for Alexandra for two years but he wants to leave after one, he can leave, provided he pays Alexandra the cost of hiring and training a replacement.

- **Inability to perform required duties.** The agency agreement also terminates if either the principal or the agent becomes unable to perform his required duties. For example, if either the principal or the agent dies, the agency agreement automatically terminates. And the agreement terminates if the activity becomes illegal. Zach hired Andrew to act as his agent importing goods from Russia. But then, after Russia attacked Ukraine, the U.S. government imposed sanctions that prohibited the importation of these items. The agency agreement automatically ended.

17-5 LIABILITY TO THIRD PARTIES

Although an agent can greatly increase his principal's ability to accomplish her goals, an agency relationship also dramatically increases the risk of legal liability to third parties.

17-5a Principal's Liability for Contracts

The principal is liable for the acts and statements of his agent if the agent had authority. In other words, the principal is as responsible as if he had performed those acts himself. **There are three types of authority: express, implied, and apparent.**

Express Authority

Express authority
Either by words or conduct, the principal grants an agent permission to act.

The principal grants express authority by words or conduct that, reasonably interpreted, cause the agent to believe the principal desires her to act on the principal's account. In other words, the principal asks the agent to do something and the agent does it. Craig calls his stockbroker, Alice, and asks her to buy 100 shares of Banshee Corp. for his account. She has *express authority* to carry out this transaction.

Implied Authority

Implied authority
The agent has authority to perform acts that are reasonably necessary to accomplish an authorized transaction, even if the principal does not specify them.

Unless otherwise agreed, authority to conduct a transaction includes authority to perform acts that are reasonably necessary to accomplish it. This is **implied authority**. The principal does not have to micromanage the agent. David has recently inherited a house from his grandmother. He hires Nell to auction off the house and its contents. She hires an auctioneer, advertises the event, rents a tent, and generally does everything necessary to conduct a successful auction. After withholding her expenses, she sends the tidy balance to David. Totally outraged, he calls her on the phone, "How dare you hire an auctioneer and rent a tent? I never gave you permission! I *refuse* to pay these expenses!"

David is wrong. A principal almost never gives an agent absolutely complete instructions. Unless some authority is implied, David would have had to say, "Open the car door, get in, put the key in the ignition, drive to the store, buy stickers, mark an auction number on each sticker …" and so forth. To solve this problem, the law assumes that the agent has authority to do anything that is reasonably necessary to accomplish her task.

Apparent Authority

Apparent authority
A principal does something to make an innocent third party believe that an agent is acting with the principal's authority, even though the agent is not authorized.

A principal can be liable for the acts of an agent who is not, in fact, acting with authority if the *principal's* conduct causes a third party reasonably to believe that the agent is authorized. This is **apparent authority**. Because the principal has done something to make an innocent third party *believe* the agent is authorized, the principal is every bit as liable to the third party as if the agent did have authority.

Two stockbrokers sold fraudulent stock out of their offices at a legitimate brokerage house, using firm email accounts and making presentations to investors in the company's conference rooms. Although the two brokers do not have *actual* or *implied* authority to sell the fraudulent stock, their employer is nonetheless liable on the grounds that the brokers *appeared* to have authority. Of course, the company has the right to recover from the two brokers in the unlikely event that they have assets.

17-5b Agent's Liability for Contracts

The agent's liability on a contract depends upon how much the third party knows about the principal. Disclosure is the agent's best protection against liability.

Fully Disclosed Principal

An agent is not liable for any contracts she makes on behalf of a *fully* disclosed principal. A principal is fully disclosed if the third party knows of his *existence* and his *identity*. Augusta acts as agent for Parker when he buys Tracey's prize-winning show horse. Tracey does not know Parker, but she figures any friend of Augusta's must be okay. She figures wrong—Parker is a charming deadbeat. He injures Tracey's horse, fails to pay the full contract price, and promptly disappears. Tracey angrily demands that Augusta make good on Parker's debt. Unfortunately for Tracey, Parker was a fully disclosed principal—Tracey knew of his *existence* and his *identity*. Augusta is not liable because Tracey knew who the principal was and could have investigated him. Tracey's only recourse is against the principal, Parker (wherever he may be).

Unidentified Principal

In the case of an unidentified principal, the third party can recover from either the agent or the principal. A principal is unidentified if the third party knew of his *existence* but not his *identity*. Suppose Augusta had simply said, "I have a friend who is interested in buying your champion." Parker is an unidentified principal because Tracey knows only that he exists, not who he is. She cannot investigate him because she does not know his name. Tracey relies solely on what she is able to learn from the agent, Augusta. Both Augusta and Parker are **jointly and severally liable** to Tracey. Thus Tracey can recover from either or both of them. She cannot, however, recover more than the total that she is owed: If her damages are $100,000, she can recover that amount from either Parker or Augusta, or partial amounts from both, but in no event more than $100,000.

Jointly and severally liable
All members of a group are liable. They can be sued as a group, or any one of them can be sued individually for the full amount owed. But the plaintiff cannot recover more than the total she is owed.

Undisclosed Principal

In the case of an *undisclosed* principal, the third party can recover from either the agent or the principal. A principal is undisclosed if the third party did not know of his existence. Suppose that Augusta simply asks to buy the horse herself, without mentioning that she is purchasing it for Parker. In this case, Parker is an undisclosed principal because Tracey does not know that Augusta is acting for someone else. Both Parker and Augusta are jointly and severally liable. As Exhibit 17.1 illustrates, the principal is always liable, but the agent is not unless the principal's identity is a mystery.

It is easy to understand why the principal and agent are liable on these contracts, but what about the third party? Is it fair for her to be liable on a contract if she does not even know the identity of the principal? The courts have found these contracts valid for reasons of commercial necessity. For instance, the United Nations headquarters in New York City is located on land purchased secretly. If sellers had known that the same person was purchasing this large block of land, the price of the real estate would have skyrocketed.

17-5c Principal's Liability for Torts

The general rule of tort liability is this: **An employer is liable for a physical tort committed by an employee acting within the scope of employment and a nonphysical tort of an employee acting with authority.** This principle of liability is called *respondeat superior,* which

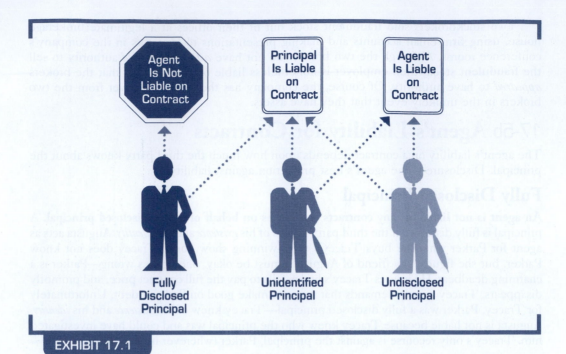

EXHIBIT 17.1

is a Latin phrase meaning "let the master answer." Under the theory of *respondeat superior*, the employer (i.e., the principal) is liable for misbehavior by the employee (that is, the agent) whether or not the employer was at fault. Indeed, the employer may be liable even if he *forbade* or tried to *prevent* the employee from misbehaving. This rule sounds harsh. But the theory is that, because the principal controls the agent, he should be able to *prevent* misbehavior. If he cannot prevent it, at least he can *insure* against the risks. Furthermore, the principal may have deeper pockets than the agent or the injured third party and thus be better able to *afford* the cost of the agent's misbehavior.

To apply the principle of *respondeat superior*, it is important to understand these terms: employee, scope of employment, nonphysical tort, and acting with authority.

Employee

There are two kinds of agents: (1) employees and (2) independent contractors. **Generally, a principal *is* liable for the physical torts of an employee but generally is *not* liable for the physical torts of an independent contractor.**

Employee or Independent Contractor?   The more control the principal has over an agent, the more likely that the agent will be considered an employee. **Therefore, when determining if agents are employees or independent contractors, courts consider whether:**

- The principal supervises details of the work.
- The principal supplies the tools and place of work.
- The agents work full time for the principal.
- The agents receive a salary or hourly wages, not a fixed price for the job.
- The work is part of the regular business of the principal.
- The principal and agents believe they have an employer-employee relationship.
- The principal is in business.

Ethics For employers, the advantages of independent contractors extend beyond agency law. Contractors cost substantially less in payroll taxes and benefits and require less paperwork. Also, companies with fewer than 50 employees are not required to provide health insurance under the Affordable Care Act.

To increase tax revenue, the federal government is aggressively auditing employers to ensure that workers are being properly classified as employees. Microsoft paid almost $100 million to settle such a case. But even apart from the legal issues, employees who are inaccurately classified as independent contractors suffer from a large tear in their financial safety net, with unemployment, social security, and health care benefits at risk. What ethical obligation do employers have? What would Mill and Kant say?

Negligent Hiring. Although, as we have seen, principals are generally not liable for the physical torts of an independent contractor, there is one exception to this rule: **A principal is liable for the physical torts of an independent contractor *if* the principal has been negligent in hiring or supervising her.** Would the car service Uber be liable if one of its drivers (an independent contractor) assaulted a passenger? Only if Uber had been negligent in hiring or supervising the driver.

Exhibit 17.2 illustrates the difference in liability between an employee and an independent contractor.

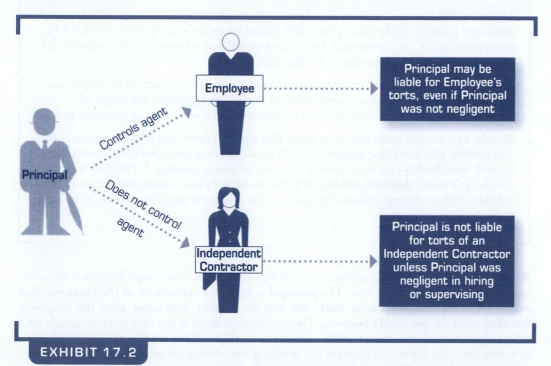

EXHIBIT 17.2

Scope of Employment

You remember that: An employer is liable for a physical tort committed by an employee acting within the scope of employment. **An employee is acting within the scope of employment if the act:**

- Is one that employees are generally responsible for,
- Takes place during hours that the employee is generally employed,
- Is part of the principal's business,

- Is similar to the one the principal authorized,

- Is one for which the principal supplied the tools, and

- Is not seriously criminal.

If an employee leaves a pool of water on the floor of a store and a customer slips and falls, the employer is liable. But if the same employee leaves water on his own kitchen floor and a friend falls, the employer is not liable because the employee is not acting within the scope of employment.

Scope of employment cases raise two major issues: authorization and abandonment.

Authorization.   **An act is within the scope of employment, even if expressly forbidden, if it is of the same general nature as that authorized or if it is incidental to the conduct authorized.** Although Jane has often told Hank not to speed when driving the delivery van, Hank ignores her instructions and plows into Bernadette. Hank was authorized to drive the van but not to speed. However, his speeding was of the same general nature as the authorized act, so Jane is liable to Bernadette.

EXAM Strategy

Question: While on a business trip, Trevor went sightseeing on his day off. Although company policy forbade talking on a cell phone while driving, Trevor answered his cell phone in his car. Distracted, he crashed into Olivia's house, causing substantial damage. Was his employer liable for the damage?

Strategy: Whenever a case involves a company's liability for the acts of an employee, begin by asking if *respondeat superior* applies. Was he acting within the scope of employment? Does it matter that it was his day off and he was violating company policy?

Result: In a similar case, the court ruled that the employer was liable because it is foreseeable that travelling employees will go sightseeing and, therefore, companies should include this potential liability as a cost of doing business.[8] The fact that the employer's policy prohibits talking on a cell phone does not protect the company from liability if an employee violates that policy. The employer should not have hired such a disobedient worker.

Abandonment.   This Exam Strategy also illustrates the second major issue in a scope-of-employment case: abandonment. **The principal is liable for the actions of the employee that occur while the employee is at work, but not for actions that occur after the employee has *abandoned* the principal's business.** The employer is liable if the employee is simply on a *detour* from company business, but the employer is not liable if the employee is on a *frolic of his own.* Suppose that Hank, the delivery van driver, speeds during his afternoon commute home. An employee is generally not acting within the scope of his employment when he commutes to and from work, so his principal, Jane, is not liable. On the other hand, if Hank stops at the Burger Box drive-in window en route to making a delivery, Jane is liable when he crashes into Anna on the way out of the parking lot because this time, he is simply making a detour. In the prior Exam Strategy, Trevor's employer was liable despite the fact that he was on his day off because he was on a business trip for the company. He would not have been in that place doing that thing if not for being on company business.

---

[8]*Potter v. Shaw,* 2004 Mass. App. LEXIS 61 (Mass. App. Ct. 2004).

Was the employee in the following case acting within the scope of his employment while driving to work? You be the judge.

You be the Judge

Facts: Staff Sergeant William E. Dreyer was a recruiter for the United States Marine Corps, working 16 to 18 hours a day, seven days a week. He was required to ask permission before using his

ZANKEL V. UNITED STATES OF AMERICA

2008 U.S. Dist. LEXIS 23655, 2008 WL 828032
United States District Court for the Western District
of Pennsylvania, 2008

Marine Corps car to commute to or from work. Late one night, Dreyer's personal car would not start, so he drove his government car home. He did not ask permission because he thought it was too late to call his boss. Dreyer believed that, had he called, his boss would have said it was okay because he had given approval in similar situations in the past. Driving to work in the government car at 6:40 the next morning on the way to an early training session, Dreyer struck and killed 12-year-old Justin Zankel.

You Be the Judge: *Was Dreyer acting within the scope of his employment when he killed Zankel? Is the government liable?*

Argument for the Zankels: At the time of the accident, Dreyer was driving a government vehicle. Although he had not requested permission to drive the car, if he had done so, permission certainly would have been granted.

Moreover, even if Dreyer was not authorized to drive the Marine Corps car, the government is still liable because his activity was of the same general nature as that authorized and it was incidental to the conduct authorized. Also, Dreyer was on the road early so that he could attend a required training session. The Marine Corps must bear responsibility for this tragic accident.

Argument for the United States: The government had a clear policy stating that recruiters were not authorized to drive a government car without first requesting permission. Dreyer had not done so.

Moreover, it is well established that an employee commuting to and from work is not within the scope of employment. If Dreyer had been driving from one recruiting effort to another, that would be a different story. But in this case, he had not yet started work for the Marine Corps, and therefore the government is not liable.

Intentional Torts

A principal is *not* liable for the *intentional* physical torts of an employee unless (1) the employee intended to serve some purpose of the employer or (2) the employer was negligent in hiring or supervising this employee. A Catholic priest engaged in a sexual relationship with one of his students. In response, the bishop in charge transferred the priest to a parish church. In this new job, the priest sexually abused a child. This child sued the Church, alleging that it was liable for the priest's intentional tort. The court held that the sexual abuse of a child did not serve any purpose of the Church—indeed, it was harmful to the Church. Nor had the Church been negligent in hiring the priest because when it hired him, it had no reason to believe that he was likely to commit this tort. However, the Church was liable for the negligence of the bishop in supervising the priest.[9]

Nonphysical Torts

So far, we have seen the rules on *physical* torts. A **nonphysical tort** is one that harms only reputation, feelings, or wallet. **Nonphysical torts (whether intentional or unintentional) are treated like a contract claim: The principal is liable only if the employee acted with express,**

Nonphysical tort
A civil wrong that harms only reputation, feelings, or wallet

---

[9]Doe v. Liberatore, 478 F. Supp. 2d 742 (M.D. Pa. 2007).

implied, or apparent authority. Suppose that Dwayne buys a house insurance policy from Andy, who is an agent of the Balls of Fire Insurance Company. Andy throws away Dwayne's policy and pockets his premiums. When Dwayne's house burns down, Balls of Fire is liable because Andy was acting with apparent authority.

EXAM Strategy

Question: Daisy was the founder of an Internet start-up company. Mac was her driver. One day, after he had dropped her at a board meeting, he went to the car wash. There, he told an attractive woman that he worked for a money management firm. She gave him money to invest. He was so excited that, on the way out of the car wash, he hit another customer's expensive car. Who is liable for Mac's misdeeds?

Strategy: In determining a principal's liability, begin by figuring out whether the agent has committed a physical or nonphysical tort. Remember that the principal is liable for physical torts within the scope of employment, but for nonphysical torts, she is liable only if the employee acted with authority.

Result: In this case, Daisy is liable for the damage to the car because that was a physical tort within the scope of employment. But she is not liable for the investment money because Mac did not have authority from her to take those funds.

17-5d Agent's Liability for Torts

The focus of the prior section was on the *principal's* liability for the agent's torts. But it is important to remember that **agents are always liable for their own torts.** Agents who commit torts are personally responsible whether or not their principal is also liable. Even if the tort was committed to benefit the principal, the agent is still liable.

This rule makes obvious sense. If the agent was not liable, he would have little incentive to be careful. Imagine Hank driving his delivery van for Jane. If he was not personally liable for his own torts, he might think, "If I drive fast enough, I can make it through that light even though it just turned red. And if I don't, what the heck, it'll be Jane's problem, not mine." Agents, as a rule, may have fewer assets than their principal, but it is important that their personal assets be at risk in the event of their negligent behavior.

If the agent and principal are *both* liable, which does the injured third party sue? The principal and the agent are *jointly and severally liable*, which means, as we have seen, that the injured third party can sue either one or both, as she chooses. If she recovers from the principal, he can sue the agent.

Chapter Conclusion

Agency is an area of the law that affects us all because each of us has been and will continue to be both an agent and a principal many times in our lives.

EXAM REVIEW

1. **CREATING AN AGENCY RELATIONSHIP** To create an agency relationship, there must be: A principal and an agent who mutually consent that the agent will act on behalf of the principal and be subject to the principal's control, thereby creating a fiduciary relationship.

2. **AN AGENT'S DUTIES TO THE PRINCIPAL** An agent owes these duties to the principal: duty of loyalty, duty to obey instructions, duty of care, and duty to provide information.

   Question: When Bess signed up for a fancy trip, she emphasized to her travel agent that she was seriously allergic to lead paint, and therefore, she could stay only in new hotels. The agent assumed that Hotel Augustine would be fine because it had been renovated at a time after lead paint was banned. However, the renovation had not removed all the lead paint, and Bess became ill after staying at the hotel.

   Strategy: An agent has four duties. Which of these might the travel agent have violated? (See the "Result" at the end of this section.)

3. **THE PRINCIPAL'S REMEDIES IN THE EVENT OF A BREACH** The principal has three potential remedies when the agent breaches her duty: recovery of damages the breach has caused, recovery of any profits earned by the agent from the breach, and rescission of any transaction with the agent.

4. **THE PRINCIPAL'S DUTIES TO THE AGENT** The principal must (1) pay the agent as required by the agreement, (2) reimburse the agent for reasonable expenses, and (3) cooperate with the agent in performing agency tasks.

5. **POWER AND RIGHT TO TERMINATE** Both the agent and the principal have the power to terminate an agency relationship, but they may not have the right. If the termination violates the agency agreement and causes harm to the other party, the wrongful party must pay damages.

6. **AUTOMATIC TERMINATION** An agency relationship automatically terminates if the principal or agent no longer can perform the required duties or if the activity becomes illegal.

7. **A PRINCIPAL'S LIABILITY FOR CONTRACTS** A principal is liable for the contracts of the agent if the agent has express, implied, or apparent authority.

8. **EXPRESS AUTHORITY** The principal grants express authority by words or conduct that, reasonably interpreted, cause the agent to believe that the principal desires her to act on the principal's account.

9. **IMPLIED AUTHORITY**   Implied authority includes authority to perform acts that are reasonably necessary to accomplish the designated task.

10. **APPARENT AUTHORITY**   A principal can be liable for the acts of an agent who is not, in fact, acting with authority if the principal's conduct causes a third party reasonably to believe that the agent is authorized.

EXAM Strategy

Question: Dr. James Leonard wrote Dr. Edward Jacobson to offer him a position at a hospital. In the letter, Leonard stated that this appointment would have to be approved by the promotion committee. Jacobson believed that the promotion committee acted only as a "rubber stamp" and its approval was certain. Jacobson accepted the offer, sold his house, and quit his old job. Two weeks later, the promotion committee voted against Jacobson, and the offer was rescinded. Did Leonard have apparent authority?

Strategy: In cases of apparent authority, begin by asking what the principal did to make the third party believe that the agent was authorized. Did the hospital do anything? (See the "Result" at the end of this section.)

11. **AN AGENT'S LIABILITY FOR A CONTRACT**   An agent is not liable for any contract she makes on behalf of a fully disclosed principal. The principal is liable. In the case of an unidentified or undisclosed principal, both the agent and the principal are liable on the contract.

12. **A PRINCIPAL'S LIABILITY FOR TORTS**   An employer is liable for a physical tort committed by an employee acting within the scope of employment and a nonphysical tort of an employee acting with authority.

13. **INDEPENDENT CONTRACTOR**   The principal is liable for the torts of an independent contractor if the principal has been negligent in hiring or supervising her.

14. **INTENTIONAL TORTS**   A principal is not liable for the intentional physical torts of an employee unless (1) the employee intended to serve some purpose of the employer or (2) the employer was negligent in hiring or supervising the employee.

15. **NONPHYSICAL TORTS**   A principal is liable for nonphysical torts of an employee (whether intentional or unintentional) only if the employee was acting with express, implied, or apparent authority.

16. **AGENT'S LIABILITY FOR TORTS**   Agents are always liable for their own torts.

2. Result: From this set of facts, there is no reason to believe that the travel agent was disloyal, disobeyed instructions, or failed to provide information. But the agent did violate his duty of care when choosing hotels for Bess. He should have made sure that there was no lead paint.

10. Result: No. Indeed, Leonard had told Jacobson that he did not have authority. If Jacobson chose to believe otherwise, that was his problem.

MATCHING QUESTIONS

Match the following terms with their definitions:

___A. Term agreement
___B. Apparent authority
___C. Agency at will
___D. Express authority
___E. Implied authority

1. When two parties make no agreement in advance about the duration of their agreement
2. When an agent has authority to perform acts that are necessary to accomplish an assignment
3. When two parties agree in advance on the duration of their agreement
4. When behavior by a principal convinces a third party that the agent is authorized, even though she is not
5. When a principal gives explicit instructions to an agent

TRUE/FALSE QUESTIONS

Circle true or false:

1. T F A principal is always liable on a contract, whether he is fully disclosed, unidentified, or undisclosed.
2. T F When a contract goes wrong, a third party can always recover damages from the agent, whether the principal is fully disclosed, unidentified, or undisclosed.
3. T F An agent may receive profits from an agency relationship even if the principal does not know about the profits, so long as the principal is not harmed.
4. T F An agent may never act for two principals whose interests conflict.
5. T F An agent has a duty to provide the principal with all information in her possession that she has reason to believe the principal wants to know, even if he does not specifically ask for it.

MULTIPLE-CHOICE QUESTIONS

1. Someone painting the outside of a building you own crashed through a window, injuring a visiting executive. Which of the following questions would your lawyer *not* need to ask to determine if the painter was your employee?
   (a) Did the painter work full time for you?
   (b) Had you checked the painter's references?
   (c) Was the painter paid by the hour or by the job?
   (d) Were you in the painting business?
   (e) Did the painter consider herself your employee?

2. Which of the following duties does an agent *not* owe to his principal?
   (a) Duty of loyalty
   (b) Duty to obey instructions
   (c) Duty to reimburse
   (d) Duty of care
   (e) Duty to provide information

3. Finn learns that, despite his stellar record, he is being paid less than other salespeople at Barry Co. So he decides to start his own company. During his last month on the Barry payroll, he tells all of his clients about his new business. He also tells them that Barry is a great company, but his fees will be lower. After he opens the doors of his new business, most of his former clients come with him. Is Finn liable to Barry?
   (a) No, because he has not been disloyal to Barry—he praised the company.
   (b) No, because Barry was underpaying him.
   (c) No, because his clients have the right to hire whichever company they choose.
   (d) Yes, Finn has violated his duty of loyalty to Barry.

4. Kurt asked his car mechanic, Quinn, for help in buying a used car. Quinn recommends a Ford Focus that she has been taking care of its whole life. Quinn was working for the seller. Which of the following statements is true?
   (a) Quinn must pay Kurt the amount of money she received from the Ford's prior owner.
   (b) After buying the car, Kurt finds out that it needs $1,000 in repairs. He can recover that amount from Quinn, but only if Quinn knew about the needed repairs before Kurt bought the car.
   (c) Kurt cannot recover anything because Quinn had no obligation to reveal her relationship with the car's seller.
   (d) Kurt cannot recover anything because he had not paid Quinn for her help.

5. Figgins is the dean of a college. He appointed Sue acting dean while he was out of the country and posted a message on the college website announcing that she was authorized to act in his place. He also told Sue privately that she did not have the right to make admissions decisions. While Figgins was gone, Sue overruled the admissions committee to admit the child of a wealthy alumnus. Does the child have the right to attend this college?
   (a) No, because Sue was not authorized to admit him.
   (b) No, because Figgins was an unidentified principal.
   (c) Yes, because Figgins was a fully disclosed principal.
   (d) Yes, because Sue had apparent authority.

6. *CPA QUESTION* A principal will not be liable to a third party for a tort committed by an agent:
   (a) unless the principal instructed the agent to commit the tort.
   (b) unless the tort was committed within the scope of the agency relationship.
   (c) if the agency agreement limits the principal's liability for the agent's tort.
   (d) if the tort is also regarded as a criminal act.

CHAPTER 17 *Agency*   331

CASE QUESTIONS

1. An elementary school custodian hit a child who wrote graffiti on the wall. Is the school district liable for this intentional tort by its employee?

2. What if the custodian hit one of the schoolchildren for calling him a name? Is the school district liable?

3. A soldier was drinking at a training seminar. Although he was told to leave his car at the seminar, he disobeyed orders and drove to a nightclub. On the way to the club, he was in an accident. Is the military liable for the damage he caused?

4. One afternoon while visiting friends, tennis star Vitas Gerulaitis fell asleep in their pool house. A mechanic had improperly installed the swimming pool heater, which leaked carbon monoxide fumes into the house where he slept, killing him. His mother filed suit against the owners of the estate. On what theory would they be liable?

5. *YOU BE THE JUDGE* **WRITING PROBLEM** Sarah went to an auction at Christie's to bid on a tapestry for her employer, Fine Arts Gallery. The good news is that she purchased a Dufy tapestry for $77,000. The bad news is that it was not the one her employer had told her to buy. In the excitement of the auction, she forgot her instructions. Fine Art refused to pay, and Christie's filed suit. Is Fine Arts liable for the unauthorized act of its agent? **Argument for Christie's:** Christie's cannot possibly ascertain in each case the exact nature of a bidder's authority. Whether or not Sarah had actual authority, she certainly had apparent authority, and Fine Arts is liable. **Argument for Fine Arts:** Sarah was not authorized to purchase the Dufy tapestry, and therefore, Christie's must recover from her, not Fine Arts.

DISCUSSION QUESTIONS

1. **ETHICS** Mercedes has just begun work at Photobook.com. What a great place to work! Although the salary is not high, the company has fabulous perks. The dining room provides great food from 7 a.m. to midnight, five days a week. There is also a free laundry and dry-cleaning service. Mercedes's social life has never been better. She invites her friends over for Photobook meals and has their laundry done for free. And because her job requires her to be online all the time, she has plenty of opportunity to stay in touch with her friends by g-chatting, tweeting, and checking Facebook updates. However, she is shocked that one of her colleagues takes paper home from the office for his children to use at home. Are these employees behaving ethically?

2. Kevin was the manager of a radio station, WABC. A competing station lured him away. In his last month on the job at WABC, he notified two key on-air personalities that if they were to leave the station, he would not hold them to their non-compete agreements. What can WABC do?

3. Jesse worked as a buyer for the Vegetable Co. Rachel offered to sell Jesse 10 tons of tomatoes for the account of Vegetable. Jesse accepted the offer. Later, Jesse discovered that Rachel was an agent for Sylvester Co. Who is liable on this contract?

4. The Pharmaceutical Association holds an annual convention. At the convention, Brittany, who was president of the association, told Luke that

Research Corp. had a promising new cancer vaccine. Luke was so excited that he chartered a plane to fly to Research's headquarters. On the way, the plane crashed and Luke was killed. Is the Pharmaceutical Association liable for Luke's death?

5. Betsy has a two-year contract as a producer at Jackson Movie Studios. She produces a remake of the movie *Footloose*. Unfortunately, it bombs, and Jackson is so furious that he fires her on the weekend the movie opens. Does he have the power to do this?

CHAPTER 18

EMPLOYMENT LAW

© Creative Travel Projects/Shutterstock.com

"On the killing beds you were apt to be covered with blood, and it would freeze solid; if you leaned against a pillar, you would freeze to that, and if you put your hand upon the blade of your knife, you would run a chance of leaving your skin on it. The men would tie up their feet in newspapers and old sacks, and these would be soaked in blood and frozen, and then soaked again, and so on, until by nighttime a man would be walking on great lumps the size of the feet of an elephant. Now and then, when the bosses were not looking, you would see them plunging their feet and ankles into the steaming hot carcass of the steer.... The cruelest thing of all was that nearly all of them—all of those who used knives—were unable to wear gloves, and their arms would be white with frost and their hands would grow numb, and then of course there would be accidents."[1]

> **... you would see them plunging their feet and ankles into the steaming hot carcass of the steer.**

---

[1] From Upton Sinclair, *The Jungle* (New York: Bantam Books, 1981), p. 80 ; a 1906 novel about the meat-packing industry.

18-1 INTRODUCTION

For most of history, the concept of career planning was unknown. By and large, people were born into their jobs. Whatever their parents had been—landowner, soldier, farmer, servant, merchant, or beggar—they became, too. Few people expected that their lives would be better than their parents'. The primary English law of employment reflected this simpler time. Unless the employee had a contract that said otherwise, he was hired for a year at a time. This rule was designed to prevent injustice in a farming society. If an employee worked through harvest time, the landowner could not fire him in the winter. Likewise, a worker could not stay the winter and then leave for greener pastures in the spring.

In the eighteenth and nineteenth centuries, the Industrial Revolution profoundly altered the employment relationship. Many workers left the farms and villages for large factories in the city. Bosses no longer knew their workers personally, so they felt little responsibility toward them. Since employees could quit their factory jobs whenever they wanted, it was thought to be only fair for employers to have the same freedom to fire a worker. That was indeed the rule adopted by the courts: Unless workers had an explicit employment contract, they were employees at will. **An *employee at will* could be fired for a good reason, a bad reason, or no reason at all.** For nearly a century, this was the basic common law rule of employment.

However evenhanded this rule may have sounded in theory, in practice, it could lead to harsh results. As the opening scenario illustrates, the lives of factory workers were grim. It was not as if they could simply pack up and leave; conditions were no better elsewhere. Courts and legislatures began to recognize that individual workers were generally unable to negotiate fair contracts with powerful employers. Since the beginning of the twentieth century, employment law has changed dramatically. Now, the employment relationship is more strictly regulated by statutes and by the common law.

Note well, though: **In the absence of a specific legal exception, the rule in the United States is that an employee at will can be fired for any reason.** But, today there are many important exceptions to this rule. They take the form of statutes and common law. Many of the statutes discussed in this chapter were passed by Congress and therefore apply *nationally*. The common law, however, comes from state courts and only applies *locally*. We will look at a sampling of cases that illustrates national trends, even though the law may not be the same in every state.

This chapter covers three topics in employment law: (1) employment security, (2) workplace freedom and safety, and (3) financial protection. Chapter 19 covers employment discrimination.

18-2 EMPLOYMENT SECURITY

18-2a Family and Medical Leave Act

The Family and Medical Leave Act (FMLA) guarantees both men and women up to 12 weeks of unpaid leave each year for childbirth, adoption, or a serious health condition of their own or in their immediate family. A family member is a spouse, child, or parent—but not a sibling, grandchild, or in-law. An employee who takes a leave must be allowed to return to the same or an equivalent job with the same pay and benefits. The FMLA applies only to companies with at least 50 workers and to employees who have been with the company full time for at least a year, which means that only about 60 percent of workers are covered by this statute.

Kevin Knussman was the first person to win a lawsuit under the FMLA. While a Maryland state trooper, he requested eight weeks of leave to care for his pregnant wife, who was suffering severe complications. His boss granted only two weeks. After Knussman's daughter was born, his boss again denied leave, saying that "God made women to have babies." Knussman ultimately recovered $40,000.[2]

Ethics Although the FMLA offers important protections, the time off it provides is unpaid. Some cities require employers to provide paid family leave, but currently, only 11 percent of private sector employees are eligible for this type of time off. The federal government provides none for its own employees, not even for childbirth. The United States is the only advanced country that does not require employers to provide paid maternity leave. Should Congress modify the FMLA to require some period of paid leave for new mothers? If so, for how long? A few weeks while they recuperate from childbirth? Or a few months to care for the newborn? What about paternity leave, which many countries require? And how about workers who take FMLA leave to deal with a serious illness? Should they be paid?

18-2b Common Law Protections

The common law employment-at-will doctrine was created by the courts. Because that rule has sometimes led to absurdly unfair results, the courts have now created a major exception to the rule—wrongful discharge.

Wrongful Discharge: Violating Public Policy

Olga Monge was a schoolteacher in her native Costa Rica. After moving to New Hampshire, she attended college in the evenings to earn a U.S. teaching degree. At night, she worked at the Beebe Rubber Co. During the day, she cared for her husband and three children. When she applied for a better job at her plant, the foreman offered to promote her if she would be "nice" and go out on a date with him. When she refused, he assigned her to a lower-wage job, took away her overtime, made her clean the washrooms, and ridiculed her. Finally, she collapsed at work, and he fired her.

At that time, an employee at will could be fired for any reason. But the New Hampshire Supreme Court decided to change the rule. It held that Monge's firing was a wrongful discharge. Under the doctrine of **wrongful discharge** an employer cannot fire a worker for a reason that violates public policy.

Although the public policy rule varies from state to state, in essence, **an employee may not be fired for: refusing to violate the law, performing a legal duty, exercising a legal right, or supporting basic societal values.**

Refusing to Violate the Law.
Larry Downs went to Duke Hospital for surgery on his cleft palate. When he came out of the operating room, the doctor instructed a nurse, Marie Sides, to give Downs enough anesthetic to immobilize him. Sides refused because she thought the anesthetic was wrong for this patient. The doctor angrily administered the anesthetic himself. Shortly thereafter, Downs stopped breathing. Before the doctors could resuscitate him, he suffered permanent brain damage. When Downs's family sued the hospital, Sides was called to testify. A number of Duke doctors told her that she would be "in trouble" if she testified. She did testify, and after three months of harassment, was fired. When she sued Duke University, the court held that the university could not fire an employee for telling the truth in court.

Wrongful discharge
An employer may not fire a worker for refusing to violate the law, performing a legal duty, exercising a legal right or supporting basic societal values.

---

[2]Eyal Press, "Family-Leave Values," *The New York Times*, July 29, 2007.

As a general rule, employees may not be discharged for refusing to break the law: Courts have protected employees who refused to participate in an illegal price-fixing scheme, fake pollution control records required by state law, or assist a supervisor in stealing from customers.

Performing a Legal Duty.
Courts have consistently held that an employee may not be fired for serving on a jury. Jury duty is an important civic obligation that employers are not permitted to sabotage.

Exercising a Legal Right.
Dorothy Frampton injured her arm while working at the Central Indiana Gas Co. Her employer (and its insurance company) paid her medical expenses and her salary during the four months she was out of work. When she discovered that she also qualified for benefits under the state's workers' compensation plan, she filed a claim and received payment. One month later, the company fired her. When she sued, the court held that the gas company had violated public policy. If workers fear that making a claim for workers' comp will get them fired, then no one will file and the whole point of the statute will be undermined.

Supporting Societal Values.
Courts are sometimes willing to protect employees who do the right thing, even if they violate the boss's orders. A company fired the driver of an armored truck because he disobeyed company policy by leaving his vehicle to go to the aid of two women who were being attacked by a bank robber. A court ruled for the driver on the grounds that, although he had no affirmative legal duty to intervene in such a situation, society values those who aid people in danger. This issue is, however, one on which the courts are divided. Not all judges would have made the same decision.

In the following case, an employee was fired for exercising her legal right to use medical marijuana. Did her employer violate public policy?

You be the Judge

Facts: The voters of Washington state passed the Medical Use of Marijuana Act (MUMA) which stated that:

ROE v. TELETECH CUSTOMER CARE MGMT. (COLO.) LLC
71 Wn.2d 736
Washington Supreme Court, 2011

Jane Roe suffered from debilitating migraine headaches that caused severe chronic pain, nausea, blurred vision, and sensitivity to light. Because other medications were not effective, she obtained a prescription for medical marijuana. It alleviated her symptoms without side effects and allowed Roe to work and care for her children. She ingested marijuana only in her home.

Humanitarian compassion necessitates that the decision to authorize the medical use of marijuana by patients with terminal or debilitating illnesses is a personal, individual decision, based upon their physician's professional medical judgment and discretion.

Qualifying patients and medical practitioners shall not be found guilty of a crime under state law for their possession and limited use of marijuana. This act is intended to provide clarification to law enforcement and to all participants in the judicial system.

Any person meeting the requirements appropriate to his or her status under this chapter shall not be penalized in any manner, or denied any right or privilege, for such actions.

Nothing in this chapter requires any accommodation of any on-site medical use of marijuana in any place of employment.

TeleTech Customer Care Mgmt. offered Roe a position as a customer service representative. Although she told the company about her medical marijuana use, it fired her for failing a required drug test.

Roe sued TeleTech for wrongful discharge, alleging that her termination had violated public policy. (She filed suit under a pseudonym because medical marijuana use is illegal under federal law.)

You Be the Judge: *Did TeleTech violate public policy when it fired Roe? Was this discharge wrongful?*

Arguments for Roe: Roe is exactly the sort of person this statute is intended to protect. Medical marijuana changed her life—now she can hold a job and care for her family. But, of course, she cannot hold a job if employers terminate her for using this legal medication. TeleTech is undermining the statute and jeopardizing its clear policies. A ruling in favor of TeleTech would inhibit other people from using medication that citizens voted to make available.

Furthermore, the statute specifically states that, "No person … shall be penalized in any manner, or denied any right or privilege, for such actions." Being fired is a substantial penalty.

No one is asking TeleTech to tolerate drug-impaired workers. Marijuana should be treated like any other medication—it cannot be used if it hurts job performance. But there is no evidence that it did so.

Arguments for TeleTech: Just because medical marijuana is legal in Washington does not mean that it is an important social right. Indeed, employers can fire workers for many *legal* behaviors, such as smoking, or being disagreeable.

The purpose of MUMA is to protect doctors and patients from criminal liability, not to create an unlimited right to use medical marijuana. The statute does not explicitly prevent employers from banning its use. And how can marijuana use be an important public policy when it is still illegal under federal law?

Contract Law

Traditionally, many employers (and employees) thought that only a formal, signed document qualified as an employment contract. Increasingly, however, courts have been willing to enforce an employer's more casual promises, whether written or verbal.

Truth in Hiring.   **Verbal promises made during the hiring process are generally enforceable, even if not approved by the company's top executives.** When the Tanana Valley Medical-Surgical Group, Inc. hired James Eales as a physician's assistant, it promised him that so long as he did his job, he could stay there until retirement age. Six years later, the company fired him without cause. The Alaska Supreme Court held that the clinic's promise was enforceable.

Employee Handbooks.   The employee handbook at Blue Cross & Blue Shield stated that employees could be fired only for just cause and then only after warnings, notice, a hearing, and other procedures. Charles Toussaint was fired without warning five years after he joined the company. The court held that **an employee handbook creates a contract.**

Some employers have responded to cases like this by including provisions in their handbooks stating that it is not a contract and can be modified at any time. Generally, these provisions have been enforced. However, employers cannot have it both ways. If a handbook states that it is not a contract, then employers cannot enforce provisions favorable to them, such as required arbitration clauses.

Tort Law

Workers have successfully sued their employers under the following tort theories.

Defamation.   **Employers may be liable for defamation when they give false and unfavorable references about an employee.** In his job as a bartender at the Capitol Grille restaurant, Christopher Kane often flirted with customers. After he was fired from his job, his ex-boss claimed that Kane had been "fired from every job he ever had for sexual misconduct." In fact, Kane had never been fired before. He recovered $300,000 in damages for this defamation.

More than half of the states, however, recognize a qualified privilege for employers who give references about former employees. A qualified privilege means that employers are liable only for false statements that they know to be false or that are primarily motivated by ill will. After Becky Chambers left her job at American Trans Air, Inc., she discovered that her former boss was telling anyone who called for a reference that Chambers "does not work good with other people," is a "troublemaker," and "would not be a good person to rehire." However, Chambers was unable to prove that her boss had been primarily motivated by ill will. Neither Trans Air nor the boss was held liable for these statements because they were protected by a qualified privilege.

Qualified privilege
Employers are liable only for false statements that they know to be false or that are primarily motivated by ill will.

> To reduce the likelihood of defamation suits, many companies refuse to provide references for former employees.

To reduce the likelihood of defamation suits, many companies refuse to provide references for former employees. They tell their managers that, when asked for a reference, they should only reveal the person's salary and dates of employment and not offer an opinion on job performance.

What about risky workers? Do employers have any obligation to warn about them? **Generally, courts have held that employers do *not* have a legal obligation to disclose information about former employees. But, in the case of violence, courts are divided.** While Jeffrey St. Clair worked as a maintenance man at the St. Joseph Nursing Home, he was disciplined 24 times for actions ranging from extreme violence to drug and alcohol use. When he applied for a job with another firm, St. Joseph refused to give any information other than St. Clair's dates of employment. After he savagely murdered a security guard at his new job, the guard's family sued, but a Michigan court dismissed the case.

A California court, however, reached the opposite decision in a school case. Officials from two junior high schools gave Robert Gadams glowing letters of recommendation, without mentioning that he had been fired for inappropriate sexual conduct with students. While an assistant principal at a new school, he molested a 13-year-old. Her parents sued the former employers. The court held that the writer of a letter of recommendation has "a duty not to misrepresent the facts in describing the qualifications and character of a former employee, if making these misrepresentations would present a substantial, foreseeable risk of physical injury to the third persons." As a result of cases such as this, it makes sense to disclose past violent behavior.

Intentional Infliction of Emotional Distress.   Under the tort of intentional infliction of emotional distress, employers may be liable for the cruel treatment of their workers. Morris Shields, a supervisor at GTE, was continuously in a rage. He would yell and scream profanity at the top of his voice while pounding his fists. He would charge at employees, stopping uncomfortably close to their faces while screaming and yelling. He regularly threatened to fire the clerks he supervised. At least once a day, he would call one of the clerks into his office and have her stand in front of him, sometimes for as long as 30 minutes, while he stared at her, read papers, or talked on the phone. Once, when Shields discovered a spot on the carpet, he made a clerk get on her hands and knees to clean it while he stood over her yelling. The Supreme Court of Texas upheld a jury award of $100,000 for the workers.

18-2c Whistleblowing

No one likes to be accused of wrongdoing even if (or, perhaps, especially if) the accusations are true. This is exactly what whistleblowers do: They are employees who disclose illegal behavior on the part of their employer. Not surprisingly, some companies, when faced with such an accusation, prefer to shoot the messenger. Rather than fixing the reported problem, they retaliate against the informer.

For eight years, medical device maker C.R. Bard paid kickbacks to doctors and hospitals to get them to buy its radioactive seeds for treating prostate cancer. To cover the cost of the kickbacks, the company inflated its bills to Medicare. Bard paid the government $48 million to settle this case. Of this amount, $10 million went to Julie Darity, a former Bard employee who was fired after she blew the whistle on the company's wrongdoing.

Whistleblowers are protected in the following situations:

Whistleblower
Someone who discloses wrongdoing

- **Defrauding the government.** Darity recovered under the federal False Claims Act, a statute that permits lawsuits against anyone who defrauds the government. The government and the **whistleblower** share any recovery. The Act also prohibits employers from firing workers who file suit under the statute.

- **Violations of securities or commodities laws.** Under the Dodd-Frank Act, anyone who provides information to the government about violations of securities or commodities laws is entitled to a portion of whatever award the government receives, provided that the award tops $1 million. If a company retaliates against tipsters, they are entitled to reinstatement, double back pay, and attorney's fees.

- **Employees of public companies.** The Sarbanes-Oxley Act of 2002 protects employees of public companies who provide evidence of fraud to investigators. A successful plaintiff must be rehired and given back pay.

- **Common law.** Most states do not permit employers to fire workers who report illegal activity. For example, a Connecticut court held a company liable when it fired a quality control director who reported to his boss that some products had failed quality tests.

EXAM Strategy

Question: When Shiloh interviewed for a sales job at a medical supply company, the interviewer promised that she would only have to sell medical devices, not medications. Once she began work (as an employee at will), Shiloh discovered that the sales force was organized around regions, not products, so she had to sell both devices and drugs. When she complained to her boss over lunch in the employee lunchroom, he said in a loud voice, "You're a big girl now—it's time you learned that you don't always get what you want." That afternoon, she was fired. Does she have a valid claim against the company?

Strategy: Shiloh is an employee at will. Does she have any protection under the law? Shiloh has had two key interactions with the company—being hired and being fired. The employer's promises made during the hiring process are enforceable. Here, the company is liable because the interviewer clearly made a promise that the company did not keep. What about the way in which Shiloh was fired? Is it intentional infliction of emotional distress? This treatment is probably not cruel enough to constitute intentional infliction of emotional distress.

Result: The company is liable to Shiloh for making false promises to her during the hiring process but not for the manner in which she was fired.

18-3 WORKPLACE FREEDOM AND SAFETY

The line between home and workplace often blurs. Employees respond to customer emails 24/7, while their behavior at home (say, drug use) can have an impact on their employer. This section deals with worker freedom: the right to personal lifestyle choices and to the public expression of opinions about the workplace.

18-3a Off-Duty Activities

In the absence of a specific law to the contrary, employers *do* have the right to fire workers for off-duty conduct. Employees have been fired or disciplined for such extracurricular activities as taking part in dangerous sports (such as sky-diving), dating coworkers, smoking, or even having high cholesterol.

Lifestyle Laws

A few states, such as California, have passed lifestyle laws that protect the right of employees to engage in *any lawful activity* when off duty. Thus, if California residents sky-dive while smoking a cigarette, they may lose their lives, but not their jobs.

Here are the rules on *particular* off-duty conduct:

- **Smoking.** In roughly 60 percent of the states, employers are not allowed to prohibit workers from smoking.

- **Illegal drugs and alcohol.** Under *federal* law, *private* employers are permitted to test job applicants and workers for alcohol and *illegal* drugs. They may sanction workers who fail the test, even if the drug or alcohol use was off duty. *State* laws on drug testing vary widely.

- **Legal medication.** The Equal Employment Opportunity Commission (EEOC), the federal agency charged with enforcing federal employment laws, prohibits testing for prescription drugs unless a worker seems impaired.

18-3b Free Speech in the Workplace

The National Labor Relations Act (NLRA) is well known as pioneer legislation that protects employees' right to unionize. However, many people do not realize that the NRLA protects *all employees* (1) who engage in collective activity (2) in connection with work conditions and (3) who are not supervisors. Under this statute, all workers (who are not supervisors) have the right to discuss work conditions, whether that discussion takes place in the lunchroom or in a chat room and whether or not the employee is engaged in union activities. When a hair salon fired two (nonunionized) hairdressers for violating the salon's "negativity policy" by complaining about work conditions, the NLRB ruled that this action was a violation of the statute. In the following case, an employer was not allowed to fire workers for complaining on Facebook.

HISPANICS UNITED OF BUFFALO, INC. AND CARLOS ORTIZ BEFORE THE NLRB

359 NLRB No. 37
National Labor Relations Board, 2012

CASE SUMMARY

Facts: Lydia Cruz-Moore and Marianna Cole-Rivera worked at Hispanics United of Buffalo (the Agency), an organization that assisted victims of domestic violence. At work and at home, by phone and by text, Cruz-Moore routinely complained to Cole-Riviera that other employees provided poor service to their clients. At home one Saturday night, Cruz-Moore texted Cole-Riviera that she intended to tell the executive director, Lourdes Iglesias, that these other employees had been performing poorly. Cole-Rivera then posted the following message on her Facebook page:

> Lydia Cruz, a coworker feels that we don't help our clients enough at [the Agency]. I about had it! My fellow coworkers how do u feel?

Four off-duty employees posted comments saying that they were upset with Cruz-Moore. She then complained to Iglesias that she felt defamed by the Facebook postings. Iglesias fired Cole-Rivera and the four coworkers on the grounds that their remarks violated the Agency's zero tolerance policy on bullying and harassment.

Issues: *Does the NLRA protect the employees' right to post these comments on Facebook? Could Iglesias fire the employees?*

Decision: The employees had the right to post the comments. Iglesias could not fire them.

Reasoning: To be protected under the NLRA, an activity must involve a group of employees and must relate to work conditions. A worker acting alone is not protected.

In this case, the activity involved the group of five workers who were responding to criticism about their job performance. Their Facebook comments plainly focused on the service they had provided to the Agency's clients. If Cruz-Moore had shared her criticisms with Iglesias, the employees may well have suffered adverse consequences.

The Agency cannot use its policy against harassment and bullying to discourage the free exercise of NLRA rights. The fact that Cruz-Moore felt offended by the Facebook postings does not justify overriding important statutory goals.

Note, however, that to be protected, the speech must involve more than one employee. The *Arizona Daily Star* fired a reporter for tweeting a series of comments, including:

> You stay homicidal, Tucson. See Star Net for the bloody deets.
> What?!?!? No overnight homicide? WTF? You're slacking Tucson.

The NLRB ruled that this tweets were not protected activity because the reporter had been acting alone, not in concert with other workers.

18-3c Lie Detector Tests

Under the Employee Polygraph Protection Act of 1988, employers may not require, or even *suggest*, that an employee or job candidate submit to a polygraph test except as part of an "ongoing investigation" into crimes that have occurred.

18-3d Guns

Employers have the right to prohibit guns in the workplace but, in almost half the states, Bring Your Gun to Work Laws prevent companies from banning firearms in the parking lot. Advocates for gun rights argue that workers have the right to protect themselves during their commutes and that, ultimately, such laws improve employee safety. However, a study found that a workplace that permits guns is five times as likely to suffer a homicide as one in which they are banned.[3]

Some executives worry about the dangers of disciplining workers in states with Bring Your Gun to Work laws. An employment lawyer reported that he had attended termination meetings in which executives had sought protection with bulletproof vests or armed guards. In one case, a company held a termination meeting in an airport conference room so that participants would have to pass through security first.[4]

EXAM Strategy

Question: To ensure that its employees did not use illegal drugs in or outside the workplace, Marvel Grocery Store required all employees to take a polygraph exam. Moreover, managers began to check employees' Facebook pages for reference to drug use. Jagger was fired for refusing to take the polygraph test. Jonathan was dismissed after revealing on his Facebook page that he was using marijuana. Has the company acted legally?

Strategy: First: As employees at will, are Jagger and Jonathan protected by a statute? The Employee Polygraph Protection Act permits employers to require a polygraph test as part of ongoing investigations into crimes that have occurred.

---

[3]Dana Loomis, Stephen W. Marshall, and Myduc L. Ta, "Employer Policies Toward Guns and the Risk of Homicides in the Workplace," *Am J Public Health*, 2005 May; 95(5): 830–832.
[4]Sara Murray, "Guns in the Parking Lot: A Delicate Workplace Issue," *The Wall Street Journal*, Oct. 15, 2013.

Second: What about Jonathan's marijuana use? No statutes protect a worker for *illegal* off-duty conduct. Can the company punish Jonathan for what he wrote on his Facebook page? Not if it relates to work conditions and involves concerted activity.

Result: Here, Marvel has no reason to believe that a crime occurred, so it cannot require a polygraph test. Jonathan's Facebook postings have nothing to do with work conditions, and illegal activity is not protected. So the company is liable to Jagger for requiring him to take the polygraph exam, but not to Jonathan for firing him over illegal drug use.

18-3e Workplace Safety

Congress passed the Occupational Safety and Health Act (OSHA) to ensure safe working conditions. Under OSHA:

- Employers are under a general obligation to keep their workplace free from hazards that could cause serious harm to employees.

- Employers must comply with specific health and safety standards. For example, health care personnel who work with blood are not permitted to eat or drink in areas where the blood is kept and must not put their mouths on any instruments used to store blood.

- Employers must keep records of all workplace injuries and accidents.

- The Occupational Safety and Health Administration (also known as OSHA) may inspect workplaces to ensure that they are safe. OSHA may assess fines for violations and order employers to correct unsafe conditions.

18-4 FINANCIAL PROTECTION

Congress and the states have enacted laws that provide employees with a measure of financial security. All of the laws in this section were created by statute, not by the courts.

18-4a Fair Labor Standards Act

The Fair Labor Standards Act (FLSA) regulates wages and limits child labor nationally. It provides that hourly workers must be paid a minimum wage of $7.25 per hour, plus time and a half for any hours over 40 in one week. These wage provisions do not apply to managerial, administrative, or professional staff. More than half the states and even some cities set a higher minimum wage, so it is important to check state guidelines as well.

One significant issue facing employers: Are unpaid internships covered by the FLSA? Eric Glatt and Alexander Footman were unpaid interns at Fox Searchlight Pictures Inc., where they worked on the movie *Black Swan*. A court ruled that they were actually employees who were entitled to wages under the FLSA. To be unpaid, an internship must:

- Provide training similar to that given in school,

- Be for the benefit of the intern,

- Not displace regular employees, and

- Not provide any immediate advantage to the employer.

The FLSA also prohibits "oppressive child labor," which means that children under 14 may work only in in agriculture, entertainment, a family business, babysitting, or newspaper delivery. Fourteen-and fifteen-year-olds are permitted to work *limited* hours after school in nonhazardous jobs, such as retail. Sixteen-and seventeen-year-olds may work *unlimited* hours in nonhazardous jobs.

18-4b Workers' Compensation

Workers' compensation statutes provide payment to employees for injuries incurred at work. In return, employees are not permitted to sue their employers for negligence. The amounts allowed (for medical expenses and lost wages) under workers' comp statutes are often less than a worker might recover in court, but the injured employee trades the certainty of some recovery for the higher risk of rolling the dice at trial.

18-4c Health Insurance

Under the Affordable Care Act, employers with 50 or more full-time employees must pay a penalty if they do not provide basic health insurance. In addition, companies that provide health insurance must cover employees' children up to the age of 26.

Losing your job does not mean that you must also give up your health insurance—at least not immediately. Under the Consolidated Omnibus Budget Reconciliation Act (COBRA), former employees must be allowed to continue their health coverage for 18 months after leaving their job. But they must pay the cost themselves, plus as much as an additional 2 percent to cover administrative expenses. COBRA applies to any company with 20 or more workers.

18-4d Social Security

The federal social security system began in 1935, during the depths of the Great Depression, to provide a basic safety net for the elderly, ill, and unemployed. **The social security system pays benefits to workers who are retired, disabled, or temporarily unemployed and to the spouses and children of disabled or deceased workers.** The social security program is financed through a tax on wages that is paid by employers, employees, and the self-employed.

Although the social security system has done much to reduce poverty among the elderly, many worry that it cannot survive in its current form. The system was designed to be "pay as you go," that is, when workers pay taxes, the proceeds do not go into a savings account for their retirement but instead are used to pay benefits to current retirees. In 1940, there were 40 workers for each retiree; currently, there are 3.3. As a result, the system now pays out more in benefits each year than it receives in tax revenues. To ensure long-term viability, some aspects of social security will have to change.

The Federal Unemployment Tax Act (FUTA) is the part of the social security system that provides support to the unemployed. FUTA establishes some national standards, but states are free to set their own benefit levels and payment schedules. While receiving payments, a worker must make a good-faith effort to look for other employment. A worker who quits voluntarily or is fired for just cause is not entitled to unemployment benefits.

Chapter Conclusion

Since the first time one person hired another, there has been tension in the workplace. The law attempts to balance the right of a boss to run a business with the right of a worker to fair treatment. Different countries balance these rights differently. The United States, for instance, guarantees its workers fewer rights than virtually any other industrialized nation. American bosses have great freedom to manage their employees. Alternatively, in Canada, France, Germany, Great Britain, and Japan, employers must show just cause before terminating workers.

Which system is best? On the one hand, being mistreated at work can be a terrible, life-altering experience; but on the other, companies that cannot lay off unproductive employees are less likely to add to their workforce, which may be one reason that Europe tends to have a higher unemployment rate than the United States.

EXAM REVIEW

1. **TRADITIONAL COMMON LAW RULE** Traditionally, an employee at will could be fired for a good reason, a bad reason, or no reason at all. This rule is now modified by common law and by statute.

2. **FMLA** The Family and Medical Leave Act guarantees workers up to 12 weeks of unpaid leave each year for childbirth, adoption, or a serious health condition of their own or in their immediate family.

3. **WRONGFUL DISCHARGE** Under the doctrine of wrongful discharge, an employer cannot fire a worker for a reason that violates public policy.

4. **PUBLIC POLICY** Generally, an employee may not be fired for refusing to violate the law, performing a legal duty, exercising a legal right, or supporting basic societal values.

5. **TRUTH IN HIRING** Verbal promises made during the hiring process are generally enforceable, even if not approved by the company's top executives.

EXAM Strategy

Question: When Phil McConkey interviewed for a job as an insurance agent with Alexander & Alexander, the company did not tell him that it was engaged in secret negotiations to merge with Aon. When the merger went through soon thereafter, Aon fired McConkey. Was Alexander liable for not telling McConkey about the possible merger?

Strategy: Was McConkey protected by a statute? No. Did the company make any promises to him during the hiring process? (See the "Result" at the end of this section.)

6. **HANDBOOKS** An employee handbook creates a contract.

7. **DEFAMATION** Employers may be liable for defamation if they give false and unfavorable references. More than half of the states, however, recognize a qualified privilege for employers who give references about former employees.

Question: Jack was a top salesperson but a real pain in the neck. He argued with everyone, especially his boss, Ross. Finally, Ross had had enough and abruptly fired Jack. But he was worried that if Jack went to work for a competitor, he might take business away. So Ross told everyone who called for a reference that Jack was a difficult human being. Is Ross liable for these statements?

Strategy: Ross would be liable for making untrue statements. (See the "Result" at the end of this section.)

8. **INTENTIONAL INFLICTION OF EMOTIONAL DISTRESS** Employers may be liable for the cruel treatment of their workers.

9. **WHISTLEBLOWERS** Whistleblowers receive some protection under both federal and state laws.

10. **OFF-DUTY ACTIVITIES** In the absence of a specific law to the contrary, employers have the right to fire workers for off-duty conduct.

11. **SMOKING** In roughly 60 percent of the states, employers cannot prohibit workers from smoking.

12. **ALCOHOL AND DRUG USE** Under federal law, private employers are permitted to test job applicants and workers for alcohol and illegal drugs. The Equal Employment Opportunity Commission prohibits testing for prescription drugs unless a worker seems impaired.

13. **FREE SPEECH** Under the NLRA, workers (who are not supervisors) have the right to discuss work conditions, whether that discussion takes place in the lunchroom or in a chat room and whether or not the employee is engaged in union activities.

14. **GUNS** Employers have the right to ban guns from the workplace but, in almost half the states, laws prevent companies from banning firearms in the parking lot.

15. **OSHA** The goal of the Occupational Safety and Health Act is to ensure safe conditions in the workplace.

16. **FLSA** The Fair Labor Standards Act regulates minimum and overtime wages. It also limits child labor.

17. **WORKERS' COMPENSATION** Workers' compensation statutes ensure that employees receive payment for injuries incurred at work.

18. **HEALTH INSURANCE** Under the Affordable Care Act, employers with 50 or more full-time employees must pay a penalty if they do not provide basic health insurance.

19. **COBRA** Former employees must be allowed to continue their health insurance for 18 months after leaving their job, but they must pay for it themselves.

20. SOCIAL SECURITY The social security system pays benefits to workers who are retired, disabled, or temporarily unemployed and to the spouses and children of disabled or deceased workers.

> **5. Result:** The court held that when Alexander hired him, it was making an implied promise that McConkey would not be fired immediately. The company was liable for not having revealed the merger negotiations.
>
> **7. Result:** These statements were true, so Ross would not be liable. Before making the statements, though, he should ask himself if he wants the burden of having to prove them true in court.

MATCHING QUESTIONS

Match the following terms with their definitions:

___A. Employee at will

___B. Public policy rule

___C. FLSA

___D. Wrongful discharge

___E. OSHA

1. A federal statute that ensures safe working conditions

2. When an employee is fired for a bad reason

3. An employee without an explicit employment contract

4. A federal statute that regulates wages and limits child labor

5. States that an employer may not fire a worker for refusing to violate the law, performing a legal duty, exercising a legal right, or supporting basic societal values

TRUE/FALSE QUESTIONS

Circle true or false:

1. T F An employee may be fired for a good reason, a bad reason, or no reason at all.

2. T F Oral promises made by the employer during the hiring process are not enforceable.

3. T F In some states, employers are not liable for false statements they make about former employees unless they know these statements are false or are primarily motivated by ill will.

4. T F The federal government has the right to inspect workplaces to ensure that they are safe.

5. T F Any employer always has the right to insist that employees submit to a lie detector test.

6. T F Federal law limits the number of hours every employee can work.

7. T F Children under 16 may not hold paid jobs.

8. T F Only workers, not their spouses or children, are entitled to benefits under the social security system.

MULTIPLE-CHOICE QUESTIONS

1. When Brook went to work at an advertising agency, his employment contract stated that he was "at will and could be terminated at any time." After 28 months with the company, he was fired without explanation. Which of the following statements is true?

   (a) The company must give him an explanation for his termination.

   (b) Because he had a contract, he was not an employee at will

   (c) He could only be fired for a good reason.

   (d) He could be fired for any reason.

   (e) He could be fired for any reason except a bad reason.

2. Under the FMLA:

   (a) both men and women are entitled to take a leave of absence from their jobs for childbirth, adoption, or a serious health condition of their own or in their immediate family.

   (b) an employee is entitled to 12 weeks of paid leave.

   (c) an employee is entitled to leave to care for any member of his household.

   (d) an employee who takes a leave is entitled to return to the exact job she left.

   (e) all employees in the country are covered.

3. During a job interview with Venetia, Jack, a promising candidate, reveals that he and his wife are expecting twins. Venetia asks him if he is planning to take a leave once the babies are born. When Jack admits that he would like to take a month off work, he can see her face fall. She ultimately decides not to hire him because of the twins. Which of the following statements are true?

   (a) Venetia has violated the FMLA.

   (b) Venetia has violated COBRA.

   (c) Both (a) and (b)

   (d) None of the above

4. Which of the following statements is true?

   (a) In about half the states, employees have the right to bring guns into their workplace.

   (b) In about half the states, employees have the right to bring guns into their workplace parking lot.

   (c) Both (a) and (b) are true.

   (d) None of the above is true.

5. A whistleblower is:

   (a) always protected by the law.

   (b) never protected by the law.

   (c) always protected when filing suit under the False Claims Act.

   (d) always protected if she is an employee of the federal government.

   (e) always protected if she works for a private company.

6. **CPA QUESTION** An unemployed CPA generally would receive unemployment compensation benefits if the CPA:

   (a) was fired as a result of the employer's business reversals.

   (b) refused to accept a job as an accountant while receiving extended benefits.

   (c) was fired for embezzling from a client.

   (d) left work voluntarily without good cause.

CASE QUESTIONS

1. Reginald Delaney managed a Taco Time restaurant in Portland, Oregon. Some of his customers told Mr. Ledbetter, the district manager, that they would not be eating there so often because there were too many black employees. Ledbetter told Delaney to fire Ms. White, who was black. Delaney did as he was told. Ledbetter's report on the incident said: "My notes show that Delaney told me that White asked him to sleep with her and that when he would not, that she started causing dissension within the crew. She asked him to come over to her house and that he declined." Delaney refused to sign the report because it was untrue, so Ledbetter fired him. What claim might Delaney make against his former employer?

2. Hugo's sister posted a message on his Facebook page asking him how his evening as a bartender had gone. He responded with complaints that he had not had a raise in five years and that his tips "sucked." He also called his customers "rednecks" and stated that he hoped they choked on glass as they drove home drunk. Can Hugo's boss fire him for these comments?

3. Catherine Wagenseller was a nurse at Scottsdale Memorial Hospital and an employee at will. While on a camping trip with other nurses, Wagenseller refused to join in a parody of the song "Moon River," which concluded with members of the group "mooning" the audience. Her supervisor seemed upset by her refusal. Prior to the trip, Wagenseller had received consistently favorable performance evaluations. Six months after the outing, Wagenseller was fired. She contends it was because she had not mooned. Should the hospital be able to fire Wagenseller for this reason?

4. **ETHICS** When Walton Weiner interviewed for a job with McGraw-Hill, Inc., he was assured that the company would not terminate an employee without "just cause." McGraw-Hill's handbook said, "[The] company will resort to dismissal for just and sufficient cause only, and only after all practical steps toward rehabilitation or salvage of the employee have been taken and failed. However, if the welfare of the company indicates that dismissal is necessary, then that decision is arrived at and is carried out forthrightly." After eight years, Weiner was fired suddenly for "lack of application." Does Weiner have a valid claim against McGraw-Hill? Apart from the legal issue, did McGraw-Hill do the right thing? Was the process fair? Did the company's behavior violate important values?

5. FedEx gave Marcie Dutschmann an employment handbook stating that: (1) she was an at will employee, (2) the handbook did not create any contractual rights, and (3) employees who were fired had the right to a termination hearing. The company fired Dutschmann, claiming that she had falsified delivery records. She said that FedEx was retaliating against her because she had complained of sexual harassment. FedEx refused her request for a termination hearing. Did the employee handbook create an implied contract guaranteeing Dutschmann a hearing?

DISCUSSION QUESTIONS

1. Debra Agis worked as a waitress in a Ground Round restaurant. The manager, Roger Dionne, informed the waitresses that "there was some stealing going on." Until he found out who was doing it, he intended to fire all the waitresses in alphabetical order, starting with the letter "A." Dionne then fired Agis. Does she have a valid claim against her employer?

2. **ETHICS** Should employers be allowed to fire smokers? Nicotine is highly addictive and many smokers begin as teenagers, when they may not fully understand the consequences of their decisions. As Mark Twain, who began smoking at 12, famously said, "Giving up smoking is the easiest thing in the world. I know because I've done it thousands of times."

3. Noelle was the principal of a charter school and an employee at will. The head administrator imposed a rule requiring cafeteria workers to stamp the hands of children who did not have sufficient funds in their lunch accounts. Some of these children were entitled to free lunches; others needed to ask their parents to replenish their accounts. Noelle directed the cafeteria workers to stop this humiliating practice. The administrator fired her. Does Noelle have a valid claim for wrongful termination?

4. When Theodore Staats went to his company's "Council of Honor Convention," he was accompanied by a woman who was not his wife, although he told everyone she was. The company fired him. Staats alleged that his termination violated public policy because it infringed upon his freedom of association. He also alleged that he had been fired because he was too successful—his commissions were so high, he outearned even the highest-paid officer of the company. Has Staats's employer violated public policy?

5. *YOU BE THE JUDGE* **WRITING PROBLEM** Nationwide Insurance Co. circulated a memorandum asking all employees to lobby in favor of a bill that had been introduced in the Pennsylvania House of Representatives. By limiting the damages that an injured motorist could recover from a person who caused an accident, this bill promised to save Nationwide significant money. Not only did John Novosel refuse to lobby, but he privately criticized the bill for harming consumers. Nationwide was definitely not on his side—it fired him. Novosel filed suit, alleging that his discharge had violated public policy by infringing his right to free speech. Did Nationwide violate public policy by firing Novosel? **Argument for Novosel:** The United States Constitution and the Pennsylvania Constitution both guarantee the right to free speech. Nationwide has violated an important public policy by firing Novosel for expressing his opinions. **Argument for Nationwide:** For all the high-flown talk about the Constitution, what we have here is an employee who refused to carry out company policy. If the employee prevails in this case, where will it all end? What if an employee for a tobacco company refuses to market cigarettes because he does not approve of smoking? How can businesses operate without loyalty from their employees?

CHAPTER 19

EMPLOYMENT DISCRIMINATION

Imagine that you are on the hiring committee of a top San Francisco law firm. You come across a resume from a candidate who grew up on an isolated ranch in Arizona. Raised in a house without electricity or running water, he had worked alongside the ranch hands his entire childhood. At the age of 16, he left home for Stanford University and from there had gone on to Stanford Law School, where he finished third in his class. You think to yourself, "This sounds like a real American success story. A great combination of hard work and intelligence." But without hesitation, you toss the resume into the wastebasket.

This is a true story. Indeed, there was a candidate with these credentials who was unable to find a job in any San Francisco law firm. The only jobs on offer were as a secretary because this candidate was a woman— Sandra Day O'Connor, who went on to become one of the most influential lawyers of her era and the first woman justice on the Supreme Court of the United States.

Before 1964, you might never have seen a female or African-American doctor, engineer, police officer, or corporate executive. When a woman or minority did get a job, it was legal to treat them differently from white men. Women, for example, could be paid less for the same job and could be fired if they got married or pregnant.

In the last four decades, Congress has enacted important legislation to prevent discrimination in the workplace.

© Creative Travel Projects/Shutterstock.com

> **This sounds like a real American success story. A great combination of hard work and intelligence. But without hesitation, you toss the resume into the wastebasket.**

19-1 EQUAL PAY ACT OF 1963

Under the Equal Pay Act, a worker may not be paid at a lesser rate than employees of the opposite sex for equal work. "Equal work" means tasks that require equal skill, effort, and responsibility under similar working conditions. Citicorp rewarded Heidi Wilson's good work with a promotion to manager but neglected to include a raise or even a bonus. She protested that the man she replaced had earned 75 percent more, but Citicorp argued that salaries were based not just on position but also on seniority and experience. Also, the economy was suffering through a recession. So Wilson requested a market analysis, but Citicorp refused. She also discovered that Citicorp had rewarded other employees with bonuses that were higher than Wilson's salary. An arbitrator awarded Wilson $340,000 in back pay.[1]

19-2 TITLE VII OF THE CIVIL RIGHTS ACT OF 1964

Under Title VII of the Civil Rights Act of 1964, it is illegal for employers to discriminate on the basis of race, color, religion, sex, or national origin. Discrimination under Title VII applies to every aspect of the employment process, from job ads to postemployment references, and includes hiring, firing, promoting, placement, wages, benefits, and working conditions of anyone who is in one or more of the so-called **protected categories** under the statute.

Protected categories
Race, color, religion, sex, or national origin

19-2a Prohibited Activities

There are four types of illegal activity under this statute: disparate treatment, disparate impact, hostile environment, and retaliation.

Disparate Treatment

To prove a disparate treatment case, the plaintiff must show that she was treated differently because of her sex, race, color, religion, or national origin. The required steps in a disparate treatment case are:

One. The plaintiff presents evidence that the defendant has discriminated against her because of a protected trait. This is called a *prima facie* case. The plaintiff is not required to prove discrimination; she need only create a *presumption* that discrimination occurred.

Prima facie
Something that appears to be true upon a first look

Sandra Guzman was an editor at *The New York Post*. She was also black, Hispanic, Puerto Rican, and female. The company fired her, while keeping on a white editor. Although an editor's position was open, the company did not offer her that job. This evidence alone is not proof of discrimination because the *Post* may have had a perfectly good, nondiscriminatory explanation. However, its behavior could have been motivated by discrimination.

Two. The defendant must present evidence that its decision was based on legitimate, nondiscriminatory reasons. The *Post* said that it had fired Guzman because the section she edited, Tempo, was unprofitable. The white editor had been kept on because she had an employment contract; Guzman did not. The company had not offered Guzman the open position because the pay was substantially less.

---

[1]Elizabeth Behrman, "Tampa woman wins lawsuit against Citicorp for pay discrimination," *The Tampa Bay Times*, April 16, 2012.

Three. To win, the plaintiff must now prove that the employer discriminated. She may do so by showing that the reasons offered were simply a *pretext* or that a discriminatory intent was more likely than not. Guzman offered evidence that Tempo was not closed until after she was fired and that it had been more successful than the rest of the *Post*. She testified that she would have taken the open job, even at a lower salary. She also alleged that many *Post* employees had made racist and sexist remarks. If Guzman can prove these facts to be true, she will win because she has offered evidence of both pretext and intent.

EXAM Strategy

Question: The appearance policy at Starwood Hotels prohibited employees from wearing hairstyles that showed excessive scalp. When Carmelita Vazquez repeatedly came to work with her hair in cornrows, Starwood fired her for violating its policy. Vazquez was African-American and Hispanic. White women were allowed to wear their hair in braids. Vazquez filed a disparate treatment claim under Title VII.

Strategy: The steps of a disparate treatment case are:

One: Vazquez has presented a *prima facie* case—she has shown that she was treated differently from similar people who are not protected under Title VII.

Two: Starwood presented evidence that its decision was based on legitimate reasons – Vazquez had violated its appearance policy.

Three: To win, Vazquez must show that Starwood's decision was a pretext or had a discriminatory intent.

Result: The court found for Vazquez, believing that Starwood did have a discriminatory intent.

Disparate Impact

Disparate impact applies if the employer has a rule that, **on its face,** is not discriminatory, but **in practice** excludes too many people in a protected group. Duke Power required all applicants to its most desirable departments to have a high school education or satisfactory scores on two tests that measured intelligence and mechanical ability. Neither test gauged the ability to perform a particular job. The pass rate for whites was much higher than for blacks, and whites were also more likely than blacks to have a high school diploma. Although Duke Power was not, on its face, discriminating against blacks, the upshot of these employment rules was that more whites got the good jobs.

The Supreme Court ruled that Duke Power was violating Title VII because its rules had a disparate impact on a protected category. The court stated:

> Nothing in [Title VII] precludes the use of testing or measuring procedures; obviously they are useful. What Congress has commanded is that any tests used must measure the person for the job and not the person in the abstract.[2]

The steps in a disparate impact case are:

One. The plaintiff must present a *prima facie* case. The plaintiff is not required to prove discrimination; he need only show a disparate impact—that the employment practice in question excludes a disproportionate number of people in a protected

---

[2]*Griggs v. Duke Power*, 401 U.S. 424 (S.Ct. 1971).

group (women and minorities, for instance). In the *Duke Power* case, a higher percentage of whites than blacks passed the tests required for one of the good jobs.

Two. The defendant must offer some evidence that the employment practice was a job-related business necessity. Duke Power would have to show that the tests predicted job performance.

Three. To win, the plaintiff must now prove either that the employer's reason is a pretext or that other, less discriminatory rules would achieve the same results.

The plaintiffs in *Duke Power* showed that the tests were not a job-related business necessity—workers who had been hired before the tests were introduced performed the jobs well. Duke Power could no longer use them as a hiring screen. If the power company wanted to use tests, it would have to find some that measured an employee's ability to perform particular jobs.

Duke Power was decided almost a half century ago. Yet, as the following case illustrates, hiring tests remain a frequent subject of litigation. Was this test fair? You be the judge.

You be the Judge

Facts: A New York State task force on teacher qualifications decided that all teachers needed a basic understanding of liberal arts and sciences. National Evaluation Systems (NES), a professional test development company, was hired to create a test to measure this knowledge.

GULINO V. BD. OF EDUC. OF THE CITY SCH. DIST. OF N.Y
907 F. Supp. 2d 492
United States District Court for the Southern District of New York, 2012

NES began by establishing two committees of teachers and professors (including some minority group members) to ensure that the test was both relevant to the job of a New York public school teacher and free from bias. The Committees reviewed a draft framework, a list of exam subtopics, and sample questions. NES then sent its draft framework and subtopics for review to 1200 New York public school teachers and education professors. It also piloted some sample questions on students at various state education colleges.

Teachers could not be licensed to teach in New York City unless they passed the test. Whites succeeded at a higher rate than African-Americans and Latinos. A group of minority teachers filed suit against the Board of Education for the City of New York (Board) alleging that the test violated Title VII.

You Be the Judge: *Did the test violate Title VII?*

Argument for the Board: Two committees of diverse teachers and professors reviewed the test to ensure that it was both relevant and free from bias. NES also consulted 12 hundred teachers and education professors. And it tested specific questions. The test was designed and approved by experts, some of whom were minorities. What more can we do?

Argument for the teachers: The fact that the test covered liberal arts and sciences does not prove that it was job related; arts and sciences is an extremely broad classification that encompasses far more than the basic knowledge teachers need to be competent in the classroom.

To show the validity of the test, NES needed to create a list of the tasks teachers perform, and then determine what subtopics and questions could be used to evaluate their ability to do those jobs. NES should have presented evidence that the knowledge required by the test improves teacher performance and student results. It failed to do so.

Hostile Work Environment

Employers violate Title VII if they permit a work environment that is so hostile toward people in a protected category that it affects their ability to work. This rule applies whether the hostility is based on race, color, religion, sex, national origin, pregnancy, age, or disability. This concept of hostile environment first arose in the context of **sexual harassment**.

Everyone has heard of sexual harassment, but few people know exactly what it is.

Sexual harassment
Involves unwelcome sexual advances, requests for sexual favors, and other verbal or physical conduct of a sexual nature

Sexual Harassment. Sexual harassment involves unwelcome sexual advances, requests for sexual favors, and other verbal or physical conduct of a sexual nature which are so severe and pervasive that they interfere with an employee's ability to work. There are two categories of sexual harassment: (1) *quid pro quo* and (2) hostile work environment.

Quid pro quo
A Latin phrase that means "one thing in return for another"

1. *Quid Pro Quo.* From a Latin phrase that means "one thing in return for another," *quid pro quo* harassment occurs if any aspect of a job is made contingent upon sexual activity. In the *Guzman* case, the plaintiff alleged that a male editor had offered a permanent reporter job to a young female copy assistant in exchange for the type of sexual activity that President Bill Clinton made famous.

2. **Hostile work environment.** An employee has a valid claim of sexual harassment if sexual talk and activity are so pervasive that they interfere with her (or his) ability to work. Courts have found that offensive jokes, intrusive comments about clothes or body parts, and public displays of pornographic pictures can create a hostile environment. Guzman claimed that a male editor had shown her a photo of a naked man while telling stories about another editor's "voracious sexual appetite."

> Everyone has heard of sexual harassment, but few people know exactly what it is.

Corning Consumer Products Co. provides a set of practical guidelines for eliminating sexual harassment. It asks employees to apply four tests in determining whether their behavior violates Title VII:

1. Would you say or do this in front of your spouse or parents?

2. What about in front of a colleague of the opposite sex?

3. Would you like your behavior reported in your local newspaper?

4. Does it need to be said or done at all?

Hostile Environment Based on Race.   Reginald Jones, who was African-American, drove a truck for UPS Ground Freight. He began finding bananas and banana peels on his truck in the terminal. Some employees wore Confederate shirts and hats. After he reported these incidents to a supervisor, two other drivers came up to him one night in the parking lot holding a crowbar. They asked him if he had reported them to the supervisor. He again reported this event and again found banana peels on his truck. When Jones sued UPS, alleging a racially hostile work environment, the trial court granted UPS's motion for summary judgment. But the appellate court overturned this decision, ruling that the case should go to a jury because these events could, indeed, have created a hostile work environment.

Hostile Environment Based on National Origin.   Title VII also prohibits a hostile environment based on national origin. While working at Steel Technologies, Inc., Tony Cerros was promoted several times. So what was the problem? Coworkers and supervisors called him names like "brown boy," "spic," and "wetback." They also told him that "if it ain't white, it ain't right," and wrote "Go Back to Mexico" on the bathroom wall. Although the company removed the bathroom graffiti, it did not investigate Cerros's complaints until he filed suit. At that point, it determined that Cerros had not faced discrimination. The trial court agreed because Cerros had, after all, been promoted. However, the appeals court overturned the decision, finding for Cerros on the grounds that he had suffered a hostile work environment, which is in itself a violation of Title VII, even if there is no evidence of adverse employment actions.

Employer Liability for a Hostile Work Environment. Employees who engage in illegal harassment are liable for their own wrongdoing. But is their company also liable? The Supreme Court has held that:

- If the victimized employee has suffered a "tangible employment action" such as firing, demotion, or reassignment, the company is liable to her for harassment by a supervisor.

- Even if the victimized employee has *not* suffered a tangible employment action, the company is liable unless it can prove that (1) it used reasonable care to prevent and correct harassing behavior; and (2) the employee unreasonably failed to take advantage of the company's complaint procedures.

Retaliation

Title VII also prohibits employers from retaliating against workers who oppose discrimination, bring a claim under the statute, or take part in an investigation or hearing. Retaliation means that the employer has done something that would deter a reasonable worker from complaining about discrimination.

19-2b Religion

Employers must make reasonable accommodation for a worker's religious beliefs unless the request would cause undue hardship for the business. What would you do in the following cases if you were the boss:

1. A Christian says he cannot work at Walmart on Sundays—his Sabbath. It also happens to be one of the store's busiest days.

2. A Jewish police officer wants to wear a beard and yarmulke as part of his religious observance. Facial hair and headgear are banned by the force.

3. Muslim workers at a meat-packing plant want to pray at sundown but break times were specified in the labor contract and sundown changes from day to day. The workers begin to take bathroom breaks at sundown, stopping work on the production line.

4. A Jehovah's Witness needs to miss one of his scheduled shifts at UPS so that he can attend the Memorial, one of that religion's most important events.

Disputes such as these are on the rise and are not easy to handle fairly. In the end, Walmart fired the Christian, but when he sued on the grounds of religious discrimination, the company settled the case. A judge ruled that the police officer could keep his beard because the force allowed other employees with medical conditions to wear facial hair, but the head covering had to go. The boss at the meat-packing plant fired the Muslim employees who walked off the job. UPS paid $70,000 to settle the Jehovah's Witness suit.

19-2c Family Responsibility Discrimination

In studies, participants repeatedly rank mothers as less qualified than other employees and fathers as most desirable, even when their credentials are exactly the same. **Family responsibility discrimination is a violation of Title VII if it involves men and women being treated differently** – say, mothers being offered less-appealing assignments than fathers or fathers being denied benefits that are available to mothers. After Dawn Gallina, an associate at a big law firm, revealed to her boss that she had a young child, he began to treat her differently from her male colleagues and spoke to her "about the commitment differential between men and women." A court ruled that her belief of illegal discrimination was reasonable.[3]

19-2d Sexual Orientation

Neither Title VII nor any other federal statute protects against discrimination based on sexual orientation. However, by executive order, the federal government does prohibit discrimination based on sexual orientation among its own employees and also among companies that work for it. **In addition, almost half the states and hundreds of cities have statutes that prohibit such discrimination.**

The Supreme Court has ruled that it is unconstitutional to withhold federal benefits from same-sex married couples. But this inconsistency in federal law means that, in many places, a gay person could be fired for claiming these benefits.

19-2e Gender Identity and Expression

David Schroer was in the Army for 25 years, including a stint tracking terrorists. The Library of Congress offered him a job as a specialist in terrorism. (Who knew that libraries needed terrorism specialists?) However, when he revealed that he was in the process of becoming Diane Schroer, the Library of Congress withdrew the offer. As you can guess, he sued under Title VII.

Traditionally, courts took the view that sex under Title VII applied only to how people were born, not what they chose to become. Employers could and did fire workers for changing sex. However, a federal court recently found the Library of Congress in violation of Title VII for withdrawing Schroer's offer. And some other courts have reached a similar result. In addition, **the Equal Employment Opportunity Commission (EEOC) ruled that discriminating against someone for being transgender is a violation of Title VII.** About one-third of the states and hundreds of cities prohibit gender identity and expression discrimination. Also, the federal government prohibits discrimination on gender identity among its employees and in companies that work for it.

19-2f Immigration

Under Title VII, it is illegal for employers to discriminate against noncitizens because "national origin" is a protected category. Therefore, employers should not ask about a job applicant's country of origin, but they are permitted to inquire if the person is authorized to work in the United States. If the applicant says, "Yes," the interviewer cannot ask for evidence until the person is hired. At that point, the employer must complete an I-9 form—Employment Eligibility Verification—within three days. This form lists the acceptable documents that can be used for verification. Employees have the right to present whichever documents they want from the list of acceptable items. The employer may not ask for some other document. The I-9 forms must be kept for three years after the worker is hired or one year after termination.

19-2g Defenses to Charges of Discrimination

Under Title VII, the defendant has three possible defenses.

Merit

A defendant is not liable if he shows that the person he favored was the most qualified. Test results, education, or productivity can all be used to demonstrate merit, provided they relate to the job in question. Harry can show that he hired Bruce for a coaching job instead of Louisa

---

[3]*Gallina v. Mintz*, 123 Fed. Appx. 558 (4th Cir. 2005).

because Bruce has a master's degree in physical education and seven years of coaching experience. On the other hand, the fact that Bruce scored higher on the National Latin Exam in the eighth grade is not a good reason to hire him over Louisa for a coaching job.

Seniority

A legitimate seniority system is legal even if it perpetuates past discrimination. Suppose that Harry has always chosen the most senior assistant coach to take over as head coach when a vacancy occurs. Since the majority of the senior assistant coaches are male, most of the head coaches are, too. Such a system does not violate Title VII.

Bona Fide Occupational Qualification

An employer is permitted to establish discriminatory job requirements if they are essential to the position in question. The business must show that it cannot fulfill its primary function unless it discriminates in this way. Such a requirement is called a **bona fide occupational qualification (BFOQ)**. Catholic schools may, if they choose, refuse to hire non-Catholic teachers; clothing companies may refuse to hire men to model women's attire. Generally, however, courts are not sympathetic to claims of BFOQ. They have, for example, almost always rejected BFOQ claims that are based on customer preference. Thus, airlines could not refuse to hire male flight attendants even if they believed that travelers prefer female attendants.

> **Bona fide occupational qualification (BFOQ)**
> An employer is permitted to establish discriminatory job requirements if they are *essential* to the position in question.

However, the courts recognize three situations in which employers may consider customer preference:

1. **Safety.** The Supreme Court ruled that a maximum security men's prison could refuse to hire women correctional officers. If a woman wanted to risk her life, that was her choice, but the court feared that an attack on her would threaten the safety of both male guards and inmates.

2. **Privacy.** An employer may refuse to hire women to work in a men's bathroom, and vice versa.

3. **Authenticity.** An employer may refuse to hire a man for a woman's role in a movie. In addition, a court ruled that Disney could fire an Asian man from the Norwegian exhibit at its Epcot international theme park, not because he was Asian, but because he was not culturally authentic. He did not have first-hand knowledge of Norwegian culture and did not speak Norwegian.

19-2h Affirmative Action

Affirmative action is not required by Title VII, nor is it prohibited. Affirmative action programs have three different sources:

1. **Litigation.** Courts have the power under Title VII to order affirmative action to remedy the effects of past discrimination.

2. **Voluntary action.** Employers can voluntarily introduce an affirmative action plan to remedy the effects of past practices or to achieve equitable representation of minorities and women.

3. **Government contracts.** The government may use affirmative action programs when awarding contracts only if (1) it can show that the programs are needed to overcome specific past discrimination; (2) they have time limits; and (3) nondiscriminatory alternatives are not available.

19-3 PREGNANCY DISCRIMINATION ACT

Under the Pregnancy Discrimination Act, an employer may not fire, refuse to hire, or fail to promote a woman because she is pregnant. An employer also violates this statute if the work environment is so hostile towards a pregnant woman that it affects her ability to do her job. And an employer must treat pregnancy and childbirth as any other temporary disability. If, for example, employees are allowed time off from work for other medical disabilities, women must also be allowed a maternity leave.

When Jennifer Hitchcock told her supervisor that she was pregnant, the woman significantly increased Hitchcock's workload and began scrutinizing her performance. This same supervisor had also counselled another worker to have an abortion because she already had two children. Within two weeks, the company fired Hitchcock on the grounds that she had made an improper assessment of a patient. When Hitchcock sued under the Pregnancy Discrimination Act, the court denied her employer's request for summary judgment because the evidence was sufficient to show that the reasons given for Hitchcock's termination were just a pretext.

The Pregnancy Discrimination Act also protects a woman's right to terminate a pregnancy. An employer cannot fire a woman for having an abortion.

19-4 AGE DISCRIMINATION

Under the Age Discrimination in Employment Act (ADEA), employers may not fire, refuse to hire, fail to promote, or otherwise reduce a person's employment opportunities because he is 40 or older. Nor may an employer require workers to retire at a certain age. (This retirement rule does not apply in some jobs, such as police officer, airline pilot, and top-level corporate executive.)

The standard of proof is tougher in an age discrimination case than in Title VII litigation. **Under the ADEA, the plaintiff must show that but for his age, the employer would not have taken the action it did.** In other words, to win a case under the ADEA, the plaintiff must show that age was not just one factor, it was the *deciding* factor.

Another issue in age discrimination cases: What happens if a company fires older workers because they are paid more? Circuit City Stores fired 8 percent of its employees because they could be replaced with people who would work for less. The fired workers were more experienced—and older. This action is legal under the ADEA. As the court put it in one case, "An action based on price differentials represents the very quintessence of a legitimate business decision."[4]

In passing the ADEA, Congress was particularly concerned about employers who relied on unfavorable stereotypes rather than job performance. The following case provides further support for the adage: "Loose lips sink ships."

REID v. GOOGLE, INC.

50 Cal. 4th 512
Supreme Court of California, 2010

CASE SUMMARY

Facts: Google's vice president of engineering, Wayne Rosing (aged 55), hired Brian Reid (52) as director of operations and director of engineering. At the time, the top executives at Google were CEO Eric Schmidt (47), vice president of Engineering Operations Urs Hölzle (38), and founders Sergey Brin (28) and Larry Page (29).

---

[4]Marks v. Loral Corp., 57 Cal. App. 4th 30 (Cal. Ct. App. 1997).

During his two years at Google, Reid's only written performance review stated that he had consistently met expectations. The comments indicated that Reid had an extraordinarily broad range of knowledge, an aptitude and orientation towards operational and IT issues, an excellent attitude, and that he projected confidence when dealing with fast-changing situations, was very intelligent and creative, and was a terrific problem solver. The review also commented that "Adapting to Google culture is the primary task. Right or wrong, Google is simply different: Younger contributors, inexperienced first line managers, and the super fast pace are just a few examples of the environment."

According to Reid, even as he received a positive review, Hölzle and other employees made derogatory age-related remarks such as his ideas were "obsolete," "ancient," and "too old to matter," that he was "slow," "fuzzy," "sluggish," and "lethargic," an "old man," an "old guy," and an "old fuddy-duddy," and that he did not "display a sense of urgency" and "lacked energy."

Nineteen months after Reid joined Google, he was fired. Google says it was because of his poor perfor-mance. Reid alleges he was told it was based on a lack of "cultural fit."

Reid sued Google for age discrimination. The trial court granted Google's motion for summary judgment on the grounds that Reid did not have sufficient evidence of discrimination. He appealed.

Issue: *Did Reid have enough evidence of age discrimination to warrant a trial?*

Decision: The trial court was overruled and summary judgment denied.

Reasoning: Google argued that the trial court should have ignored the ageist comments about Reid because they were "stray remarks," made neither by decision makers nor during the decision process. But stray remarks may be relevant, circumstantial evidence of discrimination. The jury should decide how relevant.

An ageist remark, in and of itself, does not prove discrimination. But when combined with other testimony, it may provide enough evidence to find liability.

19-5 AMERICANS WITH DISABILITIES ACT

The Americans with Disabilities Act (ADA) prohibits employers from discriminating on the basis of disability.

A disabled person is someone with a physical or mental impairment that substantially limits a major life activity or the operation of a major bodily function or someone who is regarded as having such an impairment. The definition of major life activity includes caring for oneself, performing manual tasks, seeing, hearing, eating, sleeping, walking, standing, lifting, bending, speaking, breathing, learning, reading, concentrating, thinking, communicating, and working. Cell growth and digestive, bowel, bladder, neurological, brain, respiratory, circulatory, endo-crine, reproductive, and immune system functions are also considered major life activities. However, the definition does not include the *current* use of drugs, sexual disorders, pyromania, exhibitionism, or compulsive gambling.

An employer may not refuse to hire or promote a disabled person so long as she can, with *reasonable accommodation,* **perform the** *essential functions* **of the job. An accommodation is unreasonable if it would create** *undue hardship* **for the employer.**

- **Reasonable accommodation.** This includes making facilities accessible, permitting part-time schedules, and acquiring or modifying equipment.

- **Essential functions.** After breaking her wrist, a corrections officer could not work alone on the night shift. But the court ruled she could perform the essential functions of the job because she was able to work the day shift.

- **Undue hardship.** Many courts hold that employers may use cost-benefit analysis—they are not required to make an expensive accommodation that provides little benefit. An employer was not required to lower the sink in a kitchenette for the benefit of a wheelchair-bound worker because she had access to another bathroom sink.

Disabled person
Someone with a physical or mental impairment that substantially limits a major life activity, or someone who is regarded as having such an impairment

The following case explores the employer's obligation to provide reasonable accommodation.

WILLOUGHBY V. CONN. CONTAINER CORP.

2013 U.S. Dist. LEXIS 168457, 2013 WL 6198210
United States District Court for the District of Connecticut, 2013

CASE SUMMARY

Facts: When Anthony Willoughby was diagnosed with diabetes, he notified his company's Human Resources department. Despite treatment, Willoughby experienced side effects that included swelling, dizziness, blurred vision, and frequent bathroom use. Heat caused the symptoms to worsen.

One night, Willoughby reported to work feeling unwell. For two weeks, his work assignment had required particularly strenuous activity in the heat. That night, his ankles swelled, and his vision deteriorated. When he told his supervisor, she said "do the work or go home." Later that night, the supervisor found him in a chair. Willoughby says he had passed out; she stated that he was sleeping. He presented HR with a note from a physician verifying that he had passed out due to low blood sugar. The company fired Willoughby for sleeping on the job.

Willoughby filed suit, alleging that his employer had violated the ADA by failing to provide reasonable accommodation for his disability. The company filed a motion for summary judgment

Issues: *Was Willoughby disabled? If so, did his employer provide reasonable accommodation?*

Decision: The employer violated the ADA by failing to provide reasonable accommodation for his disability. The motion for summary judgment was denied.

Reasoning: Diabetes substantially limits endocrine function. Therefore, a jury could easily find that Willoughby had a physical impairment that substantially limits one or more major life activity and, accordingly, has a disability under the ADA.

The company argues that Willoughby's claim should be dismissed because he never asked for an accommodation. An individual is required to notify the employer that he needs an accommodation, but it is also the employer's duty to accommodate an employee with an obvious disability. Once Willoughby notified the company that he had diabetes, it should have engaged with him in an interactive process to assess whether his disability could be reasonably accommodated.

19-5a The Hiring Process

An employer may not ask about disabilities before making a job offer. The interviewer may ask only whether an applicant can perform the work. Before making a job offer, an employer cannot require applicants to take a medical exam unless the exam is (1) job-related and (2) required of all applicants for similar jobs. However, drug testing is permitted. After a job offer has been made, an employer may require a medical test, but it must be related to the essential functions of the job. An employer could not test the cholesterol of someone applying for an accounting job because high cholesterol is no impediment to good accounting.

19-5b Relationship with a Disabled Person

An employer may not discriminate against someone because of his relationship with a disabled person. For example, an employer cannot refuse to hire an applicant because he has a child with Down's syndrome or a spouse with AIDS.

19-5c Obesity

According to the EEOC, just being overweight is not a disability unless it has some underlying physiological cause, such as a thyroid disorder. **However, being morbidly obese (defined as having double the normal body weight) is a disability, no matter what the cause.**

Lisa Harrison weighed 527 pounds when Family House fired her. The normal weight for someone her height—five feet, two inches tall—was between 102 and 130 pounds. The EEOC filed suit, claiming that Family House had fired her for a perceived disability and had failed to make reasonable accommodation. Family House filed a motion for summary judgment alleging that it had fired Harrison because her obesity impaired her job performance. In denying this motion, the court ruled that her severe obesity was a disability under the ADA.

19-5d Mental Disabilities

Under EEOC rules, physical and mental disabilities are to be treated the same. Physical ailments such as diabetes and deafness may sometimes be easier to diagnose, but psychological disabilities are also covered by the ADA. Among other accommodations, the EEOC rules indicate that employers should be willing to put up barriers to isolate people who have difficulty concentrating, offer flexible hours to allow for therapy, or provide detailed day-to-day feedback to those who need greater structure in performing their jobs.

19-6 GENETIC INFORMATION NONDISCRIMINATION ACT

Suppose you want to promote someone to chief financial officer, but you know that her mother and sister both died young of breast cancer. Is it legal to consider that information in making a decision? Not since Congress passed the Genetic Information Nondiscrimination Act (GINA). **Under GINA, employers may not require genetic testing, or use information about genetic makeup or family medical history as a factor in hiring, firing, or promoting employees.** Nor may health insurers use such information to decide coverage or premiums. Thus, even an employer Wellness Program cannot *require* participants to answer questions about their family medical history.

Note, however, that insurance companies may seek the results of genetic testing before issuing disability, life, or long-term care policies. At this writing, only three states prohibit the use of such information for these types of policies.[5]

19-7 HIRING PRACTICES

The hiring process is an easy place for employers to wrong. Here are pitfalls to avoid.

19-7a Interviews

Most interviewers (and students who have read this chapter) would know better than Delta Airlines interviewers, who allegedly asked applicants about their sexual orientation, birth control methods, and abortion history. The following list provides guidelines for interviewers.

[5]The states are California, Oregon and Vermont.

Don't Even Consider Asking	Go Ahead and Ask
Can you perform this function with or without reasonable accommodation?	Would you need reasonable accommodation in this job?
How many days were you sick last year?	How many days were you absent from work last year?
What medications are you currently taking?	Are you currently using drugs illegally?
Where were you born? Are you a United States citizen?	Are you authorized to work in the United States?
How old are you?	What work experience have you had?
How tall are you? How much do you weigh?	Could you carry a 100-pound weight, as required by this job?
When did you graduate from college?	Where did you go to college?
How did you learn this language?	What languages do you speak and write fluently?
Have you ever been arrested?	Have you ever been convicted of a crime that would affect the performance of this job?
Do you plan to have children? How old are your children? What method of birth control do you use?	Can you work weekends? Travel extensively? Would you be willing to relocate?
What is your corrected vision?	Do you have 20/20 corrected vision?
Are you a man or a woman? Are you single or married? What does your spouse do? What will happen if your spouse is transferred? What clubs, societies, or lodges do you belong to?	Talk about the weather!

The most common gaffe on the part of interviewers? Asking women about their child-care arrangements. That question assumes the woman is responsible for child care.

19-7b Social Media

Almost all employers now rely on social media as a part of their hiring process. These searches sometimes reveal information that is illegal for employers to act on, such as age, religion, pregnancy, or illness. Yet, sometimes they do. In one experiment, researchers replied to job postings with identical (fake) resumes that were linked to a Facebook page identifying the applicant's religion as either Christian or Muslim. Christians were more likely to obtain an interview.

Such misuse of social media has consequences. A university decided against hiring an applicant after it learned from his website that, because of his religion, he doubted the theory of evolution. The university argued that these religious views would have impeded the performance of his job, which required him to raise funds in the science community and work with university scientists. A federal judge denied the university's request for summary judgment; so the university settled the case for $125,000.

To help prevent this type of liability, some employers keep the role of "cyber-vetting" separate from that of hiring. A handful of states now prohibit employers from asking for social media passwords, and many others have such legislation pending.

EXAM Strategy

Question: For Michael, it was the job of his dreams—editor of *Literature* magazine. When Cyrus, the owner of the magazine, offered him the position, Michael accepted immediately. But he also revealed a secret few people knew—he was in the early stages of Parkinson's, a neurological disorder that affects the patient's ability to move. While that symptom is controllable with medication, about 40 percent of Parkinson's patients suffer severe dementia and eventually become unable to work. Michael had no signs of dementia—he was the host of a popular television talk show. Fifteen minutes after Michael returned to his hotel room, Cyrus called to withdraw the job offer. He said he did not like some of Michael's ideas for changing the magazine. Has Cyrus violated the ADA? Could he fire Michael if dementia set in?

Strategy: Is Michael covered by the ADA? Can he perform the essential functions of the job?

Result: Michael is covered by the ADA. He has an impairment that substantially limits a major life activity—movement. But Michael is able to perform the essential functions of the job, so Cyrus violated the law when he withdrew the offer. If Michael becomes demented in the future and can no longer run a magazine, Cyrus could fire him then.

19-8 ENFORCEMENT

The EEOC is the federal agency responsible for enforcing the Equal Pay Act, Title VII, the Pregnancy Discrimination Act, the ADEA, the ADA, and GINA.

Before a plaintiff can bring suit under one of these statutes, she must first file a complaint with the EEOC. After it receives a filing, the EEOC conducts an investigation and also attempts to mediate the dispute. If it determines that discrimination has occurred, it will typically file suit on behalf of the plaintiff. This arrangement is favorable for the plaintiff because the government pays the legal bill. If the EEOC decides not to bring the case, or does not make a decision within six months, it issues a right to sue letter, and the plaintiff may proceed on her own in court within 90 days. Under the ADEA, a plaintiff may bring suit 60 days after filing a charge with the EEOC. Many states also have their own version of the EEOC.

Remedies available to the successful plaintiff include hiring, reinstatement, retroactive seniority, back pay, front pay (to compensate for future lost wages), reasonable attorney's fees and damages up to $300,000. However, employers now often require new hires to agree in advance to arbitrate, not litigate, any future employment claims. Employees sometimes receive worse results in the arbitrator's office than in the courtroom.

Chapter Conclusion

The statutes in this chapter have changed America—it is far different now from what it was when Sandra Day O'Connor first looked for a job. People are more likely to be offered employment because of their efforts and talents rather than their age, appearance, faith, family background, or health.

EXAM REVIEW

1. **EQUAL PAY ACT**   Under the Equal Pay Act, a worker may not be paid for equal work at a lesser rate than employees of the opposite sex.

2. **TITLE VII**   Title VII of the Civil Rights Act of 1964 prohibits employers from discriminating on the basis of race, color, religion, sex, or national origin.

3. **DISPARATE TREATMENT**   To prove a disparate treatment case under Title VII, the plaintiff must show that she was treated differently because of her sex, race, color, religion, or national origin.

4. **DISPARATE IMPACT**   To prove disparate impact under Title VII, the plaintiff must show that the employer has a rule that on its face is not discriminatory, but in practice excludes too many people in a protected group.

EXAM Strategy

Question: Ladies Plus refuses to hire Eric for a job as a sales associate because his credit score is too low to meet the store's hiring standards. Men, on average, have worse credit ratings than women. Has the store violated Title VII?

Strategy: Is there evidence that men and women are being treated differently? No, the same rule applies to both. Do the rules have a disparate impact? Yes, more women have acceptable credit ratings. Is sex a protected category under Title VII? Yes. Are the standards essential for the job? Would other, less discriminatory rules have achieved the same result? (See the "Result" at the end of this section.)

5. **HOSTILE WORK ENVIRONMENT**   Employers violate Title VII if they permit a work environment that is so hostile toward people in a protected category that it affects their ability to work. This rule applies whether the hostility is based on race, color, religion, sex, national origin, pregnancy, age, or disability.

6. **SEXUAL HARASSMENT**   Sexual harassment involves unwelcome sexual advances, requests for sexual favors, or other verbal or physical conduct of a sexual nature that are so severe and pervasive that they interfere with an employee's ability to work.

7. **RETALIATION** Title VII prohibits employers from retaliating against workers who oppose discrimination, bring a claim under the statute, or take part in an investigation or hearing.

8. **RELIGION** Employers must make reasonable accommodation for a worker's religious beliefs unless the request would cause undue hardship for the business.

9. **FAMILY RESPONSIBILITY DISCRIMINATION** Men and women may not be treated differently because of their family responsibilities.

10. **SEXUAL ORIENTATION** Neither Title VII nor any other federal statute protects against discrimination based on sexual orientation. However, by executive order, the federal government does prohibit discrimination based on sexual orientation among its own employees and also among companies that work for it. In addition, almost half the states and hundreds of cities have statutes that prohibit such discrimination.

11. **GENDER IDENTITY AND EXPRESSION** Traditionally, courts ruled that employees were not protected from discrimination based on gender identity. But some federal courts, the EEOC, about one-third of the states and hundreds of cities prohibit gender identity and expression discrimination. Also, the federal government prohibits discrimination on gender identity among its employees and in companies that work for it.

12. **IMMIGRATION** Under Title VII, it is illegal for employers to discriminate against noncitizens because "national origin" is a protected category.

13. **SENIORITY** A legitimate seniority system is legal even if it perpetuates past discrimination.

14. **BONA FIDE OCCUPATIONAL QUALIFICATION (BFOQ)** An employer is permitted to establish discriminatory job requirements if they are essential to the position in question.

EXAM Strategy

Question: You are the vice president of administration at a hospital. A hospital study reveals that both male and female patients prefer to have a male neurosurgeon, while men prefer male urologists and women prefer female gynecologists. Can you act on this information when hiring doctors?

Strategy: To hire based on sex would be a violation of Title VII unless sex is a BFOQ for the job. (See the "Result" at the end of this section.)

15. **AFFIRMATIVE ACTION** Affirmative action is not required by Title VII, nor is it prohibited.

16. **PREGNANCY DISCRIMINATION** Under the Pregnancy Discrimination Act, an employer may not fire, refuse to hire or fail to promote a woman because she is pregnant.

17. **AGE DISCRIMINATION** Under the Age Discrimination in Employment Act, employers may not fire, refuse to hire, fail to promote, or otherwise reduce a person's employment opportunities because he is 40 or older.

18. **DISABILITY** Under the Americans with Disabilities Act, an employer may not refuse to hire or promote a disabled person as long as she can, with reasonable accommodation, perform the essential functions of the job. A disabled person is someone with a physical or mental impairment that substantially limits a major life activity or the operation of a major bodily function or someone who is regarded as having such an impairment. An accommodation is not reasonable if it would create undue hardship for the employer.

19. **GENETIC INFORMATION NONDISCRIMINATION ACT** Under GINA, employers with 15 or more workers may not require genetic testing, or use information about genetic makeup or family medical history as a factor in hiring, firing or promoting employees.

> **4. Result:** The store is in violation of Title VII unless it can show that (1) credit ratings directly relate to a sales associate's job performance and (2) no other requirement would accurately evaluate applicants for this work.
>
> **14. Result:** Customer preference does not justify discrimination except in cases of sexual privacy. You cannot consider sex when hiring neurosurgeons, but you can when selecting urologists and gynecologists.

MATCHING QUESTIONS

Match the following terms with their definitions:

___A. Equal Pay Act

___B. Right to sue letter

___C. ADEA

___D. Title VII

___E. ADA

1. An employee cannot be paid at a lesser rate than employees of the opposite sex for equal work
2. Statute that prohibits discrimination on the basis of race, color, religion, sex, or national origin
3. Permission from the EEOC for a plaintiff to proceed with a case
4. Statute that prohibits age discrimination
5. Statute that prohibits discrimination against the disabled

TRUE/FALSE QUESTIONS

Circle true or false:

1. T F In a disparate impact case, an employer may be liable for a rule that is not discriminatory on its face.
2. T F Title VII applies to all aspects of the employment relationship, including hiring, firing, and promotion.
3. T F If more whites than Native Americans pass an employment test, the test necessarily violates Title VII.
4. T F Employers that have contracts with the federal government are required to fill a quota of women and minority employees.
5. T F Employers do not have to accommodate an employee's religious beliefs if doing so would impose an undue hardship on the business.

MULTIPLE-CHOICE QUESTIONS

1. Which of the following steps is *not* required in a disparate treatment case?

   (a) The plaintiff must file with the EEOC.

   (b) The plaintiff must submit to arbitration.

   (c) The plaintiff must present evidence of a *prima facie* case.

   (d) The defendant must show that its action had a nondiscriminatory reason.

   (e) The plaintiff must show that the defendant's excuse was a pretext.

2. An employer can legally require all employees to have a high school diploma if:

   (a) all of its competitors have such a requirement.

   (b) most of the applicants in the area have a high school diploma.

   (c) shareholders of the company are likely to pay a higher price for the company's stock if employees have at least a high school diploma.

   (d) the company intends to branch out into the high-tech field, in which case a high school diploma would be needed by its employees.

   (e) the nature of the job requires those skills.

3. Which of the following employers has violated Title VII?

   (a) Carlos promoted the most qualified employee.

   (b) Hans promoted five white males because they were the most senior.

   (c) Luke refused to hire a Buddhist to work on a Christian Science newspaper.

   (d) Max hired a male corporate lawyer because his clients had more confidence in male lawyers.

   (e) Dylan refused to hire a woman to work as an attendant in the men's locker room.

4. Which of the following activities would *not* be considered sexual harassment?

   (a) Shannon tells Connor that she will promote him if he will sleep with her.

   (b) Kailen has a screen saver that shows various people having sex.

   (c) Paige says she wants "to negotiate Owen's raise at the Holiday Inn."

   (d) Nancy yells "Crap!" at the top of her lungs every time her Rotisserie Baseball team loses.

   (e) *Quid pro quo.*

5. Which of the following activities is legal under Title VII?

   (a) When Taggart comes to a job interview, he has a white cane. Ann asks him if he is blind.

   (b) Craig refuses to hire Ben, who is blind, to work as a playground supervisor because it is essential to the job that the supervisor be able to see what the children are doing.

   (c) Concerned about his company's health insurance rates, Matt requires all job applicants to take a physical.

(d) Concerned about his company's health insurance rates, Josh requires all new hires to take a physical so that he can encourage them to join some of the preventive treatment programs available at the company.

(e) Jennifer refuses to hire Alexis because her child is ill and she frequently has to take him to the hospital.

CASE QUESTIONS

1. When Michelle told her boss that she was pregnant, his first comment was, "Congratulations on your pregnancy. My sister vomited for months." Then he refused to speak to her for a week. A month later, she was fired. Her boss told her the business was shifting away from her area of expertise. Does Michelle have a valid claim? Under what law?

2. The Lillie Rubin boutique in Phoenix would not permit Dick Kovacic to apply for a job as a salesperson. It hired only women to work in sales because fittings and alterations took place in the dressing room or immediately outside. The customers were buying expensive clothes and demanded a male-free dressing area. Has the Lillie Rubin store violated Title VII? What would its defense be?

3. After the terrorist attacks of 9/11, the United States tightened its visa requirements. In the process, baseball teams discovered that 300 foreign-born professional players had lied about their age. (A talented 16-year-old is much more valuable than a 23-year-old with the same skills.) In some cases, the players had used birth certificates that belonged to other (younger) people. To prevent this fraud, baseball teams began asking for DNA tests on prospects and their families to make sure they were not lying about their identity. Is this testing legal?

4. Ronald Lockhart, who was deaf, worked for FedEx as a package handler. Although fluent in American Sign Language, he could not read lips. After 9/11, the company held meetings to talk about security issues. Lockhart complained to the EEOC that he could not understand these discussions. FedEx fired him. Has FedEx violated the law?

5. When the boss fired Clarence from his job at a moving company, she said it was because he could no longer lift heavy furniture, his salary was too high, and as he got older, he would have a hard time remembering stuff. Clarence is 60. Has the boss violated the law?

6. In 1961, NASA began admitting women into its astronaut training program. They performed well in the training but none of them ever served as astronauts because NASA changed its rules to require jet fighter experience for astronauts. Since women were not eligible to fly jet fighters, they could not qualify for space duty. Would these women have had a claim under Title VII?

DISCUSSION QUESTIONS

1. **ETHICS** Mary Ann Singleton was the librarian at a maximum-security prison located in Tazewell County, Virginia. About four times a week, Gene Shinault, assistant warden for operations, persistently complimented Singleton and stared at her breasts when he spoke to her. On one occasion, he measured the length of her skirt to judge its compliance with the prison's dress code and told her that it looked "real good"; constantly told her how attractive he found her; made references to his physical fitness, considering his advanced age; asked Singleton if he made her nervous (she answered "yes"); and repeatedly remarked to Singleton that if he had a wife as attractive as Singleton, he would not permit her to work in a prison facility around so many inmates. Shinault told Singleton's supervisor in her presence, "Look at her. I bet you have to spank her every day." The supervisor then laughed and said, "No. I probably should, but I don't." Shinault replied, "Well, I know I would." Shinault also had a security camera installed in her office in a way that permitted him to observe her as she worked. Singleton reported this behavior to her supervisor, who simply responded, "Boys will be boys." Did Shinault sexually harass Singleton? Whether or not Shinault violated the law, what *ethical* obligation did Singleton's supervisor have to protect her from this type of behavior?

2. When Thomas Lussier filled out a Postal Service employment application, he did not admit that he had twice pleaded guilty to charges of disorderly conduct. Lussier suffered from Post-Traumatic Stress Disorder (PTSD) acquired during military service. Because of this disorder, he sometimes had panic attacks that required him to leave meetings. He was also a recovered alcoholic and drug user. During his stint with the Postal Service, he had some personality conflicts with other employees.

Once, another employee hit him. He also had one episode of "erratic emotional behavior and verbal outburst." In the meantime, a postal employee in Ridgewood, New Jersey, killed four colleagues. The postmaster general encouraged all supervisors to identify workers who had dangerous propensities. Lussier's boss discovered that he had lied on his employment application about the disorderly conduct charges and fired him. Is the Postal Service in violation of the law?

3. Lisa T. Jackson, who was white, worked at Uncle Bubba's Seafood and Oyster House. She filed suit under Title VII, alleging that the restaurant discriminated against black employees. They had to enter through the restaurant's rear entrance and could not use the customer bathrooms. Neither of these prohibitions applied to white staff. Jackson's boss also repeatedly told racist jokes. Jackson stated that this behavior caused her great difficulty in managing the staff, and also immense emotional distress because she had biracial nieces. In addition, one of her bosses asked her how she "looked so white," given that her father was of Sicilian descent. Can Jackson recover under Title VII?

4. Peter Oiler was a truck driver who delivered groceries to Winn-Dixie stores. He revealed to his boss that in his free time he liked to dress as a woman, even though he was happily married to a woman. Oiler had been diagnosed with transvestic fetishism with gender dysphoria and a gender identity disorder. Winn-Dixie fired him for fear that, if customers found out, they would go elsewhere to buy their groceries. Does Oiler have a claim against Winn-Dixie?

5. Title VII does not prohibit discrimination against people who are unattractive. Should it be amended to include looks?

CHAPTER 20

LABOR LAW

© Creative Travel Projects/Shutterstock.com

A strike! For five weeks, the union workers have been walking picket lines at JMJ, a manufacturer of small electrical engines. An entire town of 70,000 citizens, most of them blue-collar workers, is sharply divided, right down to the McNally kitchen table. Buddy, age 48, has worked on the assembly lines at JMJ for more than 25 years. Now he's sipping coffee in the house where he grew up. His sister Kristina, age 46, is a vice president for personnel at JMJ. The two have always been close, but today, the conversation is halting.

"It's time to get back together, Buddy," Kristina murmurs. "The strike is hurting the whole company—and the town."

"Not the *whole* town, Kristina," he tries to quip lightly. "Your management pals still have fat incomes and nice houses."

"Oh yeah?" she attempts to joke, "you haven't seen our porch lately."

"Go talk to Tony Falcione." Buddy replies. "He can't pay his rent."

"Talk to the Ericksons," Kristina snaps back. "They don't even work for JMJ. Their sandwich shop is going under because none of you guys stop in for lunch. Come back to work."

"Not with that clause on the table."

That clause is management's proposal for the new union contract—one that Kristina helped draft. The company officers want the right to subcontract work; that is, to send it out for other companies to perform.

"Buddy, we need the flexibility. K-Ball is underselling us by 35 percent. If we can't compete, there won't be *any* jobs or *any* contract!"

"The way to save money is not by sending our jobs overseas, where people will work for 50 bucks a month."

"Okay, fine. Tell me how we *should* save money."

> An entire town of 70,000 citizens, most of them blue-collar workers, is sharply divided, right down to the McNally kitchen table.

"How can you sit at this table and say these things? In this house? You never would have got a fancy college degree if Dad hadn't made union wages."

"If we can't cut costs, we're out of business. *Then* what's your union going to do for you? All we're asking is the right to subcontract some of the smallest components. Everything else gets built here."

"This is just the start. Next it'll be the wiring, then the batteries, then you'll assemble the whole thing over there—and that'll be it for me. You take that clause off the table, we'll be back in 15 minutes."

"You know I can't do that."

Buddy stands up. They stare silently, sadly, at each other, and then Kristina says, in a barely audible voice, "I have to tell you this. My boss is starting to talk about hiring replacement workers."

Buddy walks out.

20-1 UNIONS DEVELOP

During the nineteenth century, as industrialization spread across America, workers found employment conditions unbearable and wages inadequate. In factories, workers, often women and children, worked 60 to 70 hours a week and sometimes more, standing at assembly lines in suffocating, dimly lit spaces, performing monotonous yet dangerous work for pennies a day. Mines were different—they were worse.

Workers began to band together into unions, but courts and Congress were hostile. From the 1800s through the 1920s, judges routinely issued injunctions against strikes, ruling that unions were either criminal conspiracies or illegal monopolies. With the economic collapse of 1929, however, and the vast suffering of the Great Depression, public sympathy shifted to the workers.

20-1a **Key Statutes**

In 1932, Congress passed the **Norris-LaGuardia Act**, which prohibited federal courts from issuing injunctions in nonviolent labor disputes. Congress was declaring that workers should be permitted to organize unions and to use their collective power to achieve legitimate economic ends.

In 1935, Congress passed the Wagner Act, generally known as the **National Labor Relations Act (NLRA)**. This is the most important of all labor laws. **Section 7 guarantees employees the right to organize and join unions, bargain collectively through representatives of their own choosing, and engage in other concerted activities.**

Section 8 reinforces these rights by outlawing unfair labor practices (ULPs). **Section 8 prohibits employers from engaging in the following ULPs:**

- Interfering with union organizing efforts,

- Dominating or interfering with any union,

- Discriminating against a union member, or

- Refusing to bargain collectively with a union.

Norris-LaGuardia Act

Prohibits federal court injunctions in peaceful labor disputes

National Labor Relations Act (NLRA)

Ensures the right of workers to form unions and encourages management and unions to bargain collectively

Later, § 8 was amended to prohibit unions from engaging in these ULPs:

- Interfering with employees who are exercising their labor rights,

- Causing an employer to discriminate against workers as a means to strengthen the union, and

- Charging excessive dues.

When a union tried to organize Starbucks workers, the company prohibited employees from discussing the union or their working conditions and posting union material on employee bulletin boards. It also punished prounion employees with unfavorable work assignments. All of these actions were ULPs.

The NLRA also established the **National Labor Relations Board (NLRB)** to administer and interpret the statute and to adjudicate labor cases. For example, when a union charges that an employer has committed a ULP—say, by refusing to bargain—the charge goes first to the NLRB.

The Board, which sits in Washington, D.C., has five members, all appointed by the president. The NLRB makes final agency decisions but has no power to *enforce* its orders. If a party refuses to comply, the NLRB must seek enforcement at a federal appeals court. Likewise, the parties can ask that an appeals court overturn an NLRB order.

In the 1950s, the public became aware that certain labor leaders were corrupt. Some officers stole money from large union treasuries, rigged union elections, and stifled opposition within the organization. In 1959, Congress responded by passing the Landrum-Griffin Act, generally called the **Labor-Management Reporting and Disclosure Act (LMRDA)**. The LMRDA requires union leadership to make certain financial disclosures and guarantees free speech and fair elections within a union.

National Labor Relations Board (NLRB)

Administers and interprets the NLRA and adjudicates labor cases

Labor-Management Reporting and Disclosure Act (LMRDA)

Requires union leadership to make financial disclosures and guarantees union members free speech and fair elections

20-1b Labor Unions Today

Organized labor is in flux in the United States. In the 1950s, about 25 percent of workers belonged to a union. Today, only about 11 percent do. That is the lowest level since 1916. Even more remarkable, membership in private sector unions has declined from 35 percent in the 1950s to 6.6 percent now.

There are four major reasons for this decline. One: More states have passed right-to-work laws that permit employees in unionized workplaces to opt out of joining the union or paying dues. Two: Some large employers (such as Boeing) have relocated to states with little union presence. Three: Employment is growing in industries, such as services, that have not traditionally been unionized. Four: Public employees (such as teachers and police officers) are much more likely to be unionized but they are generally not covered by the NLRA. Instead, state labor laws apply, which tend to provide less protection than federal statutes.

This decline in strength reduces union bargaining power. Thus, the auto unions agreed to a two-tiered structure that pays new workers little more than half the wages of long-term employees. All of these factors have contributed to stagnation in pay for the bottom half of wage earners, even as their productivity has increased dramatically.

20-2 ORGANIZING A UNION

20-2a Exclusivity

Under § 9 of the NLRA, a validly recognized union is the exclusive representative of the employees. This means that the union represents all of the designated employees, regardless of whether a particular worker *wants* to be included. The company may not bargain directly with any employee in the group, nor with any other organization representing the designated employees. A **collective bargaining unit** is the precisely defined group of employees who will be represented by a particular union.

However, a union may not exercise power however it likes: Along with a union's exclusive bargaining power goes a duty of fair representation, which requires that a union treat all members fairly, impartially, and in good faith. A union may not favor some members over others, nor may it discriminate against a member based on characteristics such as race or gender.

Collective bargaining unit
The precisely defined group of employees represented by a particular union

20-2b Organizing: Stages

A union organizing effort generally involves the following pattern.

Campaign

Union organizers talk with employees and try to persuade them to form a union. The organizers may be employees of the company, who simply chat with fellow workers about unsatisfactory conditions. Or a union may send nonemployees of the company to hand out union leaflets to workers as they arrive and depart from work.

Authorization Cards

Union organizers ask workers to sign authorization cards, which state that the particular worker requests the specified union to act as her sole bargaining representative. If a union obtains authorization cards from a sizable percentage of workers, it seeks recognition as the exclusive representative for the bargaining unit. The union may ask the employer to recognize it as the bargaining representative, but most of the time, employers refuse to recognize the union voluntarily. The NLRA permits an employer to refuse recognition.

Petition

Assuming that the employer does not voluntarily recognize a union, the union generally petitions the NLRB for an election. It must submit to the NLRB authorization cards signed by at least 30 percent of the workers. If the NLRB determines that the union has identified an appropriate bargaining unit and has enough valid cards, it orders an election.

Election

The NLRB closely supervises the election to ensure fairness. All members of the proposed bargaining unit vote on whether they want the union to represent them. If more than 50 percent of the workers vote for the union, the NLRB designates that union as the exclusive representative of all members of the bargaining unit. When unions hold elections in private corporations, they win about 60 percent of the time. Labor organizations claim that management typically uses company time to campaign against the union. Employers respond that labor loses elections because workers fear that a union will hurt them, not help them.

20-2c Organizing: Actions

What Workers May Do

The NLRA guarantees employees the right (1) to talk among themselves about working conditions and forming a union, (2) to hand out literature, and ultimately (3) to join a union.

Workers have the right to urge other employees to sign authorization cards and to push their cause vigorously. When employees hand out leaflets, the employer generally may not limit the content. In one case, a union distributed leaflets urging workers to vote against political candidates who opposed minimum-wage laws. The employer objected to the union distributing the information on company property, but the Supreme Court upheld the union's right. Even though the content of the writing was not directly related to the union, the connection was close enough that the NLRA protected the union's activity.[1]

There are, of course, limits to what union organizers may do. An employer may restrict organizing discussions if they interfere with business. A worker on a moving assembly line has no right to walk away from his task to talk with other employees about organizing a union. Likewise, management may prohibit union discussions in the presence of customers.

What Employers May Do

The employer may vigorously present antiunion views to its employees but may not use either threats or rewards to defeat a union drive. A company may not fire a worker who favors a union, nor may it suddenly grant a significant pay raise in the midst of a union campaign.

EXAM Strategy

Question: The Teamsters Union is attempting to organize the drivers at We Haul trucking company. Workers who favor a union have been using the lunchroom to hand out petitions and urge other drivers to sign authorization cards. The company posts a notice in the lunchroom: "Many employees do not want unions discussed in the lunchroom. Out of respect for them, we are prohibiting further union efforts in this lunchroom." Is this sign legal?

Strategy: The NLRA guarantees employees the right to talk among themselves about forming a union and to hand out literature. Management has the right to present antiunion views.

Result: We Haul has violated the NLRA. The company has the right to urge employees not to join the union. However, it is not entitled to block the union from its organizing campaign. Even assuming the company is correct that some employees do not want unions discussed, it has no right to prohibit such advocacy.

Appropriate Bargaining Unit

When a union petitions the NLRB for an election, the Board determines whether the proposed bargaining unit is appropriate. **The Board generally certifies a proposed bargaining unit if and only if the employees share a "community of interest."** In making this determination, the Board looks for rough similarity of training, skills, hours of work, and pay.

Managerial employees must be excluded from the bargaining unit. An employee is managerial if she is so closely aligned with management that her membership in the bargaining unit would create a conflict of interest between her union membership and her actual work. For example, a factory worker who spends one-third of his time performing assembly work but two-thirds of his time supervising a dozen other workers could not fairly be part of the bargaining unit.

Employers frequently assert that a bargaining unit is inappropriate. If the Board agrees, it dismisses the union's request for an election. Otherwise, it certifies the bargaining unit.

---

[1]*Eastex, Inc. v. NLRB*, 434 U.S. 1045 (S.Ct. 1978).

20-3 COLLECTIVE BARGAINING

The goal of bargaining is to create a new contract, which is called a **collective bargaining agreement (CBA)**. Problems can arise as union and employer advocate their respective positions. Three of the most common conflicts are (1) whether an issue is a mandatory subject of bargaining; (2) whether the parties are bargaining in good faith; and (3) how to enforce the agreement.

Collective bargaining agreement (CBA)
A contract between a union and management

20-3a Subjects of Bargaining

The NLRA *permits* the parties to bargain almost any subject they wish but *requires* them to bargain certain issues. **Mandatory subjects include wages, hours, and other terms and conditions of employment.** Either side may propose to bargain other subjects, but neither side may insist upon bargaining them.

Management and unions often disagree about whether a particular topic is mandatory. Courts generally find these subjects to be mandatory: pay, benefits, order of layoffs and recalls, production quotas, work rules (such as safety practices), retirement benefits, and in-plant food service and prices (e.g., cafeteria food). Courts usually consider these subjects to be nonmandatory: product type and design, advertising, sales, financing, corporate organization, and location of plants.

Some of the most heated disputes between management and labor are caused by a company's desire to subcontract work or to move plants to areas with cheaper costs. Is a business free to subcontract work? That depends on management's motive. A company that subcontracts in order to maintain its economic viability is probably not required to bargain first; however, **bargaining is mandatory if the subcontracting is designed to replace union workers with cheaper labor.**

Employer and Union Security

Both the employer and the union will seek clauses making their positions more secure. Management, above all, wants to be sure that there will be no strikes during the course of the agreement. For its part, the union tries to ensure that its members cannot be turned away from work during the CBA's term and that all newly hired workers will affiliate with the union. We look next at two specific union security issues.

No Strike/No Lockout. Most agreements include some form of no-strike clause, meaning that the union promises not to strike during the term of the contract. In turn, unions insist on a no-lockout clause, meaning that in the event of a labor dispute, management will not prevent union members from working. **No-strike and no-lockout clauses are both legal.**

Union Shop. In a union shop, membership in the union becomes compulsory after the employee has been hired. Thus management retains the right to hire whom it pleases, but all new employees who fit into the bargaining unit must affiliate with the union. **A union shop is generally legal**, with two limitations. First, new members need not join the union for 30 days. Second, the new members, after joining the union, can only be required to pay initiation fees and union dues. If the new hire decides he does not want to participate in the union, the union may not compel him to do so.

20-3b Duty to Bargain

The union and the employer are not obligated to reach an agreement, but they are required to bargain in good faith. In other words, the two sides must meet with open minds and make a reasonable effort to reach a contract. In the following Landmark Case, a company violated this rule.

Landmark Case

NLRB v. TRUITT MANUFACTURING CO.
351 U.S. 149
United States Supreme Court, 1956

CASE SUMMARY

Facts: A union representing workers at Truitt Manufacturing Company requested a raise of 10 cents per hour for all members. The company countered with an offer of 2.5 cents, arguing that a larger increase would bankrupt the company. The union demanded to examine Truitt's books, and when the company refused, the union complained to the NLRB.

The NLRB determined that the company had committed a ULP by failing to bargain in good faith and ordered it to allow union representatives to examine its finances. A court of appeals found no ULP and refused to enforce the Board's order. The Supreme Court granted *certiorari*.

Issues: *Did the company bargain in good faith? Did it commit a ULP?*
Decision: The company's refusal to bargain in good faith was a ULP.
Reasoning: The NLRA does not require employers and unions to reach agreement, but it does expect that they will make a good faith effort to do so. Good-faith bargaining requires that the negotiators make honest claims.

The company's ability to pay an increase in wages is an important negotiating issue. Sometimes, if a company's economic environment is particularly challenging, unions will abandon a request for raises, or even accept wage decreases. If the company's finances are an important factor in negotiations, then they require some proof of accuracy.

Bargaining to impasse
Both parties must continue to meet and bargain in good faith until it is clear that they cannot reach an agreement.

Sometimes an employer will attempt to make changes without bargaining the issues at all. However, **management may not unilaterally change wages, hours, or terms and conditions of employment without bargaining the issues to impasse. Bargaining to impasse** means that both parties must continue to meet and bargain in good faith until it is clear that they cannot reach an agreement.

The goal in requiring collective bargaining is to bring the parties together to reach an agreement that brings labor peace. In one case, the union won an election, but before bargaining could begin, management changed the schedule from five 8-hour days to four 10-hour days a week. The company also changed its layoff policy from strict seniority to merit and began laying off employees based on alleged poor performance. The court held that each of these acts violated the company's duty to bargain. The employer ultimately might be allowed to make every one of these changes, but first it had to bargain the issues to impasse.

20-3c Enforcement

Grievance
A formal complaint alleging a contract violation

Arbitration
A formal hearing before a neutral party to resolve a contract dispute between a union and a company

Virtually all collective bargaining agreements provide for their own enforcement, typically through a grievance and arbitration process. Suppose a company transfers an employee from the day shift to the night shift, and the worker believes the contract prohibits such a transfer for any employee with her seniority. The employee complains to the union, which files a **grievance**; that is, a formal complaint with the company notifying management that the union claims a contract violation. Generally, the CBA establishes some kind of informal hearing, usually conducted by a member of management, at which the employee, represented by the union, may state her case.

After the manager's decision, if the employee is still dissatisfied, the union may file for **arbitration**, that is, a formal hearing before a neutral arbitrator. In the arbitration hearing, each side is represented by its lawyer. The arbitrator is required to decide the case based on the CBA. An arbitrator finds either for the employee, and orders the company to take certain corrective action, or for the employer, and dismisses the grievance.

In the vast majority of grievances, the arbitrator's decision is final. The following case demonstrates how reluctant courts are to interfere with an arbitrator's decision.

BRENTWOOD MEDICAL ASSOCIATES V. UNITED MINE WORKERS OF AMERICA

396 F.3d 237
United States Court of Appeals for the Third Circuit, 2005

CASE SUMMARY

Facts: Brentwood Medical Associates (BMA) operated a hospital. The United Mine Workers of America represented one unit of employees, which included Denise Cope, a phlebotomist (someone who draws blood). Exercising her seniority rights, Cope changed jobs to Charge Entry Associate. A year and a half later, BMA announced it was terminating the position. Cope asked to return to her old job. This would have required "bumping" the least-senior phlebotomist out of a job. BMA refused, claiming that bumping was not allowed under the CBA. Cope filed a grievance, which an arbitrator heard.

The arbitrator ruled in Cope's favor. In his decision, he asked why, if the CBA disallowed bumping, it included the following language: "employees who exercise seniority rights and bump must have the skill to perform all of the work [in the new job]."

The problem with the quoted language was that it did not in fact exist anywhere in the CBA. BMA filed suit, asking a federal court to overturn the arbitration decision. The trial court upheld the award, and BMA appealed.

Issue: *Should the arbitration award be affirmed even though the arbitrator relied on language that cannot be found in the CBA?*

Decision: Yes, the decision is affirmed.

Reasoning: The parties wanted arbitration, bargained for it, and included it in their CBA. Full-blown judicial review of the arbitrator's decision would contravene their agreement, injecting a judicial interpretation that neither side expected.

Although the arbitrator did cite language he should not have, his decision relied on several provisions of the agreement. For example, § 1 defines seniority as "bargaining unit-wide" and not within classification. Section 2 provides that the principle of seniority is a factor in layoffs and recalls. Section 5 specifies that in filling vacancies when the qualifications of two or more applicants are relatively equal, preference will be based on seniority.

The arbitrator's award does not rest solely upon the fictitious language that he unfortunately invented. He attempted to honor the intent of the agreement.

20-4 CONCERTED ACTION

Concerted action refers to any tactics union members take in unison to gain some bargaining advantage. It is this power that gives a union strength. **The NLRA guarantees the right of employees to engage in concerted action for mutual aid or protection.** The most common forms of concerted action are strikes and picketing.

Concerted action
Tactics taken by union members to gain bargaining advantage

20-4a **Strikes**

The NLRA guarantees employees the right to strike, but with some limitations. A union has a guaranteed right to call a strike if the parties are unable to reach a collective bargaining agreement. A union may also call a strike to protest a ULP or to preserve work that the employer is considering sending elsewhere.

This right to strike can be waived. As we have seen, management will generally insist that the CBA include a no-strike clause, which prohibits the union from striking while the CBA is in force. A strike is illegal in several other situations as well; here, we mention the most important.

Cooling Off Period

Before striking to terminate or modify a CBA, a union must give management 60 days' notice. This cooling-off period is designed to give both sides a chance to reassess negotiations and to decide whether some additional compromise would be wiser than enduring a strike. Suppose a union contract expires July 1. The two sides attempt to bargain a new contract, but progress is slow. The union may strike as an economic weapon, but it must notify management of its intention to do so *and then must wait 60 days*. This 60-day period does not apply to a ULP strike.

Statutory Prohibition

Many states have outlawed strikes by public employees. The purpose of these statutes is to ensure that unions do not use public health or welfare as a weapon to secure an unfair bargaining advantage. However, even employees subject to such a rule may find other tactics to press their cause.

Sit-Down Strikes

Sit-down strike
Members stop working but remain at their job posts, blocking replacement workers

In a **sit-down strike**, members stop working but remain at their job posts, physically blocking replacement workers from taking their places. This type of strike is illegal.

Partial Strikes

A partial strike occurs when employees stop working temporarily, then resume, then stop again, and so forth. This tactic is particularly disruptive because management cannot bring in replacement workers. A union may either walk off the job or stay on it, but it may not alternate.

Ethics Suppose state law prohibits teachers from striking, but the teachers' union is angry. Their contract expired a year ago, and the Board of Education has refused any pay raises. The teachers decide they will "work to rule," meaning they will teach classes, issues grades, and so forth ... but will not write any college recommendations. Is the teachers' refusal to perform any "extras" an ethical tactic? What would Mill and Kant say?

20-4b Replacement Workers

When employees go on strike, management has the right to use replacement workers to keep the business operating. What about after the strike ends: May the employer offer the replacement workers permanent jobs, or must the company give union members their jobs back when the strike is over? It depends on the type of strike.

Economic strike
One intended to gain wages or benefits

An **economic strike** is one intended to gain wages or benefits. During an economic strike, an employer may hire *permanent* replacement workers. When the strike is over, the company has no obligation to lay off the replacement workers to make room for the strikers. However, if and when the company does hire more workers, it may not discriminate against the strikers.

After an unfair labor practices (ULP) strike, a union member is entitled to her job back, even if that means the employer must lay off a replacement worker. In the *Truitt* case, the Supreme Court ruled that the company had committed an ULP. If the union had gone out on strike, the company would have had to hire back all the union members once the strike was over, regardless of how many replacement workers it had hired.

You can see why, in the following case, the company and union argued so fiercely about the nature of the strike.

SPURLINO MATERIALS, LLC

357 NLRB No. 126
National Labor Relations Board, 2011

CASE SUMMARY

Facts: For some years, Spurlino Materials, maker of ready-mix concrete, had been locked in a stalemate with its employees' union. During this time, it had fired Gary Stevenson, one of the union's most prominent supporters. The NLRB determined that this firing was a ULP and ordered Spurlino to reinstate him. But the company filed an appeal in court. For various complex legal reasons, four years passed without a final judgment in the Stevenson case and none seemed likely for years more.

Jim Cahill, the union's president, called a union meeting where he gave a report on the Stevenson litigation. At least one person also asked about contract negotiations, but it was not a focus of the meeting. Union members then voted for a ULP strike. When a company manager found out about the strike vote, he called a meeting with union employees at which he discussed the history of the parties' contract negotiations and warned them that, if they went out on strike, they would be replaced and would not get their jobs back.

The union notified management that it was calling a ULP strike and demanded Stevenson's reinstatement. Members picketed, holding signs stating that they were on a ULP strike. Spurlino hired replacement workers and continued to operate. After a week, the union ended the strike and asked for their jobs back. Spurlino refused to recall any of the strikers because, it argued, the Stevenson issue was just a pretext: The strike had really been an economic strike about the failure of contract negotiations.

Issues: *Was this strike economic or ULP? Must Spurlino recall the striking workers?*

Decision: It was a ULP strike, and Spurlino must recall the strikers.

Reasoning: In evaluating whether an event is a ULP or economic strike, the Board examines all the facts to determine the employees' motivation for striking. As long as a ULP is one motivation, even if not the primary goal, the strike counts as a ULP action, and workers are safe from permanent replacement.

Here, there is abundant evidence that the strike was motivated, at least in part, by Spurlino's unfair labor practices. The union at all times said it was engaging in a ULP strike including when it called the meeting to take a vote, the employees voted, the union notified management, and the strikers picketed. At no time during the strike did the union make any economic demands on Spurlino. The company argues that the ULP was just a pretext, but the evidence indicates that the ULP was as important a motivation as the economic issues.

20-4c Picketing

The goal of picketing is to discourage employees, replacement workers, and customers from doing business with the company. **Picketing the employer's workplace in support of a strike is generally lawful.** However, the picketers are not permitted to use physical force to prevent someone from crossing the line. The company may terminate violent picketers and permanently replace them, regardless of the nature of the strike.

Secondary boycotts are generally illegal. A secondary boycott is a picket line established not at the employer's premises but at a different workplace. If Union is on strike against Truck Co., it is free to picket Truck Co.'s office and terminal. But Union cannot set up a picket line at a supermarket where Truck Co. delivers in an effort to pressure Truck Co. by persuading shoppers and other workers to boycott the store.

> **150 employees find the company's gate locked and armed guards standing on the other side.**

20-4d **Lockouts**

The workers have bargained with management for weeks, and discussions have turned belligerent. It is 6 a.m., the start of another day at the factory. But as 150 employees arrive for work, they are amazed to find the company's gate locked and armed guards standing on the other side. This is a **lockout**: Management has prohibited workers from entering the premises and earning their paychecks.

A lockout is generally legal if the parties have reached a bargaining impasse. Most courts consider that a lockout before impasse indicates unacceptable hostility to the union.

Lockout
Management prohibits workers from entering the premises

EXAM Strategy

Question: Union workers are striking at Cheesey, forming picket lines in front of the restaurant during the lunch and dinner hours, but at no other times. The union members chant slogans denouncing their wages and working conditions, urging diners not to enter. There is no violence, but the picketers cause many prospective customers to stay away, and Cheesey suffers a substantial drop in business. The restaurant files a charge with the NLRB, claiming that the union has committed a ULP by (1) deliberately harming its business and (2) engaging in a secondary boycott. Who will win?

Strategy: Striking workers are allowed to picket. May they *urge* non-union members to stay out of the business? May they *prohibit* others from entering? Secondary boycotts are illegal. Is this one?

Result: Striking workers may urge the public not to cross the picket line. The union may not use violence to keep people out, but this union has not done so. This is not a secondary boycott, because it has not been established at a *different* company that does business with the employer. The company's loss of business is one possible—and legal—consequence of a strike. The union has committed no ULP.

Chapter Conclusion

Contemporary clashes between union and management are less likely to stem from sweltering temperatures in a mine than from a management decision to subcontract work or from a teacher's refusal to write college recommendations. But although the flash points have changed, labor law is still dominated by issues of organizing, collective bargaining, and concerted action.

EXAM REVIEW

1. **RIGHT TO ORGANIZE** Section 7 of the National Labor Relations Act (NLRA) guarantees employees the right to organize and join unions, bargain collectively, and engage in other concerted activities.

2. **EMPLOYER INTERFERENCE** Under the NLRA, it is an unfair labor practice (ULP) for an employer to interfere with union organizing, dominate a union, discriminate against a union member, or refuse to bargain collectively.

3. **UNION INTERFERENCE** Under the NLRA, it is a ULP for a union to interfere with employees who are exercising their labor rights, cause an employer to discriminate against workers as a means to strengthen the union, or charge excessive dues.

4. **EXCLUSIVITY** Under the NLRA, a validly recognized union is the exclusive representative of the employees.

5. **WORKER RIGHTS** The NLRA guarantees employees the right (1) to talk among themselves about working conditions and forming a union, (2) to hand out literature, and ultimately (3) to join a union.

6. **EMPLOYER RIGHTS** During a union organizing campaign, an employer may vigorously present antiunion views to its employees, but it may not use threats or promises of benefits to defeat the union effort.

EXAM Strategy

Question: Power, Inc., which operated a coal mine, suffered financial losses and had to lay off employees. The United Mine Workers of America began an organizing drive. Power's general manager warned miners that if the company was unionized, it would be shut down. An office manager told one of the miners that the company would get rid of union supporters. Shortly before the election was to take place, Power laid off 13 employees, all of whom had signed union cards. A low-seniority employee who had not signed a union card was not laid off. The union claimed that Power had committed ULPs. Comment.

Strategy: The NLRA guarantees employees the right to organize. An employer may vigorously advocate against a union organizing campaign. However, it is a ULP to interfere with union organizing or discriminate against a union member. (See the "Result" at the end of this section.)

7. **APPROPRIATE BARGAINING UNIT** The National Labor Relations Board (NLRB) will certify a proposed bargaining unit only if the employees share a community of interest.

8. BARGAINING   The employer and the union must bargain over wages, hours, and other terms and conditions of employment. They must bargain in good faith, but they are not obligated to reach an agreement.

Question: Concrete Company was bargaining a CBA with the drivers' union. Negotiations went on for many months. Concrete made its final offer of $9.50 per hour, with step increases of $0.75 per hour in a year, and the same the following two years. The union refused to accept the offer, and the two sides reached an impasse. Concrete then implemented its plan, minus the step increases. Was its implementation legal?

Strategy: Management may unilaterally change wages and so forth only if the parties have reached an impasse. At all stages, the two sides must bargain in good faith. The goal of the NLRA is to achieve labor peace through productive negotiations. (See the "Result" at the end of this section.)

9. STRIKES   The NLRA guarantees employees the right to strike, with some limitations.

10. COOLING OFF PERIOD   Before striking to terminate or modify a CBA, a union must give management 60 days' notice.

11. REPLACEMENT WORKERS   During an economic strike, management may hire permanent replacement workers. After a (ULP) strike, a union member is entitled to her job back, even if that means the employer must lay off a replacement worker.

12. PICKETING   Picketing the employer's workplace in support of a strike is generally lawful, but secondary boycotts are usually illegal.

13. LOCKOUTS   Lockouts are lawful if the parties have bargained to impasse.

6. Result: Each of the acts described was a ULP. Threatening layoffs or company closure are classic examples of ULPs. Laying off those who had signed union cards, but not those who refused, was clear discrimination.

8. Result: The implementation was illegal because the company showed bad faith. Although the parties had reached an impasse, the company still did not have the right to implement a plan that it had never proposed at the bargaining table. To allow the company to implement something that it had never offered would defeat the whole purpose of bargaining.

MATCHING QUESTIONS

Match the following terms with their definitions:

___A. ULP

___B. Exclusivity

___C. Collective bargaining unit

___D. Union shop

___E. Concerted action

1. A specific group of employees that a union will represent

2. The union's right to be the sole representative of workers

3. Unlawful management interference with a union organizing effort

4. Picketing and strikes

5. The requirement that workers within specified categories join the union

TRUE/FALSE QUESTIONS

Circle true or false:

1. T F The union and management are both obligated to bargain until they reach a CBA or a court declares the bargaining futile.

2. T F Health benefits are a mandatory subject of bargaining.

3. T F The union has the right to decide the appropriate bargaining unit.

4. T F Workers are entitled to form a union whether management wants them to or not.

5. T F While organizing, workers may not discuss union issues on company property but may do so off the premises.

MULTIPLE-CHOICE QUESTIONS

1. During a union organizing drive, management urges workers not to join the union and discusses a competing company that lost business after a union was formed. Management:

    (a) committed a ULP by urging workers to reject the union, but did not do so by discussing a competing company.

    (b) committed a ULP by discussing a competing company, but did not do so by urging workers to reject the union.

    (c) committed a ULP both by urging workers to reject the union and by discussing a competitor.

    (d) committed no ULP.

    (e) has violated other sections of the NLRA.

2. Which of these rights does the NLRA *not* protect?

   (a) right to form a union

   (b) right to picket

   (c) right to strike

   (d) right to block nonunion workers from company property

   (e) right to bargain collectively

3. The CBA at Red Corp. has expired, as has the CBA at Blue Corp. At Red, union and management have bargained a new CBA to impasse. Suddenly, Red locks out all union workers. The next day, during a bargaining session at Blue, management announces that it will not discuss pay increases.

   (a) Red has committed a ULP, but Blue has not.

   (b) Blue has committed a ULP, but Red has not.

   (c) Both Blue and Red have committed ULPs.

   (d) Neither company has committed a ULP.

   (e) Red and Blue have violated labor law, but not by committing ULPs.

4. When the union went on strike, the company replaced Ashley, a union member, with Ben, a non–union member. The strike is now over, and a federal court has ruled that this was a ULP strike. Does Ashley get her job back?

   (a) The company is obligated to hire Ashley, even if that requires laying off Ben.

   (b) The company is obligated to hire Ashley *unless* that would require laying off Ben.

   (c) The company is obligated to hire Ashley only if Ben voluntarily leaves.

   (d) The company is obligated to hire Ashley only when an opening occurs.

   (e) The company has no obligation at all to Ashley.

5. When new hires are forced to join an existing union, a union shop———————— exist. This kind of arrangement———————— legal under the NLRA.

   (a) does; is

   (b) does; is not

   (c) does not; is

   (d) does not; is not

CASE QUESTIONS

1. Gibson Greetings, Inc., had a plant in Berea, Kentucky, where the workers belonged to the International Brotherhood of Firemen & Oilers. The old CBA expired, and the parties negotiated a new one, but they were unable to reach an agreement on economic issues. The union struck. At the next bargaining session, the company claimed that the strike violated the old CBA, which had a no-strike clause and which stated that the terms of the old CBA would continue in force as long as the parties were bargaining a new CBA. The company refused to bargain until the union at least agreed that by bargaining, the company was not giving up its claim of an illegal strike. The two sides returned to bargaining, but meanwhile the company hired replacement

workers. Eventually, the striking workers offered to return to work, but Gibson refused to rehire many of them. In court, the union claimed that the company had committed a ULP by (1) insisting the strike was illegal; and (2) refusing to bargain until the union acknowledged the company's position. Why is it very important to the union to establish the company's act as a ULP? *Was* it a ULP?

2. Fred Schipul taught English at the Thomaston High School in Connecticut for 18 years. When the position of English Department chairperson became vacant, Schipul applied, but the Board of Education appointed a less-senior teacher. Schipul filed a grievance based on a CBA provision that required the Board to promote the most-senior teacher where two or more applicants were equal in qualification. Before the arbitrator ruled on the grievance, the Board eliminated all department chairpersons. The arbitrator ruled in Schipul's favor. The Board then reinstated all department chairs—all but the English Department. Comment.

3. A foreman at Progressive Electric told employees that the company's president, "didn't want any union crap around here," and that "if the unions got into Progressive, Progressive would lose contracts and go out of business because Progressive couldn't afford the union wages and benefits." Is the foreman in violation of the NLRA?

4. Triec, Inc., is a small electrical contracting company in Springfield, Ohio, owned by executives Yeazell, Jones, and Heaton. Employees contacted the International Brotherhood of Electrical Workers, which began an organizing drive, and 6 of the 11 employees in the bargaining unit signed authorization cards. The company declined to recognize the union, which petitioned the NLRB to schedule an election. The company then granted several new benefits for all workers, including higher wages, paid vacations, and other measures. When the election was held, only 2 of the 11 bargaining unit members voted for the union. Did the company violate the NLRA?

5. Eads Transfer, Inc., was a moving and storage company with a small workforce represented by the General Teamsters, Chauffeurs, and Helpers Union. When the CBA expired, the parties failed to reach agreement on a new one, and the union struck. As negotiations continued, Eads hired temporary replacement workers. After 10 months of the strike, some union workers offered to return to work, but Eads made no response to the offer. Two months later, more workers offered to return to work, but Eads would not accept any of the offers. Eventually, Eads notified all workers that they would not be allowed back to work until a new CBA had been signed. The union filed ULP claims against the company. Please rule.

DISCUSSION QUESTIONS

1. The full-time faculty at Private University were responsible for determining the university's curriculum, grading system, and academic standards. PU's central administration formulated the rules on teaching loads, salaries, tenure, sabbaticals, retirement, and fringe benefits, although it often adopted the faculty's recommendations on these issues. The administration also approved all budgets. The faculty sought to form a union. Should the NLRB certify PU's faculty as a union?

2. Hoffman Plastics fired Jose Castro because he was supporting the efforts of union organizers. During NLRB hearings concerning his termination, Castro

revealed for the first time that he was in the United States illegally. He had used false documents to obtain the job at Hoffman. Despite his illegal status, the NLRB found that Hoffman's retaliatory firing violated the NLRA and ordered the company to pay Castro $66,951 in back pay. Hoffman challenged the order in court. Should Hoffman have to pay?

3. While a union was trying to organize workers at Reading Batteries, some of the employees engaged in a sit-down strike to force the company to recognize the union. At the same time, the company laid off some workers because of reduced seasonal demand. Must Reading rehire these workers when demand improves?

4. Once a union is recognized, it acts as the exclusive representative for all workers in a bargaining unit, even if some of them do not want the union to represent them. Is this reasonable? Should individual employees be able to "opt out"? Would it be unfair for workers to get all the benefit of the union without having to pay dues?

5. Union workers earn an average of $200 per week more than non-union workers. Many people believe that unions are an essential part of creating a broad middle class, while others argue that they create undeserved windfalls for members. What is your view on this issue?

© Creative Travel Projects/Shutterstock.com

UNIT 5

The Lifecycle of a Business

CHAPTER 21

STARTING A BUSINESS: LLCS AND OTHER OPTIONS

© Creative Travel Projects/Shutterstock.com

Poor Jeffrey Horning. If only he had understood business law. Horning owned a thriving construction company, which operated as a corporation—Horning Construction Company, Inc. To lighten his crushing workload, he decided to bring in two partners to handle more day-to-day responsibility. It seemed a good idea at the time.

Horning transferred the business to Horning Construction, LLC, and then gave one-third ownership each to two trusted employees, Klimowski and Holdsworth. But Horning did not pay enough attention to the legal formalities—the new LLC had no operating agreement.

Jeffrey Horning was stuck in purgatory, with two business partners he loathed and no way out.

Nothing worked out as he had planned. The two men did not take on extra work. Horning's relationship with them went from bad to worse, with the parties bickering over every petty detail and each man trying to sabotage the others. It got to the point that Klimowski sent Horning a letter full of insults and expletives. At his wit's end, Horning proposed that the LLC buy out his share of the business. Klimowski and Holdsworth refused. Really frustrated, Horning asked a court to dissolve the business on the grounds that Klimowski despised him, Holdsworth resented him, and neither of them trusted him. In his view, it was their goal "to make my remaining time with Horning, LLC so unbearable that I will relent and give them for a pittance the remainder of the company for which they have paid nothing to date."

Although the court was sympathetic, it refused to help. Because Horning, LLC, did not have an operating agreement that provided for a buyout, it had to depend upon the LLC statute, which only permitted dissolution "whenever it is not reasonably practicable to carry on the business." Unfortunately, Horning, LLC, was very successful, grossing over $25 million annually. Jeffrey Horning was stuck in purgatory, with two business partners he loathed and no way out.[1]

The law affects virtually every aspect of business. Wise (and successful) entrepreneurs know how to use the law to their advantage.

To begin, entrepreneurs must select a form of organization. The correct choice can reduce taxes, liability, and conflict while facilitating outside investment.

21-1 SOLE PROPRIETORSHIPS

A sole proprietorship is an unincorporated business owned by one person. Linda owns ExSciTe (which stands for Excellence in Science Teaching), a sole proprietorship that helps teachers prepare hands-on science experiments in the classroom using such basic items as vinegar, lemon juice, and red cabbage.

Sole proprietorship
An unincorporated business owned by one person

The advantages of a sole proprietorship are:

- **Ease of formation.** If an individual runs a business without taking any formal steps to create an organization, she automatically has a sole proprietorship. Generally, there is no need to hire a lawyer or register with the state, so costs are low.

- **Taxes.** A sole proprietorship is a **flow-through tax entity**, which means that, although Linda must pay *personal* income tax on any profit she earns, the *business* itself does not pay income taxes. The business is not even required to file a separate tax return.

Flow-through tax entity
An organization that does not pay income tax on its profits but passes them through to its owners who pay the tax at their individual rates

Sole proprietorships also have some serious disadvantages:

- **Liability.** As the owner of the business, Linda is responsible for all of its debts. If ExSciTe cannot pay its suppliers or if a student is injured by an exploding cabbage, Linda is *personally* liable.

- **Limited capital.** The owner of a sole proprietorship has limited options for financing her business. Debt is generally her only source of working capital because she has no stock or memberships to sell. For this reason, sole proprietorships work best for small businesses without large capital needs.

21-2 CORPORATIONS

Corporations are the dominant form of organization for a simple reason—they have been around for a long time, and, as a result, they are numerous, and the law that regulates them is well developed.

---

[1]*Matter of Jeffrey M. Horning v. Horning Constr. LLC*, 12 Misc. 3d 402 (N.Y. Sup. Ct. 2006).

21-2a Corporations in General

As is the case for all forms of organization, corporations have their advantages and disadvantages.

Advantages of a Corporation

Limited Liability. If a business flops, its shareholders lose their investment in the company but not their other assets. Likewise, if Emily Employee injures another motorist while driving a company van, the business is liable for any harm, but its shareholders are not personally liable.

Be aware, however, **individuals are always responsible for their *own* acts.** If Emily was careless, then she would be liable even though she was a company shareholder. If the company did not pay the judgment, Emily would have to, from her personal assets. **A corporation protects managers and investors from personal liability for the debts of the corporation and the actions of others, but not against liability for their own negligence (or other torts and crimes).**

Transferability of Interests. As we will see, partnership interests are not transferable without the permission of the other partners, whereas corporate stock can be bought and sold easily.

Duration. When a sole proprietor dies, legally so does the business. But corporations have perpetual existence: They can continue without their founders.

Disadvantages of a Corporation

But the corporate form is not perfect. Here are some disadvantages:

Logistics. **Corporations require substantial expense and effort to create and operate.** The cost of establishing a corporation includes legal and filing fees, not to mention the cost of the annual filings and taxes that states require. Corporations must also hold meetings for both shareholders and directors. Minutes of these meetings must be kept indefinitely in the company minute book.

Taxes. As we have seen, a sole proprietorship is a flow-through entity that does not pay taxes itself; all taxes are paid directly by the owner. Shortly, we will look at other flow-through entities, such as partnerships and limited liability companies (LLCs) where, again, all taxes are paid directly by the owners, and none by the business itself. In contrast, a corporation is a taxable entity, which means it must pay income taxes on its profits and also file a tax return. Shareholders must then pay tax on any dividends from the corporation. Thus, with a flow-through organization, a dollar is taxed only once before it ends up in the owner's bank account, but twice before it is deposited by a shareholder.

Exhibit 21.1 compares the single taxation of an LLC (a flow-through entity) with the double taxation of corporations. Suppose, as shown in the exhibit, that a corporation and an LLC each receives $10,000 in additional income. The corporation pays tax at a top rate of 35 percent.[2] Thus, the corporation pays $3,500 of the $10,000 in tax. The corporation pays out the remaining $6,500 as a dividend of $2,167 to each of its three shareholders. Then, the shareholders are taxed at the special dividend rate of 20 percent, which means they each pay a tax of $433.10 They are each left with $1,734. Of the initial $10,000, almost 48 percent ($4,799) has gone to the Internal Revenue Service (IRS).

---

[2]This is the federal tax rate; most states also levy a corporate tax.

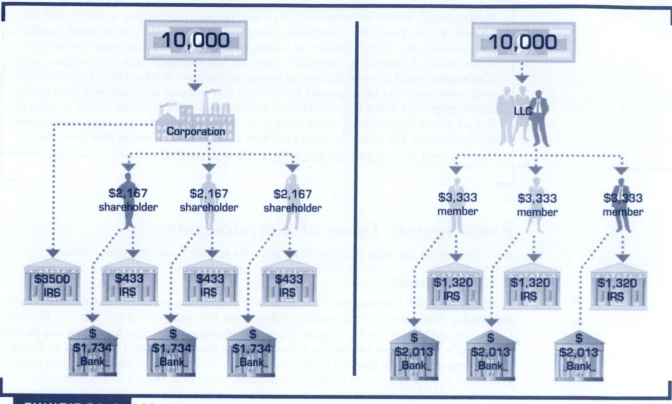

EXHIBIT 21.1   Members of an LLC pay lower taxes than shareholders.

Compare the corporation to an LLC. The LLC itself pays no taxes, so it can pass on $3,333 to each of its owners (who are called "members"). Assuming a 39.6 percent individual rate, each member pays an income tax of $1,320. As members, they pocket $2,013, which is $279 more than they could keep as shareholders. Of the LLC's initial $10,000, 39.6 percent ($3,960) has gone to the IRS, compared with the corporation's 48 percent.[3]

EXAM Strategy

Question: Consider these two entrepreneurs: Judith formed a corporation to write a blog that is unlikely to generate substantial revenues. Drexel operated his construction business as a sole proprietorship. Were these forms of organization right for these businesses?

Strategy: Prepare a list of the advantages and disadvantages of each form of organization. Sole proprietorships are best for businesses without substantial capital needs. Corporations can raise capital but are expensive to operate.

---

[3]These calculations assume the highest tax rates. As of this writing, the maximum tax rate on dividends is 20% and on regular individual income is 39.6%.

Result: Judith would be better off with a sole proprietorship—her revenues will not support the expenses of a corporation. Also, her debts are likely to be small, so she will not need the limited liability of a corporation. And no matter what her form of organization, she would be personally liable for any negligent acts she commits, so a corporation would not provide any additional protection. But for Drexel, a sole proprietorship could be disastrous because his construction company will have substantial expenses and a large number of employees. If an employee causes an injury, Drexel might be personally liable. And if his business fails, the court would take his personal assets. He would be better off with a form of organization that limits his liability, such as a corporation or a limited liability company.

21-2b Special Types of Corporations

Both the federal tax code and state laws allow for special types of corporations.

S Corporations

Congress created S corporations (aka "S corps") to encourage entrepreneurship by offering tax breaks. The name "S corporation" comes from the provision of the Internal Revenue Code that created this form of organization. **Shareholders of S corps have both the limited liability of a corporation and the tax status of a flow-through entity.** Thus, all of an S corp's profits (and losses) pass through to the shareholders, who pay tax at their individual rates. It avoids the double taxation of a regular corporation (sometimes called a "C corporation"). If, as is often the case with start-ups, the business loses money, investors can deduct these losses against their other income.

S corps do face some major restrictions:

- There can be only one class of stock.

- There can be no more than 100 shareholders.

- Shareholders must be individuals, estates, charities, pension funds, or trusts, not partnerships or corporations.

- Shareholders must be citizens or residents of the United States, not nonresident aliens.

- All shareholders must agree that the company should be an S corporation.

Close Corporations

As with S corps, a goal of close corporation statutes is to encourage entrepreneurship. But close corporations are created by state law and, therefore, these entities are not entitled to special treatment under the federal tax code unless they also register for S corp status with the IRS. Likewise, a corporation that qualifies for S Corp status with the IRS will not necessarily by treated as a close corporation under state law unless it complies with those particular requirements.

A typical **close corporation** has a small number of shareholders (usually fewer than 50), stock that is not publicly traded, and shareholders who play an active role in the management of the enterprise. Although the rules of close corporations may vary from state to state, generally these organizations share certain features:

- **Protection of minority shareholders.** As there is no public market for the stock of a close corporation, a minority shareholder who is being mistreated by the majority cannot simply sell his shares and depart. Therefore, close corporation laws typically

Close corporation

A corporation with a small number of shareholders whose stock is not publicly traded and whose shareholders play an active role in management- it is entitled to special treatment under state law.

protect minority shareholders by holding that majority shareholders owe them a fiduciary duty. In addition, the charter of a close corporation may require a unanimous vote of all shareholders to choose officers, set salaries, or pay dividends. It could grant each shareholder veto power over all important corporate decisions.

- **Transfer restrictions.** The shareholders of a close corporation often need to work closely together in the management of the company. Therefore, the charter may require that a shareholder first offer shares to the other owners before selling them to an outsider. In that way, the remaining shareholders have some control over who their new co-owners will be.

- **Flexibility.** Close corporations can typically operate without a board of directors, a formal set of bylaws, or annual shareholder meetings.

- **Dispute resolution.** The shareholders are allowed to agree in advance that any one of them can dissolve the corporation if some particular event occurs or, if they choose, for any reason at all. If the shareholders are in a stalemate, the problem can be solved by dissolving the corporation. Even without such an agreement, a shareholder can ask a court to dissolve a close corporation if the other owners behave "oppressively" or "unfairly."

EXAM Strategy

Question: While working as a plant superintendent at Rodd, Joseph bought stock in the company. On his death, he owned 20 percent, while the founder's children owned the rest. Later, Joseph's widow, Euphemia, found out that Rodd had bought back all of the children's stock, while refusing to buy any of hers. What can Euphemia do?

Strategy: Rodd meets the definition of a close corporation. What rights does that bestow on Euphemia?

Result: The court ruled that the majority shareholders had violated their fiduciary duty to her and that the company had to buy her stock, too.[4] Otherwise, Euphemia's stock was worthless.

21-3 LIMITED LIABILITY COMPANIES

An LLC offers the limited liability of a corporation and the tax status of a flow-through entity. As such, it is an extremely useful form of organization often favored by entrepreneurs because it offers the best of both worlds—limited liability and lower taxes.

21-3a Limited Liability

Members are not personally liable for the debts of the company. **They risk only their investment, as if they were shareholders of a corporation. Are the members of the LLC liable in the following case?** You be the judge.

---

[4]*Donahue v. Rodd Electrotype Co.*, 367 Mass. 578 (Mass. 1975).

You be the Judge

RIDGAWAY V. SILK
2004 Conn. Super. LEXIS 548,
2004 WL 574526
Superior Court of Connecticut, 2004

Facts: Norman Costello and Robert Giordano were members of Silk, LLC, which owned a bar and adult entertainment nightclub in Groton, Connecticut, called Silk Stockings. Anthony Sulls went drinking there one night—and drinking heavily. Although he was obviously drunk, employees at Silk Stockings continued to serve him. Costello and Giordano were working there that night. They both greeted customers (who numbered in the hundreds), supervised employees, and performed "other PR work." When Sulls left the nightclub at 1:45 a.m. with two friends, he drove off the highway at high speed, killing himself and one of his passengers, William Ridgaway, Jr.

Ridgaway's estate sued Costello and Giordano personally. The defendants filed a motion for summary judgment seeking dismissal of the complaint.

You Be the Judge: *Are Costello and Giordano personally liable to Ridgaway's estate?*

Argument for Costello and Giordano: The defendants did not own Silk Stockings; they were simply members of an LLC that owned the nightclub. The whole point of an LLC is to protect members against personal liability. The assets of Silk, LLC, are at risk, but not the personal assets of Costello and Giordano.

Argument for Ridgaway's Estate: The defendants are not liable for being members of Silk, LLC, they are liable for their own misdeeds as employees of the LLC. They were both present at Silk Stockings on the night in question, meeting and greeting customers and supervising employees. It is possible that they might actually have served drinks to Sulls, but in any event, they did not adequately supervise and train their employees to prevent them from serving alcohol to someone who was clearly drunk. The world would be an intolerable place to live if employees were free to be as careless as they wished, knowing that they were not liable because they were members of an LLC.

In deciding whether an LLC is right for your business, there are other features besides liability and tax status that you should consider.

21-3b Formation

It is easy to form an LLC; the only required document is a charter. The charter is short, containing basic information such as name and address. It must be filed with the secretary of state in the jurisdiction in which the LLC is being formed.

In addition, an LLC should have an operating agreement that sets out the rights and obligations of the members. This document is not required, but can be exceedingly helpful, as Jeffrey Horning learned in the opening scenario. The flexibility of an LLC is both the good news and the bad. Members have great choice in how to run their organization, but they are also forced to live by their (careless or bad) decisions, because courts are reluctant to interfere. In the following case, one member had to live with a bad decision. Inquiring minds want to know: Did he ever discuss the agreement with his lawyer? Did he even *have* a lawyer?

HUATUCO V. SATELLITE HEALTHCARE

2013 Del. Ch. LEXIS 298; 2013 WL 6460898
Court of Chancery of Delaware, 2013

CASE SUMMARY

Facts: The LLC statute contained some *required* provisions that applied to all LLCs and other *default* provisions that applied only to LLCs that did not have those terms in their operating agreement.

Dr. Aibar Huatuco and Satellite Health Care each owned 50 percent of an LLC (the Company) that operated dialysis centers. The LLC Agreement stated that the Company could only be dissolved if both members voted in favor. The LLC agreement further provided that the default provisions of state law did not apply to the Company.

Satellite and Huatuco had a major disagreement over management of the LLC. He wanted to dissolve the Company, but Satellite refused. With nowhere else to turn, Huatuco filed suit, asking the court to dissolve the Company, as permitted, but not required, by Delaware law. Satellite filed a motion to dismiss Huatuco's suit.

Issue: *Does Huatuco have the right to obtain dissolution of the LLC in court?*

Decision: No, Huatuco cannot force dissolution.

Reasoning: Under the LLC statute, members have the freedom to agree to whatever they want on most issues. Courts generally will not overrule the terms of an operating agreement. In this way, members can manage their businesses as they see fit.

This LLC agreement explicitly stated that the default provisions of the LLC statute did not apply. The right to seek dissolution in court is a default provision and, therefore, neither member could obtain help from a court.

The LLC agreement further stated that members could only dissolve the organization if both voted in favor. Huatuco argued that he did not know that this term was in the operating agreement. The law presumes that parties to a contract understand what they are signing. Otherwise, contracts would be subject to endless second-guessing.

Additionally, Huatuco argued that, as a matter of public policy the Court should not deprive him of the right to dissolve the LLC because no alternative exit options were available. He misread public policy, which instead supported his freedom to contract. If he did not like the terms, he should not have signed the operating agreement.

21-3c Flexibility

Unlike S corporations, LLCs can have members that are corporations, partnerships, or nonresident aliens. LLCs can also have different classes of stock. Unlike corporations, LLCs are not required to hold annual meetings or maintain a minute book.

21-3d Transferability of Interests

As a general rule, unless the operating agreement provides otherwise, existing members of an LLC cannot transfer their ownership rights, nor can the LLC admit a new member without the unanimous permission of the other members.

21-3e Duration

It used to be that LLCs automatically dissolved upon the withdrawal of a member (owing to, for example, death, resignation, or bankruptcy). The current trend in state laws, however, is to permit an LLC to continue in operation even after a member withdraws.

21-3f Going Public

Once an LLC goes public, it loses its favorable tax status and is taxed as a corporation, not a partnership. Thus, there is no advantage to using the LLC form of organization for a publicly traded company. And there are some disadvantages: Unlike corporations, publicly traded LLCs do not enjoy a well-established set of statutory and case law that is relatively consistent across the many states. For this reason, privately held companies that begin as LLCs often change to corporations when they go public.

21-3g Piercing the Company Veil

Limited liability is one of the great advantages of an LLC. However, if members abuse their rights, a court may remove their limited liability. This process is called **piercing the company veil. A court may pierce an LLC's veil if members:**

Piercing the company veil
A court holds members of an LLC personally liable for the debts of the organization.

- **Fail to observe formalities**. Members must treat the LLC like a separate organization. Thus, if an LLC enters into an agreement (particularly with a member), a legitimate contract needs to be drafted and signed.

- **Commingle assets.** This trap is the most dangerous. An LLC and its members must keep their assets separate. If courts cannot tell who owns what, they are likely to grant creditors access to the assets of both the organization and its members.

- **Fail to provide adequate capital.** In extreme cases, if an LLC is established without enough capital to run its business, then a court may look to the members' assets. One LLC had capital of only about $20,000 but proceeded to borrow millions of dollars from one of the members. That ratio looked wrong.

- **Commit fraud.** Courts are unwilling to protect fraudsters who try to use an LLC as a shield against liability.

In the following case, the defendant seemed not to have bad intent but was simply careless. Nonetheless, he was liable.

BLD Products, Ltd. v. Technical Plastics of Oregon, LLC

2006 U.S. Dist. LEXIS 89874, 2006 WL 3628062
United States District Court for the District of Oregon, 2006

Case Summary

Facts: Mark Hardie was the sole member of Technical Plastics of Oregon, LLC (TPO). He operated the business out of an office in his home. Hardie regularly used TPO's accounts to pay such expenses as landscaping and house-cleaning. TPO also paid some of Hardie's personal credit card bills, loan payments on his Ford truck, the cost of constructing a deck on his house, his stepson's college bills, and the cost of family vacations to Disneyland, as well as miscellaneous bills from GI Joe's, Wrestler's World, K-Mart, and Mattress World. At the same time, Hardie deposited cash advances from his personal credit cards into the TPO checking account. Hardie did not take a salary from TPO. When TPO filed for bankruptcy, it owed BLD Products approximately $120,000 for goods that it had purchased.

BLD filed suit asking the court to pierce TPO's company veil and hold Hardie personally liable for the organization's debts.

Issues: *Should the court pierce TPO's company veil? Should Hardie be personally liable for TPO's debts?*

Decision: Yes, this LLC's veil should be pierced. Hardie is personally liable for TPO's debts.

Reasoning: An LLC's veil can be pierced if the following three tests are met:

1. The member (that is, Hardie) controlled the LLC (in this case, TPO);

2. The member engaged in improper conduct; and

3. As a result of that improper conduct, the plaintiff (BLD) was unable to collect on a debt against the insolvent LLC.

Hardie, as the sole member and manager of TPO, clearly controlled the company. In addition, he engaged in improper conduct when he paid his personal expenses from the TPO business account. These amounts were more than occasional dips into petty cash—they indicated a disregard of TPO's separate LLC identity. Moreover, he did not keep records of these personal payments.

It is not clear whether Hardie's improper conduct prevented BLD from collecting its entire $120,000 debt. A jury will have to determine the amount that Hardie owes BLD.

21-3h Legal Uncertainty

As we have observed, LLCs are a relatively new form of organization without a consistent and widely developed body of law. As a result, members of an LLC may find themselves in the unhappy position of litigating issues of law which, although well established for corporations, are not yet clear for LLCs. Win or lose, lawsuits are expensive in both time and money.

21-3i Choices: LLC v. Corporation

When starting a business, which form makes the most sense—LLC or corporation? The tax status of an LLC is a major advantage over a corporation. Although an S corporation has the same tax status as an LLC, it also has all the annoying rules about classes of stock and number of shareholders. Once an LLC is established, it is simpler to operate—it does not, for example, have to make annual filings or hold annual meetings. However, the LLC is not right for everyone. If done properly, an LLC is more expensive to set up than a corporation because it needs to have a thoughtfully crafted operating agreement. Also, venture capitalists sometimes prefer to invest in C corporations for three reasons: (1) certain arcane tax issues best not discussed here, (2) C corporations are easier to merge, sell, or take public, and (3) the general legal uncertainty involving LLCs.

EXAM Strategy

Question: Hortense and Gus are each starting a business. Hortense's business is an Internet start-up. Gus will be opening a yarn store. Hortense needs millions of dollars in venture capital and expects to go public soon. Gus has borrowed $10,000 from his girlfriend, which he hopes to pay back soon. Should either of these businesses organize as an LLC?

Strategy: Sole proprietorships may be best for businesses without substantial capital needs and without significant liability issues. Corporations are best for businesses that will need substantial outside capital and expect to go public shortly.

Result: An LLC is not the best choice for either of these businesses. Venture capitalists will insist that Hortense's business be a corporation, especially if it is going public soon. A yarn store has few liability issues, and Gus can always buy insurance. Furthermore, he does not expect to have any outside investors. Hence, a sole proprietorship would be more appropriate for Gus's business.

21-4 SOCIAL ENTERPRISES

Almost half the states now offer charters to some type of socially conscious organization, collectively referred to as *social enterprises.* The most common forms of these organizations are benefit corporations and low-profit limited liability companies (L3Cs). Social enterprises pledge to behave in a socially responsible manner, even as they pursue profits. (Thus, they are *not* nonprofits.) Their focus is on the triple bottom line: "people, planet, and profits." In other words, they must consider some combination of their stakeholders (employees, suppliers, customers, creditors), their community, and the environment, in addition to investors.

> **Social enterprises**
> These organizations pledge to behave in a socially responsible manner

To become a socially conscious organization, typically:

- Two-thirds of shareholders (or in some states more) must approve.

- The company must agree to measure its social benefit using a standard set by an objective third party.

- On its website, the company must assess and report regularly on its societal and environmental impact.

21-5 GENERAL PARTNERSHIPS

A **partnership** is an unincorporated association of two or more co-owners who operate a business for profit. Each co-owner is called a **general partner**.

21-5a Tax Status

Partnerships are flow-through entities: The partnership itself does not pay income tax, instead the profits pass through to the partners, who report it on their personal returns.

21-5b Liability

Each partner is personally liable for the debts of the enterprise whether or not she caused them. Thus, a partner is liable for any injury that another partner or an employee causes while on partnership business as well as for any contract signed on behalf of the partnership. This form of organization can be particularly risky if the group of owners is large and the partners do not know each other.

21-5c Formation

Given the liability disadvantage, why does anyone do business as a partnership? The short answer is that very few businesses deliberately choose to be a partnership. They are more likely to drift into it unknowingly, because **a partnership is easy to form**. In fact, nothing is required in the way of forms or filings or agreements. Ideally, a partnership should have a written agreement, but it is perfectly legal without one. If two or more people do business together, sharing management, profits, and losses, they have a partnership, whether they know it or not, and are subject to all the rules of partnership law.

21-5d Raising Capital

Financing a partnership may be difficult because the firm cannot sell shares as a corporation does. **The capital needs of the partnership must be provided by contributions from partners or by borrowing.**

21-5e Management

The management of a partnership can be a significant challenge.

Management Rights

Unless the partnership agrees otherwise, partners share both profits and losses equally, and each partner has an equal right to manage the business.

In a large partnership, with hundreds of partners, too many cooks can definitely spoil the firm's profitability. That is why large partnerships are almost always run by one or a few partners who are designated as **managing partners or members of the executive committee**.

> In a large partnership, with hundreds of partners, too many cooks can definitely spoil the firm's profitability.

Management Duties

Partners have a duty to the partnership. This duty means that:

- Partners are liable to the partnership for gross negligence or intentional misconduct.

- Partners cannot compete with the partnership. Each partner must turn over to the partnership all earnings from any activity that is related to the partnership's business. Thus, law firms would typically expect a partner to turn over any fees he earned as a director of a company, but he could keep royalties from his novel on scuba diving.

- A partner may not take an opportunity away from the partnership unless the other partners consent. If the partnership wants to buy an office building and a partner hears of one for sale, she must give the partnership an opportunity to buy it before she purchases it herself.

- If a partner engages in a conflict of interest, he must turn over to the partnership any profits he earned from that activity. Thus, someone who bid on partnership assets (in this case, a racehorse) at auction without telling his partner was in violation of his duty to the partnership.

21-5f Transfer of Ownership

A partner cannot sell his share of the organization without the permission of the other partners. He can only transfer the *value* of his partnership interest, not the interest itself. He cannot, for example, transfer the right to participate in firm management or vote on firm matters. Take the case of Evan and his mother. She is a partner in the immensely profitable McBain Consulting firm. She dies, leaving him an orphan with no siblings. He overcomes his grief as best he can and goes to her office on the next Monday to take over her job and her partnership. Imagine his surprise when her partners tell him that, as her sole heir, he can inherit the *value* of her partnership but he has no right to be a partner. He is out on the sidewalk within the hour. The partners have promised him a check in the mail.

21-5g Terminating a Partnership

A partnership begins with an *association* of two or more people. Appropriately, the end of a partnership begins with a dissociation. **A dissociation occurs when a partner quits.**

Dissociation

A partner always has the *power* to leave a partnership but may not have the *right*. In other words, a partner can always dissociate, but if she has violated the partnership agreement, she will have to pay damages for any harm that her departure caused.

If the partners have agreed in advance how long the partnership will last, it is a **term partnership**. At the end of the specified term, the partnership automatically ends. If a partner leaves before the end of the term, that is a wrongful dissociation, and she may have to pay damages. A **partnership at will**, means that any of the partners can leave at any time, for any reason, without owing damages.

A dissociation is a fork in the road: **The partnership can either buy out the departing partner(s) and continue in business or wind up the business and terminate the partnership.** If the partnership chooses to terminate the business, it must follow three steps: dissolution, winding up, and termination.

Term partnership
A partnership in which the partners agree in advance how long it will last

Partnership at will
A partnership with no fixed duration- any of the partners may leave at any time, for any reason

Three Steps to Termination

Dissolution.   A partnership dissolves anytime the business cannot continue, such as when (1) a partner leaves, and the remaining partners cannot agree unanimously to continue on, (2) the partners decide to end the partnership, or (3) the partnership business becomes illegal.

Winding Up.   During the winding-up process, all debts of the partnership are paid, and the remaining proceeds are distributed to the partners.

Termination.   Termination happens automatically once the winding up is finished. The partnership is not required to do anything official.

21-6 LIMITED LIABILITY PARTNERSHIPS

A **limited liability partnership (LLP)** offers the limited liability of a corporation and the tax status of a flow-through organization. **Partners are not liable for the debts of the partnership,** but, naturally, they are liable for their own misdeeds.

To form an LLP, the partners must file a statement of qualification with state officials. LLPs must also file annual reports. It is absolutely crucial to comply with all the technicalities of the statute. Otherwise, partners lose protection against personal liability. Note the sad result for Michael Gaus and John West, who formed a Texas LLP. Unfortunately, they did not renew the LLP registration each year, as the statute required. After the registration had expired, the partnership entered into a lease. When the partners ultimately stopped paying rent and abandoned the premises, they were both were held personally liable for the rent. As the court pointed out, the statute did not contain a "substantial compliance" section, nor did it contain a grace period for filing a renewal application. Close only counts in horseshoes and hand grenades, not in LLPs.

Why would a business elect to be an LLP rather than an LLC? In some states, professionals such as lawyers and accountants are not permitted to operate as an LLC; the LLP form is their only option other than a general partnership. And sometimes lawyers just like to maintain the tradition of operating as a partnership, even if in a more modern version.

21-7 PROFESSIONAL CORPORATIONS

Professional corporations (PCs) are mostly a legacy form of organization—few businesses would now elect to be a PC. But there are still many PCs in existence because, in the past, PCs were the only option available to professionals (such as lawyers and doctors) other than a general partnership.

PCs offer the limited liability of a regular corporation. If a member of a PC commits malpractice, the corporation's assets are at risk, but not the personal assets of the innocent members. If Drs. Sharp, Payne, and Graves form a *partnership*, all the partners will be personally liable when Dr. Payne accidentally leaves her scalpel inside a patient. If the three doctors have formed a *PC* instead, Dr. Payne's Aspen condo and the assets of the PC will be at risk, but not the personal assets of the two other doctors.

PCs are a separate taxable entity not a flow-through organization. **Therefore, the tax issues can be complicated and are a major reason why most professional groups now choose to be an LLC or an LLP.**

21-8 FRANCHISES

This chapter has presented an overview of the various forms of organization. Franchises are not, strictly speaking, a separate form of organization. They are included here because they represent an important option for entrepreneurs. Most franchisors and franchisees are corporations or LLCs, although some franchisees are sole proprietorships.

All franchisors must comply with the Federal Trade Commission's (FTC) Franchise Rule. In addition, some states also impose their own requirements. Under FTC rules, a franchisor must deliver to a potential purchaser a **Franchise Disclosure Document (FDD)** at least 14 calendar days before any contract is signed or money is paid. **The FDD must provide information on:**

Franchise Disclosure Document

A disclosure document that a franchisor must deliver to a potential purchaser

- The history of the franchisor and its key executives;

- Litigation with franchisees;

- Bankruptcy filings by the company and its officers and directors;

- Costs to buy and operate a franchise;

- Restrictions, if any, on suppliers, products, and customers;

- Territory—any limitations (in either the real or virtual worlds) on where the franchisee can sell or any restrictions on other franchisees selling in the same territory;

- Business continuity—the circumstances under which the franchisor can terminate the franchisee and the franchisee's rights to renew or sell the franchise;

- Required advertising expenses; and

- A list of current franchisees and those that have left in the prior three years (a significant number of departures may be a bad sign).

The purpose of the FDD is to ensure that the franchisor discloses all relevant facts. It is not a guarantee of quality because the FTC does not investigate to make sure that the information is accurate or the business idea sound. After the fact, if the FTC discovers the franchisor has violated the rules, it may sue on the franchisee's behalf. (The franchisee does not have the right to bring suit personally against someone who violates FTC franchise rules, but it may be able to sue under state law.)

As the following case illustrates, under current law, the franchisor has much of the power in a franchise relationship.

NATIONAL FRANCHISEE ASSOCIATION v. BURGER KING CORPORATION

2010 U.S. Dist. LEXIS 123065, 2010 WL 4811912
United States District Court for the Southern District of Florida, 2010

CASE SUMMARY

Facts: The Burger King Corporation would not allow franchisees to have it their way. Instead, Burger King forced them to sell double-cheeseburgers (DCB) for $1.00, which was below cost. Burger King franchisees filed suit alleging that (1) Burger King did not have the right to set maximum prices; and (2) that even if Burger King had such a right, it had violated its obligation under the franchise agreement to act in good faith.

The court dismissed the first claim because the franchise agreement unambiguously permitted Burger King to set whatever prices it wanted. But the court allowed the plaintiffs to proceed with the second claim.

Issue: *Was Burger King acting in good faith when it forced franchisees to sell items below cost?*

Decision: Yes, Burger King was acting in good faith.

Reasoning: This case hinges on Burger King's motives. To show bad faith, plaintiffs must prove that Burger King's goal, in setting these prices, was to harm the franchisees.

For example, the franchisees could show that Burger King's motive was to weaken them so much that the company could take them over itself.

Alternatively, the plaintiffs could show (1) that no reasonable person would have set the price of a DCB at $1.00 and (2) this pricing caused severe harm to the franchises. Clearly, the plaintiffs would never have agreed to a contract that permitted unreasonable and harmful behavior.

The franchisees cannot meet any of these tests. First, there is no evidence that Burger King had any motive other than helping the franchisees. Second, selling below cost is not necessarily irrational. Indeed, there are lots of good reasons why stores might adopt such a strategy—to build customer loyalty, lure customers away from competitors, or serve as loss leaders to generate increased sales on other, higher-priced products (French fries, anyone?). Third, there is no evidence that the franchises were unprofitable or in danger of bankruptcy.

Chapter Conclusion

The process of starting a business is immensely time-consuming. Not surprisingly, entrepreneurs are sometimes reluctant to spend their valuable time on legal issues that, after all, do not contribute directly to the bottom line. No customer buys more tacos because the franchise is a limited liability company instead of a corporation. Wise entrepreneurs know, however, that careful attention to legal issues is an essential component of success. The idea for the business may come first, but legal considerations should occupy a close second place.

Exam Review

	Separate Taxable Entity	Personal Liability for Owners	Ease of Formation	Transferable Interests (Easily Bought and Sold)	Perpetual Existence	Other Features
Sole Proprietorship	No	Yes	Very easy	No, can only sell entire business	No	
Corporation	Yes	No	Difficult	Yes	Yes	
Close Corporation	Yes, for C corp; No, for S corp	No	Difficult	Transfer restrictions	Yes	Protection of minority shareholders. No board of directors required
S Corporation	No	No	Difficult	Transfer restrictions	Yes	Only 100 shareholders. Only one class of stock. All shareholders must agree to S status and must be citizens or residents of the United States. Partnerships and corporations cannot be shareholders.
Limited Liability Company	No	No	Charter is easy, but should have thoughtful operating agreement	Yes, if the operating agreement permits	Varies by state, but generally, yes	Becomes taxable entity if it goes public
General Partnership	No	Yes	Easy	No	Depends on the partnership agreement	
Limited Liability Partnership	No	No	Difficult	No	Depends on the partnership agreement	
Professional Corporation	Yes	No	Difficult		Yes, as long as it has shareholders	Complex tax issues
Franchise	All these issues depend on the form of organization chosen by participants.					

MATCHING QUESTIONS

Match the following terms with their definitions:

___A. S corporation

___B. Dissociation

___C. Close corporation

___D. Dissolution

___E. Partnership

1. The first step in the process of terminating a partnership

2. Created by federal law

3. The owners are liable for debts of organization

4. Created by state law

5. A partner leaves the partnership

TRUE/FALSE QUESTIONS

Circle true or false:

1. T F Sole proprietorships must file a tax return.

2. T F Ownership in a partnership is not transferable.

3. T F Benefit corporations are nonprofits.

4. T F In both a general partnership and a limited liability partnership, the partners are not personally liable for the debts of the partnership.

5. T F Privately held companies that begin as corporations often change to LLCs before going public.

MULTIPLE-CHOICE QUESTIONS

1. A sole proprietorship:
   (a) can easily raise capital
   (b) requires no formal steps for its creation.
   (c) must register with the secretary of state.
   (d) may sell stock.
   (e) provides limited liability to the owner.

EXAM Strategy

2. **CPA QUESTION** Assuming all other requirements are met, a corporation may elect to be treated as an S corporation under the Internal Revenue Code if it has:
   (a) both common and preferred stockholders.
   (b) a partnership as a stockholder.
   (c) 100 or fewer stockholders.
   (d) the consent of a majority of the stockholders.

   Strategy: Review the list of requirements for an S corporation. (See the "Result" at the end of this section.)

3. A limited liability company:

(a) is regulated by a well-established body of law.

(b) pays taxes on its income.

(c) cannot have members that are corporations.

(d) must register with state authorities.

(e) protects the owners from all personal liability.

4. While working part time at a Supercorp restaurant, Jenna spills a bucket of hot French fries on a customer. Who is liable to the customer?

(a) Supercorp alone

(b) Jenna alone

(c) Both Jenna and Supercorp

(d) Jenna, Supercorp, and the president of Supercorp

(e) Jenna, Supercorp, and the shareholders of Supercorp

5. A limited liability partnership:

(a) protects partners from liability for their own misdeeds.

(b) protects the partners from liability for the debts of the partnership.

(c) must pay taxes on its income.

(d) Both (a) and (b).

(e) (a), (b), and (c) are all correct.

> **2. Result:** An S corporation can have only one class of stock. A partnership cannot be a stockholder, and all the shareholders must consent to S corporation status. C is the correct answer.

CASE QUESTIONS

EXAM Strategy

1. **Question:** Alan Dershowitz, a law professor famous for his prominent clients, joined with other lawyers to open a kosher delicatessen, Maven's Court. Dershowitz met with greater success at the bar than in the kitchen—the deli failed after barely a year in business. One supplier sued for overdue bills. What form of organization would have been the best choice for Maven's Court?

Strategy: A sole proprietorship would not have worked because there was more than one owner. A partnership would have been a disaster because of unlimited liability. They could have met all the requirements of an S corporation or an LLC. (See the "Result" at the end of this section.)

EXAM Strategy

2. Question: Mrs. Meadows opened a biscuit shop called The Biscuit Bakery. The business was not incorporated. Whenever she ordered supplies, she was careful to sign the contract in the name of the business, not personally: The Biscuit Bakery by Daisy Meadows. Unfortunately, she had no money to pay her flour bill. When the vendor threatened to sue her, Mrs. Meadows told him that he could only sue the business because all the contracts were in the business's name. Will Mrs. Meadows lose her dough?

Strategy: The first step is to figure out what type of organization her business is. Then recall what liability protection that organization offers. (See the "Result" at the end of this section.)

3. Kristine bought a Rocky Mountain Chocolate Factory franchise. Her franchise agreement required her to purchase a cash register that cost $3,000, with an annual maintenance fee of $773. The agreement also provided that Rocky Mountain could change to a more expensive system. Within a few months after signing the agreement, Kristine learned that she would have to buy a new cash register that cost $20,000, with annual maintenance fees of $2,000. Does Kristine have to buy this new cash register? Did Rocky Mountain act in bad faith?

4. If you were to look online for a description of a professional corporation, you might find websites stressing that, in a PC, shareholders are still responsible for their own wrongdoing. For example: "In some states, these professionals can form a corporation, but with the distinction that each professional is still liable for his or her own wrongful professional actions." Why is this statement at best unnecessary and at worst misleading?

---

1. Result: An S corp is an easier choice because no operating agreement is required. But in the long run, it is safer to have a good operating agreement to manage disputes. An S corp could accomplish the same goal with a set of custom-tailored bylaws, but that would cost as much as an operating agreement. In a situation such as this, most enterpreneurs would choose an LLC.

2. Result: The Biscuit Bakery was a sole proprietorship. No matter how Mrs. Meadows signed the contracts, she is still personally liable for the debts of the business.

DISCUSSION QUESTIONS

1. Leonard, an attorney, was negligent in his representation of Anthony. In settlement of Anthony's claim against him, Leonard signed a promissory note for $10,400 on behalf of his law firm, an LLC. When the law firm did not pay, Anthony filed suit against Leonard personally for payment of the note. Is a member personally liable for the debt of an LLC that was caused by his own negligence?

2. Think of a business concept that would be appropriate for each of the following: a sole proprietorship, a corporation, and a limited liability company.

3. As you will see in Chapter 22, Facebook began life as a corporation, not an LLC. Why did the founder, Mark Zuckerberg, make that decision?

4. Corporations developed to encourage investors to contribute the capital needed to create large-scale manufacturing enterprises. But LLCs are often start-ups or other small businesses. Why do their members deserve limited liability? Is it fair that LLCs do not pay income taxes?

5. ETHICS Frank Brown, who is African-American, tried to buy lunch at a McDonald's at Dadeland Mall in Miami, Florida. The manager, Omar Zaveri, not only refused to serve Brown but verbally abused him, used racial slurs, and told all the other employees that he would fire them if they served Brown. This McDonald's was owned by a franchisee. Is McDonald's liable to Brown? Whether or not McDonald's is technically liable, should it pay Brown anyway?

CHAPTER 22

© Creative Travel Projects/Shutterstock.com

CORPORATIONS

On July 26, 2004, Mark Zuckerberg signed a Certificate of Incorporation for his company, which he called TheFacebook, Inc. At 11:34 a.m. on July 29, 2004, that Certificate was filed with the secretary of state for Delaware, and what is now known as Facebook began its life as a corporation. Zuckerberg had started this social networking Internet site the previous February in his dorm room at Harvard. By December 2004, Facebook had almost 1 million users. By the beginning of 2006, the company was estimated to be worth between $750 million and $2 billion. Today, Facebook is valued at more than $150 billion. As Zuckerberg built his company, what did he need to know about the law?

Zuckerberg started TheFacebook in his dorm room at Harvard. Within 10 months, it had almost 1 million users.

22-1 PROMOTER'S LIABILITY

Facebook operated for five months before it was incorporated. During this period, Zuckerberg needed to be careful to avoid liability as a promoter. A **promoter** is someone who organizes a corporation.

Zuckerberg had moved company headquarters to Palo Alto, California, before the certificate of incorporation was filed. Suppose that he found the perfect location for his headquarters and was eager to sign the lease before someone else snatched the opportunity away, but Facebook did not yet legally exist—it was not incorporated. What would happen if he signed the lease anyway? **As promoter, he would be personally liable on any contract he signed before the corporation was formed.** If Zuckerberg signed the lease before Facebook, Inc. legally existed, he would be personally liable for the rent due. After formation, the corporation could adopt the contract, in which case, both it and the promoter would be liable. **Adoption** means either that the board of directors approves the contract or the corporation accepts the benefits under the contract. The promoter can get off the hook personally only if the landlord agrees to a **novation**—that is, a new contract with the corporation alone.

Promoter
Someone who organizes a corporation

Adoption
Either the board of directors approves the contract or the corporation accepts benefits under the contract

Novation
A new contract

EXAM Strategy

Question: Warfield hired Wolfe, a young carpenter, to build his house. A week or so after they signed the contract, Wolfe filed the charter for Wolfe Construction, Inc. Warfield made payments to the corporation. Unfortunately, the work on the house was shoddy; the architect said he did not know whether to blow up the house or try to salvage what was there. Warfield sued Wolfe and Wolfe Construction, Inc. for damages. Wolfe argued that if he was liable as a promoter, then the corporation must be absolved and that, conversely, if the corporation was held liable he, as an individual, must not be. Who is liable to Warfield? Does it matter if Wolfe signed the contract in his own name or in the name of the corporation?

Strategy: Wolfe's argument is wrong. Warfield does not have to choose between suing him individually or suing the corporation. He can sue both.

Result: Wolfe is personally liable on any contract signed before the charter was filed, no matter whose name is on the contract. The corporation is liable only if it adopts the contract. Did it do so here? The fact that the corporation cashed checks that were made out to it means that the corporation is also liable. So Warfield can sue both Wolfe and the corporation.

22-2 INCORPORATION PROCESS

Because there is no federal corporation code, a company can incorporate only under state law. **No matter where a company actually does business, it may incorporate in any state.** This decision is important because the organization must live by the laws of whichever state it chooses for incorporation.

To encourage similarity among state corporation statutes, the American Bar Association drafted the Model Business Corporation Act (the Model Act) as an example. Many states use the Model Act as a guide, although Delaware does not. Therefore, this chapter provides examples from both the Model Act and Delaware. Why Delaware? Despite its small size, it has a disproportionate influence on corporate law. Over half of all public companies have incorporated there, including 60 percent of Fortune 500 companies.

22-2a Where to Incorporate?

A corporation has to pay filing fees and franchise taxes in its state of incorporation, as well as in any state in which it does ongoing business. To avoid this double set of fees, a business that will be operating primarily in one state typically selects that state for incorporation. But if a company is going to do business in several states, it might consider choosing Delaware. **Delaware offers corporations several advantages:**

- **Flexible laws that favor management.** For example, a Delaware court recently upheld the enforceability of bylaws requiring shareholders who want to sue a Delaware company to do so in Delaware. For a company, defending a lawsuit on its home turf is much more convenient and predictable, not to mention cheaper, than being sued in another state.

- **An efficient court system.** Delaware has a special court (called "Chancery Court") that hears nothing but business cases and has judges who are experts in corporate law.

- **A neutral arena.** Because very few businesses are actually based in Delaware, it is viewed as being a neutral place in which to try cases. None of the parties has a home court advantage.

22-2b The Charter

Once a company has decided where to incorporate, the next step is to prepare and file the charter (which may also be called the Articles of Incorporation or the Articles of Organization). The charter must be filed with the secretary of state.

Name

The Model Act imposes two requirements in selecting a name. First, all **corporations must use one of the following words in their name: Corporation, Incorporated, Company, or Limited. Delaware also accepts some additional terms, such as Association or Institute.** Second, under both the Model Act and Delaware law, a new corporate name must be different from that of any corporation, limited liability company, or limited partnership that already exists in that state. If your name is Freddy Dupont, you cannot name your corporation "Freddy Dupont, Inc.," because Delaware already has a company named E. I. DuPont de Nemours & Co. It does not matter that Freddy Dupont is your real name or that the existing company is a large chemical business, whereas you want to open a frozen yogurt shop. The names are too similar. Zuckerberg chose "TheFacebook" because that was what Harvard students called their freshman directory.

Address and Registered Agent

A company must have an official address in the state in which it is incorporated so that the secretary of state knows where to contact it and so that anyone who wants to sue the corporation can serve the complaint in-state. Because most companies incorporated in Delaware do not actually have an office there, they hire a registered agent to serve as their official presence in the state.

Incorporator

The **incorporator** signs the charter and files it with the secretary of state. Mark Zuckerberg was the incorporator for Facebook, but lawyers often serve this role.

Incorporator
Someone who signs the charter and files it with the secretary of state

Ethics Mark Zuckerberg was Facebook's incorporator. He was happy to have anyone and everyone know that he was behind Facebook because he was operating a legal business. Other scarier types—terrorists, drug dealers, and tax evaders—can use a corporation to hide the source and destination of illegal money. In one case, a Nevada corporation received thousands of suspicious wire transfers totaling millions of dollars, but the authorities could not identify the villains because there was no way to know who owned the company.[1]

Should states require corporations to disclose more information? What if stricter disclosure requirements caused corporations to move to other, more lenient, jurisdictions? Should states be willing to risk a decline in revenue?

Purpose

The corporation is required to give its purpose for existence. Most companies use a very broad purpose clause, such as Facebook's:

> The purpose of the Corporation is to engage in any lawful act or activity for which corporations may be organized under the General Corporation Law of Delaware.

Stock

The charter must provide three items of information about the company's stock.

Par Value. Par value does not relate to market value; it is usually some nominal figure such as 1¢ or $1 per share, or it is possible to choose no par value for stock. Facebook stock has a par value of $0.0001 per share.

Number of Shares. Before stock can be sold, it must first be authorized in the charter. The corporation can authorize as many shares as the incorporators choose, but the more shares, the higher the filing fee. The Facebook charter authorizes 10 million shares. After incorporation, a company can add authorized shares by simply amending its charter and paying the additional fee. Stock that the company has sold but later bought back is **treasury stock**.

Treasury stock
Stock that a company has sold, but later bought back

Classes of Stock. Shareholders often make different contributions to a company. Some may be involved in management, whereas others may simply contribute financially. To reflect these varying contributions, a corporation can issue different classes of stock, such as preferred or common stock. Owners of **preferred stock** are in line before common shareholders to receive dividends and any liquidation payments after a company goes into bankruptcy.

Preferred stock
The owners of preferred stock have preference on dividends and also, typically, in liquidation.

22-3 AFTER INCORPORATION

22-3a Directors and Officers

Under the Model Act, a corporation is required to have at least one director, unless (1) all the shareholders sign an agreement that eliminates the board, or (2) the corporation has 50 or fewer shareholders. Shareholders elect directors. To do so, they may hold a meeting or,

---

[1]See, for example, John A. Cassara, "Delaware, Den of Thieves", *The New York Times*, November 1, 2013.

in the more typical case for a small company, they elect directors by **written consent**. A typical written consent looks like this:

Classic American Novels, Inc.
Written Consent

The undersigned shareholders of Classic American Novels, Inc., a corporation organized and existing under the General Corporation Law of the State of Wherever, hereby agree that the following action shall be taken with full force and effect as if voted at a validly called and held meeting of the shareholders of the corporation:

Agreed: That the following people are elected to serve as directors for one year or until their successors have been duly elected and qualified:

Herman Melville
Louisa May Alcott
Mark Twain

Dated: _____   Signed: _____
                                                    Willa Cather

Dated: _____   Signed: _____
                                                    Nathaniel Hawthorne

Dated: _____   Signed: _____
                                                    Harriet Beecher Stowe

Once the shareholders have chosen the directors, **the directors must elect the officers of the corporation.** They can use a consent form if they wish. Delaware law and the Model Act simply require a corporation to have whatever officers are described in the bylaws. The same person can hold more than one office.

The written consents and any records of actual meetings are kept in a **minute book**, which is the official record of the corporation. Entrepreneurs sometimes feel they are too busy to bother with all these details, but if a corporation is ever sold, the lawyers for the buyers will *insist* on a well-organized and complete minute book—and the cost to re-create it after the fact will be substantial.

22-3b Bylaws

The **bylaws** list all the "housekeeping" details for the corporation. For example, bylaws set the date of the annual shareholders' meeting, define what a **quorum** is (i.e., what percentage of stock must be represented for a meeting to count), give titles to officers, set the number of directors, and establish the fiscal (i.e., tax) year of the corporation.

22-3c Foreign Corporations

A company is called a **domestic corporation** in the state where it was incorporated and a **foreign corporation** everywhere else. **A foreign corporation must register in any state in which it is doing business.** "Doing business" means opening an office or establishing any other ongoing presence in the state. (The process of registering is called "qualifying to do business.") To obtain the required certificate of authority, the company must register, list a registered agent, and pay annual fees and taxes on income generated in that jurisdiction.

22-4 DEATH OF THE CORPORATION

Sometimes business ideas are not successful, and the corporation fails. This death can be voluntary (the shareholders elect to terminate the corporation) or forced (by court order). Sometimes a court takes a step that is much more damaging to shareholders than simply dissolving the corporation—it removes the shareholders' limited liability.

22-4a Piercing the Corporate Veil

Pierce the corporate veil

A court holds shareholders personally liable for the debts of the corporation.

One of the major purposes of a corporation is to protect its owners—the shareholders—from personal liability for the debts of the organization. However, as was the case with LLCs, courts have the right to **pierce the corporate veil**; that is, to hold shareholders personally liable for the debts of the corporation. **Courts generally pierce a corporate veil in four circumstances:**

1. **Failure to observe formalities.** If an organization does not act like a corporation, it will not be treated like one. It must, for example, hold required shareholders' and directors' meetings (or sign consents), keep a minute book as a record of these meetings, and make all the required state filings. In addition, officers must be careful to sign all corporate documents with a corporate title, not as an individual. An officer should sign like this:

   Classic American Novels, Inc.

   By: *Stephen Crane*

   Stephen Crane, President

2. **Commingling of assets.** Nothing makes a court more willing to pierce a corporate veil than evidence that shareholders used corporate assets to pay their personal debts or mixed their assets with those of the corporation. If shareholders commingle assets, it is genuinely difficult for creditors to determine which assets belong to whom. This confusion is generally resolved in favor of the creditors—all assets are deemed to belong to the corporation.

3. **Inadequate capitalization.** If the founders of a corporation do not raise enough capital to give the business a fighting chance of paying its debts, courts may require shareholders to pay corporate obligations. For example, Oriental Fireworks Co. had hundreds of thousands of dollars in annual sales, but only $13,000 in assets. The company did not obtain any liability insurance, keep a minute book, or defend lawsuits. There was no need because the company had so few assets. But then a court pierced the corporate veil and found the owner of the company personally liable.[2]

4. **Fraud.** Corporations cannot be used to shelter fraud. If a con artist uses a corporation to steal money, the victims can go after his personal assets, even though the fraud was committed in the name of a corporation.

22-4b Termination

Terminating a corporation is a three-step process:

1. **Vote.** The directors recommend to the shareholders that the corporation be dissolved, and a majority of the shareholders agree.

2. **Filing.** The corporation files "Articles of Dissolution" with the Secretary of State.

---

[2]*Rice v. Oriental Fireworks Co.*, 75 Or. App. 627 (Or. Ct. App. 1985).

3. **Winding up.** The officers of the corporation pay its debts and distribute the remaining property to shareholders. When the winding up is completed, the corporation ceases to exist.

The Secretary of State may dissolve a corporation that fails to comply with state requirements such as paying the required annual fees. Indeed, many corporations, particularly small ones, do not bother with the formal dissolution process. They simply walk away and let the Secretary of State act. **In addition, a court may dissolve a corporation if it is insolvent or if its directors and shareholders cannot resolve conflict over how the corporation should be managed.**

22-5 MANAGEMENT DUTIES

Before the Industrial Revolution in the eighteenth and nineteenth centuries, a business owner typically supplied both capital and management. However, the cash needs of the great manufacturing enterprises spawned by the Industrial Revolution were larger than any small group of individuals could supply. To find capital, firms sought outside investors, who often had neither the knowledge nor the desire to manage the enterprise. Investors without management skills complemented managers without capital.

Corporations have two sets of managers: directors and officers.[3] Shareholders elect directors who set policy and then the directors appoint officers to implement these corporate goals.

A fundamental problem of the modern corporation is that the interests of managers, shareholders, and stakeholders often conflict. In the 2000s, the world faced two financial crises that starkly revealed these different incentives. Too often, managers earned exorbitant compensation from highly risky, short-term decisions that in the longer run left shareholders holding an empty bag. If CEOs made a risky decision that paid off, they personally earned enormous profit. If the decision failed, they might be fired, but they would have received compensation that left them wealthy beyond most people's dreams. In the two years before investment banks Bear Stearns Companies, Inc. and Lehman Brothers Holdings, Inc. failed, their top five executives took home $1.4 billion and $1 billion respectively, even as their shareholders were left with nothing.

Even worse, investigations revealed that compliant boards had been little more than rubber stamps, approving whatever the officers wanted. In anger and frustration, shareholders, Congress, the Securities and Exchange Commission (SEC), and stock exchanges undertook an unprecedented effort to rebalance corporate power.

Among those most willing to use their new power are **activist investors**—those shareholders with a large block of stock whose goal is to influence management decisions and strategic direction.

The rest of this chapter is about the balance of rights and responsibilities among managers, shareholders, and stakeholders. We begin with managers' duties and then discuss shareholders' rights.

Activist investors

Shareholders with a large block of stock whose goal is to influence management decisions

22-6 THE BUSINESS JUDGMENT RULE

The rules that govern a manager's relationship with stakeholders are different from those that regulate the relationship among managers, the corporation, and its shareholders.

---

[3]Throughout this chapter, the term "manager" includes both directors and officers.

Hostile takeovers

An attempt by an outside investor to acquire a company in the face of opposition from the target corporation's board of directors

22-6a Stakeholders

Traditionally, the law required the officers and directors of a company to focus solely on the interests of the corporation and its shareholders. But, in the 1980s, came a wave of **hostile takeovers** and communities began to realize that, when a company was acquired, they were hurt, too. A plant might be shuttered or headquarters moved. It was not just laid-off employees who suffered; real estate prices, tax receipts, charitable giving—everything did.

As a result, some states have adopted statutes that permit directors, when making a decision, to consider, for example, "both the short-term and long-term best interests of the corporation, taking into account, and weighing as the directors deem appropriate, the effects thereof on the corporation's shareholders and the other corporate constituent groups...."

These statutes *permit* managers to consider the interests of stakeholders. But the relationship with shareholders is different: Managers have an affirmative duty to protect the interests of shareholders and the corporation.

22-6b Shareholders

The officers and directors of a corporation owe a fiduciary duty to, and must act in the best interests of, both the corporation and its shareholders. This fiduciary duty rule is easy to say but more difficult to enforce. The problem is that even well-intentioned people make mistakes. It is unreasonable to hold managers liable if they mean well but still make an unprofitable decision.

Over time, the business judgment rule developed to protect officers and directors who make good faith decisions, even those that turn out badly. **The business judgment rule provides that managers are not liable for decisions they make in good faith:**

Duty of Loyalty	1. Without a conflict of interest
Duty of Care	2. With the care that an ordinarily prudent person would take in a similar situation, and
	3. In a manner they reasonably believe to be in the best interests of the corporation.

The business judgment rule is two shields in one: It protects both the manager and her decision. **If a manager has acted in good faith, a court will not hold her personally liable for any harm her decision has caused the company, nor will the court rescind her decision.** If the manager's act breached her **duty of loyalty** or her **duty of care**, then she has the burden of proving that her decision was entirely fair to the shareholders. If it was not entirely fair, she may be held personally liable and the decision can be rescinded. Exhibit 22.1 illustrates the business judgment rule.

Analysis of the business judgment rule is divided into two parts. The obligation of a manager to act without a conflict of interest is called the **duty of loyalty**. The requirements that a manager act with care and in the best interests of the corporation are referred to as the **duty of care**.

Duty of loyalty

The obligation of a manager to act without a conflict of interest

Duty of care

The requirements that a manager act with care and in the best interests of the corporation

Duty of Loyalty

The duty of loyalty prohibits managers from making a decision that benefits them at the expense of the corporation.

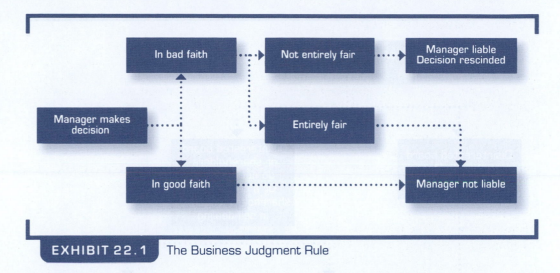

EXHIBIT 22.1   The Business Judgment Rule

Self-Dealing.   **Self-dealing means that a manager makes a decision benefiting either himself or another company with which he has a relationship.** While working at the Blue Moon restaurant, Zeke signs a contract on behalf of the restaurant to purchase bread from Rising Sun Bakery. Unbeknownst to anyone at Blue Moon, he is a part owner of Rising Sun. Zeke has engaged in self-dealing, which is a violation of the duty of loyalty.

Once a manager engages in self-dealing, the business judgment rule no longer applies. This does not mean the manager is automatically liable to the corporation or that his decision is automatically void. All it means is that the court will no longer presume that the transaction was acceptable. Instead, the court will scrutinize the deal more carefully. **A self-dealing transaction is valid in any one of the following situations:**

- **The disinterested members of the board of directors form a special committee that approves the transaction.** Disinterested directors are those who do not themselves benefit from the transaction.

- **The disinterested shareholders approve it.** The transaction is valid if the shareholders who do not benefit from it are willing to approve it.

- **The transaction was entirely fair to the corporation.** In determining fairness, the courts will consider the impact of the transaction on the corporation and whether the price was reasonable.

In the case of self-dealing by a controlling shareholder of the company, the board will still form a special committee, but a court will always examine the fairness of the transaction, no matter how the special committee votes.[4] The controlling shareholder will not be liable if the transaction was entirely fair to the corporation.

Exhibit 22.2 illustrates the rules on self-dealing.

In the case on the next page, the court ignored the recommendation of a special committee that approved an entirely unfair transaction. As a result, the directors were liable.

Special committee

Independent board members form a committee to review a self-dealing transaction and determine if it is entirely fair to the corporation.

---

[4]Courts always examine self-dealing transactions involving controlling shareholders because independent directors may not make an unbiased decision for fear of retaliation. Although boards know that, in the event of litigation, courts will look at the underlying fairness of the transaction, they often hope that a special committee's approval will influence the court's decision.

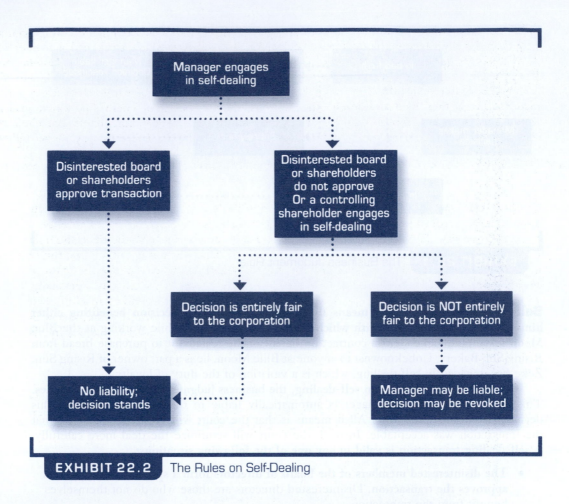

EXHIBIT 22.2   The Rules on Self-Dealing

In re S. Peru Copper Corp. Shareholder Derivative Litig.

52 A.3d 761
Court of Chancery of Delaware, 2011

CASE SUMMARY

Facts: Grupo Mexico was the controlling stockholder of Southern Peru Copper Corporation (SPC), a company whose stock was listed on the NYSE. Grupo also owned 99 percent of the stock of Minera Mexico, a company that was not publicly traded. Grupo offered to trade all its Minera stock for $3.75 billion of SPC shares. Because of Grupo's self-interest, SPC's board formed a special committee of disinterested directors to evaluate the proposal.

When called in to advise the board, Goldman Sachs ran the numbers many ways, but could not find any that valued

Minera's stock at more than $2.8 billion. Nonetheless SPC's special committee approved Grupo's offer, and the deal went ahead. SPC's minority shareholders filed suit against the directors who worked for Grupo.

Issue: *Were the board members liable for their decision?*

Decision: Yes, the board members were liable because the decision was entirely unfair.

Reasoning: The Committee members were competent, well-qualified individuals with business experience. They hired first-rate advisors. Their hands were on the oars. So why then did their boat go, if anywhere, backward?

From the get-go, the Committee's and Goldman's focus was on finding some way to make Grupo's deal look reasonable, rather than asking whether it fundamentally made sense. If they had considered other options, they would have seen how foolish this deal was. They might also have been able to negotiate better terms with Grupo.

The Committee also ignored a fundamental economic fact: SPC's stock had a market value on the NYSE and Minera's did not. The Committee should not have been willing to exchange $3.75 billion of this market-tested stock for $2.8 billion worth of shares in a struggling, privately held business. There is no way to justify this decision.

The defendants breached their fiduciary duty of loyalty and must pay $1.347 billion.

Corporate Opportunity. **Managers are in violation of the corporate opportunity doctrine if they compete against the corporation without its consent.** To avoid liability, a manager must first offer an opportunity to disinterested directors and shareholders, and only if they turn it down, does the manager have the right to take advantage of the opportunity himself. Long ago, Charles Guth was president of Loft, Inc., which operated a chain of candy stores that sold Coca-Cola. Guth purchased the Pepsi-Cola Company personally, without offering the opportunity to Loft. The Delaware court found that Guth had violated the corporate opportunity doctrine and ordered him to transfer all his shares in PepsiCo to Loft.[5] That was in 1939, and Pepsi-Cola was bankrupt; today, PepsiCo, Inc. is worth more than $100 billion.

Duty of Care

In addition to the *duty of loyalty*, managers also owe a *duty of care*. **The duty of care requires officers and directors to act in the best interests of the corporation and to use the same care that an ordinarily prudent person would in a similar situation.** To meet this duty of care:

- The decision must be legal;

- It must have a rational business purpose; and

- The manager must have made an informed decision.

Even if she violates the duty of care, a manager is not liable under the business judgment rule as long as the decision is entirely fair to the corporation.

EXAM Strategy

Question: You are the CEO of an app company. You will only allow your engineers to create apps for iPads, not for Android or Microsoft tablets because you think iPads are cooler. Some of your shareholders disagree with this policy. Is your decision protected by the business judgment rule?

Strategy: Remember that you owe a duty of care to the corporation. This means that you must have a rational business purpose for your decision.

Result: The courts are very generous in defining a rational business purpose. They would probably uphold your decision as long as it was not in some way personally benefiting you, for instance, as long as you are not a major shareholder of Apple.

---

[5]Guth v. Loft, 5 A2d 503 (Del. 1939).

22-7 SHAREHOLDER RIGHTS

> **If you own stock in Starbucks Corp., your share of stock plus $4.23 entitles you to a Caffè Vanilla Frappuccino, the same as everyone else.**

As we have seen, *directors*, not *shareholders*, have the right to manage the corporate business. Shareholders have neither the right nor the obligation to manage the day-to-day business of the enterprise. If you own stock in Starbucks Corp., your share of stock plus $4.23 entitles you to a Caffè Vanilla Frappuccino, the same as everyone else. By the same token, if the pipes freeze and the local Starbucks store floods, the manager has no right to call you, as a shareholder, to help clean up the mess.

Who are the shareholders and what rights do they have over the enterprises they own?

22-7a Who Are the Shareholders?

At one time, corporate stock was primarily owned by individuals. But now, institutional investors—pension plans, mutual funds, asset management firms, hedge funds, insurance companies, banks, foundations, and university endowments—are the most important shareholders of public companies. Not only do they own more than 70 percent of all the stock of these companies, but they are much more likely to vote their shares than individual shareholders are.

Because they have such vast amounts to invest, if they are unhappy with management, it is difficult for them to do the "Wall Street walk"—that is, sell their shares—because a sale of their large stock holdings would depress the market price. And where would they invest the proceeds? Institutional investors cannot all profit simply by trading shares among themselves. For better or worse, the fate of institutional investors hangs on the success of these large companies.

What rights do shareholders have?

22-7b Right to Information

Under the Model Act, shareholders acting in good faith and with a proper purpose have the right to inspect and copy the corporation's minute book, accounting records, and shareholder lists. A proper purpose is one that aids the shareholder in managing and protecting her investment. If, for example, Celeste is convinced that the directors of Devil Desserts, Inc., are mismanaging the company, she might demand a list of other shareholders so that she can ask them to join her in a lawsuit. This purpose is proper—although the company may not like it—and the company is required to give her the list. If, however, Celeste wants to use the shareholder list as a potential source for her new online business featuring exercise equipment, the company could legitimately turn her down.

The following case is typical: The court must decide if the shareholder is acting in his role as owner or competitor.

You be the Judge

Facts: Paul Chopra was a minority shareholder and former director of Helio Solutions, Inc. Both he and Helio were in the business of reselling Sun Microsystems products.

CHOPRA V. HELIO SOLUTIONS, INC.
2007 Cal. App. Unpub. LEXIS 5909, 2007 WL 2070387
Court of Appeal of California, 2007

Chopra suspected that (1) some of Helio's majority shareholders had purchased a building and leased it to

Helio at an excessive rent; (2) the company had broken a lease so that it could rent this building; (3) some shareholders had used assets of the corporation to secure a personal loan; (4) Helio had permitted ex-employees to take away substantial business; and (5) the company had not collected a

$1 million debt it was owed. In addition, he wanted to know if Helio was planning to issue stock and thereby dilute his ownership. Finally, he felt that his dividend of $1,952.55 was unreasonably low, given that Helio had $88 million in revenue.

To find answers to his questions, Chopra asked Helio for these documents:

1. Articles of incorporation;
2. Minutes for meetings of the board of directors and shareholders;
3. All financial statements;
4. All tax returns;
5. The general ledger with accompanying journals;
6. Income and balance sheets;
7. Schedule of accounts payable and received and inventory;
8. Depreciation schedule for fixed assets;
9. Supporting documents, including bank loans, lines of credit, accrued payroll liabilities, sales tax liabilities, other receivables, loans to officers and owners, significant prepayments or deposits, and equipment lease agreements;
10. Monthly bank statements;
11. Company credit card statements;
12. Compensation records;
13. The following contracts: life insurance policies for officers and/or stockholders, pension plan and profit sharing plans, stock purchase plans, equipment and building leases, employment and bonus agreements for owners or key employees, covenants not to compete, loan agreements and credit information, documents connected with the company's real property, option grants, and each owner's curriculum vitae;
14. A list of patents held by the company;
15. Budget projections for the current year;
16. Company brochures and/or marketing information;
17. A list of key management personnel with job titles;
18. An overview of company positions and objectives for each department manager; and
19. Information regarding contingencies and lawsuits.

Helio Solutions gave Chopra items 1–6 but refused to turn over the other material. He filed suit.

You Be the Judge: *Which of these documents must a company provide to its shareholders?*

Argument for Chopra: All these documents are necessary for assessing the value of Chopra's investment in the company and determining whether his interests as a minority shareholder are being protected. Without employee agreements and compensation information, he cannot assess the current corporate financial situation, value the business, determine if the business is being properly managed, or discover whether the majority shareholders or directors are improperly diverting corporate funds for their own benefit. He needs the contracts and agreements related to equipment and building leases to determine whether the majority shareholders had purchased a building and leased it to Helio at an excessive rate.

Argument for Helio: Chopra is simply on a fishing expedition to find information that would help him compete against Helio. He wants to use Helio's budget projections and managerial objectives so that he can beat them to the punch on some of their new initiatives. Also, many of the requests relate to specific shareholders rather than to the company. In any event, it would take weeks of work to locate and photocopy these documents. Shareholders have some rights to corporate information, but they are not entitled to unlimited access to corporate confidences and secrets.

22-7c Right to Vote

A corporation must have at least one class of stock with voting rights.

Fundamental Corporate Changes

A corporation must seek shareholder approval before undergoing any of the following fundamental changes: a merger, a sale of major assets, dissolution of the corporation, or an amendment to the charter.

Shareholder Meetings

For public corporations, annual shareholder meetings are the norm. Both the New York Stock Exchange (NYSE) and NASDAQ require them for listed companies. But companies whose stock is not publicly traded can either hold an annual meeting or use written consents from their shareholders.

Proxies

Proxy

The person whom a shareholder appoints to vote for her at a meeting of the corporation- also, the document a shareholder signs appointing this substitute voter

Shareholders have the right to appoint someone else to vote for them at a meeting. Both this person and the card the shareholder signs to appoint the substitute voter are called a **proxy**.

Along with the proxy card, the company must also give shareholders a proxy statement and an annual report. The proxy statement provides information on everything from management compensation to a list of directors who miss too many meetings. The annual report contains detailed financial data.

Election and Removal of Directors

At the annual meeting, shareholders have the right to elect directors. But "corporate democracy" in America bears little resemblance to our political democracy.

The election process begins when the nominating committee of the board of directors produces a slate of directors, with one name per opening. The NYSE and NASDAQ both require that the members of the nominating committee be independent directors, that is, people who are not employees of the company and, therefore, presumably not in the pocket of the CEO. Nonetheless, CEOs often influence the nominating committee's decisions. When Biogen-Idec needed a new director, it hired a search firm to look for the right person. Coincidentally, that person had children who attended the same school as those of the CEO.

Plurality voting

To be elected, a candidate only needs to receive more votes than her opponent, not a majority of the votes cast.

Once a slate of nominees is selected, it is placed in the proxy statement and sent to shareholders, whose only choice is to vote in favor of a nominee or to withhold their vote (i.e., not vote at all). This traditional corporate voting method is called **plurality voting**. A successful candidate does not need to receive a majority vote; he must simply receive more than any competitor. Since there are no competitors, one vote is sufficient (and that vote could be his own). Even if a large number of shareholders withhold their votes, the nominee may be embarrassed, but as long as he receives that one vote, he is elected.

However, because of pressure from shareholder activists, 80 percent of large companies now require directors to resign if fewer than half of the shares vote for them. (Among smaller companies—those in the Russell 3000 Index—three-quarters still permit plurality voting, where one vote is often sufficient to insure election.) But even if directors are rejected by shareholders, the other board members can refuse to accept their resignation. This phenomenon is so common that these directors who serve on a board with less than majority support from shareholders have a name: **zombie directors**. In one recent year, directors at 41 companies failed to get a majority vote, but all of those directors stayed on.

Zombie directors

A director who receives less than majority support from shareholders

If shareholders want to nominate their own candidates to the board, they have to prepare and distribute a proxy statement to other shareholders, and then communicate why their slate is superior, all the while fighting against the company's almost unlimited financial resources. This process is complex, expensive, and disruptive to any company. Not surprisingly, only a few shareholder groups undertake this effort each year. Recent research does indicate, however, that companies with a director elected through proxy contests outperform their peers in both the short and long run.

In the following sections, we look at other reforms that the SEC and the stock exchanges have instituted with the goal of enhancing shareholder democracy and improving corporate governance.

Proxy Access. Under new SEC rules, shareholders now have the right to require the company to take a vote at the annual meeting on changing company bylaws to permit so-called proxy access.

Under proxy access bylaws, companies are required to include in their proxy material the names of board nominees selected by large shareholders. These outsider nominees compete directly against directors nominated by the existing board. It is, therefore, possible for an outside nominee to be elected to the board without the expense and drama of preparing separate proxy materials. So far, proxy access has been approved by only a handful of companies.

Independent Directors. Congress, the SEC, and the stock exchanges have all passed rules that require some degree of independence for boards of directors. Although, as we have seen, "independence" can be in the eye of the beholder. One study found that 45 percent of directors who are technically independent have friendship ties to the CEO.

For publicly traded companies, independent directors must comprise:

- A majority of the board; and

- The entire audit, compensation, corporate governance, and nominating committees.

In addition, independent directors must meet regularly on their own without inside directors, that is, without members of the board who are also employees of the corporation.

Executive Compensation

One impact of corporate voting rules is that shareholders have been unable to control soaring executive compensation. In 1975, the top 100 CEOs earned 39 times as much as the average worker. By 2011, that ratio was over 300. See Exhibit 22.3 for an illustration of this trend. Or, to look at it another way, the average salary of the CEO of a Fortune 500 company in 1960 was twice that of the president of the United States. In 2012, the ratio was 37 to 1.

But, you say, executives are paid for performance—they only do well when their shareholders also profit. Not exactly. A recent study could find no correlation between the performance of publicly traded companies and their CEO's pay.[6] Other researchers have found a negative correlation in larger firms: The higher the pay, the worse the company does.[7] What does correlate with CEO compensation is good press: When CEOs get favorable mention in the news media, their salaries go up, but, unfortunately, not the performance of their companies.[8]

Why are executives paid so much? Another way of putting this question is: Why have directors been so reluctant to rein in this spending? Several reasons:

- **Other people's money**. It is always easy to spend other people's money. Imagine that you have the right to decide how much your next-door neighbor can spend on dinner tonight. No matter what you decide, faceless, nameless residents 10 blocks away will have to pay for the meal and, if they object to the amount you choose, they would have to pay thousands of dollars to fire you from this position. Your neighbor is not

---

[6]Cited in: Adam Davidson, "C.E.O.'s Don't Need to Earn Less: They Need to Sweat More," *The New York Times*, May 29, 2013. Also in "Executive Pay and Performance," *The Economist*, February 7, 2012.
[7]Robert Daines, Vinay B. Nair, and Lewis A. Kornhauser, "The Good, the Bad and the Lucky: CEO Pay and Skill" (August 2005). U of Penn, Inst for Law & Econ Research Paper 05-07; NYU, Law and Economics Research Paper No. 04-035. Available at SSRN: http://ssrn.com/abstract=622223.
[8]"The 'Moneyball' Approach to Hiring CEOs," Knowledge@Wharton, February 3, 2014.

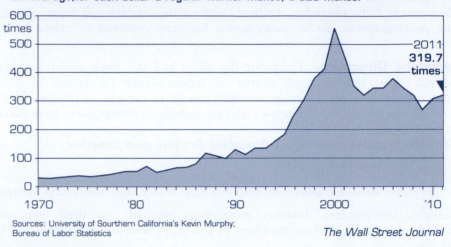

Long Division

Since 1970, the difference between what chief executives and rank-and-file employees are paid has grown.

On average, for each dollar a regular worker makes, a CEO makes:

2011
319.7 times

Sources: University of Sourthern California's Kevin Murphy; Bureau of Labor Statistics

The Wall Street Journal

EXHIBIT 22.3   CEO's Pay as a Multiple of the Average Worker's Pay, 1970–2011[9]

your best friend, but you know and like him, so why not let him have a gourmet meal at the finest restaurant in town. (Plus a fabulous bottle of wine!)

- **Nice work if you can get it.**[10] Being a director is a good job–prestigious, well-paid, with nice perks. On average, directors of public companies earn at least $250,000 a year for what is very part-time work. They know that shareholders are very unlikely to withhold a vote from them, and, should that happen, fellow board members may well let them stay on anyway. Why offend the CEO, who still has significant influence over the nomination process?

- **It is hard to see the harm.** If a company has a trillion dollar balance sheet, what harm is done if the CEO gets $10 million or $25 million or $100 million? Two things: One, economic theory teaches us that organizations should be profit-maximizing. And if that principle does not apply at the top, it sets a bad example throughout the organization. Two, CEOs who earn mind-boggling amounts of money become insulated from reality. If they have so much money that five generations of their family will never have to work, why would they care what other people, such as shareholders, think?

It is hardly surprising that managers play all sorts of games when setting compensation. For example:

- **Rationalization.** You need look no further than the *Raul* case later in this chapter for some fine examples of rationalization. When the economy is doing well and business

---

[9]Andrew Ackerman and Joann S. Lublin, "SEC Wants Boss-Employee Pay Gap On Display," *The Wall Street Journal*, Sept. 18, 2013.

[10]As Ira Gershwin put it in his song, "Nice work if you can get it, and if you get it—won't you tell me how?"

is flourishing, executives deserve generous compensation. When times are difficult, well, it is hard work cutting costs and laying off employees.

- **Competitive market.** Managers argue that their pay is set by the market. But the data do not reveal significant intercompany bidding for CEO talent: Fewer than 2 percent of CEOs have held that same post at another company.[11] And there is evidence that insider CEOs perform better than outside candidates anyway.

- **Benchmarking**. Two-thirds of the largest 1,000 U.S. companies report that they performed better than their peers. Campbell Soup used one set of benchmark companies to determine executive compensation but another set to evaluate its total shareholder return.

- **Stock prices.** In setting executive compensation, boards are highly influenced by stock prices. Yet, there is evidence that 70 percent of stock market value is a function of general market trends, not company efforts. Exhibit A: When the price of crude oil goes up, so do the profits of oil companies, and therefore the salaries of oil company CEOs.[12]

    A truly shameful example of gaming occurred after the 9/11 terrorist attack. The stock market was closed for four days and when it reopened, stocks took a bigger plunge than they had in any week since Nazi Germany invaded France early in World War II. Taking advantage of these low prices, more than double the usual number of companies granted stock options to executives, which meant their executives profited when the nation recovered.[13]

    If managers truly wanted executive compensation to mirror performance, net returns on invested capital would be a better measure of real economic value than stock prices. That is, the company's return on its capital investments, such as plants and equipment, less the opportunity cost of those investments.

The federal government has tried to change the landscape of corporate governance and executive compensation, in the following ways:

- **Disclosure**. The SEC now requires more complete disclosure of executive compensation. This disclosure includes the relationship between financial performance and executive compensation, as well as the ratio between the CEO's total pay and the median total compensation for all other company employees.

- **Clawbacks.** A public company must establish a clawback policy, whereby it can require the CEO and CFO to reimburse the company for any bonus or profits they received from selling company stock within a year of the release of flawed financials.

- **Say-on-pay**. At least once every three years, companies must take a *nonbinding* shareholder vote on the compensation of the five highest paid executives.

The following case demonstrates that a board of directors has the absolute right to ignore say-on-pay votes.

---

[11]Charles M. Elson and Craig K. Ferrere, "Executive Superstars, Peer Groups and Overcompensation: Cause, Effect and Solution," August 7, 2012. Available at SSRN: http://ssrn.com/abstract=2125979.
[12]"The 'Moneyball' Approach to Hiring CEOs," Knowledge@Wharton, February 3, 2014.
[13]Charles Forelle, James Bandler, and Mark Maremont, "Executive Pay: The 9/11 Factor," *The Wall Street Journal*, July 15, 2006.

RAUL V. RYND

929 F. Supp. 2d 333
United States District Court for the District of Delaware, 2013

CASE SUMMARY

Facts: Hercules Offshore, Inc. provided drilling services to the oil and natural gas industry. In the prior year, its revenue, assets, cash, and stock price had fallen. It had also had a significant net operating loss. In the face of these poor results, the board of directors voted to *raise* executive pay by between 40 percent and 190 percent.

In its proxy statement to shareholders, Hercules stated that its compensation plan was designed to emphasize pay for performance and align the financial interests of the executives and stockholders. In the required say-on-pay vote, Hercules shareholders were not feeling too aligned: 59 percent of them voted against the plan. The board ignored the vote.

A Hercules shareholder brought suit alleging that the board had breached its fiduciary duty. He also alleged that the compensation plan violated the company's pay-for-performance philosophy as outlined in the proxy statement.

Hercules filed a motion to dismiss.

Issue: *Did the Hercules board violate its fiduciary duty when it approved the compensation plan?*

Decision: No, the board was not in violation.

Reasoning: The say-on-pay statute specifically provides that these votes are not binding and that do not affect the board's fiduciary duties.

Although the Hercules' Proxy Statement explains that pay for performance is an important part of its compensation program, the same statement also identifies other goals, such as retaining, motivating, and rewarding executives. A generous compensation plan was critical in keeping the management team focused on creating shareholder value and preventing competitors from luring away company officers. In this light, increased executive compensation makes sense even when the Company is experiencing poor financial performance.

Chapter Conclusion

How can shareholders ensure that the corporation will operate in their best interest? How can managers make tough decisions without being second-guessed by shareholders? Balancing the interests of managers and shareholders is a complex problem the law struggles to resolve.

EXAM REVIEW

1. **PROMOTERS** Promoters are personally liable for contracts they sign before the corporation is formed unless the corporation and the third party agree to a novation.

2. **STATE OF INCORPORATION** A company may incorporate in any state. A business that will be operating primarily in one state typically selects that state for incorporation. However, if it intends to operate in several states, it may choose to incorporate in a jurisdiction known for its favorable corporate laws, such as Delaware.

3. **CHARTER**   A corporate charter must generally include the company's name, address, registered agent, purpose, and a description of its stock. It must be signed by the incorporator.

4. **ELECTION OF OFFICERS AND DIRECTORS**   Shareholders elect the directors of a corporation. The directors elect the officers.

5. **FOREIGN CORPORATION**   A corporation must register in every state in which it is doing business.

6. **PIERCING THE CORPORATE VEIL**   A court may hold a corporation's shareholders personally liable if they fail to observe legal formalities, commingle assets, inadequately capitalize the organization, or use it to commit fraud.

7. **TERMINATION**   Termination of a corporation is a three-step process requiring a shareholder vote, the filing of Articles of Dissolution, and the winding up of the enterprise's business.

8. **STAKEHOLDERS**   The laws in some states permit managers to consider the interests of stakeholders.

9. **FIDUCIARY DUTY**   The officers and directors of a corporation owe a fiduciary duty to both the corporation and its shareholders.

10. **BUSINESS JUDGMENT RULE**   If managers comply with the business judgment rule, a court will not hold them personally liable for any harm their decisions cause the company, nor will the court rescind the decision.

EXAM Strategy

> **Question:** Employees of Exxon Corp. paid some $59 million in corporate funds as bribes to Italian political parties to secure special favors and other illegal commitments. The board of directors decided not to sue the employees who had committed the illegal acts. Were these decisions protected by the business judgment rule?
>
> **Strategy:** Two decisions are at issue here: illegal payments and the decision not to sue. (See the "Result" at the end of this section.)

11. **DUTY OF LOYALTY: SELF-DEALING**   Under the duty of loyalty, managers may not enter into an agreement on behalf of their corporation that benefits them personally unless the disinterested directors or shareholders have first approved it. If the manager does not seek the necessary approval, the business judgment rule no longer applies, and the manager will be liable unless the transaction was entirely fair to the corporation.

12. **DUTY OF LOYALTY: CORPORATE OPPORTUNITY**   Under the duty of loyalty, a manager must first offer an opportunity to disinterested directors and shareholders, and only if they turn it down, does the manager have the right to take advantage of the opportunity himself.

Question: Vern owned 32 percent of Coast Oyster Co. and served as president and director. Coast was struggling to pay its debts, so Vern suggested that the company sell some of its oyster beds to Keypoint Co. After the sale, officers at Coast discovered that Vern owned 50 percent of Keypoint. They demanded that he give the Keypoint stock to Coast. Did Vern violate his duty to Coast?

Strategy: Vern has violated the duty of loyalty not once, but twice. (See the "Result" at the end of this section.)

13. **DUTY OF CARE** Under the duty of care, managers must make decisions that are legal, informed and have a rational business purpose.

14. **DIRECTORS** Directors, not shareholders, have the right to manage the corporate business.

15. **SHAREHOLDER RIGHTS** Shareholders have the right to:
    - Inspect and copy the corporation's records (for a proper purpose),
    - Approve fundamental corporate changes, such as a merger or a major sale of assets;
    - Receive annual financial statements (if their company is publicly traded); and elect and remove directors.

16. **PROXY** Virtually all publicly held companies solicit proxies from their shareholders. A proxy authorizes someone else to vote in place of the shareholder.

17. **PROXY ACCESS** Proxy access bylaws require companies to include in their proxy material the names of board nominees selected by large shareholders.

18. **INDEPENDENT DIRECTORS** For publicly traded companies, independent directors must comprise a majority of the board, and only independent directors can serve on audit, compensation, corporate governance and nominating committees.

19. **CLAWBACKS** Companies are required to establish clawback policies, whereby they can require the CEO and CFO to reimburse the company for any bonus or profits they received from selling company stock within a year of the release of flawed financials.

20. **SAY-ON-PAY** At least once every three years, companies must take a *nonbinding* shareholder vote on the compensation of the five highest paid executives.

---

10. Result: The business judgment rule would not protect the underlying illegal payments, but it did protect the decision not to sue. In other words, anyone who made an illegal payment had violated the business judgment rule, but the people who had decided not to pursue the violators had not themselves breached the business judgment rule because they had not violated the duty of care or the duty of loyalty.

12. Result: If the shareholders and directors did not know of Vern's interest in Keypoint, they could not properly evaluate the contract. By not telling them, he violated the rule against self-dealing. Also, by purchasing stock in Keypoint, Vern took a corporate opportunity. He had to turn over to Coast any profits he had earned on the transaction, as well as his stock in Keypoint.

MATCHING QUESTIONS

Match the following terms with their definitions:

___A. Duty of loyalty

___B. Duty of care

___C. Promoter

___D. Incorporator

___E. Registered agent

1. Requires managers to act as an ordinarily prudent person would in a similar situation

2. The company's representative in its state of incorporation

3. Someone who organizes a corporation

4. The person who prepares and files the charter

5. Prohibits managers from making a decision that benefits them at the expense of the corporation

TRUE/FALSE QUESTIONS

Circle true or false:

1. T F A corporation can be formed in any state or under the federal corporate code.

2. T F Managers are required to consider the best interests of stakeholders.

3. T F Most companies use a very broad purpose clause in their charter.

4. T F Shareholders own the corporation; thus they have the right to manage the corporate business.

5. T F A company must include in its proxy materials the names of all shareholder nominees for the board of directors.

MULTIPLE-CHOICE QUESTIONS

1. A promoter is liable for any contract he signs on behalf of a corporation before it is formed, unless:

(a) the corporation adopts the contract.

(b) the promoter notifies the other party that the corporation has not yet been formed.

(c) the promoter signs the contract on behalf of the corporation.

(d) the promoter forms the corporation within 72 hours of signing the contract.

(e) the other party agrees to a novation.

2. *CPA QUESTION* A corporate stockholder is entitled to which of the following rights?

(a) Elect officers

(b) Receive annual dividends

(c) Approve dissolution

(d) Prevent corporate borrowing

3. ***CPA QUESTION*** Generally, a corporation's articles of incorporation must include all of the following except:

   (a) the name of the corporation's registered agent.

   (b) the name of each incorporator.

   (c) the number of authorized shares.

   (d) quorum requirements.

4. Generally, a corporation's bylaws include all of the following except:

   (a) par value of the stock.

   (b) the date of the shareholders' meeting.

   (c) the number of directors.

   (d) the titles of officers.

   (e) the date of the fiscal year.

5. Under the duty of care, directors will be liable if they:

   (a) make a decision that has a rational business purpose.

   (b) use the same care as an ordinarily prudent person.

   (c) make informed decisions.

   (d) engage in illegal behavior that is profitable to the company.

   (e) make an informed decision that ultimately harms the company.

6. By law, a candidate for the board of a publicly traded company must:

   (a) receive a majority of the votes cast.

   (b) receive a majority vote of the shares outstanding.

   (c) receive a plurality of the votes cast.

   (d) receive a plurality of the shares outstanding.

CASE QUESTIONS

1. Michael incorporated Erin Homes, Inc., to manufacture mobile homes. He issued himself a stock certificate for 100 shares, for which he made no payment. He and his wife served as officers and directors of the organization, but during the eight years of its existence, the corporation held only one meeting. Erin always had its own checking account, and all proceeds from the sales of mobile homes were deposited there. It filed federal income tax returns each year, using its own federal identification number. John and Thelma paid $17,500 to purchase a mobile home from Erin, but the company never delivered it to them. John and Thelma sued Erin Homes and Michael, individually. Should the court "pierce the corporate veil" and hold Michael personally liable?

2. Davis signed an employment contract with William. The contract stated: "Whatever company, partnership, or corporation that William may form for the purpose of manufacturing shall succeed William and exercise the rights and assume all of William's obligations as fixed by this contract." Two months later, William formed

Auto-Soler Company. Davis entered into a new contract with Auto-Soler providing that the company was liable for William's obligations under the old contract. Neither William nor the company ever paid Davis the sums owed him under the contracts. Davis sued William personally. Does William have any obligations to Davis?

3. **ETHICS** Edgar Bronfman, Jr., dropped out of high school to go to Hollywood and write songs and produce movies. Eventually, he left Hollywood to work in the family business—the Bronfmans owned 36 percent of Seagram Co., a liquor and beverage conglomerate. Promoted to president of the company at the age of 32, Bronfman seized a second chance to live his dream. Seagram received 70 percent of its earnings from its 24 percent ownership of DuPont Co. Bronfman sold this stock at less than market value to purchase (at an inflated price) 80 percent of MCA, a movie and music company that had been a financial disaster for its prior owners. Some observers thought Bronfman had gone Hollywood, others that he had gone crazy. After the deal was announced, the price of Seagram shares fell 18 percent. Was there anything Seagram shareholders could have done to prevent what to them was not a dream but a nightmare? Apart from legal issues, was Bronfman's decision ethical? What ethical obligations did he owe Seagram's shareholders?

4. Angelica is planning to start a home security business in McGehee, Arkansas. She plans to start modestly but hopes to expand her business within five years to neighboring towns and, perhaps, within 10 years, to neighboring states. Her inclination is to incorporate her business in Delaware. Is her inclination correct?

5. Ulrick and Birger started an air taxi service in Berlin, Germany, under the name Berlinair, Inc. Birger was approached by a group of travel agents who were interested in hiring an air charter business to take German tourists on vacation. Birger formed Air Berlin Charter Co. (ABC) and was its sole owner. On behalf of ABC, he entered into a contract with the Berlin travel agents. Birger concealed his negotiations from Ulrick, even though he used Berlinair working time, staff, money, and facilities. Has Birger violated his duty to Berlinair and Ulrick?

DISCUSSION QUESTIONS

1. Corporate executives are not the only people to earn fabulous salaries. Some athletes earn even more than CEOs. What is the difference between athletes and executives (besides a hook shot)?

2. States compete for lucrative filing fees by passing corporate statutes that favor management. One proposed solution to this problem would be a federal system of corporate registration. Is this a good idea? What are the impediments to such a system?

3. Congressional Airlines was highly profitable operating flights between Washington, D.C., and New York City. The directors approved a plan to offer flights from Washington to Boston. This decision turned out to be a major mistake, and the airline ultimately went bankrupt. Under what circumstances would shareholders be successful in bringing suit against the directors?

4. An appraiser valued a subsidiary of Signal Co. at between $230 million and $260 million. Six months later, Burmah Oil offered to buy the

subsidiary at $480 million, giving Signal only three days to respond. The board of directors accepted the offer without obtaining an updated valuation of the subsidiary or determining if other companies would offer a higher price. Members of the board were sophisticated, with a great deal of experience in the oil industry. A Signal Co. shareholder sued to prevent the sale. Is the Signal board protected by the business judgment rule?

5. For several years, CSK Auto, Inc., fraudulently reported inflated earnings. During this period, Maynard Jenkins was CEO. He was not involved in the fraud, however, and he was never charged with a crime. Nonetheless, the SEC sought to claw back some of his earnings during this period. Should Jenkins be financially responsible for fraud that occurred on his watch, even though he did not participate?

CHAPTER 23

© Creative Travel Projects/Shutterstock.com

BANKRUPTCY

Three bankruptcy stories:

1. Tim's account: "It happened all at once. My daughter's basketball team qualified for the nationals at Disney World. The kids had never gone to Disney World. How could we say no? Then my car died. And I didn't get a bonus this year. Next thing you know, we had $27,000 in credit card debt. Then we had some uninsured medical bills. There was just no way we could pay all that money back."

2. Kristen had always loved flowers. When the guy who owned the local flower shop wanted to retire, it seemed a great opportunity to buy the business. Everything went really well at first. Then the recession hit, and people cut back on nonessentials like flowers. How could she pay her loans?

3. General Motors (GM), once a symbol of American business, filed for bankruptcy in 2009. At the time, its liabilities were $90 billion more than its assets. It also had 325,000 employees and even more stakeholders: retired employees, car owners, suppliers, investors, and communities in which it operated and its employees lived and paid taxes. A mere 40 days after the filing, GM emerged from bankruptcy. The next year, the company was profitable.

> The kids had never gone to Disney World. How could we say no?

Bankruptcy laws are controversial. Typically, in other countries, their goal is to protect creditors and punish debtors, but American laws are more lenient towards the bankrupt.

The General Motors example illustrates the good news about American bankruptcy. It is efficient (taking only 40 days!) and effective at reviving ailing companies. Everyone—investors, employees, the country—benefited from GM's survival. And, although Kristen's flower shop did not survive, bankruptcy laws will protect her so that she is not afraid to try entrepreneurship again. New businesses fail more often than not, but they are nonetheless important engines of growth for our country.

Tim represents the bad news in bankruptcy laws. Unfortunately, he is often the type of person who first comes to mind when people think about bankrupts. And people do not like Tim very much. They think: Why should he be rewarded for his irresponsibility, when I get stuck paying all my bills? But a more difficult bankruptcy process will probably not discourage Tim. He is the kind of guy who cares a lot about current pleasures and little about future pain. No matter what bankruptcy laws are in place, he will not say no to Disney World. Should the laws become too onerous, businesses will fail, entrepreneurs will be discouraged, and the Tims of the world will continue to spend more than they should.

But maybe America has too much of a good thing. This nation has the highest bankruptcy rate in the world. In a recent year, there was one bankruptcy filing for every 200 Americans.[1] Clearly, bankruptcy laws play a vital role in our economy. At the same time, it is important not to enable irresponsible spendthrifts. Do American bankruptcy laws strike the right balance?

23-1 OVERVIEW OF BANKRUPTCY

The U.S. Bankruptcy Code (the Code) has three primary goals:

1. To preserve as much of the debtor's property as possible,

2. To divide the debtor's assets fairly between the debtor and creditors, and

3. To divide the creditors' share of the assets fairly among them.

The following options are available under the Bankruptcy Code:

Number	Topic	Description
Chapter 7	Liquidation	The bankrupt's assets are sold to pay creditors. If the debtor owns a business, it terminates. The creditors have no right to the debtor's future earnings.
Chapter 11	Reorganization	This chapter is designed for businesses and wealthy individuals. Businesses continue to operate, and creditors receive a portion of both current assets and future earnings.
Chapter 13	Consumer reorganization	Chapter 13 offers reorganization for the typical consumer. Creditors usually receive a portion of the individual's current assets and future earnings.

---

[1]Some of these filings are by businesses, although that percentage is small. In the last 15 years, more than 95 percent of all bankruptcy filings have been by consumers.

The goal of Chapters 11 and 13 is to rehabilitate the debtor. These chapters hold creditors at bay while the debtor develops a payment plan. In return for retaining some of their assets, debtors typically promise to pay creditors a portion of their future earnings. However, when debtors are unable to develop a feasible plan for rehabilitation under Chapter 11 or 13, Chapter 7 provides for liquidation (also known as a **straight bankruptcy**). Most of the debtor's assets are distributed to creditors, but the debtor has no obligation to share future earnings.

Debtors are sometimes eligible to file under more than one chapter. No choice is irrevocable because both debtors and creditors have the right to ask the court to convert a case from one chapter to another at any time during the proceedings.

Straight bankruptcy

Also known as liquidation, this form of bankruptcy mandates that the bankrupt's assets be sold to pay creditors, but the bankrupt has no obligation to share future earnings

23-2 CHAPTER 7 LIQUIDATION

All bankruptcy cases proceed in a roughly similar pattern, regardless of chapter. We use Chapter 7 as a template to illustrate common features of all bankruptcy cases. Later on, the discussions of the other Chapters will indicate how they differ from Chapter 7.

23-2a Filing a Petition

Any individual, partnership, corporation, or other business organization that lives, conducts business, or owns property in the United States can file under the Code. (Chapter 13, however, is available only to individuals.) The traditional term for someone who could not pay his debts was **bankrupt**, but the Code uses the term **debtor** instead. We use both terms interchangeably.

A case begins with the filing of a bankruptcy petition in federal district court. Debtors may go willingly into the bankruptcy process by filing a voluntary petition, or they may be dragged into court by creditors who file an involuntary petition.

Bankrupt

Someone who cannot pay his debts and files for protection under the Bankruptcy Code

Debtor

Another term for bankrupt

Voluntary Petition

Any debtor (whether a business or individual) has the right to file for bankruptcy. It is not necessary that the debtor's liabilities exceed assets. Debtors sometimes file a bankruptcy petition because cash flow is so tight they cannot pay their debts, even though they are not technically insolvent. However, *individuals* must meet two requirements before filing:

1. Within 180 days before the filing, an individual debtor must undergo credit counseling with an approved agency.

2. Individual debtors may file under Chapter 7 only if they earn less than the median income in their state *or* they cannot afford to pay back at least $7,475 over five years.[2] Generally, all other debtors must file under Chapters 11 or 13. (These Chapters require the bankrupt to repay some debt.)

---

[2]In some circumstances, debtors with income higher than this amount may still be eligible to file under Chapter 7, but the formula is highly complex and more than most readers want to know. The formula is available at 11 USC §707(b)(2)(A). Also, you can google "bapcpa means test" and then click on the Department of Justice website. The dollar amounts are updated every three years. You can find them by googling "federal register bankruptcy revision of dollar amounts."

The voluntary petition must include the following documents:

Document	Description
Petition	Begins the case. Easy to fill out, it requires checking a few boxes and typing in name, address, and social security number
List of Creditors	The names and addresses of all creditors
Schedule of Assets and Liabilities	A list of the debtor's assets and debts
Claim of Exemptions	A list of all assets that the debtor is entitled to keep
Schedule of Income and Expenditures	The debtor's job, income, and expenses
Statement of Financial Affairs	A summary of the debtor's financial history and current financial condition. In particular, the debtor must list any recent payments to creditors and any other property held by someone else for the debtor.

Involuntary Petition

Creditors may force a debtor into bankruptcy by filing an involuntary petition. The creditors' goals are to preserve as much of the debtor's assets as possible and to ensure that all creditors receive a fair share. Naturally, the Code sets strict limits—debtors cannot be forced into bankruptcy every time they miss a credit card payment. **An involuntary petition must meet all of the following requirements:**

- The debtor must owe at least $15,325 in unsecured claims to the creditors who file.

- If the debtor has at least 12 creditors, 3 or more must sign the petition. If the debtor has fewer than 12 creditors, any of them may file a petition.

- The creditors must allege either that a custodian for the debtor's property has been appointed in the prior 120 days or that the debtor has generally not been paying debts that are due.

What does "a custodian for the debtor's property" mean? *State* laws sometimes permit the appointment of a custodian to protect a debtor's assets. The Code allows creditors to pull a case out from under state law and into federal bankruptcy court by filing an involuntary petition.

Once a voluntary petition is filed or an involuntary petition approved, the bankruptcy court issues an **order for relief**. This order is an official acknowledgment that the debtor is under the jurisdiction of the court, and it is, in a sense, the start of the bankruptcy process. An involuntary debtor must now make all the filings that accompany a voluntary petition.

Order for relief

An official acknowledgment that a debtor is under the jurisdiction of the bankruptcy court

23-2b Trustee

The trustee is responsible for gathering the bankrupt's assets and dividing them among creditors. The creditors have the right to elect a trustee, but often they do not bother. In this case, the **U.S. Trustee** makes the selection. The U.S. Attorney General appoints a U.S. Trustee for each region of the country to administer the bankruptcy law.

U.S. Trustee

Oversees the administration of bankruptcy law in a region

23-2c Creditors

After the order for relief, the U.S. Trustee calls a meeting of all of the creditors. At this meeting, the bankrupt must answer (under oath) any question the creditors pose about his financial situation. If the creditors want to elect a trustee, they do so now.

After the meeting of creditors, unsecured creditors must submit a **proof of claim**. The proof of claim is a simple form stating the name of the creditor and the amount of the claim. Secured creditors do not file proofs of claim.

23-2d Automatic Stay

A fox chased by hounds has no time to make rational long-term decisions. What that fox needs is a safe burrow. Similarly, it is difficult for debtors to make sound financial decisions when hounded night and day by creditors shouting, "Pay me! Pay me!" The Code is designed to give debtors enough breathing space to sort out their affairs sensibly. An automatic stay is a safe burrow for the bankrupt. It goes into effect as soon as the petition is filed. An **automatic stay** prohibits creditors from collecting debts that the bankrupt incurred before the petition was filed. **Creditors may not sue a bankrupt to obtain payment, nor may they take other steps, outside of court, to pressure the debtor for payment.** The following case illustrates how persistent creditors can be.

JACKSON V. HOLIDAY FURNITURE

309 B.R. 33
United States Bankruptcy Court for the Western District of Missouri, 2004

CASE SUMMARY

Facts: Soon after Cora and Frank Jackson purchased a recliner chair on credit from Dan Holiday Furniture, they filed for protection under the Bankruptcy Code. Dan Holiday received a notice of the bankruptcy, which stated that the store must stop all efforts to collect on the Jacksons' debt.

Despite this notice, a Dan Holiday collector telephoned the Jacksons' house 10 times and left a card in their door threatening repossession of the chair. Frank went to Dan Holiday to pay $230.00 toward what they owed. He told the store owner that he wanted to continue making payments despite the bankruptcy filing.

Then Frank died, and Cora did not make any payments. A collector telephoned her house 26 times in the course of a month. The store owner's sister left the following message on Cora's answering machine:

Hello. This is Judy over at Dan Holiday Furniture. And this is the last time I am going to call you. If you do not call me, I will be at your house. And I expect you to call me today. If there is a problem, I need to speak to you about it. You need to call me. We need to get this thing going. And if you think you are going to get away with it, you've got another thing coming.

The store also left seven bright yellow slips of paper in Cora's doorjamb stating that a Dan Holiday truck had stopped by to repossess her furniture. And she received a letter from the store stating, "Repossession Will Be Made and Legal Action Will Be Taken."

These threats were merely a ruse to frighten Cora. Dan Holiday did not really want the recliner back; the owner just wanted to negotiate a payment plan with her.

Cora's bankruptcy attorney contacted Dan Holiday. Thereafter, all collection activity ceased.

Issues: *Did Dan Holiday violate the automatic stay provisions of the Bankruptcy Code? What is the penalty for a violation?*

Decision: Dan Holiday was in violation of the Bankruptcy Code. The court awarded Jackson her actual damages, attorney's fees, court costs, and punitive damages.

Reasoning: Creditors who violate the automatic stay provisions must pay both actual damages (including court costs and attorney's fees) as well as punitive damages where appropriate. In this case, the court awarded actual damages of $230.00, because that is how much Dan Holiday coerced from Frank Jackson. The court also awarded the Jacksons their attorney's fees and court costs in the amount of $1,142.42.

In addition, the Jacksons were entitled to punitive damages because Dan Holiday intentionally and flagrantly violated the automatic stay provision. Dan Holiday's conduct was remarkably bad—employees called the Jackson household no less than 26 times in the course of a month.

The court did not know how much to award in punitive damages because no evidence was presented at trial about what Dan Holiday could afford. But assuming that it was a relatively small business, the court awarded $2,800 in punitive damages. That was $100 for each illegal contact with the Jacksons after Dan Holiday learned of the bankruptcy filing. This penalty was designed to sting the pocketbook of Dan Holiday and impress upon the company the importance of complying with the provisions of the Bankruptcy Code.

23-2e Bankruptcy Estate

Bankruptcy estate
The new legal entity created when a bankruptcy petition is filed- the debtor's existing assets pass into the estate

The filing of the bankruptcy petition creates a new legal entity separate from the debtor—the **bankruptcy estate**. All of the bankrupt's assets pass to the estate, except exempt property and new property that the debtor acquires after the petition is filed.

Exempt Property

The Code permits *individual* debtors (but not organizations) to keep some property for themselves. This exempt property saves the debtor from destitution during the bankruptcy process and provides the foundation for a new life once the process is over.

In this one area of bankruptcy law, the Code defers to state law. Although the Code lists various types of exempt property, it permits states to opt out of the federal system and define a different set of exemptions. However, debtors can take advantage of state exemptions only if they have lived in that state for two years prior to the bankruptcy.

Under the *federal* Code, a debtor is allowed to exempt only $22,975 of the value of her home. Many *states* exempt items such as the debtor's home, household goods, cars, work tools, disability and pension benefits, alimony, and health aids. Both Florida and Texas permit debtors to keep homes of unlimited value and a certain amount of land. But the federal statute limits this state exemption to $155,675 for any house that was acquired during the 40 months before the bankruptcy.

Voidable Preferences

Preference
When a debtor unfairly pays creditors immediately before filing a bankruptcy petition

A major goal of the bankruptcy system is to divide the debtor's assets fairly among creditors. It would not be fair if debtors were permitted to pay off some of their creditors immediately before filing a bankruptcy petition. Such a payment is called a **preference** because it gives unfair preferential treatment to a creditor. **The trustee can void any transfer to a creditor that took place in the 90-day period before the filing of a petition.**

Fraudulent Transfers

Fraudulent transfer
Occurs when a debtor gives assets to someone other than a creditor for the purpose of hindering, delaying, or defrauding creditors

Suppose that a debtor sees bankruptcy approaching across the horizon like a tornado. He knows that, once the storm hits and he files a petition, everything he owns except a few items of exempt property will become part of the bankruptcy estate. Before that happens, he may be tempted to give some of his property to friends or family to shelter it from the tornado. If he succumbs to that temptation, however, he is committing a **fraudulent transfer. A transfer is fraudulent if it is made within the year before a petition is filed and its purpose is to hinder, delay, or defraud creditors.** The trustee can void any fraudulent transfer. The debtor has committed a crime and may be prosecuted.

EXAM Strategy

Question: Eddie and Lola appeared to be happily married. But then Eddie's business failed, and he owed millions. Suddenly, Lola announced that she wanted a divorce. In what had to be the friendliest divorce settlement of all time, Eddie quickly agreed to transfer all of the couple's remaining assets to her. Are you suspicious? Is there a problem?

Strategy: Was this a voidable preference or a fraudulent transfer? What difference does it make?

Result: In a voidable preference, the debtor makes an unfair transfer to a creditor. In a fraudulent transfer, the bankrupt's goal is to hold on to assets himself. In a case similar to this one, the court ruled that the transfer was fraudulent because Eddie intended to shield his assets from all creditors.

23-2f Payment of Claims

Imagine a crowded delicatessen on a Saturday evening. People are pushing and shoving because they know there is not enough food for everyone; some customers will go home hungry. The delicatessen could simply serve whoever pushes to the front of the line, or it could establish a number system to ensure that the most deserving customers are served first. The Code has, in essence, adopted a number system to prevent a free-for-all fight over the bankrupt's assets. Indeed, one of the Code's primary goals is to ensure that creditors are paid in the proper order, not according to who pushes to the front of the line.

All claims are placed in one of three classes: (1) secured claims, (2) priority claims, and (3) unsecured claims. **The trustee pays the bankruptcy estate to the various classes of claims in order of rank**. A higher class is paid in full before the next class receives any payment at all. The debtor is entitled to any funds remaining after all claims have been paid. The payment order is shown in Exhibit 23.1.

Secured Claims

Creditors whose loans are secured by specific collateral are paid first. Secured claims are fundamentally different from all other claims because they are paid not out of the general funds of the estate but by selling a specific asset.

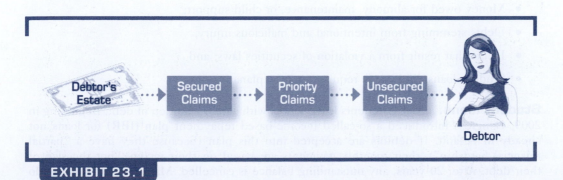

EXHIBIT 23.1

Priority Claims

Each category of priority claims is paid in order, with the first group receiving full payment before the next group receives anything. Priority claims include:

- Alimony and child support,
- Administrative expenses (such as fees to the trustee, lawyers, and accountants),
- Back wages to the debtor's employees for work performed during the 180 days prior to the date of the petition, and
- Income and property taxes.

Unsecured Claims

Last, and frequently very much least, unsecured creditors have now reached the delicatessen counter. They can only hope that some goods remain.

23-2g Discharge

Filing a bankruptcy petition is embarrassing and time consuming. It can affect the debtor's credit rating for years, making the simplest car loan a challenge. To encourage debtors to file for bankruptcy despite the pain involved, the Code offers a powerful incentive: the **fresh start**. Once a bankruptcy estate has been distributed to creditors, they cannot make a claim against the debtor for money owed before the filing, *whether or not they actually received any payment*. These prepetition debts are discharged. All is forgiven, if not forgotten.

Discharge is an essential part of bankruptcy law. Without it, debtors would have little incentive to take part. To avoid abuses, however, the Code limits both the type of debts that can be discharged and the circumstances under which discharge can take place. In addition, a debtor must complete a course on financial management before receiving a discharge.

Debts That Cannot Be Discharged

The following debts are *never* discharged, and the debtor remains liable in full until they are paid:

- Recent income and property taxes;
- Money obtained by fraud;
- Cash advances on a credit card totaling more than $925 that an individual debtor takes out within 70 days before the order of relief;
- Debts omitted from the Schedule of Assets and Liabilities;
- Money owed for alimony, maintenance, or child support;
- Debts stemming from intentional and malicious injury;
- Debts that result from a violation of securities laws; and
- Student loans. This topic requires more explanation.

Student loans.   Many students leave school with a heavy burden of debt. Beginning in 2009, Congress introduced a so-called income-based repayment plan (IBR) for loans not already in default. If debtors are accepted into this plan (because they have a "partial financial hardship"), their monthly payments are based on their income, not the size of their debt. After 20 years, any outstanding balance is cancelled. Many eligible debtors do not apply because they are unaware of this plan.

Fresh start

After the termination of a bankruptcy case, creditors cannot make a claim against the debtor for money owed before the initial bankruptcy petition was filed.

Discharge

The bankrupt no longer has an obligation to pay a debt.

Debtors who are not eligible for the IBR and who are struggling to pay their debts may seek to discharge them through bankruptcy. But student loans cannot be discharged in the bankruptcy process unless repayment would cause *undue hardship*. To demonstrate undue hardship, the debtor must show that, if he pays his loans, he cannot maintain a minimal standard of living and there is little hope for improvement in his financial situation during the term of the loan.

Debtors who have been successful in obtaining discharge tend to be in dire circumstances, with serious illnesses. Carol Todd was 63 years old and autistic. She had been unemployed for a decade and was living on Social Security disability income payments. The court discharged her $340,000 in debt.

In the following case, the debtors were not as successful.

KELLY V. MICH. FIN. AUTH. (IN RE KELLY)

496 B.R. 230
United States Bankruptcy Court for the Middle District of Florida, 2013

CASE SUMMARY

Facts: Lisa and Adam Kelly had two children. Their son, Noah, 18 months old, was born with serious birth defects that affected his physical and intellectual development. He faced large on-going medical expenses. Under their health insurance plan, the family had to pay 20 percent of the cost of their medical care.

Lisa taught Special Education in an elementary school in Florida. Her husband, Adam, had a B.A. in Fine Arts with a concentration in Digital Cinema. He worked remotely from their home for a television station in Michigan, so that he could care for Noah.

The Kellys' annual income totaled approximately $70,000; their combined educational loans exceeded $160,000. When the Kellys filed for bankruptcy, they asked the court to discharge these student loans.

Issue: *Would repayment of their student loans cause the Kellys undue hardship?*

Decision: No, they were financially able to pay these loans.

Reasoning: The Kellys are not required to live in poverty, but they must take further steps to reduce their expenditures. They have recently taken a number of trips for the holidays and to visit with family. If they reduced this travel, they could save $200 a month in gas. Likewise, they currently own two newer cars. If they really need two vehicles, they could trade down to less expensive models.

They are also spending too much on food. According to the United States Department of Agriculture, a thrifty family can live on $550 a month, assuming that all food is purchased at the grocery store and prepared at home. But the Kellys are spending $800. If they reduced this expenditure to $625, they would have more money available to pay their student loans.

Also, both of the Kellys are healthy, educated, and employed. Presumably, their income will continue to increase. In that case, they will have even more funds available to pay their loans.

Noah's medical condition presents some financial uncertainty, but courts do not discharge student loans because a debtor might have a precarious financial situation. A finding of undue hardship is an incredibly high hurdle to overcome. The Kellys have not done so.

One last note Research indicates that more people could benefit from seeking discharge. A very small percentage of debtors who file for bankruptcy ask for a discharge of their student loans.[3] Yet studies have shown that a substantial proportion of student-loan debtors who do ask for discharge receive at least partial relief from their debts. And those who receive a discharge are typically no worse off than those who never even apply.

In short, no one should enter into a student loan with the expectation that somehow he will not have to pay it back. The government makes it extremely difficult to avoid repayment. And the debtors who do escape repayment are in very unhappy situations.

---

[3]Jason Iuliano, "An Empirical Assessment of Student Loan Discharges and the Undue Hardship Standard," 86 *Am. Bankr. L.J.* 495 (2012).

However, people who find themselves in desperate circumstances need to know (1) about IBR and (2) that those who apply for discharge have a reasonable success rate. We hope you never have to use this knowledge, but now you know.

EXAM Strategy

Question: Someone stole a truck full of cigarettes. Zeke found the vehicle abandoned at a truck stop. Not being a thoughtful fellow, he took the truck and sold it with its cargo. Although Tobacco Company never found out who stole the truck originally, it did discover Zeke's role. A court ordered Zeke to pay Tobacco $50,000. He also owed his wife $25,000 in child support. Unfortunately, he only had $20,000 in assets. After he files for bankruptcy, who will get paid what?

Strategy: There are two issues: The order in which the debts are paid and whether they will be discharged.

Result: Child support is a priority claim, so that will be paid first. In a similar case, the court refused to discharge the claim over the theft of the truck, ruling that that was an intentional and malicious injury. Nor will a court discharge the child support claim. So Zeke will be on the hook for both debts, but the child support must be paid first.

Circumstances That Prevent Debts from Being Discharged

The Code also prohibits the discharge of debts under the following circumstances:

- **Business organizations**. Under Chapter 7 (but not the other Chapters), only the debts of individuals can be discharged, not those of business organizations. Once its assets have been distributed, an organization must cease operation. If the company resumes business again, it becomes responsible for all its prefiling debts.

- **Revocation**. A court can revoke a discharge within one year if it discovers the debtor engaged in fraud or concealment.

- **Dishonesty or bad-faith behavior**. The court may deny discharge altogether if the debtor has made fraudulent transfers, hidden assets, or otherwise acted in bad faith.

- **Repeated filings for bankruptcy**. A debtor who has received a discharge under Chapter 7 or 11 cannot receive another discharge under Chapter 7 for at least eight years after the prior filing. And a debtor who has received a prior discharge under Chapter 13 cannot, in most cases, receive one under Chapter 7 for at least six years.

Ethics   Banks and credit card companies lobbied Congress hard to insert the prohibition against repeat bankruptcy filings. They argued that irresponsible consumers run up debt and then blithely walk away. You might think that, if this were true, lenders would avoid customers with a history of bankruptcy. New research indicates, though, that lenders actually target those consumers, repeatedly sending them offers to borrow money. The reason is simple: These consumers are much more likely to take cash advances, which carry very high interest rates. And this is one audience that must repay its loans, for the simple reason that these borrowers cannot obtain a discharge again anytime soon.[4] Is this strategy ethical?

---

[4]See Katherine M. Porter, "Bankrupt Profits: The Credit Industry's Business Model for Postbankruptcy Lending," 93 *Iowa L. Rev.* 1369 (2008).

Reaffirmation

Sometimes debtors are willing to **reaffirm** a debt, meaning they promise to pay even after discharge. They may want to reaffirm a secured debt to avoid losing the collateral. For example, a debtor who has taken out a loan secured by a car may reaffirm that debt so that the finance company will not repossess it. Sometimes debtors reaffirm because they feel guilty or want to maintain a good relationship with the creditor. They may have borrowed from a family member or an important supplier.

Because discharge is a fundamental pillar of the bankruptcy process, creditors are not permitted to unfairly pressure the bankrupt. **A reaffirmation must be approved by the court if the debtor is not represented by an attorney or if, as a result of the reaffirmed debt, the bankrupt's expenses exceed his income.** William Grisham owed about $200,000 in debt that was not dischargeable. His expenses were $1,000 a month more than his income. He owned no real estate and was living rent free with a relative. His one asset was a truck that was worth $16,000 but he owed $17,500 on it. He asked the bankruptcy court to reaffirm that debt, presumably so that the lender would not repossess it. But the court refused on the grounds that Grisham needed a fresh start and that meant shedding as much debt as possible.

<aside>
Reaffirm

To promise to pay a debt even after it is discharged
</aside>

23-3 CHAPTER 11 REORGANIZATION

For a business, the goal of a Chapter 7 bankruptcy is euthanasia—putting it out of its misery by shutting it down and distributing its assets to creditors. Chapter 11 has a much more complicated and ambitious goal—resuscitating a business so that it can ultimately emerge as a viable economic concern, as GM did.

Both individuals and businesses can use Chapter 11. Businesses usually prefer Chapter 11 over Chapter 7 because Chapter 11 does not require them to dissolve at the end, as Chapter 7 does. The threat of death creates a powerful incentive to try rehabilitation under Chapter 11. Individuals usually file under Chapter 7 if they can meet the income requirements because then they emerge from bankruptcy debt free (except for debts that are not dischargeable). Chapter 13 is specifically designed for individuals, but is only available to those whose debt does not exceed certain limits. For consumers with even modest income and high debt, Chapter 11 is the only option.

A Chapter 11 proceeding follows many of the same steps as Chapter 7: a petition (either voluntary or involuntary), an order for relief, a meeting of creditors, proofs of claim, and an automatic stay. There are, however, some significant differences.

23-3a Debtor in Possession

Chapter 11 does not require a trustee. The bankrupt is called the **debtor in possession** and, in essence, serves as trustee. The debtor in possession has two jobs: to operate the business and to develop a plan of reorganization. A trustee is chosen only if the debtor is incompetent or uncooperative. In that case, the creditors can elect the trustee, but if they do not choose to do so, the U.S. Trustee appoints one.

<aside>
Debtor in possession

Under Chapter 11, the bankrupt, in essence, serves as trustee.
</aside>

23-3b Creditors' Committee

In a Chapter 11 case, the creditors' committee is important because typically there is no neutral trustee to watch over the committee's interests. The committee may play a role in developing the plan of reorganization. The U.S. Trustee typically appoints the seven largest *un*secured creditors to the committee, although the court has the right to require the appointment of some small-business creditors as well.

23-3c Plan of Reorganization

Once the bankruptcy petition is filed, an automatic stay goes into effect to provide the debtor with temporary relief from creditors. The next stage is to develop a plan of reorganization that provides for the payment of debts and the continuation of the business. For the first 120 days after the order for relief, the debtor has the exclusive right to propose a plan. If the shareholders and creditors accept it, then the bankruptcy case terminates. If the creditors or shareholders reject the debtor's plan, they may file their own version.

32-3d Confirmation of the Plan

All the creditors and shareholders have the right to vote on the plan of reorganization. In preparation for the vote, each creditor and shareholder is assigned to a class. Chapter 11 classifies claims in the same way as Chapter 7: (1) secured claims, (2) priority claims, and (3) unsecured claims.

The bankruptcy court will approve a plan if a majority of the debtors in *each* class votes in favor of it *and* if the "yes" votes hold at least two-thirds of the total debt in that class. So long as at least one class votes in favor of the plan, the court can still confirm it over the opposition of other classes in what is called a **cramdown** (as in, "the plan is crammed down the creditors' throats"). If the court rejects the plan of reorganization, the creditors must develop a new one.

Cramdown
When a court approves a plan of reorganization over the objection of some of the creditors

23-3e Discharge

A confirmed plan of reorganization is binding on the debtor and creditors. **The debtor now owns the assets in the bankrupt estate, free of all obligations except those listed in the plan.** Under a typical plan of reorganization, the debtor gives some current assets to creditors and also promises to pay them a portion of future earnings. In contrast, the Chapter 7 debtor typically relinquishes all assets (except exempt property) to creditors but then has no obligation to turn over future income (except for nondischargeable debts). Exhibit 23.2 illustrates the steps in a Chapter 11 bankruptcy.

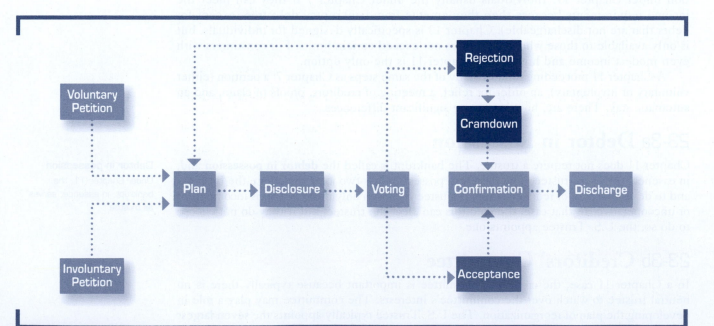

EXHIBIT 23.2

23-3f Small-Business Bankruptcy

To aid the creditors of small businesses, Congress added provisions that speed up the bankruptcy process for entities with less than $2,490,925 in debt. After the order of relief, the bankrupt has the exclusive right to file a plan for 180 days. The court must confirm or reject the plan within 45 days after its filing. If these deadlines are not met, the case can be converted to Chapter 7 or dismissed.

23-4 CHAPTER 13 CONSUMER REORGANIZATIONS

The purpose of Chapter 13 is to rehabilitate an individual debtor. It is only available to individuals with less than $383,175 in unsecured debts or $1,149,525 in secured debts. Under Chapter 13, the bankrupt consumer typically keeps most of her assets in exchange for a promise to repay some of her debts using future income. Therefore, to be eligible, the debtor must have a regular source of income. Individuals who do not qualify for Chapter 7 usually choose this chapter because it is easier and cheaper than Chapter 11.

A bankruptcy under Chapter 13 generally follows the same course as Chapter 11. The debtor files a petition, creditors submit proofs of claim, the court imposes an automatic stay, the debtor files a plan, and the court confirms the plan. But there are some differences.

23-4a Beginning a Chapter 13 Case

To initiate a Chapter 13 case, the debtor must file a voluntary petition. Creditors cannot use an involuntary petition to force a debtor into Chapter 13. In all Chapter 13 cases, the U.S. Trustee appoints a trustee to supervise the debtor. The trustee also serves as a central clearinghouse for the debtor's payments to creditors. The debtor pays the trustee who, in turn, transmits these funds to creditors. For this service, the trustee is allowed to keep up to 10 percent of the payments.

23-4b Plan of Payment

The debtor must file a plan of payment within 15 days after filing the voluntary petition. Only the bankruptcy court has the authority to confirm or reject a plan of payment. Creditors have no right to vote on it. However, to confirm a plan, the court must ensure that:

- The plan is feasible and the bankrupt will be able to make the promised payments;

- The plan does not extend beyond three years without good reason and in no event lasts longer than five years;

- If the plan does not provide for the debtor to pay off creditors in full, then all of the debtor's disposable income for the next five years must go to creditors; and

- The debtor is acting in good faith, making a reasonable effort to pay obligations.

23-4c Discharge

Once confirmed, a plan is binding on all creditors whether they like it or not. **The debtor is washed clean of all prepetition debts except those provided for in the plan.** But if the debtor violates the plan, all of the debts are revived, and the creditors have a right to recover them under Chapter 7. The debts become permanently discharged only when the bankrupt fully complies with the plan. Note, however, that any debtor who has received a discharge under Chapter 7 or 11 within the prior four years or under Chapter 13 within the prior two years is not eligible for discharge under Chapter 13.

If the debtor's circumstances change, the debtor, the trustee, or unsecured creditors can ask the court to modify the plan. Most such requests come from debtors whose income has declined. However, if the debtor's income rises, the creditors or the trustee can ask that payments increase, too.

Chapter Conclusion

Bankruptcy law is the safety net that catches those who are not able to meet their financial obligations. Bankruptcy laws cannot create assets where there are none, but they can ensure that the debtor's assets, however limited, are fairly divided between the debtor and creditors. Any bankruptcy system that accomplishes this goal must be deemed a success.

EXAM REVIEW

The following chart sets out the important elements of each bankruptcy chapter.

	Chapter 7	Chapter 11	Chapter 13
Objective	Liquidation	Reorganization	Consumer reorganization
Who May Use It	Individual or organization	Individual or organization	Individual
Type of Petition	Voluntary or involuntary	Voluntary or involuntary	Only voluntary
Administration of Bankruptcy Estate	Trustee	Debtor in possession	Trustee
Selection of Trustee	Creditors have right to elect trustee; otherwise, U.S. Trustee makes appointment	Usually no trustee	Appointed by U.S. Trustee
Participation in Formulation of Plan	No plan is filed	Both creditors and debtor can propose plans	Only debtor can propose a plan
Creditor Approval of Plan	Creditors do not vote	Creditors vote on plan, but court may approve plan without the creditors' support	Creditors do not vote
Impact on Debtor's Postpetition Income	Not affected; debtor keeps all future earnings	Must contribute toward payment of prepetition debts	Must contribute toward payment of prepetition debts

The following table sets out the waiting times before debtors can file a new bankruptcy petition:

Prior Case	To File under Chapter 7, Must Wait:	To File under Chapter 13, Must Wait:
Chapter 7	8 years	4 years
Chapter 11	8 years	4 years
Chapter 13	6 years	2 years

EXAM Strategy

1. Question: Mark Milbank's custom furniture business was unsuccessful, so he repeatedly borrowed money from his wife and her father. He promised that the loans would enable him to spend more time with his family. Instead, he spent more time in bed with his next-door neighbor. After the divorce, his ex-wife and her father demanded repayment of the loans. Milbank filed for protection under Chapter 13. What could his ex-wife and her father do to help their chances of being repaid?

Strategy: First ask yourself what kind of creditor they are: secured or unsecured? Then think about what creditors can do to get special treatment. (See the "Result" at the end of this section.)

EXAM Strategy

2. Question: After a jury ordered actor Kim Basinger to pay $8 million for breaching a movie contract, she filed for bankruptcy protection, claiming $5 million in assets and $11 million in liabilities. Under which Chapter should she file? Why?

Strategy: Look at the requirements for each Chapter. Was Basinger eligible for Chapter 13? What would be the advantages and disadvantages of Chapters 7 and 11? (See the "Result" at the end of this section.)

1. Result: The father and the ex-wife were unsecured creditors who, as a class, come last on the priority list. The court granted their request not to discharge their loans on the grounds that Milbank had acted in bad faith.

2. Result: Basinger was not eligible to file under Chapter 13 because she had debts of $11 million. She first filed under Chapter 11 in a effort to retain some of her assets, but then her creditors would not approve her plan of reorganization, so she converted to liquidation under Chapter 7.

MATCHING QUESTIONS

Match the following terms with the correct description:

___A. Discharge

___B. Fraudulent transfer

___C. Exempt property

___D. Reaffirmation

___E. Voidable preference

1. Property that individual debtors can keep for themselves
2. Debtors are not liable for money owed before the filing
3. Debtor's promise to pay a debt after discharge
4. Payment to a creditor immediately before filing
5. Payment made within the year before a petition is filed with the goal of hindering creditors

TRUE/FALSE QUESTIONS

Circle true or false:

1. T F Student loans can never be discharged.
2. T F Each of the Code's Chapters has one of two objectives—rehabilitation or liquidation.
3. T F A creditor is not permitted to force a debtor into bankruptcy.
4. T F The bankruptcy court issues an order for relief to give the debtor a chance to file a petition.
5. T F The Code permits *individual* debtors (but not organizations) to keep some property for themselves.

MULTIPLE-CHOICE QUESTIONS

1. *CPA QUESTION* Decal Corp. incurred substantial operating losses for the past three years. Unable to meet its current obligations, Decal filed a petition of reorganization under Chapter 11 of the federal Bankruptcy Code. Which of the following statements is correct?

   (a) A creditors' committee, if appointed, will consist of unsecured creditors.

   (b) The court must appoint a trustee to manage Decal's affairs.

   (c) Decal may continue in business only with the approval of a trustee.

   (d) The creditors' committee must select a trustee to manage Decal's affairs.

2. *CPA QUESTION* A voluntary petition filed under the liquidation provisions of Chapter 7 of the federal Bankruptcy Code:

   (a) is not available to a corporation unless it has previously filed a petition under the reorganization provisions of Chapter 11 of the Code.

   (b) automatically stays collection actions against the debtor except by secured creditors.

   (c) will be dismissed unless the debtor has 12 or more unsecured creditors whose claims total at least $5,000.

   (d) does not require the debtor to show that the debtor's liabilities exceed the fair market value of assets.

3. **CPA QUESTION** Unger owes a total of $50,000 to eight unsecured creditors and one fully secured creditor. Quincy is one of the unsecured creditors and is owed $6,000. Quincy has filed a petition against Unger under the liquidation provisions of Chapter 7 of the federal Bankruptcy Code. Unger has been unable to pay debts as they become due. Unger's liabilities exceed Unger's assets. Unger has filed papers opposing the bankruptcy petition. Which of the following statements regarding Quincy's petition is correct?

   (a) It will be dismissed because the secured creditor failed to join in the filing of the petition.

   (b) It will be dismissed because three unsecured creditors must join in the filing of the petition.

   (c) It will be granted because Unger's liabilities exceed Unger's assets.

   (d) It will be granted because Unger is unable to pay Unger's debts as they become due.

4. A debtor is not required to file the following document with his voluntary petition:

   (a) Budget statement for the following three years

   (b) Statement of financial affairs

   (c) List of creditors

   (d) Claim of exemptions

   (e) Schedule of income and expenditures

5. Grass Co. is in bankruptcy proceedings under Chapter 11. _____ serves as trustee. In the case of _____ , the court can approve a plan of reorganization over the objections of the creditors.

   (a) The debtor in possession; a cramdown

   (b) A person appointed by the U.S. Trustee; fraud

   (c) The head of the creditors' committee; reaffirmation

   (d) The U.S. Trustee; voidable preference

CASE QUESTIONS

1. James, the owner of an auto parts store, told his employee, Rickey, to clean and paint some tires in the basement. Highly flammable gasoline fumes accumulated in the poorly ventilated space. James threw a firecracker into the basement as a joke, intending only to startle Rickey. Sparks from the firecracker caused an explosion and fire that severely burned him. Rickey filed a personal injury suit against James for $1 million. Is this debt dischargeable under Chapter 7?

2. Mary Price went for a consultation about a surgical procedure to remove abdominal fat. When Robert Britton met with her, he wore a name tag that identified him as a doctor, and was addressed as "doctor" by the nurse. Britton then examined Price, touching her stomach and showing her where the incision would be made. Britton was not a doctor, he was the office manager. Although a doctor actually

performed the surgery on Price, Britton was present. The doctor left a tube in Price's body at the site of the incision. The area became infected, requiring corrective surgery. A jury awarded Price $275,000 in damages in a suit against Britton. He subsequently filed a Chapter 7 bankruptcy petition. Is this judgment dischargeable in bankruptcy court?

3. Lydia D'Ettore received a degree in computer programming at DeVry Institute of Technology, with a grade point average of 2.51. To finance her education, she borrowed $20,500 from a federal student loan program. After graduation, she could not find a job in her field, so she went to work as a clerk at a salary of $12,500. D'Ettore and her daughter lived with her parents free of charge. After setting aside $50 a month in savings and paying bills that included $233 for a new car and $50 for jewelry from Zales, her disposable income was $125 per month. D'Ettore asked the bankruptcy court to discharge the debts she owed for her DeVry education. Should the court do so?

4. Dr. Ibrahim Khan caused an automobile accident in which a fellow physician, Dolly Yusufji, became a quadriplegic. Khan signed a contract for the lifetime support of Yusufji. When he refused to make payments under the contract, she sued him and obtained a judgment for $1,205,400. Khan filed a Chapter 11 petition. At the time of the bankruptcy hearing, five years after the accident, Khan had not paid Yusufji anything. She was dependent on a motorized wheelchair; he drove a Rolls-Royce. Is Khan's debt dischargeable under Chapter 11?

5. After filing for bankruptcy, Yvonne Brown sought permission of the court to reaffirm a $6,000 debt to her credit union. The debt was unsecured, and she was under no obligation to pay it. The credit union had published the following notice in its newsletter:

> If you are thinking about filing bankruptcy, THINK about the long-term implications. This action, filing bankruptcy, closes the door on TOMORROW. Having no credit means no ability to purchase cars, houses, credit cards. Look into the future—no loans for the education of your children.

Should the court approve Brown's reaffirmation?

DISCUSSION QUESTIONS

1. **ETHICS** On November 5, Hawes, Inc., a small subcontractor, opened an account with Basic Corp., a supplier of construction materials. Hawes promised to pay its bills within 30 days of purchase. Although Hawes purchased a substantial quantity of goods on credit from Basic, it made few payments on the accounts until the following March, when it paid Basic over $21,000. On May 14, Hawes filed a voluntary petition under Chapter 7. Why did Hawes pay Basic in March? Does the bankruptcy trustee have a right to recover this payment? Is it fair to Hawes's other creditors if Basic is allowed to keep the $21,000 payment?

2. Look on the Internet for your state's rules on exempt property. Compared with other states and the federal government, is your state generous or stingy with exemptions? In considering a new bankruptcy statute, Congress struggled mightily over whether or not to permit state exemptions at all. Is it fair for exemptions to vary by state? Why should someone in one state fare better than his neighbor across the state line? How much should the exemption be?

3. Some states permit debtors an unlimited exemption on their homes. Is it fair for bankrupts to be allowed to keep multimillion-dollar homes while their creditors remain unpaid? But other states allow an exemption of as little as $5,000. Should bankrupts be thrown out on the street? What amount is fair?

4. What about the rules regarding repeated bankruptcy filings? (See the chart in Exam Review.) Are these rules too onerous, too lenient, or just right?

5. A bankrupt who owns a house has the option of either paying the mortgage or losing his home. The court cannot reduce the amount owed; its choice is to discharge the entire debt or leave it whole. Congress considered a bill that would permit a bankruptcy judge to adjust the terms of mortgages to aid debtors in holding onto their houses. Proponents argued that this change in the law would reduce foreclosures and stabilize the national housing market. Opponents said that it was not fair to reward homeowners for being irresponsible. How would you have voted on this bill?

6. Between back taxes, alimony, child support, and student loans, debtors can leave the bankruptcy process with hundreds of thousands of dollars in debt that has not been discharged. What kind of fresh start is that? Should limits be placed on the total debt that cannot be discharged? Is the list of non-dischargeable debts appropriate?

Government Regulation

CHAPTER 24

SECURITIES AND ANTITRUST

© Galyna Andrushko/Shutterstock.com

Sandy is a director of a public company. He tells his girlfriend, Carly, that the company is about to receive a takeover offer. Sandy does not buy any stock himself, but Carly does. When the offer is announced, the stock zooms up in price and Carly makes a huge profit.

Steve and Joe coach college wrestling teams in the same conference. One evening after a meet, they have a pleasant dinner complaining about how tight their budgets are and how difficult it is to hire an assistant coach. Under the influence of wine and whine, it occurs to them that they would both benefit by agreeing to limit what they will pay a new assistant coach. That way, neither of them will break his budget and they might even have more money for athletic scholarships. Such a great idea! They shake hands on it.

Each of these people is about to find out, in a very unpleasant way, about important laws that regulate business. Sandy and Carly have violated securities laws on insider trading. Steve and Joe have engaged in price-fixing that is prohibited by antitrust laws. They are all subject to a substantial fine and even a prison sentence.

> **Each of these people is about to find out, in a very unpleasant way, about important laws that regulate business.**

24-1 SECURITIES LAWS

There are two major securities laws: the Securities Act of 1933 (the 1933 Act) and the Securities Exchange Act of 1934 (the 1934 Act).

24-1a What Is a Security?

Both the 1933 and the 1934 Acts regulate securities. **A security is any transaction in which the buyer (1) invests money in a common enterprise and (2) expects to earn a profit predominantly from the efforts of others.**

This definition includes investments that are not necessarily called *securities*. Besides the obvious stocks or bonds, the definition of security can even include items such as orange trees. W. J. Howey Co. owned large citrus groves in Florida. It sold these trees to investors, most of whom were from out of state and knew nothing about farming. Purchasers were expected to hire someone to take care of their trees. Someone like Howey-in-the-Hills, Inc., a related company that just happened to be in the service business. Customers were free to hire any service company, but 85 percent of the acreage was covered by service contracts with Howey-in-the-Hills. The court held that Howey was selling a security (no matter how orange or tart), because the purchaser was investing in a common enterprise (the orange grove) expecting to earn a profit from Howey's farm work.

Other courts have interpreted the term *security* to include animal breeding arrangements (chinchillas, silver foxes, or beavers, take your pick); condominium purchases in which the developer promises the owner a certain level of income from rentals; and even athletes. In these deals, investors make a lump sum payment now, in return for a share of the athlete's future earnings.

Security
Any transaction in which the buyer invests money in a common enterprise and expects to earn a profit predominantly from the efforts of others

24-1b Securities Act of 1933

The 1933 Act requires that, before offering or selling securities in a public offering, the issuer must register the securities with the Securities and Exchange Commission (SEC). An **issuer** is the company that sells the stock initially.

The guiding principle of federal securities laws is that investors can make a reasonable decision on whether to buy or sell securities if they have full and accurate information about a company and the security it is selling. Given clear information, the responsibility is on the buyer to evaluate the quality of the investment. **The SEC does not, itself, evaluate or investigate the** *quality* **of any offering; it simply ascertains that, on the surface, the company has** *disclosed* **all required information about itself and its major products.** Permission from the SEC to sell securities does not mean that the company has a good product or will be successful.

When the Green Bay Packers football team sold an offering of stock to finance stadium improvements, the prospectus admitted:

> IT IS VIRTUALLY IMPOSSIBLE that any investor will ever make a profit on the stock purchase. The company will pay no dividends, and the shares cannot be sold.

This does not sound like a stock you want in your retirement fund; on the other hand, the SEC will not prevent Green Bay from selling it, or you from buying it, so long as you understand what the risks are.

Issuer
A company that sells its own stock

Liability

Under the 1933 Act, the seller of a security is liable for making any *material* **misstatement or omission, either oral or written, in connection with the offer or sale of a security.** Anyone who issues fraudulent securities is in violation of the 1933 Act, whether or not the securities are registered. Both the SEC and any purchasers of the stock can sue the issuer. In addition, the Justice Department can bring criminal charges against anyone who willfully violates this statute.

Material
Important enough to affect an investor's decision

Public Offerings

A company's first public sale of securities is called an **initial public offering** or an **IPO.** Any subsequent public sale is called a **secondary offering**.

This is the process an issuer follows for either an IPO or a secondary offering:

- **Registration statement.** To make a public offering, the company must file a **registration statement** with the SEC. The registration statement has two purposes: to notify the SEC that a sale of securities is pending and to disclose information of interest to prospective purchasers. The registration statement must include detailed information about the issuer and its business, a description of the stock, the proposed use of the proceeds from the offering, and three years of audited financial statements. Preparing for an IPO is neither fast nor cheap. A typical IPO can cost $10 million; an exceptional one as much as $40 million.

- **Prospectus.** Typically, buyers never see the registration statement; they are given the prospectus instead. (The prospectus is part of the registration statement that is sent to the SEC.) The prospectus includes all of the important disclosures about the company and the security that is to be sold, while the registration statement includes additional information that is of interest to the SEC but not to the typical investor, such as the names and addresses of the lawyers for the issuer and underwriter. All investors must receive a copy of the prospectus before purchasing stock.

- **Sales effort.** Even before the final registration statement and prospectus are completed, the investment bank representing the issuer begins its sales effort. As part of this effort, company executives and the investment bankers conduct a **road show**; that is, they travel around the country making presentations to potential investors. The investment bank cannot actually make sales during this period, but it can solicit offers. The SEC closely regulates an issuer's sales effort to ensure that it does not hype the stock by making public statements about the company before the stock is sold. The SEC delayed an offering of stock by Google, Inc., after *Playboy* magazine published an interview with its founders.

- **Going effective.** Once the SEC finishes its review of the registration statement, it sends the issuer a **comment letter** listing required changes. An issuer almost always has to amend the registration statement at least once, and sometimes more than once. Remember that the SEC does not assess the value of the stock or the merit of the investment. Its role is to ensure that the company has disclosed enough information to enable investors to make an informed decision. After the SEC has approved a final registration statement (which includes, of course, the final prospectus), the issuer and underwriter agree on a price for the stock and the date to **go effective**, that is, to begin the sale.

Emerging Growth Companies. An **emerging growth company (EGC)** is an issuer with annual gross revenues of less than $1 billion (indexed for inflation), which means virtually all companies undertaking an IPO. Under new rules, an EGC can require the SEC to keep its registration statement secret until 21 days before its road show begins.

In one recent year, the companies in about three-quarters of all IPOs opted to keep their registration statements secret until the last minute. In theory, this provision permits EGCs to keep sensitive information out of the hands of their competitors. Also, these EGCs can make any changes that the SEC requires, without damaging publicity. When Groupon went public, the SEC's questions about its unusual accounting methods damaged its reputation with investors.

But what is good for issuers may not be a boon to investors. They want to know if the SEC has criticized an issuer's accounting methodology. And the upshot of these new rules is that potential investors have less time to review company data.

Private Offerings

Registering securities with the SEC for a public offering is very time-consuming and expensive, but the 1933 Act also permits issuers to sell stock in a private offering, which is much simpler (and cheaper). Tens of thousands of these offerings take place each year while, in a recent year, there were only about 250 IPOs.

Under the 1933 Act, an issuer is not required to register securities that are sold in a *private offering*, that is, an offering with a relatively small number of investors or a limited amount of money involved.

Regulation D.   The most common and important type of private offering is under **Regulation D** (often referred to as "Reg D"). **Rule 505 under Reg D permits a company to sell up to $5 million of stock during each 12-month period, subject to the following restrictions:**

- The issuer can sell to an unlimited number of accredited investors, but to only 35 unaccredited investors. **Accredited investors** are institutions (such as banks and insurance companies) or wealthy individuals (with a net worth of more than $1 million, not counting their homes, or an annual income of more than $200,000).

- The company may not advertise the stock publicly.

- The company need not provide information to accredited investors but must make some disclosure to unaccredited investors.

Crowdfunding.   Under the new Jumpstart Our Business Startups (JOBS) Act, privately held companies can sell up to $1 million in securities in any 12-month period, provided that they do all of the following:[1]

- Sell the securities through an **approved intermediary**—a broker or a funding portal (e.g., a website) that is registered with the SEC,

- File with the SEC an initial offering statement and annual reports,

- Limit investments by individuals to no more than 10 percent of their income or net worth, and

- Prohibit resale of the stock for one year.

The SEC was opposed to this crowdfunding legislation because there will be little oversight of these companies. As we remember from the discussion in the chapter on corporations about the business judgment rule, managers will have wide latitude in how they spend the funds they raise. Investors will have little recourse for off-plan expenditures. Since few of these companies will ever go public, investors will have limited opportunities to sell their stock or realize any return on their investment.

24-1c Securities Exchange Act of 1934

Registration

Most buyers do not purchase new securities from the issuer in an IPO. Rather, they buy stock that is publicly traded in the open market. This stock is, in a sense, secondhand because other people—perhaps many others—have already owned it. The purpose of the 1934 Act is to provide investors with ongoing information about public companies (that is, companies with publicly traded stock).

Private offering
A sale of securities that involves a small number of investors or takes in a relatively modest amount of money

Regulation D
The most common and important type of private offering

Accredited investors
Are institutions (such as banks and insurance companies) or wealthy individuals (with a net worth of more than $1 million or an annual income of more than $200,000)

Approved intermediary
A broker or website that is registered with the SEC

---

[1]These amounts will be inflation-adjusted at least once every five years. This discussion reflects the SEC's proposed rules.

Under the 1934 Act, an issuer must register with the SEC if:

- It completes a public offering under the 1933 Act, or

- Its securities are traded on a national exchange (such as the New York Stock Exchange), or

- It has at least 2,000 shareholders (or 500 who are unaccredited investors) *and* total assets that exceed $10 million.

The 1934 Act requires public companies to file the following documents:

- **Annual reports** on Form 10-K, containing audited financial statements, a detailed analysis of the company's performance, and information about officers and directors. A public company must also deliver its annual report to shareholders.

- **Quarterly reports** on Form 10-Q, which are less detailed than 10-Ks and contain unaudited financials.

- **Form 8-K** to report any significant developments, such as a change in control, the resignation of a director over a policy dispute, or a change in auditing firms.

A company's CEO and CFO must certify that:

- The information in the quarterly and annual reports is true,

- The company has effective internal controls, and

- The officers have informed the company's audit committee and its auditors of any concerns that they have about the internal control system.

Liability

Section 10(b) (and Rule 10b-5) prohibit fraud in connection with the purchase and sale of any security, whether or not the security is registered under the 1934 Act. Under these rules, anyone who fails to disclose material information or makes incomplete or inaccurate disclosure is liable, provided that the statement or omission was made with **scienter**. This legal term means that someone has acted with the intent to deceive or with deliberate recklessness as to the possibility of misleading investors. Negligence is not enough to create liability. Thus, an accounting firm that certified financials in a company's annual report, knowing that it had not in fact adequately audited the firm's books, is acting with scienter and would be liable under §10(b).

In the following case, Hewlett-Packard (HP) and its executives made inaccurate statements. But did they have scienter? You be the judge.

Scienter

Acting with the intent to deceive or with deliberate recklessness as to the possibility of misleading investors

---

You be the Judge

Facts: Here is the timeline of events:

1. October: HP purchased Autonomy Corporation. Over the next few months, HP learned that Autonomy's financials were inaccurate.

2. May 23:

In re HP Secs. Litig
2013 U.S. Dist. LEXIS 168292 2013, WL 6185529 2013
United States District Court for the Northern District of California, 2013

a. HP CEO Meg Whitman hired Price WaterhouseCoopers to investigate reports of serious accounting improprieties at Autonomy.

b. On a call with analysts, Whitman said, "In my view, Autonomy is a terrific product."

3. June 5: During a press interview, Whitman stated about Autonomy's difficulties:

> In my view, this is the classic case of scaling a business from startup to grownup. You can't run the organization at $1.5 billion the same way you did at $500 million. You just can't. I know exactly how this world works. I have every confidence that Autonomy will be a very big and very profitable business.

4. August 22: On a conference call, Whitman said, "Autonomy still requires a great deal of attention and we've been aggressively working on that business."

5. September 10: HP's Form 10-Q reported that: "At the time of the Autonomy acquisition in October 2011, the fair value of Autonomy approximated the carrying value."

6. Fifteen months later, on November 20: HP announced that, because of the report it had just received from PriceWaterhouseCoopers, it was writing down the Autonomy investment by $8.8 billion.

Shareholders filed suit alleging that Whitman and HP had committed fraud under §10(b).

You Be the Judge: *Did the defendants have scienter? Did they act either intentionally or with deliberate recklessness?*

Argument for the Shareholders: Long after it knew of problems with the Autonomy purchase, HP executives made filings with the SEC and statements to investors that gave no hint of trouble. Whitman even made up a whole story about how Autonomy was just going through growing pains. She stated that "Autonomy is a terrific product"—an odd description for a fraudulent deal.

HP said in a filing that, at the time of the Autonomy acquisition in October, its fair value approximated the carrying value. The senior executives could not possibly have believed that statement to be true. In short, they deliberately duped and defrauded investors.

Argument for the Company and Its Executives: Yes, there were rumors and allegations about Autonomy, but not until November 20, when the PriceWaterhouse investigation finished, did the defendants know for sure that the deal had been a fraud. As soon as the company knew, it made the public announcement. Taking time to investigate a situation before making disclosures to the investing public is not fraudulent; it is prudent and reasonable. Besides, Whitman's statements were nothing but sales talk and, therefore, create no liability.

The Autonomy purchase was a mistake, but no one intentionally engaged in wrongdoing. HP was the one who was duped.

24-1d Insider Trading

Why is insider trading a crime? Who is harmed? **Insider trading is illegal because:**

- It undermines the integrity of stock markets. Investors will be unwilling to buy in the market unless they believe in its fundamental honesty.

- It offends our fundamental sense of fairness. No one wants to be in a poker game with marked cards.

- Investment banks typically "make a market" in stocks, meaning that they hold extra shares so that orders can be filled smoothly. These marketmakers expect to earn a certain profit, but inside traders skim some of it off. So marketmakers simply raise the commission they charge. As a result, everyone who buys and sells stock pays a slightly higher price.

The 1934 Act takes two approaches to preventing this type of trading: It bans both short-swing trading and classic insider trading.

Short-Swing Trading

Section 16 of the 1934 Act applies to officers, directors, and shareholders who own more than 10 percent of the company. The statute takes a two-pronged approach:

- First, anyone who becomes an insider must *report* this status to the SEC. Insiders must then *report* any trades in company stock within two business days.

- Second, insiders must *turn over* to the corporation any profits they make from the purchase and sale or sale and purchase of company securities in a six-month period.

Section 16 is a strict liability provision. It applies even if the insider did not actually take advantage of secret information or try to manipulate the market; if she bought and sold or sold and bought stock in a six-month period, she is liable for any profits she earned.

Suppose that Manuela buys 20,000 shares of her company's stock in June at $10 a share. In September, her (uninsured) winter house in Florida is destroyed by a hurricane. To raise money for rebuilding, she sells the stock at $12 per share, making a profit of $40,000. She has violated §16 and must turn over the profit to her company.

Classic Insider Trading

Under §10(b) of the 1934 Act, insider trading is a crime punishable by fines and imprisonment. The main elements of this crime are as follows.

Fiduciary Duty.   Any corporate insider (1) with material, nonpublic information, (2) who breaches a fiduciary duty *to his company* (3) by trading on the information is guilty of insider trading. Corporate insiders who have a fiduciary duty include board members, major shareholders, employees, and so-called temporary insiders, such as lawyers and investment bankers who are doing deals for the company. Examples:

- If the director of research for MediSearch, Inc. buys stock in the company at a time when she knows that its scientists have found a cure for Ebola but before that information is public, she is guilty of insider trading. So is a lawyer who finds out about this breakthrough because he works at the firm that is patenting MediSearch's new discovery and then buys stock before the information is public.

- Suppose, however, that while looking in a dumpster, Harry finds correspondence that reveals MediSearch's new discovery. He then buys MediSearch stock that promptly quadruples in value. Harry will be dining at the Ritz, not in federal prison, because he has no fiduciary duty to MediSearch.

Misappropriation.   Anyone (1) with material, nonpublic information, (2) who breaches a fiduciary duty to the *source of the information* (3) by trading on it is guilty of insider trading.

Misappropriation applies both to the workplace and to personal relationships. Anyone who trades on material, secret information obtained through the workplace is guilty. In addition, people in personal relationships with a fiduciary duty are guilty if they trade on material secret information obtained through that relationship. A fiduciary duty exists in a personal relationship if:

- The recipient has promised to keep the information secret;

- The communicator has a reasonable expectation that the recipient will not tell; or

- The recipient has obtained the information from her spouse, parent, child, or sibling.

James O'Hagan was a lawyer in a firm that represented a company attempting to take over Pillsbury Co. Although O'Hagan did not work on the case, he heard about it and then bought stock in Pillsbury. After the takeover attempt was publicly announced, O'Hagan sold his stock in Pillsbury at profit of more than $4.3 million.[2] The Supreme Court found Hagan guilty of misappropriation.

---

[2]O'Hagan used the profits that he gained through this trading to conceal his previous embezzlement of client funds. There is a moral here.

Tippers. Sometimes people do not trade themselves, but instead pass on information to others (such as friends and family). Anyone who reveals material nonpublic information in violation of his fiduciary duty is liable if (1) he knows the information was confidential and (2) he expected some personal gain. Essentially, any gift to a friend or family member counts as personal gain. Examples:

- W. Paul Thayer was a corporate director, deputy secretary of defense, and former fighter pilot who gave stock tips, based on information he had learned as a director, to his girlfriend in lieu of paying her rent. That counted as personal gain, and he spent a year and a half in prison.

- Amy Goodson had just found out that her employer, VeriFone, was about to be acquired by Hewlett-Packard. She confided in her husband, Floyd, that she was worried she might lose her job. But Floyd found a way to profit from this bad news—he phoned his father, who promptly bought stock in VeriFone. And promptly made a $62,000 profit. Floyd was guilty of misappropriation because he had violated his fiduciary duty to his wife.

Tippees. Even without a fiduciary relationship, those who receive tips are liable for trading on this inside information, if (1) they know the information is confidential, (2) they know that it came from an insider who was violating his fiduciary duty, and (3) the insider expected some personal gain. Examples:

- Barry Switzer, then head football coach at the University of Oklahoma, went to a track meet to see his son compete. On the bleachers, he overheard an insider talking about a company that was going to be acquired. Switzer bought the stock but was acquitted of insider trading charges because the insider had not breached his fiduciary duty. He had not tipped anyone on purpose—he had simply been careless. Also, the insider had not expected personal gain.

- In the VeriFone case involving Floyd Goodson, his father was also found guilty of insider trading. Because he knew his daughter-in-law worked for VeriFone, he was on notice that the information might have been confidential.

EXAM Strategy

Question: Paul was an investment banker who sometimes bragged about deals he was working on. One night, he told a bartender, Ryanne, about an upcoming deal. Ryanne bought stock in the company Paul had mentioned. Both were prosecuted for insider trading. Ryanne was acquitted but Paul was convicted, even though Ryanne was the one who made money. How is that possible?

Strategy: Note that there are different standards for tippers and tippees.

Result: Paul is liable if he knew the information was confidential and he expected some personal gain. A gift counts as personal gain. (The courts have an expansive definition of gifts—practically anything counts. Here, the information could be interpreted as a tip to the bartender.) Ryanne would not be liable unless she knew the information was confidential and had come from an insider who was violating his fiduciary duty.

24-1e Blue Sky Laws

Currently, all states and the District of Columbia also regulate the sale of securities. These state statutes are called **blue sky laws** (because the promises that crooks made to naïve investors "had no more substance than so many cubic feet of blue sky").

Blue sky laws
State statutes regulating securities

24-2 ANTITRUST

Congress passed the Sherman Act in 1890 to prevent extreme concentrations of economic power. Because this statute was aimed at the Standard Oil Trust, which then controlled the oil industry throughout the country, it was termed *antitrust* legislation.

Violations of the antitrust laws are divided into two categories: *per se* and **rule of reason**. *Per se* violations are automatic. Defendants charged with this type of violation cannot defend themselves by saying, "But the impact wasn't so bad" or "No one was hurt." The court will not listen to excuses, and violators may be sent to prison.

Rule of reason violations, on the other hand, are illegal only if they have an anti-competitive impact on the market. For example, mergers are illegal only if they harm competition in their industry. Those who commit rule of reason violations are typically not sent to prison because the government cannot prove intent.

Both the Justice Department and the Federal Trade Commission (FTC) have authority to enforce the antitrust laws. In addition to the government, anyone injured by an antitrust violation has the right to sue for damages. The United States is unusual in this regard—in most other countries, only the government is able to sue antitrust violators. A successful plaintiff can sue for treble (that is, triple) damages from the defendant.

> **Per se**
> An automatic breach of antitrust laws
>
> **Rule of reason**
> An action that breaches antitrust laws only if it has an anticompetitive impact

24-2a The Sherman Act

Price-Fixing

Section 1 of the Sherman Act prohibits all agreements "in restraint of trade." The most common—and one of the most serious—violations of this provision involves horizontal price-fixing. **When competitors agree on the prices at which they will buy or sell products, their price-fixing is a *per se* violation of §1 of the Sherman Act.**

The Supreme Court has referred to this type of collusion as "the supreme evil of antitrust," and it has been illegal for the better part of a century.[3] But it never seems to go away. MasterCard, Visa, JP Morgan Chase, and Bank of America recently paid a $6 billion fine for having fixed the prices they charged merchants for processing credit and debit card payments.

When Apple was about to introduce its first iPad, it wanted to be able to offer e-books, but feared it could not compete with Amazon's price of $9.99 per book. In many cases, Amazon was actually losing money on the books themselves, but was profiting from sales of the Kindle (its e-book reader). Apple was not willing to sell e-books at a loss. Apple knew that publishers disliked the $9.99 price because it hurt sales of their more expensive print books, but they had little leverage to negotiate with Amazon.

Apple approached the publishers and offered to sell their e-books at a higher price, but only if they would refuse to sell to Amazon unless that company also raised its prices. Once the publishers had all agreed to withhold their books unless Amazon raised its prices, it had no choice but to agree. Together, the publishers had accomplished what they could not do separately. As in many price-fixing cases, the participants were responding to what they viewed as overwhelming market power (in this case, on the part of Amazon). But no matter the rationalization, price-fixing is illegal. When charged with violating the law, the publishers all settled their cases, but Apple went to trial... and lost.[4]

---

[3]Verizon Communs., Inc. v. Trinko, LLP, 540 U.S. 398 (2004).
[4]United States v. Apple Inc., 952 F. Supp. 2d 638 (S.D.N.Y. 2013).

Resale Price Maintenance

Resale price maintenance (RPM), also called **vertical price fixing,** means the manufacturer sets the *minimum* prices that retailers may charge. The goal is to prevent the retailer from discounting. Why does the manufacturer care? After all, once the retailer purchases the item, the manufacturer has made its profit. The only way the manufacturer makes more money is to raise its *wholesale* price, not the *retail* price. RPM guarantees a profit margin for the *retailer*.

Manufacturers care about retail prices because pricing affects the product's image with consumers. Armani men's suits sell for around $2,000. What conclusion do you draw about the quality of those suits? Would your opinion change if you saw Armani suits being sold at discounted prices? You can understand that Armani might want to prohibit retailers from lowering the prices on its suits. Consumer advocates contend, however, that manufacturers such as Armani are simply protecting dealers from competition. Discounting may or may not harm products, but, they insist, RPM certainly hurts consumers.

Should RPM be a *per se* or rule of reason violation of the antitrust laws? The Supreme Court answered this question in the following case.

> **Resale price maintenance (RPM)**
>
> A manufacturer sets minimum prices that retailers may charge

---

LEEGIN CREATIVE LEATHER PRODUCTS, INC. v. PSKS, INC.

127 S. Ct. 2705
United States Supreme Court, 2007

CASE SUMMARY

Facts: Leegin manufactured belts and other women's fashion accessories under the brand name "Brighton." It sold these products only to small boutiques and specialty stores. Sales of the Brighton brand accounted for about half the profits at Kay's Kloset, a boutique in Lewisville, Texas.

Leegin decided it would no longer sell to retailers who discounted Brighton prices. It wanted to ensure that stores could afford to offer excellent service. It was also concerned that discounting harmed Brighton's image. Despite warnings from Leegin, Kay's Kloset persisted in marking down Brighton products by 20 percent. So Leegin cut the store off.

Kay's sued Leegin, alleging that RPM was a *per se* rule violation of the law. The trial court found for Kay's and entered judgment against Leegin for almost $4 million. The Court of Appeals affirmed. The Supreme Court granted *certiorari.* On appeal, Leegin did not dispute that it had entered into RPM agreements with retailers. Rather, it contended that the rule of reason should apply to those agreements.

Issue: *Is resale price maintenance a* **per se** *or rule of reason violation of the Sherman Act?*

Decision: RPM is a rule of reason violation.

Reasoning: To be a *per se* violation, an activity must not only be anticompetitive, it must also lack any redeeming virtue. Recent research indicates that resale price maintenance may offer some benefits:

- Retailers can provide better service. Without RPM, consumers might go *look* at a product at the retailer who hires experienced sales help or offers product demonstrations, but then go *buy* the item from a discounter who provides none of these services. In short order, the upscale retailer will either go out of business or cut back on service, and consumers will have fewer options.

- If retailers do not have to compete with others who sell the same brand, they can focus instead on competing against other brands. For example, retailers selling the same brand may pool their marketing dollars to have greater impact.

It is worth noting, though, that RPM can have an anticompetitive effect. A manufacturer with market power could, for example, use resale price maintenance to give retailers an incentive not to sell the products of smaller rivals. Courts must be diligent in recognizing and preventing any RPM that has an anticompetitive impact.

> Possessing a monopoly is not necessarily illegal; using "bad acts" to acquire or maintain one is.

Monopolization

Under §2 of the Sherman Act, it is illegal to monopolize or attempt to monopolize a market. To monopolize means to acquire control over a market in the wrong way. *Having* a monopoly is legal unless it is *gained* or *maintained* by using wrongful tactics.

To determine if a defendant has illegally monopolized, we must ask two questions:

1. **Does the company control the market?** No matter what its market share, a company does not have a monopoly unless it can exclude competitors or control prices. For example, the Justice Department sued a movie theater chain that possessed a 93 percent share of the box office in Las Vegas. But the court ruled against the Justice Department because the chain's market share decreased to 75 percent within three years. This decline indicated that the company did not control the market and that barriers to entry were low.[5]

2. **How did the company acquire or maintain its control?** If the law prohibited the mere possession of a monopoly, it might discourage companies from producing excellent products or offering low prices. So possessing a monopoly is not necessarily illegal; using "bad acts" to acquire or maintain one is. A typical bad act is sham litigation in which a competitor files baseless lawsuits for the sole purpose of harming competition. To prevent Glitzy Restaurant from opening its doors, Family Eatery files a suit against Glitzy alleging that this potential competitor has violated Family's trademark, even though Family knows the allegation is not true. That lawsuit would be a bad act.

Predatory pricing is another example of a bad act.

Predatory Pricing

Predatory pricing occurs when a company lowers its prices below cost to drive competitors out of business. Once the predator has the market to itself, it raises prices to make up lost profits—and more besides. Typically, the goal of a predatory pricing scheme is either to win control of a market or to maintain it. Therefore, it is illegal under §2 of the Sherman Act. **To win a predatory pricing case, the plaintiff must prove three elements:**

1. The defendant is selling its products *below cost.*

2. The defendant *intends* that the plaintiff go out of business.

3. If the plaintiff does go out of business, the defendant will be able to earn sufficient profits to *recover* its prior losses.

The classic example of predatory pricing is a large grocery store that comes into a small town offering exceptionally low prices that are subsidized by profits from its other branches. Once all the mom and pop corner groceries go out of business, MegaGrocery raises its prices to much higher levels.

Predatory pricing cases can be difficult to win. It is hard for Mom and Pop to prove that MegaGrocery intended for them to go out of business. It is also difficult for Mom and Pop to show that MegaGrocery will be able to make up all its lost profits once the corner grocery is out of the way. They need to prove, for example, that no other grocery chain will come to town. It is difficult to prove a negative proposition like that, especially in the grocery business, where barriers to entry are low.

[5]United States v. Syufy Enterprises, 903 F.2d 659 (9th Cir. 1990).

24-2b The Clayton Act

Mergers

The Clayton Act prohibits mergers that are anticompetitive. Companies with substantial assets must notify the Federal Trade Commission (FTC) before undertaking a merger.[6] This notification gives the government an opportunity to prevent a merger ahead of time, rather than trying to untangle one after the fact.

Tying Arrangements

A tying arrangement is an agreement to sell a product on the condition that the buyer also purchase a different (or tied) product. A tying arrangement is illegal under the Clayton Act if:

- The two products are clearly separate,

- The seller requires the buyer to purchase the two products together,

- The seller has significant power in the market for the tying product, and

- The seller is shutting out a significant part of the market for the tied product.

Six movie distributors refused to sell individual films to television stations. Instead, they insisted that a station buy an entire package of movies. To obtain classics such as *Treasure of the Sierra Madre* and *Casablanca* (the **tying product**), the station also had to purchase such forgettable films as *Gorilla Man* and *Tugboat Annie Sails Again* (the **tied product**).[7] The distributors engaged in an illegal tying arrangement. These are the questions that the court asked:

- **Are the two products clearly separate?** A left and right shoe are not separate products, and a seller can legally require that they be purchased together. *Gorilla Man*, on the other hand, is a separate product from *Casablanca*.

- **Is the seller requiring the buyer to purchase the two products together?** Yes, that is the whole point of these "package deals."

- **Does the seller have significant power in the market for the tying product?** In this case, the tying products are the classic movies. Since they are copyrighted, no one else can show them without the distributor's permission. The six distributors controlled a great many classic movies. So, yes, they do have significant market power.

- **Is the seller shutting out a significant part of the market for the tied product?** In this case, the tied products are the undesirable films like *Tugboat Annie Sails Again*. Television stations forced to take the unwanted films did not buy "B" movies from other distributors. These other distributors were effectively foreclosed from a substantial part of the market.

Tying arrangement

An agreement to sell a product on the condition that a buyer also purchase another, usually less desirable, product

Tying product

In a tying arrangement, the product offered for sale on the condition that another product be purchased as well

Tied product

In a tying arrangement, the product that a buyer must purchase as the condition for being allowed to buy another product

---

EXAM Strategy

Question: Two medical supply companies in the San Francisco area provide oxygen to homes of patients. The companies are owned by the doctors who prescribe the oxygen. These doctors make up 60 percent of the lung specialists in the area. Does this arrangement create an antitrust problem?

---

[6]For example, a notice must be filed if the transaction involves assets of $303.4 million or more (adjusted annually for inflation).

[7]United States v. Loew's Inc., 371 U.S. 38 (1962).

Strategy: Does the seller have significant power in the market for the tying product (lung patients)? Is it shutting out a significant part of the market for the tied product (oxygen)?

Result: The FTC charged the doctors with an illegal tying arrangement. Because the doctors effectively controlled such a high percentage of the patients needing the service, other oxygen companies could not enter the market.

24-2c The Robinson-Patman Act

Under the Robinson-Patman Act (RPA), it is illegal to charge different prices to different purchasers if:

- The items are the same, and

- The price discrimination lessens competition.

However, it is legal to charge a lower price to a particular buyer if:

- The costs of serving this buyer are lower, or

- The seller is simply meeting competition.

Congress passed the RPA in 1936 to prevent large chains from driving small, local stores out of business. Owners of these mom and pop stores complained that the large chains could sell goods cheaper because suppliers charged them lower prices. As a result of the RPA, managers who would otherwise like to develop different pricing strategies for specific customers or regions may hesitate to do so for fear of violating this statute. In reality, however, they have little to fear.

Under the RPA, a plaintiff must prove both that price discrimination occurred and that it lessened competition. It is perfectly permissible, for example, for a supplier to sell at a different price to its Texas and California distributors, or to its health care and educational distributors, so long as the distributors are not in competition with each other.

The RPA also permits price variations that are based on differences in cost. Thus, Kosmo's Kitchen would be perfectly within its legal rights to sell its frozen cheese enchiladas to Giant at a lower price than to Corner Grocery if Kosmo's costs are lower to do so. Giant often buys shipments the size of railroad containers, which cost less to deliver than smaller boxes.

In the following case, everyone agreed that the manufacturer was charging different prices to various competitors. But was it violating the Robinson-Patman Act?

COALITION FOR A LEVEL PLAYING FIELD, L.L.C. v. AUTOZONE, INC.

737 F. Supp. 2d 194
United States District Court for the Southern District of New York, 2010

CASE SUMMARY

Facts: Auto parts manufacturers used two distribution channels: (1) a two-step process in which they sold to big box stores, such as Walmart and AutoZone, who then sold the parts to the end users, and (2) a three-step process in which they sold to warehouse distributors (WDs) who then sold to mom and pop auto parts stores, who sold to the end users.

The WDs sued the manufacturers, alleging that they were violating the Robinson-Patman Act by selling to the big box stores at prices 40 to 50 percent less than the WDs paid.

Issue: *Did the manufacturers and big box stores violate the Robinson-Patman Act?*

Decision: No, they were not in violation.

Reasoning: The RPA does not require sellers to charge everyone the same price. For example, a seller can reduce prices in return for services that a purchaser performs. Or, a seller can charge different prices if the terms of the contract are different. A seat on the 6:00 a.m. flight from Chicago to New York is not the same as a seat on the 5:00 p.m. flight.

Although the plaintiffs have provided substantial evidence that the manufacturers charged lower prices to big box stores, they have not shown whether these discounts were justified. The big box stores provided a different mix of distribution, warehousing, marketing, and promotional services to the parts manufacturers. In the absence of any evidence to the contrary, it is plausible to assume that the services provided by the big box stores were more valuable than those offered by WDs and, therefore, justified the lower prices.

Chapter Conclusion

In this chapter, you have learned about some of the important securities and antitrust laws that affect business. They can have a profound impact on your business—and on your life.

EXAM REVIEW

EXAM Strategy

1. **SECURITY** A security is any transaction in which the buyer (1) invests money in a common enterprise and (2) expects to earn a profit predominantly from the efforts of others.

> **Question:** Jonah bought 12 paintings from Theo's Art Gallery at a total cost of $1 million. Theo told Jonah that the paintings were a safe investment that could only go up in value. (If anyone ever tells you that, run!) The gallery permitted purchasers to trade in a painting in return for any other artwork the gallery owned. In the trade-in, the purchaser would get credit for the amount of the original painting and then pay the difference if the new painting was worth more. When Jonah's paintings did not increase in value, he sued Theo for a violation of the securities laws. Were these paintings securities?
>
> **Strategy:** Are all the elements of a security present here? (See the "Result" at the end of this section.)

2. **THE 1933 ACT** The 1933 Act requires that, before offering or selling securities in a public offering, the issuer must register the securities with the Securities and Exchange Commission (SEC).

3. **LIABILTY UNDER THE 1933 ACT** The seller of a security is liable for making any material misstatement or omission, either oral or written, in connection with the offer or sale of a security.

4. **PROSPECTUS** All investors must receive a copy of the prospectus before purchasing stock in a public offering.

5. **EMERGING GROWTH COMPANY (EGC)**   An EGC is an issuer with annual gross revenues of less than $1 billion (indexed for inflation). When an EGC undertakes an IPO, it can require the SEC to keep its registration statement secret until 21 days before its road show begins.

6. **PRIVATE OFFERING**   Under the 1933 Act, an issuer is not required to register securities that are sold in a private offering, but the issuer may have to meet certain disclosure requirements.

7. **REGULATION D**   The most common and important type of private offering is under Regulation D. It permits issuers to sell stock to a small number of investors and for a limited amount of money.

8. **CROWDFUNDING**   Privately held companies can sell up to $1 million in securities through a broker or online in any twelve-month period, provided that they comply with certain requirements.

9. **THE 1934 ACT**   Under the 1934 Act, an issuer must register with the SEC if (1) it completes a public offering under the 1933 Act, or (2) its securities are traded on a national exchange (such as the New York Stock Exchange), or (3) it has 2,000 shareholders (or 500 who are unaccredited investors) *and* total assets that exceed $10 million.

10. **FILINGS UNDER THE 1934 ACT**   The 1934 Act requires public companies to make regular filings with the SEC, including annual reports, quarterly reports, and Form 8-Ks. The company CEO and CFO must certify that the information in the quarterly and annual reports is true.

11. **SECTION 16**   Insiders must report their trades in company stock within two business days. They must turn over to the corporation any profits they make from the purchase and sale or sale and purchase of company securities in a six-month period.

12. **CLASSIC INSIDER TRADING**   Any corporate insider (1) with material, nonpublic information, (2) who breaches a fiduciary duty *to his company* (3) by trading on the information is guilty of insider trading. In addition, anyone (1) with material, nonpublic information, (2) who breaches a fiduciary duty to the *source of the information* (3) by trading on the information is guilty of insider trading. Tippers and tippees may also be liable.

13. **BLUE SKY LAWS**   All states and the District of Columbia regulate the sale of securities. State securities statutes are called blue sky laws.

14. **PRICE-FIXING**   When competitors agree on the prices at which they will buy or sell products, their price-fixing is a *per se* violation of §1 of the Sherman Act.

15. **RESALE PRICE MAINTENANCE (RPM)**   Resale price maintenance means the manufacturer sets minimum prices that retailers may charge. It is a rule of reason violation of §1 of the Sherman Act.

16. **MONOPOLIZATION**   Under §2 of the Sherman Act, it is illegal to monopolize or attempt to monopolize a market. *Having* a monopoly is legal unless it is *gained* or *maintained* by using wrongful tactics.

EXAM Strategy

Question: BAR/BRI was the largest bar review company in the country, with branches in 45 states. Barpassers was a much smaller company located only in Arizona and California. BAR/BRI distributed pamphlets on campuses that falsely suggested Barpassers was near bankruptcy. Enrollments in Barpassers' courses dropped, and the company was forced to postpone plans for expansion. Did Barpassers have an antitrust claim against BAR/BRI?

Strategy: It did not matter if BAR/BRI *had* a monopoly. These "bad acts" could have helped the company *acquire* one. (See the "Result" at the end of this section.)

17. **PREDATORY PRICING**   Predatory pricing occurs when a company lowers its prices below cost to drive competitors out of business.

18. **MERGERS**   The Clayton Act prohibits mergers that are anticompetitive.

19. **TYING ARRANGEMENTS**   A tying arrangement is an agreement to sell a product on the condition that the buyer also purchase a different (or tied) product. Certain tying arrangements are illegal under the Clayton Act.

20. **ROBINSON-PATMAN ACT (RPA)**   Under the Robinson-Patman Act, it is illegal to charge different prices to different purchasers if the items are the same and the price discrimination lessens competition. However, a seller may charge different prices if these prices reflect different costs or if the seller is simply meeting competition.

> **1. Result:**   The paintings were not securities because there was no "common enterprise." The investors did not pool funds or share profits with other investors.
>
> **16. Result:**   A jury found that BAR/BRI had violated §2 of the Sherman Act by attempting to create an illegal monopoly. The jury ordered BAR/BRI to pay Barpassers more than $3 million, plus attorney's fees.

MATCHING QUESTIONS

Match the following terms with their definitions:

___A. Securities Act of 1933

___B. Section 16

___C. Sherman Act

___D. Robinson-Patman Act

___E. Securities Exchange Act of 1934

1. Prohibits price discrimination

2. Regulates companies once they have gone public

3. Prohibits price-fixing

4. Regulates the issuance of securities

5. Requires an insider to turn over profits she has earned from buying and selling or selling and buying company stock in a six-month period

TRUE/FALSE QUESTIONS

Circle true or false:

1. T F Before permitting a company to issue new securities, the SEC investigates to ensure that the company has a promising future.

2. T F Small offerings of securities do not need to be registered with the SEC.

3. T F Horizontal price-fixing is legal as long as it does not have an anticompetitive impact.

4. T F Only the federal government regulates securities offerings; the states do not.

5. T F It is legal for a company to sell its product at a price below cost so long as it does not intend to drive competitors out of business.

MULTIPLE-CHOICE QUESTIONS

1. Under Regulation D, an issuer:

   (a) may sell to no more than 1,000 accredited investors.

   (b) may sell to no more than 25 unaccredited investors.

   (c) must make disclosure to accredited investors.

   (d) must make disclosure to unaccredited investors.

   (e) may advertise the stock publicly.

2. Which of the following statements about a public offering is FALSE?

   (a) The issuer files a registration statement with the SEC.

   (b) The issuer files a prospectus with the SEC.

   (c) Company officers may make public statements about the offering before the stock is sold.

   (d) Company officers may make public statements about the offering after the stock is sold.

   (e) The issuer may solicit offers for the stock before the effective date.

3. To have an illegal monopoly, a company must:

   I.   Control the market.

   II.   Maintain its control improperly.

   III. Have a market share greater than 50 percent.

   (a) I, II, and III

   (b) I and II

   (c) II and III

   (d) I and III

   (e) Neither I, II, nor III

4. Are horizontal price-fixing and vertical price-fixing *per se* violations of the Sherman Act?

(a) Yes, Yes

(b) Yes, No

(c) No, Yes

(d) No, No

5. Reserve Supply Corp., a cooperative of 379 lumber dealers, charged that Owens-Corning Fiberglass Corp. violated the Robinson-Patman Act by selling at lower prices to Reserve's competitors. It presented proof that these prices had harmed competition. Owens-Corning admitted that it had granted lower prices to a number of Reserve's competitors to meet, but not beat, the prices of other insulation manufacturers. Is Owens-Corning in violation of the RPA?

(a) Yes, because the RPA requires that manufacturers charge all competitors the same price.

(b) Yes, because any difference in price is a *per se* violation of the RPA.

(c) Yes, because these price variations harmed competition.

(d) No, because a manufacturer is not liable under the RPA if it charges lower prices to meet competition.

Case Questions

1. You are the president of Turbocharge, Inc., a publicly traded company. You have been buying stock recently because you think the company's product—a more efficient hybrid engine—is very promising. One day, you show up at work and find your desk in the hallway. The CEO has fired you. In a huff, you sell all your company stock. The only silver lining to your cloud is that you make a large profit. Or is this a silver lining?

2. You're in line at the movie theater when you overhear a stranger say: "The FDA has just approved Hernstrom's new painkiller. When the announcement is made on Monday, Hernstrom stock will take off." Have you violated the law if you buy stock in the company before the announcement on Monday?

3. In New York City, 50 bakeries agreed to raise the retail price of bread. All the association's members printed the new price on their bread sleeves. Are the bakeries in violation of the antitrust laws?

4. Suppose that Masi Bikes insists that retailers cannot sell its Soulville 10 model for less than $1,099. The company threatens to cut off any retailers who discount that price. But bicycle stores would like to use these bikes as a loss leader—selling them at a lower price to lure customers. Is it legal for Masi to cut off retailers who discount prices?

5. Gary Griffiths was a vice president for a railroad. The CEO asked him to prepare an inventory of all the rolling stock the company owned and to arrange trips among its rail yards for a group of men in suits. Employees began asking Griffiths if the company would be sold and whether they would lose their jobs. Indeed, the company was exploring sale options. Griffiths went to visit his brother-in-law, Rex, who the next day purchased $400,000 in stock of the company. For a month, Griffiths called regularly, and each time Rex bought more stock. In total, he spent $1.14 million on company stock. After the company was sold, Rex made a substantial profit. Did Gary and Rex engage in illegal insider trading? Was the fact that men in suits were touring the rail yards material nonpublic information?

DISCUSSION QUESTIONS

1. Federal security laws are based on the assumption that investors are knowledgeable enough to assess the quality of a stock, so long as the issuer provides adequate disclosure. Is this assumption reasonable, or should securities laws provide greater protection to investors?

2. **ETHICS** David Sokol worked at Berkshire Hathaway for legendary investor Warren Buffett, who is renowned not only for his investment skills but also his ethics. Bankers suggested to both Sokol and the CEO of Lubrizol that the company might be a good buy for Berkshire. Sokol then found out that the CEO of Lubrizol planned to ask his board for permission to approach Berkshire about a possible acquisition. Sokol purchased $10 million worth of Lubrizol stock before recommending Lubrizol to Buffett. Sokol mentioned to Buffett "in passing" that he owned shares of Lubrizol. Buffett did not ask any questions about the timing or amount of Sokol's purchases. Sokol made a $3 million profit when Berkshire acquired Lubrizol. Did Sokol violate insider trading laws? Did he behave ethically? What are Buffett's ethical obligations?

3. What would you say to critics who argue that crowdfunding does not provide enough protection to investors? That the business judgment rule will permit managers to spend the money as they will. That few of these companies will ever go public, so investors will have limited opportunities to sell their stock or realize any return on their investment.

4. Resale price maintenance used to be a *per se* violation of the antitrust laws, but now it is a rule of reason violation. Will this change in the law lead to higher or lower prices for consumers? Will it provide other benefits for consumers? Do you agree with the Supreme Court's decision?

5. **ETHICS** Clarice, a young woman with a mental disability, brought a malpractice suit against a doctor at the Medical Center. As a result, the Medical Center refused to treat her on a nonemergency basis. Clarice then went to another local clinic, which was later acquired by the Medical Center. Because the new clinic also refused to treat her, Clarice had to seek medical treatment in another town 40 miles away. Has the Medical Center violated the antitrust laws? Was is it ethical to deny treatment to a patient? What Life Principles are at issue here?

CHAPTER 25

CONSUMER PROTECTION

The following online review was written by JA2009 on the consumer website my3cents.com.

In yesterday's Sunday newspaper insert, I saw that Staples was featuring an Acer laptop for $449. This laptop typically retails for $599. I immediately drove over to the nearest Staples store, and arrived 5 minutes after it opened.

Upon my arrival, I found an associate who informed me that the laptops were in stock. However, before he would get me one, he proceeded to try to sell me his "protection plan." I declined this. The sales associate walked away to, I assumed, get my computer. He returned with the store's general manager who was EXTREMELY rude, implying that I was "cheap" for not adding the plan. Moments later, the sales associate informed me that the laptop was not in stock after all. Just to summarize the timeline…it was available…I declined the approximately $150 protection plan [that] would have boosted the price of the laptop to the regular sale price…then suddenly it was unavailable.

I then called a 2nd Staples store and was told the store had multiple laptops and they should definitely be there when I arrived. I arrived exactly 8 minutes later. I found the exact person who I had spoken to and asked him if they were indeed in stock, and he indicated that they were. And then, before he goes back to get one, he asks me if I want the service plan. I responded, "No thanks." He said "fine" and walked away. 2–3 minutes later…he walks back and, just like the last store, the inventory suddenly has vanished. Half smirking, he implied that all of them had been sold in the last 8 minutes.

© Galyna Andrushko/Shutterstock.com

> **The inventory suddenly has vanished. Half smirking, he implied that all of them had been sold in the last 8 minutes.**

Why would these salespeople not sell the advertised computer? Because they knew that if they failed to sell $200 in extras, they would be in serious trouble and might even be fired.[1] This practice is classic bait and switch, and, as we will see, it is illegal.

25-1 INTRODUCTION

Congress has empowered two federal agencies to enforce consumer laws:

1. **Federal Trade Commission (FTC)** and
2. **Consumer Financial Protection Bureau (CFPB).**

25-2 SALES

Section 5 of the Federal Trade Commission Act (FTC Act) prohibits "unfair and deceptive acts or practices."

25-2a Deceptive Acts or Practices

Many deceptive acts or practices involve advertisements. **Under the FTC Act, an advertisement is deceptive if it contains an important misrepresentation or omission that is likely to mislead a reasonable consumer.** The most common deceptive claims involve—you guessed it—weight loss. Please do not believe that L'Occitane's Almond Beautiful Shape body cream will magically burn away fat.

The FTC ad rules also apply to online ads and even tweets. Tweeted ads must clearly indicate that they are, in fact, ads by including some equivalent of "ad" or "sponsored."

25-2b Unfair Practices

The FTC Act also prohibits unfair acts or practices. For example, Qchex.com set up an online system that permitted any person to draw checks on any bank account, as long as the user knew the name, account number, and routing number. Qchex did not verify that the user was authorized to withdraw funds from the account. Using this system, fraudsters wrote more than $400 million in bad checks. Even the FTC was a victim. (Helpful hint: If you are going to run a fraud, make sure the FTC stays out of your trap.) A court enjoined Qchex from continuing its business and ordered it to turn over its profits.

25-2c Abusive Acts

The CFPB has the authority to take action against anyone committing "abusive acts." American Debt Settlement Solutions, Inc. won the unenviable prize of being first to be charged under this rule. The company was running so-called debt-relief programs, enrolling people in programs that they could not afford and that did nothing to help with their debts.

25-2d Bait-and-Switch

Bait-and-switch

A practice where sellers advertise products that are not generally available but are being used to draw interested parties in so that they will buy other items.

FTC rules prohibit bait-and-switch advertisements: A merchant may not advertise a product and then disparage it (or otherwise make it unavailable) to consumers in an effort to sell a different (more expensive) item. In addition, merchants must have enough stock on hand to meet reasonable demand for any advertised product.

---

[1]As reported in David Segal, "Selling It with Extras, or Not at All," *The New York Times*, September 8, 2012.

The opening scenario describes a classic bait-and-switch. The Acer computer at $449 was the *bait*—an alluring offer that sounds almost too good to be true. Of course, it is. Once a customer asks to buy it, the company tries to sell an upgraded product at a much higher price. That is the *switch*. The real purpose of the advertisement was simply to lure interested customers into a trap to buy a more expensive item.

25-2e Merchandise Bought by Mail, by Telephone, or Online

The FTC has established the following rules for these types of sales:

- Sellers must ship an item within the time stated or, if no time is given, within 30 days after receipt of the order.

- If a company cannot ship the product when promised, it must send the customer a notice with the new shipping date and an opportunity to cancel. If the new shipping date is within 30 days of the original one and the customer does not cancel, the order is still valid.

- If the company cannot ship by the second shipment date, it must send the customer another notice. This time, however, the company must cancel the order unless the customer returns the notice, indicating that he still wants the item.

Staples, Inc. also violated these FTC rules when it told customers that they were viewing "real-time" inventory online and that products would be delivered in one day, even on weekends. In fact, the website was not updated in real time, one-day delivery only applied to customers who lived within 20 miles of a Staples store, and it never happened on weekends.

25-2f Telemarketing

The telephone rings: "Could I speak with Alexander Johannson? This is Denise from Master Chimney Sweeps." It is 7:30 p.m.; you have just straggled in from work and are looking forward to a tranquil dinner of takeout cuisine. You are known as Sandy, your last name is pronounced "Yohannson," and you do not have a chimney. A telemarketer has struck again! What can you do to protect your peace and quiet?

The FTC prohibits telemarketers from calling or texting any telephone number listed on its do-not-call registry. You can register your home and cell phone numbers with the FTC online at http://www.donotcall.gov or by telephone at (888) 382-1222. FTC rules also prohibit telemarketers from blocking their names and telephone numbers on Caller ID systems.

What is even more annoying than telemarketing calls from a live person? Robocalls—autodialed and prerecorded commercial telemarketing calls. **The Telephone Consumer Protection Act (TCPA) prohibits telemarketers from making autodialed and/or prerecorded calls or texts to cell phones and prerecorded calls to residential land lines unless the consumer unambiguously consents in writing.** Furthermore, any prerecorded telemarketing calls must provide an opt-out option so that the caller can avoid receiving any future calls from that source. If you receive any of these prohibited contacts, you can file a complaint at http://www.fcc.gov/complaints. Or you can sue and recover from $500 to $1,500 per call. Informational calls, political messages, charitable outreach, and health care messages are exempted from this ban.

25-2g Unordered Merchandise

Under §5 of the FTC Act, anyone who receives unordered merchandise in the mail can treat it as a gift. She can use it, throw it away, or do whatever else she wants with it.

There you are, watching an infomercial for Anushka products, guaranteed to fight that scourge of modern life—cellulite! Rushing to your phone, you place an order. The Anushka cosmetics arrive, but for some odd reason, the cellulite remains. A month later, another bottle arrives, like magic, in the mail. The magic spell is broken, however, when you get your credit card bill and see that, without your authorization, the company has charged you for the new supply of Anushka. This company was in violation of FTC rules because it did not notify customers that they were free to treat the unauthorized products as a gift, to use or throw out as they wished.

25-2h Door-to-Door Sales

Consumers at home need special protection from unscrupulous salespeople. In a store, customers can simply walk out, but at home, they may feel trapped. Also, it is difficult at home to compare products or prices offered by competitors. Under the FTC door-to-door rules, **a salesperson is required to notify the buyer that she has the right to cancel the transaction at any time before midnight of the third business day thereafter.** This notice must be given both orally and in writing; the actual cancellation must be in writing. The seller must return the buyer's money within 10 days.

EXAM Strategy

Question: Mantra Films sold *Girls Gone Wild* DVDs online. When customers ordered one DVD, the company would enroll them automatically in a "continuity program" and send them unordered DVDs each month on a "negative-option" basis, charging consumers' credit cards for each DVD until consumers took action to stop the shipments. Is Mantra's marketing plan legal?

Strategy: Review the various sales regulations—more than one is involved in this case.

Result: This marketing plan was deceptive because customers were not told that they would be enrolled in the continuity program. Also, Mantra could not legally bill for the unordered DVDs. Under the unordered merchandise rule, consumers had the right to treat them as gifts.

25-3 CONSUMER CREDIT

Usury statutes

Laws that limit the maximum interest rate a lender may charge

Most states limit the maximum interest rate a lender may charge consumers. These laws are called **usury statutes**. (Although, usury laws typically do not apply to credit card debt, mortgages, consumer leases, or commercial loans.) The penalty for violating usury statutes varies among the states. Depending upon the jurisdiction, the lender may forfeit the illegal interest, all interest, or, in some states, the entire loan.

25-3a Payday Loans

A woman borrows $2,600 and then makes payments on the loan for over a year, totaling $4,000. But still she owes $2,500, almost as much as she borrowed. How is that possible? Because the interest rate was so high. She borrowed from CashCall, which charged annual interest rates of between 90 percent and 350 percent. Over the four-year term of her loan, she would have repaid almost $14,000. Is that legal? In some states it is, but not in North Carolina, where this woman lived. The CFPB accused CashCall of unfair, deceptive and abusive practices and asked the court to order CashCall to return all the funds it obtained from borrowers.

Loans by CashCall and similar companies are called **payday loans** because they are made to desperate people who need money to make it to the next paycheck. These loans often carry exorbitant interest rates, with the result that the borrowers never manage to dig out from under their debt. Although these loans violate the usury laws in some states, the Internet allows unscrupulous lenders to reach desperate borrowers everywhere.

25-3b Truth in Lending Act

The federal Truth in Lending Act (TILA) does not regulate interest rates or the terms of a loan; these rules are set by state law. **In all loans covered by TILA, the lender must:**

- **Disclose all information clearly.** A TILA disclosure statement should not be a scavenger hunt. A finance company violated TILA when it loaned money to Dorothy Allen. The company made all the required disclosures but scattered them throughout the loan document and intermixed them with confusing terms that were not required by TILA.

- **Disclose the following facts:**
  - **The total of payments.** The amount the consumer will have paid by the end of the loan.
  - **The finance charge.** The finance charge is the amount, in dollars, the consumer will pay in interest and fees over the life of the loan.
  - **The annual percentage rate (APR).** This number is the actual rate of interest the consumer pays on an annual basis. Without this disclosure, it would be easy in a short-term loan to disguise a very high APR because the finance charge is low. Boris borrows $5 for lunch from his employer's credit union. Under the terms of the loan, he must repay $6 the following week. His finance charge is only $1, but his APR is astronomical—20 percent per week—which is over 1,000 percent for a year.

25-3c Home Mortgage Loans

In the first decade of this century, the United States suffered through a bubble in housing prices, followed by a dramatic crash. Like all bubbles, this one began when prices rose and people began to believe that they could not lose money. They could always sell the house for more than they had paid for it.[2] Lenders fueled this mania by giving out mortgages without first verifying the borrower's income or assets; indeed, in some cases, encouraging loans that any reasonable observer would know the borrower could not repay. When the inevitable occurred and many homeowners were unable to pay back their loans, banks began huge numbers of foreclosures, which caused prices to fall further. Bleak tracts of abandoned houses stood everywhere across America. Congress amended TILA hoping to prevent another such crash.

TILA prohibits unfair, abusive, or deceptive home mortgage lending practices. (Some of the following rules seem little more than common sense, but that was an attribute sorely missing during the bubble.) **Under TILA, lenders:**

- Must make a good faith, reasonable effort to determine whether a borrower can afford to repay the loan, considering data such as income, assets, debt, and credit history;

- May not coerce or bribe an appraiser into misstating a home's value; and

- Cannot charge prepayment penalties on adjustable rate mortgages.

---

[2]But, as the group Blood, Sweat & Tears once observed, "What goes up, must come down."

Qualified mortgages

A mortgage that complies with rules established by the CFPB that make repayment more likely

To help lenders comply with these requirements, the CFPB established criteria for what it calls **qualified mortgages** (QMs). If lenders give a QM, they are deemed to have complied with TILA because it is likely that the borrower can afford to repay the loan. **QMs:**

- Limit all of a borrower's debt (not just her mortgage) to 43 percent of her income;

- Limit up-front points and fees to 3 percent; and

- Prohibit harmful features such as:
  - Interest only periods—when the borrower is not paying down the principal of the loan and
  - Balloon payments (very large payments at the end).

25-3d Plastic: Credit, Debit, and ATM Cards

Credit Cards: Fees

During the economic crisis that began in 2008, many consumers struggled to pay their credit card bills. In response, Congress passed the Credit CARD Act. **These are the major provisions of this statute:**

- **Due dates**
  - Must be disclosed
  - Set for the same time each month and occur at the end of a business day
  - Bill must be mailed at least 21 days ahead of time

- **Increases in rates and fees**
  - Not allowed on any charges already incurred (until a cardholder has missed two consecutive payments)
  - Only permitted for future purchases and only if the credit card company provides 45 days' notice to the consumer and permits cancellation of the card

- **Late payment fees** are limited to $25 for the first event, $35 thereafter.

- **Payment must be applied to whichever debt on the card has the highest interest rate** (say, a cash advance rather than a new purchase).

- **Consumers have the right to set a fixed credit limit.** Consumers cannot be charged a fee if the company accepts charges above that limit unless the consumer has agreed to the fee. Only one overlimit fee per statement is permitted.

- **People under 21 cannot obtain a credit card unless they have income or a co-signer.**

Ethics   Each of the rules in the previous section was aimed at eliminating existing abuses. Should Congress really have to tell credit card companies that they cannot raise rates on charges already incurred? Or set a due date on a Sunday and then charge a late fee if payment arrives on Monday? What Life Principles might credit card companies use when setting policies?

Debit and ATM Cards: Fees

Debit cards are used to make purchases (they are also called **check cards**). ATM cards withdraw cash from a bank account. Although they look and feel like credit cards, legally they are a different plastic altogether. When you use a credit card, the funds do not leave your account until you pay the bill. But with both debit and ATM cards, funds are deducted immediately. Many people prefer to use debit and ATM cards because their expenditures are limited by the size of their bank accounts and they can avoid the interest fees and late charges levied on credit card overspending.

In the case of ATM and debit cards, banks cannot overdraw an account and charge an overdraft fee unless the consumer signs up for an overdraft plan. Of course, this rule means that consumers who do not "opt in" to the overdraft plan will not be able to overdraw their account, no matter how desperate they are.

Note, however, that if you do opt-in to an overdraft plan, banks can charge a flat fee (typically $20 to $30) *each time* cardholders overdraw their bank account, no matter how small the overdraft. A customer can, say, be charged $150 in overdraft fees on $50 worth of overdrafts. In that case, he has paid an interest rate of 3,520 percent.

> Although they look and feel like credit cards, legally they are a different plastic altogether.

Check cards
Another term for debit cards- used to make purchases.

Liability

Your wallet is missing, and with it your cash, your driver's license, a photo of your dog, a Groupon, and—oh, no!—all your plastic! What is your liability if the thief spends up a storm on your stolen cards? The answer depends on the type of card.

- **Credit Cards:**
  - You are liable only for the first $50 in charges the thief makes before you notify the credit card company. If the thief steals just your credit card number, but not the card itself, you are not liable for any unauthorized charges.

- **Debit and ATM Cards:**
  - If you report the loss before anyone uses your card, you are not liable for any unauthorized withdrawals.
  - If you report the theft within two days of discovering it, the bank will make good on all losses above $50.
  - If you wait until after two days, your bank will only replace stolen funds above $500.
  - If you wait more than 60 days after receipt of your bank statement, the bank is not responsible for any losses.
  - If an unauthorized transfer takes place using just your number, not your card, then you are not liable at all as long as you report the loss within 60 days of receiving the bank statement showing the loss. After 60 days, however, you are liable for the full amount.

The goal of these laws is to protect consumers. As the following case illustrates, however, that protection goes only so far. It is important for consumers to pay careful attention to the legal time limits.

KRUSER v. BANK OF AMERICA

230 Cal. App. 3d 741
Court of Appeal of California, 1991

CASE SUMMARY

Facts: Mr. and Mrs. Kruser each had an ATM card for their joint account at the Bank of America. Mr. Kruser believed his card had been destroyed. It turned out, however, that someone used it to make an unauthorized withdrawal of $20 from the account in December, which the Krusers did not notice. Perhaps because, that same month, Mrs. Kruser underwent surgery and was hospitalized for 11 days. She then spent six or seven months recuperating at home. Her recovery underwent a nasty setback, however, when she discovered in September that someone had illegally withdrawn $9,020 from the account during July and August. The Bank refused to refund the money. The Krusers sued, but the trial court granted the Bank's motion for summary judgment. The Krusers appealed.

Issue: *Did the Krusers' failure to report the unauthorized withdrawal in December prevent them from recovering the much larger amount stolen in July and August?*

Decision: The bank is not liable to the Krusers for the money stolen out of their account.

Reasoning: The Krusers argued they did not have sufficient warning that someone was illegally using their ATM card because the initial $20 theft happened long ago and was relatively insignificant. They further argued that the purpose of the law is to protect consumers, and, therefore, the bank should pay.

If the Krusers had reported the first theft, the bank would have canceled their ATM card, and the larger sum would not have been stolen. Mrs. Kruser's illness is no excuse. If she was too ill to look at the statements, Mr. Kruser could have done so.

Disputes with Merchants

You use your credit card to buy a new tablet computer at ShadyComputers, but when you take it out of the box, it will not even turn on. You have a major $600 problem. But all is not lost. **In the event of a dispute between a customer and a merchant, the credit card company cannot bill the customer if (1) she makes a good faith effort to resolve the dispute, (2) the dispute is for more than $50, and (3) the merchant is in the same state where she lives, or within 100 miles of her house.**

These are the circumstances under which a credit card company is not allowed to bill customers, but most will not seek payment from cardholders who seem to have a reasonable claim against a merchant.

Disputes with Credit Card Companies

A dispute between a consumer and a credit card company used to consist of little more than an avalanche of threatening form letters from the company that ignored any response from the hapless cardholder. Then, in 1975, Congress passed the Fair Credit Billing Act (FCBA), which provides protection for credit card holders.

The FCBA provides that, if a consumer has a complaint about a bill and writes to the credit card company within 60 days of receipt of the bill, the company must acknowledge receipt of the complaint within 30 days and, then, within two billing cycles (but no more than 90 days) investigate the complaint and respond.

25-3e Electronic Fund Transfers

The Electronic Fund Transfer Act (EFTA) protects consumers who make electronic payments using a telephone, computer, or wire transfers. This statute applies in situations where consumers ask banks to wire funds on a regular basis to pay, say, their monthly health club fee or their mortgage. An electronic fund transfer authorized in advance to recur at regular intervals is called a **preauthorized transfer. For preauthorized transactions, the bank must follow two rules:**

1. It may not make preauthorized transfers without written instructions from the consumer.

2. It must allow the consumer to stop payment of the transfer by oral or written notice up to three business days before the scheduled date.

Here is a good example of the EFTA at work: Suk Jae Chang saw a great offer online for the free poster of his choice. He just had to pay a 99¢ shipping fee. He entered his debit card data to pay the shipping cost. He also checked a box agreeing to the terms and conditions, which of course he did not read. Next thing he knew, $29.99 a month was being deducted from his bank account to pay for his membership in a poster club. The website had said nothing about the club – including how to cancel his membership. Nor did the terms and conditions. After irate consumers filed suit against the poster company, it agreed to pay back all the funds it had received.

Preauthorized transfer
Electronic fund transfer authorized in advance to recur at regular intervals

25-3f Credit Reports

Accuracy of Credit Reports

Most adults rely on credit—to acquire a house, credit cards, overdraft privileges at the bank, or even rent an apartment. About half of businesses use credit checks as part of the hiring process, although nine states now prohibit this practice. A number of statutes, including the **Fair Credit Reporting Act (FCRA)** and the **Fair and Accurate Credit Transactions Act (FACTA)** regulate credit reports. **Consumer reporting agencies** are businesses that supply consumer reports to third parties.

Consumer reporting agencies
Businesses that supply consumer reports to third parties

Under the FCRA:

- A consumer report can be used only for a legitimate business need.

- A consumer reporting agency cannot report information that is more than seven years old (10 years for bankruptcies).

- A consumer reporting agency cannot report medical information without the consumer's permission.

- An employer cannot request a consumer report on any current or potential employee without the employee's permission.

- Anyone who penalizes a consumer because of a credit report must reveal the name and address of the reporting agency that supplied the information.

- Upon request from a consumer, a reporting agency must disclose all information in his file.

- If a consumer tells an agency that some of the information in his file is incorrect, the agency must investigate. The consumer also has the right to report her side of the story.

According to the FTC, 20 percent of consumers had errors in their credit report at one of the three major reporting agencies–Equifax, Experian, and TransUnion. Victims of inaccurate reports have found it virtually impossible to get these mistakes corrected.[3] In a

---

[3]Todd Ruger, "FTC Report Finds Widespread Errors in consumer Credit Reports," *The National Law Journal*, February 11, 2013.

recent case, a jury ordered Equifax to pay $18 million to a woman who, despite two years of heroic effort, had been unsuccessful in convincing the agency to fix errors. Because of the mistakes, she had been unable to cosign a car loan for her disabled brother.[4]

Access to Credit Reports and Credit Scores

Under FACTA, consumers are entitled by law to one free credit report every year from each of the three major reporting agencies. You can order these reports at https://www.annual creditreport.com. (Note, though, that many websites with similar names *pretend* to offer a free credit report but instead enroll customers in paid programs to monitor their credit reports. Be sure to go to the right website.)

Although your credit report is valuable information, you do not know how creditors will evaluate it. For that, you need to know your **credit score** (usually called a FICO score).[5] This number (which ranges between 300 and 850) is based on your credit report and is supposed to predict your ability to pay your bills. Currently, it is not automatically included as part of your credit report, although the CFPB has urged reporting agencies to provide it for free. Anyone who penalizes you because of your score is required to give it to you for free, as well as information about how your score compares with others.

Credit score

Usually called a FICO score, this number is based on your credit report and is supposed to predict your ability to pay your bills.

25-3g Debt Collection

Have you ever fallen behind on your car payments? That is hardly a crime—but in the past, debt collectors might have *treated* you as a criminal. They might have threatened to arrest you. Or they might have changed the password on your cell-phone account and obtained your cell-phone records so that they could pose as a police officer and call your friends, relatives, and past employers to tell them there was an arrest warrant out for you, even if this was not true.

Congress passed **the Fair Debt Collection Practices Act (FDCPA) to protect consumers from abusive debt collection efforts. Under the FDCPA:**

- A collector must, within five days of contacting a debtor, send the debtor a written notice containing the amount of the debt, the name of the creditor to whom the debt is owed, and a statement that if the debtor disputes the debt (in writing), the collector will cease all collection efforts until it has sent evidence of the debt.

- Collectors may not:
  - Call or write a debtor who has notified the collector in writing that he wishes no further contact;
  - Call or write a debtor who is represented by an attorney;
  - Call a debtor before 8:00 a.m. or after 9:00 p.m.;
  - Threaten a debtor or use obscene or abusive language;
  - Call or visit the debtor at work if the consumer's employer prohibits such contact;
  - Imply that they are attorneys or government representatives when they are not, or use a false name;
  - Make any false, deceptive, or misleading statement;
  - Contact acquaintances of the debtor for any reason other than to locate the debtor (and then only once);
  - Tell acquaintances that the consumer is in debt; or
  - Collect charges in addition to the debt unless permitted by state law or any contract the debtor has signed.

---

[4]Tara Siegel Bernard, "An $18 Million Lesson in Handling Credit Report Errors," *The New York Times*, August 2, 2013.
[5]It is called a FICO score because it was developed by the Fair Isaac Corporation.

Of course, these rules do not prevent the collector from filing suit against the debtor. In the following case, a court found that a debt collector had violated the FDCPA.

BRADLEY V. FRANKLIN COLLECTION SERV.

739 F.3d 606
United States Court of Appeals for the Eleventh Circuit, 2014

CASE SUMMARY

Facts: When Melvin Bradley sought treatment at North Alabama Urology, P.C. (Urology) he signed a patient agreement, stating that: "In the event of non-payment … I agree to pay all costs of collection, including a reasonable attorney's fee." He then incurred a bill for $861.96, which he failed to pay. Urology referred his bill to Franklin Collection Service, Inc. and, in the process, added a $293.06 collection fee to Bradley's balance. The contract between Urology and Franklin provided that Urology would add $33\frac{1}{3}$ percent to a debt prior to transferring the account to Franklin and then Franklin was entitled to 30 percent of the total it collected.

Bradley challenged this fee, alleging that it violated the FDCPA.

Issue: *Did Franklin violate the FDCPA when it tried to collect a percentage-based collection fee?*

Decision: Yes, Franklin was in violation.

Reasoning: In his contract with Urology, Bradley agreed to pay the costs of collection. Yet Franklin did not provide any evidence that the $33\frac{1}{3}$ percent "collection fee" bore any relationship to the actual cost of its collection effort. Urology and Franklin cannot, by their agreement, alter the terms of Bradley's contract with Urology.

Urology could have required Bradley to sign a contract that allowed for the addition of a percentage-based fee, but it failed to do so. Therefore, Franklin violated the FDCPA when it attempted to collect from Bradley a debt that included a "collection fee" based on a percentage of the bill rather than the actual costs of collection.

25-3h Equal Credit Opportunity Act

The Equal Credit Opportunity Act (ECOA) prohibits any creditor from discriminating against a borrower because of race, color, religion, national origin, sex, marital status, age (as long as the borrower is old enough to enter into a legal contract), or because the borrower is receiving welfare. A lender must respond to a credit application within 30 days. If a lender rejects an application, it must either tell the applicant why or notify him that he has the right to a written explanation of the reasons for this adverse action.

The dealer in the following case was sleazy, but did it violate the ECOA?

TREADWAY V. GATEWAY CHEVROLET OLDSMOBILE INC.

362 F.3d 971
United States Court of Appeals for the Seventh Circuit, 2004

CASE SUMMARY

Facts: Gateway Chevrolet Oldsmobile, a car dealership, sent an unsolicited letter to Tonja Treadway notifying her that she was "pre-approved" for the financing to purchase a car. Gateway did not provide financing itself; instead, it arranged loans through banks or finance companies.

Treadway called the dealer to say that she was interested in purchasing a used car. With her permission, Gateway obtained her credit report. Based on this report, the dealer determined that Treadway was not eligible for financing. This was not surprising, given that Gateway had purchased Treadway's name from a list of people who had recently filed for bankruptcy.

Instead of applying for a loan on behalf of Treadway, Gateway told her that it had found a bank that would finance her transaction, but only if she purchased a new car and provided a co-signer. Treadway agreed to purchase a new car and came up with Pearlie Smith, her godmother, to serve as a co-signer.

Concerned as it was with customer convenience, Gateway had an agent deliver papers directly to Smith's house to be signed immediately. If Smith had read the papers before she signed them, she might have realized that she had committed herself to be the sole purchaser and owner of the car. But she had no idea that she was the owner until she began receiving bills on the car loan. After Treadway made the first payment on behalf of Smith, both women refused to pay more—Smith because she did not want a new car; Treadway because the car was not hers. The car was repossessed, but the financing company continued to demand payment.

It appears that Gateway was running a scam. The dealership would lure desperate prospects off the bankruptcy rolls and into the showroom with promises of financing for a used car, and then sell a new car to their "co-signer" (who was, in fact, the sole signer). Instead of selling a used car to Treadway, Gateway sold a new car to Smith.

Treadway filed suit against Gateway, alleging that it had violated the ECOA by not notifying her that it had taken an adverse action against her.

Issue: *Did Gateway violate the ECOA?*

Decision: Yes, Gateway failed to notify Treadway that it had taken an adverse action.

Reasoning: The ECOA requires any lender who rejects a loan application to tell the applicant the reason or notify her that she has the right to a written explanation.

By deciding not to send Treadway's application to *any* lender, Gateway effectively rejected it. But because Gateway did not tell customers that it had done the rejecting, they would naturally assume that a bank or other lender had turned them down.

If the dealership's role was secret, it would have no accountability—it could discriminate against any and all without getting caught. Gateway could simply throw the credit report of every minority applicant in the "circular file" and none would be the wiser.

EXAM Strategy

Question: Clyde goes into a Tesla dealership to investigate buying an electric sports car. He does not look as if he can afford a six-figure purchase, so the sales staff orders a credit report on him. After all, no point in wasting their time. Do they have the right to order a report on Clyde?

Strategy: The FCRA regulates the issuance of consumer reports. These reports can be used only for a legitimate business need.

Result: A car dealership cannot obtain a consumer report on someone who simply asks general questions about prices and financing or who wants to test-drive a car; nor can the dealer order a report to use in negotiations. However, a dealer has the right to a report that is needed to arrange financing requested by the consumer or to verify a buyer's creditworthiness when he presents a personal check to pay for the vehicle.

25-4 MAGNUSON-MOSS WARRANTY ACT

The Magnuson-Moss Warranty Act applies to written warranties on goods (not services) sold to consumers. This statute does *not* require manufacturers or sellers to provide a warranty on their products. It does require the seller to disclose:

- The terms of any written warranty in simple, understandable language.

- Whether the warranty is full or limited. Under a **full warranty**, the seller must promise to fix a defective product for a reasonable time without charge. If, after a reasonable number of efforts to fix the defective product, it still does not work, the consumer must have the right to a refund or a replacement without charge.

- The name and address of the person the consumer should contact to obtain warranty service.

- The parts that are covered and those that are not.

- What services the warrantor will provide, at whose expense, and for what period of time.

- A statement of what the consumer must do and what expenses he must pay.

Full warranty

The seller must promise to fix a defective product for a reasonable time without charge

25-5 CONSUMER PRODUCT SAFETY

In 1969, the federal government estimated that consumer products caused 30,000 deaths, 110,000 disabling injuries, and 20 million trips to the doctor. Toys were among the worst offenders, injuring 700,000 children a year. The Consumer Product Safety Act of 1972 (CPSA) created the Consumer Product Safety Commission (CPSC) to evaluate consumer products and develop safety standards. **Under the CPSA:**

- Manufacturers must report all potentially hazardous product defects within 24 hours of discovery.

- The Commission can impose civil and criminal penalties on those who violate its standards.

- Individuals have the right to sue for damages, including attorney's fees, from anyone who knowingly violates a consumer product safety rule.

You can find out about product recalls or file a report on an unsafe product at the Commission's website (http://www.cpsc.gov) or at saferproducts.gov.

Ethics Imagine that you are Robert Eckert, chairman and CEO of Mattel, Inc. Your company has sold millions of Jeep Wrangler Power Wheels. These toys are designed for children as young as two years old. You have just been notified that 150 of the cars have caught on fire, while thousands of others have overheated. In some cases, these toys have burned so fiercely that they have caught their garages on fire, endangering all of the home's occupants. You know that under CPSC rules, you are required to report toy defects within 24 hours. You also know that making the required report could have a significant impact on Mattel's profitability. What would you do?

Mattel decided that it ought to figure out what the problem was before reporting anything to the CPSC. In the end, it delayed months. Eckert was quoted as saying that the law was unreasonable and the company would not follow it.[6]

Is Mattel's stance ethical? What would Kant and Mill say? What Life Principle is Eckert applying? Is it ever ethical to violate the law?

---

[6]Based on an article by Nicholas Casey and Andy Pasztor, "Safety Agency, Mattel Clash over Disclosures," *The Wall Street Journal*, September 4, 2007, p. A1.

Chapter Conclusion

Virtually no one will go through life without reading an advertisement, ordering online, borrowing money, acquiring a credit report, or using a consumer product. It is important to know your rights.

Exam Review

1. **UNFAIR PRACTICES**   The Federal Trade Commission (FTC) prohibits unfair and deceptive acts or practices.

2. **THE CONSUMER FINANCE PROTECTION BUREAU (CFPB)**   The Consumer Finance Protection Bureau has the authority to take action against those committing "abusive acts" against consumers.

3. **BAIT-AND-SWITCH**   FTC rules prohibit bait-and-switch advertisements. A merchant may not advertise a product and then disparage it (or make it unavailable) to consumers in an effort to sell a different item.

4. **MERCHANDISE BOUGHT BY MAIL, BY TELEPHONE, OR ONLINE**   Under FTC rules for this type of merchandise, sellers must ship an item within the time stated or, if no time is given, within 30 days after receipt of the order.

5. **DO-NOT-CALL REGISTRY**   The FTC prohibits telemarketers from calling or texting any telephone numbers listed on its do-not-call registry.

6. **TELEPHONE CONSUMER PROTECTION ACT (TCPA)**   The Telephone Consumer Protection Act prohibits telemarketers from making autodialed and/or prerecorded calls or texts to cell phones and prerecorded calls to residential land lines unless the consumer unambiguously consents in writing.

7. **UNORDERED MERCHANDISE**   Consumers may keep as a gift any unordered merchandise that they receive in the mail.

8. **DOOR-TO-DOOR RULES**   Under the FTC door-to-door rules, a salesperson is required to notify the buyer that she has the right to cancel the transaction prior to midnight of the third business day thereafter.

9. **TRUTH IN LENDING ACT (TILA)**   In all loans regulated by TILA, the lender must disclose information clearly.

10. **MORTGAGES**   Lenders must make a good faith effort to determine whether a borrower can afford to repay the loan. They may not coerce or bribe an appraiser into misstating a home's value. Nor may they charge prepayment penalties.

11. **QUALIFIED MORTGAGES**   If lenders give a qualified mortgage, they are deemed to have complied with TILA.

12. **CREDIT CARD FEES**   Credit card companies are not allowed to increase fees and interest rates on any charges already incurred (until a cardholder has missed two consecutive payments). Such increases are only permitted for future purchases if the company gives the consumer 45 days' notice and permits cancellation of the card.

13. **DEBIT CARD FEES**   Banks may not overdraw an account and charge an overdraft fee unless the consumer signs up for an overdraft plan.

14. **LIABILITY FOR CREDIT CARDS**   Under TILA, a credit card holder is liable only for the first $50 in unauthorized charges made before the credit card company is notified that the card was stolen.

15. **LIABILITY FOR DEBIT AND ATM CARDS**   If the consumer reports the theft of a debit or ATM card within two days of discovering it, the bank will make good on all losses above $50. If the consumer waits more than two days, the bank will only replace stolen funds above $500. If the consumer waits more than 60 days after receipt of the bank statement, the bank is not responsible for any losses.

16. **CREDIT CARD DISPUTES WITH A MERCHANT**   In the event of a dispute between a customer and a merchant, the credit card company cannot bill the customer if:

    * She makes a good faith effort to resolve the dispute,

    * The dispute is for more than $50, and

    * The merchant is in the same state where she lives or is within 100 miles of her house.

17. **FAIR CREDIT BILLING ACT (FCBA)**   Under the Fair Credit Billing Act, a credit card company must promptly investigate and respond to any consumer complaints about a credit card bill.

18. **ELECTRONIC FUND TRANSFERS**   A consumer can stop payment on a transfer by oral or written notice up to three business days before the scheduled date.

19. **FAIR CREDIT REPORTING ACT (FCRA)**   Under FCRA:

    * A consumer report can be used only for a legitimate business need,

    * A consumer reporting agency cannot report obsolete information,

    * An employer cannot request a consumer report on any current or potential employee without the employee's permission, and

    * Anyone who penalizes a consumer because of a credit report must reveal the name and address of the reporting agency that supplied the negative information.

20. **THE FAIR AND ACCURATE CREDIT TRANSACTIONS ACT (FACTA)**   Under FACTA, consumers have the right to obtain one free credit report every year from each of the three major reporting agencies. Also, anyone who penalizes a consumer because of her credit score must give it to her at no charge.

21. **THE FAIR DEBT COLLECTION PRACTICES ACT (FDCPA)** A debt collector may not harass or abuse debtors.

22. **THE EQUAL CREDIT OPPORTUNITY ACT (ECOA)** The ECOA prohibits any creditor from discriminating against a borrower on the basis of race, color, religion, national origin, sex, marital status, age, or because the borrower is receiving welfare.

EXAM Strategy

Question: Kathleen, a single woman, applied for an Exxon credit card. Exxon rejected her application without giving any specific reason and without providing the name of the credit bureau it had used. When Kathleen asked for a reason for the rejection, she was told that the credit bureau did not have enough information about her to establish creditworthiness. In fact, Exxon had denied her credit application because she did not have a major credit card or a savings account, she had been employed for only one year, and she had no dependents. Did Exxon violate the law?

Strategy: Exxon violated two laws. Review the statutes in the "Consumer Credit" section of the chapter. (See the "Result" at the end of this section.)

23. **WARRANTIES** The Magnuson-Moss Warranty Act requires any seller that offers a written warranty on a consumer product to disclose the terms of the warranty in simple and readily understandable language before the sale.

24. **CONSUMER PRODUCT SAFETY** Under the Consumer Product Safety Act (CPSA) manufacturers must report all potentially hazardous product defects within 24 hours of discovery.

EXAM Strategy

Question: Joel and his brother, Joshua, were toddlers when their father left them asleep in the rear seat of his automobile while visiting a friend. A cigarette lighter was on the dashboard of the car. When Joshua woke up, he began playing with the lighter and set fire to Joel's diaper. Do the parents have a claim against the manufacturer of the lighter under the Consumer Product Safety Act?

Strategy: The CPSA regulates unsafe products. Was the cigarette lighter unsafe? (See the "Result" at the end of this section.)

---

22. Result: The court held that Exxon violated both the Fair Credit Reporting Act (FCRA) and the Equal Credit Opportunity Act (ECOA). The FCRA requires Exxon to tell Kathleen the name of the credit bureau that it used. Under the ECOA, Exxon was required to tell Kathleen the real reasons for the credit denial.

24. Result: The court held that the plaintiff did not have a claim because there was no evidence that the manufacturer had knowingly violated a consumer product safety rule.

MATCHING QUESTIONS

Match the following terms with their definitions:

___A. EFTA

___B. FDCPA

___C. FCRA

___D. ECOA

___E. TILA

1. Requires lenders to disclose the terms of a loan
2. Regulates credit reports
3. Regulates debt collectors
4. Prohibits lenders from discriminating based on race, religion, and sex
5. Regulates electronic payments

TRUE/FALSE QUESTIONS

Circle true or false:

1. T F If a store advertises a product, it is not required have enough stock on hand to fill every order.
2. T F The FTC telemarketing rules apply to calls but not texts.
3. T F Payday loans are illegal.
4. T F Under the Truth in Lending Act, it does not matter how the information is disclosed, so long as it is disclosed someplace on the first page of the loan document.
5. T F A consumer reporting agency has the right to keep information in its files secret from the consumer.

MULTIPLE-CHOICE QUESTIONS

1. If you receive a product in the mail that you did not order:
   (a) you must pay for it or return it.
   (b) you must pay for it only if you use it.
   (c) you must throw it away.
   (d) it is a gift to you.
   (e) you must return it, but the company must reimburse you for postage.

2. Zach sells Cutco Knives door to door. Which of the following statements is FALSE?
   (a) The buyer has three days to cancel the order.
   (b) Zach must tell the buyer of her rights.
   (c) Zach must give the buyer a written notice of her rights.
   (d) The seller can cancel orally or in writing.
   (e) If the seller cancels, Zach must return her money within 10 days.

3. Depending on state law, if a lender violates the usury laws, the borrower could possibly be allowed to keep:

I.   the interest that exceeds the usury limit.

II.   all the interest.

III. all of the loan and the interest.

    (a) I, II, and III
    (b) Only I
    (c) Only II
    (d) Only III
    (e) Neither I, II, nor III

4. Companies must obtain permission from a consumer before charging for overdrafts on:

(a) debit cards.

(b) credit cards.

(c) neither.

(d) both.

5. On the first of every month, your monthly rent is automatically deducted from your bank account. You are moving out and want to make sure the payments stop. What should you do?

(a) You must call the bank at least three days before the first of the month.

(b) You must write the bank at least three days before the first of the month.

(c) Either (a) or (b).

(d) You must have the landlord sign a form which you then mail or deliver to the bank at least three days before the first of the month.

CASE QUESTIONS

1. Process cheese food slices must contain at least 51 percent natural cheese. Imitation cheese slices, by contrast, contain little or no natural cheese and consist primarily of water and vegetable oil. Kraft, Inc. makes Kraft Singles, which are individually wrapped process cheese food slices. When Kraft began losing market share to imitation slices that were advertised as both less expensive and equally nutritious as Singles, Kraft responded with a series of advertisements informing consumers that Kraft Singles cost more than imitation slices because they are made from 5 ounces of milk. Kraft does use 5 ounces of milk in making each Kraft Single, but 30 percent of the calcium contained in the milk is lost during processing. Imitation slices contain the same amount of calcium as Kraft Singles. Are the Kraft advertisements deceptive?

2. Josephine was a 60-year-old ailing widow. A bill collector from Collections Accounts Terminal, Inc., called her and demanded that she pay $56 she owed to Cabrini

Hospital. She told him that Medicare was supposed to pay the bill. Shortly thereafter, Josephine received a letter from Collections that stated:

> You have shown that you are unwilling to work out a friendly settlement with us to clear the above debt. Our field investigator has now been instructed to make an investigation in your neighborhood and to personally call on your employer. The immediate payment of the full amount will spare you this embarrassment.

Has Collections violated the law?

3. Thomas worked at a Sherwin-Williams paint store that James managed. But Thomas and James had a falling out. After Thomas quit, James claimed that Thomas owed the store $121. Sherwin-Williams reported this information to the Chilton credit reporting agency. Thomas sent a letter to Chilton disputing the accuracy of the Sherwin-Williams charges. Chilton contacted James who confirmed that Thomas still owed the money. Chilton failed to note in Thomas's file that a dispute was pending. Thereafter, two of Thomas's requests for credit cards were denied. Have James and Chilton violated the Fair Credit Reporting Act?

4. In October, Renie Guimond discovered that her credit report at TransUnion incorrectly stated that she was married, used the name "Ruth Guimond," and had a credit card from Saks Fifth Avenue. After she reported the errors, TransUnion wrote her in November to say that it had removed this information. However, in March, TransUnion again published the erroneous information. The following October, TransUnion finally removed the incorrect information from her file. Guimond was never denied credit because of these mistakes. Is TransUnion liable for violating the Fair Credit Reporting Act?

5. **ETHICS** After TNT Motor Express hired Joseph Bruce Drury as a truck driver, it ordered a background check from Robert Arden & Associates. TNT provided Drury's social security number and date of birth, but not his middle name. Arden discovered that a Joseph *Thomas* Drury, who coincidentally had the same birth date as Joseph *Bruce* Drury, had served a prison sentence for drunk driving. Not knowing that it had the wrong Drury, Arden reported this information to TNT, which promptly fired Drury. When he asked why, the TNT executive refused to tell him. Did TNT violate the law? Whether or not TNT was in violation, did its executives behave ethically? Who would have been harmed or helped if TNT managers had informed Drury of the Arden report?

DISCUSSION QUESTIONS

1. Collecto, Inc. had a contract with the U.S. Department of Education to collect overdue student loans. When student loan debtors filed bankruptcy proceedings, Collecto would send them a letter with this language:****ACCOUNT INELIGIBLE FOR BANKRUPTCY DISCHARGE**** Your account is NOT eligible for bankruptcy discharge and must be resolved.

It is very difficult to discharge student loans because the debtor must show undue hardship. Did Collecto's letter violate the FDCPA?

2. **ETHICS** Should employers check credit reports as part of the hiring process? Each year retailers lose $30 *billion* a year from employee theft and $55 million because of workplace violence. Those who commit fraud are often living above their means,

but there is no evidence that workers with poor credit reports are more likely to be violent, steal from their employers, or quit their jobs. And refusing to hire someone with a low credit score creates a sad Catch-22: People have poor credit records because they are unemployed, and because they have poor credit records they continue to be unemployed. What is the right thing for an employer to do?

3. **ETHICS** The fee on a debit card overdraft can be as high or higher than the amount taken out. Instead of overdrawing their accounts, consumers would be much better off either not spending the money, using a credit card, or paying cash. Typically, the people most likely to sign up for overdraft "protection" are those who can least afford it—they have maxed out their credit cards and used up any home equity. Is it ethical for a bank to offer an overdraft plan?

4. Go to youtube.com and watch the advertisements for freecreditreport.com. Although the characters repeat the word, "free" over and over, in fact the reports are not free unless the consumer signs up for the paid credit monitoring service. At the end of the ad, a voice quickly says, "Offer applies with enrollment in Triple Advantage." Are these ads deceptive under FTC rules? Are they ethical according to your Life Principles?

5. Advertisements for Listerine mouthwash claimed that it was as effective as flossing in preventing tooth plaque and gum disease. This statement was true, but only if the flossing was done incorrectly. In fact, many consumers do floss incorrectly. However, if flossing is done right, it is more effective against plaque and gum disease than Listerine. Is this advertisement deceptive?

CHAPTER 26

ENVIRONMENTAL LAW

© Galyna Andrushko/Shutterstock.com

Michelle has owned a building on Main Street for more than 20 years. At the beginning, one of the businesses in the building was a dry-cleaning shop. The operators of the shop disposed of the cleaning fluids legally. Recent testing of the groundwater in a nearby park revealed that it was contaminated by dry-cleaning chemicals from that shop. By law, Michelle is required to pay the cost of cleaning up the chemicals, even though they were disposed of legally years ago. The cost of the cleanup will far exceed the value of the building she owns.

The cost of the cleanup will far exceed the value of the building she owns.

26-1 INTRODUCTION

This scenario is based on a true story. The environment is a complex issue. It is not enough simply to say, "We are against pollution." The question is: Who will pay? Who will pay for past damage inflicted before anyone understood the harm that pollutants cause? Who will pay for current changes necessary to prevent damage now and in the future? Will consumers insulate their homes or buy more energy-efficient appliances? Cities upgrade their public transportation systems? Developers protect wetlands? Car buyers accept the higher cost of greener technology?

The cost-benefit trade-off is particularly complex in environmental issues because those who pay the cost often do not receive the benefit. If a company dumps toxic wastes into a stream, its shareholders benefit by avoiding the expense of safe disposal. Those who fish or drink the waters pay the real cost without receiving any of the benefit. Economists use the term **externality** to describe the situation in which people do not bear the full cost of their decisions. Externalities prevent the market system from achieving a clean environment on its own. Most commonly, government involvement is required to realign costs and benefits.

As we begin our discussion of environmental law, please note that violations are a serious matter. Those who break environmental laws are liable for civil damages. In addition, some statutes, such as the Clean Water Act, the Resource Conservation and Recovery Act, and the Endangered Species Act, provide for *criminal* penalties, including imprisonment.

Externality

When people do not bear the full cost of their decisions

26-2 AIR POLLUTION

The major sources of air pollution are power plants, refineries, factories, and motor vehicles. **Airborne contaminants cause a variety of harms:**

- **Human health.** Air pollution can cause or increase the severity of serious diseases such as asthma, bronchitis, cancer, emphysema, heart disease, pneumonia, and strokes. The EPA estimates that it causes 5 percent of the deaths in America.

- **The physical environment.** Crops, forests, lakes, rivers, buildings, monuments, and vehicles are damaged.

- **Animals.** On land and in water, animals are injured and killed. The rate of extinction rises. The food chain is threatened.

  The impact of this climate change is potentially catastrophic: a devastating decline in fishing stocks, the death of major forests, and a loss of farmland worldwide. But even worse is the flooding that will result from a worldwide rise in sea levels. Hundreds of millions of people—including two-thirds of the world's megacities—are in coastal areas that could be flooded.

- **Global warming.** If current trends continue, the world's average temperature during the next 100 years will rise 2 to 6 °F, producing the warmest climate in the history of humankind. (By comparison, the planet is only 5 to 9 °F warmer than during the last Ice Age.)

Air pollution is both a national and global issue, with particularly acute externalities. Within the United States, prevailing west-to-east winds blow air pollution—and the harm it causes—across country. Internationally, burning fossil fuels in the United States causes worldwide global warming. Air pollution from China creates smog in the United States.

26-2a Clean Air Act

In the United States, air pollution is regulated by the Clean Air Act of 1963 (CAA). **Under the CAA, the EPA has the authority to regulate both the total amount of existing air pollution and its ongoing production.** Any individual state may impose stricter rules than the EPA.

The CAA's major provisions are as follows:

- **National standards.** The EPA is required to establish national air-quality standards that protect public health and provide an adequate margin of safety *without regard to cost*.

- **State implementation plans (SIPs).** After the EPA sets standards, states must produce SIPs to meet them. If a state fails to produce an acceptable SIP, the EPA develops its own plan for that state.

- **Regulation of stationary sources.** A **stationary source** is any building or facility that emits a certain level of pollution. The EPA sets limits on the amount of pollution these facilities produce and requires that they obtain permits for construction, operation, or renovation. They must also use the best available control technology (**BACT**) for every pollutant.

- **Prevention of significant deterioration (PSD) program.** Any applicant for a permit must demonstrate that its emissions will not cause an overall decline in air quality, *regardless of health impact*.

- **Motor vehicles.** The EPA has set standards for the pollution control devices in motor vehicles and also the composition of fuel.

In the following case, a power plant argued that the EPA had imposed a solution whose cost far outweighed its benefit. There is only one Grand Canyon. Should visibility there be preserved at any cost?

Stationary source
Any building or facility that emits pollution

BACT
Best available control technology

You be the Judge

**CENTRAL ARIZONA
WATER CONSERVATION
DISTRICT V. EPA**
990 F.2d 1531
United States Court of Appeals for
the Ninth Circuit, 1993

Facts: The Navaho Generating Station (NGS) is a power plant 12 miles from the Grand Canyon. To protect the views of this national treasure, the EPA ordered NGS to reduce its sulfur dioxide emissions by 90 percent. To do so would cost NGS $430 million in capital expenditures initially, and then $89.6 million annually. Average winter visibility in the Grand Canyon would be improved by at most 7 percent, but perhaps less.

NGS sued to prevent implementation of the EPA's order. A court may nullify an EPA order if it determines that the Agency's action was arbitrary and capricious.

You Be the Judge: *Did the EPA act arbitrarily and capriciously in requiring NGS to spend half a billion dollars to improve winter visibility at the Grand Canyon by at most 7 percent?*

Argument for NGS: This case is a perfect example of environmentalism run amok. Half a billion dollars for the chance of increasing winter visibility at the Grand Canyon by 7 percent? Winter visitors to the Grand Canyon would undoubtedly prefer that NGS provide them with a free lunch rather than a 7 percent improvement in visibility. The EPA order is simply a waste of money.

Argument for the EPA: How can NGS, or anyone else, measure the benefit of protecting a national treasure like the Grand Canyon? Even people who never have and never will visit it during the winter sleep better at night knowing that the canyon is protected. NGS has been causing harm to the Grand Canyon, and now it should remedy the damage.

26-2b Greenhouse Gases (GHGs) and Global Warming

Scientific evidence underlying the theory of global warming has been debated for a long time, but today scientists accept that the burning of fossil fuels produces gases that create a greenhouse effect by trapping heat in the Earth's atmosphere. The United Nations Intergovernmental Panel on Climate Change recently issued a report warning that, if governments fail to limit GHGs by 2030, profound global warming will be impossible to prevent using the technologies currently available. This report also warned that countries have not taken the steps necessary to adapt to inevitable changes.

Global warming is the most complex environmental problem of the new millennium because any solution requires international political cooperation coupled with major behavioral changes.

International Treaties

The 1997 Kyoto Protocol to the United Nations Framework Convention on Climate Change is an international treaty designed to reduce GHGs. However, China and the United States are the two largest producers of GHGs, but neither is covered by this treaty: The United States because it refused to sign; China because compliance is optional for developing countries.

The United States was the only leading industrialized nation not to sign. It had two reasons: (1) it competes against countries such as China and India, which were not bound because they are developing economies; and (2) the worldwide cost of compliance was estimated at $700 billion, of which the United States would have had to pay $450 billion. But there would have been little *short-run* benefit to the United States. As for China, it and other developing countries view cheap carbon fuels as an essential part of their efforts to raise their citizens' standard of living.

The Kyoto Protocol set emission levels for each country. However, it has had little impact on GHGs, and not just because the United States and China opted out. Many signatories withdrew from the treaty and others that stayed in exceeded their quotas.

Domestic Regulation

In 2007, **the Supreme Court ruled that, if GHGs endanger health or welfare, the EPA must regulate them.** As we have seen, the EPA already regulates car emissions. It recently issued regulations for *existing* power plants that are designed to cut GHGs from these sources to just 70 percent of 2005 levels. The EPA has also recently issued stringent regulations on GHG emissions by *new* power plants. Critics argue that these regulations are so strict, the EPA is effectively banning new coal plants. In addition, **states are able to set their own standards for air pollution, so long as they are stricter than federal rules.**

Meanwhile, companies are beginning to see their business affected by global warming. Coke has found that its supply of ingredients—beets, sugar, and citrus—is sometimes disrupted. And it was denied an operating license in India because of a water shortage. Floods shut down a Nike factory; droughts damaged the cotton production that it needed for its clothing.[1]

---

[1] Coral Davenport, "Industry Awakens to Threat of Climate Change," *The New York Times*, January 23, 2014.

Ethics   Since Tim Cook became CEO of Apple, more than three-quarters of the company's buildings worldwide have been adapted to run on sustainable energy—sun, wind, water, or geothermal. But, at its most recent annual meeting, a large shareholder asked Cook to limit Apple's environmental activities to those that also enhanced company profits. Cook responded that many environmental policies do make economic sense. But then he added, "We do a lot of things for reasons besides profit motive. We want to leave the world better than we found it." His advice to the objecting shareholder: "Get out of the stock."

Should Cook be spending shareholder money on activities that do not enhance the bottom line? If so, how should the company evaluate unprofitable activities? What metrics should it use? What are Cook's Life Principles?[2]

26-3 WATER POLLUTION: THE CLEAN WATER ACT

Water pollution is harmful to:

- **Human health.** Pathogens can cause a number of loathsome diseases, such as typhus, dysentery, and hepatitis. Chemicals are poisonous and can cause serious diseases such as cancer.

- **Animals.** Fish, shellfish, dolphins, whales, and birds die or reproduce more slowly. The food chain is disrupted.

- **The physical environment.** Damaged water systems are unable to support biodiversity in plants and animals. They are no longer attractive or useful for recreational purposes.

Sources of water pollution include:

- **Point sources.** Discharges from a single producer, such as a pipe from waste treatment plants, factories, and refineries.

- **Nonpoint sources.** Refers to pollutants that have no single source but result from events such as storm water runoff. As it flows over the ground, it brings along pesticides, fertilizer, heavy metals, animal waste, and dirt. Rain is also a nonpoint source. It carries pollutants from the air into the water.

- **Accidents.** Such as an oil spill in the Gulf of Mexico.

- **Heat.** When industrial plants use water as a coolant, they return it to the waterways at a high temperature that damages the ecosystem.

In 1972, Congress passed a statute, now called the Clean Water Act (CWA), with two ambitious goals: (1) to make all navigable water suitable for swimming and fishing by 1983, and (2) to eliminate the discharge of pollutants into navigable water by 1985.

Point sources
Discharges from a single producer

Nonpoint sources
Pollutants that have no single producer but result from events such as storm water runoff or rain

---

[2]Chris Taylor, "Tim Cook to Climate Change Deniers: Get Out of Apple Stock," *Mashable*, March 1, 2014.

26-3a Coverage

Navigable Waters

The CWA governs all navigable waters in the United States. Traditionally, the courts had interpreted this term in a way that gave the EPA the right to regulate virtually all water polluters. But the Supreme Court dramatically narrowed the definition of navigable water. The EPA is now struggling to determine which waterways are covered. It estimates that almost one-third of the nation's population drinks water fed by waterways that it may no longer have the right to regulate.

Cost-Benefit Analysis

Courts had interpreted the CWA to require the EPA to make decisions that best protected the environment without regard to cost. But then the Supreme Court ruled that using cost-benefit analysis was well within the EPA's legitimate discretion, at least, under the CWA.

26-3b Major Provisions

Under the CWA:

- **Point sources.** Any discharge into navigable water from a point source is illegal without a permit (from the EPA or a state).

- **Pollution limits.** The EPA sets limits, by industry, on the amount of each type of pollution any point source can discharge and the technology that must be used to treat it. The EPA faces a gargantuan task in determining the best available technology that each industry can use to reduce pollution.

- **National water quality standards.** The EPA must set national standards for water quality generally. Standards vary depending upon use: higher for drinking, fishing, or recreation than for irrigation or industry.

- **State plans.** Each state must develop plans to achieve these EPA standards.

  - **Water use.** States must identify how each body of water is used. For each body of water that does not meet water quality standards, the state is required to establish a set of total maximum daily loads (**TMDLs**) sufficient to bring the body into compliance with water quality standards.
  - **Nonpoint sources.** States must develop a plan for nonpoint source pollution.

- **Wetlands.** Wetlands are the transition areas between land and open water. They may look like swamps, they may even *be* swamps, but their unattractive appearance should not disguise their vital role in the aquatic world. They are natural habitats for many fish and wildlife. They also serve as a filter for neighboring bodies of water, trapping chemicals and sediments. Moreover, they are an important aid in flood control because they can absorb a high level of water and then release it slowly after the emergency is past.

  The CWA prohibits any discharge of dredge and fill material into wetlands without a permit. However, EPA regulations to implement the statute were successfully challenged in court, creating uncertainty in the agency's enforcement powers. Although, in theory, the government's official policy is no net loss of wetlands, in reality about 60,000 acres of wetlands are lost each year.

TMDLs

Total maximum daily loads of permitted pollution

- **Wastewater.** Sewer lines feed into publicly owned wastewater treatment plants, also known as municipal sewage plants. A municipality must obtain a permit for any discharge from a wastewater treatment plant. To obtain a permit, the municipality must first treat the waste to reduce its toxicity. However, taxpayers have resisted the large increases in taxes or fees necessary to fund required treatments. Since the fines imposed by the EPA are almost always less than the cost of treatment, some cities have been slow to comply.

Many of the ambitious goals set by the CWA have not been met. Its actions are often challenged in court—both by those who think its enforcement efforts are too rigorous and others who seek even stricter enforcement.

The following case demonstrates how complicated environmental issues can be. The EPA found a more efficient method for setting pollution standards. But will the court allow it? You be the judge.

You be the Judge

VA. DOT V. UNITED STATES EPA

2013 U.S. Dist. LEXIS 981, 2013 WL 53741
United States District Court
for the Eastern District of Virginia, 2013

Facts: The Accotink Creek is a 25-mile long tributary of the Potomac River. After the Commonwealth of Virginia violated the CWA by failing to set TMDLs that would enable the Creek to meet water-quality standards, EPA established its own set of TDMLs.

The Creek was unhealthy because it had too much sediment from storm water runoff. Sediment is a pollutant and, therefore, regulated by the CWA. However, it is difficult for scientists to measure and set daily pollution standards for sediment because its content varies and it is not always clear which components cause what problems and how the various ingredients react with each other. Storm water runoff is easy to assess and measure, but it is not technically classified as a pollutant.

The EPA established TDMLs for the flow rate of storm water into the Creek, but Virginia sued, alleging that the EPA had no right to regulate storm water because it is not a pollutant.

You Be the Judge: *Does the EPA have the right to limit storm water runoff (which is not a pollutant) because it carries pollutants?*

Argument for Virginia: The statute is very clear: The EPA has the right to regulate pollutants. Storm water is not a pollutant. Therefore, the EPA cannot regulate it. Beginning and end of story.

Argument for the EPA: Here is what we know: (1) how to measure and handle storm water runoff, because civil engineers deal with it all the time; (2) how much storm water will carry enough sediment to harm the Accotink Creek; (3) that to repair the Creek, Virginia has to limit storm water runoff because that is how the sediment enters the water.

What we do not know is how much of each pollutant will, on a daily basis, damage the Creek. Why spend huge amounts of time and money assessing each individual component of the sediment just to end up at the same result—limiting runoff?

Remember that the goal of the CWA is to eliminate the discharge of pollutants into navigable water. We have come up with a reasonable methodology that is very much in keeping with the goals of the CWA.

EXAM Strategy

Question: Edward lives on a ranch near Wind River. He uses water from the river for irrigation. To divert more water to his ranch, he builds a dike in the river using scrap metal, cottonwood trees, car bodies, and a washing machine. This material does not harm downstream water. Has Edward violated the CWA?

Strategy: The CWA prohibits the discharge of pollution. Was this pollution?

Result: Yes, the court ruled that the material Edward placed in the water was pollution. It was irrelevant that the material did not flow downstream.

26-4 Waste including Disposal

Do not be fooled by the name. Love Canal, in Niagara Falls, New York, was an unlovely place after 1945, when Hooker Chemical Co. dumped 21,800 tons of chemicals into the canal and on nearby land. Hooker then sold the land to the local school board to build an elementary school. Children swam in the canal. They played with hot balls of chemical residue—what they called "fire stones"—that popped up through the ground. Cancer, epilepsy, respiratory problems, and skin diseases were common in the neighborhood. Finally, a national health emergency was declared, and 800 families were relocated.[3]

In its time, what Hooker did was not unusual. Companies historically dumped waste in waterways, landfills, or open dumps. Out of sight was out of mind. Waste disposal continues to be a major problem in the United States. It has been estimated that the cost of cleaning up existing waste products will exceed $1 *trillion*. At the same time, the country continues to produce more than 6 billion tons of agricultural, commercial, industrial, and domestic waste each year. Two major statutes regulate wastes: the Resource Conservation and Recovery Act and the Comprehensive Environmental Response, Compensation, and Liability Act.

26-4a Resource Conservation and Recovery Act (RCRA)

The Resource Conservation and Recovery Act (RCRA) focuses on *preventing* future Love Canals by regulating the production, transportation, and disposal of solid wastes, both hazardous material and ordinary garbage.

Ordinary Garbage

The disposal of nonhazardous solid waste has generally been left to the states, but they must follow guidelines set by the RCRA. **The RCRA:**

- Bans new open dumps,
- Requires that garbage be sent to sanitary landfills,
- Sets minimum standards for landfills,

---

[3]William Glaberson, "Love Canal: Suit Focuses on Records from 1940s," *The New York Times*, October 22, 1990. Copyright © 1990 by The New York Times Co.

- Requires landfills to monitor nearby groundwater,

- Requires states to develop a permit program for landfills, and

- Provides some financial assistance to aid states in waste management.

Hazardous Wastes

Walmart recently paid $82 million to settle claims that it had illegally disposed of hazardous wastes. Its workers had thrown toxic products such as bleach and fertilizer into the local sewer system rather than disposing of them legally.[4]

Hazardous wastes must be tracked from creation to final disposal and disposed of at a certified facility. Anyone who creates, transports, stores, treats, or disposes of more than a certain quantity of hazardous wastes must apply for an EPA permit.

26-4b Superfund

The official name of **Superfund** is the Comprehensive Environmental Response, Compensation, and Liability Act (CERCLA). Its goal is to clean up hazardous wastes that were illegally dumped in the past.

The philosophy of Superfund is "the polluter pays." **Therefore, under Superfund, anyone who has *ever owned or operated* a site on which hazardous wastes are found, or who has *transported* wastes to the site, or who has *arranged* for the disposal of wastes that were released at the site, is liable for:**

- **The cost of cleaning up the site,**

- **Any damage done to natural resources, and**

- **Any required health assessments.**

In a "shovels first, lawyers later" approach, Congress established a revolving trust fund for the EPA to use in cleaning up sites even before obtaining reimbursement from those responsible for the damage or if the polluters cannot be found. The trust fund was initially financed by a tax on the oil and chemical industries, which produce the bulk of hazardous waste. In 1995, however, the taxes expired, and Congress refused to renew them. Since then, the EPA has had to rely on reimbursements from polluters and congressional appropriations.

Superfund

Another name for the Comprehensive Environmental Response, Compensation, and Liability Act (CERCLA)

EXAM Strategy

Question: In 1963, FMC Corp. purchased a manufacturing plant in Virginia from American Viscose Corp., the owner of the plant since 1937. During World War II, the government's War Production Board had commissioned American Viscose to make rayon for airplanes and truck tires. In 1982, inspections revealed carbon disulfide, a chemical used to manufacture this rayon, in groundwater near the plant. American Viscose was out of business by then. Who is responsible for cleaning up the carbon disulfide? Under what statute?

Strategy: Look at the statutes that govern waste disposal.

Result: Both FMC and the U.S. government are liable for cleanup under CERCLA.

---

[4]Stephanie Clifford, "Wal-Mart Is Fined $82 Million over Mishandling of Hazardous Wastes," *The New York Times*, May 28, 2013.

26-5 CHEMICALS

Chemicals are so common in consumer products such as shampoo, clothing, and furniture that babies are now born with hundreds of chemicals in their blood.

More than 85,000 chemicals are used in food, drugs, cosmetics, pesticides, and other products. Up to 3,000 new chemicals are introduced each year. Although consumers may think that these products have been safety tested, that is true for only a very small percent. Our regulatory system assumes that they are safe unless proven otherwise.

Chemicals are so common in consumer products such as shampoo, clothing, and furniture that babies are now born with hundreds of chemicals in their blood. Some of these chemicals are known to cause, among other harm, cancer, birth defects, endocrine disruption, and neurological damage.[5]

Under the Toxic Substances Control Act (TSCA):

- **Register.** Before manufacturing or importing a new chemical (or an old chemical being used for a new purpose), the manufacturer must register it with the EPA.

- **Test.** A chemical does not need to be *tested* before it is *registered*. The EPA can require a manufacturer or importer to test a chemical only if there is evidence that it is dangerous. But without testing, there is no evidence. The EPA has ordered testing in only about 200 chemicals. The agency can test chemicals itself, but if it does not block a chemical within 90 days, the company can proceed with selling it.

    If, over time, evidence develops that a particular chemical is dangerous, the manufacturer can withdraw it from the market and replace it with a similar item for which there are no data and, thus, avoid EPA testing requirements.

- **Regulate.** Once a chemical is on the market, the standard for subjecting it to regulation is very high. The EPA must show that it poses an "unreasonable risk." The agency has only ever regulated nine chemicals.

26-6 NATURAL RESOURCES

Thus far, this chapter has focused on the regulation of pollution. Congress has also passed statutes whose purpose is to preserve the country's natural resources.

26-6a National Environmental Policy Act

EIS
Environmental impact statement

The National Environmental Policy Act of 1969 (NEPA) requires all federal agencies to prepare an environmental impact statement (EIS) for every major federal action significantly affecting the quality of the human environment. An EIS is a major undertaking—often hundreds, if not thousands, of pages long. It must discuss:

- Environmental consequences of the proposed action,
- Available alternatives,

---

[5]The National Institute of Health defines endocrine disruptors as "chemicals that may interfere with the body's endocrine system and produce adverse developmental, reproductive, neurological, and immune effects in both humans and wildlife."

- Direct and indirect effects,

- Energy requirements,

- Impact on urban quality and historic and cultural resources, and

- The means to mitigate adverse environmental impacts.

Once a draft report is ready, the federal agency must hold a hearing to allow for outside comments.

The EIS requirement applies not only to actions *undertaken* by the federal government, but also to activities *regulated* or *approved* by the government. For instance, the following projects required an EIS:

- Installing a work of art by Christo and Jeanne-Claude, which consisted of 5.9 miles of fabric panels suspended above the Arkansas River;

- Expanding the Snowmass ski area in Aspen, Colorado, because approval was required by the Forest Service;

- Killing a herd of wild goats that was causing damage at the Olympic National Park (outside Seattle); and

- Creating a golf course outside Los Angeles, because the project required a government permit to build in wetlands.

The EIS process is controversial. If a project is likely to have an important impact, environmentalists almost always litigate the adequacy of the EIS. Industry advocates argue that environmentalists are simply using the EIS process to delay—or halt—any projects they oppose. In 1976, seven years after NEPA was passed, a dam on the Teton River in Idaho burst, killing 17 people and causing $1 billion in property damage. The Department of the Interior had built the dam in the face of allegations that its EIS was incomplete; it did not, for example, confirm that a large, earth-filled dam resting on a riverbed was safe. To environmentalists, this tragedy graphically illustrated the need for a thorough EIS.

Researchers have found that the EIS process generally has a beneficial impact on the environment. The mere prospect of preparing an EIS tends to eliminate the worst projects. Litigation over the EIS eliminates the next weakest group. If an agency does a good faith EIS, honestly looking at the available alternatives, projects tend to be kinder to the environment, at little extra cost.

26-6b Endangered Species Act

Worldwide, 25 percent of mammals, 22 percent of reptiles, and 13 percent of birds are threatened with extinction. This threat is largely caused by humans. **The Endangered Species Act (ESA):**

- **Requires the Department of the Interior's Fish and Wildlife Service (FWS) to:**

  ○ Prepare a list of species that are in danger of becoming extinct or likely to become endangered; and
  ○ Develop plans to revive these species.

- **Requires all federal agencies to:**

  ○ Ensure that their actions will not jeopardize an endangered species; and
  ○ Avoid damage to habitat that is critical to survival of endangered species.

- **Prohibits:**
  - ○ Any sale or transport of these species;
  - ○ Any taking of an endangered animal species (taking is defined as harassing, harming, killing, or capturing any endangered species or modifying its habitat in such a way that its population is likely to decline); and
  - ○ The taking of any endangered plant species on federal property.

No environmental statute has been more controversial than the ESA. In theory, everyone is in favor of saving endangered species. In practice, however, the cost of saving a species can be astronomical. One of the earliest ESA battles involved the snail darter—a three-inch fish that lived in the Little Tennessee River. The Supreme Court upheld a decision under the ESA to halt work on a dam that would have blocked the river, flooding 16,500 acres of farmland and destroying the snail darter's habitat. To the dam's supporters, this decision was ludicrous: stopping a dam (on which $100 million in taxpayer money had already been spent) to save a little fish that no one had ever even thought of before the dam (or damn) controversy. The real agenda, they argued, was simply to halt development. Environmental advocates argued, however, that the wanton destruction of whole species will ultimately and inevitably lead to disaster for humankind. In the end, Congress overruled the Supreme Court and authorized completion of the dam. It turned out that the snail darter survived in other rivers.

The snail darter was the first in a long line of ESA controversies that have included charismatic animals such as bald eagles, grizzly bears, bighorn sheep, and rockhopper penguins, but also more obscure fauna such as the Banbury Springs limpet and the triple-ribbed milkvetch. In 2007, a federal court moved to protect the delta smelt by ordering officials to shut down pumps that supplied as much as one-third of southern California's water. (That case was in litigation for seven years, but was ultimately upheld by the appeals court.) Opponents of the ESA argue that too much time and money have been spent to save too few species of too little importance.

Those issues involve some of the 1,400 species in the United States that have already been listed. Deciding which species make the list is also controversial. In the first four decades after Congress passed the ESA, the FWS listed species at a rate of about 35 a year. Nearly 100 species had become extinct while on the list or waiting to be listed. Ultimately, environmental groups sued to force the FWS to act faster. But as the agency began adding species to the list, business groups threatened litigation. For example, the Independent Petroleum Association of America has expressed concern over the impact on oil and gas exploration if the Gunnison Sage Grouse is listed.

The following case discusses the advantages of protecting endangered species.

Gibbs v. Babbitt

214 F.3d 483
United States Court of Appeals for the Fourth Circuit, 2000

Case Summary

Facts: The red wolf used to roam throughout the southeastern United States. Owing to wetlands drainage, dam construction, and hunting, this wolf was on the endangered species list. The FWS trapped the remaining red wolves, placed them in a captive breeding program, and then reintroduced them into wildlife refuges in North Carolina and Tennessee.

About 41 red wolves wandered from the refuges onto private property. Richard Mann shot a red wolf that he feared might attack his cattle. Mann pled guilty to taking an endangered species without a permit.

Two individuals and two counties in North Carolina filed suit against the U.S. government, alleging that the antitaking regulation as applied to the red wolves on private land exceeded Congress's power under the Interstate Commerce Clause of the U.S. Constitution.

Issue: *Is the antitaking provision of the ESA constitutional?*

Decision: The ESA is constitutional.

Reasoning: The red wolf has great impact on interstate commerce, to wit:

- Red wolves are part of the $29 billion national tourism industry. Many tourists travel each year to take part in "howling events"—evenings spent studying wolves and listening to their howls. It has been predicted that the wolves could contribute somewhere between $40 and $180 million per year to the economy of North Carolina.

- The red wolf is a subject of scientific research, which is an important industry in its own right. And this research benefits us all—approximately 50 percent of all modern medicines are derived from wild plants or animals.

- If the red wolf thrives, it could be hunted for its pelt. The American alligator is a case in point. In 1975, this alligator was nearing extinction and listed as endangered, but by 1987, conservation efforts restored the species. Now, there is a vigorous trade in alligator hides.

- Mann shot a wolf that was threatening his livestock. Killing livestock also has an impact on interstate commerce. Under the Commerce Clause, any impact counts even if negative. It is also possible that red wolves help farms by preying on animals like raccoons, deer, and rabbits that destroy their crops.

Congress has the right to decide that protecting red wolves will one day produce a substantial commercial benefit to this country and that failure to preserve it may result in permanent, though unascertainable, loss. If a species becomes extinct, we are left to speculate forever on what we might have learned or what we may have realized. If we conserve the species, it will be available for study by, and the benefit of, future generations.

Chapter Conclusion

Environmental laws have a pervasive impact on our lives. Their cost has been great, causing higher prices for everything from cars and electricity to sewage. Some argue that cost is irrelevant—that a clean environment has incalculable value for its own sake. Others insist on a more pragmatic approach and want to know if the benefits outweigh the costs.

What benefits has the country gained from environmental regulation? The EPA estimates that the CAA has saved trillions of dollars by preventing lost work and school days, illness, and premature deaths. Sixty percent of the nation's waters are safe for fishing and swimming, up from only 30 percent when the Clean Water Act was passed.

Despite this progress, as a nation we still face many intractable problems. We have not developed consensus on global warming. We have done virtually nothing to assess and regulate the thousands of chemicals that pervade our lives. Many environmental projects, (such as Superfund and the Endangered Species Act) are tangled in a thorn bush of litigation. The EPA is overwhelmed by its obligations, sometimes taking decades to issue regulations, even as Congress cuts its budget.

Although many people, including many politicians, readily acknowledge the importance of the environment to both present and future generations, when the time comes to allocate funds, change lifestyles, and make tough choices, the consensus too often breaks down, with the result that resources are spent on litigation instead of the environment.

EXAM REVIEW

1. **CLEAN AIR ACT (CAA)**   Under the CAA, the EPA has the authority to regulate both the total amount of existing air pollution and its ongoing production. The EPA must also regulate greenhouse gases.

2. **CLEAN WATER ACT (CWA)**   Under the CWA, any discharge into navigable water from a point source is illegal without a permit (from the EPA or a state). The EPA must set national standards for water quality generally, and then each state has to develop plans to achieve these standards. States must also develop a plan for nonpoint source pollution.

3. **WETLANDS**   The CWA prohibits any discharge of dredge and fill material into wetlands without a permit.

EXAM Strategy

Question: In theory, Astro Circuit Corp. in Lowell, Massachusetts, pretreated its industrial waste to remove toxic metals. In practice, however, the factory was producing twice as much wastewater as the treatment facility could handle, and therefore, it was dumping the surplus directly into the city sewer. It was David Boldt's job to keep the production line moving. Has Boldt violated the law by dumping polluted water into the city sewer? What penalties might he face?

Strategy: Whenever water is involved, look at the provisions of the CWA. (See the "Result" at the end of this section.)

4. **RESOURCE CONSERVATION AND RECOVERY ACT (RCRA)**   The RCRA establishes rules for treating both hazardous and nonhazardous forms of solid waste.

5. **COMPREHENSIVE ENVIRONMENTAL RESPONSE, COMPENSATION, AND LIABILITY ACT (CERCLA OR SUPERFUND)**   Under CERCLA, anyone who has ever owned or operated a site on which hazardous wastes are found, who has transported wastes to the site, or who has arranged for the disposal of wastes that were released at the site is liable for (1) the cost of cleaning up the site, (2) any damage done to natural resources, and (3) any required health assessments.

6. **TOXIC SUBSTANCES CONTROL ACT (TSCA)**   Under TSCA, manufacturers must register new chemicals with the EPA.

7. **NATIONAL ENVIRONMENTAL POLICY ACT (NEPA)**   NEPA requires all federal agencies to prepare an environmental impact statement (EIS) for every major federal action significantly affecting the quality of the environment.

EXAM Strategy

Question: The U.S. Forest Service planned to build a road in the Nez Perce National Forest in Idaho to provide access to loggers. Is the Forest Service governed by any environmental statutes? Must it seek permission before building the road?

Strategy: Does a road significantly affect the quality of the environment? Is an EIS required? (See the "Result" at the end of this section.)

8. ENDANGERED SPECIES ACT (ESA) The ESA requires the Fish and Wildlife Service (FWS) to list endangered species and then prohibits activities that harm them.

> **3. Result:** Although Boldt was in an unfortunate situation—he could have lost his job if he had not been willing to dump the industrial waste—he was found guilty of a criminal violation of the CWA. There are worse things than being fired—such as being fired *and* sent to prison.
>
> **7. Result:** As an agency of the federal government, the Forest Service must prepare an EIS (under the National Environmental Policy Act) for every action that significantly affects the quality of the environment. Although the road itself may not have been significant enough to require an impact statement, its purpose was to provide access for logging, which did require an EIS.

Matching Questions

Match the following terms with their definitions:

___A. EPA

___B. ESA

___C. NEPA

___D. CERCLA

___E. RCRA

1. Regulates the cleanup of hazardous wastes improperly dumped in the past
2. Establishes rules for treating newly created wastes
3. Protects red wolves
4. The agency that regulates environmental policy in the United States
5. Requires all federal agencies to prepare an environmental impact statement

True/False Questions

Circle true or false:

1. T F In establishing national standards under the Clean Air Act, the EPA need not consider the cost of compliance.
2. T F The Clean Water Act requires anyone discharging pollution into navigable water to obtain a permit from the EPA.
3. T F Any individual, business, or federal agency that significantly affects the quality of the environment must file an EIS.
4. T F The number of acres of wetlands in the United States has remained roughly constant over the past decade.
5. T F Violating the environmental laws can be a criminal offense, punishable by a prison term.

MULTIPLE-CHOICE QUESTIONS

1. Which of the following statements are true of Superfund?

   I.   Anyone who has ever owned a site is liable for cleanup costs.

   II. Anyone who has ever transported waste to a site is liable for cleanup costs.

   III. Anyone who has ever disposed of waste at a site is liable for cleanup costs.

   (a) Neither I, II, nor III
   (b) I, II, and III
   (c) I and II
   (d) II and III
   (e) I and III

2. The EPA _____ have authority to regulate greenhouse gases. The states _____ impose their own standards for these gases.

   (a) does; can
   (b) does; cannot
   (c) does not; cannot
   (d) does not; can

3. For purposes of the Clean Water Act, Farmer Brown's fields _____ a point source. A canal that collects rainwater and discharges it into the Everglades _____ a point source.

   (a) are; is
   (b) are; is not
   (c) are not; is
   (d) are not; is not

4. Which of the following statements are true?

   I.   The EPA sets national air quality standards.

   II. The EPA is not allowed to develop plans to meet air quality standards.

   III. States have no right to set their own air quality standards.

   IV. The states develop plans to meet air quality standards.

   (a) II and III
   (b) III and IV
   (c) I and IV
   (d) I, III, and IV
   (e) I and II

5. The Toxic Substances Control Act:

   (a) requires manufacturers to test for safety all chemicals before they can be used in products.

   (b) requires the EPA to test for safety all chemicals before they can be used in products.

   (c) requires the EPA to test all chemicals, even if they are already being used in products.

   (d) permits the EPA to require testing of a chemical only if there is evidence that it is dangerous.

CASE QUESTIONS

1. Tariq Ahmad decided to dispose of some of his laboratory's hazardous chemicals by shipping them to his home in Pakistan. He sent the chemicals to Castelazo (in the United States) to prepare the materials for shipment. Ahmad did not tell the driver who picked up the chemicals that they were hazardous, nor did he give the driver any written documentation. What law has Ahmad violated? What does this law require? What penalties might he face?

2. The marbled murrelet is a seabird on the list of endangered species. Pacific Lumber Co. received permission to harvest trees from land on which the murrelet nested, on the condition that it would cooperate with regulators to protect the murrelet. But before the company met this condition, it went in one weekend and cut down trees. Caught in the act, it promised no more logging until it had a plan to protect the birds. But it went in again over the long Thanksgiving weekend to take down even more trees. A federal court then ordered a permanent halt to any further logging. There was no evidence that the company had harmed the murrelet. Had it violated the law?

3. *YOU BE THE JUDGE* **WRITING PROBLEM** The Lordship Point Gun Club operated a trap and skeet shooting club in Stratford, Connecticut, for 70 years. During this time, customers deposited millions of pounds of lead shot and clay target fragments on land around the club and in the Long Island Sound. Forty-five percent of sediment samples taken from the Sound exceeded the established limits for lead. Was the Gun Club in violation of the RCRA? **Argument for the Gun Club:** The Gun Club does not *dispose* of hazardous wastes, within the meaning of the RCRA. Congress meant the statute to apply only to companies in the business of manufacturing articles that produce hazardous waste. If the Gun Club happens to produce wastes, that is only *incidental* to the normal use of a product. **Argument for the Plaintiff:** Under the RCRA, lead shot is hazardous waste. The law applies to anyone who produces hazardous waste, no matter how.

4. Shell Oil sold pesticides to B&B, which allowed these chemicals to leak into the ground. Shell was aware that the leaks were occurring. B&B ultimately went bankrupt. Is Shell liable for the costs of cleaning up this site? Under what law?

5. Before the Department of Agriculture issued regulations on genetically modified beets, what steps did it need to take under the environmental statutes?

DISCUSSION QUESTIONS

1. Life is about choices—and never more so than with the environment. Being completely honest, which of the following are you willing to do? Why?

   - Drive a smaller, lighter, more fuel-efficient car.

   - Take public transportation or ride your bike to work.

   - Vote for political candidates who are willing to impose higher taxes on pollutants.

   - Insulate your home.

   - Unplug appliances when not in use.

   - Recycle your wastes.

   - Pay higher taxes to clean up Superfund sites.

2. The Navy wanted to conduct training exercises off the coast of California for sonar submarines. Scientists were concerned that the sounds emitted by the sonar would harm marine mammals, such as whales, dolphins, and sea lions. Environmental groups filed suit, asking that the Navy prepare an EIS. The Navy responded that these training exercises were important for national security and therefore it did not have to prepare an EIS. Was the Navy correct?

3. The Commonwealth of Virginia refused to prepare TMDLs for polluted Accotink Creek. When the EPA prepared its own set of TMDLs, Virginia sued to avoid compliance. Should Virginia be allowed to determine how much pollution to permit in its own waters? Alternatively, is it ethical

for Virginia to refuse to comply with the law and to prolong the dispute with litigation?

4. **ETHICS** Externalities pose an enormous problem for the environment. Often, the people making decisions do not bear the full cost of their choices. And businesses tend to fight efforts to make them pay these externalities. For example, CropLife America lobbied against a bill that would support research on the effects of chemicals on children. On the other hand, Nike resigned its seat on the board of the United States Chamber of Commerce in response to the Chamber's active lobbying against legislation that would regulate greenhouse gases. But Nike decided to remain a member of the group. What ethical obligation do American companies have to support environmental legislation that may impose higher costs? Do they have an obligation to look out for the greater good, or should they focus on maximizing their shareholder returns? What Life Principles would you apply? What would Kant and Mill say?

5. Is cost-benefit analysis an effective tool in environmental disputes? How do we measure the costs and benefits? How do we know what benefits we might gain from saving endangered species, or improving visibility at the Grand Canyon? Should you survey people to ask them how much it is worth? Or just think in terms of lives saved or sick days avoided? Or should we protect the environment regardless of cost?

CHAPTER 27

ACCOUNTANTS' LIABILITY

© Galyna Andrushko/Shutterstock.com

The accounting firm Arthur Andersen prided itself on its ethics. Old-timers would tell new recruits the legend of the firm's founder: How in 1914, the young Arthur Andersen had refused a client's request to certify a dubious earnings report. Although Andersen knew his firm would be fired and he might not be able to meet payroll, he nonetheless stood on principle. He was vindicated a few months later, when the client went bankrupt.

The firm collapsed in disgrace, the first major accounting firm ever to be convicted of a crime.

For its first 35 years, Andersen was primarily in the business of auditing public companies. Although its partners did not become rich, they made a good living. Then the firm entered the consulting business. Soon the consultants in the firm were generating much higher profits—and earning much higher salaries—than the auditors. Audits were fast becoming loss leaders to attract consulting business. Lower prices led to lower quality, as Andersen (and other auditors) felt they could not afford to invest as many hours in their audits. And the audits were becoming less effective because partners were increasingly afraid to deliver bad news for fear of losing both audit and consulting fees.[1]

To save money, the firm began to force partners to retire at 56. This system reduced the general level of experience and expertise. At the same time, accounting was becoming more complicated. Predictably, mistakes happened, lawsuits were filed, settlements were made.

Andersen's name was soiled by its role in a number of financial disasters, such as Global Crossing and WorldCom. And then there was Enron. Andersen opened an office in Enron's headquarters staffed with more than 150 Andersen employees. When the federal government began investigating Enron's bankruptcy, panicked Andersen employees shredded documents, leading to the firm's conviction on a criminal charge of obstructing justice. And

---

[1]Later in this chapter, the Winstar case provides a good example of this point.

so, the firm that began as a model of ethics in the accounting profession collapsed in disgrace, the first major accounting firm ever to be convicted of a crime.[2] The conviction was ultimately overturned by the Supreme Court, but by then it was too late. Andersen was dead.

Worse was to come. As more accounting irregularities came to light involving other companies and other auditors, and as scores of major companies restated (i.e., lowered reports of) their earnings, investors doubted they could rely on public financial statements. In the month following the Andersen verdict in June 2002, the stock market went into a tailspin, losing 20 percent of its value.

27-1 INTRODUCTION

27-1a Sarbanes-Oxley

After the stock market tumbled, Congress acted to restore investor confidence by passing the Sarbanes-Oxley Act of 2002 (SOX). The major provisions of SOX as it relates to auditors are as follows.

The Public Company Accounting Oversight Board

Public Company Accounting Oversight Board (PCAOB)
The PCAOB regulates public accounting firms.

Congress established the **Public Company Accounting Oversight Board (PCAOB)** to ensure that investors receive accurate and complete financial information. The board has the authority to regulate public accounting firms, establishing everything from audit rules to ethics guidelines. All accounting firms that audit public companies must register with the board, and the board must inspect them regularly. The PCAOB has the authority to revoke an accounting firm's registration or prohibit it from auditing public companies. The PCAOB recently reported that it had found flaws in one-third of the audits performed by the Big Four accounting firms.[3]

Reports to the Audit Committee

Under SOX, auditors must report to the audit committee of the client's board of directors, not to senior management. The accountants must inform the audit committee of any (1) significant flaws they find in the company's internal controls, (2) alternative options that the firm considered in preparing the financial statements, and (3) accounting disagreements with management.

Consulting Services

SOX prohibits accounting firms that audit public companies from providing consulting services to those clients on topics such as bookkeeping, financial information systems, human resources, and legal issues (unrelated to the audit). Auditing firms cannot base their employees' compensation on sales of consulting services to clients.

---

[2]Based in part on information in Ken Brown and Ianthe Jeanne Dugan, "Andersen's Fall from Grace Is a Tale of Greed and Miscues," *The Wall Street Journal*, June 7, 2002, p. 1.
[3]The Big Four are: Deloitte Touche Tohmatsu, Ernst & Young, KPMG, and PricewaterhouseCoopers.

SOX rules on these issues apply only in the United States. Globally, the Big Four earn between a sixth and a quarter of their income from consulting. It seems that consulting income will continue to be important to accounting firms because the audit market is mature while the consulting industry has significant growth potential.

Conflicts of Interest

An accounting firm cannot audit a company if one of the client's top officers has worked for that accounting firm within the prior year and was involved in the company's audit. In short, a client cannot hire one of its auditors to ensure a friendly attitude.

Term Limits on Audit Partners

After five years with a client, the lead audit partner must rotate off the account for at least five years. Other partners must rotate off an account every seven years for at least two years.

27-1b Consolidation in the Accounting Profession

The Big Four audit 98 percent of all companies in the United States with revenues over $1 billion. In such a concentrated industry, you would expect audit fees to rise. But instead, the audit fees that companies pay per dollar of revenue earned have declined even as SOX has required auditors to do more work. Industry observers have asked: Are auditors in fact doing all the work they are supposed to? Or are auditors taking risks because they believe that regulators are afraid to kill a Big Four firm? Should the Big Four be broken into smaller firms to enhance competition?

Ethics   The PCAOB is considering a new rule that would require accounting firms to disclose the name of the supervising accountant for each audit. Researchers have found that, in countries that have instituted such a requirement, the quality of audits has improved. Moreover, companies with more lenient auditors paid a price—their stock traded at a lower value and they paid higher interest rates on borrowed money. The accounting profession has fought hard against this proposal.[4]

What response should the accounting profession make to the PCAOB proposed rule on disclosing an auditor's name? To whom do accounting firms owe an obligation? What would Kant and Mill say?

27-1c Audits

Audits are a major source of potential liability for accountants, so it is important to understand what an auditor does.

Accountants serve two masters—company management and the investing public. Management hires the accountants, but investors and creditors rely upon them to offer an independent evaluation of the financial statements that management issues.

When conducting an audit, accountants verify information provided by management. Since it is impossible to check each and every transaction, they verify a *sample* of various types of transactions. If these are accurate, they assume all are. To verify transactions, accountants use two mirror image processes—vouching and tracing.

---

[4]Based on an article by Floyd Norris, "Accounting World, Still Resisting Sunlight," *The New York Times*, October 24, 2013.

Vouching

Auditors choose a transaction listed in a company's books and check backwards for original data to support it.

In **vouching**, accountants choose a transaction listed in the company's books and check backwards to make sure that there are original data to support it. They might, for example, find in accounts payable a bill for the purchase of 1,000 reams of photocopy paper. They would check to ensure that all the paper had actually arrived and that the receiving department had properly signed and dated the invoice. The auditors would also check the original purchase order to ensure that the acquisition had been properly authorized.

Tracing

An auditor takes an item of original data and tracks it forward to ensure that it has been properly recorded throughout the bookkeeping process.

In **tracing**, the accountant begins with an item of original data and traces it forward to ensure that it has been properly recorded throughout the bookkeeping process. For example, the sales ledger might report that 1,000 copies of a software program were sold to a distributor. The accountant checks the information in the sales ledger against the original invoice to ensure that the date, price, quantity, and customer's name all match. The auditor then verifies each step along the paper trail until the software leaves the warehouse.

In performing their duties, accountants must follow two sets of rules: (1) generally accepted accounting principles (GAAP); and (2) generally accepted auditing standards (GAAS). **GAAP** are the rules for preparing financial statements, and **GAAS** are the rules for conducting audits. These two sets of standards include broadly phrased general principles, as well as specific guidelines and illustrations. The application and interpretation of these rules require acute professional skill.

GAAP

"Generally accepted accounting principles" are the rules for preparing financial statements.

GAAS

"Generally accepted auditing standards" are the rules for conducting audits.

Proposed Changes

The PCAOB has recently proposed new rules that could make audit reports more useful to investors. Under these proposals, auditors would be required to discuss "critical audit matters" (CAMs); that is, any particularly difficult and troubling issues raised by the audit. For example, a CAM might be significant assets that are hard to value or a lack of sufficient evidence to support a valuation.

The proposed rules also require auditors to evaluate other parts of the annual report, such as Management's Discussion and Analysis, for any material omission or misstatement. And accounting firms would have to reveal in the financial statements how long they have audited a particular company, so that investors could assess their independence.

IFRS

"International financial reporting standards" are a set of international accounting principles that the SEC allows foreign companies to use.

In 2007, the Securities and Exchange Commission (SEC) began allowing *foreign* companies to use **international financial reporting standards (IFRS)** instead of GAAP.[5] Since, then, the SEC has been considering the possibility of requiring *U.S.* companies to use IFRS instead of GAAP. As business becomes more international, there is something to be said for a worldwide, consistent set of accounting rules. If U.S. firms used IFRS (as most countries now do), cross-country comparisons would be easier. It may be, too, that foreign companies and investors would be more willing to invest in the United States if everyone used international accounting rules. Many accounting firms and multinational companies have urged adoption of IFRS in the United States. Although, at this writing, it is possible that the SEC will *permit* U.S. companies to use IFRS, it seems unlikely that the agency will *require* them to do so.

The downside? Domestic companies are concerned about the cost of such a major change. Also, some of the IRFS standards are less detailed; for example, they provide less direction about the way in which companies report earnings. And countries that use the IFRS interpret them differently or create their own exceptions. As a result, some commentators worry that cross-company comparisons would be *more* difficult because observers will

---

[5]IFRS are established by the International Accounting Standards Board, a privately funded organization located in London.

not know how each country and each company interpreted the guidelines. Also, companies must report financial information to other places besides the SEC, such as to business partners, banks, and other regulators. Unless everyone accepts IFRS, companies could end up having to prepare two sets of financials.

Opinions

After an audit is complete, the accountant issues an opinion on the financial statements that indicates how accurately those statements reflect the company's true financial condition. The auditor has four choices:

1. **Unqualified opinion.** Also known as a **clean opinion,** this indicates that the company's financial statements fairly present its financial condition in accordance with GAAP. A less-than-clean opinion is a warning to potential investors and creditors that something may be wrong.

2. **Qualified opinion.** This opinion indicates that although the financial statements are generally accurate, there is nonetheless an outstanding, unresolved issue. For example, the company may face potential liability from environmental law violations, but the liability cannot yet be estimated accurately.

3. **Adverse opinion.** In the auditor's view, the company's financial statements do not accurately reflect its financial position. In other words, the company is lying about its finances.

4. **Disclaimer of opinion.** Although not as damning as an adverse opinion, a disclaimer is still not good news. It is issued when the auditor does not have enough information to form an opinion.

Clean opinion
An unqualified opinion. The company's financial statements fairly present its financial condition in accordance with GAAP.

27-2 LIABILITY TO CLIENTS

27-2a Contract

A written contract between accountants and their clients is called an **engagement letter.** The contract has both express and implied terms. The accountant *expressly* promises to perform a particular project by a given date. The accountant also *implies* that she will work as carefully as an ordinarily prudent accountant would under the circumstances. If she fails to do either, she has breached her contract and may be liable for any damages that result.

Engagement letter
A written contract by which a client hires an accountant

27-2b Negligence

An accountant is liable for negligence to a client who can prove both of the following elements:

- **The accountant breached his duty to his client by failing to exercise the degree of skill and competence that an ordinarily prudent accountant would under the circumstances.** For example, if the accountant fails to follow GAAP or GAAS, he has almost certainly breached his duty.

- **The accountant's violation of duty caused harm to the client.** In the following case, the accounting firm had clearly breached its duty. But had this wrongdoing actually caused harm to the client?

You be the Judge

Facts: Oregon Steel Mills, Inc., was a publicly traded company whose financial statements were audited by Coopers & Lybrand, LLP. When Oregon sold the stock in one of its subsidiaries, Coopers advised Oregon that the transaction should be reported as a $1 million gain. This advice was wrong, and Coopers was negligent in giving it.

Two years later, Oregon began a public offering of additional shares of stock. It intended to sell these shares to the public on May 2. Shortly before Oregon filed the stock offering with the SEC, Coopers told the company that the sale of its subsidiary had been misreported and that it would have to revise its financial statements. As a result, the offering was delayed from May 2 to June 13. During this period of delay, the price of the stock fell.

Oregon filed suit against Coopers, seeking as damages the difference between what Oregon actually received for its stock and what it would have received if the offering had occurred on May 2—an amount equal to approximately $35 million.

You Be the Judge: *Did Coopers' negligence cause the loss to Oregon?*

OREGON STEEL MILLS, INC. V. COOPERS & LYBRAND, LLP
336 Ore. 329
Supreme Court of Oregon, 2004

Argument for Oregon: Coopers was negligent in giving advice to Oregon. As a result, Oregon had to delay its securities offering for six weeks. During this time, the market price of Oregon stock fell, with the result that the company sold the new stock for $35 million less than it would have received on the original sale date. Someone is going to suffer a $35 million loss. It should be Coopers, which caused the loss, rather than Oregon, which was blameless.

Argument for Coopers: It is true that Coopers was negligent, the market price of the stock fell, and Oregon suffered a loss. However, to recover for negligence, the plaintiff must show that the loss was reasonably foreseeable.[6] When Coopers made its error, no one could foresee that, as a result, Oregon would suffer a loss two years later because its securities offering was delayed by six weeks. At the time of its mistake, Coopers did not know when the offering would take place, nor that one date would be more favorable than another. The decline in stock price was unrelated to Oregon's financial condition or Coopers' conduct. Coopers is not liable.

27-2c Common Law Fraud

An accountant is liable for fraud if (1) she makes a false statement of a material fact, (2) she either knows it is not true or recklessly disregards the truth, (3) the client justifiably relies on the statement, and (4) the reliance results in damages. For example, Kurt deliberately inflated numbers in the financial statements he prepared for Tess so that she would not discover that he had made some disastrous investments for her. Because of these errors, Tess did not realize her true financial position for some years, which caused her to make some poor investment choices. Kurt committed fraud.

A fraud claim is an important weapon because it permits the client to ask for punitive damages, which can be substantially higher than a compensatory claim.

27-2d Breach of Trust

Accountants occupy a position of enormous trust because financial information is often sensitive and confidential. Clients may put as much trust in their accountant as they do in their lawyer, clergy, or psychiatrist. **Accountants have a legal obligation to (1) keep all client**

---

[6]See Chapter 8 for a discussion of negligence.

information confidential and (2) use client information only for the benefit of the client. For example, Alexander Grant & Co. did accounting work for Consolidata Services, Inc. (CDS), a company that provided payroll services. The two firms had a number of clients in common. When Alexander Grant discovered discrepancies in CDS's client funds accounts, it notified those companies that were clients of both firms. Not surprisingly, these mutual clients fired CDS, which then went out of business. The court held that Alexander Grant had violated its duty of trust to CDS.[7]

> **Clients may put as much trust in their accountant as they do in their lawyer, clergy, or psychiatrist.**

EXAM Strategy

Question: Zapper, Inc., hired the accounting firm PriceTouche to determine if building an apartment building was financially feasible. After PriceTouche determined that the building would be profitable, Zapper started construction. Before the structure was complete, it burned to the ground. Although Zapper rebuilt it, the apartment building turned out not to be profitable, at least in part because of the delay in construction. Is PriceTouche liable to Zapper?

Strategy: There are three potential bases for liability—contract, negligence, and breach of trust. Which apply here?

Result: If PriceTouche did not perform as carefully as an ordinarily prudent accountant would under the circumstances, then it has violated its contract with Zapper and would be liable under contract law. It would also be negligent. But it would only be liable if its negligence caused the harm. It might be that the apartment building was not profitable because of the delays caused when it burned down during construction. If this is the case, PriceTouche would not be liable for negligence. There is no breach of trust because it has not violated client confidentiality.

27-3 LIABILITY TO THIRD PARTIES

No issue in the accounting field is more controversial than liability to third parties (those who are not clients, but nonetheless rely on audits, such as creditors and investors). Plaintiffs argue that auditors owe an important duty to a trusting public. The job of the auditor, they say, is to provide an independent, professional source of assurance that a company's audited financial statements are accurate. If the auditors do their job properly, they have nothing to fear. The accounting profession says in response that, if everyone who has ever been harmed, even remotely, by a faulty audit can recover damages, there will soon be no auditors left.

---

[7]Wagenheim v. Alexander Grant & Co., 19 Ohio App. 3d 7 (App. Ct., Ohio 1983).

27-3a **Negligence**

Accountants who fail to exercise due care are liable to (1) anyone they knew would rely on the information and (2) anyone else in the same class. Suppose, for example, that Adrienne knows she is preparing financial statements for the BeachBall Corp. to use in obtaining a bank loan from the First National Bank of Tucson. If Adrienne is careless in preparing the statements and BeachBall bursts, she will be liable to First Bank. Suppose, however, that the company takes its financial statements to the Last National Bank of Tucson instead. She would also be liable because Last Bank is in the same class as First Bank. Once Adrienne knows that a bank will rely on the statements she has prepared, the identity of the particular bank should not make any difference to her when doing her work.

Suppose, however, that BeachBall uses the financial statements to persuade a landlord to rent it a manufacturing facility. In this case, Adrienne would not be liable because the landlord is not in the same class as First Bank, for whom Adrienne knew she was preparing the documents.

In the following case, a potential employee relied on audited financial statements that proved to be faulty. Was the accounting firm liable?

ELLIS V. GRANT THORNTON

530 F.3d 280
United States Court of Appeals for the Fourth Circuit, 2008

CASE SUMMARY

Facts: For five years, the First National Bank of Keystone issued a lot of risky mortgage loans on which the borrowers defaulted. Keystone management also lied about the value of the loans. When the Office of the Comptroller of the Currency (OCC) first began to smell trouble, it required Keystone to hire a nationally recognized, independent accounting firm to audit its books. The bank hired Grant Thornton (GT) who assigned Stan Quay as the lead partner on the account. But he was negligent in conducting the audit and failed to notice a discrepancy of $515 million between the reported and actual value of the loans.

As Quay was finishing his audit, the board began talking with Gary Ellis about becoming president of the bank. Ellis already had a perfectly good job, so he was understandably reluctant to move to a bank that the OCC was investigating. To reassure him, the Keystone board suggested he talk with Quay and look at the bank's financials. Quay told Ellis that Keystone would receive a clean, unqualified opinion.

Quay did ultimately issue a clean opinion reporting shareholder's equity of $184 million when, in fact, the bank was insolvent. The first page of the report stated: "This report is intended for the information and use of the Board of Directors and Management of The First National Bank of Keystone and its regulatory agencies and should not be used by third parties for any other purpose." A week later, the Board voted to hire Ellis, who then quit his job elsewhere to join Keystone.

Five months later, the OCC declared Keystone insolvent and shut it down. Ellis was out of work. He filed suit against GT, seeking compensation for his lost wages. The district court ruled in favor of Ellis and granted him $2.5 million in damages. GT appealed.

Issue: *Was GT liable to Ellis for its negligence in preparing Keystone's financial statements?*

Decision: GT was not liable.

Reasoning: GT prepared its audit for the benefit of Keystone and the OCC. It did not know that Ellis, or any other potential employee, would be relying on the report. Keystone did not pay GT to review the bank's financial position with potential employees and, indeed, the accountants did not know about Ellis's involvement until *after* it had decided to issue the clean opinion. GT was not aware that it might be held liable for Ellis's lost wages. If the accountant is unaware of the risk, it cannot be held liable.

27-3b Fraud

Courts consider fraud to be much worse than negligence because it is *intentional*. Therefore, the penalty is heavier. **An accountant who commits fraud is liable to any foreseeable user of the work product who justifiably relies on it.** TechDisk manufactured disk drives. When customers placed more orders than the company could fill, executives feared that shareholders would flee the company if they found out about the shortage. So they boosted their sales numbers by shipping out bricks wrapped up to look like disk drives. Company accountants deliberately altered the financial statements to pretend that the bricks were indeed computer parts. These accountants would be liable to any foreseeable users—including investors, creditors, and customers.

27-3c Securities Act of 1933

The Securities Act of 1933 (1933 Act) requires a company to register securities before offering them for sale to the public. To do this, the company files a registration statement with the SEC. This registration statement must include audited financial statements. **If investors lose money, auditors are liable for any important misstatement or omission in the financial statements that they prepare for the registration statement**

The plaintiff must prove only that (1) the registration statement contained an important misstatement or omission and (2) she lost money. Ernst & Young served as the auditor for FP Investments, Inc., a company that sold tax shelter partnerships. These partnerships were formed to cultivate tropical plants in Hawaii. The prospectus for this investment neglected to mention that the partnerships did not have enough cash on hand to grow the plants. The investors lost their money. A jury ordered Ernst & Young to pay damages of $18.9 million.[8]

However, auditors can avoid liability by showing that they made a reasonable investigation of the financial statements in a registration statement. This investigation is called **due diligence**. Typically, auditors will not be liable if they can show that they complied with GAAP and GAAS.

Due diligence
An investigation of the registration statement

27-3d Securities Exchange Act of 1934

Under the Securities Exchange Act of 1934 (1934 Act), public companies must file an annual report containing audited financial statements and quarterly reports with unaudited financials.

Fraud

In these filings under the 1934 Act, an auditor is liable for making (1) a misstatement or omission of an important fact, (2) knowingly or recklessly, (3) that the plaintiff relies on in purchasing or selling a security. Note that accountants are liable only if they have acted knowingly or recklessly with an intent to deceive, manipulate or defraud. This requirement is called **scienter**. The following Landmark Case established this principle of liability.

Scienter
An action is done knowingly or recklessly with an intent to deceive, manipulate, or defraud

---

[8]Hayes v. Haushalter, 1994 U.S. App. LEXIS 23608 (9th Cir. 1994).

Landmark Case

ERNST & ERNST V. HOCHFELDER

425 U.S. 185
United States Supreme Court, 1976

CASE SUMMARY

Facts: For 19 years, Ernst & Ernst audited a small brokerage firm, First Securities Company of Chicago (First Securities). Leston B. Nay was president of the firm and owned 92 percent of its stock. He convinced some customers to invest funds in "escrow" accounts that would yield a high rate of return. And, indeed, from 1942 through 1966, they did. The investments were unusual in that the customers wrote their checks to Nay personally, not to First Securities. None of these escrow accounts appeared in First Securities' records.

As you perhaps have guessed, there were no escrow accounts. Nay was spending much of the customers' money on himself. The fraud came to light when he killed himself.

In investigating the fraud, customers discovered that Nay had had a rigid rule prohibiting anyone else from ever opening mail addressed to him, even if it arrived in his absence. The customers alleged that if Ernst had done a proper audit, they would have found out about this mail rule, which would have led to an investigation of Nay and discovery of the fraud.

The customers sued Ernst under the 1934 Act. The accounting firm filed a motion for summary judgment, alleging that liability under this statute requires scienter; that is, an intent to deceive, manipulate, or defraud. Ernst admitted that it had been negligent but denied any *intentional* wrongdoing. The trial court granted Ernst's motion, the Court of Appeals reversed, and the Supreme Court granted *certiorari*.

Issue: *Was Ernst liable under the 1934 Act when it acted negligently but not intentionally?*

Decision: Liability under the 1934 Act requires scienter. Ernst was not liable.

Reasoning: The language of the statute prohibits the use or employment of "any manipulative or deceptive device or contrivance." These words indicate that the goal of the statute was to prohibit intentional misconduct.

A look at the legislative history of the statute confirms this interpretation. A spokesman for the drafters interpreted this provision thus: "Thou shalt not devise any cunning devices." It is difficult to believe that any lawyer or legislator would use these words if the intent was to create liability for merely negligent acts or omissions.

This landmark case establishes the need for scienter. The following case provides an example of what scienter is. As you read the case, you might ask yourself why Grant Thornton accountants were willing to do what they did.

GOULD V. WINSTAR COMMUNS., INC.

692 F.3d 148
United States Court of Appeals for the Second Circuit, 2011

CASE SUMMARY

Facts: Grant Thornton (GT) audited Winstar, a broadband communications company that provided businesses with wireless Internet connectivity. Winstar was one of GT's largest and most important clients, but only 12 percent of the company's fees came from auditing, the rest were for consulting projects. Winstar asked that the partner in charge of its audit be replaced and also threatened to fire GT. In response, Winstar assigned two auditors who had no experience with telecommunications companies.

When Winstar's real revenues fell, it began to report fake ones. For example, it reported that a large percentage of its revenue was from equipment sales to Lucent Technologies, a strategic partner. Equipment sales were not part of Winstar's core business, and there was little documentation that these sales had taken place. Winstar also engaged in round-trip transactions in which it overpaid other companies for goods and services and, in return, those companies bought unneeded equipment from Winstar.

GT warned that these transactions were wrong, but ultimately issued an unqualified audit opinion. A year later, Winstar filed for bankruptcy protection. Winstar investors filed suit against GT under §10(b). GT filed a motion for summary judgment, which the trial court granted on the grounds that the firm had not acted with scienter. Plaintiffs appealed.

Issues: *Did GT act with scienter? Was it liable under §10(b)?*

Decision: Yes, GT acted with scienter and was liable under §10(b).

Reasoning: A finding of scienter requires evidence of deliberate illegal behavior. This standard is met (1) when conduct was so unreasonable that the defendant must have known it would cause harm or (2) when a defendant ignores obvious signs of fraud.

The evidence that GT consciously ignored Winstar's fraud goes beyond a mere failure to uncover wrongdoing. There was evidence that GT learned of and advised against the use of indisputably deceptive accounting schemes, but eventually acquiesced in the schemes by issuing an unqualified audit opinion.

The trial court found in favor of GT at least partly because its accountants had spent so much time and reviewed so many documents. But even great effort does not protect accountants who have nonetheless violated security laws.

Whistleblowing

Auditors who suspect that a client has committed an illegal act must notify the client's board of directors. If the board fails to take appropriate action, the auditors must issue an official report to the board. If the board receives such a report from its auditors, it must notify the SEC within one business day (and send a copy of this notice to its accountant). If the auditors do not receive this copy, they must notify the SEC themselves.

Joint and Several Liability

Traditionally, liability under the 1934 Act was **joint and several**. When several different participants were potentially liable, a plaintiff could sue any one defendant or any group of defendants for the full amount of the damages. If a company committed fraud and then went bankrupt, its accounting firm might well be the only defendant with assets. Even if the accountants had caused only, say, 5 percent of the damages, they could be liable for the full amount.

Congress amended the 1934 Act to provide that accountants are liable *jointly and severally* only if they *knowingly* violate the law. Otherwise, the defendants are *proportionately* liable, meaning that they are liable only for the share of the damages that they themselves caused.

Joint and several
All members of a group are liable. They can be sued as a group, or any of them can be sued individually for the full amount of the damages. But the plaintiff may not recover more than 100 percent of her damages.

27-4 CRIMINAL LIABILITY

Some violations by accountants are criminal acts for which the punishment may be a fine and imprisonment:

- The Justice Department has the right to prosecute willful violations under either the 1933 Act or the 1934 Act.

- The Internal Revenue Code imposes various criminal penalties on accountants for wrongdoing in the preparation of tax returns.

- Many states prosecute violations of their securities laws.

EXAM Strategy

Question: When Benjamin hired Howard to prepare financial statements for American Equities, he gave Howard a handwritten sheet of paper entitled "Pro Forma Balance Sheet." It contained a list of real estate holdings and the balance sheets of two corporations that Benjamin claimed were owned by American Equities. From this one piece of paper, without any examination of books and records, Howard prepared an Auditor's Report for the company. Benjamin used the Auditor's Report to sell stock in American Equities. Has Howard committed a criminal offense?

Strategy: Wilful violations of the securities laws are criminal offenses.

Result: A court held that Howard's actions were willful. He was found guilty of a criminal violation.

27-5 OTHER ACCOUNTANT-CLIENT ISSUES

27-5a The Accountant-Client Relationship

The SEC has long been concerned about the relationship between accountants and the companies they audit. Its rules require accountants to maintain independence from their clients. **For example, an auditor or her family must not maintain a financial or business relationship with a client.**

SEC rules on independence specifically prohibit accountants or their families from owning stock in a company that their firm audits. To take one woeful example, the SEC discovered that most of PricewaterhouseCoopers's partners were in violation of this rule, including half of the partners who were charged with enforcing it. Even worse, the firm had been caught violating the same rule only a few years before. The SEC notified 52 of the firm's clients that there were potential concerns about the integrity of their financial statements and even requested that some of the companies select a new auditor.

SEC rules of practice specify that an accountant who engages in "unethical or improper professional conduct" may be banned from practice before the SEC. Auditors who are banned or suspended cannot perform the audits that are required by the 1933 and 1934 Acts—quite a professional blow.

27-5b Accountant-Client Privilege

Traditionally, an accountant-client privilege did not exist under federal law. Accountants were under no obligation to keep confidential any information they received from their clients. In one notorious case, the IRS suspected that the owner of a chain of pizza parlors was under-reporting his income. The agency persuaded the owner's certified public accountant, James Checksfield, to spy on him for eight years. (The IRS agreed to drop charges against Checksfield, who had not paid his own taxes for three years.) Thanks to the information that Checksfield passed to the IRS, his client was indicted on criminal charges of evading taxes.

Then Congress passed the Internal Revenue Service Restructuring and Reform Act, which provides limited protection for tax advice that accountants give their clients. That is the good news. The bad news is the word *limited*. This privilege applies only in civil cases involving the IRS or the U.S. government. It does not apply to criminal cases, civil cases not involving the U.S. government, or cases with other federal agencies such as the SEC, nor does it apply to advice about tax shelters. Thus, this new accountant-client privilege would not have protected Checksfield's client because he was charged with a criminal offense.

Working Papers

When working for a client, accountants use the client's own documents and also prepare working papers of their own—notes, memoranda, and research. In theory, each party owns whatever it has prepared itself. Thus, accountants own the working papers they have created. In practice, however, the client controls even the accountant's working papers. **The accountant (1) cannot show the working papers to anyone without the client's permission (or a valid court order) and (2) must allow the client access to the working papers.** Under the Sarbanes-Oxley Act, accountants for public companies must keep all audit work papers for at least seven years.

Chapter Conclusion

Accountants serve many masters and, therefore, face numerous potential conflicts. Clients, third parties, and the government all rely on their work. The wrong decision may destroy the client, impoverish its shareholders, and subject its auditors to substantial penalties.

Exam Review

1. **THE PUBLIC COMPANY ACCOUNTING OVERSIGHT BOARD (PCAOB)** The PCAOB regulates public accounting firms.

2. **THE SARBANES-OXLEY ACT (SOX)**

   - Requires an accounting firm to make regular and complete reports to the audit committees of its clients;

   - Prohibits accounting firms that audit public companies from providing consulting services to those companies on certain topics, such as bookkeeping, financial information systems, human resources, and legal issues (unrelated to the audit);

   - Prohibits an accounting firm from auditing a company if one of the company's top officers has worked for the firm within the last year and was involved in the company's audit; and

   - Provides that a lead audit partner cannot work for a client in any auditing role for more than five years at a time.

3. **OPINIONS** After an audit is complete, the accountant issues an opinion that indicates how accurately the financial statements reflect the company's true financial condition. The auditor has four choices:

   - Unqualified opinion

   - Qualified opinion

   - Adverse opinion

   - Disclaimer of opinion

4. **LIABILITY TO CLIENTS FOR NEGLIGENCE**   Accountants are liable to their clients for negligence if:

- They breach their duty to their clients by failing to exercise the degree of skill and competence that an ordinarily prudent accountant would under the circumstances; and

- The violation of this duty causes harm to the client.

EXAM Strategy

CPA Question: A CPA's duty of due care to a client most likely will be breached when a CPA:

(a) Gives a client an oral instead of a written report.

(b) Gives a client incorrect advice based on an honest error judgment.

(c) Fails to give tax advice that saves the client money.

(d) Fails to follow generally accepted auditing standards.

Strategy: Accountants are not liable for every error they make, only if they fail to act like an ordinarily prudent accountant. (See the "Result" at the end of this section.)

5. **LIABILITY TO CLIENTS FOR COMMON LAW FRAUD**   Accountants are liable for fraud if:

- They make a false statement of a material fact;

- They know it is not true or recklessly disregard the truth;

- The client justifiably relies on the statement; and

- The reliance results in damages.

6. **BREACH OF TRUST**   Accountants have a legal obligation to:

- Keep all client information confidential; and

- Use client information only for the benefit of the client.

7. **LIABILITY TO THIRD PARTIES FOR NEGLIGENCE**   Accountants who fail to exercise due care are liable to (1) any third party they knew would rely on the information and (2) anyone else in the same class.

8. **LIABILITY TO THIRD PARTIES FOR FRAUD**   An accountant who commits fraud is liable to any foreseeable user of the work product who justifiably relies on it.

EXAM Strategy

Question: When Jeff said he did not want to invest in Edge Energies limited partnerships, the general partner suggested he call Jackson, the partnerships' accountant. Jackson told Jeff that Edge partnerships were a "good deal," that they were "good moneymakers," and "they were expecting something like a two-year payoff." In fact, Jackson knew that the operators were mismanaging these ventures and that the partnerships were bad investments. Jeff relied on Jackson's recommendation and invested in Edge. He subsequently lost his entire investment. Is Jackson liable to Jeff?

Strategy: Whenever there is intentional wrongdoing, think fraud. (See the "Result" at the end of this section.)

9. **SECURITIES ACT OF 1933** If investors lose money, auditors are liable for any important misstatement or omission in the financial statements that they provide for a registration statement.

10. **SECURITIES EXCHANGE ACT OF 1934** Under the 1934 Act, an auditor is liable for making (1) any misstatement or omission of a material fact in financial statements, (2) knowingly or recklessly, (3) that the plaintiff relies on in purchasing or selling a security. To be liable, an auditor must have acted with scienter.

11. **WHISTLEBLOWING** Auditors who suspect that a client has committed an illegal act must notify the client's board of directors.

12. **JOINT AND SEVERAL LIABILITY** Under the 1934 Act, accountants are liable jointly and severally only if they knowingly violate the law. Otherwise, they are proportionately liable.

13. **CRIMINAL LIABILITY** The Justice Department has the right to prosecute willful violations under the 1933 Act and the 1934 Act. The Internal Revenue Code imposes various criminal penalties on accountants for wrongdoing in the preparation of tax returns.

14. **AUDITOR INDEPENDENCE** An auditor or her family must not maintain a financial or business relationship with a client.

15. **ACCOUNTANT-CLIENT PRIVILEGE** A *limited* accountant-client privilege exists under federal law for tax advice that accountants give their clients.

16. **WORKING PAPERS** An accountant cannot show working papers to anyone without the client's permission (or a valid court order) and must allow the client access to the working papers.

---

4. Result: The correct answer is (d) because an ordinarily prudent accountant follows GAAS.

8. Result: Jackson was liable to Jeff for fraud because Jeff was a foreseeable user of the information and justifiably relied on it.

MATCHING QUESTIONS

Match the following terms with their definitions:

___A. GAAS

___B. Tracing

___C. Qualified opinion

___D. GAAP

___E. Vouching

___F. Unqualified opinion

1. Rules for preparing financial statements

2. When accountants check backward to ensure there are data to support a transaction

3. Clean opinion

4. Rules for conducting audits

5. When accountants check a transaction forward to ensure it has been properly recorded

6. When there is some uncertainty in the financial statements

TRUE/FALSE QUESTIONS

Circle true or false:

1. T F Auditors are liable under the 1933 Act only if they intentionally misrepresent financial statements.

2. T F Auditors generally are not liable if they follow GAAP and GAAS.

3. T F Under the 1934 Act, accountants are liable for negligent behavior.

4. T F If auditors discover that company officers have committed an illegal act, they must always report this wrongdoing to the SEC.

5. T F Under federal law, accounting firms may not provide any consulting services to companies that they audit.

MULTIPLE-CHOICE QUESTIONS

1. To be successful in a suit under the Securities Act of 1933, the plaintiff must prove:

Important Mistake in the Registration Statement	Plaintiff Lost Money
(a) No	Yes
(b) No	No
(c) Yes	No
(d) Yes	Yes

2. For an accountant to be liable to a client for conducting an audit improperly, the accountant must have:
   (a) acted with intent.
   (b) been a fiduciary of the client.
   (c) failed to exercise due care.
   (d) executed an engagement letter.

3. Which of the following statements about Sarbanes-Oxley is FALSE?
   (a) All accounting firms that audit public companies must register with the PCAOB.
   (b) Auditors must report to the CEO of the company they are auditing.
   (c) Auditing firms cannot base their employees' compensation on sales of consulting services to clients.
   (d) An accounting firm cannot audit a company if one of the client's top officers has worked for that firm within the prior year and was involved in the company's audit.
   (e) Every five years, the lead audit partner must rotate off an audit account.

4. For a client to prove a case of fraud against an accountant, the following element is *not* required:

   (a) The client lost money.

   (b) The accountant made a false statement of fact.

   (c) The client relied on the false statement.

   (d) The accountant knew the statement was false.

   (e) The accountant was reckless.

5. Dusty is trying to buy an office building to house his growing consulting firm. When Luke, a landlord, asks to see a set of financials, Dusty asks his accountant, Ellen, to prepare a set for Luke. Dusty shows these financials to a number of landlords, including Carter. Dusty rents from Carter. Ellen has been careless, and the financials are inaccurate. Dusty cannot pay his rent, and Carter files suit against Ellen. Which of the following statements is true?

   (a) Carter will win because Ellen was careless.

   (b) Carter will win because Ellen was careless and she knew that landlords would see the financials.

   (c) Carter will lose because Ellen did not know that he would see the financials.

   (d) Carter will lose because he had no contract with Ellen.

6. Ted prepared fraudulent financial statements for the Arbor Corp. Lacy read these statements before purchasing stock in the company. When Arbor goes bankrupt, Lacy sues Ted.

   (a) Lacy will win because it was foreseeable that she would rely on these statements.

   (b) Lacy will win because Ted was negligent.

   (c) Lacy will lose because she did not rely on these statements.

   (d) Lacy will lose because it was not foreseeable that she would rely on these statements.

CASE QUESTIONS

1. After reviewing Color-Dyne's audited financial statements, the plaintiffs provided materials to the company on credit. These financial statements showed that Color-Dyne owned $2 million in inventory. The audit failed to reveal, however, that the company had loans outstanding on all of this inventory. The accountant did not know that the company intended to give the financial statements to plaintiffs or any other creditors. Color-Dyne went bankrupt. Is the accountant liable to plaintiffs?

2. Penelope purchased securities offered by Hughes Homes, Inc., which sold manufactured housing. During its audit, Deloitte found that Hughes's internal controls had flaws. As a result, the accounting firm adjusted the scope of its audit to perform independent testing to verify the accuracy of the company's financial records. Satisfied that the internal controls were functional, Deloitte issued a clean opinion. After Hughes went bankrupt, Penelope sued Deloitte for violating the 1933 Act. She alleged that Deloitte's failure to disclose that it had found flaws in Hughes's internal control system was a material omission. GAAS did not require disclosure. Is Deloitte liable?

3. The British Broadcasting Corp. (BBC) broadcast a TV program alleging that Terry Venables, a former professional soccer coach, had fraudulently obtained a £1 million loan by misrepresenting the value of his company. Venables had been a sportscaster for the BBC but had switched to a competing network. The source of the BBC's story was "confidential working papers" from Venables's accountant. According to the accountant, the papers had been stolen. Who owns these working papers? Does the accountant have the right to disclose the content of working papers?

4. Medtrans, an ambulance company, was unable to pay its bills. In need of cash, it signed an engagement letter with Deloitte to perform an audit that could be used to attract investors. Unfortunately, the audit had the opposite effect. The unaudited statements showed earnings of $1.9 million, but the accountants calculated that the company had actually lost about $500,000. While in the process of negotiating adjustments to the financials, Deloitte resigned. Some time passed before Medtrans found another auditor, and, in that interim, a potential investor withdrew its $10 million offer. Is Deloitte liable for breach of contract?

5. A partnership of doctors in Billings, Montana, sought to build a larger office building. When it decided to finance this project using industrial revenue bonds under a complex provision of the Internal Revenue Code, it hired Peat Marwick to do the required financial work. The deal was all set to close when it was discovered that the accountants had made an error in structuring the deal. As a result, the partnership was forced to pay a significantly higher rate of interest. When the partnership sued Peat for breach of contract, the accounting firm asked the court to dismiss the claim on the grounds that the client could only sue for the tort of negligence not for breach of contract. Peat argued that it had performed its duties under the contract. The statute of limitations had expired for a tort case, but not for a contract case. Should the doctors' case be dismissed?

DISCUSSION QUESTIONS

1. **ETHICS** Pete, an accountant, recommended that several of his clients invest in Competition Aircraft. These clients passed this recommendation on to Arlene, who did invest. Unfortunately, Competition was a fraudulent company that pretended to sell airplanes. After the company went bankrupt, she sought to recover from Pete. Is Pete liable to Arlene? Whether or not Pete faces legal liability, is it a good idea for accountants to recommend investments to clients? Does that practice create any potential conflicts of interest?

2. Should the IFRS be adopted in the United States? What result would be best for companies? For investors?

3. Are the SOX rules on consulting services sufficiently strict? Should auditing firms be prohibited from performing *any* consulting services for companies that they audit?

4. Some argue that investors have unrealistic expectations about what an audit can accomplish, especially at the prices companies are willing to pay their accountants. Critics respond that this view is just another way of saying: "Given how much money accounting firms want to earn each year, they may not spend as much time as they should on an audit, especially in a complex situation." Arthur Andersen got in trouble, in part, because of its desire to maintain high levels of profitability. Is there a solution to this dilemma?

5. Under the 1934 Act, accountants are only liable if they act with scienter. Make an argument that they should be liable for negligence. What do you think is the right standard?

Property

CHAPTER 28

INTELLECTUAL PROPERTY

© Olga Danylenko/Shutterstock.com

Cooper is a producer at a small indie film company in Los Angeles. He puts together packages that have a script, a director, and actors. He then finds investors who pay to make the movie and distributors who purchase the right to release it in cinemas, on TV, and on DVD. (Although most people think that box office results are what count, the reality is that, historically, over half of most movies' revenue have come from home entertainment options such as DVD rentals and sales.)

Cooper is pretty excited about two packages he has put together: one stars established actor Robert de Niro, and the other features an up-and-coming director working with movie star Clive Owen. But his excitement has turned to disappointment—shockingly, he cannot find anyone willing to invest in either movie. Cooper hears the same thing from everyone: "DVD sales are way down, so we know we won't get the payback we used to. We can't afford to invest in as many movies."

On a flight to New York in search of investors, Cooper finds himself sitting next to a man who is watching a movie on his computer. Cooper knows this movie has not even been released to DVD yet. Clearly, the man has downloaded it from an illegal website. Cooper slowly crushes the plastic cup in his hand. What's wrong with that guy? Doesn't he know that movies cost money to make? Doesn't he realize people like him are killing an industry?

> On a flight to New York, Cooper finds himself sitting next to a man who is watching a movie on his computer .... Clearly, the man has downloaded it from an illegal website.

28-1 INTRODUCTION

For much of history, land was the most valuable form of property. It was the primary source of wealth and social status. Today, intellectual property is a major source of wealth. New ideas—for manufacturing processes, computer programs, medicines, books—bring both affluence and influence.

Although both can be valuable assets, land and intellectual property are fundamentally different. The value of land lies in the owner's right to exclude, to prevent others from entering it. Intellectual property, however, has little economic value unless others use it. This ability to share intellectual property is both good news and bad. On the one hand, the owner can produce and sell unlimited copies of, say, a software program; but on the other hand, the owner has no easy way to determine if someone is using the program for free. The high cost of developing intellectual property, combined with the low cost of reproducing it, makes it particularly vulnerable to theft.

Because intellectual property is nonexclusive, many people see no problem in using it for free. But when consumers take intellectual property—movies, songs, and books—without paying for it, they ensure that fewer of these items will be produced.

Some commentators suggest that the United States has been a technological leader partly because its laws have always provided strong protection for intellectual property. The Constitution provided for patent protection early in the country's history.

28-2 PATENTS

A patent is a grant by the government permitting the inventor exclusive use of an invention for a certain time period. During this period, no one may make, use, or sell the invention without permission. In return, the inventor publicly discloses information about the invention that anyone can use upon expiration of the patent.

Patent
A grant by the government permitting the inventor exclusive use of an invention for a specified period

28-2a Types of Patents

There are three types of patents: design patents, plant patents, and utility patents.

Design Patents

A design patent protects the appearance, not the function, of an item. Design patents are granted to anyone who invents a new, original, and ornamental design for an article. These types of patents protect the design of products ranging from Star Wars action figures to Coca-Cola bottles, Nike shoes to Ferrari chassis. Design patents last 14 years from the date of issuance.

Plant Patents

Anyone who creates a new type of plant can patent it, provided that the inventor is able to reproduce it asexually—through grafting, for instance, rather than by planting its seeds. For example, one company patented its unique heather plant.

Plant patents are not without controversy. Monsanto, a multinational biotechnology company, patented a genetically modified canola seed designed to resist certain herbicides. When the wind blew some of those patented seeds into an unsuspecting farmer's field and these grew into herbicide-resistant plants, the farmer decided to save some seeds for future plantings. Monsanto sued the farmer and won because the farmer had infringed Monsanto's plant patent by using it without permission.

Utility Patents

Whenever people use the word "patent" by itself, they are referring to a utility patent. In fact, about 94 percent of all patents are utility patents. For this reason, we will focus the rest of our patent discussion on them.

Utility patents are available to those who invent (or significantly improve) any of the following:

Type of Invention	Example
Mechanical invention	A hydraulic jack used to lift heavy aircraft
Electrical invention	A prewired, portable wall panel for use in large, open-plan offices
Chemical invention	The chemical 2-chloroethylphosphonic acid used as a plant growth regulator
Process	A method for applying a chemical compound to an established plant such as rice in order to inhibit the growth of weeds selectively; the application can be patented separately from the actual chemical
Machine	A device that enables a helicopter pilot to control all flight functions (pitch, roll, and heave) with one hand
Composition of matter	A sludge used as an explosive at construction sites; the patent specifies the water content, the density, and the types of solids contained in the mixture

28-2b Requirements for a Patent

To receive a patent, an invention must be:

Novelty
An invention must be new to be patentable.

- **Novel.** An invention is not patentable if it has already been (1) patented, (2) described in a printed publication, (3) in public use, (4) on sale, or (5) otherwise available to the public any place in the world. For example, an inventor discovered a new use for existing chemical compounds but was not permitted to patent it because the compounds had already been described in prior publications, though the new uses had not.[1] Note, however, that a disclosure does not count under this provision if it was made by the inventor in the one year prior to filing the application.

Nonobviousness
An invention must be unexpected to be patentable.

- **Nonobvious.** An invention is not patentable if it is obvious to a person with ordinary skill in that particular area. To determine if an invention is obvious, the Patent and Trademark Office (PTO) and courts look at the difference between it and existing technologies to see if that difference would be unexpected to someone skilled in the field (at the time of patenting). For example, if a four-legged stool with a square seat already exists, the patent application for four-legged stool with a circular seat would be denied because it is, duh, obvious. Changing the shape of the seat may be new and useful, but it is not unexpected enough to earn a patent.

Utility
An invention must be useful for its stated purpose to be patentable.

- **Utility.** To be patented, an invention must be useful. It need not necessarily be commercially valuable, but generally, it must *do* something. This requirement is the least restrictive: An invention will only be denied a patent if it has absolutely no practical utility. For example, the PTO has granted a patent for a comb in the shape of a bacon strip. To the PTO, useful does not mean *socially beneficial;* it simply means capable of some use.

[1]In re Schoenwald, 964 F.2d 1122 (Fed. Cir. 1992).

- **Patentable subject matter**. Not every innovation is patentable. A patent is not available solely for an idea, but only for its tangible application. Thus, patents are not available for laws of nature, scientific principles, mathematical algorithms, mental processes, intellectual concepts, or formulas such as $a^2+b^2=c^2$.

EXAM Strategy

Question: In 1572, during the reign of Queen Elizabeth I of England, a patent application was filed for a knife with a bone rather than a wooden handle. Would this patent be granted under current U.S. law?

Strategy: Was a bone handle novel, nonobvious, and useful?

Result: It was useful—no splinters from a bone handle. It was novel—no one had ever done it before. But the patent was denied because it was obvious.[2]

28-2c The Limits of Patentable Subject Matter: Living Organisms

Technology and business are constantly challenging patent law and the limits of what is patentable, especially when it comes to living things. Under what conditions are life forms patentable?

In 1980, the Supreme Court ruled that living organisms could be patented. The case of *Diamond v. Chakrabarty* involved genetically engineered bacteria that were used to treat oil spills. Those challenging the patent argued that living things could not be patented. The Court held that the bacteria—and other living organisms—could be patented if they are different from anything found in nature and a product of human ingenuity. That is, if they were made or significantly modified by humans. *Diamond v. Chakrabarty* made famous the phrase that patentable subject matter included "anything under the sun that is made by man." But, seriously, *anything*?

As a result of this ruling, the PTO began issuing patents on human genetic material. A total of 20 percent of all genes were patented, and the companies that owned these patents were valued at billions of dollars. But it was just a matter of time before patents on human genes were challenged in court. And that is exactly what occurred in the following groundbreaking Supreme Court case.

ASSOCIATION FOR MOLECULAR PATHOLOGY V. MYRIAD GENETICS, INC.

569 U.S. ___, 133 S. Ct. 2107
United States Supreme Court, 2013

CASE SUMMARY

Facts: Mutations in two genes known as BRCA1 and BRCA2 can dramatically increase the risk of breast and ovarian cancer. Myriad Genetics, Inc. (Myriad) obtained a number of patents on these genes. One patent gave Myriad the exclusive right to isolate an individual's naturally occurring BRCA1 and BRCA2 genes. Another

---

[2]Sakraida v. Ag Pro, Inc., 425 U.S. 273 (1976).

patent granted Myriad the exclusive right to synthetically create variants of BRCA1 and BRCA2 in the laboratory (cDNA).

A group of researchers filed a lawsuit seeking a declaration that Myriad's patents were invalid. The district court struck down the patents on the grounds that they covered products of nature. The appeals court reversed, holding that both DNA and cDNA were patentable. The Supreme Court granted *certiorari*.

Issues: *Is naturally-occurring DNA patentable? Is manmade cDNA patentable?*

Decision: No, naturally occurring DNA is not patentable, but manmade cDNA is patentable.

Reasoning: Laws of nature, natural phenomena, and abstract ideas are not patentable because they are the basic tools of science and technology. Allowing patents on what is found in nature would inhibit future innovation and would be at odds with the very point of patents, which is to promote creation.

In this case, Myriad did not create anything. Yes, it did find an important and useful gene, but separating that gene from its surrounding genetic material is not an act of invention. Just because Myriad's work was innovative, does not mean that the genes were new creations. Myriad simply located what nature made, which is not enough for patent protection.

cDNA is different because the lab technician creates something new when making cDNA. As a result, cDNA is not a "product of nature" and is patentable.

In short, Myriad's patent on DNA is invalid because DNA is a product of nature. However, its patent on cDNA is valid because this material is different from anything found in nature.

Ethics A chimera is a combination of two different animals' cells that creates a third animal with a genetic blend of the two. In 1984, the PTO granted a chimera patent for a "geep," a combination of a goat and a sheep created in a lab.

The America Invents Act states that "no patent may issue on a claim directed to or encompassing a human organism."[3] But the law does not define "human organism." Clearly it prohibits human cloning, because that process creates a human being, but how about other engineered animals containing human DNA? How about human-animal chimeras made in a lab (maybe called a "heep")? At what point is an invention *too human* to patent?

28-2d Patent Application and Issuance

To obtain a patent, the inventor must file a complex application with the PTO. If a patent examiner determines that the application meets all legal requirements, the PTO will issue the patent. If an examiner denies a patent application for any reason, the inventor can appeal that decision to the Patent Trial and Appeal Board in the PTO and from there to the Court of Appeals for the Federal Circuit in Washington.

Priority Between Two Inventors

When two people invent the same product, who is entitled to the patent—the first to invent or the first to file an application? Before 2013, the person who invented and first put the invention into practice has priority over the first filer. But in 2013 the law changed so that the first person to *file* a patent application has priority. This change brought the United States into conformity with most of the rest of the world.

---

[3]Leahy-Smith America Invents Act § 33.

Prior Sale

An inventor must apply for a patent within one year of selling the product commercially. The purpose of this rule is to encourage prompt disclosure of inventions. It prevents someone from inventing a product, selling it for years, and then obtaining a 20-year monopoly with a patent.

Infringement

A patent holder has the exclusive right to make, use, or sell the patented invention during the term of the patent. A holder can prohibit others from using any product that is substantially the same, license the product to others for a fee, and recover damages from anyone who uses the product without permission.

As permitted under the America Invents Act, the PTO has set up a *Track One* system that permits inventors to buy their way to the head of the line by paying an additional fee of $4,800 (for large companies) and $2,400 (for small). Track One applications are supposed to be decided within one year. Only 10,000 Track One applications will be accepted in any given year.

International Patent Treaties

Suppose you have a great idea that you want to protect around the world. **The Paris Convention for the Protection of Industrial Property requires each member country to grant to citizens of other member countries the same rights under patent law as its own citizens enjoy.** Thus, the patent office in each member country must accept and recognize all patent and trademark applications filed with it by anyone who lives in any member country. For example, the French patent office cannot refuse to accept an application from an American, as long as the American has complied with French law.

The **Patent Cooperation Treaty (PCT)** is a step toward providing more coordinated patent review across many countries. Inventors who pay a fee and file a so-called PCT patent application are granted patent protection in the 148 PCT countries for up to 30 months. During this time, they can decide how many countries they actually want to file in.

28-3 COPYRIGHTS

The holder of a copyright owns the *particular expression* of an idea, but not the underlying idea or method of operation. Abner Doubleday could have copyrighted a book setting out his particular version of the rules of baseball, but he could not have copyrighted the rules themselves, nor could he have required players to pay him a royalty.

Unlike patents, the ideas underlying copyrighted material need not be novel. For example, three movies—*Like Father Like Son*, *Vice Versa*, and *Freaky Friday*—are about a parent and child who switch bodies. The movies all have the same plot, but there is no copyright violation because their *expressions* of the basic idea are different.

A work is copyrighted *automatically* once it is in tangible form. For example, when a songwriter puts notes on paper, the work is copyrighted without further ado. But if she whistles a happy tune without writing it down, the song is not copyrighted, and anyone else can use it without permission. Registration with the Copyright Office of the Library of Congress is necessary only if the holder wishes to bring suit to enforce the copyright. Although authors still routinely place the copyright symbol (©) on their works, such a precaution is not necessary in the United States. However, some lawyers still recommend using the copyright symbol because other countries recognize it. Also, the penalties for intentional copyright infringement are heavier than for unintentional violations, and the presence of a copyright notice is evidence that the infringer's actions were intentional.

In the following case, you can imagine the author's frustration when a celebrity stole her thunder and her sales by writing a book on the very same topic. But did the celebrity violate copyright law?

LAPINE V. SEINFELD

375 Fed. Appx. 81
United States Court of Appeals for the Second Circuit, 2010

CASE SUMMARY

Facts: Missy Chase Lapine wrote a book called *The Sneaky Chef: Simple Strategies for Hiding Healthy Foods in Kids' Favorite Meals,* which was about how to disguise vegetables so that children would eat them. Her strategy was to add pureed vegetables to food that children like, such as macaroni and cheese. (We are not making this up.) Four months later, Jessica Seinfeld, the wife of comedian Jerry Seinfeld, published a book entitled *Deceptively Delicious: Simple Secrets to Get Your Kids Eating Good Food,* which featured recipes involving pureed vegetables in (guess what?) macaroni and cheese and other kid-friendly foods.

Lapine filed suit against Seinfeld, alleging violation of her copyright in *The Sneaky Chef.*

Issue: *Did Seinfeld violate Lapine's copyright in* **The Sneaky Chef?**

Decision: No, Seinfeld did not violate Lapine's copyright.

Reasoning: While it is true that the two books have a similar subject matter, no one can copyright the *idea* of

stockpiling vegetable purees for secret use in children's food. It is a fundamental principle of our copyright doctrine that ideas, concepts, and processes are not protected from copying.

As for the *expression* of the ideas in Lapine's work, it is true that the two books take a vaguely similar approach, including their titles, illustrations, health advice, recipes, and language about children's healthy eating. But any book with this subject matter would be likely to do the same. These features follow naturally from the work's theme rather than from the author's creativity.

In any event, the total concept and feel of the two books is different. *Deceptively Delicious* lacks an extensive discussion of child behavior, food philosophy, and parenting. Its recipes are simpler. And it uses brighter colors and more photographs than *The Sneaky Chef.*

In short, Lapine cannot copyright the *idea* of the book. And because the books look so different, it is clear that Seinfeld has not stolen the *expression* of Lapine's idea.

28-3a Copyright Term

Copyright term
The term for a copyright in the United States is the life of the author plus 70 years.

More than 300 years ago, on April 10, 1710, Queen Anne of England approved the first copyright statute. Called the Statute of Anne, it provided copyright protection for 14 years, which could be extended by another 14 years if the copyright owner was still alive when the first term expired. Many credit the Statute of Anne with greatly expanding the burst of intellectual activity that we now refer to as the Enlightenment.

American law adopted these same time limits, which stayed in effect until the twentieth century. Since then, copyright holders have fought aggressively to lengthen the copyright period. These efforts have been led by the Walt Disney Company, which wants to protect its rights in Mickey Mouse. **Today, a copyright is valid until 70 years after the death of the work's last living author or, in the case of works owned by a corporation, the copyright lasts 95 years from publication or 120 years from creation, whichever is shorter.** Once a copyright expires, anyone may use the material. Mark Twain died in 1910, so anyone may now publish *Tom Sawyer* without permission and without paying a copyright fee.

28-3b Infringement

Anyone who uses copyrighted material without permission is violating the Copyright Act. **To prove a violation, the plaintiff must present evidence that the work was original** and that either:

- The infringer actually copied the work; or

- The infringer had access to the original and the two works are substantially similar.

Damages can be substantial. In a recent case, a jury ordered SAP to pay Oracle $1.3 billion for copyright infringement of Oracle's software.

28-3c First Sale Doctrine

Suppose you buy a textbook that, in the end, you never read. (Unlikely, we know.) Under the **first sale doctrine,** you have the legal right to sell that textbook. **The first sale doctrine permits a person who owns a lawfully made copy of a copyrighted work to sell or otherwise dispose of the copy**. This exception to copyright is essential to commerce. If there were no first sale doctrine, people would not be able to rent movies or sell their used cars (or anything else). eBay might not exist. And museums and libraries would certainly be out of business, because any display or distribution of a copyrighted work would constitute infringement.

Note, however, that the first sale doctrine does not permit the owner to make a copy and sell it. If you read the textbook and then decide to sell it, that is legal. But it is not legal to scan the textbook onto your iPad and then sell the original or any copy of it.

First sale doctrine
Permits the owner of a copyrighted work to sell it

28-3d Fair Use

The **fair use doctrine** permits limited use of copyrighted material without permission of the author. We have all benefited from this doctrine. However, the boundaries between legal use and copyright violation can be subtle so it is important to pay attention to the following four factors, which determine whether a use is a fair one.

Fair use doctrine
Permits limited use of copyrighted material without permission of the author

1. **The purpose and character of the use.** When copyrighted material is used for purposes such as criticism, parody, comment, news reporting, scholarship, research, or education, it is more likely to be a fair use. For example, the Supreme Court upheld 2 Live Crew's right to create a parody of the song, "Pretty Woman."

2. **The nature of the copyrighted work.** Facts receive less protection than fiction. If we were not permitted to use, say, the facts described in a textbook, education would be stifled.

3. **The amount and proportion of the work that is used.** Digitally sampled songs use a riff from a classic song.[4] Faculty members show a short clip of a Hollywood film in class. A reviewer quotes a passage from a book without the author's permission. How do we know if these are acceptable uses? Less is more. Or, in the copyright context, less is more likely to be fair use. Some faculty had been in the habit of routinely preparing lengthy course packets of copyrighted material without permission of the authors. A federal court held that this practice violated the copyright laws because the material was more than one short passage and because it was sold to students.[5]

---

[4]Sampling is the act of using small portions of other sound recordings (a beat, a rhythm break, spoken or sung words) in constructing a new song.
[5]758 F. Supp. 1522 (S.D.N.Y. 1991).

4. **The effect of the use upon the potential market.** Courts generally do not permit a use that will deprive the copyright owner of income or compete with the original work. For example, when users conduct an Internet search for a picture, search engines bring up indexed thumbnail-sized images from various sites. A commercial photographer sued Google, claiming that its search results showing his photos violated his copyright in the images.[6] The court held that the Google search results were a fair use because the thumbnails did not harm the market or value of the original photographs. Instead, they were attracting potential buyers for the photos.

28-3e Digital Music and Movies

One of the major challenges for legal institutions in regulating copyrights is simply that modern intellectual property is so easy to copy. Many consumers are in the habit of violating the law by downloading copyrighted material—music, movies and books—for free. They seem to believe that if it is easy to steal something, then the theft is somehow acceptable. In one survey of adolescents and teenagers, 75 percent agreed with the statement, "file sharing is so easy to do, it's unrealistic to expect people not to do it."[7]

The entertainment world used to turn a blind eye, but illegal downloading is threatening the viability of recording companies, movie studios, and publishers. And the music industry is striking back. The Recording Industry Association of America (RIAA) developed a strategy of aggressively suing those who download large amounts of music illegally. In addition, a coalition of entertainment businesses sued Grokster, Ltd., and StreamCast Networks, Inc., two companies in the business of distributing free peer-to-peer software that allowed computer users to share electronic files. Although this software can be used for legal purposes (such as sharing the very briefs in that case), nearly 90 percent of the files available for download through Grokster or StreamCast were copyrighted. Even worse, the two companies encouraged the illegal uses of their software. For example, the chief technology officer of StreamCast said that "the goal is to get in trouble with the law and get sued. It's the best way to get in the news." The Supreme Court ruled that anyone who distributes a product or software and then promotes its use for the purpose of infringing copyrights is liable for the resulting acts of infringement by third parties.[8]

The Digital Millennium Copyright Act

Tom Tomorrow drew a cartoon that was syndicated to 100 newspapers, but by the time the last papers received it, the cartoon had already gone zapping around cyberspace. Because his name had been deleted, some editors thought he had plagiarized it.

In response to incidents such as this, Congress passed the **Digital Millennium Copyright Act (DMCA),** which provides that:

- **It is illegal to delete copyright information, such as the name of the author or the title of the article.** It is also illegal to distribute false copyright information. Thus, anyone who emailed Tom Tomorrow's cartoon without his name on it, or who claimed it was his own work, would be violating the law.

Digital Millennium Copyright Act

U.S. statute that updated copyright law for the Internet age

---

[6]Kelly v. Arriba Soft Corporation, 336 F. 3d 811 (9th Cir. 2003).
[7]http://pewinternet.org/Reports/2009/9-The-State-of-Music-Online-Ten-Years-After-Napster/The-State-of-Music-Online-Ten-Years-After-Napster.aspx?view=all#footnote25, or google "pew 10 years after napster."
[8]Metro-Goldwyn-Mayer Studios Inc. v. Grokster, Ltd.,545 U.S. 913 (2005).

- **It is illegal to circumvent encryption or scrambling devices that protect copyrighted works.** For example, some software programs are designed so that they can only be copied once. Anyone who overrides this protective device to make another copy is violating the law.

- **It is illegal to distribute tools and technologies used to circumvent encryption devices.** If you help others to copy that software program, you have violated the statute.

- **Internet service providers (ISPs) are not liable for posting copyrighted material so long as they are unaware that the material is illegal and they remove it promptly after receiving notice that it violates copyright law.** Thus, when Viacom sued YouTube for allowing copyrighted material to be posted online, the court ruled for YouTube. General awareness that many postings infringed copyright law did not impose a duty on YouTube to monitor its videos. Its only requirement was to respond when notified of infringement. YouTube had done just that, removing Viacom's property within one day of receiving its "takedown notice."[9]

28-4 TRADEMARKS

A trademark is any combination of words and symbols that a business uses to identify its products or services and distinguish them from others. Trademarks are important to both consumers and businesses. Consumers use trademarks to distinguish between competing products. People who feel that Adidas shoes fit their feet best can rely on the Adidas trademark to know they are buying the shoes they want. A business with a high-quality product can use a trademark to develop a loyal base of customers who are able to distinguish its product from another.

Trademark
Any combination of words and symbols that a business uses to identify its products or services and distinguish them from others

28-4a Ownership and Registration

Under common law, the first person to use a mark in trade owns it. Registration under the federal Lanham Act is not necessary. However, registration has several advantages:

- Even if a mark has been used in only one or two states, registration makes it valid nationally.

- Registration notifies the public that a mark is in use, which is helpful because anyone who applies for registration first searches the Public Register to ensure that no one else has rights to the mark.

- The holder of a registered trademark generally has the right to use it as an Internet domain name.

Under the Lanham Act, the owner files an application with the PTO in Washington, D.C. The PTO will accept an application only if the owner has already used the mark attached to a product in interstate commerce or promises to use the mark within six months after the filing. In addition, the applicant must be the *first* to use the mark in interstate commerce. Initially, the trademark is valid for 10 years, but the owner can renew it for an unlimited number of 10-year terms as long as the mark is still in use.

---

[9]Viacom Int'l, Inc. v. YouTube, Inc., 718 F. Supp. 2d 514 (S.D.N.Y., 2010).

28-4b Valid Trademarks

Words (Reebok), symbols (Microsoft's flying window logo), phrases (Nike's "Just do it"), shapes (Apple's iPod), sounds (NBC's three chimes), colors (UPS's brown), and even scents (grass-scented tennis balls) can be trademarked. To be valid, a trademark must be distinctive—that is, the mark must clearly distinguish one product from another.

The following categories are not distinctive and *cannot* be trademarked:

- **Similar to an existing mark.** To avoid confusion, the PTO will not grant a trademark that is similar to one already in existence on a similar product. Once the PTO had granted a trademark for "Pledge" furniture polish, it refused to trademark "Promise" for the same type of product.

- **Generic trademarks.** No one is permitted to trademark an item's ordinary name—"shoe" or "book," for example. Sometimes, however, a word begins as a trademark and later becomes a generic name. *Zipper, escalator, aspirin, linoleum, thermos, yo-yo, band-aid, ping-pong,* and *nylon* all started out as trademarks, but eventually became generic. Once a name is generic, the owner loses the trademark because the name can no longer be used to distinguish one product from another—all products are called the same thing. That is why Xerox Corp. encourages people to say, "I'll photocopy this document," rather than "I'll xerox it." Jeep, Rollerblade, and TiVo are names that began as trademarks and may now be generic. What about "app store"? Microsoft has sued Apple, disputing its right to trademark this term. Meanwhile, Facebook has trademarked "face," "book," "like," "wall," and "poke." The goal is not to prevent consumers from using these terms, but rather to warn off other companies.

- **Descriptive marks.** Words cannot be trademarked if they simply describe the product—such as "low-fat," "green," or "crunchy." Descriptive words can be trademarked, however, if they do not describe that particular product because they then become distinctive rather than descriptive. "Blue Diamond" is an acceptable trademark for nuts so long as the nuts are neither blue nor diamond-shaped.

- **Names.** The PTO generally will not grant a trademark in a surname because other people are already using it and have the right to continue. No one could register "Obama" as a trademark.

- **Scandalous or immoral trademarks.** The PTO refused to register a mark that featured a nude man and woman embracing.[10] This author once had a client who wanted to apply for a trademark for marijuana: "Sweet Mary Jane, she never lets you down." However, the client was unwilling to admit to affixing the name to his product and shipping it in interstate commerce. Medical marijuana is legal in 23 states today, but the PTO refuses to register marijuana trademarks.

28-4c Infringement

To win an infringement suit, the trademark owner must show that the defendant's trademark is likely to deceive customers about who has made the goods or provided the services. In the *Seinfeld* case, the court ruled there was no trademark infringement because consumers would not be confused by the names or covers of the two books. On the other hand, auction website eBay did prevent a seller of perfumes from using the name Perfumebay. The court ruled that the use of "ebay" confused consumers.[11]

---

[10]In re McGinley, 660 F.2d 481 (C.C.P.A. 1981).
[11]Perfumebay.com, Inc. v. eBay, Inc., 506 F.3d 1165 (9th Cir. 2007).

The following case raises an issue of confusion in cyberspace. Once again, the Internet is challenging intellectual property laws that were not conceived with this technology in mind.

You be the Judge

NETWORK AUTOMATION, INC. v. ADVANCED SYSTEMS CONCEPTS, INC.

637 F. 3d 1137
United States Court of Appeals for the Ninth Circuit, 2011

Facts: Network Automation and Advanced Systems Concepts sold competing software that they both advertised on the Internet. Systems sold its product under the trademarked name Active-Batch. Customers paid between $995 and $10,995 for these software programs.

Google AdWords is a program that sells "keywords," which are search terms that trigger the display of a sponsor's advertisement. Although ActiveBatch was Systems' trademark, Network purchased it as a keyword. This purchase meant that anyone who googled "ActiveBatch" would see a web page where the top results were links to Systems's own website and various articles about the product. But in the "Sponsored Sites" section of the page, users saw Network's ad. This ad did not use the word "ActiveBatch."

You Be the Judge: *Has Network violated Systems's trademark by purchasing ActiveBatch as a Google keyword?*

Argument for Systems: By purchasing ActiveBatch as a Google keyword, Network is deliberately confusing customers about whose product it really is. Few customers analyze the web address of an ad to make sure they are going to the right website. Customers could easily assume that whatever web address comes up belongs to the rightful owner.

When customers search for a generic term, they know that they will encounter links from a variety of sources, but when they look for a trade name, they expect to be linked only to that specific product. The use of another company's trade name can create tremendous confusion.

Argument for Network: Today, most consumers are sophisticated about the Internet. They skip from site to site, ready to hit the Back button whenever they are not satisfied with a site's contents. Consumers do not form any firm expectations about the sponsorship of a website until they have seen the landing page—if then.

Even if Systems's arguments were true for consumer purchases, the typical customer for this software is a sophisticated businessperson buying an expensive product. These purchasers are likely to be very careful and will not be confused by Google ads.

In the end, Network's intent was not to confuse consumers but rather to allow them to compare its product to ActiveBatch. That goal is a completely appropriate use of a trademark.

28-4d International Trademark Treaties

Under the **Paris Convention,** if someone registers a trademark in one country, then he has a grace period of six months during which he can file in any other country using the same original filing date. Under the **Madrid Agreement,** any trademark registered with the international registry is valid in all signatory countries. (The United States is a signatory.) The **Trademark Law Treaty** simplifies and harmonizes the process of applying for trademarks around the world. Now, a U.S. firm seeking international trademark protection need file only one application, in English, with the PTO, which sends the application to the World Intellectual Property Organization (WIPO), which transmits it to each country in which the applicant would like trademark protection.

EXAM Strategy

Question: Jerry Falwell was a nationally known Baptist minister whose website was falwell.com. One of his most outspoken critics registered the website fallwell.com— note the misspelling—to criticize the minister's views on homosexuality. This site has a disclaimer indicating that it was not affiliated with Reverend Falwell. The minister sued fallwell.com, alleging a violation of trademark law and the anti cybersquatting statute. Was there a violation?

Strategy: To win a trademark claim, the reverend must show that there was some confusion between the two sites. To win the cybersquatting claim, he must show bad faith on the part of fallwell.com.

Result: The reverend lost on both counts. The court ruled that there was no confusion—fallwell.com had a clear disclaimer. Also, there was no indication of bad faith. The court was reluctant to censor political commentary.

28-5 TRADE SECRETS

Trade secrets—such as the formula for Coca-Cola—can be a company's most valuable asset. It has been estimated that the theft of trade secrets costs U.S. businesses $100 billion a year. Under the Uniform Trade Secrets Act (UTSA), **a trade secret is a formula, device, process, method, or compilation of information that, when used in business, gives the owner an advantage over competitors who do not know it.** In determining if information is a trade secret, courts consider:

Trade secret
A formula, device, process, method, or compilation of information that, when used in business, gives the owner an advantage over competitors.

- How difficult (and expensive) was the information to obtain? Was it readily available from other sources?

- Does the information create an important competitive advantage?

- Did the company make a reasonable effort to protect it?

Although a company can patent some types of trade secrets, it may be reluctant to do so because patent registration requires that the formula be disclosed publicly. In addition, patent protection expires after 20 years. Some types of trade secrets cannot be patented— customer lists, business plans, and marketing strategies.

The following case deals with a typical issue: How much information can employees take with them when they start their own, competing business?

POLLACK V. SKINSMART DERMATOLOGY AND AESTHETIC CENTER P.C.

68 Pa. D. & C. 4th 417
Common Pleas Court of Philadelphia County, Pennsylvania, 2004

CASE SUMMARY

Facts: Dr. Andrew Pollack owned the Philadelphia Institute of Dermatology (PID), a dermatology practice. Drs. Toby Shawe and Samy Badawy worked for PID as independent contractors, receiving a certain percentage of the revenues from each patient they treated. Natalie Wilson was Dr. Pollack's medical assistant.

Pollack tentatively agreed to sell the practice to Shawe and Badawy. But instead of buying his practice, the two doctors decided to start their own, which they called Skinsmart. They executed a lease for the Skinsmart office space, offered Wilson a job, and instructed PID staff members to make copies of their appointment books and printouts of the patient list. Then they abruptly resigned from PID. Wilson called PID patients to reschedule procedures at Skinsmart. The two doctors also called patients and sent out a mailing to patients and referring physicians to tell them about Skinsmart.

Pollack filed suit, alleging that the two doctors had misappropriated trade secrets.

Issue: *Did Shawe and Badawy misappropriate trade secrets from PID?*

Decision: Yes, the two doctors misappropriated trade secrets.

Reasoning: The right to protect trade secrets must be balanced against the right of individuals to pursue whatever occupation they choose. For this reason, secrets will only be protected if they are the particular information of the employer, not general secrets of the trade. Pollack must also demonstrate that the trade secrets had value and importance to his business and that he either discovered or owned the secrets.

Against this backdrop, it is clear the patient list is a trade secret, worthy of protection. Patient information is confidential and is not known to anyone outside the practice. Pollack relied upon the patient list as the core component of his practice. For this reason, it is valuable. He made substantial effort to compile the list over a number of years. It contained 20,000 names with related information. He spent money on computers, software, and employees to keep and maintain the list. He also sought to protect the secrecy of the information. Within PID's offices, the information was not universally known or accessible. Not every staff member, including the practicing physicians, could pull the records. Wilson did not have access to them, and the doctors relied on other PID employees to access the patient list.

Chapter Conclusion

For many individuals and companies, intellectual property is the most valuable asset they will ever own. As its economic value increases, so does the need to understand the rules of intellectual property law.

EXAM REVIEW

	Patent	Copyright	Trademark	Trade Secrets
Protects:	An invention that is the tangible application of an idea	The tangible expression of an idea, but not the idea itself	Words and symbols that a business uses to identify its products or services	Information that, when used in business, gives its owner an advantage over competitors
Requirements for protections:	Application approved by the PTO	Automatic once it is in tangible form	Must be used on the product in interstate commerce	Must be kept confidential
Duration:	20 years	70 years after death of the author or, for a corporation, 95 years from publication or 120 years from creation, whichever is shorter	10 years, but can be renewed an unlimited number of times	As long as it is kept confidential

MATCHING QUESTIONS

Match the following terms with their definitions:

___A. Patent

___B. Copyright

___C. Trade secrets

___D. Trademark

___E. Paris Convention

1. Protects the particular expression of an idea
2. A word that a business uses to identify a product
3. Extends patent protection overseas
4. Grants the inventor exclusive use of an invention
5. Compilation of information that would give its owner an advantage in business

TRUE/FALSE QUESTIONS

Circle true or false:

1. T F Once you have purchased a CD and copied it onto your iPod, it is legal to give the CD to a friend.
2. T F A provisional patent lasts until the product is used in interstate commerce.
3. T F In the case of corporations, copyright protection lasts 120 years from the product's creation.
4. T F Under the fair use doctrine, you have the right to make a photocopy of a chapter of this textbook for a classmate.
5. T F The first person to file the application is entitled to a patent over someone else who invented the product first.

MULTIPLE-CHOICE QUESTIONS

1. To receive a patent, an invention must meet all of the following tests, except:
   (a) it has not ever been used anyplace in the world.
   (b) it is a new idea.
   (c) it has never been described in a publication.
   (d) it is nonobvious.
   (e) it is useful.

2. After the death of Babe Ruth, one of the most famous baseball players of all time, his daughters registered the name "Babe Ruth" as a trademark. Which of the following uses would be legal without the daughters' permission?
   I. Publication of a baseball calendar with photos of Ruth
   II. Sales of a "Babe Ruth" bat

III. Sales of Babe Ruth autographs

(a) Neither I, II, nor III

(b) Just I

(c) Just II

(d) Just III

(e) I and III

3. To prove a violation of copyright law, the plaintiff does not need to prove that the infringer actually copied the work, but she does need to prove:

I.   the item has a © symbol on it.

II. the infringer had access to the original.

III. the two works are similar.

(a) I, II, and III

(b) II and III

(c) I and II

(d) I and III

(e) Neither I, II, nor III

4. Eric is a clever fellow who knows all about computers. He:

I.   removed the author's name from an article he found on the Internet and sent it via email to his lacrosse team, telling them he wrote it.

II. figured out how to unscramble his roommate's cable signal so they could watch cable on a second TV.

III. taught the rest of his lacrosse team how to unscramble cable signals.

Which of these activities is legal under the Digital Millennium Copyright Act?

(a) I, II, and III

(b) Neither I, II, nor III

(c) II and III

(d) Just III

(e) Just I

5. Which of the following items *cannot* be trademarked?

(a) A color

(b) A symbol

(c) A phrase

(d) A surname

(e) A shape

6. Donald Trump wanted to copyright the phrase "You're Fired!" which he used on his reality show, *The Apprentice*. He:

(a) can copyright it only if he registers it.

(b) can copyright it only if it is in a tangible form.

(c) cannot copyright it because it is not novel.

(d) none of the above.

CASE QUESTIONS

1. While in college, David invented a new and useful machine to make macaroni and cheese (he called it the "Mac n'Cheeser"). It was like nothing on the market, but David did not apply for a patent. At that time, he offered to sell his invention to several kitchen products companies. His offers were all rejected, and he never sold the invention. Years later, he decided to apply for a utility patent. Is David entitled to a utility patent?

2. Rebecca Reyher wrote (and copyrighted) a children's book entitled *My Mother Is the Most Beautiful Woman in the World.* The story was based on a Russian folktale told to her by her own mother. Years later, the children's TV show *Sesame Street* televised a skit entitled "The Most Beautiful Woman in the World." The *Sesame Street* version took place in a different locale and had fewer frills, but the sequence of events in both stories was identical. Has *Sesame Street* infringed Reyher's copyright?

3. **ETHICS** After Edward Miller left his job as a salesperson at the New England Insurance Agency, Inc., he took some of his New England customers to his new employer. At New England, the customer lists had been kept in file cabinets. Although the company did not restrict access to these files, it said there was an understanding to the effect that "you do not peruse my files and I do not peruse yours." The lists were not marked "confidential" or "not to be disclosed." Did Miller steal New England's trade secrets? Whether or not he violated the law, was it ethical for him to use this information at his new job? What is your Life Principle?

4. In the documentary movie *Expelled: No Intelligence Allowed*, there was a 15-second clip of "Imagine," a song by John Lennon. The purpose of the scene was to criticize the song's message. His wife and sons, who held the copyright, sued to block this use of the song. Under what theory did the movie makers argue that they had the right to use this music? Did they win?

5. Roger Schlafly applied for a patent for two prime numbers. (A prime number cannot be evenly divided by any number other than itself and 1. Examples of primes are 2, 3, 5, 7, 11, 13.) Schlafly's numbers are a bit longer—one is 150 digits, the other is 300. His numbers, when used together, can help perform the type of mathematical operation necessary for exchanging coded messages by computer. Should the PTO issue this patent?

6. Sequenom developed a noninvasive prenatal diagnostic test to assess the risk of Down syndrome and other chromosomal abnormalities in fetuses. The test analyzes DNA from the fetus that is found in the mother's blood. Prior to this test, women had to undergo invasive tests that carried a slight risk of miscarriage. The PTO awarded Sequenom a patent on the test, but other diagnostic testing companies sued to invalidate the patent. Is Sequenom's patent valid?

EXAM Strategy

7. Question: A man asked a question of the advice columnist at his local newspaper. His wife had thought of a clever name for an automobile. He wanted to know if there was any way they could own or register the name so that no one else could use it. If you were the columnist, how would you respond?

Strategy: McMahon cannot copyright an idea—only the *expression* of an idea. (See the "Result" at the end of this section.)

EXAM Strategy

8. Question: Frank B. McMahon wrote one of the first psychology textbooks to feature a light and easily readable style. He also included slang and examples that appealed to a youthful student market. Charles G. Morris wrote a psychology textbook that copied McMahon's style. Has Morris infringed McMahon's copyright?

Strategy: McMahon cannot copyright an idea—only the *expression* of an idea. (See the "Result" at the end of this section.)

<u>**7. Result:**</u>   The couple could not trademark the name unless they had already or were intending to attach it to a product used in interstate commerce. So unless they had plans to manufacture a car, they could not trademark the name.

<u>**8. Result:**</u>   The style of a textbook is an idea and not copyrightable. Thus, Morris could write a book with funny stories, just not the same stories told in the same way as in McMahon's book. Morris did not infringe McMahon's copyright.

DISCUSSION QUESTIONS

1. **ETHICS** Virtually any TV show, movie, or song can be downloaded for free on the Internet. Most of this material is copyrighted and was very expensive to produce. Most of it is also available for a fee through such legitimate sites as iTunes. What is your ethical obligation? Should you pay $1.99 to download an episode of *Big Bang Theory* from iTunes or take it for free from an illegal site? What is your Life Principle?

2. For much of history, the copyright term was limited to 28 years. Now it is as long as 120 years. What is a fair copyright term? Some commentators argue that because so much intellectual property is stolen, owners need longer protection. Do you agree with this argument?

3. Should Amazon be able to patent the One-Click method of ordering? What about Facebook's patent on a process that "dynamically provides a news feed about a user of a social network"? Were these inventions novel and nonobvious? What should the standard be for business method patents?

4. Fredrik Colting wrote a book entitled *60 Years Later: Coming Through the Rye*, a riff on J. D. Salinger's famous *Catcher in the Rye*. Colting's book imagined how Salinger's protagonist, Holden Caulfield, would view life as a 76-year-old. Alice Randall wrote a novel entitled *The Wind Done Gone*, which retells the Civil War novel *Gone with the Wind* from the perspective of Scarlett O'Hara's (imagined) black half-sister. Both Colting and Randall were sued, and both alleged fair use. Should they win?

5. Music stars Beyoncé and Jay-Z named their newborn daughter Blue Ivy and then rushed to trademark the name, because they planned to use it in commerce. Their application was partially denied because a wedding planner in Massachusetts was already using "Blue Ivy" as the name of her business. Is this the correct outcome? Should people have priority in protecting personal names? Should a small business have priority over what would surely have been a much larger, more profitable use of this name?

6. The America Invents Act allows inventors to "buy" their way to the front of the line and expedite review of their inventions through a Track One application. This clearly favors those applicants who can pay. Do you agree with this practice? Why or why not?

CHAPTER 29

REAL PROPERTY AND LANDLORD-TENANT LAW

© Olga Danylenko/Shutterstock.com

Some men have staked claims to land for its oil; others, for its gold. But Paul Termarco and Gene Murdoch are staking their claim to an island using ... hot dogs. Their quest to market frankfurters in the New Jersey wilderness has made their children blush with embarrassment, their wives shrug in bewilderment, and strangers burst into laughter. But for three years, the two friends from West Milford have sold chili dogs, cheese dogs, and the ever-traditional, hold-everything-but-the-mustard hot dogs from a tiny island in Greenwood Lake. Now it seems as though everyone knows about "Hot Dog Island."

"People love it," said Termarco. "They say, 'Thank you for being here.' I always say, 'No. Thank you.'"

> But Paul Termarco and Gene Murdoch are staking their claim to an island using ... hot dogs.

The personalized service and the inexpensive prices (hot dogs cost $1.75; chili dogs, cheese dogs, and sauerkraut, $2) have cultivated a base of regulars. "I think it's great. It's better than going to a restaurant for two hours and spending a lot of money," said Joan Vaillant, who frequently jet-skis to the island for hot dogs slathered in mustard.

At two-eighths of an acre, the island's pile of craggy rocks, scrubby bushes, and a few ash trees are difficult to spot. Termarco doesn't mind. "Not everyone can say they own an island," he boasted. Termarco and Murdoch decided to claim the slip of land after chatting with a local restaurateur a few years ago. Termarco had just finished suggesting that the man expand his lakeside business to the island when Murdoch kicked his friend under the table.

"We left thinking, 'We can do this ourselves,'" said Murdoch, who rushed to the township offices the following day to see who owned the island. Property records showed that the state owned the lake and lake floor, but nobody owned the island. An attorney told them about the law of adverse possession written in the 1820s. If Murdoch and Termarco could show that they used the island for five years, it would be theirs. As crazy as the scheme sounded, Murdoch figured it was worth trying.[1]

Can two friends acquire an island simply by pretending they own it? Possibly. The law of adverse possession permits people to obtain title to land by using it if they meet certain criteria, which we examine later in the chapter. Real property law can provide surprises.

29-1 NATURE OF REAL PROPERTY

Property falls into three categories: real, personal, and intellectual. Real property, which is the focus of this chapter, usually consists of the following:

- **Land.** Land is the most common and important form of real property. In England, land was historically the greatest source of wealth and social status, far more important than industrial or commercial enterprises. As a result, the law of real property has been of paramount importance for nearly 1,000 years, developing very gradually to reflect changing conditions. Some real property terms sound medieval for the simple reason that they *are* medieval. By contrast, the common law of torts and contracts is comparatively new.

- Real property usually also includes anything underground ("subsurface rights"), and some amount of airspace above land ("air rights").

- **Buildings.** Buildings are real property. Houses, office buildings, apartment complexes, and factories all fall in this category.

- **Plant life.** Plant life growing on land is real property whether the plants are naturally occurring, such as trees, or cultivated crops. When a landowner sells his property, plant life is automatically included in the sale, unless the parties agree otherwise. A landowner may also sell the plant life separately if he wishes. A sale of the plant life alone, without the land, is a sale of goods. (Goods, as you may recall, are movable things.)

- **Fixtures.** Fixtures are goods that have become attached to real property. A house (which is real property) contains many fixtures. The furnace and heating ducts were goods when they were manufactured and when they were sold to the builder because they were movable. But when the builder attached them to the house, the items became fixtures. By contrast, neither the refrigerator nor the grand piano is a fixture.

When an owner sells real property, the buyer normally obtains the fixtures unless the parties specify otherwise. Sometimes it is difficult to determine whether something is a fixture. The general rule is this: **An object is a fixture if a reasonable person would consider the item to be a permanent part of the property,** taking into account attachment, adaptation, and other objective manifestations of permanence:

- **Attachment.** If an object is attached to property in such a way that removing it would damage the property, it is probably a fixture. Heating ducts could be removed from a house, but only by ripping open walls and floors, so they are fixtures.

---

[1]Leslie Haggin, "Pair Stake Their Claim to Hot Dog Island," *Record* (Bergen, NJ), September 5, 1994, p. A12. Excerpted with permission of the *Record*, Hackensack, NJ.

- **Adaptation.** Something that is made or adapted *especially for attachment* to the particular property is probably a fixture, such as custom-made bookshelves fitted in a library.

- **Other manifestations of permanence.** If the owner of the property clearly intends the item to remain permanently, it is probably a fixture. Suppose a homeowner constructs a large concrete platform in his backyard, then buys a heavy metal shed and bolts it to the platform. His preparatory work indicates that he expects the shed to remain permanently, and a court would likely declare it a fixture.

29-2 CONCURRENT ESTATES

Concurrent estates

Two or more people owning property at the same time

When two or more people own real property at the same time, they have **concurrent estates**. The most common forms of concurrent estates are tenancy in common, joint tenancy, and tenancy by the entirety.

29-2a Tenancy in Common

Tenancy in common

Two or more people holding equal interest in a property, but with no right of survivorship

The most common form of concurrent estate is **tenancy in common**. Suppose Patricia owns a house. Patricia agrees to sell her house to Quincy and Rebecca. When she **conveys** the deed (that is, transfers the deed) "to Quincy and Rebecca," those two now have a tenancy in common. This kind of estate can also be created in a will. If Patricia had died still owning the house and left it in her will to "Sam and Tracy," then Sam and Tracy would have a tenancy in common. Tenancy in common is the "default setting" when multiple people acquire property. Co-owners are automatically considered tenants in common unless another type of interest (joint tenancy, tenancy by the entirety) is specified.

A tenancy in common might have two owners, or 22, or any number. The tenants in common do not own a particular section of the property; they own an equal interest in the entire property. Quincy and Rebecca each own a 50 percent interest in the entire house.

Any co-tenant may convey her interest in the property to another person. Thus, if Rebecca moves 1,000 miles away, she may sell her 50 percent interest in the house to Sidney.

Partition

Since any tenant in common has the power to convey her interest, some people may find themselves sharing ownership with others they do not know or, worse, dislike. What to do? Partition, or division of the property among the co-tenants. Any co-tenant is entitled to demand partition of the property. If the various co-tenants cannot agree on a fair division, a co-tenant may request a court to do it. **All co-tenants have an absolute right to partition.**

Partition by kind

A court's equal division of a property among co-tenants

A court will normally attempt a **partition by kind**, meaning that it actually divides the land equally among the co-tenants. If three co-tenants own a 300-acre farm and the court can divide the land so that the three sections are of roughly equal value, it will perform a partition in kind, even if one or two of the co-tenants oppose partition. If partition by kind is impossible because there is no fair way to divide the property, the court will order the real estate sold and the proceeds divided equally.

29-2b Joint Tenancy

Joint tenancy

Two or more people holding equal interest in a property, with the right of survivorship

Joint tenancy is similar to tenancy in common but is used less frequently. The parties, called *joint tenants*, again own a percentage of the entire property and also have the absolute right of partition. The primary difference is that a **joint tenancy** includes the right of survivorship. Recall that a tenant in common, by contrast, has the power to leave his interest in the real estate to his heirs. Because a joint tenant cannot leave the property to his heirs, courts do not favor this form of ownership. The law presumes that a concurrent estate is a tenancy in common; a court will interpret an estate as a joint tenancy only if the parties creating it clearly intended that result.

Joint tenancy has one other curious feature. Although joint tenants may not convey their interest by will, they may do so during their lifetime. If Frank and George own vacation property as joint tenants, Frank has the power to sell his interest to Harry. But as soon as he does so, the joint tenancy is **severed**, that is, broken. Harry and George are now tenants in common, and the right of survivorship is destroyed.

EXAM Strategy

Question: Thomas, aged 80, has spent a lifetime accumulating unspoiled land in Oregon. He owns 16,000 acres, which he plans to leave to his five children. He is not so crazy about his grandchildren. Thomas cringes at the problems the grandchildren would cause if some of them inherited an interest in the land and became part-owners along with Thomas's own children. Should Thomas leave his land to his children as tenants in common or joint tenants?

Strategy: When a co-tenant dies, her interest in property passes to her heirs. When a joint tenant dies, his interest in the property passes to the surviving joint tenants.

Result: Thomas is better off leaving the land to his children as joint tenants. That way, when one of his children dies, that child's interest in the land will go to Thomas's surviving children, not to his grandchildren.

29-3 ADVERSE POSSESSION

Recall Paul Termarco and Gene Murdoch, who opened this chapter by trying to sell us a hot dog from the middle of a New Jersey lake. The pair had their sights set on more than mustard and relish: They hoped that by using the island as if they owned it, they *would* own it. They were relying on the doctrine of adverse possession. **Adverse possession allows someone to take title to land if she demonstrates possession that is (1) exclusive; (2) notorious; (3) adverse to all others; and (4) continuous.**

Adverse possession
Allows someone to take title to land without paying for it, if she meets four specific standards

29-3a Entry and Exclusive Possession

The user must take physical possession of the land and must be the only one to do so. If the owner is still occupying the land, or if other members of the public share its use, there can be no adverse possession.

29-3b Open and Notorious Possession

The user's presence must be visible and generally known in the area, so that the owner is on notice that his title is contested. This ensures that the owner can protect his property by ejecting the user. Someone making secret use of the land gives the owner no opportunity to do this, and hence acquires no rights in the land.

29-3c A Claim Adverse to the Owner

The user must clearly assert that the land is his. He does not need to register a deed or take other legal steps, but he must act as though he is the sole owner. If the user occupies the land with the owner's permission, there is no adverse claim, and the user acquires no rights in the property.

29-3d Continuous Possession for the Statutory Period

State statutes on adverse possession prescribe a period of years for continuous use of the land. Originally, most states required about 20 years to gain adverse possession, but the trend has been to shorten this period. Many states now demand 10 years, and a few require only five years of use. The reason for shortening the period is to reward those who make use of land.

Regardless of the length required, the use must be continuous. In a residential area, the user would have to occupy the land year round for the prescribed period. In a wilderness area generally used only in the summer, a user could gain ownership by seasonal use.

How did Murdoch and Termarco fare? They certainly entered on the land and established themselves as the exclusive occupants. Their use has been open and notorious, allowing anyone who claimed ownership to take steps to eject them from the property. Their actions have been adverse to anyone else's claim. If the two hot dog entrepreneurs have grilled those dogs for the full statutory period, they should take title to the island.

In the following case, the couple claiming adverse possession have taken up residence in a ghost town.

RAY V. BEACON HUDSON MOUNTAIN CORP.

88 N.Y.2d 154
Court of Appeals of New York, 1996

CASE SUMMARY

Facts: In 1931, Rose Ray purchased a cottage in a mountaintop resort town in the Adirondacks, at the same time agreeing to rent the land on which the structure stood. The long-term lease required her to pay the real estate taxes and provided that when the tenancy ended, the landlord would buy back the cottage at fair market value. In 1960, the landlord terminated the lease of everyone in the town, so Ray and all other residents packed up and left. She died in 1962, without ever getting a penny for the cottage. The next year, Mt. Beacon Incline Lands, Inc., bought all rights to the abandoned 156-acre resort.

Robert and Margaret Ray, the son and daughter-in-law of Rose Ray, reentered the cottage and began to use it one month per year, every summer from 1963 to 1988. They paid taxes, insured the property, installed utilities, and posted NO TRESPASSING signs.

In 1978, Beacon Hudson bought the resort in a tax foreclosure sale. Finally, in 1988, the Rays filed suit, claiming title to the cottage by adverse possession. Beacon Hudson counterclaimed, seeking to eject the Rays. The trial court ruled for the couple. The appellate court reversed, stating that the Rays had been absent too frequently to achieve adverse possession. The Rays appealed to New York's highest court.

Issue: *Did the Rays acquire title by adverse possession?*

Decision: The Rays acquired title by adverse possession. Reversed.

Reasoning: To obtain property by adverse possession, the claiming party must prove continuous possession, among other elements. However, the actual occupancy need not be constant. The claimant must simply use the land as ordinary owners would.

Beacon Hudson argues that the Rays cannot demonstrate continuous possession because they only occupied the property one month per year. However, that argument fails to consider the Rays' other acts of control over the premises. The couple maintained and improved the cottage and installed utilities. They also repelled trespassers, posted the land, and padlocked the cottage. These acts demonstrated continuous control of the property.

The Rays' seasonal use of the cottage, along with the improvements described, put the owner on notice of the couple's hostile and exclusive claim of ownership, especially considering that all neighboring structures had collapsed due to vandalism and neglect. The Rays have obtained title by adverse possession.

29-4 LAND USE REGULATION

29-4a Zoning

Zoning statutes are state laws that permit local communities to regulate building and land use. The local communities, whether cities, towns, or counties, then pass zoning ordinances that control many aspects of land development. For example, a town's zoning ordinance may divide the community into an industrial zone where factories may be built, a commercial zone in which stores of a certain size are allowed, and several residential zones in which only houses may be constructed. Within the residential zones, there may be further divisions—for example, permitting two-family houses in certain areas and requiring larger lots in others.

Zoning statutes
State laws that permit local communities to regulate land use

Ethics Many people abhor "adult" businesses, such as strip clubs and pornography shops. Urban experts agree that having a large number of these concerns in a neighborhood often causes crime to increase and property values to drop. Nonetheless, many people patronize such businesses, which can earn a good profit. Should a city have the right to restrict adult businesses? Some cities have passed zoning ordinances that prohibit adult businesses from all residential neighborhoods, from some commercial districts, or from being within 500 feet of schools, houses of worship, daycare centers, or other sex shops (to avoid clustering). Owners and patrons of these shops have protested, claiming the restrictions unfairly deny access to a form of entertainment that the public obviously desires. Who are the stakeholders? What are the consequences of these restrictions?

29-4b Eminent Domain

Eminent domain is the power of the government to take private property for public use. A government may need land to construct a highway, an airport, a university, or public housing. All levels of government—federal, state, and local—have this power. But the Fifth Amendment to the United States Constitution states: "nor shall private property be taken for public use, without just compensation." The Supreme Court has held that this clause, the Takings Clause, applies not only to the federal government, but also to state and local governments. So, although all levels of government have the power to take property, they must pay the owner a fair price.

A "fair price" generally means the reasonable market value of the land. Generally, if the property owner refuses the government's offer, the government will file suit seeking **condemnation** of the land; that is, a court order specifying what compensation is just and awarding title to the government.

A related issue arose in the following case. A city used eminent domain to take property on behalf of *private developers*. Was this a valid public use? The *Kelo* decision was controversial, and in response, some states passed statutes prohibiting eminent domain for private development.

Eminent domain
The power of the government to take private property for public use

Condemnation
A court order awarding title of real property to the government in exchange for just compensation

KELO v. CITY OF NEW LONDON, CONNECTICUT

545 U.S. 469
United States Supreme Court, 2005

CASE SUMMARY

Facts: New London, Connecticut, was declining economically. The city's unemployment rate was double that of the state generally, and the population was at its lowest point in 75 years. In response, state and local officials targeted a section of the city called Fort Trumbull for revitalization. Located on the Thames River, Fort Trumbull comprised

115 privately owned properties and 32 additional acres of an abandoned naval facility. The development plan included one section for a waterfront conference hotel and stores; a second one for 80 private residences; and one for research facilities.

The state bought most of the properties from willing sellers. However, nine owners of 15 properties refused to sell, and they filed suit. The owners claimed that the city was trying to take land for *private* use, not public, in violation of the Takings Clause. The case reached the United States Supreme Court.

Issue: *Did the city's plan violate the Takings Clause?*

Decision: No, the plan was constitutional. Affirmed.

Reasoning: The Takings Clause allows for some transfers of real property from one private party to another, so long as

the land will be used by the public. For example, land may be taken to allow for the construction of a railroad even if private railroad companies will be the primary beneficiaries of the transfer.

New London's economic development plan aimed to create jobs and increase the city's tax receipts. The Supreme Court had not previously considered this type of public use, but it now determined that economic development is a legitimate public purpose. New London did not violate the Takings Clause.

Dissent by Justice O'Connor: Any public benefit in this case would be incidental and secondary. Under the majority's opinion, the government can now take private property for *any* purpose. This case will most likely benefit those with inside access to government officials at the expense of small property owners.

29-5 LANDLORD-TENANT LAW

Landlord-tenant law is really a combination of three areas of law: property, contract, and negligence. We begin our examination of landlord-tenant law with an analysis of the different types of tenancy.

When an owner allows another person temporary, exclusive possession of the property, the parties have created a landlord-tenant relationship. The owner is the **landlord**, and the person allowed to possess the property is the **tenant**. The landlord has conveyed a **leasehold** interest to the tenant, meaning the right to temporary possession. Courts also use the word *tenancy* to describe the tenant's right to possession. A leasehold may be commercial or residential.

Leasehold
A right to possess real property temporarily

29-5a Three Legal Areas Combined

Property law influences landlord-tenant cases because the landlord is conveying rights in real property to the tenant. She is also keeping a reversionary interest in the property, meaning the right to possess the property when the lease ends. Contract law plays a role because the basic agreement between the landlord and tenant is a contract. **A lease is a contract that creates a landlord-tenant relationship.** And negligence law increasingly determines the liability of landlord and tenant when there is an injury to a person or property.

29-5b Lease

The Statute of Frauds generally requires that a lease be in writing. Some states will enforce an oral lease if it is for a short term, such as one year or less, but even when an oral lease is permitted, it is wiser for the parties to put their agreement in writing because a written lease helps to avoid many misunderstandings. At a minimum, a lease must state the names of the parties, the premises being leased, the duration of the agreement, and the rent. But a well-drafted lease generally includes many provisions, called *covenants* and *conditions*. A **covenant** is simply a promise by either the landlord or the tenant to do something or refrain from doing something. For example, most leases include a covenant concerning the tenant's payment of a security deposit and the landlord's return of the deposit, a covenant describing how the tenant may use the premises, and several covenants about who must maintain and repair the property, who is liable for damage, and so forth. Generally, tenants may be fined

Covenant
A promise to do or refrain from doing something

but not evicted for violating lease covenants. A **condition** is similar to a covenant, but it allows for a landlord to evict a tenant if there is a violation. In many states, conditions in leases must be clearly labeled as "conditions" or "evictable offenses."

29-6 TYPES OF TENANCY

There are four types of tenancy: a tenancy for years, a periodic tenancy, a tenancy at will, and a tenancy at sufferance. The most important feature distinguishing one from the other is how each tenancy terminates. In some cases, a tenancy terminates automatically, while in others, one party must take certain steps to end the agreement.

29-6a Tenancy for Years

Any lease for a stated, fixed period is a tenancy for years. If a landlord rents a summer apartment for the months of June, July, and August of next year, that is a tenancy for years. A company that rents retail space in a mall beginning January 1, 2015, and ending December 31, 2018, also has a tenancy for years. A tenancy for years terminates automatically when the agreed period ends.

29-6b Periodic Tenancy

A periodic tenancy is created for a fixed period and then automatically continues for additional periods until either party notifies the other of termination. This is probably the most common variety of tenancy, and the parties may create one in either of two ways. Suppose a landlord agrees to rent you an apartment "from month to month, rent payable on the first." That is a periodic tenancy. The tenancy automatically renews itself every month unless either party gives adequate notice to the other that she wishes to terminate. A periodic tenancy could also be for one-year periods—in which case it automatically renews for an additional year if neither party terminates—or for any other period.

29-6c Tenancy at Will

A tenancy at will has no fixed duration and may be terminated by either party at any time. Typically, a tenancy at will is vague, with no specified rental period and with payment, perhaps, to be made in kind. The parties might agree, for example, that a tenant farmer could use a portion of his crop as rent. Since either party can end the agreement at any time, it provides no security for either landlord or tenant.

29-6d Tenancy at Sufferance

A tenancy at sufferance occurs when a tenant remains on the premises, against the wishes of the landlord, after the expiration of a true tenancy. Thus, a tenancy at sufferance is not a true tenancy because the tenant is staying without the landlord's agreement. The landlord has the option of seeking to evict the tenant or of forcing the tenant to pay rent for a new rental period.

29-7 LANDLORD'S DUTIES

29-7a Duty to Deliver Possession

The landlord's first important duty is to **deliver possession** of the premises at the beginning of the tenancy; that is, to make the rented space available to the tenant. In most cases, this presents no problems, and the new tenant moves in. But what happens if the previous tenant has refused to leave when the new tenancy begins? In most states, the landlord is legally required to remove the previous tenant. In some states, it is up to the new tenant either to evict the existing occupant or begin charging him rent.

29-7b Quiet Enjoyment

Quiet enjoyment
The right to inhabit the property in peace

All tenants are entitled to quiet enjoyment of the premises, meaning the right to use the property without the interference of the landlord. Most leases expressly state this covenant of quiet enjoyment. And if a lease includes no such covenant, the law implies the right of quiet enjoyment anyway, so all tenants are protected. If a landlord interferes with the tenant's quiet enjoyment, he has breached the lease, entitling the tenant to damages.

The most common interference with quiet enjoyment is an eviction, meaning some act that forces the tenant to abandon the premises. Of course, some evictions are legal, as when a tenant fails to pay the rent. But some evictions are illegal. There are two types of eviction: actual and constructive.

29-7c Actual Eviction

If a landlord prevents the tenant from possessing the premises, he has actually evicted her. Suppose a landlord decides that a group of students are "troublemakers." Without going through lawful eviction procedures in court, the landlord simply waits until the students are out of the apartment and changes the locks. By denying the students access to the premises, the landlord has actually evicted them and has breached their right of quiet enjoyment.

29-7d Constructive Eviction

If a landlord substantially interferes with the tenant's use and enjoyment of the premises, he has constructively evicted her. Courts construe certain behavior as the equivalent of an eviction. In these cases, the landlord has not actually prevented the tenant from possessing the premises, but has instead interfered so greatly with her use and enjoyment that the law regards the landlord's actions as equivalent to an eviction. Suppose the heating system in an apartment house in Juneau, Alaska, fails during January. The landlord, an avid sled-dog racer, tells the tenants he is too busy to fix the problem. If the tenants move out, the landlord has constructively evicted them and is liable for all expenses they suffer.

To claim a constructive eviction, the tenant must vacate the premises. The tenant must also prove that the interference was sufficiently serious and lasted long enough that she was forced to move out. A lack of hot water for two days is not fatal, but lack of any water for two weeks creates a constructive eviction.

29-7e Duty to Maintain Premises

In most states, a landlord has a duty to deliver the premises in a habitable condition and a continuing duty to maintain the habitable condition. This duty overlaps with the quiet enjoyment obligation, but it is not identical. The tenant's right to quiet enjoyment focuses primarily on the tenant's ability to use the rented property. The landlord's duty to maintain the property focuses on whether the property meets a particular legal standard. The required standard may be stated in the lease, created by a state statute, or implied by law.

Lease

The lease itself generally obligates the landlord to maintain the exterior of any buildings and the common areas. If a lease does not do so, state law may imply the obligation.

Building Codes

Many state and local governments have passed building codes that mandate minimum standards for commercial property, residential property, or both. The codes are likely to be stricter for residential property and may demand such things as minimum room size, sufficient hot water, secure locks, proper working kitchens and bathrooms, absence of insects and rodents, and other basics of decent housing. Generally, all rental property must comply with the building code whether the lease mentions the code or not.

Implied Warranty of Habitability

Students Maria Ivanow, Thomas Tecza, and Kenneth Gearin rented a house from Les and Martha Vanlandingham. The monthly rent was $900. But the roommates failed to pay any rent for the final five months of the tenancy. After they moved out, the Vanlandinghams sued. How much did the landlords recover? Nothing. The landlords had breached the implied warranty of habitability.

The implied warranty of habitability requires that a landlord meet all standards set by the local building code, or that the premises be fit for human habitation. Most states, though not all, imply this warranty of habitability, meaning that the landlord must meet this standard whether the lease includes it or not.

The Vanlandinghams breached the implied warranty. The students had complained repeatedly about a variety of problems. The washer and dryer, which were included in the lease, frequently failed. A severe roof leak caused water damage in one of the bedrooms. Defective pipes flooded the bathroom. The refrigerator frequently malfunctioned, and the roommates repaired it several times. The basement often flooded, and when it was dry, rats and opossums lived in it. The heat sometimes failed.

In warranty of habitability cases, a court normally considers the severity of the problems and their duration. In the case of Maria Ivanow and friends, the court abated (reduced) the rent 50 percent. The students had already paid more than the abated rent to the landlord, so they owed nothing for the last five months.[2]

Duty to Return Security Deposit

Most landlords require tenants to pay a security deposit, to be used to finance repairs in case the tenant damages the premises. **In many states, a landlord must either return the security deposit soon after the tenant has moved out or notify the tenant of the damage and the cost of the repairs.** A landlord who fails to do so may owe the tenant damages of two or even three times the deposit.

Your authors are always grateful when plaintiffs volunteer to illustrate half a dozen legal issues in one lawsuit. The landlord in the following case demonstrates problems of security deposit, quiet enjoyment, constructive eviction, and, well, see how many you can count.

> One tenant slept with blankets over her head, to keep heat in and bugs out.

HARRIS V. SOLEY

2000 Me. 150
Supreme Judicial Court of Maine, 2000

CASE SUMMARY

Facts: Near Labor Day, Andrea Harris, Kimberly Nightingale, Karen Simard, and Michelle Dussault moved into a large apartment in the Old Port section of Portland, Maine. The apartment had been condemned by the city of Portland, but Joseph Soley, the landlord, assured the tenants that all problems would be repaired before they

---

[2]*Vanlandingham v. Ivanow*, 246 Ill. App. 3d 348 (Ill. Ct. App. 1993).

moved in. Not quite. When the women arrived, they found the condemnation notice still on the door, and the apartment an uninhabitable mess. Soley's agent told the tenants that if they cleaned the unit themselves, they would receive a $750 credit on their first month's rent of $1,000. So the four rented a steam cleaner, bought supplies, and cleaned the entire apartment. Unfortunately, their problems had only begun.

The tenants suffered a continuous problem with mice and cockroaches, along with a persistent odor of cat urine. They ultimately discovered a dead cat beneath the floorboards. During October, the apartment had no heat. One tenant slept with blankets over her head, to keep heat in and bugs out. In November, the women submitted a list of complaints to Soley, including a broken toilet, an inoperable garbage disposal, and a shattered skylight, as well as a leaking roof and cockroach infestation. Snow began to fall into the living room through the skylight.

Soley made no repairs, and the women stopped paying the rent. He phoned them several times, aggressively demanding payments. The tenants found another place to live, but before they had moved, Soley's agents broke into the apartment and took many of their belongings. The tenants located Soley at the restaurant he owned and asked for their possessions back, but he refused to return the belongings unless they paid him $3,000. He threatened them by saying that he knew where their families lived.

The tenants sued, claiming breach of contract, conversion [wrongful taking of property], intentional infliction of emotional distress, wrongful eviction, and wrongful retention of a security deposit. Soley refused to respond to discovery requests, and eventually the trial court gave a default judgment for the plaintiffs. The judge instructed the jury that all allegations were deemed true, and their job was to award damages. The jury awarded damages for each of the claims, including $15,000 to each tenant for emotional distress and a total of *$1 million* in punitive damages. Soley appealed.

Issue: *Are the tenants entitled to such large damages?*

Decision: The tenants are entitled to all damages. Affirmed.

Reasoning: Soley argues that the identical awards to all four tenants indicates the verdict is a result of irrational thinking, passion, and prejudice. However, the jury could reasonably have found that the emotional distress suffered by each tenant deserved comparable compensation, even if the harm was not identical to each. Among the factual findings from the trial court was this statement:

The plaintiffs were shaken up, infuriated, violated, intimidated, and in fear for their physical safety. The conduct of [Soley] was so extreme and outrageous as to exceed all possible bounds of decency. Defendant acted intentionally, knowingly, willfully, wantonly, and with malice.

The jury was entirely justified in awarding substantial punitive damages. The tenants had to endure insect and rodent infestation, dead animals, and falling snow. Soley refused to repair conditions that made the apartment unfit for human habitation, violently removed the tenants' property, destroyed some of their belongings, and threatened the young women. His conduct was utterly intolerable, and the verdict is reasonable.

29-8 TENANT'S DUTIES

29-8a Duty to Pay Rent

Rent is the compensation the tenant pays the landlord for use of the premises, and paying the rent is the tenant's foremost obligation. The lease normally specifies the amount of rent and when it must be paid. Typically, the landlord requires that rent be paid at the beginning of each rental period, whether that is monthly, annually, or otherwise.

If the tenant fails to pay rent on time, the landlord has several remedies. She is entitled to apply the security deposit to the unpaid rent. She may also sue the tenant for nonpayment of rent, demanding the unpaid sums, cost of collection, and interest. Finally, the landlord may evict a tenant who has failed to pay rent.

State statutes prescribe the steps a landlord must take to evict a tenant for nonpayment. Typically, the landlord must serve a termination notice on the tenant and wait for a court hearing. At the hearing, the landlord must prove that the tenant has failed to pay rent on time. If the tenant has no excuse for the nonpayment, the court grants an order evicting him. The order authorizes a sheriff to remove the tenant's goods and place them in storage, at the tenant's expense. However, if the tenant was withholding rent because of unlivable conditions, the court may refuse to evict.

EXAM Strategy

Question: Leo rents an apartment from Donna for $900 per month, both parties signing a lease. After six months, Leo complains about defects, including bugs, inadequate heat, and window leaks. He asks Donna to fix the problems, but she responds that the heat is fine and that Leo caused the insects and leaks. Leo begins to send in only $700 for the monthly rent. Donna repeatedly phones Leo, asking for the remaining rent. When he refuses to pay, she waits until he leaves for the day, then has a moving company place his belongings in storage. She changes the locks, making it impossible for him to re-enter. Leo sues. What is the likely outcome?

Strategy: A landlord is entitled to begin proper eviction proceedings against a tenant who has not paid rent. However, the landlord must follow specified steps, including a termination notice and a court hearing. Review the consequences for actual eviction, described in the section "Quiet Enjoyment."

Result: Donna has ignored the legal procedures for evicting a tenant. Instead, she engaged in *actual eviction*, which is quick and, in the short term, effective. However, by breaking the law, Donna has ensured that Leo will win his lawsuit. He is entitled to possession of the apartment, as well as damages for rent he may have been forced to pay elsewhere, injury to his possessions, and the cost of retrieving them. He may receive punitive damages as well. Bad strategy, Donna.

29-8b Duty to Mitigate

Pickwick & Perkins, Ltd., was a store in the Burlington Square Mall in Burlington, Vermont. Pickwick had a five-year lease but abandoned the space almost two years early and ceased paying rent. The landlord waited eight months before renting the space to a new tenant and then sued, seeking the unpaid rent. Pickwick defended on the grounds that Burlington had failed to **mitigate damages,** that is, to keep its losses to a minimum by promptly seeking another tenant. The winner? Pickwick, the tenant. Today, most (but not all) courts rule that **when a tenant breaches the lease, the landlord must make a reasonable effort to mitigate damages.** Burlington failed to mitigate, so it also failed to recover its losses.

Mitigation
The duty to keep losses at a minimum

29-8c Duty to Use Premises Properly

A lease normally lists what a tenant may do in the premises and prohibits other activities. For example, a residential lease allows the tenant to use the property for normal living purposes, but not for any retail, commercial, or industrial purpose. A tenant may never use the premises for an illegal activity, such as gambling or selling drugs, whether or not the lease mentions the issue. A tenant may not disturb other tenants, and a landlord has the right to evict anyone who unreasonably disturbs neighbors.

A tenant is liable to the landlord for any significant damage he causes to the property. The tenant is not liable for normal wear and tear. If, however, he knocks a hole in a wall or damages the plumbing, the landlord may collect the cost of repairs, either by using the security deposit or, if necessary, by suing.

29-9 Change in the Parties

Sometimes the parties to a lease change. This can happen when the landlord sells the property or when a tenant wants to turn the leased property over to another tenant.

29-9a Sale of the Property

Generally, the sale of leased property does not affect the lease but merely substitutes one landlord, the purchaser, for another, the seller. The lease remains valid, and the tenant enjoys all rights and obligations until the end of the term. The new landlord may not raise the rent during the period of the existing lease or make any other changes in the tenant's rights.

EXAM Strategy

Question: Julie, an MBA student, rents an apartment from Marshall for $1,500 a month. The written lease will last for two years, until Julie graduates. Julie moves in and enjoys the apartment. However, after 10 months, Marshall sells the building to Alexia, who notifies Julie that the new rent will be $1,750, effective immediately. If Julie objects, Alexia will give her one month to leave the apartment. Julie comes to you for advice. What are her options?

Strategy: What effect does the sale of leased property have on existing leases?

Result: Generally, the sale of leased property does not affect the lease but merely substitutes one landlord, the purchaser, for another, the seller. Alexia has no right to raise the rent during Julie's tenancy. Julie is entitled to the apartment, for $1,500 per month, until the lease expires.

29-9b Assignment and Sublease

Assignment

Process under which the original tenant transfers all of his rights and duties to a new tenant

A tenant who wishes to turn the property over to another tenant will attempt to assign the lease or to sublet it. In an **assignment**, the tenant transfers all of his legal interest to the other party. If a tenant validly assigns a lease, the new tenant obtains all rights and liabilities under the lease. The new tenant is permitted to use and enjoy the property and must pay the rent. **However, the original tenant remains liable to the landlord unless the landlord explicitly releases him, which the landlord is unlikely to do.** This means that if the new tenant fails to pay the rent on time, the landlord can sue *both* parties, old and new, seeking to evict both and to recover the unpaid rent from both.

A landlord generally insists on a covenant in the lease prohibiting the tenant from assigning without the landlord's written permission. Some states permit a landlord to deny permission for any reason at all, but a growing number of courts insist that a landlord act reasonably and grant permission to sublease unless he has a valid objection to the new tenant.

29-10 Injuries

29-10a Tenant's Liability

A tenant is generally liable for injuries occurring within the premises she is leasing, whether that is an apartment, a store, or something else. If a tenant fails to clean up a spill on the kitchen floor, and a guest slips and falls, the tenant is liable. If a merchant negligently installs display shelving that tips onto a customer, the merchant pays for the harm. Generally, a tenant is not liable for injuries occurring in common areas over which she has no control, such as exterior walkways. If a tenant's dinner guest falls because the building's common stairway has loose steps, the landlord is probably liable.

29-10b Landlord's Liability

Historically, the common law held a landlord responsible only for injuries that occurred in the common areas, or those due to the landlord's negligent maintenance of the property. Increasingly, though, the law holds landlords liable under the normal rules of negligence law. In many states, a landlord must use reasonable care to maintain safe premises and is liable for foreseeable harm. For example, most states now have building codes that require a landlord to maintain structural elements in safe condition. States further imply a warranty of habitability, which mandates reasonably safe living conditions.

29-10c Crime

Landlords may be liable in negligence to tenants or their guests for criminal attacks that occur on the premises. Courts have struggled with this issue and have reached opposing results in similar cases. The very prevalence of crime sharpens the debate. What must a landlord do to protect a tenant? Courts typically answer the question by looking at four factors:

1. **Nature of the crime.** How did the crime occur? Could the landlord have prevented it?

2. **Reasonable person standard.** What would a reasonable landlord have done to prevent this type of crime? What did the landlord actually do?

3. **Foreseeability.** Was it reasonably foreseeable that such a crime might occur? Were there earlier incidents or warnings?[3]

4. **Prevalence of crime in the area.** If the general area, or the particular premises, has a high crime rate, courts are more likely to hold that the crime was foreseeable and the landlord responsible.

In the following case, the court held that a landlord was required to take reasonable steps to protect a tenant, even when some of the threats occurred in cyberspace. Should the landlord be responsible?

LINDSAY P. v. TOWNE PROPERTIES ASSET MANAGEMENT CO., LTD.

2013-Ohio-4124
Court of Appeals of Ohio, 2013

CASE SUMMARY

Facts: Lindsay[3] and her young daughter lived above Rhonda Schmidt, in an apartment complex operated by Towne Properties (TP). Schmidt's boyfriend, Courtney Haynes, often stayed in Schmidt's apartment. The couple blared rap music and fought loudly, often waking Lindsay's child.

Lindsay frequently complained to TP about her downstairs neighbors. In retaliation, Haynes banged on her door and threatened her. Terrified, Lindsay reported Haynes to TP and they suggested she file a police report so they would have the documentation necessary to "take care of it."

Late one night, Haynes sent Lindsay a Facebook message. It read: "You will really like having a friend so close that can satisfy you in so many great ways" and had a link to a pornographic website.

---

[3]The court refers to Lindsay by her first name alone to protect her privacy.

Lindsay immediately told TP managers and begged them to let her out of her lease. TP refused, but offered to move her to an available first-floor unit, where they assured her she would be safe. TP promised to "keep an eye" on Haynes for Lindsay.

Meanwhile, TP advised Schmidt that since Haynes was not on her lease, he would have to leave. In response, Schmidt insisted on adding him to the lease, and TP agreed. In the process, TP divulged that Lindsay was moving to another unit.

A few days later, Haynes broke into Lindsay's new apartment and raped her. Lindsay sued TP, alleging that it was negligent. The trial court dismissed the case, reasoning that TP had no duty to protect Lindsay from a random criminal act. Lindsay appealed.

Issue: *Could the landlord be liable for the tenant's injuries?*

Decision: Yes. The evidence suggests that TP did not take reasonable steps to protect its tenant. Reversed.

Reasoning: Generally, landlords do not have a duty to protect their tenants from third party criminal acts. However, such a duty exists when the landlord should have reasonably foreseen the criminal activity and failed to take reasonable precautions to prevent it.

Haynes' criminal activity was certainly foreseeable. TP was aware of his dangerous propensities and his menacing behavior toward Lindsay. It knew that Lindsay had good reason to feel threatened by Haynes. It also reassured Lindsay, telling her it was "taking care of it," promising to "keep an eye on" Haynes, and guaranteeing it was taking precautions.

But it did not take such precautions. TP did not let Lindsay out of her lease. It moved her to a first-floor apartment even though she expressed concern for her safety. It even informed Haynes that Lindsay was moving and began the process of adding him to Schmidt's lease.

Chapter Conclusion

Real property law is ancient but forceful. Although real property today is not the dominant source of wealth that it was in medieval England, it is still the greatest asset that most people will ever possess—and therefore, it is worth understanding the law that applies to it. Landlord-tenant law places many special obligations on both parties. The current trend is clearly for expanded landlord liability, but how far that will continue is impossible to divine.

EXAM REVIEW

1. **REAL PROPERTY** Real property includes land, buildings, air and subsurface rights, plant life, and fixtures. A fixture is any good that has become attached to other real property.

EXAM Strategy

Question: Paul and Shelly Higgins had two wood stoves in their home. Each rested on, but was not attached to, a built-in brick platform. The downstairs wood stove was connected to the chimney flue and was used as part of the main heating system for the house. The upstairs stove, in the master bedroom, was purely decorative. It had no stovepipe connecting it to the chimney. The Higginses sold their house to Jack Everitt, and neither party said anything about the two stoves. Is Everitt entitled to either stove? Both stoves?

Strategy: An object is a fixture if a reasonable person would consider the item to be a permanent part of the property, taking into account attachment, adaptation, and other objective manifestations of permanence. (See the "Result" at the end of this section.)

2. CONCURRENT ESTATES When two or more people own real property at the same time, they have a concurrent estate.

3. ADVERSE POSSESSION Adverse possession permits the user of land to gain title if he can prove entry and exclusive possession, open and notorious possession, a claim adverse to the owner, and continuous possession for the required statutory period.

EXAM Strategy

Question: In 1966, Arketex Ceramic Corp. sold land in rural Indiana to Malcolm Aukerman. The deed described the southern boundary as the section line between sections 11 and 14 of the land. Farther south of this section line stood a dilapidated fence running east to west. Aukerman and Arketex both believed that this fence was the actual southern boundary of his new land, though in fact it lay on Arketex's property.

Aukerman installed a new electrified fence, cleared the land on "his" side of the new fence, and began to graze cattle there. In 1974, Harold Clark bought the land that bordered Aukerman's fence, assuming that the fence was the correct boundary. In 1989, Clark had his land surveyed and discovered that the true property line lay north of the electric fence. Aukerman filed suit, seeking a court order that he had acquired the disputed land by adverse possession. The statutory period in Indiana is 20 years. Who wins?

Strategy: There are four elements to adverse possession. Has Aukerman proved them? (See the "Result" at the end of this section.)

4. REGULATION Real property law generally permits a government to regulate property and, in some cases, to take it for public use.

5. LANDLORD-TENANT RELATIONSHIP When an owner of a freehold estate allows another person temporary, exclusive possession of the property, the parties have created a landlord-tenant relationship.

6. TENANCIES Any lease for a stated, fixed period is a tenancy for years. A periodic tenancy is created for a fixed period and then automatically continues for additional periods until either party notifies the other of termination. A tenancy at will has no fixed duration and may be terminated by either party at any time. A tenancy at sufferance occurs when a tenant remains, against the wishes of the landlord, after the expiration of a true tenancy.

7. QUIET ENJOYMENT All tenants are entitled to the quiet enjoyment of the premises, without the interference of the landlord.

8. CONSTRUCTIVE EVICTION A landlord may be liable for constructive eviction if he substantially interferes with the tenant's use and enjoyment of the premises.

9. IMPLIED WARRANTY OF HABITABILITY The implied warranty of habitability requires that a landlord meet all standards set by the local building code and/or that the premises be fit for human habitation.

10. **RENT**   The tenant is obligated to pay the rent, and the landlord may evict for nonpayment. The modern trend is to require a landlord to mitigate damages caused by a tenant who abandons the premises before the lease expires.

EXAM Strategy

Question: Loren Andreo leased retail space in his shopping plaza to Tropical Isle Pet Shop for five years, at a monthly rent of $2,100. Tropical Isle vacated the premises 18 months early, turned in the key to Andreo, and acknowledged liability for the unpaid rent. Andreo placed a FOR RENT sign in the store window and spoke to a commercial real estate broker about the space. But he did not enter into a formal listing agreement with the broker, or take any other steps to rent the space, for about nine months. With approximately nine months remaining on the unused part of Tropical's lease, Andreo hired a commercial broker to rent the space. He also sued Tropical for 18 months' rent. Comment.

Strategy: When a tenant abandons leased property early, the landlord is obligated to mitigate damages. Did Andreo? (See the "Result" at the end of this section.)

11. **DAMAGES TO PROPERTY**   A tenant is liable to the landlord for any significant damage that he causes to the property.

12. **ASSIGNMENT**   A tenant typically may assign a lease or sublet the premises only with the landlord's permission, but the current trend is to prohibit a landlord from unreasonably withholding permission.

EXAM Strategy

Question: Doris Rowley rented space from the city of Mobile, Alabama, to run the Back Porch Restaurant. Her lease prohibited assignment or subletting without the landlord's permission. Rowley's business became unprofitable, and she asked the city's real estate officer for permission to assign her lease. She told the officer that she had "someone who would accept if the lease was assigned." Rowley provided no other information about the assignee. The city refused permission. Rowley repeated her requests several times without success, and finally she sued. Rowley alleged that the city had unreasonably withheld permission to assign and had caused her serious financial losses as a result. Comment.

Strategy: A landlord may not unreasonably refuse permission to assign a lease. Was the city's refusal unreasonable? (See the "Result" at the end of this section.)

13. **MAINTENANCE OF THE PROPERTY**   Many courts require a landlord to use reasonable care in maintaining the premises and hold her liable for injuries that were foreseeable.

14. **CRIME**   Landlords may be liable in negligence to tenants or their guests for criminal attacks on the premises. Courts determine liability by looking at factors such as the nature of the crime, what a reasonable landlord would have done to prevent it, and the foreseeability of the attack.

1. Result: A buyer normally takes all fixtures. The downstairs stove was permanently attached to the house and used as part of the heating system. The owner who installed it *intended* that it remain, and it was a fixture; Everitt got it. The upstairs stove was not permanently attached and was not a fixture; the sellers could take it with them.

3. Result: Aukerman wins. He considered himself to be the owner, as had Arketex for 8 years and Clark for 15. All the owners had maintained the land and kept everyone else off for more than 20 years.

10. Result: For about nine months, Andreo made no serious effort to lease the store. The court rejected his rent claim for that period, permitting him to recover unpaid money only for the period that he made a genuine effort to lease the space.

12. Result: A landlord is allowed to evaluate a prospective assignee, including its financial stability and intended use of the property. Mobile could not do that because Rowley provided no information about the proposed assignee. Mobile wins.

MATCHING QUESTIONS

Match the following terms with their definitions:

___A. Constructive eviction

___B. Adverse possession

___C. Fixture

___D. Tenancy at will

___E. Tenancy at sufferance

1. A landlord's substantial interference with a tenant's use and enjoyment of the premises

2. Goods that have become attached to real property

3. A tenancy without fixed duration, which either party may terminate at any time

4. A method of acquiring ownership of land without ever paying for it

5. A tenant remains on the premises after expiration of true tenancy

TRUE/FALSE QUESTIONS

Circle true or false:

1. T F If one joint tenant dies, his interest in the property passes to surviving joint tenants, not to his heirs.

2. T F The federal government has the power to take private property for public use, but local governments have no such power.

3. T F A landlord could be liable for a constructive eviction even if he never asked the tenant to leave.

4. T F A nonrenewable lease of a store, for six months, establishes a tenancy for years.

5. T F A landlord may charge a tenant for normal wear and tear on an apartment, but the charges must be reasonable.

MULTIPLE-CHOICE QUESTIONS

1. **CPA QUESTION** On July 1, 2015, Quick, Onyx, and Nash were deeded a piece of land as tenants in common. The deed provided that Quick owned one-half the property and Onyx and Nash owned one-quarter each. If Nash dies, the property will be owned as follows:

   (a) Quick $\frac{1}{2}$, Onyx $\frac{1}{2}$

   (b) Quick $\frac{5}{8}$, Onyx $\frac{3}{8}$

   (c) Quick $\frac{1}{3}$, Onyx $\frac{1}{3}$, Nash's heirs $\frac{1}{3}$

   (d) Quick $\frac{1}{2}$, Onyx $\frac{1}{4}$, Nash's heirs $\frac{1}{4}$

2. Marta places a large, prefabricated plastic greenhouse in her backyard, with the steel frame bolted into concrete that she poured specially for that purpose. She attaches gas heating ducts and builds a brick walkway around the greenhouse. Now, the town wants to raise her real property taxes, claiming that her property has been improved. Marta argues that the greenhouse is not part of the real property. Is it?

   (a) The greenhouse is not part of the real property because it was prefabricated.

   (b) The greenhouse is not part of the real property because it could be removed.

   (c) The greenhouse cannot be part of the real property if Marta owns a fee simple absolute.

   (d) The greenhouse is a fixture and is part of the real property.

3. **CPA QUESTION** Which of the following forms of tenancy will be created if a tenant stays in possession of the leased premises without the landlord's consent, after the tenant's one-year written lease expires?

   (a) Tenancy at will

   (b) Tenancy for years

   (c) Tenancy from period to period

   (d) Tenancy at sufferance

4. **CPA QUESTION** A tenant renting an apartment under a three-year written lease that does not contain any specific restrictions may be evicted for:

   (a) counterfeiting money in the apartment.

   (b) keeping a dog in the apartment.

   (c) failing to maintain a liability insurance policy on the apartment.

   (d) making structural repairs to the apartment.

5. Michael signs a lease for an apartment. The lease establishes a periodic tenancy for one year, starting September 1 and ending the following August 31. Rent is $800 per month. As August 31 approaches, Michael decides he would like to stay another year. He phones the landlord to tell him this, but the landlord is on vacation and Michael leaves a message. Michael sends in the September rent, but on September 15, the landlord tells him the rent is going up to $900 per month. He gives Michael the choice of paying the higher rent or

leaving. Michael refuses to leave and continues to send checks for $800. The landlord sues. Landlord will:

(a) win possession of the apartment because the lease expired.

(b) win possession of the apartment because Michael did not renew it in writing.

(c) win possession of the apartment because he has the right to evict Michael at any time, for any reason.

(d) win $1,200 (12 months times $100).

(e) lose.

CASE QUESTIONS

1. **ETHICS** Lisa Preece rented an apartment from Turman Realty, paying a $300 security deposit. Georgia law states: "Any landlord who fails to return any part of a security deposit which is required to be returned to a tenant pursuant to this article shall be liable to the tenant in the amount of three times the sum improperly withheld plus reasonable attorney's fees." When Preece moved out, Turman did not return her security deposit, and she sued for triple damages plus attorney's fees, totaling $1,800. Turman offered evidence that its failure to return the deposit was inadvertent and that it had procedures reasonably designed to avoid such errors. Is Preece entitled to triple damages? Attorney's fees? What is the rationale behind a statute that requires triple damages? Is it ethical to force a landlord to pay $1,800 for a $300 debt?

2. Philip Schwachman owned a commercial building and leased space to Davis Radio Corp. for use as a retail store. In the same building, Schwachman leased other retail space to Pampered Pet, a dog grooming shop. Davis Radio complained repeatedly to Schwachman that foul odors from Pampered Pet entered its store and drove away customers and workers. Davis abandoned the premises, leaving many months' rent unpaid. Schwachman sued for unpaid rent and moved for summary judgment. What ruling would you make on the summary judgment motion?

3. Nome 2000, a partnership, owned a large tract of wilderness land in Alaska. The Fagerstrom family had used the property for camping and vacationing since about 1944. In 1966, Charles and Peggy Fagerstrom marked off an area for a cabin and brought material to build the cabin, but they never did so. In about 1970, they built a picnic area on the land, and in about 1974, they placed a camper trailer on the land, where it remained until the lawsuit. In 1987, Nome 2000 sued to eject the Fagerstroms from the land. The Fagerstroms had used the land only during the summer months. No one lived in the area during the winter months, when it was virtually uninhabitable. Has the family adversely possessed the land from Nome 2000?

4. *YOU BE THE JUDGE* **WRITING PROBLEM** Frank Deluca and his son David owned the Sportsman's Pub on Fountain Street in Providence, Rhode Island. The Delucas applied to the city for a license to employ topless dancers in the pub. Did the city have the power to deny the Delucas' request? **Argument for the Delucas:** Our pub is perfectly legal. Further, no law in Rhode Island prohibits topless dancing. We are morally and legally entitled to present this entertainment. The city should not use some phony moralizing to deny customers what they want. **Argument for Providence:** This section of Providence is zoned to prohibit topless dancing, just as it is zoned to

bar manufacturing. There are other parts of town where the Delucas can open one of their sleazy clubs if they want to, but we are entitled to deny a permit in this area.

5. Kenmart Realty sued to evict Mr. and Ms. Alghalabio for nonpayment of rent and sought the unpaid monies, totaling several thousand dollars. In defense, the Alghalabios claimed that their apartment was infested with rats. They testified that there were numerous rat holes in the walls of the living room, bedroom, and kitchen, that there were rat droppings all over the apartment, and that on one occasion, they saw their toddler holding a live rat. They testified that the landlord had refused numerous requests to exterminate. Please rule on the landlord's suit.

DISCUSSION QUESTIONS

1. **ETHICS** During the Great Recession, home foreclosures hit an all-time high. In many instances, banks ended up as property managers, a job for which they were ill-prepared. As a result, many homes were abandoned for long periods. Some people who knew a little bit about adverse possession decided to take advantage: They shamelessly occupied vacant homes, claiming them as their own, changing locks, purchasing electricity—and waiting for the statutory period to pass. The new residents argued that they were not hurting anyone and acting within the bounds of the law. Examine the squatters' ethics. What do you think of their behavior? Does your opinion vary if the squatters were the home's former owners? What if the banks were ignoring the home? What would Kant and Mill say?

2. Leslie buys a house from Jamal. Consider the following items in the house.

– A ceiling fan	– A bathtub
– The carpeting	– A floor lamp
– A dishwasher	– A television

Which of the above are Jamal's personal property? Which are real property? Which will Jamal get to take when he moves, and which will Leslie own?

3. Donny Delt and Sammy Sigma are students and roommates. They lease a house in a neighborhood near campus. Few students live on the block.

The students do not have large parties, but they often have friends over at night. The friends sometimes play loud music in their cars, and they sometimes talk loudly when going to and from their cars. Also, beer cans and fast food wrappers are often left in the street by departing late-night guests.

Neighbors complain about being awakened in the wee hours of the morning. They are considering filing a nuisance lawsuit against Donny and Sammy. Would such an action be reasonable? Do you think Donny and Sammy are creating a nuisance? If so, why? If not, where is the line—what amount of late-night noise does amount to a nuisance?

4. Imagine that you sign a lease and that you are to move into your new apartment on August 15. When you arrive, the previous tenant has not moved out. In fact, he has no intention of moving out. Should the landlord be in charge of getting rid of the old tenant, or should you have the obligation to evict him?

5. When landlords wrongfully withhold security deposits, they can often be sued for three times the amount of the security deposit. Is this reasonable? Should a landlord have to pay $3,000 for a $1,000 debt? What if you fail to pay a rent on time? Should you have to pay three times the amount of your normal rent? If your answers to the two situations presented here are different, why are they different?

CHAPTER 30

PERSONAL PROPERTY AND BAILMENT

© Olga Danylenko/Shutterstock.com

> "It is his love, it is his passion," Cameron argued. "It is his *fault* for not locking the garage," Ferris responded.

Ferris Bueller was not really sick. Neither were his sidekicks, Cameron and Sloane. But the trio concocted an elaborate plan for the perfect "day off" from the doldrums of their senior year of high school. And no day off would be complete without a joyride. So Ferris persuaded the stiff Cameron to take his father's prized 1961 Ferrari 250 GT California for a field trip into downtown Chicago. A similar Ferrari sold at auction for $11 million, setting a record for the world's priciest car. "It is his love, it is his passion," Cameron argued. "It is his *fault* for not locking the garage," Ferris responded.

As one would, the teenagers decided to deposit the vehicle with a parking valet service. (Parking in downtown Chicago is a doozy.) But Cameron was nervous. "No, not here," he uttered. *Why?* "It could get wrecked, stolen, scratched, it could get breathed on wrong," he fretted. Ferris consoled him by generously "dropping" the parking attendant a five-dollar bill.

"Relax. You guys got nothin' to worry about. I'm a professional," said the wily attendant with a glimmer in his eye.

After a long day full of adventures, the friends returned to collect the car, only to discover that its mileage has gone from 124.5 to 329. The attendants enjoyed a better joyride than theirs. Cameron would have a lot of explaining to do.[1]

---

[1]Adapted from the classic 1986 John Hughes film *Ferris Bueller's Day Off.*

This chapter is about a lot of stuff, things, possessions, in other words, personal property. And the duties incurred in giving it, finding it, and loaning it.

Personal property
All tangible property other than real property

Personal property means all tangible property other than real property. In Chapter 29, we saw that real property is land and things firmly attached to it, such as buildings, crops, and minerals. All other physical objects are personal property—a toothbrush, a share of stock, a 1961 Ferrari 250 GT California.

In this chapter, we look at several ways in which personal property can be acquired. We will then turn to disputes over found property. And finally, we examine bailments, which occur when the owner of personal property permits another to possess it.

30-1 GIFTS

Gift
A voluntary transfer of property from one person to another, without consideration

Donor
A person who gives property away

Donee
A person who receives a gift of property

A gift is a voluntary transfer of property from one person to another without any consideration. Recall from Chapter 11 that, for consideration to exist, parties must make an exchange. But a gift is a one-way transaction, without anything given in return. The person who gives property away is the **donor**, and the one who receives it is the **donee**.

A gift involves three elements:

1. The donor *intends to transfer* ownership of the property to the donee *immediately*;

2. The donor *delivers* the property to the donee; and

3. The donee *accepts* the property.

If all three elements are met, the donee becomes the legal owner of the property. If the donor later says, "I've changed my mind, give that back!" the donee is free to refuse.

30-1a Intention to Transfer Ownership

The donor must intend to transfer ownership to the property right away, immediately giving up all control of the item. Notice that the donor's intention must be to give title to the donee. Merely proving that the owner handed you property does not guarantee that you have received a gift; if the owner only intended that you use the item, there is no gift, and she can demand it back.

The donor must also intend the property to transfer immediately. A promise to make a gift in the future is unenforceable. Promises about future behavior are governed by contract law, and a contract is unenforceable without consideration. If Sarah hands Lenny the keys to a $600,000 yacht and says, "Lenny, it's yours," then it *is* his, since Sarah intends to transfer ownership right away. But if Sarah says to Max, "Next week, I'm going to give you my yacht," Max has not received a gift because Sarah did not intend an immediate transfer. Nor does Max have an enforceable contract since there is no consideration for Sarah's promise.

Revocable gifts
Are not gifts at all because the donor can take them back

A **revocable gift** is governed by a special rule, and it is actually not a gift at all. Suppose Harold tells his daughter Faith, "The mule is yours from now on, but if you start acting silly again, I'm taking her back." Harold has retained some control over the animal, which means he has not intended to transfer ownership. There is no gift, and no transfer of ownership. Harold still owns the mule.

30-1b Delivery

Physical Delivery

The donor must deliver the property to the donee. Generally, this involves physical delivery. If Anna hands Eddie a Rembrandt drawing, saying, "I want you to have this forever," she has satisfied the delivery requirement. But such a dramatic statement is not necessary.

Constructive Delivery

Physical delivery is the most common and the surest way to make a gift, but it is not always required. **A donor makes constructive delivery by transferring ownership without a physical delivery.** Most courts permit constructive delivery only when physical delivery is impossible or extremely inconvenient. Suppose Anna wants to give her niece Jen a blimp, which is parked in a hangar at the airport. The blimp will not fit through the doorway of Jen's dorm. Anna may simply deliver to Jen the certificate of title and the keys to the blimp.

30-1c *Inter Vivos* Gifts and Gifts *Causa Mortis*

A gift can be either *inter vivos* or *causa mortis*. An **inter vivos gift** means a gift made "during life," that is, when the donor is not under any fear of impending death. The vast majority of gifts are *inter vivos*, involving a healthy donor and donee. Shirley, age 30 and in good health, gives Terry an eraser for his birthday. This is an *inter vivos* gift, which is absolute. The gift becomes final upon delivery, and the donor may not revoke it. If Shirley and Terry have a fight the next day, Shirley has no power to erase her gift.

A **gift *causa mortis*** is one made in contemplation of approaching death. The gift is valid if the donor dies as expected, but it is revoked if he recovers. Suppose Lenny's doctors have told him he will probably die of a liver ailment within a month. Lenny calls Jane to his bedside and hands her a fistful of cash, saying, "I'm dying; these are yours." Jane sheds a tear and then sprints to the bank. If Lenny dies within a few weeks, Jane gets to keep the money. But note that this gift is revocable. Since a gift *causa mortis* is conditional (upon the donor's death), the donor has the right to revoke it at any time before he dies. If Lenny telephones Jane the next day and says that he has changed his mind, he gets the money back. Further, if the donor recovers and does not die as expected, the gift is automatically revoked.

Inter vivos gift
A gift made during the donor's life, with no fear of impending death

Gift *causa mortis*
A gift made in contemplation of approaching death

EXAM Strategy

Question: Julie does good deeds for countless people, and many are deeply grateful. On Monday, Wilson tells Julie, "You are a wonderful person, and I have a present for you. I am giving you this baseball, which was the 500th home run hit by one of the greatest players of all time." He hands her the ball, which is worth nearly half a million dollars.

Julie's good fortune continues on Tuesday, when another friend, Cassandra, tells Julie, "I only have a few weeks to live. I want you to have this signed first edition of *Ulysses*. It is priceless, and it is yours." The book is worth about $200,000. On Wednesday, Wilson and Cassandra decide they have been foolhardy, and both demand that Julie return the items. Must she do so?

> **Strategy:** Both of these donors are attempting to revoke their gifts. An *inter vivos* gift cannot be revoked, but a gift *causa mortis* can be. To answer the question, you must know what kind of gifts these were.
>
> **Result:** A gift *causa mortis* is one made in fear of approaching death, and this rule applies to Cassandra. Such a gift is revocable any time before the donor dies, so Cassandra gets her book back. A gift *inter vivos* is one made without any such fear of death. Most gifts fall in this category, and they are irrevocable. Wilson was not anticipating his demise, so his was a gift *inter vivos*. Julie keeps the baseball.

30-1d Acceptance

The donee must accept the gift. This rarely leads to disputes, but if a donee should refuse a gift and then change her mind, she is out of luck. Her repudiation of the donor's offer means there is no gift, and she has no rights in the property.

The following case offers a combination of love, alcohol, and diamonds—always a volatile mix.

You be the Judge

ALBINGER V. HARRIS
2002 Mont. 118
Montana Supreme Court, 2002

Facts: Michelle Harris and Michael Albinger lived together, on and off, for three years. Their roller-coaster relationship was marred by alcohol abuse and violence. When they announced their engagement, Albinger gave Harris a $29,000 diamond ring, but the couple broke off their wedding plans. Harris returned the ring. Later, they reconciled and resumed their marriage plans, and Albinger gave his fiancee the ring again. This cycle repeated several times over the three years. Each time they broke off their relationship, Harris returned the ring to Albinger; and each time they made up, he gave it back to her.

On one occasion, Albinger held a knife over Harris as she lay in bed, threatening to chop off her finger if she did not remove the ring. He beat her and forcibly removed the ring. Criminal charges were brought but then dropped when, inevitably, the couple reconciled. Another time, Albinger told her to "take the car, the horse, the dog, and the ring and get the hell out." Finally, mercifully, they ended their stormy affair, and Harris moved to Kentucky—keeping the ring.

Albinger sued for the value of the ring. The trial court found that the ring was a conditional gift, made in contemplation of marriage, and ordered Harris to pay its full value. She appealed. The Montana Supreme Court had to decide, in a case of first impression, whether an engagement ring was given in contemplation of marriage. (In Montana and in many states, neither party to a broken engagement may sue for breach of contract.)

You Be the Judge: *Who owns the ring?*

Argument for Harris: The problem with calling the ring a "conditional gift" is that there is no such thing. The elements of a gift are intent, delivery, and acceptance, and Harris has proven all three. Once a gift has been accepted, the donor has no more rights in the property and may not demand its return. Hundreds of years of litigation have resulted in only one exception to this rule—a gift *causa mortis*—and despite some cynical claims to the contrary, marriage is not death. What is more, to create a special rule for engagement rings would be blatant gender bias because the exception would only benefit men. This court should stick to settled law and permit the recipient of a gift to keep it.

Argument for Albinger: The symbolism of an engagement ring is not exactly news. For decades, Americans have given rings—frequently diamond—in contemplation of marriage. All parties understand why the gift is made and what is expected if the engagement is called off: the ring must be returned. Albinger's intent, to focus on one element, was conditional—and Michelle Harris understood that. Each time the couple separated, she gave the ring back. She knew that she could wear this beautiful ring in anticipation of their marriage, but that custom and decency required its return if the wedding was off. We are not asking for new law, but for confirmation of what everyone has known for generations: There is no wedding ring when there is no wedding.

The following chart distinguishes between a contract and a gift.

A Contract and a Gift Distinguished

A Contract:

Lou: I will pay you $2,000 to paint the house, if you promise to finish by July 3.
　　　　Abby: I agree to paint the house by July 3, for $2,000.

Lou and Abby have a contract. Each promise is consideration in support of the other promise. Lou and Abby can each enforce the other's promise.

A Gift:

Lou hands Phil two opera tickets, while saying: I want you to have these two tickets to *Rigoletto*.
　　　　Phil: Hey, thanks.

This is a valid *inter vivos* gift. Lou intended to transfer ownership immediately and delivered the property to Phil, who now owns the tickets.

Neither Contract nor Gift:

Lou: You're a great guy. Next week, I'm going to give you two tickets to *Rigoletto*.
　　　　Jason: Hey, thanks.

There is no gift because Lou did not intend to transfer ownership immediately, and he did not deliver the tickets. There is no contract because Jason has given no consideration to support Lou's promise.

30-2 FOUND PROPERTY

As you stagger to your 8 a.m. class, there is a gleam of light, not in your mind (which is vacant), but right there on the sidewalk. A ring! You stop in at the local jewelry shop, where you learn the ruby marvel is worth just over $70,000. Is it yours to keep?

The primary goal of the common law has been to get found property back to its proper owner. The finder must make a good-faith effort to locate the owner. In some states, the finder is obligated to notify the police of what she has found and entrust the property to them until the owner can be located or a stated period has passed. A second policy has been to reward the finder if no owner can be located. But courts are loath to encourage trespassing, so finders who discover personal property on someone else's land generally cannot keep it. Those basic policies yield various outcomes, depending on the nature of the property. The common-law principles follow, although some states have modified them by statute.

Abandoned property

Property that the owner has knowingly discarded because she no longer wants it

Lost property

Property accidentally given up

Mislaid property

Property the owner has intentionally placed somewhere and then forgotten

- **Abandoned property** is something that the owner has knowingly discarded because she no longer wants it. A vase thrown into a garbage can is abandoned. Generally, a finder is permitted to keep abandoned property, provided he can prove that the owner intended to relinquish all rights.

- **Lost property** is something accidentally given up. A ring that falls off a finger into the street is lost property. Usually, the finder of lost property has rights superior to all the world except the true owner. If the true owner comes forward, he gets his property back; otherwise, the finder may keep it. However, if the finder has discovered the item on land belonging to another, the landowner is probably entitled to keep it.

- **Mislaid property** is something the owner has intentionally placed somewhere and then forgotten. A book deliberately placed on a bus seat by an owner who forgets to take it with her is mislaid property. Generally, the finder gets no rights in property that has simply been mislaid. If the true owner cannot be located, the mislaid item belongs to the owner of the premises where the item was found.

The following case has contributed significantly to modern legal ideas on found property. It may seem to come from a Charles Dickens novel, but it actually happened. A villainous goldsmith sought to take advantage of a poor chimney sweep's boy. Would he get away with it? Read on.

Landmark Case

ARMORIE V. DELAMIRIE

93 ER 664
Middlesex, 1722

CASE SUMMARY

Facts: Before Parliament banned the practice in 1840, many English chimney sweeps forced young children to climb the narrow flues and do the cleaning. Armorie was one such boy. But fortune smiled on him, and he found a jeweled ring. To discover its value, he carried the ring to a local goldsmith.

Armorie handed the ring to the goldsmith's apprentice, who removed the jewels from the ring and pretended to weigh it. He called out to the goldsmith that the ring was worth three halfpence. The goldsmith then offered that amount to Armorie.

Not being a fool, Armorie refused the offer and demanded that the ring be returned. The apprentice gave him the ring, but without the jewels.

Issue: *Did the chimney sweep boy have a legal right to retain possession of the found jewels?*

Decision: Yes, he had a right to the jewels.

Reasoning: Someone who finds property has a right to keep it unless the true owner claims it. In this case, the chimney sweep found the jewels, so they belonged to him. The goldsmith wrongfully withheld the stones from Armorie. The judge instructed the jury to award damages and to assume that the missing stones had been of the highest quality.

30-3 BAILMENT

A bailment is the rightful possession of goods by someone who is not the owner. The one who delivers the goods is the **bailor**, and the one in possession is the **bailee**. In the chapter opener, Cameron is the reluctant bailor and the joy-riding valet is the bailee. Such bailments are common. Suppose you are going out of town for the weekend and lend your motorcycle to Stan. You are the bailor, and your friend is the bailee. When you check your suitcase with the airline, you are again the bailor, and the airline is the bailee. If you rent a car at your destination, you become the bailee, while the rental agency is the bailor. In each case, someone other than the true owner has rightful, temporary possession of personal property. **Parties generally create a bailment by agreement.** In each of the examples above, the parties consented to the bailment. In two cases, the agreement included payment, which is common but not essential. When you buy your airline ticket, you pay for your ticket, and the price includes the airline's agreement, as bailee, to transport your suitcase. When you rent a car, you pay the bailor for the privilege of using it. By loaning your motorcycle, you engage in a bailment without either party paying compensation.

A bailment without any agreement is called a constructive, or involuntary bailment. Suppose you find a wristwatch in your house that you know belongs to a friend. You are obligated to return the watch to the true owner, and until you do so, you are the bailee, liable for harm to the property. This is called a constructive bailment because, with no agreement between the parties, the law is construing a bailment.

Bailment
The rightful possession of goods by one who is not the owner, usually by mutual agreement between the bailor and bailee

Bailor
The one who delivers the goods

Bailee
The one who possesses the goods

Involuntary bailment
A bailment that occurs without an agreement between the bailor and bailee

30-3a Control

To create a bailment, the bailee must assume physical control of an item with intent to possess. A bailee may be liable for loss or damage to the property, and so it is not fair to hold him liable unless he has taken physical control of the goods, intending to possess them.

Disputes about whether someone has taken control often arise in parking lot cases. When a car is damaged or stolen, the lot's owner may try to avoid liability by claiming it lacked control of the parked auto and therefore was not a bailee. If the lot is a "park and lock" facility, where the car's owner retains the key and the lot owner exercises *no control at all*, there is probably no bailment and no liability for damage.

By contrast, when a driver leaves her keys with a parking attendant, the lot clearly is exercising control of the auto, and the parties have created a bailment. The lot is probably liable for loss or damage in that case.

The following case examines whether a bailment was created during one of history's greatest tragedies. It was not quite a parking or car rental agreement, but was it a bailment?

DAVID L. DE CSEPEL V. REPUBLIC OF HUNGARY

714 F.3d 591
United States District Court for the District of Columbia, 2013

CASE SUMMARY

Facts: Baron Herzog was a Hungarian who had amassed one of Europe's largest private art collections. But the Herzog family was Jewish, and during World War II, the Hungarian government worked with the Nazis to confiscate all the property of Hungarian Jews. The government turned many pieces in the Herzog collection over to Hungarian museums; others were sent to Germany. The Herzog family was forced to flee or face extermination.

At the end of the war, the Herzog heirs were dispersed all over the world. They claim that, at that time, they arranged for Hungary to retain possession of the collection so that the works could stay in Hungary. But when the Herzogs requested the collection's return, Hungary refused.

The Herzogs sued Hungary for return of the art. They argued that the postwar arrangement formed a bailment, whereby Hungary promised to safeguard their property and return it to them on demand. Hungary denied that such a deal existed. It asked the court to dismiss the lawsuit. The district court denied the motion, and Hungary appealed.

Issue: *Did the parties create a valid bailment agreement?*

Decision: Yes, there is enough evidence to suggest that the parties formed a bailment.

Reasoning: The question is whether the postwar agreement created a valid bailment contract. If such a bailment was created, Hungary was merely the keeper, not the owner, of the artwork during the time of the family's exile. If there was no such agreement, Hungary has a claim of ownership in the expropriated collection.

Hungary argues that there was no bailment agreement because one of the key elements to bailment formation was absent: consent. Since the Herzogs were under duress when they made the postwar deal, a valid bailment could not have been created.

The court disagreed. If there was duress, then the contract would be voidable *by the Herzogs* (who suffered the duress) not by Hungary. It is up to the Herzogs to decide whether or not to enforce the bailment contract, and they have decided to do so.

EXAM Strategy

Question: Jack arrives at Airport Hotel's valet parking area in a Ferrari, just as Kim drives up in her rustbucket car. A valet drives Kim's car away, but the supervisor asks Jack to park the Ferrari himself, in the hotel's lot across the street. Jack parks as instructed, locking the Ferarri and keeping the keys. During the night, both vehicles are stolen. The owners sue for the value of their vehicles— about $2,000 for Kim's clunker and $350,000 for Jack's Ferrari. Each owner will win if there was a bailment but lose if there was not. Can either or both prove a bailment?

Strategy: To create a bailment, the bailee must assume physical control with intent to possess.

Result: When the valet drove Kim's car away, the hotel assumed control with intent to possess. The parties created a bailment, and the hotel is liable. But Jack loses. The hotel never had physical control of the Ferarri. Employees did not park the vehicle, and Jack kept the keys. Jack's Ferarri was a "park and lock" case, with no bailment.

Ethics Many companies post their parking policies on the Internet, often including a disclaimer stating that use of their facility creates no bailment or liability. Find such a statement, and analyze it. Why does the owner claim (or hope) that no bailment exists? If a parked car is damaged, will a court honor the disclaimer? Does the facility operator have any control of the cars as they enter, or while parked, or as they leave? Do you consider the facility's policy fair, or is it an unjust effort to escape responsibility?

30-3b Rights of the Bailee

The bailee's primary right is possession of the property. **Anyone who interferes with the bailee's rightful possession is liable to her.** The bailee is typically, though not always, permitted to use the property. When a farmer loans his tractor to a neighbor, the bailee is entitled to use the machine for normal farm purposes. But some bailees have no authority to use the goods. If you store your furniture in a warehouse, the storage company is your bailee, but it has no right to curl up in your bed.

A bailee may or may not be entitled to compensation, depending on the parties' agreement. A warehouse will not store your furniture for free, but a friend might.

> **If you store your furniture in a warehouse, the storage company is your bailee, but it has no right to curl up in your bed.**

30-3c Duties of the Bailee

The bailee is strictly liable to redeliver the goods on time to the bailor or to whomever the bailor designates. Strict liability means there are virtually no exceptions. Rudy stores his $6,000 drum set with Melissa's Warehouse while he is on vacation. Blake arrives at the warehouse and shows a forged letter, supposedly from Rudy, granting Blake permission to remove the drums. If Melissa permits Blake to take the drums, she will owe Rudy $6,000, even if the forgery was a high-quality job.

Due Care

The bailee is obligated to exercise due care. **The level of care required depends upon who receives the benefit of the bailment.** There are three possibilities:

1. **Sole benefit of bailee.** If the bailment is for the sole benefit of the bailee, the bailee is required to use **extraordinary care** with the property. Generally, in these cases, the bailor loans something for free to the bailee. Since the bailee is paying nothing for the use of the goods, most courts consider her the only one to benefit from the bailment. If your neighbor loans you a power lawn mower, the bailment is probably for your sole benefit. You are liable if you are even slightly inattentive in handling the lawn mower, and you can expect to pay for virtually any harm done.

2. **Mutual benefit.** Most bailments benefit both parties. When Ferris and his friends parked the Ferrari with the valet, they benefited from the convenience, and the parking service profited from the fee they paid. When the bailment is for the mutual benefit of bailor and bailee, the bailee must use **ordinary care** with the property. Ordinary care is what a reasonably prudent person would use under the circumstances. It is certainly *not* what the valet attendant exercised in the opening scenario.

3. **Sole benefit of bailor.** When the bailment benefits only the bailor, the bailee must use only **slight care.** This kind of bailment is called a *gratuitous bailment*, and the bailee is liable only for gross negligence. Michelle enters a pie-eating contest and asks you to hold her $29,000 diamond engagement ring while she competes. You put the ring in your pocket. Michelle wins the $20 first prize, but the ring has disappeared. This was a gratuitous bailment, and you are not liable to Michelle unless she can prove gross negligence on your part. If the ring dropped from your pocket or was stolen, you are not liable. If you used the ring to play catch with friends, you are liable.

Burden of Proof

In an ordinary negligence case, the plaintiff has the burden of proof to demonstrate that the defendant was negligent and caused the harm alleged. In bailment cases, the burden of proof is reversed. **Once the bailor has proven the existence of a bailment and loss or harm to the goods, a presumption of negligence arises,** and the burden shifts to the bailee to prove adequate care. This is a major change from ordinary negligence cases. Georgina rents Sam her sailboat for a month. At the end of the month, Sam announces that the boat is at the bottom of Lake Michigan. If Georgina sues Sam, she only needs to demonstrate that the parties had a bailment and that he failed to return the boat. The burden then shifts to Sam to prove that the boat was lost through no fault of his own. If he cannot meet that burden, Georgina recovers the full value of the boat.

30-3d Rights and Duties of the Bailor

The bailor's rights and duties are the reverse of the bailee's. The bailor is entitled to the return of his property on the agreed-upon date. He is also entitled to receive the property in good condition and to recover damages for harm to the property if the bailee failed to use adequate care.

30-3e Liability for Defects

Depending upon the type of bailment, the bailor is potentially liable for known or even unknown defects in the property. **If the bailment is for the sole benefit of the bailee, the bailor must notify the bailee of any known defects.** Suppose Megan lends her stepladder to Dave. The top rung is loose, and Megan knows it, but she forgets to tell Dave. The top rung crumbles, and Dave falls onto his girlfriend's iguana. Megan is liable to Dave and the girlfriend unless the defect in the ladder was obvious. Notice that Megan's liability is not only to the bailee, but also to any others injured by the defects. Megan would not be liable if she had notified Dave of the defective rung.

 In a mutual-benefit bailment, the bailor is liable not only for known defects, but also for unknown defects that the bailor could have discovered with reasonable diligence. Suppose RentaLot rents a power sander to Dan. RentaLot does not realize that the sander has faulty wiring, but a reasonable inspection would have revealed the problem. When Dan suffers a serious shock from the defect, RentaLot is liable to him, even though it was unaware of the problem.

30-3f Common Carriers and Contract Carriers

A carrier is a company that transports goods for others. It is a bailee of every shipment entrusted to it. There are two kinds of carriers: common carriers and contract carriers. The distinction is important because each type of company has a different level of liability.

 A **common carrier** makes its services available on a regular basis to the general public. For example, a trucking company located in St. Louis that is willing to haul freight for anyone, to any destination in the country, is a common carrier. **Generally, a common carrier is strictly liable for harm to the bailor's goods.** A bailor needs only establish that it delivered property to the carrier in good condition and that the cargo arrived damaged. The carrier is then liable unless it can show that it was not negligent *and* that the loss was caused by an act of God (such as a hurricane) or some other extraordinary event, such as war. These defenses are difficult to prove, and in most cases, a common carrier is liable for harm to the property.

 A common carrier, however, is allowed to limit its liability by contract. For example, a common carrier might offer the bailor the choice of two shipping rates: a low rate, with a maximum liability, say, of $10,000, or a higher shipping rate, with full liability for

Common carrier
A company that transports goods and makes its services regularly available to the general public

any harm to the goods. In that case, if the bailor chooses the lower rate, the limitation on liability is enforceable. Even if the bailor proves a loss of $300,000, the carrier owes merely $10,000.

A **contract carrier** does not make its services available to the general public, but engages in continuing agreements with particular customers. Assume that Steel Curtain Shipping is a trucking company in Pittsburgh that hauls cargo to California for two or three steel producers and carries manufactured goods from California to Pennsylvania and New York for a few West Coast companies. Steel Curtain is a contract carrier. **A contract carrier does not incur strict liability.** The normal bailment rules apply, and a contract carrier can escape liability by demonstrating that it exercised due care of the property.

> **Contract carrier**
>
> A company that transports goods for particular customers

30-3g Innkeepers

Hotels, motels, and inns frequently act as bailees of their guests' property. Most states have special innkeeper statutes that regulate liability.

Hotel patrons often assume that anything they bring to a hotel is safe. But some state innkeeper statutes impose an absolute limit on a hotel's liability. Other statutes require guests to leave valuables in the inn's safe deposit box. And even that may not be enough to protect them fully. For example, a state statute might require the guest to register the nature and value of the goods with the hotel. If a guest fails to follow the statutory requirements, he receives no compensation for any losses suffered.

Chapter Conclusion

Personal property law plays an almost daily role in all of our lives. The manager of a parking lot, the finder of lost property, and the operator of an airport security system must all realize that they may incur substantial liability for personal property, whether they intend to accept that obligation or not. Understanding personal property can be worth a lot of chips—but do not leave them lying around your hotel room.

Exam Review

1. **GIFTS** A gift is a voluntary transfer of property from one person to another without consideration. The elements of a gift are intention to transfer ownership immediately, delivery, and acceptance.

2. **FOUND PROPERTY** The finder of property must attempt to locate the true owner unless the property was abandoned. The following principles generally govern:

   - Abandoned property—the finder may keep it.

   - Lost property—the finder generally has rights superior to everyone but the true owner, except that if she found it on land belonging to another, the property owner generally is entitled to it.

   - Mislaid property—generally, the finder has no rights in the property.

Question: The government accused Carlo Francia and another person of stealing a purse belonging to Frances Bainlardi. A policeman saw Francia sorting through the contents of the purse, which included a photo identification of Bainlardi. Francia kept some items, such as cash, while discarding others. At trial, Francia claimed that he had thought the purse was lost or abandoned. Besides the fact that Francia's accomplice was holding burglary tools, what is the weakness in Francia's defense?

Strategy: The finder of property must attempt to locate the true owner unless the property was abandoned. Is there any likelihood that the purse was abandoned? If it was not abandoned, did Francia attempt to locate the owner? (See the "Result" at the end of this section.)

3. **BAILMENT**   A bailment is the rightful possession of goods by one who is not the owner. The one who delivers the goods is the bailor and the one in possession is the bailee. To create a bailment, the bailee must assume physical control with intent to possess.

4. **BAILEE'S RIGHTS**   The bailee is always entitled to possess the property, is frequently allowed to use it, and may be entitled to compensation.

5. **REDELIVERY**   The bailee is strictly liable to redeliver the goods to the bailor.

6. **DUE CARE**   The bailee is obligated to exercise due care. The level of care required depends upon who receives the benefit of the bailment: If the bailee is the sole beneficiary, she must use extraordinary care; if the parties mutually benefit, the bailee must use ordinary care; and if the bailor is the sole beneficiary of the bailment, the bailee must use only slight care.

7. **PRESUMPTION OF NEGLIGENCE**   Once the bailor has proven the existence of a bailment and loss, a presumption of negligence arises, and the burden shifts to the bailee to prove adequate care.

Question: Lonny Joe owned two rare 1955 Ford Thunderbird automobiles, one red and one green, both in mint condition. He stored the cars in his garage. His friend Stephanie wanted to use the red car in a music video, so Lonny Joe rented it to her for two days, for $300 per day. When she returned the red car, Lonny Joe discovered a long scratch along one side. That same day, he noticed a long scratch along the side of the green car. He sued Stephanie for harm to the red car. Lonny Joe sued an electrician for damage to the green car, claiming that the scratch occurred while the electrician was fixing a heater in the garage. Explain the different burdens of proof in the two cases.

Strategy: In an ordinary negligence case, the plaintiff must prove all elements by a preponderance of the evidence. However, in a bailment, a *presumption* of negligence arises. To answer this question, you need to know whether Lonny Joe established a bailment with either or both defendants. (See the "Result" at the end of this section.)

8. **BAILOR'S RESPONSIBILITY** The bailor must keep the property in suitable repair, free of any hidden defects. If the bailor is in the business of renting property, the bailment is probably subject to implied warranties.

9. **COMMON CARRIERS** Generally, a common carrier is strictly liable for harm to the bailor's goods. A contract carrier incurs only normal bailment liability.

10. **INNKEEPER LIABILITY** The liability of an innkeeper is regulated by state statute. A guest intending to store valuables with an innkeeper must follow the statute to the letter.

---

2. Result: Abandoned property is something that the owner has knowingly discarded because she no longer wants it. The burden is on the finder to prove that the property was abandoned, which will be impossible in this case since no one would throw away cash and credit cards. Because the purse contained photo identification, Francia could easily have located its owner. He made no attempt to do so and his defense is unpersuasive.

7. Result: Lonny Joe had no bailment with the electrician because the electrician never assumed control of the car. To win that case, Lonny Joe must prove that the electrician behaved unreasonably and caused the scratch. However, when Lonny Joe rented Stephanie the red car, the parties created a bailment, and the law presumes Stephanie caused the damage unless she can prove otherwise. That is a hard burden, and Stephanie will likely lose.

MATCHING QUESTIONS

Match the following terms with their definitions:

___A. Extraordinary care

___B. *Inter vivos* gift

___C. Ordinary care

___D. Gift *causa mortis*

___E. Slight care

1. A gift made with no fear of death, cannot be revoked

2. Required level of care in a bailment made for the sole benefit of the bailee

3. A gift made in contemplation of approaching death, can be revoked

4. Required level of care in a bailment made for the mutual benefit of bailor and bailee

5. Required level of care in a bailment made for the sole benefit of the bailor

TRUE/FALSE QUESTIONS

Circle true or false:

1. T F A gift is unenforceable unless both parties give consideration.

2. T F A gift *causa mortis* is automatically revoked if the donor dies shortly after making it.

3. T F A bailee always has the right to possess the property.

4. T F A finder of lost property generally may keep the property unless the true owner comes forward.

5. T F A common carrier is strictly liable for harm to the bailor's goods.

MULTIPLE-CHOICE QUESTIONS

1. **CPA QUESTION** Which of the following requirements must be met to create a bailment?

   I.   Delivery of personal property to the intended bailee

   II. Possession by the intended bailee

   III. An absolute duty on the intended bailee to return or dispose of the property according to the bailor's directions

   (a) I and II only

   (b) I and III only

   (c) II and III only

   (d) I, II, and III

2. Martin is a rich businessman in perfect health. On Monday morning, he tells his niece, Stephanie, "Tomorrow I'm going to give you my brand-new Tesla sports car." Stephanie is ecstatic. That afternoon, Martin is killed in a car accident. Does Stephanie get the car?

   (a) Stephanie gets the car because this is a valid *inter vivos* gift.

   (b) Stephanie gets the car because this is a valid gift *causa mortis.*

   (c) Stephanie gets the car because there is no reason to dispute that Martin made the promise.

   (d) Stephanie gets the car unless Martin left a wife or children.

   (e) Stephanie does not get the car.

3. Margie has dinner at Bill's house. While helping with the dishes, she takes off her Rolex watch and forgets to put it back on when she leaves for the night. Bill finds the watch in the morning and decides to keep it.

   (a) This is abandoned property, and Bill is entitled to it.

   (b) This is lost property, and Bill is entitled to it.

   (c) This is lost property, and Margie is entitled to it.

   (d) This is mislaid property, and Bill is entitled to it.

   (e) This is mislaid property, and Margie is entitled to it.

4. Arriving at a restaurant, Max gives his car keys to the valet. When the valet returns the car three hours later, it has a large, new dent. The valet says he did not cause it. Max sues the valet service.

   (a) The burden is on the valet service to prove it did not cause the dent.

   (b) The burden is on Max to prove that the valet service caused the dent.

   (c) The valet service is strictly liable for harm to Max's car.

   (d) The valet service has no liability to Max, regardless of how the dent was caused.

   (e) The valet service is only liable for gross negligence.

5. Car Moves hauls autos anywhere in the country. Valerie hires Car Moves to take her Porsche from Chicago to Los Angeles. The Porsche arrives badly damaged because the Car Moves truck was hit by a bus. The accident was caused by the bus driver's negligence. If Valerie sues Car Moves for the cost of repairs, what will happen?

(a) Valerie will win.

(b) Valerie will win only if she can prove Car Moves was partly negligent.

(c) Valerie will win only if she can prove that Car Moves agreed to strict liability.

(d) Valerie will lose because Car Moves did not cause the accident.

(e) Valerie will lose because this was a bailment for mutual benefit.

CASE QUESTIONS

1. While in her second year at the Juilliard School of Music in New York City, Ann Rylands had a chance to borrow for one month a rare Guadagnini violin, made in 1768. She returned the violin to the owner in Philadelphia, but then she telephoned her father to ask if he would buy it for her. He borrowed money from his pension fund and paid the owner. Ann traveled to Philadelphia to pick up the violin. She had exclusive possession of the violin for the next 20 years, using it in her professional career. Unfortunately, she became an alcoholic, and during one period when she was in a treatment center, she entrusted the violin to her mother for safekeeping. At about that time, her father died. When Ann was released from the center, she requested return of the violin, but her mother refused. Who owns the violin?

2. Ronald Armstead worked for First American Bank as a courier. His duties included making deliveries between the bank's branches in Washington, D.C. During a delivery, Armstead illegally parked the bank's station wagon near the entrance of one branch. In the rear luggage section of the station wagon vehicle's trunk were four locked bank dispatch bags containing checks and other valuable documents. Armstead had received tickets for illegal parking at this spot on five occasions. Shortly after Armstead entered the bank, a tow truck operated by Transportation Management, Inc., drove away with the station wagon in tow. One-and-a-half hours later, a bank employee paid for the car's release, but one dispatch bag, containing documents worth $107,000, was missing. First American sued Transportation Management. The towing company sought summary judgment, claiming it could not be liable. Was it correct?

3. Eileen Murphy often cared for her elderly neighbor, Thomas Kenney. He paid her $25 per day for her help and once gave her a bank certificate of deposit worth $25,000. She spent the money. Murphy alleged that shortly before his death, Kenney gave her a large block of shares in three corporations. He called his broker, intending to instruct him to transfer the shares to Murphy's name, but the broker was ill and unavailable. So Kenney told Murphy to write her name on the shares and keep them, which she did. Two weeks later, Kenney died. When Murphy presented the shares to Kenney's broker to transfer ownership to her, the broker refused because Kenney had never endorsed the shares as the law requires—that is, signed them over to Murphy. Was Murphy entitled to the $25,000? To the shares?

4. Artist James Daugherty painted six murals on the walls of the public high school in Stamford, Connecticut. Many years later, the city began to restore its high school. The architect and school officials agreed that the Daugherty murals should be preserved. They arranged for the construction workers to remove the murals to prevent harm. By accident, the workers rolled them up and placed them near the trash dumpsters for disposal. A student found the murals and took them home, and he later notified the federal government's General Services Administration (GSA) of his find. The GSA arranged to transport the murals to an art restorer named Hiram Hoelzer for storage and eventual restoration when funds could be arranged. Over *19 years* went by before anyone notified the Stamford School system where the murals were. In the meantime, neither the GSA nor anyone else paid Hoelzer for the storage or restoration. By 1989, the murals were valued at $1.25 million by Sotheby's, an art auction house. Hoelzer filed suit, seeking a declaration that the murals had been abandoned. Were they abandoned? What difference would that make when determining ownership?

5. Marjan International Corp. sells handmade Oriental rugs. V. K. Putman, Inc., is a Montana trucking company. Marjan delivered valuable rugs to Putman for shipment from New York City to Tacoma, Washington. Unfortunately, there were several delays in transit. The truck driver encountered snowstorms and closed roads. His truck also overheated and required repairs in a garage. Before the driver resumed the trip, he stopped to pick up and load other goods. When the truck finally arrived in Tacoma, two bales of rugs were missing. Marjan sued on the grounds that Putman was a common carrier, but Putman claimed it was a contract carrier. What difference does it make whether Putman was a common carrier or a contract carrier, and how is that determined?

DISCUSSION QUESTIONS

1. Ann is Becky's best friend. Tomorrow, Ann will move across the country to start a new job. Feeling sentimental on a night of goodbyes, Becky gives Ann a necklace that has been in Becky's family for 50 years. "You've always liked this, and I want you to have it," she says. Ann accepts the necklace. Early the next morning, Becky reconsiders. She finds Ann at the airport and sees her wearing the necklace. "Ann, my grandmother gave me that necklace. I'm sorry, but I want it back," she pleads. "You know," Ann replies with a smile, "I think I'm going to keep it." Is Ann legally required to return the necklace? Is she ethically required to return the necklace?

2. "Finders keepers, losers weepers" is a common children's rhyme. Does the law mirror its sentiment?

3. **ETHICS** Famous artists Georgia O'Keefe and Alfred Stieglitz donated 101 artworks to Fisk University in the 1940s. But the gift had two conditions: The pieces could not be sold and had to be displayed as one collection. Over 50 years later, Fisk could not pay to maintain the collection and decided to sell two of the pieces. Proceeds of the sale would go to restore its endowment and build a new science building. The Georgia O'Keefe Foundation sued to stop the sale, arguing that the artists would have opposed it. Should the law permit this sale? Do you agree with Fisk's actions? What duties do gift recipients have to donors? What would Kant and Mill say?[2]

4. After a baseball game, Randy cannot find his car in the stadium parking lot. For the life of him, he

[2]Based on Georgia O'Keefe Foundation v. Fisk University, 312 S.W.3d 1 (2009).

cannot remember where he parked. He wanders down row after row for an hour, and then another hour. Eventually, he gives up and calls a cab. Is Randy's car lost, abandoned, or mislaid? If Randy never returns to reclaim the car, who owns it?

5. Dan checks into a nice beachfront hotel. He does not want to expose his $10,000 Patek Phillipe wristwatch to salt water, and so he leaves it in the dresser in the room. When he returns from the beach, the watch is gone. He is shocked to learn that the hotel is not legally responsible for the value of his watch. Is the law reasonable in such cases? Should the hotel be liable? Why or why not?

CHAPTER 31

ESTATE PLANNING

© Olga Danylenko/Shutterstock.com

Pablo Picasso created hundreds of paintings and sculptures, as well as thousands of drawings and sketches. The famous artist's personal life was unconventional, featuring a series of wives, mistresses, and children, both legitimate and illegitimate. Despite this large group of feuding heirs, he died in France without a will.

After four years of litigation, the French court decided that his estate would be shared by his widow, Jacqueline (who later committed suicide); two grandchildren by his legitimate child, Paulo (who died of cirrhosis of the liver); and his three illegitimate children, Maya, Claude, and Paloma. But by the time the decision was reached, legal fees had swallowed up all the cash in the estate.[1]

> Despite having a large group of feuding heirs, Picasso died without a will.

---

[1]Adapted from Lynn Barber, "A Perfectly Packaged Picasso," *The Independent*, December 9, 1990, p. 8.

31-1 INTRODUCTION

There is one immutable law of the universe: "You can't take it with you." But you can control where your assets go after your death. Or you can decide not to bother with an estate plan and leave all in chaos behind you.

31-1a Definitions

Like many areas of the law, estate planning uses its own terminology:

- **Estate planning.** The process of giving away property after (or in anticipation of) death.

- **Estate.** The legal entity that holds title to assets after the owner dies and before the property is distributed.

- **Decedent.** The person who has died.

- **Testator** or **testatrix.** Someone who has signed a valid will. *Testatrix* is the female version (from the Latin).

- **Intestate.** To die without a will.

- **Heir.** Technically, the term *heir* refers to someone who inherits from a decedent who died intestate. *Devisee* means someone who inherits under a will. However, common parlance and many courts use *heir* to refer to anyone who inherits property, and we follow that usage in this chapter.

- **Issue.** A person's direct descendants, such as children and grandchildren.

- **Probate.** The process of carrying out the terms of a will.

- **Executor** or **executrix.** A personal representative *chosen by the decedent* to carry out the terms of the will. An *executrix* is a female executor.

- **Administrator** or **administratrix.** A personal representative appointed *by the probate court* to oversee the probate process for someone who has died intestate (or without appointing an executor). As you can guess, an *administratrix* is a female administrator.

- **Grantor** or **settlor.** Someone who creates a trust.

- **Donor.** Someone who makes a gift or creates a trust.

31-1b Purpose

Estate planning has two primary goals: to ensure that property is distributed as the owner desires and to minimize estate taxes. Although tax issues are beyond the scope of this chapter, they are an important element of estate planning, often affecting not only how people transfer their property but, in some cases, to whom. For instance, wealthy people may set up trusts as a means of passing on money tax-free. Or they may give money to charity, at least in part, to minimize the taxes on the rest of their estate.

31-1c Probate Law

The federal government and many states levy estate taxes (although traditionally, state taxes have been much lower). But only the states, and not the federal government, have probate codes to regulate the creation and implementation of wills and trusts. These codes vary from state to state. This chapter, therefore, speaks only of general trends among the states. Certainly, anyone who is preparing a will must consult the laws of the relevant state.

To make probate law more consistent, the National Conference of Commissioners on Uniform State Laws drafted a Uniform Probate Code (UPC). However, fewer than half of the states have adopted it.

31-2 WILLS

Will

A legal document that disposes of the testator's property after death

A will is a legal document that disposes of the testator's property after death. It can be revoked or altered at any time until death. Virtually every adult, even those with modest assets, should have a will to:

- Ensure that their assets are distributed in accordance with their wishes.

- Provide guardians for minor children. If parents do not appoint a guardian before they die, a court will. Presumably, the parents are best able to make this choice.

- Select a personal representative to oversee the estate. If the decedent does not name an executor in a will, the court will appoint an administrator. Generally, people prefer to have someone they know, rather than a court, in charge of their property.

- Avoid unnecessary expenses. Those who die intestate often leave behind issues for lawyers to resolve. A properly drafted will can also reduce the estate tax bill.

31-2a Requirements for a Valid Will

Generally speaking, a person may leave his assets to whomever he wants. However, the testatrix must be:

- **Of legal age** (which is 18).

- **Of sound mind.** That is, she must be able to understand what a will is, more or less what she owns, who her relatives are, and how she is disposing of her property.

- **Acting without undue influence.** Undue influence means that one person has enough influence over another to persuade her to do something against her free will.

In the following case, an elderly man disowned his family. Was he acting under undue influence? You be the judge.

You be the Judge

Facts: Wayne Ulrich lived alone on a farm. His only relatives were his brother, Raymond (who lived next door) and Raymond's two adult daughters. When he was 68, he made a will leaving everything to his nieces and their children.

He then met Susan Sorenson, who was a customer at his farm. Ten years after he met her, he suddenly broke off all communication with his brother and closest friends, wrongly accusing them of having stolen a canister of prunes from his house.

IN RE ESTATE OF ULRICH
2013 Minn. App. Unpub. LEXIS 770;
2013 WL 4404717
Court of Appeals of Minnesota, 2013

Wayne asked Sorenson for help with personal grooming and household chores. He attended Sorenson family events and began to look upon her as a daughter. He also had daily help from a home healthcare assistant.

Two years later, when Wayne was 80 years old, Sorenson took him to visit a lawyer she had selected. He asked the lawyer to draft a power of attorney giving Sorenson authority over his affairs and a will leaving everything to her. He believed that she would take care of him and keep him out of a nursing home.

Because Wayne's request was so unusual, the lawyer insisted that he meet privately with two other attorneys at the firm to assess his competence and any undue influence. Wayne explained that Sorenson was like family to him and his nieces would inherit from their father. All three lawyers stated that Wayne was a competent, very strong-willed person who made his own decisions.

When Wayne ultimately entered a nursing home, Sorenson visited him and bought what he needed. She also wrote herself $256,000 worth of checks from Wayne's accounts, claiming they were gifts from him.

After Wayne died, one of his nieces sued, alleging that Wayne's will was invalid because of Sorenson's undue influence.

You Be the Judge: *When Wayne altered his will, was he acting under undue influence?*

Argument for Wayne's niece: When Wayne Ulrich changed his will, he was a confused old man, isolated from his family and long-time friends. Did he really think someone had stolen a canister of prunes from him? Wayne was clearly afraid of having to go into a nursing home and

was depending on Sorenson to keep him at home. (Not that she did.)

Sorenson selected the lawyer who drafted the documents and even drove Wayne to his appointment. Three lawyers said he was competent, but they had an incentive to say so. And competence is not the same thing as acting with free will. How could they assess, in one visit, her influence over him?

Argument for Sorenson: No one has alleged that Wayne was demented or unaware of what he was doing. And when he changed his will, he was not isolated—home health care aides visited him regularly.

At that point, Sorenson had taken care of Wayne for more than a decade. He considered her his family and, indeed, she acted like a daughter. He knew that his brother would be able to provide for his nieces and their children.

Sorenson was not in the room when Wayne met with the lawyers. Three of them interviewed him before allowing him to sign the documents. Wayne was the opposite of confused or persuadable: He was a hard-headed man who had the right to change his will.

A testator must comply with the legal requirements for executing a will:

- It must be in writing.

- The testator must sign it or direct someone else to sign it for him, if he is too weak.

- Generally, two witnesses must also sign the will. Under the UPC, a notarized will does not require any witnesses, but only a few states have passed this amendment.

- No one named in a will should also serve as a witness because, in many states, a witness may not inherit under a will.

The importance of abiding by the legal technicalities cannot be overstated. No matter what the testator's intent, courts generally do not enforce a will unless each requirement of the law has been fully met.

Holographic Will

Some states recognize a **holographic will**, which is a will that is handwritten and signed by the testatrix, but not witnessed. **A holographic will *must* be in a testator's own handwriting—it cannot be typed or written by someone else.**

Suppose Rowena is on a plane that suffers engine trouble. For 15 minutes, the pilot struggles to control the plane. Despite his efforts, it crashes, killing everyone aboard. During those 15 minutes, Rowena writes on a Post-it note, "This is my last will and testament. I leave all my assets to the National Gallery of Art in Washington, D.C.," and then signs her name. This note is found in the wreckage of the plane. Her previous will, signed and witnessed in a lawyer's office, left everything to her beau, Ivan. If Rowena resides in one of the majority of states that accepts a holographic will, then Ivan is out of luck and the National Gallery will inherit all. One court has, indeed, accepted as a will a handwritten Post-it note that had not been witnessed.

Holographic will
A will that is handwritten and signed by the testator, but not witnessed

Nuncupative Will

Nuncupative will
An oral will

A few states will also accept a **nuncupative will** for personal property but not for real estate. This is the formal term for an oral will. **For a nuncupative will to be valid:**

- The testatrix must know she is dying,

- There must be two witnesses, and

- These witnesses must know that they are listening to her will.

Suppose that Rowena survives the airplane crash for a few hours. Instead of writing a will on the plane, she whispers to a nurse in the hospital, "I'd like all my property to go to the Angell Memorial Cat Hospital." This oral will is valid if there are two witnesses and Rowena also says the equivalent of, "I'm dying. Please witness my oral will." The cat hospital, however, is only entitled to her personal property. Ivan would inherit her farm under the written will she executed in her lawyer's office.

31-2b Spouse's Share

In community property states, a spouse can override the will and claim one-half of all marital property acquired during the marriage, except property that the testator inherited or received as a gift.[2] Although this rule sounds easy and fair, implementation can be troublesome. If a couple has been married for many years and has substantial assets, it can be very difficult to sort out what is and is not community property. Suppose that the testatrix inherited a million dollars 20 years before her death. She and her husband both earned sizable incomes during their careers. How can a court tell what money bought which asset? Anyone in a situation such as this should keep detailed records.

In most non–community property states, a spouse can override the will and claim some percentage of the decedent's estate (which varies by state). The UPC provides a complex formula that depends on how long the couple was married and what percentage of marital assets each owned.

31-2c Children's Share

Parents are not required to leave assets to their children. They may disinherit their children for any reason.[3] In most states, this is true even if the children are minors whom the testator was obligated to support while alive.

Pretermitted child
A child who is left nothing under the parent's will

However, the law presumes that a **pretermitted child** (that is, a child left nothing under the parent's will) was omitted by accident unless the parent clearly indicates in the will that he has omitted the child on purpose. To do so, he must either leave her some nominal amount, such as $1, or specifically write in the will that the omission was intentional: "I am making no bequest to my daughter because she has chosen a religion of which I disapprove."

If a pretermitted child is left out by accident, she is generally entitled to the same share she would have received if her parent had died intestate, that is, without a will. Does this rule make sense? How likely is it that a parent with sufficient mental capacity to make a valid will would *forget* a child? Do you think the father in the following case simply forgot?

---

[2]Arizona, California, Idaho, Louisiana, Nevada, New Mexico, Texas, and Washington all have community property laws; Wisconsin's system is a variation of the same principle.
[3]Except in Louisiana, whose laws are based on the French model.

In re Estate of Josiah James Treloar, Jr.

151 N.H. 460
New Hampshire Supreme Court, 2004

CASE SUMMARY

Facts: Josiah James Treloar, Jr.'s first will left his estate to his wife unless she died before he did, in which case one piece of land was to go to his daughter Evelyn, another to his son, Rodney, and the rest of his estate was to be divided equally among Evelyn, Rodney, and another daughter, Beverly.

After his daughter Evelyn died, Josiah executed a new will. To help his lawyer in preparing this document, Josiah gave him a copy of the old will with handwritten changes, including Evelyn's name crossed out. The new will left the estate to Rodney and Beverly equally. Evelyn's children and her husband, Leon, got nothing, although Leon was named as executor. Josiah referred to Leon as "my son-in-law."

Under New Hampshire law, all *issue* (including children and grandchildren) can qualify as pretermitted heirs. The law assumes that if the testator does not leave anything to his issue or does not refer to them in his will, it is because he has forgotten them. They are therefore entitled to a share of his estate. If Josiah had mentioned Evelyn, then the assumption would be that he had not forgotten her or her children.

Evelyn's children argued that they were entitled to a share of Josiah's estate because he had not left her or them out on purpose. Josiah's attorney was serving as executor (not Leon). When he refused to pay the children, they sued.

Issue: *Are Evelyn's children entitled to a share of Josiah's estate?*

Decision: Yes, Evelyn's children are entitled to a share of the estate.

Reasoning: Most people leave their money to their children and grandchildren. Therefore, when a parent omits one or more of these heirs from his will, the law in New Hampshire assumes that it was a mistake unless he clearly specifies *in the will* that he had left them out on purpose. In this case, it seemed that Josiah had not forgotten Evelyn or her children. After all, he had crossed her name out of the old will he had given his lawyer to use as a basis for the new document. He also listed her husband, Leon, as executor. Presumably, he remembered that Leon was married to Evelyn.

Nonetheless, it is not the court's job to try to figure out what Josiah did or did not remember. The law is clear—indirectly alluding to the children or grandchildren is not sufficient. Because Josiah did not specifically refer to Evelyn or her children within the four corners of the will, it is presumed he forgot them, and therefore they are entitled to a share of his estate.

As we have observed before, the laws regarding wills are very precise. It seems highly unlikely that Josiah remembered his son-in-law but forgot the daughter to whom the son-in-law had been married. No matter—the will did not meet the requirements of the statute, so Evelyn's children were in luck.

In drafting a will, lawyers use the term issue instead of children. Issue means all direct descendants, such as children, grandchildren, great-grandchildren, and so on. If the will leaves property to "my children" and one child dies before the testator, the child's children would not inherit their parent's share. But if the will says "to my issue" and one child dies first, her children will inherit her share.

The will must also indicate whether issue are to inherit per stirpes or per capita. Per stirpes means that each *branch* of the family receives an equal share. Thus, each child of the decedent receives the same amount, and, if a child has already died, her heirs inherit her share. **Per capita** means that each *heir* receives the same amount. If the children have died, then each grandchild inherits the same amount.

Suppose that Gwendolyn has two children, Lance and Arthur. Lance has one child; Arthur has four. Both sons predecease their mother. If Gwendolyn's will says "per stirpes,"

Issue
A person's direct descendants, such as children and grandchildren

Per stirpes
Each branch of the family receives an equal share

Per capita
Each heir receives the same amount

Lance's child will inherit her father's entire share, which is half of Gwendolyn's estate. Arthur's four children will share their father's portion, so each will receive one-eighth ($\frac{1}{4} \times \frac{1}{2}$). If Gwendolyn's will says, "per capita," each of her grandchildren will inherit one-fifth of her estate. Although it might sound fairer to give all grandchildren the same inheritance, most people choose a per stirpes distribution on the theory that they are treating their *children* equally. The following chart illustrates the difference between per stirpes and per capita.

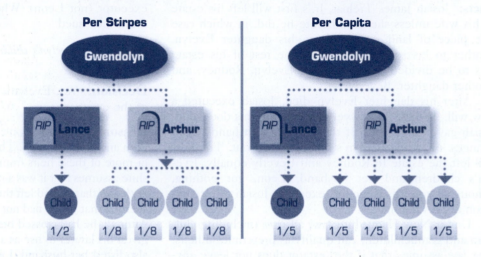

31-2d Digital Assets

Most people own digital assets with substantial value, both sentimental and financial, such as photos, music, movies, websites, social media accounts, email, and software. If the owner dies, some of this content (such as family photos) should be shared with loved ones, but other items (use your imagination) are best kept private. The rules on the inheritance of digital assets are based on:

- **Service provider policies.** Some of those terms and conditions (which we all agree to without reading), specify what happens after death (although many do not). For example:
  - Google has set up an Inactive Account Management system ("Inactive" is Googlese for "dead"). You can tell Google what to do when you become inactive: Either it can delete your whole account, or you can specify who will have access to what.
  - Facebook will, at the request of a family member and upon proof of death, either convert a user's timeline to a "memorial page" or deactivate it altogether. It will not reveal passwords.

- **Federal statutes.** A court ruled that, under the Electronic Communications Privacy Act, Facebook had the right to enforce its terms of service and withhold information from the family of woman who had died. Her family was trying to determine if her fall from a building had been suicide.[4]

---

[4]The ECPA is discussed at greater length in Chapter 9 on privacy and cyberlaw.

- **State statutes.** A handful of states have passed laws giving executors the right to access some digital assets (such as email, social media accounts, and texts).

- **Court decisions.** A court in Michigan required Yahoo to provide the family of a dead Marine with copies of the emails in his account.

What can you do to protect your digital life after death? Some options include:

- State in your will who has access to what.

- Share usernames and passwords with those you want to have access.

31-2e Amending a Will

A testator can generally revoke or alter a will at any time prior to death. In most states, he can revoke a will by destroying it, putting an *X* through it, writing "revoked" (or some synonym) on it, or signing a new will. He can also execute an amendment—called a **codicil**—to change specific terms of the will while keeping the rest of it intact. A codicil must meet all the requirements of a will, such as two witnesses. Suppose that Uncle Herman, who has a long and elaborate will, now wants his sterling silver Swiss Army knife to go to Cousin Larry rather than Niece Shannon. Instead of redoing his whole will, he can ask his lawyer to draw up a codicil changing only that one provision.

Codicil
An amendment to a will

31-2f Intestacy

When singer John Denver died unexpectedly in a plane accident, he had had several marriages, children, and platinum albums. His estate was worth $20 million. What he did not have was a will, as is the case with two-thirds of Americans. **When someone dies intestate, the law steps in and determines how to distribute the decedent's property.** Although, in theory, intestacy laws are based on what most people would prefer, in practice, they are not. The vast majority of married people, for instance, leave all their assets to their surviving spouse. Most intestacy laws do not. In some states, if a married person dies intestate, some portion of her property (one-half or two-thirds) goes to her spouse, and the remainder to her issue (including grandchildren). Few people would actually want grandchildren to take a share of their estate in preference to their spouse.

31-2g Power of Attorney

A **power of attorney** is a document that permits the **attorney-in-fact** to act for the principal. (An attorney-in-fact need not be a lawyer.) Typically, a power of attorney expires if the principal revokes it, becomes incapacitated, or dies. But a **durable power** is valid even if the principal can no longer make decisions for herself.

Lawyers generally recommend that their clients execute a durable power of attorney, particularly if they are elderly or in poor health. The power of attorney permits the client not only to choose an attorney-in-fact, but also to give advance instructions, such as "loan money to my son, Billy, if ever he needs it." If a client becomes incompetent and has no power of attorney, a court will appoint a guardian. As a general rule, it is better to make choices yourself rather than leave them to a court.

Power of attorney
A document that allows one person to act for another

Attorney-in-fact
The person who has the authority under a power of attorney to act for the principal

Durable power
A power of attorney that remains valid even if the principal becomes incapacitated

31-2h Probate

The testatrix cannot implement the terms of the will from beyond the grave, so she appoints an executor for this task. Typically, the executor is a family member, lawyer, or close friend. If the decedent does not select an executor, the probate court appoints an administrator to fulfill the same functions. Both the executor and the administrator are entitled to reasonable compensation—typically between 1 and 5 percent of the estate's value, although family members and friends often waive the fee.

31-2i Property Not Transferred by Will

A will does not control the distribution of joint property, retirement benefits, or life insurance. As explained in Chapter 29, property that is held in a joint tenancy automatically passes to the surviving owner, regardless of provisions in the decedent's will. Pension plans, other retirement benefits, and life insurance are also excluded from the decedent's estate and pass to whomever is named as beneficiary in the plans or policies themselves.

31-2j Anatomical Gifts

The demand for transplants of organs, such as hearts, corneas, kidneys, livers, pituitary glands, and even skin, is much greater than the supply. **You can register to be an organ donor:**

- Under the Uniform Anatomical Gift Act (UAGA), by putting a provision in your will or by signing an organ donation card in the presence of two witnesses;

- Using a smartphone app such as DonateLives or Organ Donor ECard; or

- In some states, by signing up when you apply for or renew a driver's license.

The UAGA also provides that, unless a decedent has affirmatively indicated her desire not to be a donor, family members have the right to make a gift of her organs after death.

31-2k End of Life Health Issues

Living Wills

Living wills or advance directives

In the event that a person is unable to make medical decisions, this document indicates her preferences and may also appoint someone else to makes these decisions for her.

Experts estimate that more than 75 percent of the population will not be capable of making their own medical decisions at the end of their lives. **Living wills (also called advance directives) allow people to**:

- Appoint a **health care proxy** to make decisions for them in the event that they become incompetent;

Health care proxy

Someone who is authorized to make health care decisions for a person who is incompetent

- Refuse, in advance, medical treatment that would, in their view, unreasonably prolong their lives, such as artificial feeding, cardiac resuscitation, or mechanical respiration; and

Physician-assisted death or assisted suicide

The process of hastening death for a terminally ill patient at the request of the patient

- Resolve disputes among family members. Terri Schiavo was only 26 years old when her heart stopped beating one evening, causing brain damage that put her in a persistent vegetative state. Her husband said she would not have wanted to live that way and asked to have her feeding tube removed; her parents disagreed and fought him through the courts. Even Congress intervened to try to keep the tube in place. Her husband ultimately prevailed, and the tube was removed, but only after 15 years of litigation and public uproar. If Schiavo had had a living will, her family would have had more privacy, fewer legal bills, and, perhaps, greater peace.

> **If Schiavo had had a living will, her family would have had more privacy, fewer legal bills, and, perhaps, greater peace.**

Physician-Assisted Death

Doctors are legally permitted to shorten a patient's life by withholding treatment. Four states – Montana, Oregon, Vermont, and Washington—also allow doctors to prescribe a lethal dose of medication for use by a terminal patient who is suffering intolerably. This process is called **physician-assisted death** or **assisted suicide**.

EXAM Strategy

Question: Tim's will leaves all his money to his cat, Princess Ida. After he dies, his widow and children claim that they are entitled to a share of his estate. Is this true? Will Princess Ida be living like royalty?

Strategy: The answer is different for his wife and children.

Result: Tim's wife is definitely entitled to some percentage of his assets (which varies by state). His children have no automatic right to a share of his estate so long as he indicated in his will that they had been left out on purpose.

31-3 TRUSTS

Trusts are an increasingly popular method for managing assets, both during life and after death. A **trust** is an entity that separates legal and beneficial ownership. It involves three people: the **grantor** (also called the settlor or donor), who creates and funds it; the **trustee**, who manages the assets; and the **beneficiary**, who receives the financial proceeds. A grantor can create a trust during her lifetime or after her death through her will.

31-3a Advantages and Disadvantages

These are among the advantages of a trust:

- **Control.** The grantor can control her assets after her death. In the trust document, she can direct the trustees to follow a specific investment strategy, and she can determine when and how much each beneficiary receives.
    - Suppose the grantor has a husband and children. She wants to provide her husband with adequate income after her death, but she does not want him to spend so lavishly that nothing is left for the children. Nor does she want him to spend all her money on his second wife. The grantor could create a trust in her will that allows her husband to spend the income and, upon his death, gives the principal to their children.
    - To obtain payments from a trust set up by real estate tycoon Leona Helmsley, her grandchildren had to visit their father's grave. She also left a trust for her dog, Trouble.[5]

- **Caring for children.** Minor children cannot legally manage property on their own, so parents or grandparents often establish trusts to take care of these assets until the children grow up.

- **Tax savings.** Although tax issues are beyond the scope of this chapter, it is worth noting that trusts can reduce estate taxes. For example, many married couples use a **marital trust**, and parents or grandparents can establish *generation-skipping trusts* to reduce the estate tax bill.

Trust
An entity that separates the legal and beneficial ownership of assets

Grantor
Someone who creates and funds a trust- also called a *settler* or *donor*

Trustee
Someone who manages the assets of a trust

Beneficiary
Someone who receives the financial proceeds of a trust

Marital trust
A legal entity created for the purpose of reducing a married couple's estate taxes

---

[5]Laura Saunders, "How to Control Your Heirs from the Grave," *The Wall Street Journal*, August 10, 2012.

- **Privacy.** A will is filed in probate court and becomes a matter of public record. Anyone can obtain a copy of it. Some companies are even in the business of providing copies to celebrity hounds. Jacqueline Kennedy Onassis's will is particularly popular. Trusts, however, are private documents and are not available to the public.

- **Probate.** Because a will must go through the often-lengthy probate process, the heirs may not receive assets for some time. Assets that are put into a trust *before the grantor dies* do not go through probate; the beneficiaries have immediate access to them.

Domestic Asset Protection Trusts (DAPTs)

A trust whose purpose is to prevent creditors of the beneficiary from taking the assets

- **Protecting against creditors.** About a quarter of the states permit so-called **Domestic Asset Protection Trusts (DAPTs).** Creditors have no right to reach any assets that a donor has placed in a DAPT, but the donor can spend the assets, as long as he has the trustees' permission. Hartwell has an unfortunate alcohol and drug problem, but he is no fool. When he inherited millions on his twenty-first birthday, he placed them all in an asset protection trust. Later he married, had children, and got divorced. He also was in a car accident that caused the death of a young investment banker. Both his ex-wife and the banker's husband sued him, looking for financial support. But they are both out of luck. His assets are protected from all creditors. The downside: He can only spend trust assets with the trustee's permission, and they may not always agree on what constitutes reasonable payouts to him.

The major *disadvantage* of a trust is expense. Although it is always possible for the grantor to establish a trust himself with the aid of software or online tools, trusts are complex instruments with many potential pitfalls. Do-it-yourself trusts are a recipe for disaster. In addition to the legal fees required to establish a trust, the trustees may have to be paid. Professional trustees typically charge an annual fee of about 1 percent of the trust's assets. Family members usually do not expect payment. Also, trust income taxes can be higher than if the assets are held by an individual.

31-3b Types of Trusts

Depending upon the goal in establishing a trust, a grantor has two choices.

Living Trust

Living trust or *Inter vivos* trust

A trust established while the grantor is still alive

Revocable

A trust that the grantor can terminate or change at any time

Testamentary trust

A trust that goes into effect when a grantor dies

Also known as an ***inter vivos* trust, a living trust** is established while the grantor is still alive. In the typical living trust, the grantor serves as trustee during his lifetime. He maintains total control over the assets and avoids a trustee's fee. If the grantor becomes disabled or dies, the successor trustee, who is named in the trust instrument, takes over automatically. All of the assets stay in the trust and avoid probate. Most (but not all) living trusts are **revocable**, meaning that the grantor can terminate or change the trust at any time.

Testamentary Trust

A **testamentary trust** is created by a will. It goes into effect when the grantor dies. Naturally, it is irrevocable because the grantor is dead. The grantor's property must first go through probate on its way to the trust.

Living trusts are particularly popular with older people because they want to ensure that their assets will be properly managed if they become disabled. Younger people typically opt for a testamentary trust because the probability they will become disabled any time soon is remote. Also they want to avoid the effort of transferring their assets to the trust in the short term.

31-3c **Trust Administration**

The primary obligation of trustees is to carry out the terms of the trust. They may exercise any powers expressly granted to them in the trust instrument and any implied powers reasonably necessary to implement the terms of the trust, unless that power has been specifically prohibited. **In carrying out the terms of the trust, the trustees have a fiduciary duty to the beneficiary. This fiduciary duty includes:**

- **A Duty of loyalty.** In managing the trust, the trustees must put the interests of the beneficiaries first. They must disclose any relevant information to the beneficiaries. They may not commingle their own assets with those of the trust, do business with the trust (unless expressly permitted by the terms of the trust), or favor one beneficiary over another (unless permitted by the trust documents).

- **A Duty of care.** The trustee must act as a reasonable person would when managing the assets of another. The trustee must make careful investments, keep accurate records, and collect debts owed the trust.

31-3d **A Trust's Term**

There are three possible outcomes for a trust: decanting, termination, or perpetual life.

Decanting

Decanting means pouring the assets out of one trust into another. This process can be used for two purposes: changing the terms of the original trust or distributing all of the trust assets to the beneficiaries. About half the states permit decanting, so long as the trustee has the power to make unlimited distributions to the beneficiaries.

   A trustee might want to decant a trust so that the assets can be moved to a state with more favorable trust laws. Or to change the payment schedule to beneficiaries—either to delay distributions if need be (say, the beneficiary is still in that cult) or hasten payments if appropriate (in time to start tuition payments). Typically, the trustee does not need approval from the beneficiaries.

> **Decanting**
> Pouring the assets out of one trust into another

Termination

A trust ends upon the occurrence of any of these events:

- On the date indicated by the grantor.

- If the trust is revocable, when revoked by the grantor. Even if the trust is irrevocable, the grantor and all the beneficiaries can agree to revoke it.

- When the purpose of the trust has been fulfilled. If the grantor established the trust to pay college tuition for his grandchildren, the trust ends when the last grandchild graduates.

Perpetual Trusts

The **Rule Against Perpetuities** provides that a trust must end within 21 years of the death of some named person who was alive when the trust was created. This rule has been the law in England and the United States since the seventeenth century. Its goal is to ensure that trusts do not last forever.

   However, more than half the states now permit so-called **perpetual** or **dynasty trusts**—trusts that do last forever. These trusts avoid estate taxes and generally allow donors to control their money forever.

> **Rule Against Perpetuities**
> Provides that a trust cannot last forever

> **Perpetual** or **dynasty trusts**
> A trust that lasts forever

EXAM Strategy

Question: Maddie set up a trust for her children, with Field as trustee. Field decided to sell a piece of trust real estate to his wife, without obtaining an appraisal, attempting to market the property, or consulting a real estate agent. Maddie was furious and ordered him not to make the sale. Can she stop him? Would she have to go to court?

Strategy: The answer depends upon what type of trust she has established.

Result: If the trust is revocable, Maddie can simply terminate it and take the property back. If it is irrevocable, she could still prevent the sale by going to court because Field has violated the duties he owes to the beneficiaries. He has violated the duty of loyalty by selling trust property to his wife. He has violated the duty of care by failing to act as a reasonable person would in managing the assets of another.

Chapter Conclusion

Most people do not like to think about death, especially their own. And they particularly do not want to spend time and money thinking about it in a lawyer's office. However, responsible adults understand how important it is not to leave their financial affairs in chaos when they do eventually die.

EXAM REVIEW

1. **WILL** A legal document that disposes of the testator's property after death.

2. **HOLOGRAPHIC WILL** A will that is handwritten and signed by the testator but not witnessed.

3. **NUNCUPATIVE WILL** The formal term for an oral will.

EXAM Strategy

Question: If you were in an emergency situation and desperately wanted to prepare a new will, under what circumstances would a holographic will be preferable to the nuncupative option?

Strategy: The two types of wills have different requirements for witnesses. (See the "Result" at the end of this section.)

4. **SURVIVING SPOUSE AND CHILDREN**   A spouse is entitled to a certain share of the decedent's estate. Children have no automatic right to share in a parent's estate so long as the parent indicates in his will that the pretermitted children have been left out on purpose.

EXAM Strategy

> **Question:** Josh was a crotchety fellow, often at odds with his family. In his will, he left his son an autographed copy of his book, *A Guide to Federal Prisons*. He completely omitted his daughter, instead leaving the rest of his substantial estate to the Society for the Assistance of Convicted Felons. Which child fared better?
>
> **Strategy:** Pretermitted children fare differently from those named in the will. (See the "Result" at the end of this section.)

5. **PER STIRPES VS. PER CAPITA**   In a will, a per stirpes distribution means that each *branch* of the family receives an equal share. Per capita means that each *heir* receives the same amount.

6. **REVOCATION OF A WILL**   A testator may generally revoke or alter a will at any time prior to death.

7. **INTESTACY**   When someone dies without a will. In this event, the law determines how the decedent's property will be distributed.

8. **PROPERTY NOT COVERED BY A WILL**   A will does not control the distribution of joint property, retirement benefits, or life insurance.

9. **LIVING WILL**   A living will allows people to appoint a health care proxy and/or refuse medical treatment that would prolong life.

10. **PHYSICIAN-ASSISTED DEATH**   Physician-assisted death occurs when a doctor prescribes a lethal dose of medication for use by a terminal patient who is suffering intolerably.

11. **TRUST**   A trust is an entity that separates legal and beneficial ownership.

12. **TRUST'S TERM**   There are three possible outcomes for a trust: decanting, termination, or perpetual life.

> **3. Result:**   A holographic will does not require witnesses; a nuncupative will requires two.
>
> **4. Result:**   Because the son was not totally omitted from the will, he is entitled to nothing more than the book, while the daughter who received nothing under the will actually gets more than her brother—she receives whatever share she would be entitled to if Josh had died intestate.

MATCHING QUESTIONS

Match the following terms with their definitions:

___A. Executrix

___B. Intestate

___C. Codicil

___D. Administrator

___E. Heir

___F. Issue

1. Someone who inherits assets

2. An amendment to a will

3. Children and grandchildren

4. Dying without a will

5. A personal representative appointed by the probate court to oversee the probate process

6. A personal representative chosen by the decedent to carry out the terms of a will

TRUE/FALSE QUESTIONS

Circle true or false:

1. T F There is no need to have a will unless you have substantial assets.

2. T F A holographic will does not need to be witnessed.

3. T F A nuncupative will does not need to be witnessed.

4. T F Only a handful of states permit an executor access to the decedent's digital assets.

5. T F A trustee must obtain approval from the beneficiaries before decanting a trust.

MULTIPLE-CHOICE QUESTIONS

1. *CPA QUESTION* A decedent's will provided that the estate was to be divided among the decedent's issue per capita and not per stirpes. If there are two surviving children and three grandchildren who are children of a predeceased child at the time the will is probated, how will the estate be divided?

(a) 1/2 to each surviving child

(b) 1/3 to each surviving child and 1/9 to each grandchild

(c) 1/4 to each surviving child and 1/6 to each grandchild

(d) 1/5 to each surviving child and grandchild

2. Hallie is telling her cousin Anne about the will she has just executed. "Because of my broken arm, I couldn't sign my name, so I just told Bertrand, the lawyer, to sign it for me. Bertrand was also the witness to the will." Anne said, "You made a big mistake:

I.   You should have made at least some sort of mark on the paper."

II. The lawyer is not permitted to witness the will."

III. You did not have enough witnesses."

Which of Anne's statements is true?

(a) I, II, and III

(b) Neither I, II, nor III

(c) Just I

(d) Just II

(e) Just III

3. Owen does not want to leave any money to his son, Kevin. What must he do to achieve this goal?

I.   Nothing. If he dies without a will, Kevin will inherit nothing.

II. Make a will that omits Kevin entirely.

III. Leave Kevin $1 in his will.

(a) I, II, or III

(b) II or III

(c) Just I

(d) Just II

(e) Just III

4. Lauren, a resident of Kansas, appointed her husband to be her health care proxy. Now that she is dying of cancer and suffering terribly, she is begging her husband and her doctors to give her an overdose of drugs. Which of the following statements is true?

I.   If she goes into a coma, her husband has the right to direct her doctors to withhold treatment.

II. Her doctor has the right to prescribe her a lethal dose of medication.

III. Her husband has the right to provide her with enough medication to kill her.

(a) I, II, and III

(b) Neither I, II, nor III

(c) Just I

(d) Just II

(e) Just III

5. Blake tells his client that there are five good reasons to set up a trust. Which of the following is *not* a good reason?

(a) To pay his grandchildren's college tuition if they go to the same college he attended

(b) To save money, since a trust is cheaper than a will

(c) To make sure the money is invested properly

(d) To avoid probate

(e) To safeguard his privacy

CASE QUESTIONS

1. If your grandparents were to die leaving a large estate, and all of their children were also dead, would you have a larger inheritance under a per stirpes or a per capita distribution?

2. When William Cook died, his will left all of his property to his brother Eugene. There were two other pieces of paper in the safe with the will. One said that that his stamp collection should go to his housekeeper, Bertha. This document was signed by two witnesses—the gardener and the cook. It was dated after the will. There was also a piece of paper stating that he would like all of his assets to go to his sister's daughter, Evangeline. Who will get what?

3. Kevin Fitzgerald represented the down-and-out Mission Hill and Roxbury districts in the Massachusetts House of Representatives. A priest alerted him that Mary Guzelian, a street person who roamed his district, had trash bags in her ghetto apartment stuffed with cash, bonds, and bankbooks. Fitzgerald visited the apartment with his top aide, Patricia McDermott. Two weeks later, Guzelian signed a will, drafted by one of Fitzgerald's acquaintances, that left Guzelian's $400,000 estate to Fitzgerald and McDermott. Fitzgerald claimed not to know about the will until Guzelian's death four years later. Guzelian, 64, suffered from chronic paranoid schizophrenia and severe health problems. Would Guzelian's sister have a claim on Guzelian's estate?

4. When Bill died, he left all of his property in a trust to take care of his wife, Doris, for the rest of her life. On her death, the money would go to their son, Rob. The Bank of Tulsa was the trustee. Fifty years later, Rob needed money, so he began writing checks out of Doris's checking account. She knew about the checks, but she could never say no to him. At the rate at which Rob was spending her money, the trust funds would all be gone within a couple of years. What was the bank's responsibility? Was it obligated to let Doris have as much money as she wanted?

5. When Sheryl founded a Silicon Valley company, she placed half of her stock in a trust for her children. They were entitled to the assets in the trust when they turned 21. The company has just gone public, and the stock in the trust is now worth $150 million. She does not want her children, who are 12 and 10 years old, to have that much money when they turn 21. Is there anything she can do?

6. When Gregg died, his will left his money equally to his two children, Max and Alison, whom he explicitly named. Max had died a few years earlier, leaving behind a widow and four children. Who will get Gregg's money?

DISCUSSION QUESTIONS

1. **ETHICS** Is an asset protection trust ethical? Should wealthy people be able to avoid paying legitimate creditors? What about perpetual trusts that avoid estate taxes forever? Legislators pass such laws to attract trust business from out of state. Trusts generate billions of dollars in fees each year. If you were a state legislator, how would you vote when this legislation came up for approval? If you

had substantial assets, would you put them in such a trust? What Life Principles apply here?

2. Should you have a will? *Do* you have one?

3. Billionaire Warren Buffett said that children should inherit enough money so that they can do anything, but not so much that they can do nothing. Is it good for people to inherit money? How much? At what age? How much would you like to leave your children?

4. The rules on wills are very exact. If the testator does not comply precisely, then the will is invalid. Suppose a man discovers that his daughter has broken virtually every law in this book—she has engaged in insider trading, price-fixing, and fraud, to name just a few. At his birthday party, the man says to the videographer, in front of 100 witnesses, "I have an appointment with my lawyer tomorrow. but in the meantime, you should know that I want all of my assets to go to the Home for Little Wanderers, the orphanage that raised me." On his way home that night, he dies in a car accident. Under his will, his daughter inherits all, and a court would undoubtedly enforce that will, despite all the evidence about the man's real wishes. Is that right? Courts are often called upon to make difficult decisions about facts. In the case of disputed wills, why not let the courts decide what the decedent really wanted?

5. What should intestacy laws provide? To whom would most people want their assets to automatically go?

CHAPTER 32

INSURANCE

Jamie needs insurance advice. When he bought a 3-D television at Shopping World for $1,000, the salesperson offered him a two-year service plan for $80. Should he buy it? What about renter's insurance for his apartment? And then his mother suggested he get a term life insurance policy while he is young and the rates are low. Is that a good idea? When he applies for health insurance, should he admit to being a social smoker? And what about the travel insurance available at the airport in case his flight home crashes?

© Olga Danylenko/Shutterstock.com

When he applies for health insurance, should he admit to being a social smoker?

How should Jamie evaluate his options? To answer these questions, it is important to understand the economics of the insurance industry. Suppose that you have recently purchased a $500,000 house. The probability your house will burn down in the next year is 1 in 1,000. That is a low risk, but the consequences would be devastating, especially since you could not afford to rebuild. Instead of bearing that risk yourself, you take out a fire insurance policy. You pay an insurance company $1,200 in return for a promise that, if your house burns down in the next 12 months, the company will pay you $500,000. The insurance company sells the same policy to 1,000 similar homeowners, expecting that on average, one of these houses will burn down. If all 1,000 policyholders pay $1,200, the insurance company takes in $1.2 million each year but expects to pay out only $500,000. It will put some money aside in case two houses burn down, or even worse, a major forest fire guts a whole tract of houses. It must also pay overhead expenses, such as marketing and administration. And, of course, shareholders expect profits.

When purchasing insurance, it is important to remember that insurance companies have a lot of data on people like you so they can predict accurately the probability that a calamity will befall you. They then price their premiums so that they will make a profit. For that reason, most people who buy insurance pay more in premiums than they ultimately receive from the policy. If that were not the case, insurance companies would go out of business. So why should you buy insurance? To protect yourself from disasters—no matter how improbable—that you simply cannot afford.

To review Jamie's situation:

Televisions are reliable and unlikely to need repairs in the first two years. These service plans are remarkably profitable—for the seller. Stores often make a larger profit from the insurance than from the product itself.

Does Jamie need rental insurance? Not to replace the $10 couch he bought off craigslist, but he should consider buying a policy that would protect him from liability if someone is injured in his apartment.

If he buys life insurance, term is the cheapest form—but does he need it? Whom is he protecting? He has no spouse or children. He is not supporting his mother. It seems that he does not need life insurance now.

When applying for health insurance, he must admit that he is a smoker (even if just "social"). Otherwise, the health insurance company can cancel his policy if he becomes ill. It is a bad idea to lie on *any* insurance application because then the policy is voidable.

As for travel insurance, those last-minute policies are almost always a bad deal. And if Jamie needs to protect someone, he should have life insurance that covers him all the time, not just on his trip home.

32-1 INTRODUCTION

Insurance has its own terminology, so it is important to begin by defining key terms:

- **Person.** An individual, corporation, partnership, or any other legal entity.

- **Insurance.** A contract in which one person, in return for a fee, agrees to guarantee another against loss caused by a specific type of danger.

- **Insurer.** The person who issues the insurance policy and serves as guarantor.

- **Insured.** The person whose loss is the subject of the insurance policy.

- **Owner.** The person who enters into the insurance contract and pays the premiums.

- **Premium.** The consideration that the owner pays under the policy.

- **Beneficiary.** The person who receives the proceeds from the insurance policy.

The beneficiary, the insured, and the owner can be, but are not necessarily, the same person. If a homeowner buys fire insurance for her house, she is the insured, the owner, and the beneficiary because she bought the policy and receives the proceeds if her house burns down. If a mother buys a life insurance policy on her son that is payable to his children in the event of his death, then the mother is the owner, the son is the insured, and the grandchildren are the beneficiaries.

32-2 INSURANCE CONTRACT

An insurance policy must meet all the common law requirements for a contract. There must be an offer, acceptance, and consideration. The owner must have legal capacity; that is, he must be an adult of sound mind. Fraud, duress, and undue influence invalidate a policy. In theory, insurance contracts need not be in writing because the Statute of Frauds does not apply to any contract that can be performed within one year, and it is possible that the house may burn down or the car may crash within a year. Some states, however, specifically require insurance contracts to be in writing.

32-2a Offer and Acceptance

The purchaser of a policy makes an offer by delivering an application and a premium to the insurer. The insurance company then has the option of either accepting or rejecting the offer. **It can accept by oral notice, by written notice, or by delivery of the policy. It also has a fourth option—a written binder.** A **binder** is a short document acknowledging receipt of the application and premium. It indicates that a policy is *temporarily* in effect, but it does not constitute *final* acceptance. The insurer still has the right to reject the offer once it has examined the application carefully.

Kyle buys a house on April 1 and wants insurance right away. The insurance company issues a binder to him the same day. If Kyle's house burns down on April 2, the insurer must pay, even though it has not yet issued the final policy. If, however, there is no fire, but on April 2, the company decides Kyle is a bad risk, it has the right to reject his application at that time.

Binder
A short document acknowledging receipt of an application and premium for an insurance policy

32-2b Limiting Claims by the Insured

Insurance policies can sometimes look like a quick way to make easy money. More than one person suffering from overwhelming financial pressure has insured a building to the hilt and then burned it down for the insurance money. Unbelievably, more than one parent has killed a child to collect the proceeds of a life insurance policy. Therefore, the law has created a number of rules to protect insurance companies from fraud and bad faith on the part of insureds.

Insurable Interest

An insurance contract is not valid unless the owner has an insurable interest in the subject matter of the policy. Here is a tragic example of why an insurable interest is important. To celebrate their engagement, Deana Wild and James Coates took a sightseeing trip along the California coast with Coates's mother, Virginia Rearden. They seemed to be just one big happy family. Tragically, Wild slipped while walking along the edge of a cliff at Big Sur and fell to her death. That would have been the end of the story except that, the day before, Rearden had taken out a $35,000 life insurance policy on Wild, naming Coates and Rearden as beneficiaries. When the insurance company investigated, it learned that Coates was married to someone else. Therefore, he could not be Wild's fiancé, and neither he nor Rearden had an insurable interest in Wild. It also turned out that Rearden had taken out the policy without Wild's knowledge. Ultimately, a jury determined that Rearden had pushed Wild over the cliff and convicted her of first degree murder. She was sentenced to life in prison without parole.

These are the rules on insurable interest:

- **Definition.** A person has an insurable interest if she would be harmed by the danger that she has insured against. If Jessica takes out a fire insurance policy on her own barn, she will presumably be reluctant to burn it down. However, if she buys a policy on Nathan's barn, she will not mind—she may even be delighted—when fire sweeps through the building. It is a small step to saying that she might even burn the barn down herself.

- **Amount of loss.** The insurable interest can be no greater than the actual amount of loss suffered. If the barn is worth $50,000, but Jessica insures it (and pays premiums) for $100,000, she will recover only $50,000 when it burns down. The goal is to make sure that Jessica does not profit from the policy.

- **Life insurance.** A person always has an insurable interest in his own life and the life of his spouse or fiancée. Parents and minor children also have an insurable interest in each other. Creditors have a legitimate interest in someone who owes them money. For some states, the standard is that you have an insurable interest in someone if the person is worth more to you alive than dead.

- **Work relationships.** Business partners, employers, and employees have an insurable interest in each other if they would suffer some financial harm from the death of the insured. For example, companies sometimes buy **key person life insurance** on their officers as compensation if they were to die.

Key person life insurance
Companies buy insurance on their officers as compensation were they to die

In the following case, one family entity owned properties, while a different family company managed them. When a hurricane blew, who had an insurable interest? You be the judge.

You be the Judge

Facts: The Banta family controlled a complex network of companies. One family company owned three apartment complexes in Florida. A different family business, Banta Properties, Inc. (Properties), managed these three complexes in return for 4 percent of the gross income. Properties bought $11 million in property insurance on the three complexes from Arch Specialty Insurance. Two months later, Hurricane Wilma badly damaged all three.

As a result of the hurricane damage, the apartments lost $39,000 in rents. Properties' share of those rents was $1,600. It filed an insurance claim for $6.1 million, which was the cost to repair the damage that Wilma had caused to the apartments. Arch refused to pay, claiming that Properties had no insurable interest in the complexes because it did not own them.

BANTA PROPS. V. ARCH SPECIALTY INS. CO.
2014 U.S. App. LEXIS 1419; 2014 WL 274478
United States Court of Appeals
for the Eleventh Circuit, 2014

Florida law defines an insurable interest as an "actual, lawful, and substantial economic interest" in keeping the property "free from loss, destruction, or pecuniary damage or impairment."

You Be the Judge: *Did Banta Properties have an insurable interest in the three apartment complexes?*

Argument for Properties: Yes, Properties meets the Florida definition of insurable interest because it had "a substantial economic interest" in keeping the property free from damage. If the properties were out of commission, Properties lost substantial management fees.

Also, Properties paid premiums on the full value of the apartments. It is only fair for it to receive what it paid for. This situation is different from, say, fire insurance, where the insured may be tempted to burn down a building. No one can cause a hurricane, thus Properties had no adverse incentives. Arch is just being a poor loser—it was unlucky and is trying to avoid paying what it owes.

Argument for Arch: An insurable interest is the amount of the insured's potential loss. Properties' potential loss was $39,000—the entire amount of its management fees for a year. Its actual loss was $1,600. But Properties is claiming $6.1 million in damages, hugely more than it could have, or actually did, lose.

The Banta family, with its complicated ownership structure, needed to be more careful when purchasing insurance to ensure that only those entities with an insurable interest actually bought the policies.

Misrepresentation

Insurers have the right to void a policy if, during the application process, the insured makes a material misstatement or conceals a material fact. The policy is voidable whether the misstatement was oral or in writing, and in many states, whether it was intentional or unintentional. **Material** means that the misstatement or omission affected the insurer's decision to issue the policy or set a premium amount. Note that a lie can void a policy even if it does not relate to the actual loss.

Material
Important to the insurer's decision to issue a policy or set a premium amount

Brian Hopkins submitted an application to Golden Rule Insurance Co. for medical and life insurance. In filling out the application, he answered "no" to questions asking whether he had had any of the following conditions: heart murmur, growths, skin disorders, immune deficiencies, sexually transmitted diseases, or any disorders of the glands. In fact, he had had all of the above. Two years later, Hopkins died of AIDS. Golden Rule rescinded Hopkins's policies because his application contained material misrepresentations.

EXAM Strategy

Question: During a visit to a hospital emergency room for treatment of a gunshot wound to his chest, John Cummings tested positive for cocaine. Six months later, he applied for a life insurance policy, which was to benefit his mother. The application asked if he had, within the prior five years, used any controlled drugs without a prescription by a physician. Cummings answered, "No." A year after the policy was issued, Cummings died of a gunshot wound. Was the policy valid?

Strategy: If the insured makes a material misstatement during the application process, the insurer has the right to void a policy, whether or not the misstatement relates to the cause of death.

Result: Cummings's mother argued that the policy was valid because her son had not died from taking drugs. The gunshot wound was unrelated to his cocaine use. However, an insurer has a right to void a policy if the insured makes *any* material misstatement. Here, the misstatement was material because the insurance company would not have issued the policy, or would have charged a much higher premium, if it had known about the cocaine. As a result, the company had the right to void the policy.

32-2c Bad Faith by the Insurer

Insurance policies often contain a *covenant of good faith and fair dealing.* Even if the policy itself does not *explicitly* include such a provision, an increasing number of courts (but not all) *imply* this covenant. **An insurance company can violate the covenant of good faith and fair dealing by:**

- Fraudulently inducing someone to buy a policy,

- Refusing to pay a valid claim, or

- Refusing to accept a reasonable settlement offer that has been made to an insured.

When an insurance company violates the covenant of good faith and fair dealing, it becomes liable for both compensatory and punitive damages.

Fraud

In recent years, a number of insurance companies have paid serious damages to settle fraud charges involving the sale of life insurance. The companies trained their salespeople to tell elderly customers that a new policy was better when, in fact, it was much worse. State Farm Insurance agreed to pay its customers $200 million to settle such a suit. Officials in Florida ordered Prudential Insurance Company of America to pay as much as $2 billion in damages after they determined that, for more than a decade, the company had deliberately cheated its customers. Prudential also trained agents to target the elderly.

> The companies trained their salespeople to tell elderly customers that a new policy was better when, in fact, it was much worse.

Ethics Presumably, the agents knew that defrauding elderly people was wrong. Why did they do it? What ethics traps did they face? How could you protect yourself from being in that situation?

Refusing to Pay a Valid Claim

Perhaps because juries feel sympathy for those who must deal with an immovable bureaucracy, damage awards are often sizable when an insurance company has refused to pay a legitimate claim. A jury in Ohio entered a $13 million verdict against Buckeye Union Insurance Co. for its bad faith refusal to pay a claim. An Ohio sheriff stopped the automobile of 19-year-old Eugene Leber. As the sheriff approached Leber's car, he slipped on ice and his gun discharged. By incredibly bad luck, the bullet struck Leber, permanently paralyzing him from the rib cage down. The insurance company recognized that it was liable under the policy, but it nonetheless fought the case for *16* years.

Consumers complain that insurance companies often "lowball"—that is, they make an unreasonably low offer to settle a claim. Some insurance companies even set claims quotas that limit how much their adjusters can pay out each year, regardless of the merits of each individual claim. If juries continue to award multimillion-dollar verdicts, insurance companies may reassess such a strategy.

In the following case, the insurance company ultimately paid the claim, but not fast enough to satisfy the jury.

GOODSON V. AMERICAN STANDARD INSURANCE COMPANY OF WISCONSIN

89 P.3d 409
Colorado Supreme Court, 2004

CASE SUMMARY

Facts: Dawn Goodson and her two children were in an automobile accident while driving someone else's car. The owner was insured by American Standard Insurance Company of Wisconsin.

To treat injuries that she and her children suffered in the accident, Goodson sought care from a chiropractor. She submitted these bills, totalling about $8,000, to American Standard. The insurance company offered a number of erroneous reasons why it would not pay the claims: that the chiropractor was not a member of American Standard's preferred provider organization; that the policy was not in effect at the time of the accident; and that Goodson and her children needed to undergo an independent medical evaluation to determine whether their injuries were related to the accident and whether their medical treatment was reasonable and necessary. In the end, American Standard did pay Goodson's bills, but it took 18 months to do so.

Goodson filed suit against American Standard, alleging that its delay was a bad faith breach of the insurance contract. Although the delay had not actually cost Goodson any money, it had caused her substantial emotional distress. The jury awarded Goodson and her children $75,000 in actual damages and an additional $75,000 in punitive damages. The appeals court overturned the verdict. Goodson appealed to the state supreme court.

Issue: *Can Goodson recover damages for the emotional distress caused by American Standard's delay in paying her claim?*

Decision: Yes, Goodson can recover both compensatory and punitive damages.

Reasoning: An insurer that violates its duties of good faith and fair dealing is liable for both compensatory and punitive damages. Compensatory damages include emotional distress, pain and suffering, inconvenience, fear and anxiety, and impairment of the quality of life.

The goal of punitive damages is to punish the insurer and deter wrongful conduct by other companies. To recover punitive damages, the insured must show that the insurer acted with fraud, malice, or wilful and wanton conduct.

Goodson suffered emotional distress as a result of the company's delay. Her worries about the medical bills left her anxious, fearful, stressed, and concerned about whether she would have to pay the bills herself. The whole point of buying insurance is to enjoy peace of mind. The fact that the company finally paid the bill, after 18 months of unreasonable delays, does not undo the distress caused by the bad faith conduct.

Refusing to Accept a Settlement Offer

An insurer also violates the covenant of good faith and fair dealing when it wrongfully refuses to settle a claim. Suppose that Dmitri has a $100,000 automobile insurance policy. After he injures Tanya in a car accident, she sues him for $5 million. As provided in the policy, Dmitri's insurance company defends him against Tanya's claim. She offers to settle for $100,000, but the insurance company refuses because it only has $100,000 at risk anyway. It may get lucky with the jury. Instead, a jury comes in with a $2 million verdict. The insurance company is only liable for $100,000, but Dmitri must pay $1.9 million. A court might well find that the insurance company had violated its covenant of good faith and fair dealing.

EXAM Strategy

Question: Geoff takes out renters' insurance with Fastball Insurance Co. On the application where it asks if he has any pets, he fills in "poodle." Although he does not know it, his "poodle" is really a Portuguese water dog. The two breeds look a lot alike. A month later, his apartment is robbed. Fastball investigates and discovers that Geoff does not have a poodle after all. It denies his claim. Geoff files suit. What result?

Strategy: There are two issues here: Was Geoff's answer on the application a *material* misstatement? Was Fastball's denial in bad faith?

Result: Geoff's misrepresentation was not material—the difference between these two breeds of dog would not have affected liability on the renter's policy. If he had said he had an attack dog such as a Doberman, perhaps the premium would have been lower because the dog would scare off intruders (or higher because the dog would also attack friends and neighbors), but poodles and Portuguese water dogs are equally friendly. Fastball would be liable for refusing to pay this legitimate claim.

32-3 TYPES OF INSURANCE

Insurance is available for virtually any risk. Bruce Springsteen insured his voice and Heidi Klum her legs. When Kerry Wallace shaved her head to promote the *Star Trek* films, she bought insurance in case her hair failed to grow back. Afraid of alien abduction? There is insurance for that, too. And an amateur dramatics group took out insurance to protect against the risk that a member of the audience might die laughing. Most people, however, get by with six different types of insurance: property, life, health, disability, liability, and automobile.

32-3a Property Insurance

Property insurance (also known as **casualty insurance**) covers physical damage to real estate, personal property (boats, furnishings), or inventory from causes such as fire, smoke, lightning, wind, riot, vandalism, or theft.

Property or Casualty insurance
Covers physical damage to real estate, personal property, or inventory from causes such as fire, smoke, lightning, wind, riot, vandalism, or theft

32-3b Life Insurance

Life insurance is really death insurance—it provides for payments to a beneficiary upon the death of the insured. The purpose is to replace at least some of the insured's income to protect her family or her employer.

Term Insurance

Term insurance is the simplest, cheapest life insurance option. It is purchased for a specific period, such as 1, 5, or 20 years. If the insured dies during the period of the policy, the insurance company pays the policy amount to the beneficiary. If the owner stops paying premiums, the policy terminates, and the beneficiary receives nothing. As the probability of death rises with age, so do the premiums. A $200,000 10-year term policy on a 25-year-old nonsmoking woman in good health costs as little as $95 annually; at age 60, the same policy costs about $400. Term insurance is the best choice for someone who simply wants to protect his family by replacing his income if he dies young.

Whole Life Insurance

Whole life (also called *straight life*) insurance is designed to cover the insured for his entire life. A portion of the premiums pays for insurance, and the remainder goes into savings. This savings portion is called the cash value of the policy. The company pays dividends on this cash value and typically, after some years, the dividends are large enough to cover the premium so that the owner does not have to pay any more. The cash value accrues without being taxed until the policy is cashed in. The owner can borrow against the cash value, in many cases at a below-market rate. In addition, if the owner cancels the policy, the insurance company will pay her the policy's cash value. When the owner purchases the policy, the company typically sets a premium that stays constant over the life of the policy. A healthy 25-year-old nonsmoking woman pays annual premiums of roughly $1,900 per year on a $200,000 policy.

The advantage of a whole life policy is that it forces people to save. It also has some significant disadvantages:

- The investment returns from the savings portion of whole life insurance have traditionally been mediocre. Mutual funds may offer better investment opportunities.

- A significant portion of the premium for the first year goes to pay overhead and commissions. Agents have a great incentive to sell whole life policies, rather than term, because their commissions are much higher.

- Unless the customer holds a policy for about 20 years, it will typically generate little cash value. Half of all whole life policyholders drop their policies in the first seven or eight years. At that point, the policy has generated little more than commissions for the agent.

- Whole life insurance provides the same amount of insurance throughout the insured's life. Most people need more insurance when they have young children and less as they approach retirement age.

Universal Life

Universal life insurance is a flexible combination of whole life and term. The owner can adjust the premiums over the life of the policy and also adjust the allocation of the premiums between insurance and savings. The options are sometimes so complex that customers have difficulty understanding them.

Annuities

As life expectancy has increased, people have begun to worry as much about supporting themselves in their old age as they do about dying young. **Annuities** are the reverse of life insurance—they make payments *until* death, whereas life insurance pays *after* death. In the basic annuity contract, the owner makes a lump-sum payment to an insurance company in return for a fixed annual income for the rest of her life, no matter how long she lives. If she dies tomorrow, the insurance company makes a huge profit. If she lives to be 95, the company loses money. But whatever happens, she knows she will have an income until the day she dies.

In a **deferred annuity contract**, the owner makes a lump-sum payment now but receives no income until some later date, say, in 10 or 20 years when he retires. From that date forward, he will receive payments for the rest of his life.

Annuities
Provides payment to a beneficiary during his lifetime

Deferred annuity contract
The owner makes a lump sum payment now, but receives no income until a later date

32-3c Health Insurance

The Affordable Care Act requires most Americans to obtain health insurance.

Traditional health insurance plans are *pay for service*. The insurer pays for virtually any treatment that any doctor orders. The good news under this system is that policyholders have the largest possible choice of doctor and treatment. The bad news is that doctors and patients have an incentive to overspend on health care because the insurance company picks up the tab. Complexity and quantity are rewarded, not outcomes. It has been estimated that as many as one-third of the medical procedures performed in pay-for-service plans have little medical justification, which in the end is not good for the patient. As a surgeon once said, "There is no condition so bad I can't make it worse by operating."

Instead of, or in addition to, pay-for-service plans, many insurers offer *managed care plans*. There are many variations on this theme, but they all work to limit treatment choices. In some plans, the patient has a primary care physician who must approve all visits to specialists. In **health maintenance organizations**, known as **HMOs,** the patient can be treated only by doctors in the organization unless there is some extraordinary need for an outside specialist. Patients are sometimes resentful of these constraints.

Neither type of plan is perfect. In pay-for-service plans, doctors have an incentive to overtreat. In managed care plans, they may have an incentive to undertreat. A study revealed that managed care plans tend to treat mental illness primarily with drugs. A combination of drugs and therapy tends to be more successful, but it is also more expensive.

Under the Affordable Care Act, the government is encouraging what it calls *value-based care*. The idea is that medical providers should be paid based on patient outcomes, not quantity and complexity of services performed. Thus, doctors could receive a bonus for reducing avoidable hospital readmissions. Conversely, hospitals may not be paid to treat preventable conditions, such as bedsores. The government is now funding a series of pilot programs to determine which methods are most effective at improving the efficiency of the medical system.

Managed care plans
Health insurance plans that limit treatment choices to reduce costs

Health Maintenance Organization (HMOs)
Generally, patients can only be treated by doctors who are employees of the organization.

Value-based care
Payment to medical providers is based on patient outcomes, not quantity and complexity of services performed.

32-3d Disability Insurance

Disability insurance replaces the insured's income if he becomes unable to work because of illness or injury. Perhaps you are thinking, "That will never happen to me." In fact, the average person is seven times more likely to be disabled for at least 90 days than she is to die before age 65. A significant percentage of all mortgage foreclosures are caused by an owner's disability. Everyone should have disability insurance to replace between 60 and 75 percent of their income. (There is no need for 100 percent replacement because expenses while unemployed are lower.) Many employers provide disability protection.

Disability insurance
Replaces the insured's income if he becomes unable to work because of illness or injury

32-3e Liability Insurance

Most insurance—property, life, health, disability—is designed to reimburse the insured (or her family) for any harm she suffers. **Liability insurance** is different. **Its purpose is to reimburse the insured for any liability she incurs by (accidentally) harming someone else.** Personal liability insurance covers tort claims by:

- Those injured on property owned by the insured—the mail carrier who slips and falls on the front sidewalk, or the parents of the child who drowns in the pool,

- Those injured by the insured away from home or business—the jogger knocked down by an insured who loses control of his skateboard, and

- Those whose property is damaged by the insured—the owner whose stone wall is pulverized by the insured's swerving car.

Liability insurance
Reimburses the insured for any liability she incurs by accidentally harming someone else

These are the types of claims covered in a *personal* liability policy. **Business** liability policies may also protect against other sorts of claims:

- Professional malpractice on the part of an accountant, architect, doctor, engineer, or lawyer;

- Product liability for any injuries caused by the company's products; and

- Employment practices liability insurance to protect employers against claims of sexual harassment, discrimination, and wrongful termination on the part of an employee. Note that this insurance typically does not protect the person who actually commits the wrongdoing—the sexual harasser, for instance—but it does protect the innocent insureds, such as the company itself.

32-3f Automobile Insurance

An automobile insurance policy is a combination of several different types of coverage that, depending on state law, are either mandatory or optional. **These are the basic types of coverage:**

- **Collision** covers the cost of repairing or replacing a car that is damaged in an accident.

- **Comprehensive** covers fire, theft, and vandalism—but not collision.

- **Liability** covers harm that the owner causes to other people or their property—such as their bodies, cars, or stone walls. Most states require drivers to carry liability insurance.

- **Personal injury protection** pays the medical expenses and lost wages of the owner, his passengers, and anyone living in his house or authorized to drive the car.

- **Uninsured motorist** covers the owner and anyone else in the car who is injured by an uninsured motorist.

Chapter Conclusion

Life is a risky business. Cars crash, people die, houses burn. So what can we do? Buy insurance and get on with our lives, knowing that we have prepared as best we can.

EXAM REVIEW

1. **INSURANCE CONTRACT** An insurance policy must meet all the common law requirements for a contract—offer, acceptance, consideration, and legal capacity.

2. **INSURABLE INTEREST** A person has an insurable interest if she would be harmed by the danger that she has insured against.

3. **MATERIAL MISREPRESENTATION** Insurers have the right to void a policy if the insured makes a material misstatement or conceals a material fact.

EXAM Strategy

Question: When Mark applied for life insurance with Farmstead, he indicated on the application that he had not received any traffic tickets in the preceding five years. In fact, he had received several such citations for driving while intoxicated. Two years later, Mark was shot to death. When Farmstead discovered the traffic tickets, it denied coverage to his beneficiary. Was Farmstead in the right?

Strategy: A misrepresentation is material if it affects the insurer's decision to issue a policy or set a premium amount. (See the "Result" at the end of this section.)

4. BAD FAITH BY INSURER   Many courts have held that insurance policies contain a covenant of good faith and fair dealing and have found insurance companies liable for compensatory and punitive damages if they commit fraud, refuse to pay legitimate claims in a timely manner, or wrongfully refuse to settle a claim.

EXAM Strategy

Question: Pamela Stone was in a car accident. Her policy did not cover any damages she suffered if she was more than 50 percent to blame. The insurance company investigated and determined that the accident was at least 60 percent her fault, so it refused to pay her claim. When Stone sued the company, the jury determined she was only 45 percent at fault. Did the insurance company violate its covenant of good faith and fair dealing?

Strategy: The insurance company violated its covenant of good faith and fair dealing if it was unreasonable when it failed to pay Stone's claim. Was it unreasonable? (See the "Result" at the end of this section.)

5. PROPERTY INSURANCE   Property insurance covers physical damage to real estate, personal property (boats, furnishings), or inventory from causes such as fire, smoke, lightning, wind, riot, vandalism, or theft.

6. ANNUITIES   Annuities are the reverse of life insurance policies; they make payments *until* death.

7. HEALTH INSURANCE   The Affordable Care Act requires most Americans to obtain health insurance. Health insurance is available in pay-for-service plans, managed care plans, or HMOs. Some doctors and hospitals are now experimenting with value-based care.

8. DISABILITY INSURANCE   Disability insurance replaces the insured's income if he becomes unable to work because of illness or injury.

9. LIABILITY INSURANCE   Liability insurance reimburses the insured for any liability that she incurs by accidentally harming someone else.

10. AUTOMOBILE INSURANCE   Basic automobile insurance includes: collision, comprehensive, liability, personal injury protection, and uninsured motorist.

3. Result: If Mark had told the truth, Farmstead still would have issued the policy, but the premium would have been higher. Therefore, it can deny coverage even though his lie was not about something that was a factor in his death.

4. Result: No, it was not unreasonable. The two parties had a good faith disagreement about the validity of the claim. The insurance company had to pay the claim, but not any penalty for violating the covenant of good faith and fair dealing.

MATCHING QUESTIONS

Match the following terms with their definitions:

___A. Insured

___B. Insurer

___C. Owner

___D. Beneficiary

___E. Insurable interest

1. The person who issues the insurance policy

2. The person who receives the proceeds from the insurance policy

3. If the person who takes out the policy would be harmed by the danger that she has insured against

4. The person who enters into the policy and pays the premiums

5. The person whose loss is the subject of an insurance policy

TRUE/FALSE QUESTIONS

Circle true or false:

1. T F If the insured makes any false statement in the application process, the insurance policy is voidable.

2. T F Even after an insurance company issues a binder, it can still revoke the policy.

3. T F You should primarily buy insurance to protect against harm that you cannot afford to repair.

4. T F You are more likely to die before 65 than to become disabled before 65.

5. T F An annuity is simply a type of life insurance.

MULTIPLE-CHOICE QUESTIONS

1. Lucas has bought the following insurance this week:

I.   A life insurance policy on his brother;

II. A life insurance policy on the partner in his accounting practice; and

III. A fire insurance policy on the fitness club he belongs to, so that if it burns down, he will receive a large enough payment to enable him to join a different club

In which of these policies does he have an insurable interest?

(a) I, II, and III

(b) Neither I, II, nor III

(c) I and II

(d) I and III

(e) II and III

2. If Chip helps out his daughter Sarah by buying a policy to insure her apartment, then _____ is the insured, _____ is the beneficiary, and _____ is the owner.

(a) Sarah, Sarah, Sarah,

(b) Chip, Chip, Chip

(c) Sarah, Chip, Chip

(d) Sarah, Sarah, Chip

3. If you are a smart consumer, you will:

I. insure against as many different kinds of risks as you can so that no matter what happens, you will be protected.

II. select as low a deductible as possible so that no matter what happens, you will not have to pay large sums out of pocket.

III. buy flight insurance when you take long airplane flights so that your family will be protected if your plane crashes.

(a) I, II, and III

(b) Neither I, II, nor III

(c) I and II

(d) Just I

(e) Just II

4. An insurance company does *not* violate its covenant of good faith and fair dealing if it:

(a) charges elderly customers higher premiums than it charges younger customers.

(b) tells potential customers that their premiums will decline when that is not true.

(c) tells potential customers that their returns on a whole life policy are certain to be higher than an equivalent amount invested in the stock market.

(d) refuses to pay a valid claim until after four years of litigation.

(e) refuses to accept a settlement offer on behalf of an insured that was reasonable, but not in the company's best interest.

5. Which of the following policies are you likely to *need* in your lifetime?

   I.   Service plan on an appliance
   II. Whole life insurance
   III. Disability insurance
   IV. Health insurance

   (a) All of the above
   (b) None of the above
   (c) II, III, and IV
   (d) III and IV
   (e) IV

CASE QUESTIONS

1. *YOU BE THE JUDGE* **WRITING PROBLEM** Linda and Eddie had two children before they were divorced. Under the terms of their divorce, Eddie became the owner of their house. When he died suddenly, their children inherited the property. Linda moved into the house with the children and began paying the mortgage, which was in Eddie's name alone. She also took out fire insurance. When the house burned down, the insurance company refused to pay the policy because she did not have an insurable interest. Do you agree? **Argument for the Insurance Company:** Linda did not own the house; therefore, she had no insurable interest. **Argument for Linda:** She was harmed when the house burned down because she and her children had no place to live. She was paying the mortgage, so she also had a financial interest.

2. Armeen ran a stop sign and hit the Smiths' car, killing their child. He had $1.5 million in insurance. The Smiths offered to settle the case for that amount, but Liberty State, Armeen's insurance company, refused and proposed $300,000 instead. At trial, the jury awarded the Smith's $1.9 million, which meant that Armeen was liable for $400,000 rather than the zero dollars he would have had to pay if Liberty had accepted the Smiths' offer. What is Liberty's liability? Under what theory?

3. Dannie Harvey sued her employer, O. R. Whitaker, for sexual harassment, discrimination, and defamation. Whitaker counterclaimed for libel and slander, requesting $1 million in punitive damages. Both Whitaker and Harvey were insured by Allstate, under identical homeowner's policies. This policy explicitly promised to defend Harvey against the exact claim Whitaker had made against her. Harvey's Allstate agent, however, told her that she was not covered. Because the agent kept all copies of Harvey's insurance policies in his office, she took him at his word. She had no choice but to defend against the claim on her own. Whitaker mounted an exceedingly hostile litigation attack, taking 80 depositions. After a year, Allstate agreed to defend Harvey. However, instead of hiring the lawyer who had been representing her, it chose another lawyer who had no expertise in this type of case and was a close friend of Whitaker's attorney. Harvey's new lawyer refused to meet her or to attend any depositions. Harvey and Whitaker finally settled. Whitaker had spent $1 million in legal fees, Harvey $169,000, and Allstate $2,513. Does Harvey have a claim against Allstate?

4. Clyde received a letter from his automobile insurance company notifying him that it would not renew his policy that was set to expire on February 28. Clyde did not obtain another policy, and in a burst of astonishing bad luck, at 2:30 a.m. on March 1, he struck another vehicle, killing two men. Later that day, Clyde applied for insurance coverage. As part of this application, he indicated that he had not been involved in any accident in the last three years. The new policy was effective as of 12:01 a.m. on March 1. Will the estates of the two dead men be able to recover under this policy?

5. Jason lived in an apartment with Miri, to whom he was not married. When he applied for homeowners insurance, the form asked their marital status. He checked the box that said "married." Later, the apartment was robbed, and Jason filed a claim with his insurance company. When the company discovered that Jason and Miri were not married, it refused to pay the claim on the grounds that he had made a material misrepresentation. Jason argued that the misrepresentation was not material because the insurance company would have issued the policy no matter how he answered that question. Is Jason's policy valid?

DISCUSSION QUESTIONS

1. Suzy Tomlinson, 74, met a tragic end—she drowned, fully clothed, in her bathtub after a night out partying with 36-year-old J. B. Carlson. He had taken her home at 1 a.m. and was the last person to see her alive. The two were not only party buddies—Suzy was on the board of directors of a company J. B. had started. Her family was stunned to find out that she had a $15 million life insurance policy, with the proceeds payable to a company J. B. controlled. He said it was a key person policy. He wanted to protect the company if Suzy died because she had frequently introduced him to potential investors. Is the life insurance policy valid?

2. Tomlinson's family sued the insurance company, claiming that the policy was valid, but that they were the beneficiaries, not J. B. Is the family entitled to the proceeds of the policy? Should they be?

3. **ETHICS** Most people who rent cars do not need to buy the extra coverage that the rental agencies offer because credit cards already provide this type of insurance. However, this coverage is very profitable for the rental companies. If you were the manager of a car rental agency, how aggressive would you be in encouraging your agents to sell these policies? Would you pay them a commission or base their salaries on the number of policies

they sold? Or train them to remind customers that their credit card company might provide coverage? What is your Life Principle on this issue? What would Kant and Mill say?

4. **ETHICS** Donna and Carl Nichols each bought term life insurance from Prudential Insurance Company of America. These policies contained a provision stating that if the insured became disabled, the premiums did not have to be paid, and the policy would still stay in effect. This term is called a *waiver of premium*. Carl became totally disabled, and his premiums were waived. Some years later, two Prudential sales managers convinced the Nicholses to convert their term life insurance policies into whole life policies. They promised that, once Carl made the conversion, he would only have to pay premiums on the new policy for a six-month waiting period. They even wrote "WP to be included in this policy" on the application form. "WP" stood for waiver of premium benefit. Only after the new policy was issued did the Nicholses learn that Prudential would not waive the premium. The Nicholses had exchanged a policy on which they owed nothing further for a policy on which they now had to pay premiums that they could not afford. Do the Nicholses have a claim against Prudential? Regardless of the legal outcome, did Prudential have an ethical obligation to the Nicholses?

5. Jason applied for a homeowners policy through CPM Insurance Services, Inc. An employee of CPM filled out the application form using information provided by Jason's housemate, Tricia. The two-page form asked: "Does applicant or any tenant have any animals or exotic pets?" The CPM employee checked an adjacent box stating that the answer was "No." At the time, Jason owned two dogs, a Doberman and a German shepherd. Although Jason had not read this part of the form, he nonetheless signed the application attesting that he had read it and that the answers were true. When Jason was sued by someone who claimed to have been bitten by one of his dogs, CPM rescinded his policy for material misrepresentation. In his defense, Jason said that the question about pets was confusing. He thought it applied only to exotic animals, not dogs. Also, he had not filled out the form, a CPM employee had. Is Jason's policy with CPM valid?

THE CONSTITUTION OF THE UNITED STATES

Preamble

We the People of the United States, in Order to form a more perfect Union, establish Justice, insure domestic Tranquility, provide for the common defense, promote the general Welfare, and secure the Blessings of Liberty to ourselves and our Posterity, do ordain and establish this Constitution for the United States of America.

ARTICLE I

Section 1.

All legislative Powers herein granted shall be vested in a Congress of the United States, which shall consist of a Senate and House of Representatives.

Section 2.

The House of Representatives shall be composed of Members chosen every second Year by the People of the several States, and the Electors in each State shall have the Qualifications requisite for Electors of the most numerous Branch of the State Legislature.

No Person shall be a Representative who shall not have attained to the Age of twenty five Years, and been seven Years a Citizen of the United States, and who shall not, when elected, be an Inhabitant of that State in which he shall be chosen.

Representatives and direct Taxes shall be apportioned among the several States which may be included within this Union, according to their respective Numbers, which shall be determined by adding to the whole Number of free Persons, including those bound to Service for a Term of Years, and excluding Indians not taxed, three fifths of all other Persons. The actual Enumeration shall be made within three Years after the first Meeting of the Congress of the United States, and within every subsequent Term of ten Years, in such Manner as they shall by Law direct. The number of Representatives shall not exceed one for every thirty Thousand, but each State shall have at Least one Representative; and until such enumeration shall be made, the State of New Hampshire shall be entitled to chuse three, Massachusetts eight, Rhode Island and Providence Plantations one, Connecticut five, New-York six, New Jersey four, Pennsylvania eight, Delaware one, Maryland six, Virginia ten, North Carolina five, South Carolina five, and Georgia three.

When vacancies happen in the Representation from any State, the Executive Authority thereof shall issue Writs of Election to fill such vacancies.

The House of Representatives shall chuse their Speaker and other Officers; and shall have the sole Power of Impeachment.

Section 3.

The Senate of the United States shall be composed of two Senators from each State, chosen by the Legislature thereof, for six Years; and each Senator shall have one Vote.

Immediately after they shall be assembled in Consequence of the first Election, they shall be divided as equally as may be into three Classes. The Seats of the Senators of the first Class shall be vacated at the Expiration of the second Year, of the second Class at the Expiration of the fourth Year, and of the third Class at the Expiration of the sixth Year, so that one third may be chosen every second Year; and if Vacancies happen by Resignation or otherwise, during the Recess of the Legislature of any State, the Executive thereof may make temporary Appointments until the next Meeting of the Legislature, which shall then fill such Vacancies.

No Person shall be a Senator who shall not have attained to the Age of thirty Years, and been nine Years a Citizen of the United States, and who shall not, when elected, be an Inhabitant of that State for which he shall be chosen.

The Vice President of the United States shall be President of the Senate, but shall have no Vote, unless they be equally divided.

The Senate shall chuse their other Officers, and also a President pro tempore, in the Absence of the Vice President, or when he shall exercise the Office of President of the United States.

The Senate shall have the sole power to try all Impeachments. When sitting for that Purpose, they shall be on Oath or Affirmation. When the President of the United States is tried, the Chief Justice shall preside: And no Person shall be convicted without the Concurrence of two thirds of the Members present.

Judgment in Cases of Impeachment shall not extend further than to removal from Office, and disqualification to hold and enjoy any Office of honor, Trust or Profit under the United States: but the Party convicted shall nevertheless be liable and subject to Indictment, Trial, Judgment and Punishment, according to Law.

Section 4.

The Times, Places and Manner of holding Elections for Senators and Representatives, shall be prescribed in each State by the Legislature thereof: but the Congress may at any time by Law make or alter such Regulations, except as to the Places of chusing Senators.

The Congress shall assemble at least once in every Year, and such Meeting shall be on the first Monday in December, unless they shall by Law appoint a different Day.

Section 5.

Each House shall be the Judge of the Elections, Returns and Qualifications of its own Members, and a Majority of each shall constitute a Quorum to do Business; but a smaller Number may adjourn from day to day, and may be authorized to compel the Attendance of absent Members, in such Manner, and under such Penalties as each House may provide.

Each House may determine the Rules of its Proceedings, punish its Members for disorderly Behaviour, and, with the Concurrence of two thirds, expel a Member.

Each House shall keep a Journal of its Proceedings, and from time to time publish the same, excepting such Parts as may in their Judgment require Secrecy; and the Yeas and Nays of the Members of either House on any question shall, at the Desire of one fifth of those Present, be entered on the Journal.

Neither House, during the Session of Congress, shall, without the Consent of the other, adjourn for more than three days, nor to any other Place than that in which the two Houses shall be sitting.

Section 6.

The Senators and Representatives shall receive a Compensation for their Services, to be ascertained by Law, and paid out of the Treasury of the United States. They shall in all Cases, except Treason, Felony and Breach of the Peace, be privileged from Arrest during their Attendance at the Session of their respective Houses, and in going to and returning from the same; and for any Speech or Debate in either House, they shall not be questioned in any other Place.

No Senator or Representative shall, during the Time for which he was elected, be appointed to any civil Office under the Authority of the United States, which shall have been created, or the Emoluments whereof shall have been encreased during such time; and no Person holding any Office under the United States, shall be a Member of either House during his Continuance in Office.

Section 7.

All Bills for raising Revenue shall originate in the House of Representatives; but the Senate may propose or concur with Amendments as on other Bills.

Every Bill which shall have passed the House of Representatives and the Senate, shall, before it become a Law, be presented to the President of the United States; If he approve he shall sign it, but if not he shall return it, with his Objections to that House in which it shall have originated, who shall enter the Objections at large on their Journal, and proceed to reconsider it. If after such Reconsideration two thirds of that House shall agree to pass the Bill, it shall be sent, together with the Objections, to the other House, by which it shall likewise be reconsidered, and if approved by two thirds of that House, it shall become a Law. But in all such Cases the Votes of both Houses shall be determined by Yeas and Nays, and the Names of the Persons voting for and against the Bill shall be entered on the Journal of each House respectively. If any Bill shall not be returned by the President within ten Days (Sundays excepted) after it shall have been presented to him, the Same shall be a Law, in like Manner as if he had signed it, unless the Congress by their Adjournment prevent its Return, in which Case it shall not be a Law.

Every Order, Resolution, or Vote to which the Concurrence of the Senate and House of Representatives may be necessary (except on a question of Adjournment) shall be presented to the President of the United States; and before the Same shall take Effect, shall be approved by him, or being disapproved by him, shall be repassed by two thirds of the Senate and House of Representatives, according to the Rules and Limitations prescribed in the Case of a Bill.

Section 8.

The Congress shall have Power to lay and collect Taxes, Duties, Imposts and Excises, to pay the Debts and provide for the common Defence and general Welfare of the United States; but all Duties, Imposts and Excises shall be uniform throughout the United States;

To borrow Money on the credit of the United States;

To regulate Commerce with foreign Nations, and among the several States, and with the Indian Tribes;

To establish an uniform Rule of Naturalization, and uniform Laws on the subject of Bankruptcies throughout the United States;

To coin Money, regulate the Value thereof, and of foreign Coin, and fix the Standard of Weights and Measures;

To provide for the Punishment of counterfeiting the Securities and current Coin of the United States;

To establish Post Offices and post Roads;

To promote the Progress of Science and useful Arts, by securing for limited Times to Authors and Inventors the exclusive Right to their respective Writings and Discoveries;

To constitute Tribunals inferior to the supreme Court;

To define and punish Piracies and Felonies committed on the high Seas, and Offenses against the Law of Nations;

To declare War, grant Letters of Marque and Reprisal, and make Rules concerning Captures on Land and Water;

To raise and support Armies, but no Appropriation of Money to that Use shall be for a longer Term than two Years;

To provide and maintain a Navy;

To make Rules for the Government and Regulation of the land and naval Forces;

To provide for calling forth the Militia to execute the Laws of the Union, suppress Insurrections and repel Invasions;

To provide for organizing, arming, and disciplining, the Militia, and for governing such Part of them as may be employed in the Service of the United States, reserving to the States respectively, the Appointment of the Officers, and the Authority of training the Militia according to the discipline described by Congress;

To exercise exclusive Legislation in all Cases whatsoever, over such District (not exceeding ten Miles square) as may, by Cession of particular States, and the Acceptance of Congress, become the Seat of the Government of the United States, and to exercise like Authority over all Places purchased by the Consent of the Legislature of the State in which the Same shall be, for the Erection of Forts, Magazines, Arsenals, dock-Yards, and other needful Buildings;—And

To make all Laws which shall be necessary and proper for carrying into Execution the foregoing Powers, and all other Powers vested by this Constitution in the Government of the United States, or in any Department or Officer thereof.

Section 9.

The Migration or Importation of such Persons as any of the States now existing shall think proper to admit, shall not be prohibited by the Congress prior to the Year one thousand eight hundred and eight, but a Tax or Duty may be imposed on such Importation, not exceeding ten dollars for each Person.

The Privilege of the Writ of Habeas Corpus shall not be suspended, unless when in Cases of Rebellion or Invasion the public Safety may require it.

No Bill of Attainder or ex post facto Law shall be passed.

No Capitation, or other direct, Tax shall be laid, unless in Proportion to the Census or Enumeration herein before directed to be taken.

No Tax or Duty shall be laid on Articles exported from any State.

No Preference shall be given by any Regulation of Commerce or Revenue to the Ports of one State over those of another; nor shall Vessels bound to, or from, one State, be obliged to enter, clear, or pay Duties in another.

No Money shall be drawn from the Treasury, but in Consequence of Appropriations made by Laws; and a regular Statement and Account of the Receipts and Expenditures of all public Money shall be published from time to time.

No Title of Nobility shall be granted by the United States: And no Person holding any Office of Profit or Trust under them, shall, without the Consent of the Congress, accept of any present, Emolument, Office, or Title, of any kind whatever, from any King, Prince, or foreign State.

Section 10.

No State shall enter into any Treaty, Alliance, or Confederation; grant Letters of Marque and Reprisal; coin Money; emit Bills of Credit; make any Thing but gold and silver Coin a Tender in Payment of Debts; pass any Bill of Attainder, ex post facto Law, or Law impairing the Obligation of Contracts, or grant any Title of Nobility.

No State shall, without the Consent of the Congress, lay any Imposts or Duties on Imports or Exports, except what may be absolutely necessary for executing its inspection Laws: and the net Produce of all Duties and Imposts, laid by any State on Imports or Exports, shall be for the Use of the Treasury of the United States; and all such Laws shall be subject to the Revision and Controul of the Congress.

No State shall, without the Consent of Congress, lay any Duty of Tonnage, keep Troops, or Ships of War in time of Peace, enter into any Agreement or Compact with another State, or with a foreign Power, or engage in War, unless actually invaded, or in such imminent Danger as will not admit of delay.

ARTICLE II

Section 1.

The executive Power shall be vested in a President of the United States of America. He shall hold his Office during the Term of four Years, and, together with the Vice President, chosen for the same Term, be elected, as follows:

Each State shall appoint, in such Manner as the Legislature thereof may direct, a Number of Electors, equal to the whole Number of Senators and Representatives to which the State may be entitled in the Congress: but no Senator or Representative, or Person holding an Office of Trust or Profit under the United States, shall be appointed an Elector.

The Electors shall meet in their respective States, and vote by Ballot for two Persons, of whom one at least shall not be an Inhabitant of the same State with themselves. And they shall make a list of all the Persons voted for, and of the Number of Votes for each; which List they shall sign and certify, and transmit sealed to the Seat of the Government of the United States, directed to the President of the Senate. The President of the Senate shall, in the presence of the Senate and House of Representatives, open all the Certificates, and the Votes shall be counted. The Person having the greatest Number of Votes shall be the President, if such Number be a Majority of the whole Number of Electors appointed; and if there be more than one who have such Majority, and have an equal Number of Votes, then the House of Representatives shall immediately chuse by Ballot one of them for President; and if no Person have a Majority, then from the five highest on the List the said House shall in like Manner chuse the President. But in chusing the President, the Votes shall be taken by States, the Representation from each State having one Vote; A quorum for this Purpose shall consist of a Member or Members from two thirds of the States, and a Majority of all the States shall be necessary to a Choice. In every Case, after the Choice of the President, the Person having the greatest Number of Votes of the Electors shall be the Vice President. But if there should remain two or more who have equal Votes, the Senate shall chuse from them by Ballot the Vice President.

The Congress may determine the Time of Chusing the Electors, and the Day on which they shall give their Votes; which Day shall be the same throughout the United States.

No Person except a natural born Citizen, or a Citizen of the United States, at the time of the Adoption of this Constitution, shall be eligible to the Office of President; neither shall any Person be eligible to that Office who shall not have attained to the Age of thirty five Years, and been fourteen Years a Resident within the United States.

In Case of the Removal of the President from Office, or of his Death, Resignation, or Inability to discharge the Powers and Duties of the said Office, the Same shall devolve on the Vice President, and the Congress may by Law provide for the Case of Removal, Death, Resignation or Inability, both of the President and Vice President, declaring what Officer shall then act as President, and such Officer shall act accordingly, until the Disability be removed, or a President shall be elected.

The President shall, at stated Times, receive for his Services, a Compensation, which shall neither be encreased nor diminished during the Period for which he shall have been elected, and he shall not receive within that Period any other Emolument from the United States, or any of them.

Before he enter on the Execution of his Office, he shall take the following Oath or Affirmation:—"I do solemnly swear (or affirm) that I will faithfully execute the Office of President of the United States, and will to the best of my Ability, preserve, protect and defend the Constitution of the United States."

Section 2.   The President shall be Commander in Chief of the Army and Navy of the United States, and of the Militia of the several States, when called into the actual Service of the United States; he may require the Opinion, in writing, of the principal Officer in each of the executive Departments, upon any Subject relating to the Duties of their respective Offices, and he shall have Power to grant Reprieves and Pardons for Offenses against the United States, except in Cases of Impeachment.

He shall have Power, by and with the Advice and Consent of the Senate, to make Treaties, providing two thirds of the Senators present concur; and he shall nominate, and by and with the Advice and Consent of the Senate, shall appoint Ambassadors, other public Ministers and Consuls, Judges of the supreme Court, and all other Officers of the United States, whose Appointments are not herein otherwise provided for, and which shall be established by Law: but the Congress may by Law vest the Appointment of such inferior Officers, as they think proper, in the President alone, in the Courts of Law, or in the Heads of Departments.

The President shall have Power to fill up all Vacancies that may happen during the Recess of the Senate, by granting Commissions which shall expire at the End of their next Session.

Section 3.   He shall from time to time give to the Congress Information of the State of the Union, and recommend to their Consideration such Measures as he shall judge necessary and expedient; he may, on extraordinary Occasions, convene both Houses, or either of them, and in Case of Disagreement between them, with Respect to the Time of Adjournment, he may adjourn them to such Time as he shall think proper, he shall receive Ambassadors and other public Ministers; he shall take Care that the Laws be faithfully executed, and shall Commission all the Officers of the United States.

Section 4.   The President, Vice President and all civil Officers of the United States, shall be removed from Office on Impeachment for, and Conviction of, Treason, Bribery, or other high Crimes and Misdemeanors.

ARTICLE III

Section 1.   The judicial Power of the United States, shall be vested in one supreme Court, and in such inferior Courts as the Congress may from time to time ordain and establish. The Judges, both of the supreme and inferior Courts, shall hold their Offices during good Behaviour, and shall, at Times, receive for their Services, a Compensation, which shall not be diminished during their Continuance in Office.

Section 2.   The judicial Power shall extend to all Cases, in Law and Equity, arising under this Constitution, the Laws of the United States, and Treaties made, or which shall be made, under their Authority;—to all Cases affecting Ambassadors, other public Ministers and Consuls;—to all Cases of admiralty and maritime Jurisdiction;—to Controversies to which the United States shall be a Party;—to controversies between two or more States;—between a State and Citizens of another State;—between Citizens of different States;—between Citizens of the same State claiming Lands under Grants of different States; and between a State, or the Citizens thereof, and foreign States, Citizens or Subjects.

In all Cases affecting Ambassadors, other public Ministers and Consuls, and those in which a State shall be Party, the supreme Court shall have original Jurisdiction. In all the other Cases before mentioned, the supreme Court shall have appellate Jurisdiction, both as to Law and Fact, with such Exceptions, and under such Regulations as the Congress shall make.

The Trial of all Crimes, except in Cases of Impeachment, shall be by Jury; and such Trial shall be held in the State where the said Crimes shall have been committed; but when not committed within any State, the Trial shall be at such Place or Places as the Congress may by Law have directed.

Section 3.   Treason against the United States, shall consist only in levying War against them, or in adhering to their Enemies, giving them Aid and Comfort. No Person shall be convicted of Treason unless on the Testimony of two Witnesses to the same overt Act, or on Confession in open Court.

The Congress shall have Power to declare the Punishment of Treason, but no Attainder of Treason shall work Corruption of Blood, or Forfeiture except during the Life of the Person attainted.

ARTICLE IV

Section 1.   Full Faith and Credit shall be given in each State to the public Acts, Records, and judicial Proceedings of every other State. And the Congress may by general Laws prescribe the Manner in which such Acts, Records and Proceedings shall be proved, and the Effect thereof.

Section 2.   The Citizens of each State shall be entitled to all Privileges and Immunities of Citizens in the several States.

A Person charged in any State with Treason, Felony, or other Crime, who shall flee from Justice, and be found in another State, shall on Demand of the executive Authority of the State from which he fled, be delivered up, to be removed to the State having Jurisdiction of the Crime.

No Person held to Service or Labour in one State, under the Laws thereof, escaping into another, shall, in Consequence of any Law or Regulation therein, be discharged from such Service or Labour, but shall be delivered up on Claim of the Party to whom such Service or Labour may be due.

Section 3.   New States may be admitted by the Congress into this Union; but no new State shall be formed or erected within the Jurisdiction of any other State; nor any State be formed by the Junction of two or more States, or Parts of States, without the Consent of the Legislatures of the States concerned as well as the Congress.

The Congress shall have Power to dispose of and make all needful Rules and Regulations respecting the Territory or other Property belonging to the United States; and nothing in this Constitution shall be so construed as to Prejudice any Claims of the United States, or of any particular State.

Section 4.   The United States shall guarantee to every State in this Union a Republican Form of Government, and shall protect each of them against Invasion; and on Application of the Legislature, or of the Executive (when the Legislature cannot be convened) against domestic Violence.

ARTICLE V

The Congress, whenever two thirds of both Houses shall deem it necessary, shall propose Amendments to this Constitution, or, on the Application of the Legislatures of two thirds of the several States, shall call a Convention for proposing Amendments, which, in either Case, shall be valid to all Intents and Purposes, as Part of this Constitution, when ratified by the Legislatures of three fourths of the several States, or by Conventions in three fourths thereof, as the one or the other Mode of Ratification may be proposed by the Congress; Provided that no Amendment which may be made prior to the Year One thousand eight hundred and eight shall in any Manner affect the first and fourth Clauses in the Ninth Section of the first Article; and that no State, without its Consent, shall be deprived of its equal Suffrage in the Senate.

ARTICLE VI

All Debts contracted and Engagements entered into, before the Adoption of this Constitution, shall be as valid against the United States under this Constitution, as under the Confederation.

This Constitution, and the Laws of the United States which shall be made in Pursuance thereof; and all Treaties made, or which shall be made, under the Authority of the United States, shall be the supreme Law of the Land; and the Judges in every State shall be bound thereby, any Thing in the Constitution or Laws of any State to the Contrary notwithstanding.

The Senators and Representatives before mentioned, and the Members of the several State Legislatures, and all executive and judicial Officers, both of the United States and of the Several States, shall be bound by Oath or Affirmation, to support this Constitution; but no religious Test shall ever be required as a Qualification to any Office or public Trust under the United States.

ARTICLE VII

The Ratification of the Conventions of nine States, shall be sufficient for the Establishment of this Constitution between the States so ratifying the Same.

Amendment I [1791].

Congress shall make no law respecting an establishment of religion, or prohibiting the free exercise thereof; or abridging the freedom of speech, or the press; or the right of the people peaceably to assemble, and to petition the Government for a redress of grievances.

Amendment II [1791].

A well regulated Militia, being necessary to the security for a free State, the right of the people to keep and bear Arms, shall not be infringed.

Amendment III [1791].

No Soldier shall, in time of peace be quartered in any house, without the consent of the Owner, nor in time of war, but in a manner to be prescribed by law.

Amendment IV [1791].

The right of the people to be secure in their persons, houses, papers, and effects, against unreasonable searches and seizures, shall not be violated, and no Warrants shall issue, but upon probable cause, supported by Oath or Affirmation, and particularly describing the place to be searched, and the persons or things to be seized.

Amendment V [1791].

No person shall be held to answer for a capital, or otherwise infamous crime, unless on a presentment or indictment of a Grand Jury, except in cases arising in the land or naval forces, or in the Militia, when in actual service in time of War or public danger; nor shall any person be subject for the same offense to be twice put in jeopardy of life or limb; nor shall be compelled in any criminal case to be a witness against himself, nor be deprived of life, liberty, or property, without due process of law; nor shall private property be taken for public use, without just compensation.

Amendment VI [1791].

In all criminal prosecutions, the accused shall enjoy the right to a speedy and public trial, by an impartial jury of the State and district wherein the crime shall have been committed, which district shall have been previously ascertained by law, and to be informed of the nature and cause of the accusation; to be confronted with the Witnesses against him; to have compulsory process for obtaining witnesses in his favor, and to have the Assistance of counsel for his defence.

Amendment VII [1791].

In suits at common law, where the value in controversy shall exceed twenty dollars, the right of trial by jury shall be preserved, and no fact tried by a jury, shall be otherwise re-examined in any Court of the United States, than according to the rules of the common law.

Amendment VIII [1791].

Excessive bail shall not be required, no excessive fines imposed, nor cruel and unusual punishments inflicted.

Amendment IX [1791].

The enumeration in the Constitution, of certain rights, shall not be construed to deny or disparage others retained by the people.

Amendment X [1791].

The powers not delegated to the United States by the Constitution, nor prohibited by it to the States, are reserved to the States respectively, or to the people.

Amendment XI [1798].

The judicial power of the United States shall not be construed to extend to any suit in law or equity, commenced or prosecuted against one of the United States by Citizens of another State, or by Citizens or Subjects of any Foreign State.

Amendment XII [1804].

The Electors shall meet in their respective states and vote by ballot for President and Vice-President, one of whom, at least, shall not be an inhabitant of the same state with themselves; they shall name in their ballots the person voted for as President, and in distinct ballots the person voted for as Vice-President, and they shall make distinct lists of all persons voted for as President, and of all persons voted for as Vice-President, and of the number of votes for each, which lists they shall sign and certify, and transmit sealed to the seat of the government of the United States, directed to the President of the Senate;—The President of the Senate shall, in the presence of the Senate and House of Representatives, open all the certificates and the votes shall then be counted;—The person having the greatest number of votes for President, shall be the President, if such number be a majority of the whole number of Electors appointed; and if no person have such majority, then from the persons having the highest numbers not exceeding three on the list of those voted for as President, the

House of Representatives shall choose immediately, by ballot, the President. But in choosing the President, the votes shall be taken by states, the representation from each state having one vote; a quorum for this purpose shall consist of a member or members from two-thirds of the states, and a majority of all the states shall be necessary to a choice. And if the House of Representatives shall not choose a President whenever the right of choice shall devolve upon them, before the fourth day of March next following, then the Vice-President shall act as President, as in the case of the death or other constitutional disability of the President. The person having the greatest number of votes as Vice-President, shall be the Vice-President, if such number be a majority of the whole number of Electors appointed, and if no person have a majority, then from the two highest numbers on the list, the Senate shall choose the Vice-President; a quorum for the purpose shall consist of two-thirds of the whole number of Senators, and a majority of the whole number shall be necessary to a choice. But no person constitutionally ineligible to the office of President shall be eligible to that of the Vice-President of the United States.

Amendment XIII [1865].

Section 1. Neither slavery nor involuntary servitude, except as a punishment for crime whereof the party shall have been duly convicted, shall exist within the United States, or any place subject to their jurisdiction.

Section 2. Congress shall have power to enforce this article by appropriate legislation.

Amendment XIV [1868].

Section 1. All persons born or naturalized in the United States, and subject to the jurisdiction thereof, are citizens of the United States and of the State wherein they reside. No State shall make or enforce any law which shall abridge the privileges or immunities of citizens of the United States; nor shall any State deprive any person of life, liberty, or property, without due process of law; nor deny to any person within its jurisdiction the equal protection of the laws.

Section 2. Representatives shall be apportioned among the several States according to their respective numbers, counting the whole number of persons in each State, excluding Indians not taxed. But when the right to vote at any election for the choice of electors for President and Vice President of the United States, Representatives in Congress, the Executive and Judicial officers of a State, or the members of the Legislature thereof, is denied to any of the male inhabitants of such State, being twenty-one years of age, and citizens of the United States, or in any way abridged, except for participation in rebellion, or other crime, the basis of representation therein shall be reduced in the proportion which the number of such male citizens shall bear the whole number of male citizens twenty-one years of age in such State.

Section 3. No person shall be a Senator or Representative in Congress, or elector of President and Vice President, or hold any office, civil or military, under the United States, or under any State, who, having previously taken an oath, as a member of Congress, or as an officer of the United States, or as a member of any State legislature, or as an executive or judicial officer of any State, to support the Constitution of the United States, shall have engaged in insurrection or rebellion against the same, or given aid or comfort to the enemies thereof. But Congress may by a vote of two-thirds of each House, remove such disability.

Section 4. The validity of the public debt of the United States, authorized by law, including debts incurred for payment of pensions and bounties for services in suppressing insurrection or rebellion, shall not be questioned. But neither the

United States nor any State shall assume or pay any debt or obligation incurred in aid of insurrection or rebellion against the United States, or any claim for the loss or emancipation of any slave; but all such debts, obligations and claims shall be held illegal and void.

Section 5. The Congress shall have power to enforce, by appropriate legislation, the provisions of this article.

Amendment XV [1870].

Section 1. The right of citizens of the United States to vote shall not be denied or abridged by the United States or by any State on account of race, color, or previous condition of servitude.

Section 2. The Congress shall have power to enforce this article by appropriate legislation.

Amendment XVI [1913].

The Congress shall have power to lay and collect taxes on incomes, from whatever source derived, without apportionment among the several States, and without regard to any census or enumeration.

Amendment XVII [1913].

The Senate of the United States shall be composed of two Senators from each State, elected by the people thereof, for six years; and each Senator shall have one vote. The electors in each State shall have the qualifications requisite for electors of the most numerous branch of the State legislatures.

When vacancies happen in the representation of any State in the Senate, the executive authority of each State shall issue writs of election to fill such vacancies; *Provided*, That the legislature of any State may empower the executive thereof to make temporary appointments until the people fill the vacancies by election as the legislature may direct.

This amendment shall not be construed as to affect the election or term of any Senator chosen before it becomes valid as part of the Constitution.

Amendment XVIII [1919].

Section 1. After one year from the ratification of this article the manufacture, sale, or transportation of intoxicating liquors within, the importation thereof into, or the exportation thereof from the United States and all territory subject to the jurisdiction thereof for beverage purposes is hereby prohibited.

Section 2. The Congress and the several States shall have concurrent power to enforce this article by appropriate legislation.

Section 3. This article shall be inoperative unless it shall have been ratified as an amendment to the Constitution by the legislatures of the several States, as provided in the Constitution, within seven years from the date of the submission hereof to the States by the Congress.

Amendment XIX [1920].

The right of citizens of the United States to vote shall not be denied or abridged by the United States or by any State on account of sex.

Congress shall have power to enforce this article by appropriate legislation.

Amendment XX [1933].

Section 1. The terms of the President and Vice President shall end at noon on the 20th day of January, and the terms of Senators and Representatives at noon on the 3d day of January, of the years in which such terms would have ended if this article had not been ratified; and the terms of their successors shall then begin.

Section 2. The Congress shall assemble at least once in every year, and such meeting shall begin at noon on the 3d day of January, unless they shall by law appoint a different day.

Section 3. If, at the time fixed for the beginning of the term of the President, the President elect shall have died, the Vice President elect shall become President. If a President shall not have been chosen before the time fixed for the beginning of his term, or if the President elect shall have failed to qualify, then the Vice President elect shall act as President until a President shall have qualified; and the Congress may by law provide for the case wherein neither a President elect nor a Vice President elect shall have qualified, declaring who shall then act as President, or the manner in which one who is to act shall be selected, and such person shall act accordingly until a President or Vice President shall have qualified.

Section 4. The Congress may by law provide for the case of the death of any of the persons from whom the House of Representatives may choose a President whenever the right of choice shall have devolved upon them, and for the case of the death of any of the persons from whom the Senate may choose a Vice President whenever the right of choice shall have devolved upon them.

Section 5. Sections 1 and 2 shall take effect on the 15th day of October following the ratification of this article.

Section 6. This article shall be inoperative unless it shall have been ratified as an amendment to the Constitution by the legislatures of three-fourths of the several States within seven years from the date of its submission.

Amendment XXI [1933].

Section 1. The eighteenth article of amendment to the Constitution of the United States is hereby repealed.

Section 2. The transportation or importation into any State, Territory, or possession of the United States for delivery or use therein of intoxicating liquors, in violation of the laws thereof, is hereby prohibited.

Section 3. This article shall be inoperative unless it shall have been ratified as an amendment to the Constitution by conventions in the several States, as provided in the Constitution, within seven years from the date of the submission hereof to the States by the Congress.

Amendment XXII [1951].

Section 1. No person shall be elected to the office of the President more than twice, and no person who has held the office of President, or acted as President, for more than two years of a term to which some other person was elected President shall be elected to the office of the President more than once. But this Article shall not apply to any person holding the office of President when this Article was proposed by the Congress, and shall not prevent any person who may be holding the office of President, or acting as President, during the term within which this Article becomes operative from holding the office of President, or acting as President during the remainder of such term.

Section 2. This article shall be inoperative unless it shall have been ratified as an amendment to the Constitution by the legislatures of three-fourths of the several States within seven years from the date of its submission to the States by the Congress.

Amendment XXIII [1961].

Section 1. The District constituting the seat of Government of the United States shall appoint in such manner as the Congress may direct:

A number of electors of President and Vice President equal to the whole number of Senators and Representatives in Congress to which the District would be entitled if it were a State, but in no event more than the least populous State; they shall be in addition to those appointed by the States, but they shall be considered, for the purposes of the election of President and Vice President, to be electors appointed by a State; and they shall meet in the District and perform such duties as provided by the twelfth article of amendment.

Section 2. The Congress shall have power to enforce this article by appropriate legislation.

Amendment XXIV [1964].

Section 1. The right of citizens of the United States to vote in any primary or other election for President or Vice President, for electors for President or Vice President, or for Senator or Representative in Congress, shall not be denied or abridged by the United States or any State by reason of failure to pay any poll tax or other tax.

Section 2. The Congress shall have power to enforce this article by appropriate legislation.

Amendment XXV [1967].

Section 1. In case of the removal of the President from office or of his death or resignation, the Vice President shall become President.

Section 2. Whenever there is a vacancy in the office of the Vice President, the President shall nominate a Vice President who shall take office upon confirmation by a majority vote of both Houses of Congress.

Section 3. Whenever the President transmits to the President pro tempore of the Senate and the Speaker of the House of Representatives his written declaration that he is unable to discharge the powers and duties of his office, and until he transmits to them a written declaration to the contrary, such powers and duties shall be discharged by the Vice President as Acting President.

Section 4. Whenever the Vice President and a majority of either the principal officers of the executive departments or of such other body as Congress may by law provide, transmit to the President pro tempore of the Senate and the Speaker of the House of Representatives their written declaration that the President is unable to discharge the powers and duties of his office, the Vice President shall immediately assume the powers and duties of the office as Acting President.

Thereafter, when the President transmits to the President pro tempore of the Senate and the Speaker of the House of Representatives his written declaration that no inability exists, he shall resume the powers and duties of his office unless the Vice President and a majority of either the principal officers of the executive department or of such other body as Congress may by law provide, transmit within four days to the President pro tempore of the Senate and the Speaker of the House of Representatives their written declaration that the President is unable to discharge the powers and duties of his office. Thereupon Congress shall decide the issue, assembling within forty-eight hours for that purpose if not in session. If the Congress, within twenty-one days after receipt of the latter written declaration, or, if Congress is not in session, within twenty-one days after Congress is required to assemble, determines by two-thirds vote of both Houses that the President is unable to discharge the powers and duties of his office, the Vice President shall continue to discharge the same as Acting President; otherwise, the President shall resume the powers and duties of his office.

Amendment XXVI [1971].

Section 1. The right of citizens of the United States, who are eighteen years of age or older, to vote shall not be denied or abridged by the United States or by any State on account of age.

Section 2. The Congress shall have power to enforce this article by appropriate legislation.

Amendment XXVII [1992].

No law, varying the compensation for the services of the Senators and Representatives, shall take effect, until an election of Representatives shall have intervened.

Uniform Commercial Code

The Uniform Commercial Code can be found at:

http://www.law.cornell.edu/ucc/ucc.table.html or http://www.law.cornell.edu

CHAPTER 1

MATCHING QUESTIONS

A. Statute → (3) A law passed by Congress or a state legislature

C. Common law → (1) Law created by judges

E. United States Constitution → (4) The supreme law of the land

TRUE/FALSE QUESTIONS

1. T **F** The idea that current cases must be decided based on earlier cases is called legal positivism.

3. T **F** Congress established the federal government by passing a series of statutes.

5. **T** F Law is different from morality, but the two are closely linked.

MULTIPLE-CHOICE QUESTIONS

1. **Answer:** (b) England

3. **Answer:** (a) Common law

5. **Answer:** (d) The Amendments

CASE QUESTIONS

1. Union organizers at a hospital wanted to distribute leaflets to potential union members, but hospital rules prohibited leafleting in areas of patient care, hallways, cafeterias, and any areas open to the public. The National Labor Relations Board (NLRB) ruled that these restrictions violated the law and ordered the hospital to permit the activities in the cafeteria and coffee shop. The NLRB cannot create common law or statutory law. What kind of law was it creating?

Answer: The NLRB is an administrative agency and creates administrative law. Congress created the NLRB to oversee all aspects of federal law regulating labor–management relations. The NLRB frequently makes rulings like the one described here.

3. **ETHICS** The greatest of all Chinese lawgivers, Confucius, did not esteem written laws. He believed that good rulers were the best guarantee of justice. Does our legal system rely primar-ily on the rule of law or the rule of people? Which do you instinctively trust more?

Answer: In a sense, legal realists share some ideas with the great Chinese lawgiver. The realists argue that what is written matters far less than who enforces the laws. Confucius also put primary emphasis on having wise leaders. The danger, of course, with relying on a government of people, rather than laws, is that it is difficult to get wise, honest people to lead society and basically impossible to find anyone remotely as good as Confucius.

5. *Kuene v. Pub Zone* and *Soldano v. O'Daniels* both involve attacks in a bar. Should they come out in the same way? If so, which way—in favor of the injured plaintiffs or owner-defendants? Or, should they have different outcomes? What are the key facts that lead you to believe as you do?

Answer: Answers will vary.

CHAPTER 2

MATCHING QUESTIONS

A. Shareholder model → (3) Requires business decisions that maximize the owners' return on investment

C. Utilitarianism → (1) Requires doing "the greatest good for the greatest number"

E. John Rawls → (2) Thought that society should try to make up for people's different life prospects.

TRUE/FALSE QUESTIONS

1. T **F** Immanuel Kant was a noted utilitarian thinker.

3. T **F** Modern China has experienced slower economic growth than did England during the Industrial Revolution.

5. T **F** John Rawls believed that everyone should have the same income.

MULTIPLE CHOICE QUESTIONS

1. **Answer:** (a) shareholder; did

3. **Answer:** (c) Immanuel Kant

5. **Answer:** (b) Even people who do not believe in God are more likely to behave honestly after reading the Ten Commandments.

CASE QUESTIONS

1. The Senate recently released a report on wrongdoing at JP Morgan Chase. It found that bank executives lied to investors and the public. Also, traders, with the knowledge of top management, changed risk limits to facilitate more trading and then violated even these higher limits. Executives revalued the bank's investment portfolio to reduce apparent losses. JP Morgan's internal investigation failed to find this wrongdoing. Into what ethics traps did these JP Morgan employees fall ? What options did the executives and traders have for dealing with this wrongdoing?

Answer: Money, rationalization, conformity, following orders, lost in a crowd; loyalty, exit, voice

3. I oversee the internal audit function at my company. We hold periodic bid competitions to get the lowest price we can. At the moment, we are using Firm A. Recently, one of the partners at A offered me box seats to a Red Sox game. I love the Red Sox, and even more importantly, I could have taken my father who, even though he has always been a big Sox fan, has never been to a game. However, I knew that we would soon be asking A to bid against the other Big Four firms for the right to do next year's audit. I was torn about what I should do. What pitfalls does this person face ? Would something as minor as Red Sox tickets affect his decision about which audit firm to use?

Answer: This is a conflict of interest. The evidence is that we can be swayed by even small gifts. And, indeed, the small gifts are surprisingly influential because the recipients do not make a conscious effort to overcome any bias they may create.

5. In Japan, automobile GPS systems come equipped with an option for converting them into televisions so that drivers can watch their favorite shows, yes, while driving. "We can't help but respond to our customers' needs," says a company spokesperson. Although his company does not recommend the practice of watching while driving, he explained that it is the driver's responsibility to make this decision. Is it right to sell a product that could cause great harm to innocent bystanders? What would Mill and Kant say?

Answer: Answers will vary.

CHAPTER 3
MATCHING QUESTIONS

A. GATT → (4) A treaty that governs trade

C. TRIPS → (5) A treaty that governs intellectual property

E. ICJ → (2) The World Court

TRUE/FALSE QUESTIONS

1. T **F** The ICC makes international law.

3. **T** F The CISG requires parties to negotiate internationally in good faith.

5. T **F** The WTO settles disputes involving individuals, businesses, or countries.

MULTIPLE-CHOICE QUESTIONS

1. **Answer:** (a) Operating a factory dangerously

3. **Answer:** (b) Two-thirds of the Senate

5. **Answer:** (c) Yes, Austria is violating the WTO's most favored nation rules.

CASE QUESTIONS

1. A Saudi Arabian government-run hospital hired American Scott Nelson to be an engineer. The parties signed the employment agreement in the United States. On the job, Nelson reported that the hospital had significant safety defects. For this, he was arrested, jailed, and tortured for 39 days. Upon his release to the United States, Nelson sued the Saudi government for personal injury. Can Nelson sue Saudi Arabia ?

Answer: Based on *Saudi Arabia v. Nelson* (U.S. S. Ct. 1993). The Supreme Court found that FSIA applied to immunize Saudi Arabia from the suit. While employing someone is a commercial activity, the Court reasoned that the injury stemmed from his arrest. Since a private citizen cannot jail someone, this is purely a governmental activity.

3. Asante, located in California, purchased electronic parts from PMC, whose offices were in Canada. When Asante sued PMC for breach of contract, it alleged that California sales law should apply. PMC argued that the CISG automatically applied because both Canada and the United States have ratified the treaty. Who is right?

Answer: CISG applies. The two parties are located in two member countries, and the parties did not opt out.

5. Many European nations are fearful of the effects of genetically modified foods, so they choose to restrict their importation. The EU banned the entry of these foods and subjected them to strict labeling requirements. Does this policy contravene the principles of WTO/GATT ?

Answer: The United States challenged this practice, and the WTO ruled that GM food had to be allowed into the EU. The WTO held that no scientific evidence supported the EU's fears, and therefore the regulation unduly burdened trade.

CHAPTER 4
MATCHING QUESTIONS

A. Statute → (5) A law passed by a legislative body

C. Judicial review → (1) The power of federal courts to examine the constitutionality of statutes and acts of government

E. *Stare decisis* → (3) The rule that requires lower courts to decide cases based on precedent

TRUE/FALSE QUESTIONS

1. **T** F The government may not prohibit a political rally, but it may restrict when and where the demonstrators meet.

3. **T** F The government has the right to take a homeowner's property for a public purpose.

5. T **F** A bystander who sees someone in peril must come to that person's assistance, but only if he can do so without endangering himself or others.

MULTIPLE-CHOICE QUESTIONS

1. **Answer:** (d) is void, based on the Commerce Clause.

3. **Answer:** (c) The President may veto the bill, but Congress may attempt to override the veto.

5. **Answer:** (c) A federal agency demands various internal documents from a corporation.

CASE QUESTIONS

1. In the early 1970s, President Nixon became embroiled in the Watergate dispute. He was accused of covering up a criminal break-in at the national headquarters of the Democratic Party. Nixon denied any wrongdoing. A United States District Court judge ordered the President to produce tapes of conversations held in his office. Nixon knew that complying with the order would produce damaging evidence, probably destroying his presidency. He refused, claiming executive privilege. The case went to the Supreme Court. Nixon strongly implied that even if the Supreme Court ordered him to produce the tapes, he would refuse. What major constitutional issue did this raise?

Answer: The constitutional issue is judicial review. Since *Marbury v. Madison*, 5 U.S. 137 (1803), federal courts have insisted that they have the power to review acts of the other two branches. The Supreme Court ruled that while there was a limited executive privilege, it did not include the right to withhold evidence in a criminal investigation. When the Supreme Court did in fact order Nixon to produce the tapes, he hesitated … but obeyed. The tapes he produced destroyed his credibility and his political base, and he became the first President to resign his office. But the principle of judicial review was affirmed.

3. *YOU BE THE JUDGE* **WRITING PROBLEM** An off-duty, out-of-uniform police officer and his son purchased some food from a 7-Eleven store and were still in the parking lot when a carload of teenagers became rowdy. The officer went to speak to them, and the teenagers assaulted him. The officer shouted to his son to get the 7-Eleven clerk to call for help. The son entered the store, told the clerk that a police officer needed help, and instructed the clerk to call the police. He returned 30 seconds later and repeated the request, urging the clerk to say it was a Code 13. The son claimed that the clerk laughed at him and refused to do it. The policeman sued the store. **Argument for the Store**: We sympathize with the policeman and his family, but the store has no

liability. A bystander is not obligated to come to the aid of anyone in distress unless the bystander created the peril, and obviously the store did not do so. The policeman should sue those who attacked him. **Argument for the Police Officer:** We agree that in general a bystander has no obligation to come to the aid of one in distress. However, when a business that is open to the public receives an urgent request to call the police, the business should either make the call or permit someone else to do it.

Answer: The Maryland high court established another exception to the bystander rule. "It is evident … that a shopkeeper has a legal duty to come to the assistance of an endangered business visitor if there is no risk of harm to the proprietor or its employees." The police officer was a business invitee because he had bought food, and the clerk was obligated to take reasonable affirmative steps to protect him. *Southland Corp. v. Griffith*, 332 Md. 704, 633 A.2d 84 (1993).

5. The federal Defense of Marriage Act (DOMA) defined marriage as a union between a man and a woman. As a result, same-sex couples were not eligible for the federal marriage benefits given to heterosexual couples. Edith Windsor and Thea Spyer had been together for 40 years, and married for two, when Spyer died. Because of DOMA, the federal government did not treat Windsor as a surviving spouse for purposes of estate taxes, so she was presented with a tax bill of $363,000. If she had been married to a man, she would not have owed any taxes. Windsor challenged the statute, claiming the government had violated her right to equal protection. Should she win?

Answer: This case is based on *U.S. v. Windsor*, 570 U.S. ___ (2013), 133 S.Ct. 2675. The Supreme Court held that restricting interpretation of "spouse" to apply only to heterosexual unions was unconstitutional under the Due Process Clause of the Fifth Amendment.

CHAPTER 5
MATCHING QUESTIONS

A. Arbitration → (5) A form of ADR that leads to a binding decision

C. Mediation → (2) A form of ADR in which the parties themselves craft the settlement

E. Deposition → (3) A pretrial procedure involving oral questions answered under oath

TRUE/FALSE QUESTIONS

1. T **F** One advantage of arbitration is that it provides the parties with greater opportunities for discovery than litigation does.

3. **T** F If we are listening to witnesses testify, we must be in a trial court.

5. **T** F In a lawsuit for money damages, both the plaintiff and the defendant are generally entitled to a jury.

MULTIPLE-CHOICE QUESTIONS

1. **Answer:** (e) any lawsuit based on a federal statute.

3. **Answer:** (c) the plaintiff must prove her case by a preponderance of the evidence.

5. **Answer:** (d) the power of a court to hear a particular case.

CASE QUESTIONS

1. State which court(s) have jurisdiction as to each of these lawsuits:

(a) Pat wants to sue his next-door neighbor Dorothy, claiming that Dorothy promised to sell him the house next door.

(b) Paula, who lives in New York City, wants to sue Dizzy Movie Theatres, whose principal place of business is Dallas. She claims that while she was in Texas on holiday, she was injured by their negligent maintenance of a stairway. She claims damages of $30,000.

(c) Phil lives in Tennessee. He wants to sue Dick, who lives in Ohio. Phil claims that Dick agreed to sell him 3,000 acres of farmland in Ohio, worth over $2 million.

(d) Pete, incarcerated in a federal prison in Kansas, wants to sue the United States government. He claims that his treatment by prison authorities violates three federal statutes.

Answer:

(a) The state trial court of general jurisdiction may hear the case. There is no federal court jurisdiction.

(b) The general trial court of Texas only. There is no federal court diversity jurisdiction because the money sought is less than $75,000.

(c) Ohio's general trial court has jurisdiction. United States District Court has concurrent jurisdiction, based on diversity. The parties live in different states, and the amount in question is over $75,000.

(d) United States District Court has federal question jurisdiction, based on the federal statutes at issue. The general trial court of Kansas has concurrent jurisdiction.

3. Claus Scherer worked for Rockwell International and was paid over $300,000 per year. Rockwell fired Scherer for alleged sexual harassment of several workers, including his secretary, Terry Pendy. Scherer sued in United States District Court, alleging that Rockwell's real motive in firing him was his high salary.

Rockwell moved for summary judgment, offering deposition transcripts of various employees. Pendy's deposition detailed instances of harassment, including comments about her body, instances of unwelcome touching, and discussions of extramarital affairs. Another deposition, from a Rockwell employee who investigated the allegations, included complaints by other employees as to Scherer's harassment. In his own deposition, which he offered to oppose summary judgment, Scherer testified that he could not recall the incidents alleged by Pendy and others. He denied generally that he had sexually harassed any-

one. The district court granted summary judgment for Rockwell. Was its ruling correct?

Answer: Yes. The court of appeals affirmed. *Scherer v. Rockwell International Corp.*, 975 F.2d 356, 1992 U.S. App. LEXIS 22080 (7th Cir. 1992). "When questioned about the specific instances of sexual harassment, he did not deny that the incidents occurred, but instead stated that he could not recall. In other sections of his deposition, he stated that he generally denied having sexually harassed any coworker… Scherer may not defeat Rockwell's properly supported summary judgment motion without offering any evidence from which a jury could determine that the alleged sexual harassment did not actually occur and by merely asserting that the jury might disbelieve Rockwell's witness because of Rockwell's motive and desire to get out of the contract."

5. Raul lives in Georgia. He creates custom paintings and sells them at a weekly art fair near Atlanta. Sarah lives in Vermont. While on vacation in Georgia, she buys one of Raul's paintings for $500. Soon after she returns home, she decides the painting is ugly, calls Raul, and demands a refund. Raul refuses. Sarah wants to sue him in Vermont. Raul has never been to Vermont, and has never sold a painting to anyone else from Vermont. Do Vermont courts have personal jurisdiction over Raul? Why or why not?

Answer: No. Raul is not a resident and cannot be served a Vermont summons in Georgia. The Vermont long arm statute will not be effective because Raul has not had minimum contacts with the state.

CHAPTER 6
MATCHING QUESTIONS

A. Larceny → (5) The trespassory taking of personal property

C. Money laundering → (3) Using the proceeds of criminal acts to promote crime

E. Embezzlement → (2) Fraudulently keeping property already in defendant's possession

TRUE/FALSE QUESTIONS

1. T **F** Both the government and the victim are entitled to prosecute a crime.

3. **T** F A misdemeanor is a less serious crime, punishable by less than a year in jail.

5. T **F** An affidavit is the government's formal charge of criminal wrongdoing.

MULTIPLE-CHOICE QUESTIONS

1. **Answer:** (c) Both are guilty of embezzlement; Cheryl is also guilty of violating RICO.

3. **Answer:** (b) embezzlement.

5. **Answer:** (d) that based on all of the information presented, it is likely that evidence of crime will be found in the place mentioned.

CASE QUESTIONS

1. *YOU BE THE JUDGE* **WRITING PROBLEM** An undercover drug informant learned from a mutual friend that Philip Friedman "knew where to get marijuana." The informant asked Friedman three times to get him some marijuana, and Friedman agreed after the third request. Shortly thereafter, Friedman sold the informant a small amount of the drug. The informant later offered to sell Friedman three pounds of marijuana. They negotiated the price and then made the sale. Friedman was tried for trafficking in drugs. He argued entrapment. Was Friedman entrapped? **Argument for Friedman:** The undercover agent had to ask three times before Friedman sold him a small amount of drugs. A real drug dealer, predisposed to commit the crime, leaps at an opportunity to sell. **Argument for the Government:** Government officials suspected Friedman of being a sophisticated drug dealer, and they were right. When he had a chance to buy three pounds, a quantity only a dealer would purchase, he not only did so, but he bargained with skill, showing a working knowledge of the business. Friedman was not entrapped—he was caught.

Answer: Friedman argued entrapment, claiming that there was no evidence of his predisposition to traffic in drugs. The Alabama Supreme Court ruled against him. The court noted that Friedman admitted to occasional use of marijuana, that he had been able quickly to locate marijuana to resell to the agent, and that he showed a sophisticated knowledge of the drug when bargaining over the price of three pounds. The court held that there was no evidence of entrapment. *Friedman v. State*, 654 So.2d 50, 1994 Ala. Crim. App. LEXIS 179 (1994).

3. Shawn was caught stealing letters from mailboxes. After pleading guilty, he was sentenced to two months in prison and three years' supervised release. One of the supervised release conditions required him to stand outside a post office for eight hours wearing a signboard stating, "I stole mail. This is my punishment." He appealed this requirement on the grounds that it constituted cruel and unusual punishment. Do you agree?

Answer: The appeals court affirmed the sentence on the grounds that it did not violate standards of decency. *United States v. Gementera*, 379 F.3d 596 (2004)

5. While driving his SUV, George Xinos struck and killed a pedestrian. He then fled the scene of the crime. A year later, the police downloaded information from his car's onboard computer, which they were able to use to convict him of the crime. Should this information have been admissible at trial?

Answer: A California court ruled that Xinos did have a reasonable expectation of privacy and the data was not admissible in court, because the computer had simply been recording his movements on a public road. *People v. Xinos*, 192 Cal. App. 4th 637 (Cal. App. 6th Dist. 2011)

7. *The New York Times* reported that Walmart paid bribes to obtain building permits in Mexico. If true, would these acts violate the FCPA?

Answer: Not if those payments were simply speeding up a process that would inevitably have resulted in the permits being issued. But, as is often the case with bribery, what may have started as simple facilitating payments ultimately became clear wrongdoing. Among other offenses, Walmart is alleged to have paid bribes to avoid compliance with zoning laws, or the requirement for construction licenses, and environmental permits. These payments would be illegal.

CHAPTER 7
MATCHING QUESTIONS

A. Interference with a contract → (4) Deliberately stealing a client who has a contract with another

C. Defamation → (6) Using a false statement to damage someone's reputation

E. Punitive damages → Money awarded to punish the wrongdoer.

G. Commercial exploitation → (5) Violation of the exclusive right to use one's own name, likeness, or voice

TRUE/FALSE QUESTIONS

1. T **F** A store manager who believes a customer has stolen something may question him but not restrain him.

3. **T** F A defendant cannot be liable for defamation if the statement, no matter how harmful, is true.

5. **T** F A beer company that wishes to include a celebrity's picture in its magazine ads must first obtain the celebrity's permission.

MULTIPLE-CHOICE QUESTIONS

1. **Answer:** (d) opinion.

3. **Answer:** (c) intentional infliction of emotional distress.

5. **Answer:** (b) Antonio and the state could start separate criminal cases against Hank.

CASE QUESTIONS

1. Caldwell was shopping in a K-Mart store, carrying a large purse. A security guard observed her look at various small items such as stain, hinges, and antenna wire. On occasion, she bent down out of sight of the guard. The guard thought he saw Caldwell put something in her purse. Caldwell removed her glasses from her purse and returned them a few times. After

she left, the guard approached her in the parking lot and said that he believed she had store merchandise in her pocketbook but was unable to say what he thought was put there. Caldwell opened the purse, and the guard testified he saw no K-Mart merchandise in it. The guard then told Caldwell to return to the store with him. They walked around the store for approximately 15 minutes, while the guard said six or seven times that he saw her put something in her purse. Caldwell left the store after another store employee indicated she could go. Caldwell sued. What kind of suit did she file, and what should the outcome be?

Answer: Caldwell sued for false imprisonment. The jury found in her favor, and the Court of Appeals affirmed. *Caldwell v. K-Mart*, 306 S.C. 27, 410 S.E.2d 21, 1991 S.C. App. LEXIS 135 (S.C. Ct. App.1991). From this evidence, a finder of fact could draw various inferences about whether K-Mart's actions in investigating were conducted for a reasonable time and in a reasonable manner. The initial stop in the parking lot was probably justified, but the actions of the guard in walking Caldwell through the store and continuing to accuse her of taking merchandise were not justified as part of a reasonable investigation.

3. For many years, Johnny Carson was the star of a well-known television show, *The Tonight Show*. For about 20 years, he was introduced nightly on the show with the phrase, "Here's Johnny!" A large segment of the television-watching public associated the phrase with Carson. A Michigan corporation was in the business of renting and selling portable toilets. The company chose the name "Here's Johnny Portable Toilets," and coupled the company name with the marketing phrase, "The World's Foremost Commodian." Carson sued. What claim is he making? Who should win, and why?

Answer: The Court of Appeals ruled for Carson. *Carson v. Here's Johnny Portable Toilets, Inc.*, 698 F.2d 831 (6th Cir. 1983). The company was clearly and deliberately appropriating Carson's identity in connection with its name and product. To violate the right of commercial exploitation, the defendant need not use a plaintiff's actual name. A nickname or phrase will violate his rights if it clearly identifies the plaintiff. This one does, and Carson wins.

5. Lou DiBella was an executive responsible for programming boxing shows on HBO cable network. DiBella signed Bernard Hopkins, the then-middleweight world boxing champion, to participate in a fight televised by HBO. After DiBella's departure from the network, he and Hopkins entered into an agreement in which Hopkins paid $50,000 for DiBella's promotional services. Months later, Hopkins publicly accused DiBella of taking bribes and "selling" spots in HBO fights, calling him greedy, filthy, and unethical. DiBella sued Hopkins for libel. What did DiBella have to prove to be successful in his claim?

Answer: The district court found for DiBella. It found he was a public figure by virtue of his success in boxing, but that the statements had been made with malice. The court also found that Hopkins made a defamatory statement that was false and communicated to others. The Second Circuit affirmed, and the Supreme Court denied cert.

CHAPTER 8
MATCHING QUESTIONS

A. Breach → (3) A defendant's failure to perform a legal duty

C. Compensatory damages → (1) Money awarded to an injured plaintiff

E. Negligence → (4) A tort in which an injury or loss is caused accidentally

TRUE/FALSE QUESTIONS

1. T **F** There are five elements in a negligence case, and a plaintiff wins who proves at least three of them.

3. T **F** Some states are comparative negligence states, but the majority are contributory negligence states.

5. **T** F A defendant can be liable for negligence even if he never intended to cause harm.

7. **T** F Under strict liability, an injured consumer could potentially recover damages from the product's manufacturer and the retailer who sold the goods.

MULTIPLE-CHOICE QUESTIONS

1. **Answer:** (c) Injury caused by a tiger that escapes from a zoo.

3. **Answer:** (d) Dolly wins $70,000.

5. **Answer:** (d) was engaged in the business of selling the product.

CASE QUESTIONS

1. At approximately 7:50 p.m., bells at the train station rang and red lights flashed, signaling an express train's approach. David Harris walked onto the tracks, ignoring a yellow line painted on the platform instructing people to stand back. Two men shouted to Harris, warning him to get off the tracks. The train's engineer saw him too late to stop the train, which was traveling at approximately 66 mph. The train struck and killed Harris as it passed through the station. Harris's widow sued the railroad, arguing that the railroad's negligence caused her husband's death. Evaluate the widow's argument.

Answer: Harris was a trespasser, and as a result the railroad had no duty of due care to him. The railroad would be liable only if it caused Harris's death by reckless or intentional conduct. There was no evidence of either. The widow was not permitted to introduce evidence of negligence, because even if the railroad had been negligent, it would be not be liable. *Harris v. Mass. Bay Transit Authority* (D. Mass. 1994), Mass. Lawyer's Weekly, Feb. 7, 1994, p.15.

3. Randy works for a vending machine company. One morning, he fills up a vending machine that is on the third floor of an

office building. Later that day, Mark buys a can of Pepsi from that machine. He takes the full can to a nearby balcony and drops it three floors onto Carl, a coworker who recently started dating Mark's ex-girlfriend. Carl falls unconscious. Is Randy a cause in fact of Carl's injury? Is he a proximate cause? What about Mark?

Answer: Randy's behavior (filling the vending machine) did lead to the harm, but since he did not do anything wrong, he did not breach his duty. Therefore, his actions were not either a factual cause or a proximate cause. If his behavior had been wrongful, it would have been a factual cause. Randy's behavior cannot be a proximate cause because Mark's behavior was not foreseeable. Mark's behavior, however, is both a factual cause and a proximate cause because Mark's behavior did lead to Carl's injury, and it was foreseeable that his action (dropping the can) would lead to Carl's injury.

5. Ryder leased a truck to Florida Food Service; Powers, an employee, drove it to make deliveries. He noticed that the door strap used to close the rear door was frayed, and he asked Ryder to fix it. Ryder failed to do so in spite of numerous requests. The strap broke, and Powers replaced it with a nylon rope. Later, when Powers was attempting to close the rear door, the nylon rope broke, and he fell, sustaining severe injuries to his neck and back. He sued Ryder. The trial court found that Powers's attachment of the replacement rope was a superseding cause, relieving Ryder of any liability, and granted summary judgment for Ryder. Powers appealed. How should the appellate court rule?

Answer: The case was reversed and remanded for trial. *Powers v. Ryder Truck*, 625 So. 2d 979, 1993 Fla. App. LEXIS 10729 (Fla. Dist. Ct. App. 1993). Whether an event is a superseding cause is a jury question, unless it is so bizarre as to be entirely unforeseeable by the defendant. Here, even if Powers was negligent in attaching a nylon rope, that negligence was not so bizarre as to be unforeseeable by Ryder.

CHAPTER 9
MATCHING QUESTIONS

A. ECPA → (1) Regulates employers' access to employee email

C. FISA → (5) Regulates government spying

E. CDA → (2) Protects ISPs from liability for content that they did not create

TRUE/FALSE QUESTIONS

1. **T** F The First Amendment to the Constitution protects bloggers who post insults about other people.

3. **T** F The FTC requires websites to establish a privacy policy and then abide by it.

5. **T** F Employers can read employees' emails sent on work computers.

MULTIPLE-CHOICE QUESTIONS

1. **Answer:** (d) None of the above

3. **Answer:** (d) All of the above

5. **Answer:** (e) None

CASE QUESTIONS

1. **ETHICS** Facebook implemented a new policy on gun sales: It now removes certain posts about guns, notifies gun sellers of gun laws, and limits the visibility of gun posts to users over 18. Proponents contend that Facebook's actions go a long way toward ending illegal firearms sales over social media. But critics worry that Facebook is meddling in legitimate businesses—and a contentious political issue. Is Facebook's gun policy susceptible to legal challenge? Does Facebook have a duty to its users? To its advertisers? To society? What is that duty?

Answer: Students will discuss the pros and cons of Facebook's actions. One relevant legal issue is the extent to which Facebook exercises editorial control over its postings. Taking down postings or changing them in some way can be interpreted as editing, which implicates its immunity under the CDA.

3. Over the course of 10 months, Joseph Melle sent more than 60 million unsolicited email advertisements to AOL members. What charges could be brought against him?

Answer: Melle was charged with violating the Computer Fraud and Abuse Act. He agreed to a permanent injunction prohibiting him from sending more spam over the AOL network.

5. Barrow was a government employee. Because he shared his office computer with another worker, he brought in his personal computer from home to use for office work. No other employee accessed it, but it was connected to the office network. The computer was not password protected, nor was it regularly turned off. When another networked computer was reported to be running slowly, an employee looked at Barrow's machine to see if it was the source of the problem. He found material that led to Barrow's termination. Had Barrow's Fourth Amendment rights been violated?

Answer: The court ruled no, that Barrow did not have a reasonable expectation of privacy. *United States v. Barrows*, 481 F.3d 1246 (10th Cir. 2007)

CHAPTER 10
MATCHING QUESTIONS

A. Implied contract → (4) An agreement based on the words and actions of the parties

C. Offeree → (1) A party that receives an offer

E. Bilateral contract → (2) An agreement based on one promise in exchange for another

TRUE/FALSE QUESTIONS

1. T **F** To be enforceable, all contracts must be in writing.

3. T **F** If an offer demands a reply within a stated period, the offeree's silence indicates acceptance.

5. T **F** An agreement to sell cocaine is a voidable contract.

MULTIPLE-CHOICE QUESTIONS

1. **Answer**: (a) unilateral contract.

3. **Answer**: (c) Both I and II

5. **Answer**: (d) All of the above

CASE QUESTIONS

1. **ETHICS** John Stevens owned a dilapidated apartment that he rented to James and Cora Chesney for a low rent. The Chesneys began to remodel and rehabilitate the unit. Over a four-year period, they installed two new bathrooms, carpeted the floors, installed new septic and heating systems, and rewired, replumbed, and painted. Stevens periodically stopped by and saw the work in progress. The Chesneys transformed the unit into a respectable apartment. Three years after their work was done, Stevens served the Chesneys with an eviction notice. The Chesneys counterclaimed, seeking the value of the work they had done. Are they entitled to it? Comment on the law and the ethics.

Answer: Yes, they are entitled to the value of their work, said the court in *Chesney v. Stevens*, 435 Pa. Super. 71, 644 A.2d 124.0 (Pa. Super. Ct. 1994). They have neither an express nor an implied contract for the work. Stevens did nothing to create either. But he was aware of the work they were doing, and he should know that they would reasonably expect compensation. It would be unjust, said the court, to permit him to keep the benefit without paying anything, and so the Chesneys won their case of quasi-contract, receiving *quantum meruit* damages for the value of their work.

3. The Tufte family leased a 260-acre farm from the Travelers Insurance Co. Toward the end of the lease, Travelers mailed the Tuftes an option to renew the lease. The option arrived at the Tuftes' house on March 30, and gave them until April 14 to accept. On April 13, the Tuftes signed and mailed their acceptance, which Travelers received on April 19. Travelers claimed there was no lease and attempted to evict the Tuftes from the farm. May they stay?

Answer: Yes, they may. Using the mail to accept is reasonable, since Travelers chose that medium to send its offer. Acceptance is effective on dispatch, meaning that the Tuftes accepted Travelers' offer on April 13, within the deadline. They have a binding lease. *Travelers Insurance Co. v. Tufte*, 435 N.W.2d 824 (Minn. Ct. App. 1989).

5. Raul makes an offer to Tina. He says, "I'll sell you this briefcase for $100." Describe four ways in which this offer might be terminated.

Answer: Tina could accept the offer and purchase the briefcase. Tina could outright reject the offer. Tina could make a counter-offer. Or, Raul could withdraw the offer. If the offer has an expiration date, it would automatically terminate on that date if it had not been accepted or rejected before then.

CHAPTER 11

MATCHING QUESTIONS

A. Fraud → (3) The intention to deceive the other party

C. Part performance → (5) Entry onto land, or improvements made to it, by a buyer who has no written contract

E. Consideration → (2) The idea that contracts must be a two-way street

TRUE/FALSE QUESTIONS

1. **T** F A contract may not be rescinded based on puffery.

3. **T** F Non-compete clauses are suspect because they tend to restrain free trade.

5. **T** F A court is unlikely to enforce an exculpatory clause included in a contract for surgery.

MULTIPLE-CHOICE QUESTIONS

1. **Answer**: (b) Hang gliding

3. **Answer**: (c) fraud.

5. **Answer**: (d) Kyle wins because Chuck allowed him to dig the foundation.

CASE QUESTIONS

1. Brockwell left his boat to be repaired at Lake Gaston Sales. The boat contained electronic equipment and other personal items. Brockwell signed a form stating that Lake Gaston had no responsibility for any loss to any property in or on the boat. Brockwell's electronic equipment was stolen, and other personal items were damaged; he sued. Is the exculpatory clause enforceable?

Answer: According to the North Carolina Supreme Court, no. The court held that boat repairing is in the public interest and that it is against public policy for a company in that business to use an exculpatory clause to escape liability for its own negligence. The clause was void, and Brockwell won. Note that while most states would extend public policy to cover auto repairs, not all states would include boat repairs. *Brockwell v. Lake Gaston Sales & Service*, 105 N.C. App. 226, 412 S.E.2d 104 (N.C. Ct. App. 1992).

3. **ETHICS** Richard and Michelle Kommit traveled to New Jersey to have fun in the casinos. While in Atlantic City, they used their MasterCard to withdraw cash from an ATM conveniently located in the pit, which is the gambling area of a casino. They ran up debts of $5,500 on the credit card and did not pay. The Connecticut National Bank sued for the money. What argument should the Kommits make? Which party, if any, has the moral high ground here? Should a casino offer ATM services in the gambling pit? If a credit card company allows customers to withdraw cash in a casino, is it encouraging them to lose money? Do the Kommits have any ethical right to use the ATM, attempt to win money by gambling, and then seek to avoid liability?

Answer: They should and did claim that they borrowed the money to gamble. They argued correctly that a gambling debt is unenforceable in Connecticut. The appellate court remanded the case so that the trial court could determine whether the bank knew that the money was borrowed for gambling. If the bank knew the intended use of the money (which a court could but need not infer from the location of the ATM), the debt is void. *Connecticut National Bank of Hartford v. Kommit*, 31 Mass. App. Ct. 348, 577 N.E.2d 639 (Mass. Ct. App. 1991). As to which party has the high ground, of course, the answer is that it is a tie for last place. Clearly, the credit card company *is* encouraging people to gamble by placing its ATM in the gambling pit. Just as certainly, the Kommits are trying to have it both ways, gambling in the hopes of a quick gain, then attempting to avoid liability by invoking this legal principle. Generally, when faced with two parties who are both less than saintly, courts attempt to make rulings that will be in the best interests of society, in the long term.

5. Lonnie Hippen moved to Long Island, Kansas, to work at an insurance company owned by Griffiths. After he moved there, Griffiths offered to sell Hippen a house he owned, and Hippen agreed in writing to buy it. He did buy the house and moved in, but two years later, Hippen left the insurance company. He then claimed that at the time of the sale, Griffiths had orally promised to buy back his house at the selling price if Hippen should happen to leave the company. Griffiths defended based on the statute of frauds. Hippen argued that the statute of frauds did not apply because the repurchase of the house was essentially part of his employment with Griffiths. Comment.

Answer: Hippen's claim fails. The purchase—or repurchase—of a house is the classic interest in land, and any such promise must be in writing to be enforceable. *Hippen v. First National Bank*, 1992 U.S. Dist. LEXIS 6029 (D. Kan. 1992).

CHAPTER 12
MATCHING QUESTIONS

A. Material → (1) A type of breach that substantially harms the innocent party

C. Discharged → (2) When a party has no more obligations under a contract

TRUE/FALSE QUESTIONS

1. T **F** Contract dates and deadlines are strictly enforceable unless the parties agree otherwise.

3. **T** F Courts award the expectation interest more often than any other remedy.

MULTIPLE-CHOICE QUESTIONS

1. **Answer:** (d) Bob owes Hardknuckle Bank money.

3. **Answer:** (e) legally irrelevant.

5. **Answer:** (b) Museum will win if, when the parties made the deal, Sue Ellen knew the importance of the date.

CASE QUESTIONS

1. Darin bought his fiancée Sarah a three-carat diamond ring for $43,121 from Mandarin Gems. Later, Mandarin supplied Erstad with a written appraisal valuing the engagement ring at $45,500. Years later, the couple divorced, and Sarah kept the ring. When she had the ring reappraised, another gemologist assessed its value at only $20,000.

Sarah sued Mandarin for breach of contract, but the jeweler defended by saying that it had never made a contract with her. Does Sarah have contract rights against Mandarin?

Answer: The court held that Sarah was an intended done beneficiary. At the time of purchasing the ring, Darin had made clear to Mandarin that its purpose was as an engagement right for Sarah. Even though Sarah was not a party to the contract between Darin and Mandarin, she had a right to enforce it.

3. Evans built a house for Sandra Dyer, but the house had some problems. The garage ceiling was too low. Load-bearing beams in the "great room" cracked and appeared to be steadily weakening. The patio did not drain properly. Pipes froze. Evans wanted the money promised for the job, but Dyer refused to pay. Comment.

Answer: This case creates an issue of substantial performance. The court held that the low garage ceiling was a minor problem and would not defeat substantial performance. But the cracked beams were very serious and might require major reconstruction. The water collecting in the patio could seep under the house and destroy the foundation. The freezing pipes posed a danger of bursting. The contractor had failed to substantially perform and was not entitled to his contract price. He was owed only the value of work completed, if any. *Evans & Associates v. Dyer*, 246 Ill. App. 3d 231, 615 N.E.2d 770, 1993 Ill. App. LEXIS 826 (Ill. App. Ct. 1993).

5. **ETHICS** The National Football League (NFL) owns the copyright to the broadcasts of its games. It licenses local television stations to telecast certain games and maintains a "blackout rule," which prohibits stations from broadcasting home games that are not sold out 72 hours before the game starts. Certain home games of the Cleveland team were not sold out, and the NFL blocked local broadcast. But several bars in the Cleveland area were able to pick up the game's signal by using special antennas. The NFL

wanted the bars to stop showing the games. What did it do? Was it unethical of the bars to broadcast the games that they were able to pick up? Apart from the NFL's legal rights, do you think it had the moral right to stop the bars from broadcasting the games?

Answer: It sued and obtained an injunction, based on a violation of the NFL's copyright in the broadcasts. The permanent injunction prohibited the bars from showing any blacked out games without written permission. *NFL v. Rondor, Inc.*, 840 F. Supp. 1160 (N.D. Ohio 1993).

CHAPTER 13
MATCHING QUESTIONS

A. Assignment of rights → (6) Transfer of benefits under a contract

C. Covenant → (5) Promise about what a party will do in the future

E. Conditional promise → (1) Promises that a party agrees to perform only if the other side has first done what it promised

TRUE/FALSE QUESTIONS

1. T **F** The same states must be named in the Choice of Law and Choice of Forum provisions.

3. **T** F A severability provision asks the court simply to delete the offending clause and enforce the rest of the contract.

5. **T** F Unless the contract provides otherwise, both sides in a contract dispute pay their own legal fees.

MULTIPLE-CHOICE QUESTIONS

1. **Answer:** (b) 6 percent

3. **Answer:** (e) The parties reside in different jurisdictions.

5. **Answer:** (c) Yes, because the language is ambiguous and should be interpreted against the insurance company.

CASE QUESTIONS

1. Zoe has been offered a job as CIO at Appsley Co, but first she has to negotiate a contract with the CEO, Phil. Do a role play with another student in your class, in which one of you takes the role of Zoe and the other is Phil. What terms do you each want? Draft the contract. Now compare your results with others in the class. Who has negotiated the best deal? Who has written the best contract?

Answer: Answers will vary.

3. Slimline and Distributor signed a contract which provided that Distributor would use reasonable efforts to promote and sell Slimline's diet drink. Slimline was already being sold in Warehouse Club. After the contract was signed, Distributor stopped conducting in-store demos of Slimline. It did not repackage the product as Slimline and Warehouse requested. Sales of Slimline continued to

increase during the term of the contract. Slimline sued Distributor, alleging a violation of the agreement. Who should win?

Answer: The issue is whether Distributor used "reasonable efforts." The fact that sales increased is irrelevant.

5. Laurie's contract to sell her tortilla chip business to Hudson contained a provision that she must continue to work at the business for five years. One year later, she quit. Hudson refused to pay her the amounts still owing under the contract. Laurie alleged that he is liable for the full amount because her breach was not material. Is Laurie correct?

Answer: The purpose of the contract was for Hudson to build up the business and make a profit. Laurie's departure interfered with that goal. The court ruled that the breach was material, and Hudson did not have to pay the sums still owing under the contract.

CHAPTER 14
MATCHING QUESTIONS

A. Additional terms → (2) Generally become part of a contract between merchants

C. Merchantability → (1) An implied warranty that goods are fit for their ordinary purpose

TRUE/FALSE QUESTIONS

1. T **F** In a contract for the sale of goods, the offer may include any terms the offeror wishes; the offeree must accept on exactly those terms or reject the deal.

3. **T** F The description of products in promotional materials can create express warranties.

MULTIPLE-CHOICE QUESTIONS

1. **Answer:** (b) Leasing an automobile worth $35,000

3. **Answer:** (c) Seller is liable because the disclaimer was invalid.

5. **Answer:** (b) II only

CASE QUESTIONS

1. Nina owns a used car lot. She signs and sends a fax to Seth, a used car wholesaler who has a huge lot of cars in the same city. The fax says, "Confirming our agrmt—I pick any 15 cars fr yr lot—30% below blue book." Seth reads the fax, laughs, and throws it away. Two weeks later, Nina arrives and demands to purchase 15 of Seth's cars. Is he obligated to sell?

Answer: Probably. Under UCC §2-201(2), a signed memo between merchants that would be binding against the sender is sufficient to satisfy the Statute of Frauds against the recipient if he reads it and fails to object within 10 days.

3. Lewis River Golf, Inc., grew and sold sod. It bought seed from defendant, O. M. Scott & Sons, under an express warranty. But the sod grown from the Scott seeds developed weeds, a breach of Scott's warranty. Several of Lewis River's customers sued, unhappy with the weeds in their grass. Lewis River lost most of its customers, cut back its production from 275 acres to 45 acres, and destroyed all remaining sod grown from Scott's seeds. Eventually, Lewis River sold its business at a large loss. A jury awarded Lewis River $1,026,800, largely for lost profits. Scott appealed, claiming that a plaintiff may not recover for lost profits. Comment.

Answer: Scott is wrong. Lost profits and goodwill are both consequential damages, and both are potentially recoverable. The court can measure lost profits by contracts actually cancelled, by the decreased sod production, and by diminished sales. Goodwill refers *to future business* lost, and for that a court can rely on financial forecasts made by experts, based on the buyer's history of sales. A buyer expecting to resell may obtain the loss of profit caused by the seller's breach. The court affirmed Lewis River's verdict. *Lewis River Golf, Inc. v. O. M. Scott & Sons*, 120 Wash. 2d 712,845 P.2d 987 (1993).

5. When Whitehouses decided to breed horses, they went horse shopping at the Lange's ranch. Although the Whitehouses had owned horses, they had no experience in horse breeding. Knowing the buyers would breed the horse, the Langes suggested a particular mare. After the sale, the Whitehouses discovered that this mare was infertile and sued for breach of warranty. Will the buyers win? If so, under which UCC warranty?

Answer: *Whitehouse v. Lange*, 128 Idaho 129 (1996).

Because the court found this use of the horse to be nonordinary, the buyers were entitled to an implied warranty of fitness.

CHAPTER 15
MATCHING QUESTIONS

A. Drawer → (2) The person who issues a draft

C. Issuer → (5) The maker of a promissory note or the drawer of a draft

E. Holder → (4) Anyone in possession of an instrument if it is indorsed to her

TRUE/FALSE QUESTIONS

1. T **F** The possessor of a piece of commercial paper always has an unconditional right to be paid.

3. T **F** To be negotiable, bearer paper must be indorsed and delivered to the transferee.

5. **T** F A promissory note may be valid even if it does not have a specific due date.

MULTIPLE-CHOICE QUESTIONS

1. **Answer:** (c) deliver the paper.

3. **Answer:** (b) it is signed only by the drawee.

5. **Answer:** (e) The due date was specified as "three months after Donna graduates from college."

CASE QUESTIONS

1. Kay signed a promissory note for $220,000 that was payable to Investments, Inc. The company then indorsed the note over to its lawyers to pay past and future legal fees. Were the lawyers holders in due course?

Answer: The lawyers could not be holders in due course unless they had given value for the note. The answer depends on whether the prior legal fees had real value.

3. In the prior question, who are the drawer, drawee, and payee of this check?

Answer: Shelby Case is the drawer; Last National Bank of Alvin is the drawee; Dana Locke is the payee.

5. Duncan Properties, Inc. agrees to buy a car from Shifty for $25,000. The company issues a promissory note in payment. The car that Duncan bought is defective. If Shifty still has the note, does Duncan have to pay it?

Answer: No, because Shifty is just a holder, not a holder in due course, so all the contract defenses are valid against him.

7. Abe gives the note to his daughter, Prudence, for her birthday. Is Prudence a holder in due course? Does Duncan have to pay Prudence?

Answer: Prudence is not a holder in due course because she did not give value. However, under the Shelter Rule, Duncan must still pay her.

CHAPTER 16
MATCHING QUESTIONS

A. Attachment → (5) Steps necessary to make a security interest valid against the debtor, but not against third parties

C. Perfection → (2) Steps necessary to make a security interest valid against the whole world

E. Priority → (4) The order in which creditors will be permitted to seize the property of a bankrupt debtor

TRUE/FALSE QUESTIONS

1. **T** F A party with a perfected security interest takes priority over a party with an unperfected interest.

3. **T F** When a debtor defaults, a secured party may seize the collateral and hold it, using reasonable care, but may not sell or lease it.

5. **T F** Without an agreement of the parties, there can be no security interest.

MULTIPLE-CHOICE QUESTIONS

1. **Answer:** (c) A buyer in the ordinary course of business

3. **Answer:** (c) Consumers

5. **Answer:** (e) Millie has an attached, perfected security interest in the ring.

CASE QUESTIONS

Notice Concerning Article 9 Revision: The following cases and problems were decided under the former Article 9. In each instance, the outcome would be the same under the revised code, although the relevant sections of Article 9 have been renumbered and probably rewritten.

1. The Copper King Inn, Inc., had money problems. It borrowed $62,500 from two of its officers, Noonan and Patterson, but that did not suffice to keep the inn going. So Noonan, on behalf of Copper King, arranged for the inn to borrow $100,000 from Northwest Capital, an investment company that worked closely with Noonan in other ventures. Copper King signed an agreement giving Patterson, Noonan, and Northwest a security interest in the inn's furniture and equipment. But the financing statement that the parties filed made no mention of Northwest. Copper King went bankrupt. Northwest attempted to seize assets, but other creditors objected. Is Northwest entitled to Copper King's furniture and equipment?

Answer: No. Northwest's name was omitted from the financing statement. Minor omissions are acceptable, but the court held that this was not minor. It is essential that any potential creditors be able to learn all existing creditors. This is especially true where one secured party, Northwest, has a close working relationship with the debtor's officers, a relationship that could harm other creditors. Even though no one was deceived in this case, the financing statement was still misleading, and therefore Northwest has no security interest. *In re Copper King Inn, Inc.*, 918 F.2d 1404, 1990 U. S. App. LEXIS 19624 (9th Cir. 1990).

3. When Corona leased farmland to a strawberry farmer named Armando Munoz Juarez, it claimed a security interest in his strawberry crop. Corona's financing statement listed the farmer's name as "Armando Munoz," even though his state-issued ID card identified his last name as "Juarez." When the farmer contracted to sell strawberries to Frozsun, it filed its own financing statement securing the strawberries. This statement listed the debtor's name as "Armando Juarez." When the farmer defaulted, both Corona and Frozsun claimed an interest in the same strawberries. Which party prevails—Corona or Frozsun? Why?

Answer: Frozsun prevails because Corona did not list the debtor's name correctly on the financing statement. The UCC requires the debtor's name to be the same as on his driver's license or state-issued ID.

5. The state of Kentucky filed a tax lien against Panbowl Energy, claiming unpaid taxes. Six months later, Panbowl bought a powerful drill from Whayne Supply, making a down payment of $11,500 and signing a security agreement for the remaining debt of $220,000. Whayne perfected the next day. Panbowl defaulted. Whayne sold the drill for $58,000, leaving a deficiency of just over $100,000. The state filed suit, seeking the $58,000 proceeds. The trial court gave summary judgment to the state, and Whayne appealed. Who gets the $58,000?

Answer: Whayne had a properly perfected PMSI, and it took priority over the tax lien. Whayne gets the $58,000.

CHAPTER 17

MATCHING QUESTIONS

A. Term agreement → (3) When two parties agree in advance on the duration of their agreement

C. Agency at will → (1) When two parties make no agreement in advance about the duration of their agreement

E. Implied authority → (2) When an agent has authority to do acts that are necessary to accomplish an assignment

TRUE/FALSE QUESTIONS

1. **T F** A principal is always liable on a contract, whether he is fully disclosed, unidentified, or undisclosed.

3. **T F** An agent may receive profits from an agency relationship even if the principal does not know about the profits, as long as the principal is not harmed.

5. **T F** An agent has a duty to provide the principal with all information in her possession that she has reason to believe the principal wants to know, even if he does not specifically ask for it.

MULTIPLE-CHOICE QUESTIONS

1. **Answer:** (b) Had you checked the painter's references?

3. **Answer:** (d) Yes, Finn has violated his duty of loyalty to Barry.

5. **Answer:** (d) Yes, because Sue had apparent authority.

CASE QUESTIONS

1. An elementary school custodian hit a child who wrote graffiti on the wall. Is the school district liable for this intentional tort by its employee?

Answer: Yes, because the custodian thought he was serving the purpose of his employer.

3. A soldier was drinking at a training seminar. Although he was told to leave his car at the seminar, he disobeyed orders and drove to a nightclub. On the way to the club, he was in an accident. Is the military liable for the damage he caused?

Answer: No, he was not acting within the scope of employment.

5. *YOU BE THE JUDGE* WRITING PROBLEM Sarah went to an auction at Christie's to bid on a tapestry for her employer, Fine Arts Gallery. The good news is that she purchased a Dufy tapestry for $77,000. The bad news is that it was not the one her employer had told her to buy. In the excitement of the auction, she forgot her instructions. Fine Art refused to pay, and Christie's filed suit. Is Fine Arts liable for the unauthorized act of its agent? **Argument for Christie's**: Christie's cannot possibly ascertain in each case the exact nature of a bidder's authority. Whether or not Sarah had actual authority, she certainly had apparent authority, and Fine Arts is liable. **Argument for Fine Arts:** Sarah was not authorized to purchase the Dufy tapestry, and therefore Christie's must recover from her, not Fine Arts.

Answer: Sarah had apparent authority, and Fine Arts is liable *Christie, Manson & Woods International, Inc. v. Nardin Fine Arts Gallery*, Supreme Court of New York, IA Part 49, *New York Law Journal*, 3/15/1994, p. 21.

CHAPTER 18

MATCHING QUESTIONS

A. Employee at will. → (3) An employee without an explicit employment contract

C. FLSA → (4) A federal statute that regulates wages and limits child labor

E. OSHA → (1) A federal statute that ensures safe working conditions

TRUE/FALSE QUESTIONS

1. T **F** An employee may be fired for a good reason, a bad reason, or no reason at all.

3. **T** F In some states, employers are not liable for false statements they make about former employees unless they know these statements are false or are primarily motivated by ill will.

5. T **F** Any employer has the right to insist that employees submit to a lie detector test.

7. T **F** Children under 16 may not hold paid jobs.

MULTIPLE-CHOICE QUESTIONS

1. **Answer:** (e) He could be fired for any reason except a bad reason.

3. **Answer:** (a) Venetia has violated the FMLA.

5. **Answer:** (c) always protected when filing suit under the False Claims Act.

CASE QUESTIONS

1. Reginald Delaney managed a Taco Time restaurant in Portland, Oregon. Some of his customers told Mr. Ledbetter, the district manager, that they would not be eating there so often because there were too many black employees. Ledbetter told Delaney to fire Ms. White, who was black. Delaney did as he was told. Ledbetter's report on the incident said: "My notes show that Delaney told me that White asked him to sleep with her and that when he would not that she started causing dissension within the crew. She asked him to come over to her house and that he declined." Delaney refused to sign the report because it was untrue, so Ledbetter fired him. What claim might Delaney make against his former employer?

Answer: Ledbetter committed a wrongful discharge when he fired Delaney for refusing to commit the tort of defamation. *Delaney v. Taco Time International, Inc.*, 297 Or. 10, 681 P.2d 114 (1984).

3. Catherine Wagenseller was a nurse at Scottsdale Memorial Hospital and an employee at will. While on a camping trip with other nurses, Wagenseller refused to join in a parody of the song "Moon River," which concluded with members of the group "mooning" the audience. Her supervisor seemed upset by her refusal. Prior to the trip, Wagenseller had received consistently favorable performance evaluations. Six months after the outing, Wagenseller was fired. She contends that it was because she had not mooned. Should the hospital be able to fire Wagenseller for this reason?

Answer: The Arizona Supreme Court ruled that the hospital had violated public policy by firing Wagenseller for refusing to break the law (indecent exposure). *Wagenseller v. Scottsdale Memorial Hosp.*, 147 Ariz. 370 (Ariz. 1985)

5. **ETHICS** To ensure that its employees did not use illegal drugs in or outside the workplace, Marvel Grocery Store required all employees to take a polygraph exam. Moreover, managers began to check employees' Facebook pages for reference to drug use. Jagger was fired for refusing to take the polygraph test. Jonathan was dismissed after revealing on his Facebook page that he was using marijuana. Has the company acted legally?

Answer: Here, Marvel has no reason to believe that a crime occurred, so it cannot require a polygraph test. Jonathan's Facebook postings have nothing to do with work conditions, and illegal activity is not protected. So the company is liable to Jagger for requiring him to take the polygraph exam, but not to Jonathan for firing him over illegal drug use.

CHAPTER 19

MATCHING QUESTIONS

A. Equal Pay Act → (1) Statute that prohibits an employee from being paid at a lesser rate than employees of the opposite sex for equal work

C. ADEA → (4) Statute that prohibits age discrimination

E. ADA → (5) Statute that prohibits discrimination against the disabled

TRUE/FALSE QUESTIONS

1. **T** F In a disparate impact case, an employer may be liable for a rule that is not discriminatory on its face.

3. T-**F** If more whites than Native Americans pass an employment test, the test violates Title VII.

5. **T** F Employers do not have to accommodate an employee's religious beliefs if doing so would impose an undue hardship on the business.

MULTIPLE-CHOICE QUESTIONS

1. **Answer:** (b) The plaintiff must submit to arbitration.

3. **Answer:** (d) Max hired a male corporate lawyer because his clients had more confidence in male lawyers.

5. **Answer:** (b) Craig may refuse to hire Ben, who is blind, to work as a playground supervisor because it's essential to the job that the supervisor be able to see what the children are doing.

CASE QUESTIONS

1. When Michelle told her boss that she was pregnant, his first comment was, "Congratulations on your pregnancy. My sister vomited for months." Then he refused to speak to her for a week. A month later, she was fired. Her boss told her the business was shifting away from her area of expertise. Does Michelle have a valid claim? Under what law?

Answer: Under the Pregnancy Discrimination Act of 1978, an employer may not fire a woman because she is pregnant.

3. After the terrorist attacks of 9/11, the United States tightened its visa requirements. In the process, baseball teams discovered that 300 foreign-born professional players had lied about their age. (A talented 16-year-old is much more valuable than a 23-year-old with the same skills.) In some cases, the players had used birth certificates that belonged to other (younger) people. To prevent this fraud, baseball teams began asking for DNA tests on prospects and their families, to make sure they were not lying about their identity. Is this testing legal?

Answer: There have not been any cases yet, but commentators speculate that the testing would violate the Genetic Information Nondiscrimination Act. It seems clear the teams would be in violation if they used the information to predict whether a player is susceptible to disease.

5. When the boss fired Clarence from his job at a moving company, she said it was because he could no longer lift heavy furniture; his salary was too high and, as he got older, he would have a hard time remembering stuff. Clarence is 60. Has the boss violated the law?

Answer: It is legal to fire someone who can't perform the job requirements or because his salary is too high. There may have been some age discrimination, but there is no evidence that age was the deciding factor. Therefore, the firing was legal.

CHAPTER 20
MATCHING QUESTIONS

A. ULP → (3) Unlawful management interference with a union organizing effort

C. Collective bargaining unit → (1) A specific group of employees that a union will represent

E. Concerted action → (4) Picketing and strikes

TRUE/FALSE QUESTIONS

1. T **F** The union and management are both obligated to bargain until they reach a CBA or a court declares the bargaining futile.

3. T F The union has the right to decide the appropriate bargaining unit.

5. T **F** While organizing, workers may not discuss union issues on company property, but may do so off the premises.

MULTIPLE-CHOICE QUESTIONS

1. **Answer:** (d) committed no ULP.

3. **Answer:** (b) Blue has committed a ULP, but Red has not.

5. **Answer:** (a) does; is

CASE QUESTIONS

1. Gibson Greetings, Inc., had a plant in Berea, Kentucky, where the workers belonged to the International Brotherhood of Firemen & Oilers. The old CBA expired, and the parties negotiated a new one, but were unable to reach an agreement on economic issues. The union struck. At the next bargaining session, the company claimed that the strike violated the old CBA, which had a no-strike clause and which stated that the terms of the old CBA would continue in force as long as the parties were bargaining a new CBA. The company refused to bargain until the union at least agreed that by bargaining, the company was not giving up its claim of an illegal strike. The two sides returned to bargaining, but meanwhile the company hired replacement workers. Eventually, the striking workers offered to return to work, but Gibson refused to rehire many of them. In court, the union claimed that the company had committed a ULP by (1) insisting the strike was illegal; and (2) refusing to bargain until the union acknowledged the company's position. Why is it very important to the union to establish the company's act as a ULP? *Was* it a ULP?

Answer: The strike was initially over pay and was thus an economic strike. If the company committed a ULP by refusing to bargain until the validity of the strike was resolved, then it converted the dispute into a ULP strike. In that case, all striking workers would be entitled to their jobs back, even if it meant laying off replacement workers. However, the court ruled that the company had *not* committed a ULP. Gibson claimed in good faith that the strike was illegal. The strike remained an economic one, and the striking workers were *not* guaranteed their jobs back (though they had to be rehired without discrimination if openings appeared). *Gibson Greetings v. NLRB*, 53 F.3d 385, 1995 U.S. App. LEXIS 11788 (D.C. Cir. 1995).

3. A foreman at Progressive Electric told employees that the company's president, "didn't want any union crap around here," and that "if the unions got into Progressive, Progressive would lose contracts and go out of business because Progressive couldn't afford the union wages and benefits." Is the foreman in violation of the NLRA?

Answer: The court ruled that these statements alone might not constitute an ULP but when combined with the company's refusal to hire any union members, the company was in violation. *Progressive Electric, Inc. v. National Labor Relations Board*, 453 F. 3d 538 (D.C. Cir. 2006)

5. Eads Transfer, Inc., was a moving and storage company with a small workforce represented by the General Teamsters, Chauffeurs, and Helpers Union. When the CBA expired, the parties failed to reach agreement on a new one, and the union struck. As negotiations continued, Eads hired temporary replacement workers. After 10 months of the strike, some union workers offered to return to work, but Eads made no response to the offer. Two months later, more workers offered to return to work, but Eads would not accept any of the offers. Eventually, Eads notified all workers that they would not be allowed back to work until a new CBA had been signed. The union filed ULP claims against the company. Please rule.

Answer: The union is correct. Eads *locked out* its employees by refusing to allow them back to work. A lockout is a legitimate weapon with which a company may apply economic pressure on a union to force agreement on a CBA. But the company must *notify* the union of the lockout before it begins, so that the union understands the position and may bargain or respond accordingly. Without such notice, the lockout doesn't serve to bring the parties together, which is the purpose of the NLRA. *Eads Transfer, Inc. v. NLRB*, 989 F.2d 373, 1993 U.S. App. LEXIS 6872 (9th Cir. 1993).

CHAPTER 21
MATCHING QUESTIONS

A. S corporation → (2) Created by federal law

C. Close corporation → (4) Created by state law

E. Partnership → (3) The owners are liable for the debts of the organization

TRUE/FALSE QUESTIONS

1. T **F** Sole proprietorships must file a tax return.

3. T **F** Benefit corporations are nonprofits.

5. T **F** Privately held companies that begin as corporations often change to LLCs before going public.

MULTIPLE-CHOICE QUESTIONS

1. **Answer:** (b) requires no formal steps for its creation.

3. **Answer:** (d) must register with state authorities.

5. **Answer:** (b) protects the partners from liability for the debts of the partnership.

CASE QUESTIONS

1. Alan Dershowitz, a law professor famous for his prominent clients, joined with other lawyers to open a kosher delicatessen, Maven's Court. Dershowitz met with greater success at the bar than in the kitchen—the deli failed after barely a year in business. One supplier sued for overdue bills. What form of organization would have been the best choice for Maven's Court?

Answer: A sole proprietorship would not have worked, because there was more than one owner. A partnership would have been a disaster because of unlimited liability. An LLP was a possibility, as long as the owners did not anticipate selling their shares. A limited liability partnership would have worked, too. An S corporation would have been possible because the owners could have deducted their losses on this investment from their (substantial) other income and still enjoyed limited liability. The owners would probably not have been troubled by the restraints of an S corporation—only one class of stock, for example—but the technicalities involved in forming and maintaining an S corporation can be vexing. Like many start-ups today, Maven's Court probably would have been an LLC or an S corporation.

3. Kristine bought a Rocky Mountain Chocolate Factory franchise. Her franchise agreement required her to purchase a cash register that cost $3,000, with an annual maintenance fee of $773. The agreement also provided that Rocky Mountain could change to a more expensive system. Within a few months after signing the agreement, Kristine learned that she would have to buy a new cash register that cost $20,000, with annual maintenance fees of $2,000. Does Kristine have to buy this new cash register? Did Rocky Mountain act in bad faith?

Answer: Yes, she had to buy the system—the agreement permitted Rocky Mountain to change systems. It was not a bad faith decision, as bad faith involves a subterfuge or evasion of contractual duties.

CHAPTER 22

MATCHING QUESTIONS

A. Duty of loyalty → (5) Prohibits managers from making a decision that benefits them at the expense of the corporation

C. Promoter → (3) Someone who organizes a corporation

E. Registered agent → (2) The company's representative in its state of incorporation

TRUE/FALSE QUESTIONS

1. T **F** A corporation can be formed in any state or under the federal corporate code.

3. **T** F Most companies use a very broad purpose clause in their charter.

5. T **F** A company must include in its proxy materials the names of all shareholder nominees for the board of directors.

MULTIPLE-CHOICE QUESTIONS

1. **Answer:** (e) the other party agrees to a novation.

3. **Answer:** (d) quorum requirements.

5. **Answer:** (d) engage in illegal behavior that is profitable to the company.

CASE QUESTIONS

1. Michael incorporated Erin Homes, Inc., to manufacture mobile homes. He issued himself a stock certificate for 100 shares, for which he made no payment. He and his wife served as officers and directors of the organization, but, during the eight years of its existence, the corporation held only one meeting. Erin always had its own checking account, and all proceeds from the sales of mobile homes were deposited there. It filed federal income tax returns each year, using its own federal identification number. John and Thelma paid $17,500 to purchase a mobile home from Erin, but the company never delivered it to them. John and Thelma sued Erin Homes and Michael, individually. Should the court "pierce the corporate veil" and hold Michael personally liable?

Answer: The appeals court pierced the corporate veil and held the shareholder liable because the corporation had grossly inadequate capitalization and had disregarded corporate formalities, and because the shareholder was actively participating in the operation of the business. *Laya v. Erin Homes, Inc.*, 177 W. Va. 343, 352 S.E.2d 93 (1986).

3. **ETHICS** Edgar Bronfman, Jr., dropped out of high school to go to Hollywood and write songs and produce movies. Eventually, he left Hollywood to work in the family business—the Bronfmans owned 36 percent of Seagram Co., a liquor and beverage conglomerate. Promoted to president of the company at the age of 32,

Bronfman seized a second chance to live his dream. Seagram received 70 percent of its earnings from its 24 percent ownership of DuPont Co. Bronfman sold this stock at less than market value to purchase (at an inflated price) 80 percent of MCA, a movie and music company that had been a financial disaster for its prior owners. Some observers thought Bronfman had gone Hollywood, others that he had gone crazy. After the deal was announced, the price of Seagram shares fell 18 percent. Was there anything Seagram shareholders could have done to prevent what to them was not a dream but a nightmare? Apart from legal issues, was Bronfman's decision ethical? What ethical obligations did he owe Seagram's shareholders?

Answer: The Seagram shareholders have little choice other than the "Wall Street walk." Seagram will not merge with MCA, so shareholder approval of the purchase is not necessary. The sale of DuPont stock is not significant enough to require shareholder approval. It is unlikely that a court would hold that Seagram had violated the business judgment rule. Floyd Norris, "Bronfman Follies: From Oil to Movies," *The New York Times*, April 8, 1995, p. D1; Laura Landro and Eben Shapiro, "Seagram Sells Stake in DuPont So It Can Buy Control of MCA," *The Wall Street Journal*, April 7, 1995, p. l.

5. Ulrick and Birger started an air taxi service in Berlin, Germany, under the name Berlinair, Inc. Birger was approached by a group of travel agents who were interested in hiring an air charter business to take German tourists on vacation. Birger formed Air Berlin Charter Co. (ABC) and was its sole owner. On behalf of ABC, he entered into a contract with the Berlin travel agents. Birger concealed his negotiations from Ulrick, even though he used Berlinair working time, staff, money, and facilities. Birger defended his behavior on the grounds that Berlinair could not afford to enter into a contract with the travel agents. Has Birger violated the corporate opportunity doctrine?

Answer: Whether or not Berlinair could afford the opportunity, Birger had the obligation to offer it to the company. *Klinicki v. Lundgren*, 298 Or. 662, 695 P.2d 906 (1995).

CHAPTER 23

MATCHING QUESTIONS

A. Discharge → (2) Debtors are not liable for money owed before the filing

C. Exempt property → (1) Property that individual debtors can keep for themselves

E. Voidable preference → (4) Payment to a creditor immediately before filing

TRUE/FALSE QUESTIONS

1. T **F** Student loans can never be discharged.

3. T **F** A creditor is not permitted to force a debtor into bankruptcy.

5. **T** F The Code permits *individual* debtors (but not organizations) to keep some property for themselves.

MULTIPLE-CHOICE QUESTIONS

1. **Answer:** (a) A creditors' committee, if appointed, will consist of unsecured creditors.

3. **Answer:** (d) It will be granted because Unger is unable to pay Unger's debts as they become due.

5. **Answer:** (a) the debtor in possession/a cramdown

CASE QUESTIONS

1. James, the owner of an auto parts store, told his employee, Rickey, to clean and paint some tires in the basement. Highly flammable gasoline fumes accumulated in the poorly ventilated space. James threw a firecracker into the basement, as a joke, intending only to startle Rickey. Sparks from the firecracker caused an explosion and fire that severely burned him. He filed a personal injury suit against James for $1 million. Is this debt dischargeable under Chapter 7?

Answer: Injuries caused by a stupid accident are dischargeable, not those caused intentionally or maliciously. James's behavior was foolish, but his debt to Rickey was dischargeable because the injury was not intentional or malicious.

3. Lydia D'Ettore received a degree in computer programming at DeVry Institute of Technology, with a grade point average of 2.51. To finance her education, she borrowed $20,500 from a federal student loan program. After graduation she could not find a job in her field, so she went to work as a clerk at a salary of $12,500. D'Ettore and her daughter lived with her parents free of charge. After setting aside $50 a month in savings and paying bills that included $233 for a new car and $50 for jewelry from Zales, her disposable income was $125 per month. D'Ettore asked the bankruptcy court to discharge the debts she owed for her DeVry education. Should the court do so?

Answer: The court refused to discharge D'Ettore's debts. It reasoned that anyone who can afford to buy jewelry and a new car, while saving money, could also afford to pay her educational loans. If there was hardship, it was clearly caused by her extravagant purchases. *In re D'Ettore* 106 Bankr. 715 (Bankr. M.D. Fla. 1989).

5. After filing for bankruptcy, Yvonne Brown sought permission of the court to reaffirm a $6,000 debt to her credit union. The debt was unsecured, and she was under no obligation to pay it. The credit union had published the following notice in its newsletter:

> *If you are thinking about filing bankruptcy THINK about the long-term implications. This action, filing bankruptcy, closes the door on TOMORROW. Having no credit means no ability to purchase cars, houses, credit cards. Look into the future—no loans for the education of your children.*

Should the court approve Brown's reaffirmation?

Answer: The court refused to approve the reaffirmation because the credit union's threats constituted duress. *In re Brown*, 95 Bankr. 35, 1989 Bankr. LEXIS 543 (Bankr. E.D. Va. 1989).

CHAPTER 24
MATCHING QUESTIONS

A. Securities Act of 1933 → (4) Regulates the issuance of securities

C. Sherman Act → (3) Prohibits price-fixing

E. Securities Exchange Act of 1934 → (2) Regulates companies once they have gone public

TRUE/FALSE QUESTIONS

1. T **F** Before permitting a company to issue new securities, the SEC investigates to ensure that the company has a promising future.

3. T **F** Horizontal price-fixing is legal as long as it does not have an anticompetitive impact.

5. **T** F It is legal for a company to sell its product at a price below cost as long as it does not intend to drive competitors out of business.

MULTIPLE-CHOICE QUESTIONS

1. **Answer:** (d) must make disclosure to unaccredited investors.

3. **Answer:** (b) I and II.

5. **Answer:** (d) No, because a manufacturer is not liable under the RPA if it charges lower prices to meet competition.

CASE QUESTIONS

1. You are the president of Turbocharge, Inc., a publicly traded company. You have been buying stock recently because you think the company's product—a more efficient hybrid engine—is very promising. One day, you show up at work and find your desk in the hallway. The CEO has fired you. In a huff, you sell all your company stock. The only silver lining to your cloud is that you make a large profit. Or is this a silver lining?

Answer: You are in violation of Section 16. Even though you acted without any bad intent, you must turn over all your profits to the company.

3. In New York City, 50 bakeries agreed to raise the retail price of bread. All the association's members printed the new price on their bread sleeves. Are the bakeries in violation of the antitrust laws?

Answer: Four directors of the association were indicted on antitrust charges. They were charged with violating the Sherman Act by fixing prices and allocating markets. Seth Faison, "Detectives Posing as Bakers Charge 4 with Price Fixing," *The New York Times*, July 14, 1994, p. A13.

5. Gary Griffiths was a vice president for a railroad. The CEO asked him to prepare an inventory of all the rolling stock the company owned and to arrange trips among its rail yards for a group of men in suits. Employees began asking Griffiths if the company would be sold and whether they would lose their jobs. Indeed, the company was exploring sale options. Griffiths went to visit his brother-inlaw, Rex, who the next day purchased $400,000 in stock of the company. For a month, Griffiths called regularly, and each time Rex bought more stock. In total, he spent $1.14 million on company stock. After the company was sold, Rex made a substantial profit. Did Gary and Rex engage in illegal insider trading? Was the fact that men in suits were touring the rail yards material nonpublic information?

Answer: The court found both men liable. Although there was no direct evidence that Gary passed on confidential information, circumstantial evidence was sufficient. Gary was a tipper and Rex a tippee. SEC v. Steffes, 805 F.Supp 2d 601 (N.D. Ill. 2011).

CHAPTER 25
MATCHING QUESTIONS

A. EFTA → (5) Regulates electronic payment

C. FCRA → (2) Regulates credit reports

E. TILA → (1) Requires lenders to disclose the terms of a loan

TRUE/FALSE QUESTIONS

1. **T** F If a store advertises a product, it is not required to have enough stock on hand to fill every order.

3. T **F** Payday loans are illegal.

5. T **F** A consumer reporting agency has the right to keep information in its files secret from the consumer.

MULTIPLE-CHOICE QUESTIONS

1. **Answer:** (d) it is a gift to you.

3. **Answer:** (a) I, II, and III

5. **Answer:** (c) Either (a) or (b)

CASE QUESTIONS

1. Process cheese food slices must contain at least 51 percent natural cheese. Imitation cheese slices, by contrast, contain little or no natural cheese and consist primarily of water and vegetable oil. Kraft, Inc. makes Kraft Singles, which are individually wrapped process cheese food slices. When Kraft began losing market share to imitation slices that were advertised as both less expensive and equally nutritious as Singles, Kraft responded with a series of advertisements informing consumers that Kraft Singles cost more than imitation slices because they are made from 5 ounces of milk.

Kraft does use 5 ounces of milk in making each Kraft Single, but 30 percent of the calcium contained in the milk is lost during processing. Imitation slices contain the same amount of calcium as Kraft Singles. Are the Kraft advertisements deceptive?

Answer: The court agreed with the FTC that Kraft's ads were deceptive. *Kraft, Inc. v. FTC*, 970 F.2d 311, 1992 U.S. App. LEXIS 17575 (7th Cir. 1992).

3. Thomas worked at a Sherwin-Williams paint store that James managed. But Thomas and James had a falling out. After Thomas quit, James claimed that Thomas owed the store $121. Sherwin-Williams reported this information to the Chilton credit reporting agency. Thomas sent a letter to Chilton disputing the accuracy of the Sherwin-Williams charges. Chilton contacted James who confirmed that Thomas still owed the money. Chilton failed to note in Thomas's file that a dispute was pending. Thereafter, two of Thomas's requests for credit cards were denied. Have James and Chilton violated the Fair Credit Reporting Act?

Answer: Once Chilton received notice of the dispute, it was obligated to reverify the accuracy of the information. It was not enough simply to ask James, because Chilton knew that James and Thomas had had a dispute. If no one else could verify the report, Chilton should have deleted it. James was not in violation because the information he provided was essentially true–Thomas's account at Sherwin-Williams was delinquent. *Pinner v. Schmidt*, 805 F.2d 1258 (5th Cir. 1986).

5. **ETHICS** After TNT Motor Express hired Joseph Bruce Drury as a truck driver, it ordered a background check from Robert Arden & Associates. TNT provided Drury's social security number and date of birth, but not his middle name. Arden discovered that a Joseph Thomas Drury, who coincidentally had the same birthdate as Joseph Bruce Drury, had served a prison sentence for drunk driving. Not knowing that it had the wrong Drury, Arden reported this information to TNT, which promptly fired Drury. When he asked why, the TNT executive refused to tell him. Did TNT violate the law? Whether or not TNT was in violation, did its executives behave ethically? Who would have been harmed or helped if TNT managers had informed Drury of the Arden report?

Answer: The Fair Credit Reporting Act required TNT to ask Drury's permission before requesting a consumer report. Then, before firing him, TNT was required to give him a copy of the report and a description of his rights under this statute. *Drury v. TNT Holland Motor Express, Inc.*, 885 F. Supp. 161, 1994 U.S. Dist. LEXIS 11583 (D.Ct. 1994).

CHAPTER 26
MATCHING QUESTIONS

A. EPA → (4) The agency that regulates environmental policy in the United States

C. NEPA → (5) Requires all federal agencies to prepare an environmental impact statement

E. RCRA → (2) Establishes rules for treating newly created wastes

TRUE/FALSE QUESTIONS

1. **T** F In establishing national standards under the Clean Air Act, the EPA need not consider the cost of compliance.

3. T F Any individual, business, or federal agency that significantly affects the quality of the environment must file an EIS.

5. **T** F Violating the environmental laws can be a criminal offense, punishable by a prison term.

MULTIPLE-CHOICE QUESTIONS

1. **Answer:** (b) I, II, and III

3. **Answer:** (c) does not; cannot

5. **Answer:** (d) permits the EPA to require testing of a chemical only if there is evidence that it is dangerous.

CASE QUESTIONS

1. Tariq Ahmad decided to dispose of some of his laboratory's hazardous chemicals by shipping them to his home in Pakistan. He sent the chemicals to Castelazo (in the United States) to prepare the materials for shipment. Ahmad did not tell the driver who picked up the chemicals that they were hazardous, nor did he give the driver any written documentation. What law has Ahmad violated? What penalties might he face?

Answer: Ahmad was convicted of transporting hazardous waste in violation of the Resource Conservation and Recovery Act. He was subject to criminal penalties under the Act. *United States v. Ahmad*, 1995 U.S. App. LEXIS 28350 (9th Cir. 1995).

3. *YOU BE THE JUDGE* **WRITING PROBLEM** The Lordship Point Gun Club operated a trap and skeet shooting club in Stratford, Connecticut, for 70 years. During this time, customers deposited millions of pounds of lead shot and clay target fragments on land around the club and in Long Island Sound. Forty-five percent of sediment samples taken from the Sound exceeded the established limits for lead. Was the Gun Club in violation of the RCRA? **Argument for the Gun Club**: The Gun Club does not dispose of hazardous wastes, within the meaning of the RCRA. Congress meant the statute to apply only to companies in the business of manufacturing articles that produce hazardous waste. If the Gun Club happens to produce wastes, that is only incidental to the normal use of a product. **Argument for the Plaintiff:** Under the RCRA, lead shot is hazardous waste. The law applies to anyone who produces hazardous waste, no matter how.

Answer: The court held that the Gun Club was in violation of the RCRA because it was disposing of lead shot that was clearly hazardous waste as defined by the statute. It ordered the Gun Club to clean up the site and also to obtain a permit for the operation of a hazardous waste disposal site. *Connecticut Coastal Fishermen's Assoc. v. Remington Arms Co.*, 989 F.2d 1305, 1993 U.S. App. LEXIS 6424 (2nd Cir. 1993).

5. Before the Department of Agriculture issued regulations on genetically modified beets, what steps did it need to take under the environmental statutes?

Answer: The Department had to conduct an EA (environmental assessment) to determine if an EIS (environmental impact statement) was necessary.

CHAPTER 27
MATCHING QUESTIONS

A. GAAS → (4) Rules for conducting audits

C. Qualified opinion → (6) When there is some uncertainty in the financial statements

E. Vouching → (2) When accountants check backwards to ensure there are data to support a transaction

TRUE/FALSE QUESTIONS

1. T **F** Auditors are liable under the 1933 Act only if they intentionally misrepresent financial statements.

3. T **F** Under the 1934 Act, accountants are liable for negligent behavior.

5. T **F** Under federal law, accounting firms may not provide any consulting services to companies that they audit.

MULTIPLE-CHOICE QUESTIONS

1. **Answer:** (d) Yes; Yes

3. **Answer:** (b) Auditors must report to the CEO of the company they are auditing.

5. **Answer:** (b) Carter will win because Ellen was careless and she knew that landlords would see the financials.

CASE QUESTIONS

1. After reviewing Color-Dyne's audited financial statements, the plaintiffs provided materials to the company on credit. These financial statements showed that Color-Dyne owned $2 million in inventory. The audit failed to reveal, however, that the company had loans outstanding on all of this inventory. The accountant did not know that the company intended to give the financial statements to plaintiffs or any other creditors. Color-Dyne went bankrupt. Is the accountant liable to plaintiffs?

Answer: The accountant was not liable. 356 S.E.2d 198 (Ga. 1987).

3. The British Broadcasting Corp. (BBC) broadcast a TV program alleging that Terry Venables, a former professional soccer coach, had fraudulently obtained a £1 million loan by misrepresenting the value of his company. Venables had been a sportscaster for the BBC but had switched to a competing network. The source

of the BBC's story was "confidential working papers" from Venables's accountant. According to the accountant, the papers had been stolen. Who owns these working papers? Does the accountant have the right to disclose the content of working papers?

Answer: Although, in theory, the accountant owns the working papers, he may not disclose confidential client information without the client's permission. Ian Burrell and Adrian Levy, "Venables to Sue BBC Chief over 'Stolen' Papers," *Sunday Times*, July 16, 1995, Home News section.

5. A partnership of doctors in Billings, Montana, sought to build a larger office building. When it decided to finance this project using industrial revenue bonds under a complex provision of the Internal Revenue Code, it hired Peat Marwick to do the required financial work. The deal was all set to close when it was discovered that the accountants had made an error in structuring the deal. As a result, the partnership was forced to pay a significantly higher rate of interest. When the partnership sued Peat for breach of contract, the accounting firm asked the court to dismiss the claim on the grounds that the client could only sue for the tort of negligence, not for breach of contract. Peat argued that it had performed its duties under the contract. The statute of limitations had expired for a tort case, but not for a contract case. Should the doctors' case be dismissed?

Answer: The doctors could file suit either in tort or in contract. It was implied in the contract that Peat would act like a reasonably careful accountant under the circumstances. When Peat was negligent, it violated the contract. *Billings Clinic v. Peat Marwick Alain & Co.*, 797 P.2d 899, 1990 Mont. LEXIS 241 (Mont. 1990).

CHAPTER 28
MATCHING QUESTIONS

A. Patent → (4) Grants the inventor exclusive use of an invention

C. Trade secrets → (5) Compilation of information that would give its owner an advantage in business

E. Paris Convention → (3) Extends patent protection overseas

TRUE/FALSE QUESTIONS

1. T **F** Once you have purchased a CD and copied it onto your iPod, it is legal to give the CD to a friend.

3. **T** F In the case of corporations, copyright protection lasts 120 years from the product's creation.

5. T **F** The first person to file the application is entitled a patent over someone else who invented the product first.

MULTIPLE-CHOICE QUESTIONS

1. **Answer:** (a) it has not ever been used anyplace in the world.

3. **Answer:** (b) II and III

5. **Answer:** (d) A surname

CASE QUESTIONS

1. While in college, David invented a new and useful machine to make macaroni and cheese (he called it the "Mac n'Cheeser"). It was like nothing on the market, but David did not apply for a patent. At that time, he offered to sell his invention to several kitchen products companies. His offers were all rejected, and he never sold the invention. Years later, he decided to apply for a utility patent. Is David entitled to a utility patent ?

Answer: No, while the Mac n'Cheeser was new, useful, and nonobvious at the time it was invented, David's disclosure to the kitchen products companies years before renders it not novel now. Inventors have a grace period of one year once disclosure is made to apply for a patent. That time lapsed. Patent rejected.

3. **ETHICS** After Edward Miller left his job as a salesperson at the New England Insurance Agency, Inc., he took some of his New England customers to his new employer. At New England, the customer lists had been kept in file cabinets. Although the company did not restrict access to these files, it said there was an understanding to the effect that "you do not peruse my files and I do not peruse yours." The lists were not marked "confidential" or "not to be disclosed." Did Miller steal New England's trade secrets? Whether or not he violated the law, was it ethical for him to use this information at his new job? What is your Life Principle?

Answer: Answers will vary. The court held that these customer lists were not trade secrets because New England had not made sufficient effort to keep them secret. *New England Ins. v. Miller*, 1991 Conn. Super. LEXIS 817 (1991).

5. Roger Schlafly applied for a patent for two prime numbers. (A prime number cannot be evenly divided by any number other than itself and 1. For example, 2, 3, 5, 7, 11, 13.) Schlafly's numbers are a bit longer—one is 150 digits, the other is 300. His numbers, when used together, can help perform the type of mathematical operation necessary for exchanging coded messages by computer. Should the PTO issue this patent?

Answer: The PTO patented these numbers because they were useful, they had never been used before by anyone else, and their use for this particular technique was not obvious. Simson Garfinkel, "A Prime Argument in Patent Debate," *Boston Globe*, April 6, 1995, p. 69.

CHAPTER 29
MATCHING QUESTIONS

A. Constructive eviction → (1) A landlord's substantial interference with a tenant's use and enjoyment of the premises

C. Fixture → (2) Goods that have become attached to real property

E. Tenancy at sufferance → (3) A tenant remains on the premises after expiration of true tenancy

TRUE/FALSE QUESTIONS

1. **T** F If one joint tenant dies, his interest in the property passes to surviving joint tenants, not to his heirs.

3. **T** F A landlord could be liable for a constructive eviction even if he never asked the tenant to leave.

5. T **F** A landlord may charge a tenant for normal wear and tear on an apartment, but the charges must be reasonable.

MULTIPLE-CHOICE QUESTIONS

1. **Answer:** (d) Quick 1/2, Onyx 1/4, Nash's heirs 1/4

3. **Answer:** (d) Tenancy at sufferance

5. **Answer:** (e) lose.

CASE QUESTIONS

1. **ETHICS** Lisa Preece rented an apartment from Turman Realty, paying a $300 security deposit. Georgia law states: "Any landlord who fails to return any part of a security deposit which is required to be returned to a tenant pursuant to this article shall be liable to the tenant in the amount of three times the sum improperly withheld plus reasonable attorney's fees." When Preece moved out, Turman did not return her security deposit, and she sued for triple damages plus attorney's fees, totaling $1,800. Turman offered evidence that its failure to return the deposit was inadvertent and that it had procedures reasonably designed to avoid such errors. Is Preece entitled to triple damages? Attorney's fees?

Answer: The court held the defendant liable for $900 (treble damages) and an additional $900 in attorney's fees. The rationale for treble damages is that, historically, landlords often willfully refuse to refund security deposits, knowing that most tenants will not bother to sue. That was obviously unethical. By trebling the damages, state legislatures have given landlords a financial incentive to be fair. By permitting attorney's fees, such laws ensure that injured tenants have access to court and a remedy. *Preece v. Turman Realty Co., Inc.*, 228 Ga. App. 609, 492 S.E.2d 342, 1997 Ga. App. LEXIS 1216 (Ga. App. 1997).

3. Nome 2000, a partnership, owned a large tract of wilderness land in Alaska. The Fagerstrom family had used the property for camping and holidays since about 1944. In 1966, Charles and Peggy Fagerstrom marked off an area for a cabin and brought material to build the cabin, but never did so. In about 1970, they built a picnic area on the land, and in about 1974, they placed a camper trailer on the land, where it remained until the lawsuit. In 1987, Nome 2000 sued to eject the Fagerstroms from the land. The Fagerstroms had used the land only during the summer months. No one lived in the area during the winter months, when it was virtually uninhabitable. Has the family adversely possessed the land from Nome 2000?

Answer: The Fagerstroms win and take title to the land by adverse possession. Their use, and their ancestors' use, was open and notorious, and adverse to the claim of the true owner. The owner of the land had many years in which it could have ejected the Fagerstroms, but failed to do so. Although the Fagerstroms used the land only in the summer, that is sufficient to obtain title when it is the normal use for land in the given area. *Nome 2000 v. Fagerstrom*, 799 P.2d 304, 1990 Alaska LEXIS 107 (Alaska 1990).

5. Kenmart Realty sued to evict Mr. and Ms. Alghalabio for nonpayment of rent and sought the unpaid monies, totaling several thousand dollars. In defense, the Alghalabios claimed that their apartment was infested with rats. They testified that there were numerous rat holes in the walls of the living room, bedroom, and kitchen, that there were rat droppings all over the apartment, and that on one occasion they saw their toddler holding a live rat. They testified that the landlord had refused numerous requests to exterminate. Please rule on the landlord's suit.

Answer: The Alghalabios' defense was *breach of the implied warranty of habitability*. The landlord failed to maintain the premises in a livable condition, and the tenants are therefore entitled to an abatement of rent. The amount of abatement depends upon the severity of the problems. In this case, the infestation was so severe, and lasted so long, that the court found the rent 100 percent abated for all months the tenants did not pay. By the time of trial, the Alghalabios had voluntarily moved out. The landlord recovered no money. *Kenmart Realty v. Alghalabio, New York Law Journal*, Dec. 19, 1994, p. 25 (N.Y. City Court 1994).

CHAPTER 30
MATCHING QUESTIONS

A. Extraordinary care → (2) Required level of care in a bailment made for the sole benefit of the bailee

C. Ordinary care → (4) Required level of care in a bailment made for the mutual benefit of bailor and bailee

E. Slight care → (5) Required level of care in a bailment made for the sole benefit of the bailor

TRUE/FALSE QUESTIONS

1. T **F** A gift is unenforceable unless both parties give consideration.

3. **T** F A bailee always has the right to possess the property.

5. **T** F A common carrier is strictly liable for harm to the bailor's goods.

MULTIPLE-CHOICE QUESTIONS

1. **Answer:** (d) I, II, and III.

3. **Answer:** (e) This is mislaid property, and Margie is entitled to it.

5. **Answer:** (a) Valerie will win.

CASE QUESTIONS

1. While in her second year at the Juilliard School of Music in New York City, Ann Rylands had a chance to borrow for one month a rare Guadagnini violin, made in 1768. She returned the violin to the owner in Philadelphia, but then she telephoned her father to ask if he would buy it for her. He borrowed money from his pension fund and paid the owner. Ann traveled to Philadelphia to pick up the violin. She had exclusive possession of the violin for the next 20 years, using it in her professional career. Unfortunately, she became an alcoholic, and during one period when she was in a treatment center, she entrusted the violin to her mother for safekeeping. At about that time, her father died. When Ann was released from the center, she requested return of the violin, but her mother refused. Who owns the violin?

Answer: Ann does. Ann's father made a valid *inter vivos* gift of the violin while Ann was still a student. He intended to transfer ownership to her immediately, and made delivery by permitting her to pick up the violin. From that point on, Ann owned it. *Rylands v. Rylands*, 1993 Conn. Super. LEXIS 823 (Conn. Super. Ct. 1993).

3. Eileen Murphy often cared for her elderly neighbor, Thomas Kenney. He paid her $25 per day for her help and once gave her a bank certificate of deposit worth $25,000. She spent the money. Murphy alleged that shortly before his death, Kenney gave her a large block of shares in three corporations. He called his broker, intending to instruct him to transfer the shares to Murphy's name, but the broker was ill and unavailable. So Kenney told Murphy to write her name on the shares and keep them, which she did. Two weeks later, Kenney died. When Murphy presented the shares to Kenney's broker to transfer ownership to her, the broker refused because Kenney had never endorsed the shares as the law requires—that is, signed them over to Murphy. Was Murphy entitled to the $25,000? To the shares?

Answer: Murphy gets the $25,000. There was delivery, acceptance, and adequate evidence that Kenney intended the items as gifts. Murphy is not entitled to the shares, though, because without the endorsement there is no delivery, an essential element. Kenney lived for two weeks after instructing Murphy to write her name on the shares and during that time should have endorsed them to her, or caused a broker to do so. *In Re Estate of Kenney*, 1993 Ohio App. LEXIS 2481, Ohio Ct. App., 1993).

5. Marjan International Corp. sells handmade oriental rugs. V. K. Putman, Inc., is a Montana trucking company. Marjan delivered valuable rugs to Putman for shipment from New York City to Tacoma, Washington. Unfortunately, there were several delays in transit. The truck driver encountered snow storms and closed roads. His truck also overheated and required repairs in a garage. Before the driver resumed the trip, he stopped to pick up and load other goods. When the truck finally arrived in Tacoma, two bales of rugs were missing. Marjan sued on the grounds that Putman was a common carrier, but Putman claimed it was a contract carrier. What difference does it make whether Putman was a common carrier or a contract carrier, and how is that determined?

Answer: A common carrier is one that makes its services available on a regular basis to the general public. A common carrier is strictly liable for any loss to the goods, unless the carrier can demonstrate that the harm was caused by an act of God, an enemy of the state, a public authority, the shipper itself, or the nature of the goods themselves. Most such defenses fail. A contract carrier, however, is an ordinary bailee, who will escape liability if it used ordinary care. Here, Putman made its services available to the general public on a regular basis and was thus a common carrier. It was liable for the full value of the lost rugs. *Marjan International Corp. v. V. K. Putman, Inc.*, 1993 U.S. Dist. LEXIS 18243 (S.D.N.Y. 1993).

CHAPTER 31

MATCHING QUESTIONS

A. Executrix → (5) A personal representative chosen by the decedent to carry out the terms of a will

C. Codicil → (2) An amendment to a will

E. Heir → (1) Someone who inherits assets

TRUE/FALSE QUESTIONS

1. T **F** There is no need to have a will unless you have substantial assets.

3. T **F** A nuncupative will does not need to be witnessed.

5. T **F** A trustee must obtain approval from the beneficiaries before decanting a trust.

MULTIPLE-CHOICE QUESTIONS

1. **Answer:** (d) 1/5 to each surviving child and grandchild

3. **Answer:** (e) Just III.

5. **Answer:** (b) To save money, since a trust is cheaper than a will

CASE QUESTIONS

1. If your grandparents were to die leaving a large estate, and all of their children were also dead, would you have a larger inheritance under a per stirpes or a per capita distribution?

Answer: Answers will vary. It depends on the number of siblings you have in relation to the number of children in each of the other branches of the family. For example, if the decedents had two children, under per stirpes distribution, they would each inherit half the estate. If the children were dead, their children (the grandchildren of the decedents) would split the parents' portions. So, if you were an only child, you would get half the estate. If you had three siblings, you would get ¼ of half, or 1/8 of the estate. In the same example, but under per capita, each grandchild would get 1/5 of the estate. So, per stirpes is better if you have few siblings; per capita is better if your sibling group is larger than the average sibling group in the extended family.

3. Kevin Fitzgerald represents the down-and-out Mission Hill and Roxbury Districts in the Massachusetts House of Representatives. A priest alerted him that Mary Guzelian, a street person who roamed his district, had trash bags in her ghetto apartment stuffed with cash, bonds, and bankbooks. Fitzgerald visited the apartment with his top aide, Patricia McDermott. Two weeks later, Guzelian signed a will, drafted by one of Fitzgerald's acquaintances, that left Guzelian's $400,000 estate to Fitzgerald and McDermott. Fitzgerald claimed not to know about the will until Guzelian's death four years later. Guzelian, 64, suffered from chronic paranoid schizophrenia and severe health problems. Would Guzelian's sister have a claim on Guzelian's estate?

Answer: The probate court overturned Guzelian's will and ordered Fitzgerald and McDermott to pay the entire estate to Guzelian's sister. The lawyer who drafted the will was suspended from practice for three years. Patricia Nealon, "Probate Judge Orders Rep. Fitzgerald, Two Others to Repay Guzelian Estate," *Boston Globe*, November 9, 1994, p. B1.

5. When Sheryl founded a Silicon Valley company, she placed half of her stock in a trust for her children. They were entitled to the assets in the trust when they turned 21. The company has just gone public, and the stock in the trust is now worth $150 million. She does not want her children, who are 12 and 10 years old, to have that much money when they turn 21. Is there anything she can do?

Answer: She can ask the trustee to decant the assets into a different trust that would place limits on the children's income.

CHAPTER 32
MATCHING QUESTIONS

A. Insured → (5) The person whose loss is the subject of an insurance policy

C. Owner → (4) The person who enters into the policy and pays the premiums

E. Insurable interest → (3) If the person who takes out the policy would be harmed by the danger that she has insured against

TRUE/FALSE QUESTIONS

1. T **F** If the insured makes any false statement in the application process, the insurance policy is voidable.

3. **T** F You should primarily buy insurance to protect against harm that you cannot afford to repair.

5. T **F** An annuity is simply a type of life insurance.

MULTIPLE-CHOICE QUESTIONS

1. **Answer:** (e) II and III

3. **Answer:** (b) Neither I, II, nor III

5. **Answer:** (d) III and IV

CASE QUESTIONS

1. ***YOU BE THE JUDGE* WRITING PROBLEM** Linda and Eddie had two children before they were divorced. Under the terms of their divorce, Eddie became the owner of their house. When he died suddenly, their children inherited the property. Linda moved into the house with the children and began paying the mortgage, which was in Eddie's name alone. She also took out fire insurance. When the house burned down, the insurance company refused to pay the policy because she did not have an insurable interest. Do you agree? **Argument for the Insurance Company:** Linda did not own the house; therefore, she had no insurable interest. **Argument for Linda:** She was harmed when the house burned down because she and her children had no place to live. She was paying the mortgage, so she also had a financial interest.

Answer: Linda had an insurable interest because she had made a substantial financial contribution by paying the mortgage. Also, the house was owned by her children and as their guardian, she had an insurable interest in the house. *Motorists Mutual v. Richmond*, 676 S.W.2d 478 (Ky. Ct. App. 1984).

3. Dannie Harvey sued her employer, O. R. Whitaker, for sexual harassment, discrimination, and defamation. Whitaker counterclaimed for libel and slander, requesting $1 million in punitive damages. Both Whitaker and Harvey were insured by Allstate, under identical homeowner's policies. This policy explicitly promised to defend Harvey against the exact claim Whitaker had made against her. Harvey's Allstate agent, however, told her that she was not covered. Because the agent kept all copies of Harvey's insurance policies in his office, she took him at his word. She had no choice but to defend against the claim on her own. Whitaker mounted an exceedingly hostile litigation attack, taking 80 depositions. After a year, Allstate agreed to defend Harvey. However, instead of hiring the lawyer who had been representing her, it chose another lawyer who had no expertise in this type of case and was a close friend of Whitaker's attorney. Harvey's new lawyer refused to meet her or to attend any depositions. Harvey and Whitaker finally settled. Whitaker had spent $1 million in legal fees, Harvey $169,000, and Allstate $2,513. Does Harvey have a claim against Allstate?

Answer: Harvey sued Allstate for a violation of the covenant of good faith and fair dealing. A jury awarded her $94,000 plus attorney's fees. *Harvey v. Allstate Insurance Co.*, 1993 U.S. App. LEXIS 33865 (10th Cir. 1993).

5. Jason lived in an apartment with Miri, to whom he was not married. When he applied for homeowner's insurance, the form asked their marital status. He checked the box that said "married." Later, the apartment was robbed, and Jason filed a claim with his insurance company. When the company discovered that Jason and Miri were not married, it refused to pay the claim on the grounds that he had made a material misrepresentation. Jason argued that the misrepresentation was not material because the insurance company would have issued the policy no matter how he answered that question. Is Jason's policy valid?

Answer: This representation was material because it would have changed the amount of the premiums Jason had to pay. The policy is invalid.

A

Abandoned property Property that the owner has knowingly discarded because she no longer wants it.

Accredited investors Are institutions (such as banks and insurance companies) or wealthy individuals (with a net worth of more than $1 million or an annual income of more than $200,000).

Activist investors A shareholder with a large block of stock whose goal is to influence management decisions.

Additional terms Raise issues not covered in the offer.

Adjudicate To hold a formal hearing about an issue and then decide it.

Administrative law judge (ALJ) An agency employee who acts as an impartial decision maker.

Adoption Either the board of directors approves the contract or the corporation accepts benefits under the contract.

Adversary system A system based on the assumption that if two sides present their best case before a neutral party, the truth will be established.

Adverse possession Allows someone to take title to land without paying for it, if she meets four specific standards.

Affirm To allow a court decision to stand as is; to uphold a lower court's ruling.

After-acquired property Items that the debtor obtains after the parties have made their security agreement.

Agent In an agency relationship, the person who is acting on behalf of a principal.

Agreement on Trade Related Aspects of Intellectual Property (TRIPs) A treaty on intellectual property.

Alternative dispute resolution Resolving disputes out of court, through formal or informal processes.

Ambiguity When a provision in a contract is unclear by accident.

Annuities Provides payment to a beneficiary during his lifetime.

Answer The defendant's response to the complaint.

Apparent authority A principal does something to make an innocent third party believe that an agent is acting with the principal's authority, even though the agent is not authorized.

Appellant The party filing an appeal of a trial verdict.

Appellate courts Higher courts, which generally accept the facts provided by trial courts and review the record for legal errors.

Appellee The party opposing an appeal.

Approved intermediary A broker or website that is registered with the SEC.

Arbitration A binding process of resolving legal disputes by submitting them to a neutral third party; a form of ADR in which a neutral third party has the power to impose a binding decision; a formal hearing before a neutral party to resolve a contract dispute between a union and a company.

Arson The malicious use of fire or explosives to damage or destroy real estate or personal property.

Assault An action that causes another person to fear an imminent battery.

Assignee The person receiving an assignment.

Assignment A transfer of contract rights to a third party; a contracting party transfers his rights under a contract to someone else.

Assignment of rights A transfer of benefits under a contract to another person.

Assignor The person making an assignment.

Assumption of the risk A person who voluntarily enters a situation of obvious danger cannot complain if she is injured.

Attachment A three-step process that creates an enforceable security interest.

Attorney-in-fact The person who has the authority under a power of attorney to act for the principal.

Authenticate To sign a document or to use any symbol or encryption method that identifies the person and clearly indicates she is adopting the record as her own.

Automatic stay Prohibits creditors from collecting debts that the bankrupt incurred before the petition was filed.

B

BACT Best available control technology.

Bailee The one who possesses the goods.

Bailment The rightful possession of goods by one who is not the owner, usually by mutual agreement between the bailor and bailee.

Bailor The one who delivers the goods.

Bait-and-switch A practice where sellers advertise products that are not generally available but are being used to draw interested parties in so that they will buy other products.

Bankrupt Someone who cannot pay his debts and files for protection under the Bankruptcy Code.

Bankruptcy estate The new legal entity created when a bankruptcy petition is filed. The debtor's existing assets pass into the estate.

Bargained for When something is sought by the promisor and given by the promisee in exchange for their promises.

Bargaining to impasse Both parties must continue to meet and bargain in good faith until it is clear that they cannot reach an agreement.

Battery A harmful or offensive bodily contact.

Bearer paper An instrument payable "to bearer".

Behavioral marketing or **Behavioral targeting** The practice of aiming certain advertisements at consumers based on their online behavior.

Bench trial There is no jury; the judge reaches a verdict.

Beneficiary Someone who receives the financial proceeds of a trust.

Beyond a reasonable doubt The government's burden in a criminal prosecution; the very high burden of proof in a criminal trial, demanding much more certainty than required in a civil trial.

Bilateral contract A contract where both parties make a promise.

Bill A proposed statute.

Binder A short document acknowledging receipt of an application and premium for an insurance policy.

Blue sky laws State statutes regulating securities.

Bona fide occupational qualification (BFOQ) An employer is permitted to establish discriminatory job requirements if they are *essential* to the position in question.

Breach of duty A defendant breaches his duty of due care by failing to behave the way a reasonable person would under similar circumstances.

Breach of the peace Any action that disturbs public tranquility and order.

Burden of proof The obligation to convince the jury that a party's version of the case is correct.

Buyer in ordinary course of business (BIOC) Someone who buys goods in good faith from a seller who routinely deals in such goods.

Bylaws A document that specifies the organizational rules of a corporation such as the date of the annual meeting and the required number of directors.

C

Capacity The legal ability to enter into a contract.

Categorical imperative An act is only ethical if it would be acceptable for everyone to do the same thing.

Check An instrument in which the drawer orders the drawee bank to pay money to the payee.

Check cards Another term for debit cards. Used to make purchases.

Children's Online Privacy Protection Act COPPA is a federal statute protecting the privacy of children online.

Choice of forum Determines the state in which any litigation would take place.

Choice of law provisions Determines which state's laws will be used to interpret the contract.

Civil law Regulates the rights and duties between parties.

Class action A suit filed by a group of plaintiffs with related claims.

Close corporation A corporation with a small number of shareholders whose stock is not publicly traded and whose shareholders play an active role in management. It is entitled to special treatment under state law.

Codicil An amendment to a will.

Collateral Property that is subject to a security interest.

Collective bargaining agreement (CBA) A contract between a union and management.

Collective bargaining unit The precisely defined group of employees represented by a particular union.

Comment letter A letter from the SEC to an issuer with a list of changes that must be made to the Registration Statement.

Commerce Clause Gives Congress the power to regulate commerce with foreign nations and among states.

Commercial exploitation Prohibits the unauthorized use of another person's likeness or voice for business purposes.

Common carrier A company that transports goods and makes its services regularly available to the general public.

Common law Legal precedents created by appellate courts.

Communications Decency Act of 1996 (CDA) Provides ISPs immunity from liability when information was provided by an end user.

Comparative negligence A plaintiff may generally recover even if she is partially responsible.

Compensatory Are those that flow directly from the contract.

Compensatory damages Are intended to restore the plaintiff to the position he was in before the defendant's conduct caused injury.

Complaint The pleading that starts a lawsuit, this is a short statement of the facts alleged by the plaintiff and his or her legal claims.

Compliance program A plan to prevent and detect improper conduct at all levels of a company.

Concerted action Tactics taken by union members to gain bargaining advantage.

Concurrent estates Two or more people owning property at the same time.

Condemnation A court order awarding title of real property to the government in exchange for just compensation.

Conditional Promises that a party agrees to perform only if the other side has first done what it promised.

Conforming goods Satisfy the contract terms.

Consequential Damages resulting from the unique circumstances of the injured party.

Consequential damages Damages that result from the unique circumstances of the plaintiff. Also known as *special damages*.

Consideration The inducement, price, or promise that causes a person to enter into a contract and forms the basis for the parties' exchange.

Consumer credit contract A contract in which a consumer borrows money from a lender to purchase goods and services from a seller who is affiliated with the lender.

Consumer reporting agencies Businesses that supply consumer reports to third parties.

Contract A promise that the law will enforce.

Contract carrier A company that transports goods for particular customers.

Contributory negligence A plaintiff who is even *slightly* negligent recovers nothing.

Copyright term The term for a copyright in the United States is the life of the author plus 70 years.

Corporate social responsibility An organization's obligation to contribute positively to the world around it.

Counteroffer An offer made in response to a previous offer.

Covenant A promise in a contract; a promise to do or refrain from doing something.

Cover To reasonably obtain substitute goods because another party has not honored a contract.

Credit score Usually called a FICO score, this number is based on your credit report and is supposed to predict your ability to pay your bills.

Creditor beneficiary When the contracting party intended the benefit in fulfillment of some duty or debt, the beneficiary is a creditor beneficiary.

Criminal law Concerns behavior so threatening that society outlaws it altogether.

Criminal procedure The process by which criminals are investigated, accused, tried, and sentenced.

Cross-examine A lawyer asks questions of an opposing witness.

Customary international law International rules that have become binding through a pattern of consistent, longstanding behavior.

D

Debtor A person who has original ownership interest in the collateral; another term for bankrupt.

Default judgment A decision that the plaintiff in a case wins without going to trial.

Defendant The person being sued.

Deferred annuity contract The owner makes a lump sum payment now, but receives no income until a later date.

Delegatee A person who receives an obligation under a contract from someone else.

Delegation A transfer of contract duties to a third party.

Delegation of duties A transfer of obligations in a contract.

Delegator A person who gives his obligation under a contract to someone else.

Delegator A person who gives his obligation under a contract to someone else.

Deontological From the Greek word for *obligation*. The duty to do the right thing, regardless of the result.

Deponent The person being questioned in a deposition.

Difference principle Rawls' suggestion that society should reward behavior that provides the most benefit to the community as a whole.

Different terms Contradict those in the offer.

Direct examination A lawyer asks questions of his or her own witness.

Disability insurance Replaces the insured's income if he becomes unable to work because of illness or injury.

Disabled person Someone with a physical or mental impairment that substantially limits a major life activity, or someone who is regarded as having such an impairment.

Disaffirm To give notice of refusal to be bound by an agreement.

Discharge The bankrupt no longer has an obligation to pay a debt.

Disclaimer A statement that a particular warranty does not apply.

Discovery The pretrial opportunity for both parties to gather information relevant to the case.

Diversity cases A lawsuit in which the plaintiff and defendant are citizens of different states and the amount in dispute exceeds $75,000.

Domestic Asset Protection Trusts (DAPTs) A trust whose purpose is to prevent creditors of the beneficiary from accessing the assets.

Domestic corporation A corporation operating in the state in which it was incorporated.

Donee A person who receives a gift of property.

Donee beneficiary When the contracting party intended the benefit as a gift, the beneficiary is a donee beneficiary.

Donor A person who gives property away.

Double jeopardy A criminal defendant may be prosecuted only once for a particular criminal offense.

Draft The drawer of this instrument orders someone else to pay money.

Drawee The person who pays a draft. In the case of a check, the bank is the drawee.

Drawer The person who issues a draft.

Due diligence An investigation of the registration statement.

Durable power A power of attorney that remains valid even if the principal becomes incapacitated.

Duty of care The requirements that a manager act with care and in the best interests of the corporation.

Duty of loyalty The obligation of a manager to act without a conflict of interest.

E

Economic strike One intended to gain wages or benefits.

EIS Environmental impact statement.

Electronic Communications Privacy Act The ECPA is a federal statute governing the privacy of wire and electronic communications.

Element A fact that a plaintiff must prove to win a lawsuit.

Embezzlement The fraudulent conversion of property already in the defendant's possession.

Emerging growth company (EGC) An issuer with annual gross revenues of less than $1 billion.

Eminent domain The power of the government to take private property for public use.

Engagement letter A written contract by which a client hires an accountant.

Equal Protection Clause Requires that the government must treat people equally.

Ethics How people should behave.

Ethics decision Any choice about how a person should behave that is based on a sense of right and wrong.

Exculpatory clause A contract provision that attempts to release one party from liability in the event the other party is injured.

Executed contract An agreement in which all parties have fulfilled their obligations.

Executory contract A binding agreement in which one or more of the parties has not fulfilled its obligations.

Express authority Either by words or conduct, the principal grants an agent permission to act.

Express contract An agreement with all important terms explicitly stated.

Express warranty A guarantee, created by the words or actions of the seller, that goods will meet certain standards.

Externality When people do not bear the full cost of their decisions.

Extraterritoriality The power of one country's laws to reach activities outside of its borders.

F

Factual cause The defendant's breach led to the ultimate harm.

Fair use doctrine Permits limited use of copyrighted material without permission of the author.

False imprisonment The intentional restraint of another person without reasonable cause or consent.

Federal question case A claim based on the United States Constitution, a federal statute, or a federal treaty.

Federal Sentencing Guidelines The detailed rules that judges must follow when sentencing defendants convicted of federal crimes.

Federalism A double-layered system of government, with the national and state governments each exercising important but limited powers.

Felony A serious crime, for which a defendant can be sentenced to one year or more in prison.

Fiduciary relationship One of trust in which a trustee acts for the benefit of the beneficiary, always putting the interests of the beneficiary before his own.

Fifth Amendment Ensures due process.

Financing statement A document that the secured party files to give the general public notice that it has a secured interest in the collateral.

First Amendment Protects freedom of speech.

Fixtures Goods that have become attached to real estate.

Flow-through tax entity An organization that does not pay income tax on its profits but passes them through to its owners who pay the tax at their individual rates.

***Force majeure* event** A disruptive, unexpected occurrence for which neither party is to blame that prevents one or both parties from complying with a contract.

Foreign corporation A corporation operating in a state in which it was not incorporated.

Foreign enforcement Means that the court system of a country will assist in enforcing or collecting on the verdict awarded by a foreign court.

Foreign Intelligence Surveillance Act FISA is a federal statute governing domestic spying.

Foreign recognition Means that a foreign judgment has legal validity in another country.

Foreign Sovereign Immunities Act A U.S. statute that provides that American courts generally cannot hear suits against foreign governments.

Fourteenth Amendment Guarantees equal protection of the law.

Fourth Amendment Protects against illegal searches; prohibits unreasonable searches and seizures of individuals by the government.

Franchise Disclosure Document A disclosure document that a franchisor must deliver to a potential purchaser.

Fraud Deception for the purpose of obtaining money or property; injuring someone by deliberate deception; intending to induce the other party to contract, knowing the words are false or uncertain that they are true.

Fraudulent transfer Occurs when a debtor gives assets to someone other than a creditor for the purpose of hindering, delaying, or defrauding creditors.

Fresh start After the termination of a bankruptcy case, creditors cannot make a claim against the debtor for money owed before the initial bankruptcy petition was filed.

Full warranty The seller must promise to fix a defective product for a reasonable time without charge.

G

GAAP "Generally accepted accounting principles" are the rules for preparing financial statements.

GAAS "Generally accepted auditing standards" are the rules for conducting audits.

Gap-fillers UCC rules for supplying missing terms.

General Agreement on Trade in Services (GATS) A treaty on transnational services.

General partner One of the owners of a general partnership.

Gift A voluntary transfer of property from one person to another, without consideration.

Gift *causa mortis* A gift made in contemplation of approaching death.

Go effective The SEC authorizes a company to begin the public sale of its stock.

Good faith An honest effort to meet both the spirit and letter of a contract.

Goods Are things that are movable, other than money and investment securities.

Grand jury A group of ordinary citizens that decides whether there is probable cause the defendant committed the crime with which she is charged.

Grantor Someone who creates and funds a trust. Also called a *settler* or *donor*.

Grievance A formal complaint alleging a contract violation.

Guilty A judge or jury's finding that a defendant has committed a crime.

H

Hacking Gaining unauthorized access to a computer system.

Health care proxy Someone who is authorized to make health care decisions for a person who is incompetent.

Holder For order paper, anyone in possession of the instrument if it is payable to or indorsed to her. For bearer paper, anyone in possession.

Holder in due course Someone who has given value for an instrument, in good faith, without notice of outstanding claims or other defenses.

Holding A court's decision.

Holographic will A will that is handwritten and signed by the testator, but not witnessed.

Hostile takeover An attempt of by an outside investor to acquire a company in the face of opposition from the target corporation's board of directors.

I

IFRS "International financial reporting standards" are a set of international accounting principles that U.S. companies may ultimately be required to follow in preparing financial statements.

Ijtihad The process of Islamic legal and religious reasoning.

Implied authority The agent has authority to perform acts that are reasonably necessary to accomplish an authorized transaction, even if the principal does not specify them.

Implied contract A contract where the words and conduct of the parties indicate that they intended an agreement.

Implied warranties Guarantees created by the Uniform Commercial Code and imposed on the seller of goods.

Implied warranty of fitness for a particular purpose If the seller knows that the buyer plans to use the goods for a particular purpose, the seller generally is held to warrant that the goods are in fact fit for that purpose.

Implied warranty of merchantability Goods must be of at least average, passable quality in the trade.

Incidental beneficiary A party who benefits from the contract although the contract was not designed for their benefit.

Incidental damages Are the relatively minor costs that the injured party suffers when responding to the breach.

Incoterms A series of three-letter codes used in international contracts for the sale of goods.

Indictment The government's formal charge that the defendant has committed a crime and must stand trial.

Indorsement The signature of the payee.

Initial public offering A company's first public sale of securities.

Injunction A court order to do something or to refrain from doing something.

Intentional infliction of emotional distress Extreme and outrageous conduct that causes serious emotional harm.

Intentional torts Involve harm caused by deliberate action.

Inter vivos gift A gift made during the donor's life, with no fear of impending death.

Interest A legal right in something.

International Court of Justice The judicial branch of the United Nations.

Internet service providers (ISPs) Companies like Verizon and Comcast that connect users to the Internet.

Intrusion A civil cause of action that applies when a person intrudes on another's affairs or space in an offensive way.

Invitee A person who has a right to be on property because it is a public place or a business open to the public.

Involuntary bailment A bailment that occurs without an agreement between the bailor and bailee.

Issue A person's direct descendants, such as children and grandchildren.

Issuer The maker of a promissory note or the drawer of a draft; a company that sells its own stock.

J

Joint and several All members of a group are liable. They can be sued as a group, or any of them can be sued individually for the full amount of the damages. But the plaintiff may not recover more than 100 percent of her damages.

Joint tenancy Two or more people holding equal interest in a property, with the right of survivorship.

Jointly and severally liable All members of a group are liable. They can be sued as a group, or any one of them can be sued individually for the full amount owed. But the plaintiff cannot recover more than the total she is owed.

Judicial review Refers to the power of federal courts to declare a statute or governmental action unconstitutional and void.

Jurisdiction A court's power to hear a case and bind the parties to its determination.

K

Key person life insurance Companies buy insurance on their officers as compensation were they to die.

L

Labor-Management Reporting and Disclosure Act (LMRDA) Requires union leadership to make financial disclosures and guarantees union members free speech and fair elections.

Leasehold A right to possess real property temporarily.

Liability insurance Reimburses the insured for any liability she incurs by accidentally harming someone else.

Libel Written defamation.

Licensee A person on property for her own purposes, but with the owner's permission.

Life Principles The rules by which you live your life.

Life prospects The opportunities one has at birth, based on one's natural attributes and initial place in society.

Litigation The process of resolving disputes in court.

Living trust or **Inter vivos trust** A trust established while the grantor is still alive.

Living wills or **Advance directive** In the event that a person is unable to make medical decisions, this document indicates her preferences and may also appoint someone else to makes these decisions for her.

Lockout Management prohibits workers from entering the premises.

Long-arm statute Statutes that may broaden a state court's jurisdiction.

Lost property Property accidentally given up.

M

Maker The issuer of a promissory note.

Marital trust A legal entity created for the purpose of reducing a married couple's estate taxes.

Material Important enough to affect an investor's decision.

Material Important to the insurer's decision to issue a policy or set a premium amount.

Material breach A violation of a contract that defeats an essential purpose of the agreement.

Mediation A form of ADR in which a neutral third party guides the disputing parties toward a voluntary settlement.

Merchant Someone who routinely deals in the particular goods involved.

Minute book A book that contains a record of a corporation's official meetings.

Mirror image rule A contract doctrine that requires acceptance to be on exactly the same terms as the offer.

Misdemeanor A less serious crime, often punishable by less than a year in a county jail.

Mislaid property Property the owner has intentionally placed somewhere and then forgotten.

Misrepresentation A statement that is factually wrong.

Mitigate To keep damages as low as possible.

Modify To let a court decision stand, but with changes.

Money laundering Using the proceeds of criminal acts either to promote crime or conceal the source of the money.

Moral relativism A belief that a decision may be right even if it is not in keeping with our own ethical standards.

Moral universalism A belief that some acts are always right or always wrong.

Most favored nation WTO/GATT requires that favors offered to one country must be given to all member nations.

Motion A formal request to the court.

Mutual mistake Occurs when both parties negotiate based on the same fundamental factual error.

N

National Labor Relations Act (NLRA) Ensures the right of workers to form unions and encourages management and unions to bargain collectively.

National Labor Relations Board (NLRB) Administers and interprets the NLRA and adjudicates labor cases.

National treatment The principle of nondiscrimination between foreigners and locals.

Negotiation An instrument has been transferred to the holder by someone other than the issuer.

Net neutrality The principle that all information flows on the Internet must receive equal treatment.

New York Convention Widely accepted treaty on the court enforcement of arbitral awards.

Nonphysical tort A civil wrong that harms only reputation, feelings, or wallet.

Nonpoint sources Pollutants that have no single producer but result from events such as storm water runoff or rain.

Norris-LaGuardia Act Prohibits federal court injunctions in peaceful labor disputes.

North American Free Trade Agreement (NAFTA) A treaty that reduced trade barriers among Canada, the United States, and Mexico.

Novation A new contract.

Nuncupative will An oral will.

O

Obligee The person who has an obligation coming to her.

Obligor The person obligated to do something under a contract.

Offer In contract law, an act or statement that proposes definite terms and permits the other party to create a contract by accepting those terms.

Offeree The party in contract negotiations who receives the first offer.

Offeror The party in contract negotiations who makes the first offer.

Order for relief An official acknowledgment that a debtor is under the jurisdiction of the bankruptcy court.

Order paper An instrument that includes the words "pay to the order of" or their equivalent.

P

Partition by kind A court's equal division of a property among co-tenants.

Partnership An unincorporated association of two or more co-owners who operate a business for profit.

Partnership at will A partnership with no fixed duration. Any of the partners may leave at any time, for any reason.

Patent A grant by the government permitting the inventor exclusive use of an invention for a specified period.

Payday loans Small loans with high interest rates made to people who need money to make it to the next paycheck.

Payee Someone who is owed money under the terms of an instrument.

Per capita Each heir receives the same amount.

Per se An automatic breach of antitrust laws.

Per stirpes Each branch of the family receives an equal share.

Perfection A series of steps the secured party must take to protect its rights in the collateral against people other than the debtor.

Perpetual or **Dynasty trusts** A trust that lasts forever.

Personal property All tangible property other than real property.

Personal services Any service that must be performed by the promisor.

Physician-assisted death or assisted suicide The process of hastening death for a terminally ill patient at the request of the patient.

Pierce the corporate veil A court holds shareholders personally liable for the debts of the corporation.

Piercing the company veil A court holds members of an LLC personally liable for the debts of the organization.

Plaintiff The person who is suing.

Plea bargain An agreement in which the defendant pleads guilty to a reduced charge, and the prosecution recommends to the judge a relatively lenient sentence.

Pleadings The documents that begin a lawsuit, consisting of a complaint, the answer, and sometimes a reply.

Plurality voting To be elected, a candidate only needs to receive more votes than her opponent, not a majority of the votes cast.

Point sources Discharges from a single producer.

Power of attorney A document that allows one person to act for another.

Preauthorized transfer Electronic fund transfer authorized in advance to recur at regular intervals

Precedent Earlier decisions by a court on similar or identical issues, on which subsequent court decisions can be based.

Preference When a debtor unfairly pays creditors immediately before filing a bankruptcy petition.

Preferred stock The owners of preferred stock have preference on dividends and also, typically, in liquidation.

Preponderance of the evidence The standard of proof required for a civil case.

Pretermitted child A child who is left nothing in the parent's will.

Prima facie From the Latin, meaning "from its first appearance." Something that appears to be true upon a first look.

Principal In an agency relationship, the person for whom an agent is acting.

Private international law International rules and standards applying to cross-border commerce.

Private offering A sale of securities that involves a small number of investors or takes in a relatively modest amount of money.

Probable cause It is likely that evidence of crime will be found in the place to be searched.

Procedural due process Ensures that before the government takes liberty or property, the affected person has a fair chance to oppose the action.

Promisee The person to whom a promise is made.

Promisor The person who makes the promise.

Promissory estoppel A doctrine in which a court may enforce a promise made by the defendant even when there is no contract.

Promissory note The maker of the instrument promises to pay a specific amount of money.

Promoter Someone who organizes a corporation.

Proof of claim A form stating the name of an unsecured creditor and the amount of the claim against the debtor.

Property or **Casualty insurance** Covers physical damage to real estate, personal property, or inventory from causes such as fire, smoke, lightning, wind, riot, vandalism, or theft.

Protected categories Race, color, religion, sex, or national origin.

Proximate cause Refers to a party who contributes to a loss in a way that a reasonable person could anticipate.

Proxy The person whom a shareholder appoints to vote for her at a meeting of the corporation. Also, the document a shareholder signs appointing this substitute voter.

Public Company Accounting Oversight Board (PCAOB) The PCAOB regulates public accounting firms.

Public disclosure of private facts A civil cause of action that may apply when an individual discloses another's private information without consent.

Public international law Rules and norms governing relationships among states and international organizations.

Punitive damages Punishment of the defendant for conduct that is extreme and outrageous.

Purchase money security interest (PMSI) An interest taken by the person who sells the collateral or advances money so the debtor can buy it.

Q

Qualified mortgages A mortgage that complies with rules established by the CFPB that make repayment more likely.

Qualified privilege Employers are liable only for false statements that they know to be false or that are primarily motivated by ill will.

Quantum meruit "As much as he deserved." The damages awarded in a quasi-contract case.

Quasi-contract A legal fiction in which, to avoid injustice, the court awards damages as if a contract had existed, although one did not.

Quid pro quo A Latin phrase that means "one thing in return for another."

Quorum The percentage of stock that must be represented for a meeting to count.

R

Racketeer Influenced and Corrupt Organizations Act (RICO) A powerful federal statute, originally aimed at organized crime, now used in many criminal prosecutions and civil lawsuits.

Racketeering acts Any of a long list of specified crimes, such as embezzlement, arson, mail fraud, and wire fraud.

Reaffirm To promise to pay a debt even after it is discharged.

Reasonably Ordinary or usual under the circumstances.

Reciprocal promises Promises that are each enforceable independently.

Record Information written on paper or stored in an electronic or other medium.

Regional trade agreements (RTAs) Treaties that reduce trade restrictions and promote common policies among member nations.

Registration statement The document that an issuer files with the SEC to initiate a public offering of securities.

Regulation D The most common and important type of private offering.

Remand To send a case back down to a lower court.

Representations and warranties Statements of fact about the past or present.

Res ipsa loquitur Means "the thing speaks for itself" and refers to cases where the facts *imply* that the defendant's negligence caused the harm.

Resale price maintenance (RPM) A manufacturer sets minimum prices that retailers may charge.

Rescind To cancel a contract; to terminate a contract by mutual agreement.

Rescission The undoing of a contract, which puts both parties in the positions they were in when they made the agreement.

Restitution When a guilty defendant must reimburse the victim for the harm suffered.

Restitution Restoring an injured party to its original position.

Reverse To rule that the loser in a previous case wins, with no new trial; to declare the lower court's ruling wrong and void.

Reverse and remand To nullify a lower court's decision and return a case to trial.

Revocable A trust that the grantor can terminate or change at any time.

Revoked Cancellation of the offer.

Road show As part of the IPO sales process, company executives and investment bankers make presentations to potential investors.

Rule Against Perpetuities Provides that a trust cannot last forever.

Rule of reason An action that breaches antitrust laws only if it has an anticompetitive impact.

S

Scienter Acting with the intent to deceive or with deliberate recklessness as to the possibility of misleading investors.

Scrivener's error A typo.

Secondary offering Any public sale of securities by a company after the initial public offering.

Secured party A person or company that holds a security interest.

Security Any transaction in which the buyer invests money in a common enterprise and expects to earn a profit predominantly from the efforts of others.

Security agreement A contract in which the debtor gives a security interest to the secured party.

Security interest An interest in personal property or fixtures that secures the performance of an obligation.

Sexual harassment Involves unwelcome sexual advances, requests for sexual favors, and other verbal or physical conduct of a sexual nature.

Shari'a law Islamic law.

Single recovery principle Requires a court to settle a legal case once and for all, by awarding a lump sum for past and future expenses.

Sit-down strike Members stop working but remain at their job posts, blocking replacement. workers.

Sixth Amendment Demands fair treatment for defendants in criminal prosecutions.

Slander Oral defamation.

Sole discretion The *absolute* right to make any decision on an issue.

Sole proprietorship An unincorporated business owned by one person.

Spam Unsolicited commercial email.

Special committee Independent board members form a committee to review a self-dealing transaction and determine if it is entirely fair to the corporation.

Specific performance Compels parties to perform the contract they agreed to when the contract concerns the sale of land or some other unique asset.

Stare decisis The principle that precedent is binding on later cases; the principle that legal conclusions must be reached after an analysis of past judgments; means "let the decision stand" and describes a court's tendency to follow earlier cases.

Stationary source Any building or facility that emits pollution.

Statute of Frauds Requires certain contracts to be in writing.

Statute of limitations Limits the time within which an injured party may file suit.

Statute A law passed by Congress or by a state legislature.

Straight bankruptcy Also known as liquidation, this form of bankruptcy mandates that the bankrupt's assets be sold to pay creditors, but the bankrupt has no obligation to share future earnings.

Strict liability A high level of liability assumed by people or corporations who engage in activities that are very dangerous.

Subpoena An order to appear at a particular time and place.

Subpoena *duces tecum* An order to require a person to produce certain documents or things.

Summary judgment A ruling that no trial is necessary because essential facts are not in dispute. More than 90 percent of all lawsuits are settled before trial.

Summons The court's written notice that a lawsuit has been filed.

Superfund Another name for the Comprehensive Environmental Response, Compensation, and Liability Act (CERCLA).

T

Takings Clause Prohibits a state from taking private property for public use without just compensation.

Tenancy in common Two or more people holding equal interest in a property, but with no right of survivorship.

Term partnership A partnership in which the partners agree in advance how long it will last.

Testamentary trust A trust that goes into effect when a grantor dies.

Third party beneficiary Someone who is not a party to a contract but stands to benefit from it.

Tied product In a tying arrangement, the product that a buyer must purchase as the condition for being allowed to buy another product.

TMDLs Total maximum daily loads of permitted pollution.

Tort A violation of a duty imposed by the civil law.

Tortious interference with a contract Occurs when a defendant deliberately harms a contractual relationship between two other parties.

Tracing An auditor takes an item of original data and tracks it forward to ensure that it has been properly recorded throughout the bookkeeping process.

Tracking tools A computer program that tracks information about Internet users.

Trade secret A formula, device, process, method, or compilation of information that, when used in business, gives the owner an advantage over competitors.

Trademark Any combination of words and symbols that a business uses to identify its products or services and distinguish them from others.

Treasury stock Stock that a company has sold, but later bought back.

Treaty An agreement between two or more states governed by international law.

Treble damages A judgment for three times the harm actually suffered.

Trespasser A person on someone else's property without consent.

Trial courts First level of courts to hear disputes.

Trust An entity that separates the legal and beneficial ownership of assets.

Trustee Someone who manages the assets of a trust.

Tying arrangement An agreement to sell a product on the condition that a buyer also purchase another, usually less desirable, product.

Tying product In a tying arrangement, the product offered for sale on the condition that another product be purchased as well.

U

U.S. Trustee Oversees the administration of bankruptcy law in a region.

Ultrahazardous activity A defendant engaging in such acts is virtually always liable for resulting harm.

Unenforceable agreement A contract where the parties intend to form a valid bargain but a court declares that some rule of law prevents enforcing it.

Unilateral contract A contract where one party makes a promise that the other party can accept only by doing something.

Unilateral mistake Occurs when only one party negotiates based on a factual error.

United States Constitution The supreme law of the United States.

User-generated content Any content created and made publicly available by end users.

Usury statutes Laws that limit the maximum interest rate a lender may charge.

V

Vagueness When a provision in a contract is deliberately left unclear.

Valid contract A contract that satisfies all the law's requirements.

Value The holder has *already* done something in exchange for the instrument.

Veil of ignorance The rules for society that we would propose if we did not know how lucky we would be in life's lottery.

Void agreement An agreement that neither party may legally enforce.

Voidable contract An agreement that, because of some defect, may be terminated by one party, such as a minor, but not by both parties.

Vouching Auditors choose a transaction listed in a company's books and check backwards for original data to support it.

W

Warrant Written permission from a neutral officer to conduct a search.

Warranty A contractual assurance that goods will meet certain standards.

Whistleblower Someone who discloses wrongdoing.

Will A legal document that disposes of the testator's property after death.

World Trade Organization (WTO) An international organization whose mandate is to lower trade barriers.

Written consent A signed document that takes the place of a shareholders' or directors' meeting.

Wrongful discharge An employer may not fire a worker for a reason that violates basic social rights, duties, or responsibilities.

Z

Zoning statutes State laws that permit local communities to regulate land use.

TABLE OF CASES

A

ABKCO Music, Inc. v. Harrisongs Music, Ltd., 317 n. 7

Albinger v. Harris, 570

Andreason v. Aetna Casualty & Surety Co., 180 n. 1

Antuna v. Nescor, Inc., 285

Armorie v. Delamirie, 572

Association for Molecular Pathology v. Myriad Genetics, Inc., 531

B

Baer v. Chase, 184

Banta Props. v. Arch Specialty Ins. Co., 605

Based on Daniell v. Ford Motor Co., 135 n. 1

Based on Georgia O'Keefe Foundation v. Fisk University, 582 n. 2

Based on Hebert v. Enos, 140 n. 3

Bi-Economy Market, Inc. v. Harleysville Ins. Co. of New York, 229

Blasco v. Money Services Center, 280

BLD Products, LTC. v. Technical Plastics of Oregon, LLC, 396

Boeken v. Philip Morris, Incorporated, 127

Bradley v. Franklin Collection Serv., 481

Brentwood Medical Associates v. United Mine Workers of America, 377

Brumberg v. Cipriani USA, Inc., 141

Brunswick Hills Racquet Club Inc. v. Route 18 Shopping Center Associates, 224

C

Carafano v. Metrosplash.Com, Inc., 157

Carey v. Davis, 68 n. 3

Carnero v. Boston Scientific Corporation, 49

CCB Ohio, LLC v. Chemque, Inc., 268

Central Arizona Water Conservation District v. EPA, 493

Chapa v. Traciers & Associates, Inc., 305

Chelsea Chaney v. Fayette County Public School District, 161

Chopra v. Helio Solutions, Inc., 418

Coalition for a Level Playing Field, L.L.C. v. AutoZone, Inc., 464

Colby v. Burnham,

Commonwealth v. James, 315 n. 3

Conseco Finance Servicing Corp. v. Lee, 302

Creative Ventures, LLC v. Jim Ward & Associates, 284

D

Dacor Corp. v. Sierra Precision, 266 n. 12

Daniell v. Ford, 146

David L. de Csepel v. Republic of Hungary, 573

Demasse v. ITT Corporation, 179

Dick Broadcasting Co. v. Oak Ridge FM, Inc., 248

Doe v. Liberatore, 325 n. 9

Donahue v. Rodd Electrotype Co., 393 n. 4

Donald L. Harmon v. Delaware Harness Racing Commission, 180

E

Eastex, Inc. v. NLRB, 374 n. 1

Edwards v. Arthur Andersen LLP, 198 n. 2

Ehling v. Monmouth-Ocean Hosp. Serv. Corp., 163

Ellis v. Grant Thornton, 516

Ernst & Ernst v. Hochfelder, 518

Estate of Josiah James Treloar, Jr., In re, 589

Estate of Ulrich, In re, 586

F

Forestal Guarani S.A. v. Daros International, Inc., 47

Foster v. Ohio State University, 186 n. 2

G

Gallina v. Mintz, 356 n. 3

Gibbs v. Babbitt, 502

Goodman v. Wenco Foods, Inc., 267

Goodson v. American Standard Insurance Company Of Wisconsin, 608

Gould v. Winstar Communs., Inc., 518

Gulino v. Bd. of Educ. of the City Sch. Dist. of N.Y., 353

Guth v. Loft, 417 n. 5

H

Harris v. Soley, 555

Hawkins v. McGee, 227

Hayes v. Haushalter, 517 n. 8

Heritage Technologies, L.L.C. v. Phibro-Tech, Inc., 245

Hernandez v. Arizona Board of Regents, 137

Hispanics United of Buffalo, Inc. and Carlos Ortiz before the NLRB, 340

Hobbs v. Duff, 197 n. 1

HP Secs. Litig, *In re*, 456

Huatuco V. Satellite Healthcare, 394

I

International Shoe Co. v. State of Washington, 82

J

Jackson v. Holiday Furniture, 435

Jane Doe and Nancy Roe v. Lynn Mills, 125

Jannusch v. Naffziger, 261

Jones v. Clinton, 88

Juzwiak v. John/Jane Doe, 156

K

Kelly v. Mich. Fin. Auth. (In re Kelly), 439

Kelo v. City of New London, Connecticut, 551

Kennedy v. Louisiana, 61

Kim v. Son, 196

King v. Head Start Family Hair Salons, Inc., 199

Kiobel v. Royal Dutch Petroleum Co., 38 n. 1

Kruser v. Bank of America, 478

Kuehn v. Pub zone, 8

L

Lapine v. Seinfeld, 534

Leegin Creative Leather Products, Inc. v. PSKS, Inc., 461

Legends are Forever, Inc. v. Nike, Inc., 87

Lindsay P. v. Towne Properties Asset Management Co., Ltd, 559

M

Marks v. Loral Corp., 358 n. 4

Matter of Jeffrey M. Horning v. Horning Constr. LLC, 389 n. 1

Metro-Goldwyn-Mayer Studios Inc. v. Grokster, Ltd., 536 n. 8

Miranda v. Arizona, 105

Mr. W Fireworks, Inc. v. Ozuna, 177

N

Nadel v. Tom Cat Bakery, 185

National Federation of Independent Business v. Sebelius, 59

National Franchisee Association v. Burger King Corporation, 401

Network Automation, Inc. v. Advanced Systems Concepts, Inc., 539

New Jersey Department of Environmental Protection v. Alden Leeds, Inc., 144

New York Central & Hudson River R.R. Co., v. United States, 109 n. 6

New York Times Co. v. Sullivan, 123

NLRB v. Truitt Manufacturing Co., 376

O

Oregon Steel Mills, Inc. v. Coopers & Lybrand, LLP, 514

P

Palsgraf v. Long Island Railroad, 136

Perfumebay.com, Inc. v. eBay, Inc., 536 n. 11

Pollack v. Skinsmart Dermatology and Aesthetic Center P.C., 540

Potter v. Shaw, 324 n. 8

Pure Power Boot Camp, Inc. v. Warrior Fitness Boot Camp, LLC, 316

Q

Quake Construction, Inc. v. American Airlines, Inc., 242

R

R. J. Reynolds Tobacco Co. v. Food and Drug Administration, 70

Rathke v. Corrections Corporation of America, Inc., 219

Raul v. Rynd, 424

Ray v. Beacon Hudson Mountain Corp., 550

Reid v. Google, Inc., 358

Rice v. Oriental Fireworks Co., 412 n. 2

Ridgaway v. Silk, 394

Roe v. TeleTech Customer Care Mgmt. (Colo.) LLC, 336

Roe v. Wade, 4

Roser, *In re*, 304

S

Sakraida v. Ag Pro, Inc., 531 n. 2

Saudi Basic Industries Corporation v. Mobil Yanbu Petrochemical Company, Inc. and Exxon Chemical Arabia, Inc., 42

See Justice Brennan's dissent in United States v. Leon, 104 n. 4

Sherwood v. Walker, 205

Soldano v. O'daniels, 11

Sony PS3 "Other OS" Litigation, *In re*, 265

S. Peru Copper Corp. Shareholder Derivative Litig, *In re*, 416

Spurlino Materials, LLC, 379

Stanford v. Kuwait Airways Corp., 316 n. 4

T

Texas v. Johnson, 63

The People v. Han, 102 n. 2

Treadway v. Gateway Chevrolet Oldsmobile Inc., 481

U

United States – Measures Affecting the Cross-Border Supply of Gambling and Betting Services, 45

United States v. Alfonso Lopez, Jr., 4 n. 2

United States v. Apple Inc., 460 n. 4

United States v. Leon, 104 n. 4

United States v. Loew's Inc., 463 n. 7

United States v. Nosal, 109

United States v. Syufy Enterprises, 462 n. 5

V

Va. DOT v. United States EPA, 497

Vanlandingham v. Ivanow, 555 n. 2

Verizon Communs., Inc. v. Trinko, LLP, 460 n. 3

Viacom Int'l, Inc. v. YouTube, Inc., 537 n. 9

W

Wagenheim v. Alexander Grant & Co., 515 n. 7

Wightman v. Consolidated Rail Corporation, 143 n. 4

Willoughby v. Conn. Container Corp., 360

Z

Zankel v. United States of America, 325

A

abandonment, 324–325
abusive acts, 472
acceptance, 186–188
    of gifts, 570–571
    of insurance contract, 604
access, 164, 421, 480
accidents, 495
accountant-client liability, 513–515,
    520–521
accountant-client privilege, 520–521
accountant-client relationship, 520
accountants' liability, 509–521
    audits and, 511–513
    to clients, 513–515, 520–521
    consolidation and, 511
    criminal, 519–520
    introduction to, 510–513
    Sarbanes-Oxley Act of 2002, 510–511
    to third parties, 515–519
accounting records, 418
accredited investors, 455
accuracy of credit reports, 479–480
achieving purpose, 319
acts, 101, 110, 472
actual eviction, 554
adaptation to real property, 548
additional terms, 263
address for charter, 409
adequate capital, 396, 412
adjudication, 60, 71
administrative law, 6, 69–71
administrative law judge (ALJ), 71
administrator, 585
administratrix, 585
adopted treaties, 43
adoption, 408
advance directives, 592
adversary system, 90
adverse opinion, 513
adverse possession, 549–550
Aetna, 180
affirmation, 9, 93
affirmative action, 357
Affordable Care Act, 343, 611
after-acquired property, 297

age, 481, 586
Age Discrimination in Employment Act
    (ADEA), 358–359
agency, 314–326
    breaches of duty by, 318–319
    consent of, 315
    consumer reporting, 479
    control in, 315–316
    creating relationships in, 315–316
    laws of, 3
    liability of, 321, 326
    principals, duties of/to, 316–319
    terminating relationships in, 319–320
    third party liabilities, 320–326
    at will, 319
agents
    defined, 315
    employees as, 322–323
    independent contractor as, 322–323
    registered, 409
Aggravated Identity Theft statute, 107
Agreement on Trade Related Aspects of
    Intellectual Property (TRIPs),
    45–46
agreements, 183–188. See also Contracts;
    Promise
    acceptance of, 186–188
    attachment of security interest and,
      295–296
    bailment by, 573
    collective bargaining, 375
    for interest in land, 207–208
    meeting of the minds on, 183
    mutual, 319
    non-compete, 197–199
    offer, 183–186
    rescinding, 202
    security, 293
    term, 319
    that cannot be performed within one
      year, 208
    unenforceable, 177, 207
    valid, 177
    void, 177
    voidable, 177
    written, 240
air pollution, 492–495

Akers, John, 19
alcohol, 340
altered instrument, 282
alternative design, 147
alternative dispute resolution (ADR),
    79–80
Amazon, 460
ambiguities, 244, 279–280
American Bar Association, 408
American Chemistry Council, 28
American Law Institute, 259
Americans with Disabilities Act (ADA),
    359–361
anatomical gifts, 592
animals, 492, 495
annual percentage rate (APR), 475
annual reports, 456
annuities, 610
answer, 85
antitrust, 460–465
    Clayton Act, 463–464
    Robinson-Patman Act, 464
    Sherman Act, 460–462
apparent authority, 320–321
appeal court options, 93
appeals, 92–93, 104
appellant, 83
appellate courts, 83–84
appellee, 83
Apple, 30, 460, 538
application for patents, 532–533
appointment, 60
appropriate bargaining unit, 374
appropriate behavior, 318
approved intermediary, 455
arbitral award, 51
arbitration, 51, 79–80, 251, 376–377
Ariely, Dan, 23
Armed Services, 66
arraignment, 104
arrest, 104–106
arson, 108
Article 9 of Uniform Commercial Code,
    293, 294–295
assault, 124
assets, 396, 412
assignee, 220

assignment, 220–221, 251, 558
assignor, 220
assisted suicide, 592
assumption of risk, 142
attachment, 295–297, 547
attorney fees, 251
attorney-in-fact, 591
auctions, 107
audits, 510, 511–513
authentication, 293, 357
authority, 320–321
authorization, 324
authorization cards, 373
automated teller machine (ATM) cards, 477
automatic stay, 435
automobile, 103
automobile insurance, 612
award, 51
awareness, 164

B

bad-faith behavior, 440
bad-faith by insurer, 607–608
bailee, 573, 575–576
bailment, 573–577
    by agreement, 573
    common carriers, 576–577
    constructive, 573
    contract carriers, 576–577
    control, 573
    defined, 573
    innkeepers, 577
    involuntary, 573
bailor, 573, 576
bait-and-switch advertisements, 472–473
Bank of America, 460
bankrupt, defined, 433
bankruptcy, 431–444
    Chapter 11, 441–443
    Chapter 7, 433–441
    Chapter 13, 443–444
    overview of, 432–433
    repeated filings for, 440
    small-business, 443
bankruptcy estate, 436–437
bargained for, 196
bargaining
    collective, 375–377
    for consideration, 196

to impasse, 376
legitimate, 197
plea, 104
battery, 124
bearer paper, 279
Beatles, 317
behavior
    appropriate, 318
    bad-faith, 440
    ethical, 19
    unethical, 30–31
behavioral marketing, 160
behavioral targeting, 160
being objective, 23
benchmarking, 423
bench trial, 100
beneficiary, 218–219, 593, 603–604
best available control technology
        (BACT), 493
beyond a reasonable doubt, 91, 100
Big Egos and Talents, Inc. (BEAT), 317
bilateral contract, 176
bilateral treaty, 43
bill, 5, 66
binder, 604
blind spots, 25
Bloomingdale's, 31
blue sky laws, 459
boilerplates, 250–251
Boisjoly, Roger, 24
bona fide occupational qualification
        (BFOQ), 357
Bonds, Barry, 25
borrowing, ethics of, 26
Boston Marathon, 26
boycotts, secondary, 379
breach, 137
    in contract, 248–249
    of duty, 139, 318–319
    good faith, 248
    material, 248
    of the peace, 305
    performance and, 225
    of trust, 514–515
Bring Your Gun to Work Laws, 341
British Petroleum (BP), 112
building, 547
building codes, 555–556
bumper-to-bumper warranty, 265
burden of proof, 90–91, 100, 576
Bureau of Land Management, 69

business
    buyers in ordinary course of, 302
    crime committed by, 109–112
    crime that harms, 106–109
    liability policies, 612
    organization of, 440
    sale of, 198
    society, role in, 18
    torts in, 128–129
business judgment rule, 413–417
business lifecycle
    bankruptcy, 431–444
    corporations, 407–424
    starting a business, 388–402
business prevention department. *See*
    Lawyer
buyers in ordinary course of business
        (BIOC), 302
buyer's protection, 300–303
buyer's remedies, 47, 264
bylaws for incorporation, 411
bystander cases, 68

C

campaign for unions, 373
capacity, 201–202
capital, 396, 398, 412
Carey, Ed, 68
caring for children, 593
case analysis, 8–10
CashCall, 474–475
categorical imperative, 20
causality insurance, 609
causation, 139–141
Challenger space shuttle, 24
changes in parties, 558
Chapter 11 bankruptcy, 441–443
Chapter 7 bankruptcy, 433–441
    automatic stay, 435
    bankruptcy estate, 436–437
    creditors, 434–435
    discharge, 438–441
    filing petition, 433–434
    payment of claims, 437–438
    trustee, 434
Chapter 13 bankruptcy, 443–444
charter, 394, 409–410
Charter of the United Nations, 39–40
check, 277
checks and balances, 5

chemicals, 500
Chevron, 50
child/children
    caring for, 593
    labor, 45
    pretermited, 588
    share, 588–590
Children's Online Privacy Protection Act
    (COPPA) of 1998, 165
choice, 164
    ethical, 18
    of forum, 51, 250
    of language, 51
Circuit City Stores, 358
Citicorp, 351
civil cases, 100–101
civil law, 6, 42
claims, 437–438
    insurance contract, limitations for,
        604–606
    notices of, 283
    outstanding, 282–283
    owners, 549
    payment of, 437–438
    proof of, 435
    refusing to pay valid, 607–608
class actions, 86
classic insider trading, 458–459
clawbacks, 423
Clayton Act, 463–464
Clean Air Act (CAA), 70, 493
clean opinion, 513
Clean Water Act (CWA), 495–497
clients, 240–241
closed corporations, 392–393
closing, 252
closing arguments, 92
Coca-Cola, 30, 417, 494, 529, 540
codicil, 591
collateral, 293
    debtor rights in, 295–296
    disposition of, 305
    taking possession of, 304–305
    types of, 295
collective bargaining, 375–377
collective bargaining agreement (CBA),
    375
collective bargaining unit, 373
collision, 612
color, 351, 481
comment letter, 454

Commerce Clause, 59, 60
commercial activity, 41
commercial exploitation, 129
commercial goods, 47
commercial paper, 276
    fundamental "rule" of, 277–285
    negotiability of, 277–280
commingling assets, 396, 412
committee for creditors, 441
committee reports on audit, 510
committee work, 66–67
commodities laws, 339
common carriers, 576–577
common law, 5, 41, 67–69, 339
    bystander cases, 68
    on contract law, 182, 337
    defined, 67
    on found property, 571–572
    fraud, 514
    hallmarks of, 41
    for insurance contracts, 604
    protections, 335–338
    stare decisis, 67–68
    on tort law, 337–338
    on wrongful discharge, 334–336
communication, 122, 188
Communications Decency Act (CDA) of
    1996, 157
comparative negligence, 142–143
compensation, 343
compensatory damages, 125–126, 228
competition, 23, 317
competitive market, 423
complaint, 84–85
compliance program, 112
comprehensive coverage, 612
Comprehensive Environmental
    Response, Compensation,
    and Liability Act (CERCLA),
    498–499
Computer Fraud and Abuse Act of 1986
    (CFAA), 108–109
concerted action, 377–380
concurrent estates, 548–549
condemnation, 551
condition, 553
conditional covenants, 249
conditions of employment, 375
conduct, off-duty, 318, 340
confidential information, 198
confirmation of plans, 442

conflict of interest, 23, 317, 511
conforming goods, 264
conformity, 24
congressional power, 59
conscious uncertainty, 205
consent, 164
    of agency, 315
    fraud, 202–204
    mistake, 204–205
    reality of, 202–206
    searches without a warrant, 103
consequential damages, 228–229, 264
consideration, 195–197
Consolidated Omnibus Budget
    Reconciliation Act (COBRA), 343
consolidation, 511
conspiracy, 101–102
constitutional law, 3, 58–65
    Fifth Amendment, 63–65
    Fourteenth Amendment, 65
    government power, 58–59
    powers granted by, 59–61
    protected rights, 62–63
Constitution of United States, 4–5
constructive bailment, 573
constructive delivery, 569
constructive eviction, 554
consulting services, 510–511
consumer credit, 474–482
    ATM cards, 477
    contract for, 284
    credit cards, 476–478
    credit reports, 479–480
    debit cards, 477
    debt collection, 480–481
    electronic fund transfers, 478–479
    Equal Credit Opportunity Act, 481
    home mortgage loans, 475–476
    payday loans, 474–475
    plastic cards, 477–479
    Truth in Lending Act, 475
consumer exception, 284–285
consumer expectation, 147
Consumer Financial Protection Bureau
    (CFPB), 472
consumer goods, 268, 299–300
consumer product safety, 483
Consumer Product Safety Act of 1972
    (CPSA), 483
Consumer Product Safety Commission
    (CPSC), 483

consumer protection, 158–159, 471–484
  consumer credit, 474–482
  consumer product safety, 483
  Federal Trade Commission Act, 158–159
  introduction to, 472
  Magnuson-Moss Warranty Act, 482–483
  sales, 472–474
  spam, 159
consumer reorganizations. *See* Chapter 13bankruptcy
consumer reporting agencies, 479
contaminants. *See* Pollution
contemporary laws, 4–6
contemporary trends, 147
continuous possession for statutory period, 550
contract. *See also* Agreements; Promise
  accountant-client liability, 513
  ambiguity in, 244
  bilateral, 176
  boilerplates in, 250–251
  breach in, 248–249
  carriers, 576–577
  consumer credit, 284
  covenants in, 246–248
  deferred annuity, 610
  defined, 176
  drafting, 241
  elements of, 175–176
  executed, 177
  executory, 177
  express, 178
  fairness of, 47
  flexibility of, 47
  forming, 174–188
  government, 357
  implied, 178
  for insurance, 604–609
  intention of creating, 263
  interference with, 128–129
  introductory paragraph in, 246
  liability for, 320–321
  mistakes in, 241–246
  modification of, 250–251
  negotiable instruments, 275–285
  opting out of, 47
  other important issues in, 176
  performance of, 217–232
  practical, 239–252

prices for, 265
prohibition of, 221, 222
quasi-, 179, 181
representations in, 249–250
requirements for, 194–210
rescinding, 222
sales, 258–269
secured transactions, 292–306
structure of, 246–252
title of, 246
types of, 176–181
typos in, 244–246
unilateral, 176
vagueness in, 241–243
valid, 177
voidable, 177, 201
warranties in, 249–250
in writing, 206–210
contract laws, 3, 182–183, 337
contractor, 322–323
contract requirements, 194–210
  capacity, 201–202
  consideration, 195–197
  legality, 197–200
  reality of consent, 202–206
contributory negligence, 142–143
control, 241, 315–316, 573, 593
Controlling the Assault of Non-Solicited Pornography and Marketing Act (CANSPAM), 159
convention, 43
Convention on Contracts for the International Sale of Goods (CISG), 40, 43, 46–47
Convention on the Recognition and Enforcement of Foreign Arbitral Awards, 40, 51
conveying of deed, 548
Cook, Tim, 495
cooling off period, 378
Copyright Office of the Library of Congress, 533
copyrights, 533–537
  for digital music, 536–537
  fair use doctrine for, 535–536
  first sale doctrine for, 535
  infringement of, 535
  for movies, 536–537
  term for, 534
corporate opportunity, 417

corporate social responsibility (CSR), 31–32
corporations, 407–424. *See also* Incorporation
  advantages of, 390
  business judgment rule, 413–417
  closed, 392–393
  compliance programs for, 112
  death of, 412–413
  disadvantages of, 390–391
  duration of, 390
  fines on, 112
  foreign, 411
  limited liability companies *vs.*, 397
  limited liability of, 390
  logistics in, 390
  management duties, 413
  piercing the corporate veil, 412
  promoter's liability, 408
  punishing, 112
  S, 392
  shareholder rights, 418–424
  special types of, 392–393
  starting, 389–393
  taxes on, 390–391
  termination of, 412–413
  transferability of interests in, 390
costs of unethical behavior, 19
counter-offer, 186
court, 80–84, 93
court decisions, 591
covenant, 246–249, 552, 607
cover, 264
coverage, 496
cramdown, 442
credit cards, 476–478
creditor
  beneficiary of, 218–219
  Chapter 7 bankruptcy, 434–435
  committee for, 441
  priorities of, 303–304
  protection for, 594
credit reports, 479–480
credit scores, 480
crime, 99–112
  civil cases *vs.*, 100–101
  committed by businesses, 109–112
  criminal procedures for, 101–106
  fear of, 100
  injuries, 559
  nature of, 559

prevalence of, 559
that harms businesses and customers, 106–109
criminal cases, 100–101
criminal law, 6
criminal liability, 109, 519–520
criminal procedures, 101–106
after arrest, 104–106
defined, 101
gathering of evidence, 102–104
state of mind, 101–102
critical audit matters (CAMs), 512
cross-examination, 91
crowdfunding, 455
cruel and unusual punishment, 105
cultural moral relativism, 22
currency, choice of, 51
customary international law, 48
customers, 29, 106–109
cyberlaw, 154–166
consumer protection, 158–159
Internet regulation, 155–158
privacy in digital world, 160–166

D

damages, 125–128, 137, 318
compensatory, 125–126, 228
consequential, 228–229, 264
direct, 228
economic, 128
incidental, 228, 230, 264–265
mitigation of, 557
negligence, 141–142
non-economic, 128
punitive, 126–127
reliance, 230
tort reform, 128
treble, 110
data mining, 160
Davis, Frank, 68
death, 412–413, 592
debit cards, 477
debt collection, 480–481
debtor, 293, 433
in possession, 441
rights of, 295–296
decanting, 595
decedent, 585
deception, 107, 472
decisions, 9, 17–19, 93, 591

deed, conveying of, 548
defamation, 122–123, 337–338
defamatory statement, 122
default, 304–305
default judgment, 85
defective products, 144–146
defects, notices of, 282–283
defendant, 9, 91–92
defenses, 142–143
to charges of discrimination, 356–357
against holder in due course, 283–284
deferred annuity contract, 610
definiteness, problems with, 183–184
definite time, 278
defrauding of government, 338
delegatee, 221
delegation, 220–222, 251
delegator, 221
delivery, 264, 568–569
deontological ethics, 20–21
deponent, 86
depositions, 86
descriptive trademarks, 538
design, 145, 147, 529
destruction of subject matter, 186
difference principle, 21
different terms, 263
digital assets, 590–591
Digital Millennium Copyright Act (DMCA), 536–537
digital music, 536–537
direct damages, 228
direct examination, 91
directors, 418
in incorporation, 410–411
independent, 421
zombie, 420
disability insurance, 611
disabled persons, relationships with, 360
disaffirmance, 201
discharge, 176, 222–226, 438
Chapter 11bankruptcy, 442
Chapter 7 bankruptcy, 438–441
Chapter 13bankruptcy, 443–444
debts that cannot be, 438–440
reaffirmation of, 441
disclaimers, 268, 513
disclosures, 162, 423
discovery, 86–88
discrimination, 356–357
dishonesty, 440

dishonored instrument, 282
disinheritance, 588
disparate impact, 352–353
disparate treatment, 351–352
disposal, 498–499
disposition, 305
dispute resolution, 393
disputes, 283, 478
dissociation, 399
dissolution, 399
diversity cases, 83
documents, 86
Dodd, Tyler, 26
Dodd-Frank Act, 339
Domestic Asset Protection Trusts (DAPTs), 594
domestic corporation, 411
domestic regulation of air pollution, 494
donee, 568
donee beneficiary, 219
donor, 568, 585
do-not-call registry, 473
door-to-door sales, 474
double jeopardy, 104
Downey Jr., Robert, 317
draft, 277
drawee, 277
drawer, 277
dredge, 496
drugs, 340
due care, 575
due diligence, 517
Due Process Clause, 64, 81
Duke Power, 352–353
durable power, 591
duties
of bailee, 575–576
of bailor, 576
breaches of, 318–319
of care, 318, 414, 417 595
to collective bargaining, 375–376
customs, 44
delegation of, 221–222, 251
of due care, 137–139
fiduciary, 316, 458, 595
legal, 336
of loyalty, 316–318, 414–417, 595
management, 398–399
to obey instructions, 318
to provide information, 318

duties (*continued*)
  required, 320
  types of, 222
Dylan, Bob, 25
dynasty trusts, 595

E

economic damages, 128
economic strike, 378
economic terms of exchange, 196
e-discovery, 87
efficient court system, 409
Eighth Amendment, 105
election, 373, 420–421
Electronic Communications Privacy Act
    (ECPA) of 1986, 164–166, 590
Electronic Fund Transfer Act (EFTA),
    478–479
electronic fund transfers, 478–479
electronic signatures, 209–210
Electronic Signatures in Global and
    National Commerce Act (E-SIGN),
    210
element, 122
embezzlement, 108
emergencies, 103
emerging growth company (EGC), 454
eminent domain, 551
emotional distress, intentional infliction
    of, 338
employee at-will, 334
employees
  as agents, 322–323
  handbooks, 337
  organizations responsibility, 28–29
employer, 355, 374–375
employment
  abandonment of, 324–325
  authorization of, 324
  conditions of, 375
  contracts for, 198–199
  scope of, 323–325
employment discrimination, 350–364
  Age Discrimination in Employment
      Act, 358–359
  Americans with Disabilities Act, 359–361
  EEOC enforcement, 363
  Equal Pay Act of 1963, 351
  Genetic Information
      Nondiscrimination Act, 361

hiring practices, 361–363
  Pregnancy Discrimination Act, 358
  Title VII of Civil Rights Act of 1964,
      351–357
employment law, 333–344
  defined, 3
  employment security, 334–339
  financial protection, 342–343
  introduction to, 334
  workplace freedom and safety,
      339–342
employment security, 334–339
  common law protections, 335–338
  Family and Medical Leave Act,
      334–335
  whistleblowing, 338–339
Endangered Species Act (ESA), 501–502
end of life health issues, 592–593
enforceable only to quantity stated, 262
enforcement, 50, 363, 376–377
engagement letter, 513
entering into force, 43
entrapment, 101
entry, 549
environmental impact statement (EIS),
    500–501
environmental law, 491–503
  air pollution, 492–495
  chemicals, 500
  disposal, 498–499
  introduction to, 492
  natural resources, 500–503
  waste, 498–499
  water pollution, 495–498
Environmental Protection Agency
    (EPA), 6, 60, 69–70, 83, 493–494,
    496–497, 500
Equal Credit Opportunity Act (ECOA),
    481
Equal Employment Opportunity
    Commission (EEOC), 340, 356, 361,
    363
Equal Pay Act of 1963, 351
Equal Protection Clause, 65
Equifax, 479–480
equitable interest, 226, 231–232
Ernst & Young, 517
essential functions, 359
estate, 548–549, 585
estate planning, 584–596
  defined, 585

introduction to, 585–586
  probate law and, 585–586
  purpose of, 585
  terminology for, 585
  trusts, 593–596
  wills, 586–593
Estee Lauder, 31
ethical behavior, 19
ethical choices, 18
ethical theories, 19–22
ethics, 16–31
  of borrowing, 26
  businesses role in society, 18
  defined, 17
  deontological, 20–21
  introduction to, 17–18
  lying, 25–26
  principles of, 26–30
  theories of, 19–22
  unethical behavior, 30–31
  utilitarian, 20
  in workplace, personal, 26
ethics decisions, 17–19
ethics traps, 22–25
euphemisms, 24
European Union (EU), 44
eviction, 554
evidence
  gathering of, 102–104
  physical, 86
  preponderance of the, 91
  valid, 87
examination, 86–87, 91
exchange, 195–197
exclusionary rule, 103–104
exclusive possession, 549
exclusivity, 372–373
exculpatory clauses, 199–200
executed contract, 177
executive compensation, 421–423
executive power, 60
executor, 585
executor of estate, 209
executory contract, 177
executrix, 585
exempt property, 436
existing trademarks, 538
expectation interest, 226–230
expectation of consumer, 147
Experian, 479
expiration of offer, 186

express authority, 320
express contract, 178
Extell Development Corporation, 244
externally, 492
extraterritoriality, 48–51
Exxon Valdez, 128

F

Facebook, 590
factual cause, 139
factural clause, 137
failure to warn, 145
Fair and Accurate Credit Transactions
    Act (FACTA), 479–480
Fair Credit Billing Act (FCBA), 478
Fair Credit Reporting Act (FCRA), 479
Fair Debt Collection Practices Act
    (FDCPA), 480
Fair Information Practices (FIPS), 164
Fair Labor Standards Act (FLSA),
    342–343
fairness of contract, 47
fair use doctrine, 535–536
False Claims Act, 339
false imprisonment, 123
false statements, 110
falsity, 122
Family and Medical Leave Act (FMLA),
    334–335
family responsibility discrimination,
    355–356
fear of crime, 100
Federal Aviation Administration, 69
Federal Communications Commission
    (FCC), 155
federal courts, 83–84
federalism, 4, 59
federal privacy statutes, 164–166
federal question cases, 83
Federal Sentencing Guidelines, 112
federal statutes, 590
Federal Trade Commission (FTC),
    69–71, 158–159, 165, 284, 400–401,
    460, 463, 472
Federal Trade Commission Act (FTC
    Act), 158–159, 472
Federal Unemployment Tax Act
    (FUTA), 343
fees for attorney, 251
felonies, 101

Ferrari, 529
FICO score, 480
fiduciary duty, 316, 458, 595
fiduciary relationship, 315, 316
Fifth Amendment, 5, 62–65
filing
    for bankruptcy, 440
    perfection, 297–299
    petition, 433–434
    secured transactions, 299
fill material, 496
finance charges, 475
financial protection, 342–343
financing statement, 293, 298–299
fines on corporations, 112
First Amendment, 5, 62–63, 156
first sale doctrine, 535
Fish and Wildlife Service (FWS),
    501–502
fitness of particular purpose, 267–268
fixtures, 293, 547
flexibility, 47, 67, 395, 409
flow-through tax entity, 389
following orders, 24
force majeure event, 252
Ford Motor Company, 129
foreign corporations, 411
Foreign Corrupt Practices Act (FCPA),
    111–112
foreign enforcement, 50
Foreign Intelligence Surveillance Act
    (FISA), 165–166
Foreign Intelligence Surveillance Court
    (FISC), 166
foreign judgments, 50–51
foreign policy, 60
foreign recognition of international law,
    48–51
Foreign Sovereign Immunities Act
    (FSIA), 41
foreseeability, 559
foreseeable consequence, 229
forged instrument, 282
formalities, 395, 412
Form 8-K, 456
forum, choice of, 51, 250
found property, 571–572
Fourteenth Amendment, 62, 65
Fourth Amendment, 5, 62, 102–104, 161
Franchise Disclosure Document (FDD),
    400–401

franchises, 400–401
fraud, 106–107
    bad faith by insurer, 607
    common law, 514
    consent, 202–204
    defined, 107, 124, 202
    innocent misrepresentation, 204
    intentional misrepresentation of facts,
        202–203
    international torts, 124
    Internet, 107
    justifiable reliance, 203
    mail, 107
    materiality, 203
    plaintiff's remedies for, 203
    reckless misrepresentation of facts,
        202–203
    sheltering, 412
    third parties liability, 517
    wire, 107
fraudulent transfers, 436
freedom of speech, 5, 62–63, 156,
    340–341
fresh start, 438
Friedman, Milton, 18
Front Page Test, 21
full performance, 207
full warranty, 483
fundamental corporate changes, 419
fundamental rights, 5
fundamental "rule" of commercial paper,
    277–285
future property, 297

G

Gap, 30
gap-fillers, 263
garbage, 498–499
gathering of evidence, 102–104
gender identity and expression, 356
General Agreement on Tariffs and Trade
    (GATT), 44
General Agreement on Trade in Services
    (GATS), 45–46
General Assembly, 39
generally accepted auditing principles
    (GAAP), 512, 517
generally accepted auditing standards
    (GAAS), 512, 517
general partner, 398

general partnerships, 398–399
generation-skipping trusts, 593
generic trademarks, 538
Genetic Information Nondiscrimination
    Act (GINA), 361
Geneva Conventions, 48
gift *causa mortis*, 569
gifts, 568–571
    acceptance of, 570–571
    anatomical, 592
    defined, 568
    delivery of, 568–569
    elements of, 568
    intention to transfer ownership, 568
    inter vivos, 569
    revocable, 568
global warming, 492, 494
going effective, 454
going public, 395
good faith, 224, 282
good faith breach, 248
goods
    commercial, 47
    conforming, 264
    consumer, 268, 299–300
    defined, 182, 259
    delivery of, 264
    nonconforming, 264
    quantity of, 262
    sale of, 261–262
Goodson, Floyd, 459
Google, 536, 590
government
    branches, 4
    contracts with, 357
    defrauding of, 338
    power of, 58–59
government regulation
    antitrust, 460–465
    consumer protection, 471–484
    securities laws, 453–459
Grand Canyon, 493
grantor, 585, 593
gravity of danger, 147
Great Depression, 343
greenhouse gases (GHGs), 494
grievance, 376
Grokster, 536
gross negligence, 200
guilty, 100
Gun-Free School Zones Act, 4

guns, 341–342
Guth, Charles, 417

H

hacking, 108–109
hazardous waste, 499
health care proxy, 592
health insurance, 343, 611
health maintenance organizations
    (HMOs), 611
heat, 495
heir, 585
Hewlett-Packard (HP), 456
higher liability, 138
highest liability, 138
hiring
    of illegal workers, 111
    lawyer, 241
    negligent, 323
    practices for, 361–363
    process for, 360
    truth in, 337
holder, 282
holder in due course, 277, 281–284
holding, 9
holographic wills, 587
home mortgage loans, 475–476
hostile takeovers, 414
hostile work environment, 353–355
hours, 375
human health, 492, 495

I

IBM, 19
identity theft, 107
Identity Theft and Assumption
    Deterrence Act of 1998, 107
illegal drugs, 340
illegal workers, 111
immigration, 356
Immigration and Customs Enforcement,
    69
immoral trademarks, 538
immunity, 41
impairment, 201–202, 359
implied authority, 320
implied contract, 178
implied warranty, 266–268, 556
impossibility, 226

imprisonment, false, 123
incidental beneficiary, 219
incidental damages, 228, 230, 264–265
income-based repayment plan (IBR),
    438–439
incomplete instrument, 282
incorporation, 409–411. *See also*
    Corporations
incorporator, 409
Incoterms rules, 40
independent contractor, 322–323
independent directors, 421
indictment, 104
individual moral relativism, 22
indorsement, 281
Industrial Revolution, 30
information
    confidential, 198, 317
    duty to provide, 318
    shareholder rights, 418
infringement, 533, 535, 538–539
initial public offering (IPO), 454
injunction, 232
injuries, 558–560
injury, 122
innkeepers, 577
innocent misrepresentation, 204
in practice, 352
insider trading, 457–459
instructions, duty to obey, 318
instrument, 282
insurabel interest, 604–605
insurance, 602–612
    annuities as, 610
    automobile, 612
    causality, 609
    contract for, 604–609
    defined, 603
    disability, 611
    health, 611
    introduction to, 603–604
    liability, 611–612
    life, 592, 605, 609–610
    property, 609
    straight life, 610
    term, 609–610
    types of, 609–612
    universal life, 610
    whole life, 610
insured, 603
insurer, 603, 607–608

integration, 251
integrity, 164
intellectual property, 528–541
  copyrights on, 533–537
  introduction to, 529
  laws, 3
  patents on, 529–533
  trademarks on, 537–540
  trade secrets on, 540–541
intentional infliction of emotional
    distress, 124–125, 338
intentional misrepresentation of facts,
    202–203
intentional physical torts, 325
intention of creating contract, 263
intention to transfer ownership, 568
interest
  conflict of, 317
  defined, 226
  equitable, 226
  expectation, 226
  in land, 207–208
  reliance, 226
  restitution, 226, 231
  substantial, 222
  third-party, 176
interference with contract, 128–129
intermediary, approved, 455
Internal Revenue Code, 519
Internal Revenue Service (IRS), 6, 64,
    390–391, 520
Internal Revenue Service Restructuring
    and Reform Act, 520–521
international air pollution treaties, 494
International Chamber of Commerce
    (ICC), 40–41
international contract clauses, 51
International Court of Justice (ICJ), 40
international financial reporting standards
    (IFRS), 512–513
international law, 38–52, 39–41
  actors in, 39–41
  clauses in international contracts, 51
  customary, 48
  custom principles of, 48
  defined, 39
  extraterriotoriality and, 48–51
  foreign recognition of, 48–51
  general principles of, 48
  International Chamber of Commerce,
    40–41

International Court of Justice, 40
international legal systems, 41–43
public *vs.* private, 39
sources of, 43–48
sovereign nations, 41
treaties as, 43–47
United Nations, 39–40
U.S. law and, application of, 48–50
international legal systems, 41–43
International Monetary Fund (IMF),
    40
international patent treaties, 533
international torts, 122–125
international trademarks treaties, 539
Internet, 107, 155–158
Internet service providers (ISPs), 155,
    537
interpretive rules, 70
interrogatories, 86
interstate, 585
interstate commerce, 59
interviews, 361–362
inter vivos gifts, 569
inter vivos trusts, 594
intestacy, 591
intoxication, 202
introductory paragraph in contract, 246
intrusion, 163
invention, 530
inventor priority, 532
investigation, 71
investors, accredited, 455
invitations to bargain, 183
invitee, 138
involuntary bailment, 573
involuntary petition, 434
Islamic law, 42
issuance of patents, 532–533
issue, 585, 589
issuer, 277

J

Jackson, Michael, 317
Jehovah's Witness, 355
Johnson & Johnson, 112
joint and several liability, 321, 326, 519
joint property, 592
joint tenancy, 548–549
JP Morgan Chase, 460

judgment, 85
  foreign, 50–51
  summary, 88–90
judicial power, 60–61
judicial review, 60
jurisdiction, 80–81
jury rights, 100
Justice Department, 519
justifiable reliance, 203

K

Kant, Immanuel, 20
key person life insurance, 605
Klum, Heidi, 609
Koran, 42
Kuwait Airways (KA), 315–316
Kyoto Protocol to the United Nations
    Framework Convention on Climate
    Change, 494

L

labor law, 370–380. *See also* Unions
  collective bargaining, 375–377
  concerted action, 377–380
Labor-Management Reporting and
    Disclosure Act (LMRDA), 372
land, 207–208, 547, 551–552
landlord, 552
  duties of, 553–555
  liability of, 138, 559
landlord-tenant law, 552–553
  changes in parties, 558
  injuries, 558–560
  landlord's duties, 553–556
  lease, 552–553
  tenancy, 553
  tenant's duties, 556–557
language, 51, 249
Lanham Act, 537
larceny, 106
lawful arrest, 103
Lawrence, Jennifer, 317
laws
  administrative, 69–71
  agency, 3
  choice of, 51, 250
  civil, 6–7, 42
  classifications of, 6–7
  commodities, 339

(continued)

common, 67–69
constitutional, 3, 58–65
contemporary, 4–6
contract, 182–183, 337
criminal, 6–7
cyber, 154–166
employment, 333–344
environmental, 491–503
fascination with, 3
flexibility of, 409
fundamental areas of, 79
ideas about, 3
importance of, 3
intellectual property, 3
international, 38–52
introduction to, 2–11
Islamic, 42
labor, 370–380
landlord-tenant, 552–553
morality and, 7
power of, 3
probate, 585–586
refusing to violate, 335–336
securities, 453–459
shari'a, 42
statutory, 66–67
tort, 337–338
United States and, 48–50
lawyer, 240–241
lease, 552–553, 555
leasehold, 552
legal age, 586
legal capacity, 201
legal duties, 336
legal environment. *See also* Laws
    alternative dispute resolution (ADR), 79–80
    appeals, 92–93
    corporate social responsibility, 31–32
    court systems, 80–84
    crime, 99–112
    ethics, 16–32
    litigation, 84–92
legality, 197–200
legal medication, 340
legal rights, exercising, 336
legal uncertainty, 396
legislation, 60
legislative rules, 70
legitimate bargain, 197

liabilities. *See also* Limited liability
    accountant-client, 513–515, 520–521
    accountants', 509–521
    of agency, 321, 326
    ATM cards, 477
    automotive, 612
    bailor, for defects by, 576
    business policies for, 612
    for contracts, 320–321
    of credit cards, 477
    criminal, 109, 519–520
    of debit cards, 477
    of general partnerships, 398
    higher, 138
    highest, 138
    joint and several, 519
    of landlord, 559
    landowner's, 138
    lowest, 138
    mid-level, 138
    of plastic cards, 477
    product, 145–147
    promoter's, 408
    Securities Act of 1933, 453
    Securities Exchange Act of 1934, 456
    of sole proprietorships, 389
    third party, 320–326
liability insurance, 611–612
libel, 122
libel per se, 122
licensee, 138
lie detector tests, 341
life insurance, 592, 605, 609–610
Life Principles, 17–18, 25
life prospects, 21
likelihood of danger, 147
limited capital, 389
limited liability
    of corporations, 390
    of limited liability companies, 393–394
    partnerships, 400
limited liability companies (LLCs), 393–397
    corporation *vs.*, 397
    duration of, 395
    flexibility of, 395
    formation of, 394
    going public, 395
    legal uncertainty of, 396
    limited liability of, 393–394
    piercing the company veil, 395–396
    transferability of interests in, 395

limited liability partnerships (LLPs), 400
liquidation. *See* Chapter 7 bankruptcy
litigation, 84–90, 357
    alternative dispute resolution *vs.*, 79
    defined, 79
    pleadings, 84–90
litigator, 79
living trusts, 594
living wills, 592
Locke, Richard, 30
lockouts, 380
Loft, Inc., 417
logistics, 390
long-arm statute, 81
losing privacy online, 160–161
lowest liability, 138
loyalty, 31, 316–318, 414–417, 595
lying, 25–26

M

Madrid Agreement, 539
Magnuson-Moss Warranty Act, 482–483
mailbox rule, 188
mail fraud, 107
maker, 276
managed care plans, 611
management duties, 398–399, 413
management of general partnerships, 398–399
managing partners, 398
marital status, 481
marital trusts, 593
market/marketing, 160, 423
marriage, 209
MasterCard, 460
material, 496, 606
material breach, 248
materiality, 203
material misstatement, 453
McGrath, Victoria, 26
mediation, 79
MediSearch, Inc., 458
meeting of the minds, 183
members of the executive committee, 398
mental disabilities, 361
mental examination, 86–87
mental impairment, 201–202, 359
merchandise, 473–474
merchantability, 266–267

merchant disputes, 478
merchant exception, 262
merchants, 260
mergers, 463
merit of discrimination, 356–357
Merkel, Angela, 165
Microsoft, 538
Midler, Bette, 129
mid-level liability, 138
Mill, John Stuart, 20
minority shareholders, 392–393
minors, 201
minute book, 418
mirror image rule, 186–187
misappropriation, 458
misdemeanors, 101
misrepresentation, 202–204, 606
misstatement, 453
mistake, 204–205
mitigation, 232, 557
Model Business Corporation Act (the
    Model Act), 408, 418
modifying decisions, 93
money, 22, 111
monopolization, 462
Monsanto, 529
morality, 7
moral relativism, 21–22
moral universalism, 21–22
mortgage loans, 475–476
Morton-Thiokol, Inc., 24
"most favored nation," 44
motions, 87
motor vehicles, 493
movies, 536–537
Muhammed, 42
multilateral treaty, 43
music, 536–537
mutual agreement, 319
mutual benefit, 575
mutual mistake, 204–205

N

names, 409, 538
NASA, 24
NASDAQ, 420
national air-quality standards, 493
National Conference of Commissioners
    on Uniform State Laws, 259

National Environmental Policy Act
    (NEPA), 500–501
National Labor Relations Act (NLRA),
    340, 371–374, 377
National Labor Relations Board (NLRB),
    372–374
national origin, 351, 354–356, 481
National Security Agency (NSA), 165
national treatment, 44
national water quality standards, 496
natural resources, 500–503
navigable waters, 496
NBC, 538
negligence, 136–142, 513
    breach of duty, 139
    causation, 139–141
    comparative, 142–143
    contributory, 142–143
    damages, 141–142
    duty of due care, 137–139
    gross, 200
    product liability, 145
    third parties liability, 516
negligent design, 145
negligent hiring, 323
negligent manufacture, 145
negotiable commercial paper, 278
negotiable instruments, 275–285. *See also*
    Commercial paper
    consumer exception and, 284–285
    holder in due course for, 281–284
    negotiation with, 281
    types of, 276–277
    value of, 282
negotiable paper, 277
negotiation, 277–281
net neutrality, 155
neutral arena, 409
New York Convention, 40, 51
New York Stock Exchange (NYSE), 420
NFL, 142
Nike, 30, 529, 538
no expectation of privacy, 103
no-lockout clauses, 375
non-compete agreements, 197–199
non-compete clauses, 251
nonconforming goods, 264
non-economic damages, 128
nonobvious invention, 530
nonpoint sources, 495–496
nontariff barriers, 44

Norris-LaGuardia Act, 371
North American Free Trade Agreement
    (NAFTA), 45
no-strike out clauses, 375
note, 276
nothing less than perfection, 297
notices, 164, 252, 282–283
notorious possession, 549
novation, 408
novel invention, 530
nuncupative wills, 588

O

Obama, Barack, 158
obesity, 361
objective test, 282
obligor, 220
Occupational Safety and Health Act
    (OSHA), 342
Occupational Safety and Health
    Administration (OSHA), 71, 342
off-duty activities, 339–340
off-duty conduct, 318, 340
offer, 604, 608
    agreements, 183–186
    counter-, 186
    defined, 183
    destruction of subject matter, 186
    expiration of, 186
    invitations to bargain, 183
    problems with definiteness, 183–184
    rejection of, 186
    revocation of, 185
    termination of, 185–186
offeree, 183
offeror, 183
officers, 410–411
Onassis, Jacqueline Kennedy, 163, 594
on its face, 352
opening statements, 90
open possession, 549
opinions, 203, 513
opportunity, 417
oppressive child labor, 342–343
opting out, 47
options, 93
order paper, 279
orders
    court, 6
    following, 24

orders (*continued*)
  to pay, 278
  protective, 87
  for relief, 434
ordinary garbage, 498–499
organ donation, 592
organization
  of business, 440
  responsibility of, 27–30
  socially conscious, 397
outside benefits, 317
outstanding claims, 282–283
overdue instrument, 282
overseas workers, 29–30
owner/ownership, 537, 549, 568, 603

P

paper, 277, 279
Paris Convention, 539
partial strikes, 378
participation, 164
partition, 548
partner, 398
partnership, 398–400
part performance, 208
party rights after assignment, 221
patentable subject matter, 531
Patent and Trademark Office (PTO),
    530–533, 537, 539
Patent Cooperation Treaty (PCT), 533
patents, 529–533
  application for, 532–533
  design, 529
  issuance of, 532–533
  limits on, 531–532
  plant, 529
  requirements for, 530–531
  types of, 529–530
  utility, 530
payable on demand, 278
payday loans, 474–475
payee, 276
pay for service, 611
payment, 437–438, 443
peace, breach of the, 305
Pepsi-Cola Company, 417
per capita, 589–590
perfected security interest, 302
perfection, 293, 297–300

performance, 176
  assignment, 220–221
  breach and, 225
  of contracts, 217–232
  delegation of duties, 221–222
  discharge and, 222–226
  full, by seller, 207
  good faith and, 224
  impossibility and, 226
  part, by buyer, 208
  remedies, 226–232
  sales and, 264–265
  specific, 231
  statute of limitations and, 225
  strict, 223
  substantial, 222–223
  third party beneficiary, 218–219
  Uniform Commercial Code, 265
periodic tenancy, 553
permanence, 548
perpetual trusts, 595
per se, 460
person, 603
personal injury protection, 612
personal jurisdiction, 80–81
personal liability insurance, 611
personal property, 295
  defined, 568
  found property as, 571–572
  gifts as, 568–571
personal services, 220
per stirpes, 589–590
petition, 373, 433–434
phising, 107
physical delivery, 568–569
physical environment, 492, 495
physical evidence, 86
physical examination, 86–87
physical impairment, 359
physical torts, 322–323, 325
physician-assisted death, 592
picketing, 379
piercing the company veil, 395–396
piercing the corporate veil, 412
Pillsbury Co., 458
plaintiff, 9, 91, 203
plain view searches, 102
plans/planning, 442–443
  estate, 584–596
  managed care, 611
  state implementation, 493

plants, 529, 547
plastic cards, 477–478
plea bargaining, 104
pleadings, 84–90
  answer, 85
  class actions, 86
  complaint, 84–85
  defined, 84
  discovery, 86–88
  summary judgment, 88–90
plurality voting, 420
point sources, 495–496
pollution
  in air, 492–495
  water, 495–498
Pope Benedict XVI, 21–22
Porter, Michael, 31
positive ethical behavior, 19
possession, 296, 299, 441
  adverse, 550–549
  landlord's duties to deliver, 553–554
  notorious, 549
  open, 549
power
  of attorney, 591
  congressional, 59
  durable, 591
  executive, 4, 60
  government, 58–59
  granted, 59–61
  judicial, 4, 60–61
  to leave partnerships, 399
  legislative, 4
  separation of, 58–59
practical contracts, 239–252
  drafting, 241
  lawyer, 240–241
  mistakes in, 241–246
  structure of, 246–252
preauthorized transfer, 479
precedent, 93
predatory pricing, 462
predictability, 67
prediction error, 205
preferences, 436
preferred stock, 410
Pregnancy Discrimination Act, 358
premises, 554–555, 557
premium, 603
preponderance of the evidence, 91
present day unions, 371–372

pretermited child, 588
prevention of significant deterioration (PSD), 493
price-fixing, 460
prices
    for contract, 265
    retail, 461
    stock, 423
    wholesale, 461
prima facie, 351–353
Princeton Theological Seminary, 25
principals, 315
    agency, duties of, 319
    agency, duties to, 316–319
    competition with, 317
    conflict of interest between, 317
    control of, 315
    fully disclosed, 321
    liability of, 320–326
    remedies of, 318–319
    secretly dealing with, 317–318
    undisclosed, 321
    unidentified, 321
principles
    difference, 21
    of ethics, 26–30
    single recovery, 126
priorities, 303–304, 438
prior sale, 533
privacy, 357, 594
    behavioral marketing, 160
    data mining, 160
    in digital world, 160–166
    Fair Information Practices, 164
    federal statutes, 164–166
    federal statutes on, 164–166
    Fourth Amendment on, 161
    losing, 160–161
    reasonable expectation of, 161
    regulation of online, 161–166
    social media, 160
    torts, 162–163
    workplace, 161
private international law, 39
private offerings, 455
probable cause, 102
probate, 585
    law, 585–586
    trusts, 594
    wills, 591
problems with definiteness, 183–184

procedural due process, 64
product liability, 145–147
products, 144, 463, 483
professional corporations (PCs), 400
professionals, 138–139
profits, 318
prohibited activities, 351–355
prohibition of contract, 221, 222
promise, 208–209, 249. *See also* Agreements; Contracts
promisee, 218
promisor, 218
promissory estoppel, 179–180
promissory note, 276
promoter, 408
promoter's liability, 408
proof of claim, 435
property
    abandoned, 572
    after-acquired, 297
    exempt, 436
    found, 571–572
    future, 297
    insurance for, 609
    intellectual, 528–541
    joint, 592
    lost, 572
    mislaid, 572
    personal, 295
    real, 547–552
    sale of, 558
    wills, not transferred by, 592
prosecution, 100
prospectus, 454
protected rights, 62–63
protection
    buyers, 300–303
    common law, 335–338
    consumer, 158–159, 471–484
    financial, 342–343
protective order, 87
proxies, 420–421, 592
proximate cause, 137, 139–141
Public Company Accounting Oversight Board (PCAOB), 510–511
public disclosure, 162
public disclosure tort, 162
public international law, 39
publicly traded companies, 421
public offerings, 454
public policy, 221–222, 335–336

puffery, 203
punishment, 105, 112
punitive damages, 126–127
purchase money, 300
purchase money security interest (PMSI), 300
purpose, 319, 410

Q
qualified mortgages (QMs), 476
qualified opinion, 513
qualified privilege, 337
quantity of goods, 262
quantum meruit, 181
quarterly reports, 456
quasi-contract, 179, 181
Queen Anne of England, 534
quid pro quo, 354
quiet enjoyment, 554
quiet exit, 31
quorum, 411

R
race, 351, 354, 481
Racketeer Influenced and Corrupt Organizations Act (RICO), 110
racketeering acts, 110
raising capital, 398
ramanding the case, 9
ratified treaties, 43
rationalization, 23, 422–423
Rawls, John, 21
Rawlsian justice, 21
real property
    adaptation to, 548
    adverse possession, 549–550
    attachment to, 547
    buildings as, 547
    concurrent estates, 548–549
    fixtures as, 547
    land as, 547
    land use regulation, 551–552
    nature of, 547–548
    permanence and, 548
    plant life as, 547
reasonable accommodation, 359
reasonable certainty, 210
reasonable expectation of privacy, 161
reasonable person standard, 559

reasonably, 248

reciprocal promise, 249

reckless misrepresentation of facts, 202–203

record, 293, 418

Recording Industry Association of America (RIAA), 536

Reebok, 538

reframing, 24

regional trade agreements (RTAs), 45

registered agent, 409

registration, 455–456, 500, 537

registration statement, 454

regulation, 6, 161–166
  of air pollution, 494
  of chemicals, 500
  land use, 551

Regulation D, 455

rejection of offer, 186

relationship, 315–316, 360

relativism, 21–22

reliance damages, 230

reliance interest, 226, 230–231

religion, 351, 355, 481

remanding decisions, 93

remedies, 176, 226–232
  buyer's, 47, 264
  equitable interests and, 231–232
  expectation interest and, 227–230
  mitigation of damages and, 232
  for plaintiff's, 203
  of principals, 318–319
  reliance interest and, 230–231
  restitution interest and, 231
  sales and, 264–265
  seller's, 264–265
  Uniform Commercial Code, 264–265

removal of directors, 420–421

rent, 556–557

reorganization, 442. *See also* Chapter 11 bankruptcy

repeated filings for bankruptcy, 440

replacement workers, 378–379

reports
  annual, 456
  credit, 479–480
  quarterly, 456

repossession, 293

representations in contract, 249–250

required duties, 320

resale price maintenance (RPM), 461

rescinding agreements, 202

rescinding contracts, 222

rescission, 231, 319

res ipsa loquitur, 141

Resource Conservation and Recovery Act (RCRA), 498–499

respondeat superior, 321–322

restitution, 100, 201

restitution interest, 226, 231

retail price, 461

retaliation, 355

retirement benefits, 592

reversal of decision, 9, 93

revocable gifts, 568

revocable trusts, 594

revocation, 185, 440

rights
  assignment of, 220–221, 251
  of bailee, 575
  of bailor, 576
  to cure, 264
  of debtor, 295–296
  to jury, 90, 100
  to a lawyer, 106
  legal, 336
  of management, 398
  protected, 62–63
  shareholder, 418–424
  unconditional, 278
  to vote, 419–423

risk, assumption of, 142

risk-utility test, 147

road show, 454

Robinson-Patman Act (RPA), 464

Royal Dutch Petroleum (RDP), 38

Rule Against Perpetuities, 595

rules/ruling
  affirmation of, 9
  business judgment, 413–417
  Incoterms, 40
  making, 70
  of reason, 460

S

safety, 357, 483

sales, 258–269
  abusive acts in, 472
  bait-and-switch advertisements for, 472–473
  of business, 198

  of commercial goods, 47
  consumer protection, 472–474
  deceptive acts/practices in, 472
  door-to-door, 474
  effort of, 454
  formation of contract for, 260–263
  of goods, 210, 261–262
  of merchandise bought by mail/ telephone/online, 473
  performance, 264–265
  prior, 533
  remedies, 264–265
  telemarketing, 473
  unfair practices in, 472
  Uniform Commercial Code, development of, 259–260
  of unordered merchandise, 473–474
  warranties, 265–268

Sarbanes-Oxley Act of 2002 (SOX), 339, 510–511

say-on-pay, 423

scandalous trademarks, 538

scienter, 456, 517–518

S corporations, 392

scrivener's error, 244

searches and seizures, 161

searches without a warrant, 102–103

Sears, 284

secondary boycotts, 379

Secretariat, 39

Secretary of State, 413

secretly dealing with principal, 317–318

secured claims, 437

secured party, 293

secured transactions, 292–306
  Article 9 of Uniform Commercial Code on, 294–295
  attachment of security interest, 295–297
  buyers protection, 300–303
  creditors priorities, 303–304
  default, 304–305
  filing, 299
  perfection, 297–300
  termination, 306
  terminology for, 293–294

securities, 164, 339, 453
  employment, 334–339

Securities Act of 1933, 453–455, 517

Securities and Exchange Commission (SEC), 6, 453–455, 512–513, 519–521
Securities Exchange Act of 1934, 455–457, 517–519
securities laws, 453–459
  blue sky laws, 459
  insider trading, 457–459
  Securities Act of 1933, 453–455
  Securities Exchange Act of 1934, 455–457
security agreement, 293
Security Council, 40
security deposit, 555
security interest, 293, 299–300
  attachment of, 295–297
  perfected, 302
  purchase money, 300
self-dealing, 415
self-incrimination, 105
seller's remedies, 264–265
seniority, 357
separation of powers, 58–59
seriousness of danger, 147
service provider policies, 590
settlement offer, 608
settlor, 585
severability, 251–252
severed joint tenancy, 549
sex, 351, 481
sexual harassment, 353–354
sexual orientation, 356
shareholder, 18
  business judgment rule, 414–417
  defined, 418
  duty of care, 417
  duty of loyalty, 414–417
  lists for, 418
  meetings for, 420
  minority, 392–393
  rights to, 418–424
shari'a law, 42
sheltering fraud, 412
Sherman Act, 460–462
shochu, 44
shoplifting, 123
short-swing trading, 457–458
short-term perspective, 25
signatures, 209–210
single recovery principle, 126
sit-down strikes, 378

Sixth Amendment, 5, 62, 106
slander, 122
slander per se, 122
small-business bankruptcy, 443
smoking, 340
Snowden, Edward, 165
social enterprises, 397
socially conscious organization, 397
social media, 160, 362–363
social security, 343
society, 18–19, 27–28
sole benefit, 575
sole discretion, 248
sole proprietorships, 389
sound mind, 586
sources, 493, 495–496
sovereign immunity, 41
sovereign nations, 41
sovereignty, 41
spam, 159
special committee, 415
Specialized Agencies, 40
special types of corporations, 392–393
specific performance, 231
speech, freedom of, 5, 62–63, 156
Spielberg, Steven, 317
spouse's share, 588
Springsteen, Bruce, 609
stakeholders, 18, 414
standards
  national air-quality, 493
  national water quality, 496
  reasonable person, 559
stare decisis, 5, 41, 67–68
starting a business, 388–402
  corporations, 389–393
  franchises, 400–401
  general partnerships, 398–399
  limited liability companies, 393–397
  limited liability partnerships, 400
  professional corporations, 400
  social enterprieses, 397
  sole proprietorships, 389
starting corporations, 389–393
Star Trek, 609
Star Wars, 529
state courts, 80–83
state for incorporation, 409
state implementation plans (SIPs), 493
statement
  communication of, 122

defamatory, 122
  financing, 293, 298–299
  making false, 110
  registration, 454
state of mind, 101–102
state plans, 496
state statutes, 591
stationary source, 493
Statute of Frauds, 206–207, 261–262, 552
statutes, 5
  Aggravated Identity Theft, 107
  defined, 5, 66
  federal, 590
  federal privacy, 164–166
  of limitations, 225
  long-arm, 81
  state, 591
  for unions, 371–372
  usury, 474
  zoning, 551
statutory law, 66–67
statutory prohibition, 378
Steel Technologies, Inc., 354
Stewart, Martha, 110
stock, 410, 423
stop and frisk, 102
straight bankruptcy, 433–441
straight life insurance, 610
StreamCast Networks, Inc., 536
strict liability, 143–146
strict performance, 223
strikes, 377–378
student loans, 438–440
subjective test, 282
subjects of collective bargaining, 375
sublease, 558
subpoena, 71
subpoena duces tecum, 71
substantial change, 220
substantial interest, 222
substantial performance, 223
summary judgment, 88–90
summons, 81
Superfund, 499
superseding cause, 139
Switzer, Barry, 459

T

taking possession, 304–305
taking responsibility, 24

Takings Clause, 64–65
targeting behavioral, 160
taxes, 44, 389–391, 593
Telecommunications Act of 1996, 155
telemarketing, 473
Telephone Consumer Protection Act
     (TCPA), 473
tenancy, 548–549, 553
tenant, 552
   duties of, 556–557
   liability of, 558–559
term agreement, 319
termination, 306
   of corporations, 412–413
   general partnerships, 399
   of offer, 185–186
   of partnership, 399
   relationships in agency, 319–320
   of trusts, 595
   wrongful, 319–320
term insurance, 609–610
term partnership, 399
testamentary trusts, 594
testator, 585, 587
testatrix, 585
testing chemicals, 500
Texaco, 50
theories of ethics, 19–22
third parties liability, 515–519
   fraud, 517
   negligence, 516
   Securities Act of 1933, 517
   Securities Exchange Act of 1934,
      517–519
third party beneficiary, 218–219
third party interests, 176
third party liability, 320–326
tied product, 463
tippees, 459
tippers, 459
title of contract, 246
Title VII of Civil Rights Act of 1964,
     351–357
   affirmative action, 357
   defenses to charges of discrimination,
      356–357
   family responsibility discrimination,
      355–356
   gender identity and expression, 356
   immigration, 356
   prohibited activities, 351–355

religion, 355
sexual orientation, 356
tort
   business, 128–129
   cyberlaw and privacy, 154–166
   damages, 128
   intentional, 325
   international, 122–125
   of intrusion, 163
   liability for, 321–326
   negligence, strict liability, and product
      liability, 135–148
   nonphysical, 325–326
   physical, 322–323, 325
   public disclosure, 162
tort law, 3, 337–338
torture, 48
total maximum daily loads (TMDLs),
     496
Toxic Substances Control Act (TSCA),
     500
tracing, 512
tracking tools, 160
Track One system, 533
Trademark Law Treaty, 539
trademarks, 537–540
   defined, 537
   descriptive, 538
   existing, 538
   generic, 538
   immoral, 538
   infringement on, 538–539
   international treaties for, 539
   ownership and, 537
   registration and, 537
   scandalous, 538
   valid, 538
trade secrets, 198, 540–541
trading, 44, 457–459
transfers
   electronic fund, 478–479
   fraudulent, 436
   of interests, 390, 395
   of ownership, 399
   preauthorized, 479
   restrictions, 393
transgender, 356
TransUnion, 479
treasury stock, 410
treaties, 43–47
   adopted, 43

Agreement on Trade Related Aspects
     of Intellectual Property, 45–46
   bilateral, 43
   defined, 43
   entering into force, 43
   General Agreement on Tariffs and
      Trade, 44
   General Agreement on Trade in
      Services, 45–46
   international air pollution, 494
   as international law, 43–47
   international patent, 533
   international trademarks, 539
   multilateral, 43
   ratified, 43
   regional trade agreements, 45
   Trademark Law, 539
   United Nations Convention on
      Contracts for the International Sale
      of Goods, 46–47
treble damages, 110
trespasser, 138
trespassing, 138
trial, 90–92, 100, 104
trial courts, 80–83
trust, 19
trustee, 434, 593
trust instincts, 25
trusts, 514–515, 593–595
Truth in Lending Act (TILA), 475
tying arrangements, 463–464
tying product, 463
typos in contract, 244–246

U

ultrahazardous activity, 144
unconditional promise, 278
unconditional rights, 278
undue hardship, 359
undue influence, 586
unenforceable agreements, 177, 207
unethical behavior, 19, 30–31
unfair and deceptive acts or practices, 472
unfair labor practices (ULPs), 371–372,
     378–379
unfair practices, 472
Uniform Anatomical Gift Act (UAGA),
     592
Uniform Commercial Code (UCC)
   acceptance, 187

Article 9 of, 293, 294–295
on contract formation, 260–263
contract laws, 182
development of, 259–260
merchants, 260
on performance, 265
on remedies, 264–265
Section 2-104 of, 260
Section 2-201 of, 261–262
Section 2-204 of, 260–261
Section 2-207 of, 263
Statute of Frauds, 261–262
Uniform Electronic Transactions Act
    (UETA), 210
Uniform Foreign Money Judgments
    Recognition Act, 50
Uniform Trade Secrets Act (UTSA), 540
unilateral contract, 176
unilateral mistake, 204
uninsured motorist, 612
unintentional tort. *See* Negligence
unions, 371–375
union shop, 375
United Nations, 39–40
United Nations Intergovernmental Panel
    on Climate Change, 494
UN Commission on International Trade
    Law (UNCITRAL), 40
UN Educational, Scientific, and Cultural
    Organization (UNESCO), 40
United States
    Constitution, 4–5
    Courts of Appeals, 83
    foreign judgments, recognition and
        enforcement of, 50–51
    law and, 48–50
U.S. Attorney General, 434
U.S. Bankruptcy Code (the Code), 432
U.S. Department of Education, 276
U.S. Department of Interior, 501
U.S. Department of Justice, 460, 462
U.S. Product Safety Commission, 71
U.S. Supreme Court, 83–84
U.S. Trustee, 434
universalism, 21–22
universal life insurance, 610
University of Oklahoma, 459
unordered merchandise, 473–474
unqualified opinion, 513
unreasonable non-compete clauses, 251
unreasonable searches and seizures, 161

unsecured claims, 438
unsolicited bulk email (UBE), 159
unsolicited commercial email (UCE), 159
UPS, 538
UPS Ground Freight, 354
USA Today, 155
user-generated content, 155–158
usury statutes, 474
utilitarian ethics, 20
Utilitarianism (Mill), 20
utility, 530

V

vagueness in contract, 241–243
valid agreements, 177
valid contract, 177
valid evidence, 87
valid trademarks, 538
value, 195
    of attachment of security interest, 296
    consideration, 195–196
    defined, 282
    mutual mistake of, 205
    of negotiable instruments, 282
    of product, 147
    societal, 336
vehicles, 493
veil of ignorance, 21
verdict, 92
VeriFone, 459
Verizon, 155
vertical price fixing, 461
vetos, 5
Visa, 460
voicing your opinions, 31
voidable agreements, 177
voidable contract, 177, 201
voidable preferences, 436
void agreements, 177
voluntary act, 101
voluntary action, 357
voluntary petition, 433–434
vote/voting, 412
    plurality, 420
    rights to, 419–423
    shareholder rights, 419–424
vouching, 512

W

wages, 375
waiver, 41
Wallace, Kerry, 609
Walmart, 355
warranties, 265–268
    bumper-to-bumper, 265
    in contract, 249–250
    defined, 265
    express, 265
    full, 483
    gathering of evidence, 102
    implied, 266–268
    searches without a, 102–103
waste, 498–499
wastewater, 497
water, 496–497
water pollution, 495–498
welfare, 481
wetlands, 496
whistleblower, 338–339
whistleblowing, 338–339, 519
whole life insurance, 610
wholesale price, 461
William the Conqueror, 41
wills
    amending, 591
    anatomical gifts, 592
    children's share, 588–590
    defined, 586
    digital assets, 590–591
    drafting, 589
    end of life health issues, 592–593
    executing, 587
    holographic, 587
    intestacy, 591
    living, 592
    nuncupative, 588
    power of attorney, 591
    probating, 591
    property not transferred by, 592
    requirements for valid, 586–587
    revoking, 591
    spouse's share, 588
winding-up process, 413
wire fraud, 107
workers
    compensation, 343
    illegal, 111
    overseas, 29–30

workers (*continued*)
    replacement, 378–379
working papers, 521
workplace
    ethics, 26
    freedom, 339–342
    privacy, 161
    safety, 342
World Bank, 40
World Court. *See* International Court of
    Justice (ICJ)

World Food Program, 32
World Health Organization (WHO),
    40
World Intellectual Property Organization
    (WIPO), 40, 539
world's legal system. *See* International
    legal systems
World Trade Organization (WTO), 44
World Wide Web, 155
writing contracts, 206–210
written agreement, 240

wrongful discharge, 334–336
wrongful termination, 319–320

X

Xerox Corp., 538

Z

zombie directors, 420
zoning statutes, 551